T0392011

PRINTING AND MISPRINTING

PRINTING AND MISPRINTING

A Companion to Mistakes and In-House Corrections
in Renaissance Europe (1450–1650)

Edited by

GERI DELLA ROCCA DE CANDAL,

ANTHONY GRAFTON,

AND

PAOLO SACHET

Great Clarendon Street, Oxford, OX2 6DP,
United Kingdom

Oxford University Press is a department of the University of Oxford.
It furthers the University's objective of excellence in research, scholarship,
and education by publishing worldwide. Oxford is a registered trade mark of
Oxford University Press in the UK and in certain other countries

© Geri Della Rocca de Candal, Anthony Grafton, and Paolo Sachet 2023

The moral rights of the authors have been asserted

All rights reserved. No part of this publication may be reproduced, stored in
a retrieval system, or transmitted, in any form or by any means, without the
prior permission in writing of Oxford University Press, or as expressly permitted
by law, by licence or under terms agreed with the appropriate reprographics
rights organization. Enquiries concerning reproduction outside the scope of the
above should be sent to the Rights Department, Oxford University Press, at the
address above

You must not circulate this work in any other form
and you must impose this same condition on any acquirer

Published in the United States of America by Oxford University Press
198 Madison Avenue, New York, NY 10016, United States of America

British Library Cataloguing in Publication Data
Data available

Library of Congress Control Number: 2022921889

ISBN 978-0-19-886304-5

DOI: 10.1093/oso/9780198863045.001.0001

Printed and bound by
CPI Group (UK) Ltd, Croydon, CR0 4YY

Cover image: Constantinus Lascaris, *De octo partibus orationis*, [Florence, Filippo I Giunta, 1515].
Courtesy of: Oxford, Lincoln College, to which the editors are most grateful.

Links to third party websites are provided by Oxford in good faith and
for information only. Oxford disclaims any responsibility for the materials
contained in any third party website referenced in this work.

FOREWORD

H. R. WOUDHUYSEN

The conference, 'Printing and Misprinting: Typographical Mistakes and Publishers' Corrections (1450–1650)', that took place at Lincoln College, Oxford, on 20 and 21 April 2018, laid the foundations for this book. The College of the Blessed Virgin Mary and All Saints, Lincoln, was instituted in 1427 by Richard Fleming, Bishop of Lincoln, with the intention of training men in theology. They were to 'counteract the forces of heresy and error' ('*haereses et errores*') and 'to overcome those who with their swinish snouts imperil the pearls of true theology' — Fleming was particularly concerned to marshal forces against Lollards, followers of the teaching of John Wyclif.[1] A conference devoted to misprinting, mistakes, and corrections was well suited to a college that was founded to combat the terrible twins of heresy and error. Even when limited to the first two centuries of printing, the scope of the subject of printing and misprinting is enormous. '*Humanum est errare*' ('to err is human') and errors beget other errors. *Printing and Misprinting* provides a valuable map of the early history of the subject and a language with which to describe its multitudinous manifestations.

One of the earliest uses of the term 'misprinting' in English occurs in the second part of Thomas More's *The Confutation of Tyndale's Answer*, published in 1533. Robert Barnes had claimed that a text of St Augustine's was to be found in his sermon 99, *De Tempore*. More responded by reporting 'in whyche sermon I fynde it not'. He went on to say,

> And leste there myghte haue ben some ouersyghte, eyther in hym self or in the prenter, by mysse wrytynge or by mysse prentyng those fygurs of algorysme, bycause the fygure of .9. & the fygure of .6. be all in maner one yf they be contrary turned: I assayed them euery way / and sought & red ouer not onely .99. sermon whyche he assygneth, but also .96.69. and 66 / and I fynde his texte in none of all those places / and than to go seke tohse wordes thorowout all saynt Austayns wurkes, were a great longe besynesse. For surely it semeth that the man hath alledged hys texte in a wrong place, of purpose bycause he wolde not haue it founden.[2]

More shows a characteristically acute awareness of both the mechanical sources of error (in script and in print) and of the possible uses of deliberate error for ulterior motives. What is also pleasing is to find in this passage an example of the sort of typographic error ('tohse') that is regularly found in books set and printed in the hand-press period and, in fact, in

---

[1] V. Green, *The Commonwealth of Lincoln College 1427–1977*, Oxford, 1979, p. 6.

[2] Thomas More, *The second parte of the confutacion of Tyndals answere*, London, William Rastell, 1533, f° (USTC 502567), sig. 2T1v. Part of the passage is quoted in the *OED* misprint v. 1 from Thomas More, *The workes*, London, John Cawod, John Walley, and Richard Tottel, 1557, f° (USTC 505459), sig. C6v.

all periods. It is not unknown for printers deliberately to create errors when they or their colleagues felt that they or their trade were being unfairly represented.

If the verb was available to More in the 1530s, the noun 'misprinting' soon followed. In the preface to the reader before his translation of Cicero's *Tusculanae Disputationes*, John Dolman explained that there was nothing dark or obscure in his version, while apologising for

> the misprinting of manye wordes, and the yll printing of some greeke wordes, in latin letters, & of the verses also, otherwyse then they shoulde be red. But the blame thereof I vtterlye refuse. Inasmuch as, euerye man knoweth, that it doth nothinge pertayne vnto me. Neuertheles, as for the firste, whych contayneth the misprintinge of wordes, thou shalt finde them, all corrected, in the ende of the booke. So that if thou list to reade it, without desire of faulte findinge: thou mayst firste, amende all those faultes, with thy pen, in the margeant of thy booke, whiche in the ende of the booke be corrected.[3]

While not actually pointing a finger at the printer, Dolman makes it quite clear where he feels the blame for these errors lies and shows how they can be remedied. Trouble with setting Greek and the layout of poetry are hardly unfamiliar matters to modern scholars. In fact, the 'Faultes escaped in printing' in Dolman's book are not especially extensive ('for bed, read beard,'), but are carefully laid out and supplemented by a list of 'Wordes left out' ('betwixt, is, and, written, bring in, not').[4]

The universal problem of misprinting makes the relatively late emergence of the individual instance of the misprint, the cause of authorial fury and despair, all the more surprising. The earliest citation for this sense in the *OED* is from Byron, whose ability to spell and to punctuate left something to be desired and whose handwriting was confessedly not of the best. In November 1813, he is quoted as claiming, 'I can't survive a single mis*print* — it *choaks* me to see words misused by the Printers'; the novelty of the word is evident from its unusual and partial italicisation. Eight years later, he is on more familiar ground when complaining, 'The *misprinting* was shameful — such nonsense! — in some of the clearest passages too.'[5] Byron employed others to see his writings through the press, but he knew enough about the technical processes of book production to joke about them. 'The proof' of *The Age of Bronze*, he told his publisher John Hunt in March 1823, 'is called "a proof in Slips" and certainly the "slips" are the most conspicuous part of it.'[6] The slips in Byron's slip proof are related to a slip as 'A mistake or fault [...] an unintentional error or blunder', which is related to a slip of the pen or a slip of the tongue.[7] Such mistakes are errors, errata and corrigenda, faults, escapes (a sixteenth-century usage), and typos (the term is late nineteenth century).[8]

---

[3] *Those fyue questions, which Marke Tullye Cicero, disputed in his manor of Tusculanum*, transl. John Dolman, London, Thomas Marsh, 1561, 8° (USTC 505856), sigs C5v–6r. Dolman anticipates the *OED*'s first citation for 'misprinting' as a noun from John Selden's commentary on Michael Drayton's *Poly-Olbion* (1612).

[4] *Those fyue questions* (n. 3 above), sigs E7r–8v.

[5] *OED* misprint n.; misprinting n. in misprint v.

[6] G. Byron, *Letters and Journals*, ed. L. A. Marchand, 12 vols, London, 1973–1982, 10.117.

[7] *OED* slip n.³ 10c, d. For 'slip' as 'A proof pulled on a long slip of paper, for revision before the type is made up into pages', see *OED* slip n.² 10d, where the first citation is from Blackwood's *Edinburgh Magazine* in 1818.

[8] *OED* escape n.¹ 6a; *OED* typo n. 2, with a first citation from Israel Zangwill's *Children of the Ghetto* (1892).

The taxonomy of misprinting is the subject matter of this book, in which its causes and remedies are extensively discussed in a wide range of printed matter, including illustrations, music, play-texts, and newspapers. In all of this, it is worth remembering how complicated and difficult it is to set, print, and distribute type and how fallible men and women are in their ability to undertake such work. Bad copy from an author or scribe produces bad work by compositors; in stopping the press to make corrections, in setting paste slips, in making pen-and-ink corrections to printed works, or even in reprinting a book, new errors are often introduced; corrected proofs are only as good as their corrector; and authors are not the best readers of their own work. Even, perhaps especially, in an age when electronic copy from authors is expected by publishers, misprinting and mistakes, in academic as well as in trade books, are legion. It comes as a shock when reading a fairly serious recently published biography to see that an editor's marginal query about the argument of the opening of a chapter has been incorporated in the body of the text or to pause over a repetition in a new novel by a much-celebrated author to try to detect some significant meaning where none was (probably) intended.

Just as the uncovering and public exposure of forgeries have advanced our knowledge and understanding of literary history and the history of books (in their widest senses), so the examination of misprinting provides a window into how works were translated into print and how they were received and understood. By their very nature, translations — however accurate and professional they are — can only be approximate versions of their originals. A world of books without misprints would be a dull place indeed. In his important book about narrative, *The Genesis of Secrecy*, Frank Kermode included a striking tribute at the end of the acknowledgements:

> My wife scrutinized the text with extraordinary care, and purged it of many infelicities. Keith Walker, who loves error, read the proofs and caught more mistakes than I did.[9]

To love error is not to place it above truth and accuracy, for by exposing and correcting error and heresy, as Richard Fleming believed, our understanding of this world and perhaps the next are greatly enhanced.

Lincoln College
13 February 2022

---

[9] F. Kermode, *The Genesis of Secrecy: On the Interpretation of Narrative*, Cambridge (MA) and London, 1978, p. xii.

CONTENTS

List of Illustrations xi
List of Contributors xxiii

Introduction 1
GERI DELLA ROCCA DE CANDAL, ANTHONY GRAFTON, AND
PAOLO SACHET

1. From Copy to Cancels: Matthew Parker and the Quest for Error 7
ANTHONY GRAFTON

PART I TYPE, PROOFS, AND ILLUSTRATIONS

2. Fallen Type: The Benefits of a Printer's Error 33
CLAIRE BOLTON

3. Proof Sheets as Evidence of Early Pre-Publication Procedures 51
RANDALL HERZ

4. Kludging Type: Some Workarounds in Early English Print 70
JAMES MISSON

5. Misprinting Illustrated Books 80
ILARIA ANDREOLI, CAROLINE DUROSELLE-MELISH, AND
ROGER GASKELL

PART II HUMANISM

6. Printing and Politics in Italian Humanism: Manuscript and Stop-Press
Corrections in Poliziano's *Coniurationis commentarium* 107
MARTA CELATI

7. *Manus Manutii*: A Preliminary Checklist of Typographical and
Manuscript Interventions in Aldine Incunabula (1495–1500) 121
GERI DELLA ROCCA DE CANDAL

CONTENTS

8. Aldus as Proofreader: The Case of the *Thesaurus Cornu copiae* (1496) 165
PAOLO SACHET

9. Managing Misprints: Jan Moretus I's Diverse Approaches to Correcting Errors 198
DIRK IMHOF

PART III RELIGION

10. Misprinting the Word and the Image of God (Paris, 1498–1538) 215
FRANÇOIS DUPUIGRENET DESROUSSILLES

11. The Collective Editorial Strategy of the Unity of the Brethren 233
VERONIKA SLADKÁ

12. Biblical Misprints: Error and Correction in an Early Yiddish Epic 248
RACHEL WAMSLEY

13. 'Before the Law': Jewish Correctors of Early Printed Books 261
PAVEL SLÁDEK

14. 'But to whose charge shall I lay it? Your Printer is all readie loaden': The Rhetoric of Printers' Errors in Early Modern Religious Disputes 278
MATTHEW DAY

PART IV SCIENCE

15. Controlling Errors in the First Printed Book of Astronomical Tables: Regiomontanus's *Ephemerides* (Nuremberg, 1474) 295
RICHARD L. KREMER

16. Misprinting Aristotle: The Birth and Life of a Frankenstein's Fish 325
GRIGORY VOROBYEV

17. Conrad Gessner as Corrector: How to Deal with Errors in Images 345
ANTHONY GRAFTON

PART V POETRY, MUSIC, AND THEATRE

18. Fernando de Herrera *Contra Errata*: A Re-evaluation of his Edition of
    Garcilaso de la Vega   369
    PABLO ALVAREZ

19. Marketing a Misprint: Christopher Tye's *The Actes of the Apostles* and
    Early English Music Publishing   385
    ANNE HEMINGER

20. Misprinting and Misreading in *The Comedy of Errors*   399
    ALICE LEONARD

21. Making Sense of Error in Commercial Drama: The Case of
    Edward III   415
    AMY LIDSTER

PART VI WIDESPREAD AND EPHEMERAL CIRCULATION

22. Drawn Corrections and Pictorial Instability in Devotional Books from
    the Workshop of Gerard Leeu   431
    ANNA DLABAČOVÁ

23. Learning from Mistakes: Paper and Printing Defects in Sixteenth-Century
    Italian Popular Books   446
    LAURA CARNELOS

24. Printing under Pressure: Mistakes in the Earliest Newspapers   463
    JAN HILLGÄRTNER

    Appendix A: Glossary of Printing and Misprinting   481
    Appendix B: Glossary Translation Tables   504
    Index of Subjects   566
    Index of Names   568

LIST OF ILLUSTRATIONS

1.1 A Parkerian reader singles out what he describes as a deliberate omission in a manuscript of Hrabanus Maurus, *De ecclesiasticis officiis.* Cambridge, Corpus Christi College, MS 11, fol. 45*v.* Courtesy of: Oxford, Corpus Christi College. — 14

1.2 A reader censors a passage on the privileges and prerogatives of the see of Canterbury in Matthew Parker, *De antiquitate ecclesiae Britannicae*, London, John Day, 1572, f° (USTC 507554), p. 29. Princeton, William H. Scheide Library, WHS 20.11. Courtesy of: Princeton, William H. Scheide Library. — 18

1.3 A reader completes a correction by excision of a passage on the privileges and prerogatives of the see of Canterbury in Parker, *De antiquitate* (see Fig. 1.2.), p. 39. Princeton, William H. Scheide Library, WHS 20.11. Courtesy of: Princeton, William H. Scheide Library. — 19

2.1 Fallen type with halo of space around the fallen letter, found in Johannes Gerson, *Opera*, Cologne, Johann Kölhoff, 1483–1484, f° (ISTC ig00185000), vol. IV, fol. XLVIII*r*. Oxford, Bodleian Library, Bod Auct. 5Q 5.51. (MEI 02014894). Courtesy of: Oxford, Bodleian Library. — 36

2.2 A broken foot from a piece of type in *Missale Cracoviense*, Mainz, Peter Schöffer, 10 Nov. 1484, f° (ISTC im00658000), fol. 166*r*. Berlin, Staatsbibliothek, f° Ink 1544 (MEI 02014968). Courtesy of: Berlin, Staatsbibliothek. — 41

2.3 A piece of fallen type with a sloping foot found in Angelus Politianus, *Opera*, Aldus Manutius, Venice, 1498, f° (ISTC ip00886000), sig. b2*v*. Oxford, Bodleian Library, Byw. F 4.1. (MEI 00204488). Courtesy of: Oxford, Bodleian Library. — 43

2.4 Repair on de Gregoriis' woodcut printer's mark, most likely covering the damage caused by a piece of fallen type, in Hieronymus, *Commentaria in Bibliam*, Venice, Johannes and Gregorius de Gregoriis, de Forlivio, 1497–1498, f° (ISTC ih00160000), sig. ppp8*r*. Oxford, Bodleian Library, Auct. 6Q 1.2 (MEI 02014901). Courtesy of: Oxford, Bodleian Library. — 46

xii LIST OF ILLUSTRATIONS

2.5 Piece of type from the modern experiment, with hole drilled through, lying on the set text. The nick in the side of the letter was formed in the mould. Courtesy of: Claire Bolton.   47

2.6 Fine impression from the piece of fallen type, showing the halo effect around the type letter and the raised circle from the drilled hole. Courtesy of: Claire Bolton.   47

3.1. An early sixteenth-century pressroom. Geoffrey of Monmouth, *Historia Regum Britanniae*, Paris, Josse Bade and Yves Cavellat, 1508, 4° (USTC 143331), title-page. Augsburg, Staats- und Stadtbibliothek, 4 Gs 765. Courtesy of: Augsburg, Staats- und Stadtbibliothek.   52

3.2.a–c A proof sheet with manuscript corrections, recycled in a binding (a) as the verso of the front pastedown (c). Erlangen and Nuremberg, Universitätsbibliothek, H62/INC 1246. Courtesy of: Erlangen and Nuremberg, Universitätsbibliothek.   54

3.3 Proof sheet of *Biblia* [German], Nuremberg, Anton Koberger, 13 February 1483, f° (ISTC ib00632000), fol. VIIr. Göttingen, Niedersächsische Staats- und Universitätsbibliothek, Sammlung Dziatzko 1. Courtesy of: Göttingen, Niedersächsische Staats- und Universitätsbibliothek.   56

3.4 Proof sheet of Koberger's German Bible (see Fig. 3.3), fol. VIIr. Detail: col. a, ll. 1–4. Courtesy of: Göttingen, Niedersächsische Staats- und Universitätsbibliothek.   57

3.5 Proof sheet of Koberger's German Bible (see Fig. 3.3), fol. VIIr. Detail: col. a, ll. 28–33. Courtesy of: Göttingen, Niedersächsische Staats- und Universitätsbibliothek.   57

3.6 Proof sheet of *Epistolae et Evangelia* [German], Ulm, Conrad Dinckmut, 28 February [14]83, f° (ISTC ie00082000), fol. 31r. Memmingen, Wissenschaftliche Stadtbibliothek, 2° 3.115, as rear pastedown. Courtesy of: Memmingen, Wissenschaftliche Stadtbibliothek.   59

3.7 Proof sheet of *Epistolae et Evangelia* (see Fig. 3.6.), fol. 31r. Detail: ll. 2–26. Courtesy of: Memmingen, Wissenschaftliche Stadtbibliothek.   60

3.8 Proof sheets of Aesopus, *Vita et Fabulae*, Ulm, Johann Zainer, about 1476/1477, f° (ISTC ia00116000), fol. 170r. Tübingen, Universitätsbibliothek, 2 Ke XVIII 4 b.2 (Nr. 13). Courtesy of: Tübingen, Universitätsbibliothek.   61

3.9 Proof sheets of Aesopus, *Vita et Fabulae* (see Fig. 3.8.), fol. 170r. Courtesy of: Tübingen, Universitätsbibliothek.   62

3.10 Aesopus, *Vita et Fabulae*, Ulm, Johann Zainer, about 1476/1477, f° (ISTC ia00116000), fol. 170v. Detail, ll. 11–14. Munich, Bayerische

| | Staatsbibliothek, Rar 762. Courtesy of: Munich, Bayerische Staatsbibliothek. | 62 |

3.11 Layout manuscript of Aesopus, *Vita et Fabulae*. MS Munich, Bayerische Staatsbibliothek, Cgm 1137, fol. 259*v*. Courtesy of: Munich, Bayerische Staatsbibliothek. 63

3.12 Aesopus, *Vita et Fabulae* (see Fig. 3.10.), fol. 272*r*. Courtesy of: Munich, Bayerische Staatsbibliothek. 64

3.13 Layout manuscript of Aesopus, *Vita et Fabulae* (see Fig. 3.11.), fol. 249*v*. Detail: ll. 16–18. Courtesy of: Munich, Bayerische Staatsbibliothek. 66

4.1 *The volume of the bokes called Apocripha*, London, John Day and William Seres, 1549, 8° (USTC 504307), sig. D3*v*. Oxford, Bodleian Library, 8° P 269 Th. Courtesy of: Oxford, Bodleian Library. 71

4.2 *Diues et Pauper*, London, Richard Pynson, 1493, f° (ISTC ip00117000), sig. e3*v*. Oxford, Bodleian Library, Arch. G d.23. Courtesy of: Oxford, Bodleian Library. 73

4.3 *The first Sonday in Aduent'* of *The boke of common praier*, London, Richard Grafton, 1552, f° (USTC 504687), sig. A1*r*. Oxford, Bodleian Library, C.P. 1552 d.4. Courtesy of: Oxford, Bodleian Library. 73

4.4 James Whytstons, *De justicia & sanctitate belli*, London, Richard Pynson, 1512, 4° (USTC 501215), fol. 51*v*. Oxford, Bodleian Library, Arch. A e. 48. Courtesy of: Oxford, Bodleian Library. 77

5.1 'The artist has not fully followed the intention of the author concerning the vases'. Jacques Besson, *Le cosmolabe*, Paris, Philippe Gaulthier Rouillé, 1567–1569, 4° (USTC 16555), p. 239. Cambridge (MA), Houghton Library, *FC5.C3975.B585. Courtesy of: Cambridge (MA), Houghton Library. 83

5.2.a–b Apollonius, *Conicorum*, Florence, 1661, pp. 415 and 12. The errata list on p. 415 points out a missing line NQ and letter D from the end of the parabola on the left in the diagram on p. 12. Roger Gaskell Rare Books. Courtesy of: Roger Gaskell. 84

5.3.a–b *Biblia* [Italian], [Venice, Adam de Ambergau], 1 Oct. 1471, f° (ISTC ib00639000), fols 10*v*–11*r*. Manchester, John Rylands Library, Inc. 3071. Courtesy of: Manchester, John Rylands Library. 86

5.4.a Autograph manuscript of Copernicus, *De revolutionibus orbium coelestium*. Kraków, Biblioteka Jagiellońska, BJ Rkp. 10,000 III, fol. 119*v*. Courtesy of: Kraków, Biblioteka Jagiellońska. 88

5.4.b Nicolaus Copernicus, *De revolutionibus orbium coelestium*, Nuremberg, Johann Petreius, 1543, f° (USTC 678038), fol. 111*r*. The erratum for this diagram ('in hac figura connectantur EM, EL, lineis rectis') is itself an error, as it should read 'in this figure connect CM, CL with straight lines'. These lines can be seen by comparison with the manuscript and have been omitted in the woodcut. Kansas City, Linda Hall Library, QB41 .C64 1543 quarto. Courtesy of: Kansas City, Linda Hall Library.   89

5.5.a Autograph of Copernicus, *De revolutionibus* (see Fig. 5.4.a), fol. 74*r*. Courtesy of: Kraków, Biblioteka Jagiellońska.   90

5.5.b Copernicus, *De revolutionibus* (see Fig. 5.4.b), fol. 66*v*. The figure-of-eight path of the pole in the manuscript appears as two ovals in the woodcut. Courtesy of: Kansas City, Linda Hall Library.   90

5.6.a Autograph of Copernicus, *De revolutionibus* (see Fig. 5.4.a), fol. 9*v*. Courtesy of: Kraków, Biblioteka Jagiellońska.   91

5.6.b Copernicus, *De revolutionibus* (see Fig. 5.4.b), fol. 9*v*. Compared with the manuscript, the labels for the spheres of Mars, Jupiter, Saturn, and the fixed stars are moved out and the orbit of the moon is shown graphically instead of verbally. Courtesy of: Kansas City, Linda Hall Library.   91

5.7 Blaming the block-cutter. Nicholas Culpeper, *Catastrophe magnatum*, London, 1652, sig. E4*r*. Washington DC, Folger Shakespeare Library, call no. 261279. Courtesy of: Washington, Folger Shakespeare Library.   93

5.8.a-b Vitruvius, *I dieci libri dell'architettura*, Venice, Francesco Marcolini, 1556, f° (USTC 863689). In this copy, the original leaf signed B3r (on the left) has been retained in addition to the replacement leaf with a woodcut showing a different temple plan. Einsiedeln, Stiftung Bibliothek Werner Oechslin, A04f. Courtesy of: Einsiedeln, Stiftung Bibliothek Werner Oechslin.   96

5.9.a-b Jean Cousin, *Livre de Perspective*, Paris, J. le Royer, 1560, f° (USTC 23189), sigs C3*v*–C4*r*, with inserted slip providing two alternative diagrams making the same point as that printed on the left-hand page. It would need to be turned over to read the text on the right-hand page. Cambridge (MA), Houghton Library, Typ 515.6.301 (A). Courtesy of: Cambridge (MA), Houghton Library.   97

6.1 Angelus Politianus, *Pactianae coniurationis commentariolum*, [Florence, Nicolaus Alamanus], 1478, 4° (ISTC ip00892500). Exemplar R_1: Rome, Biblioteca dell'Accademia Nazionale dei Lincei e Corsiniana, 52.E.62, sig. [a5]*r* (detail). Courtesy of: Rome, Biblioteca Corsiniana.   113

6.2 Angelus Politianus, *Pactianae coniurationis commentariolum*, 1478. Exemplar F_1: Florence, Biblioteca Nazionale Centrale, E.6.3.26, sig. [a5]*r* (detail). Courtesy of: Florence, Biblioteca Nazionale Centrale.   114

6.3 Angelus Politianus, *Pactianae coniurationis commentariolum*, 1478. Exemplar R₁: Rome, Biblioteca dell'Accademia Nazionale dei Lincei e Corsiniana, 52.E.62, sig. [a9]*v*. Courtesy of: Rome, Biblioteca Corsiniana. 116

6.4 Angelus Politianus, *Pactianae coniurationis commentariolum*, 1478. Exemplar F₁: Florence, Biblioteca Nazionale Centrale, E.6.3.26, sig. [a9]*v*. Courtesy of: Florence, Biblioteca Nazionale Centrale. 116

7.1 Proof sheet of Dioscorides, *De materia medica* [Greek], Venice, Aldus Manutius, 1499, f° (ISTC id00260000), sig. θ2*r*. Leeuwarden, Tresoar, 1165 Gnk. Courtesy of: Leeuwarden, Tresoar. 148

8.1.a–d The four combinations of the emendation in Θησαυρὸς, Κέρας Ἀμαλθείας, καὶ κῆποι Ἀδώνιδος. *Thesaurus Cornu copiae & Hortus Adonidis*, Venice, Aldus Manutius, 1496, f° (ISTC it00158000), f. 6*v*, ll. 25–6. A: Provo (UT), The Harold B. Lee Library, 1496 no.1. B: Oxford, Bodleian Library, Auct R 1.4. C: Oxford, Bodleian Library, Byw. G 3.16. D: Kraków, Biblioteka Jagiellońska, BJ Cam. L. X. 11. Courtesy of: Provo (UT), The Harold B. Lee Library; Oxford, Bodleian Library; Kraków, Biblioteka Jagiellońska. 181

8.2–4 Anomalous emendations in the *Thesaurus* (see Figs. 8.1.a–d), f. 6*v*, ll. 25–6. Fig. 8.2: Alba Iulia, Biblioteca Batthyaneum, SR Inc. VI 45. Fig. 8.3: Shrewsbury, Shrewsbury School, INC 43 E.VI.16. Fig. 8.4: Paris, Bibliothèque nationale de France, RES-X-30. Courtesy of: Alba Iulia, Biblioteca Batthyaneum; Shrewsbury, Shrewsbury School; Paris, Bibliothèque nationale de France. 182

9.1 Thomas Willeboirts Bosschaert, *Portrait of Balthasar Moretus*, oil painting. Antwerp: Museum Plantin-Moretus, V.IV.3. Courtesy of: Antwerp, Museum Plantin-Moretus — UNESCO, World Heritage. 201

9.2 Letter by Balthasar Moretus to Jan Bernaerts from June or July 1599. Antwerp, Museum Plantin-Moretus, Arch. 12, *Copie de lettres de Jean Moretus I, 1598–1607*, p. 79. Courtesy of: Antwerp, Museum Plantin-Moretus — UNESCO, World Heritage. 203

9.3 Payments for printing Frédéric Jamot, *Varia poëmata Graeca & Latina*, Antwerp, Jan Moretus, 1593, 4° (USTC 406950) between 29 August and 3 October 1592 and for the errata on 21 November 1592. Antwerp, Museum Plantin-Moretus, Arch. 786, *Ouvriers 1590–1610*, fol. 30*r*. Courtesy of: Antwerp, Museum Plantin-Moretus — UNESCO, World Heritage. 205

9.4 Justus Lipsius's poem in Martín Anton Delrio, *Florida Mariana*, Antwerp, Jan Moretus, 1598, 8° (USTC 4070391598), p. 12. Antwerp, Museum Plantin-Moretus, A 1230. Courtesy of: Antwerp, Museum Plantin-Moretus — UNESCO, World Heritage. 209

10.1 Woodcut representing the coronation of an English king in *Bible historiée*, ed. Jean de Rély, Paris, Antoine Vérard, [between 8 May 1498 and 25 Oct. 1499], f° (ISTC ib00623000), fol. 87r. Paris, Bibliothèque nationale de France, A 270. Courtesy of: Paris, Bibliothèque nationale de France.   217

10.2 Tempera painting representing the payment of the tithe. *Bible historiée* (see Fig. 10.1), fol. 87r. Paris, Bibliothèque nationale de France, Vélins 100. Courtesy of: Paris, Bibliothèque nationale de France.   219

10.3 Adam receives the forbidden fruit. *Historiarum veteris instrumenti et Apocalypsis icones ad vivum expressae*, Paris, [François Regnault], 1538, 8° (USTC 147431), sig. a3r. Paris, Bibliothèque de la Société d'histoire du Protestantisme francais, André 246. Courtesy of: Paris, Sociètè d'histoire du Protestantisme francais.   224

10.4 Adam and Eve chased out of the garden of Eden. *Historiarum veteris instrumenti* (see Fig. 10.3), sig. a4r. Paris, Bibliothèque de la Société d'histoire du Protestantisme francais, André 246. Courtesy of: Paris, Sociètè d'histoire du Protestantisme francais.   225

10.5 The illustration of Ruth 1 with incorrect heading. *Historiarum veteris instrumenti* (see Fig. 10.3), sig. e8v. Paris, Bibliothèque de la Société d'histoire du Protestantisme francais, André 246. Courtesy of: Paris, Sociètè d'histoire du Protestantisme francais.   227

10.6 The forgotten illustration related to Ex. 1. *Historiarum veteris instrumenti* (see Fig. 10.3), sig. []1r. Paris, Bibliothèque de la Société d'histoire du Protestantisme francais, André 246. Courtesy of: Paris, Sociètè d'histoire du Protestantisme francais.   229

11.1 Proof sheets showing the first stage of corrections of *Pjsně duchownj ewangelistské*, [Ivančice, Tiskárna bratrská — printer of Czech Brothers], 1572, 8° (USTC 568910). Brno, Moravský zemský archiv, Fond G 21 Staré tisky, sign. II/181, fols 9v, 16r. Courtesy of: Brno, Moravský zemský archiv.   240

11.2 Cibulka's signature on the title-page of Jan Blahoslav, *Musica*, [Ivančice, Tiskárna bratrská—printer of Czech Brothers], 1569, 8° (USTC 567053). Wrocław University Library, 330760. Courtesy of: Wrocław, University Library.   243

11.3 Cibulka's corrections in *Musica* (see Fig. 11.2), fol.11r. Wrocław University Library, 330760. Courtesy of: Wrocław, University Library.   244

12.1 *Lamed*-ascender and absent *sheva* below the *shin* in the line above. *Shmuel Bukh*, Augsburg, [Schwarz], 1544, 4° (not in USTC), fol. 5v,

v. 64. Munich, Bayerische Staatsbibliothek, A.hebr.1070 u#Beibd.1. Courtesy of: Munich, Bayerische Staatsbibliothek.   253

12.2 *Gimel*-descender and partial *qamats. Shmuel Bukh* (see Fig. 12.1), fol. 2*r*, v. 5. Munich, Bayerische Staatsbibliothek, A.hebr.1070 u#Beibd.1. Courtesy of: Munich, Bayerische Staatsbibliothek.   253

12.3 Two types of *gimel* in 'Agag King of Amalek'. *Shmuel Bukh* (see Fig. 12.1), fol. 16*v*, v. 270. New York, YIVO Institute for Jewish Research Library, Rare Book Collection, Augsburg 1544 (photocopy). Courtesy of: New York, YIVO Institute for Jewish Research Library.   253

12.4 Two square *gimel* in 'Agag' and one *mashket gimel* in 'King'. *Shmuel Bukh*, Kraków, Prostitz, 1593, 4° (not in USTC), fol. 1*v*, v. 17. 20. Vienna, Österreichishe Nationalbibliothek, 20. H. 27. ALT PRUNK. Courtesy of: Vienna, Österreichishe Nationalbibliothek.   257

15.1 Johannes Regiomontanus, *Kalendarium* [Latin], Nuremberg, Johannes Regiomontanus, c. 1474, 4° (ISTC iroo092000), sigs [a1]*v*–[a2]*r*. Munich, Bayerische Staatsbibliothek, 4 Inc.s.a. 1552. Courtesy of: Munich, Bayerische Staatsbibliothek.   298

15.2 Johannes Regiomontanus, *Ephemerides [1475–1506]*, Nuremberg, Johannes Regiomontanus, 1474, 4° (ISTC iroo104500), sigs [a2]*v*–[a3]*r*. Munich, Bayerische Staatsbibliothek, Rar. 299. Courtesy of: Munich, Bayerische Staatsbibliothek.   298

15.3 Regiomontanus, *Ephemerides* (see Fig. 15.2), sig. [a2]*r*. Munich, Bayerische Staatsbibliothek, Rar. 299. Courtesy of: Munich, Bayerische Staatsbibliothek.   299

15.4 Imposition problem for the December 1484 aspects page in Regiomontanus, *Ephemerides* (see Fig. 15.2). BSB (1) for December 1483, partly corrected by owner to correspond to December 1484 (left); BSB (2) for December 1484 (right). Munich, Bayerische Staatsbibliothek, 4 L.impr.c.n.mss.74 and Rar. 299. Courtesy of: Munich, Bayerische Staatsbibliothek.   307

15.5 Two hands for the glossed instructions, planetary positions, July 1498 in Regiomontanus, *Ephemerides* (see Fig. 15.2). Hand A, Leipzig BSM (above); Hand B, Padua (below). Leipzig, Deutsches Buch- und Schriftmuseum der Deutschen Nationalbibliothek, Klemm-Sammlung, II 24,5a; Padua, Biblioteca Universitaria, Sec. XV 544. Courtesy of: Leipzig, Deutsches Buch- und Schriftmuseum der Deutschen Nationalbibliothek, and Padua, Biblioteca Universitaria.   308

15.6 Second differences of daily printed lunar longitudes, 30 April to 18 August 1475. Courtesy of: Richard L. Kremer.   311 xviii   LIST OF ILLUSTRATIONS

15.7   Positions for January 1502 in Regiomontanus, *Ephemerides* (see Fig. 15.2), emending a printed '5' to a manuscript '4' but for the incorrect date. The 10-minute correction is needed for the 4th of the month, not the 3rd. Munich, Bayerische Staatsbibliothek, Rar. 299. Courtesy of: Munich, Bayerische Staatsbibliothek.   312

15.8   Positions for January 1485 in Regiomontanus, *Ephemerides* (see Fig. 15.2). Budapest ELTE 'uncorrected' (left); Madrid 'corrected' (right). Budapest, ELTE University Library and Archives, Inc. 815; Madrid, Patrimonio Nacional, Real Biblioteca, i/210. Courtesy of: Budapest, ELTE University Library and Archives, and Madrid, Patrimonio Nacional, Real Biblioteca.   313

15.9   Eclipse page for 1485 in Regiomontanus, *Ephemerides* (see Fig. 15.2). Budapest ELTE 'uncorrected' (left); BSB (2) 'corrected' (right). Budapest, ELTE University Library and Archives, Inc. 815; Munich, BSB Rar. 299. Courtesy of: Budapest, ELTE University Library and Archives, and Munich, Bayerische Staatsbibliothek.   313

15.10   Individual errors by year. Note the decline, after 1494, in errors unrelated to the Moon. Courtesy of: Richard L. Kremer.   316

15.11   Seeking Regiomontanus's computational algorithm for lunar positions, 1–23 January 1475. Courtesy of: Richard L. Kremer.   318

15.12   Knife-and-pen correction for 30 June 1483, in an 'uncorrected' copy of Regiomontanus, *Ephemerides* (see Fig. 15.2). Vatican City, Biblioteca Apostolica Vaticana, Stamp.Ross. 1947. Courtesy of: Vatican City, Biblioteca Apostolica Vaticana.   319

16.1   Gaza's translation of Aristotle's *Historia*, 610b3-7. MS Vatican City, Biblioteca Apostolica Vaticana, Vat. lat. 2094, fol. 135r, ll. 18–22. Courtesy of: Vatican City, Biblioteca Apostolica Vaticana.   327

16.2   Aristoteles, *De animalibus*, Venice, Johannes de Colonia and Johannes Manthen, 1476, f° (ISTC ia00973000), sig. n2v, ll. 3–6. Munich, Bayerische Staatsbibliothek, 2 Inc.c.a. 448 m. Courtesy of: Munich, Bayerische Staatsbibliothek.   328

16.3.a–b   Aristoteles and Theophrastus, *De natura animalium* [...] *De historia plantarum*, Venice, Aldo Manuzio, 1504, f° (USTC 810,862), fol. 47r and sig. a4r. Vienna, Österreichische Nationalbibliothek, 22.L.2 ALT PRUNK. Courtesy of: Vienna, Österreichische Nationalbibliothek.   329

16.4.a–b   Similar execution of *mu* and *beta* in MS Vatican City, Biblioteca Apostolica Vaticana, Vat. gr. 1339, a: 'ἐκ μὲν τῆς' ('from the'), fol. 109v, l. 16; b: 'ἀποβάλλειν' ('to throw away'), ibid., l. 10. Courtesy of: Vatican City, Biblioteca Apostolica Vaticana.   336

LIST OF ILLUSTRATIONS xix

17.1 This marginal correction to Gessner's *Nomenclator* is by the author. Where he had written that frogs were viviparous, he changes this to oviparous in the margin. Conrad Gessner, *Nomenclator aquatilium animantium*, Zurich, Christoph Froschauer, 1560, f° (USTC 678237), p. 117. Zurich, Zentralbibliothek, NNN 44, 3. Courtesy of: Zurich, Zentralbibliothek. 354

17.2 In his working copy, Gessner notes problems in his figure of the opossum, drawn from André Thevet. Conrad Gessner, *Icones animalium quadrupedum viviparorum et oviparorum*, Zurich, Christoph Froschauer, 1560, f° (USTC 6649365), p. 127. Zurich, Zentralbibliothek, NNN 44/F. Courtesy of: Zurich, Zentralbibliothek. 355

17.3 The feet are wrongly depicted in Gessner's image of a merops (bee-eater), as his note indicates. Conrad Gessner, *Icones avium omnium, quae in historia avium Conradi Gesneri describuntur*, Zurich, Christoph Froschauer, 1560, f° (USTC 6649378), p. 98. Zurich, Zentralbibliothek, NNN 44, 2. Courtesy of: Zurich, Zentralbibliothek. 357

17.4 Gessner indicates that his image of a semivulpa (fox-ape) does not match the description in his text. Gessner, *Icones animalium* (see Fig. 17.2), p. 90. Zurich, Zentralbibliothek, NNN 44/F. Courtesy of: Zurich, Zentralbibliothek. 358

17.5 This image vividly records Gessner's struggle to provide an accurate image of the civet. Gessner, *Icones animalium* (see Fig. 17.2), p. 72. Zurich, Zentralbibliothek, NNN 44/F. Courtesy of: Zurich, Zentralbibliothek 360

17.6 In the *additiones* to his *Icones animalium* (see Fig. 17.2), p. 126, Gessner gives a second, improved image of the civet, but remarks that it too is imperfect. Zurich, Zentralbibliothek, NNN 44/F. Courtesy of: Zurich, Zentralbibliothek. 361

17.7 Gessner included this image of a lynx in the text of the *Icones animalium* (see Fig. 17.2), p. 74, though he considered its face inaccurate. Zurich, Zentralbibliothek, NNN 44/F. Courtesy of: Zurich, Zentralbibliothek. 363

17.8 This improved image of the lynx, supplied by John Caius, found its place in Gessner's additions to the *Icones animalium* (see Fig. 17.2), p. 127. Zurich, Zentralbibliothek, NNN 44/F. Courtesy of: Zurich, Zentralbibliothek. 364

18.1 Title-page of Garcilaso de la Vega, *Obras con Anotaciones de Fernando de Herrera*, Alonso de la Barrera, Seville, 1580, 4° (USTC 336,469). Ann Arbor (MI), University of Michigan Library, PQ 6391 .A1 1580. Courtesy of: Ann Arbor (MI), University of Michigan Library. 372

LIST OF ILLUSTRATIONS

18.2.a–c In-house corrections in de la Vega, *Obras* (see Fig. 18.1). a: p. 504 [i.e., 405]. Madrid, Biblioteca Nacional de España, U/1110. b–c: pp. 504 [i.e., 405] and 359. Madrid, Biblioteca Histórica Marqués de Valdecilla, Universidad Complutense, FLL 26159. Courtesy of: Madrid, Biblioteca Nacional de España and Biblioteca Histórica Marqués de Valdecilla, Universidad Complutense.   375

18.3.a–c In-house corrections in de la Vega, *Obras* (see Fig. 18.1). a: p. 34. Madrid, Biblioteca Nacional de España, R/5384. b: p. 255. Madrid, Biblioteca Nacional de España R/30901. c: p. 376, Madrid, Biblioteca Histórica Marqués de Valdecilla, Universidad Complutense, FLL 26159. Courtesy of: Madrid, Biblioteca Nacional de España and Biblioteca Histórica Marqués de Valdecilla, Universidad Complutense.   376

18.4 A reader's correction in de la Vega, *Obras* (see Fig. 18.1), p. 376. Madrid, Biblioteca Nacional de España, R/5063. Courtesy of: Madrid, Biblioteca Nacional de España.   378

19.1 Beginning of the musical setting for Chapter 1 in the second edition of Christopher Tye, *The Actes of the Apostles, translated into Englyshe Metre*, London, William Seres, 1553, 8° (USTC 504928 and 504886). London, British Library, K.4.c.4. Courtesy of: London, British Library.   389

19.2 Beginning of the musical setting for Chapter 2 in the first edition of Christopher Tye, *The Actes of the Apostles, translated into Englyshe Metre*, London, William Seres, 1553, 8° (USTC 504933). Cambridge, Cambridge University Library, Syn.8.55.85. Courtesy of: Cambridge, Cambridge University Library.   391

19.3 Beginning of the musical setting for Chapter 3 in the first edition of Tye, *The Actes of the Apostles* (see Fig. 19.2). Cambridge, Cambridge University Library, Syn.8.55.85. Courtesy of: Cambridge, Cambridge University Library.   392

19.4 Beginning of the musical setting for Chapter 3 in Tye, *The Actes of the Apostles*, second edition (see Fig. 19.1). London, British Library, G.12146. Courtesy of: Cambridge, Cambridge University Library.   396

20.1 The 'Nursery' Copy of Shakespeare First Folio, p. 86 (misnumbered as p. 88). Hand 1 deletes 'Erotes', adds 'Seracuse' above, and places 'Se' after 'Dromio'. On this page, the same hand adds an 'E:' to all the speech prefixes of Antipholus, presumably for 'Erotes'. Realising that 'E:' was ambiguous and would be confused with 'Ephesus', Hand 1 deleted 'E:' and added 'S', presumably for 'Syracuse'. Edinburgh, Edinburgh University Library, EUL JY 438. Courtesy of: Edinburgh, Edinburgh University, Centre for Research Collections.   405

20.2 The 'Nursery' Copy of Shakespeare First Folio, p. 88. Hand 1 substituted 'Errotis' with 'Seracus:' and also added 'E:' to all the speech prefixes related to Antipholus (of Syracuse). Realising the mistake, Hand 1 either wrote 'S' over 'E:' or deleted 'E:' and wrote 'S' next to it. Edinburgh, Edinburgh University Library, EUL JY 438. Courtesy of: Edinburgh, Edinburgh University, Centre for Research Collections. 406

21.1 Thomas Dekker, *Satiro-mastix*, London, Edward White, 1602, 4° (USTC 3000771), sig. A4*v*. Austin, The Harry Ransom Center, University of Texas, Wh D39 602s WRE. Courtesy of: Austin, The Harry Ransom Center, University of Texas. 416

21.2 Anon., *The Raigne of King Edward the Third*, London, [Thomas Scarlet] for Cuthbert Burby, 1596, 4° (USTC 513018) = Q1 *Edward III*, sig. E1*v*. Washington, DC, Folger Shakespeare Library, STC 7501. Courtesy of: Washington, DC, Folger Shakespeare Library. 422

21.3 Anon., *The Raigne of King Edward the Third*, London, Simon Stafford for Cuthbert Burby, 1599, 4° (USTC 513866) = Q2 *Edward III*, sig. I1*r*. Washington, DC, Folger Shakespeare Library, STC 7502. Courtesy of: Washington DC, Folger Shakespeare Library. 425

22.1 Woodcut of 'The Soul kneeling before the Christ Child nailed to the Tree of the Cross' converted into 'Amor piercing the Child's Side' through details added by hand in this copy of *Van die gheestlike Kintscheÿt ihesu ghemoraliseert*, Antwerp, Gerard Leeu, 16 Feb. 1488, 8° (ISTC ik00022000), sig. n1*v*. The drawn emendations are partly concealed by the red paint. The Hague, Koninklijke Bibliotheek, 150 F 10. Courtesy of: The Hague, Koninklijke Bibliotheek. 436

22.2 Woodcut of 'The Soul kneeling before the Christ Child nailed to the Tree of the Cross' at the start of the final prayer of the Soul to the Child in *Van die gheestlike Kintscheÿt ihesu ghemoraliseert* (see Fig. 22.1), sig. o1*v*. The Hague, Koninklijke Bibliotheek, 150 F 10. Courtesy of: The Hague, Koninklijke Bibliotheek. 437

22.3 Woodcut of 'The Soul kneeling before the Christ Child nailed to the Tree of the Cross' converted into 'Amor piercing the Child's Side' in a copy of *Van die gheestlike Kintscheÿt ihesu ghemoraliseert* (see Fig. 22.1), sig. n1*v*. The details added by hand are fully visible. Washington, DC, Library of Congress, Incun. 1488 .V3. Courtesy of: Washington, DC, Library of Congress. 438

22.4 Woodcut of 'Amor piercing the Christ Child's side' in a copy of *Van die gheestlike Kintscheÿt ihesu ghemoraliseert* (see Fig. 22.1), sig. n1*v*. Gouda, Streekarchief Midden-Holland, 2306 G 5. Courtesy of: Gouda, Streekarchief Midden-Holland. 439

22.5 In-house correction in a copy of the *Boeck vanden leven Jhesu Christi*, Antwerp, Gerard Leeu, 3 Nov. 1487, f° (ISTC il00353000), sig. kk1*r*.

| | Maastricht, Stadsbibliotheek, 6000 E 6. Courtesy of: Maastricht, Stadsbibliotheek. | 442 |

23.1 A raised type in the middle of the page preventing the ink from reaching the adjacent types. Note also the imperfect register in the last line. *La rapresentatione di santa Agata vergine & martire. Nuouamente ristampata*, Florence, 1558, 4° (PT00000067; USTC 801089), sig. A6*v*. Venice, Fondazione Giorgio Cini, FOAN TES 1061. Courtesy of: Venice, Fondazione Giorgio Cini. — 453

23.2 Inked shoulders are particularly marked on the last two letters of 'rapresentatione' and 'vergine'. Most probably, the sheet was slightly moved during printing, leaving a sort of double impression (smudged types). The woodcut is also crooked. *La rapresentatione di santa Agata* (see Fig. 23.1), sig. A1*r*. Venice, Giorgio Cini Foundation, FOAN TES 1061. Courtesy of: Venice, Fondazione Giorgio Cini. — 456

23.3 The ink bled from the recto giving a dirty aspect to the page. The margin on the left side shows an inked smudge running along the text. *La rapresentatione di santa Agata* (see Fig. 23.1), sig. A1*v*. Venice, Giorgio Cini Foundation, FOAN TES 1061. Courtesy of: Venice, Fondazione Giorgio Cini. — 457

24.1 Pagination inserted upside down in *Vom 31 Marty. Fol. 201 Die Europäische RELATION No 26 1693*, [Altona, Anna de Löw and Heinrich Heuss, 1693], 4° (USTC N214-4305), p. 208. Courtesy of: Bremen, Staats- und Universitätsbibliothek. — 466

24.2 Example of a misplaced type in the *Europaeische Zeitung* from 5 February 1684. — 467

24.3.a–b Varying type sizes in the main body of text in a newspaper issue from 1620. Courtesy of: Bremen, Staats- und Universitätsbibliothek. — 468

24.4 Mistakes on a title-page of Hake's newspaper. Courtesy of: Bremen, Staats-und Universitätsbibliothek. — 472

24.5 Gabelkover's corrections to the proof sheets of the *Zeittung*. Courtesy of: Bremen, Staats- und Universitätsbibliothek. — 477

A.1 The printing press and the forme. Courtesy of: Raikhan Musrepova. — 483

LIST OF CONTRIBUTORS

Pablo Alvarez is Curator at the Special Collections Research Center, University of Michigan Library.

Ilaria Andreoli is Scientific Coordinator at the Institut National d'Histoire de l'Art, Paris, and Lecturer in History and Techniques of Book Illustration at the University of Normandy, Caen.

Claire Bolton is a printer and an independent scholar who lives between Australia and the UK.

Laura Carnelos is Library Curator of Early Modern Books and Manuscripts, Eton College Library.

Marta Celati is Senior Researcher in Medieval and Humanist Literature at the University of Pisa.

Matthew Day is Deputy Dean for Research and Innovation of the Faculty of Arts, Humanities and Social Sciences, Anglia Ruskin University.

Geri Della Rocca de Candal is a bank consultant and independent scholar based in Milan.

Anna Dlabačová is an Assistant Professor at the Centre for the Arts in Society, Leiden University.

François Dupuigrenet Desroussilles is Professor of Medieval and Early Modern Christian History, Florida State University.

Caroline Duroselle-Melish is Associate Librarian for Collection Care and Development and Andrew W. Mellon Curator of Early Modern Books and Prints at the Folger Shakespeare Library.

Roger Gaskell is an antiquarian bookseller based in the UK.

Anthony Grafton is Henry Putnam University Professor of History, Princeton University.

Anne Heminger is Assistant Professor of Music, The University of Tampa.

Randall Herz is Lecturer at the Institut für Fremdsprachen und Auslandskunde, Erlangen.

xxiv   LIST OF CONTRIBUTORS

Jan Hillgärtner is an independent scholar based in Leiden.

Dirk Imhof is Curator of Rare Books and Archives at the Plantin-Moretus Museum, Antwerp.

Richard L. Kremer is Professor Emeritus of History at Dartmouth College.

Alice Leonard is a Permanent Research Fellow at the Centre for Arts, Memory and Communities, Coventry University.

Amy Lidster is Departmental Lecturer in English Language and Literature, University of Oxford.

James Misson is a Reseacher for the Oxford English Dictionary.

Paolo Sachet is Ambizione Fellow at the Institut d'histoire de la Réformation, University of Geneva.

Pavel Sládek is Associate Professor of Hebrew and Jewish Studies, Charles University, Prague.

Veronika Sladká is Researcher of Book History in the Department of the Historical Bibliography, Czech Academy of Sciences Library.

Grigory Vorobyev is a Postdoctoral Researcher at Ghent University.

Rachel Wamsley is an independent scholar based in Jerusalem.

INTRODUCTION

GERI DELLA ROCCA DE CANDAL,
ANTHONY GRAFTON, AND PAOLO SACHET

THE kingdom of error in early modern Europe was as vividly real as the Kingdom of Satan. It was located not in the bowels of the earth but on its surface, in the shops of printers. The most learned and painstaking writers, printers, and correctors found themselves constantly embroiled, like modern Laocoons, in struggles with error-ridden copy, type, proofs, and finished books. 'I am learning', Balthasar Moretus wrote in 1602 to his favourite author, Justus Lipsius, 'that if error is the normal condition in any area, it is certainly so in correcting printed books'.[1] Even extraordinary efforts could not prevent mistakes from taking place. In the 1730s, the engraver John Pine set out to produce an edition of Horace that would be not only handsome, but impeccable. Following precedents that had been adopted in Asia for quite different reasons, he took the text of a 1701 edition by James Talbot, one of Richard Bentley's many enemies at Trinity College, Cambridge, and engraved each page, to prevent the errors caused by the use of moveable type.[2] As Pine explained in his short preface,

> The form of printing carried out with fixed letters cut into brass plates is more handsome than that produced by moveable metal type. It also has another advantage: so long as the plates are engraved without errors, whatever they depict on the paper must be immaculately corrected. The course of events in the printing house is different. There, while the press is being worked, letters are commonly pushed down or fall out.[3]

[1] Balthasar Moretus to Justus Lipsius, 12 February 1602, Antwerp, Museum Plantin-Moretus, Arch. 12, fols 198, 14: 'et si usquam in re alia, in typographica hac correctione labi hominis proprium esse disco.'
[2] Pine followed the text in *Quinti Horatii Flacci Opera ad optimorum exemplarium fidem recognita*, ed. J. Tabot, Cambridge, 1701. Talbot's first edition appeared 1699. On Talbot, see R. Unwin, '"An English Writer on Music": James Talbot, 1664–1708', *The Galpin Society Journal*, 40, 1987, pp. 53–72. Though Bentley did not see Talbot's edition as significant, it was certainly better than one of its competitors, the edition published in 1701 by William Baxter, whose many errors drew the ire of John Locke. See F. Waldmann, 'Locke, Horace and a *Syllabus Errorum*', *Locke Studies*, 15, 2015, pp. 3–29.
[3] *Quinti Horatii Flacci Opera*, 2 vols, London, 1733–1737, I, sig. b1r: 'Impressio, quam characteres immobiles aeneis tabulis incisi faciunt, eam ex metallicis typis mobilibus ductam non solum nitore superat: sed illud commodi etiam habet, ut, modo tabulae sine mendis sint insculptae, quidquid per easdem in charta repraesentatur, non possit esse non perquam emendatum; cum in typographia aliter eveniat, ubi, dum prelum exercetur, literae haud raro aut deprimuntur, aut intercidunt.'

Geri Della Rocca de Candal, Anthony Grafton, and Paolo Sachet, *Introduction*. In: *Printing and Misprinting*. Edited by Geri Della Rocca de Candal, Anthony Grafton, and Paolo Sachet, Oxford University Press. © Geri Della Rocca de Candal, Anthony Grafton, and Paolo Sachet (2023). DOI: 10.1093/oso/9780198863045.003.0001

This project evoked immense enthusiasm. The Prince of Wales and throngs of noblemen subscribed to the first volume, the Kings of England and France to the second, and the finished book was very handsome. Unfortunately, however, Homer nodded. Pine illustrated his edition with fine images of many antiquities. In reproducing a Roman coin, he slipped and engraved 'POST EST' in place of 'POTEST'. The error had to be corrected in a second impression.[4]

'To err is human'. As a material and mechanical process, as an effort to give old and new texts a permanent, reliable, and accessible form, early printing made no exception to this general rule. Conventional wisdom treats printing as a technological triumph that spread freedom and knowledge. In fact, the history of the book is largely a story of errors and adjustments. Mistakes of many kinds regularly crept in while texts were transferred from manuscript to printed forms, and various emendation strategies were adopted when printers and their workers spotted them. In practice, the 'Gutenberg galaxy' turned into something like a black hole which sucked texts in and mangled them. Publishers, editors, and authors reacted to these failures in highly creative ways. They aimed at impeccability in both style and contents, developed time- and money-efficient ways to cope with mistakes, and soon came to link formal accuracy with authoritative and reliable information. Most of these features remained standard in the publishing industry until present days, despite such worrying recent developments as the decline of copy-editing and the spread of 'fake news'. Yet none of these strategies functioned perfectly: control and correction not only prevented, but generated errors.

In spite of its pervasiveness, early modern misprinting has so far received only passing mentions in scholarship and it has never been treated together with proofreading in a systematic way. Even specialised manuals — from McKerrow, Bowers, Haebler, and Gaskell up to Greetham and Tanselle — refrained from describing the causes and types of errors in detail.[5] In recent times, a few bibliographers, including Lotte Hellinga, Neil Harris, Randall McLeod, Edoardo Barbieri, A. S. G. Edwards, and Ann Blair, have started working on specific issues. Room remains, however, for a comprehensive account.

In-house correction has benefited from a slightly higher degree of attention, though the procedures used in printing shops have often been idealised as smooth and consistent. While the two most authoritative and recent companions to the book world adopt a novel global perspective and offer up-to-date insights into economic, social, and didactic aspects of printing, they include only short entries on cancel, erasure, errata, manuscript corrections, overprinting, and proofs.[6]

---

[4] See the online entry, '*Monumentum aere perennius*: John Pine's Horace', University of Missouri, https://library.missouri.edu/specialcollections/exhibits/show/engraved/horace, accessed 30 September 2022.

[5] R. B. McKerrow, *An Introduction to Bibliography for Literary Students*, Oxford, 1927; F. Bowers, *Principles of Bibliographical Description*, Princeton, 1949; K. Haebler, *The Study of Incunabula*, transl. L. E. Osborne, New York, 1933 (originally published in German in 1925 and 1932); P. Gaskell, *A New Introduction to Bibliography*, Oxford, 1972; D. C. Greetham, *Textual Scholarship: An Introduction*, New York, 1992; G. T. Tanselle, *Descriptive Bibliography*, Charlottesville (VA), 2020.

[6] M. F. Suarez and H. Woudhuysen (eds), *The Oxford Companion to the Book*, Oxford, 2010; L. Howsam (ed.), *The Cambridge Companion to the History of the Book*, Cambridge, 2015. D. Duncan and A. Smyth (eds), *Book Parts*, Oxford, 2019, includes A. Smyth, 'Errata Lists', pp. 251–61,

More often than not, scholars have concentrated on the people involved and their efforts to impose new standards of usage and style, rather than on their methods for dealing with typographical and textual mistakes. Percy Simpson's *Proof-Reading in the Sixteenth, Seventeenth and Eighteenth Centuries* (1935, repr. 1970 and 1976), a rich if chaotic array of anecdotes of and about correctors, exemplifies the first tendency. In indispensable studies, D. F. McKenzie, David McKitterick, George Hoffman, Paolo Trovato, and Brian Richardson have traced the links between correction and the social history of texts and languages, especially for English, French, and Italian literatures in the early modern period.[7] One of the editors of this Companion has treated the attitudes and practices of learned *correctores* in some detail. But he also points out that many unresolved problems await further investigation, notably outside the market for scholarly books.[8]

Misprinting and correction are far from being as well integrated in book studies and intellectual history as they are, for example, in classical and medieval philology.[9] Literary scholars, in particular, have studied textual mistakes as well as efforts to correct them.[10] Recent books by Alice Leonard, one of the contributors to this volume, Adam Smyth, and Jennifer Richards provide further illumination, taking new paths from the narrower view championed by such pioneers as Fredson Bowers, Charlton Hinman, and W. W. Greg, who examined errors because they were useful for reconstructing an *Urtext*.[11]

Textual and non-textual misprints and corrections, after all, are not obviously attractive topics. Often, those who have studied them have been inspired to do so by stumbling on or reading about an individual case. Yet there are millions of the former and thousands

---

while S. Werner, *Studying Early Printed Books, 1450–1800: A Practical Guide*, Hoboken (NJ), 2019, briefly discusses 'Corrections and Changes' at pp. 61–4.

[7] D. F. McKenzie, *Bibliography and the Sociology of Texts*, Cambridge, 1999; D. F. McKenzie, *Making Meaning: 'Printers of the Mind' and Other Essays*, ed. P. D. McDonald and M. F. Suarez, Amherst (MA), 2002; D. McKitterick, *Print, Manuscript and the Search for Order, 1450–1830*, Cambridge, 2013; G. Hoffman, 'Writing Without Leisure: Proofreading as Labour in the Renaissance', *The Journal of Medieval and Renaissance Studies*, 25, 1995, pp. 17–31; P. Trovato, *Con ogni diligenza corretto: la stampa e le revisioni editoriali dei testi letterari italiani, 1470–1570*, Bologna, 1991; B. Richardson, *Printing, Writers and Readers in Renaissance Italy*, Cambridge, 1999. For broader overviews, see, among others, F. Janssen, 'Authors Want to Read Proofs! From Erasmus to Schopenhauer', *Bulletin du Bibliophile*, 1, 2012, pp. 33–50 and C. Clavería Laguarda, *Los correctores: tipos duros en imprentas antiguas*, Zaragoza, 2019.

[8] A. Grafton, *The Culture of Correction in Renaissance Europe*, London, 2011 and A. Grafton, *Inky Fingers: The Making of Books in Early Modern Europe*, Cambridge (MA), 2020.

[9] See, e.g., S. Timpanaro, *La genesi del metodo del Lachmann*, Florence, 1963 (new edn. Turin, 2010); B. Cerquiglini, *Éloge de la variante: Histoire critique de la philologie*, Paris, 1989; G. Most (ed.), *Editing Texts/Texte edieren*, Göttingen, 1998; C. Macé, *Textual Scholarship*, http://www.textualscholarship.org/ index.html, accessed 30 September 2022. Also see: P. Trovato, *Everything you Always Wanted to Know About Lachmann's Method: A Non-Standard Handbook of Genealogical Textual Criticism in the Age of Post-Structuralism, Cladistics, and Copy-Text*, rev. edn, Padua, 2017.

[10] See J. McGann, *A Critique of Modern Textual Criticism*, Chicago and London, 1983 (rev. edn. Charlottesville (VA), 1992); J. Loewenstein, *Ben Jonson and Possessive Authorship*, Cambridge, 2002; and S. Lerer, *Error and the Academic Self: The Scholarly Imagination, Medieval to Modern*, New York, 2002. Cf. also J. Ziolkowski, 'Metaphilology', *Journal of English and Germanic Philology*, 104/2, 2005, pp. 239–72.

[11] A. Leonard, *Error in Shakespeare: Shakespeare in Error*, London, 2020; A. Smyth, *Material Texts in Early Modern England*, Cambridge, 2018; J. Richards, *Voice and Books in the English Renaissance: A New History of Reading*, Oxford, 2019. On the strengths and drawbacks of the methodology adopted by Bowers, Hinman, and Greg, see G. T. Tanselle, *Bibliographical Analysis: An Historical Introduction*, Cambridge, 2009, pp. 6–30.

of the latter in the products of early printing — 'Saul has slain his thousands, and David his tens of thousands'. Printing multiplied the copies of a given text by the hundreds, but it sprayed out misprints in vastly greater numbers. The traditional systems of correction, many of them inherited from scribes, could not dam the flood of mistakes loosed by the new system of production, or even keep it in bounds. Early printing was not a smooth, modern process, but a barely ordered chaos. Only negligible fractions of these early errors and corrections have so far been identified or studied: less the tip of an iceberg than a single ice cube perched on that tip. Most scholars and students working at any level on early modern books still lack a method for recognising and recording mistakes and publishers' corrections. They often end up overlooking their presence and missing their relevance as sources of information.

This book provides the first comprehensive and interdisciplinary guide to the complex relationships among textual production in print, technical and human errors, and more or less successful attempts at emendation. The twenty-four specialist contributions present new evidence on what we can learn from misprints in relation to publishers' practices, printing and pre-publication procedures, and editorial strategies between 1450 and 1650. They focus on texts, images, and mise-en-page in incunabula, sixteenth- and early seventeenth-century books issued throughout Europe, from the stately creations of humanist printers to humble vernacular pamphlets. Through a series of case studies and comparative analyses, the authors tackle the entire spectrum of errors, their sources, and the ways of dealing with them. Their source material includes manuscripts, proof sheets and printed copies retaining preparatory interventions for new editions; extant copies of a faulty edition which was corrected by the publisher more or less systematically; different faulty editions by the same publisher and/or of the same text; printed errata; and contemporary paratextual material, scholarly correspondence and treatises discussing typographical mistakes and publisher's corrections. A detailed appendix provides the first account of the various misprints and corrections one can encounter while studying books as material objects and vehicle of texts.

The methodology employed in the book combines textual and material bibliography with history of information, scholarship, and ideas. This integrated approach makes possible a well-rounded investigation of the subject and aims at maximum accessibility to non-specialist readers. Its chief innovations take four forms.

1) The extended timespan, embracing the first two centuries of Western printing, is designed to overcome the divisions, traditional in book studies, among manuscripts, incunabula, and later publications. This book treats *editiones principes* and early scientific publications side by side with illustrated sixteenth-century books, Shakespeare's plays, and the precursors of modern newspapers.

2) This volume also attends to genres well outside the classical and vernacular masterpieces that have been the object of most previous studies. It covers examples of religious, scientific, and popular literature, and images, numerals, and music, as well as texts, and broadens our understanding of the practices used in varied provinces of the world of early printing.

3) Another strength of the volume is its geographical and linguistic range. From Spain to Poland, Renaissance Europe is represented in all its magnificent variety of peoples and pursuits, including religious minorities and the eastern parts of the continent.

4) Numerous illustrations, detailed appendices and indexes, and efforts to avoid jargon and refer to evidence in consistent, transparent ways aim to make this book accessible to students as well as scholars.

This collection chiefly addresses academic readers, at both an institutional and an individual level. Still, it is intended as a resource not only for book historians and analytical bibliographers, but also for a broader readership. We hope that it will find users in many institutions, among scholars, librarians, and students interested in classical and early modern literature (from Homer to Shakespeare), religious history (Christianity and Hebraism), art history (book illustrations), history of science (astronomy and zoology), popular culture (devotion and chap books) and information (early gazettes), and the intellectual history of Renaissance Europe.

The chapters are thematically arranged, with each session following an internal chronological order. This ensures maximum clarity and readability. Chapter 1 serves as an introduction. It offers a case study that suggests the range of ways in which error haunted all involved in making books. The chapters in Part I address four technical problems that early modern printers had to deal with, from proofreading to inclusion and arrangement of images. Part II focuses on celebrated humanist printers, active in Florence, Venice, and Antwerp, and their Latin, Greek, and Hebrew books. The various challenges involved in printing sacred texts and related commentaries are examined in Part III, which draws comparisons among the practices of Catholics, Protestants, and Jews. Errors and emendations in astronomical and zoological treatises are fully explored for the first time in Part IV, with special attention to the tables and figures that appear in so many early modern books, but few of which have yet been fully studied.[12] Part V concentrates on vernacular poetry, music, and theatre, three genres which are often characterised by textual fluidity and, especially for music, required complex printing abilities. Finally, Part VI examines the attitudes toward errors and the practices of emendation characteristic of printers of popular literature, ranging from devotional books to early newspapers. Their tendency to value time and productivity over precision and correctness had, on occasion, dramatic results.

The volume ends with two appendices and indexes for subjects and names. Appendix A comprises a glossary detailing for the first time the many cases of misprinting and correction, while Appendix B offers tables of translation of the glossary's entry words into a number of different languages.

As children of Ford and Taylor, we tend to imagine early modern workplaces as orderly, even though well-known documents like Thomas Platter's autobiography and innovative historical works by Natalie Zemon Davis, Robert Darnton, and others should have taught us to know better.[13] The evidence collected and sifted here enables us to understand the texture of working lives in the printer's shop in a new way. Our material shows that in-house quality control was sporadic at best. By studying the problems that arose in the course of

---

[12] For a notable exception see S. Kusukawa, *Picturing the Book of Nature: Image, Text and Argument in Sixteenth-Century Human Anatomy and Medical Botany*, Chicago and London, 2011.

[13] T. Platter, *Lebensbeschreibung*, ed. A. Hartmann, 2nd edn. rev. by U. Dill, Basel, 1999, pp. 119–20, and discussed in Gaskell, *A New Introduction* (n. 5 above), pp. 48–9; N. Zemon Davis, *Society and Culture in Early Modern France: Eight Essays*, Stanford, 1975, Chapter 1; R. Darnton, *The Great Cat Massacre and Other Episodes in French Cultural History*, New York, 1984 (rev. edn., New York, 2009), Chapter 2.

everyday work, we not only see that theory and practice often did not match, but also gain a deeper mastery of the ways in which books were produced.

Many years ago, the eldest editor of this volume met Sir Roger Mynors, appropriately in Duke Humfrey's library. When the subject of errors came up, Sir Roger said that even in the most recent iteration of his OUP edition of Vergil, new typographical errors had appeared. On a visit to the Clarendon Press, he requested an explanation. The press officials produced a compositor, whom Sir Rogers described as a small man with a strong Oxfordshire accent. Asked about the errors, he told a story. He himself had never dared to enter the premises of the Press on Walton Street on a Saturday night. Colleagues who had done so, however, had witnessed pieces of type dancing. Presumably, they had escaped from the locked formes, and some of them had eventually climbed back into the wrong positions. Anyone who hopes to understand the world and work of hand-press printers — and some of their more recent successors — should meditate on this tale.

We are grateful to the OUP editorial team for helping us get this Companion into the best possible shape. Unlike most of our early modern colleagues, we will not blame the printer for the mistakes that might still be found in the book.

CHAPTER 1

FROM COPY TO CANCELS

Matthew Parker and the Quest for Error

ANTHONY GRAFTON

THE NIGHTMARE OF ERROR

ERRORS haunted early modern scholars as well as compositors and pressmen.* But not all errors were treated equally in the courts of learned opinion. In the mid 1530s, Erasmus annoyed Joachim Camerarius. He called attention to the German humanist's historical and metrical errors in a now lost letter to a mutual friend, Helius Eobanus Hessus.[1] Camerarius gave the great man a retort courteous in the form of a short treatise, nicely entitled *Erratum*. Liberally scattering examples across the pages, he showed that all great writers, from antiquity to his own time, had committed errors of usage and fact, ascription and quotation. Erasmus himself had attributed verses to the wrong authors, ascribed anecdotes to the wrong heroes, and detected errors in accurate citations. Still, Camerarius dismissed these as '*erratula*': 'minor errors, which creep past the guard of the greatest scholars when they are not paying attention, especially on great subjects and in long texts'.[2] Like his own slips, they were not the sort of error that should incite scholars to wage war with one another, as the Italian humanists of the late fifteenth century had done.

---

* A tip of the old fedora to Madeline McMahon, Bill Sherman, Jeffrey Todd Knight and my fellow editors, for help of many kinds. The following abbreviations are used: BL = London, British Library; CCCC = Cambridge, Corpus Christi College; LPL = London, Lambeth Palace Library.

[1] See P. Bietenholz and T. Deutscher (eds), *Contemporaries of Erasmus: A Biographical Register of the Renaissance and Reformation*, 3 vols, Toronto, Buffalo (NY), and London, 1985, I, p. 248, s.v. Joachim Camerarius, by I. Guenther. For the metrical error in question see *The Correspondence of Erasmus: Letters 2472 to 2634, April 1531–March 1532*, transl. C. Fantazzi, ed. J. Estes, Toronto, Buffalo (NY) and London, 2018, p. 47, n. 11.

[2] J. Camerarius, 'Erratum, in quo circiter quadraginta loca autorum cum veterum, tum recentium notantur', in *In hoc libello cura et diligentia Ioachimi Camerarii Qu. perfecta, haec insunt*, Nuremberg, Johann Petreius, 1535, 8° (USTC 665810), fol. 17*r–v*, at 17*v*: 'Sunt ista erratula, quae obrepunt doctissimis viris minime animadvertentibus, maximeque adeo in grandi argumento ac longo opere.'

Anthony Grafton, *From Copy to Cancels*. In: *Printing and Misprinting*. Edited by Geri Della Rocca de Candal, Anthony Grafton, and Paolo Sachet, Oxford University Press. © Anthony Grafton (2023). DOI: 10.1093/oso/9780198863045.003.0002

8   PRINTING AND MISPRINTING

Guillaume Budé, by contrast, had made worse mistakes, especially when criticising Cicero and others. One of them particularly irritated Camerarius. In 1518 and 1519 Erasmus and Budé had waged a long epistolary quarrel. At one point, Budé reproached Erasmus for misrepresenting — even fabricating — a passage in an earlier letter from him: 'in quoting the words of my letter, you make out that I put "you say" in the present tense instead of "you will say", as though I had actually invented words from some earlier letter of yours.'[3] In fact, Budé insisted, his original draft showed that he had used a rhetorical figure, setting out what he thought Erasmus might write in a future reply: 'everywhere in my draft it has the future tense "you will say"'.[4] Camerarius mocked this defence unmercifully, using the language of sin, light, and darkness to emphasise the seriousness of this mechanical mistake:

> What sort of thing is it that this immensely brilliant and literate man defends when subjected to insult by Erasmus, claiming that it reads differently, and correctly, in the draft that he has at home? What could have been more trivial or more vulgar than this argument, as though it would not be an *erratum* if a text that reached the light in a faulty form was correct in the shadows? For not only is ignorance a sin, but so is error, negligence, drowsiness, to be fooled, to be led away from the truth in any way. These are all clearly shameful, though some are more dishonourable and shameful than others.[5]

Though Camerarius scented an error in transmission behind Budé's self-defence, a banalising scribal slip made in copying a letter, he took it not as a forgivable *erratulum* but as an ugly example of the deepest scholarly incompetence — the sort of error characteristic of scholars who affected carelessness and spontaneity in their writing.[6] His little treatise amused his friend Eobanus Hessus, but its attacks on celebrities alarmed him: 'Keep away from the one with the black buttocks [a periphrasis for Hercules, i.e. a formidable enemy]', he warned Camerarius.[7] Errors — especially errors for which great men disclaimed responsibility — were a touchy subject. The scholar's duties including taking care to see that his words reached the public in the correct form.

---

[3] *Opus epistolarum Des. Erasmi Roterodami*, ed. P. S. Allen, H. M. Allen, and H. W. Garrod, 12 vols, Oxford, 1906–1958, III, ep. 915, p. 479: 'Illud calumniae plenum pene per oblivionem omisi, quod verba tu epistolae meae repetens, *inquis* in praesenti pro *inquies* scripsisse me confingis: quasi vero scilicet superioris tuae epistolae verba ementitus sim'; translation from *The Correspondence of Erasmus, Volume Six: Letters 842–992 (1518–1519)*, transl. R. A. B. Mynors and D. F. S. Thompson, Toronto and Buffalo (NY), 1982, p. 235.

[4] *Opus epistolarum Erasmi* (n. 3 above), III, p. 459: 'ubique enim inquies in futuro in scheda mea scriptum est'; translation from *Correspondence of Erasmus, Volume Six* (n. 3 above), p. 235.

[5] Camerarius, 'Erratum' (n. 2 above), fol. 18r–v: 'Iam quale est hoc quod suggillante Erasmo sic defendit maximo vir ingenio, & admirabili literarum facultate, ut aliter & recte quidem in autographo quod domi habeat legi affirmet? Quid enim hac argumentatione fieri levius aut vulgarius potuisset? Ac quasi hoc ipsum non erratum fuerit, vitiosum in lucem emissum quod in umbra bene se haberet. Neque enim sola ignoratio peccatum est, sed error etiam, negligentia, oscitantia, falli, quocunque modo abduci a vero, quae profecto sunt turpia omnia, &si est aliud alio inhonestius & magis dedecorosum.'

[6] Ibid., fol. 18v: 'Quare miror quorundam etiam doctorum negligentiae quasi affectationem, iactantium & celeritatem & incuriam suam, & ut dicunt extemporalitatem in scribendo.'

[7] Helius Eobanus Hessus to Joachim Camerarius, 18 July 1535, in Joachim Camerarius, *Narratio de H. Eobano Hesso*, Nuremberg, Johann vom Berg and Ulrich Neuber, 1553, 8° (USTC 676766), sig. M5r: 'Librum tuum nondum satis potui perlegere, aspexi tamen & risi, quod tanta tibi res cum aliorum erratis sit. Vide ne in Melampygum incidas.'

Correction Before Print

No Renaissance scholar hated and feared errors more than Matthew Parker (1504–1575). He spent endless hours hunting them in his manuscripts and the proofs of his books, asked friends for help in rooting them out, and corrected them during and after the process of printing. In doing so, like the distinguished Spanish cleric Benito Arias Montano and the still more distinguished Italian Franciscan Felice Peretti, Pope Sixtus V, he acted as a corrector of the press. Like them, he never worked for a printer: printers worked for him. Parker served as Archbishop of Canterbury from 1559 until his death.[8] In that capacity, he paid a number of London printers — especially John Day — to produce complex and demanding texts: the enormous Bishops' Bible, first printed in 1568 by Richard Jugge; the homilies of Abbot Aelfric of Eynsham; the life of King Alfred ascribed to Asser; the chronicles of Matthew Paris, printed by Reginald Wolfe, and others; and the history of the English church in Latin, entitled *De antiquitate Britannicae ecclesiae*, which bears Parker's name and the date 1572 on its title-page.[9] An impresario of print, Parker seems the opposite of the poor devils of literature who wore out their eyes reading proofs.[10]

Yet Parker spent much of his life on a highly personal effort to find and correct errors, and in doing so he often did correctors' work. His choices of errors to attack help us to understand exactly what constituted errata in the minds of sixteenth-century authors and printers. One of the central tasks that the correctors performed took place long before trial sheets came off the press; it happened when they worked through copy before it was printed, inserting punctuation, correcting spelling, and emending errors, as well as adding the book and chapter divisions and tables of contents that made printed books user-friendly and attractive to buyers. During this process they sometimes discovered and corrected prestigious authors' errors of taste and fact. The correctors in Oporinus's shop in Basel, for example, radically changed the orthography of Theodor Bibliander's chronology when they printed its second edition — so radically that he insisted on attaching corrigenda in which he damned their impertinence and restored the correct spelling of many words.[11]

Parker laboured in the same vineyard, with better results. Between 1570 and 1573, he helped William Lambarde shape his pioneering antiquarian work, *The Perambulation of Kent*. Parker, or a secretary, corrected one manuscript. He also sent a copy to Burghley himself for further correction.[12] Later he sent Burghley a draft of Lambarde's prefatory letter to Thomas Wotton. Lambarde, he explained, 'doth repute it to be imperfect, and worthy

---

[8] On Parker see in general V. J. K. Brook, *A Life of Archbishop Parker*, Oxford, 1962; D. Crankshaw and A. Gillespie, 'Parker, Matthew (1504–1575)', in *Oxford Dictionary of National Biography*, 2004, https://doi.org/10.1093/ref:odnb/21327, accessed 5 June 2020.

[9] For Parker's relations with his printers see E. Evenden, *Patents, Pictures and Patronage: John Day and the Elizabethan Book Trade*, Aldershot, 2008; F. Heal, 'The Bishops and the Printers, Henry VII to Elizabeth', in M. Heale (ed.), *The Prelate in England and Europe, 1300–1560*, Suffolk and Rochester, 2014, pp. 142–69 (142–5).

[10] A. Grafton, *The Culture of Correction in Renaissance Europe*, London, 2011.

[11] Ibid., 155–6. For a more normal instance of correction at this stage, see U. Leu, 'Buchdruck im Dienst der Reformation. Die Zusammenarbeit zwischen dem Zürcher Drucker Christoph Froschauer d. Ä. und den Reformatoren Huldrych Zwingli sowie Heinrich Bullinger', *Bibliothek und Wissenschaft*, 49, 2016, pp. 173–97 (189–92).

[12] M. McMahon, 'Licking the "Beare Whelpe": William Lambarde and Matthew Parker revise the *Perambulation of Kent*', *Journal of the Warburg and Courtauld Institutes*, 81, 2018, pp. 154–71.

of further reformation'.[13] Neither Parker nor Burghley was worried about Lambarde's eminently respectable book, which reserved fierce criticism for the superstitious rituals that had once flourished in Kent, such as the pilgrimage cults of Thomas Becket and the Rood of Boxley.[14] These Elizabethan grandees cultivated their own culture of criticism, apparently for its own sake.

Parker not only corrected others, but also invited correction from them. When he sent Lambarde's *Perambulation* to Burghley, he accompanied it with another, much larger, book: a printed text of his own project, the *De antiquitate ecclesiae Britannicae*.[15] In his covering letter he made clear that, though he had agreed to criticise Lambarde's text, he claimed no superior learning or expertise. In fact, he had also asked Lambarde to serve as 'a judge of some of my small travails' — to correct, that is, some of his writings.[16] The book that he sent Burghley looked complete: it was not only printed but also 'bound by my man', the French binder Jean de Planche.[17] The copy in question, now in Cambridge University Library, is especially splendid. Its illustration of Cambridge is beautifully coloured. Errata have not only been collected in a printed list but also painstakingly corrected by hand in the text.[18]

Yet Parker insisted that the book was not complete. He and Lambarde were both modest authors who had deliberately refused to release their books until they had been sufficiently edited:

> I think the rather we both used this foresight, to suppress our labours in *nonum annum*, as Horace counselleth, rather than to suffer an undigested and tumultuous collection to be gazed on of many folks.[19]

Parker's modesty was genuine, as was his desire for substantive collaboration and correction. Even when he had *De antiquitate* printed, he did not consider it sufficiently free from error to be published, in any conventional sense.[20] As he explained to Burghley, he had not given copies of his book 'to four men in the whole realm, and peradventure [it] shall never come to sight abroad'.[21] Many flaws still required correction — or, perhaps, demanded the destruction of the whole text (the remedy that Horace recommended for fatally

---

[13] M. Parker, *Correspondence*, ed. J. Bruce and T. T. Perowne, Cambridge, 1853, p. 441.

[14] See McMahon, 'Licking the "Beare Whelpe"' (n. 12 above), and A. Grafton, 'From Production to Reception: Reading the *Perambulation*', *Journal of the Warburg and Courtauld Institutes*, 81, 2018, pp. 172–88.

[15] Matthew Parker, *De antiquitate ecclesiae Britannicae & privilegiis ecclesiae Cantuariensis cum Archiepiscopis eiusdem 70*, London, John Day, 1572, f° (USTC 507554).

[16] Parker, *Correspondence* (n. 13 above), p. 435.

[17] Ibid.

[18] E. Evenden and T. Freeman, *Religion and the Book in Early Modern England: The Making of Foxe's 'Book of Martyrs'*, Cambridge, 2011, p. 225. The copy in question is Cambridge, Cambridge University Library, Sel.3.229.

[19] Parker, *Correspondence* (n. 13 above), p. 425, alluding to Horace, *Ars Poetica*, 386–90.

[20] Cf. Cyril Connolly, the dominant critic and editor in London in the thirties and forties, who informed an author that his work 'was good enough to print but not good enough to publish' in his magazine, *Horizon*. J. Maclaren-Ross, *Memoirs of the Forties*, London, 1965, 77–8.

[21] Parker, *Correspondence* (n. 13 above), p. 425.

flawed poems): 'To keep it by me I yet purpose, whiles I live, to add and to amend as occasion shall serve me, or utterly to suppress it and to bren it'.[22]

Error, for Parker as for professional correctors, was a broad category. In this case, he asked Burghley to make a judgment on a question of taste. He loved heraldry, as the famous initials with his arms in the Bishops' Bible made clear. For the *De antiquitate*, he had had a sheet prepared on which the arms of the English dioceses appeared, not only printed but illuminated. Like Horace's author, Parker realised, in the cold light of day and in the context of Puritan criticism of clerical wealth and Papism, that this might occasion criticism, even justified criticism. Accordingly, as he explained, he had had his printer and binder take care to make the leaf in question easy to remove:

> You may note many vanities in my doings, but I thought it not against my profession to express my times, and give some testimony of my fellow-brothers, of such of my coat as were in place in her Majesty's reign, and when I was thus placed; and though ye may rightly blame an ambitious fantasy for setting out our church's arms in colours, yet ye may relinquish the leaf and cast it into the fire, as I have joined it but loose in the book for that purpose, if you so think it meet.[23]

He even told Burghley that 'ye may, if it so please you (without great grief to me) cast the whole book the same way'.[24] 'Nescit vox missa reverti', warned Horace, "a word once spoken cannot be taken back," in the poem to which Parker himself alluded (*Ars poetica* 390). Well instructed, Parker sought Cecil's help to ensure that he would not endure post-publication shaming. In the end, the leaf remained, and Parker distributed a few copies of *De antiquitate* to the good and the great. One, swathed in embroidered velvet and gleaming with gold and silver, went to Queen Elizabeth.[25] But Parker meant what he said when he told Burghley that he was not ready to release the book for wider circulation 'though some men, smelling of the printing it, seem to be very desirous cravers of the same'.[26] The hunt came first.

From Copy Preparation to Textual Criticism

Pre-production error hunting demanded intense and protracted effort, since it involved the detection of mechanical and historical as well as aesthetic errors. Soon after Parker took office, he learned that a scholar who had taught Hebrew at Wittenberg, Matthias Flacius Illyricus, was collecting medieval manuscripts with which to write a Protestant history of the church. Taking advice from a pioneering bibliographer of English writers, John Bale, Parker and his secretaries — above all John Joscelyn — set out to build their own collection

[22] Ibid., p. 426.
[23] Ibid., p. 425.
[24] Ibid.
[25] London, BL, C.24.b.8. See also Heal, 'The Bishops and the Printers' (n. 9 above), p. 143.
[26] Parker, *Correspondence* (n. 13 above), pp. 426–7.

12 PRINTING AND MISPRINTING

of evidence.[27] From this in turn they hoped to draw a history that revealed the purity of the original English church, founded by King Lucius at the end of the second century with the help of Pope Eleutherius; its continuing piety and lack of superstition in the early Middle Ages; and its ruin at the hands of Augustine of Canterbury and other emissaries of Roman corruption — not to mention the Norman rulers of England. Bishops ransacked their cathedral libraries and archives, Parker's secretaries travelled and copied, and soon the floors of Lambeth palace were heaped with insular, Anglo-Saxon, and Anglo-Norman manuscripts, many of them of great splendour.[28]

Parker and his men did more than collect these manuscripts: they corrected them. Some of their notes were purely technical. They added titles and pagination. They assessed age and quality. A codex containing the lives of the hermits Paul and Guthlac bears a declaration in red chalk in Parker's bold, clumsy writing: 'this book was written before the Conquest'.[29] They inserted headnotes that indicated the nature and uses of particular texts. In a manuscript of William of Malmesbury's *History of the Kings of England* now in the Scheide Library in Princeton, as in many others, Parker himself added page numbers in red chalk. Joscelyn noted missing passages and inserted replacements for them, neatly written, in all cases but one, on paper, so that no one could take them for part of the original.[30]

Sometimes they went further. Joscelyn, for example, confronted a curious statement in the Anglo-Saxon Chronicle, as transmitted by a manuscript now in the British Library, Cotton MS Tiberius B IV. After a defeat at the hands of the Britons, the narrative ran, 'then he [Julius Caesar] let his army abide with the Scots'. Jocelyn corrected this obvious historical error with a sharp and elegant note.

> Everything on this leaf is translated word for word from the first two chapters of Bede's *Ecclesiastical History*. But the first author, whoever he was, of this history, seems not to have understood what Bede meant with this Latin idiom: 'he sent his legions off into winter quarters [in Hyberna]'. For this is how he translated them into English: ꝥ þa he forlet his here gebidan mid Scottum, that is, he then allowed his forces or his army to remain in Scotland, that is in Ireland [in Hybernia], whose inhabitants are Scots. The man was fooled by the similarity of the words Hybernia and Hyberna.[31]

---

[27] N. Jones, 'Matthew Parker, John Bale and the Magdeburg Centuriators', *Sixteenth Century Journal*, 12, 1981, pp. 35–49; M. McMahon, 'Matthew Parker and the Practice of Church History', in N. Hardy and D. Levitin (eds), *Confessionalism and Erudition in Early Modern Europe: An Episode in the History of the Humanities*, Oxford, 2020, pp. 116–53.

[28] R. I. Page, *Matthew Parker and His Books*, Kalamazoo (MI), 1993; M. Budny, *Insular, Anglo-Saxon, and Early Anglo-Norman Manuscript Art at Corpus Christi College, Cambridge: An Illustrated Catalogue*, 2 vols, Kalamazoo (MI) and Cambridge, 1997; T. Graham, 'Matthew Parker's Manuscripts: an Elizabethan Library and its Uses', in E. Leedham-Green and T. Webber (eds), *The Cambridge History of Libraries in Britain and Ireland*, 3 vols, Cambridge, 2006, I, pp. 322–41; J. Summit, *Memory's Library: Medieval Books in Early Modern England*, Chicago, 2008, Chapter 3.

[29] CCCC, MS 389, fol. 1r: 'Hic liber scriptus ante conquestum'; quoted by Graham, 'Matthew Parker's Manuscripts' (n. 28 above), p. 333.

[30] Princeton, William H. Scheide Library, Scheide MS 159, pp. 294 ('hic desunt quaedam'), 210 ('et hic quoque desunt nonnulla'), 365 ('hic deest nova historia ad robertum comitem glocestrie. W. Malmesbury').

[31] London, BL, Cotton MS Tiberius B IV, fol. 3v: 'Quae continentur in hoc folio sunt omnia ad verbum translata e primis duobus capitibus ecclesiasticae historiae Bedae. sed autor primus, quisquis fuit,

After Joscelyn had emended this and other manuscripts, he stowed extracts in common-place books, ready for use in the *De antiquitate*.[32] Yet the search for errors and omissions continued in these collections, as Joscelyn compared his extracts and drew new inferences from them.[33] In this case — as in many others — the work done to make a learned book as accurate as possible merged into textual criticism as practiced by the retrospective heroes of modern histories of philology.

THE HUNT FOR DELIBERATE ALTERATIONS

Parker himself searched for every imaginable sort of error in his manuscripts. Mechanical errors that had taken place in their transmission and aesthetic ones that diminished their appeal both bothered him, and he assembled a skilled staff to repair them. Most serious of all, though, were the errors that Parker saw as ideological in origin: they revealed the efforts of corrupt clerics to conceal the true Christian doctrines that the sources had attested. Good clerics, Parker thought, corrected scribal errors to free texts from corruption. Lanfranc, though burdened with duties of state, had 'corrected the texts of the Old and New Testament, which the scribes had corrupted, and published them in an emended and pure form'.[34] Parker drew this account from his manuscript of the *Actus pontificum Cantuariensis ecclesiae* by the twelfth-century Benedictine Gervase of Canterbury.[35]

Other manuscripts in his collection, however, were still disfigured by the sorts of errors that Lanfranc had set right. Worse still, the evidence suggested that these were sometimes deliberate falsifications. The Carolingian theologian Hrabanus Maurus discussed the nature of the sacrament in his treatise *De ecclesiasticis officiis*. Parker owned a manuscript of this text. In the margin of the passage in question, a sixteenth-century reader makes an accusation: 'there is an omission here, which the scribe seems to have made deliberately' (Fig. 1.1).[36]

The missing passage in question has also been entered in the margin above. Parker and his men recorded this discovery for later use. In 1570, they printed an edition of a chronicle compiled originally at St Albans and then extended by many writers, the

---

huius historiae, minime videtur intellexisse hunc apud Bedam latine loquendi modum, scilicet legiones in Hyberna dimisit. nam haec verba in hunc modum facit anglica. ¶ þa he forlet his here gebidan mid Scottum, id est, tum autem permisit ut suae copiae vel suus exercitus remaneret apud scottos, hoc est in Hybernia, cuius incollae sunt Scotti. Similitudo horum verborum Hybernia et Hyberna decepit hominem.'

[32] See McMahon, 'Matthew Parker and the Practice of Church History' (n. 27 above).

[33] E.g., London, BL, Cotton MS Vitellius D. VII, fol. 59*v*: 'Ex superiore Gregorij pontificis Romani epistola quamvis de hoc certum et exploratum habeamus pallium Augustino missum esse ad Londinensem civitatem: non fuisse tamen eam archiepiscoporum primariam sedem ait Willms Malmesburiensis, qui nobis etiam causam reddit, cur Londinium potius quam Doroverniam archipraesul atque honore et praeeminentia decorarit.'

[34] Parker, *De antiquitate* (n. 15 above), p. 97: 'itaque veteris atque novi Testamenti libros, a scriptoribus corruptos correxit, & emendatos atque sinceros aedidit.'

[35] CCCC, MS 438, fol. 229*v*.

[36] CCCC, MS 11, fol. 45*v*, col. 1: 'hic desunt. ex industria ut videtur, scriptoris.'

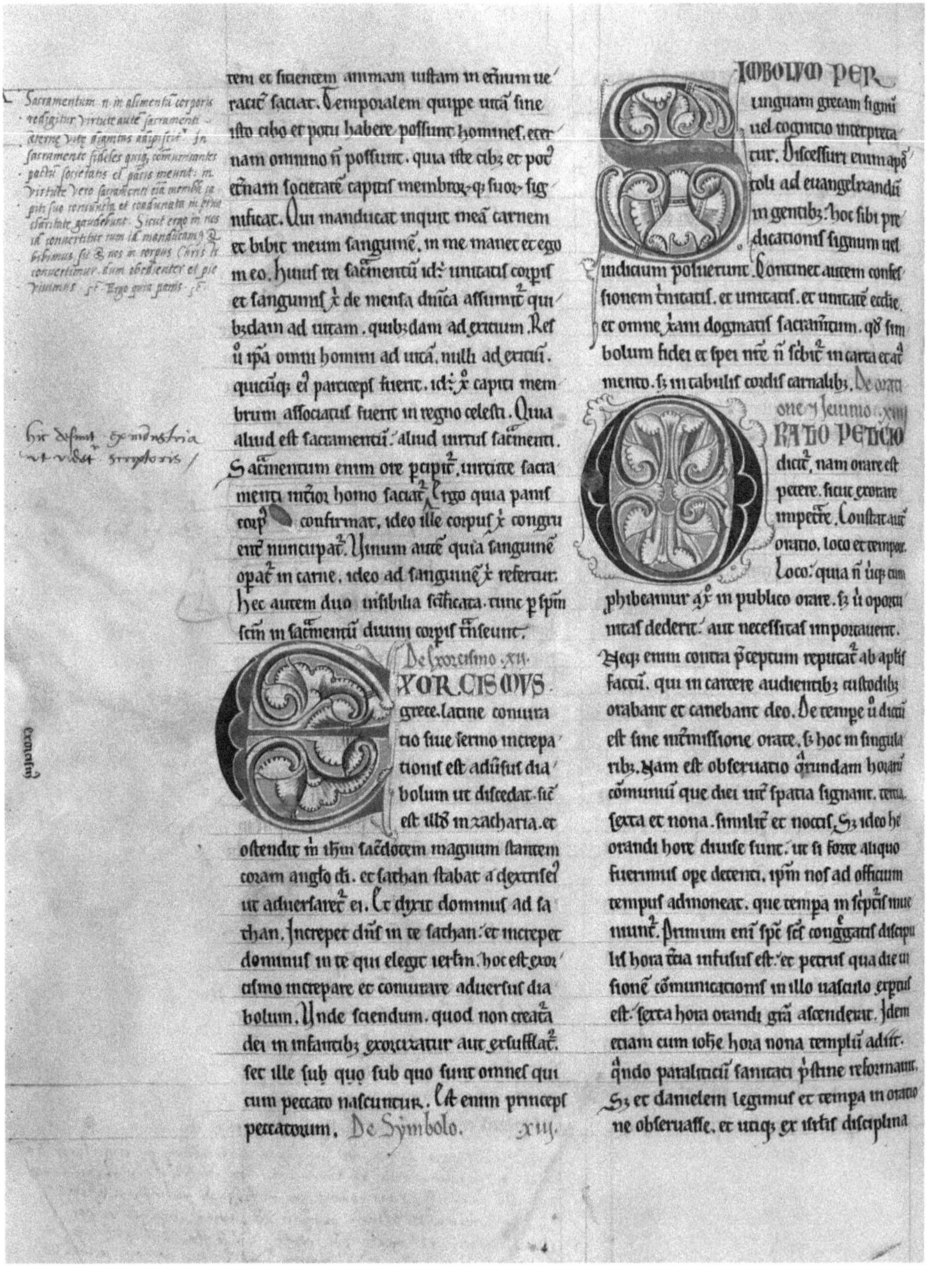

FIG. 1.1. A Parkerian reader singles out what he describes as a deliberate omission in a manuscript of Hrabanus Maurus, *De ecclesiasticis officiis*. Cambridge, Corpus Christi College, MS 11, fol. 45*v*.

Flores historiarum. Parker's chaplain, Edmund Guest, the bishop of Rochester, drafted the preface.[37] He described the work as based on a 'very ancient manuscript of the history', and

[37] A handwritten contents list on the verso of the blank before the title-page in London, BL, C.123.g.2. identifies the text as 'Roffensis praefat'.

radically different from the known text.[38] Many texts, after all, had undergone radical alteration over time at the hands of Catholics determined to suppress inconvenient truths. Bale had criticised monks for losing or concealing books. Guest raised the philological stakes in the preface:

> For such was the wickedness of those times, so unrestrained was the passion for concealing the truth, that in order to blind the minds of men, they did not hesitate to insert, erase or change whole sentences in the old writers, and much less when it came to individual words, just as each one wished.[39]

He also described Parker's manuscript of Hrabanus and treated it as a case in point of the old church's general effort 'to blind the minds of men'. Happily, he explained, the full text could be found 'in every old copy put into circulation before the time of William the Conqueror' — that is, in the time of the purer Saxon church.[40] Error, in other words, was a pervasive fact of textual culture, whether it was owed to scribal error, physical damage, lapses in taste, or efforts to suppress the truth. Parker and his men had sharpened their nibs early in the process of historical research because their definition of error — and their explanation for the causes of its most serious examples — was as much ideological as mechanical.

---

[38] *Flores historiarum*, London, Thomas Marsh, 1570, f° (USTC 507164), sig. a2r: 'Huius recognitionis causam si desideras: hinc ortam intellige, quod nuper incidimus in vetustissimum illius historiae exemplar, non solum elaboratius scriptum, sed in multis locis ita undique absolutum, ut merito videri possit ab ipso authore primo sic emissum. Neque hoc novum videri debet, aut ulla admiratione dignum, quod plerosque authores ea affici iniuria cernas, ut eorum scripta (posteritatis dolo) ab origine reddantur degenera: Cum eo impudentiae prorupere nonnulli, ut eisdem addendo et subtrahendo, quoslibet, licet pios, pro suo cuiusque arbitrio, quaeque vel nephanda patrocinari cogerent.' Parker's chief source, which he enriched eclectically, and arbitrarily, with extracts from other sources, is now Eton College Library, MS Bl.3.9., written in the early fourteenth century. For this manuscript see H. R. Luard, 'Preface', in H. R. Luard's edition of *Flores historiarum*, 3 vols, London, 1890, I, pp. xv–xvi. For Parker's edition and his methods see ibid., pp. xliv–xlviii.

[39] *Flores historiarum* 1570 (n. 38 above), sig. a2r: 'Tanta enim fuit olim temporum nequitia, tam effrenata veritatis supprimendae cuiusque libido, ut nihil dubitarint ad occecandas hominum mentes, veterum scriptorum, vel universas periodos, multo minus verbula intrudere, extinguere, commutare, prout cuique libitum fuerat, quae quidem mens mala et animus malus non in istiusmodi solum Authorum veterum monumentis reperientur, sed in hiis etiam authoribus qui de rebus divinis maxime seriis et sacris scripsere'.

[40] Ibid., sig. a2r–v: 'Quid queso hisce maioribus propositum erat, qui Rabani Magnentii Mauri, natione Scoti, abbatis Fuldensis, opera, adhuc fere ante septingentos annos scripta, in publicum exponi decernentes, quam tenebris perstringere hominum mentes, in illius, quem edidit, libri de universo sive de rerum naturis (adhuc ni fallor inexcusi) cap. xi. lib. 5. De ecclesiasticis officiis? Qui nequiter, et iniuriose ab hisce verbis (Sacramentum ore percipitur, virtute sacramenti interior homo satiatur) hanc subsequentem sententiam (Sacramentum enim in alimentum corporis redigitur, virtute autem sacramenti aeternae vitae dignitas adipiscitur) etc. quasi spuriam et illegitimam penitus abrasere. Cum tamen haec sententia, priori coniuncta, in quolibet veteri exemplari (ante Gulielmi conquestoris tempora edito) passim reperiatur'. The passage described here as missing is added in the margin of CCCC, MS 11, fol. 45v.

Printing a Correct Text: Dreams and Realities

In most cases, Parker's printers worked in their usual premises. The queen's printer, Richard Jugge, who produced the magnificent first lectern edition of the Bishops' Bible for Parker, had his press in Saint Paul's churchyard — probably too far from Lambeth to allow continuous examination of proofs. Errors resulted. Parker told Burghley that the 'printer hath honestly done his diligence'. But he also noted that 'it may be that in so long a book things have scaped, which may be lawful to every man, *cum bona venia*, to amend when they find them'; after all, he admitted, in the words of Vergil, '*non omnia possumus omnes*' — we can't all do everything.[41] In fact, Parker knew that errors had remained in the printed sheets, and in very prominent places. Two correction slips adorn Parker's own preface to the New Testament.[42] Working at a distance made the hunt for error less effective.

When it came to Parker's history of the English church, accordingly, he decided to go to work in a different way — one that would give him control over every aspect of book production. The title-page of the *De antiquitate* states that the book was 'excusum Londoni in aedibus Johannis Daij' — printed at London in the house of John Day. But the premises in question were special. The archbishop's son John gave a copy of the *De antiquitate,* now in the Bodleian Library, to the ecclesiastical lawyer Richard Cosin, on 1 January 1593/1594. He described the book as 'compiled and printed under the auspices and at the expense of Matthew, recently Archbishop of Canterbury, in his own house in Lambeth'.[43] Parker had one or more presses installed in Lambeth Palace, and Day printed the book in the same complex of buildings that housed its primary sources, Parker's library.[44]

De antiquitate is fissured with ambiguities.[45] Parker and his associates believed that the English church had already begun going downhill at the end of the sixth century, when Augustine set up his headquarters in Canterbury (then called Durovernum). Yet *De antiquitate* also praised individual bishops. Lanfranc even emerged as a kind of model for Parker himself. The title-page of Parker's book referred not only to the antiquity of the British church, but also to the 'privileges of the church of Canterbury'. Not surprisingly, Lanfranc was not the only archbishop who defended these effectively and attracted Parker's favourable attention. What arc did this history of the British church actually follow: decline and fall or paths of glory?

---

[41] Parker, *Correspondence* (n. 13 above), pp. 336–7, quoting Vergil, *Eclogues* 8.63.

[42] *The holie Bible*, London, Richard Jugge, 1568, f° (USTC 506837), verso of the title-page to the New Testament. The slips appear in both BL copies, C.35.l.14. and 1.e.2.

[43] Oxford, Bodleian Library, A.19.9 Th., flyleaf: 'Hunc librum dono dedit Richardo Cosin Johannes Parker armiger filius primogenitus Matthaei Parker, nuper Cantuariensis Archiepiscopi, cuius auspicijs et sumptibus liber iste et collectus et impressus est proprijs in aedibus Lamethae positis'.

[44] It was, of course, more normal for printers to invite authors to live and/or work in their shops, and sometimes to boast of this as a sign of the quality of the end product. The title-page of Sebastian Münster's *Institutiones grammaticae in hebraeam linguam*, Basel, Johann Froben, 1524, 8° (USTC 661237) notes, 'Opus est recens, atque chartatim emendatum ab ipso autore in officina Frobeniana. Anno M.D. XXIIII.'

[45] See now McMahon, 'Matthew Parker and the Practice of Church History' (n. 27 above).

The material history of *De antiquitate* is even stranger than its text. Samuel Drake, the clerical antiquary whose 1729 edition printed much supplementary information about the book, recorded the basic facts on its title-page.[46] His edition, he explained, rested on '21 copies printed in 1572, which differ from one another in the most remarkable way'.[47] No two copies of the book, as he found, seem to be identical. All of them promise on their title-pages the lives of '70 archbishops of Canterbury'. In fact, though, some — for example, the Scheide Library copy in Princeton — end with the life of number 69, Cardinal Reginald Pole, the restorer of Catholicism. Others include a life numbered 70, entitled 'Matthaeus'. This concludes with Parker's epitaph, composed by Walter Haddon, but not with the archbishop's death since he was, awkwardly, still alive when the book was completed.

Some copies include a detailed history of Cambridge, which emphasises Parker's benefactions. Others lack it. Within the text of the *De antiquitate* itself, moreover, distinctive oddities abound. The *De antiquitate*, as should be clear by now, touched on a good many hot button issues, and some readers responded to the text's treatment of them by altering it physically. On p. 29 of the first section, for example, begins a long description of 'The privileges and prerogatives of the see of Canterbury' — not a title or a subject to appeal to the more Puritanical reader. An owner of the Scheide copy in Princeton made his opinion clear (Figs 1.2 and 1.3).[48]

He cut page 29 where its approving discussion of the virtues of the Anglo-Saxon church ended, glued the mutilated page to a blank, and then cut out all the succeeding pages up to page 39. There too he covered the first two lines, which dealt with the archbishop's court, with a cancel slip. Historians of censorship have shown how energetically Catholic censors in Italy practiced this kind of ideologically driven correction, using ink, paper, and paste to turn material texts into strangely decorated caricatures of their original selves.[49] It is striking, to say the least, to see Protestant readers do much the same. Parker emphasised more than once that he knew his book needed criticism. In a letter printed by Drake, to an unknown friend Parker wrote that he was communicating *De antiquitate* 'to such, as should probably allow, or disallow that, which I should set down: which prudence I think very necessary in matters of story: *Quia plus vident oculi, quam oculus* [eyes see more than one eye]'.[50] The reader of the Scheide copy, whose view of the *De antiquitate* led him to mutilate his copy, paradoxically suited his action to Parker's words, and he was not alone.

---

[46] See J. Westby-Gibson, 'Drake, Samuel (1687/1688–1753)', rev. by J. A. Marchand, in *Oxford Dictionary of National Biography*, 2004: https://doi.org/10.1093/ref:odnb/8031, accessed 5 June 2020.

[47] M. Parker, *De antiquitate Britannicae ecclesiae*, ed. S. Drake, London, 1729, title-page: 'e xxi exemplarium 1572 excusorum, sibique mutuo sorte plane singulari discrepantium, collatione, integra nunc primum numerisque absoluta omnibus historia'. Drake's text is in fact a composite that should not be cited except to illuminate his methods or draw on the materials he collected.

[48] Princeton, William H. Scheide Library, 20.11.

[49] H. Marcus, *Forbidden Knowledge: Medicine, Science and Censorship in Early Modern Italy*, Chicago and London, 2020, Chapter 6. See also G. Fragnito, *Rinascimento perduto. La letteratura italiana sotto gli occhi dei censori (secoli XV–XVII)*, Bologna, 2019, with earlier bibliography on this much investigated subject.

[50] *De antiquitate*, ed. Drake (n. 47 above), sig. [*4]v.

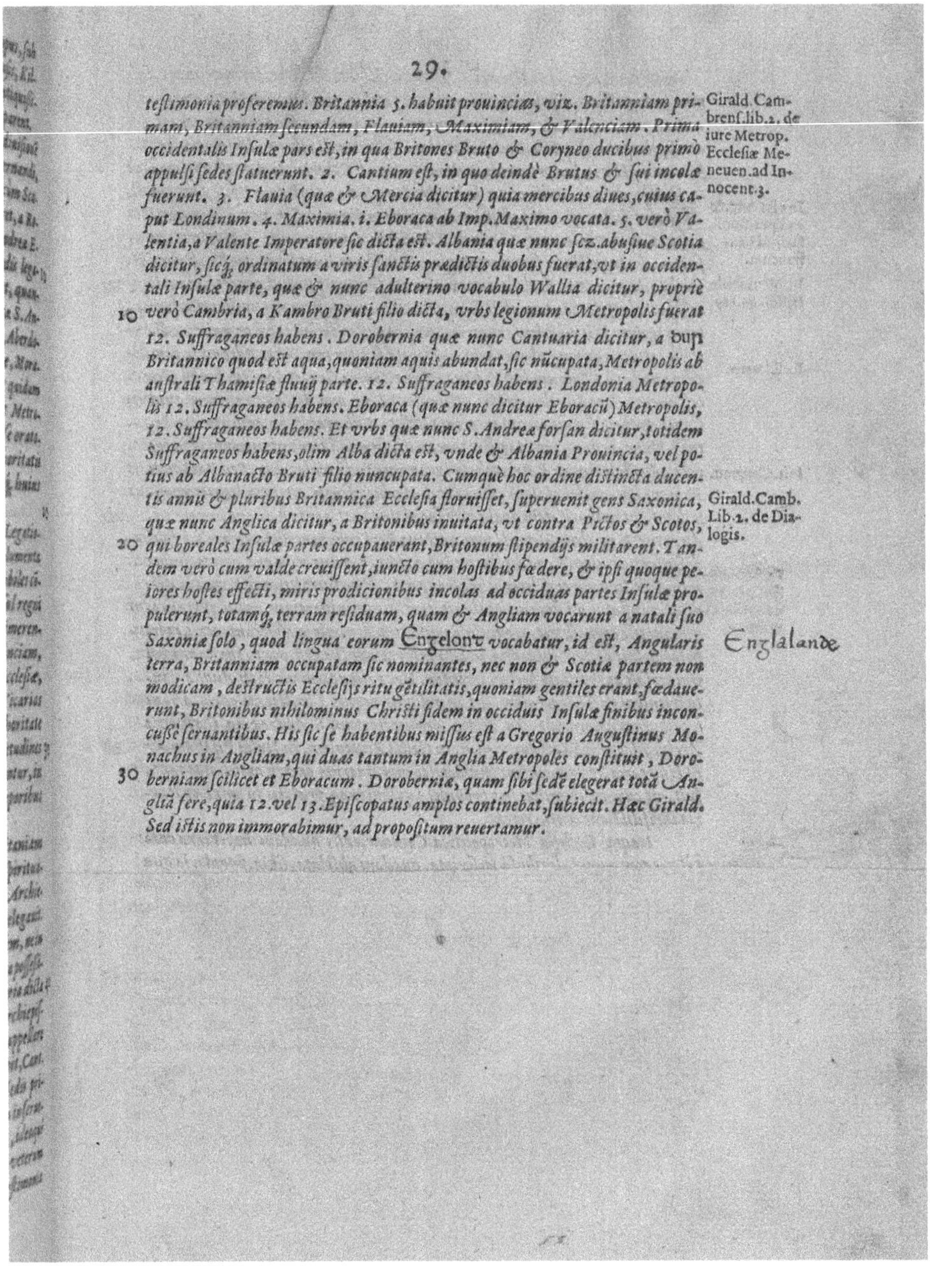

FIG. 1.2. A reader censors a passage on the privileges and prerogatives of the see of Canterbury in Matthew Parker, *De antiquitate ecclesiae Britannicae*, London, John Day, 1572, f° (USTC 507554), p. 29. Princeton, William H. Scheide Library, WHS 20.11.

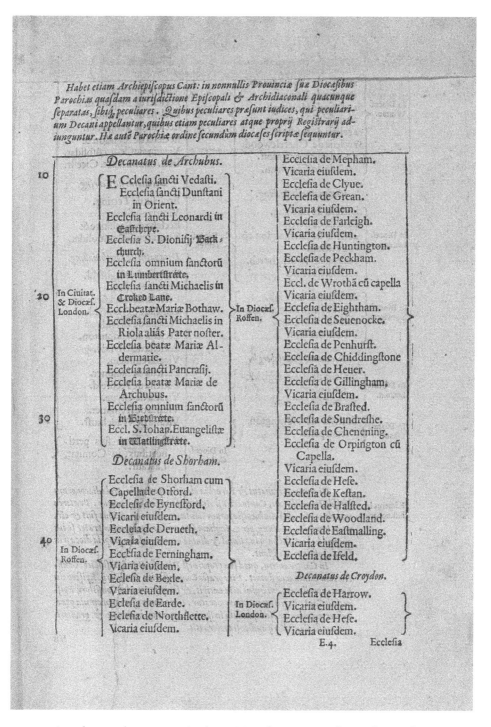

FIG. 1.3. A reader completes a correction by excision of a passage on the privileges and prerogatives of the see of Canterbury in Parker, *De antiquitate* (see Fig. 1.2.), p. 39. Princeton, William H. Scheide Library, WHS 20.11.

Correcting the Proofs: Errors, Corrections, and Revisions

But most of the correcting took place before Parker's paper boats set sail. Two copies, (Oxford, Bodleian Library, Rawl. 593 and BL C.24.b.6.) differ in multiple ways from the rest. Their evidence takes us inside Lambeth Palace, back to the original stage of correction carried out there, and it suggests that having the press under the archbishop's roof was not a sovereign remedy for error. Consider two examples, both from Rawl. 593 in the Bodleian Library. On page 97, someone has found and corrected a factual omission. The text refers in passing to a palace that Gilbert, bishop of Rochester, had built, which was surrounded by a wall. The annotator first writes 'Johanne Fischero' between the lines of the text and then explains himself in the margin: 'muro cinctum lateritio nuper per J. Fisherum' — the palace was recently surrounded with a brick wall by John Fisher. This correction found its way into most of the printed copies of the book. The text usually reads: 'in qua sibi palacium (nuper muro latericio per Io. Fisherum cinctum) extruxit' — in which he built himself a palace, recently surrounded with a brick wall by John Fisher. Evidently, then, Rawl. 593 — like the printed versions of Asser — represents a first stage in the printing of the text: page proofs.

A second example qualifies this diagnosis. On the first page of the life of Lanfranc in Rawl. 593, the text describes how Thomas of York came to Lanfranc to be consecrated: 'Hora statuta est, qua Thomas quaestionem seu examinationem subiret: qua Lanfrancus cum suis Suffraganeis in choro lineis induti stabant, Thomam expectabant' (The hour was appointed, when Thomas was to be tested. Lanfranc stood with his suffragans, wearing linen, in a group, they awaited Thomas). The staccato final pair of clauses was clearly faulty. In the margin, a corrector changed 'expectabant' to 'expectantes' (Lanfranc stood with his suffragans, wearing linen, in a group, awaiting Thomas). But this correction ended up only in the errata, not the text, of the copies in which the first mistake was set right. It is not clear, accordingly, just how long the process of error-hunting lasted, or what exact relation it bore to the printing of the text.

Another case, also in the life of Lanfranc, shows just how substantial the changes made in the course of production could be. The life of Lanfranc turned in part on the great rivalry between Canterbury and York. In the earliest version of *De antiquitate*, Parker printed a document, the 1072 Accord of Windsor, which was meant to settle the questions at issue between the dioceses. He gave the text in full, including all the names of signatories.[51] Then he changed his mind. In the standard version, the list of names is sharply abridged, and a printed marginal gloss informs the reader that the rest can be found 'in the archives'.[52] It is not clear what inspired this change. William of Malmesbury, a favourite historian of the Parker circle, quoted the Accord of Windsor more than once — in one case with the full list of witnesses, in another with an abridged list.[53] It is possible that Jocelyn decided to

---

[51] This version of the printed *De antiquitate* appears in London, BL, C.24.b.6, where the Accord is printed at pp. 94–5.

[52] In the standard text of the *De antiquitate* (e.g., London, BL, C.24.b.7. and C.24.b.8, 95), the list of signatures after the Accord ends with the following statement: 'Ego Gulielmus London. Episcopus consensi, cum multis alijs Episcopis et Abbatibus, ut in Archivis patet.'

[53] See McMahon, 'Matthew Parker and the Practice of Church History' (n. 27 above).

follow William's example. But it is also possible that Parker himself came to see the full list of names as a dry and pointless interruption to the life of his favourite predecessor: a new literary mistake.

The different fates of these two errors square the circle: they explain why the *De antiquitate*, though produced in circumstances that made correction easy, exists in so few copies and in such different states. Bringing production into Lambeth Palace did not impose stricter control; on the contrary, it gave free rein both to Parker's own neuroses and to the diverse tastes of his collaborators. They combed through the text again and again — at times printing was interrupted to enable substantive corrections — but the whole text, as it stands, was never subjected to a final polishing.

Not surprisingly, it was in the most delicate section of all — the life of Augustine of Canterbury — that the most significant errors were identified in the course of printing. How could Parker and his men hope to show that Augustine and Gregory, his master, had been anything but heroes, as portrayed by Bede, bent on bringing Christianity to a world full of obdurate pagans and insular Christians? They did their best. They stuffed the text with primary source quotations, many of them from texts a couple of centuries removed from Augustine himself. Every one of these, in one way or another, documented the degeneration of the church in Augustine's time and after: the rise of luxury, the multiplication of ceremonies, and the proliferation of superstitions. And yet, they realised as they read through the first printed state of the text, their documentation was not yet complete. All copies of the standard text have two additional leaves inserted into gathering A. The four additional pages — inelegantly numbered 4a through 4d — offer further quotations to the same effect.[54]

These revisions caused new problems. The preface to the *De antiquitate* evoked the form of church history created, in the fourth century, by Eusebius of Caesarea: the historian of a church must cite documents in the words of their authors in order both to show that his narrative is well founded and to endow it with the flavour of an older, purer time — a kind of confessional historicism.[55] On these new pages, the text's makers heaped up primary sources. But a casual reader could easily be forgiven for failing to identify them. Consider page 6 of the life of Augustine. A break appears in the text and a new section begins with a title: '*De vasculis. Ca. 18*'. This turns out to be a polemical set of statements about church vessels:

> When Boniface, martyr and bishop, was asked about these, he answered: Once upon a time golden priests used wooden chalices. Now, by contrast, wooden priests use golden chalices. Zephyrinus, the sixteenth bishop of Rome, ordered that mass be celebrated with glass patens. After that Pope Urban V at last made all sacred appurtenances silver. For in this as in other forms of worship, over time the church has become more and more rich in adornment.[56]

---

[54] For another uncomely Parkerian correction, see Luard, 'Preface' (n. 38 above), pp. xlvii–xlviii.

[55] On this characteristic of ecclesiastical history as founded by Eusebius see A. Momigliano, 'Pagan and Christian Historiography in the Fourth Century A.D.', in A. Momigliano (ed.), *The Conflict Between Paganism and Christianity in the Fourth Century*, Oxford, 1963, pp. 79–99. For the slow uptake of Eusebius's documentary methods in early modern Europe see A. Grafton, 'Mixed Messages: The Early Modern Reception of Eusebius as a Church Historian', *International Journal of the Classical Tradition*, 27, 2020, pp. 332–60.

[56] Parker, *De antiquitate* (n. 15 above), second pagination, pp. 5–6.

What is this text? Where are its other seventeen chapters? And what does Chapter 18 document? A very careful reader might have noticed the last sentence before the break, which answered some of these questions: 'Let us describe the transformation of chalices into wooden vessels, using the Council of Tribur, at the start of the reign of emperor Arnulf'.[57] This was meant to identify the Chapter 18 in question as part of the proceedings of a local council held at Tribur, near Mainz, in May 895. The Catholic scholar Johannes Cochlaeus had printed this text in 1525.[58] What looked like a new section heading in the text actually introduced a ninth-century document. But beyond the cryptic headline, the structure of the page did nothing to explain or highlight this document, and the same is true of the rest.

Parker wrote to his unnamed friend that he intended to reprint his book in a corrected form.[59] The evidence confirms that he not only planned, but actually began, a systematic revision. Four copies of the *De antiquitate* contain a second version, printed, of the life of Augustine. One of these is LPL, MS 959 — a copy of the *De antiquitate* so heavily annotated and richly supplemented by Parker's associates that it has undergone metamorphosis into a manuscript. A note on the first page of the new text states that Parker commissioned George Acworth to compose it.[60] Acworth was indeed a lawyer and one of Parker's associates.[61] The core of his version of the life of Augustine resembles the original, though it has some curious additional matter. For example, Acworth introduced the story, told by Polydore Virgil and others, of how Augustine's English hearers at Rochester threw fish tails at him and were divinely punished by growing tails of their own.[62] He insisted that he told this fish story only in order to ridicule it.[63]

For the most part, though, what preoccupied Acworth was mise-en-page: less how to transform the text, which remained recognisably the same, than how to make clear, as Day's original setting had not, which parts of it were by whom, so that a reader could navigate them without becoming lost. Acworth devised a complex system, probably based on the recently published chronicles of Theodore Bibliander, which he cited, and Heinrich Pantaleon, to coordinate the different components of his narrative and set them in a chronological frame.[64] Both books emulated the *Chronicle* of Eusebius and Jerome. They used parallel

---

[57] Ibid., p. 5.

[58] *Acta et decreta Concilii Triburiensis*, ed. J. Cochlaeus, Mainz, Johann Schöffer, 1525, 4° (USTC 608645), sig. D1r. On this council see C. Carroll, 'The Last Great Carolingian Church Council: The Tribur Synod of 895', *Annuarium Historiae Conciliorum*, 33/1, 2001, pp. 9–25.

[59] Parker, *De antiquitate*, ed. Drake (n. 47 above), sig. [*4]v.

[60] LPL, MS 959, fol. 18r: 'Thes 24 pages of Augustins life, were thus begun, by George Acworth, d. of the Law at yᵉ appointment of Matthew Parker Archb. of Cant.'

[61] R. Fritze, 'Acworth, George', in *Oxford Dictionary of National Biography*, 2004, https://doi.org/10.1093/ref:odnb/78, accessed 1 June 2020; L. G. H. Horton-Smith, *George Acworth: A Full Account of His Life* […], [St Albans], 1953.

[62] See McMahon, 'Licking the "Beare Whelpe"' (n. 12 above), p. 162.

[63] LPL, MS 959, fol. 24r (p. 13 of the 'vita'): 'Ex qua quidem perantiqua sane & nonnullis monumentis serio tanquam re gesta celebrata fabula, non modo apud nostrates, sed apud exteros vicinos percrebuit, Cantios monstri similes esse atque caudatos. Nonnulli etiam id toti Anglorum genti ascribunt, tanquam poenam & ignominiam primae huic Roffensium contumaciae diuinitus illatam, ne posteritati quidem ob delicti atrocitatem remissam.'

[64] Theodore Bibliander, *Temporum a condito mundo usque ad eius ultimam aetatem supputatio partitioque exactior*, Basel, Johann Oporinus, 1558, f° (USTC 693137); Heinrich Pantaleon, *Chronographia Christianae ecclesiae, in qua dilucide patrum et doctorum praecipuorum ordo, cum omnium haeresum origine et multiplici innovatione ceremoniarum, decretorum, et rituum in ecclesia, per imperatores,*

columns to show which emperors, bishops, liturgical practices, and heretical doctrines had flourished at any given time. In the new version of Augustine's life, columns describing the wider political and ecclesiastical situation — the degeneration of the church, the flourishing of heresies, the rise of Islam and of Talmudic Judaism — flanked the central narrative. Quotations in the central text were set in Italic, the text itself in Roman type. Glosses inset in the central text block identified their sources. The section on Chapter 18 of the Council of Tribur now became beautifully legible as a supporting document. A lead-in identified the passage as a 'decretum'; Italic type set it off from the exposition and a prominent gloss named its source. Like Parker's letter to his unidentified friend, the note about George Acworth's work in Lambeth claimed that Parker intended to have the whole work rewritten: '& the lives of all ye Archb. shold have in this course bene perfected in a generall storie. but deth prevented it'.[65] There is every reason to believe this statement — and to infer that every page would have been subjected to close inspection for errors in layout, as well as in content, and to redesign. Parker wrote to his unnamed friend that:

> I accept well your diligence for comparing my writings with your records. And if you espie any more suche, signifie them unto me. For I purpose, before I do evulgate [publish] my books, to suffer them to be expended, and to be printed again, where they be faulty; which was the principal cause to send to you again for the book of *Westminster*; which I will return corrected.[66]

'Expending' the original text meant not only collating it with its sources and other texts, but also examining it for lapses in stylistic and typographical clarity.

A number of factors caused the basic mass of text to be pushed and tweaked in so many different directions. The book was the product of many authors. Most modern catalogues and bibliographies identify Parker as the author, as I have done up to now. He himself sometimes claimed the book as his own. Writing to his unnamed friend, he noted that 'I did of purpose keep back my book of my Canterbury predecessors'.[67] Samuel Drake inferred from this text and the letter to Burghley quoted above that Parker was the book's author. But the bulk of the evidence points in a very different direction. John Parker, Matthew's son, as we saw, described the work as 'collected and printed' in Lambeth. The perfect participle 'collectum' — here rendered 'compiled' — appears without a subject. Both the meaning of the word and its grammatical place suggest the same conclusion. John regarded the book as the work of multiple authors who collected materials and wrote them up.[68]

Further testimonies identify some of the compilers. In a remark on the printed title-page in LPL, MS 959, Parker's secretary John Joscelyn staked his claim: 'This Historie was collected & penned by John Joscelyn one of ye sons of Sr. Tho. Joscelyn. knight by y^e

---

principes, concilia, aut pontifices Romanos, a Christi nativitate ad nostra tempora usque ostenditur: ad S. Patrum et omnium bonorum authorum lectionem rerumque ecclesiasticarum et civilium cognitionem utilis et necessaria, 2nd edn, Basel, Nikolaus Brylinger, 1561, f° (USTC 622495).

[65] LPL, MS 959, fol. 18r.

[66] Parker, *De antiquitate*, ed. Drake, sig. [*4]r–v.

[67] Ibid., sig. [*4]r.

[68] On this and what follows, see McMahon, 'Matthew Parker and the Practice of Church History' (n. 27 above).

appointment & oversight of Matthwe Parker Archbp. of Cant. ye saide John being inter-tained in ye said Archb: howse, as one of his Antiquaries'.[69] Joscelyn's notebooks in the British Library contain rough drafts for passages in the *De antiquitate* and confirm that he composed at least parts of the text. Some well-informed scholars — for example, James Ussher — treated Joscelyn as the real author of the book.[70] But like the notes in Parker's manuscripts, those in the copies of his book reveal a large cast of characters at work, many of them hard to identify. One anonymous marginal note in LPL, MS 959, for example, makes a remark about the authorship of another one: 'That is the hand of Doctor Yale, unless I'm wrong. I have an autograph of his in my hands as I write.' 'I seriously doubt it', rejoins a second annotator: 'For the hand of John Parker is very similar'.[71] The *De antiquitate* was a collaborative work, produced by a team. In that it resembles a number of other large-scale early modern historical enterprises, from the Nuremberg Chronicle, designed by Hartmann Schedel, to the Magdeburg Centuries, another church history, called into being by Flacius Illyricus.[72] Like Heinrich Münzer, who served as both content provider and corrector for the Nuremberg Chronicle, the content providers of the *De Antiquitate* were also its correc-tors.[73] Their combined but sometimes conflicting efforts, made all too easy to repeat by the presence of the press in Parker's house, left the book a shapeless mass.

No document reveals the endlessness of the Lambeth error hunt more vividly than LPL, MS 959. It shows that the hunt for error went on even after Parker's book had appeared and he himself had died. Joscelyn and others enriched the printed text of the *De antiquitate*, in its fullest form, with further materials of the most varied kinds: extracts from texts that con-firmed arguments, medieval documents — with their seals, and more. They even included a printed broadside, created by Parker's express order, that listed the expenses for the enthronement of one of his medieval predecessors.[74] And they entered minute typographi-cal and factual corrections, as when they changed the source reference for a letter from 'Ex Florileg'. to 'Ex Archetypo'.[75] The correctors could not stop correcting. Perhaps they were not aiming at a final state. In other cases as well, the authors of massive compilatory works

---

[69] LPL, MS 959, fol. 36r.

[70] James Ussher, 'De Britannicarum ecclesiarum primordiis', in James Ussher, *Britannicarum eccle-siarum antiquitates*, Dublin, Societas bibliopolarum, 1639, 4° (USTC 3020617), p. 90: 'Ita Balaeus: atque eum hic secutus Matthaeus Parkerus (vel Iohannes Iosselinus potius) in libro de Antiquitate Britanni-cae Ecclesiae.' Cf. ibid., p. 45: 'Collector Britannicarum antiquitatum (quas evulgandas curavit Matthaeus Parkerus Cantuariensis archepiscopus) [...].' The seventeenth-century polymath and philologist Thomas Marshall transcribed the former passage and noted the latter on the title-page of his copy of the 1605 Hanau edition of the *De antiquitate* (USTC 2118262), now at Oxford, Lincoln College Library, Senior Library, B.2.34.

[71] LPL, MS 959, fol. 132r: 'manus Domini Yale, ni fallor. autographum Yalei iam prae manibus habeo' — 'valde dubito. Manus enim Johannis Parker est perquam similis'.

[72] On the Nuremberg Chronicle see B. Posselt, *Konzeption und Kompilation der Schedelschen Weltchronik*, Wiesbaden, 2015; on the Magdeburg Centuries see H. Bollbuck, *Wahrheitszeugnis, Gottes Auftrag und Zeitkritik: die Kirchengeschichte der Magdeburger Zenturien und ihre Arbeitstechniken*, Wiesbaden, 2014.

[73] On Münzer see the classic study by E. P. Goldschmidt, *Hieronymus Münzer und seine Bibliothek*, London, 1938.

[74] LPL, MS 959, fol. 186v, entitled *Provisiones & Emptiones circa dictam Intronizationem*. A manuscript note on the broadside records that it was 'Printed by the Command of Abp Parker with other Memoirs, of the same kind'.

[75] Ibid., fol. 54v.

continued working on them for years after publication. Conrad Gessner, for example, no sooner sent a work through the press than he began to annotate it. He added new materials when he could. But he also went over old prose, polishing it anew; identified the authors of materials that he had quoted anonymously in earlier drafts; and summarised the letters of his informants.[76] One idea of authorship in the early modern period — one that sorted well with collaborative methods and a passion for correction — was apparently 'the journey, not the arrival, matters'.[77]

The Mole and the Critic: Defending the Text After Printing

Still, LBL, MS 959 was not only the product of an endless, hopeless effort to perfect the work of the long-dead Parker. It stemmed from a very specific effort to counter slanders of Parker that had entered the public world of print — slanders that appeared in a work designed to publicise what its author treated as errors in Parker's text and in his life. In 1574 an anonymous press, probably that of Froschauer at Zurich, printed a little book with a long title: *The Life of the 70 Archbishopp off Canterbury presentlye sitting Englished, and to be added to the 69. Lately sett forth in Latin.*[78] This was a clever satire: a translation of the life of Parker composed for the *De antiquitate*, accompanied by sarcastic glosses, now ascribed to John Stubbe and, perhaps, some friends.[79] Where Parker was described as 'entred in all the rites of holye orders', a gloss corrected the text: 'Poope holye'.[80] Where he was credited with having 'applied all his mynde to the studye of divinitie', a gloss deflated his biographer's rhetoric: 'As the course of his liffe hath declared, for he gott therby a benefice or two'.[81] Where the hospitality of Parker's feasts was praised, the glossator gloomily summoned up those 'whose God is their belly. Phil. 3. 19'.[82] And where the text mentioned I John 2:17, the line that Parker had inscribed on the walls and windows of his palace ('And the world passeth away, and the lust thereof'), the glossator pointed out that 'the Pharisees did the like in the hem of their garments. The worlde laughethe at it'.[83] The notes, in other words, performed

---

[76] For a case in point see A. Grafton, 'Philological and Artisanal Knowledge Making in Renaissance Natural History: A Study in Cultures of Knowledge', *History of Humanities*, 3/1, 2018, pp. 39–55.

[77] J. T. Knight, *Bound to Read: Compilations, Collections and the Making of Renaissance Literature*, Philadelphia, 2013, pp. 40–51, esp. pp. 47–51.

[78] John Stubbe [Stubbs], *The Life of the 70 Archbishopp off Canterbury presentlye sitting Englished, and to be added to the 69. Lately sett forth in Latin*, [Zurich, Christoph Froschauer?], 1574, 8° (not in USTC; ESTC S114022).

[79] See L. Berry, 'Introduction', in *John Stubbs's* Gaping Gulf *with Letters and Relevant Documents*, ed. L. Berry, Charlottesville (VA), 1968, pp. ix–lxi, at pp. xxiv–xxv. Natalie Mears suggests that the translation may have been a collaboration by Stubbe, Vincent Skinner, and Michael Hickes: N. Mears, 'Stubbe [Stubbs], John (c. 1541–1590)', in *Oxford Dictionary of National Biography*, 2004, https://doi.org/10.1093/ref:odnb/26736, accessed 5 June 2020.

[80] Stubbe, *The Life* (n. 78 above), sig. A3r.

[81] Ibid.

[82] Ibid., sig. B1v.

[83] Ibid., sig. [B6]v.

yet another act of correction: they skewered errors of description in the text and errors in the conduct it described — at one and the same time.

The translator identified his source. The Latin original, he explained, had been 'written by a man off his [Parker's] owne, I thincke his secretarie.' Characteristically, it bore 'the stampe of his owne armes, descended as he saith off his auncient howse, entremaried with those off his sea, which is a supersticious pall all double croised or perced thorowe with that Arch-pastorall or Archpapisticall staffe'.[84] This text was entitled not 'Matthaeus', as the printed ones were, but 'Historiola'. As the commentator took care to note, 'this word (historiola) is written with his [Parker's] owne hand in redde oker letters uppon the browe of the boke.'[85] These details show that the translator worked not from the final version of the life of Parker but from an earlier draft by Joscelyn, which had been entitled 'Historiola'. Another copy of this survives in the Corpus Christi College Library, Cambridge. It too has Parker's arms, impaled as the translator describes, in its first initial.[86] The copy that the translator himself used had been examined by Parker himself, since it bore a title in red chalk in his characteristic handwriting. The source, in other words, was genuine and came from Parker's own circle.

It seems likely that one of those working with the texts and printing press in Lambeth Palace was a mole: a Puritan, he removed a preliminary draft of the seventieth life from Lambeth so that the translator could use it. Correction could hardly have gone farther: Stubbe, in effect, corrected not only Parker's enterprise, but also his understanding and portrayal of his own work as an Anglican archbishop. Stubbe's short but sour book very likely inspired the compilation of LPL, MS 959. When the compilers added lists of Parker's expenses and, for comparative purposes, those of his predecessors, they were not collecting random details but mounting a defence against the change that his belly had been his God. Joscelyn, for example, inserted a list of Parker's outgoings in London from 1559 to 1563. 'This', he noted, 'written by ArchBp Parker hym self Who best knew what hym self did'.[87] The defensiveness of the tone — and the annotation — are unmistakable.

Correction engendered correction. Of course, the corrector also needed correction: all known copies of Stubbe's book have two identical ink corrections, probably made by the author in Froschauer's shop. 'If the red slayer think he slays, Or if the slain think he is slain, They know not well the subtle ways I keep, and pass, and turn again'. What was error in Parker's palace? An art form? An obsession? Was hunting it in all its forms the way to perfect a project or to postpone its completion indefinitely? All of the above. David Wakelin points out a paradox: 'early printed books were [...] riddled with errors [...]. Nonetheless, the early makers and users of printed books sometimes seem to have dreamed that they could make them creditable, accurate and stable'.[88] The dream held Parker and his men in its grip, even as errors of every kind multiplied around them. Once dipped into the ink well, the bent nib never ceased in its unhappy course.

---

[84] Ibid., sig. E5*r–v*.
[85] Ibid., sig. E5*v*.
[86] CCCC, MS 489, p. 105.
[87] LPL, MS 959, fol. [332]*r*.
[88] D. Wakelin, *Scribal Correction and Literary Craft: English Manuscripts, 1375–1510*, Cambridge, 2014, p. 5.

BIBLIOGRAPHY

PRIMARY SOURCES

MANUSCRIPTS

Cambridge, Corpus Christi College, MS 11
Cambridge, Corpus Christi College, MS 359
Cambridge, Corpus Christi College, MS 438
London, British Library, Cotton MS Tiberius B IV
London, British Library, Cotton MS Vitellius D. VII
London, Lambeth Palace Library, MS 959
Princeton, William H. Scheide Library, Scheide MS 159

PRINTED BOOKS

Acta et decreta Concilii Triburiensis, ed. J. Cochlaeus, Mainz, Johann Schöffer, 1525, 4° (USTC 608645).

Bibliander, Theodore, *Temporum a condito mundo usque ad eius ultimam aetatem supputatio partitioque exactior*, Basel, Johann Oporinus, 1558, f° (USTC 693137).

Camerarius, Joachim, 'Erratum, in quo circiter quadraginta loca autorum cum veterum, tum recentium notantur', in *In hoc libello cura et diligentia Ioachimi Camerarii Qu. perfecta, haec insunt*, Nuremberg, Johann Petreius, 1535, 8° (USTC 665810).

Camerarius, Joachim, *Narratio de H. Eobano Hesso*, Nuremberg, Johann vom Berg and Ulrich Neuber, 1553, 8° (USTC 676766).

Erasmus, Desiderius, *The Correspondence of Erasmus, Volume Six: Letters 842–992 (1518–1519)*, transl. R. A. B. Mynors and D. F. S. Thompson, Toronto and Buffalo (NY), 1982.

Erasmus, Desiderius, *The Correspondence of Erasmus: Letters 2472 to 2634, April 1531–March 1532*, transl. C. Fantazzi, ed. J. Estes, Toronto, Buffalo (NY), and London, 2018.

Erasmus, Desiderius, *Opus epistolarum Des. Erasmi Roterodami*, ed. P. S. Allen, H. M. Allen, and H. W. Garrod, 12 vols, Oxford, 1906–1958.

Flores historiarum, London, Thomas Marsh, 1570, f° (USTC 507164). Copy discussed: London, British Library, C.123.g.2.

The holie Bible, London, Richard Jugge, 1568, f° (USTC 506837). Copies discussed: London, British Library, C.35.l.14 and 1.e.2.

Münster, Sebastian, *Institutiones grammaticae in hebraeam linguam*, Basel, Johann Froben, 1524, 8° (USTC 661237).

Pantaleon, Heinrich, *Chronographia Christianae ecclesiae, in qua dilucide patrum et doctorum praecipuorum ordo, cum omnium haeresum origine et multiplici innovatione ceremoniarum, decretorum, et rituum in ecclesia, per imperatores, principes, concilia, aut pontifices Romanos, a Christi nativitate ad nostra tempora usque ostenditur: ad S. Patrum et omnium bonorum authorum lectionem rerumque ecclesiasticarum et civilium cognitionem utilis et necessaria*, 2nd edn, Basel, Nikolaus Brylinger, 1561, f° (USTC 622495).

Parker, Matthew, *Correspondence*, ed. J. Bruce and T. T. Perowne, Cambridge, 1853.

Parker, Matthew, *De antiquitate Britannicae ecclesiae*, Hanau, 1605, (USTC 2118262). Copy discussed: Oxford, Lincoln College Library, Senior Library, B.2.34.

Parker, Matthew, *De antiquitate Britannicae ecclesiae*, ed. S. Drake, London 1729.

Parker, Matthew, *De antiquitate ecclesiae Britannicae & privilegiis ecclesiae Cantuariensis cum Archiepiscopis eiusdem 70*, London, John Day, 1572, f° (USTC 507554). Copies discussed: Cambridge, Cambridge University Library, Sel.3.229; Oxford, Bodleian Library, A.19.9 Th.; London, British Library, C.24.b.6., C.24.b.7., and C.24.b.8.; Princeton, William H. Scheide Library, 20.11.

Stubbe [Stubbs], John, *The Life of the 70 Archbishopp off Canterbury presentlye sitting Englished, and to be added to the 69. Lately sett forth in Latin*, [Zurich, Christoph Froschauer?], 1574, 8° (not in USTC; ESTC S114022).

Ussher, James, 'De Britannicarum ecclesiarum primordiis', in Ussher, James, *Britannicarum ecclesiarum antiquitates*, Dublin, Societas bibliopolarum, 1639, 4° (USTC 3020617), pp. 1-972.

SECONDARY LITERATURE

Berry, L., 'Introduction', in *John Stubbs's* Gaping Gulf *with Letters and Relevant Documents*, ed. L. Berry, Charlottesville (VA), 1968, pp. ix-lxi.

Bietenholz, P., and Deutscher, T. (eds), *Contemporaries of Erasmus: A Biographical Register of the Renaissance and Reformation*, 3 vols, Toronto, Buffalo (NY), and London, 1985.

Bollbuck, H., *Wahrheitszeugnis, Gottes Auftrag und Zeitkritik: die Kirchengeschichte der Magdeburger Zenturien und ihre Arbeitstechniken*, Wiesbaden, 2014.

Brook, V. J. K., *A Life of Archbishop Parker*, Oxford, 1962.

Budny, M., *Insular, Anglo-Saxon, and Early Anglo-Norman Manuscript Art at Corpus Christi College, Cambridge: An Illustrated Catalogue*, 2 vols, Kalamazoo (MI) and Cambridge, 1997.

Carroll, C., 'The Last Great Carolingian Church Council: The Tribur Synod of 895', *Annuarium Historiae Conciliorum*, 33/1, 2001, pp. 9-25.

Evenden, E., *Patents, Pictures and Patronage: John Day and the Elizabethan Book Trade*, Aldershot, 2008.

Evenden, E., and Freeman, T., *Religion and the Book in Early Modern England: The Making of Foxe's "Book of Martyrs"*, Cambridge, 2011.

Fragnito, G., *Rinascimento perduto. La letteratura italiana sotto gli occhi dei censori (secoli XV–XVII)*, Bologna, 2019.

Goldschmidt, E. P., *Hieronymus Münzer und seine Bibliothek*, London, 1938.

Grafton, A., *The Culture of Correction in Renaissance Europe*, London, 2011.

Grafton, A., 'From Production to Reception: Reading the *Perambulation*', *Journal of the Warburg and Courtauld Institutes*, 81, 2018, pp. 172–88.

Grafton, A., 'Mixed Messages: The Early Modern Reception of Eusebius as a Church Historian', *International Journal of the Classical Tradition*, 27, 2020, pp. 332–60.

Grafton, A., 'Philological and Artisanal Knowledge Making in Renaissance Natural History: A Study in Cultures of Knowledge', *History of Humanities*, 3/1, 2018, pp. 39–55.

Graham, T., 'Matthew Parker's Manuscripts: an Elizabethan Library and its Uses', in E. Leedham-Green and T. Webber (eds), *The Cambridge History of Libraries in Britain and Ireland*, 3 vols, Cambridge, 2006, I, pp. 322–41.

Heal, F., 'The Bishops and the Printers, Henry VII to Elizabeth', in M. Heale (ed.), *The Prelate in England and Europe, 1300–1560*, Suffolk and Rochester, 2014, pp. 142–69.

Horton-Smith, L. G. H., *George Acworth: A Full Account of His Life* […], [St Albans], 1953.

Jones, N., 'Matthew Parker, John Bale and the Magdeburg Centuriators', *Sixteenth Century Journal*, 12, 1981, pp. 35–49.

Knight, J. T., *Bound to Read: Compilations, Collections and the Making of Renaissance Literature*, Philadelphia, 2013.

Leu, U., 'Buchdruck im Dienst der Reformation. Die Zusammenarbeit zwischen dem Zürcher Drucker Christoph Froschauer d. Ä. und den Reformatoren Huldrych Zwingli sowie Heinrich Bullinger', *Bibliothek und Wissenschaft*, 49, 2016, pp. 173–97.

Luard, H. R., 'Preface', in *Flores historiarum*, ed. H. R. Luard, 3 vols, London, 1890.

McMahon, M., 'Licking the "Beare Whelpe": William Lambarde and Matthew Parker revise the *Perambulation of Kent*', *Journal of the Warburg and Courtauld Institutes*, 81, 2018, pp. 154–71.

McMahon, M., 'Matthew Parker and the Practice of Church History', in N. Hardy and D. Levitin (eds), *Confessionalism and Erudition in Early Modern Europe: An Episode in the History of the Humanities*, Oxford, 2020, pp. 116–53.

Maclaren-Ross, J., *Memoirs of the Forties*, London, 1965.

Marcus, H., *Forbidden Knowledge: Medicine, Science and Censorship in Early Modern Italy*, Chicago and London, 2020.

Momigliano, A., 'Pagan and Christian Historiography in the Fourth Century A.D.', in A. Momigliano (ed.), *The Conflict Between Paganism and Christianity in the Fourth Century*, Oxford, 1963, pp. 79–99.

Oxford Dictionary of National Biography, Oxford, 2004.

Page, R. I., *Matthew Parker and His Books*, Kalamazoo (MI), 1993.

Posselt, B., *Konzeption und Kompilation der Schedelschen Weltchronik*, Wiesbaden, 2015.

Summit, J., *Memory's Library: Medieval Books in Early Modern England*, Chicago, 2008.

Wakelin, D., *Scribal Correction and Literary Craft: English Manuscripts, 1375–1510*, Cambridge, 2014.

PART I

TYPE, PROOFS, AND ILLUSTRATIONS

CHAPTER 2

FALLEN TYPE

The Benefits of a Printer's Error

CLAIRE BOLTON

FALLEN type letters, with their clear provenance, can shed light on the shape and size of types used by a printer in a town on a certain date. This paper describes a number of prominent examples recorded online in *Material Evidence in Incunabula* (MEI), a database created to gather copy-specific information on fifteenth-century editions.[1] The early decades of typography displayed a high degree of experimentalism in the development of type casting, setting and printing methods, but since there is very limited technical documentary information and no known handbooks dating from that period, hard evidence on the shape and dimensions of early type letters can help fill this gap. These findings are compared to a collection of late-fifteenth-/early-sixteenth-century type letters found near Lyon in the river Saône in 1868. Finally, a practical experiment involving printing with a piece of fallen type on the forme is described, while the results concerning paper shrinkage when measuring fallen type is discussed.[2]

The most familiar part of a type letter is the face, whose inked mark on paper is what readers see when leafing through a printed book. However, the face is only a very small section of the type letter; the remainder, the type body, hardly ever appears on a page. In a perfect piece, this rectangular body with smooth sides and right-angled corners supports the letter and holds it in position in the forme and within a word, with the correct amount of space between it and adjoining letters. While we are acquainted with the physical shape of modern type letters, little, if anything, is known about the features of type bodies at the dawn of Western printing.

---

[1] Unless otherwise stated, references made in this essay discuss specific copies, not editions in general; all examples found in incunabula are listed in MEI (https://data.cerl.org/mei/_search), a resource available under the umbrella of the Consortium of European Research Libraries (CERL).

[2] I would like to express my gratitude to all the colleagues and friends who have contributed their discoveries of fallen type, identified the specimens in their collections, answered my queries and provided photographic reproductions; this has very much been a collective effort. Anyone who happens to find further examples of fallen type is encouraged to contact me with bibliographic references, copy information (i.e. shelfmark and leaf), type height measurement, and a picture if possible.

Claire Bolton, *Fallen Type*. In: *Printing and Misprinting*. Edited by Geri Della Rocca de Candal, Anthony Grafton, and Paolo Sachet, Oxford University Press. © Claire Bolton (2023). DOI: 10.1093/oso/9780198863045.003.0003

A sensational discovery first contributed to shed some dim light on the issue. In 1868, an array of type letters dating from the late fifteenth to early sixteenth century were rescued from the bed of the river Saône in Lyon. They were in two sets of 21 and 212 pieces and were classified, measured, and recorded by Maurice Audin in the mid twentieth century,[3] yet their wide variety in height, depth, and shape produced more questions than answers. A further example of a fifteenth-century type letter, slightly crusted and bent, was found during an archaeological excavation in Basel in 1995.[4] This is regarded as a specimen of Type 19: 62G, [c. 9 point], probably used by Johann Amerbach between 1486 and 1500.

Cases of fallen type can compensate for the paucity of these physical examples. Fallen type is a term used to describe type letters that have accidentally fallen on top of the inked type forme during the printing process, leaving an impressed mark on the printed page. Occurrences of pieces of fallen type impressions are rare and so is their recording in catalogues and secondary literature. Regarded as printers' errors, they were first discussed in 1875 by J. P. A. Madden, who described a case found in the copy of Johann Nider's *De moralis lepra* held in the Bibliothèque Municipale of Versailles.[5]

While fallen type are usually not inked, in two instances there is evidence that they were inked when lying on the forme — it seems that they had fallen on the forme during inking, perhaps having been sucked out by the sticky ink dabber. Both examples, incidentally, are broken pieces of type, suggesting that they may have snapped when being pulled out of the forme: the broken part fell back and was subsequently inked.[6] Some show light inky smudges, while others are almost clean.

EVIDENCE FROM THE 'COLLECTION' BROUGHT TOGETHER IN MEI

Since Madden's discovery, other examples have been found and promptly discussed in scholarship, though the discovery of fallen type letters over the last 150 years has been slow. Most recently, I have listed in MEI all known examples from the incunable period, retrievable under the search key 'data.copyType:n'. Albeit small, the corpus finally allows comparisons and lays the ground for conclusions.

As part of the MEI listings, efforts were made to personally examine and/or obtain up-to-date images of all the examples as described by other, earlier scholars. This has not always

[3] M. Audin, 'Types du XVe siècle', *Gutenburg-Jahrbuch*, 29, 1954, pp. 84–100 and his *Les types lyonnais primitifs, conservés au département des imprimés*, Paris, 1955.

[4] P. F. Tschudin, 'Ein buchgewerblicher Fundkomplex der Inkunabelzeit aus Basel', *Gutenberg-Jahrbuch*, 77, 2002, pp. 84–9, describes the type letter and other print-related artefacts found in the St. Alban-Vorstadt area.

[5] Johannes Nider, *De morali lepra*, [Cologne], Conrad Winters de Homborch, [between 17 Mar. and 20 Sept. 1479], 8° (ISTC in00191000; MEI 02104966). See J. P. A. Madden, *Lettres d'une bibliographe: quatrième série*, Paris, 1875, p. 230.

[6] A broken piece of type, 7 mm high, in Augustinus, *De civitate dei*, Naples, Mathias Moravus, 1477, f° (ISTC ia01237000; MEI 02014904), and another broken letter in Jacobus de Voragine, *The golden legend*, Westminster, William Caxton, [between 20 Nov. 1483 and Mar. 1484], f° (ISTC ij00148000; MEI 02019511).

been possible for all of them, and currently two remain without a clear or recent image: the Bonn copy of the *Catholicon*,[7] and the copy of Günther Zainer's edition of Johannes Friburgensis' *Summa confessorum* formerly belonging to Detlef Mauss.[8]

To date, fifty-four different examples of fallen type letters and spacing are known to survive among incunabula, as detailed in Table 2.1; there are, however, four exceptions. Particular marks in the Madrid and Darmstadt copies of the *Catholicon* and the Darmstadt *Sententiarum*,[9] originally thought to be evidence of fallen type and thus included in MEI on account of their mentions in earlier literature, have since turned out to be the result of thin strips of paper or card masking the type letters.[10] A true example has a 'halo' of unprinted type letters surrounding it, because the fallen type letter, lying on the forme, has stopped some of the inked letters in the forme making contact with the paper (see Fig. 2.1).[11] A similar non-type example is cited by Adolf Schmidt.[12]

The MEI collection includes a variety of type sizes and shapes dating from c. 1456 to 1498.[13] They come from thirty-eight different printers working in nineteen different cities. Five of the printers occur more than once and three have more than one example of fallen

Table 2.1 General figures.

Copies with fallen type	45
Number of fallen pieces	54 (some copies show more than one fallen letter)
Broken or unclear examples	10
Pieces of spacing	1
Slips of paper/card (i.e., not type)	3/4

[7] Johannes Balbus, *Catholicon*, [Mainz, Printer of the *Catholicon*], '1460' [not before 1469], f° (ISTC ib00020000; MEI 02014963).

[8] D. Mauss, 'Johannes Friburgensis: *Summa confessorum* (1476)', *Gutenberg-Jahrbuch*, 68, 1993 pp. 62–5 (62 and image 1 at p. 64). Also see the chart in Appendix 1. Mauss died in 2009 and his collection has since been sold. The copy is Johannes Friburgensis, *Summa confessorum*, [Augsburg, Günther Zainer], 1476 [not after 1 Feb.], f° (ISTC ij00316000; MEI 02014905).

[9] A. Schmidt, 'Untersuchungen über die Buchdruckertechnik des 15. Jahrhunderts', *Zentralblatt für Bibliothekswesen*, 14, 1897, pp. 57–65 (64–5), concerning a copy of Petrus Lombardus, *Sententiarum libri IV*, [Strasbourg, Printer of Henricus Ariminensis (Georg Reyser?), about 1476)], f° (ISTC ip00479100; MEI 02014947).

[10] It has not yet been possible to check on the Bonn copy of the *Catholicon* (MEI 02014963) cited in L. Hellinga, 'Slipped Lines and Fallen Type in the Mainz *Catholicon*', *Gutenberg-Jahrbuch*, 67, 1992, pp. 35–40. The image resolution in the article is poor, but it is doubtful that this copy will show a fallen type letter.

[11] J.-B. Krumenacker, 'Un Virgile plein de caractère: découverte d'un cas de caractères tombés de la forme en groupe', *Gutenberg-Jahrbuch*, 92, 2017, pp. 64–70 (69), also mentions the 'halo' or '*aureole*' effect of white space around a fallen type letter, as does N. Harris, 'Un caractère tombé de la Bible d'Estienne', in *Guide déraisonne des collections du Musée de l'Imprimerie et de la communication graphique*, Lyon, 2014, pp. 12–15, republished in English as 'A fallen sort in the 1540 Estienne Bible', *Gutenberg-Jahrbuch*, 90, 2015, pp. 99–104.

[12] Schmidt, 'Untersuchungen über die Buchdruckertechnik' (n. 9 above).

[13] Type continued to fall long after 1500, the latest one recorded so far being in one of the two Folger Shakespeare Library's copies of Richard Eburne, *The maintenance of the ministery*, London, [Thomas

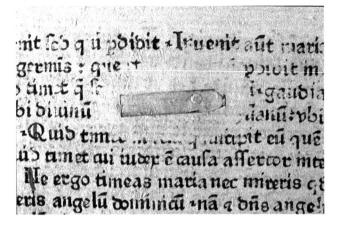

FIG. 2.1. Fallen type with halo of space around the fallen letter, found in Johannes Gerson, *Opera*, Cologne, Johann Kölhoff, 1483–1484, f° (ISTC ig00185000), vol. IV, fol. XLVIIIr. Oxford, Bodleian Library, Bod Auct. 5Q 5.51. (MEI 02014894).

type. Three distinct editions by both Johann Zainer and Johann Schönsperger contain fallen type, and Zainer has two pieces on the same page in one edition. Baptista de Tortis also has two fallen pieces on a page, as does Matthias Huss. Antoine Lambillon has five fallen type letters in a row. William Caxton and Günther Zainer have a fallen type letter in two different editions. Johann Mentelin has two pieces on two different pages, in one copy, and another example on a different page in a second copy of the same edition. Some examples are clearer than others; those that lie in the margin, off the edge of the set text — thus lying lower than the text — are often not so clear.

Type Heights

Type heights are a perennial problem for printers. To be used together to set a page of text, all the letters have to be exactly the same height to enable even inking and printing. A worn type letter, or one that is cast to a different height from the rest, is unusable. A difference in height of 0.10 mm might not make a difference, but more than that could cause serious problems.[14] It should be noted that the problem of printing slightly varying type heights in a fount would be less noticeable when working with damped paper, on a wooden press, and with a tympan (the metal frame that holds and supports the sheet of paper during the printing process) with soft packing, than when working with an iron press and firm packing.

As seen in Table 2.2, during the incunable period many printers produced their own type using their own moulds. The mould dictates the type height, as well as body width and

Creede] for Eleazar Edgar, 1609, 4° (USTC 3003922), https://collation.folger.edu/2016/03/fallen-type/, accessed 3 February 2021.

[14] To compare, a variation in height between letters of 0.05 and 0.75 mm was found in some modern founts, with no significant impact on to the quality of the printed letter on the pages.

depth, before the final dressing of the feet of the cast letters to ensure they are all the same height.[15] Type height can be increased with a small sliver of paper underneath, though it is generally safer to throw away a low or badly worn piece of type. We can confidently assume that a printer would try to use the same type height for all his various founts. As today, he would also have to be aware of different type heights when acquiring stock from other printers or typefounders.

Olivier Deloignon, in an article about Mentelin's fallen type examples, gave a brief summary of the Saône type heights.[16] He noted that the majority of the letters were high compared with the modern standard UK and US height of 0.918 inches (23.32 mm) and the Didot type height used in France and Germany of 23.56 mm. A large majority of the 233 Saône type letters are over 24 mm high; forty examples are around 24.0 mm in height, eleven are 26.3 mm, fifty-four are 25.3 mm high, and fifty-six are over 27 mm high, with the remainder being at various odd sizes in between. The Saône type letters vary in height by almost 5 mm from the shortest to the tallest. Within the groupings of type letters from the same fount there was a difference of 0.10 and 0.15 mm in height.[17]

In comparison, the fallen type examples in the MEI collection are somewhat shorter. Of the thirty-seven examples that can be measured, there are three at 24 mm high, two from Cologne printers and one from Lyon. Seven 25 mm examples come from Lyon (two), Milan, Naples, Paris, Utrecht, and Venice. There are two examples of 26 mm high type from Strasbourg and Venice, and one measuring about 26.5 mm from Venice. The seven 27 mm high examples come from Cologne, Mainz, and Basel (one each), and from Venice (four). The other eighteen type letters in the collection are all less than 24 mm high, two of these being from Lyon: a 22 mm high letter from Nicolaus Philippi and Marcus Reinhart[18] and a 23 mm high letter from Matthias Huss (see Table 2.2).[19] None of the fallen type letters from Lyon are taller than 25 mm high.

CHRONOLOGY

There may be a chronological trend to type heights: slight evidence points towards earlier type in the 1470s being shorter and later type in the 1490s being taller, though the small

---

[15] The method of dressing is described in some detail by various authors: J. Southward, *Practical Printing*, 3rd edn, London, 1887, I, p. 24; J. Moxon, *Mechanick Exercises on the Whole Art of Printing (1683–4)*, 2nd edn, ed. H. Davis and H. Carter, New York, 1978, pp. 179–90; and L. A. Legros and J. C. Grant, *Typographical Printing Surfaces*, London, 1916, pp. 20–2.

[16] O. Deloignon, 'Un double 'accident typographique' dans la *Concordantiae Bibliorum* de Konrad von Halberstadt, Strasbourg, avant 1474', *Gutenberg-Jahrbuch*, 91, 2015, pp. 81–92 (83 and footnote).

[17] See also Audin, 'Types du XVe siècle' (n. 3 above).

[18] Robertus Caracciolus, *Sermones de adventu*, [Lyon, Nicolaus Philippi and Marcus Reinhart, about 1479], f° (ISTC ic00140000; MEI 02014967). See M. Perrier, 'Enquête autour d'un recueil de trois incunables issu de la bibliothèque d'un amateur', PhD dissertation, Lyon, ENSSIB, 2014, https://www. enssib.fr/bibliotheque-numerique/notices/64938-enquete-autour-d-un-recueil-de-trois-incunables-issu-de-la-bibliotheque-d-un-amateur,accessed 17 January 2021.

[19] *Biblia latina*, [Lyon], Matthias Huss, 1494, f° (ISTC ib00596000; MEI 02014974). The *Gesamtkatalog der Wiegendrucke*'s description of this edition (GW 04273) lists two instances of fallen type letters.

Table 2.2 Fallen type height with printer, place, and year (where the impression is complete enough to measure).

Type height (mm)	Printer	Place, Year
c. 16 (spacing)	Johann Schönsperger	Augsburg, 1485
c. 20	William Caxton	Westminster, 1483
c. 20.5	Johann Mentelin	Strasbourg, 1474
c. 21	Günther Zainer (2)	Augsburg, 1476 and 1477
c. 21	Johann Schönsperger	Augsburg, 1482
c. 21	Johann Zainer (4)	Ulm, 1474, 1480, and 1481
c. 21	Berthold Ruppel	Basel, 1478–1479
c. 22	Erhard Ratdolt	Venice, 1480
c. 22	N. Philippi and M. Reinhart	Lyon, 1479
c. 22	Johann Schönsperger	Augsburg, 1486
c. 22	Theodoric Rood	Oxford, 1483/1484
c. 22	Carolus de Darleriis	Cremona, 1496
c. 23	Printer of the 1481 *Legenda aurea*	Strasbourg, 1482
c. 23	P. Gérard and J. Dupré	Abbeville, 1487
c. 24	Conrad Winters	Cologne, 1479
c. 24	Nicolaus Götz	Cologne, 1475
c. 24	Antoine Lambillon (5)	Lyon, 1492
c. 25	Matthias Huss (2)	Lyon, 1494
c. 25	L. Pachel and U. Scinzenzeler	Milan, 1483
c. 25	Azriel ben Joseph A. Gunzenhauser	Naples, 1492
c. 25	Georges Wolf	Paris, 1498
c. 25	N. Ketelaar and G. de Leempt	Utrecht, 1474
c. 25	J. and G. de Gregoriis	Venice, 1497–1498
c. 26	Adolf Rusch	Strasbourg, 1480
c. 26	Simon Bevilaqua	Venice, 1498
c. 26.5	Nicolaus de Frankfordia	Venice, 1498
c. 27	Baptista de Tortis (2)	Venice, 1490
c. 27	Aldus Manutius	Venice, 1498
c. 27	J. Fust and P. Schöffer	Mainz, 1457
c. 27	Johann Kölhoff	Cologne, 1483–1484
c. 27	Johann Bergmann	Basel, 1498

sample available suggests caution. Having said that, there are at least a couple of anomalies that stand out. One fallen type example, measuring 26 mm, is in Adolf Rusch's edition of the *Biblia latina cum glossa*, printed in 1480 in Strasbourg.[20] One wonders why Rusch's type for this edition was so much taller compared to other Strasbourg or Basel examples (other Strasbourg fallen type letters were c. 21 mm and 23 mm high). This anomaly might be explained because the four type founts used for this edition were all cast especially for Rusch by Johann Amerbach in Basel, though it is also worth remembering that the only other contemporary fallen type from Basel measures c. 21 mm high.

The other example is in Erhard Ratdolt's edition of Werner Rolewinck's *Fasciculus temporum*, issued in Venice in 1480, and measures only 22 mm, whereas other printers based in Venice have type of 27 mm in height;[21] perhaps Ratdolt had purchased this type from Augsburg where he had connections (see Table 2.3).

Shorter letters appear to have been cast in Ulm, Augsburg, Strasbourg, and Basel, against taller ones produced in Cologne, Paris, Naples, and Venice, though further evidence would be helpful to buttress these claims.

These measurements might suggest that many of the Saône type letters, where the majority were over 24 mm high, had been imported, or cast some years later — the few examples of sixteenth-century fallen type are all taller, between 24 mm to 27 mm high. Or perhaps when buying type or purchasing/making moulds they were influenced by printers working in Italy. At present, there are probably not enough examples to make any definitive statements.

TYPE BODY PARTS

Being able to see an outline of the type bodies has shown the variation in the different body shapes of type letters. There are type letters with sloping shoulders and square shoulders, with flat feet, grooved feet, and sloping feet, as well as pierced type, and again the fallen type examples can be compared with the Lyon type letters.

Sloping shoulders

Type with sloping shoulders is unusual and most of the fallen types have square shoulders. Sloping shoulders are only known to exist in examples from three printers: two from Cologne, Nicolas Götz and Conrad Winters, from 1475 and 1479, and one from Philippi and Reinhart in Lyon from 1479. Filing or paring down the square shoulders of the type body to a slope helps to remove the possibility of making inked marks on the pages. However, the filing process is time consuming, so it is perhaps not surprising that, so far, evidence of this has been identified only in the works of three printers. Sloping shoulders are also very rare

---

[20] *Biblia latina*, [Strasbourg, Adolf Rusch, for Anton Koberger at Nuremberg, not after 1480], f° (ISTC ib00607000; MEI 02014893).

[21] Werner Rolewinck, *Fasciculus temporum*, Venice, Erhard Ratdolt, 24 Nov. 1480, f° (ISTC ir00261000; MEI 02014895).

Table 2.3 Type height by year of printing and printers.

Year	Height (mm)	Printer	Place
1474	c. 21	Johann Zainer	Ulm
1474	c. 21	Johann Mentelin (3)	Strasbourg
1474	c. 25	N. Ketelaar and G. de Leempt	Utrecht
1475	c. 24	Nicolaus Götz	Cologne
1476	c. 21	Günther Zainer	Augsburg
1477	c. 21	Günther Zainer	Augsburg
1478–1479	c. 21	Berthold Ruppel	Basel
1479	c. 22	N. Philippi and M. Reinhart	Lyon
1479	c. 24	Conrad Winters	Cologne
1480	c. 26	Adolf Rusch	Strasbourg
1480	c. 22	Erhard Ratdolt	Venice
1480	c. 21	Johann Zainer (2)	Ulm
1481	c. 21	Johann Zainer	Ulm
1482	c. 21	Johann Schönsperger	Augsburg
1482	c. 23	Printer of the 1481 *Legenda aurea*	Strasbourg
1483	c. 20	William Caxton	Westminster
1483	c. 25	L. Pachel and U. Scinzenzeler	Milan
1483–1484	c. 27	Johann Kölhoff	Cologne
1483/1484	c. 22	Theodoric Rood	Oxford
1486	c. 22	Johann Schönspeger	Oxford
1487	c. 23	P. Gérard and J. Dupré	Abbeville
1487	c. 26.5	Nicolaus de Frankfordia	Venice
1490	c. 27	Baptista de Tortis (2)	Venice
1492	c. 25	Azriel ben Joseph A. Gunzenhauser	Naples
1492	c. 24	Antoine Lambillon (5)	Lyon
1494	c. 23	Matthias Huss (2)	Lyon
1496	c. 22	Carolus de Darleriis	Cremona
1497–1498	c. 25	J. and G. de Gregoriis	Venice
1498	c. 25	Georges Wolf	Paris
1498	c. 26	Simon Bevilaqua	Venice
1498	c. 27	Johann Bergman de Olpe	Basel
1498	c. 27	Aldus Manutius	Venice

in the Lyon type collection, with perhaps only two examples, although further inspection of the letters themselves might lead to finding a few more sloping shoulders.

Flat feet

The shape of the foot of a piece of type is another aspect that is revealed by some of the fallen type impressions. The hand-casting process known today leaves a tang of waste metal, attached to the foot of the piece of type, that remains from the pouring process through the jet, or mouthpiece, of the mould. The tang is broken off at the foot, and then any rough edges are removed by being planed, or filed, along with all the other letters in the fount. This method leaves a slight groove in the foot. The feet of many of the fallen letters in the MEI collection cannot be seen, or seen clearly. However, thirteen of them show completely flat feet, and five show a slight grove in the centre of their foot which could show where the tang has been removed. Harry Carter noted one of these latter examples, from 1484 (see Fig. 2.2): he postulated the earliest types were cast with flat feet and stated that having a different method of casting by pouring the metal through a jet was a refinement.[22]

FIG. 2.2. A broken foot from a piece of type in *Missale Cracoviense*, Mainz, Peter Schöffer, 10 Nov. 1484, f° (ISTC im00658000), fol. 166r. Berlin, Staatsbibliothek, f° Ink 1544 (MEI 02014968).

---

[22] H. Carter, *A View of Early Typography up to about 1600* (reprinted with an introduction by J. Mosley), London, 2002, pp. 18–19. Carter noted a broken piece of type, showing only the foot, in the Berlin Staatsbibliothek's copy of the *Missale Cracoviense*: Mainz, Peter Schöffer, 10 Nov. 1484, f° (ISTC im00658000; MEI 02014968).

The thirteen fallen type letters that show completely flat feet may have been cast in a different kind of mould, one not known today. More recently, Stan Nelson, with a lifetime of experience of hand mould making and hand typecasting, has commented on the difference between completely flat feet and feet with a groove. He maintains that the use of a plane or a plough and dressing bench to trim the feet of printing type did not exist during the earliest period of typecasting, and that 'the lack of a foot-groove proves only the absence of the dressing bench and its plough, and nothing more'. He adds that the existence of flat feet tells us nothing about the shape of the early moulds.[23] To date, it is not known how early letters were cast with flat feet. To add to the confusion, there are also type letters with sloping feet.

Sloping feet

At first sight the idea of type letters with sloping feet seems strange. Type letters fall over with flat feet, so trying to make them stand on pointed feet seems against all reason. However, once set in a stick and then locked up in the forme, there should be no problem with their ability to print evenly. In the MEI collection, there are eight examples of fallen type with sloping feet, about 25%; four of them come from Venice and from the 1490s (see Table 2.2); the others come from Milan, Abbeville, Paris, and Naples — the earliest being from Milan in 1483. Interestingly, two other later examples of fallen type letters with sloping feet have been found: one from 1540 in Paris and another from 1564 in Lyon. This suggests that this was a fairly long-lived method of type making.[24]

90% of the type from the river Saône have sloping feet (see Fig. 2.3).[25] Of those that Audin could collate as being perhaps from the same fount, he stated that the angle of the foot slope was the same for all letters. However, the angle of slope altered from fount to fount. He noted that while the flat part of the foot of each letter was smooth (as cast from a mould), the sloped edge was rough, and stated categorically that all the sloped edges had been made after casting.[26] The letters with sloping feet in the MEI collection all show signs of a rough edge along the slope.

Audin suggests that most likely the type letters were cast over height and then, as part of the dressing process, had a corner taken off the foot, followed by the flat section of foot being filed exactly to the required height. He postulated that this would require much less work in filing down and would make it easier to get the correct height more precisely.

Conversely, Nelson suggested that the sloped edge on the foot might have come from a different style of mould being used — one with a hemispherical mouthpiece and where the metal was poured in at the corner of the foot rather than centrally: the jet would be broken off from the corner at an angle, leaving a sloping foot, ready for dressing.[27]

---

[23] S. Nelson, 'Reconsidering a Conclusion: Were Early Types Cast or Cut to Height?', *Journal of the Printing Historical Society*, 25, 2016, pp. 7–24 (12).

[24] N. Harris, 'Un caractère tombé' (n. 11 above).

[25] Audin, 'Types du XVe siècle' (n. 3 above), p. 94.

[26] Audin, 'Types du XVe siècle' (n. 3 above), p. 95.

[27] I am grateful to Stan Nelson for sharing his expertise on the matter.

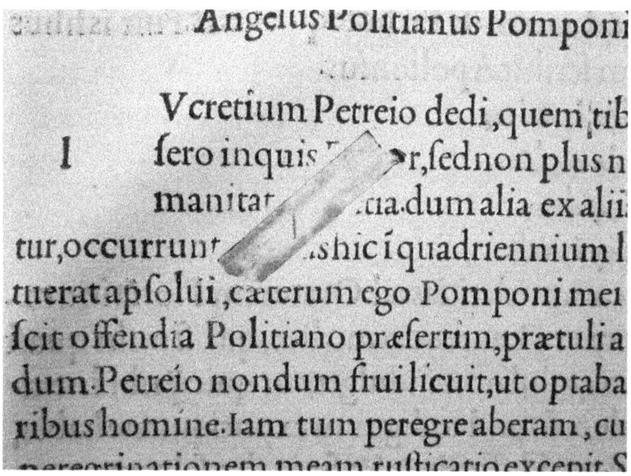

FIG. 2.3. A piece of fallen type with a sloping foot found in Angelus Politianus, *Opera*, Aldus Manutius, Venice, 1498, f° (ISTC ip00886000), sig. b2v. Oxford, Bodleian Library, Byw. F 4.1. (MEI 00204488).

Holes and perforations

There are so far seventeen examples of fallen type with a circle in the impression in the side of the body, most probably caused by an indent or hole in the type. Some examples occur more than once in an edition, and the pierced, fallen type examples come from seven different places and from eleven different printers between the dates 1474 to 1486 (see Table 2.4). With the exception of one example from Lyon and one from Basel, all the other fallen type letters with holes are from Germany. We might infer that the printers Philippi and Reinhart in Lyon had brought some of their type from Germany.

The practice of drilling holes through the type body is supported by documentary evidence. For instance, Abbot Melchior, when ordering his type for the new press at Saints Ulrich and Afra in Augsburg, specified that the fount of 80,000 letters should be bored through and planed.[28] Surely one does not bore holes through 80,000 letters without a reason. The most obvious explanation is related to threading, but then it begs the question that, if the letters were threaded when being printed, how did they fall out of the forme. And indeed there are occasional sightings of blind impressed lengths of wire or string on which such letters might have been threaded.[29] A good example of an impressed mark made by

[28] R. Schmidt, 'Die Klosterdruckerei von St. Ulrich und Afra in Augsburg (1472 bis kurz nach 1474)', in H. Gier and J. Janota (eds), *Augsburger Buchdruck und Verlagswesen: von den Anfängen bis zur Gegenwart*, Wiesbaden, 1997, pp. 141–53.

[29] W. Partridge, 'The Typesetting and Printing of the Mainz *Catholicon*', *The Book Collector*, 35, 1986, pp. 21–51 (31, fig. 14). L. Hellinga, 'Analytical Bibliography and the Study of Early Printed Books with a Case-Study of the Mainz *Catholicon*', *Gutenberg-Jahrbuch*, 64, 1989, pp. 47–96 (76), after a discussion with James Mosley, restates Mosley's suggestion that wire might have been used to hold lines of type together.

Table 2.4 Fallen type with a hole through the body.

Year	Place	Printer
1474	Strasbourg (3)	Johann Mentelin
1474	Ulm	Johann Zainer
1475	Cologne	Nicolaus Götz
1477	Augsburg	Günther Zainer
1478–1479	Basel	Berthold Ruppel
1479	Cologne	Conrad Winters de Homborch
1479	Lyon	N. Philippi and M. Reinhart
1480	Ulm (2)	Johann Zainer
1480	Strasbourg	Adolf Rusch
1481	Ulm	Johann Zainer
1482	Augsburg	Johann Schönsperger
1482	Strasbourg	Printer of the 1481 *Legenda aurea*
1483–1484	Cologne	Johann Kölhoff
1486	Augsburg	Johann Schönsperger

wire or cord can be seen on the last page in the Bodleian Library's copy of Thomas Aquinas, *De articulis fidei*, [Mainz, Printer of the *Catholicon*, about 1469].[30]

Type Falling on its Front (or back)

Almost all of the examples are of type letters having fallen on their sides, which is understandable, as the sides are generally wider than the front and back of the type body. However, two instances are known, both from Lyon printers and both displaying more than one fallen letter, where the type letters have fallen on their front or back. On both occasions, the fallen letters are different widths from each other and from the type body used for setting the text.

One example, from a 1492 printing of Vergil's *Opera* by Antoine Lambillon, shows five letters, on their fronts, that had formed the printed word 'Pecus' as a marginal note. When they fell, they were lying on the two marginal notes below them; thus, all three marginal

---

[30] Thomas Aquinas, *De articulis fidei et ecclesiae sacramentis*, [Mainz, Printer of the Catholicon, about 1469], 4° in divided half sheets (ISTC it00273000; MEI 00209002).

notes on that page were obliterated.[31] It is possible to see the differences in width of each of the letters, though not to tell whether the letters had sloping feet or not, because they are lying on their fronts (even though the letter 's' might be on its side with a sloping foot). The other is from Matthias Huss's 1494 printing of the *Biblia latina,* where the widths of the type bodies of the fallen type examples are again not the depth of the type bodies being used.[32] It can be presumed that they also have fallen on their front or back.

Fallen Spacing

Along with all the fallen type examples, there survives one example of fallen spacing.[33] It comes from a book printed by Schönsperger in 1485 and measures 16 mm high. This height can be compared with a fallen letter printed by Schönsperger the following year that is 22 mm high — the spacing was cast 6 mm shorter than the type letters — about 25% lower than the type height. The Lyon spacing examples were generally 20% lower than the type letters of the same type body size. There was no hole through the piece of spacing. A later piece of fallen spacing has been found, also measuring c. 16 mm high. It is on the last leaf in the single known copy, currently in Paris, BnF, of Thomas Artus's *Les Hermaphrodites,* dated 1605.[34]

Woodblocks

Four of the examples are from a type letter that has fallen on a woodblock illustration, leaving a type-shaped indentation on the block. They have been found in two separate 1498 editions of Brant's *Ship of fools,* one from Paris and the other from Basel;[35] one in Simon Bevilaqua's *Biblia latina,* also printed in 1498, in Venice;[36] and one in Johannes and Gregorius de Gregoriis' printer's device in their 1497–1498 *Commentaria in Bibliam* (see Fig. 2.4).[37] In the latter case, the damage was presumably repaired with a plug, leaving a faint rectangular, type-sized, outline, while in all the others the damage was ignored and the

---

[31] J.-B. Krumenacker, 'Un Virgile plein de caractères' (n. 11 above), pp. 64–70.

[32] *Biblia latina* (n. 19 above).

[33] Spaces are cast from the same type metal, and to the same body size, to be used to separate words and fill out the lines. They are cast to a lower height than the letters to ensure they do not print.

[34] Thomas Artus, *Les Hermaphrodites,* [s.l. (France), s.n.], 1605, 12° (USTC 6017686).

[35] Sebastian Brant, *Stultifera navis,* Paris, [Johann Philippi, de Cruzenach], for E., J. and G. De Marnef, 8 Mar. 1498, 4° (ISTC ib01092000; MEI 02014899); Sebastian Brant, *Stultifera navis,* Basel, Johann Bergmann, de Olpe, 1 Mar. 1498, 4° (ISTC ib01091000; MEI 02014900).

[36] *Biblia latina,* Venice, Simon Bevilaqua, 8 May 1498, 4° (ISTC ib00603000; MEI 02024308).

[37] Hieronymus, *Commentaria in Bibliam,* Venice, Johannes and Gregorius de Gregoriis, de Forlivio, 1497–1498, f° (ISTC ih00160000; MEI 02014901). The block with the printer's device was most probably repaired, arguably a consequence of the relevance of this particular block for the printers.

FIG. 2.4. Repair on de Gregoriis' woodcut printer's mark, most likely covering the damage caused by a piece of fallen type, in Hieronymus, *Commentaria in Bibliam*, Venice, Johannes and Gregorius de Gregoriis, de Forlivio, 1497–1498, f° (ISTC ih00160000), sig. ppp8r. Oxford, Bodleian Library, Auct. 6Q 1.2 (MEI 02014901).

printer carried on with the rest of the print run. Interestingly, unlike the type letters fallen on text and discussed above, all these examples, fallen on woodblocks, appear in more than one copy of their editions: this might be because woodblocks were expensive and rather time-consuming to repair or replace.

Re-creating Fallen Type: an Experiment

As part of my investigation, a practical experiment was conducted to print some text with a piece of pierced, fallen type lying on the forme. Clearly, I could not recreate all the fifteenth-century conditions, some of which remain shrouded in mystery to this day, but it was hoped that it would be possible to recreate an example of fallen type as close in appearance as possible to one from the fifteenth century.

Damped paper made from linen fibres was used, along with a soft packing in the tympan. Printing took place with an iron hand press using Monotype-cast text and some Monotype letters of different thicknesses to be used as fallen type examples. It might be worth noting that Monotype type letters are made from a slightly softer metal than founders' type and could have produced different results than harder, founders' type. A hole was drilled though the type letters with a 2 mm drill.

A very successful example of fallen type was produced on the paper, with a crisp white circle made from damp paper being pressed into the hole, matching well with the fifteenth-century examples (see Figs 2.5 and 2.6).

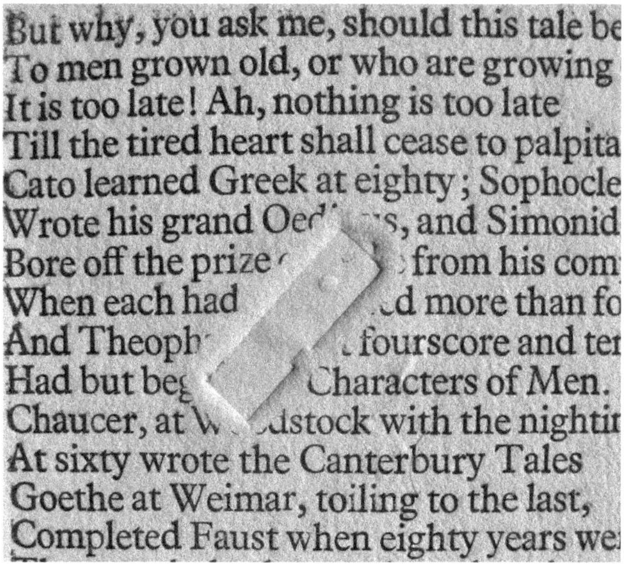

2: FALLEN TYPE 47

FIG. 2.5. Piece of type from the modern experiment, with hole drilled through, lying on the set text. The nick in the side of the letter was formed in the mould.

FIG. 2.6. Fine impression from the piece of fallen type, showing the halo effect around the type letter and the raised circle from the drilled hole.

During the fifteenth century, in the event of text over a number of lines being crushed under fallen type, replacing the damaged letters as well as the fallen type would have been almost compulsory: despite the interruption to the printing schedule, a printer could not ignore an error of this magnitude. In the modern experiment the thinnest of the fallen type letters was cracked in half by the process.[38]

The experiment also gave a chance to compare the size of the blind impressed letter with the actual piece of type used to make the impression, and to measure the impressed mark when the paper was damp and when it was dry. The metal type letter was 23.36 mm high (measured with a micrometre). The impressed mark was about 23.00 mm long on dry paper and about 23.35 mm long on damped paper — it was only possible to make this measurement by eye with a fine scale, so the measurements are perhaps not as exact as with a micrometre. There was a difference of about 0.35 mm between the impressions on wet and on dry paper, about 1.5%.[39] This is important when measuring the type heights of all the fallen type examples — some allowance should be made for paper shrinkage after printing. It can be useful to have the resources to measure fallen type impressions to three decimal points, yet that measurement still cannot be completely accurate because of the shrinkage of the paper as it dries.

The Importance of Fallen Type

Although in the past they have been mostly treated as a curiosity, these examples of fallen type are highly relevant historical artefacts. Apart from the obvious importance of showing the type height and the shape of the body — the parts of a piece of type not usually seen on the page — each piece of fallen type comes with solid provenance information such as date, printer, and place of printing.

As more fallen type examples emerge, we can get a better understanding of the variety of type heights in incunable print shops. If the current knowledge of type heights is irregular, and mostly limited to specific geographical areas, with more examples it should become possible to attribute the origins of various type founts to different towns with more certainty. This could lead to a better understanding of the origins of the printing material used by some early typographers: for instance, the case of Ratdolt printing in Venice with type that was of Augsburg height suggests that he was not necessarily using local Venetian material. The extent to which type travelled, on occasion even great distances, would greatly add to our understanding of the circulation, marketing, and use of printing supplies. Likewise, a larger corpus would enable us to narrow down the span of years for the use of type with holes drilled through, type with sloping shoulders, and type with various flat, grooved, and sloping feet. Finally, it would help to contextualise the exceptional finding of the Saône types.

---

[38] Two of the letters found by Deloignon, 'Un double "accident typographique"' (n. 16 above), pp. 84–6, had been cracked by the printer Johann Mentelin during the printing process, an indication of the pressure produced by a fifteenth-century press.

[39] The shrinkage of paper in relation to the measurement of type sizes is discussed in F. Bowers, 'Bibliographical Evidence from the Printer's Measure', *Studies in Bibliography*, 2, 1949–1950, pp. 154–69, and by A. Pollard, *Catalogue of Books Printed in the Fifteenth Century now in the British Museum*, London, 1908, I, pp. xx–xxi.

BIBLIOGRAPHY

PRIMARY SOURCES

See Table 2.2.

SECONDARY LITERATURE

Audin, M., 'Types du XVe siècle', *Gutenburg-Jahrbuch*, 29, 1954, pp. 84–100.

Audin, M., *Les types lyonnais primitifs, conservés au département des imprimés*, Paris, Bibliothèque Nationale, 1955.

Bowers, F., 'Bibliographical Evidence from the Printer's Measure', *Studies in Bibliography*, 2, 1949–1950, pp. 154–69.

Carter, H., *A View of Early Typography up to about 1600* (reprinted with an introduction by J. Mosley), London, 2002.

Deloignon, O., 'Un double "accident typographique" dans la *Concordantiae Bibliorum* de Konrad von Halberstadt, Strassburg', *Gutenberg-Jahrbuch*, 91, 2015, pp. 81–92.

Harris, N., 'Un caractère tombé de la Bible d'Estienne', in *Guide déraisonne des collections du Musée de l'Imprimerie et de la communication graphique*, Lyon, 2014, pp. 12–15. Also in English as 'A fallen sort in the 1540 Estienne Bible', *Gutenberg-Jahrbuch*, 90, 2015, pp. 99–104.

Hellinga, L., 'Analytical Bibliography and the Study of Early Printed Books with a Case-Study of the Mainz *Catholicon*', *Gutenberg-Jahrbuch*, 64, 1989, pp. 47–96.

Hellinga, L., 'Slipped Lines and Fallen Type in the Mainz *Catholicon*', *Gutenberg-Jahrbuch*, 67, 1992, pp. 35–40.

Krumenacker, J.-B., 'Un Virgile plein de caractères. Découverte d'un cas de caractères tombé de la forme engroupe', *Gutenberg-Jahrbuch*, 92, 2017, pp. 64–70.

Legros, L. A., and Grant, J. C., *Typographical Printing Surfaces*, London, 1916.

Madden, J. P. A., *Lettres d'une bibliographe*, série 4, Paris, 1875.

Mauss, D., 'Johannes Friburgensus: Summa confessorum (1476)', *Gutenberg-Jahrbuch*, 68, 1993, pp. 62–5.

Moxon, J., *The Mechanick Exercises on the Whole Art of Printing*, 2nd edn, ed. H. Davis and H. Carter, New York, 1978.

Nelson, S., 'Reconsidering a Conclusion: Were Early Types Cast or Cut to Height?', *Journal of the Printing Historical Society*, 25, 2016, pp. 7–24.

Partridge, W., 'The Typesetting and Printing of the Mainz *Catholicon*', *The Book Collector*, 1986, 35, pp. 21–51.

Perrier, M., 'Enquête autour un receuil de trois incunables issu de la bibliothèque d'un amateur', PhD dissertation, Lyon, ENSSIB, 2014: https://www.enssib.fr/bibliotheque-numerique/notices/64938-enquete-autour-d-un-recueil-de-trois-incunables-issu-de-la-bibliotheque-d-un-amateur.

Pollard, A., *Catalogue of Books Printed in the Fifteenth Century now in the British Museum*, London, 1908.

Schmidt, A., 'Untersuchungen über die Buchdruckertechnik des 15. Jahrhunderts', *Zentralblatt für Bibliothekswesen*, 14 (1897), pp. 57–65.

Schmidt, R., 'Die Klosterdruckerei von SS. Ulrich und Afra in Augsburg (1472 bis kurz nach 1474)', in H. Gier and J. Janota (eds), *Augsburger Buchdruck und Verlagswesen von den Anfängen bis zur Gegenwart*, Wiesbaden, 1997, pp. 141–53.

Southward, J., *Practical Printing*, 3rd edn, London, 1887.

Tschudin, P. F., 'Ein buchgewerblicher Fundkomplex der Inkunabelzeit aus Basel,' *Gutenburg-Jahrbuch*, 77, 2002, pp. 84–9.

CHAPTER 3

PROOF SHEETS AS EVIDENCE OF EARLY PRE-PUBLICATION PROCEDURES

RANDALL HERZ

INTRODUCTION

PROOF sheets, being a waste by-product of the early hand press era, have never been regarded as attractive objects of research. Yet they can provide insight into the pre-press procedures used in early fifteenth-century printing and are also witness to the efforts of early printers to produce well-edited books. In this paper four case studies will be presented that illuminate various aspects of these efforts.

A proof, or trial print, is an impression made of the newly imposed pages ready for printing. It is used to find and correct mistakes prior to printing the full run. In the hand press era proofs were an integral part of printing and accompanied each stage of text production. A proof of two conjugate leaves for the Gutenberg Bible survives, as well as proof sheets from the Mainz press of Johann Fust and Peter Schöffer, all documenting their use in the earliest years of printing.[1] To prepare a book for print, the tasks of the compositor and corrector were closely interwoven. Early modern printers' manuals describe their work as follows: the compositor set the text and initiated the proof, the corrector examined it for misprints and then returned it to the compositor to make corrections to the forme.[2]

---

[1] See Bloomington (IN), Lilly Library, BS75 1454a vault (one sheet of the forty-two-line Gutenberg Bible, one half with recto and verso sides printed, the other half unprinted), described and digitised at http://www.dlib.indiana.edu/omeka/lilly/items/show/79; see ISTC ib00526500, for a proof of a forty-line Bible using the types of the thirty-six-line Bible; for proof sheets from the printing shop of Fust and Schöffer from 1459–1460, see ISTC id00403000; ip01062000; ic00710000.

[2] J. Moxon, *Mechanick Exercises on the Whole Art of Printing (1683–4)*, ed. H. Davis and H. Carter, London, 1958; on the cycle of proofing, see ibid., pp. 233, 238–9, 246–50, 368–9; see also P. Gaskell, *A New Introduction to Bibliography*, New Castle (DE), 2006, pp. 110–16.

Randall Herz, *Proof Sheets as Evidence of Early Pre-Publication Procedures.* In: *Printing and Misprinting.*
Edited by Geri Della Rocca de Candal, Anthony Grafton, and Paolo Sachet, Oxford University Press. © Randall Herz (2023).
DOI: 10.1093/oso/9780198863045.003.0004

FIG. 3.1. An early sixteenth-century pressroom. Geoffrey of Monmouth, *Historia Regum Britanniae*, Paris, Josse Bade and Yves Cavellat, 1508, 4° (USTC 143331), title-page. Augsburg, Staats- und Stadtbibliothek, 4 Gs 765.

In the fifteenth century, a compositor worked directly from manuscript or printed copy. In the woodcut illustrations from this period, he is depicted seated at the type case, setting the forme from a page of copy inserted in the so-called *visorium* (Fig. 3.1).[3] Indeed, it was common practice to remove the copy from its binding before composition began.

No matter how carefully the compositor might proceed, errors inevitably crept into his work. No wonder — he set each line of text letter by letter, inserting each upside down and from right to left into his composing stick! Once he had set the pages required for a printing forme, a proof was made. After a quick check to ensure that general features were in order, the proof sheet was collated against the source text, marked, and returned to the compositor to carry out the corrections. The latter opened the metal frame, the chase, which kept the typeset pages locked in place, and, using an instrument such as a bodkin, lifted one by one each faulty letter and character from the typeset page and replaced them with the correct ones. This round of pulling a proof and proofreading was undoubtedly the most important pre-press procedure. According to the theoretical model, two more rounds would follow.

Whether they actually took place, however, depended on several factors, among which were time, manpower, and whether the commissioner of the book was also its author.

---

[3] The earliest depictions show compositors sitting in the pressroom near the press: *Danse macabre*, Lyon, [Matthias Huss], 18 Febr. 1499/1500, f° (ISTC id00020500), sig. b1r; Geoffrey of Monmouth, *Historia regum Britanniae*, Paris, Josse Bade, 1508, 4° (USTC 143331), title-page; see also the variations with a view into the printing room in the title-pages of Cicero, *Orationes*, Paris, Josse Bade, 1511, f° (USTC 187193) and *Sermones de Sanctis S. Antonii a Padua*, Paris, Josse Bade, 1521, 8° (USTC 145464). See also Jost Amman's illustration in Hans Sachs, *Eygentliche Beschreibung aller Stände auff Erden*, Frankfurt am Main, Georg Raben for Sigmund Feyerabend, 1568, 4° (VD16 S244, not in USTC), sig. F3r, and the title-page of Hieronymus Hornschuch, *Orthotypographia, Hoc Est: Instructio, operas typographicas correcturis*, Leipzig, Michael Lantzenberger, 1608 (USTC 2001806), 8°.

3: PROOF SHEETS AS EVIDENCE OF EARLY PRE-PUBLICATION PROCEDURES

Thus, in the second round, proofs could be made for the author to review during printing. Although fifteenth-century specimens of authors' proofs have yet to be identified, both historical accounts and anecdotal evidence suggest they were made. When Hans Tucher, the author of a popular account of travel to the Holy Land first published in Augsburg in 1482, commissioned a revised edition of his book within just weeks of the publication of the faulty first edition, he closely followed its printing in the Nuremberg printing shop. There is a gap of half of a line in the last line of page 16 in gathering f of the Nuremberg edition, leaving the reader to scramble to the top of the next page to continue reading. Tucher had discovered, apparently upon reviewing a proof of the page, several fill words which had been inserted by the Augsburg printer to offset a printing miscalculation and which the Nuremberg printer had inadvertently preserved. Tucher had the insertion struck just as the page was about to go to print.[4] Like the Nuremberg patrician, authors from such diverse backgrounds as the Carthusian monk Werner Rolewinck (*Fasciculus temporum*), the Ulm physician and humanist Heinrich Steinhöwel (*Aesopus*), and even printer-translator William Caxton, all of whom used the new art of printing to promote their literary projects, closely followed or were personally involved in the printing of their works.[5] Indeed, Steinhöwel is likely responsible for the changes in punctuation made at the proof stage of *Aesopus* discussed in the case study below.

Finally, a press proof was made immediately prior to the full print run. It was the third and final proof, a kind of quality control stage to ensure that all details of the typeset pages were correct before proceeding with printing.

Additional proof sheets could also be made as required in the course of printing: further proofs were regularly pulled following changes made at intermediary stages. Many surviving proofs contain a distribution of text which differs considerably from the final printed version, evidence that corrections were still being made during printing.[6] Red printing for missals or legal texts also required an additional proof to be made to ensure that chapter headlines, majuscules, and paragraph signs, etc., all printed in red, had been properly carried out.[7]

Once the printing of a book had been completed, proofs were no longer of use and were discarded. The majority which have come down to us survived solely through fifteenth- and early sixteenth-century bookbinders who made use of them as binding material (Fig. 3.2).

The proof sheets were used or, better, recycled as pastedowns in the upper and lower covers of books. The unprinted blank side of the proof was ideally suited for this purpose, while the printed side was glued down on the wooden boards of the binding.

---

[4] For Tucher's involvement in the publication of his travel book, see R. Herz, 'From Manuscript Copy to the Printed Book: Hans Tucher's Palestine Account of 1482', *Archiv für Geschichte des Buchwesens*, 69, 2014, pp. 1–19 (esp. 11).

[5] See: V. Zapf, 'Werner Rolevinck', *Deutsches Literatur-Lexikon, Das Mittelalter*, Berlin and Boston, 2010, cols 847–53; P. Amelung, *Der Frühdruck im deutschen Südwesten 1473–1500*, Stuttgart, 1979, pp. 15–148; and L. Hellinga, *William Caxton and Early Printing in England*, London, 2010.

[6] A list of such proofs is lacking.

[7] A preliminary list is drawn in R. Herz, 'Setzermarkierungen und Korrekturblätter in deutschen Inkunabeloffizinen', *Gutenberg-Jahrbuch*, 93, 2018, pp. 92–136, (135–6, Anhang IV).

FIG. 3.2.a–c. A proof sheet with manuscript corrections, recycled in a binding (a) as the verso of the front pastedown (c). Erlangen and Nuremberg, Universitätsbibliothek, H62/INC 1246.

This is not the place to give a detailed account of the history of research into proof sheets. It must suffice here to say that a decisive impulse for their study was given by the German incunabulist Konrad Haebler, who in a lecture of 1908 drew attention to binding material as a potential source of as yet unrecorded incunabula.[8] Paul Needham and Lotte Hellinga made important contributions to this area of research in the 1970s.[9] More recently the team of Falk Eisermann and Oliver Duntze at the *Gesamtkatalog der Wiegendrucke* (GW) in Berlin published a comprehensive article on printer's waste in 2015,[10] and in 2016 Renzo Baldasso called for renewed research into proof sheets.[11] Interest in proof sheets has thus re-emerged in recent years, and it is worth noting that the study of binding waste and proof sheets has helped to expand to our knowledge of the corpus of texts published by fifteenth-century printers. Many 'lost' editions are known only through surviving proof sheets.[12] The four case studies which follow hope to make a small contribution to the ongoing investigations into this promising field of investigation.

---

[8] K. Haebler, 'Makulatur-Forschung', *Zentralblatt für Bibliothekswesen*, 25, 1908, pp. 535–44.
[9] P. Needham, 'The Cambridge Proof Sheets of Mentelin's Bible', *Transactions of the Cambridge Bibliographical Society*, 9, 1986, pp. 1–35; L. Hellinga, 'Proofreading and Printing in Mainz in 1459', in L. Hellinga, *Texts in Transit: Manuscript to Proof and Print in the Fifteenth Century*, Leiden, 2014, pp. 102–55.
[10] O. Duntze and F. Eisermann, 'Fortschritt oder Fidibus? Zur Bestimmung, Bewahrung und Bedeutung von Inkunabelfragmenten', in H. P. Neuheuser et al. (eds), *Fragment und Makulatur. Überlieferungsstörungen und Forschungsbedarf bei Kulturgut in Archiv und Bibliotheken*, Wiesbaden, 2015, pp. 281–307.
[11] R. Baldasso, 'The Variant Typesetting of the *Editio Princeps* of Augustinus, De civitate Dei, 1467 (Subiaco: Conradus Sweynheym and Arnoldus Pannartz, 12 June 1467)', *Gutenberg-Jahrbuch*, 91, 2016, pp. 33–41.
[12] The search phrase 'known only' in ISTC brings up 15 editions of which we are aware exclusively through proof sheets, including: Vegetius, *De re militari*, [Augsburg, Günther Zainer, 1477–1478?], f° (ISTC iv00106200); *Horae ad usum Romanum*, [Paris, Jean Bonhomme, about 1486–1490], 16° (ISTC ih00357470); *Book of Courtesy*, [Westminster, Wynkyn de Worde, about 1493], 4° (ISTC ib01029600).

Proofreading in a Fifteenth-century Printing House

While fifteenth-century press proofs have survived in great numbers, surviving sheets with handwritten corrections are very rare. A recent survey based on the ISTC and GW counted twenty-one specimens with corrections for the German-speaking regions vis-à-vis hundreds of press proofs. Since that survey, more have come to light.[13] They exist for the entire incunabula period, from c. 1459 to 1501, though they are distributed unevenly from region to region and with many leaps and gaps in time.

Let us examine a proof sheet with manuscript corrections which gives insight into fifteenth-century proofreading. It is from the Nuremberg printing house run by Anton Koberger, who by the late 1470s had established himself on the international book market as one of the leading southern German printer/publishers, a position he held until he closed his printing shop in 1503 to concentrate solely on the book trade.[14] While his printing house specialised in high-quality Latin editions of law and theology, it also published a small number of books in German, among which was a two-volume edition of a beautifully illustrated Bible — the ninth in the series of German Bibles — completed on 13 February 1483.[15]

Fig. 3.3 shows a trial sheet of sig. [b3]r from this bible. The leaf, kept in the Dziatzko collection in the Niedersächsische Staats- und Universitätsbibliothek Göttingen, is one of just two proof sheets currently known for this Bible[16] and one of just three specimens of corrector's proof which are presently recorded for Koberger's press. To put this into perspective: hundreds of so-called press proofs survive today for his press, but these contain, as one would expect at that late stage, the final state of text as it appears in print — meticulously edited.

The Göttingen sheet is a highly instructive example of fifteenth-century proofreading. At this point, the compositor had set gathering b of the first volume and had already made several proofs. These were now in the hands of the corrector who had begun to inspect them for mistakes. The sheet shows how thoroughly fifteenth-century proofreaders worked. One would expect nothing less in an establishment as reputable as the Koberger printing house.

In this case, however, the proofreader had much work to do: the sheet, containing Chapter 4 of Genesis (here labelled as the First Book of Moses), is marred with misprints,

---

[13] Herz, 'Setzermarkierungen' (n. 7 above), pp. 119–22. The newly discovered proof sheets are from the presses of Anton Koberger (*Pantheologia*, 1474) in Würzburg, UB, in I.t.f. 30; Conrad Dinckmut (*Epistolae et Evangelia*, 1483) in Memmingen, Wissenschaftliche Stadtbibliothek (Wiss. StB), 2° 3.115, (see below pp. 58–60); and Heinrich Quentell (*Doctrinale* (?), after 1494) in Göttingen, Niedersächsische Staats- und Universitätsbibliothek (SUB), Frag. Impr. 01102-01105.

[14] See H.-O. Keunecke, 'Anton Koberger (c. 1445–1513)', in C. Sauer (ed.), *Anton Koberger. Zum 500. Todestag des Druckers der Schedelschen Weltchronik*, Nuremberg, 2013, pp. 6–13 (esp. 9).

[15] *Biblia*, Nuremberg, Anton Koberger, 17 Febr. 1483, f° (ISTC ib00632000).

[16] A second leaf, a specimen of press proof, is kept today in Munich, Bayerische Staatsbibliothek (BSB), 2 Inc.c.a. 1162 b (sig. [m1]r = fol. 83r). The leaf was pasted down inside the upper cover of Astesanus de Ast, *Summa de casibus conscientiae*, Nuremberg, Koberger, 11 May 1482, f° (ISTC ia01170000).

FIG. 3.3. Proof sheet of *Biblia* [German], Nuremberg, Anton Koberger, 13 February 1483, f° (ISTC ib00632000), fol. VIIr. Göttingen, Niedersächsische Staats- und Universitätsbibliothek, Sammlung Dziatzko 1.

ranging from omissions and misspelled words to typographical errors such as turned and foul-case letters. Let us have a look at the proofreader's marks used at one of the leading printing shops in the year 1483 (Figs 3.4 and 3.5). Many of the symbols used there are ones still familiar to us today, even after the advent of computer-aided editing. For example, in

3: PROOF SHEETS AS EVIDENCE OF EARLY PRE-PUBLICATION PROCEDURES   57

FIG. 3.4. Proof sheet of Koberger's German Bible (see Fig. 3.3), fol. VIIr. Detail: col. a, ll. 1–4.

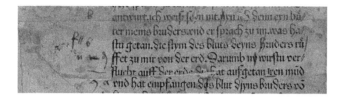

FIG. 3.5. Proof sheet of Koberger's German Bible (see Fig. 3.3), fol. VIIr. Detail: col. a, ll. 28–33.

col. a, l. 1, we encounter the familiar symbol for *deleatur* (✑), requiring the deletion of letter *t* after capital *C* in *Ctapiel* and reinserting it between the vowels *i* and *e* (i.e. Capitel). The proofreader marked a letter or character in a line of text and wrote the correction for it in the margin. In our example, the Nuremberg corrector found three misprints in line 3 of the chapter summary.

He made a stroke on each and entered the correction in the margin, proceeding from right to left, i.e. in the opposite order in which the mistakes appear in the text, moving his quill quickly and efficiently between misprint and margin. This is the sign of a seasoned proofreader working with routine skill. The first correction nearest the margin is the letter *ü*, a German vowel used to form the plural *brüder* (brothers). To its left is the next, the name of Noah's son *Abel*, which the compositor had omitted; a perpendicular stroke in the text marks where the name is to be inserted. Furthest to the left is the word *flüchtig* (fugitive), replacing the word *flach* (flat!) and meaningfully correcting the sentence to read that Cain slew his brother Abel and was fugitive.

Apart from misspellings and omissions, the page also contains many examples of the typographical errors frequently occurring in early printing. In col. a, l. 2, the letter *h* has been corrected to *b* (i.e. to *bruder*), giving us an example of foul case. While redistributing the type from a previous forme, the letter had been mistakenly put in the case box for the letter *b* (see also col. a, l. 30). The proof shows that proper word division was also a concern in early printing. The division of *Rüffet* (to call or summon; col. a, l. 30f.) should have occurred after the first letter *f*, similar to the rule of word division for English words with a double consonant. As with all of our examples, the proofreader has indicated the correction in the line of text and in the margin adjacent to it.

A recurring problem in early printing is present in col. b, l. 5, where the letter *i* is not aligned with the adjacent letters. It is highlighted in the text with an underline and a horizontal stroke in the margin (occurring also in col. b, l. 5 and 13). Another problem that plagued early printing is also present here: in col. a, l. 45, the spacing lead used to maintain space between words has slipped upwards, creating an unsightly vertical mark between the words; here, as above, a horizontal stroke is used to mark the misprint. Lastly, the

58   PRINTING AND MISPRINTING

sheet also contains five cases of turned letters (*u* for *n* in col. b, ll. 5 (twice), 41–2, 44). All of the proofreader's marks found here were, with little regional variation, in common use in fifteenth-century German and other European printing houses. Many of them continued to be used well into the seventeenth century and are mentioned in Hornschuch's handbook for correctors, *Orthotypographia*, published in 1608.[17]

A CASE OF EYE-SKIP

A proof sheet from an Ulm printing shop provides an example of a type of error most often associated with scribal practice rather than printing (Fig. 3.6).

The sheet is from a richly illustrated volume printed by Conrad Dinckmut, which, despite its Latin title *Epistolae et Evangelia*, contains the gospels and epistles for the church year in German translation. It was completed on 28 February 1483.[18]

The sheet, today in a semi-detached state, is the pastedown in the lower cover of Pelegrinus de Oppeln's sermons, issued in Ulm before 1479.[19] Printed on both sides, it was cut in half for use as a pastedown and contains fol. 41*r–v*, corresponding to the first leaf of gathering f. The other half of the sheet appears to be lost.

The proof contains the text of the gospel for the third Sunday before Lent. It provides an example of an eye-skip (Fig. 3.7). About three-quarters into line 25 the line reads: '[…] zu den ersten. un[d] do die pfe[n]nig ./ aber do ‖ […]'. Before the word *pfennig*, the compositor omitted eleven words, probably corresponding to a full line of text in the copy he was working from. The corrector discovered the omission and indicated the location where the text was to be restored with brackets and a pointer in the margin adjacent to the line. In the final printed version, the text now reads: '[…] zu den ersten. Vn[d] do die kame[n] zu der ‖ aylften stu[n]d ware[nt] ko[m]men da nam yetlicher sin pfe[n]nig ./'

A few lines later in l. 29, there are three misprints in the literals, likely due to another lapse in concentration.[20] The eye-skip, however, had a more serious consequence. Keeping to the line count per page (35 lines), but having skipped over a line of text, the compositor set the first line of the text intended for the next page, and as he did, he managed again to omit a word (the article *der*). Presumably the eye-skip went unnoticed because the compositor, as was standard practice, was not working linearly, i.e. from p. 1 to p. 2, but by forme: he set the conjugate page of the forme next, p. 16, before setting the two pages needed for the back of the sheet, pp. 2 and 15. As he set p. 2, he omitted the article again in line 1.

---

[17] Hornschuch, *Orthotypographia* (n. 3 above), pp. 16–19.

[18] *Epistolae et Evangelia* [German], Ulm, Conrad Dinckmut 28 February [14]83, f° (ISTC ie00082000). On the printer, see P. Amelung, *Der Frühdruck im deutschen Südwesten 1473–1500*, Stuttgart, 1979, pp. 149–72. I am grateful to Claire Bolton for drawing my attention to this proof sheet.

[19] Peregrinus de Oppeln, *Sermones de tempore et sanctis*, [Ulm, Johann Zainer the Elder], not after 1479, f° (ISTC ip00267000). This copy is at Memmingen, Wiss. StB, 2° 3.115.

[20] *balt* to *bait*; *nemacht* to *gemacht*; *haët* to *habēt*, all in line 29 in the proof, in line 30 in the printed edition.

3: PROOF SHEETS AS EVIDENCE OF EARLY PRE-PUBLICATION PROCEDURES 59

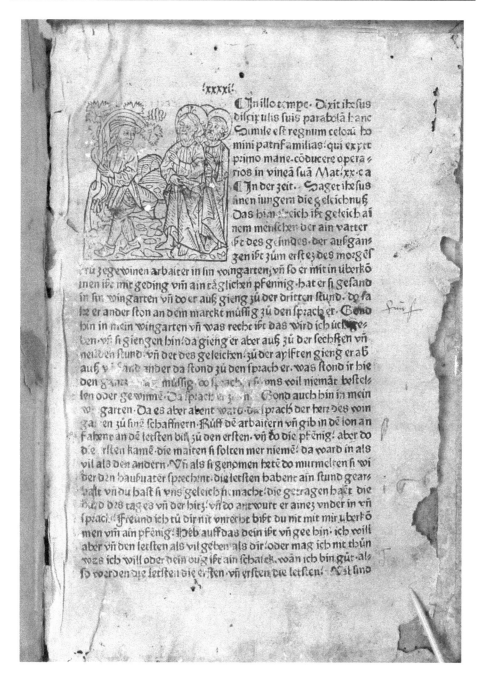

FIG. 3.6. Proof sheet of *Epistolae et Evangelia* [German], Ulm, Conrad Dinckmut, 28 February [14]83, f° (ISTC ie00082000), fol. 31r. Memmingen, Wissenschaftliche Stadtbibliothek, 2° 3.115, as rear pastedown.

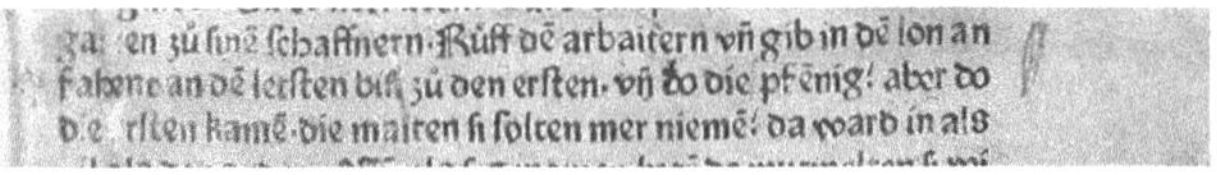

60 PRINTING AND MISPRINTING

FIG. 3.7. Proof sheet of *Epistolae et Evangelia* (see Fig. 3.6.), fol. 31r. Detail: ll. 2–26.

CORRECTIONS TO PUNCTUATION

A Tübingen proof sheet opens a view to an area of proofreading which is often overlooked in early book studies (Fig. 3.8).[21]

In the fifteenth century a unified system of orthography or punctuation did not yet exist in the European vernaculars, which mostly relied on local scribal practices according to region and dialect. In this context, it is noteworthy when, in the sense-for-sense translations by the Ulm physician and early German humanist Heinrich Steinhöwel (1410/1411–1479),[22] we find a standardised system of punctuation in use. It is found in all of the editions of his translations published by Johann Zainer, the printer Steinhöwel brought to Ulm for this purpose. Apart from *De claris mulieribus* and three editions of *Historia Griseldis*, it is also present in Steinhöwel's last and perhaps most celebrated translation, that of the Aesopian fables, which appeared in Zainer's printing house around 1476/1477.[23]

The Tübingen leaf is from this work and is witness to the high editorial standards used in preparing the publication. It is printed on one side only and, though there are no correction marks on it, it is one of perhaps three or four proofs pulled especially for the corrector's use. The leaf contains a section of the 'Fabel von dem wolf vnd hungrigen hund' (no. 12) from the *Fabulae extravagantes*, which is printed on fols 170v–171r in the edition (Figs 3.9 and 3.10). As a result of editing in the preceding folios, this segment moves from l. 1 in the proof state to l. 7 in the final printed state and spills over slightly onto the next page. At first glance the text appears unchanged, as in both states each line begins and ends with the same word. A closer inspection, however, reveals more than fifty changes, most of which pertain to punctuation (thirty-one corrections). The editorial changes can be seen in a comparison of a passage in the proof and final states:

> [...] vnd blödikait deß lybes ‖ S odas die hirtten vn[d] daz husgesind gemainlich ‖ ersen he[n]/so sprechen sie? fürwar wäre vnser hunde ‖ genugsamlich gespyset ./ der wolff het vnser lemlin ‖ [...].[24]
>
> (Proof, ll. 5–8)

---

[21] Tübingen, Universitätsbibliothek (UB), Ke XVIII 4 b.2 (Nr. 13).

[22] See G. Dicke, 'Heinrich Steinhöwel', in W. Stammler et al. (eds), *Die deutsche Literatur des Mittelalters. Verfasserlexikon*, 2nd edn, IX, Berlin and New York, 1995, 258–78. See also Amelung, *Frühdruck* (n. 18 above), pp. 15–148.

[23] Aesopus, *Vita et Fabulae*, with a German translation by Heinrich Steinhöwel, Ulm, Johann Zainer, [c. 1476–1477], f° (ISTC ia00116000). See Aesopus, *Vita et Fabulae / Der Ulmer Aesop von 1476/77* (facsimile edition and commentary), ed. P. Amelung, Ludwigsburg, 1995.

[24] '[...] and the body's inertia ‖ As the shepherds and household members saw that, they spoke: truly, if our hound had had enough to eat, the wolf wouldn't have [taken] our baby lamb [...]'. The rough translation is mine.

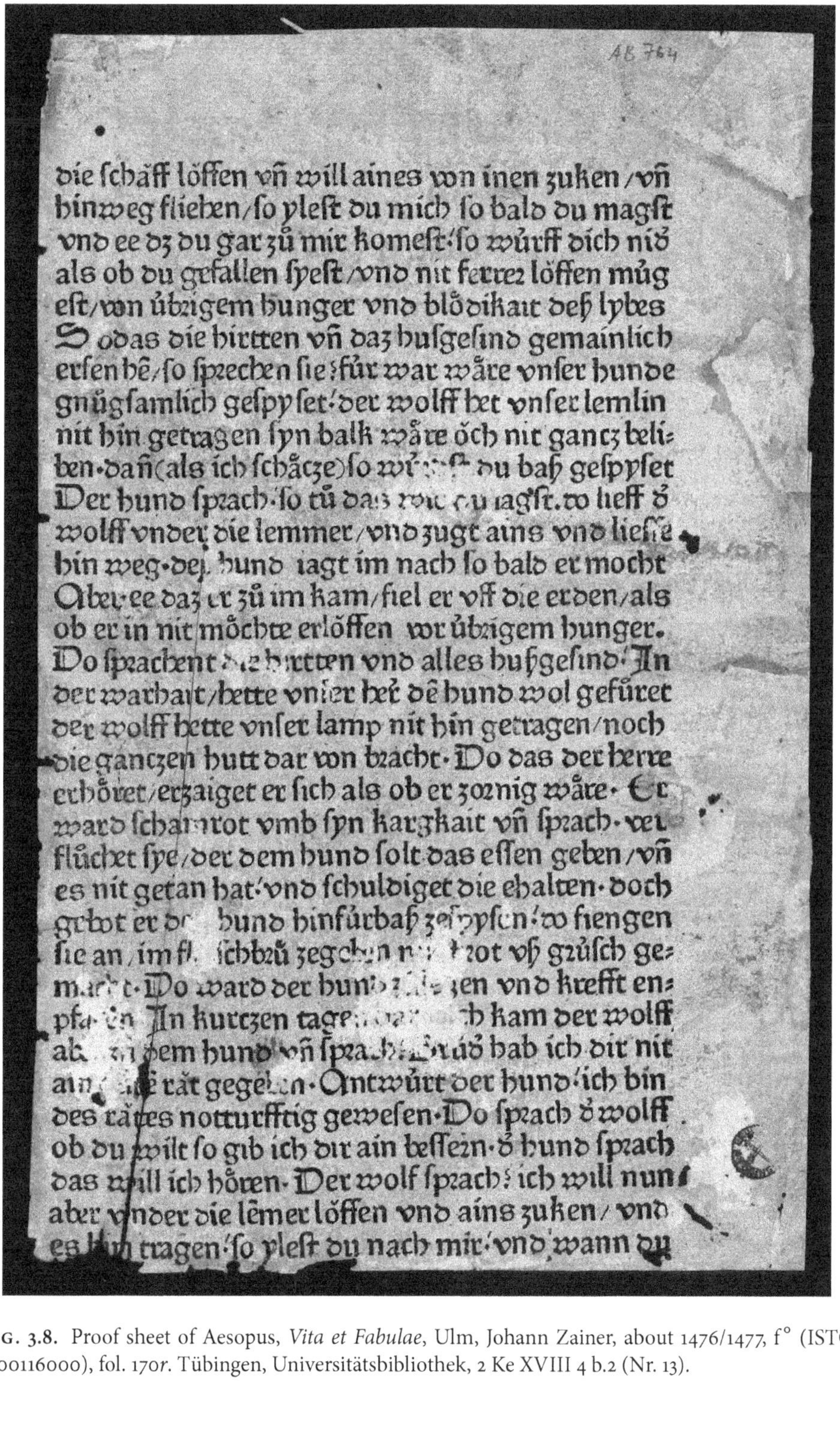

FIG. 3.8. Proof sheet of Aesopus, *Vita et Fabulae*, Ulm, Johann Zainer, about 1476/1477, f° (ISTC ia00116000), fol. 170*r*. Tübingen, Universitätsbibliothek, 2 Ke XVIII 4 b.2 (Nr. 13).

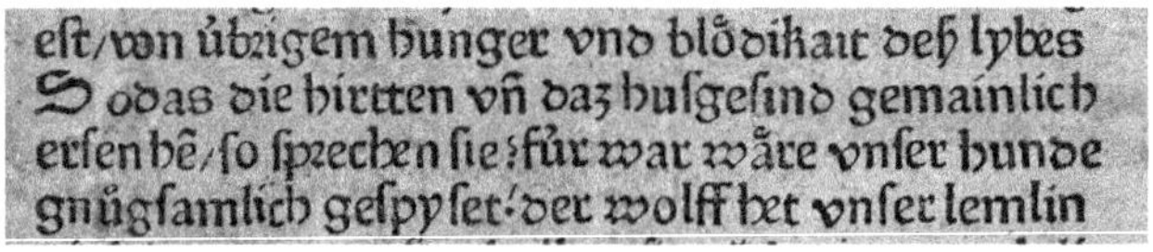

62 PRINTING AND MISPRINTING

> est/von übrigem hunger vnd blödikait deß lybes
> So odas die hirtten vñ daz husgesind gemainlich
> ersenhē/so sprechen sie;für war wäre vnser hunde
> gnügsamlich gespyset/der wolff het vnser lemlin

FIG. 3.9. Proof sheet of Aesopus, *Vita et Fabulae* (see Fig. 3.8.), fol. 170r.

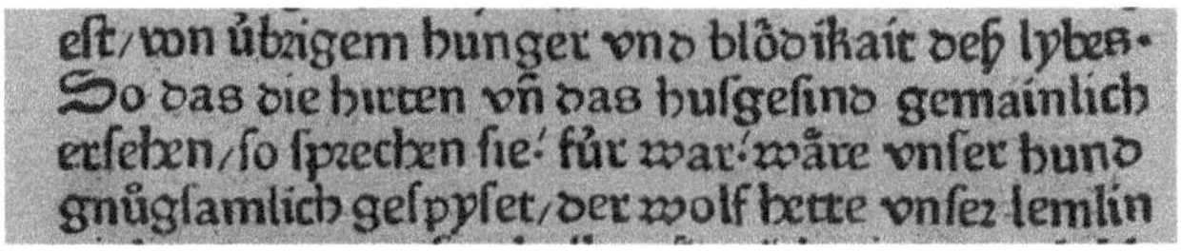

> est/von übrigem hunger vnd blödikait deß lybes·
> So das die hirten vñ das husgesind gemainlich
> ersehen/so sprechen sie· für war·wäre vnser hund
> gnügsamlich gespyset/der wolf hette vnsez lemlin

FIG. 3.10. Aesopus, *Vita et Fabulae*, Ulm, Johann Zainer, about 1476/1477, f° (ISTC ia00116000), fol. 170v. Detail, ll. 11–14. Munich, Bayerische Staatsbibliothek, Rar 762.

It was corrected to:

> [...] vnd blödikait deß lybes · ‖ So das die hirten vn[d] das husgesind gemainlich ‖ ersehen/so sprechen sie ./ für war ./ wäre vnser hund ‖ genugsamlich gespyset/der wolff hette vnser lemlin ‖ [...].

> (*Aesopus*, 1476, fol. 170v, ll. 11–14)

Let us first consider the corrections which were made to the literals.

In the printed edition, the space separating the letters *S* and *o* in *So* has been removed, the tilted letter *o* straightened, and the space between *So* and *das* has been restored. It now correctly reads: *So das* [...]. Further, the redundant *t* in *hirtten* has been removed and the typographical jumble *erseh hē* has been corrected to *ersehen* (i.e. saw).

With respect to the corrections in punctuation, a direct line can be drawn from here to the guidelines Steinhöwel set forth in his translation of *De claris mulieribus*.[25] In the last chapter, a kind of editorial postscript, Steinhöwel offers a summary of the system of punctuation used in the edition, beginning with the most important ones which ensure a correct reading of text: a slash (*virgel*); then a mark similar to an inverted semicolon (./), which he calls a *punctlin mit ainem besicz gezognen strychlin*; and an interpunct (*periodus*). Accordingly, we see that the following changes have been made in the passage above: after *lybes*, an interpunct (·) has been inserted to mark the end of the sentence; after *sprechen sie*, a spurious question mark has been changed to a *punctlin* (./) to separate the clauses; it is also inserted after *für war*, similar to the English rule of using a comma to set off an adverb or adverbial phrase at the start of a main clause. Furthermore, Steinhöwel also mentions a parenthesis (*zwey mönlun gegen ainander gehalten*), a question mark (*ain frag*), and a colon (*Teilungsstrich*) for dividing words across a line — the first two signs appearing in the proof sheet at ll. 7, 10 and 32 (Figs 3.11 and 3.12). All of the emendations would have been indicated on the corrector's proof — had it survived. As a final note, all of these punctuation marks

---

[25] [Heinrich Steinhöwel], 'Was die puncten bedüten vn[d] wie man darnach lesen sol das .C. capitel', in Giovanni Boccaccio, *De claris mulieribus. Von etlichen frowen*, Ulm, Johann Zainer, not before 1473, f° (ISTC ib00720000), fols 139v–140v.

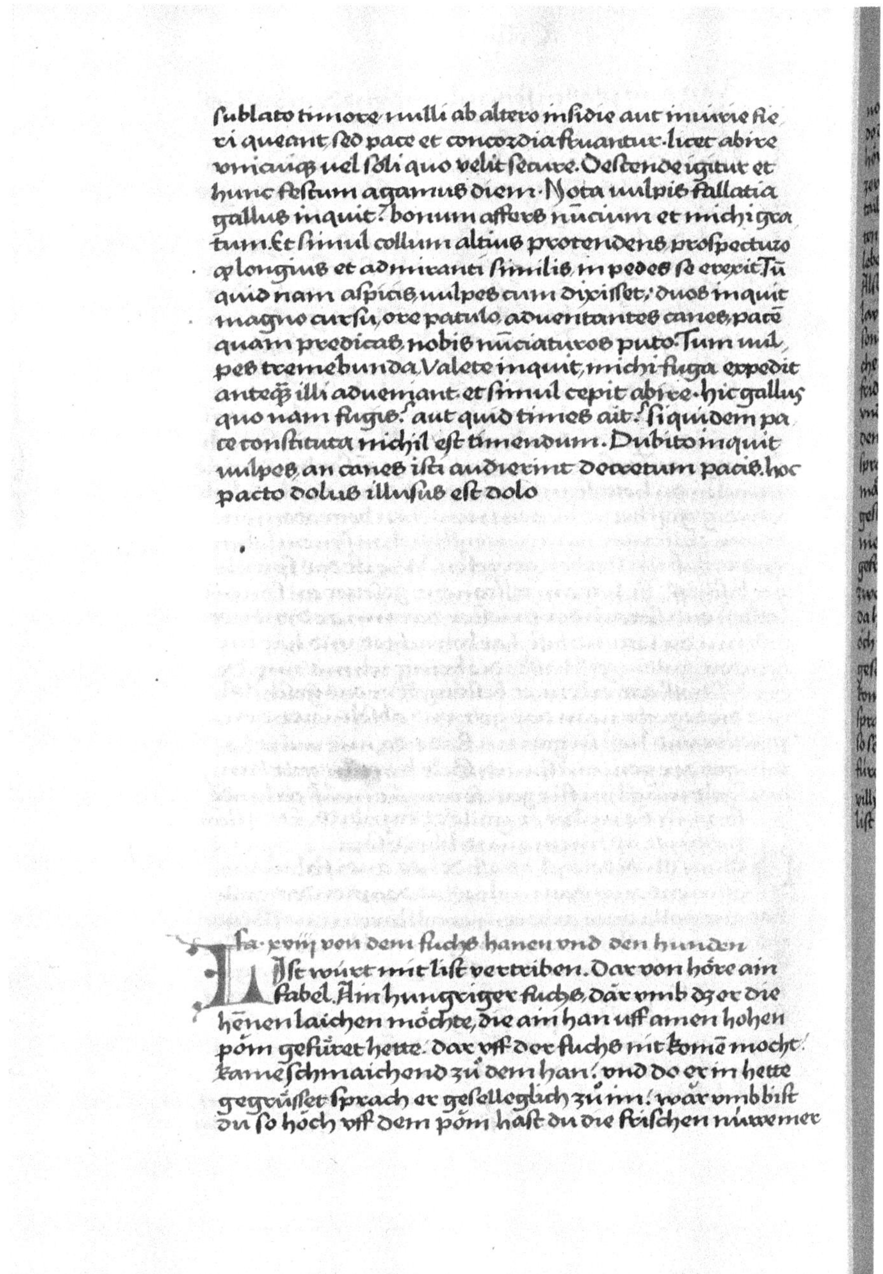

FIG. 3.11. Layout manuscript of Aesopus, *Vita et Fabulae*. Munich, Bayerische Staatsbibliothek, Cgm 1137, fol. 259v.

Collecte
magno cursu/ore patulo/aduentantes canes pace
quaz predicas nobis nuntiaturos puto. Tum vul
pes tremebunda·valete inquit/ mihi fuga expedit
anteqq illi adueniant·et simul cœpit abire·hic gallꝰ
quo nam fugis ?aut qd times ait ?siquidẽ pace con
stituta nihil est timendũ·Dubito inqt vulpes/an
canes isti audierint decretum pacis·Hoc pacto vo
lus illusus est volo.

⁌·xviii· Von dem fuchs/hannen vñ den hunden
Ist wúrt mit list vertribẽ·dar von hö
re ain fabel· Ain hungriger fuchs daz
vmb dz er die hennen laichen möchte/
die ain han vff ainen hohen böm gefü
ret hette·dar vff der fuchs nit komen
mocht·kame schmaichend zů dem han. vnd do er
in hette gegrüsset sprach er geselleglich zů im·wār
vmb bist du so hóch vff dẽ böm hast du die frischẽ
nüwe mer noch nit gehöret die menglichẽ so hail
sam sint·vñ do der han geantwúrt/er hette gancz
nichtz dar vō gehöret/sprach er·Ich bin vß gesant

FIG. 3.12. Aesopus, *Vita et Fabulae* (see Fig. 3.10.), fol. 272r.

3: PROOF SHEETS AS EVIDENCE OF EARLY PRE-PUBLICATION PROCEDURES

are present in Steinhöwel's autograph manuscript of *Spiegel des menschlichen Lebens* and were rigorously followed in the Zainer editions of his translations.[26]

A CASE OF MISE-EN-PAGE

In addition to the proof from Zainer's edition of *Aesopus*, a fragment of seventeen leaves from the printer's copy for this work has survived.[27] It is one of only two known surviving fragments of manuscript copy associated with Steinhöwel's publishing activity. The Munich fragment contains fables XII–XVIII from the *Fabulae collectae*, the last of five collections of fables included in the *Aesopus* first edition, and is all that remains of a presumably once voluminous manuscript. With 205 woodcut illustrations contained on 288 leaves, the Ulm edition, dating to c. 1476/1477, was one of the most richly illustrated books in the early incunabula period.[28] It was the last of Steinhöwel's projects to be completed before his death.

The original manuscript, from which the fragment derives, was made expressly for use as printer's copy. It is the so-called 'clean copy', i.e. it was written in a clear, regular scribal hand which allowed the printer to make accurate computations concerning the length and quire structure of the book and ensured good readability as the compositor set the pages from it. Most importantly, we observe here how text and image were physically arranged in preparation for the printed edition. It is an example of an early layout manuscript, also referred to as mise-en-page. In the printed edition, the fables are presented in a fixed sequence: first in Latin, followed by a woodcut illustration and the German translation. This corresponds to the mise-en-page of the manuscript fragment. Each fable begins with the Latin text, followed by a space or placeholder for the illustration (which remains approximately the same size throughout), followed by the German translation. Like the layout manuscripts for Hartmann Schedel's *Liber chronicarum*,[29] the arrangement of text and image is already specified, even though the level of sophistication of design in the *Aesopus* edition is far from that of Schedel's work. Whereas layout manuscripts usually contain a detailed page-by-page model which the compositors had to follow precisely, in the case of the *Aesopus* manuscript only the sequence of text and image was fixed. Only as the printer cast off the pages to determine the page breaks did the final page layout emerge.

The master printer proceeded by counting off thirty-one to thirty-two lines of manuscript text and making a horizontal stroke in the outer margin adjacent to that line (Fig. 3.13). The mark told the compositor where the page division was to occur. There was no mystery to his

---

[26] Munich, BSB, Cgm 1137, fols 265r–362r. For the Zainer editions, see: Giovanni Boccaccio, *De claris mulieribus*, Ulm, about 1474, f° (ISTC ib00720000); Francesco Petrarca, *Historia Griseldis*, Ulm, printed in folio three times: about 1473 (ISTC ip00403000), 1473/1474 (ISTC ip00404000), not before 1474 (ISTC ip00404100); as well as Zainer's edition of Boccaccio's *Decamerone* (trans. Arigo), Ulm, about 1476, f° (ISTC ib00730000); later editions are listed in ISTC.

[27] Munich, BSB, Cgm 1137, fols 247r–260r.

[28] Aesopus, *Vita et Fabulae* (n. 23 above).

[29] Nuremberg, Stadtbibliothek (StB), Cent. II, 98, 1r–324v; the edition was printed by Anton Koberger, Nuremberg, 12 July 1493, f° (ISTC is00307000). See C. Reske, *Die Produktion der Schedelschen Weltchronik in Nürnberg*, Wiesbaden, 2000.

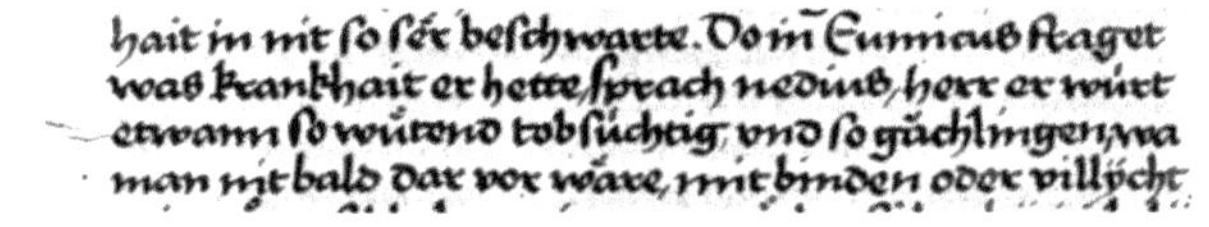

*hait in mit so sēr beschwarte. Do in Eunicus klaget
was krankhait er hette, sprach nedius, herr er wirt
etwann so wütend tobsüchtig, und so gächlingen, ywa
man nit bald dar vor wäre, mit binden oder villycht*

FIG. 3.13. Layout manuscript of Aesopus, *Vita et Fabulae* (see Fig. 3.11.), fol. 249*v*. Detail: ll. 16–18.

method, as the page length was based on a ratio of manuscript line to printed line, in effect a one-to-one ratio, as here 31/32 manuscript lines were equivalent to c. 32/33 lines of printed text. For illustrated pages the formula was 18 to 19 manuscript lines plus an additional 13 lines, the space needed for a woodcut illustration.

Despite a potentially disastrous mistake — the master printer overlooked a woodcut at the outset of the final gathering (signed as d), resulting in a series of twenty falsely marked page divisions — the compositor was able to compensate for this and correctly finish setting the text by using the established line count of 31/32.[30] As he finished setting each page, the compositor made a blind marking with a piece of lettertype or stylus where he stopped. He would know from the mark where to resume work after tying up the typeset page and putting it aside.

These blind markings provide invaluable clues about how the compositor worked, i.e. whether he was setting page by page in sequence or whether he was setting the pages required for a sheet, a method known as forme printing associated with the two-pull press. Determining the sequence in which the pages were set also tells us whether Zainer was printing on a simple press or a two-pull press.[31] Evidence of copy fitting at the end of several pages suggest that Zainer was already using a two-pull press.

Conclusion

From the beginning, early printing houses made great efforts to produce well-edited and attractive books. This was achieved in no small part through a correcting cycle which involved pulling proofs at multiple junctures during printing. The most important one was the corrector's proof. Between it and the final press-proof, others, including the author's proof, could be made to review any further changes which occurred at intermediate stages. From a modern standpoint, the most instructive proof sheets are those which contain handwritten corrections. They document the thoroughness and care with which texts were prepared for printing and give insight into the kinds of errors and misprints which affected early printing, which also included eye-skip. The use of a standardised system of punctuation in the Ulm editions of Heinrich Steinhöwel's literary translations at a time when regional scribal practice still prevailed is remarkable and reflects budding reform efforts at punctuation in early printing across Europe. Finally, a surviving fragment of the manuscript

---

[30] See Herz, 'Setzermarkierungen' (n. 7 above), pp. 109–11, 114–15.
[31] This is the topic of a forthcoming article in which I shall discuss two other instances of printer's copy in addition to Munich, BSB, Cgm 1137.

used in Zainer's workshop to set Steinhöwel's *Aesopus* provides an opportunity to study the relationship between the exemplar used as copy and the typographical realisation of the text.

The case studies presented in this article show just how fruitful the study of proof sheets can be. It thus remains a desideratum for rare book library departments to continue their efforts to identify proofs in their collections and report the findings to ISTC and GW.[32] Each newly discovered specimen adds a little more to our knowledge of pre-press procedures and underlines the high editorial standards of the earliest printers.

Bibliography

PRIMARY SOURCES

Manuscripts

Munich, Bayerische Staatsbibliothek (BSB), Cgm 1137
Nuremberg, Stadtbibliothek (StB), Cent. II, 98

Printed books

Aesopus, *Vita et Fabulae*, with a German translation by Heinrich Steinhöwel, Ulm, Johann Zainer, [c. 1476–1477], f° (ISTC ia00116000).
Antonio da Padova, *Sermones de sanctis*, Paris, Josse Bade, 1521, 8° (USTC 145464).
Ast, Astesanus de, *Summa de casibus conscientiae*, Nuremberg, 11 May 1482, f° (ISTC ia01170000).
Biblia [German], Nuremberg, Anton Koberger, 17 Febr. 1483, f° (ISTC ib00632000).
Biblia latina, 42 lines, [Mainz, Printer of the forty-two-line Bible (Johann Gutenberg) and Johannes Fust, about 1455], f° (ib00526000).
Boccaccio, Giovanni, *De claris mulieribus/Von etlichen frowen*, transl. Heinrich Steinhöwel, Ulm, Johann Zainer, not before 1473, f° (ISTC ib00720000).
Book of Courtesy, [Westminster, Wynkyn de Worde, about 1493], 4° (ISTC ib01029600).
Cicero, *Orationes*, Paris, Josse Bade, 1511, f° (USTC 187193).
Danse macabre, Lyon, [Matthias Huss], 18 Febr. 1499/1500, f° (ISTC id00020500).

---

[32] See also Herz, 'Setzermarkierungen' (n. 7 above), pp. 92–136.

Epistolae et Evangelia [German], Ulm, Conrad Dinckmut, 28 Febr. [14]83, f° (ISTC ie00082000).

Horae: ad usum Romanum, [Paris, Jean Bonhomme, about 1486–1490], 16° (ISTC ih00357470).

Hornschuch, Hieronymus, *Orthotypographia, Hoc Est: Instructio, operas typographicas correcturis*, Leipzig, Michael Lantzenberger, 1608, 8° (USTC 2001806).

Monmouth, Geoffrey of, *Historia Regum Britanniae*, Paris, Josse Bade, 1508, 4° (USTC 143331).

Oppeln, Peregrinus de, *Sermones de tempore et sanctis*, [Ulm, Johann Zainer], not after 1479, f° (ISTC ip00267000).

Sachs, Hans, *Eygentliche Beschreibung aller Stände auff Erden*, Frankfurt am Main, Georg Raben for Sigmund Feyerabend, 1568, 4° (USTC 655780).

Schedel, Hartmann, *Liber chronicarum*, Nuremberg, Anton Koberger for Sebald Schreyer and Sebastian Kammermeister, 12 July 1493, f° (ISTC is00307000).

Vegetius, Flavius Renatus, *De re militari*, [Augsburg, Günther Zainer, 1477–1478?], f° (ISTC iv00106200).

Wyle, Nicolaus von, *Translationen*, [Esslingen, Conrad Fyner, after 5 April 1476], f° (ISTC iw00072000).

SECONDARY LITERATURE

Aesopus, *Vita et Fabulae/Der Ulmer Aesop von 1476/77* (facsimile edition and commentary), ed. P. Amelung, Ludwigsburg, 1995.

Amelung, P., *Der Frühdruck im deutschen Südwesten 1473–1500*, Stuttgart, 1979.

Baldasso, R., 'The Variant Typesetting of the *Editio Princeps* of Augustinus, *De civitate dei* 1467 (Subiaco: Conradus Sweynheym and Arnoldus Pannartz, 12 June 1467)', *Gutenberg-Jahrbuch*, 91, 2016, pp. 33–41.

Dicke, G., 'Heinrich Steinhöwel', in W. Stammler et al. (eds), *Die deutsche Literatur des Mittelalters. Verfasserlexikon*, 2nd edn, IX, Berlin and New York, 1995, pp. 258–78.

Duntze, O., and Eisermann, F., 'Fortschritt oder Fidibus? Zur Bestimmung, Bewahrung und Bedeutung von Inkunabelfragmenten', in H. P. Neuheuser et al. (eds), *Fragment und Makulatur. Überlieferungsstörungen und Forschungsbedarf bei Kulturgut in Archiv und Bibliotheken*, Wiesbaden, 2015, pp. 281–307.

Gaskell, P., *A New Introduction to Bibliography*, New Castle (DE), 2006.

Haebler, K., 'Makulatur-Forschung', *Zentralblatt für Bibliothekswesen*, 25, 1908, pp. 535–44.

Hain, L., *Repertorium typographicum: in quo libri omnes ab arte typographica inventa usque ad annum MD. Typis expressi ordine alphabetico vel simpliciter enumerantur vel adcuratius recensentur*, 2 vols, Stuttgart, 1826–1838.

Hellinga, L., 'Proofreading and Printing in Mainz in 1459', in L. Hellinga, *Texts in Transit: Manuscript to Proof and Print in the Fifteenth Century*, Leiden, 2014, pp. 102–55.

Herz, R., 'From Manuscript Copy to the Printed Book: Hans Tucher's Palestine Account of 1482', *Archiv für Geschichte des Buchwesens*, 69, 2014, pp. 1–19.

Herz, R., 'Setzermarkierungen und Korrekturblätter in deutschen Inkunabeloffizien', *Gutenberg-Jahrbuch*, 93, 2018, pp. 78–124.

Keunecke, H.-O., 'Anton Koberger (c. 1445–1513)', in C. Sauer (ed.), *Anton Koberger. Zum 500. Todestag des Druckers der Schedelschen Weltchronik*, Nuremberg, 2013, pp. 6–13.

Kyriß, E., *Verzierte gotische Einbände im alten deutschen Sprachgebiet*, Stuttgart, 1951–1958.

Moxon, J., *Mechanick Exercises on the Whole Art of Printing (1683–4)*, ed. H. Davis and H. Carter, London, 1958.

Needham, P., 'The Cambridge Proof Sheets of Mentelin's Bible', *Transactions of the Cambridge Bibliographical Society*, 9, 1986, pp. 1–35.

Reske, C., *Die Produktion der Schedelschen Weltchronik in Nürnberg*, Wiesbaden, 2000.

Schneider, K., *Die deutschen Handschriften der Bayerischen Staatsbibliothek. Die mittelalterlichen Handschriften aus Cgm 888–4000*, Wiesbaden, 1991.

CHAPTER 4

KLUDGING TYPE
Some Workarounds in Early English Print

JAMES MISSON

INTRODUCTION

THE twentieth-century typographer Jan Tschichold knew that, despite aspirations towards perfect geometry, book designers must sometimes settle for a 'close approximation of the ideal'.[1] Early modern printers would have empathised: all too often, the limits of their equipment prevented their texts from materialising as they'd like. Take John Lyon, who printed Richard Bristow's *A reply to Fulke* in 1580.[2] Lyon wanted to create a visual dialogue between Bristow and Fulke's words by setting them in different typefaces, but when it came to it, he was 'forst to vse one Character' for the two different kinds of text (as he explains in his preface to the work, 'The Printer to the Reader'). Lyon rounds off his apology for the text's expediently flat appearance with some sage wisdom: 'Remember that when man can not do as he would, he must do as he may'.[3]

DEFINING KLUDGE

The spirit of Lyon's aphorism informs a practice seen occasionally in early books, and especially those printed in England. Having run out of type, printers would make up for the deficit by repurposing type sorts to stand in for other letters. Here, the binary of printing and misprinting is blurred: in using type for purposes other than that for which it was designed, such instances are *deliberate* misprints. Fig. 4.1 shows an especially visible example. The decorative initial V is upside down — a transformation made all the more obvious by its

---

[1] J. Tschichold, *The Form of the Book*, London, 1991, p. 55.
[2] Richard Bristow, *A reply to Fulke, in defense of m. D. Allens scroll of articles*, East Ham, John Lyon, 1580, 4° (USTC 414235).
[3] John Lyon, 'The Printer to the Reader', in Bristow, *A reply to Fulke* (n. 2 above), p. 416.

James Misson, *Kludging Type*. In: *Printing and Misprinting*. Edited by Geri Della Rocca de Candal, Anthony Grafton, and Paolo Sachet, Oxford University Press. © James Misson (2023). DOI: 10.1093/oso/9780198863045.003.0005

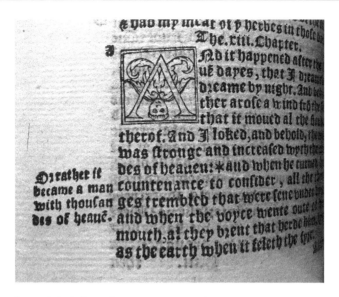

FIG. 4.1. *The volume of the bokes called Apocripha*, London, John Day and William Seres, 1549, 8° (USTC 504307), sig. D3v. Oxford, Bodleian Library, 8° P 269 Th.

decoration. At first glance, this could be mistaken for a turned letter, a common form of misprint, but in this case a mistake seems unlikely, given the size of the initial and the orientation of the face. In fact, this is a V deliberately playing the role of the letter A. Faced with a lack of As, the compositor had a dilemma: alter the text, or use a letter incorrectly. Print or misprint?

Perhaps because of how rare and idiosyncratic such instances are, this practice has received little attention, which makes defining it difficult. Contemporary letterpress printers sometimes use the terms *bodge* and *botch* to refer to similar techniques. I prefer the term *kludge* — a word used sometimes in computer science, but which is equally applicable to the earlier information technology of printing. A kludge is any improvised solution to a problem that appropriates tools or materials to new, unintended uses. In an article published in 1962 entitled 'How to Design a Kludge', Jackson Granholm offers an ironically self-deprecating definition: 'Kludge, n.: An ill-assorted collection of poorly-matching parts, forming a distressing whole'.[4] To this, the *Oxford English Dictionary* adds: 'a machine, system, or program that has been improvised or "bodged" together'.[5]

Kludge Typologies

The most common forms of typographical kludge in early English books can be divided into four categories: rotation, combination, modification, and substitution. We have already

[4] J. W. Granholm, 'How to Design a Kludge', *DATAMATION*, 8, February 1962, pp. 30–1 (30).
[5] 'Kludge, n.' *OED Online*, Oxford University Press, (December 2018), www.oed.com/view/Entry/103870, accessed 20 February 2019.

seen the first of these in Fig. 4.1: rotational kludges rely on the resemblance between letters when turned upside down or on their side. Lotte Hellinga notes an instance of this in her description of Pynson's edition of *Dives and Pauper*, printed in 1492.[6] The book's chapters begin with large decorative initials, and, due to what Hellinga describes as 'a heavy run on d', the compositor occasionally resorts to an upside-down Q instead of a d.[7] In other books, we find Zs likewise rotated 90 degrees to use as Ns,[8] and Vs for As, such as the one in Fig. 4.1.[9] In cases of rotation, the same properties of type that make turned letters possible — its movability, its ability to tessellate — have been exploited to rewrite and reread letter-forms, but this often comes at the expense of detail. The V in Fig. 4.1, for instance, achieves a close resemblance to an A, but without its crossbar. While that may have no serious consequences for legibility, some rotational kludges stretch the imagination of the reader: in an edition of *Domestycal or housholde sermons* the compositor has resorted to using a decorative initial K, rotated 90 degrees anticlockwise, to represent a Y, beginning the word 'Ye'.[10] Its tenuous resemblance to a Y might warrant its description as 'distressing', as Granholm puts it — it certainly leans heavily on its verbal context in order to be understood.

Individual sorts can also be combined to approximate an unavailable letter. Again, this sometimes lays a heavy burden of interpretation on the reader, as with the example in the third line of Fig. 4.2 (in the word 'skylles'). Here, an l and an r have been combined to represent a k.[11] For comparison, a non-kludged k, with an upright stem and strokes connecting, can be seen just above it, in line 2. Sometimes, however, the technique of combination is used extremely convincingly, as in one of Reginald Wolfe's kludges. While setting one of his colophons, the compositor has run out of Italic Ws, and so Wolfe's Latin surname, 'Wolfium', begins instead with an *l* followed by a *V*: '*lVolfium*'.[12] In context, the combination's resemblance to *W* is close enough that the kludge barely impedes reading, or might even go unnoticed.

Perhaps the least common form of kludge involves temporary modifications being made to the type in order to form other letters. Peter Blayney identifies this practice in a Bible printed by John Day and William Seres in 1549,[13] which employed 'improvisations such as [...] packing the bottom arm of an E with some unknown substance to make it resemble an F'.[14] As these are decorative initials, the actual letterform is comprised of white, uninked

---

[6] *Diues et Pauper*, London, Richard Pynson, 1493, f° (ISTC ip00117000).

[7] L. Hellinga (ed.), *Catalogue of Books Printed in the XVth Century now in the British Library. BMC Part XI: England*, 't Goy Houten, 2007, p. 272.

[8] For instance, the initial on fol. iir of Erasmus, *Prouerbes or Adagies, gathered oute of the Chiliades of Erasmus*, London, Nicolas Hill for Richard Kele, 1552, 8° (USTC 504748); or fol. ccr of Thomas Littleton, *Lyttelton tenures in Englysshe*, London, William Middelton, 1544, 8° (USTC 503532).

[9] An Italic *V* is inverted, becoming an Italic *A*, for instance, in the running title '*The first Sonday in Aduent*' in *The boke of common praier*, London, Richard Grafton, 1552, f° (USTC 504687).

[10] Christoph Hegendorph, *Domestycal or housholde sermons, for a godly housholder*, Ipswich, John Oswen, 1548, 8° (USTC 504068), sig. F3*v*.

[11] Harry Carter refers to this r as a 'ragged r' (sometimes called *r rotunda* or *zed-moid r*)—a variant form of black-letter r resembling the numeral 2. H. Carter, *A View of Early Typography*, London, 2002, p. 62.

[12] The same combination can be seen in the words 'Wedensdaye' and 'Whitsondaie' in the running titles of *The boke of common praier* (n. 9 above), sigs H1*v* and K3*v*.

[13] *The Byble*, London, [Steven Mierdman] for John Day and William Seres, 1549, f° (USTC 504300), sigs Cc2*v* and Gg5*v*.

[14] P. W. M. Blayney, *The Stationers' Company and the Printers of London, 1501–1557*, Cambridge, 2013, p. 677.

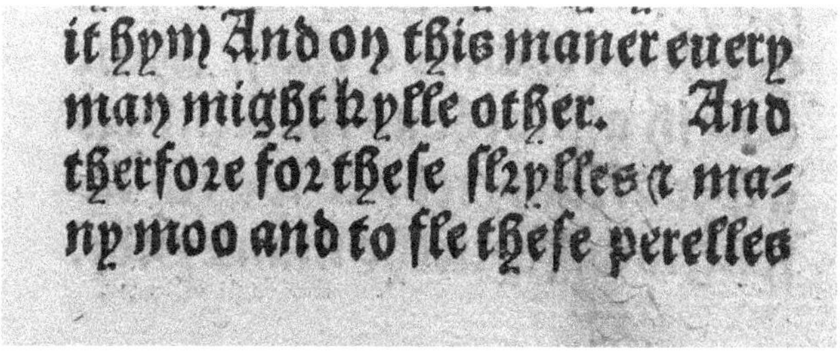

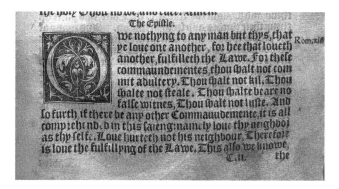

FIG. 4.2. *Diues et Pauper*, London, Richard Pynson, 1493, f° (ISTC ip00117000), sig. e3v. Oxford, Bodleian Library, Arch. G d.23.

FIG. 4.3. *'The first Sonday in Aduent'* of *The boke of common praier*, London, Richard Grafton, 1552, f° (USTC 504687), sig. A1r. Oxford, Bodleian Library, C.P. 1552 d.4.

space, defined by its inked outline and decoration that surrounds it, carved in relief. Packing its lower arm, then, fills in a gap in the piece of type, raising that portion up to type height, where it is inked and makes an impression on the page. The same technique is found in the *Book of Common Prayer*: packing has been added to several initial Qs in order to remove their tails, thereby turning them into Os (the results are not perfect, and traces of the Qs' tails remain, as shown in Fig. 4.3).[15]

While kludging via rotation, combination, or modification depends on adapting different sorts from the same font as the missing letter, the fourth and final category, substitution, brings in letters from other fonts. It is here that it becomes difficult to distinguish between printing and misprinting: type sorts could accidentally migrate between similar-looking typefaces when, after a forme was printed, the type was distributed back into the type case.[16] When the type was used again, the interloping letter might escape the notice of the compositor. These are sometimes known as 'wrong-face' or foul-case letters, because, as Adrian Weiss puts it, 'they contaminate the stylistic purity of the typefont'.[17] But the

[15] E.g., *The boke of common praier* (n. 9 above), sigs a3v and [Aa5r].
[16] P. Gaskell, *A New Introduction to Bibliography*, Oxford, 1972, p. 53.
[17] A. Weiss, 'Casting Compositors, Foul Cases, and Skeletons: Printing in Middleton's Age', in G. Taylor and J. Lavagnino (eds), *Thomas Middleton and Early Modern Textual Culture*, Oxford, 2007, pp. 195–225 (217).

kludges discussed so far raise the possibility that at least some of these 'contaminations' may have been purposeful, drafted in to augment the font. From the Elizabethan period, many such examples are of little consequence to the reader, mixing Roman typefaces that differ only subtly in their design, but before this period substitutions occurred between broader families of type, mixing black letter, Roman, and Italic. So, we find a Roman Z in an otherwise black-letter text in proper nouns such as 'Zabulon' and 'Zachee',[18] a Roman w embedded in the Italic word '*newe*',[19] and a black-letter W on a title-page listing the author's name in Roman, 'Wylliam Barkar'.[20] In each case, the 'fouling' is clearly discernible: the contrast in typeface leaves a denser or lighter concentration of ink, disrupting the evenness of the page's typographical colour.[21]

Kludges that adapt a font and kludges that import from another font both do the job, but they are conspicuous in their deviation, and there is a necessary compromise to each: those instances which replace a letter from the same font jeopardise the legibility of the text; but the alternative, a letter from a different font, disturbs the aesthetic coherence of the page. But all of these compromises have been deemed worthwhile for the sake of faithfully rendering the text. They could therefore even be considered a defence against misprinting, and where misprints might bear testament to the compositors' inattention, these all reflect instances of their *hyper*-attention, where they've had to think outside the box (or the type case). It is therefore more appropriate to read these occasions not as faults, and not with any of the negative connotations of 'fouling', but as evidence of ingenuity. This is intended by their characterisation as 'kludges': the discourse that surrounds the term typically carries with it a wry reverence for craftsmanship. As Granholm writes in his article, 'the building of a Kludge is not work for amateurs. There is a certain, indefinable, masochistic finesse that must go into true Kludge building'.[22] While the etymology of the word is disputed, a commonly cited folk-etymology incorporates this finesse, connecting it to the Yiddish קלוג (*klug*) and German *klug*, meaning 'clever'. Kludging typography, then, isn't a mark of naive, amateurish, or shoddy workmanship, but a creative exploitation of a tool's potential beyond its normative, prescribed use, founded on an expert's intimacy with those tools.

By looking more closely at some of these examples, we can better understand the conditions that made them necessary. As most are solutions to running out of type, their circumstances typically involve a font being drained by unusually high frequencies of certain letters — sometimes known as 'sort-pressure'.[23] They are therefore not just consequences of the form of the tools, but also of the form of the text. Richard Pynson's 1493 edition of *Dives and Pauper*, mentioned above, provides an illustrative example. The text is a dialogue between a rich man and a poor man, discussing questions of religion and morality. In the book, the speech of both characters is preceded by a heading bearing their

---

[18] *The Boke of common praier* (n. 9 above), sigs [P6]*v*, Q4*v*.

[19] *The late expedicion in Scotlande*, London, Reginald Wolfe, 1544, 8° (USTC 503483), sig. C[4]*v*.

[20] Xenophon, *The bookes of Xenophon*, transl. W. Barker, London, Reginald Wolfe, [1552], 8° (USTC 504782), sig. *r*.

[21] The term 'colour' is used by typographers to refer to the density of darkness on the page taken as a whole. Achieving a balanced and even colour eliminates visual distractions from reading: as Robert Bringhurst puts it, 'once the demands of legibility and logical order are satisfied, *evenness of color* is the typographer's normal aim.' R. Bringhurst, *The Elements of Typographic Style*, Vancouver, 2005, p. 25.

[22] Granholm, 'How to Design a Kludge' (n. 4 above), p. 30.

[23] Weiss, 'Casting Compositors' (n. 17 above), p. 218.

character name, as in a play. Each chapter typically begins with Dives, the rich man, asking a question or making a statement, followed by Pauper's answer, producing a Socratic dynamic between the characters that is maintained for the duration of the text. With Dives typically prompting these dialogues, the majority of these headings therefore require a decorative initial D. But while the font has been designed to accommodate an average number of Ds, this text features far more than the average. The compositor is therefore forced to improvise, and for much of the book, an upside-down Q makes up for the lack of Ds. Dives' characterisation as the dialogue's instigator therefore manifests on the page as a typographical irregularity. In a similar fashion, those modified Qs standing in for Os in the *Book of Common Prayer* are a product of its form and style. The vocative 'O God', or 'O Lord', the form of address conventionally used at the beginning of many of the prayers, causes a higher than typical sort-pressure on the decorative initial Os. These Qs are therefore modified to meet the demands of the text. So, as in *Dives and Pauper*, the *Book of Common Prayer*'s textual stylistics affects its appearance on the page.

Another example from *Dives and Pauper* elucidates the decisions of the compositor in handling an uncooperative text. As seen above, there are instances in this book in which the letters l and r appear together to approximate the shape of the black-letter k. The example shown in Fig. 4.2 appears in the word 'skylles'. Some readers may find the kludge unconvincing — certainly the pair would not be recognisable as a k without its context. But the compositor seems to have acknowledged this by giving the context of the kludge some stability: when reading the book, we realise that this kludge only ever occurs in the same word, 'skylles', or derivations such as 'skilfull'. These words appear frequently throughout the text, 'skill' being one of its major themes, a Middle English word used to refer to the reasons or rationalisations behind certain virtuous behaviours — the behaviours that Dives and Pauper are attempting to establish via their dialogue.[24] Furthermore, the compositor purposefully acclimatises the reader to this kludge: in the sentence in which it first appears, the word 'skilles' appears twice — the first time using a conventional k, and again soon after using the l and r. This is therefore a process of controlled misreading: readers are guided in their reinterpretation of the letterforms, and they learn to read the kludge as a k for the duration of the book. That this solution is applied to most instances of one word demonstrates a programmatic application of the kludge, designed as a response to the text's thematically (and therefore textually) dominant concept. Unlike other kludges, this is not, therefore, an ad hoc solution or improvisation; here, the compositor has pre-empted a deficit of the letter k, and mitigated the sort-pressure by adapting their practice to the demands of the text. Such a plan is only possible with the knowledge that this word appears frequently enough in the text to take the pressure off the font's k: again, the nature of a text's content determines its irregular appearance.

As a final example of the relationship between a text's form and its kludges, I turn to another of Pynson's books: his 1509 edition of Sebastian Brant's *Stultifera navis*, or *Ship of Fools*, translated by Alexander Barclay.[25] The book uses a mixture of Roman and black-letter type, conventionally setting Latin in the former and English in the latter, maintaining

---

[24] 'Skil', in *Middle English Dictionary*, http://quod.lib.umich.edu/cgi/m/mec/med-idx?type=id&id=MED40677, accessed 28 February 2019.
[25] Sebastian Brant, *Stultifera nauis*, transl. A. Barclay, London, Richard Pynson, 1509, f° (USTC 501050).

a visual as well as linguistic distinction between the text and its translation. To this end, Pynson is using his newly acquired Roman type — the first of its kind available in England. So, on the verso of the first leaf, the Latin preface and dedication is set in Roman, with a shorter paragraph in English black letter below it. But within the light block of Latin text, two patches of denser colour are immediately obvious. Two black-letter Ds are used towards the end of the paragraph in the words 'Discipuli' and 'Dece[m]bris' — the only Ds in the Latin text, standing out in stark contrast to the lighter Roman text that surrounds it.

Reading the book for the first time, this might surprise us, as no Roman Ds are used in the text before these kludges, nor is there any discernible textual reason for the switch. Why, then, is the kludge necessary? The answer becomes apparent two pages later, on the recto of the fourth leaf, one of the contents pages. The chapter titles are here listed in Latin, most of them beginning with the conventional Latin 'De' (*of*, *concerning*, or *about*) preceding the topic of the chapter: 'De predestinatione', for instance. The contents, then, have drained the font of Roman Ds. As the book is a folio, this page was printed at the same time and on the same sheet of paper as the first leaf — the one on which our kludged Ds appear. The compositor has run out of Roman Ds whilst setting the contents, which has consequences for the subsequent typesetting of the preface. From this example, we can witness the non-linear methods of printing by forme, and the fact that a text's appearance can be altered by that which is yet to come. We also gain a sense of where kludging falls in the rhythm of the printing process: the substitution was only necessary while printing this first sheet. After all copies of it were printed, the type was distributed and the replenished case ready to print subsequent sheets.

Besides this general principle of the non-sequential nature of printing, we might also deduce some specific details about Pynson's new Roman font from this kludge. On the contents page, we can see the point at which the Roman Ds run out, where the compositor switches to black letter, in the twentieth line of the second column. By counting their instances up to this point, we can see from this page that Pynson's new Roman font contained at least thirty-six uppercase Ds. There is, of course, the possibility that others are in use elsewhere, e.g. in standing type, but if we assume that this is a low number (no other part of the book relies so heavily on Roman D), then thirty-six offers a reasonable approximation. We can also apply this principle to the Roman x, which is also exhausted by the contents page, with the compositor occasionally switching to a black-letter x. The Roman x appears ninety-seven times across the sheet, giving another reasonable stock approximation, assuming the same conditions as above.

The examples given so far show that kludges occur when there is a tension between a text and its materials. The text's form, style, and content can thereby influence its own visual appearance. Whether a dialogue, contents page, or prayer, as the fonts are pushed to their limits, the repetition inherent to these forms disturbs the aesthetics of the page. But this is not only a product of the text's forms, but also of their language, because, as Sarah Werner describes, a font's sorts would be 'distributed in proportion to the frequency with which they were used'.[26] The number of, say, Ss required for Dutch texts is far fewer than for French texts, and fonts were manufactured accordingly. This is problematic for early English books, whose printers were using equipment manufactured on the

---

[26] S. Werner, *Studying Early Printed Books*, Chichester and Hoboken (NJ), 2019, p. 40.

continent — and therefore designed to accommodate Latin and continental languages. The sort-pressure on k in *Dives and Pauper* is caused not only by the frequency of the word 'skylles', but also by the overall frequency of the letter k in Middle English — a frequency not accounted for by Pynson's fonts, which were probably products of France and therefore designed for French and Latin, in which k appears only occasionally in loan words.[27] Harry Carter sees in this detail evidence for England's lack of typefounding skills, writing that a 'lower-case l followed by ragged r deputising for k in several early London founts is evidence that not a single letter was cut and struck here'.[28] It likewise stands to reason that those decorative initials used for the *Book of Common Prayer* would have spare Qs to modify and substitute for Os, despite that letter's rare use in English: the font's proportions were presumably designed with Latin texts in mind and the pronouns and prepositions — *quis, quid, quoniam* — commonly found in these texts' beginnings.

While the kludges discussed above are consequences of a font running out of sorts, English's most frequent kludge is caused by a complete absence of sorts. A font designed for Latin might have an abundance of Qs, but the absence of the letter W from the Latin alphabet meant that it was often not represented at all. It is this absence that makes early English printers, in their application of continental technology to vernacular English, especially adroit kludgers. With a few exceptions, English books in the first half of the sixteenth century adhered to the convention of printing the vernacular in black letter and Latin in Roman — the same convention that lasted in Germany even up until the beginnings of the twentieth century.[29] This convention was both reflected in and sustained by a material obstacle: in lacking Ws, Roman fonts excluded Germanic languages like English; the hardware couldn't support the software. Whilst this was not generally a problem, it makes itself known when printing proper nouns, demonstrated in James Whytstons' *De justicia & sanctitate belli*, shown in Fig. 4.4.

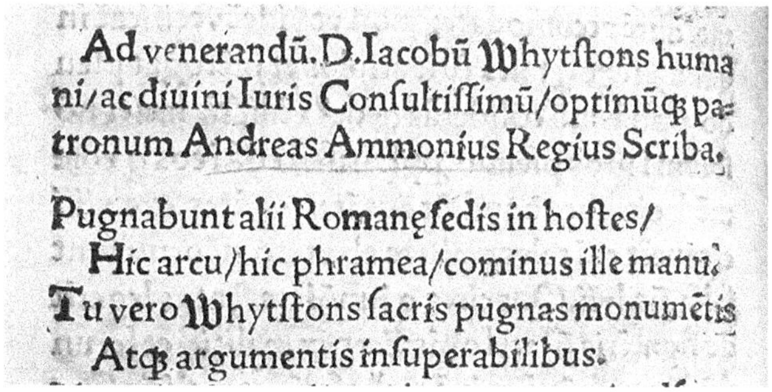
Ad venerandũ.D.Iacobũ Whytſtons humani/ac diuini Iuris Conſultiſſimũ/optimũq; patronum Andreas Ammonius Regius Scriba.

Pugnabunt alii Romanę ſedis in hoſtes/
Hic arcu/hic phramea/cominus ille manu.
Tu vero Whytſtons ſacris pugnas monumẽtis
Atq; argumentis inſuperabilibus.

FIG. 4.4. James Whytstons, *De justicia & sanctitate belli*, London, Richard Pynson, 1512, 4° (USTC 501215), fol. 51*v*. Oxford, Bodleian Library, Arch. A e. 48.

[27] On the French source of fonts used in England during this period, see L. Hellinga, 'Printing Types and Other Typographical Materials', in *BMC XI* (n. 7 above), pp. 335–44.

[28] Carter, *A View of Early Typography* (n. 11 above), p. 63.

[29] S. K. Galbraith, '"English" Black-Letter Type and Spenser's *Shepheardes Calender*', *Spenser Studies*, 23, 2008, pp. 13–40.

CONCLUSIONS

Remember that when you cannot do as you would, you must do as you may. Kludges represent a compositor's solution to a problematic tension between their equipment and the form and language of the text they are printing. They are the visible consequences of reifying an otherwise abstract text. In making these tensions conspicuous, some kludges can even be read as indexes of a linguistic identity. Rather than dismissing them as deficiencies, we can admire these kludges as creative, applied 'misprints' that demonstrate the compositors' resolute fidelity to their copy-text — what might at first glance appear to be a mistake proves itself to be a precaution against error. Jackson Granholm's attitude to kludging should therefore inspire our own: 'Whatever weird shape your final product may assume, after a year or so of careful kludgecraft, there is one thing to keep always in mind: Don't apologise for it!'[30]

BIBLIOGRAPHY

PRIMARY SOURCES

Articuli ad narrationes nouas pertimentes formati, London, Robert Redman, 1539 (USTC 503039).
The boke of common praier, London, Richard Grafton, 1552, f° (USTC 504687).
Brant, Sebastian, *Stultifera nauis*, transl. A. Barclay, London, Richard Pynson, 1509, f° (USTC 501050).
Bristow, Richard, *A reply to Fulke, in defense of m. D. Allens scroll of articles*, East Ham, John Lyon, 1580, 4° (USTC 414235).
The Byble, London, [Steven Mierdman] for John Day and William Seres, 1549, f° (USTC 504300).
Diues et Pauper, London, Richard Pynson, 1493, f° (ISTC ip00117000).
Erasmus, Desiderius, *Prouerbes or Adagies, gathered oute of the Chiliades of Erasmus*, London, Nicolas Hill for Richard Kele, 1552, 8° (USTC 504748).
Hegendorph, Christoph, *Domestycal or housholde sermons, for a godly housholder*, Ipswich, John Oswen, 1548, 8° (USTC 504068).
The late expedicion in Scotlande, London, Reginald Wolfe, 1544, 8° (USTC 503483).
Littleton, Thomas, *Lyttelton tenures in Englysshe*, London, William Middelton, 1544, 8° (USTC 503532).
The volume of the bokes called Apocripha, London, John Day and William Seres, 1549, 8° (USTC 504307).
Whytstons, James, *De justicia & sanctitate belli*, London, Richard Pynson, 1512, 4° (USTC 501215).
Xenophon, *The bookes of Xenophon*, transl. W. Barkar, London, Reginald Wolfe, [1552], 8° (USTC 504782).

---

[30] Granholm, 'How to Design a Kludge' (n. 4 above), p. 31.

SECONDARY LITERATURE

Blayney, P. W. M., *The Stationers' Company and the Printers of London, 1501–1557*, Cambridge, 2013.

Bringhurst, R., *The Elements of Typographic Style*, Vancouver, 2005.

Carter, H., *A View of Early Typography*, London, 2002.

Galbraith, S. K, '"English" Black-Letter Type and Spenser's *Shepheardes Calender*', *Spenser Studies*, 23, 2008, pp. 13–40.

Gaskell, P., *A New Introduction to Bibliography*, Oxford, 1972.

Granholm, J. W., 'How to Design a Kludge', *DATAMATION*, 8, February 1962, pp. 30–1.

Hellinga, L. (ed.), *Catalogue of Books Printed in the XVth Century now in the British Library. BMC Part XI: England*, t' Goy Houten, 2007.

Middle English Dictionary, https://quod.lib.umich.edu/m/middle-english-dictionary/dictionary.

OED Online, https://www.oed.com/.

Tschichold, J., *The Form of the Book*, London, 1991.

Weiss, A., 'Casting Compositors, Foul Cases, and Skeletons: Printing in Middleton's Age', in G. Taylor and J. Lavagnino (eds), *Thomas Middleton and Early Modern Textual Culture*, Oxford, 2007, pp. 195–225.

Werner, S., *Studying Early Printed Books*, Chichester and Hoboken (NJ), 2019.

CHAPTER 5

MISPRINTING ILLUSTRATED BOOKS

ILARIA ANDREOLI, CAROLINE DUROSELLE-MELISH, AND ROGER GASKELL

No less than with verbal texts, inaccuracies in images are an inevitable consequence of the production of printed books.* An anonymous author in the early seventeenth century sets out the potential pitfalls:

> Such as have any experience in the mystery of printing can easily tell, how a ragged coppy, absence of the author, and want of a carefull corrector, by reason of farr distance of place, doe usually bring forth slipps, and oversights to the offence of the author, reader and printer himself.[1]

These difficulties,[2] which form the staple excuses for errata, are only compounded by the mysteries of printing pictures with letterpress texts. This is because the book printer generally relied on independent block cutters and engravers to supply the printing surface, unlike the text, the setting and correcting of which was done in house.

---

* We are grateful to David McKitterick and Ed Potten for their valuable comments on early drafts of this chapter. The following abbreviations will be used throughout: Davies *Fairfax Murray French*: H. W. Davies, *Catalogue of a Collection of Early French Books in the Library of C. Fairfax Murray*, London, 1910, facsimile reprint 1961; Davies *Fairfax Murray German*: H. W. Davies, *Catalogue of a Collection of Early German Books in the Library of C. Fairfax Murray*, London, 1913, facsimile reprint 1962. Mortimer *French*: R. Mortimer, *French 16th Century Books*, 2 vols, Cambridge (MA), 1964; Mortimer *Italian*: R. Mortimer, *Italian 16th Century Books*, 2 vols, Cambridge (MA), 1974.

[1] *A short dialogue proving that the ceremonyes, and some other corruptions now in question are defended,* [Amsterdam], s.n., 1605, 4° (USTC 1506131), sig. K1v, quoted by H. S. Bennett, *English Books and Readers*, 3 vols, Cambridge, 1952–1970, III, p. 210.

[2] R. B. McKerrow, *An Introduction to Bibliography for Literary Students*, 2nd impression with corrections, Oxford, 1928, indexes errors under 'misreading copy', 'failure of memory', 'muscular error', 'foul case', 'faulty correction', 'imposition', 'perfecting', 'folding', and 'progressive corruption of text'.

Ilaria Andreoli, Caroline Duroselle-Melish, and Roger Gaskell, *Misprinting Illustrated Books.* In: *Printing and Misprinting.* Edited by Geri Della Rocca de Candal, Anthony Grafton, and Paolo Sachet, Oxford University Press. © Ilaria Andreoli, Caroline Duroselle-Melish, and Roger Gaskell (2023). DOI: 10.1093/oso/9780198863045.003.0006

In the period under discussion, visual, non-textual elements were either printed from relief surfaces, for the most part wood blocks printed with the type, or from intaglio plates, mostly copperplates printed separately. In either case the author may have had recourse to a professional draughtsman and the finished drawing may have been copied and adapted for the benefit of the print maker, who then had to convert the lines on paper to a printable block or plate. Errors could be introduced at any of these stages in a process which was obviously different from that of setting the text in type. Once the printer had received the printing matrix, further mistakes could be made in the integration of text and image, as well as in the actual printing of the plate. In this chapter we consider errors — and their correction — in images in terms of production from the original drawing to the printed book. We therefore examine errors in the original, errors introduced in copying and transfer, errors in making the matrix, errors of imposition (combining text and image), and errors of printing.

Textual error in printed books has been studied intensively for many years in the service of textual criticism. The extensive literature on compositorial practices, proofreading and correction, errata lists and reader's manuscript corrections includes a few scattered examples of errors in images.[3] Several of our examples come from H. S. Bennett's *English Books and Readers*, a work too often overlooked by book historians.[4] However, the first extended essay on the bibliographical issues surrounding the integration of text and image is David McKitterick's aptly titled chapter, 'Pictures in motley', in his *Print Manuscript and the Search for Order*.[5] McKitterick details the ways that printed images start to appear in printed books and the attendant technological challenges which result in variation from copy to copy and the scope for error.[6]

Errors, particularly but not exclusively imposition errors — that is, blocks or plates printed upside down or in the wrong place — reveal themselves through bibliographical analysis. Here we are fortunate in having the remarkable catalogues by Hugh W. Davies of the Fairfax Murray collections of French and German books from the fifteenth and early sixteenth centuries, and Ruth Mortimer's catalogues of sixteenth-century French and Italian books at Harvard. Both catalogues provide extensive details about the illustrations of, between them, around 2,000 editions, often comparing more than one copy, revealing 'at press' correction and other differences.[7]

Before looking at sources of error from drawing to printing, it is worth pausing to consider the ways that authors and printers have drawn attention to error. Both textual references and errata lists reveal much about the place of picture printing in the production history of the books.

---

[3] P. Simpson, *Proof-Reading in the Sixteenth, Seventeenth and Eighteenth Centuries*, London, 1970; A. Blair, 'Errata Lists and the Reader as Corrector', in S. A. Baron, E. N. Lindquist, and E. F. Shevlin (eds), *Agent of Change: Print Culture Studies after Elizabeth L. Eisenstein*, Amherst (MA), 2007, pp. 21–41. On errors and correction in general, see, prior to this Companion, A. Grafton, *The Culture of Correction in Renaissance Europe*, London, 2011; D. McKitterick, *Print, Manuscript and the Search for Order, 1450–1830*, Cambridge, 2013, Chapter 4. 'A house of errors', pp. 97–138.

[4] Bennett, *English Books and Readers* (n. 1 above).

[5] McKitterick, *Print, Manuscript* (n. 3 above), Chapter 3, pp. 53–96.

[6] For the problems of printing engravings with text see R. Gaskell, 'Printing House and Engraving Shop: A Mysterious Collaboration', *The Book Collector*, 53, 2004, pp. 213–51, and his 'Printing House and Engraving Shop, Part II: Further Thoughts on "Printing and Engraving Shop: A Mysterious Collaboration"', *The Book Collector*, 67, 2018, pp. 788–97.

[7] Davies *Fairfax Murray French* and *German*; Mortimer *French* and *Italian*.

Errors Signalled in the Text and Errata Lists

Jacques Besson is at pains to tell the reader that the woodcut of the water clock in *Le cosmolabe* (Paris, 1567) is wrong, as he points out in the caption (Fig. 5.1):

> Figure of the clepsydre [water clock], in which the painter has not fully followed the intention of the author concerning the vases, but this will be easy to correct for those who have a little understanding of this science, while waiting for a second edition.[8]

Here the blame is put on the artist. Besson failed to notice the error when the drawing was sent to the block cutter; he only picked it up when the block had been cut, too late to have a new cut made but before the text was set in type and the sheet printed off. Similarly, Andreas Vesalius points out in *De humani corporis fabrica* (Basel, 1543) that guide letters have been left out of an image, but he is not sure if this was his own omission or the fault of the block cutter.[9] In any case, rather than risk spoiling the block by having it corrected, he adds a new image showing where the guide letters should be.[10] We might speculate that if Vesalius had discovered the error in the block while still in Venice, he would have had a new one cut before the blocks were sent to Basel. More likely, therefore, it was noticed as he was overseeing the printing in Basel and he had the extra block made there. In his analysis of annotations to the Vesalius woodcuts, Dániel Margócsy and his co-authors blame the block cutters for this and other errors in the lettering.[11] But were the block cutters really to blame, or was the drawing provided defective? In most cases like this we can only guess, but it is important to consider the possible sources of error.

More commonly, inaccuracies in the illustrations were discovered during the printing of the book. In well-set-up print shops, the text was corrected in-house, and occasionally a proof was also sent to the author.[12] But there was generally little time available before the sheet needed to be put to press, and textual errors that had been detected were put right as stop-press corrections or gathered in errata lists printed at the end of the book or in the preliminaries (the last sheets to be printed) or in a separately printed errata sheet.

---

[8] Jacques Besson, *Le cosmolabe*, Paris, Philippe Gaulthier Rouillé, 1567–1569, 4° (USTC 16555), p. 239: 'Figure de la Clepsydre, en laquelle le Pintre n'a suyui toutaleme[n]t l'intention de l'Auteur touchant les vases, mais cela sera facile à corriger à ceux qui auront tant soit peu la connoissance de cette scie[n]e, en atte[n]dant une seconde impression.' The translation is ours. There was no second edition of this work.

[9] 'I have inadvertently left out *l* and *m* in the first figure; I may have done so in assigning the symbols because I thought I had put them on the left side, or perhaps I did in fact use them but the block cutter did not notice them.' Translation taken from A. Vesalius, *On the Fabric of the Human Body*, transl. W. F. Richardson, San Francisco, 1998–2009, III, p. 210.

[10] S. Kusukawa, *Picturing the Book of Nature: Image, Text, and Argument in Sixteenth-Century Human Anatomy and Medical Botany*, Chicago, 2012, pp. 96–7 and fig. 4.4.

[11] D. Margócsy, M. Somos, and S. N. Joffe, *The Fabrica of Andreas Vesalius: A Worldwide Census, Ownership, and Annotations of the 1543 and 1555 editions*, Leiden and Boston, 2018, p. 39.

[12] P. Gaskell, *A New Introduction to Bibliography*, reprinted with corrections, Cambridge, 1979, pp. 110–16.

FIG. 5.1. 'The artist has not fully followed the intention of the author concerning the vases'. Jacques Besson, *Le cosmolabe*, Paris, Philippe Gaulthier Rouillé, 1567–1569, 4° (USTC 16555), p. 239. Cambridge (MA), Houghton Library, *FC5.C3975.B585.

FIG. 5.2.a–b. Apollonius, *Conicorum,* Florence, 1661, pp. 415 and 12. The errata list on p. 415 points out a missing line NQ and letter D from the end of the parabola on the left in the diagram on p. 12. Roger Gaskell Rare Books.

Woodblocks themselves could not be corrected during the run, but imposition errors were regularly corrected at press when it was noticed that a block had been printed upside down or in the wrong place. Other errors had to be printed as errata.

Setting unfamiliar languages was often given as an excuse for error, and Henry Billingsley's apology for the extensive errata to text and diagrams in his English translation of Euclid printed by John Day in London in 1570 makes the same point for mathematics:

> Marvaile not (gentle reader) that faultes here following, have escaped in the correction of this booke. For, that the matter in it contained is straunge to our Printers here in England, not having bene accustomed to Print many, or rather any books containing such matter, which causeth them to be unfurnished of a corrector skilfull in that art: I was forced, to my great travaile and paine, to correcte the whole booke my selfe.[13]

---

[13] Euclid, *The elements of geometrie*, London, John Day, 1570, f° (USTC 507133), sig. 3E2v, 'Faultes escaped'. Billingsley goes on to chide the printer for not making all the corrections he had marked on the proof. Quoted from Bennett, *English Books and Readers* (n. 1 above), II, p. 287, who transcribes the full passage (modernising u/v). Percy Simpson mentions the Billingsley case but is otherwise silent on the subject of correcting diagrams. However, his transcript of fees paid to Sheldonian Press and Clarendon Press correctors includes an entry for correcting John Wallis's *Opera mathematica* in 1695, at 1s 6d per sheet. This was at the lower end of the scale for the period. Corrections for most books were charged at 1s 6d or 2s per sheet. If the Oxford correctors had any special skill in correcting mathematical texts,

Because Billingsley had to be both press corrector and author, more errors were printed than might ordinarily be expected. In fact, diagrams and their lettering are particularly prone to error, and errors in diagrams are the most common mistakes in visual material recorded in errata lists. Billingsley's extensive corrections to the diagrams are interspersed with the textual errata, while an edition of Apollonius's *Conics* printed at Florence in 1661 has a separate section of 'Errata in figuris'.[14] These are corrections to lettering and verbal descriptions of how to correct diagrams by altering or adding curves or lines, using the familiar language of geometry (Fig. 5.2.a–b). More complex figures have to be given visually, sometimes asking the reader to cut out an image and paste it over an incorrect figure in the text, as in Oronce Finé's *La théorique des cieux et sept planètes* (Paris, 1567).[15]

ERRORS IN DRAWING, COPYING, AND TRANSFER

The first Bible to be printed in Italian is a translation by Niccolò Malermi, published in Venice by Wendelin of Speyer in August 1471.[16] This *Biblia italica* has no illustrations, but half a page was left blank at the head of Genesis, as if the need for illustration of some sort had been felt. A few months later, on 1 October 1471, Adam de Ambergau finished printing, also in Venice, a new edition of the *Biblia italica*.[17] The text, in Roman font, is organised in a single block, but in the double-page spread at the beginning of Genesis the text is interrupted by seven white spaces, created by the indentation of the text with respect to the margins. The first space was reserved for the initial 'N' of 'Nell'inizio' ('In the beginning') and the other six were to accommodate scenes from the Creation. This curious choice of mise-en-page is most likely due to the desire to decorate the pages not so much with miniatures but rather with woodcuts. In the well-known copy of the John Rylands University Library (Fig. 5.3.a–b), the spaces are actually occupied by an illuminated initial and six scenes from the Creation.[18]

As already recognised by Essling, the outlines of human and animal figures are indicated by the imposition, following the printing of the text, of woodcut matrices, subsequently completed, like the landscapes, in tempera.[19] The repetitive pose of God the Father facing right on the second, third, fourth, and fifth days was undoubtedly obtained through

---

they were not charging extra for it. We doubt if they did. Wallis could probably not rely on the printing house correctors any more than Billingsley could. Simpson, *Proof-Reading* (n. 2 above), Appendix I, 'Fees paid to Sheldonian Press and Clarendon Press Correctors from 1691 to 1806'. For another case study on numerals and misprinting, see Richard Kremer's contribution in this Companion.

[14] Apollonius Pergaeus, *Conicorum lib. V. VI. VII*, Florence, 1661, ed. Giovanni Alfonso Borelli, p. 415.

[15] Blair, 'Errata Lists' (n. 3 above), pp. 30–1.

[16] *Biblia*, transl. Nicolò Malermi, Venice, Vindelinus de Spira, 1 Aug. 1471, f° (ISTC ib00640000).

[17] *Biblia*, [Venice, Adam de Ambergau], 1 Oct. 1471, f° (ISTC ib00639000).

[18] Manchester, John Rylands Library, Spencer 3071.

[19] V. Masséna, prince d'Essling, *Les livres illustrés vénitiens de la fin du 15ᵉ siècle et du commencement du 16ᵉ*, 3 vols, Florence and Paris, 1907–1914, I, no. 131 and III, pp. 56–7; A. Pollard, 'The Woodcut Design for Illumination for Illumination of Venetian Borders (1469–1473)', in A. Pollard (ed.), *Bibliographica: Papers on Books, their History and Art*, III, London, 1897, pp. 122–8; M. Sander, *Le livre à figures italien depuis 1467 jusqu'à 1530*, 6 vols, Milan, 1942–1943, no. 985; L. Armstrong, 'The Hand Illumination of Venetian Bibles in the Incunable Period', in K. Jensen (ed.), *Incunabula and Their Readers*, London, 2003,

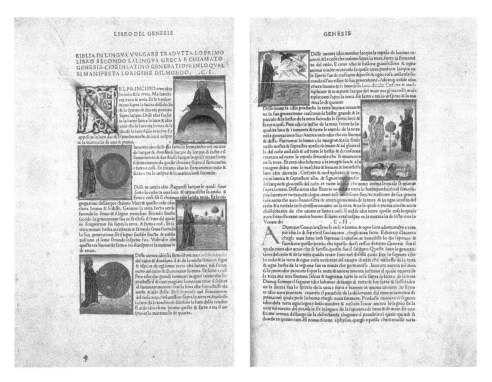

FIG. 5.3.a-b. *Biblia* [Italian], [Venice, Adam de Ambergau], 1 Oct. 1471, f° (ISTC ib00639000), fols 10v–11r. Manchester, John Rylands Library, Inc. 3071.

the impression of the same block, as evidenced by the portion of the cloak that goes beyond the red handwritten frame. For the sixth day, that of the creation of Adam and Eve, God the Father blesses the two of them with his left hand, which probably indicates that the block cutter did not take into account the need to reverse the preparatory drawing to produce the correct direction of the image when printed. A slight trace of the outlines of the wooden matrix is also visible in the figures of Adam and Eve and in the group of animals at their feet. The printer must have had the woodblocks made with the idea of being able to use them on several copies of the print run, but as happened with other experiments attempted in Venice with woodblock frames to be applied later to the printing of the text, this semi-mechanical illustration method was soon abandoned and impressions of the blocks are not seen in any other copy.

Besson laid the blame squarely on his artist for not following his intentions. More obliquely, Antonio Manetti (1423–1497) points out that the woodcut illustrations of Hell in his commentary on Dante's *Inferno* are defective:

pp. 83–113, 229–36 (91–3) and E. Barbieri, 'Un "nuovo" caso di silominiatura: l'esemplare perugino della Bibbia volgare dell'ottobre 1471', *La Bibliofilia*, 122/1, 2020, pp. 23–30.

5: MISPRINTING ILLUSTRATED BOOKS   87

> All these illustrations (as you can see) lack many things and many things are placed almost (as one says familiarly) '*alla burchia*' [at random, in the style of the nonsense poetry of Burchiello], because of the lack of space and the difficulty of the work.[20]

This suggests that, while the drawing was correct, it needed to be reduced in size and was not easy for the block cutter to interpret.

Errors in the diagrams in Nicolaus Copernicus's *De revolutionibus* may have been introduced in the process of copying, but they also hint at editorial interventions. The text as printed by Johannes Petreius at Nuremberg in 1543 differs significantly from the manuscript in Copernicus's own hand, probably completed before 1539 and now in the Jagiellonian library in Kraków.[21] Noel Swerdlow has postulated that two further manuscripts would have been prepared before the printed edition.[22] The first, a working copy prepared by Copernicus, possibly aided by Georg Joachim Rheticus; the second, a scribal copy which Rheticus took to Nuremberg to see through the press. The unstated implication in Swerdlow's account is that the scribal copy was the printer's copy. Five corrections to diagrams are included in the printed list of errata, out of a total of 108 corrections. The printed errata only cover the first three quarters of the book,[23] but contemporary readers' additional errata provide another three corrections to diagrams and as many as 157 textual errors.[24] Between them, these eight entries related to diagrams correct three wrong letters, a letter in the wrong position, a missing letter, and three missing lines or circles (Fig. 5.4.a–b).[25]

---

[20] Dante Alighieri, *Commedia di Dante insieme con uno dialogo circa el sito forma et misure dello inferno*, Florence, Filippo Giunta, 1506, 8° (USTC 808765), sigs O8*v*–P1*r*: 'In tutti questi disegni (come uoi hauete potuto notare) ma[n] cono molte cose, & molte ce ne sono poste quasi (come uulgarmente si dice) alla burchia rispecto alla scarsita delli spatii & alla impossibilita della opera.' The translation is ours. The book was printed posthumously, showing that Manetti was writing his text after having had the blocks cut, but before arranging for printing.

[21] Nicolaus Copernicus, *De revolutionibus orbium coelestium*, Nuremberg, Johann Petreius, 1543, f° (USTC 678038); Biblioteka Jagiellońska, BJ Rkp. 10,000 III, digitised at https://jbc.bj.uj.edu.pl/dlibra/metadatasearch?action=AdvancedSearchAction&type=-3&val1=dig:%22NDIGORP000663%22.

[22] N. M. Swerdlow, 'On Establishing the Text of *De Revolutionibus*', *Journal for the History of Astronomy*, 12, 1981, pp. 35–46.

[23] It is often the case that errata lists do not include errors in the last few sheets, suggesting that they were being collected as the book went through the press, not as Ann Blair writes 'once the printing was completed', and the Copernicus errata sheet covers 146 out of 196 leaves, 74% rather than 'midway' through the book. Blair 'Errata lists' (n. 3 above), pp. 22, 28.

[24] The errata leaf is found in about a quarter of copies, bound either before f. 1 or at the end of the book. The five errata to the diagrams are as follows:'30 r pro K in polo antarctico, repone H, figurae primae; 91 r in hac figura coniunge DI & OI lineis rectis; 111 r in hac figura connectantur EM, EL, lineis rectis; 125 r in hac figura RE circumfere[n]tia, à dextris accipienda erat; 142 r in hac figura pro T, lege R.' Extended errata entered in manuscript in 8 copies are listed in O. Gingerich, *An Annotated Census of Copernicus' De Revolutionibus (Nuremberg, 1543 and Basel, 1566)*, Leiden and Boston, 2002, pp. 362–5 (in Gingerich's translation): '112 recto, on the diagram, change the position of F to the line EC; 123 recto, on the diagram, for L read C; 158 recto, add X to the diagram.'

[25] The erratum for the diagram on f. 111*r* re-inserts the lines CM and CL which are omitted in the woodcut. Ironically, the printed erratum is erroneous, misprinting the lines as 'EM, EL,' having mis-read the *c* in the centre of the circle as *e* and then converted it to uppercase. Gingerich lists the errors in the errata leaf but misses this one. Gingerich, *Annotated Census* (n. 24 above), p. 365.

FIG. 5.4.a. Autograph manuscript of Copernicus, *De revolutionibus orbium coelestium*. Kraków, Biblioteka Jagiellońska, BJ Rkp. 10,000 III, fol. 119v.

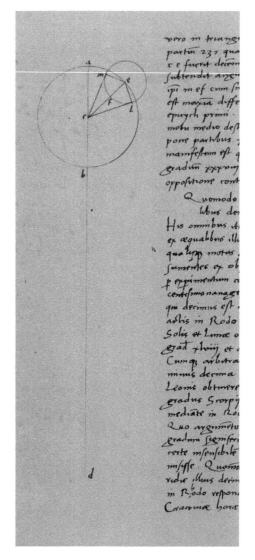

The errors signalled in the printed and manuscript errata in *De revolutionibus* seem to be the result of carelessness or, in the case of the wrong letters, the conversion of the lowercase letters used in the manuscript to the uppercase letters which were cut on the block. Comparing the manuscript with the printed book one can readily see how a *l* became a C and a *r* became a T. A misreading of the diagram rather than of the lettering is seen where the figure-of-eight path of the pole has been misinterpreted as two distinct ovals

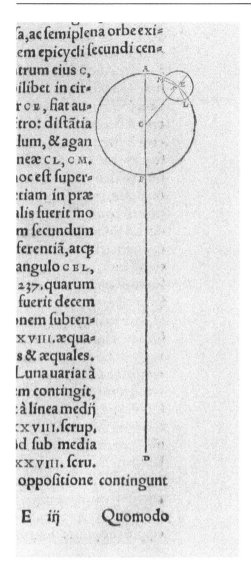

FIG. 5.4.b. Nicolaus Copernicus, *De revolutionibus orbium coelestium*, Nuremberg, Johann Petreius, 1543, f° (USTC 678038), fol. 111r. The erratum for this diagram ('in hac figura connectantur EM, EL, lineis rectis') is itself an error, as it should read 'in this figure connect CM, CL with straight lines'. These lines can be seen by comparison with the manuscript and have been omitted in the woodcut. Kansas City, Linda Hall Library, QB41 .C64 1543 quarto.

(Fig. 5.5.a–b), making the printed diagram unintelligible.[26] These errors might have been introduced either in making a copy of the diagrams for the block cutter or in transferring them to the block for cutting.

Conversely, errors introduced into Copernicus's famous diagram of the solar system seem hard to ascribe solely to copying. The diagram differs from the autograph manuscript in two important ways. First, the legends for Mars, Jupiter, Saturn, and the fixed stars are all moved

---

[26] M. Kemp, 'Temples of the Body and Temples of the Cosmos: Vision and Visualization in the Vesalian and Copernican Revolutions', in B. S. Baigrie (ed.), *Picturing Knowledge: Historical and Philosophical Problems Concerning the Use of Art in Science*, Toronto and Buffalo (NY), 1996, pp. 40–85, 966–7.

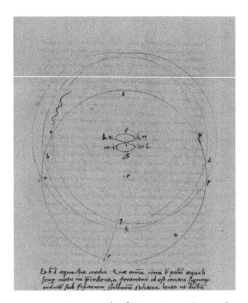
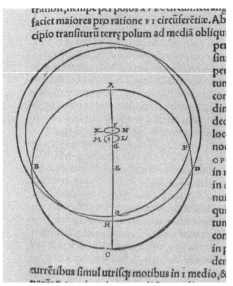

FIG. 5.5.a. Autograph of Copernicus, *De revolutionibus* (see Fig. 5.4.a), fol. 74r.

FIG. 5.5.b. Copernicus, *De revolutionibus* (see Fig. 5.4.b), fol. 66v. The figure-of-eight path of the pole in the manuscript appears as two ovals in the woodcut.

above the lines defining the spheres, rather than between them (Fig. 5.6.a–b). This has the effect of making the sphere of the fixed stars appear to be unbounded, as though a visual hint of an infinite universe, a highly contentious issue. Furthermore, it is no longer clear if the planets move along the lines or, as Copernicus meant, in the areas between the lines, the two-dimensional rendering of spheres.[27] The error was repeated in copies of the diagram, leading to a misunderstanding of the Copernican system.[28]

The second difference is that in the autograph manuscript the moon is only indicated verbally, 'Telluris c[u]m luna. an. re.', but in the woodcut there is an image of the moon in a circle round the earth, now shown as a dot labelled 'Terra', and the text is expanded to 'Telluris cum orbe Lunari annua revolutio' (The annual revolution of the earth, together with the moon). This is not something that would have been changed in scribal copying; it must have been an intervention made by Copernicus or by Rheticus.[29]

---

[27] The diagram is now internally inconsistent in that Mercury and Venus are labelled within their spheres and there is an empty sphere between the spheres of Earth and Mars.

[28] According to Gerd Grasshoff, 'this error was continuously repeated over many centuries and gave rise to the misinterpretation that the Copernican system was simpler (regarding the number of circles) than the Ptolemaic system.' G. Grasshoff, 'Michael Maestlin's Mystery: Theory Building with Diagrams', *Journal for the History of Astronomy*, 43, 2012, pp. 57–73 (66).

[29] Swerdlow, 'On Establishing the Text' (n. 22 above), does not consider a separate copy of the diagrams made for the block cutter, but it is most unlikely that they would have had the fair copy from which the text was presumably set.

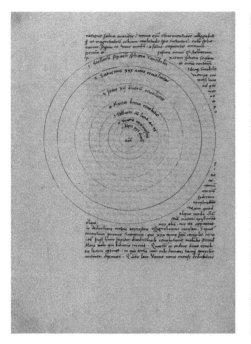 

FIG. 5.6.a. Autograph of Copernicus, *De revolutionibus* (see Fig. 5.4.a), fol. 9v.

FIG. 5.6.b. Copernicus, *De revolutionibus* (see Fig. 5.4.b), fol. 9v. Compared with the manuscript, the labels for the spheres of Mars, Jupiter, Saturn, and the fixed stars are moved out and the orbit of the moon is shown graphically instead of verbally.

Errors in Copying Printed Images

Reversing an image in copying was a standard procedure (not necessary but easier), leading to a series of left-handed swordsmen in a German edition of Aesop.[30] The narrative of the pictures in Giorgio de' Rusconi's edition of Ovid (1517) runs backwards, as Mortimer explains: 'The majority of the Rusconi copies are reversed. The cutter was not generally aware that reversing the design also reversed the sequence of events when several scenes were combined on one block'.[31]

Direct copies of woodcuts could be astonishingly accurate because, as was presumably the case in the above examples, the original printed image was pasted to the new block and the block cutter could follow every detail exactly. On the other hand, when an image was

---

[30] Davies *Farifax Murray German*, no. 17 describing Aesopus, *Fabulae*, Antwerp, Gerard Leeu, 1486, f° (ISTC ia00114000) and noting that the blocks were first used in H. Knoblochtzer's Strasburg edition c. 1481–1482, f° (ISTC ia00113000).

[31] Mortimer *Italian*, no. 338 describing Ovid, *Metamorphosis*, Venice, Giorgio de' Rusconi, 1517, f° (USTC 763005).

copied from one medium to another, and especially if it was, as we would say, 'reformatted', errors were more likely. An engraved building plan in the Giunta 1569 Venice edition of Mercuriale's *De arte gymnastica* was rendered as two woodcuts on consecutive pages when the same press reprinted the work in 1573 (the first fully illustrated edition, famous for its woodcuts of gymnasts). In the woodcut plan, there were errors in the relative positions and proportions of architectural features. The errors were blamed on the block cutter in a note following the list of textual errata at the end of the book.[32]

ERRORS IN MAKING THE MATRIX

It was conventional to blame the block cutter for errors, although it may not have been the cutter himself who committed them but a draughtsman who copied the drawing onto the block in the way shown in the famous triple portrait in Leonhart Fuchs's *De historia stirpium* (Basle, 1542).[33] As if to forestall criticism, the *Formschneider* or block cutter in Hans Sachs's book of trades says, 'I am a good block cutter and anything you draw for me with a pen on a plank of wood I will cut with my knife.'[34] Still, the block cutter gets the blame, rather in the same way that the 'printer' is blamed for typographic errors that might be the fault of the compositor or corrector. But to err is human, so the reader may pardon the blunders (Fig. 5.7).[35]

As with copying from existing prints, new blocks could also be prepared for cutting by pasting the pen-and-ink diagram onto the block, as Philibert de l'Orme explains in his architectural treatise (Paris, 1567). It was customary, he says, for the block cutters to dampen, and sometimes warm, the paper on which the diagrams were drawn before pasting them to the block for cutting. This would deform the paper so that the resulting woodcuts would be inaccurate. In addition, some lines, figures, and numbers do not correspond to the text because when the blocks were being cut de l'Orme was otherwise occupied — a standard

---

[32] Girolamo Mercuriale, *De arte gymnastica libri sex*, Venice, Lucantonio II Giunta, 1573, 4° (USTC 763167), in Mortimer *Italian*, no. 302. The woodcut in question is on sig. B4r, the note in the errata list on V2r.

[33] Leonhart Fuchs, *De historia stirpium commentarii insignes*, Basel, Michael Isengrin, 1542, f° (USTC 602520), sig. 3f5r; this 'Pictoris operis' shows the artist, Albertus Meyer, drawing a plant in a vase, Heinrich Füllmaurer transferring the drawing to the woodblock, and the 'Sculptor' Vitus Rudolph Speckle.

[34] We paraphrased from Hans Sachs, *Eygentliche beschreibung aller Staende auff erden hoher und nidriger*, Frankfurt am Main, [Georg Rab I for Sigmund Feyerabend], 1568, 4o (USTC 655780), sig. f1r: 'Ich bin ein Formen schneider gut, / Als was man mir für reissen thut, / it der federn auff ein form bret / Das schneid ich denn mit meim geret / Wenn mans denn druckt so find sich scharff / Die Bildnuß, wie sie der entwarff, / Die steht, denn druckt auff dem papyr, / Künstlich denn auß zustreichen schier.'

[35] Nicholas Culpeper, *Catastrophe magnatum, or, the fall of monarchie a caveat to magistrates, deduced from the eclipse of the sunne, march 29, 1652, with a probable conjecture of the determination of the effects*, London, printed for T. Vere and Nath. Brooke, 1652, sig. E4r.

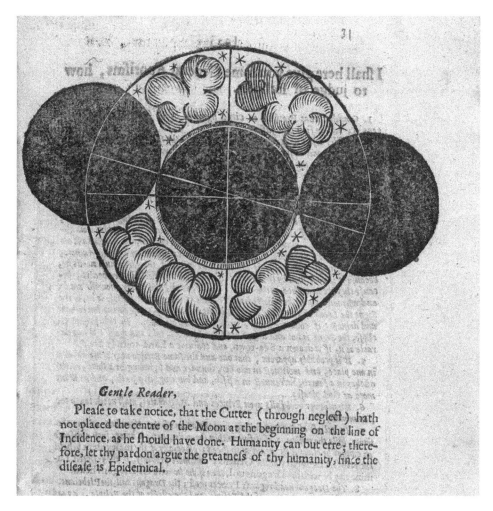

FIG. 5.7. Blaming the block-cutter. Nicholas Culpeper, *Catastrophe magnatum*, London, 1652, sig. E4r. Washington DC, Folger Shakespeare Library, call no. 261279.

trope, in this case offered with the unassailable justification that he was in the service of the king.[36]

A similar excuse for errors introduced in making the matrix, this time engraved copperplate, is given by Anthony Ashley in his edition of Lucas Wagenaer's *The Mariners Mirrour* (London, 1588). Ashley explains that he had been unable to oversee the production of the maps owing to his duties as an officer of the Privy Council and 'the Negligent gravers' got away with their mistakes.[37]

---

[36] Philibert De L'Orme, *Le premier tome de l'architecture*, Paris, Frédéric Morel, 1567, f° (USTC 24434), fols 5r and 6v.

[37] Bennett, *English Books and Readers* (n. 1 above), II, p. 282 citing Lucas Janssen Wagenaer, *The mariners mirrour*, London, [J. Charlewood, 1588?], f° (USTC 51102), sig. ¶1r.

IMPOSITION ERRORS

Having considered erroneous images and mistakes introduced in copying, block cutting, and engraving, we turn now to errors introduced during the printing process. The most common, and the most obvious, are imposition errors. Many examples where imposition errors are obscured — and so drawn to our attention — by paste-on cancels are indexed by Davies and Mortimer. The earliest, reported by Davies, is in Johann Schobsser's printing of *Auslegung des Lebens Jesu Christi* (Augsburg, c. 1490–1494), but the practice no doubt starts earlier.[38] Here, the woodcut of the Samaritan Woman (*Von dem haideschen fröwlin*) on sig. e6*v* is pasted over the Woman taken in Adultery (*Von dem fröwlin begriffen in dem eebruch*) which also appears in the correct place on sig. g4*v*, fifteen leaves further on. Davies describes both the Fairfax Murray and the Huth copies, in both cases with very similar contemporary colouring: the covered-up Woman taken in Adultery is uncoloured in both copies. Davies notes that Schreiber listed the cuts on sigs e6*v* and g4*v* as identical, commenting, 'in other words the correction had not been made in his copy'. Or, we might add, the printer or binder had failed to paste the cancel image or it had later become detached. As we will see, many errors were corrected during production, but without further evidence it would be wrong to assume that the absence of a paste-on cancel implies an earlier state.

In the *Auslegung* one block was printed twice in error; in many other cases blocks were interchanged, as in the Aldine Caesar of 1513.[39] The blocks for the views of Uxellodunum and Massilia were transposed, and rather than go to the expense of paste-on cancels, the woodcuts, which can no longer be identified by the adjacent text, were captioned in manuscript. Publishers' pen-and-ink correction to text is not uncommon and in this case, as with many other interventions in the Aldine Press, it was made by Aldus himself.[40]

If blocks were omitted, either by accident or because they had not yet been delivered to the printer, a space could be left so that they could be printed separately, and cut and pasted in at a later stage, or they could simply be printed at the end of the book.[41]

Because printing intaglio plates into the spaces left in letterpress required a special rolling press run by independent and specialised print shops, it is perhaps less surprising

---

[38] Davies *Fairfax Murray German*, no. 110 and p. 814.

[39] Mortimer *Italian*, no. 96.

[40] Cf. the dubitative stance taken by McKitterick, *Print, Manuscript* (n. 3 above), p. 87, with the contributions by Geri Della Rocca de Candal and Paolo Sachet to this Companion. A much more elaborate way of correcting a misplaced block is discussed by François Dupuigrenet Desroussilles in this Companion.

[41] Pasted-in illustrations can be found in Marcolini's *Le Sorti*, Venice, Francesco Marcolini, 1540, f° (USTC 840720), where some cards of the play are corrected with pasted ones, others with ink (see Mortimer *Italian*, no 279), and in Petrus Peña and Matthias de l'Obel, *Stirpium adversaria nova*, London, Thomas Purfoot, 1570–1571, f° (USTC 19595). The sheets were re-issued several times in London and Antwerp with the paste-on cancels applied in the same way, perhaps suggesting that it was done in the London printing house. R. W. Chapman, *Cancels*, London and New York, 1930, notes that paste-on cancels of odd words or lines were applied to flat sheets, rather than being pasted in to folded sheets at a later stage (with thanks to David McKitterick for pointing this out). In Vincenzo Cartari, *Les images des dievx anciens*, Lyon, Guichard Julliéron for Etienne Michel, 1581, 4° (USTC 6474), a block was omitted and printed at the end with a note explaining the error on sig. 4L3*v* (Mortimer *French*, no. 128). See also François Dupuigrenet Desroussilles' essay in this Companion for a particularly enigmatic edition of a picture Bible, in which two missing woodcuts were printed recto and verso of a single leaf bound at end.

that plates got printed in the wrong position.[42] A particularly instructive example analysed by Mortimer is Francesco Ferretti, *Diporti notturni* (Ancona, 1580).[43] The second of three double-page engravings is a battle formation, printed in this edition to correct an illustration printed in the Venice 1568 and 1577 editions of the same author's *Osservanza militare*.[44] The other engravings are maps of islands with engraved captions and sea monsters, the text on facing pages of letterpress. In one Harvard copy, cancel engravings are pasted over wrongly placed maps on five pages, while in another the copperplates have been printed in their correct positions.[45] In Enea Vico's *Le imagini delle donne auguste* (Venice, 1557) a whole series of mis-impositions and paste-on cancels are seen in different copies, including a correction to one plate made by pasting a circular portrait medallion onto the engraving.[46]

This demonstrates the variability inherent in books with engraved illustrations. If the engraving is incorporated in the text, the letterpress is printed first, in a single impression, before the sheets are sent out to the rolling press printer. The plates can then be printed in the spaces left for them, not necessarily in one run. In some cases, engravings were added in batches as copies were required.[47] Where engravings are bound in as plates there is even more flexibility, as printing is completely independent of the letterpress. Unlike woodcuts, copperplates can fairly readily be reworked or corrected so that states of plates, printed at different times, can vary from copy to copy.

AUTHORS' AND PRINTERS' CORRECTIONS DURING AND AFTER PRINTING

One of the most elaborately produced books illustrated with woodcuts, Daniele Barbaro's Italian edition of Vitruvius (Venice, 1556), was almost bound to run into trouble.[48] Three erroneous — or are they? — woodcuts had to be corrected, and this was done in a number of different ways: paste-on cancels just covering the image; a paste-on cancel for the whole page; and cancellation of a whole bifolium. Both these last two methods were used for correcting the same image, the plan of a temple, in different copies. At Harvard, one copy has a paste-on cancel covering the whole of page B3r, including the headline and signature; but

---

[42] Gaskell, 'Printing House and Engraving Shop' (n. 6 above).

[43] Francesco Ferretti, *Diporti notturni*, Ancona, Francesco Salvioni, 1580, 8° (USTC 829285). See Mortimer *Italian*, no. 184.

[44] The engraving is printed on sig. E2v and the explanation on sigs E1v–E2r.

[45] On sigs G2r, H1r, H5r, I1r and I7r.

[46] Enea Vico, *Le imagini delle donne auguste intagliate in istampa di rame*, Venice, Enea Vico and Vincenzo Valgrisi, 1557, 4° (USTC 863205); see Mortimer *Italian*, no 532.

[47] E.g., Christophe Plantin paid the rolling press printer Mynken Liefrinck to print the engravings for 100 of 600 copies of the Polyglot Bible in 1572. K. Bowen and D. Imhof, *Christopher Plantin and Engraved Book Illustrations in Sixteenth-Century Europe*, Cambridge, 2008, p. 102.

[48] Vitruvius, *I dieci libri dell'architettura*, Venice, Francesco Marcolini, 1556, f° (USTC 863689). There are double-page woodcuts which disturb the regularity of the gatherings; images too large for the page required pasted-on extensions; one has a revolving pointer; two woodcuts of Roman theatres are mounted on threads and can be rotated to show how they could form one amphitheatre.

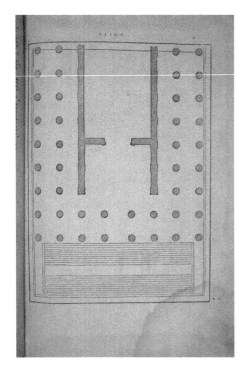 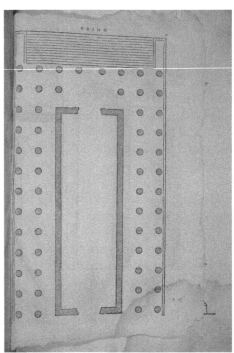

FIG. 5.8.a–b. Vitruvius, *I dieci libri dell'architettura*, Venice, Francesco Marcolini, 1556, f° (USTC 863689). In this copy, the original leaf signed B3r (on the left) has been retained in addition to the replacement leaf with a woodcut showing a different temple plan. Einsiedeln, Stiftung Bibliothek Werner Oechslin, A04f.

in the second copy, the bifolium B3-4 is cancelled, the text on sig. B4v being a new setting of type.[49]

Two other images have paste-on cancels just covering the image in both copies. In the woodcut originally printed at sig. B3r, the temple has no porch and one flight of steps, while in the replacement there is a porch and two flights of steps (Fig. 5.8.a–b).[50]

This is not then an error, there is no question of a copyist or block cutter making such a significant change: it must be, as Michael Waters points out, that Barbaro 'rejected' one plan and replaced it with another.[51] Most descriptions of the book describe this as a 'correction' (as indeed Waters does), or the 'wrong block' (Mortimer), but this example shows that we should be cautious about attributing all alterations to mistakes rather than authorial changes. In the same way, textual errata can both correct misprints and allow space for the author's afterthoughts.

[49] Mortimer *Italian*, no. 547.
[50] Both original and replacement are retained in the copy in Einsiedeln, Stiftung Bibliothek Werner Oechslin, digitised at http://echo.mpiwg-berlin.mpg.de/MPIWG:HVAZH321, accessed 14 January 2021.
[51] M. J. Waters, 'A Renaissance without Order: Ornament, Single-Sheet Engravings, and the Mutability of Architectural Prints', *Journal of the Society of Architectural Historians*, 71, 2012, pp. 488–523 (520, n. 69).

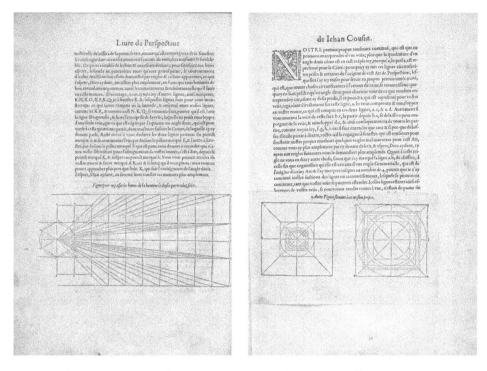

FIG. 5.9.a–b. Jean Cousin, *Livre de Perspective,* Paris, Jean le Royer, 1560, f° (USTC 23189), sigs C3v–C4r, with inserted slip providing two alternative diagrams making the same point as that printed on the left-hand page. It would need to be turned over to read the text on the right-hand page. Cambridge (MA), Houghton Library, Typ 515.6.301 (A).

Modern bibliographers are not the only ones to have been led astray by a paste-on cancel. Jean Cousin provided an additional pair of diagrams for his *Livre de perspective* (Paris, 1560),[52] clearly labelled 'Autre Figure servant à ce mesme propos' (Another figure for the same purpose). In some copies, this is tipped in facing the original diagram on sig. C3v, as was surely intended, so that the original and extra diagrams can both be seen (Fig. 5.9.a–b). In other copies, it has been pasted over the original diagram, which can now no longer be seen.[53]

Images inappropriate to the text are found in the first edition of Lodovico Dolce, *Le Trasformationi*, a translation into Italian verse of Ovid's *Metamorphosis*, with episodes illustrated by eighty-eight woodblocks (Venice, 1553). Many of them are employed two or three times and some are inserted in the wrong place. To these are added six Old Testament blocks of a smaller format at sigs G2v, G4v, I4v, T1r, T2v, and T6v.[54]

---

[52] Jean Cousin, *Livre de Perspective*, Paris, Jean le Royer, 1560, f° (USTC 23189); Mortimer *French*, no. 157.

[53] Copies with the slip tipped in are at Harvard, Houghton Library, Typ 515.6.301(A), and Washington, DC, National Gallery of Art, 1985.61.481; paste slips are found in a second Harvard copy, Typ 515.6.301(B), and at Paris, Beaux-Arts, Masson 403, and Los Angeles, Getty Center, 54035.

[54] Ovid, *Le Trasformationi*, Venice, Gabriele Giolito, 1553, 4° (USTC 845802 and 845803); M. D. Henkel, 'Illustrierte Ausgaben von Ovids Metamorphosen im XV., XVI., und XVII. Jahrhundert',

98   PRINTING AND MISPRINTING

It is not possible to identify a precise editorial plan in this arrangement. Even though each canto always begins with an image, they are sometimes not suitable for the text. The reason for the biblical insertions and the repetitions is probably to be found in the fact that, for some cantos, the illustrations of Ovidian argument available to the printer, Gabriele Giolito, were not sufficient; for canto XXIX, in particular, he did not even have one at hand. Evidence shows that the author of the woodblocks, probably the architect and printer Giovanni Antonio Rusconi, had provided several blocks for the first twenty-three cantos, roughly up to the twelfth book of Ovid, but then he had worked sparingly and perhaps also with great haste to get to the end: from the twenty-fourth onwards, the initial woodcut is the only print of the canto.

However, in 1552 nine blocks of the *Transformationi* had already been used in a Giolito edition of the Boccaccio's *Decameron* edited by the same Lodovico Dolce (Venice, 1552, at sigs D3r, E6v, K7r, L1v, L4r, L5r–v and P5v).[55] By this date, therefore, the block cutter must have already been well advanced with his work, since the later illustration in Ovid's text is that representing the story of Ceix and Alcyon, corresponding to Ovid's book XI and canto XXIII of the Italian translation.

The six biblical woodcuts included in the *Trasformationi* are actually part of a series of 135 prints for which Giolito had requested the privilege in 1543. They were intended for a vernacular Bible never printed by Giolito which was to be used by his heirs for the 1588 Vulgate. Nine of these had already been used by the publisher in the *Decameron* edited by Dolce in 1552, where there are, as already noted, also nine *Transformationi* woodcuts. In the second edition of the latter (1553), described on the title-page as 'newly reprinted, corrected and expanded in several places', Giolito reduced the biblical woodblocks to one (the pharaoh and the plague of frogs), eliminated many repetitions, added ornamental blocks to the sides of the woodblocks, corrected the positioning errors, and added four new illustrations. In a postscript to the reader, Giolito admitted the imperfection of the first edition (sig. X1r–v) and states that 1,800 or more copies of the first edition had been sold in four months. In the subsequent editions of 1555, 1557, 1558, and 1561, the last edited by Dolce, there are no more substantial changes regarding the illustrations, even if in the editions of 1557 and 1558 the one with Orfeo singing, perhaps temporarily lost, is missing.[56]

Finally, a group of Ludovico Ariosto's *Orlando furioso* small blocks appears amongst the seventy-three woodcuts of Olaus Magnus's *Historia de gentibus septentrionalibus*, though not in the Venice 1565 edition of the Italian translation of this work.[57]

Vorträge der Bibliothek Warburg, 7, 1926–1927, pp. 58–144 (83–4); Mortimer *Italian*, nos 72 and 342; B. Guthmüller, 'Nota su Giovanni Antonio Rusconi illustratore delle *Trasformationi* del Dolce', in *Miscellanea di studi in onore di Vittore Branca*, III/2: *Umanesimo e Rinascimento a Firenze e Venezia*, Florence, 1983, pp. 771–9; E. Michael, 'Some Sixteenth-Century Venetian Bible Woodcuts Inspired by Holbein's *Icones*', *Print Quarterly*, 7, 1990, pp. 239–47 (246–7); C. Coppens and A. Nuovo, 'The Illustrations of the Unpublished Giolito Bible', in M. Lamberigts and A. den Hollander (eds), *Lay Bibles in Europe 1450–1800*, Leuven, 2006, pp. 119–41.

[55] Giovanni Boccaccio, *Il Decamerone*, 2 vols, Venice, Gabriele Giolito and brothers, 1552, 4° (USTC 814838).

[56] All 4° format: USTC 845810, 845814, 845820, and 845831.

[57] Cf. Olaus Magnus, *Historia de gentibus septentrionalibus*, Rome, Giovanni Maria Viotti in aedibus Sanctae Brigittae, 1555, f° (USTC 839655) and his *Historia delle genti et della natura delle cose settentrionali*, Venice, Domenico Nicolini da Sabbio for Lucantonio Giunta; f° (USTC 839658); Mortimer *Italian*, no. 270.

Errors in Printing

We saw that Manetti excused the difficulty that his readers might have had in understanding his woodcuts, which were not as he would have liked 'because of the lack of space and the difficulty of the work'. Illustrators were always constrained by the limitations of the chosen medium and this could lead, if not to substantive error, at least to a lack of clarity. This is demonstrated by the problem of the hidden guide letters in the woodcuts in Vesalius's *De humani corporis fabrica* printed at Basel by Johann Oporinus in 1543.[58] As is well known, when the blocks were re-used for the second edition (1555), the area round many of the guide letters was cut away to make them more visible. Vesalius himself was aware that printing the woodcuts was going to be challenging. The blocks were cut in Venice and shipped to Basel with a covering letter in which Vesalius asks Oporinus to make sure that the impressions of the blocks matched the block cutter's proofs which accompanied them. He explains that 'if this is done then no symbol, however hidden in the shading, will escape the notice of a reader who has eyes and uses them'.[59] In fact, this was probably impossible, as the block cutters in Venice would have proofed the blocks either by rubbing or using a hand-held roller to produce much finer impressions than would be obtained when the blocks were printed in combination with type on a common press. A block cutter in Basel was therefore employed to cut away the shading round the guide letters so that when printed the lettering stood out in a pool of white space.[60]

Conclusions

There is more than scholarly good fun to the comedy of errors in illustrated books that we have assembled from examples picked from different printing towns in Europe. Although our collection of case studies represents an invitation for future research in a subject that has never been treated before, rather than a synthesis that would be extremely premature, we can formulate at the moment of parting three general observations.

In this chapter we have discussed errors that were recognised by the book's author or printer and revealed by textual comments, errata lists, printed cancels, or publishers' manuscript corrections. Individual readers, in an age when reading pen-in-hand was expected, would also make corrections. However, although more attention is now being given to book illustration and the study of annotated books is now central to book history, there has been no systematic survey of annotations to illustrations. Such a survey should help improve our understanding of the reception of early modern book illustration. In a

---

[58] Andreas Vesalius, *De humani corporis fabrica*, Basel, [Johann Oporinus, 1543], f° (USTC 606035).

[59] Ibid., sig. *5r; translation taken from Vesalius, *On the Fabric* (n. 9 above), I, p. lx. See above p. 82 for the cutting of these blocks.

[60] On the problems of printing woodcuts with letterpress and the impossibility of matching the block cutter's proof, see J.-M. Papillon, *Traité historique et pratique de la gravure en bois*, Pairs, 1766, II, p. 359. We may perhaps gain some idea of how the proofs would have looked from the impressions made from the original blocks for the Bremer Presse *Icones anatomicae* (1943), printed with extensive use of overlays.

typical errata list, the reader is asked to correct misprints in the text or images with a pen, thus in a sense completing the production process of the book.[61] But these paratexts are also rhetorical. As Ann Blair points out, acknowledging errors forestalls criticism, blaming the printer exculpates the author, and flattering the reader deflects criticism.[62] Thus Besson says that the error in his image 'will be easy to correct for those who have a little understanding of this science'. As both Bennett and Blair have observed, in the great majority of surviving copies, the requests to 'mend with a pen' have not been observed.[63] Furthermore, annotators seem to have been less concerned with marking illustrations than text.[64] In both cases, we think the picture is much more complicated than the raw figures suggest: surely, more research is needed.

Illustrated books during the sixteenth and the seventeenth century were part of a technical system that was intrinsically error-prone, at least in the eyes of the twenty-first-century reader. The processes of having images in printed books multiplied occasions for error at every stage of production, from the transfer of original drawings onto the surface of the woodblocks, or the translation of drawings into the syntax of engraving, to imposition and printing. Many errors mentioned in this chapter are systemic, but we have focused on those that were recognised as such by contemporaries, ignoring those that were below the toleration level of the early modern public and were only pointed out by modern scholars. We have also ignored the mistakes involved in early trial and error technical attempts, such as the soon-abandoned introduction of intaglio illustrations in typographically composed sheets in Florence at the end of the fifteenth century,[65] or the use of hand-printed woodblocks in the blank spaces of some copies of the 1472 Verona Valturius.[66] During the 'classical' period under consideration here, illustrated books offered more occasions for misprinting than the non-illustrated ones, for example using images inappropriate to the subject of the text, or, in technical writing, where the image or lettering does not match the text.

What is more specific to early modern illustrated books is that, beyond proper misprints, they offer historians, and art historians in particular, a rare opportunity to examine what sixteenth and seventeenth century readers considered as an erroneous image. If we envisage early modern images globally, be they paintings, frescoes, stained glass, ceramics, statues, or single-sheet prints, they were seldom confronted with anything that could call their truth

---

[61] McKitterick *Print, Manuscript* (n. 3 above), pp. 139–65.

[62] Blair, 'Errata lists' (n. 3 above), p. 34.

[63] For English books, Bennett remarks, 'Having looked over some thousands of books from the beginning of printing until 1640, I think that it would be safe to say that in 75% of them there is no sign that any corrections were made, and of the remainder, few readers persevered beyond the first fifty or sixty pages. To find a volume in which all the errata are noticed and corrected in the text is rare indeed.' Bennett, *English Books and Readers* (n. 1 above), III, pp. 207–8. Similarly, Blair notes: 'In my experience, however, corrections of this mechanical kind are surprisingly uncommon.' Blair 'Errata lists' (n. 3 above), p. 38.

[64] As noted above (n. 24), Owen Gingerich in his census of Copernicus records that the additional errata lists of readers found only three errors in the diagrams and 157 in the text.

[65] In Dante Alighieri, *La Commedia*, Florence, Nicolaus Laurentii Alamanus, 30 Aug. 1481, f° (ISTC id00029000), it is also possible that the printers stopped printing the intaglios in the sheets because Botticelli had fallen behind with the drawings — apparently the first ones may not have been delivered until 1482. D. Landau and P. Parshall, *The Renaissance Print*, New Haven (CT) and London, 1994, p. 108.

[66] Valturius, *De re militari*, [Verona], Johannes Nicolai de Verona, 1472, f° (ISTC iv00088000).

into question. Images in books, on the contrary, immediately entered into a complex relationship with an array of texts, from the main text to captions and references of all kinds, that implied the truth of the image. This is particularly obvious in Bibles because biblical illustrations had to bear the weight of the word of God, to the point that Puritans, following the example of John Calvin, successfully pressed for the exclusion from their Bibles of any illustration, except for maps: illustration was regarded as a form of idolatry, deflecting attention from divine truth.[67] If illustrations were admitted, as in Lutheran and Catholic Bibles, any discrepancy between text and illustration could have serious theological implications. Misprinting the image of God was just as bad as misprinting his word. But misprinting the illustrated texts of botany, medicine, or astronomy raised the same type of difficulty, which reinforces the need for the extra level of care that authors and printers took in chasing misprints in scientific books.

BIBLIOGRAPHY

PRIMARY SOURCES

MANUSCRIPTS

MS Kraków, Biblioteka Jagiellońska, BJ Rkp. 10000 III: Copernicus, Nicolaus, *De revolutionibus orbium coelestium*, c. 1520–1541, digitised at https://jbc.bj.uj.edu.pl/dlibra/metadatasearch?action= AdvancedSearchAction&type=–3&val1=dig:%22NDIGORP000663%22

PRINTED BOOKS

A short dialogue proving that the ceremonyes, and some other corruptions now in question are defended, [Amsterdam], s.n., 1605, 4° (USTC 1506131).
Aesopus, *Fabulae*, Strasburg, Heinrich Knoblochtzer, c. 1481–1482, f° (ISTC ia00113000).
Aesopus, *Fabulae*, Antwerp, Gerard Leeu, 1486, f° (ISTC ia00114000).

---

[67] See R. S. Luborsky and E. M. Ingram, *A Guide to English Illustrated Books 1536–1603*, Tempe (AZ), 1998, I, pp. 83–5 and nos 2063–193. P. Collison defended the idea of a growing iconophobia in the English Reformation, particularly in Bibles: 'From Iconoclasm to Iconophobia', in P. Marshall (ed.), *The Impact of the English Reformation 1500–1640*, London, 1997, pp. 278–307. His position was contested by D. J. Davis, *Seeing Faith, Printing Pictures: Religious Identity in the English Reformation*, Leiden, 2013, pp. 213–17.

102   PRINTING AND MISPRINTING

Alighieri Dante, *La Commedia*, Florence, Nicolaus Laurentii Alamanus, 30 Aug. 1481, f° (ISTC id00029000).

Alighieri Dante, *Commedia di Dante insieme con uno dialogo circa el sito forma et misure dello inferno*, Florence, Filippo Giunta, 1506, 8° (USTC 808765).

Apollonius Pergaeus, *Conicorum lib. V. VI. VII*, ed. G. A. Borelli, Florence, 1661.

Besson, Jacques, *Le cosmolabe*, Paris, Philippe Gaulthier Rouillé, 1567–1569, 4° (USTC 16555).

Biblia, [Venice, Adam de Ambergau], 1 Oct. 1471, f° (ISTC ib00639000).

Biblia, transl. Nicolò Malermi, Venice, Vindelinus de Spira, 1 Aug. 1471, f° (ISTC ib00640000).

Boccaccio, Giovanni, *Il Decamerone*, 2 vols, Venice, Gabriele Giolito and brothers, 1552, 4° (USTC 814838).

Cartari, Vincenzo, *Les images des dievx anciens*, Lyon, Guichard Julliéron for Etienne Michel, 1581, 4° (USTC 6474).

Copernicus, Nicolaus, *De revolutionibus orbium coelestium*, Nuremberg, Johann Petreius, 1543, f° (USTC 678038).

Cousin, Jean, *Livre de Perspective*, Paris, Jean le Royer, 1560, f° (USTC 23189).

Culpeper, Nicholas, *Catastrophe magnatum, or, the fall of monarchie a caveat to magistrates, deduced from the eclipse of the sunne, march 29, 1652, with a probable conjecture of the determination of the effects*, London, T. Vere and Nath. Brooke, 1652.

De L'Orme, Philibert, *Le premier tome de l'architecture*, Paris, Frédéric Morel, 1567, f° (USTC 24434.

Euclid, *The elements of geometrie*, London, John Day, 1570, f°, (USTC 507133).

Ferretti, Francesco, *Diporti notturni*, Ancona, Francesco Salvioni, 1580, 8° (USTC 829285).

Fuchs, Leonhart, *De historia stirpium commentarii insignes*, Basel, Michael Isengrin, 1542, f° (USTC 602520).

Magnus, Olaus, *Historia de gentibus septentrionalibus*, Rome, Giovanni Maria Viotti in aedibus Sanctae Brigittae, 1555, f° (USTC 839655).

Magnus, Olaus, *Historia delle genti et della natura delle cose settentrionali*, Venice, Domenico Nicolini da Sabbio for Lucantonio Giunta, f° (USTC 839658).

Marcolini, Francesco, *Le Sorti*, Venice, Francesco Marcolini, 1540, f° (USTC 840720).

Mercuriale, Girolamo, *De arte gymnastica libri sex*, Venice, Lucantonio II Giunta, 1573, 4° (USTC 763167).

Ovid, *Le Trasformationi*, Venice, Gabriele Giolito, 1553, 4° (USTC 845802 and 845803).

Ovid, *Le Trasformationi*, Venice, Gabriele Giolito, 1555, 4° (USTC 845810).

Ovid, *Le Trasformationi*, Venice, Gabriele Giolito, 1557, 4° (USTC 845814).

Ovid, *Le Trasformationi*, Venice, Gabriele Giolito, 1558, 4° (USTC 845820).

Ovid, *Le Trasformationi*, Venice, Gabriele Giolito, 1561, 4° (USTC 845831).

Ovid, *Metamorphosis*, Venice, Giorgio de' Rusconi, 1517, f° (USTC 763005).

Papillon, J.-M., *Traité historique et pratique de la gravure en bois*, Pairs, 1766.

Peña, Petrus and de l'Obel, Matthias, *Stirpium adversaria nova*, London, Thomas Purfoot, 1570–1571, f° (USTC 19595).

Sachs, Hans, *Eygentliche beschreibung aller Staende auff erden hoher und nidriger*, Frankfurt am Main, [Georg Rab I for Sigmund Feyerabend], 1568, 4° (USTC 655780).

Valturio, Roberto, *De re militari*, [Verona], Johannes Nicolai de Verona, 1472, f° (ISTC iv00088000).

Vesalius, Andreas, *De humani corporis fabrica*, Basel, [Johann Oporinus, 1543], f° (USTC 606035).

Vesalius, Andreas, *De humani corporis fabrica*, Basel, [Johann Oporinus, 1555], f° (USTC 606036).

Vesalius, Andreas, *Icones anatomicae*, New York and Munich, 1934 [i.e. 1935].

Vesalius, Andreas, *On the Fabric of the Human Body*, transl. W. F. Richardson, San Francisco, 1998–2009.

Vico, Enea, *Le imagini delle donne auguste intagliate in istampa di rame*, Venice, Enea Vico and Vincenzo Valgrisi, 1557, 4° (USTC 863205).

Vitruvius, *I dieci libri dell'architettura*, Venice, Francesco Marcolini, 1556, f° (USTC 863689).

Wagenaer, Lucas Janssen, *The mariners mirrour*, London, [J. Charlewood, 1588?], f° (USTC 51102].

SECONDARY LITERATURE

Armstrong, L., 'The Hand Illumination of Venetian Bibles in the Incunable Period', in K. Jensen (ed.), *Incunabula and Their Readers*, London, 2003, pp. 83–113, 229–36.

Barbieri, E., 'Un "nuovo" caso di silominiatura: l'esemplare perugino della Bibbia volgare dell'ottobre 1471', *La Bibliofilia*, 122/1, 2020, pp. 23–30.

Bennett, H. S., *English Books and Readers*, 3 vols, Cambridge, 1952–1970.

Blair, A., 'Errata Lists and the Reader as Corrector', in S. A. Baron, E. N. Lindquist, and E. F. Shevlin (eds), *Agent of Change: Print Culture Studies after Elizabeth L. Eisenstein*, Amherst (MA), 2007, pp. 21–41.

Bowen, K., and Imhof, D., *Christopher Plantin and Engraved Book Illustrations in Sixteenth-Century Europe*, Cambridge, 2008.

Chapman, R. W., *Cancels*, London and New York, 1930.

Collison, P., 'From Iconoclasm to Iconophobia', in P. Marshall (ed.), *The Impact of the English Reformation 1500–1640*, London, 1997, pp. 278–307.

Coppens, C. and Nuovo, A., 'The Illustrations of the Unpublished Giolito Bible', in M. Lamberigts and A. den Hollander (eds), *Lay Bibles in Europe 1450–1800*, Leuven, 2006, pp. 119–41.

Davies, H. W., *Catalogue of a Collection of Early French Books in the Library of C. Fairfax Murray*, London, 1910, facsimile reprint 1961.

Davies, H. W., *Fairfax Murray German Catalogue of a Collection of Early German Books in the Library of C. Fairfax Murray*, London, 1913, facsimile reprint 1962.

Davis, D. J., *Seeing Faith, Printing Pictures: Religious Identity in the English Reformation*, Leiden, 2013, pp. 213–17.

Gaskell, P., *A New Introduction to Bibliography*, reprinted with corrections, Cambridge, 1979, pp. 110–16.

Gaskell, R., 'Printing House and Engraving Shop: A Mysterious Collaboration', *The Book Collector*, 53, 2004, pp. 213–51.

Gaskell, R., 'Printing House and Engraving Shop, Part II: Further Thoughts on "Printing and Engraving Shop: A Mysterious Collaboration"', *The Book Collector*, 67, 2018, pp. 788–97.

Gingerich, O., *An Annotated Census of Copernicus' De Revolutionibus (Nuremberg, 1543 and Basel, 1566)*, Leiden and Boston, 2002.

Grafton, A., *The Culture of Correction in Renaissance Europe*, London, 2011.

Grasshoff, G., 'Michael Maestlin's Mystery: Theory Building with Diagrams', *Journal for the History of Astronomy*, 43, 2012, pp. 57–73.

Guthmüller, B., 'Nota su Giovanni Antonio Rusconi illustratore delle *Trasformationi* del Dolce', in *Miscellanea di studi in onore di Vittore Branca*, III/2: *Umanesimo e Rinascimento a Firenze e Venezia*, Florence, 1983, pp. 771–9.

Henkel, M. D., 'Illustrierte Ausgaben von Ovids Metamorphosen im XV., XVI., und XVII. Jahrhundert', *Vorträge der Bibliothek Warburg*, 7, 1926–1927, pp. 58–144.

Kemp, M., 'Temples of the Body and Temples of the Cosmos: Vision and Visualization in the Vesalian and Copernican Revolutions', in B. S. Baigrie (ed.), *Picturing Knowledge: Historical and Philosophical Problems Concerning the Use of Art in Science*, Toronto and Buffalo (NY), 1996, pp. 40–85, 966–7.

Kusukawa, S., *Picturing the Book of Nature: Image, Text, and Argument in Sixteenth-Century Human Anatomy and Medical Botany*, Chicago, 2012.

Landau, D., and Parshall, P., *The Renaissance Print*, New Haven (CT) and London, 1994.

Luborsky, R. S., and Ingram, E. M., *A Guide to English Illustrated Books 1536–1603*, Tempe (AZ), 1998.

McKerrow, R. B., *An Introduction to Bibliography for Literary Students*, 2nd impression with corrections, Oxford, 1928.

McKitterick, D., *Print, Manuscript and the Search for Order, 1450–1830*, Cambridge, 2013.

Margócsy, D., Somos, M., and Joffe, S. N., *The* Fabrica *of Andreas Vesalius: A Worldwide Census, Ownership, and Annotations of the 1543 and 1555 editions*, Leiden and Boston, 2018.

Masséna, V., prince d'Essling, *Les livres illustrés vénitiens de la fin du 15ᵉ siècle et du commencement du 16ᵉ*, 3 vols, Florence and Paris, 1907–1914.

Michael, E., 'Some Sixteenth-Century Venetian Bible Woodcuts Inspired by Holbein's *Icones*', *Print Quarterly*, 7, 1990, pp. 239–47.

Mortimer, R., *French 16th Century Books*, 2 vols, Cambridge (MA), 1964.

Mortimer, R., *Italian 16th Century Books*, 2 vols, Cambridge (MA), 1974.

Pollard, A., 'The Woodcut Design for Illumination of Venetian borders (1469–1473)', in A. Pollard (ed.), *Bibliographica: Papers on Books, their History and Art*, III, London, 1897, pp. 122–8.

Sander, M., *Le livre à figures italien depuis 1467 jusqu'à 1530*, 6 vols, Milan, 1942–1943.

Simpson, P., *Proof-Reading in the Sixteenth, Seventeenth and Eighteenth Centuries*, London, 1970.

Swerdlow, N. M., 'On Establishing the Text of *De Revolutionibus*', *Journal for the History of Astronomy*, 12, 1981, pp. 35–46.

Waters, M. J., 'A Renaissance without Order: Ornament, Single-Sheet Engravings, and the Mutability of Architectural Prints', *Journal of the Society of Architectural Historians*, 71, 2012, pp. 488–523.

PART II

HUMANISM

CHAPTER 6

PRINTING AND POLITICS IN ITALIAN HUMANISM

Manuscript and Stop-Press Corrections in Poliziano's Coniurationis commentarium

MARTA CELATI

INTRODUCTION

THE decisive impact that the invention of the art of printing had on the European historical scene emerged already in the first years of its diffusion and affected both the cultural and political horizon, two dimensions that were often interconnected. These complex phenomena, relevant to various geographical areas with different specificities, characterise in particular the Italian context and its lively cultural milieu; this is reflected by the high number of print shops that set up their activities throughout the peninsula in the late fifteenth century. Besides Venice and Rome, which (for different reasons) provided exceptionally dynamic markets for printers and fostered the proliferation of printing enterprises,[1] Florence saw the extensive growth of print shops, often run by printers who were keen on experimenting with innovative publishing methods and procedures.[2] A significant case

---

[1] On the printing press in fifteenth-century Italy see, in particular, C. Dondi (ed.), *Printing R-Evolution 1450–1500: Fifty Years that Changed Europe*, Venice, 2018; L. Hellinga, *Texts in Transit: Manuscript to Proof and Print in the Fifteenth Century*, Leiden and Boston, 2014; P. Veneziani, *Tracce sul foglio: saggi di storia della tipografia*, ed. P. Piacentini, Rome, 2007; and, with a wider chronological perspective, B. Richardson, *Print Culture in Renaissance Italy: The Editor and the Vernacular Text, 1470–1600*, Cambridge, 2004. More specifically on Venice: C. Dondi and N. Harris, 'Best Selling Titles and Books of Hours in a Venetian Bookshop of the 1480s: The *Zornale* of Francesco de Madiis', *La Bibliofilia*, 115, 2013, pp. 63–82; on Rome: C. Bianca et al. (eds), *Scrittura, biblioteche e stampa a Roma nel Quattrocento. Atti del I seminario, 1–2 giugno 1979*, Vatican City, 1980; M. Miglio, P. Farenga, and A. Modigliani (eds), *Scrittura, biblioteche e stampa a Roma nel Quattrocento. Atti del II seminario, 6–8 maggio 1982*, Vatican City, 1983; M. Miglio and O. Rossini (eds), *Gutenberg e Roma: le origini della stampa nella città dei Papi (1467–1500)*, Naples, 1997.

[2] On printing in fifteenth-century Florence see R. Ridolfi, *La stampa in Firenze nel secolo XV*, Florence, 1958; D. E. Rhodes, *Gli annali tipografici fiorentini del XV secolo*, Florence, 1988; P. Trovato, 'Il libro toscano nell'età di Lorenzo. Schede e ipotesi', in *La Toscana al tempo di Lorenzo il Magnifico. Politica,*

108   PRINTING AND MISPRINTING

study of these developing practices in the first Florentine print shops is the *editio princeps* of Poliziano's *Coniurationis commentarium*, published in 1478 by Niccolò di Lorenzo della Magna, a German printer also known as Niccolò Tedesco, or by his Latin name Nicolaus Alamanus.[3] This chapter examines the four extant copies of this edition, focusing on the intricate network of mistakes, stop-press corrections, and manuscript emendations that appear in these volumes. This investigation can help us gain a clearer understanding of the editorial and printing operations performed by one of the most active printers in Florence between the late 1470s and the mid 1480s, of his role in the Medici environment, and more specifically, of the process of publication of Poliziano's work and its crucial political implications.

A WORK OF PROPAGANDA

The *Coniurationis commentarium* is the most famous literary account of the Pazzi conspiracy, the plot to assassinate the Medici brothers in the cathedral of Florence on 26 April 1478, when Giuliano de' Medici was murdered while Lorenzo managed to save himself. This work, written by one of the main scholars in the Laurentian entourage, is the first historical narrative of the events and the most pivotal and sophisticated piece of pro-Medici propaganda in the aftermath of the conspiracy.[4] The key political function that Poliziano's text was intended to play in the critical situation that followed the plot is evidenced by its

economia, cultura, arte, Pisa, 1996, II, pp. 525–63; C. Bianca, 'Le dediche a Lorenzo de' Medici nell'editoria fiorentina', in F. Bausi and V. Fera (eds), *Laurentia laurus: per Mario Martelli*, Messina, 2004, pp. 51–89; and Richardson, *Print Culture* (n. 1 above).

[3] Angelus Politianus, *Pactianae coniurationis commentariolum*, [Florence, Nicolaus Alamanus], 1478, 4° (ISTC ip00892500); Rom.; 10 unnumbered leaves; 152×102 mm.; watermark *fleur* (*Briquet* 6374: Lucca 1477). Rhodes, *Gli annali tipografici* (n. 2 above), no. 516; Ridolfi, *La stampa* (n. 2 above), p. 20; A. Lenzuni (ed.), *All'ombra del lauro. Documenti librari della cultura in età laurenziana (Firenze, Biblioteca Medicea Laurenziana, 4 maggio–30 giugno 1992)*, Milan, 1992, p. 124; Bianca, 'Le dediche' (n. 2 above), p. 61. A preliminary analysis of this edition (which has been revised and expanded in the present chapter with substantial variations and additions in light of a new examination of the extant copies and new studies) is in M. Celati, 'L'*editio princeps* fiorentina del *Coniurationis commentarium* di Angelo Poliziano e il tipografo Niccolò Tedesco: nuove acquisizioni', *Archivum Mentis*, 2, 2013, pp. 161–80. On Niccolò della Magna: Ridolfi, *La stampa* (n. 2 above), pp. 49–62; R. Ridolfi, 'Le ultime imprese tipografiche di Niccolò tedesco', *La Bibliofilia*, 67, 1965, pp. 143–51; L. Boeninger, 'Ein deutscher Frühdrucker in Florenz: Nicolaus Laurentii de Alemania', *Gutenberg Jarhbuch*, 77, 2002, pp. 94–109; and P. Scapecchi, 'Niccolò di Lorenzo', in *Dizionario biografico degli Italiani*, LXXVIII, 2013, pp. 414–15.

[4] The most recent edition of the text is Angelo Poliziano, *Coniurationis commentarium*, transl. and ed. M. Celati, Alessandria, 2015; for an analysis of the political perspective of the text see also M. Celati, *Conspiracy Literature in Early Renaissance Italy: Historiography and Princely Ideology*, Oxford, 2021, Chapter 4. The first critical edition, based on the print tradition of the text, is Angelo Poliziano, *Della congiura dei Pazzi (Coniurationis commentarium)*, ed. A. Perosa, Padova, 1958. On the historical circumstances of the conspiracy: R. Fubini, *Italia quattrocentesca: politica e diplomazia nell'età di Lorenzo de' Medici*, Milan, 1994, pp. 87–106, 253–327; L. Martines, *April Blood: Florence and the Plot Against the Medici*, Oxford and New York, 2003; T. Daniels, *La congiura dei Pazzi: i documenti del conflitto fra Lorenzo de' Medici e Sisto IV. Le bolle di scomunica, la* Florentina Synodus, *e la* Dissentio insorta *tra la Santità del Papa e i Fiorentini. Edizione critica e commento*, Florence, 2013, pp. 9–21.

immediate publication in Florence, probably between summer and autumn 1478, as we shall see. In the same months, with the collaboration of intellectuals very close to him, Niccolò della Magna published all the principal texts and documents through which Lorenzo de' Medici's cultural policies were articulated (different works that were aimed at displaying and, at the same time, supporting the Medici regime): in particular, the *Florentina synodus*, a juridical-religious text composed by Gentile Becchi, the archbishop of Arezzo, who had been Lorenzo's personal tutor;[5] and Bartolomeo Scala's *Excusatio Florentinorum*, a document containing the official reconstruction of the events, written by the chancellor of Florence and published after 11 August 1478.[6] Both these works were intended to defend the Medici leader against the allegations made by Pope Sixtus IV, one of the main instigators of the attack, together with the king of Naples, Ferdinand I of Aragon. Indeed, in June the Pope had issued three bulls promulgating the excommunication of Lorenzo and an interdict against Florence, in response to the harsh reprisal that was carried out against the members of the church who had taken part in the plot. These bulls too were immediately published in Rome.[7] Thus the production and quick publication of this wide-ranging corpus of texts reveals the fundamental role played by the printing press in this delicate political scenario, since the main documents and works concerning the Pazzi conspiracy enjoyed a wide circulation through this new and powerful means of communication. The second version of Poliziano's *Commentarium* was also published in Rome by Johannes Bulle in two distinct but virtually identical editions in 1480.[8] Especially in the delicate context that followed the violent attack against the Medici, both parties immediately understood the extraordinary potential that the introduction of the art of printing in their territories offered, and tried to employ it with the aim of spreading their versions of the events and defending their positions.

In particular, the channels of Florentine propaganda made extensive use of print shops to disseminate various kinds of writings, with the goal of reaching an audience as diversified as possible. On the one hand, the official texts were published by Niccolò della Magna, who, as we shall see, was often committed to print works by humanists of the Medici entourage; on the other hand, the anonymous *Lamento in morte di Giuliano*, a vernacular text intended for a less educated readership, was published in October 1478 by the print shop of San Jacopo di Ripoli, which was getting increasingly involved in the publication of popular works.[9] Significantly, the editor of this edition of the *Lamento* has been identified

---

[5] *Florentina Synodus ad veritatis testimonium et Sixtianae caliginis dissipationem*, [Florence, Nicolaus Alamanus, after 20 July 1478], f° (ISTC if00207300). A modern edition is in Daniels, *La congiura dei Pazzi* (n. 4 above), where the publication of the text is dated after the end of August 1478. See also Fubini, *Italia quattrocentesca* (n. 4 above), pp. 264–8.

[6] Scala Bartholomaeus, *Excusatio florentinorum ob poenas de sociis Pactianae in Medices coniurationis*, [Florence, Nicolaus Alamanus, after 10 August 1478], 8° (ISTC is00300700). The text is now published in Bartolomeo Scala, *Humanistic and Political Writings*, ed. A. Brown, Tempe (AZ), 1997, pp. 199–202.

[7] ISTC is00545000 and is00545550. A modern edition is now in Daniels, *La congiura dei Pazzi* (n. 4 above).

[8] Angelus Politianus, *Coniurationis commentarium*, [Rome, Johannes Bulle, 1480], 4° (edn 1: ISTC ip00892600; edn 2: ISTC ip00892000). See M. Celati, 'La seconda redazione del *Coniurationis commentarium* di Angelo Poliziano e l'edizione romana di Johannes Bulle', *Humanistica*, 11/1–2, 2016, pp. 283–92.

[9] *Tradimento per la morte di Giuliano de' Medici*, [Florence, S. Jacobum de Ripoli, 1478], 4° (ISTC it00421600); Rhodes, *Gli annali tipografici* (n. 2 above), no. 390. The text is now published in F. Flamini,

as Bartolomeo Fonzio, another distinguished intellectual in Lorenzo's circle.[10] Fonzio also cooperated with Niccolò della Magna on some occasions and was one of the main links between this print shop and the Ripoli press. The two printing houses collaborated between 1480 and 1483, as is testified by a contract signed by Fonzio himself on behalf of Niccolò della Magna on 11 November 1480.[11] But in 1478 both shops were already involved in projects that shared similar purposes. In particular, all the editions related to the Pazzi plot show that the printing activity in support of Florence and the Medici was a well-coordinated major feature of the period, aimed at reaching different targets through various kinds of texts: historical, popular, doctrinal, and juridical. Among these publications, the *editio princeps* of Poliziano's *Commentarium* offers a perfect opportunity to study some publishing practices adopted by one of Florence's main proto-typographers and involving particular procedures of correction.

Mistakes and In-House Corrections

The edition consists in a small quarto volume of ten leaves, in Roman type (the type always used by Niccolò della Magna),[12] and the title of the text in this first version is *Pactianae coniurationis commentariolum*.[13] All four extant copies have been examined thoroughly and are referred to here in abbreviated form: two of these are now in Rome, R_1 in the Biblioteca Corsiniana (52.E.62), and R_2 in the Biblioteca Casanatense (Inc. 1432); the other two copies are both in Florence, in the Biblioteca Nazionale Centrale, F_1 = E.6.3.26; F_2 = M.6.21. All copies display a layered series of typos, stop-press corrections, manuscript emendations, and in at least two cases, a change in the date of publication.[14]

The misprints that have been corrected in the text are all minor spelling mistakes and not significant errors. This strongly suggests that Poliziano was not involved in the proofreading

---

'Versi in morte di Giuliano de' Medici', *Il Propugnatore*, 2, 1889, pp. 318–30. After the plot, other editions of this poem were printed by the print shop of San Iacopo di Ripoli: in one of these incunables the text is published with the title *Tradimento per la morte di Giuliano* (ISTC it00421600). For other editions that are now lost: Rhodes, *Gli annali tipografici* (n. 2 above), 'Appendice I', p. 125. On this print shop: E. Nesi, *Il Diario della Stamperia di Ripoli*, Florence, 1903; M. Conway, *The Diario of the Printing Press of San Jacopo di Ripoli, 1476-1484: Commentary and Transcription*, Florence, 1999.

[10] On this edition: Nesi, *Il Diario* (n. 9 above), p. 17; S. Caroti and S. Zamponi, *Lo scrittoio di Bartolomeo Fonzio umanista fiorentino. Documenti sulle arti del libro*, Milan, 1974, pp. 13, 179; B. Maracchi Biagiarelli, 'Editori di incunaboli fiorentini', in *Contributi alla storia del libro italiano, miscellanea in onore di Lamberto Donati*, Florence, 1969, pp. 211–20 (214–17) .

[11] The contractors were Fonzio, Niccolò della Magna, Domenico da Pistoia, and Bartolo di Domenico di Guido: the document is published in D. Marzi, *I tipografi tedeschi in Italia durante il sec. XV*, in O. Hartwing (ed.), *Festschrift zum fünfhundertjährigen Geburtstage von Johann Gutenberg*, Leipzig, 1900, pp. 568–9; see also Maracchi Biagiarelli, 'Editori' (n. 10 above), pp. 212–17.

[12] On Niccolò della Magna's predilection for Roman type: Ridolfi, 'Le ultime imprese' (n. 3 above), p. 144.

[13] On this title and its change in the final version of the text see M. Celati, 'Introduzione', in Poliziano, *Coniurationis commentarium* (n. 4 above), pp. 24–6.

[14] It is worth mentioning that sigs [a3]*r–v* and 8*r–v* in R_1 are not the original printed leaves but the text has been copied by an unknown hand, which imitated rather faithfully the Roman types of the edition. Probably this operation was carried out due to the loss of the original printed leaves that might have been caused by the re-binding of this copy (indeed the binding is modern and not the original).

6: PRINTING AND POLITICS IN ITALIAN HUMANISM   111

process, or other additional and more significant mistakes (harder to detect for anyone other than the author) would presumably have been spotted and amended. These more substantial errors were probably already present in the manuscript that arrived in the print shop (and perhaps also in the copy that could have been prepared as the printer's copy) and was transcribed from an archetype, or more generally from a copy coming from the author (the existence of an archetype is proved by some mistakes attested by the whole manuscript and print tradition of the text).[15] As for pre-publishing practices, it is worth mentioning that a printer's copy used by Niccolò della Magna has been identified for the *editio princeps* of Leon Battista Alberti's *De re aedificatoria* published posthumously in 1485 and edited by Poliziano himself.[16] In a case similar to that of the *Commentarium*, Poliziano (this time as the editor) did not prepare or work on the printer's copy of Alberti's treatise (none of the casting off signs and corrections on this manuscript can be ascribed to his hand), and it has been proved that he did not do any proofreading at any printing stage (although someone else did, as some errors in the manuscript version are corrected in the printed volumes).[17] As for the *Commentarium*, the copy that contains stop-press corrections is R_1; but, significantly, the other copies of the edition all display manuscript emendations that correct the same mistakes. This twofold correcting process occurred in four instances, always in specific kinds of typos where a word is misspelled by skipping a letter. In R_1 these letters are introduced by stop-press corrections, while in all other copies they are added in the line space by handwritten emendations; the only exception is the last misprint in the list below, which is eliminated only in R_1 with a stop-press correction and in F_2 by hand, while the other two copies retain the mistake:[18]

1) sig. [a2]*v, refrebat / referebat*
2) sig. [a2]*v, uerint / fuerint*
3) sig. [a9]*r, suis / suris*
4) sig. [a9]*r, artculis / articulis*

Presumably these typos were detected through an operation of proofreading carried out during the printing process and were then amended in some sheets by stop-press corrections, altering the form and introducing the missing types,[19] while on the sheets already printed the mistakes were corrected by hand (and in the case of F_2 the corrections were executed more accurately than in the others exemplars, since one of these errors is still present

---

[15] See Poliziano, *Della congiura* (n. 4 above), pp. XIII–XX; the new philological analysis of the whole tradition of the text (of both manuscripts and printed editions) has attested the existence of an archetype: on this tradition see Celati, 'Introduzione' (n. 13), pp. 27–33; and M. Celati, *Angelo Poliziano, 'Coniurationis commentarium'. Edizione critica, introduzione e commento.* PhD dissertation, Pisa, University of Pisa, 2013.

[16] Leo Baptista Alberti, *De re aedificatoria*, Florence, Nicolaus Alamanus, 29 Dec. 1485, f° (ISTC ia00215000). See S. Fiaschi, 'Una copia di tipografia finora sconosciuta: Il Laurenziano Plut. 89 sup. 113 e l'*Editio princeps* del *De re aedificatoria*', *Rinascimento*, 41, 2001, pp. 267–84; Hellinga, *Texts in Transit* (n. 1 above), pp. 83–4. On this edition see also: Bianca, 'Le dediche' (n. 2 above), pp. 51–89; Lenzuni (ed.), *All'ombra del lauro* (n. 3 above), pp. 125–6.

[17] See Fiaschi, 'Una copia di tipografia' (n. 16 above), pp. 278–80.

[18] In all lists of misprints and corrections in this chapter, the amended version always follows the mistake.

[19] On stop-press corrections see, in particular, C. Fahy, *Saggi di bibliografia testuale*, Padua, 1988, pp. 82–8, and A. Grafton, *The Culture of Correction in Renaissance Europe*, London, 2011, pp. 108, 206.

in F_1 and R_2).[20] It is clear that all of these corrections can be considered as part of the same procedure of emendation performed in the print shop and were aimed at cancelling even very small mistakes in the edition. This suggests that Poliziano's *Commentarium* was published very quickly, in order to disseminate the Florentine 'official' version of the events as soon as possible: some of the mistakes present in the edition were probably caused by this need for a speedy publication and, for this very same reason, the pages with the typos could not be reprinted (even though this is just a pamphlet of ten leaves) but were amended by handwritten emendations. Although this turns out to be a hasty publication, at the same time this edition needed to be as correct as possible, if even minor typos were eliminated with either stop-press corrections, for the leaves that had still to be printed,[21] or manuscript changes.[22] Significantly, the practice of introducing stop-press corrections was also adopted by the same printer in the aforementioned edition of Alberti's *De re aedeficatoria*, since some copies of the work display a few variants in one of the pages of both the first and last gathering, which were reset during printing.[23] Moreover, in this incunable, the multi-stage operations of preparation of the printer's copy, proofreading, and correction in print were probably carried out by more than one person: a shared procedure that may also have been followed for the *Commentarium*. In this case the manuscript emendations could have been inserted on the sheets by the printer himself, and/or by one of his assistants, possibly a professional corrector (although there is no information on the identity of Niccolò della Magna's assistants). These professional figures, the correctors, were already often employed in fifteenth-century print shops (especially as collaborators of foreign proto-typographers for the publication of both humanist and vernacular works) and were also frequently in charge of preparing the printer's copy and executing corrections during (and after) printing,[24] a twofold role that a corrector may have also played in the edition of Poliziano's *Commentarium*.

This procedure of handwritten emendations is substantiated by another group of manuscript signs that appear in all four copies of Poliziano's work. In four instances, the typos have been eliminated through the same handwritten amendments that, significantly, were executed in the exact same way in all exemplars (and they do not consist in the simple addition of a missing letter, as for the misprints described above, but in different kinds of changes):

---

[20] On the practice of manuscript correction of all (or several) copies of a printed edition, which is more frequent in the age of incunables, see the glossary appended to this Companion.

[21] A famous similar case is the edition of Ariosto's *Orlando Furioso* published in 1553, where minor spelling mistakes were emended by stop-press corrections (for example, the change of *soave* in *suave*): Fahy, *Saggi* (n. 19 above), p. 109; see also C. Fahy, *L'Orlando furioso del 1532: profilo di una edizione*, Milan, 1989.

[22] For this procedure: C. F. Bühler, 'Stop-press and Manuscript Corrections in the Aldine Edition of Benedetti's *Diaria de Bello Carolino*', *The Papers of the Bibliographical Society of America*, 43, 1949, pp. 365–73; his, 'Manuscript Corrections in the Aldine Edition of Bembo's *De Aetna*', *The Papers of the Bibliographical Society of America*, 45, 1951, pp. 136–42; and his, 'Pen corrections in the first edition of Paolo Manuzio's *Antiquitatum Romanorum liber de legibus*', *Italia medioevale e umanistica*, 5, 1962, pp. 165–70.

[23] On these variants see Fiaschi, 'Una copia di tipografia' (n. 19 above), pp. 278–9; Hellinga, *Texts in Transit* (n. 1 above), pp. 83–4.

[24] On correctors and the context in which they worked see B. Richardson, *Printing, Writers and Readers in Renaissance Italy*, Cambridge, 1999; Grafton, *The Culture* (n. 19 above); and his *Humanists with Inky Fingers: The Culture of Correction in Renaissance Europe*, Florence, 2011, pp. 27–49.

1) sig. [a4]*v, pue / puero* ('ro' add. *post* 'e')
2) sig. [a5]*r, ne Iuliani / ne in Iuliani* ('in' add. in line space)
3) sig. [a5]*r, arcipret / incideret* ('arcipret' del. by erasure, 'incideret' add. *supra*)
4) sig. [a5]*r, vexillifeum / vexilliferum* ('r' add. in line space)

In particular, corrections nos 2–3 appear in the same line on sig. [a5]*r* and are introduced in the very same manner in all copies (Figs 6.1–6.2): in the first case, the preposition 'in' is added in the line space with an identical abbreviation (an 'i' with a *titulus* for the 'n'); in the second case, the wrong form 'arcipret' is eliminated by erasure and then the right verb 'incideret' replaces it in all copies with the same abbreviation for the syllable 'de', which is obtained from the 'p' type of the original erroneous word (however, the result of this handwritten emendation is not equally good in all copies, especially in R$_1$, where the original incorrect letters are still quite noticeable). Thus, this further group of homogeneous variants can be traced back to the same planned and systematic operation carried out after printing, revealing a specific practice of correction adopted in this print shop. All these amendments were executed in series and aimed at perfecting the edition of a text that had to be distributed rapidly but in an adequate form, suitable for a text that had to be read as the first and most authoritative account of the Pazzi plot. Thus these emendations can be regarded as an integral part of the volumes published, which would have been 'imperfect' without them.[25]

A confirmation of the publishing approach adopted by this proto-typographer (as far as the correcting and editing practice is concerned) can be provided by the agreement signed in 1483 by Niccolò della Magna himself and Antonio di Luca di Berto, the *speziale* who funded the edition of the *volgarizzamento* of Pope Gregory I's *Moralia, sive Expositio in Job* (which was not completed until 15 June 1486).[26] This document demonstrates the attention paid to misprints and the thorough correcting procedures that were required from the printer, who, according to this contract, had to amend even small mistakes in this incunable:

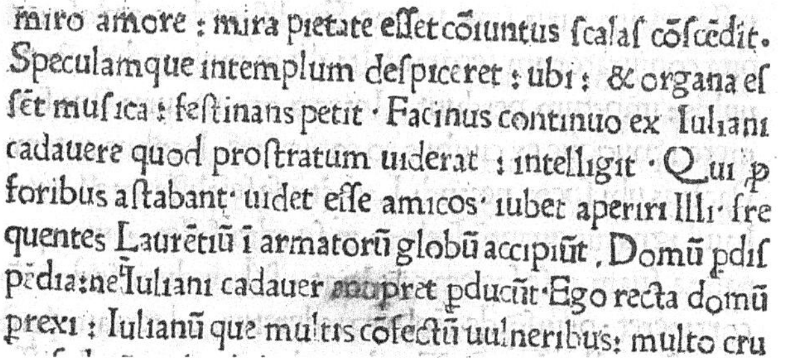

FIG. **6.1.** Angelus Politianus, *Pactianae coniurationis commentariolum*, [Florence, Nicolaus Alamanus], 1478, 4° (ISTC ipo0892500). Exemplar R$_1$: Rome, Biblioteca dell'Accademia Nazionale dei Lincei e Corsiniana, 52.E.62, sig. [a5]*r* (detail).

---

[25] For an analogous case: Bühler, 'Pen corrections' (n. 22 above), pp. 169–70.
[26] ISTC ig00435000.

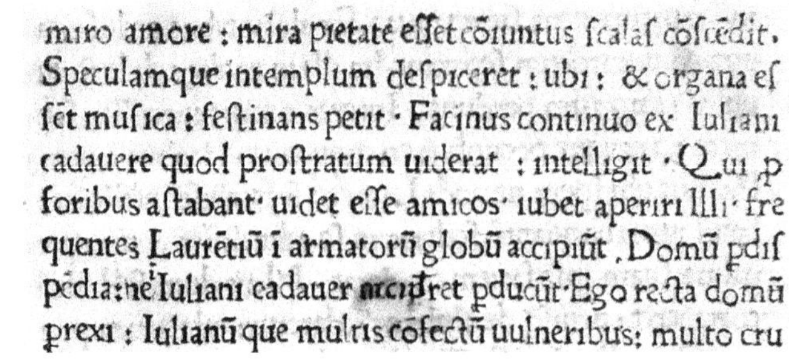

114 PRINTING AND MISPRINTING

miro amore : mira pietate eſſet cōiuntus ſcalaſ cōſuedit.
Speculamque intemplum deſpiceret : ubi : & organa eſ
ſet muſica : feſtinans petit · Facinus continuo ex Iuliani
cadauere quod proſtratum uiderat : intelligit · Qui p
foribus aſtabant· uidet eſſe amicos· iubet aperiri Illi· fre
quentes Laurētiū i armatorū globū accipiūt . Domū pdiſ
pedia:neĪuliani cadauer acriſret pducūt·Ego recta domū
prexi : Iulianūque multis cōfectū uulneribus: multo cru

FIG. 6.2. Angelus Politianus, *Pactianae coniurationis commentariolum*, 1478. Exemplar F₁: Florence, Biblioteca Nazionale Centrale, E.6.3.26, sig. [a5]r (detail).

decto Nicholò debba fare e curare con ogni diligentia che tali libri venghino netti e di buona lettera e corretti d'ogni e qualunche cosa a somma perfezione; e in caso avessino alcuno man-camento fatto per lui o suoi gharzoni, che tale mancamento decto Nicholò l'abbia a sodisfare di suo proprio.[27]

However, the copies of the *editio princeps* of Poliziano's work also display other manuscript corrections that are harder to classify since they are not present in all extant copies. In this case, only the emendations that have been added in three copies and that were executed in the same manner can be almost certainly traced back to the correction carried out in the print shop: a proofreading that probably was not performed carefully enough on all the sheets in the four copies. Conversely, a few handwritten changes that appear only on two copies (or in some cases even on a single one) and are characterised by a different execution were more probably added independently by owners of the single books.[28]

EMENDING THE DATE OF PUBLICATION?

In this complex stratification of corrections, a further change figures in the date of pub-lication. The edition has no colophon, and the only information provided is the year of publication, 1478, at the end of the text, on sig. [a9]v. However, as already mentioned, it is possible to place the date of publication in a narrower time frame, between the end of summer and autumn 1478, when the other main pro-Medici works on the conspiracy were also published. If we consider both historical and textual elements, the *terminus post quem*

---

[27] '[…] the aforementioned Niccolò must take every care and diligence that these books turn out clean, typographically pleasant, and correct in every detail, to the highest standard of perfection; in the case of any deficiency due either to him or his assistants, he must set it right at his own expense.' The contract is published in Ridolfi, 'Le ultime imprese' (n. 3 above), pp. 146–8.

[28] The following handwritten variants are displayed in three copies (R₁, R₂, and F₂): *lature/ latuere* (sig. [a7]v); *virgiliae / vigiliae* (sig. [a9]v); *succurre / succurrere* (sig. [a9]v). On the different level of precision in the correction of printed copies see Bühler, 'Pen Corrections' (n. 22 above), p. 169.

for the composition of the *Commentarium* has been identified as 23 May 1478, since in the first version of the text Poliziano mentions the *provvisione* that was issued by the Florentine government against the Pazzi on that day.[29] As for the *terminus ante quem*, it is likely that Poliziano finished writing his work before the first days of August,[30] since, due to the plague, he left Florence on 12 August and temporarily relocated to Pistoia,[31] followed in autumn by travels between Fiesole, Careggi, and Cafaggiolo. As Poliziano lived in a condition of uncertainty (also due to the critical political situation) and was unsure as to when he could go back to Florence, he probably completed his work on such a burning issue and gave it to the printer before leaving for Pistoia. However, if we examine the edition, a change appears in the date of publication ('1478') on two out of the four extant copies, R_1 and F_1: here the indication of the year of publication appears to have been tampered with, using pen and ink (and causing a great deal of confusion), to read '1479', possibly to 'refresh' the copy or, alternatively, to remove a typographical error that read 'M. CCCC. LXXVIIII.', and therefore change the date to 'M. CCCC. LXXVIII.', as it should have been and in fact as it reads in the other two copies (Figs 6.3–6.4). So it is possible to formulate two hypotheses to explain this alteration, though neither of the two provides a completely satisfactory answer.[32] This change could be the result of a somewhat clumsy correction of a typographical mistake (a hypothesis that seems the most likely), or it could be an attempt to 'refresh' the date with the intent of disseminating some copies in 1479, in order to put onto the market some seemingly 'fresh' books. In this latter case, however, some problems must have occurred with the indication of the date '1479', perhaps because of the use of the calendar *ab Incarnatione Domini*, according to which the new year in Florence started on 25 March; consequently the date '1479' would be apt only for the copies sold after 25 March and this might have caused the change of '1479' into '1478'.[33]

Apart from conjectural elements and in light of both the historical considerations mentioned above and this alteration of the date in the edition, it is likely that the publication was quite close to the end of 1478, probably in the autumn or at the end of the summer (as for most of the other texts on the plot). Moreover, what seems certain is that the printer and his collaborators put considerable effort into publishing this edition, especially into correcting it, and they answered to the needs of the Florentine government, which had to react quickly

---

[29] See Poliziano, *Coniurationis commentarium* (n. 4 above), p. 87; and Celati, *Conspiracy Literature* (n. 4 above), pp. 184–5. On the document (Florence, Archivio di Stato, *Provvisioni, Registri*, vol. 169, fols 24r–26v), see Poliziano, *Della congiura* (n. 4 above), p. 61; and Martines, *April Blood* (n. 4 above), pp. 137–41.

[30] See Poliziano, *Della congiura* (n. 4 above), pp. VI–VIII.

[31] For this date: A. Chiappelli, 'Sopra due avvenimenti notevoli nella vita pistoiese dell'anno 1478', *Bullettino Storico Pistoiese*, 31, 1929, pp. 94–111 (94).

[32] Thanks to the examination of all copies carried out through more sophisticated techniques of analysis, it has been possible to reconsider this complex case and previous conjectures — see Celati, *Conspiracy Literature* (n. 4 above), p. 160 — and make two hypotheses. I would like to thank Geri Della Rocca de Candal, Anthony Grafton, and Paolo Sachet for their advice and help in the examination of this issue.

[33] Mistakes in the date of publication due to the use of different calendars were frequent, especially in the age of incunables: see Marzi, 'I tipografi' (n. 11 above), pp. 508–9; more generally, the practice of storing some copies of an edition bearing a different date, so as to sell them the following year, was often the cause of inconsistencies in the indication of the publishing date, though this practice became common among printers mainly from the sixteenth century: see, e.g., Fahy, *Studi* (n. 19 above), pp. 169–211.

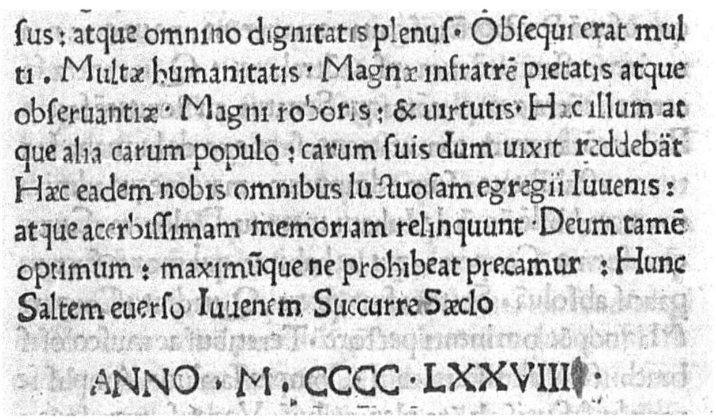

> fus : atque omnino dignitatis plenuſ· Obſequi erat mul
> ti . Multæ humanitatis · Magnæ infratrē pietatis atque
> obſeruantiæ· Magni roboris ; & uirtutis· Hæc illum at
> que alia carum populo ; carum ſuis dum uixit reddebāt
> Hæc eadem nobis omnibus lu ꞁtuoſam egregii Iuuenis :
> atque acerbiſſimam memoriam relinquunt ·Deum tamē
> optimum ; maximūque ne prohibeat precamur ; Hunc
> Saltem euerſo Iuuenem Succurre Sæclo
>
> ANNO · M . CCCC · LXXVIII ·

FIG. 6.3. Angelus Politianus, *Pactianae coniurationis commentariolum*, 1478. Exemplar R_1: Rome, Biblioteca dell'Accademia Nazionale dei Lincei e Corsiniana, 52.E.62, sig. [a9]*v*.

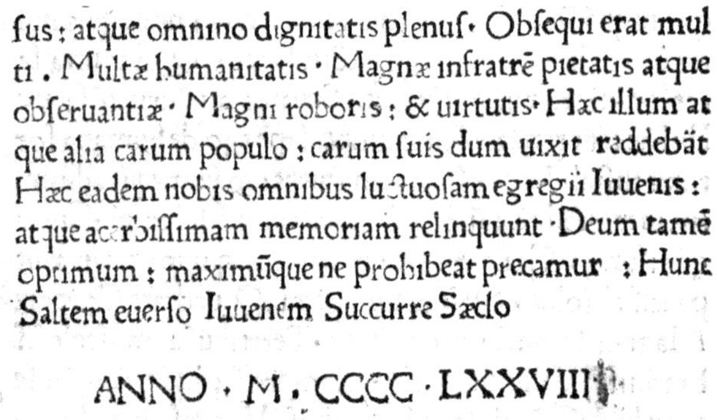

> fus : atque omnino dignitatis plenuſ· Obſequi erat mul
> ti . Multæ humanitatis · Magnæ infratrē pietatis atque
> obſeruantiæ· Magni roboris ; & uirtutis· Hæc illum at
> que alia carum populo ; carum ſuis dum uixit reddebāt
> Hæc eadem nobis omnibus lu ꞁtuoſam egregii Iuuenis :
> atque acerbiſſimam memoriam relinquunt ·Deum tamē
> optimum ; maximūque ne prohibeat precamur ; Hunc
> Saltem euerſo Iuuenem Succurre Sæclo
>
> ANNO · M . CCCC · LXXVIII ·

FIG. 6.4. Angelus Politianus, *Pactianae coniurationis commentariolum*, 1478. Exemplar F_1: Florence, Biblioteca Nazionale Centrale, E.6.3.26, sig. [a9]*v*.

and effectively to the escalation of the diplomatic conflict, when, after June, the papal bulls against Lorenzo and Florence were disseminated by print. This would prove Niccolò della Magna's involvement in a delicate publishing operation. More generally, his participation in ambitious publishing initiatives (in some cases surrounded by crucial ideological overtones) is confirmed by other editions of his and by the trajectory of his typographical activity in Florence. It is not known exactly when he arrived in Italy from Germany, but in 1471 he probably worked as a scribe in Lendinara (close to Rovigo), before moving to Mantua and then to Florence. Here della Magna became one of the most distinguished printers and, between 1474 and 1486, published around forty-seven known editions, mainly of humanistic texts, some of them renowned for their illustrations.[34] Indeed, he was involved in some of the most groundbreaking publishing projects in Florence: the most emblematic examples are the edition of the *Geographia* by Francesco Berlinghieri in 1482[35] and the very famous

[34] On the overall output of this printer see bibliography at n. 3 above.

[35] ISTC ib00342000; Ridolfi, *La stampa* (n. 2 above), pp. 49–62; P. Veneziani, 'Vicende tipografiche della *Geografia* di Francesco Berlinghieri', *La Bibliofilia*, 84, 1982, pp. 195–208.

edition of Landino's *Commentary* on Dante's *Commedia*, published on 30 August 1481, with engravings by Baccio Baldini, on the basis of drawings by Sandro Botticelli (a presentation copy of which, printed on parchment, was offered to Lorenzo).[36] More generally, Niccolò della Magna's work reveals a pioneering attitude and his intention to explore the full potential of the new printing medium. Thus, it seems no accident that he printed all the core political texts concerning the Pazzi conspiracy (although there is no evidence of a formal commission of these works by the Florentine government), a choice that can be also traced back to his closeness to Lorenzo's cultural entourage, since, during his activity, Niccolò published a large number of works by humanists in the Medici circle. Moreover, he was the only printer who was commissioned to publish chancery documents and official texts from the *Signoria*. In particular, between 1480 and 1486 he printed the *Uffici della Città*, the *Stratto dei Gabellieri*, and some official orations: texts that had a key bearing on civic life in Florence.[37]

Conclusions

This brief overview of Niccolò della Magna's work helps us contextualise his involvement in important projects that also were relevant from a political perspective: a commitment that is openly attested by the production of the *editio princeps* of the *Commentarium*. As we have seen, the stop-press corrections and manuscript emendations executed in series in this edition are probably the result of the need to emend misprints caused by a rapid publication. The urgent political need for a prompt diffusion of the first account of the Pazzi plot, along with the high cost of paper, meant that it was not possible to reprint the sheets containing mistakes and thus several ink corrections were added systematically, so as to reduce the imperfections in the text. Thus the *Commentarium* proves to have been conceived, composed, and published as an authoritative and influential work that, also in light of its printing history, can be considered a piece of 'official historiography' which was composed by one of the most distinguished Florentine humanists.[38] More generally, the analysis of this edition illuminates the crucial role of the new art of printing in the precarious historical unfolding of the Pazzi conspiracy in Florence. Here the political conflict was fought not only with actual weapons but also with sophisticated cultural, literary, and this time also publishing means, a practice that, from that period onwards, would often be exploited in the following centuries.

---

[36] Dante Alighieri, *La Commedia (comm. Christophorus Landinus)*, Florence, Nicolaus Alamanus, 30 August 1481, f° (ISTC id00029000). See Maracchi Biagiarelli, 'Editori' (n. 10 above), pp. 214–17; R. Cardini, 'Landino e Dante', *Rinascimento*, 30, 1990, pp. 175–90; G. Tanturli, 'La Firenze laurenziana davanti alla propria storia letteraria', in G. C. Garfagnini (ed.), *Lorenzo Magnifico e il suo tempo*, Florence, 1992, pp. 1–38; P. Scapecchi, 'Cristoforo Landino, Niccolò di Lorenzo e la *Commedia*', in S. Gentile (ed.), *Sandro Botticelli: pittore della Divina Commedia*, Milan, 2000, I, pp. 44–7.

[37] On the edition of these official documents: Bianca, 'Le dediche' (n. 2 above), p. 70; Ridolfi, *La stampa* (n. 2 above), p. 20.

[38] On the political outlook of the text: Celati, 'Introduzione' (n. 13 above), pp. 12–26.

BIBLIOGRAPHY

·····································

PRIMARY SOURCES

Alberti, Leo Baptista, *De re aedificatoria*, Florence, Nicolaus Alamanus, 29 Dec. 1485, f° (ISTC ia00215000).

Alighieri, Dante, *La Commedia (comm. Christophorus Landinus)*, Florence, Nicolaus Alamanus, 30 August 1481, f° (ISTC id00029000).

Daniels, T., *La congiura dei Pazzi: i documenti del conflitto fra Lorenzo de' Medici e Sisto IV. Le bolle di scomunica, la* Florentina Synodus, *e la* Dissentio insorta *tra la Santità del Papa e i Fiorentini. Edizione critica e commento*, Florence, 2013.

Flamini, F., 'Versi in morte di Giuliano de' Medici', *Il Propugnatore*, 2, 1889, pp. 318–30.

Florentina Synodus ad veritatis testimonium et Sixtianae caliginis dissipationem, [Florence, Nicolaus Alamanus, after 20 July 1478], f° (ISTC if00207300).

Tradimento per la morte di Giuliano de' Medici, [Florence, S. Jacobum de Ripoli, 1478], 4° (ISTC it00421600).

Politianus, Angelus, *Pactianae coniurationis commentariolum* [Florence, Nicolaus Alamanus], 1478, 4° (ISTC ip00892500).

Politianus, Angelus, *Coniurationis commentarium* [Rome, Johannes Bulle, 1480], 4° (edn 1: ISTC ip00892600; edn 2: ISTC ip00892000).

Poliziano, Angelo, *Coniurationis commentarium*, transl. and ed. M. Celati, Alessandria, 2015.

Poliziano, Angelo, *Della congiura dei Pazzi (Coniurationis commentarium)*, ed. A. Perosa, Padua, 1958.

Scala, Bartholomaeus, *Excusatio florentinorum ob poenas de sociis Pactianae in Medices coniurationis*, [Florence, Nicolaus Alamanus, after 10 August 1478], 8° (ISTC is00300700).

Scala, Bartolomeo, *Humanistic and Political Writings*, ed. A. Brown, Tempe (AZ), 1997.

SECONDARY LITERATURE

·····································

Bianca, C., 'Le dediche a Lorenzo de' Medici nell'editoria fiorentina', in F. Bausi and V. Fera (eds), *Laurentia laurus: per Mario Martelli*, Messina, 2004, pp. 51–89.

Bianca, C., et al. (eds), *Scrittura, biblioteche e stampa a Roma nel Quattrocento. Atti del I seminario, 1–2 giugno 1979*, Vatican City, 1980.

Boeninger, L., 'Ein deutscher Frühdrucker in Florenz: Nicolaus Laurentii de Alemania', *Gutenberg Jarhbuch*, 77, 2002, pp. 94–109.

Bühler, C. F., 'Stop-press and Manuscript Corrections in the Aldine Edition of Benedetti's *Diaria de Bello Carolino*', *The Papers of the Bibliographical Society of America*, 43, 1949, pp. 365–73.

Bühler, C. F., 'Manuscript Corrections in the Aldine Edition of Bembo's *De Aetna*', *The Papers of the Bibliographical Society of America*, 45, 1951, pp. 136–42.

Bühler, C. F., 'Pen corrections in the first edition of Paolo Manuzio's *Antiquitatum Romanorum liber de legibus*', *Italia medioevale e umanistica*, 5, 1962, pp. 165–70.

Cardini, R., 'Landino e Dante', *Rinascimento*, 30, 1990, pp. 175–90.

Caroti, S., and Zamponi, S., *Lo scrittoio di Bartolomeo Fonzio umanista fiorentino. Documenti sulle arti del libro*, Milan, 1974.

Celati, M., *Angelo Poliziano, 'Coniurationis commentarium'. Edizione critica, introduzione e commento*, PhD dissertation, Pisa, University of Pisa, 2013.

Celati, M., *Conspiracy Literature in Early Renaissance Italy: Historiography and Princely Ideology*, Oxford, 2021.

Celati, M., 'L'*editio princeps* fiorentina del *Coniurationis commentarium* di Angelo Poliziano e il tipografo Niccolò Tedesco: nuove acquisizioni', *Archivum Mentis*, 2, 2013, pp. 161–80.

Celati, M., 'Introduzione', in Angelo Poliziano, *Coniurationis commentarium*, transl. and ed. M. Celati, Alessandria, 2015, pp. 1–43.

Celati, M., 'La seconda redazione del *Coniurationis commentarium* di Angelo Poliziano e l'edizione romana di Johannes Bulle', *Humanistica*, 11/1–2, 2016, pp. 283–92.

Chiappelli, A., 'Sopra due avvenimenti notevoli nella vita pistoiese dell'anno 1478', *Bullettino Storico Pistoiese*, 31, 1929, pp. 94–111.

Conway, M., *The Diario of the Printing Press of San Jacopo di Ripoli, 1476–1484: Commentary and Transcription*, Florence, 1999.

Dondi, C. (ed.), *Printing R-Evolution 1450–1500: Fifty Years that Changed Europe*, Venice, 2018.

Dondi, C., and Harris, N., 'Best Selling Titles and Books of Hours in a Venetian Bookshop of the 1480s: The *Zornale* of Francesco de Madiis', *La Bibliofilia*, 115, 2013, pp. 63–82.

Fahy, C., *Saggi di bibliografia testuale*, Padua, 1988.

Fahy, C., *L'Orlando furioso del 1532: profilo di una edizione*, Milan, 1989.

Fiaschi, S., 'Una copia di tipografia finora sconosciuta: Il Laurenziano Plut. 89 sup. 113 e l'*Editio princeps* del *De re aedificatoria*', *Rinascimento*, 41, 2001, pp. 267–84.

Fubini, R., *Italia quattrocentesca: politica e diplomazia nell'età di Lorenzo de' Medici*, Milan, 1994.

Grafton, A., *The Culture of Correction in Renaissance Europe*, London, 2011.

Grafton, A., *Humanists with Inky Fingers: The Culture of Correction in Renaissance Europe*, Florence, 2011.

Hellinga, L., *Texts in Transit: Manuscript to Proof and Print in the Fifteenth Century*, Leiden and Boston, 2014.

Lenzuni, A., (ed.), *All'ombra del lauro. Documenti librari della cultura in età laurenziana (Firenze, Biblioteca Medicea Laurenziana, 4 maggio–30 giugno 1992)*, Milan, 1992.

Maracchi Biagiarelli, B., 'Editori di incunaboli fiorentini', in *Contributi alla storia del libro italiano, miscellanea in onore di Lamberto Donati*, Florence, 1969, pp. 211–20.

Martines, L., *April Blood: Florence and the Plot against the Medici*, Oxford and New York, 2003.

Marzi, D., *I tipografi tedeschi in Italia durante il sec. XV*, in O. Hartwing (ed.), *Festschrift zum fünfhundertjährigen Geburtstage von Johann Gutenberg*, Leipzig, 1900, pp. 568–9.

Miglio, M., and Rossini, O. (eds), *Gutenberg e Roma: le origini della stampa nella città dei Papi (1467–1500)*, Naples, 1997.

Miglio, M., Farenga P., and Modigliani A. (eds), *Scrittura, biblioteche e stampa a Roma nel Quattrocento. Atti del II seminario, 6–8 maggio 1982*, Vatican City, 1983.

Nesi, E., *Il Diario della Stamperia di Ripoli*, Florence, 1903.

Richardson, B., *Print Culture in Renaissance Italy: The Editor and the Vernacular Text, 1470–1600*, Cambridge, 2004.

Richardson, B., *Printing, Writers and Readers in Renaissance Italy*, Cambridge, 1999.

Ridolfi, R., *La stampa in Firenze nel secolo XV*, Florence, 1958.

Ridolfi, R., 'Le ultime imprese tipografiche di Niccolò tedesco', *La Bibliofilia*, 67, 1965, pp. 143–51.

Rhodes, D. E., *Gli annali tipografici fiorentini del XV secolo*, Florence, 1988.

Scapecchi, P., 'Cristoforo Landino, Niccolò di Lorenzo e la *Commedia*', in S. Gentile (ed.), *Sandro Botticelli: pittore della Divina Commedia*, Milan, 2000, I, pp. 44–7.

Scapecchi, P., 'Niccolò di Lorenzo', in *Dizionario biografico degli Italiani*, LXXVIII, 2013, pp. 414–15.

Tanturli, G., 'La Firenze laurenziana davanti alla propria storia letteraria', in G. C. Garfagnini (ed.), *Lorenzo Magnifico e il suo tempo*, Florence, 1992, pp. 1–38.

Trovato, P., 'Il libro toscano nell'età di Lorenzo. Schede e ipotesi', in *La Toscana al tempo di Lorenzo il Magnifico. Politica, economia, cultura, arte*, Pisa, 1996, II, pp. 525–63.

Veneziani, P., *Tracce sul foglio: saggi di storia della tipografia*, ed. P. Piacentini, Rome, 2007.

Veneziani, P., 'Vicende tipografiche della *Geografia* di Francesco Berlinghieri', *La Bibliofilia*, 84, 1982, pp. 195–208.

CHAPTER 7

··

MANUS MANUTII

A Preliminary Checklist of Typographical and Manuscript Interventions in Aldine Incunabula (1495–1500)

··

GERI DELLA ROCCA DE CANDAL

In memoriam: Carlo Argenton (1982–2018)

INTRODUCTION

··

'ERRARE humanum est; perseverare' … not quite.* The purpose of this paper is twofold: first, it intends to offer what admittedly remains a very preliminary checklist of manuscript

---

* This contribution owes much to a series of earlier works specifically discussing printing errors, most notably those by Curt F. Bühler (1905–1985), a great pioneer in the study of early misprints, manuscript alterations, and typographical variants. Other essential works on early Aldine typographical issues, by Neil Harris and Randall McLeod, also proved extremely useful, and I take the opportunity to express my gratitude to both of them, as well as to John Lancaster, for all the support they have provided in the preparation of this chapter. I am also grateful to Stephen Parkin (London, British Library), John McQuillen (New York, Morgan Library), Dunja Sharif (Oxford, Bodleian Library), Julia Bührle, and Nathalie Coilly and Patrick Morantin (Paris, Bibliothèque nationale de France) for helping me in getting hold of reproductions of copies from their respective collections, often beyond the call of duty. Finally, I wish to express my sincerest gratitude to David Speranzi (Florence, Biblioteca Nazionale Centrale), for generously sharing his great expertise on Manutius's handwriting; to Ester Camilla Peric, for her advice on Aldine prices and collations; to Raikhan Musrepova, for helping me with some experimental digital collations (and for bearing with endless ramblings on typographical issues); and, most importantly, to Paolo Sachet, for the constant and nurturing exchange of ideas, and without whose gentle prodding this chapter would never have seen the light.

Abbreviations used: A-M: *The Aldine Press, Catalogue of the Ahmanson-Murphy Collection of Books by or Relating to the Press in the Library of the University of California, Los Angeles: Incorporating Works Recorded Elsewhere*, Berkeley - London, 2001; BMC: *Catalogue of Books Printed in the XVth Century now in the British Museum* [British Library], 13 parts, London, 1963–2007; Bod-inc: *A Catalogue of Books Printed in the Fifteenth Century now in the Bodleian Library*, 6 vols, Oxford, 2005; CIBN: *Bibliothèque*

Geri Della Rocca de Candal, *Manus Manutii*. In: *Printing and Misprinting*. Edited by Geri Della Rocca de Candal, Anthony Grafton, and Paolo Sachet, Oxford University Press. © Geri Della Rocca de Candal (2023). DOI: 10.1093/oso/9780198863045.003.0008

122   PRINTING AND MISPRINTING

and stop-press corrections in the thirty-five editions issued by the Aldine press during its first six years of activity,[1] that is, between 1495 and 1500. Aldus Manutius (c. 1450–1515), arguably the best-known printer in Renaissance Venice, built part of his fame on the ability to promote himself as a publisher who could offer the highest editorial standards. But not even the most careful of printers could avoid typographical mistakes, particularly at the dawn of what would become a long and celebrated career. And while a vast majority of errors went unspotted, or at any rate uncorrected,[2] others were. Of these, some were solved while printing was still underway, taking the form of stop-press emendations or, occasionally, larger typographical resets. But if the printing process was completed, corrections had to be inserted by means of erasures, stamped letters, printed paste slips, or by pen and ink, in which case they are almost always found to be in Manutius's own hand. Finally, in some cases misprints were not corrected, but errata lists were produced. The second purpose of this paper, and in a sense its true ambition, is to assess Manutius's approach to correcting, its development over time, and most importantly, its meaning and significance within the Aldine press's activities. Inevitably, a thorough examination of the second point would deserve a more extensive study, but it is nonetheless possible, through this first analysis, to put forward a few initial observations on the matter.

In order to prepare this checklist and to answer the research questions, I have inspected at least twenty copies per edition — and often several more — for a total of over one thousand copies.[3] Yet misprints are like stars in the sky: as many as one can spot, they ultimately remain a negligible fraction of the whole. Corrections, on the other hand, are easier to identify, particularly when they are performed by hand, and this study has in fact resulted in the discovery of a number of previously unrecorded ones.[4] As painstaking as the task may

---

Nationale: Catalogue des Incunables, 2 vols, Paris, 1981–2014; GW: *Gesamtkatalog der Wiegendrucke*, Stuttgart, 1968–ongoing: https://www.gesamtkatalogderwiegendrucke.de/; ISTC: *Incunabula Short Title Catalogue*: https://data.cerl.org/istc/_search; Renouard: A.-A. Renouard, *Annales de l'imprimerie des Alde, ou histoire des trois Manuce et de leurs éditions*, Paris, 1834, 3rd edn.

[1] The number rises to forty-one if one includes the trial sheet of Athenaeus's *Deipnosophistae*, the sale catalogue of 1498 (*Libri Graeci Impressi*), Fortiguerra's *Lex Neacademiae*, and three editions of uncertain attribution: Cicero's *Synonyma*, the *Vita S. Josephi*, and the *Frottola Nova*. With regards to the latter three, it should be noted that their presence in this chapter is not an endorsement of attribution — far too many heads have rolled for this — but merely a tribute to an age of inclusiveness. The *Vita* and the *Frottola*, at any rate, survive in single copies (i.e. it cannot be determined whether they contain typographical recompositions) and do not have MS corrections; Cicero's *Synonyma* survives in twelve copies, also without MS corrections, and I did not detect any typographical recomposition.

[2] For a sample of these, see Piero Vettori's volumes of the Aldine Aristoteles (Munich, Bayerische Staatsbibliothek (BSB), 2 Inc.c.a. 3161 n3, n4.1, and n5, all digitally available via *GW* and *ISTC*): excluding the emendations to the Greek text, which Vettori clearly carried out by collating his volumes against one or more manuscripts, it is instructive to look at the sheer number of corrections to the running titles, the leaf numbers, and other paratextual materials, bearing in mind that, even in the case of such a careful reader, only a limited amount of misprints were actually corrected.

[3] I have seen fewer than twenty copies only when an edition has a particularly low survival rate and in the case of the *Thesaurus Cornu Copiae*, specifically discussed by Paolo Sachet in this Companion. A minority of copies I have inspected neither personally nor through digital scans, but after a fruitful correspondence and thanks to the reproductions sent to me by a number of colleagues, librarians, curators, and friends, several of whom are listed at the beginning of this chapter.

[4] Many however remain to be identified, and I would be grateful if anyone who found other corrections or variants were to inform me via e-mail (gdrdec@gmail.com): may this chapter be, in other words,

sound, it is only thanks to the careful inspection of as many copies as possible that one can find more corrections and, most importantly, the occasional, unexpected surprise: it was only while checking the seventh copy of Dioscorides that I found a genuine proof sheet with what almost certainly are Manutius's own final corrections. This discovery alone, arguably the most important unforeseen consequence of this research, inevitably encouraged further investigation, and sure enough, two further proof sheets eventually cropped up. This, in turn, will help shed even more light on Manutius's early editorial practices.

Chronological List and Alphabetical List

To make the results of this research more accessible, I have drafted two lists. The first contains a chronological synopsis of Aldine incunabula, with information useful for comparative purposes on three levels:

i) General information, i.e. format, number of leaves, number of sheets, paper stocks, lines per page, type area (the latter three based on *A-M*), the presence (or not) of these editions in the 1498, 1503, and 1513 Aldine sale catalogues (and, if so, their price), collation (based on *Bod-inc*), language, known existence of printer's copy (based on Sicherl's work), and number of extant copies (based on *GW*).

ii) The presence/absence of specific binding and reading implements, such as register, foliation, running titles, and catchwords.

iii) Finally, and with particular attention to editorial and printing processes, information on typographical variants, manual corrections of various sorts (manuscript emendations, erasures, paste slips, stamped letters, etc.), errata lists, and *integrantia* sheets.[5]

Each particular case, however, requires a more elaborate explanation: the second list, arranged alphabetically, is designed specifically to help navigate some of the intricacies of early misprinting and, in particular, as a guide for anyone handling Aldine incunabula and interested in learning whether they contain corrections; if so, of what type; and, if manuscript, in whose hand.

The 'Erratic' Presence of Errata Lists

In the case of several mistakes of medium and minor entity, errata lists offered a remarkably simple solution, *de facto* outsourcing the task of correcting to the reader. Yet Manutius's use of errata lists, at least in the early days, seems to have been erratic. The first of these appeared

---

a mere starting point towards a comprehensive mapping of Aldine editorial revisions, both manuscript and typographical.

[5] Occasional miscalculations in the print run resulted in shortages of one or more sheets. To make up for these shortages, inevitably discovered after the original formes had already been broken up, printers could resort to setting new formes. The sheets resulting from this second, limited print run are known as *integrantia*.

as early as March 1495 in Manutius's first dated edition, Lascaris's *Erotemata*. After that, other lists were issued in Musaeus's *De Herone et Leandro*; Leonicenus's *De Morbo Gallico*; Maiolus's *Epiphyllides* and *De Gradibus Medicinarum*; Bolzanius's *Institutiones*; Perottus's *Cornucopiae*; and Columna's *Hypnerotomachia Poliphili*. In all other incunabula editions, and regardless of the number of corrections required — in some instances, substantial — Manutius preferred to avoid this solution.

Although there seems to be no specific fil rouge connecting the editions with errata lists, nonetheless some trends appear discernible: (i) none of the major Greek-only editions have these lists: the only ones are Lascaris's *Erotemata* and Bolzanius's *Institutiones*, both of which, however, are bilingual educational texts (Greek and Latin); (ii) the few errata lists are more commonly found in quartos, despite two notable exceptions (Perottus's *Cornucopiae* and Columna's *Hypnerotomachia*); (iii) these lists are only present in editions connected to living, or at any rate modern, authors.[6] Generally speaking, the impression is that although Manutius would — reluctantly — endure the presence of errata lists in some of his minor editions, they were not perceived as particularly desirable in high-end humanistic editions. The example of the *Thesaurus Cornu Copiae* (n. 8), studied in depth by Paolo Sachet in this Companion, is instructive: the large number of minor misprints that were corrected by hand could have easily been included in a list of errata, yet the overwhelming impression is that Manutius went out of his way to avoid having to draft one, insisting on much lengthier manuscript emendations.

OTHER TYPES OF CORRECTIONS

If there were mistakes requiring corrections, but not enough to warrant the production of an errata list, or if, for whatever other reason, it was decided that a list was either not necessary or not appropriate, then the issue had to be dealt with in a different fashion. Stop-press typographical recomposition could of course only be performed if the presses were still at work on a particular forme, in which case correcting a mistake would not be a problem, at least in the sheets that had not yet been printed. But if the printing had already been completed, corrections had to be performed sheet by sheet and, depending on the type of problem, they could take the form of erasures, paste slips, stamped integrations, or, more frequently, manuscript interventions. For more serious mishaps, entire sheets could be reset to replace faulty ones: these reset sheets are known as *cancellans/cancellantia* and *cancellandum/cancellanda* respectively. Other than this, Manutius does not seem to have adopted other styles of correction, or at any rate very rarely, including overprinting and the rarer technique of whiting out a mistake with paint and, again, printing over it. Thus, depending on the exact moment when a misprint was spotted and the decision to correct it taken, there could be five possible outcomes:[7]

---

[6] The one exception being Musaeus, but what appears in this text is not, strictly speaking, a list of errata, but rather a brief note informing the reader about two lines that should be added to the main text.

[7] I am not considering here the instances of manual corrections inadvertently skipped, an almost inevitable outcome when correcting dozens or even hundreds of sheets.

i)   Almost all copies with stop-press alterations: when a minor misprint was identified and typographically corrected after the first few prints. This is perhaps the most common condition, but also the hardest to detect: to do so, one should carefully collate all the copies of an edition, and even so, this would only lead to the identification of variant settings among *extant* copies.

ii) Some copies with stop-press alterations, others unaltered: when a misprint was not considered serious enough to deserve correction in the sheets that had already been printed, or when manual correction was unfeasible (e.g. the five reset sheets in Theocritus).

iii) Some copies with stop-press alterations, others with manual interventions: when a misprint, spotted during the printing process, was deemed serious enough to warrant its correction in both printed and unprinted sheets.

iv) All copies with manual interventions: when a misprint was spotted immediately after (or at any rate too late during) the printing process, but before distribution and sale.

v)   Some copies with manual interventions, others uncorrected: when a misprint was spotted after the printing process, and after some of the copies had already been sold or otherwise distributed.

In the case of Aldine incunabula, it would appear that all solutions were used interchangeably, and it is not uncommon for combinations of different solutions to coexist in the same edition. Part of the reason for this is understandable: the nature and the timing of detection of different misprints called for different solutions. But the impression is that there was also a degree of experimentalism in the way mistakes were dealt with.

MANUTIUS'S HAND

Looking in particular at manuscript corrections, two observations immediately come to mind. The first is that corrections made at the Aldine press are usually quite easy to identify thanks to their neat and distinctive full brown colour, suggesting that the ink used for handwriting at the press was more or less the same throughout the period. The second, and by far the most impressive, is that almost all the manuscript corrections appear to have been made by Manutius himself. There are confirmed exceptions, such as Bembus's handwriting in some of the copies of his *De Aetna Dialogus*, or the enigmatic 'Hand B' in the *Psalterium* (see below), and of course there are cases in which the hand cannot be confirmed with absolute certainty; but in all other circumstances a simple comparison with Greek and Latin specimens of Manutius's handwriting confirms that it was always Manutius who personally made the corrections.[8] This inevitably raises questions about the availability, at the press,

---

[8] See Manutius's autograph copy of the *Grammaticae Institutiones Graecae* (MS Milan, Veneranda Biblioteca Ambrosiana, P 35 sup.). On his Greek handwriting see D. Speranzi, 'La scrittura di Aldo e il suo ultimo carattere greco (con uno sconosciuto esemplare di tipografia)', in N. Vacalebre (ed.), *Five Centuries Later. Aldus Manutius: Culture, Typography and Philology*, Florence, 2018, pp. 29–60. On Manutius's Latin handwriting see, for instance, the 1499 receipt for the loan of four manuscripts and a printed book to prepare his edition of St Catherine's *Epistole*, published in 1500 (MS Venice, Biblioteca Nazionale Marciana, It. XI, 207), and his first will, dated 1506 (Venice, Archivio di Stato, *Notarile, Testamenti*, env. 765, no. 260).

of individuals able to assist in this task and, more importantly, about Manutius's character, a character increasingly reminiscent of a perfectionist and a control freak (a bad combination), effectively unable to entrust the task of correcting to his assistants, regardless of their presence and skill. At least, however, it helps understand Manutius's endless rants about being constantly overworked. It may be no coincidence, in other words, that his own Greek grammar, on which he had worked for years, was only first published shortly after his death.

CONCLUSIONS

The purpose of this preliminary checklist is not so much to identify the entirety of alterations or variations present among Aldine incunabula (as I am sure that plenty more remain to be discovered), nor is it to investigate printing techniques beyond a certain degree of detail: for that one should definitely rely on the work of specialists far more capable than me, such as Neil Harris or Randal McLeod. Rather, the intention is to provide the reader with a general overview of the sheer quantity of misprints present in early Aldine editions and the variety of ways in which Manutius and his collaborators dealt with them. As mentioned earlier, it was not uncommon for several styles of correction to coexist within the same edition, and this, by itself, provides solid evidence that in the early years of the Aldine press misprints were tackled with a high degree of experimentalism. But while in some cases it is easier to understand what encouraged the adoption of a particular solution, in others it is hard to appreciate the rationale behind certain choices. This holds particularly true for the occurrences in which Manutius opted for stop-press corrections but did not feel the need to intervene on the sheets that had already been printed. One legitimately wonders why sometimes he went to great lengths to correct relatively minor misprints over hundreds of copies, while on other occasions, even after spotting a major misprint, he limited his action to a stop-press alteration, neglecting to intervene on the copies that had already been printed. One can only conjecture that Manutius's ability to keep pace with all the corrections that required his attention was indirectly proportional to the degree of pressure under which he was operating at any particular moment.

Misprints are an almost inevitable feature of any early edition, and for this very reason they are not intrinsically interesting: the abundant presence of corrections in Aldine incunabula, however, is. These corrections, for instance, add new layers to the philological and bibliographical question of what really defines an 'ideal copy', since, to this day, the vast majority of them have been dismissed as being produced by later readers, and never considered legitimate authorial or editorial interventions.[9] Some will certainly argue that this is further proof of Manutius's editorial care. This is probably true, except for the fact that, if he was so keen on editorial perfection, why then not allow for more time to revise the proof sheets, and thus avoid — or at least substantially reduce — the number of misprints in his editions? This, in turn, would have avoided stopping the presses too frequently and saved the time needed for the lengthy exercise of applying manual corrections to hundreds of copies. By glancing at the sheer number of corrections in these editions (see the chronological list), it is evident that proofreading consistently and invariably continued into the printing process, and that this delay was not occasional — it was the rule. At the very

---

[9] This point, additionally, provides a rock-solid argument in favour of always examining as many copies as possible.

least eighteen out of thirty-five editions had to undergo time-consuming manual corrections, twenty-nine out of thirty-five if one considers editions that required only stop-press alterations or errata lists. Nonetheless, a flicker of discernible progress does appear on the horizon: except for the Greek *Horae* (seven sheets, issued in December 1497) and Leonicenus's *De Tiro seu Vipera* (a pamphlet of two sheets, dated c.1498), the four remaining editions that do not appear to contain any correction (Dioscorides, S. Catharina Senensis, Lucretius, and the tiny *Introductio utilissima Hebraice*) all concentrate between late 1499 and 1500. This possibly suggests that Manutius was improving his technique to deal with misprints, though to make sure that this reading is correct, the case study should expand, in the future, to include all the editions produced up to 1515.

But returning to the earlier years, the question remains: was it really so unattainable to spare some extra time for proofreading, if only to ensure that, at a later stage, a much larger amount of time did not have to be wasted on corrections? Apparently not. This circumstance seems to lend at least some degree of credit to the theory that the 'opulentus sed sordidissimus' Andreas Torresanus might not have been merely a silent partner in Manutius's printing venture (as was, for instance, Pierfrancesco Barbarigo), but, on the contrary, an active general partner.[10] It is not in fact inconceivable that one disadvantage of Manutius's many qualities was his own perfectionism, a fairly unhealthy trait from a business point of view, and that perhaps, to counter this inclination, the financial success of the Aldine venture also rested, to some degree, on the shoulders of an experienced partner, someone with a clear say and a more pragmatic attitude — maybe not so much on the general publishing strategy, but rather on daily management and operations, and to ensure a regular printing schedule. Perhaps, I muse, it is also in this light that one could read Manutius's *festina lente*: an elegant classicising oxymoron, but also a cry of affliction, cleverly cloaked in bittersweet humour.

Be that as it may, the sheer number of misprints, alterations, and interventions observed in this handful of editions should serve as a reminder that Renaissance print shops were far from the idealised, almost clockwork descriptions that one still occasionally finds in modern secondary literature, and Manutius's was no exception. Most of the corrections in the checklist that follows are effectively irrelevant, but by seeing them all together, and remembering that plenty more are yet to be discovered, we gain at least a sense of the magnitude of this correcting process, and the amount of time it must have involved. By all means, early typographers endeavoured to organise their work and avoid misprints to the best of their possibilities, but printing was, simply put, a highly complex and messy business, and errors of all sorts lurked around the press, just like the skeletons of a well-known typographical *danse macabre*.[11]

---

[10]   See N. Harris, 'Aldo Manuzio, il libro e la moneta', in T. Plebani (ed.), *Aldo al Lettore: viaggio intorno al mondo del libro e della stampa in occasione del V centenario della morte di Aldo Manuzio*, Venice and Milan, 2016, pp. 79–110. For Erasmus's caustic description of Torresanus see the very first lines of the dialogue *Opulentia Sordida*, in Desiderius Erasmus, *Opera Omnia*, I/3, Amsterdam, 1972, pp. 681–5.

[11]   *Danse macabre*, [Lyon, Matthias Huss], 18 Feb. 1499 [/1500?], f° (ISTC id00020500), sig. b1r. This woodcut is also the earliest known representation of a printing press: https://dpul.princeton.edu/scheide/catalog/ms35td33q, accessed 16 February 2021.

Chronological Checklist of Corrections

N.	TEXT	DATE	ISTC / GW	GW COPIES	F.	LEAVES	SHEETS	PAPER STOCK (AHMANSON-MURPHY)	LINES (A-M)	TYPE AREA (AHMANSON-MURPHY)	LANG.	GREEK TYPE (A-M)	ROMAN TYPE + OTHERS (A-M)	PRICE IN 1498	PRICE IN 1503	PRICE IN 1513
1	Galeo-myomachia	[c.1494/95]	ig00040000 / M01795	14	4°	10	2.5	Keys 1	24+1	177 (171) x 101	GREEK	GR1:146		N/A	N/A	N/A
2	Lascaris, Erotemata	28/02/1495* - 08/03/1495	ii00068000 / M17107	92	4°	166	41.5	Bull's Head 1; Scales 1-2	24+1	Greek: 149 x 101 Latin: 155 (149) x 102	GREEK / LATIN	GR1:146	R1:124	4 marcelli	N/A*	N/A*
3	Musaues, De Herone et Leandro	[<01/11/1495 + c.1497?]	im00880000 / M25737	53	4°	22	5.5	Scales 2 + Scales 20-23	20+1	(144) x 103 Latin: 139 (136) x 100	GREEK / LATIN	GR1:146	R1:130; + [GR2:114]	1 marcello	10 soldi	1 lira
4	Aristoteles, Opera I	01/11/1495	ia00959000 / 2334	350	f°	234	117	Hat 1; Scales 3-7	30+1	224 (219) x 125	GREEK	GR1:146	R2:81; R1:108	1½ ducati	1 ducato 3 lire	9 lire 6 soldi
5	Gaza, Grammatica introductiva	25/12/1495	ig00110000 / 10562	218	f°	198	99	Hat 1	31+1	233 (266) x 137	GREEK	GR1:146	R3:83	1 ducato	1 ducato	6 lire 4 soldi
6	Theocritus, Idyllia	??/02/1496*	it00144000 / M45831	202	f°	140	70	Bull's Head 2; Hat 1-2	30+1	223 (218) x 110	GREEK	GR1:146	R3:83	8 marcelli	4 lire	4 lire
7	Bembus, De Aetna Dialogus	??/02/1496*	ib00304000 / 3810	37	4°	30	7.5	Scales 8	22+1	129 (126) x 77	LATIN		R4:114	N/A	N/A	N/A
8	Thesaurus Cornu Copiae	[??/08/1496]	it00158000 / 7571	169	f°	280	140	Hat 1-2	1+30+1	233 (219) x 131	GREEK	GR1:146	R4:115	1½ ducati	1 ducato 3 lire	9 lire 6 soldi
9	Benedictus, Diaria de Bello Carolino	[>27/08/1496]	ib00320400 / 863	72	4°	68	17	Bird 1; Cross 1; Hat 1	25+1	147 (141) x 87	LATIN		R4:114	N/A	N/A	N/A
10	Aristoteles, Opera III	29/01/1497	ia00959000 / 2334	350	f°	468	234	Crown 4; Orb 1-2; Scales 9-14, 16-17, 24-26	1+30+1	236 (219) x 129	GREEK	GR1:146	R4:114	2½ ducati	2 ducati 3 lire	15 lire 8 soldi
11	Aristoteles, Opera II	??/02/1497	ia00959000 / 2334	350	f°	300	150	Anchor 1; Bull's Head 7-8; Crown 5-6; Letters 1; Orb 1; Scales 9, 25, 31-35	1+30+1	236 (220) x 128	GREEK	GR1:146	R4:114	2 ducati	2 ducati	12 lire 8 soldi
12	Aristoteles, Opera IV	01/06/1497	ia00959000 / 2334	350	f°	520	260	Bull's Head 3; Crown 1-2; Orb 1; Scales 9-10	1+30+1	236 (218) x 132	GREEK	GR1:146	R4:114	3 ducati	3 ducati	18 lire 12 soldi
13	Leonicenus, DeMorbo Gallico	??/06/1497	il00165000 / M17947	82	4°	30	7.5	Orb 2	33+1	150 (146) x 117 (95)	LATIN	GR2:114	R5:87; R3:83	N/A	N/A	N/A
14	Maiolus, Epiphyllides	??/07/1497	im00083000 / M20060	57	4°	158	39.5	Bull's Head 4; Orb 1-2; Scales 9-14	33+1	148 (144) x 97	LATIN		R5:87	N/A	2 lire	N/A
15	Maiolus, De Gradibus	??/07/1497	im00084000 / M20071	52	4°	58	14.5	Bull's Head 4; Scales 13	33+1	147 (144) x 97	LATIN	GR2:114	R5:87	Sold with Epyphillides		
16	Jamblichus, De Mysteriis	??/09/1497	ij00216000 / M11750	291	f°	186	93	Scales 6, 9, 15	1+37+1	224 (212) x 132	LATIN		R4:114	N/A	3 lire	N/A
17	Horae	05/12/1497	ih00391000 / 13396	33	16°	112	7	Mount; Letters 'bc'	13+1	77 (73) x 50	GREEK	GR2:114	R4:114	2 marcelli	1 lira	N/A
18	Manutius, Brev. Introductio ad Litteras Graecas	[c.??/12/1497]	im00226400 / M12563	6	16°	16	1	?	12+1	74 (68) x 50	LATIN / GREEK	GR2:114	R4:114	N/A	N/A	N/A
19	Crastonus, Lexicon	??/12/1497	ic00960000 / 7814	169	f°	244	122	Crown 3; Orb 2; Scales 10, 16-19	42+1	241 (238) x 139, two columns	GREEK / LATIN	GR2:114	R4:114; R5:87	1 ducato	1 ducato	6 lire 4 soldi
20	Bolzanius, Institutiones	??/01/1498*	iu00066000 / M48900	131	4°	212	53	Crown 4; Scales 10, 16, 25	27+1	159 (153) x 101	LATIN / GREEK	GR2:114	R4:114	4 marcelli	1 lira 10 soldi	N/A
21	Aristoteles, Opera V	05/06/1498	ia00959000 / 2334	350	f°	330	165	Anchor 1; Bull's Head 7-8; Crown 5-6; Letters 1; Orb 1; Scales 9, 25, 31-35	1+30+1	237 (218) x 127	GREEK	GR1:146	R4:114	2 ducati	4 ducati	12 lire 8 soldi

N.	COLLATION	PRINTER'S COPY (SICHERL)	REGIS-TER	FOLIA-TION	RUN. TITLE	CATCH WORD	TYPO-GRAPHIC VARIANTS	HAND INTER-VENTIONS	ERRATA LIST	KNOWN INTE-GRANTIA	NOTES
1	α¹⁰						✓	✓			
2	a–r² f⁴ A–C⁸ [D]²						✓		[D]1r-2r	✓	SALE CATALOGUES: the editions for sale in 1503 and 1513 are the second and the third, printed respectively in c. 1501–1503 and 1512. REGISTER: contains the list of gatherings, but not the register.
3	α¹⁰ b¹², interleaved	✓					✓	✓	b1v		PRINTER'S COPY (Latin only, Manutius's hand): Sicherl, *Aldus Manutius*, pp. 11–30; Hellinga, *Texts in Transit*, 'List', pp. 67-101, n. 38.
4	A–K⁸ L–N⁶ a–c⁸ d–e⁶ f–q⁸ r– f⁶	✓	✓				✓	✓			PRINTER'S COPY (parts only): Sicherl, *Aldus Manutius*, pp. 31–113; Hellinga, *Texts in Transit*, 'List', pp. 67–101, n. 36. GW COPIES: see detailed edition description.
5	a⁶ bβ–lΛ⁸ ²a⁸ b¹⁰ AA–LL⁸ MM⁴		✓			✓*	✓	✓		✓	CATCHWORD: only in gatherings a and b, halfway through the volume, leaves 1–4 + a8.
6	A.A.–Δ.D⁸ E.e.–Θ.G⁸ AA.αα–ΔΔ.δδ⁸EE.εε⁸ ZZ.ζζ¹⁰ α.a–β.b⁸ γ.c¹⁰		✓		✓		✓	✓		✓	CATCHWORD: throughout, leaves 1–3, except α.a–γ.c (Hesiod, Theogonia), which has none.
7	A–C⁸ D⁸						✓	✓			
8	*¹⁰ αa–zψ⁸ ξπω⁴ AA–DΔ³ EE⁶ FZ–GH⁸ HΘ⁵ lI⁸ KK⁶ LΛ³		✓	✓		✓	✓	✓		✓	CATCHWORD: last leaf.
9	a–h⁸ i⁴						✓	✓			
10	aaαα–iiii¹⁰ κκ¹⁰ llλλ–zzηψψ¹⁰ ξξξτωω¹⁰AA–PP¹⁰ ˣPP² ΣΣ–ΦΦ¹⁰ XX⁸ ϗ⁶	✓	✓	✓	✓	✓	✓	✓		✓	CATCHWORD: throughout, occasionally missing, usually leaves 5 or 6. PRINTER'S COPY (parts only): Sicherl, *Aldus Manutius*, pp. 31–113; Hellinga, *Texts in Transit*, 'List', pp. 67–101, n. 36. GW COPIES: see detailed edition description.
11	₊⁸ ᷣ⁸ ᷤ⁸ oς³ aα–rς⁴ sπ–zψ⁶ ξτω⁴ A–B⁸ CΓ⁶ DΔ–HΘ⁴ lI⁸ K⁶	✓	*	✓	✓	✓	✓				REGISTER: only the list of gatherings. CATCHWORD: throughout, occasionally missing, more frequently towards end of the volume. FOLIATION: introduction gatherings not numbered.CATCHWORD: absent in the first gatherings after the intro (aα1–εε7); gathering ηη has catchwords on the rectos too. PRINTER'S COPY (parts only): Sicherl, *Aldus Manutius*, pp. 31–113; Hellinga, *Texts in Transit*, 'List', pp. 67–101, n. 36. GW COPIES: see detailed edition description.
12	Φ⁴ aaaaαα–iiiii κκκ llλλ–zzηψψ⁸ ξξξτωωω⁸ AAA–BBB⁸ CCCΓΓΓ⁸ DDDΔΔΔ¹⁰ AAAaaa–MMMmmm⁸ NNNnnn–ΞΞΞοοο¹⁰ αa–δd⁸ εε¹⁰ aa–bβ⁸ AAAαaα–OOOξξξ⁸ PPPοοο¹⁰	✓		✓	✓	✓	✓				REGISTER: only the list of gatherings. CATCHWORD: throughout, occasionally missing, usually leaf 4 (or 5 in gatherings of 10 leaves). PRINTER'S COPY (parts only): Sicherl, *Aldus Manutius*, pp. 31–113; Hellinga, *Texts inTransit*, 'List', pp.67–101, n. 36. GW COPIES: see detailed edition description.
13	a–c⁸ d⁴ [e]²								[e]1r-v		
14	a⁴ b–f⁸ g¹⁰ ²a–i² A–D⁸		✓				✓		I1r-2v*		ERRATA LIST: shared with Maiolus, De Gradibus.
15	A–G⁸ I²		*						I1r-2v		REGISTER: only the list of gatherings.
16	a–i⁸ k⁴ L–M⁸ N–Z⁸ ꝛ¹⁰	✓	✓	✓	✓	✓	✓	✓			CATCHWORD: throughout. PRINTER'S COPY: Hellinga (2014),' List', no.37.
17	α–ξ⁸					✓				✓	SALE CATALOGUES: the edition for sale in 1513 is the second, printed in 1505. CATCHWORD: [α–λ1–8; μ8; ν1–3, 5, 7–8; ξ1].
18	a–b⁸							✓			LINES, TYPE AND TYPE AREA: edition not in Ahmanson-Murphy, I have thus provided or partly integrated the information.
19	a–k⁸ l¹⁰ A–K⁸ L¹⁰ M⁸ N¹⁰ O⁸ p–r⁸ f⁸ t⁸		✓			✓	✓	✓			FOLIATION: the Vobabulista in appendix refers to page numbers of the Lexicon, but readers are invited to number the pages by themselves. CATCHWORD: Only last leaf of quires, from O5 all.
20	a¹⁰ b–z⁸ Ꝛ⁸ A⁶ B¹⁰ [C]²					✓			[C]1r-2v + ²a1r-2v / [¶]1r-3v		ERRATA LIST: the gathering of errata exists in three variants. The most common, [C]², is occasionally accompanied,but almost never substituted, by either one of the two variants, ²a² and [¶]⁴. CATCHWORD: usually leaves 2, 6 and 8, with occasional omissions.
21	aaaa–iiii¹⁰ κκκκ⁴ λλλλ–φφφφ¹⁰ χχχχ⁴ ψψψψ¹² ωωωω¹⁰ AAAA–BBBB¹⁰ ΓΓΓΓ¹⁰ ΔΔΔΔ–IIII¹⁰ KKKK¹²		✓	✓	✓	✓	✓				SALE CATALOGUES: in 1503 the price is set at 4 ducats, which seems to be a mistake: in 1513 it is back to the equivalent of 2 ducats. CATCHWORD: throughout, occasionally missing fol. 5 (in gatherings of 10 leaves). GW COPIES: see detailed edition description.

130 PRINTING AND MISPRINTING

N.	TEXT	DATE	ISTC / GW	GW COPIES	F.	LEAVES	SHEETS	PAPER STOCK (AHMANSON-MURPHY)	LINES (A–M)	TYPE AREA (AHMANSON-MURPHY)	LANG.	GREEK TYPE (A–M)	ROMAN TYPE + OTHERS (A–M)	PRICE IN 1498	PRICE IN 1503	PRICE IN 1513
22	Aristophanes, Comoediae Novem	15/07/1498	ia00958000 /2333	254	f°	348	174	Bull's Head 9–10; Hat 3; Letters 1;Mount 1; Scales 10; 36–38	1+42+1	255 (241) x 156, gloss layout	GREEK	GR1:146; GR2:114	R4:114	2½ ducati	2 ducati 3 lire	16 lire 10 soldi
23	Politianus, Opera	??/07/1498	ip00886000 /M34727	332	f°	452	226	Bull's Head 9–13; Crown 7; Hat 3–4; Letters 1; Mount 1; Scales 22a, 25, 36–39	1+38+1	224 (216) x 128	LATIN	GR2:114	R4:114; HEB	N/A	1 ducato	9 lire 6 soldi
24	Reuchlin, Oratio	01/09/1498	ir00153500 /M37878	5	4°	12	3	Scales 79/80	23+1	137 (131) x 76	LATIN		R4:114	N/A	N/A	N/A
25	Psalterium	[<01/10/1498]	ip01033000 /M36248	120	4°	150	37.5	Crown 8; Orb 1	20+1	151 (145) x 92	GREEK	GR1:146; GR2:114		4 marcelli	2 lire	1 lira
26	Leonicenus, De Tiro seu Vipera	[c.1498?]	il00169000 /M17952	8	4°	8	2	?	26+1	?	LATIN	GR2:114	R4:114	N/A	N/A	N/A
27	Epistolae diversorum philosophorum	[29]03/1499 – [>17/04/1499]	ie00064000 /9367	302	4°	404	101	Anchor 2; Bull's Head 4–5, 9,14; Crown 8–12; Letters 1; Scales 11, 14–19, 23,29, 31, 35, 37–38, 40–46	26+1	152 (147) x 100	GREEK	GR2:114	R4:114	N/A	1 ducato	6 lire 4 soldi
28	Firmicus, Mathesis	??/06/1499 – [17]/10/1499	if00191000 /9981	350	f°	376	188	v.1 Hat 5–6; Scales 51–52. v.2Anchor 2; Bull's Head 15–18; Hat 6;Scales 47, 51–53	Latin: 1+39+1 Greek: 40+1	239 (223) x 132;Latin: 236 (222) x 133; Greek: 232 (227) x 130	LATIN / GREEK	GR2:114	R4:114; R2a:82	N/A	1 ducato	6 lire 4 soldi
29	Perottus, Cornucopiae	??/07/1499	ip00296000 /M31090	94	f°	372	186	Hat 5–6; Scales 42; 44, 49–50	1+59+1	252 (244) x 150, five columns	LATIN		R4:114; R2a:82	N/A	3 lire	N/A
30	Dioscorides, De Materia Medica	[>08/07/1499]	id00260000 /8435	106	f°	184	92	Anchor 2; Hat 5; Scales 47–48	1+40+1	244 (230) x 134	GREEK	GR2:114 ;GR3:84	R4b:115	N/A	1 ducato	5 lire
31	Amaseus, Vaticinium	20/09/1499	ia00550000 /1596	32	4°	12	3	Hat 5/6; Scales 56	28+1	164 (159) x 103	LATIN		R4b:115	N/A	N/A	N/A
32	Columna, Hypneroto-machia	??/12/1499	ic00767000 /7223	261	f°	234	117	Anchor 1; Bull's Head 17; Scales 2, 32, 47	39+1	227 (222) x 132	ITAL	GR2:114 ; GR3:84	R4b:115; R2a:82; HEB	N/A	N/A	N/A
33	Catharina Senensis, Epistole	[>19]/09/1500	ic00281000 /6222	179	f°	422	211	Hat 9; Scales 32, 54–55	1+40+1	239 (229) x 134	ITAL		R4b:115; R2a:82; I1:80	N/A	1 ducato	N/A
34	Lucretius, De Rerum Natura	??/12/1500	il00335000 / M19135	72	4°	108	27	Hat 9–10; Scales 56–57	37+1	156 (153) x 87	LATIN	GR2:114	R4b:115; R2a:82	N/A	1 lira	N/A
35	Manutius, Introductio util. Hebraice	[c.1500?]	im00226600 / M1256310	2	16°	16	1	?	12	?	LATIN / GREEK	GR2:114	R4b:115; HEB	N/A	N/A	N/A
36	Cicero, Synonyma[?]	[c.1497?]	ic00691000 /7036		4°	36	9	Hat (Briquet 3424–6); Scales 84 (similar)	35+1	157 (152) x 99, three columns			R5:87	N/A	N/A	N/A
37	Athenaeus, Deipnosophistae	[<15/04/1498]	ia01175000 /0276210N		f°	1	½	?	34	224 x 132		GR2:114		N/A	N/A	N/A
38	Manutius, Libri Graeci Impressi	[>01/10/1498]	im00226700 / M20275		Bds de	1	1	Hat 4?	63	358 x 245		GR2:114	R4:114	N/A	N/A	N/A
39	Vita S. Josephi [?]	[<01/06/1499]	ij00479700 / M5081220		4°	8	2	?	26+1	154 (148) x 105			R4:114	N/A	N/A	N/A
40	Frottola Nova [?]	[c.1499?]	if00325630 /10413		4°	2	1	No watermark	42	172 x 123			R2a:82; I1:80	N/A	N/A	N/A
41	Fortiguerra, Lex Neacademiae	[c.1500/01?]	if00272500 /1022710N		Bds de	1	1	?	51	291 x 142		GR2:114		N/A	N/A	N/A

N.	COLLATION	PRINTER'S COPY (SICHERL)	REGISTER	FOLIATION	RUN. TITLE	CATCH WORD	TYPOGRAPHIC VARIANTS	HAND INTERVENTIONS	ERRATA LIST	KNOWN INTEGRANTIA	NOTES
22	[π]⁸ α–γ⁸ δ¹⁰ ε–ξ⁸ ο¹⁰ π–υ⁸ φ⁸χ–ω⁸ A–E⁸ Z⁸ H–Λ⁸ M⁸ N–O⁸ Π¹⁰ P–Σ⁸ T⁶	✓	✓		✓	✓	✓	✓			FOLIATION: Vecce 'Aldo e l'invenzione dell'indice', p. 117, is mistaken when he claims that this edition is foliated. CATCHWORD: throughout, occasionally missing (different leaves). PRINTER'S COPY (parts only): Sicherl, Aldus Manutius, pp. 114–154 (125–133); Hellinga, Texts in Transit, 'List', pp. 67–101, n. 39.
23	a–p⁸ q–r¹⁰ f–t⁸ A–I⁸ K⁶ L–P⁸ Q–R¹⁰ S⁶ T¹⁰ V⁶ X–Y¹⁰ Z⁸ θ¹⁰ aa¹⁰ iteru aa–iteru bb⁸ bb–hh⁸ ii⁶ xx¹⁰		✓		✓	✓	✓	✓		✓	CATCHWORD: throughout.
24	a¹²							✓			PAPER STOCK, LINES, TYPE AND TYPE AREA: edition not in Ahmanson-Murphy; I have thus provided or partly integrated the information.
25	α–θ⁸ ι⁶ κ–υ⁸		*		✓	✓	✓				REGISTER: only the list of gatherings. CATCHWORD: always 8, frequently but inconsistently also 2 and 6.
26	A⁴										LINES, TYPE AND TYPE AREA: edition not in Ahmanson-Murphy; I have thus provided or partly integrated the information.
27	*⁸ α–ε¹² ς¹² ζ–η⁸ θ¹⁰ ι–τ⁸ ττ⁸ υ–ω⁸ A–Γ⁸ Δ⁴ ²α–ε⁸ ²ζ–η⁸ ²θ–ρ⁸ ²σ⁶	✓	✓		✓	✓					CATCHWORD: throughout, occasionally missing (different leaves). PRINTER'S COPY (parts only): Sicherl, Aldus Manutius, pp. 155–190; Hellinga, Texts in Transit, 'List', pp. 67–101, n. 40.
28	*⁸ a–g¹⁰ h¹² aa–hh¹⁰ ii–kk⁸; A–D¹⁰ E¹² F⁶ G–M¹⁰ N⁸ ²N¹⁰ O–S¹⁰ T⁸		✓		✓*	✓	✓			✓	RUNNING TITLE: only Firmicus and Manilius. CATCHWORD: usually first half of gathering + last leaf, from Aratus all leaves.
29	[π–5π]⁸ a–z¹⁰ A–H¹⁰ I¹²		*	✓		✓				[5π]4r–v	SALE CATALOGUES: the edition for sale in 1513 is the second, printed in 1513. REGISTER: contains the list of gatherings, but not the register. FOLIATION: first case of page (i.e. not leaf) numbering + lines too. CATCHWORD: half quire and last leaf.
30	*⁸ α–ο⁸ π¹⁰ A–Δ⁸ E⁶ ²α¹⁰		*		✓	✓					CATCH WORD: present throughout, but in almost each gathering with an omission or two, usually at the centre (leaves 4, 5,6). CORRECTIONS: at least two copies, probably more, contain proof-sheets.
31	a⁶ b⁴						✓	✓			PAPER STOCK, LINES, TYPE AND TYPE AREA: edition not in Ahmanson-Murphy; I have thus provided or partly integrated the information.
32	[π]⁴ a–y⁸ z¹⁰ A–E⁸ F⁸		*			✓	✓	✓	F4r	✓	PAPER STOCK: I have corrected Ahmanson-Murphy's mistaken description. REGISTER: Harris, 'Blind Impressions', pp. 113-7, has shown that the register and a longer colophon had been prepared, but never used. CATCHWORD: throughout, usually only 1-4 and 8, but with occasional variations, part. in gatherings r–z.
33	*¹⁰ a–y⁸ A–G⁸ H¹⁰ I–N⁴ O¹⁰ P–Z⁸ AA–FF⁸		*	✓		✓					REGISTER: only the list of gatherings. CATCHWORD: throughout, usually only 1-4 and 8, but with occasional variations, part. in the early gatherings.
34	[π]⁸ a–m⁸ n⁶		*			✓					CATCHWORD: throughout (except very few, second half of volume).
35	[π]¹⁶						N/A				LINES AND TYPE: edition not in Ahmanson-Murphy; I have thus provided or partly integrated the information.
36	A–D⁸ E⁴										LINES AND TYPE: edition not in Ahmanson-Murphy; I have thus provided or partly integrated the information.
37	N/A		N/A	N/A	N/A	N/A	N/A		N/A		LINES AND TYPE: edition not in Ahmanson-Murphy; I have thus provided or partly integrated the information.
38	N/A		N/A	N/A	N/A	N/A		✓	N/A		LINES AND TYPE: edition not in Ahmanson-Murphy; I have thus provided or partly integrated the information.
39	a⁸						N/A				LINES AND TYPE: edition not in Ahmanson-Murphy; I have thus provided or partly integrated the information.
40	[π]²						N/A				LINES AND TYPE: edition not in Ahmanson-Murphy; I have thus provided or partly integrated the information.
41	N/A		N/A	N/A	N/A	N/A	N/A		N/A		LINES AND TYPE: edition not in Ahmanson-Murphy; I have thus provided or partly integrated the information.

132 PRINTING AND MISPRINTING

ALPHABETICAL CHECKLIST OF CORRECTIONS

A few important notes about the following list:

- The editions are arranged alphabetically by author, except in the case of texts that are usually known by their title (e.g. *Epistolae Diversorum Philosophorum, Galeomyomachia, Horae, Psalterium, Thesaurus Cornu Copiae*, etc.); the list includes the three editions of uncertain attribution mentioned in the introduction.
- Whilst for manual interventions the observations listed below are the result of my own inspections or derived from dedicated secondary literature, typographical alterations are for the most part taken from six bibliographical resources (though always checked and occasionally corrected): four major incunabula catalogues (*GW, BMC, Bod-inc, CIBN*) and the two most comprehensive Aldine catalogues (*Renouard* and *A-M*). In other words, I have endeavoured to provide a common platform to harmonise the information on typographical alterations, but I did not actively attempt to find new variants.
- The copies listed in the footnotes are the ones that I have examined, either in person or digitally (the latter are listed in **bold** and are easily retrievable through *GW* or *ISTC*). For the sake of brevity I have shortened the names of libraries, but their full institutional names can be found on *ISTC*. I only provide shelfmarks in case of rare variants/corrections or if there is a risk of confusion between copies in the same institution.
- Original research concentrates in particular on three editions (Amaseus, *Galeomyomachia* and Reuchlin), with other new findings scattered throughout the list. Conversely, in the case of Bembus, Benedictus, Columna, *Horae* (with Manutius's *Brevissima Introductio*), Maiolus, Musaeus, and the *Thesaurus Cornu copiae*, the information I provide is mostly derivative from other scholars' work, duly referenced.
- *Var. A* and *Var. B* (and, rarely, *Var. C*) are used when corrections are generated by means of typographical recompositions, either through stop-press alterations (usually adopted for minor faults), or more substantial resets, for whatever reason. In particular, *Var. A* is used here to indicate *first* state and *Var. B second* state — supposedly the 'correct' one, regardless of its frequency or philological value by modern standards — even if this is occasionally at odds with the labels adopted in some major catalogues.[12] In rare instances, if there is also an intermediate state, *Var. C* is then used to represent the latter of the three. Finally, when establishing a reasonable order or priority proved too hard, I have used **Var. X, Var. Y**, and **Var. Z**.
- **No corrections**: when an edition is described as having 'no corrections' it simply means that I have been unable to detect any evidence of corrections, but this of course does not mean that there are not. The same applies to other, more specific, indicators, such

---

[12] On *CIBN*, in particular, see n. 16 below.

as the presence of typographical variants or *integrantia*. There surely are: they simply have not been discovered yet.

- **Abbreviations and statistics**: MS = manuscript; SP = stop-press; ER = erasure; ST = stamp; PS = paste slip; EF = expected frequency. The latter, in particular, only refers to the frequency of corrections. So, for instance, if there are three copies of *Var. A* and nine copies of *Var. B*, the EF is 75%. If, however, two copies of *Var. A* have manuscript corrections, then the EF would be 92%. The data on corrections is further broken down into percentiles. So, for instance, in the first example one has EF 75% (SP 100%), while in the second one has EF 92% (SP 82%; MS 18%). Rare variants and *integrantia* are likely to be statistically overrepresented. Please note that percentiles within the same edition do not always match: this is often due to the presence of washed or defective copies. In summary, it is clear that the statistics shown below are not intended to provide precision, but rather to offer a general indication of what one might expect when looking at a copy.
- **Transcription:** I have endeavoured to transcribe the text as faithfully as possible, including mistakes.

Amaseus, *Vaticinium* (n. 31)

Sample: 15/32 copies (47%).[13] Five interventions: three MS only, two SP+MS. MS interventions: Aldus Manutius. Bibliography: Tosi.[14]

1) **a4v**, line 11 (correction): *Var. A*: «locudletes»; *Var. B*: «locupletes». EF: 100% (SP 7%; MS 93%).

2) **a7v**, line 14 (correction): «properage mino» > «proper agemino». EF: 87% (MS 100%).

3) **a8r**, line 6 (correction): «aera//» > «æra//». EF: 40% (MS 100%).

4) **b2v**, line 26 (correction): «& arma Boemos.//» > «& ad arma Boemos.//». EF: 93% (MS 100%).

5) **b3v**, line 8 (correction): *Var. A*: «consurgunt»; *Var. B*: «consurgant». EF: 93% (SP 43%; MS 57%).

In the copy Paris, BnF, Rés. Vélins 2110, on vellum, all but one error (3) are corrected, and all using pen and ink, clearly showing that this dedication copy was among the first to come out

---

[13] Copies examined: Paris, BnF; Bergamo, Mai; **Florence, BNCF**; Lucca, BS; Milan, Amb.; Rome, Aless.; Turin, BNU; Venice, Correr; Venice, Marc. (4); London, BL; New York, Morgan; **Vatican City, BAV**.

[14] P. A. Tosi, *Notizia di una edizione sconosciuta del poema romanzesco La Spagna colla descrizione di un opuscolo impresso da Aldo Manuzio nell'anno M.CCCC.XCIX*, Milan, 1835, mentions two copies: one in the author's hands (now London, BL), and one in Paris (now Paris, BnF). Since there is relatively little research on this Aldine pamphlet, let alone on its corrections (possibly because its existence was only first discussed in bibliographical literature as late as 1835, i.e. after the third and last edition of A.-A. Renouard, *Annales de l'imprimerie des Alde*, Paris, 1834), I am currently in the process of writing a short dedicated piece, looking in particular at the style and incidence of each correction.

134   PRINTING AND MISPRINTING

of the press. Conversely, a vellum dedication copy of Benedictus's *Diaria de Bello Carolino* bears evidence to the fact that it was among the last to be printed (see below).

Aristophanes, *Comoediae novem* (n. 22)

Sample: 42/254 copies (17%).[15] Six interventions: five SP, one SP+MS.[16]

1) [π]3*r*, signature (correction): *Var. A*: no signature; *Var. B*: «3». EF: 30% (SP 100%).
2) θ8*r*, main text, last two lines (correction): *Var. A*: «//Δι. Χώρει δευρὶ δεῖξον σαυτὸν//ΧΟΡΟΫ//»; *Var. B*: «//ΧΟΡΟΫ//Δι. Χώρει δευρὶ δεῖξον σαυτὸν//». Inversion of the last two lines into the correct order. EF: 97% (SP 100%).
3) κ5*r*, scholia, last line (correction): *Var. A* has five additional lines, ending: «//προσέθηκε τοῦτο.//»; *Var. B* ends: «δι-//πλῆ ἔξω νενευκυῖα.//». Erroneous ink-ing of five lines of bearer type originally from ι6*r*: the first three are lines 2–4 of the scholium that begins with «Τεκούσασ»; the last two are from the scholium above.[17] EF: 88% (SP 100%).
4) ο2*v*, catchword (correction): *Var. A*: «Καθαπτὸς»; *Var. B*: «Διόνυσος». EF: 64% (SP 100%).
5) Σ2*r*, scholia, last line (correction): *Var. A* has four additional lines, ending: «ἀρτίως κε-//χεσμένον.//»; *Var. B* ends: «//ἑαυτῶν οὐσίαν.//». Erroneous repetition of a scholium that, notwithstanding some minor textual variations, appears in its correct position on the verso of the same leaf (Σ2*v*). EF: 85% (SP 100%).
6) Σ4*r*, signature (correction): *Var. A*: « Σiii»; *Var. B*: « Σiiii». EF: 76% (SP 92%; MS 8%).

Interestingly, none of the sheets of the first state of this edition appear to have been corrected by hand, as in other early Aldine editions, with the single exception of intervention (6) in the copy Stanford (CA), UL. It is also peculiar that in all six instances the emendations concentrate in the bottom lines of the page. In two instances there are additional scholia that do not belong: in the first case (3), bearer type from earlier formes is inadvertently inked; in the second (5), a scholium that correctly appears on the verso of the same leaf appears here too, erroneously.

---

[15] Copies examined: **Buenos Aires, BN**; Vienna, ÖNB (3); Chantilly, Condé; Paris, BnF (7); Paris, Mazarine; Berlin, SB (2); **Munich, BSB**; Lesbos, EHS; Lesbos, Leimonos Monastery; Florence, BNCF; Florence, Laur.; Florence, Ricc.; Genoa, Durazzo; Milan, Amb. (2); Milan, Braid.; Milan, Triv.; Turin, BNU (2); Venice, Marc.; Leiden, UL; Kraków, Jagiellonian; Soria, BP; London, BL (4); Oxford, Bod. (3); **Boston, PL; Stanford (CA), UL; Charlottesville (VA), UVA.**

[16] I have drawn Aristophanes' SP corrections from *CIBN* A-503. Here and elsewhere, however, I have inverted *CIBN*'s order of labels A and B according to the style used in this chapter (i.e., *Var. B* representing the second state). A further typographical variant, described by *CIBN* as occurring in the penultimate line of the scholia on Z3*r* (reported there as *Var. A*: «διο//»; *Var. B*: «διοι//», though the correct version would be, in this case, the latter), is not listed here because it is, in fact, a frisket bite.

[17] I am grateful to Enrico Emanuele Prodi for his aid in identifying the origin of these flying scholia.

Aristoteles, *Opera* I (n. 4)

Sample: 40/350 copies (11%).[18] Six interventions: two SP, two SP+MS, one ER+MS, one SP+(ER+MS/ST).[19] MS interventions: Aldus Manutius. Bibliography: McLeod.[20]

1) **A3r**, line 21 (correction): *Var. A*: «//οικε»; *Var. B*: «//Ἔ οικε». In *Var. A* erasure of «Ἔ» erroneously printed on the line above and placed in its right position by stamp or MS. EF: 100% (SP 57%; ER+ST 26%; ER+MS 17%).

2) **B1v**, line 14 (correction): «μέν» > «και». «μέν» erased and overwritten. EF: 100% (ER+MS 100%).

3) **N3v**, lines 5, 6 (twice), 7, 9, 10, 20, 24, 28 (corrections).[21] A series of nine minor emendations, corrected either SP or MS. When MS, the most noticeable of these are an erasure overwritten by MS «οἷον» (line 24) and the numeral «γ'» replaced by «β'» (line 28). EF: 100% (SP 61%; MS 39%).

4) **a7r**, last line (correction): *Var. A*: «ἐπιστήμαις· ἀποδεικτικαῖς.//»; *Var. B*: «ἀποδεικτικαῖς ἐπιστήμαις·//». Inversion of the last two words to the correct order. EF: 89% (SP 100%).

5) **b5r**, lines 25–30 (revision): line 30, *Var. A*: « [...]//τη ἡ αὐτὴ τῇ πρότερον ἐλάττων ἀεὶ ἀληθής ἐστιν· ἡ δὲ μείζων//»; *Var. B*: « [...]//δὲ ᾱ Δ ἀντιστρέφεσθαι· καὶ ἡ ἀπάτη ἡ αὐτὴ τῇ πρότερον·//». Reset (spacing out) after the elimination of the last seven words. In *Var. A* the words in excess are subpuncted. EF: 100% (SP 54%; MS 46%).

6) **c7v**, last line (correction): *Var. A*: «αἴτιον;,»; *Var. B*: «αἴτιον;», redundant comma removed. EF: 34% (SP 100%).

The large number of minor corrections concentrating in N3v (3) is clear evidence of the inadvertent skipping of a round of revisions in one of the pages of a proof sheet, which was then erroneously sent back to the pressmen.[22] The other pages of the sheet do not appear to be affected. The SP correction of b5r (5) involves the removal of a fragment of Philoponus's

---

[18] It is worth reminding, here, that the Aldine Aristotle was issued in five parts between 1495 and 1498. The set is considered a single edition by both *GW* and *ISTC* surviving in c. 350 copies, but this figure includes both single parts and entire sets. In light of the near impossibility of reporting the exact number of copies of each part of the set due to catalodraphic inconsistencies, for statistical purposes I will assume here that each part survives in c. 350 copies. Copies examined (part I): **Vienna, ÖNB**; Chantilly, Condé; Paris, BnF (3); Berlin, SB (2); **Munich, BSB**; Lesbos, EHS; Florence, BNCF, Magl. B.3.31; Genoa, Durazzo; Milan, Amb. (7); Milan, Braid.; Milan, Poldi Pezzoli; Milan, Triv.; Rome, Urban.; Leiden, UL (3); Kraków, Jagiellonian; **Madrid, BN**; **Uppsala, UB**; **Zurich, ZB**; Glasgow, UL (2); London, BL (4); Oxford, Bod. (3); **Vatican City, BAV (2)**.

[19] SP+(ER+MS/ST) represents a particularly elaborate combination of corrections: in some copies the error is rectified by stop-press (SP), while in the ones that had already been printed the mistake is erased with a chisel (ER), and then rectified either by pen (MS) or stamp (ST).

[20] On the typographical production of this volume and the whole set of Manutius's Aristoteles see the exceptionally detailed work by Randall McLeod, 'The Invisible Book', *New College Notes*, 14/6, 2021, pp. 1–95. Timothy Perry is responsible for the identification of Philoponus.

[21] Among digitised copies, see Munich, BSB (MS) and Zurich, ZB (SP).

[22] Similar instances are found in Columna (2, 5, 7, 12-14) and Theocritus (2–7).

scholia, «ἐλάττων, ἀεὶ ἀληθής ἐστιν· ἡ δὲ μείζων» that was mistakenly included in Aristotle's text. In copies of *Var. A* Philoponus's words are usually found subpuncted, a common means in Renaissance textual philology to inform the reader that a passage is to be ignored.[23]

Aristoteles, *Opera* II (n. 11)

Sample: 36/350 copies (10%).[24] Three SP interventions.

1) HΘ1r, running title (correction): *Var. A*: «περὶ λίθων»; *Var. B*: «περὶ ἀνέμων». EF: 77% (SP 100%).
2) K1r, foliation & signature (correction): *Var. A*: «73» & «κ»;[25] *Var. B*: «263» & «K». EF: 48% (SP 100%).
3) K2r, foliation & signature (correction): *Var. A*: «74» & «κii»; *Var. B*: «264» & «KKii»;[26] *Var. C*: «264» & «Kii». EF: *Var. A*: 30%; *Var. B*: 3% (SP 100%); *Var. C*: 67% (SP 100%).

The corrections (2, 3) were almost certainly applied at the same time, but then the sheets were mixed, so that at present it is possible to find them in multiple combinations. Leaves 200-30 (B1-EE8) are also interesting for they display a significant number of «z» used as «2» in the foliation, quite clearly an Aldine use of kludging.[27]

Aristoteles, *Opera* III (n. 10)

Sample: 34/350 copies (9%).[28] Eleven interventions: six SP, two SP+MS, one PS+MS, one MS, one MS+ER. MS interventions: Aldus Manutius. Bibliography: Della Rocca de Candal.[29]

1) aaαα8r, foliation (correction): *Var. Y*: unfoliated. *Var: Z*: «10». Neither is correct, but this correction is probably connected to the one below (2). EF: 60% (SP 100%).

---

[23] See 'espungere', in S. Rizzo, *Il lessico filologico degli umanisti*, Rome, 1973, p. 284.

[24] Copies examined (part II): **Vienna, ÖNB**; Chantilly, Condé; Paris, BnF (3); Berlin, SB (3); **Munich, BSB**; Lesbos, EHS; Florence, BNCF, Magl. B.3.32; Genoa, Durazzo; Milan, Amb. (5); Milan, Braid.; Milan, Poldi Pezzoli; Milan, Triv.; Rome, Urban.; **Venice, Marc.**; Leiden, UL; Kraków, Jagiellonian; **Madrid, BN**; **Uppsala, UB**; **Zurich, ZB**; Glasgow, UL (2); London, BL (3); Oxford, Bod. (3); **Vatican City, BAV** (2).

[25] *CIBN* A-504 reports the foliation of one of its copies as being «273», but closer inspection has demonstrated that the initial «2» has been added in black ink by a later hand.

[26] On the existence of 'intermediate' variants, here, in Aristoteles III (6), and in Jamblichus (2) see n. 98 below.

[27] On type kludging see James Misson's contribution in this Companion.

[28] Copies examined (part III): **Vienna, ÖNB**; Chantilly, Condé; Paris, BnF (3); Berlin, SB (2); **Munich, BSB**; Lesbos, EHS; Florence, BNCF, Magl. B.3.33; Florence, Maruc.; Genoa, Durazzo; Milan, Amb. (5); Milan, Braid.; Milan, Poldi Pezzoli; Milan, Triv.; Rome, Urban.; Leiden, UL; Kraków, Jagiellonian; **Zurich, ZB**; Glasgow, UL (2); London, BL (3); Oxford, Bod. (3); **Vatican City, BAV** (2).

[29] See below, under *Psalterium*.

2) **aaaa10r**, foliation, plus last five lines (correction): *Var. A*: unfoliated + «ἀγνώριστα γάρ ἦν //»; *Var. B*: «10» + last line « ἀγνώριστα γάρ ἦν μάλιστα//». Reset of the last five lines to insert the missing «μάλιστα». EF: 73% (SP 100%).[30]

3) **ff̄ζ̄9r**, foliation (correction): *Var. A*: unfoliated; *Var. B*: «49». EF: 97% (SP 100%).

4) **κκ10v**, lower margin (correction): paste slip integration of the missing line and replacement of the catchword (MS in some copies). EF: 89% (PS 91%; MS 9%).[31]

5) **oo̅ξ̄10r**, foliation (correction): «25» > «140». EF: 93% (SP 29%; MS 71%).

6) **γγχχ10r**, foliation (correction): *Var. A*: «112»; *Var. B*: «221»; *Var. C*: «220». EF: 33%. EF: *Var. A*: 50%; *Var. B*: 3% (SP 100%); *Var. C*: 47% (SP 100%).

7) **&&ωω3r**, signature (correction): «&&ωω ιιιι» > «&&ωω ιιι». EF: 96% (MS 92%; ER 8%).

8) **BB2r**, signature (correction): *Var. A*: «ΓΓ2»; *Var. B*: «BB2». EF: 100% (SP 65%; MS 35%).

9) **ΘΘ6r**, foliation (correction): *Var. A*: «13»; *Var. B*: «136». EF: 40% (SP 100%).

10) **KK5r**, signature (correction): «ΙΙ» > «KK». EF: 92% (MS 100%).

11) **XX7v** colophon, line 10 (correction): *Var. A*: «οἰκεία»; *Var. B*: «οἰκία». EF: 71% (SP 100%).

The paste slip on κκ10v (4) integrates a whole line of text gone amiss between gatherings, a correction very similar to the one that appears in the *Psalterium*. Unlike the *Psalterium*, however, in this case most copies have been integrated with a paste slip (sixty-two out of seventy-six copies, at the time of writing), while only a small number are left uncorrected (eight) or have the line added in pen, in Manutius's hand (six), including three copies on vellum.[32] The paste slips exist in at least thirteen different settings, pointing at the fact that, in order to produce the slips more efficiently, a forme was prepared with the same line plus the updated catchword below, repeated all together over and over again, presumably fifteen times (each page of the volume usually bearing thirty lines).

Known *cancellanda/integrantia*: ff̄ζ̄1.10, ff̄ζ̄2.9, AA5.6, and EE1.10: typographical reset of four sheets without textual variants of interest.[33] In the first two instances, the *integrantia* are identifiable as follows: ff̄ζ̄9r, lines 7–8: *Var. A*: « [...] καὶ τὰ//θήλεα [...]»; *Var. B*: « [...] θήλεα//καὶ [...]»; ff̄ζ̄10v, lines 26–7: *Var. A*: « [...] ὁ ἄρ-//ρην [...]»; *Var. B*: « [...] ὁ ἄρ-//ην [...]». In the latter two, the *integrantia* are identifiable by the absence of foliation. EF: 5%.

The gathering **PP**, with an additional sheet, is evidence of a major typographical mishap: the compositors must have skipped a page in their calculations, eventually finding themselves forced to add one extra sheet at the beginning of the gathering in order to include a single missing page (an expensive waste of paper), though in some copies the blank conjugate is now missing.

---

[30] In this passage the text differs in a number of ways from modern editions, which read: "Ἄγνωστα γάρ ἐστι μάλιστα'.

[31] I have examined this particular correction in another article, and the statistics are thus based on 76 copies (c. 22% of the total). See below, under *Psalterium*.

[32] It is likely, however, that manuscript integrations would have been the obvious choice for vellum copies, since paper slips on parchment would have resulted in a somewhat odd effect.

[33] The former two are in Paris, BnF, Rés. Vélins 466; the latter two in Oxford Bod., Auct. 1R 2.9(1).

Aristoteles, *Opera* IV (n. 12)

Sample: 37/350 copies (11%).[34] Two SP interventions.[35]

1) ✠ **2r** (preliminary gathering), signature (correction): *Var. A*: no signature; *Var. B*: « ✠ ». EF: 58% (SP 100%).
2) γγγχχχ**1r**, foliation (correction): *Var. A*: «158»; *Var. B*: «169». EF: 24% (SP 100%).

Aristoteles, *Opera* V (n. 21)

Sample: 30/350 copies (9%).[36] Six SP interventions.[37]

1) ββββ**2r**, signature (correction): *Var. A*: «βββ II»; *Var. B*: «ββββ II». EF: 85% (SP 100%).
2) ζζζζ**7v**, lines 25–9 and catchword (correction): *Var. A*: «[…] κακὸν ἰατρον· καὶ//» + «κακὸν»; *Var. B*: «[…] κακὸν ἰα-//» + «τρόν». Reset (spacing out) of the last five lines after the elimination of the «καὶ κακὸν» in excess from last line. EF: 54% (SP 100%).
3) φφφφ**6r**, foliation (correction): *Var. A*: «100»; *Var. B*: «200». EF: 20% (SP 100%).
4) ωωωω**5r**, foliation (correction): *Var. A*: «217»; *Var. B*: «214». EF: 48% (SP 100%).
5) EEEE**8r**, foliation (correction): *Var. A*: «293»; *Var. B*: «263». EF: 96% (SP 100%).
6) KKKK**6r**, foliation (correction): *Var. A*: «310»; *Var. B*: «311». EF: 92% (SP 100%).

Athenaeus, *Deipnosophistae* (n. 37)

Sample: 1/1 copy (100%).[38] No interventions. Bibliography: Bühler.[39]
Trial page, surviving in a single loose half-sheet, printed on one side only. One wonders why such a specimen would have to be printed in the first place, though; since the setting

---

[34] Copies examined (part IV): **Vienna, ÖNB; Vienna, UB**; Bourges, BM; Paris, BnF (4); **Munich, BSB**; Lesbos, EHS; Florence, BNCF, Magl. B.3.34; Genoa, Durazzo; Milan, Amb. (2); Milan, Braid.; Milan, Poldi Pezzoli; Milan, Triv.; Rome, Urban.; Leiden, UL; Kraków, Jagiellonian (2); **Madrid, BN; Zurich, ZB**; Glasgow, UL (3); London, BL (3); Oxford, Bod. (7); **Vatican City, BAV (2)**.

[35] *CIBN* A-504 also reports a variant setting of the signature at LLLλλλ4r, with a colon mistakenly inserted in the signature («LLLλλλ ii:i»), but the copy that should contain an example of this (Rés. R. 316) does not seem to contain this variant, and I have found no further examples.

[36] Copies examined (part V): **Vienna, ÖNB**; Paris, BnF (5); **Munich, BSB**; Lesbos, EHS; Genoa, Durazzo; Milan, Amb. (3); Milan, Braid.; Milan, Poldi Pezzoli; Milan, Triv.; Rome, Urban.; **Venice, Marc.**; Leiden, UL; **Utrecht, BU**; Kraków, Jagiellonian; **Zurich, ZB**; Glasgow, UL (2); London, BL (3); Oxford, Bod. (2); **Vatican City, BAV (2)**.

[37] In Paris, BnF, Rés. R. 321, the last line of γγγγ7r reads «//Τέλοσ//του//» rather than «//Τέλοσ//του//Γ΄.//», but this is not a variant: the digitised Venice, Marc. copy clearly shows the upper half of the «//Γ΄.//», suggesting that the frisket was out of place. Incidentally, in the same Paris copy the outer forme of δδδδ4.7 is not printed, and the text is supplied by hand. Perhaps this copy was assembled with second-rate sheets. See the similar case of two copies of Lascaris discussed below.

[38] Single known copy: New York, Morgan.

[39] C. F. Bühler, 'Aldus Manutius and the Printing of Athenaeus', *Gutenberg-Jahrbuch*, 30, 1955, pp. 104–6.

and printing of a trial page are not really relevant in the decision of whether to go ahead with a publication (or not), other factors may have been at play.

Bembus, *De Aetna Dialogus* (n. 7)

Sample: 28/37 copies (76%).[40] At least twenty-six interventions: twenty-five MS, one SP. MS interventions: Pietro Bembo + possibly Aldus Manutius. Bibliography: Bühler and Nuvoloni.[41]

1) A1*v*, lines 12/13 (revision): «aemulatio tuorum studiorum Angele//nos non excitare» > «aemulatio tuorum nos studiorum Angele//non excitare». MS «nos» interlineated after «tuorum», though on occasion the printed «nos» after «Angele» is not struck out. EF: 57% (MS 100%).
2) A2*r*, line 8 (correction): «interrogaremus» > «interrogaremur». EF: 89% (MS 100%).
3) A2*r*, line 18 (correction): «ripam» > «ripa». EF: 54% (MS 100%).
4) A4*v*, line 11 (correction): «sibi» > «tibi». EF: 36% (MS 100%).
5) A6*v*, line 21 (correction): «debeamus» > «debebamus». EF: 25% (MS 100%).
6) A8*v*, lines 5/6 (revision): «Socratem modo aut» added after «non»; «modo aut Aristotelem» deleted after «Platonem». As with (1) above, not always the printed «modo aut Aristotelem» is struck out as it should. EF: 39% (MS 100%).
7) B1*r*, line 10 (correction): «es» > «esses». EF: 54% (MS 100%).
8) B1*v*, line 18 (correction): «aquila» > «aquula». EF: 61% (MS 100%).
9) B4*v*, line 19 (correction): «feritate» > «fertilitate». EF: 54% (MS 100%).
10) C8*v*, line 17 (correction): «subiit» > «subit». EF: 43% (MS 100%).
11) D1*r*, line 4 (correction): «inocuparunt» > «inoccuparunt». EF: 37% (MS 100%).
12) D3*v*, line 10 (correction): «natura» > «naturae». EF: 32% (MS 100%).
13) D6*r*, line 8 (revision): «Antinoique» > «Alcinoique». EF: 43% (MS 100%).

A) B2*r*,[42] line 3 (correction): *Var. A*: « qnia »; *Var. B*: « quia ». EF: 57% (SP 100%).
B) D2*v*, line 6 (correction): «usque» > «ususque». EF: 42% (MS 100%).
C) D2*v*, lines 5 and 7 (integration): «meminit Strabo» > «Plinius et Strabo meminere»; «illius» > «illorum». EF: 33% (MS 100%).

[40] Copies examined: I am counting here twenty copies inspected by Bühler, the majority of which I have also inspected myself — Vienna, ÖNB; Paris, BnF (2); **Munich, BSB**; Florence, BNCF, Nenc. inc. 76; Florence, Laur.; Milan, Amb.; Milan, Braid.; Modena, Est.; Rome, Aless.; Venice, Marc. (2); London, BL (4); New York, Morgan (2); New York, Neergaard (now New Haven (CT), Beinecke); San Marino (CA), Huntington — plus Chantilly, Condé; Berlin, SB; **Stuttgart, LB**; Florence, BNCF, Nenc. Ald. 1.1.40; Cambridge, Trin.; Cambridge, UL; Oxford, Bod.; Cambridge (MA), Houghton.

[41] For this entry I have drawn almost entirely upon the works of Bühler and Nuvoloni: C. F. Bühler, 'Manuscript Corrections in the Aldine Edition of Bembo's *De Aetna*', *The Papers of the Bibliographical Society of America*, 45/1, 1951, pp. 136–42; L. Nuvoloni, 'Bembo ritrovato: varianti e correzioni d'autore nel *De Aetna* aldino della University Library di Cambridge', *L'Ellisse*, 6, 2011, pp. 205–10.

[42] Bühler's list contains thirteen corrections, plus three additional ones of which he had become aware at a later stage in his research and thus listed separately and alphabetically. To these latter three I have attached the ten interventions described by Nuvoloni, for a total of twenty-six corrections. Other copies handled directly by Bembo might contain further interventions.

140 PRINTING AND MISPRINTING

D) A7r, line 15 (correction): «itineris» > «itinere». EF: 4% (MS 100%).

E) A7r, line 19 (correction): «sicelidesque» > «sicilidesque». EF: 4% (MS 100%).

F) B6v, lines 8/9 (revision): «fru-//ges» > «segetes». EF: 4% (MS 100%).

G) B6v, lines 21/22 (revision): «quod verbum ab optimo deductum esse credo, quia nisi optimi non vincerent» > whole sentence struck out. EF: 4% (MS 100%).

H) C1r, line 16 (integration): «ut ma//nus» > «ut solo admotae ma//nus». EF: 4% (MS 100%).

I) C2v, line 13 (revision): «et» > «aut». EF: 4% (MS 100%).

J) C7r, lower margin (integration): «neque enim puto huius ignarum rei tamquam dormientem//spectatorem sic te ex eo spectaculo rediisse» to be inserted between lines 14 and 15. EF: 8% (MS 100%).

K) C7r, line 15 (integration): «quidem fieri» > «quidem pater fieri». EF: 4% (MS 100%).

L) D2r, line 14 (correction): «solet» > «solent». EF: 8% (MS 100%).

M) D2r, line 15 (revision): «videntibus» > «inspectantibus». EF: 8% (MS 100%).

The young Bembo was heavily involved in the production of this booklet, so while some of the alterations listed above are corrections of misprints, others are authorial revisions, and on occasion it is hard to draw a clear line between the two. Nuvoloni was the first to realise that the hand in the copy Cambridge, UL, Inc.4.B.3.134[4580], responsible for four textual integrations that do not appear in any of the copies examined by Bühler (but all accepted in later editions), matches Bembo's hand from another manuscript. Other copies have interventions in a hand that may or may not be Manutius's. Further research is required, systematically examining all copies, to ascertain frequency and authorship of these corrections and to better understand, if possible, the relation between author and printer at the press.

Benedictus, *Diaria de Bello Carolino* (n. 9)

Sample: 25/72 copies (35%).[43] Twenty-two interventions: eighteen MS, three SP, one SP+MS. MS interventions: Aldus Manutius. Bibliography: Bühler.[44]

1) a4r, line 11 (revision): «Alph» > «ph^r». EF: 96% (MS 100%).

2) a6r, line 13 (correction): «decreuisse» > «decreuisse?». EF: 92% (MS 100%).

3) a6r, line 16 (correction): «foedera» > «foederae».[45] EF: 87% (MS 100%).

---

[43] Copies examined: I am counting here fifteen copies inspected by Bühler, many of which I have also inspected myself — Paris, BnF; Milan, Amb., Inc.1259; Rome, Cas.; Venice, Marc.; London, BL (2); Baltimore, Walters; Cleveland, AMD (now Bethesda (MD), NLMed); New York, Morgan (2); New York, NYPL; San Marino (CA), Huntington; Washington DC, Congress; Vatican City, BAV (2) — plus Chantilly, Condé; Berlin, SB; **Munich, BSB**; Genoa, Durazzo; Milan, Amb., Inc.910; Milan, Triv.; Oxford, Bod.; Cambridge (MA), Houghton (2).

[44] For this entry, too, I have relied heavily on Bühler's work: C. F. Bühler, 'Stop-Press and Manuscript Corrections in the Aldine Edition of Benedetti's *Diaria de Bello Carolino*', *The Papers of the Bibliographical Society of America*, 43/4, 1949, pp. 365–73.

[45] In the copy Genoa, Durazzo, a wrong correction appears before the word that precedes «foedera», perhaps a result of the seriality of these insertions.

4) **a6v**, line 5 (correction): *Var A*: «golli»; *Var. B*: «galli».[46] EF: 80% (SP 90%; MS 10%).

5) **a8v**, lines 10/11 (correction): «Marci se//sedem» > «Marci//sedem». EF: 84% (MS 100%).

6) **b1r**, line 2 (correction): «Temporariū» > «Teporariū». EF: 80% (MS 100%).

7) **b1r**, line 4 (correction): «adeo» > «à deo». EF: 68% (MS 100%).

8) **b4v**, lines 1–5 (revision): «Gallus interea Senas uenit: & a factiosis ci-//uibus in urbem exceptus est. & arcem occu-//pauit. deinde ad Calendas Iunias Romam//uenit. Amissa opportunitate frustratus intacta//Roma, Pisas venit» > «Gallus interea ad Calendas Iunias Romam uenit. Amissa opportunitate frustratus intacta Roma, Senas uenit: & a factiosis ciuibus in urbem exceptus est. & arcem occupauit. Pisas deinde venit».[47] EF: 80% (MS 100%).

9) **c5v**, line 2 (revision): «Angelo sctī angeli» > «Angelo de scto angelo». EF: 92% (MS 100%).

10) **c7v**, line 14 (correction): *Var. A*: «eneæ»; *Var. B*: «aeneæ». EF: 52% (SP 100%).

11) **d1r**, line 6 (correction): «capte» > «capti». EF: 14% (MS 100%).

12) **d7v**, lines 18/19 (revision): *Var. A*: «statuerunt. Ac ad inces-//sendos à tergo, remorandosq;. Petrum duo-//»; *Var. B*: ««statuerunt: miserūtq; ad//incessendos à tergo, remorandosq; Petrū duo-//». EF: 92% (SP 100%).

13) **d7v**, line 22 (correction): *Var. A*: «præde»; *Var. B*: «prædæ». EF: 92% (SP 100%).

14) **e1r**, line 22 (revision): «Tortonam» > «Dertonam». EF: 92% (MS 100%).

15) **e1r**, line 24 (correction): «soederatis» > «foederatis». EF: 92% (MS 100%).

16) **e6v**, line 12 (correction): «sueuiorum» > «sueuorum». EF: 96% (MS 100%).

17) **g5r**, last line (correction): «diributorium» > «distributorium» (?).[48] EF: 92% (MS 100%).

18) **g6r**, line 13 (correction): «seditionémq» > «seditionéq». EF: 96% (MS 100%).

19) **g7r**, line 15 (correction): *Var. A*: «insigna uiderūt: quæ oppidanis im-//»; *Var. B*: «insignia uiderūt: quæ oppidanis im//». EF: 32% (SP 87%; MS 13%).

20) **h3v**, line 9 (revision): «prætentarūt» > «nunciarunt». EF: 96% (MS 100%).

21) **i1v**, line 13 (correction): «restitueret ac» > «reuocaret restitueretq». EF: 92% (MS 100%).

22) **i2v**, line 1 (correction): «noluerit» > «nolueritis». EF: 92% (MS 100%).

As with Bembo's edition of a few months prior, this early Aldine booklet is riddled with misprints. These have all been carefully recorded and described by Curt Bühler in an excellent article published in 1949, so that there is little for me to add. One point worth mentioning is that, as is the case with Amaseus's *Vaticinium*, one of the surviving copies of this edition is also on vellum (London, BL, C.8.h.14). Unlike the *Vaticinium*, however, the vellum copy of the *Diaria* must have been among the last to be printed, since it contains all the SP corrections (but none of the MS). With regards to the hand, the corrections are too minimal to allow for any attribution to be made with a great degree of confidence, though personally

---

[46] This correction is usually stop-press, but MS in New York, Morgan, PML 365.

[47] The mistake in the order of these lines is probably the consequence of an inversion in the transition to print of two manuscript lines from the printer's copy.

[48] The reading of this correction is uncertain, but it appears in later editions of the *Diaria*, and is cautiously supported by Bühler. Personally, however, I am not fully convinced: the first «u» of «diributorium» is quite clearly deleted and replaced by what appears to be an «i», suggesting that the actual reading might in fact be different.

Bolzanius, *Institutiones* (n. 20)

Sample: 42/131 (31%).[49] No interventions. Three lists of errata: *Var. A*: [C]1r-2v; *Var. B*: ²a1r-2v; *Var. C*: [*]1r-3v.

Three versions of the list of errata are known to exist: (i) *Var. A* ('common'), 2 leaves containing 4 pages of corrections (28 lines per page), found in 29 of the 40 copies examined (73%); (ii) *Var. B* (*Marciana*), 2 leaves containing 4 pages of corrections (35 lines per page), found in three copies (7%), all of which bound either before or after a copy of *Var. A*;[50] (iii) *Var. C* (*Parisina*), 4 leaves containing 6 pages of corrections (37 lines per page), also in three copies (7%), two of which in conjunction with *Var. A* and one alone.[51] Finally, there are five copies with no errata lists (13%).[52] In the first lines of all three variants, the reader is instructed to locate the leaf as indicated in the list, but the specific line of the correction is found counting from the first line of the *opening*: since the edition has twenty-seven lines per page, lines 28–54 are thus found in the actual page indicated in the list, while lines 1–27 are on the verso of the previous leaf (so, for instance, 'e1, line 20' is 'd8, line 20', while 'c1, line 46', is 'c1, line 19'). Several corrections are shared between the three lists, but the 'common' version (*Var. A*), despite being shorter, contains a few errata that do not appear in the other two (e.g., c2.53, e1.20, e5.16, f1.4, g3.2, etc.). Similarly, both *Var. B* and *Var. C* contain corrections that do not appear in *Var. A* (e.g., a4.15, b3.5, c6.27, d3.18, e.6.25, etc.); the difference between *Var. B* and *Var. C* is that the latter contains all the errata listed in *Var. B*, plus several more (e.g., c3.42, c4.40, d2.48, e8.1, f1.17, etc.). It follows that *Var. C* is an improved version of *Var. B*, while *Var. A* appears to be somewhat independent.[53] More research is needed to compare these lists, understand why there are as many as three, what was the point in producing two longer lists for what clearly was a relatively small number of copies, and why *Var. B* and *Var. C* frequently appear in combination with *Var. A*. Some

---

[49] Copies examined: **Vienna, ÖNB**; Bourges, BM; Chantilly, Condé; Paris, BnF (3); Berlin, SB (3); **Munich, BSB**; Florence, BNCF (2); Florence, Laur.; Florence, Maruc.; Genoa, Durazzo; Milan, Amb.; Milan, Braid.; Milan, Poldi Pezzoli; Milan, Triv.; Treviso, BC; Turin, BNU (3); Venice, Marc.; Kraków, Jagiellonian; **Sevilla, BU**; **Basel, UB**; **Zurich, ZB**; London, BL (3); Manchester, JRUL (2); Oxford, Bod. (2); **Boston, PL**; Los Angeles, UCLA; Vatican City, BAV (4); Stallebrass, private collection.

[50] In Venice, Marc., and Berlin, SB, Inc 4490b, *Var. B* is bound after *Var. A*, while in Milan, Triv., it is bound before.

[51] Paris, BnF, Rés. X. 1310, bound after *Var. A*; Manchester, JRUL, 18551 *Var. C* only. Florence, BNCF, Magl. A.5.17, does not contain errata lists, but manuscript emendations in the copy suggest that the reader had access to both *Var. A* and *Var. C*.

[52] The copies without errata lists are Munich, BSB; Milan, Amb.; Turin, BNU (2); Vatican City, BAV, Inc.IV.628. Lists of errata would occasionally be removed when the corrections had been inserted in the text, but if a copy contains no corrections it is hard to tell whether the list was discarded, lost, or in fact never included in the copy in the first place, for whatever reason (not yet produced, misplaced, etc.). To observe some examples of errata corrections copied into the text by readers, see, among digitised copies, Vienna, ÖNB, and Zurich, ZB.

[53] A preliminary examination, based on the first six gatherings (a–f), shows that, out of 88 errata (aggregated between the three lists), 30 are shared between *Vars. A, B, C* (34%), 35 are shared between *Var. B* and *Var. C* only (40%), 5 are unique to *Var. A* (5.5%), and 18 are unique to *Var. C* (20.5%).

help in this direction might come from the sales history of the volume: despite appearing in both the Aldine catalogues of 1498 and 1503, as early as 1499 Erasmus had complained that he had been unable to locate a single copy of the book.[54] Yet in the copy currently in Florence, Marucelliana, there are two inscriptions, both dated 1506, in which the otherwise unknown Angelo Manni from Siena claims to have received the book as a gift from Aldus himself, in whose shop he worked as a proofreader.[55] Thus, somehow, in 1506 a copy was still easily available. Incidentally, this is one of the two only instances of Aldine incunabula known to have been personally donated by Manutius, together with a copy of Politianus, currently in Oxford, Bod.[56]

Catharina Senensis, S., *Epistole* (n. 33)

Sample: 19/179 (11%).[57] No interventions.

Cicero, *Synonyma* [uncertain attribution] (n. 36)

Sample: 4/12 (33%).[58] No interventions.

Columna, *Hypnerotomachia Poliphili* (n. 32)

Sample: 54/261 copies (21%).[59] Sixteen interventions: four resets, ten SP, one ER+ST, one MS+ER+(ER+MS/ST). MS interventions: uncertain. List of errata: F4r. Bibliography: Hofer,

---

[54] Erasmus's letter is mentioned in Renouard, *Annales* (n. 14 above), p. 12.

[55] a1r (title-page): 'Angelj Manni Senen[sis] venetijs 1506 ex officina impressoria aldi manutij'. B9r: 'Aldus manutius donauit angelo man[n]o senen[si] correctori suo anno d[o]m[ini] M°.D°.VI°. Calen[dis] maij venetijs'. Little is known about Angelo Manni, but I am grateful to Sara Centi and Rosa De Pierro who have identified a probable match: a public notary active in Siena between 1529 and 1541. It is not inconceivable that, as a young student, perhaps imbued with humanistic ideals, he worked for some time as a proofreader in the Aldine shop.

[56] See n. 125 below.

[57] Copies examined: Paris, BnF (2); **Munich, BSB**; Bergamo, Mai; **Florence, Acad. Crusca**; Florence, BNCF (2); Milan, Amb.; Milan, Braid.; Milan, Poldi Pezzoli; Milan, Triv. (2); **Rome, Cas.**; **Madrid, BN**; London, BL (3); Oxford, Bod. (2).

[58] Copies examined: **Munich, BSB**; London, BL; New York, Morgan; Vatican City, BAV.

[59] Copies examined: **Vienna, ÖNB**; **Liège, BU**; Chantilly, Condé; **Montpellier, BV**; **Nîmes, BM**; Paris, Arsenal (2); Paris, BnF (4); **Toulouse, BM**; **Berlin, SB** (2); **Munich, BSB**; **Wolfenbüttel, HAB**; **Jerusalem, NLI**; Florence, Ricc., Ed. Rare 69; **Florence, Ridolfi**; Genoa, Durazzo; Lucca, BS; Milan, Amb. (2); Milan, Braid. (2); Milan, Poldi Pezzoli; Milan, Triv. (2); **Venice, Marc.**; Venice, Quer.; **Madrid, BN** (4); **Madrid, RAH**; **Sevilla, BU**; Glasgow, UL; London, BL (4); Oxford, Bod. (2); **Utrecht, UB**; **Boston, PL**; Charlottesville (VA), UVA; **Houston (TX), Menil**; Los Angeles, UCLA; New York, Morgan (2); **Pittsburgh (PA), CMU**; Princeton, Firestone; **Washington DC, Congress**; Lucchini, private collection. In the calculations of expected frequencies and other statistics, I am incorporating part of the copy-specific information gathered from two excellent articles by Neil Harris on the *Hypnerotomachia* (see n. 60 below). Since the overlap between the lists of inspected copies is relatively limited, the overall sample

144   PRINTING AND MISPRINTING

Mardersteig, Harris ('Rising Quadrats'), Harris ('Blind impressions'), Harris ('Un appunto'), Harris ('Nine Reset Sheets').[60]

1) [π]1.4, outer forme (reset): e.g. [π]4v, line 1, *Var A*: «//Andreas Maro Brixianus//»; *Var B*: «//Matthæi Vicecomitis Brix.//». EF: 1%.[61]

2) [π]2v, lines 5, 22, 25 (corrections): three SP emendations inserted simultaneously. Line 5: *Var. A*: «//In labriyntheis»; *Var. B*: «//In labyrintheis»; line 22: *Var. A*: «//Hic hortis»; *Var. B*: «//Hinc hortis»; line 25: *Var. A*: «//Hinc fons»; *Var. B*: «//Hic fons». EF: 58% (SP 100%).

3) [π]4r, line 19 (revision?, <u>only in *Var. B* of correction 1 above</u>): *Var. A*: «//gli mari»; *Var. B*: «//li mari». EF: 1%.

4) a1r (second title-page), line 5 (correction): «SANEQUE» > «SANEQUAM». EF: 93% (100% ER+ST).[62]

5) a1v, lines 17, 21 (corrections):[63] two SP emendations inserted simultaneously. Line 17: *Var. A*: «ingeniofo iuditio»; *Var. B*: «īgeniofo iudicio»; line 21: *Var. A*: «premio [...] talento»; *Var. B*: «præmio [...] talēto». EF: 95% (SP 100%).

rises to approximately 100 copies (I was greatly helped by the fact that, since the publication of Harris's articles between 2002 and 2006, at least twenty-six copies of the *Hypnerotomachia* have been digitised).

[60] P. Hofer, 'Variant Copies of the 1499 Poliphilus', *Bulletin of The New York Public Library*, 36/7, 1932, pp. 475–86; G. Mardersteig, 'Osservazioni tipografiche sul Polifilo nelle edizioni del 1499 e 1545', in *Contributi alla storia del libro italiano: miscellanea in onore di Lamberto Donati*, Florence, 1969, pp. 221–42; N. Harris, 'Rising Quadrats in the Woodcuts of the Aldine *Hypnerotomachia Poliphili* (1499)', *Gutenberg-Jahrbuch*, 77, 2002, pp. 158–67; N. Harris, 'The Blind Impressions in the Aldine *Hypnerotomachia Poliphili* (1499)', *Gutenberg-Jahrbuch*, 79, 2004, pp. 93–146; N. Harris, 'Un appunto per l'identità improbabile del filologo', in P. Botta (ed.), *Filologia dei testi a stampa (area iberica)*, Modena, 2005, pp. 505–16; N. Harris, 'Nine Reset Sheets in the Aldine *Hypnerotomachia Poliphili* (1499)', *Gutenberg-Jahrbuch*, 81, 2006, pp. 245–75.

[61] This unique variant of title-page and preliminary material, currently only found in Berlin, SB, Inc 4508a, is almost certainly a consequence of this being a presentation copy (to Matteo Visconti). I am inclined to believe that it was completed separately and after the other sheets: for instance, the preliminary text by Andrea Marone, usually found on[π]4v, is here transferred to the title-page ([π]1r), yet the lines of Marone's text appear to have been reset. Also, since in Berlin, SB, there are two copies (both digitised), one on paper and one of the three known to exist on vellum, this has led to some confusion: it is worth reminding that the rare variant setting is — counterintuitively — a *paper* copy.

[62] The mistake is not corrected in either of the three vellum copies (Berlin, SB; Chatsworth, Devonshire Coll.; New York, NYPL Spencer Coll.), and at least in one paper copy, Milan, Poldi Pezzoli. In the digitsied copy Vienna, ÖNB, the final 'M' is not stamped in, and in the copy Madrid, RAH, the 'E' is erased but the letters 'AM' are not stamped in. With the exception of the vellum copies, these shortcomings are probably the result of hasty work.

[63] Though listed here as two separate items to ease identification, it is clear that the SP corrections on a1v and a8v (7) were inserted at the same time. Similarly to [π]2v (2), s3v (12), u4v (13) and u5r (14), also in the *Hypnerotomachia*, and to Aristoteles I (3) and Theocritus (2–7), these all appear to be examples of uncorrected proof sheet erroneously sent back to the pressmen (all the more likely when the 'clusters' of corrections appear in conjugate leaves). I am grateful to Neil Harris for making me aware of the SP corrections on a1v and a8v (5, 7), discussed in his article 'Un appunto' (n. 60 above), p. 509–10, and on s3v (12): these latter corrections were not published, but presented at the conference *Il libro antico fra bibliografia e catalogo. Lo stato della questione*: Udine, 10–12 December 2002. I take the opportunity to mention here that the variant «PVELLAE» / «ELLAE», in the woodcut of q3r, is not included in this list because it is not the consequence of a SP correction, bur rather of two letters being pulled out during the printing process. The case is discussed in Harris, 'Rising Quadrats' (n. 60 above), pp. 165–6.

6) **a2.7,** whole sheet (*cancellandum/cancellans*): e.g. a2r, line 20, *Var. A*: «gli dui caballi del//suo Mulo»; *Var. B*: «gli dui caballi del//uehiculo suo cum il Mulo». EF: 99%.[64]

7) **a8r,** lines 2, 3, 5, 16, 18, 30, 32 (corrections): seven SP emendations inserted simultaneously. E.g. line 3, *Var. A*: «Cynnocephalo»; *Var. B*: «Cynocephalo». EF: 95% (SP 100%).

8) **a8v,** catchword (integration): *Var. A*: no catchword; *Var. B*: «piu oltra». EF: 51% (SP 100%).

9) **k6r,** reset of the first 7/8 lines (cause unclear):[65] e.g. line 1, *Var. X*: «dl primo. ImPo//»; *Var. Y*: «dl primo. ImPo//»;[66] *Var. Z*: «del primo. Im//». EF: *Var. X*: 60%; *Var. Y*: 1%; *Var. Z*: 39%.

10) **r3r,** signature (correction): *Var. A*: «qiii»; *Var. B*: «riii». EF: 93% (SP 100%).

11) **n7v,** woodcut (correction): *Var. A*: «//QVEM Q.//»; *Var. B*: «//QVEN Q.//». *Var. A* only seems to appear in vellum copies. EF: 99% (SP 100%).[67]

12) **s3v,** lines 4, 9, 34 (corrections): three SP emendations inserted simultaneously. Line 4: *Var. A*: «uanitate diffundeuasi. Im//»; *Var. B*: «suauitate diffundeuasi. Im//; Line 9: *Var. A*: «//gli fieri»; *Var. B*: «//gli fiori»; Line 34: *Var. A*: «//gli fœlicitāti»; *Var. B*: «//gli fœlici cāti». EF: 77% (SP 100%).

13) **u4v,** lines 9, 10/11, 19, 27 (corrections): five SP emendations inserted simultaneously. E.g. line 9, *Var. A*: «Cydamīo»; *Var. B*: «Cyclamīo». EF: 80% (SP 100%).

14) **u5r,** lines 28, 29 (corrections): three SP emendations inserted simultaneously. E.g. line 28, *Var. A*: «Cydamino»; *Var. B*: «Cyclamīo». EF: 80% (SP 100%).

15) **z6r,** last line (correction): *Var. A*: «sedili diaspre di//»; *Var. B*: «sedili de diasprea//». EF: 34% (SP 100%).

16) **C1r,** signature (correction): «E» > «C». EF: 46% (MS 76%; ER 8%; ER+ST 8%; ER+MS 8%).[68]

Compared to other Aldine incunabula, it is hard to tell whether the *Hypnerotomachia Poliphili* actually went through a more tormented production history or, having received more bibliophilic attention and scholarly scrutiny, this in turn has led to the discovery of a higher-than-average number of imperfections, resets, and *integrantia*. Since Philip Hofer's 1932 article, scholars and collectors have been aware of the presence of a number of major

[64] Evidence that this rare variant precedes rather than follows the common setting — unlike the several *integrantia* of this edition (see below) — comes from the fact that, of the three copies known to exist in large paper, that Harris has shown to have been among the first to be printed, all of them have the *cancellandum*. See Harris, 'Nine Reset Sheets' (n. 60 above), p. 252, n. 16.

[65] Along with a few others in the *Hypnerotomachia*, this sheet was put through the press more than once, though it is not always possible to understand the need to resort to this lengthy and painstaking expedient. Harris, 'Blind impressions' (n. 60 above), pp. 123–8.

[66] There is no visible difference between *Var. X* and *Var. Y*, but there is a difference in the blind impressions, indicating that the variants are three, not two. *Var. Y*, only found in the three known vellum copies, certainly comes after *Var. X*, whereas the position of *Var. Z* is harder to assess. See Harris, 'Blind impressions' (n. 60 above), pp. 124–6.

[67] Interestingly, in a few copies (e.g. Lucca, BS; Utrecht, UB; Houston (TX), Menil) the second leg of the 'M', cut out to correct the mistake, is supplied in manuscript. Although it cannot be excluded that the operation took place at the press, it seems more likely that subsequent readers, confronted with a woodcut letter that appeared incomplete, decided to fix it. It should be noted, in fact, that 'trahit sua quemque voluptas' (Vergil, *Eclogues*, 2.65) is a more common reading compared to the one with 'quenque', prompting a degree of caution with regards to the order of events involved in this correction.

[68] See n. 19 above for more details on a similarly elaborate correction.

resets in the *Hypnerotomachia*, but only recently has their actual nature come to light: most of them are in fact *integrantia*, and not, as originally suggested by Hofer, *cancellanda*. For an updated list and further details regarding these resets and other corrections see Harris, whose work reverses and inevitably supersedes the interpretation furnished by Hofer. The only case of an actual *cancellandum* sheet is a2.7 (4). For a full list of the c. 100 SP corrections contained in the *Hypnerotomachia* — for the most part of little or no textual significance — readers will have to wait for a forthcoming publication by Neil Harris. The copy Minneapolis, IArt, 67.60.56, also contains a faint impression of two fallen sorts (b8*v*). At present this is the single known instance of fallen type among Aldine incunabula together with the Politianus copy Oxford, Bod., Byw. F 4.1 (see below).[69]

Known *cancellanda/integrantia*: b1.8, c3.6, f2.7, s1.8, s2.7, s3.6, u4.5, C2.7, C3.6, F1.4, all *integrantia*. The list that follows is a very synthetic summary of the descriptions of the nine *integrantia* offered by Neil Harris in his very detailed 'Nine reset sheets', plus one (s3.6) of which he has informed me during a private exchange. Anyone with more than a cursory interest in these variants and their meaning is strongly encouraged to refer to Harris's work.

A) **b1.8**: e.g. b1*v*, catchword, *Var A*: no catchword; *Var B*: «Ritorniamo». EF: 3%.
B) **c3.6**: e.g. c3*v*, line 1, *Var A*: «gradatione»; *Var B*: «graditione». EF: 7%.
C) **f2.7**: e.g. f2*r*, line 5, *Var A*: «rotundatione»; *Var B*: «roiundatione». EF: 3%.
D) **s1.8**: e.g. s8*v*, line 1, *Var A*: «Niente»; *Var B*: «niente». EF: 4%.
E) **s2.7**: e.g. s7*v*, lines 3/4, *Var A*: «ſemidiame-//tro»; *Var B*: «ſemediame-//tro». EF: 3%.
F) **s3.6**: e.g. s6*r*, last line, *Var A*: «descripte.cusi»; *Var B*: «descripte,cusi». EF: 2%.
G) **u4.5**: e.g. u4*r*, line 3, *Var A*: «inannulava»; *Var B*: «innanulava». EF: 6%.
H) **C2.7**: e.g. C2*v*, line 1, *Var A*: «Et»; *Var B*: «&». EF: 6%.
I) **C3.6**: e.g. C3*r*, line 1, *Var A*: «Animaaduertissi cautamente,»; *Var B*: «animaaduertissi cautamente». EF: 6%.
J) **F1.4**: e.g. F1*v*, line 5, *Var A*: «DICE»; *Var B*: «DICE,». In this last *integrans* the compositor reset the text but neglected to do the same with the paratext, so that the list of errata and colophon are missing. EF: 4%.

Crastonus, *Lexicon* (n. 19)

Sample: 23/169 copies (14%).[70] Four interventions: three MS, one SP+MS. MS interventions: uncertain.

1) g4*r*, signature (correction): «g iii» > «g iiii». EF: 100% (MS 100%).
2) i3*r*, signature (correction): «i ɪɪ» > «i ɪɪɪ». EF: 100% (MS 100%).
3) M1*r*, signature (correction): «N» > «M». EF: 100% (MS 100%).
4) N4*r*, signature (correction): *Var. A*: «N iii»; *Var. B*: «N iiii». EF: 100% (SP 24%; MS 76%).

---

[69] On fallen type see Claire Bolton's contribution in this Companion.
[70] Copies examined: **Vienna, ÖNB**; **Liège, BU**; Chantilly, Condé; Paris, BnF (3); Berlin, SB; **Jena, ULB**; **Munich, BSB**; Lucca, BS; Milan, Amb.; Milan, Braid.; Milan, Poldi Pezzoli; Milan, Triv.; Turin, BNU.; Venice, Marc. (2); Leiden, UL; Glasgow, UL; London, Wellcome; Oxford, Bod. (2); **Vatican City, BAV**.

Dioscorides, *De Materia Medica* (n. 30)

Sample: 36/106 copies (33%).[71] No interventions.

Some copies contain a gathering ($^2α$) at the end of the volume with additional scholia for Nicander's *Alexipharmaca*, suggesting that the gathering was added at a later stage, when a number of copies had already been sold (EF: 50%). **Proof sheets**: in three of the copies examined (Vienna, ÖNB, Ink 17.D.8; Paris, Mazarine, Inc 1248; Leeuwarden, Tresoar, 1165 Gnk), I have also found proof sheets (one per each volume) with minor corrections to the text, all of which seem to be in Manutius's hand. The Paris copy has corrections only on the inner forme of the conjugate leaves η2.7, while the one in Leeuwarden (incidentally, with Erasmus's ownership inscription) has them only on the outer forme of θ2.7 (Fig. 7.1).[72] Somewhat differently, the Vienna copy only has corrections on the recto and verso of Δ6, but not on its conjugate Δ3 (or there were no mistakes to be corrected there). That these are actual proof sheets and not normal MS corrections becomes evident by combining three arguments: (i) all the other examined copies have these errors typographically corrected; (ii) the corrections are very visible, and have carets and marks on the side of the page to clearly signal their position; (iii) two of the three copies are otherwise perfectly clean (the exception being the copy Paris, Mazarine). I am not aware of the existence of other known proof sheets by Aldus Manutius, and at any rate fifteenth-century proof sheets with corrections are generally considered to be exceedingly rare, as Randall Herz has shown in his chapter of this Companion. The fact that as many as three have been found in just over thirty copies of the Dioscorides can only but raise hopes that more will be found, encouraging a systematic examination of all extant copies. The question remains, however, as to how and why exactly proof sheets ended up in these copies: presumably by mistake, but one also wonders whether perhaps they acted as makeshift *integrantia*. Had, for instance, the print run of a sheet been found to be short of a single copy (e.g., η2.7, θ2.7, and Δ3.6), it is possible that, rather than resetting the whole sheet to produce an *integrans*, a proof sheet was used instead.

Epistolae Diversorum Philosophorum (n. 27)

Sample: 33/302 copies (11%).[73] Two SP interventions.

1) **2r*, signature (integration): *Var. A*: no signature; *Var. B*: «*ii». EF: 71% (SP 100%).
2) Δ2v, line 4 (correction): *Var. A*: «υ ἐννενηϰοστω»; *Var. B*: «ῦ ἐννενηϰοστῶ». EF: 89% (SP 100%).

---

[71] Copies examined: **Vienna, ÖNB**; Chantilly, Condé; Paris, BnF (2); Paris, Mazarine (2); Berlin, SB; **Jena, ULB**; **Munich, BSB**; Athens, Laskaridis; Florence, BNCF; Florence, Laur.; Florence, Maruc.; Florence, Ricc.; Milan, Amb. (3); Milan, Braid.; Rome, Cors.; Venice, Marc. (2); **Leeuwarden, Tresoar**; Leiden, UL (2); Kraków, Jagiellonian; **Madrid, BN**; Salamanca, BU; Edinburgh, UL; London, Wellcome; Oxford, Bod. (3); **Bethesda (MD), NLMed**; **Vatican City, BAV** (4).

[72] I am grateful to Ids de Jong for providing a reproduction of the proof sheet in the copy Leeuwarden, Tresoar.

[73] Copies examined: **Vienna, ÖNB**; Copenhagen, KB; Paris, BnF (4); Heidelberg, UB (2); **Munich, BSB**; Thessaloniki, UL; Dublin, NLI; Florence, BNCF (3); Milan, Amb. (2); Milan, Braid. (2); Milan, Poldi Pezzoli; Milan, Triv.; Turin, BNU (3); Wrocław, BU; **Madrid, BR, I/45**; **Sevilla, BU**; London, Wellcome; Oxford, Bod. (3); **Boston, PL**; Della Rocca de Candal, private collection.

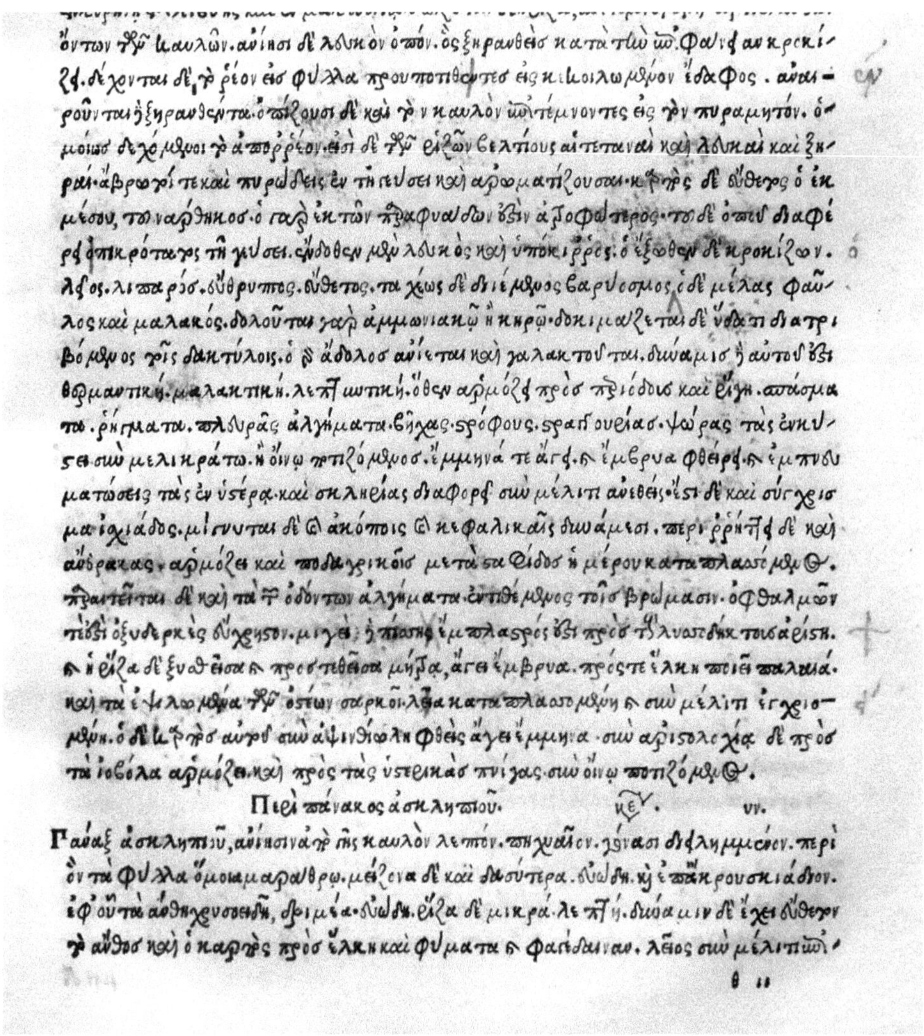

FIG. 7.1. Proof sheet of Dioscorides, *De materia medica* [Greek], Venice, Aldus Manutius, 1499, f°
(ISTC id00260000), sig. θ2r. Leeuwarden, Tresoar, 1165 Gnk.

Firmicus, *Mathesis* (n. 28).

Sample: 39/350 copies (11%).[74] Nine interventions: one reset, three corrections SP only, one
ER+ST, two SP+(ER+ST),[75] one SP+MS, one ER only.

---

[74] Copies examined: **Vienna, FBAstronomie; Vienna, ÖNB; Vienna, UB**; Chantilly, Condé; Paris,
BnF (5); Paris, Mazarine (2); Berlin, SB; **Freiburg, UB; Munich, BSB; Wolfenbüttel, HAB**; Florence,
BNCF, Nenc. Ald. 1.7.7; Florence, Ricc.; Milan, Amb. (5); Milan, Braid.; Milan, Triv.; Turin, BNU; Venice,
Correr; Leiden, UL (3); Wrocław, Ossolineum; **Sevilla, BU**; Glasgow, UL (3); Oxford, Bod. (3); **San
Fernando (CA), Observ.; Vatican City, BAV**.

[75] See n. 19 above for more details on a similarly elaborate correction.

1) *1.6, outer forme reset (revision?): e.g. *1r, last line: *Var. A*: «britanno interp̄te.//»;[76] *Var. B*: «Britanno interprete.//». EF: 95% (SP 100%).

2) ee10r, last two lines (correction): *Var. A*: «aut in ♌ iuba//aut in ♍ fronte»; *Var. B*: «aut in ♍//fronte». EF: 42% (SP 100%).

3) B7r, first and last line (correction): *Var. A*: «//Ternaq; Bissenis quadrate» and «//Quadrati si forte uoles»; *Var. B*: «//Quorum proposito» and «//Aut trinis paribus». EF: 71% (SP 100%).[77]

4) E5r, signature (correction): *Var. A*: «Ev»; *Var. B*: «E [blank space] v». EF: 37% (SP 100%).

5) G1r, signature (correction): *Var. A*: «A»; *Var. B*: «G». EF: 100% (SP 35%; ER+ST 65%).

6) G2r, signature (correction): «Aii» > «Gii». EF: 100% (ER+ST 100%).

7) H1r, signature (correction): *Var. A*: «Bi»; *Var. B*: «H». EF: 100% (SP 43%; ER+ST 57%).

8) I3r, signature (correction): «Eiii» > «Iiii». EF: 100% (ER 100%).

9) S4r, signature (correction): *Var. A*: «Siii»; *Var. B*: «Siiii». EF: 97% (SP 50%; MS 50%).

There is an unusually high concentration of signature corrections in Firmicus. The correction in B7r (3) provides yet another example of how problematic the transition between two leaves (let alone two gatherings, though this is not the case) could be, as seen in at least four other early Aldine editions.[78] A set-off impression of ²N8*v* appears on [π]2r of the vellum copy of Columna's *Hypnerotomachia Poliphili*, Berlin, SB, 4° Inc 4508 (digitised), though it is likely that when the ink transfer took place the vellum sheets had yet to be printed.

Known *cancellanda/integrantia*: in the copy Glasgow, UL, Hunterian Bh.2.2, gatherings * and N (both of six sheets) are entirely reset without textual variants of interest. Distinctive features of these *integrantia* gatherings, labelled *Var. B* (EF: 5% each), are: * gathering, e.g. *2r, last line, *Var. A*: «quod//»; *Var. B*: «quod ego//»; N gathering, e.g. N3r, line 2, *Var. A*: «//Et meditata»; *Var. B*: «//Et mediata».

Fortiguerra, *Lex Neacademiae* (n. 41)

Sample: 1/1 copy (100%).[79] No interventions.

The single extant copy of this document survives in a binding in Vatican City, BAV.

---

[76] At present the only specimen that I have been able to examine of this variant setting is in the copy Wrocław, Ossolineum.

[77] In this particular instance (part of Manilius's *Astronomica*, in verses), the last verse of B6*v* was inadvertently repeated at the top of B7*r*, and consequently the text on B7*r* also ended one verse short. The mistake was corrected by removing the repeated verse at the top and adding the missing one at the bottom.

[78] Aristoteles III (κκ10v: corrected); Benedictus (last line of g1r repeated at the top of g1v: not corrected); Bolzanius (last line of f7r repeated at the top of f7v: not corrected but included in two of the three variant errata lists, B and C); *Psalterium* (11r: corrected; ρ1r: not corrected).

[79] Single known copy: **Vatican City, BAV**.

Frottola nova [uncertain attribution] (n. 40)

Sample: 1/1 copy (100%).[80] No interventions.

Galeomyomachia (n. 1)

Sample: 9/14 copies (64%).[81] Eight interventions:[82] four ER (or MS strokes), four SP. MS interventions: uncertain.

1) a1*r*, lines 4/5 (correction): «παιδεύ//χεσθαι» > «παιδεύ//εσθαι» («χ» erased or struck out). EF: 66% (ER 50%; MS 50%).
2) a1*r*, line 15 (correction): *Var. A*: «δέ»; *Var. B*: «δὲ». EF: 44% (SP 100%).
3) a1*r*, line 20 (correction): «ου» erased or struck out. EF: 22% (ER 100%).
4) a1*v*, line 17 (correction): «ου» erased or struck out.[83] EF: 25% (ER 50%; MS 50%).
5) a2*v*, line 1 (correction): *Var. A*: «//Κρε. Τί τὸν»; *Var. B*: «//Τί τὸν», removal of the redundant name of the character (Κρεΐλλος). EF: 37% (SP 100%).[84]
6) a2*v*, line 6 (correction): *Var. A*: «πεπλησμένοι,//»; *Var. B*: «πεπλησμένοι·//», comma replaced by middle dot. EF: 37% (SP 100%).
7) a3*r*, line 15 (correction): «ἀδελφῆς ἡ ἐλθόντα» > «ἀδελφῆς ἐλθόντα» («ἡ» erased or struck out). EF: 33% (ER 67%; MS 33%).
8) a9*r*, line 5 (correction): *Var. A*: «ἀπεκρύβη·//»; *Var. B*: «ἀπεκρύβη//», removal of a middle dot. EF: 37% (SP 100%).

Compared to Lascaris's *Erotemata*, many copies of this edition have serious typographical flaws, including bad inking and imperfect setting, possibly suggesting that this was the earliest Aldine edition to be printed. This option seems all the more credible considering its length, perfect for a first trial, and the fact that the title does not appear in the 1498 sale catalogue: either the print run was very small, or it was intended for private circulation — or both.

---

[80] Single known copy: **Venice, Marc.**

[81] Copies examined: **Vienna, ÖNB**; Paris, Mazarine; Florence, Laur.; Milan, Triv.; **Venice, Marc.**; Glasgow, UL; London, BL (2); New York, Morgan.

[82] Vienna, ÖNB, has all the corrections (all MS), plus other unique corrections, either fixing minor textual errors or making faulty or badly inked type more legible. Since these corrections do not occur in any other copy, I am inclined to believe that they were made by a particularly attentive reader. I shall list them anyway: a1*v*, ll. 3 and 8; a2*r*, ll. 6, 8 and 14; a3*v*, l. 16; a4*r*, ll. 7 and 9; a4*v*, l. 16; a6*r*, l. 22; a7*v*, l. 4; a8*v*, l. 6. The same reader is probably responsible for adding a stroke in a1*r*, line 20 (2), over the erased «ου».

[83] Vienna, ÖNB, struck out; London, BL, erased.

[84] In the copy Paris, Mazarine, however, the «//Κρε.» has not been removed, but the initial «Κ», markedly risen above the line, suggests that perhaps there was some technical fault at play, rather than an intentional action.

Gaza, *Grammatica Introductiva* (n. 5)

Sample: 61/218 copies (27%).[85] Six interventions: one reset, one replacement of a woodcut capital and decoration, three MS corrections, one SP.[86] MS interventions: Aldus Manutius.

1) a1*v*, page reset (revision?): e.g. line 12, *Var. A*: «seorsum quae [blank space] appellan-tur ab activis pas-//»; *Var. B*: «seorsu[m] quae μεσα appel//». EF: 98%.

2) a1*v*, line 13 (integration, <u>only in *Var. B* above</u>): «πάθη». EF: 100% (MS 100%).

3) a1*v*, third from last line (correction, <u>only in *Var. B* above</u>) «φιλομέναθής» > «φιλομαθής». EF: 100% (MS 100%).

4) a8*v*, line 9 (correction): «τέθειμαι» > «τέθεμαι» correct version added on the margin. EF: 100% (MS 100%).[87]

5) h4*v*, woodcut capital and border-piece (replacement): *Var. A*: 'Λ' with strap-work set; *Var. B*: 'Λ' made out of a woodcut 'A' with leaf-work set. EF: 63% (SP 100%).

6) AA1*r*, signature (correction): *Var. A*: no signature; *Var. B*: «AA». EF: 75% (SP 100%).

The three known MS interventions in this edition (2, 3, 4) are all on the first sheet (a1.8), presumably also the last one to be printed. The one on a8*v* (4) is particularly useful in that it provides an excellent specimen of Manutius's hand. The other two appear in Manutius's Latin preface (a1*v*). It is interesting to observe that the Latin text contains two Greek words, but for neither of these Aldine types were used: the first («μεσα», line 12) employs fonts of the Jensonian family,[88] while the second («πάθη», line 13) is added by hand. An apparently straightforward explanation for this odd occurrence is that by the time the compositors had reached the point in which the first Greek word had to be inserted, they realised that the Latin typeface was shorter than the Greek, and thus the latter would not fit. Since recomposing twelve lines of Latin text for a single Greek word would not have been worth the effort, the decision was made to use sorts from an old Greek typecase, probably belonging to Andreas Torresanus. It is unclear why the same solution was not adopted to add «πάθη» as well, but in this case Manutius intervened personally and inserted the missing word. The two penultimate lines of the preface contain a Greek exhortation by Isocrates, and since here there is no Latin, the Aldine Greeks can finally make their appearance. A different

---

[85] Copies examined: **Vienna, ÖNB**; Bourges, BM; Chantilly, Condé; Paris, BnF (4); Paris, Mazarine (2); Berlin, SB (2); **Jena, ULB; Munich, BSB**; Bergamo, Mai; Florence, BNCF (3); Florence, Laur.; Genoa, Durazzo; Milan, Amb. (6); Milan, Braid.; Milan, Poldi Pezzoli; Milan, Triv.; Rome, Cas.; Turin, BNU (2); Venice, Marc. (2); Leiden, UB (2); Kraków, Jagiellonian; **Uppsala, UB; Zurich, ZB**; Glasgow, UL; London, BL (4); Oxford, Bod. (2); Windsor, Eton; Cambridge (MA), Houghton (3); Dallas (TX), SMU Bridwell; Los Angeles, UCLA; Provo (UT), BYU; Vatican City, BAV (7); Brussels, Arenberg Auctions (lot 1205, auction D3, 12/12/2020); Bortolani, private collection.

[86] Some slight discrepancies in the transcription of the title (a1*r*) among different catalographic descriptions, and in particular at the end of line 3, 'sane quam pulchrum.' (spelled «ſanequāpulchtū.//»), probably encouraged by the presence of a typo ('pulchtum' for 'pulchrum') and by a slightly too liberal use of the term 'variant', has inadvertently led to a bibliographical misunderstanding, but it is worth clarifying that there are in fact no known variant states for this title-page.

[87] In the copy Milan, Ambrosiana, Inc.1189, the correction has been erased and then overwritten by a later hand.

[88] As far as I can tell, this is the only known instance in which Aldus uses Greek types not designed for his own press.

mistake, however, found its way into one of the two lines (3): in place of the sort for «μ», the compositor erroneously used the ligature for «μέν», leading to the misprint being corrected by hand.

The explanation above is however complicated by the existence of a variant setting of Manutius's Latin preface (1) with minor textual variations, presumably representing the earlier of the two states, perhaps a proof sheet, and thus labelled *Var. A*. The variant setting survives in at least one copy, currently in a private collection,[89] but should not be considered a *cancellandum*, since the reset is limited to a single page. It is easy to distinguish it from the common setting (*Var. B*) because in place of both Greek words there are two blank spaces, neither of which is integrated by hand. Similarly, Isocrates' exhortation contains the same mistake (3) as in *Var. B*, and this misprint too is left uncorrected.

The replacement of a woodcut capital on h4v (5) — and, consequently, of a border-piece — may have been caused by damage to the woodcut used originally, a legitimate 'Λ', which came with a strap-work set. The alternative 'Λ' is in fact an 'A' with the central stroke cut out, and appears to have been used here as a makeshift replacement for 'Λ'.[90] For consistency, since the style of this second woodcut is floral, the border-piece was replaced too.

Known *cancellanda/integrantia*: the sheet **AA1.8** appears in two settings without textual variants of interest.[91] Although the rarer of the two settings is probably an *integrans*, the order of priority between the two variants is not certain, so it shall be labelled *Var. Z* (EF: 7%), identifiable by the different arrangement of the first two lines of AA1r: *Var. Y*: «//ΒΊΟΣ ἈΠΟΛΛΩΝΊΟΥ ἈΛΕΞΑΝΔΡΈΩΣ//ΤΟῦ ΓΡΑΜΜΑΤΙΚΟῦ.//»; *Var. Z*: «//ΒΊΟΣ ἈΠΟΛΛΩΝΊΟΥ ἈΛΕΞΑΝΔΡΈΩΣ ΤΟῦ//ΓΡΑΜΜΑΤΙΚΟῦ.//». The signature «AA» (6) always appears in *Var. Z*, and is only occasionally missing in *Var. Y*.

Horae ad Usum Romanum (n. 17)

Sample: 23/33 copies (70%).[92] No interventions. Bibliography: Bühler and Dondi.[93]

Known *cancellanda/integrantia*: the sheet that makes up gathering κ is reset without textual variants of interest.[94] Bühler did not exclude the possibility of this being an *integrans*

---

[89] *BMC*, V, 553–4, reports, rather vaguely, a variant setting, but neither mentions the source of this information, nor describes a specific copy. I am grateful to Paolo Sachet for bringing to my attention the existence of the Bortolani copy.

[90] See James Misson's contribution in this Companion for other examples of woodcut kludges.

[91] I have seen this variant setting in three copies: Vienna, ÖNB, Ink 1.H.158 (digitised); Paris, BnF, Rés. X. 24; Brussels, Arenberg Auction (see above, list of copies).

[92] Copies examined: Chantilly, Condé (A); Paris, BnF (B); Paris, Mazarine (B); Berlin, SB (A); Göttingen, SUB (A); Athens, Gennadius (A); Parma, Pal. (A); Moscow, SL (A); London, BL (A); **Oxford, Bod.** (A); Oxford, Keble (A); Austin (TX), HRHRC (A); Baltimore, Walters (A); Cambridge (MA), Houghton (A); Los Angeles, UCLA (A); New York, Morgan (2: 1 A, 1 B); **Princeton, Firestone** (A); San Marino (CA), Huntington (A); Washington DC, Congress (A); **Vatican City, BAV, Inc.VI.6** (A) and Stamp.Ross.987 (B); Giustiniani, private collection (A).

[93] C. F. Bühler, 'Notes on Two Incunabula Printed by Aldus Manutius', *Papers of the Bibliographical Society of America*, 36, 1942, pp. 18–26; C. Dondi, *Printed Books of Hours from Fifteenth-Century Italy*, Florence, 2016, pp. 415–38.

[94] The existence of a *Var. C*, mentioned in some descriptions, appears to be a catalographic misunderstanding.

but preferred the hypothesis of a *cancellandum*. I, however, am more inclined to believe that this is an *integrans*, and, for the sake of consistency with the other cases of *integrantia* described in this chapter, I have inverted Bühler's labelling of the two states accordingly.[95] At present, having examined over two thirds of the extant copies, and including additional information from Dondi, twenty-five copies are found in the first state (*Var. A*), against four belonging to the later *Var. B* (14%). Identification of the two variants is not difficult: in examining the last word in the first and second line of κ6*r* (a repetition of «Ψαλ//»), *Var. B* is readily identifiable by the use, in both cases, of a capital 'Ψ', while in *Var. A* the capital letter is only used in the second line.

Jamblichus, *De Mysteriis Aegyptiorum, Chaldaeorum, Assyriorum* (n. 16)

Sample: 37/291 (12%).[96] Three interventions: two SP, one SP+MS.[97] MS interventions: uncertain.

1) **a2*r***, signature (correction): *Var. A*: «aiii»; *Var. B*: «aii». EF: 58% (SP 100%).
2) **K1*v***, catchword (correction): *Var. A*: «damnare»; *Var. B*: no catchword;[98] *Var. C*: «neq;». In *Var. A* «damnare» appears to be always struck through. EF: *Var. A*: 42% (MS 100%); *Var. B*: 11% (SP 100%); *Var. C*: 47% (SP 100%).
3) **K2*r***, last line (correction): *Var. A*: «abente//»; *Var. B*: «absente//». EF: 83% (SP 100%).

Lascaris, *Erotemata* (n. 2)

Sample: 29/91 copies (32%).[99] Three SP interventions. List of errata: [D]1*r*-2*r*.

---

[95] I do however appreciate that Bühler's labels are now commonly used in *GW*, *ISTC*, and other resources, and I do not expect this to change.

[96] Copies examined: **Liège, BU**; Bourges, BM (2); Chantilly, Condé; Paris, BnF (3); Paris, Mazarine; **Düsseldorf, ULB**; **Munich, BSB**; Florence, Maruc.; Florence, Ricc.; Milan, Amb. (2); Milan, Braid.; Milan, Poldi Pezzoli; Rome, Cas.; Turin, BNU (6); Venice, Correr; Leiden, UL; **Cordoba, BP**; **Madrid, BN**; **Sevilla, BU**; **Zurich, ZB**; Glasgow, UL; London, BL (2); Oxford, Bod. (3); **Bethesda (MD), NLMed**; Los Angeles, UCLA.

[97] The existence of a variant title-page is cautiously reported by *CIBN* J-147, based on a possible discrepancy with M.-L. Polain, *Catalogue des livres imprimés au quinzième siècle des bibliothèques de Belgique*, Brussels, 4 vols, 1932–1978, III, no. 2236. On lines 13–14 of a1*r*, it is reported, in place of «de platonis difiniti-//onibus·//», one might find «de platonis diffiniti-//onibus·//». But this variant is merely a catalographic misunderstanding, and the title-page of the copy Brussels, KBR, is identical in appearance to all others.

[98] In the copies Milan, Braid., and Cordoba, BP, there is neither «damnare» nor «neq;», and closer inspection confirms that there is no evidence of erasure either. One might speculate that when these particular sheets went under the press «damnare» had already been removed from the forme, but «neq;» had not yet been added. Similar circumstances of 'intermediate' corrections — leading to the existence of three variants — are also visible in Aristoteles II and III.

[99] Copies examined: **Vienna, ÖNB**; Chantilly, Condé; Paris, BnF (2); Berlin, SB (2); **Munich, BSB**; Florence, BNCF (2); Florence, Laur.; Genoa, Durazzo; Milan, Amb.; Milan, Braid.; Milan, Triv.; Turin, BNU; Kraków, Jagiellonian; Uppsala, UL; Glasgow, UL; London, BL (3); Manchester, JRUL (2); Oxford, Bod. (2); Los Angeles, UCLA; Vatican City, BAV (3).

1) **a5r**, last line (correction): *Var. A*: «tenuis//»; *Var. B*: «tenuis A-//». EF: 50% (SP 100%).
2) **a6v**, line 9 (correction): *Var. A*: «Πρώτι»; *Var. B*: «Πρώτη». EF: 59% (SP 100%).
3) **B5r**, last line (revision): *Var. A*: «Et serva haec facere quae odium prohibent.»; *Var. B*: «Et cave haec facere quae odium tenent.». EF: 60% (SP 100%).

Lascaris' *Erotemata* has a list of errata, but at least in one instance (2) one of the misprints is also found corrected by SP. MS corrections found in copies of this editions do not appear to be linked to the press, but only to the activity of diligent readers who transferred the corrections from the errata into the main text.[100]

Known *cancellanda/integrantia*: the sheet that makes up gathering f, of four leaves only, appears in a variant setting without textual variants of interest (EF: 4%). It is unclear whether this is a *cancellandum* or an *integrans*, but the latter seems more likely, and it might therefore be labelled *Var. Z*. Distinctive features of this variant setting are visible on f4v, where the colophon is of fourteen lines, arranged in a cul-de-lampe, and the date is given as 28 February 1495. In *Var. Y*, substantially more common, the colophon is of six lines and the date appears as 28 February 1494, i.e. *more veneto*. A *cancellandum/integrans* is also reported for gathering b in at least one copy (Florence, BNCF, Magl. E.6.18).[101]

Leonicenus, *De Morbo Gallico* (n. 13)

Sample: 24/82 (29%).[102] No interventions. List of errata: [e]1r–v.

Among the copies that I have examined, the list of errata is only present in ten (43%), suggesting either that the list was drawn up when the number of copies in stock was low, or that, in light of the somewhat ephemeral fashion with which this particular list was included (a single leaf), over the centuries some copies ended up being detached from the rest of the volume, and eventually lost.

Leonicenus, *De Tiro seu Vipera* (n. 26)

Sample: 4/8 copies (50%).[103] No interventions.

---

[100] A copy bearing evidence of a reader inserting the corrections listed in the errata is, for instance, Oxford, Bod., Byw. P 1.22. This copy, incidentally, also contains multiple set-offs: '[…] it seems likely that the present copy was put together from remaining second-rate sheets, reflecting a demand for the text at a point when stocks of it were running low.' See *Bod-inc* L-041.

[101] This last copy, however, is unusual in many ways: (i) gathering b is entirely reset with a different Roman typeface (of the R4 family, used c. 1496–1499) and it consists of ten leaves, or two and a half sheets, rather than the usual eight; (ii) gathering c is supplied by hand; (iii) b10v is also supplied by hand. The causes that led to this curious outcome remain obscure and call for further research, but it is quite evident that this incomplete copy was made up, at least in part, while still in the print shop.

[102] Copies examined: Chantilly, Condé; Paris, BnF (2); Berlin, SB; **Jena, ULB; Munich, BSB**; Florence, BNCF; Florence, Laur.; Milan, Amb.; Milan, Braid.; Milan, Triv.; Turin, BNU; Venice, Marc.; **Madrid, BU; Salamanca, BU**; London, BL (3); London, Wellcome (2); Oxford, Bod. (2); **Boston (MA), Countway LMed**; Los Angeles, UCLA.

[103] Copies examined: Florence, Laur.; London, BL; New York, Morgan; **Vatican City, BAV**.

Lucretius, *De Rerum Natura* (n. 34)

Sample: 16/72 copies (22%).[104] No interventions.

Maiolus, *De Gradibus Medicinarum* (n. 15)

Sample: 21/52 (40%).[105] No interventions. List of errata: I1r–2v.

Intended for purchase in conjunction with Maiolus's *Epiphyllides* or independently.[106] This is made clear by the combination of: (i) the errata list, covering both texts; (ii) *De Gradibus Medicinarum* is clearly described as part of *Epiphyllides* in Manutius's catalogue of 1503, the first in which these two texts make an appearance. The errata lists, however, are not very common, and 'are shown by the type, which contains admixtures from 80 Ital., to be considerably later than the rest of the book'.[107]

Maiolus, *Epiphyllides* (n. 14)

Sample: 24/57 (42%).[108] Three SP interventions.[109] List of errata: see above, Maiolus, *De Gradibus Medicinarum*. Bibliography: Labarre.[110]

1) **a1r**, title (revision): *Var. Y*: «//Epiphyllides in dialecticis.//»; *Var. Z*: «//Epiphyllides .i. Botryuncu//li & Racemuli in//dialecticis». EF: 10% (SP 100%).
2) **b1r**, lines 1/2, preface heading (correction): *Var. A*: «//Caput primum. [...] ad cō//stituendum [...] sit opus.//»; *Var. B*: «//Incipit eiusdem Prefatio in opus cuius titulus epiphyllides.//». EF: 18% (SP 100%).
3) **b2r**, line 5 (correction): *Var. A*: «//Incipit eiusdē Prefatio in opus cuius titulus ē epiphyllides//»; *Var. B*: «//Caput primum. [...] ad cō//stituendum [...] sit opus.//». EF: 18% (SP 100%).

---

[104] Copies examined: Paris, BnF; **Munich, BSB**; Milan, Amb.; Milan, Braid.; Milan, Triv.; Venice, Marc.; **Madrid, BN**; London, BL (4); Oxford, Bod. (2); Los Angeles, UCLA; Vatican City, BAV (2).

[105] Copies examined: Chantilly, Condé; Paris, BnF (2); Paris, Mazarine (2); Berlin, SB; **Munich, BSB**; Florence, BNCF; Milan, Amb.; Rome, Cas.; Rome, Cors.; Kraków, Jagiellonian; **Madrid, BU**; **Zaragoza, BU**; London, BL; London, Wellcome; Oxford, Bod.; Bethesda (MD), NLMed; Los Angeles, UCLA; Vatican City, BAV (2).

[106] Having examined 23 copies of *Epiphyllides* and 20 of *De Gradibus Medicinarum*, in eight instances both texts appear in the same volume (Paris, BnF, Rés.R.1439–1440 Paris, Mazarine (2); Milan, Amb.; Rome, Cas.; Oxford, Bod., Auct. 2R 3.6; Vatican City, BAV (2)), suggesting that the majority circulated independently, though some volumes are likely to have been split by collectors or booksellers at a later stage.

[107] *BMC*, V, 557. Of the combined forty-three copies, I have found six errata lists: once after *Epiphyllides* (Munich, BSB, but bound before Averroes), thrice after *De Gradibus Medicinarum* (Paris, BnF, Rés.4°Te148.1; London, BL; Bethesda (MD), NLMed), and twice among the eight volumes in which both texts are bound together (Paris, BnF, Rés.R.1439–1440; Rome, Cas.).

[108] Copies examined: Chantilly, Condé; Paris, BnF (2); Paris, Mazarine (3); Berlin, SB; **Munich, BSB**; Florence, BNCF; Lucca, BS; Milan, Amb.; Milan, Braid. (2); Rome, Cas.; Kraków, Jagiellonian; Lisbon, BN; London, BL; Oxford, Bod. (2); Los Angeles, UCLA (2); Vatican City, BAV (2); London, Christie's (lot 56, auction 10455 15/07/2015).

[109] For these corrections I am reliant on Labarre and his comparison of the two copies in Paris, BnF (*Var. Y*: Rés.p.R.325; *Var. Z*: Rés.R.1439).

[110] A. Labarre, 'Variantes de trois incunables', *Gutenberg-Jahrbuch*, 54, 1979, pp. 96–7.

As shown by Albert Labarre, the stop-press corrections (2, 3) were almost certainly performed together to fix the inversion of the title of the preface (b1r) with that of the first paragraph (b2r). For the title variant (1), aside from being in a different gathering (a1r) and, strictly speaking, not a correction, it is harder to establish priority. But since the less common corrected variants of (2, 3) happen to crop up with the longer and rarer version of the title-page in two out of the three copies in which they appear (Paris, BnF, Rés.R.1439; Los Angeles, UCLA, A 1 M285e), it is plausible that all three represent the second state. As in the edition of Aristophanes, the copies that bear evidence to the first state — which also happen to be the majority, indicating that the stop-press corrections took place fairly late during the printing process — do not appear to have any MS corrections.

Manutius, *Brevissima Introductio ad Litteras Graecas* (n. 18)

Sample: 4/6 copies (66%).[111] Two MS interventions. MS interventions: uncertain, probably Aldus Manutius. Bibliography: Bühler.[112]

1) **a5v**, line 4 (correction): «ὀφελήματα» > «ὀφειλήματα». EF: 100% (MS 100%).
2) **a5v**, last line (correction): «ρῆσαι» > «ρῦσαι». EF: 100% (MS 100%).

In this minuscule volume, probably intended for purchase in conjunction with the *Horae* or independently, there are two minor mistakes on the same page, corrected by pen and ink in all three copies examined, though it is not possible to tell whether this is Manutius's hand or not. The fact, however, that Manutius was also the author of the text makes it somewhat more likely that he was also responsible for the corrections. The first of the two, the addition of the «ι» in «ὀφειλήματα», went unnoticed even to Bühler, who however did spot «ρῦσαι» (2) a few lines below.

Manutius, *Introductio utilissima Hebraice* (n. 35)

Sample: 1/2 copies (50%).[113] No interventions.

Manutius, *Libri Graeci Impressi* (n. 38)

Sample: 2/2 copies (100%).[114] One intervention (MS and ER+MS+ST). MS interventions: Aldus Manutius.

1) Last line of the broadsheet: «venditur Marcello.» > «venditur Marcellis duobus.» EF: 100% (MS 50%; ER+MS+ST 50%).

---

[111] Copies examined: Paris, Mazarine; **Munich, BSB**; New York, Morgan (2).
[112] See n. 93 above, *Horae*.
[113] Copy examined: **Stuttgart, LB**.
[114] Copies examined: **Vienna, ÖNB; Paris, BnF**.

The price of the *Horae* is raised from one to two *marcelli* (or, rather, it was mistakenly set at the wrong price). In the copy Vienna, ÖNB, the correction is in Manutius's hand, while in the copy Paris, BnF, it is obtained by erasing the final «o.», replacing it with a manuscript «is», and then adding a stamped «duobus.».

Musaeus, *Opusculum de Herone et Leandro* (n. 3)

Sample: 26/53 copies (49%).[115] Nine interventions: five MS corrections, three SP+MS, one SP only. List of errata: b1*v*. MS interventions: uncertain, probably Aldus Manutius. Bibliography: Bühler and Speranzi.[116]

1) α1*r*, line 3 (correction): *Var. A*: «παλαίοτατον»; *Var. B*: «παλαιότατον». EF: 92% (SP 4%; MS 96%).
2) α1*r*, line 5 (correction): «ἐντυπησομένοις» > «ἐντυπωσομένοις». EF: 92% (SP 4%; MS 96%).
3) α3*v*, line 14 (correction): «Ὣις ὁι» > «Ὣις ἡ». EF: 88% (MS 100%).
4) α7*v*, line 9 (correction): «Οι μὲν» > «Ἡ μὲν» («Ὁι» occasionally rubbed out). EF: 88% (MS 100%).
5) b2*r*, line: 17 (correction): «inuidiam» > «iniuriam».[117] EF: 100% (MS 100%).
6) b3*r*, line 9 (correction): *Var. A*: «uero oppidū ille Abydi//»; *Var. B*: «ille uero oppidū Abydi//». EF: 100% (SP 43%; MS 57%).
7) b3*r*, signature (correction): *Var. A*: «c»; *Var. B*: «b3». EF: 95% (SP 45%; MS 55%).
8) b9*r*, line 12 (correction): *Var. A*: «Hanc»; *Var. B*: «Haec».[118] EF: 95% (SP 26%; MS 74%).
9) b9*r*, line 19 (correction): *Var. A*: «lirora»; *Var. B*: «littora». EF: 56% (SP 100%).[119]

The volume is designed for the gatherings to be interleaved (α containing the Greek text, b Musurus's Latin translation), but since it is also often found with the Greek text and its Latin translation bound separately (and quite possibly also sold separately), I have listed the corrections by gathering. Once again, the MS corrections are too minor to ascertain their authorship, though in correction (6) of the copy Paris, BnF, the handwriting of «ille» appears, once again, to be Manutius's. The list of errata contained in this volume is not,

[115] Copies examined: I am counting here the fifteen copies inspected by Bühler, most of which I have also inspected myself — Paris, BnF (3); Milan, Amb.; Venice, Marc.; London, BL (2); New York, Morgan (2); San Marino (CA), Huntington; Titusville (PA), Scheide Collection (now Princeton, Firestone); New Haven (CT), Beinecke; Washington DC, Congress; Vatican City, BAV (2) — plus **Vienna, ÖNB**; Chantilly, Condé; Paris, BnF, Mss Rothschild IV.4(bis).31; Paris, Mazarine; Berlin, SB; **Munich, BSB**; Milan, Braid.; **Madrid, BN**; Oxford, Bod. (2); Cambridge (MA), Houghton. Once again, as with Bembus's *De Aetna* and Benedictus's *Diaria*, I am indebted to Bühler's work on this edition, drawing directly from his list of corrections.

[116] C. F. Bühler, 'Aldus Manutius and his First Edition of the Greek Musaeus', *La Bibliofilía*, 52/2, 1950, pp. 123–7; D. Speranzi, 'Intorno all'aldina di Museo', in M. Infelise (ed.), *Aldo Manuzio: la costruzione del mito /Aldus Manutius and the Making of the Myth*, Venice, 2016, pp. 126–41.

[117] The leaf is mistakenly signed «b», but this mistake is not corrected.

[118] The stop-press correction must be fairly rare, since Bühler only seems to have seen MS corrections. One example is found in Oxford, Bod., Auct. 1R 5.13.

[119] This is the only correction for this edition that is not listed by Bühler.

158   PRINTING AND MISPRINTING

strictly speaking, a list: rather, it contains two textual emendations, two distinct lines to be added to the Greek text, with their respective translations, quite likely the result of a collation with a second manuscript witness after the main text had been printed: «οὐδὲ περικτιόνων τις ἐλείπετο τῆμος ἑορτῆς» (v. 49), to be added after «οὐ Λιβάνου θυόεντος ἐνὶ πτερύγεσσι χορεύων» (a3r, line 16), and «δεῦρ᾿ ἴθι μυστιπόλευε γαμήλια θεσμὰ θεαίνης» (v. 142) after «Κύπριδος ὡς ἱέρεια μετέρχεο Κύπριδος ἔργα» (a5v, line 8).

Perottus, *Cornucopiae* (n. 29)

Sample: 12/94 copies (13%).[120] No interventions. List of errata: [5π]4r–v.

Politianus, *Opera* (n. 23)

Sample: 48/332 copies (14%).[121] Four interventions: one MS correction, one SP, two sets of paste slips replacing incorrect running titles (SP correction in one case). MS interventions: uncertain.

1) a1r, title, line 1 (revision): *Var. Y*: «& alia//»; *Var. Z*: «et alia//». EF: 94% (SP 100%).
2) b5r–c2r, running titles (corrections). In two copies (Northampton (MA), Smith College; Vatican City, BAV, Inc.II.153), six incorrect running titles are fixed by means of paste slips.[122] EF: 5% (PS 100%).
3) dd2r, signature (correction): «cc ii» > «dd ii». EF: 100% (MS 100%).
4) Y1or–Z2r, running titles (corrections). In the same copies mentioned above (2), three more incorrect running titles are found corrected with paste slips. In a few other copies, however, these three running titles also display other forms of alteration: in both copies Bergamo, Mai, the incorrect running titles are struck out, and in one of the two (Inc.3.151) the correct titles are added in MS, in a hand that might very cautiously be attributed to Manutius; in the copy Lugano, BC, the incorrect running title on Y1or alone has a SP correction. EF: 11% (SP 20%; MS 40%; PS 40%).[123]

Aside from Aristoteles III, this edition seems to be the only other Aldine incunabulum to make use of paste slips, though in this case their use appears to be very limited. The copy

---

[120] Copies examined: Paris, BnF; **Munich, BSB**; **Florence, BNCF**; Milan, Amb.; Milan, Braid.; Milan, Poldi Pezzoli; **Venice, Marc.**; **Nijmegen, UB**; London, BL (2); Oxford, Bod. (2).

[121] Copies examined: **Rio de Janeiro, BN**; Bourges, BM; Chantilly, Condé; Paris, BnF (5); Paris, Mazarine; Berlin, SB (2); **Munich, BSB**; Bergamo, Mai (2); Florence, BNCF (4); Florence, Maruc.; Genoa, Durazzo; Lucca, BS; Milan, Amb.; Milan, Braid.; Milan, Triv.; Rome, Cas.; Turin, BNU (3); Venice, Marc.; Kraków, Jagiellonian (3); **Santiago, BU**; **Sevilla, BU**; **Lugano, BC**; **Zurich, ZB**; Glasgow, UL (2); London, BL (4); Oxford, Bod. (2); Los Angeles, UCLA; Northampton (MA), Smith College; Vatican City, BAV (2).

[122] I am very grateful to John Lancaster for bringing this correction to my attention.

[123] These percentiles are aggregated, i.e., they represent the occurrence of at least one intervention among the three running titles, as in the case of the SP correction.

Oxford, Bod., Byw. F 4.1, also contains fallen type (b2*v*),[124] while the other copy Oxford, Bod., Auct. 2R 2.18, displays rare evidence of being a gift from Aldus himself.[125]

Known *cancellanda/integrantia*: **V2.5**, *integrans*, without textual variants of interest. The *integrans* is identifiable as follows: V2*r*, line 1, *Var. A*: « […] cutē suo colore roseā red//dit […]»; *Var. B*: « […] cutem suo colore roseā red-//dit […]» (EF 4%).[126]

Psalterium (n. 25)

Sample: 133/136 copies (98%). Two interventions: one SP+MS, one SP. MS interventions: Aldus Manutius + unidentified hand. Bibliography: Della Rocca de Candal.[127]

1) α1*r*, title (revision): *Var. A*: «Ψαλτήριον» (red ink); *Var. B*: «ΨΑΛΤΗΡΙΟΝ» (black ink). EF: 95% (SP 100%).
2) 11*r*, upper margin (correction): addition of a missing line of text. EF: 99% (SP 15%; MS 85%).

I have examined almost all known instances of this particular correction (133 out of 136 copies) and I discuss them in a separate article, in which I have also compared other cases of lines 'lost' between gatherings in early Aldine editions: in particular, another line missing in the *Psalterium* (ρ1*r*) — which however remained undetected and thus uncorrected — and one in Aristoteles III, fixed in most copies by means of a paste slip, are discussed. In the case of the *Psalterium*, 15% of extant copies are typographically recomposed, using a smaller typeface to fit in the missing line, while the remaining corrections are found in three different MS versions: two partial corrections, one by Manutius (11.5%), the other by an unidentified collaborator (8.5%), and the complete correction, only in Manutius's hand, representing the majority of copies (63%). This correction is particularly significant because it sheds light on the single known instance of Manutius working alongside one of his collaborators to correct a mistake.

Reuchlin, *Oratio ad Alexandrum* VI (n. 24)

Sample: 5/5 copies (100%).[128] Two interventions: one MS, one ER. MS interventions: Aldus Manutius.

---

[124] On fallen type see n. 69 above.

[125] α1*r* and L1*r*: 'Liber Conuentus Sanctj marcj d[e] flor[enti]a ord[inis] pred[icatorum]. ex liberalitate Aldj Mannucij Romanj pro quo tenemur orare'. On this copy, see the recent article by P. Scapecchi, 'Aldo e San Marco in un esemplare del Poliziano aldino conservato alla Bodleian Library', *La Bibliofilía*, 123, 2021, pp. 285–90. For the only other Aldine incunabulum known to be a personal gift from Manutius himself, see n. 55 above.

[126] I have only seen *Var. B* in Oxford, Bod., Auct. 2R 2.18. On this *integrans*, *Bod-inc* P-422 reports: 'Sheppard notes that sheet V2 is differently set in type 114 R*'.

[127] G. Della Rocca de Candal, 'Lost in Transition: A Significant Correction in Aldus Manutius's *Psalterion* (1496/98)', *The Library*, 7th ser., 23/2, 2022, pp. 155–79.

[128] Copies examined: Darmstadt, ULB; **Munich, BSB**; Stuttgart, LB; Zurich, ZB; Austin (TX), HRHRC.

1) **a3ν**, line 2 (correction): «qui» > «quasi». EF: 60% (MS 100%).
2) **a12ν**, line 12 (revision): «Dixi,» > erased. EF: 60% (ER 100%).

This edition was perhaps produced on commission and specifically intended for exportation, which would explain why four out of the five surviving copies are today found in Germany. Munich, BSB, and Austin, UL, have neither of the two corrections; Darmstadt, ULB, Stuttgart, LB, and Zurich, ZB, have both. The erasure of «Dixi,» seems intended to avoid the misunderstanding of the colophon (which comes right after) as the date and place where the speech was originally delivered.

Theocritus, *Idyllia* (n. 6)

Sample: 47/202 copies (23%).[129] Seven interventions: one major reset (five sheets), six SP+MS corrections. MS interventions: Aldus Manutius. Bibliography: Sicherl.[130]

1) Z.F1.6, Z.F2.5, θ.G1.6, θ.G2.5, θ.G3.4, five sheets (*cancellanda*/*cancellantia*): e.g. *Var. A*: the *technopaegnion* (poem shaped as an object, in this case a syrinx/pan flute)[131] is on θ.G4ν; *Var. B*: the same poem, framed in this case within a woodcut syrinx, on θ.G6r. EF: 34%.
2) θ.G5r, first column, line 17 (correction, <u>only in *Var. A* above</u>): «//ΦοΦεῖτο» > «//Φοβεῖτο», replacement of «Φ» with «β». EF: 100% (MS 100%, i.e. always corrected in sheets of the first state).
3) θ.G5r, second column, line 21 (correction, <u>only in *Var. A* above</u>): «ἐπιλούσαι//» > «ἐπιλῦσαι//», replacement of «ού» with «ῦ». EF: 100% (MS 100%, i.e. always corrected in sheets of the first state).
4) θ.G5r, second column, line 22 (correction, <u>only in *Var. A* above</u>): «ἐπηκολῦθει//» > «ἐπηκολούθει//», replacement of «ῦ» with «ού». EF: 100% (MS 100%, i.e. always corrected in sheets of the first state).
5) EE.εε6ν, line 3 (correction): *Var. A*: «κικλίζειν·//»; *Var. B*: «κιχλίζειν·//», replacement of «κ» with «χ». EF: 100% (SP 60%; MS 40%).
6) EE.εε6ν, lines 4/5 (correction): *Var. A*: «σφηκὸς και//λισσῶν»; *Var. B*: « σφηκὸς και με//λισσῶν », addition of «με». EF: 100% (SP 60%; MS 40%).
7) EE.εε6ν, lines 18/19 (correction): *Var. A*: «Ἐπὶ ὀρνίθων κακ//άζειν»; *Var. B*: «Ἐπὶ ὀρνίθων κακ//κάζειν», addition of second «κ».[132] EF: 100% (SP 60%; MS 37%; 3% ST).

---

[129] Copies examined: **Vienna, ÖNB**; Chantilly, Condé; Paris, BnF (3); Paris, Mazarine; Rouen, BM; Berlin, SB; **Jena, ULB**; **Munich, BSB**; Florence, BNCF; Florence, Laur.; Florence, Ricc.; Genoa, Durazzo; Milan, Amb. (2); Milan, Braid.; Milan, Poldi Pezzoli; Treviso, BC; Turin, BNU; Venice, Marc.; Leiden, UB; Gdansk, Acad; Kraków, Jagiellonian; Torun, BU; **Madrid, BU**; Edinburgh, NLS; Glasgow, UL; London, BL (8); London, Wellcome; Oxford, Bod. (3); Los Angeles, UCLA; Vatican City, BAV (6).

[130] M. Sicherl, *Griechische Erstausgaben des Aldus Manutius: Druckvorlagen, Stellenwert, kultureller Hintergrund*, Paderborn, 1997, pp. 341–7.

[131] In both variants the poem is dedicated to Pan («Τῷ Πανὶ») and called «Σύριγξ», though in *Var. A* it is also preceded by the title «Ἤχημα Μουσέων ἢ Θεοκρίτου Σύριγξ».

[132] In the copy Vienna, ÖNB, the «κ» appears to be stop-press, but it is more likely to be stamped, and adjoined to the rest of the word by means of a pen stroke.

Five sheets of Theocritus exist in an entirely reset form with substantial textual differences.[133] Based on the analysis of typeface and paper, I surmise that the reset sheets were produced during the second half of 1498. The most plausible explanation for this major change is that after getting hold, presumably in 1498, of a second manuscript witness with superior textual readings (MS Vatican City, Biblioteca Apostolica Vaticana, Vat. Gr. 1379), Manutius became aware of some severe flaws in these two particular gatherings; he therefore decided to replace the sheets in all the copies he still had access to. Since Theocritus was still in Manutius's sale catalogue as late as 1513, one wonders why, then, only one third of copies have the reset sheets: knowing about Manutius's large distribution network, both national and international, it would not be inconceivable to imagine that by late 1498 the majority of copies had already been distributed among booksellers in Italy and abroad.

Interventions (2, 3, 4 and 5, 6, 7), two clusters of three corrections on two distinct pages, suggest that, once again, as in Aristoteles I (3) and Columna (2, 5, 7, 12–14), an uncorrected proof sheet was mistakenly sent back to the pressman. Gathering ZZ.ζζ is more often than not found before AA.αα (and thus after Θ.G) following the order of texts as given in the title (EF: 56%). This might prove of some use towards a better understanding of how early binding processes worked, particularly considering that the book was almost entirely in Greek, and one can hardly imagine that binders in western Europe, except perhaps for a very limited few, were familiar with it, suggesting that buyers must have been actively involved in guiding the work of the binderies.

Known *cancellanda/integrantia*: the sheet δ.d4.5 appears in a second setting without textual variants of interest.[134] Presumably the rarer of the two represents an *integrans*, and should therefore be labelled *Var. B* (EF: 2%). It is identifiable looking at δ.d5v, line 2: *Var. A*: «ἄλλῳ κακὰ τεύχων//»; *Var. B*: «ἄλλῳ κακὰ τεύχ~//».

Thesaurus Cornu Copiae (n. 8)

Sample: 187/193 copies (97%).[135] Sixteen interventions: thirteen MS, three SP.[136] MS interventions: Aldus Manutius. Bibliography: Paolo Sachet's contribution in this Companion.

---

[133] M. Lowry, *The World of Aldus Manutius: Business and Scholarship in Renaissance Venice*, Oxford, 1979, pp. 233–4; Sicherl, *Aldus Manutius* (see n. 130 above), p. 342. Further, *BMC*, V, 554–5, correctly indicates that on Z.F5r (*Var. A*) the text of the idyll is 'interrupted after line 13 «σκέτλιος ... ἀπόλλων», the place of the remainder being taken by line 35-end of the Ἐπιτάφιος Βίωνος, which had already appeared in its right place on E.E2r.' The work (Ἐπιτάφιος Βίωνος) is indeed the same, but the textual variants are too many for this to be a mere copy: it is clear that the two versions of the Ἐπιτάφιος Βίωνος that appear in *Var. A* come either from two distinct manuscripts, or from a single manuscript that already contained the repeated text. This also excludes Lowry's weak conjecture of the intentionality of Manutius's action: 'so he filled out the gap by inserting a section of the earlier "Lament for Bion".' Quite evidently, as Sicherl argues, 'als der Band bereits ausgegeben war, kam Aldus der Vat. Gr. 1379 in die Hände; aus ihm ersah er, daß Μεγάρα 1–13 fälschlich mit Ἐπιτάφιος Βίωνος 35–126 zu einem Gedicht vereinigt war, er diesen aber bereits ganz nach Theokrit 18 gedruckt hatte.'

[134] I have found this variant setting in one copy: Oxford, Bod., Auct. 1R 3.3.

[135] See Sachet's list in appendix to his contribution in this Companion, enlarging the *GW* sample.

[136] In the lower margin of Kκ4v four lines, recovered from an earlier forme and used as bearers, are erroneously inked in a few of copies (EF: 81%).

162 PRINTING AND MISPRINTING

1) **aa3r** (fol. 3r), foliation (correction): *Var. A*: «ζ»; *Var. B*: «3». EF: 34% (SP 100%).

2) **aa6v** (fol. 6v), line 23 (revision): «Λητῷ ※ Λητὶ» > «Λϊτῷ ※ Λϊτὶ»: 84% (MS 100%).

3) **aa6v** (fol. 6v), lines 25-6 (revision): «//Αἰδὼ ὅτε ἐστιν εὐθεῖα, ὀξύνεται· ὡς λητὼ σαπφώ, ὅτε δέ'στιν αἱ//τιατικὴ, περισπᾶται· οἷον αἰδῶ, λητῶ.//» > both lines struck out and replaced with the cross-reference «ζήτει φύλλον 268». EF: 87% (MS 100%).

4) **cγ7r** (fol. 23r), penultimate line (correction): «Αρῶ» > «Αρπῶ». EF: 94% (MS 100%).

5) **lλ2r** (fol. 82r), line 9 (correction): «εἰως» > «εἰς». EF: 94% (MS 100%).

6) **Nν4v** (fol. 100v), last line (correction); *Var. A*: «ἐμηλε»; *Var. B*: «Μέμηλε». EF: 55% (SP 100%).

7) **&ω3r** (fol. 187r), foliation (correction): «191» > «187». EF: 97% (MS 100%).

8) **&ω4r** (fol. 188r), foliation (correction): «192» > «188». EF: 97% (MS 100%).

9) **BB1r** (fol. 197r), last line (correction): «ἀόριστος//»[137] > word struck out at the end of line. EF: 91% (MS 100%).

10) **CΓ3r** (fol. 207r), last line (correction): «μετὰ δὲ ἐτέ//» > words struck out at the end of line. EF: 98% (MS 100%).

11) **DΔ1r** (fol. 213r), foliation (correction): «203» > «213». EF: 93% (MS 100%).

12) **FZ1r** (fol. 227r), line 21 (correction): «ἔΓΚΚΙΤΙΚᾺ» > «ἔΓΚΛΙΤΙΚᾺ». EF: 100% (MS 100%).

13) **GH2v** (fol. 236v), line 16 (correction): «ἀναπεμπταῖον» > «ἀναπεμπτέον». EF: 91% (MS 100%).

14) **GH2v** (fol. 236v), line 21 (correction): «δευκαλίονως» > «δευκαλίωνος». EF: 91% (MS 100%).

15) **GH3r** (fol. 237r), lines 1-2 (revision): *Var. A*: «καὶ κῶοι καὶ πελοποννήσιοι καὶ κρίσκοι καὶ σικελοί; καὶ λίβυες; καὶ οἱ τὴν ἤπειρον λεγουμένην οἰκοῦντες»; *Var. B*: «καὶ κρῆτες καὶ πελοποννήσιοι καὶ σικελοί; καὶ λίβυες; καὶ οἱ τὴν παλαιὰν ἤπειρον οἰκοῦντες». EF: 57% (SP 100%).

16) **GH3r** (fol. 237r), line 6 (correction): «οὕτως» > «οὗτος». EF: 90% (MS 100%).

The edition contains a large number of corrections, of different nature and scattered throughout the whole volume, most of which are manuscript, and apparently all in Manutius's hand — the main one (3) certainly is. For a thorough description of these corrections see Sachet's chapter in this Companion.

Known *cancellanda/integrantia*: i14.5, BB1.8, both are *integrantia* without textual variants of interest. i14.5 (EF: 4%); BB1.8 (EF: 5%). For further details, see Sachet's chapter in this Companion.

Vita S. Josephi [uncertain attribution] (n. 39)

Sample: 1/1 copy (100%).[138] No interventions.

---

[137] The word is heavily abbreviated.
[138] Single known copy: **Paris, BnF**.

BIBLIOGRAPHY

PRIMARY SOURCES

See Table 7.1

SECONDARY LITERATURE

The Aldine Press, Catalogue of the Ahmanson-Murphy Collection of Books by or Relating to the Press in the Library of the University of California, Los Angeles: Incorporating Works Recorded Elsewhere, Berkeley and London, 2001.

Bibliothèque Nationale: Catalogue des Incunables, 2 vols, Paris, 1981–2014.

Bühler, C. F., 'Aldus Manutius and his First Edition of the Greek Musaeus', *La Bibliofilía*, 52/2, 1950, pp. 123–7.

Bühler, C. F., 'Aldus Manutius and the Printing of Athenaeus', *Gutenberg-Jahrbuch*, 30, 1955, pp. 104–6.

Bühler, C. F., 'Manuscript Corrections in the Aldine Edition of Bembo's *De Aetna*', *The Papers of the Bibliographical Society of America*, 45/1, 1951, pp. 136–42.

Bühler, C. F., 'Notes on Two Incunabula Printed by Aldus Manutius', *The Papers of the Bibliographical Society of America*, 36/1, 1942, pp. 18–26.

Bühler, C. F., 'Stop-Press and Manuscript Corrections in the Aldine Edition of Benedetti's *Diaria de Bello Carolino*', *The Papers of the Bibliographical Society of America*, 43/4, 1949, pp. 365–73.

A Catalogue of Books Printed in the Fifteenth Century now in the Bodleian Library, 6 vols, Oxford, 2005.

Catalogue of Books Printed in the XVth Century now in the British Museum [British Library], 13 parts, London, 1963–2007.

Davies, M., and Harris, N., *Aldo Manuzio: l'uomo, l'editore, il mito*, Rome, 2019.

Della Rocca de Candal, G., 'Lost in Transition: A Significant Correction in Aldus Manutius's *Psalterion* (1496/98)', *The Library*, 7th ser., 23/2, 2022, pp. 155–79.

Dondi, C., *Printed Books of Hours from Fifteenth-Century Italy*, Florence, 2016.

Erasmus, *Opera Omnia Desiderii Erasmi Roterodami*, I/3, Amsterdam and London, 1972.

Gesamtkatalog der Wiegendrucke, Stuttgart, 1968–ongoing: https://www.gesamtkatalogderwiegendrucke.de/

Harris, N., 'The Blind Impressions in the Aldine *Hypnerotomachia Poliphili* (1499)', *Gutenberg-Jahrbuch*, 79, 2004, pp. 93–146.

Harris, N., 'Aldo Manuzio, il libro e la moneta', in T. Plebani (ed.), *Aldo al Lettore: viaggio intorno al mondo del libro e della stampa in occasione del V centenario della morte di Aldo Manuzio*, Venice and Milan, 2016, pp. 79–110.

Harris, N., 'Nine Reset Sheets in the Aldine *Hypnerotomachia Poliphili* (1499)', *Gutenberg-Jahrbuch*, 81, 2006, pp. 245–75.

Harris, N., 'Un appunto per l'identità improbabile del filologo', in P. Botta (ed.), *Filologia dei testi a stampa (area iberica)*, Modena, 2005, pp. 505–16.

Harris, N., 'Rising Quadrats in the Woodcuts of the Aldine *Hypnerotomachia Poliphili* (1499)', *Gutenberg-Jahrbuch*, 77, 2002, pp. 158–67.

Hellinga, L., *Texts in Transit: Manuscript to Proof and Print in the Fifteenth Century*, Leiden and Boston, 2014.

Hofer, P., 'Variant Copies of the 1499 Poliphilus', *Bulletin of the New York Public Library*, 36/7, 1932, pp. 475–86.

Incunabula Short Title Catalogue: https://data.cerl.org/istc/_search

Labarre, A., 'Variantes de trois incunables', *Gutenberg-Jahrbuch*, 54, 1979, pp. 96–7.

Lowry, M., *The World of Aldus Manutius: Business and Scholarship in Renaissance Venice*, Oxford, 1979.

McLeod, R., 'The Invisible Book', *New College Notes*, 14/6, 2021, pp. 1–95.

Manutius, A., *The Greek Classics*, ed. N. Wilson, Cambridge (MA), 2016.

Mardersteig, G., 'Osservazioni tipografiche sul Polifilo nelle edizioni del 1499 e 1545', in *Contributi alla storia del libro italiano: miscellanea in onore di Lamberto Donati*, Florence, 1969, pp. 221–42.

Neveu, V., *Catalogues régionaux des incunables des Bibliothèques Publiques de France, XVII: Haute-Normandie*, Geneva, 2005.

Nuvoloni, L., 'Bembo ritrovato: varianti e correzioni d'autore nel *De Aetna* aldino della University Library di Cambridge', *L'Ellisse*, 6, 2011, pp. 205–10.

Polain, M.-L., *Catalogue des livres imprimés au quinzième siècle des bibliothèques de Belgique*, 4 vols, Brussels, 1932–1978.

Renouard, A.-A., *Annales de l'imprimerie des Alde, ou histoire des trois Manuce et de leurs éditions*, Paris, 1834, 3rd edn.

Rizzo, S., *Il lessico filologico degli umanisti*, Rome, 1973.

Scapecchi, P., 'Aldo e San Marco in un esemplare del Poliziano aldino conservato alla Bodleian Library', *La Bibliofilía*, 123, 2021, pp. 285–90.

Sicherl, M., *Griechische Erstausgaben des Aldus Manutius: Druckvorlagen, Stellenwert, kultureller Hintergrund*, Paderborn, 1997.

Speranzi, D., 'Intorno all'aldina di Museo', in M. Infelise (ed.), *Aldo Manuzio: la costruzione del mito/Aldus Manutius and the Making of the Myth*, Venice, 2016, pp. 126–41.

Speranzi, D., 'La scrittura di Aldo e il suo ultimo carattere greco (con uno sconosciuto esemplare di tipografia)', in N. Vacalebre (ed.), *Five Centuries Later. Aldus Manutius: Culture, Typography and Philology*, Florence, 2018, pp. 29–60.

Tosi, P. A., *Notizia di una edizione sconosciuta del poema romanzesco La Spagna colla descrizione di un opuscolo impresso da Aldo Manuzio nell'anno M.CCCC.XCIX*, Milan, 1835.

Vecce, C., 'Aldo e l'invenzione dell'indice', in D. S. Zeidberg (ed.), *Aldus Manutius and Renaissance Culture: Essays in Memory of Franklin D. Murphy: Acts of an International Conference, Venice and Florence, 14–17 June 1994*, Florence, 1998, pp. 109–41.

CHAPTER 8

ALDUS AS PROOFREADER

The Case of the Thesaurus Cornu copiae *(1496)*

PAOLO SACHET

INTRODUCTION

IN the thriving market for the classics across Renaissance Europe, novelty, thoroughness, and elegance all contributed to the lasting success of an edition. At the turn of the fifteenth century, Aldus Manutius was arguably the first printer to combine the three elements, promptly achieving fame throughout the continent. His Greek and Latin publications, featuring many long-awaited *editiones principes*, were marked not only by neat type and mise-en-page, but also by a general aura of correctness, amplified by Aldus's own emphatic statements in the introductory apparatus.[1] By the mid sixteenth century, his care in issuing a sound text had attained legendary status within the circles of scholars and bookmen;[2]

---

[1] Aldus's paratexts are edited in *Aldo Manuzio editore. Dediche, prefazioni, note ai testi*, ed. G. Orlandi, 2 vols, Milan, 1976 and translated into English in A. Manutius, *The Greek Classics*, ed. N. G. Wilson, Cambridge (MA), 2016 and his *Humanism and the Latin Classics*, ed. J. N. Grant, Cambridge (MA), 2017.

[2] E.g., Anton Francesco Doni, *La seconda parte de marmi*, Venice, nell'Accademia Peregrina per Francesco Marcolini, 1552, 4° (USTC 827617), pp. 20–1: 'Sento contar miracoli della sua [of Aldus] liberalità verso gli huomini dotti [...], *dell'infinita diligentia et patientia in volere egli stesso sempre rivedere et correggere le proprie stampe*. Odo dire da gli huomini del medesimo essercitio, fra i quali, per lo più, suole essere sempre invidia, che da che cominciò la stampa de libri non fu mai uno suo pari; et fin che durerà il mondo, ardiscon dire, che non verrà chi lo aguali, non pur chi lo vinca'. ('I hear miraculous accounts of his [Aldus's] generosity towards scholars, of *his infinite diligence and patience in wanting to revise and correct his books himself*. Workers in the same business, among whom jealousy is often the norm, tell me that no one has compared to him since the beginning of printing and they dare say that no one will ever match or outdo him as long as the world lives'.) Emphasis and translation are mine. More concisely, Aldus was hailed as 'ristaurato[r?] d'una corretta e bella stampa, tenendo di molti virtuosi per correzione de' buoni autori' ('restorer of a correct and neat form of printing, employing many erudite men in the emendation of the best authors') in the unpublished *Storia generale* written by Giovan Girolamo de' Rossi between 1557 and 1563 (MS Florence, Private archive of the Perra family, f. [509*v*]); I owe this second quotation to the courtesy of Marcello Simonetta, who is preparing an annotated edition of de' Rossi's monumental work.

Paolo Sachet, *Aldus as Proofreader*. In: *Printing and Misprinting*. Edited by Geri Della Rocca de Candal, Anthony Grafton, and Paolo Sachet, Oxford University Press. © Paolo Sachet (2023). DOI: 10.1093/oso/9780198863045.003.0009 and even outside those circles, the quality of his output rapidly earned proverbial status as a synonym for exactitude, precision, and conformity to high expectations.[3]

Modern criticism has often questioned Aldus's claims of accuracy, which inevitably crumble when judged by current methodological standards.[4] When compared to the significantly lower quality of early Renaissance presses, however, the publication process of the Aldine print shop stood out for high standards and innovative solutions to textual problems. This was due not only to preliminary editorial work and stop-press corrections, but also to Aldus's efforts at post-printing revision. These included what we may call, in today's terms, a final proofreading before shipping the still unbound copies to retailers and customers.

This concluding phase is usually overlooked by bibliographical scholarship, on account of the lack of evidence until errata leaves became common editorial practice over the sixteenth century.[5] Yet, as Geri Della Rocca de Candal has shown in this Companion, Aldus appears to be one of the most consistent correctors of his publications during as well as after printing, and in the early days of his activity this painstaking work left behind a few remarkable traces. A thorough copy-specific analysis of the Aldine Greek *Thesaurus* will show how this neglected and often unspotted group of sources can shed new light on the way in which early modern humanist printers, and Aldus in particular, handled texts on and off the press, implementing different strategies to cope with the numerous mechanical failures and human errors endemic in the hand-press world.

A FEW MISSING ARCHETYPES

In the summer of 1496, Aldus worked hard on issuing a bulky collection of Greek grammatical treatises. Published in August, the book was entitled *Thesaurus Cornu copiae & Hortus Adonidis* to emphasise the abundance and eclectic nature of the information it provided. It fell perfectly in line with Aldus's didactic purpose. Especially at the dawn of his printing enterprise, he published a handful of teaching tools to spread the knowledge of ancient Greek, while slogging away at the *editio princeps* of Aristotle. In this specific case, the target audience embraced advanced learners as well as proficient humanists, since the volume

---

[3] In briefing Cardinal Marcello Cervini on the political situation in Poland on 10 July 1545 (Florence, Archivio di Stato, *Cervini*, vol. 15, fol. 81*r*), the papal nuntio Fabio Mignanelli used the following periphrasis to confess that his premonition had come as true as one of Aldus's books, i.e. 'right as expected': 'Chi teme male indivina facilmente. Questo dico perché quella paura che io havevo [...] *è riuscita stampa d'Aldo* [...].' The emphasis is mine.

[4] See in particular M. Sicherl, *Griechische Erstausgaben des Aldus Manutius: Druckvorlagen, Stellenwert, kultureller Hintergrund*, Padeborn, 1997. For the occasional complaints voiced in Aldus's lifetime, such as those by Urceo Codro in Bologna, see M. Davies, 'Aldo Manuzio, uomo ed editore', in M. Davies and N. Harris, *Aldo Manuzio. L'uomo, l'editore, il mito*, Rome, 2019, pp. 13–53, at pp. 31–2.

[5] S. Lerer, *Error and the Academic Self: The Scholarly Imagination, Medieval to Modern*, New York, 2002, pp. 15–54; A. Blair, 'Errata Lists and the Reader as Corrector', in S. A. Baron, E. N. Lindquist, and E. F. Shevlin (eds), *Agent of Change: Print Culture Studies after Elizabeth L. Eisenstein*, Amherst (MA), 2007, pp. 21–41; as well as the language-based analyses provided by Pavel Sládek and Matthew Day in this Companion.

consists of several lists of mostly poetic and rare words, whose declension, conjugation, and accentuation are minutely analysed, often including dialectal variations.[6]

Work on the project had gone on for some time and seemingly predated the launch of Aldus's business in 1494/1495. Probably exaggerating, in his preface Aldus declared that 1496 was the seventh year of his Herculean efforts at printing Greek.[7] Be that as it may, the inception of the *Thesaurus* can surely be traced back to a leading figure of Italian Renaissance scholarship, Angelo Poliziano, and especially to his teaching of the Greek language in Florence and his interest in Homer. The *Eclogai*, the core of the Aldine edition, which takes up the first 177 numbered leaves, was compiled by two of Poliziano's pupils, Guarino Favorino and the lesser-known Carlo Antinori. Supposedly, they relied on Eustathius's Homer commentaries. In fact, they drew most of their material from a codex that belonged to their teacher: an expanded version of the Byzantine lexicon known as *Etymologicum Simeonis*.[8] Favorino, who did the lion's share of the work, submitted the text of the *Eclogai* to Poliziano and prepared a neat manuscript version of it on parchment with the help of a professional scribe. This he presented to Piero de' Medici, Lorenzo's son, sometime between 1493 and 1494. In this illuminated copy, still held at the Laurenziana Library in Florence, we can read Poliziano's wholehearted consent to publication in print, which was apparently imminent. At the very least, it had been fully planned.[9] The prospective publisher involved at this early stage might have already been Aldus, by then well known as a *grammaticus* in the Venetian milieu and beyond.[10] The other obvious choice, the Greek press established in Florence by Lorenzo Alopa and Janos Lascaris in mid 1494, was almost certainly ruled out

---

[6] Θησαυρὸς, Κέρας Ἀμαλθείας, καὶ κῆποι Ἀδώνιδος. *Thesaurus Cornu copiae & Hortus Adonidis*, Venice, Aldus Manutius, 1496, f° (ISTC it00158000; hereafter *Thesaurus*), esp. Aldus's presentation of the book as a tool to retrieve roots of difficult words whatever their local and poetical variation at sig. *iir–v*. See Davies, 'Aldo Manuzio' (n. 4 above), pp. 26–8, 33–5. For the broader pedagogical context, cf. P. Botley, *Learning Greek in Western Europe, 1396–1529: Grammars, Lexica and Classroom Texts*, Philadelphia, 2010 (with a brief insight into the *Thesaurus* at pp. 84–5) and F. Ciccolella and L. Silvano (eds), *Teachers, Students, and Schools of Greek in the Renaissance*, Leiden and Boston, 2017.

[7] *Thesaurus*, sig. *iir*.

[8] MS Florence, Biblioteca Laurenziana, San Marco 303. See *Etymologicum Symeonis Γ´-E*, ed. D. Baldi, Turnhout, 2013. On Antinori, see *Aldo Manuzio editore* (n. 1 above), II, p. 321, n. 14.

[9] MS Florence, Biblioteca Laurenziana (Bibl. Laur.), Plut. 55.18, fol. 1r–v: 'Ego vero te ut edas quam maxime exhortor [...]. Mitto autem ad te graecum quoque epigramma nostrum [...] ut (si tibi videbitur) in fronte ipsa operis imprimatur.' ('I certainly encourage you to publish it [...]. Furthermore, I send you a Greek epigram of mine [...] so that it can be printed at the beginning of this work, if you deem it worthy.') The letter was also published by Aldus in the *Thesaurus*, sig. *iiiv*. On the accompanying Greek epigrams by Poliziano, Arsenios (Aristoboulos) Apostolios, Scipione Carteromaco, and Aldus himself, see A. Poliziano, *Liber epigrammatum graecorum*, ed. F. Pontani, Rome, 2002, pp. 191–200. On the date of composition of the *Thesaurus*, see G. Ucciardello, '1523. Guarini Favorini *Magnum Dictionarium Graecum*', in C. Bianca et al. (eds), *Le prime edizioni greche a Roma (1510–1526)*, Turnhout, 2017, pp. 171–204 (178, 180).

[10] Davies, 'Aldo Manuzio' (n. 4 above), pp. 14–15, 20–3, as well as A. Scaglione, 'The Humanist as Scholar and Poliziano's Conception of the "Grammaticus"', *Studies in the Renaissance*, 8, 1961, pp. 49–70. Aldus's Latin grammar was published by Andrea Torresano in 1493 (ISTC im00226500), while the Greek grammar he had improved for some twenty years came out posthumously in 1515 (USTC 840308); see R. Black, 'Aldo Manuzio Grammarian' and B. Richardson 'Aldo Manuzio and the Uses of Translation', both in P. D. Accendere and S. U. Baldassari (eds), *Collectanea manutiana. Studi critici su Aldo Manuzio*, Florence, 2017, pp. 69–92 and 145–69, with earlier bibliography.

in light of the recent clash between Poliziano and Lascaris over personal matters as well as the development of Greek studies.[11]

The lavish dedication copy never left the Medici private library, not even during the troubled decades following the collection's confiscation by the Florentine Republic and temporary relocation to Rome in 1508. It thus cannot be regarded as the source text.[12] Another copy of Favorino's work — not necessarily identical to the codex in Laurenziana — somehow arrived on Aldus's desk and was used by the compositor to set the text. Regrettably, this manuscript does not appear to have escaped the fate often met by printers' copies: disposal or reuse as filler for bindings.

Since direct relations between Favorino and Aldus are only attested in 1504, a mediator probably stepped in to facilitate the transition of the *Eclogai* from Florence to Venice. The most likely candidates are Poliziano himself — he had been in touch with Manutius since the early 1480s and met him in Venice in 1491 — and Scipione Carteromaco, another of Poliziano's protégés, who settled in Padua in 1493 and worked at Aldus's side in the preparation of Aristotle's *Organon* for print in late 1495.[13]

It seems likely that Favorino had little or no control over the text which came out of the Aldine press. Until 1496, he was busy teaching at the Florentine *Studium* and apparently he never set foot in Venice.[14] Aldus candidly declared that he and Urbano Bolzanio, both skilled grammarians and Hellenists, had partly reworked the texts, checking sources, cutting and pasting, as though they were its co-authors.[15]

---

[11] Poliziano, *Liber epigrammatum* (n. 9 above), pp. XXIII–XXIV, XLVI–XLVIII. The Alopa-Lascaris partnership was greatly impaired by the fall of the Medici in November 1494 and dissolved two years later: see N. Barker, *Aldus Manutius and the Development of Greek Script and Type in the Fifteenth Century*, 2nd edn, New York, 1992, pp. 39–42, 45.

[12] Cf. the inventory compiled on 20 October 1495 in E. Piccolomini, *Intorno alle condizioni e alle vicende della libreria medicea privata*, Florence, 1875, pp. 66–94, esp. p. 73, and the catalogue drawn in Rome between 1508 and 1510, a copy of which was penned by Favorino himself in his capacity as librarian to Cardinal Giovanni de' Medici. The latter document is discussed in S. Gentile and D. Speranzi, 'Antichi cataloghi. Gli inventari dei manoscritti greci della libreria medicea privata', in P. Degni, P. Eleuteri, and M. Maniaci (eds), *Greek Manuscript Cataloguing: Past, Present, and Future*, Turnhout, 2018, pp. 15–38; see ibid., pp. 20–1 for the peculiar entry related to the *Thesaurus*. MS Florence, Bibl. Laur., Plut. 55.18 seems to be incorrectly described as the archetype of the Aldine edition by Piero Scapecchi in L. Bigliazzi et al. (eds), *Aldo Manuzio tipografo, 1494–1515*, Florence, 1994, p. 35, entry no. 9.

[13] See Davies, 'Aldo Manuzio' (n. 4 above), pp. 20–1, and F. Piovan, 'Forteguerri (Carteromaco), Scipione', in *Dizionario biografico degli Italiani*, XLIX, Rome, 1997, pp. 163–7. A Greek sonnet by Carteromaco forms part of the initial paratext in both the MS Florence, Bibl. Laur., Plut. 55.18, and the *Thesaurus*, with some author's changes in the printed version (Ucciardello, '1523', p. 180, n. 26), while the Aldine edition also shows a Greek letter from Cateromaco to Favorino (*Thesaurus*, sig. *ivv). A hint of Aldus-Favorino lost correspondence can be found in H. Rupprich (ed.), *Der Briefwechsel des Conrad Celtis*, Munich, 1934, p. 569. Poliziano's *Opera omnia*, published in 1498 (ISTC ip00886000), offers a further proof of the close ties between the humanist's most affectionate pupils and Aldus.

[14] Ucciardello, '1523' (n. 13 above), pp. 178–9, provides Favorino's most updated biography.

[15] *Thesaurus*, sig. *iiir: 'Secundus vero labor meus fuit: qui ea omnia recognovi non parvo labore, cum iis conferens, unde excerpta voluminibus fuerant. Multa enim addidi, plurima immutavi adiuvante interdum Urbano divi Francisci fratre optimo [...]' ('The second part of the task was mine; with considerable effort I checked it all by comparison with the sources of the excerpts. I made many additions and innumerable alterations, with intermittent help from Urbano, an excellent Franciscan brother [...]'). The translation is drawn from Wilson, *The Greek Classics* (n. 1 above), p. 33.

In addition to Favorino's *Eclogai*, Aldus explained, he decided to include in his publication eighteen treatises by ancient and Byzantine grammarians, from Herodianus to Eustathius.[16] In the absence of critical editions and systematic analyses, it is even harder to establish the textual sources of these additional parts. Such tracts were scattered throughout the manuscript tradition and appeared sparsely in many *Sammelbände* assembled by fifteenth-century Hellenists.[17] Some appear in a miscellany written by Bolzanio himself, though only further investigation will reveal whether the latter and the Aldine edition are connected, and how.[18]

A SINGLE EDITION AND A
BIBLIOGRAPHICAL GHOST

The Aldine Greek *Thesaurus* has drawn attention for its extracts from Homeric commentaries, the relation with Poliziano, and Aldus's extensive prefatory letter. This contains his announcement of the Aristotle volumes that would appear after the *Organon*, as well as an intriguing discussion on the similarities between the dialects of ancient Greece and those spoken in Italy in the late fifteenth century.[19]

From a bibliographical viewpoint, however, the *Thesaurus* is an untouched treasure, full of hidden gems in the form of unspotted mistakes in and around the text. A well-known mistake, for example, has to do with the alleged second edition issued by Aldus in 1504 with half the number of leaves. Had this edition ever been published, it would probably have contained textual improvements, and could have provided a useful source for textual comparison.

Unfortunately, the notorious 1504 edition is a ghost which has haunted the secondary literature from Zeno and Fabricius in the Enlightenment down to recent contributions.[20] Although no one has seen a copy of it, the *notitia* was uncritically granted credibility because it first appeared in that great milestone of early modern bibliography, Conrad Gessner's

---

[16] Ibid.

[17] Six of them, all devoted to enclitics, were edited by Immanuel Bekker in his *Anecdota Graeca*, III, Berlin, 1821, pp. 1142–58, improving Aldus's text by means of five Parisian manuscript witnesses. In *Grammatici Graeci*, Leipzig, 1823, Karl Wilhelm Dindorf republished Favorino's *Eclogai* (pp. 73–455) and made the unfulfilled promise to edit the other treatises (p. xxiv).

[18] Cf. O. L. Smith, 'Urbano da Belluno and Copenhagen GkS 1965, 4o', *Scriptorium*, 23, 1978, pp. 57–9 and C. Giacomelli, 'Un autografo di frate Urbano Bolzanio, umanista bellunese. Con appunti sulla sua biblioteca greca', *Italia medioevale e umanistica*, 58, 2017, pp. 243–79 (255, 257).

[19] *Aldo Manuzio editore* (n. 1 above), no. VI, and Wilson, *The Greek Classics* (n. 1 above), no. VI. A. Lemke, *Aldus Manutius and his Thesaurus Cornucopiae of 1496*, Syracuse (NY), 1958, provides another translation into English.

[20] See Zeno's review of the 1712 reprint of Favorino's *Magnum Dictionarium* in *Giornale de' letterati d'Italia*, XIX, 1714, pp. 89–129 (102–10, postulating a double-column layout) and J. A. Fabricius, *Bibliotheca graeca*, XIII, Hamburg, 1726, p. 616, up until A. Guida, 'Il *Dictionarium* di Favorino e il *Lexicon Vindobonense*', *Prometheus*, 8, 1982, pp. 264–86 (270). F. O. Mencke, *Historia vitae et in literas meritorum Angeli Politiani*, Leipzig, 1736, p. 510 — also recalled by Pontani in Poliziano, *Liber epigrammatum* (n. 9 above), p. LXXX — had disputed the existence of the 1504 edition, clearly to no avail.

170   PRINTING AND MISPRINTING

Bibliotheca Universalis. Nevertheless, several pieces of evidence suggest that Gessner relied on mistaken information, possibly passed on to him by someone else. First, the Zuricher scholar did not mention the 1496 edition at all. Second, the date 1504 could easily have resulted from a misreading of the Roman numerals in the colophon of the *princeps* at fol. 270r: the form 'M.IIII.D.' used by Aldus was misconstrued as MDIIII. Third, Gessner strangely described the book as made up of 140 leaves, as compared to the 280 of the *princeps*. Gessner's alleged arrangement would have required either squeezing the already dense text into two columns per page, by means of smaller type, or using a format twice as large as the original — a tall folio obtained from chancery sheets, the average copy size being about 315×205 mm. Both solutions would have been highly impractical, if not irrational. Perhaps this mistake sprang from a note that gave the pagination as 280, a figure Gessner halved in order to reach the likely foliation of a book he had never laid eyes on.[21]

Errors tend to be repeated over time. In fact, a copy of the *Thesaurus* allegedly bearing the imprint 1504 was recorded in 1781 by the Jesuit scholar György Pray in his catalogue of the University Library of Buda. He labelled it misleadingly as 'an exceedingly rare book'.[22] This record prompted Theodor Graesse to reinstate the second edition by Aldus, defying the most authoritative Aldine bibliographer of all, Antoine-Augustin Renouard, who had rejected it as imaginary.[23] To untangle the mystery, it seemed worth enquiring at the Budapest University Library. As it happens, their only copy of the *Thesaurus* (Inc605) was part of the first and only print run issued in 1496.[24] In his zeal, Pray too must have misread the date of publication, just as Gessner (or his informant) had done more than two centuries earlier.

---

[21] Conrad Gessner, *Bibliotheca Universalis*, Zurich, Froschauer, 1545, f° (USTC 616753), fol. 622v. Gessner's annotated copy in Zurich, Zentralbibliothek, Dr M 3 does not bear any sign of correction of these factual mistakes, so that we can be fairly certain that they did not stem from misprinting and that the author thought the entry was correct. Intriguingly, at fol. 622r, Gessner also described rather sketchily the *princeps* of Favorino's *Magnum ac perutile dictionarium*, Rome, Zacharias Kallierges, 1523, f° (USTC 828891), providing no date or publisher and only guessing the place of publication ('Romae opinor'); this means he did not check or have access to the Greek colophon of the edition (Favorino, *Magnum dictionarium*, fol. 544r). The *Thesaurus* was also included as the second entry in the catalogue of the Aldine output drawn by Gessner (probably relying on a lost catalogue issued by Paolo Manuzio about 1534) in his *Pandectarum sive partitionum universalium* [...] *libri XXI*, Zurich, Christoph Froschauer, 1548, f° (USTC 682395), fol. 107v; as the list only provides title and format, it cannot be established whether this record stands for the *princeps* or the alleged second edition, though its position just after the first dated book issued by Aldus in 1495 hints towards the first possibility. Josias Simler, in his *Epitome bibliothecae Conradi Gesnero*, Zurich, Christoph Froschauer, 1555, f° (USTC 652948), fol. 177v, referred once again to the *Thesaurus* as printed only in 1504. On Gessner's methodology, see, most recently, F. Sabba, *La Bibliotheca Universalis di Conrad Gesner. Monumento della cultura europea*, Rome, 2012, esp. pp. 153–4, and K. Yukishima, 'Gessner's *Bibliotheca Universalis* and The Aldine Press', in U. B. Leu and P. Opitz (eds), *Conrad Gessner (1516–1565): Die Renaissance der Wissenschaften/The Renaissance of Learning*, Oldenburg, 2019, pp. 29–40. See also P. Nelles, 'Reading and Memory in the Universal Library: Conrad Gessner and the Renaissance Book', in D. Beecher and G. Williams (eds), Ars reminiscendi: *Mind and Memory in Renaissance Culture*, Toronto, 2009, pp. 147–69.

[22] G. Pray, *Index rariorum librorum bibliothecae Universitatis regiae Budensis*, II, Buda, 1791, p. 400: 'Liber admodum rarus.' It should be noted, however, that Pray made extensive use of the category of rarity, using it for most of the ancient books he described.

[23] Cf. J. G. T. Graesse, *Trésor de livres rares et précieux*, VI/2, Dresden, 1867, p. 130, and A.-A. Renouard, *Annales de l'imprimerie des Alde*, Paris, 1834, p. 48, no. 8.

[24] I am grateful to Geri Della Rocca de Candal for checking this copy on my behalf.

METHODOLOGY

The complex editorial history of the *Thesaurus* is not documented by surviving printer's copy or later editions, which could verify — or indeed contradict — the claims that Aldus and his assistants made about the work they performed. Are the details of their efforts doomed to oblivion? Happily, they are not. Evidence resurfacing from extant copies fills much of the gap. As Bühler and Della Rocca de Candal have made clear, copy-specific analysis is the best methodology for studying publishers' corrections in the hand-press period.[25] The presence in more than two or three copies of the same pen marks, often made by the same hand and using the same ink, points to a revision made directly at the print shop.[26]

Digital enhancements in the research tools for incunabula have enabled us to adopt a more systematic approach, which involves investigation of all extant products of the original print run — or almost all. The worldwide lists of copies provided by the *Gesamtkatalog der Wiegendrucke* (GW) and the *Incunabula Short Title Catalogue* (ISTC) are of great help in weighing and organising copy-specific research. For the *Thesaurus*, the task is quite arduous. It entails examining over 175 copies out of a print run that probably amounted, at a cautious estimate, to 500 or more.[27] As is often the case with early modern books, a complete census remains a mirage. Many copies are forever lost, some may be inaccessible for contingent reasons, and others will eventually appear. In the course of my investigation, I was able to add a significant number of hitherto untraced copies to the known ones, and to update the locations of some that had already been recorded. There are now 193 known copies.[28] At present, I have been able to examine 97% of them, in person, online, or through images

[25] See Della Rocca de Candal's contribution in this Companion, esp. pp. 121–3. Other relevant outcomes were highlighted in D. Pearson, 'The Importance of the Copy Census as a Methodology in Book History', in B. Wagner and M. Reed (eds), *Early Printed Books as Material Objects: Proceeding of the Conference Organized by the IFLA Rare Books and Manuscripts Section (Munich, 19–21 August 2009)*, Berlin, 2010, pp. 321–8.

[26] Nevertheless, even in copies of early Greek imprints, it can occasionally happen that one detects some annotations that resemble each other in various copies because they were penned in similar readership contexts, such as classrooms: G. Della Rocca de Candal, Y. Kokkonas, and R. Olocco, 'Experimenting with Greek Typography: The Undated Vicenza Chrysoloras [1477]', *Thesaurismata*, 48, 2018, pp. 97–116 (111–16).

[27] For comparison, see A. Nuovo, *The Book Trade in the Italian Renaissance*, Leiden and Boston, 2013, pp. 99–109, esp. the case of the Greek lexicon *Suidas*, printed in Milan in 1499 (ISTC is00829000), with an overoptimistic print run of 800 copies.

[28] See Table 8.1. As of 10 October 2022, GW lists 172 copies, three of which are said to be in private collections, while ISTC registers 177 copies scattered in 140 holding institutions. From both calculations, one should deduct the alleged fourth copy of the Houghton Library in Harvard, which James Capobianco, reference librarian, confirmed is likely to be a ghost. Of the forty-seven copies described in *Material Evidence in Incunabula*, two are not to be found either in GW or in ISTC: Athens, Laskaridis Foundation, INC040 (MEI 02015126), and Meteora, Varlaam monastery, VARL. INC. 2 (MEI 00201330). By contrast, Vilnius, University Library, Ink. 239 is a copy of another book, incorrectly described in MEI 02014943. All new findings have been communicated to the administrators of the three databases, along with a few improvements. The alleged copy 2 Inc.s.a. 5017-2#Tafel 80, consisting of a single leaf and described in the online catalogue of the incunables held in Munich, Bayerische Staatsbibliothek (BSB), is in fact a cataloguing mistake: https://inkunabeln.digitale-sammlungen.de/Ausgabe_T-159.html, accessed 10 October 2022.

172 PRINTING AND MISPRINTING

kindly supplied by institutions and colleagues.[29] The very consistent data they contain yields some reasonably well-grounded observations.

Mistakes and Corrections

In attempting to elucidate the causes of textual failure and strategies to cope with it, we should bear in mind that fifteenth-century printed books in folio format did not result from a linear process of composition. Their gatherings were most usually made up not by simply folding a printed sheet into two leaves, but by assembling two or more folded printed sheets to obtain groups of four, six, eight, ten, or twelve leaves. We can take as an example a gathering of eight leaves (henceforth A), like most of those that comprise the *Thesaurus*. A could not have been set up leaf after leaf (A1, A2, A3, A4, A5, A6, A7, A8), because in folios the forme allows for two leaves per sheet, or better two pages per sheet-side. Similarly, printing sheet by sheet with consecutive couples of conjugate leaves (1–2, 3–4, 5–6, 7–8) would have produced a disordered text after each of the four sheets was folded and inserted into the following one to form the gathering. In the best-case scenario, leaves in A would have been (mis)arranged in this series: 1, 3, 5, 7–8, 6, 4, 2. To obtain a tidy gathering, Aldus's compositors set the formes normally from the outer to the inner, in the following order: 1r–8v and 1v–8r; 2r–7v and 2v–7r; 3r–6v and 3v–6r; 4r–5v and 4v–5r. In our example, it is only in the final combination (4v–5r) that the sequences of text and typesetting coincide. The way in which the text appeared in the copy and in the printed gathering differed completely from that adopted for the formes by the compositor, who, we should remember, also had to set the text from right to left.[30]

What we knew (plus an additional reset)

It is time to take a closer look at the *Thesaurus* in search of corrections that attest various forms of effective proofreading throughout the printing process. In each case, I shall try to unveil the reason for the mistakes, the methods used to correct them, and the stage at which the text was emended. Two mistakes corrected by hand were first described in *BMC*,

---

[29] The list of helpers to which I am most indebted would be too long to be reported here. In the light of their continuous engagement, I am particularly grateful to Anthony Grafton and to eight fellow book lovers, Geri Della Rocca de Candal, Madeline McMahon, Lorenzo Coccoli, Sam Kennerley, Shanti Graheli, Claudia Daniotti, Anna Gialdini and Laura Nuvoloni.

[30] The detailed register of the *Thesaurus* at fols 269r–270r outlines the book structure; instead of providing binders and readers with catchwords from one gathering to another, it lists incipits of the leaves that make up the first half of each gathering, except the preliminary *10. Between the 1490s and early 1500s, Aldus is thought to have used up to six two-pull presses, employing about fifteen pressmen: M. Lowry, *The World of Aldus Manutius: Business and Scholarship in Renaissance Venice*, Oxford, 1979, p. 95. On the difference between one- and two-pull machinery, see L. Hellinga, *Text in Transit: Manuscript to Proof and Print in the Fifteenth Century*, Leiden and Boston, 2014, pp. 13–17.

as a result of comparing the four copies currently in London, British Library.[31] At fol. 197r, line 30, the final heavily abbreviated word ἀόριστος (aorist) is crossed out, since the passage examines the active, middle, and passive forms of the verb ἐγείρω (to rouse) in the perfect tense, not aorist.[32] This mistake could have been in the manuscript copy used for this treatise, but it could also have resulted from an error made by the compositor while he was about to complete the set-up of the page.

At fol. 207r, l. 30, the final two words and part of a third (μετὰ δὲ ἐτέ[-]) are struck out. Here, the compositor's eye seems to have skipped a line in reading the archetype, tricked by the close repetition of ὀξύνονται, a form of the verb ὀξύνω (to sharpen or, in a grammatical context, to take the acute accent). The misprint may be classified as an incipient case of *saut du même au même* due to haplography, the full consequences of which the compositor managed to avoid. In setting fol. 207v (after he had laid out the conjugate page of 207r, i.e. 210v), he went back to the correct reading and inserted the three words (μετὰ δὲ ἑτέρας) at the beginning of line 2.

The incidence of both manuscript corrections is extremely high: the first appears in nearly 91% of the inspected copies, the second in all but three of them.[33] Their prevalence indicates that these errors were identified after the leaves had gone through the press. On account of their similarity and proximity in the text, we might speculate that they were emended roughly at the same time, presumably when assembling the two gatherings in question (BB and CΓ) made the fault more apparent, or even at a later stage, when the whole book was once again proofread.

In this light, it is noteworthy that the slightly lower frequency of the correction at fol. 197r is connected, in half of the instances, to the presence of a reset of the whole sheet. The reset text does not bear any sign of correction, but shows countless variations in characters (allographs), with no effect on meaning and a negligible impact on the line length.[34] Such

---

[31] *Catalogue of Books Printed in the XVth Century now in the British Museum*, V: *Venice*, London, 1924, p. 555. The shelfmarks of the BL copies are: IB.24415; IB.24416;C.15.c.11; and G.7630.

[32] Thus, the right abbreviation should here be that for παρακείμενος (perfect), which can take up roughly the same small amount of space as that of ἀόριστος. Since the earlier sentence does have παρακείμενος as subject, however, there was no need to repeat it, while the pending article ὁ could easily have been linked to the following abbreviated adjective μέσος at the beginning of fol. 197v and regarded as a demonstrative pronoun: 'the middle one' instead of 'the middle perfect'.

[33] Chatsworth, Devonshire Collection (DC), Dev/002804, in which intrusive whitewashing may have erased traces of this and other printer's corrections (see Table 8.1); Florence, Biblioteca Marucelliana, R.A.631, where other relevant manuscript emendations discussed hereafter do not appear; and Saint Petersburg, National Library of Russia, 8.10.1.4.

[34] Changes concern especially the letters β, π, γ, σ, μ, η, ω, as well as the many ligatures and abbreviations. The only minor variations in text, from the more common variant to the reset, are: fol. 197r, l. 8: λέλειφα into λέλοιφα, λέλοιβα into λέλειβα, both presumptive second perfect forms of the Homeric verb λείβω (to pour); ibid., l. 11: ὠφέλικα correctly into ὠφέληκα; fol. 204v, l. 26: ἕκαστος into ἕκαστο, probably due to poor inking. No discernible patterns in graphic choice can back the suggestive hypothesis that the two formes stemmed from two different compositors with different graphic habits. On the eclectic features of Aldus's Greek types, see Aldus's *vade mecum* in appendix to Constantinus Lascaris, *Erotemata*, Venice, Aldus Manutius, 28 Feb. 1494/1495 and 8 Mar. 1495, 4° (ISTC il00068000), sigs A1r–B1r, with allographs at sig. A2r, as well as D. Baldi, 'Aldo Manuzio e le peculiarità greche: le abbreviazioni', in G. Comiati (ed.), *Aldo Manuzio editore, umanista e filologo*, Milan, 2019, pp. 119–50; a comparative picture is offered by W. H. Ingram, 'The Ligatures of Early Printed Greek', *Greek, Roman and Byzantine Studies*, 7/4, 1966, pp. 371–89. The rare variant was first recorded in M.-L. Polain, *Catalogue des*

174   PRINTING AND MISPRINTING

crucial elements imply that no stop-press procedures were used. Rather, the forme was reset anew as an *integrans* to supply a few copies of this sheet. Presumably they had turned out to be missing from the original print run when gatherings were put together. Yet, this must have happened slightly after the final word of fol. 197*r* had been emended manually in the original print run. Copies with the *integrans* do not show the handwritten correction. Moreover, they are also marred by a new, appalling error in foliation which can be seen at fol. 204*r*, numbered as '4'. Since, however, eight copies lack both correction and reset, we need to accept the possibility that some leaves in the pile of the sheet 197+204 were accidentally left uncorrected. In one of these uncorrected copies, now held in the Corsiniana Library in Rome (56.H.15), a trained eye can spot an intriguing array of blind-printed types in the margin of the previous page (fol. 196*v*). This deserves further investigation. It may or may not account for an exceptional composition.

A handful of copies bear another hitherto unknown case of *integrantia* at the sheet 68+69. Here, too, no significant textual error was emended, while nearly every word was written with alternative characters, a fact that strongly suggests the compositor worked on it after the original forme had long been dismantled.[35] Additionally, we could infer that the printer's copy was not followed obsequiously where graphic variants were concerned. Aldus's compositors were skilled enough to harness allographs, ligatures, and abbreviations as they needed or even pleased, just as professional scribes did.

One last reset at fol. 76*v*, well known to earlier scholars, provides further insight into the compositor's pace in relation to printing and proofreading processes.[36] The page in question closes the section of Favorino's *Eclogai* devoted to the letter *eta*. Its text should end at l. 24, with a substantial amount of blank space afterwards. Yet, in three-quarters of the extant copies, four anomalous lines materialised in the lower margin as ll. 27–30. Altogether, they make little sense, but there seems to be a thread. In fact, they correspond to ll. 26, 28–30 of fol. 74*v*, here misarranged as ll. 28–30, 26. The mistake resulted from how large blank areas were commonly handled. Together with wooden spacing material, a few text lines were inserted at the end of the forme to tighten it up and balance the pressure of the platen. Known as bearer type, these were never intended to appear on the page. In our case, the compositor borrowed four lines from the closest forme at hand, that is, the one that comprised the conjugate pages 74*v* and 79*r* and was in the process of being dismantled after

---

livres imprimés au quinzième siècle des bibliothèques de Belgique, 5 vols, Bruxelles, 1932–1978, no. 3687. For a kindred explanation of post-production resets, see G. Della Rocca de Candal in this Companion, pp. 137, 145–7, 149, 152–5, 159, 161–2.

[35] Textual departures from the more common variant to the reset version are the following: fol. 68*r*, l. 24: ποικίλλεται incorrectly into ποικίλεται; fol. 68*v*, l. 30: με correctly into με-; fol. 69*r*, l. 9: οἷον incorrectly into οἰον; ibid., l. 10: οἷον incorrectly into οιο; ibid., l. 15: οἷον incorrectly into οἷον; fol. 69*v*, l. 9: ἤδειν into ἴδειν; ibid., l. 14: ἐπεκτάσει into ἐκτάσει, the two words being practically synonyms; ibid., l. 27 τὸ into καὶ. The three changes at fol. 69*r*, concerning the same word, may be the unwanted outcome of a combination of worn types and poor inking. Misalignment in the reset, denoting a certain hastiness in the operation, can be seen at: fol. 68*r*, l. 27: the *alpha* in κα-; fol. 68*v*, l. 20: the πο in ποιοῦσιν; fol. 69*r*, l. 14: the final dash. Foliation at the top of the reset fols 68*r* and 69*r* also suffered of misalignment, resulting in the shave of the upper part of digits. By contrast, fol. 68*v*, l. 8 in common variant has a misaligned πε in κατ'ἐπέκτασιν. See Table 8.1 for the incidence of this *integrans*.

[36] Polain, *Catalogue* (n. 34 above), no. 3687. The information was incorrectly reported in *Bibliothèque Nationale. Catalogue des incunables*, II/4, Paris, 1985, no. T-109, with sig. Kχ4*v* (i.e. fol. 76*v*) twice misprinted as KK4*v* (i.e. fol. 260*v*).

8: ALDUS AS PROOFREADER   175

printing. He first grabbed lines 28–30 from fol. 74*v* and patched them in so as to complete fol. 76*v*. Then he realised a fourth line was required, returned to fol. 74*v*, and picked l. 26, presumably because l. 27 had already been dismantled. We can picture the compositor subsequently passing the forme on to the pressmen with instructions on which parts were to be inked. The beater, however, automatically spread ink on all text lines, so that in most copies they all ended up reproduced on paper. At some point, the press was stopped, the four lines used as bearer type were covered by the frisket so that no marks, including blind impression, were left on the page.[37]

Be that as it may, it is suggestive that many copies — nearly a fifth of the inspected body — bear the correct impression of fol. 76*v* without the final four lines. An error of this magnitude would be immediately apparent to anyone checking preliminary proofs. If proofs for this and the conjugate page (fol. 78*r*) were indeed pulled, clearly no corrector had laid eyes on them before the printing operations were in full swing. It seems clear that the three systematic readings of proofs called for in theory and attested in some later cases, in practice did not take place in Aldus's shop.[38] It also seems that no correction was deemed necessary for the numerous faulty copies pulled out of the press. Perhaps the mistake was so conspicuous that Aldus resolved not to spoil the page even further. Nevertheless, there might be exceptions to the rule, as the copies currently at the Angelica Library in Rome and the Columbia University bear two and three slashes respectively, with traits and ink akin to those found in the other manuscript corrections in the *Thesaurus*.[39]

Additional manuscript corrections

Six handwritten emendations which were not made in so prominent a place have gone unnoticed. Hidden between the lines, the minimal changes address typos in both declensions and roots due to incorrect vowels, consonants, ligatures, and accents. Notwithstanding their apparent similarities, these errors stemmed from three different errors on the compositor's part: omission and misspelling, as well as textual misunderstanding. The emendations

[37] R. McLeod, 'The Invisible Book', *New College Notes*, 14, 2021, pp. 1–95 and R. Stein [i.e. R. McLeod], 'When the Poet Gives Empty Leaves', *Journal of Early Modern Studies*, 11, 2022, pp. 117-200 describe this and other instances detected in the Aldine output, delving into details about composition rhythm and more complex technical matters.

[38] Three rounds of proofs are attested by witnesses at a slightly later date: J. Gerritsen, 'Printing at Froben's: An Eye-Witness Account', *Studies in Bibliography*, 44, 1991, pp. 144–63. Sixteenth-century correctors routinely complained that the pressmen did not give them time to read proofs before they began to print. See, e.g., A. Grafton, *The Culture of Correction in Renaissance Europe*, London, 2011, pp. 143–208 and his *Inky Fingers: The Making of Books in Early Modern Europe*, Cambridge (MA) and London, 2020, pp. 29–55.

[39] Rome, Biblioteca Angelica, Inc. 709 and New York, Butler Library, Goff T158, the latter showing sparse annotations and corrections by a later hand. The four supernumerary lines at fol. 76*v* were marked as incorrect by three keen, nearly contemporary annotators: Guillaume Budé in Paris, Bibliothèque nationale de France (BnF), RES-X-25; an anonymous English scholar in Bloomington (IN), Lilly Library, PA253.T41 M29 1496; another anonymous scholar, probably French or Italian, who carefully crossed out all lines in New Haven (CT), Beinecke Library, BEIN Zi +5551 Copy 2. The copy in Edinburgh, National Library of Scotland (NLS), Inc.194* bears a more discreet correction which was probably made by one of the two early Italian readers who signed the volume at the head of the title-page.

176   PRINTING AND MISPRINTING

also look consistent. They were carefully inserted by the same hand, which recalls, even in the ink employed, those at fols 197r and 207r. Likewise, they appear to be the result of a belated proofreading, which certainly followed the completion of printing for the leaves involved, if not for the entire volume.

The first correction, or rather set of corrections, appears at fol. 6v, l. 23 in over 84% of inspected copies. A vowel has been corrected twice, transforming both occurrences of the feminine name Leto (Λητ-) into the adjective λῑτ-, meaning frugal, while a grave accent has been turned into a circumflex with the addition of a subscribed *iota* (ὡ into ῷ) in the first occurrence of the word. At least nine copies show a barely perceptible variation: no diaeresis appears on the *iotas* and the superfluous symbol ※ between the two λῑτ- is expunged with a vertical stroke.[40] A couple of lines below (ll. 25–6), the name Leto appears twice, and we may wonder whether this caused confusion. However, the compositor seems to have reported faithfully what he saw in front of him — at least if the Laurenziana manuscript can be regarded as a close approximation to the lost printer's copy for Favorino's *Eclogai*.[41] We shall come back to this and other complexities encapsulated in fol. 6v of the Aldine *Thesaurus* at the end of this chapter.

Leafing through the edition, we stumble upon another typo in the middle of line 9 at fol. 82r: 'εἰως', a strange fusion of three common prepositions, ἕως (until), ὡς (how), and εἰς (towards). Here, a peculiar series of kindred letters and sounds, correctly reading 'ε εἰς ῑ; ὡς', as in the Laurenziana manuscript, may have confused the compositor.[42] Some time after the printing of this sheet was completed, the mistake was spotted and emended. The *omega* was crossed out with a vertical stroke, while a round line links the *iota* and *sigma* underneath. This solution is more intrusive than the other manuscript corrections, which are usually disguised more effectively. The ink used in this case is also slightly darker than usual. This correction can be found in 93.5% of copies.[43]

Subsequent cases all affect treatises following Favorino's work, so that the Laurenziana manuscript can no longer offer the modest help it has given us thus far. A prominent misspelling crops up in the *Thesaurus* at line 21 of fol. 227r, at the start of a chapter title, which was, as usual, composed in capital letters. The opening word reads ″ΕΓΚΚΙΤΙΚᾺ, though the second K should be a L to convey the actual meaning (i.e., enclitics). The fault was probably triggered by the proximity of *kappa* and *lambda* not only in this specific instance, but in the Greek alphabet, an order most likely reflected in the disposition of case compartments for capitals.[44] Remarkably, this is the only emendation found in all inspected copies of the

---

[40] Shrewsbury, Shrewsbury School, INC 43 E.VI.16; Copenhagen, Royal Library, Inc. Haun. 3874; Paris, BnF, RES-X-30; Athens, National Library of Greece, ΕΦ. 1316[.b]; Genoa, Biblioteca Durazzo, L.III.10; Kraków, Jagiellonian Library, BJ Cam., L.X.11; New Haven (CT), Beinecke Library, BEIN Zi +5551 Copy 2; New York, Butler Library, Goff T158; Vatican City, Biblioteca Apostolica Vatican (BAV), Inc.II.592.

[41] Cf. MS Florence, Bibl. Laur., Plut. 55.18, fol. 13r–v.

[42] Ibid., fol. 115v.

[43] In New Haven (CT), Beinecke Library, BEIN Zi +5551 Copy 2, the nearly contemporary reader who extensively annotated the copy somehow overemphasised this Aldine correction, crossing the printed word out and writing the correct εἰς above it.

[44] Unlike lower cases, in the first Aldine Greek type capitals, except for *pi*, were all consistently designed and cast in a single shape. Thus, my hypothesis does not conflict with the theory that there may have been separate compartments for allographs, as posited below. See Barker, *Aldus Manutius* (n. 11 above), pp. 43, 63, 128.

8: ALDUS AS PROOFREADER 177

edition.[45] Yet, the *lambda* added by hand above the crossed *kappa* was written in some cases as a lower case in others as a capital letter. Very tentatively, we may infer from this alternation that the correcting process was divided into two stages or more, as we might expect of a lengthy operation to be repeated on the entire print run.

A little later in the book, two consecutive, albeit not conjugate, pages contain three manuscript corrections. Fol. 236*v*, l. 16, bears a non-existent word, ἀναπεμπταῖον, which was ingeniously retouched into ἀναπεμπτέον (the gerundive of ἀναπέμπω) by transforming the circumflex accent into an έ after crossing out the diphthong αι underneath it. It seems that the compositor picked the wrong type, possibly misreading an abbreviation in the printer's copy. Four lines below, a confusion of two 'o' sounds, *omicron* and *omega*, in the name Deucalion was also emended, turning δευκαλίονως into δευκαλίωνος. The two interventions were most likely done in conjunction, as they can be found together in a remarkably high number of copies (89% of the inspected body). Three other copies lack the first correction but retain the second,[46] while the opposite happened only in Inkunabel 1408 of the National Library of Sweden. These exceptions are probably due to scattered moments of inattention on the part of the corrector, though it is also possible they reflect an unexpected precedence of the second correction over the first in terms of time.

The next page (fol. 237*r*) has another typo at line 6: the compositor mistook two very similar words for one another, necessitating a pen modification to turn οὕτως (so) into οὗτος (this) which was inserted in as many as 169 copies. There is no doubt that the emendation is a result of post-printing proofreading. In this particular case, a crucial element comes to our aid: a previously undetected stop-press variant in the first two lines of fol. 237*r*, introduced midway during the print run and present in slightly over half of the inspected copies.[47] The manuscript correction, present in over 90% of them, appears in equal proportion among copies of variant A and B.[48] The very common concurrence of this correction and the two

[45] Some degree of uncertainty remains for the incomplete yet annotated copy in Edinburgh, NLS, Inc.194, in which the *lambda* was inelegantly written over the printed *kappa*. The Aldine correction is clearly visible despite white washing in the copy in Bremen, Staats- und Universitätsbibliothek (SUB), VI.9.b.35.

[46] BSB, 2 Inc.c.a. 3399a; Cambridge (MA), Houghton Library, Inc 5551(B); Provo (UT), Harold B. Lee Library, 1496 no. 1. In two copies, this printer's correction was retouched by later annotators: Paris, BnF, RES-X-28, and Chicago, Newberry Library, QH41.R94 1711.

[47] I owe this valuable finding to Geri Della Rocca de Candal. The two variants, with differences marked in bold, read: (A) **καὶ** [abbreviated] **κῶοι** καὶ πελοποννήσιοι **καὶ κρίσκοι καὶ** [abbreviated] σικελοί; καὶ λίβυες; **καὶ** [abbreviated] οἱ τὴν ἤπειρον **λεγουμένην** οἰκοῦντες; (B) **καὶ** [unabbreviated] **κρῆτες** καὶ πελοποννήσιοι **καὶ** [unabbreviated] σικελοί; καὶ λίβυες; **καὶ** [unabbreviated] οἱ τὴν **παλαιὰν** ἤπειρον οἰκοῦντες. The presence of κρίσκοι, a non-existent word possibly stemming from Κρισαῖοι, the citizen of Krisa in Phocis, suggests that variant A was the first to be set and the one regarded as incorrect. Another proof of that can be drawn from the final register. At fol. 270*r*, it records the unabbreviated καὶ as the first word of fol. 237*r* (i.e. GH 3*r*); this is exactly how variant B, thus the corrected one, starts. Lest it confuse the owner of a copy with variant A, however, Aldus decided to omit the following words, unlike all other cases in which the incipit begins with a καὶ or a similarly short element, such as an article: cf., in particular, at fols 269*r*–*v*, the register for cγιr (καὶ δαπαρῶ [misreporting for δαπανῶ, the correct reading of fol. 17*r*]) and ρρ4r (καὶ τὸ φῶς).

[48] Out of the 171 copies in which I was able to check retrospectively the presence of variant A or B, the correction is missing in eight copies of the first group and in six of the second.

emendations on the preceding page suggests they all sprang from a single intervention, most probably made following the assemblage of gathering GH[8]. In two copies only, corrections at fol. 236*v* are not followed by that at fol. 237*r*.[49] More conclusive evidence of their simultaneous origin can be drawn from the Batthyaneum copy in Alba Iulia (SR Inc. VI 45), where rawer variations of the three corrections appear in darker ink, albeit by the usual hand.

Coping with leaf numbers

A further group of printed and manuscript emendations concerns foliation. It should be noted that no Aldine imprint prior to the *Thesaurus* had numbered leaves, though the expedient was increasingly used by earlier and contemporary printers, including Aldus' partner, Andrea Torresano.[50] Aldus himself adopted this improvement in text division only in volumes II–V (1497–1498) of the Aristotle, in Catherine of Siena's epistles (1500), and then more consistently following the Lucian and Origen editions of 1503.[51] Foliation evidently played an important part in the architecture of the *Thesaurus*. It was the object of careful revision, a practice that remained unusual even in later centuries. Three misprints were identified at fols 187*r*, 188*r*, 213*r*, which had erroneously been numbered as 191, 192, and 203, respectively, and were retouched by pen, evidently by the same hand and most frequently with the same ink.[52] We can postulate that the emendations were made some time after the two gatherings involved (&ω[4] and ΔD[8]) had been assembled and the sequence of leaves had become clearly visible. As few as 3% of inspected copies lack these manuscript corrections altogether.[53] Moreover, the emendations at the non-conjugate fols 187–8 always appear together, except in the copies held at Holkham Hall and Chatsworth, which show no sign of the first one even after thorough scrutiny under UV light. A slightly anomalous correction at fol. 187*r*, with a manuscript '7' more pronounced than usual, can still be traced

[49] Stuttgart, Württembergische Landesbibliothek (WL), Inc.fol.15493, and Rome, Biblioteca Casanatense, Vol. INC. 1925.

[50] Leaf numbers were printed for the first time in the middle of the outer margin in a leaflet by Werner Rolewinck, *Sermo in festo praesentationis beatissimae Mariae virginis*, [Cologne, Arnold ter Hoernen], 1470, 4° (ISTC ir00304000); the following year, ter Hoernen applied the innovation to a larger book, adding at the beginning of most copies a detailed table of contents with instruction on how to interpret the reference to foliation: Adrianus Carthusiensis, *De remediis utriusque fortunae*, Cologne, Arnold ter Hoernen, 8 February 1471, 4° (ISTC ia00055000). I am grateful to Martin Davies for sharing his insightful notes on the subject. See the thorough chronological analysis of M. M. Smith, 'Printed Foliation: Forerunner to Printed Page-Numbers', *Gutenberg-Jahrbuch*, 63, 1988, pp. 54–70 (esp. 67–9 for printers based in Venice), and the later examples in D. Sawyer, 'Page Numbers, Signatures, and Catchwords', in D. Duncan and A. Smyth (eds), *Book Parts*, Oxford, 2019, pp. 139–49. Foliation with Roman numerals became ever more common in Venetian production from the late 1480s. To the best of my knowledge, Torresano first employed it in Hieronymus, *Epistolae*, Venice, Andrea Torresano, 15 May 1488, f° (ISTC ih00170000). An Italian precursor of Aldus in the use of Arabic numerals was Jacopo Sannazzaro da Riva with his Hilarion, *Legendarium*, printed in Milan in April 1494 (ih00268500).

[51] See G. Della Rocca de Candal in this Companion, pp. 128–31.

[52] The 0 in 203 was struck out, while the 1 was added above as a Roman numeral (i).

[53] Rome, Biblioteca Corsiniana, 56.H.15; Amsterdam, Universiteitsbibliotheek (UB), Inc. 4; Providence (RI), John Carter Brown Library, [no shelfmark]; Bryn Mawr (PA), Bryn Mawr College, Goodhart Collection, T-158 f; and Washington DC, Library of Congress (LoC), Incun.1496.T39.

back to the Aldine print shop with a high degree of likelihood.[54] By contrast, some seven copies do not show the retouching on fol. 213r.[55]

As for the origin of the mistakes, the compositor was clearly unfamiliar with adding Arabic numerals in the outer upper corners of rectos and was still coping with this novelty. He ended up inverting two of them in numbering fol. 23r. In all the copies in which I was able to check the whole printed foliation, no correction of this tiny flaw, whether in manuscript or print, was made, presumably because it caused no inconvenience.[56]

A second printed numeral suggests a few additional observations. A peculiar character resembling an inverted five appear in the numeration of rectos of fols 35, 45, 50–2, 57, 59, 154, 175, 185, 205, 225, 235, and 250. A closer inspection confirms that this is a distinctive sort, rather inelegant by modern standards but perfectly consistent with the conventions of handwriting in mid-fifteenth-century Italy. Shortly after the publication of the *Thesaurus*, Aldus discarded this character in favour of the version we are more acquainted with.[57] While the old-fashioned five was placed upside-down in all copies in numbering fol. 145r, an inverted modern five only appears in the Palatina copy of the Biblioteca Nazionale Centrale in Florence (Pal.E.8.1.1. (str. 970)) at fol. 158r: a prompt stop-press intervention rotates the type into the correct position, so that the number would appear upright in the text. The Palatina copy contains, accordingly, one of the very first specimens of the sheet 155+158 to be printed, though this does not imply that the whole copy was produced very early on in the print run, as we shall argue below.[58]

---

[54] Rastatt, Historische Bibliothek, D 32* (F) and Stuttgart, WL, Inc.fol.15493.

[55] Durham, University Library, SA 0124; Rouen, Bibliothèque municipale (BM), Montbret g 2441; Stuttgart, WL, Inc.fol.15493; Madrid, Biblioteca Nacional de España, Inc/710; Austin (TX), Harry Ransom Humanities Research Center (HRHRC), q PA 231 T54 1496 ALDINE Copy 1; New Haven (CT), Beinecke Library, BEIN Zi +5551 Copy 1; and Vatican City, BAV, Inc.II.591. Oxford, Christ Church, e.2.52 was corrected later on in red pencil, while a slightly different form of the Aldine emendation can be seen in Lyon, Bibliothèque municipale, Rés Inc 268, and Paris, BnF, RES-X-30. Copies in Florence, Biblioteca Marucelliana, R.A.631, and Milan, Biblioteca Nazionale Braidense, AO.XIII.10, retain the standard correction plus what seems to be adjustments by later annotators; the same holds true for the copy in Milan, Veneranda Biblioteca Ambrosiana, INC. 382, where the overwriting was made in pencil, most likely by a twentieth-century librarian.

[56] As the importance of this information came to my attention fairly late in the research, I managed to verify consistently printed foliation only in about sixty copies. Since all show exactly the same pattern, the rest of the extant print run can be expected to conform. Struggles with foliation can also be seen in the second, third, and fourth volume of Aristotle, all printed within a year after the *Thesaurus*: Della Rocca de Candal in this Companion, pp. 135–8.

[57] See the various specimens in G. F. Hill, *The Development of Arabic Numerals in Europe*, Oxford, 1915, pp. 12–3, 46–7, 108–21. In the foliated editions produced prior to 1500 — that is volumes III–V of Aristoteles, *Opera*, f° (ISTC ia00959000), issued between 1496 and 1498 — Aldus never employed the old-fashioned five, developing instead other variants of the modern version, which also appeared as part of a different set of types in the pagination of Niccolò Perotti, *Cornucopiae linguae latinae*, Venice, Aldus Manutius, July 1499, f° (ISTC ip00296000). Leaves in Catherine of Siena, *Epistole*, Venice, Aldus Manutius, [not before 19] September 1500, f° (ISTC ic00281000), were numbered by means of Roman numerals. Most copies of Petrarch, *Le cose volgari*, Venice, Aldus Manutius, 1501, 8° (USTC 847779), have manuscript foliation added in the Aldine print shop after printing: C. H. Clough, 'Pietro Bembo's Edition of Petrarch and His Association with the Aldine Press', in D. S. Zeidberg (ed.), *Aldus Manutius and Renaissance Culture: Essays in Memory of Franklin D. Murphy: Acts of an International Conference, Venice and Florence, 14–17 June 1994*, Florence, 1998, pp. 47–80 (72).

[58] The text of fol. 158r and the conjugate page (fol. 155v) is identical in all copies, including the Palatina.

180   PRINTING AND MISPRINTING

We can pinpoint a final inconsistency in foliation, again attesting to the compositor's uneasiness with Arabic numerals. Fol. 3r occasionally shows an odd-looking three which is simply one of the different Aldine types for the Greek letter *zeta*. A comparison between copies showing the two different numberings reveals that no other type was changed in the page or in the conjugate in the forme (fol. 6v). Thus, we can rest assured that the use of *zeta* was regarded as an unintentional mistake. The correction was made by stopping the press as soon as the issue was detected, that is, after approximately one-fifth of the sheets had already been produced.[59] This in turn raises a further consideration. The compositor appears to have picked not a random type or variant of *zeta*, but precisely the one resembling a 3. Circumstances do not suggest that this type was accidentally placed in the wrong compartment of the typecase: the neat Arabic numerals, ostensibly cut by Francesco Griffo, just like the Latin and Greek series used in the edition, had probably just reached the Aldine premises. It may follow that this and every other variant of *zeta* were kept in their own separate cases. We can apply this conclusion to all the allographs in the set, envisaging a systematically divided typecase with all the related advantages and drawbacks.

An elaborate intervention and the corrector's identity

So far, misprints and corrections in the *Thesaurus* resemble those in several other early Aldine editions, which were also meticulously emended. If anything, what stands out is the large number of them in a single book. The most relevant in-house correction, however, has yet to be discussed. Pick a random copy of the *Thesaurus* and return to fol. 6v. In 86.6% of copies, ll. 25–6, just below the different interlinear emendations mentioned above, were rather flamboyantly crossed out and the words 'ζήτει φύλλον 268' were added. This looks, at first, like a Greek marginal note by a contemporary learned reader with a confident ductus. But comparison with a few other copies reveals that this is another printer's intervention.

As Fig. 8.1.a–d shows, deletion and annotation, always carried out with scrupulous accuracy, appear in four different combinations: (A) a pen stroke along the two lines of text and a cross reference written after a full stop; (B) three slashes stretching from the first to the second line and a cross reference in the outer margin; (C) a pen stroke along the two lines and a cross reference in the outer margin; (D) three or four wavy slashes from the first to the second line and a cross reference after the full stop. The order reflects their frequency, A appearing in 73 copies, B in 47, C in 35, D only in 7. Establishing their internal chronology is a more slippery undertaking, though the sheer graphic consistency of each of the four combinations points towards a laborious process divided into four phases at least, possibly over a couple of days or more. The repetitive yet delicate task very occasionally resulted in slips. One of the copies in the Marciana (Aldina 100) shows an incomplete emendation, lacking the leaf number '268'. The Batthyaneum copy (SR Inc. VI 45) had to be recorrected

---

[59] Nearly 34% of the inspected copies have the *zeta* variant. It seems clear that the *zeta* was not used as a kludge in the temporary absence of a '3' or it would have not been corrected in most copies. See Misson's contribution in this Companion. A kindred case of confusion between look-alike letters and numerals is to be found in the Aldine Aristoteles, in which a Roman 'z' is occasionally used instead of a 2; see G. Della Rocca de Candal's contribution in this Companion, p. 136.

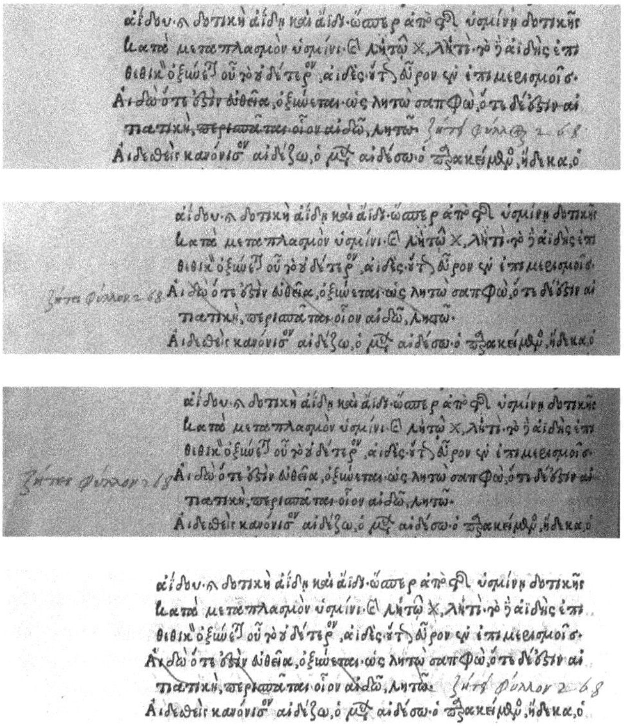

FIG. 8.1.a–d. The four combinations of the emendation in Θησαυρὸς, Κέρας Ἀμαλθείας, καὶ κῆποι Ἀδώνιδος. *Thesaurus Cornu copiae & Hortus Adonidis*, Venice, Aldus Manutius, 1496, f° (ISTC it00158000), f. 6v, ll. 25–6. A: Provo (UT), The Harold B. Lee Library, 1496 no.1. B: Oxford, Bodleian Library, Auct R 1.4. C: Oxford, Bodleian Library, Byw. G 3.16. D: Kraków, Biblioteka Jagiellońska, BJ Cam. L. X. 11.

due to a mishap: the first time, the leaf number came out as '28', so that — presumably after some muttering — a '6' had to be supplied. The second figure was adjusted accordingly and a new '8' was added soon after (Fig. 8.2). In fact, it is extraordinary that so few errors were made, given that the same correction was entered in hundreds and hundreds of copies.

Additional elements reinforce the impression that the process was fragmented and open up perspectives on possible links among the four combinations. In particular, B and D may well have been implemented one after the other; D always appears along with a minor variant of the set of in-house manuscript adjustments a few lines above on the same page, that showing no dieresis on *iotas* and the crossed asterisk ⚹ on which we have touched before. Once, however, this variant is found together with B.[60] The copy currently at Shrewsbury School (INC 43 E.VI.16) offers another, slightly ambiguous hint: here we can see the shift B/D, even though the horizontal stroke running through the second half of l. 25 may also be connected to C (Fig. 8.3); the passage from B to D (or vice versa) is more apparent in

---

[60] Vatican City, BAV, Inc.II.592. I seize the opportunity to thank Matteo Colombo, who kindly helped me put some order into the many data collected over time from the copies of the *Thesaurus*, thus enabling me to pinpoint combinations of different corrections.

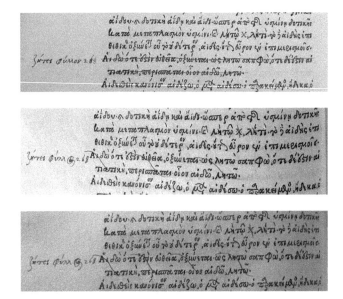

FIGS 8.2–4. Anomalous emendations in the *Thesaurus* (see Fig. 8.1.a–d), f. 6v, ll. 25–6. Fig. 8.2: Alba Iulia, Biblioteca Batthyaneum, SR Inc. VI 45. Fig. 8.3: Shrewsbury, Shrewsbury School, INC 43 E.VI.16. Fig. 8.4: Paris, Bibliothèque nationale de France, RES-X-30.

Paris, BnF, RES-X-30, in which the four wavy slashes were combined with the instruction entered in the outer margin (Fig. 8.4). What is certain is that the unstable nature of D and its infrequent occurrence mark it as a more temporary solution than the other three.

Given their mutual similarities, it is also possible that A and C were connected, though it cannot be proven with certainty. Their sole difference is the position of the inner reference to leaf 268, which looks more elegant after the full stop as it merges into the page layout, yet, at a cognitive level, is harder to catch sight of. Very tentatively, we might guess that Aldus first went for the elegant solution (A) and later moved to the more effective one (C), relocating the annotation to the outer margin. This second option was to reveal its own limitations, too: later owners could easily mistake it for a marginal annotation by an anonymous earlier reader, and it was washed out at the behest of numerous eighteenth- and nineteenth-century collectors who craved an Aldine still as clean as when it emerged from the press. If only they had known that they were deleting an inscription written by their hero right in the print shop![61]

---

[61] London, British Library, IB.24415, was washed at fols 6v and 82r; Bremen, SUB, VI.9.b.35 at fols 6v and 227r; Uppsala, Universitetsbibliotek, Ink. 35b:23 exclusively at fol. 6v. Two copies were washed only with regard to this specific emendation, maintaining all the others, including those two lines above: Amsterdam, UB, Inc. 144; The Hague, Museum Meermanno — House of the Book, 004 E 02; Vienna, Österreichische Nationalbibliothek (ÖNB), Ink 9.D.5, and Austin (TX), HRHRC, Uzielli 7 were washed similarly, though the corrections at fol. 6v, l. 23 was originally absent in both of them. In Chatsworth, DC, Dev/002804, the emendation was so carefully removed that it is hard to assign it to the proper category, and yet the ones on the upper lines were retained. The correction in Rostock, Universitätsbibliothek, Cc-1360, partly faded away due to severely yellowed margins and damp stains.

The neat handwriting remains evidently the same in all four combinations. David Speranzi has at last provided a thorough palaeographical analysis of Aldus's distinctive Greek *cursus*. The *specimena* gathered by Speranzi leave no room for doubt: the corrector of fol. 6*v* is unmistakeably Aldus himself, as the *zeta* in the form of a three, the large eyelet of the *phi*, and the understated ligature of the double *lambdas* certify.[62] The strong resemblance of this correction with all the others described — especially when the numbers and letters employed were the same, such as the eights at fols 191*r* and 192*r* or the lower *lambda* at fol. 227*r* — suggests that Aldus was personally responsible for them. This matches what Della Rocca de Candal has shown for the vast majority of emendations found in the output of the Aldine press through the 1490s.

In spite of variations, the meaning of the correction at f. 6*v* remains stable and crystal clear: benevolent reader, ignore this passage and 'ζήτει φύλλον 268', i.e. 'examine leaf 268', one of the very last in the text. The instruction is enlightening for our purpose, as it could obviously have been drafted only after the whole volume had been printed, probably except for the preliminaries. It thus provides incontestable evidence that Aldus carried out a final revision on the *Thesaurus*, even after all the work he and Bolzanio claimed that they had done to prepare the text for printing. Incidentally, the correction at l. 23 of the same page must have been inserted at the same time, as it is always found in conjunction with the one discussed here.[63] As often as not, copies lacking both of them retain either all or most of the others, which were probably made at a slightly earlier stage.

A question related to the major emendation at fol. 6*v* remains to be answered: why was Aldus compelled to intervene so dramatically in Favorino's work when the volume had already been printed? It all comes down to a shameful problem of accents. The expunged passage illustrates how the accusative of the word αἰδώ (meaning 'shame', indeed) requires a circumflex (i.e., αἰδῶ), in line with kindred names, such as Sappho and Leto. It openly contradicts the information provided in the closing treatise on feminine names ending with *omega*, on fol. 268*r*. Aldus must have spotted this aporia only in the final proofreading, buried among thousands of lemmata, and resolved to act in order to spare careful readers, who would collate the varied texts as they worked through the book, from bewilderment.

Yet Aldus's subtle, meticulous work on this passage appears to tear down barriers that usually separated proofreading, philological improvements, and authorial intervention. It is hard to say into which of these categories this correction falls. What is more, one must wonder if this is only the tip of an iceberg that has accidentally remained visible. How frequently was the same operation performed without leaving traces of what may have been more substantial inconsistencies between the various components of the *Thesaurus*, either on the missing printer's copy or, more straightforwardly, in the course of printing? What is certain is that, in this case, Aldus's frame of mind as a grammarian and publisher prevailed

---

[62] Cf. D. Speranzi, 'La scrittura di Aldo e il suo ultimo carattere greco (con uno sconosciuto esemplare di tipografia)', in N. Vacalebre (ed.), *Five centuries later: Aldus Manutius: Culture, Typography and Philology*, Florence, 2018, pp. 29–60. Fig. 8.1.a shows how the annotation usually looks, including abbreviations. Minor variants can be found here and there, notably a taller *tau* or the group ει and ον written in full (as in Fig. 8.1.b–c). Occasionally, the *zeta* sprang from Aldus's pen in the form of a two (e.g., Oxford, Merton College, 112.D.7).

[63] The only four exceptions to this pattern, most likely due to oversight, are: Vienna, ÖNB, Ink 9.D.5; Windsor, Royal Library, RCIN 1057944; Pisa, Biblioteca universitaria, Inc.14.1; and Austin (TX), HRHRC, Uzielli 7.

over his usually exacting philological standards. This correction betrays his chief priority: tailoring a technical work as a consistent learning tool in spite of its miscellaneous contents. He deemed this more important than offering a series of mostly ancient Greek treatises in what would have been, by contemporary standards, critically sound editions.

CONCLUSION

The investigation of misprints and printer's corrections in the Aldine Greek *Thesaurus* has brought to light a number of thought-provoking phenomena which yield insights into the arrangement of the typecase as well as the interlocked processes of production and correction. Most importantly, it has unveiled the tensions that could arise between the need to continue printing and the effort to provide careful proofreading in what is usually believed to be a well-organised print shop. Post-production revision became all the more crucial to compensate for the many discrepancies and inaccuracies that inevitably stemmed from the multiple demands of the compositor's job and the mechanical process of printing. The *Thesaurus* offers plenty of evidence with regard to this elusive, somewhat belated phase of proofreading. Nevertheless, we should resist the temptation to treat printed copies of a single edition as though they were manuscript witnesses of a text, and to dream of pinpointing the precise moment in which mistakes and corrections occurred. We cannot reconstruct either the 'original' printer's copy or the ideal printed copy through a Lachmannian *stemma exemplarium errorumque*. The difficulty of inferring printing order remains insurmountable. This is mostly due to the fact that we cannot determine the various ways in which sheets were combined during gathering assemblage, and that we lack detailed information on how printed sheets were hung, pressed, piled up, and stored in each shop — if we can even assume that there were established practices in the first place.[64]

In sifting through Aldus's groundbreaking output, we should constantly bear in mind another form of in-house correction, that which involved intentional textual improvements. In other words, we need to consider the aims of single publications on the one hand, and, on the other, the ambiguous vocation of a humanist printer, torn between attaining philological rigour and meeting economic and publishing goals. Examining the ways in which Aldus and his heirs coped with both routine misprinting and last-minute afterthoughts in other publications, particularly those issued during the sixteenth century, can provide new, valuable evidence to help us appreciate their complex strategies. The same probably holds true for the production of other learned printers across Europe, from the Estienne to the Elzevir families, which also awaits scrutiny.

---

[64] The copy which happens to be the less corrected is in Rome, Biblioteca Corsiniana, 56.H.15, including only the emendations at fols 82r, 207r and 227r and the correct impression of fol. 76v. This does not imply it was the first to be produced. By contrast, one can speculate which were the last copies to be assembled due to the presence of *integrantia*. By their own nature, these were pulled to integrate the short print runs of sheets usually noticed in the assemblage phase, thus once printing operations had been completed since a while. A further indication may come from the coexistence of more than one *integrans* in the same copy: in the *Thesaurus*, the two known cases of *integrantia* appear together in two third of the occurrences (see Table 8.1).

Musurus described the correction process of the Aldine press as an infinite battle against the Lernean Hydra: the more mistakes were cut out of the text, the more grew back.[65] The case of the *Thesaurus* enables us to watch Aldus closely as he fights against error, pen in hand, as though he was wielding a sword to slash off the monster's heads. This was a highly time-consuming and demanding exercise, especially for as busy an entrepreneur as Aldus, who had to run a very ambitious publishing business, perhaps the most ambitious of his time. In an anecdote, Erasmus recalled Aldus's impressive ability to concentrate on going over proofs even amid the chaos that reigned in the print shop. To Erasmus's question about why Aldus was taking such pains to check proofs after he, the author, had done so, the latter proudly replied 'studeo' (here both 'I am being diligent' and 'I am studying').[66]

A considerable share of Aldus's time must have been devoted to making manuscript corrections. Many of his collaborators, including Greek native-speakers and skilled Western Hellenists, could have stepped in with no difficulty, but clearly Aldus regarded this as his own territory and duty, part of the humanist art of *castigatio*, and not as a shameful task, unworthy of his intellectual status. The latter stance became common among sixteenth-century master printers, including, most likely, Aldus's namesake and grandson, who, in the course of his frequent ups and downs, was forced to act as a corrector in the recently established Vatican Press a hundred years or so after 1496.[67]

---

[65] Aristophanes, *Comoediae novem*, Venice, Aldus Manutius, 15 July 1498, f° (ISTC ia00958000), sig. π2r.

[66] Desiderius Erasmus, *Apologia adversus rhapsodias calumniosarum querimoniarum Alberti Pii*, Basel, Hieronymus Froben and Nikolaus Episcopius, 1531, 4° (USTC 635481), p. 58, referring to his stay with Aldus for the publication of the second edition of his *Adagia* in 1508 (USTC 828220): 'Aldus saepenumero praedicabat se admirari, qui tantum scriberem ex tempore, idque inter tumultus circumstrepentium. Operis mei formas extremas castigavi, tantum in hoc si quid vellem mutare. Nam opus alioqui suum habebat castigatorem conductum nomine Seraphinum. *Aldus post me legit, quum rogarem quur hoc laboris caperet, interim, inquit, studeo*' ('Aldus quite often expressed his amazement that I could compose so much extempore, and do so in the midst of the confusion and noise going on around me. I corrected the final proofs of my work only to the extent of making revisions if I wished to, for the work had a corrector apart from me, a man named Seraphinus hired for the purpose. *Aldus read it after I did it. When I asked why he took on this job, he said "I am studying at the same time"*'). The emphasis is mine, while the English translation is taken from *Collected Works of Erasmus*, LXXIV, ed. N. H. Minnich and transl. D. Sheerin, Toronto, 2005, pp. 163–4. See also the vivid picture of the Aldine premises in Lowry, *The World of Aldus* (n. 30 above), pp. 92–7, building on this and other more famous accounts by Erasmus.

[67] See the indirect, possibly biased, account by Aldo the Younger's partner, Niccolò Manassi: '[…] ai pari del signor Aldo [the Younger] non era poco aver gratia che egli volesse sostener col suo nome quel titolo di sopra intendente alla stampa vaticana non che esser correttor attuale di stampe, come questi mecanici, […] et che molti Prencipi averebbono avuto gratia dargli provisione per valersi del suo nome solo senza operare' ('[…] for Aldo [the Younger]'s peers, it was remarkable that he was prepared to elevate with his name the task of superintending the Vatican Press and actively correcting proofs as manual labourers do […] several princes would have been keen to give him a pension with no obligation, only to make use of his name'). My translation. A full transcription and detailed analysis of this and other letters by Manassi is given in A. Nuovo, 'The End of the Manutius Dynasty, 1597', in J. Kraye and P. Sachet (eds), *The Afterlife of Aldus: Posthumous Fame, Collectors and the Book Trade*, London, 2018, pp. 45–78 (75). See also Dirk Imhof's contribution in this Companion, showing how inserting manuscript corrections in the print runs of the Plantin press under Jan Moretus I was a task entrusted to young apprentices ('pueri'), and the dismissive comments with which Montaigne hide his meticulous reading of the proofs of his *Essais* in G. Hoffman, 'Writing Without Leisure: Proofreading as Labour in the Renaissance', *The Journal of Medieval and Renaissance Studies*, 25, 1995, pp. 17–31. For a historical overview of proofreading

186 PRINTING AND MISPRINTING

Notwithstanding Aldus's pride in personally reading and correcting his proofs, the memory of the pain that he felt while inserting the elaborate emendation at fol. 6*v* in the *Thesaurus* probably stayed with him for a long time. Perhaps it was still vivid when he published the *editio princeps* of Pindar's odes in 1513. There he inserted, quite intentionally, a typographical pun, turning the word αἰδῶ into his own name, ἀλδῶ, in a verse evoking Zeus's favour.[68] At the time of the *Thesaurus*, Aldus was less playful. After carrying on rounds of checks and counterchecks well into post-production, in the end he surrendered. He could not provide a flawless text of all the treatises. In wrapping up the preface, he resorted, somewhat inappropriately, to philological arguments, blaming the faulty manuscript copies for the mistakes (and misprints!) that still marred the edition: 'Mendosorum enim est exemplarium culpa, non mea'. Readers were consequently asked to be merciful as, in Horace's words, perfection is not of this world.[69] It could not be attained even at the Aldine press, at least through the rather chaotic revision process revealed here — one perhaps too grandiose ever to be brought to a successful completion.

ADDENDA

A quest for errors and corrections is potentially never-ending: completion often depends on where the bar is set. After writing this chapter and attentively leafing through a great many copies of the *Thesaurus*, I became aware of two other emendations inserted in the Aldine print shop in this publication. The belated discovery worked against the possibility of checking their presence in the extant portion of the original print run. Nevertheless, I was able to look, retrospectively, at enough copies to form a solid hypothesis on their nature and offer here a well-balanced description. Both pertain to Favorino's *Eclogai*, allowing for comparison with the Laurenziana manuscript Plut.55.18.

First comes a tiny variant at f. 100*v* which had already been noted in some American OPACs, including Yale Library's catalogue (https://search.library.yale.edu/catalog/1306596). At the beginning of the last line of the page (l. 30), some 55% of copies bear a printed capital *mu*, so that the lemma discussed was turned from the non-existent 'ἔμηλε' into 'Μέμηλε', the third singular person of the Attic perfect of μέλω ('to care for'). By means of this stop-press emendation, the correct reading of the Homeric term in *Iliad*, 2.25 was reinstated. Coming close to setting the end of the page, the compositor either misread the source text or simply forgot to add the outdented capital. The Laurenziana manuscript shows a straightforward 'Μέμηλε' at f. 141*r*, with the capital letter as glaringly rubricated as

---

long before and after Aldus, see P. Sachet, 'Proofreaders', in A. Blair et al. (eds), *Information: A Historical Companion*, Princeton, 2021, pp. 709–12.

[68] Pindarus, [*Odes*], Venice, Aldus Manutius and Andrea Torresano, 1513, 8° (USTC 848778), p. 62: 'Ζεῦ τέλειε, ἀλδῶ τε δίδοι / καὶ τύχαν τερπνῶν γλυκεῖαν'. The emphasis is mine. The variation is too peculiar and fitting in the context to be a coincidence due to a misprint, though Aldus's name in Greek is a paroxytone noun of second declension, taking the acute accent on the *alpha* (cf. *Thesaurus*, sig. *4r*). See D. F. Bauer, 'Problems in the Aldine Pindar', *Princeton University Library Chronicle*, 76, 2015, pp. 417–45 (440–3).

[69] *Thesaurus*, sig. *3r–v*. The passage, drawn from Horace, *Ars poetica*, 351–3, curiously continues with reference to repeated errors made by inattentive copyists (ibid., 354–5).

8: ALDUS AS PROOFREADER   187

all the others in the book. The frequency of the correction suggests that the error was caught midway in the printing of the forme containing this page and f. 101r.

The second emendation is more interesting for the purpose of this study. It concerns f. 23r and was pinpointed by Grigory Vorobyev while he was kindly inspecting the copy at the National Library of Russia in Saint Petersburg on my behalf. The initial word of l. 29, 'Ἀρῶ', bears a *pi* added in manuscript above the *rho*, thus resulting into 'Ἀρπῶ', i.e. the correct, albeit peculiar, form of ἁρπάζω ('to seize') which is examined in this passage. Since the error is also visible in the Laurenziana manuscript at f. 34v, the one to blame, in this case, is the copyist, who was probably fooled by the many contracted forms of the verb ἀρόω ('to plough') listed in the previous lemma. With five exceptions — London, BL, IB.24415; Oxford, Christ Church, e.2.52; Rouen, BM, Montbret g 2441; New Haven (CT), Beinecke Library, BEIN Zi +5551 Copy 1; and Washington DC, LoC, Incun. 1496 .T39 — the correction was found in all the ninety-three copies I managed to scrutinise. The *pi* was written in two alternative ways and with the occasional use of a caret underneath the word to highlight the insertion of the letter; in the Shrewsbury copy, the spirit on the capital *alpha* was also, and correctly, emended by the same hand. The handwriting is always compatible with Aldus's. In the light of this evidence, we can safely attribute the intervention to Aldus himself. Most likely, he acted during the final proofreading, in line with what he did for f. 227r.

A finding list of the in-house corrections

The following table details the occurrences of in-house corrections in nearly all the print run of the *Thesaurus cornu copiae* (Venice, Aldus Manutius, 1496) known to have survived to these days. '1' means that a correction is present, while its absence is denoted by a blank space. 'n/a' and '?' indicate, respectively, information that could not be checked due to missing leaves in the copy or information that has not been verified as yet. More than a dozen copies which were not listed in ISTC, GW, or MEI have surfaced during the investigation. They include three extra copies in Paris, BnF; a third copy in Athens, the National Library of Greece; a second copy in Cambridge, Trinity College, Salamanca, and Moscow, the Russian State Library; the copy in Basel, Bern, Blickling Hall, St Petersburg; three copies on the antiquarian market, the first inspected in London at Sokol Books (Borghese-Ambrogio provenance, sold at Christie's, *Valuable Books and Manuscripts including Cartography*, 15 July 2015, lot 53), the second inspected in London at PrPh (Macclesfield provenance, sold at Sotheby's, *Music and Continental Books and Manuscripts*, 8 December 2009, lot 173), and the third of unknown provenance inspected in Milan while on sale at Sotheby's, *Antiquarian Books including a Series of Views of Milan*, 4 October 2022, lot. 232. By contrast, the fourth copy recorded in both ISTC and GW in the Houghton Library was confirmed to be a ghost, while that listed in Madrid, Fundación March appears to be no longer in this private collection.

188 PRINTING AND MISPRINTING

	Country, Place	Institution, Copy	In-House Corrections (folio no., line no.)				
			3r	6v, 23	6v, 25–6	6v, 25–6 combin.	68r reset
1	Austria, Vienna	ÖNB	1		1	C	
2	Belgium, Brussels	RL		1	1	B	
3	Belgium, Gent	UL	1	1	1	A	
4	Czech Republic, Prague	NL		1	1	A	
5	Denmark, Copenhagen	RL		1	1	D	
6	France, Besançon	BM		1	1	A	
7	France, Chantilly	Musée Condé	1	1	1	A	
8	France, Lyon	BM (Rés inc 268)		1	1	A	
9	France, Lyon	BM (Rés inc 272)		1	1	A	1
10	France, Montpellier	BIU		1	1	B	
11	France, Nantes	BM	1	1	1	A	
12	France, Paris	BnF (RES-X-25)		1	1	A	1
13	France, Paris	BnF (RES-X-28)		1	1	B	
14	France, Paris	BnF (RES-X-29)	1	1	1	A	
15	France, Paris	BnF (RES-X-30)		1	1	D	
16	France, Paris	BnF (RES-X-31)		1	1	A	
17	France, Paris	BnF (FOL-BL-80 (2))		1	1	C	
18	France, Paris	BnF (FOL-BL-81)	1	1	1	A	
19	France, Paris	BnF (FOL-BL-82)	1	1	1	A	
20	France, Paris	BnF (Rothschild III.7.15)	1	1	1	A	
21	France, Paris	Inst. de France		1	1	A	
22	France, Paris	Mazarine		1	1	A	
23	France, Paris	Sorbonne		1	1	B	
24	France, Poitiers	BM		1	1	B	
25	France, Rouen	BM	1				
26	France, Toulouse	BM	1	1	1	A	
27	Germany, Berlin	SBB (Inc 4486)	1				
28	Germany, Berlin	SBB (Inc 4486a)	1	1	1	A	
29	Germany, Bonn	ULB		1	1	C	
30	Germany, Bremen	SUB		1	1	B	
31	Germany, Dessau	LB	1	1	1	A	
32	Germany, Erfurt	UB	1				
33	Germany, Giessen	UB		1	1	B	
34	Germany, Göttingen	SUB	1	1	1	A	
35	Germany, Halle	ULB		1	1	A	
36	Germany, Heidelberg	UB		1	1	C	
37	Germany, Jena	ULB	1	1	1	B	
38	Germany, Konstanz	Heinrich-Suso-Gymnasium	n/a	n/a	n/a	n/a	n/a
39	Germany, Leipzig	UB		1	1	A	
40	Germany, Marburg	UB	1				
41	Germany, Munich	BSB (2 Inc.c.a. 3399)		1	1	A	
42	Germany, Munich	BSB (2 Inc.c.a. 3399a)		1	1	B	
43	Germany, Munich	BSB (2 Inc.c.a. 3399b)		1	1	A	
44	Germany, Münster	ULB		1	1	B	
45	Germany, Nuremberg	StB	1	1	1	C	1
46	Germany, Oldenburg	LB	1	1	1	A	
47	Germany, Rastatt	Ludwig-Wilhelm-Gymnasium	1				
48	Germany, Rostock	UB		1	1	C	
49	Germany, Stuttgart	Würt. LB	1				
50	Germany, Weimar	HAAB					
51	Germany, Wesel	StArch		1	1	B	
52	Germany, Zittau	StB		1	1	B	
53	Greece, Athens	Gennadius	1	1	1	A	
54	Greece, Athens	Laskaridis		1	1	B	
55	Greece, Athens	NL (ЕФ. 1316)	1	1	1	A	
56	Greece, Athens	NL (ЕФ. 1316a)	1	1	1	C	
57	Greece, Athens	NL (ЕФ. 1316[.b])		1	1	D	
58	Greece, Athos	Vatopedi Monastery	Copy not seen				
59	Greece, Meteora	Varlaam Monastery	Copy not seen				
60	Greece, Patmos	St John Monastery (no. 5(1))		1	1	A	
61	Greece, Patmos	St John Monastery (no. 5(2))	1	1	1	A	

	In-House Corrections (folio no., line no.)								
	76v bearer type	82r	197r	197r reset	207r	227r	187r/188r, 213r	236v, 16 & 21	237r, 6
1	1	1	1		1	1	1	1	1
2	1	1	1		1	1	1	1	1
3	1	1	1		1	1	1	1	1
4	1	1	1		1	1	1	1	1
5	1	1	1		1	1	1	1	1
6	1	1	1		1	1	1	1	1
7			1		1	1	1	1	1
8	1	1	1		1	1	1	1	1
9	1	1		1	1	1	1	1	1
10	1	1	1		1	1	1	1	1
11	1	1	1		1	1	1	1	1
12	1	1		1	1	1	1	1	1
13	1	1	1		1	1	1	1	1
14		1	1		1	1	1	1	1
15	1	1	1		1	1	1	1	1
16	1	1	1		1	1	1	1	1
17	1	1	1		1	1	1	1	1
18	1	1	1		1	1	1	1	1
19	1	1	1		1	1	1	1	1
20	1	1	1		1	1	1	1	1
21	1	1	1		1	1	1	1	1
22	1	1	1		1	1	1	1	1
23	1	1	1		1	1	1	1	1
24	1	1	1		1	1	1	1	1
25	1	1	1		1	1	1		
26	1	1	1		1	1	1	1	1
27		1	1		1	1	1	1	1
28	1	1	1		1	1	1	1	1
29	1	1	1		1	1	1	1	1
30	1	1	1		1	1	1	1	1
31	1	1	1		1	1	1	1	1
32		1	1		1	1	1	1	1
33	1	1	1		1	1	1	1	1
34		1	1		1	1	1	1	1
35		1			1	1	1	1	1
36	1	1	1		1	1	1	1	1
37	1	1	1		1	1	1	1	1
38	n/a	n/a	1		1	1		1	1
39		1	1		1	1	1	1	1
40		1	1		1	1	1	1	1
41	1	1	1		1	1	1	1	1
42	1	1	1		1	1	1	1	1
43	1	1	1		1	1	1	1	1
44		1	1		1	1	1	1	1
45	1	1	1		1	1	1	1	1
46		1	1		1	1	1	1	1
47		1	1		1	1	1	1	1
48	1	1	1		1	1	1	1	1
49		1	1		1	1	1	1	
50	1	1	1		1	1	1	1	1
51	1	1	1		1	1	1	1	1
52	1	1	1		1	1	1	1	1
53		1	1		1	1	1	1	1
54	1	1	1		1	1	1	1	1
55	1	1	1		1	1	1	1	1
56	1	1	1		1	1	1	1	1
57	1	1	1		1	1	1	1	1
58	Copy not seen								
59	Copy not seen								
60	1		1		1	1	1	1	1
61	1	1	1		1	1	1	1	1

190   PRINTING AND MISPRINTING

	Country, Place	Institution, Copy	In-House Corrections (folio no., line no.)				
			3r	6v, 23	6v, 25–6	6v, 25–6 combin.	68r reset
62	Hungary, Budapest	UL		1	1	A	
63	Ireland, Dublin	Marsh's Library	1	1	1	A	1
64	Ireland, Dublin	Trinity College (Q.bb.21)		1	1	B	
65	Ireland, Dublin	Trinity College (SS.dd.29)	1	1	1	A	
66	Italy, Bologna	BU	1	1	1	A	
67	Italy, Ferrara	Ariostea		1	1	B	
68	Italy, Florence	BNCF (Magl. A.1.16,)		1	1	B	
69	Italy, Florence	BNCF (Pal. E.8.1.1 (str. 970))		1	1	C	
70	Italy, Florence	Laurenziana		1	1	B	
71	Italy, Florence	Marucelliana	1				
72	Italy, Genoa	Bibl. Durazzo		1	1	D	
73	Italy, Genoa	BU	n/a	n/a	n/a	n/a	n/a
74	Italy, Milan	Ambrosiana		1	1	A	
75	Italy, Milan	Braidense					1
76	Italy, Milan	Museo Poldi Pezzoli		1	1	A	
77	Italy, Modena	Estense		1	1	A	
78	Italy, Naples	BU (Inc. 123)	1	1	1	A	
79	Italy, Naples	BU (Inc. 266)	1	1	1	A	
80	Italy, Perugia	Augusta		1	1	A	
81	Italy, Pisa	BU			1	C	
82	Italy, Rome	Angelica		1	1	B	
83	Italy, Rome	Casanatense (Vol. INC. 101)	1	1	1	C	
84	Italy, Rome	Casanatense (Vol. INC. 1925)		1	1	B	
85	Italy, Rome	Corsiniana (56.H.15)	1				
86	Italy, Turin	BU (XV.III.106)	1	1	1	A	
87	Italy, Turin	BU (RIS. 33.7)	1	1	1	A	
88	Italy, Venice	Marciana (ALDINE 100)		1	1	C	
89	Italy, Venice	Marciana (ALDINE 224)	1	1	1	C	
90	Malta, Valletta	NL	1	1	1	A	
91	The Netherlands, Amsterdam	UB (Inc. 4)	1				
92	The Netherlands, Amsterdam	UB (Inc. 144)		1	1	B	
93	The Netherlands, Leiden	UB	1	1	1	A	
94	The Netherlands, The Hague	Museum Meermanno		1	1	B	
95	The Netherlands, The Hague	RL		1	1	A	
96	Poland, Gdańsk	Polish Academy of Sciences		1	1	B	
97	Poland, Krakow	Jagiellonian (Cam. L. X. 11)		1	1	D	1
98	Poland, Krakow	Jagiellonian (Dr. Inc. 2256 III)	1	1	1	C	
99	Romania, Alba Iulia	Batthyaneum	1	1	1	C	
100	Romania, Bucharest	Romanian Academy	Copy not seen				
101	Russia, Moscow	RSL, Ald.2.58	Copy not seen				
102	Russia, Moscow	RSL, inc/794	Copy not seen				
103	Russia, St Petersburg	NL (8.10.1.4.)		1	1	A	
104	Spain, Madrid	BNE (Inc/710)					
105	Spain, Madrid	BNE (Inc/1881)	1	1	1	A	
106	Spain, Madrid	BNE (Inc/2048)		1	1	A	
107	Spain, Madrid	BU		1	1	A	
108	Spain, Madrid	Escorial	1	1	1	A	
109	Spain, Madrid	March Private Lib.	Copy not seen and currently untraced				
110	Spain, Salamanca	BU (BG/I. 238)		1	1	B	
111	Spain, Salamanca	BU (BG/I. 322)		1	1	A	
112	Sweden, Stockholm	RL		1	1	B	
113	Sweden, Uppsala	UB		1	1	C	
114	Switzerland, Basel	UB		1	1	C	
115	Switzerland, Bern	UB		1	1	B	
116	Switzerland, Zurich	ZB		1	1	B	
117	UK, Blickling	Blickling Hall		1	1	C	
118	UK, Cambridge	St John's College	1	1	1	C	
119	UK, Cambridge	Trinity College (N.3.74)					
120	UK, Cambridge	Trinity College (N.3.75)		1	1	A	
121	UK, Cambridge	UL (Inc.3.B.3.134 [1807])		1	1	B	
122	UK, Cambridge	UL (Inc.3.B.3.134 [1808])		1	1	B	
123	UK, Chatsworth	Devonshire Collection		1	1	B?	
124	UK, Coleraine	Ulster UL		1	1	C	
125	UK, Durham	UL (SA 0124)					
126	UK, Durham	UL (SA 0125)		1	1	B	
127	UK, Edinburgh	NLS (Inc.194)					
128	UK, Edinburgh	NLS (Inc.194*)		1	1	A	

In–House Corrections (folio no., line no.)								
	76v bearer type	82r	197r	197r reset	207r	227r	187r/188r, 213r	236v, 16 & 21	237r, 6
62	1	1	1		1	1	1	1	1
63	1	1		1	1	1	1	1	1
64	1	1	1		1	1	1	1	1
65	1	1	1		1	1	1	1	1
66	1	1	1		1	1	1	1	1
67	1	1	1		1	1	1	1	1
68	1	1	1		1	1	1	1	1
69	1	1	1		1	1	1	1	1
70		1	1		1	1	1	1	1
71	1	1			1	1	1	1	1
72	1	1	1		1	1	1	1	1
73	n/a	n/a	1		1	1	1	1	1
74	1	1	1		1	1	1	1	1
75	1	1		1	1	1	1	1	1
76		1	1		1	1	1	1	1
77	1	1	1		1	1	1	1	1
78	1	1	1		1	1	1	1	1
79	1	1	1		1	1	1	1	1
80		1	1		1	1	1	1	1
81	1	1	1		1	1	1	1	1
82	1	1	1		1	1	1	1	1
83	1	1	1		1	1	1	1	1
84	1		1		1	1	1	1	
85		1			1	1			
86	1	1	1		1	1	1	1	1
87	1	1		1	1	1	1	1	1
88		1	1		1	1	1	1	1
89	1	1	1		1	1	1	1	1
90	1	1	1		1	1	1	1	1
91	1	1			1	1			
92	1	1	1		1	1	1	1	1
93	1	1	1		1	1	1	1	1
94	1	1	1		1	1	1	1	1
95	1	1	1		1	1	1	1	1
96	1	1	1		1	1	1	1	1
97	1	1	1		1	1	1	1	1
98	1	1	1		1	1	1	1	1
99	1	1	1		1	1	1	1	1
100	Copy not seen								
101	Copy not seen								
102	Copy not seen								
103	1	1	1			1	1	1	1
104	1	1	1		1	1	1		
105	1	1	1		1	1	1	1	1
106	1	1	1		1	1	1	1	1
107	1	1	1		1	1	1	1	1
108	1	1	1		1	1	1	1	1
109	Copy not seen and currently untraced								
110	1	1	1		1	1	1	1	1
111	1	1	1		1	1	1	1	1
112	1	1	1		1	1	1	1	1
113	1	1	1		1	1	1		
114	1	1	1		1	1	1	1	1
115	1	1	1		1	1	1	1	1
116	1	1	1		1	1	1	1	1
117	1	1	1		1	1	1	1	1
118	1	1	1		1	1	1	1	1
119		1	1		1	1	1	1	1
120	1		1		1	1	1	1	1
121	1	1	1		1	1	1	1	1
122	1	1	1		1	1	1	1	1
123	1	1			1	1			
124		1	1		1	1	1		1
125	1	1	1		1	1	1		
126	1	1	1		1	1	1	1	1
127	1	1	1		1	1	1		
128	1	1	1		1	1	1	1	1

192 PRINTING AND MISPRINTING

	Country, Place	Institution, Copy	In–House Corrections (folio no., line no.)				
			3r	6v, 23	6v, 25–6	6v, 25–6 combin.	68r reset
129	UK, Eton	Eton College		1	1	A	
130	UK, Glasgow	UL		1	1	B	
131	UK, Lampeter	UL		1	1	C	
132	UK, Leeds	UL		1	1	A	
133	UK, Liverpool	UL	1	1	1	A	
134	UK, London	BL (C.15.c.11)		1	1	B	
135	UK, London	BL (G.7630)		1	1	A	
136	UK, London	BL (IB.24415)		1	1	B	
137	UK, London	BL (IB.24416)	1	1	1	A	1
138	UK, London	King's College		1	1	A	
139	UK, London	Royal College of Physicians		1	1	C	
140	UK, London	Senate House		1	1	B	
141	UK, London	St Paul's School		1	1	B	
142	UK, Manchester	Chetham's	1	1	1	1	
143	UK, Manchester	Rylands UL		1	1	C	
144	UK, Oxford	All Souls College		1	1	B	
145	UK, Oxford	Balliol College		1	1	B	
146	UK, Oxford	Bodleian Library (Auct R 1.4)		1	1	B	
147	UK, Oxford	Bodleian Library (Byw. G 3.16)	1	1	1	C	
148	UK, Oxford	Christ Church					
149	UK, Oxford	Corpus Christi College		1	1	C	
150	UK, Oxford	Merton College		1	1	A	
151	UK, Oxford	New College		1	1	B	
152	UK, Oxford	Queen's College		1	1	B	
153	UK, Oxford	University College		1	1	A	
154	UK, Shrewsbury	Shrewsbury School		1	1	D/B	
155	UK, St Andrews	UL		1	1	A	
156	UK, Wells-next-the-Sea	Holkham Hall		1	1	B	
157	UK, Windsor	RL	1		1	C	
158	USA, Austin TX	HRHRC (T54 1496 ALDINE Copy 1)					
159	USA, Austin TX	HRHRC (T54 1496 ALDINE Copy 2)		1	1	C	
160	USA, Austin TX	HRHRC (Uzielli 7)			1	C	
161	USA, Baltimore	Walters Art Museum		1	1	A	
162	USA, Bloomington (IN)	Lilly Library		1	1	B	
163	USA, Bryn Mawr (PA)	Goodhart Medieval Library	1				
164	USA, Cambridge (MA)	Houghton (Inc 5551(A))		1	1	A	
165	USA, Cambridge (MA)	Houghton (Inc 5551(B))		1	1	C	
166	USA, Cambridge (MA)	Houghton (WKR 3.4.5)		1	1	A	
167	USA, Chicago	Newberry		1	1	A	1
168	USA, Claremont (CA)	Honnold Library		1	1	A	
169	USA, Los Angeles	UCLA	1	1	1	A	
170	USA, Middletown (CT)	Wesleyan UL	1	1	1	A	
171	USA, New Haven (CT)	Beinecke (BEIN Zi +5551 Copy 1)					
172	USA, New Haven (CT)	Beinecke (BEIN Zi +5551 Copy 2)		1	1	D	
173	USA, New Haven (CT)	Beinecke (BEIN Zi +5551 Copy 3)		1	1	B	
174	USA, New York	Butler Library		1	1	D	
175	USA, New York	Morgan Library and Museum		1	1	B	
176	USA, New York	NYPL		1	1	C	
177	USA, Princeton (NJ)	Firestone		1	1	A	
178	USA, Providence (RI)	John Carter Brown	1				
179	USA, Provo (UT)	Harold B. Lee Library	1	1	1	A	
180	USA, San Francisco	Public Library	1	1	1	C	
181	USA, San Marino (CA)	Huntington	1	1	1	C	
182	USA, Syracuse (NY)	Syracuse UL	1	1	1	C	
183	USA, Urbana (IL)	Univ. of Illinois Library	1				
184	USA, Washington DC	LoC (Incun. 1496 .T39)	1				
185	USA, Washington DC	LoC (Incun. 1496 .T39 Vollbehr Coll)	1	1	1	C	
186	Vatican City	BAV (Inc.II.591)	1				
187	Vatican City	BAV (Inc.II.592)		1	1	B	
188	Vatican City	BAV (Inc.II.707)		1	1	B	
189	Vatican City	BAV (Stamp.Barb.CCC.V.1)	1	1	1	C	
190	Vatican City	BAV (Stamp.Ross.899)		1	1	B	
191	Antiquarian market	Borghese-Ambrogio copy	1	1	1	A	?
192	Antiquarian market	Macclesfield copy	?	1	1	A	?
193	Antiquarian market	Sotheby's Milan, 4 October 2022		1	1	A	
	Total number of occurrences		63	158	162		8
	Frequency (in percentage)		33.6	84.4	86.6		4.2

	In-House Corrections (folio no., line no.)								
	76v bearer type	82r	197r	197r reset	207r	227r	187r/188r, 213r	236v, 16 & 21	237r, 6
129	1	1	1		1	1	1	1	1
130	1	1	1		1	1	1	1	1
131			1		1	1	1	1	1
132	1	1	1		1	1	1	1	1
133	1		1		1	1	1	1	1
134	1		1		1	1	1	1	1
135	1	1	1		1	1	1	1	1
136	1	1	1		1	1	1	1	1
137	1	1		1	1	1	1	1	1
138	1	1	1		1	1	1	1	1
139		1	1		1	1	1	1	1
140	1	1	1		1	1	1	1	1
141		1	1		1	1	1	1	1
142	1	1	1		1	1	1	1	1
143	1	1	1		1	1	1	1	1
144	1	1	1		1	1	1	1	1
145	1	1	1		1	1	1	1	1
146	1	1	1		1	1	1	1	1
147		1	1		1	1	1	1	1
148	1	1	1		1	1	1		
149		1	1		1	1	1	1	1
150	1	1	1		1	1	1	1	1
151	1	1	1		1	1	1	1	1
152	1	1	1		1	1	1	1	1
153	1		1		1	1	1	1	1
154	1	1	1		1	1	1	1	1
155	1	1	1		1	1	1	1	1
156	1	1	1		1	1	1	1	1
157	1	1	1		1	1	1	1	1
158	1	1	1		1	1	1		
159	1	1	1		1	1	1	1	1
160		1	1		1	1	1	1	1
161	1	1	1		1	1	1	1	1
162	1	1	1		1	1	1	1	1
163		1			1	1			
164		1	1		1	1	1	1	1
165	1	1	1		1	1	1	1	1
166	1	1	1		1	1	1	1	1
167	1	1		1	1	1	1	1	1
168	1		1		1	1	1	1	1
169	1	1	1		1	1	1	1	1
170	1	1	1		1	1	1	1	1
171	1	1	1		1	1	1		
172	1	1	1		1	1	1	1	1
173	1	1	1		1	1	1	1	1
174	1	1	1		1	1	1	1	1
175	1	1	1		1	1	1	1	1
176	1	1	1		1	1	1	1	1
177		1	1		1	1	1	1	1
178		1			1	1			
179		1		1	1	1	1	1	1
180	1	1	1		1	1	1	1	1
181	1	1	1		1	1	1	1	1
182	1	1	1		1	1	1	1	1
183		1	1		1	1	1	1	1
184		1			1	1			
185	1		1		1	1	1	1	1
186		1		1	1	1	1		
187	1	1	1		1	1	1	1	1
188	1	1	1		1	1	1	1	1
189	1	1	1		1	1	1	1	1
190	1	1	1		1	1	1	1	1
191	1	1	1		1	1	1	1	1
192	1	?	1		1	1	1	?	?
193	1	1	1		1	1	1	1	1
	152	175	170	9	184	187	181	171	169
	81.2	93.5	90.9	4.8	98.3	100	96.7	91.4	90.3

BIBLIOGRAPHY

PRIMARY SOURCES

MANUSCRIPTS AND ARCHIVAL DOCUMENTATION

Florence, Archivio di Stato, *Cervini*, vol. 15.
Florence, Biblioteca Laurenziana, Plut. 55.18 and San Marco 303.
Florence, Private archive of the Perra family, Giovan Girolamo de' Rossi's *Storia generale* (1557–1563).

PRINTED BOOKS

Aristophanes, *Comoediae novem*, Venice, Aldus Manutius, 15 July 1498, f° (ISTC ia00958000).

Aristoteles, *Opera*, Venice, Aldus Manutius, 1495–1498, f° (ISTC ia00959000).

Carthusiensis, Adrianus, *De remediis utriusque fortunae*, Cologne, Arnold ter Hoernen, 8 February 1471, 4° (ISTC ia00055000).

Catherine of Siena, *Epistole*, Venice, Aldus Manutius, [not before 19] September 1500, f° (ISTC ic00281000).

Doni, Anton Francesco, *La seconda parte de marmi*, Venice, nell'Accademia Peregrina per Francesco Marcolini, 1552, 4° (USTC 827617).

Erasmus, Desiderius, *Adagiorum chiliades tres*, Venice, Aldus Manutius, 1508, f° (USTC 828220).

Erasmus, Desiderius, *Apologia adversus rhapsodias calumniosarum querimoniarum Alberti Pii*, Basel, Hieronymus Froben and Nikolaus Episcopius, 1531, 4° (USTC 635481).

Favorino, Guarino, *Magnum ac perutile dictionarium*, Rome, Zacharias Kallierges, 1523, f° (USTC 828891).

Gessner, Conrad, *Bibliotheca Universalis*, Zurich, Froschauer, 1545, f° (USTC 616753); Gessner's annotated copy in Zurich, Zentralbibliothek, Dr M 3.

Gessner, Conrad, *Pandectarum sive partitionum universalium* [...] *libri XXI*, Zurich, Christoph Froschauer, 1548, f° (USTC 682395).

Hieronymus, *Epistolae*, Venice, Andrea Torresano, 15 May 1488, f° (ISTC ih00170000).

Hilarion, *Legendarium*, Milan, Jacopo Sannazzaro da Riva, 16 Apr. 1494, 4° (ISTC ih00268500).

Lascaris, Constantinus, *Erotemata*, Venice, Aldus Manutius, 28 Feb. 1494/1495 and 8 Mar. 1495, 4° (ISTC il00068000).

Manutius, Aldus, *Grammaticae institutiones Graecae*, Venice, Aldus Manutius's heirs and Andrea Torresano, 1515, 4° (USTC 840308).

Manutius, Aldus, *Institutiones grammaticae*, Venice, [Andrea Torresano], 1493, 4° (ISTC im00226500).

Perotti, Niccolò, *Cornucopiae linguae latinae*, Venice, Aldus Manutius, July 1499, f° (ISTC ip00296000).

Petrarca, Francesco, *Le cose volgari*, Venice, Aldus Manutius, 1501, 8° (USTC 847779).

Pindarus, [*Odes*], Venice, Aldus Manutius and Andrea Torresano, 1513, 8° (USTC 848778).

Poliziano, Angelo, *Opera*, Venice, Aldus Manutius, 1498, f° (ISTC ip00886000).

Rolewinck, Werner, *Sermo in festo praesentationis beatissimae Mariae virginis*, [Cologne, Arnold ter Hoernen], 1470, 4° (ISTC iro0304000).

Simler, Josias, *Epitome bibliothecae Conradi Gesnero*, Zurich, Christoph Froschauer, 1555, f° (USTC 652948).

Suidas, Milan, Johannes Bissolus and Benedictus Mangius for Demetrius Chalcondylas, 1499, f° (ISTC iso0829000).

Θησαυρὸς, Κέρας Ἀμαλθείας, καὶ κῆποι Ἀδώνιδος. Thesaurus Cornu copiae & Hortus Adonidis, Venice, Aldus Manutius, 1496, f° (ISTC it00158000).

SECONDARY LITERATURE

Aldo Manuzio editore. Dediche, prefazioni, note ai testi, ed. G. Orlandi, 2 vols, Milan, 1976.

Baldi, D., 'Aldo Manuzio e le peculiarità greche: le abbreviazioni', in G. Comiati (ed.), *Aldo Manuzio editore, umanista e filologo*, Milan, 2019, pp. 119–50.

Barker, N., *Aldus Manutius and the Development of Greek Script and Type in the Fifteenth Century*, 2nd edn, New York, 1992.

Bauer, D. F., 'Problems in the Aldine Pindar', *Princeton University Library Chronicle*, 76, 2015, pp. 417–45.

Bekker, I., *Anecdota Graeca*, III, Berlin, 1821.

Bibliothèque Nationale. Catalogue des incunables, II/4, Paris, 1985.

Bigliazzi, L., et al. (eds), *Aldo Manuzio tipografo, 1494–1515*, Florence, 1994.

Black, R., 'Aldo Manuzio Grammarian', in P. D. Accendere and S. U. Baldassari (eds), *Collectanea manutiana. Studi critici su Aldo Manuzio*, Florence, 2017, pp. 69–92.

Blair, A., 'Errata Lists and the Reader as Corrector', in S. A. Baron, E. N. Lindquist, and E. F. Shevlin (eds), *Agent of Change: Print Culture Studies after Elizabeth L. Eisenstein*, Amherst (MA), 2007, pp. 21–41.

Botley, P., *Learning Greek in Western Europe, 1396–1529: Grammars, Lexica and Classroom Texts*, Philadelphia, 2010.

Catalogue of Books Printed in the XVth Century now in the British Museum, V: *Venice*, London, 1924.

Ciccolella, F., and Silvano, L. (eds), *Teachers, Students, and Schools of Greek in the Renaissance*, Leiden and Boston, 2017.

Clough, C. H., 'Pietro Bembo's Edition of Petrarch and His Association with the Aldine Press', in D. S. Zeidberg (ed.), *Aldus Manutius and Renaissance Culture: Essays in Memory of Franklin D. Murphy: Acts of an International Conference, Venice and Florence, 14–17 June 1994*, Florence, 1998, pp. 47–80.

Davies, M., 'Aldo Manuzio, uomo ed editore', in M. Davies and N. Harris, *Aldo Manuzio. L'uomo, l'editore, il mito*, Rome, 2019, pp. 13–53.

Della Rocca de Candal, G., Kokkonas, Y., and Olocco, R., 'Experimenting with Greek Typography: The Undated Vicenza Chrysoloras [1477]', *Thesaurismata*, 48, 2018, pp. 97–116.

Etymologicum Symeonis Γ-E, ed. D. Baldi, Turnhout, 2013.

Fabricius, J. A., *Bibliotheca graeca*, XIII, Hamburg, 1726.

Gentile, S., and Speranzi, D., 'Antichi cataloghi. Gli inventari dei manoscritti greci della libreria medicea privata', in P. Degni, P. Eleuteri, and M. Maniaci (eds), *Greek Manuscript Cataloguing: Past, Present, and Future*, Turnhout, 2018, pp. 15–38.

Gerritsen, J., 'Printing at Froben's: An Eye-Witness Account', *Studies in Bibliography*, 44, 1991, pp. 144–63.

Giacomelli, C., 'Un autografo di frate Urbano Bolzanio, umanista bellunese. Con appunti sulla sua biblioteca greca', *Italia medioevale e umanistica*, 58, 2017, pp. 243–79.

Graesse, J. G. T., *Trésor de livres rares et précieux*, VI/2, Dresden, 1867.

Grafton, A., *The Culture of Correction in Renaissance Europe*, London, 2011.

Grafton, A., *Inky Fingers: The Making of Books in Early Modern Europe*, Cambridge (MA) and London, 2020.

Grammatici Graeci, ed. K. W. Dindorf, Leipzig, 1823.

Guida, A., 'Il *Dictionarium* di Favorino e il *Lexicon Vindobonense*', *Prometheus*, 8, 1982, pp. 264–86.

Hellinga, L., *Text in Transit: Manuscript to Proof and Print in the Fifteenth Century*, Leiden and Boston, 2014.

Hill, G. F., *The Development of Arabic Numerals in Europe*, Oxford, 1915.

Hoffman, G., 'Writing Without Leisure: Proofreading as Labour in the Renaissance', *The Journal of Medieval and Renaissance Studies*, 25, 1995, pp. 17–31.

Ingram, W. H., 'The Ligatures of Early Printed Greek', *Greek, Roman and Byzantine Studies*, 7/4, 1966, pp. 371–89.

Lemke, A., *Aldus Manutius and his Thesaurus Cornucopiae of 1496*, Syracuse (NY), 1958.

Lerer, S., *Error and the Academic Self: The Scholarly Imagination, Medieval to Modern*, New York, 2002, pp. 15–54.

Lowry, M., *The World of Aldus Manutius: Business and Scholarship in Renaissance Venice*, Oxford, 1979.

McLeod, R., 'The Invisible Book', *New College Notes*, 14, 2021, pp. 1–95.

Manutius, A., *The Greek Classics*, ed. N. G. Wilson, Cambridge (MA), 2016.

Manutius, A., *Humanism and the Latin Classics*, ed. J. N. Grant, Cambridge (MA), 2017.

Mencke, F. O., *Historia vitae et in literas meritorum Angeli Politiani*, Leipzig, 1736.

Nelles, P., 'Reading and Memory in the Universal Library: Conrad Gessner and the Renaissance Book', in D. Beecher and G. Williams (eds), Ars reminiscendi: *Mind and Memory in Renaissance Culture*, Toronto, 2009, pp. 147–69.

Nuovo, A., *The Book Trade in the Italian Renaissance*, Leiden and Boston, 2013.

Nuovo, A., 'The End of the Manutius Dynasty, 1597', in J. Kraye and P. Sachet (eds), *The Afterlife of Aldus: Posthumous Fame, Collectors and the Book Trade*, London, 2018, pp. 45–78.

Pearson, D., 'The Importance of the Copy Census as a Methodology in Book History', in B. Wagner and M. Reed (eds), *Early Printed Books as Material Objects: Proceeding of the Conference Organized by the IFLA Rare Books and Manuscripts Section (Munich, 19–21 August 2009)*, Berlin, 2010, pp. 321–8.

Piccolomini, E., *Intorno alle condizioni e alle vicende della libreria medicea privata*, Florence, 1875.

Piovan, F., 'Forteguerri (Carteromaco), Scipione', in *Dizionario biografico degli Italiani*, XLIX, Rome, 1997, pp. 163–7.

Polain, M.-L., *Catalogue des livres imprimés au quinzième siècle des bibliothèques de Belgique*, 5 vols, Bruxelles, 1932–1978.

Poliziano, A., *Liber epigrammatum graecorum*, ed. F. Pontani, Rome, 2002.

Pray, G., *Index rariorum librorum bibliothecae Universitatis regiae Budensis*, II, Buda, 1791.

Renouard, A.-A., *Annales de l'imprimerie des Alde*, Paris, 1834.

Richardson, B., 'Aldo Manuzio and the Uses of Translation', in P. D. Accendere and S. U. Baldassari (eds), *Collectanea manutiana. Studi critici su Aldo Manuzio*, Florence, 2017, pp. 145–69.

Rupprich, H., (ed.), *Der Briefwechsel des Conrad Celtis*, Munich, 1934.

Sabba, F., *La Bibliotheca Universalis di Conrad Gesner. Monumento della cultura europea*, Rome, 2012.

Sachet, P., 'Proofreaders', in A. Blair et al. (eds), *Information: A Historical Companion*, Princeton, 2021, pp. 709–12.

Sawyer, D., 'Page Numbers, Signatures, and Catchwords', in D. Duncan and A. Smyth (eds), *Book Parts*, Oxford, 2019, pp. 139–49.

Scaglione, A., 'The Humanist as Scholar and Poliziano's Conception of the "Grammaticus"', *Studies in the Renaissance*, 8, 1961, pp. 49–70.

Sicherl, M., *Griechische Erstausgaben des Aldus Manutius: Druckvorlagen, Stellenwert, kultureller Hintergrund*, Padeborn, 1997.

Smith, M. M., 'Printed Foliation: Forerunner to Printed Page-Numbers', *Gutenberg-Jahrbuch*, 63, 1988, pp. 54–70.

Smith, O. L., 'Urbano da Belluno and Copenhagen GkS 1965, 4o', *Scriptorium*, 23, 1978, pp. 57–9.

Stein, R. [i.e. McLeod, R.], 'When the Poet Gives Empty Leaves', *Journal of Early modern Studies*, 11, 2022, pp. 117-200

Speranzi, D., 'La scrittura di Aldo e il suo ultimo carattere greco (con uno sconosciuto esemplare di tipografia)', in N. Vacalebre (ed.), *Five centuries later: Aldus Manutius: Culture, Typography and Philology*, Florence, 2018, pp. 29–60.

Ucciardello, G., '1523. Guarini Favorini *Magnum Dictionarium Graecum*', in C. Bianca et al. (eds), *Le prime edizioni greche a Roma (1510–1526)*, Turnhout, 2017, pp. 171–204.

Yukishima, K., 'Gessner's *Bibliotheca Universalis* and The Aldine Press', in U. B. Leu and P. Opitz (eds), *Conrad Gessner (1516–1565): Die Renaissance der Wissenschaften/The Renaissance of Learning*, Oldenburg, 2019, pp. 29–40.

Zeno, A., [Review of Guarino Favorino, *Magnum Dictionarium*, Venice, 1712], *Giornale de' letterati d'Italia*, XIX, 1714, pp. 89–129.

CHAPTER 9

MANAGING MISPRINTS

*Jan Moretus I's Diverse Approaches
to Correcting Errors*

DIRK IMHOF

INTRODUCTION

THE Antwerp publisher Jan Moretus I was very proud of the high quality of his editions and, in particular, of the correctness of the texts he published. Some authors preferred to make use of his press precisely for that reason. When the English theologian Thomas Stapleton wrote to Moretus on 27 August 1589 about the publication of his *Promptuarium morale*, a collection of sermons, he explained that he had chosen Moretus not only for the high quality of his type and paper, but also because he had noticed that Moretus's Latin texts were always more correct than editions from Paris.[1]

In 1599, when other Antwerp publishers had printed a *Missale Romanum* and Moretus wrote to the archbishop to defend his privilege for printing liturgical books for the clergy in the Netherlands, he also underscored this correctness of the text. He was aware, he explained, that even if someone took the utmost care, typographical errors were unavoidable. Therefore, the printer who most succeeded in avoiding errors rightly deserved praise. But when he had looked quickly at a copy of a *Missale* just printed by his competitors, he had scarcely read two pages and had already found six or seven mistakes. These

---

[1] '[…] ante omnia desideravi tuis potissimum typis hoc opus evulgari, non solum quia elegantissimos habes, chartaque uteris plerumque selectissima, sed etiam quia quantum observare potui, correctiores multo Latini libri ex vestra officina prodeant quam ex Lutetianis' ('[…] above all I wished that this work would be printed with your type, not only because you have the most attractive type and you generally use the most select paper, but also because to the best of my knowledge, texts in Latin are produced much more accurately by your press than by Parisian printers'): Antwerp, Museum Plantin-Moretus, Arch. 93, *Recueils de lettres Aug. Sabbetius–Ger. Symont*, pp. 563–6; *Correspondance de Christophe Plantin*, ed. M. Rooses and J. Denucé, 9 vols, Antwerp and Gent, 1883–1920, no. 1494. Henceforth, documents from the Plantin-Moretus Museum are referred to as 'MPM, Arch.' followed by their individual number; at times, rectos and versos are not specified as original 'foliation' was applied to openings instead of leaves. The titles of the documents are taken from J. Denucé, *Inventaire des archives Plantiniennes*, Antwerp, 1926.

Dirk Imhof, *Managing Misprints*. In: *Printing and Misprinting*. Edited by Geri Della Rocca de Candal, Anthony Grafton, and Paolo Sachet, Oxford University Press. © Dirk Imhof (2023). DOI: 10.1093/oso/9780198863045.003.0010 were not small ones, but ones that would confuse devout priests.[2] This would not happen with editions from the Plantin press.

Jan Moretus I, Christopher Plantin's son-in-law, managed the Plantin press after Plantin's death in 1589. Despite the efforts of some of his relatives and competitors who endeavoured to divide and weaken the press, he was able to maintain the business as a whole and retain important privileges for the printing of the Bible and reformed liturgical texts that his father-in-law had previously obtained. He even succeeded in expanding the activities of the press such that it became a flourishing company once again after its decline following the fall of Antwerp in 1585.[3] Among the c. 700 editions he published between 1589 and 1610, he was best known for his liturgical editions, which were widely sought after throughout Europe due to their high quality, as well as the numerous influential editions of Justus Lipsius on Roman history and philosophy. In addition, Moretus also published the well-known atlases by Abraham Ortelius, historical treatises such as the *Annales ecclesiastici* by the Italian cardinal Cesare Baronio, and numerous editions of classical authors.[4]

If it was true that he conscientiously endeavoured to avoid printing errors in his editions, how did he manage to meet the high standard that he had set for himself? What made the Plantin press different from other publishers who had proofreaders as well? The exceptionally extensive array of preserved archival documents of the Plantin-Moretus press makes it possible to discern how Jan Moretus proceeded in printing books and how he dealt with the inevitable errors that were made in every edition that was printed.

A Proofreader in the Family

At first glance, Jan Moretus seems to have followed the same practices as his fellow publishers by relying on proofreaders to catch potential errors during the printing process and to compile a list of errata to be added to the end of the book containing any that had been overlooked. Initially, Moretus had three proofreaders in his service: the old Cornelis Kiliaan, who began working for Plantin in 1558 and was employed until 1604; Jan Gheesdael, who

---

[2] Letter to Mathias Hovius, 19 March 1599: 'Agnosco equidem nullam in correctione hac typographica cautionem tantam esse potest ut omnem caveamus errorem, sed qui quam potest maximè caverint, eos demum mereri laudem iure omnes censeant. Quod ad Keerbergii et Nutii missale, nihil temere iis detractum à me velim, sed ut heri aut nundiustertius exemplar eius mihi primùm comparavi, ac binas dumtaxat pagellas, ubi Proprium missarum incipit, inspexi, repperi supra sex aut septem errores, atque inter eos unum atque alterum haud leves, et qui facile pium sacerdotem interturbent' ('I know that in this typographical correction no precaution can guarantee that there will be no errors, but everyone agrees that he who takes as many precautions as possible, rightly deserves praise. As for Van Keerbergen's and Nutius's missals, I would not want to criticise them without a reason, but, having acquired a copy of it yesterday or the day before and inspected only the two pages where the 'Proprium missarum' starts, I found more than six or seven mistakes among where significant ones that would easily confuse a faithful priest'): MPM, Arch. 12, *Copie de lettres de Jean Moretus I, 1598–1607*, p. 66.
[3] After several years of Calvinist government, the city of Antwerp surrendered to the troops of Alessandro Farnese in August 1585. This marked the breakup between the Southern and Northern Netherlands.
[4] On Jan Moretus I, see D. Imhof, *Jan Moretus and the Continuation of the Plantin Press: A Bibliography of the Works Published and Printed by Jan Moretus I in Antwerp (1589–1610)*, 2 vols, Leiden, 2014.

occasionally drank too much and left the press in 1591; and Olivier a Fine, who left dissatisfied after a number of years.[5] They were succeeded by others in the course of the years, such as François Harduinus, who came in 1593, or the Scottish proofreader Alexander Stratton, who began in 1608. While the duration of their employment varied from several months to several years, Jan Moretus could at least be certain that one would always remain, namely his second son Balthasar, who (together with his brother Jan Moretus II) would ultimately succeed his father in 1610 and continue to run the press until 1641 (Fig. 9.1).[6] Since Balthasar was a youth, Jan Moretus had trained him to be proofreader at the press. On 18 October 1590, when Balthasar was sixteen years old, Jan Moretus wrote to the Spanish theologian Benito Arias Montano that Balthasar was attending the last year of the Latin school in Antwerp and added: 'We hope that he will be valuable some day at the press as a proofreader'.[7] After his Latin school Balthasar studied in Justus Lipsius's *contubernium* in Leuven for several months to improve his Latin. He returned to Antwerp in January 1593. From then on, he worked as a proofreader at his father's press and became increasingly involved in maintaining contact with authors and following up on the printing of their editions.

Balthasar Moretus went about his work as a proofreader by conscientiously reading the manuscripts that the authors had sent in for publication, not only to see if they were fit to be published by the Plantin press, but also if they were well-enough prepared to be printed.[8] He preferred to have the manuscript as it was written by the author himself above a manuscript copied by a secretary, even if this secretary wrote neatly and carefully. On 8 January 1603 he wrote to the Jesuit Claude Dausque, who apparently had sent a neatly written manuscript, that their main concern was a correct manuscript rather than a neat one because they had observed that authors did not see errors anymore when their secretary rewrote the manuscript. Better a correct manuscript from the author himself than one attractively rewritten by a secretary.[9]

---

[5] After the last payment to the proofreader Olivier a Fine on 25 September 1593, Jan Moretus noted: 'est parti malcontent et sans dire adieu' ('he left displeased and without saying goodbye'): MPM, Arch. 786, *Ouvriers 1590–1610*, fol. 15.

[6] On Balthasar Moretus I see D. Imhof, '*Ex arte et decore typographica*: Balthasar Moretus I, Publisher of Baroque Books', in D. Imhof (ed.), *Balthasar Moretus and the Passion of Publishing*, Kontich, 2018, pp. 12–28.

[7] MPM, Arch. 10, *Copie de lettres de Plantin 1579–1589*, fol. 285r–v; transcription in Benito Arias Montano, *Correspondencia conservada en el Museo Plantin-Moretus de Amberes*, ed. A. Dávila Pérez, Madrid, 2002, II, no. 128, pp. 761–8: 'Unus filiorum superstitum, qui est seniori proximus, dextera manu et latere integro impotens, natus est tempore primi tumultus Antverpiensis, quo matrem cum prole tunc amittere metuebam, sed conservavit Deus, qui quae magis salutifera mihi novit. Ingenio is valet sinistraque manu scribit eleganter; ad Rhetoricam pervenit in studiis. Speramus ipsum quandoque in typographia nobis profuturum in munere correctoris obeundo' ('One of my surviving sons, the second oldest, cannot use his right hand nor his side. He was born in the period of the first disturbances in Antwerp, when I feared that I would lose mother and child. God, who knows what is more beneficial for me, preserved him. He has a healthy intellect and writes neatly with his left hand. At the moment he is in the 'Rhetorica' class. We hope that one day he will be useful in our press as a proofreader').

[8] He maintained this habit of reading the texts that authors sent him once he had succeeded his father as head of the press and continued to do so until shortly before his death in 1641.

[9] MPM, Arch. 12, *Copie de lettres de Jean Moretus I, 1598–1607*, p. 219: 'Porro ut de venusta exemplaris scriptione obiter respondeam, haud eam tantopere a nobis requiri R.T. intelligat, prout distinctam ac emendatam. Usu enim edocti sumus plurima ab amanuensibus subinde peccari, quae auctores, etsi relegant, minus animadvertant. Adeo ut correctam auctorum quam venustam amanuensium manum multo

FIG. 9.1. Thomas Willeboirts Bosschaert, *Portrait of Balthasar Moretus*, oil painting. Antwerp: Museum Plantin-Moretus, V.IV.3.

Regularly, Balthasar sent the manuscript back to an author with the message that it needed to be written correctly (in one instance, he asked that at least punctuation should be added!).[10] In addition, he requested that the citations be quoted correctly from the right

---

malimus' ('Moreover, as to the attractively written manuscript, you ought to understand that we do not really need that as much as a clear and corrected one. Over time we have learned that clerks often make many mistakes that authors do not notice when they go back over the text. This is why we prefer a correct manuscript by the author above an attractive written one by a clerk').

[10] See Balthasar's letter from 7 December 1607 to the doctor Thomas Fienus: 'Vidi libellum tuum et argumentum probo [...]. At, quod ultro fateris, valde adhuc inconcinnum atque imparatum praelo offendo. Nulla interpunctionis ratio observata est, exigua etiam alibi orthographiae' ('I looked at your booklet and I like its contents [...]. However, as you will readily admit, it would be an affront to the business of printing to bring out something as clumsy and ill prepared as this. No rule for punctuation has been observed and only rarely for the orthography'): MPM, Arch. 135, *Copie de Lettres 1607–1615*, p. 9.

editions, especially for those concerning biblical references.[11] When the copy had been handed over to the press, he read it carefully looking for possible errors in the text. In Balthasar's correspondence there are many letters with his lists of *dubia* and discussions about the correct grammatical use of Latin or Greek words. An example is his letter to Jan Bernaerts, who in 1595 had published the text of the Latin poet Statius, followed by a commentary, *Ad P. Statii Papinii, Silvarum libros, commentarius* in 1599 (Fig. 9.2).[12] In addition to complaining about the poor quality of the manuscript and the many errors, he also wrote concerning matters of interpretation. For example, in a letter from June or July 1599 Balthasar remarks that the word 'Oethaea' had not in his opinion been interpreted correctly.[13]

Balthasar similarly questioned the work of other authors, such as Peter Pantin, who published a Greek biography on St Thecla in 1608. In a letter from 27 March 1608, which was written when printing was almost finished, Balthasar Moretus still had some questions regarding some words in the dedication.[14] As Balthasar grew older and his knowledge of Latin and Greek improved, his remarks on the texts that authors sent also grew in number.[15] Although he may have been hypercritical, it was definitively better for a publisher to ameliorate the text before it was printed than to add corrections afterwards.

THE AUTHORS AT PLAY

For both Bernaerts' and Pantin's publications, the gatherings were sent to the author the moment they were printed. They could then inspect the sheets and send their remarks. Only, in the case of Justus Lipsius the sheets were sent to him in Leuven for correction and returned to Antwerp before they were printed in full. For example, on 15 December 1600, during the printing of the 1601 quarto edition of his collected letters, the *Epistolarum selectarum III centuriae*, Balthasar Moretus wrote him: 'I hope that you have received the sheet that I have sent for correction via Peter Colibrant this week and that you will send it

---

[11] See Balthasar's letter to the Jesuit Jean Roberti, who in 1609 offered his work *Mysticae Ezechielis quadrigae* for publication: 'Exemplar inprimis accurate emendandum est tum Graece tum Latine: et conferendus diligenter textus Latinus cum editione Sixtina [i.e. Clementina]: textus Graecus cum editione Plantiniana, sive quae seorsim exstat, sive potius quae in Regiis Bibliis' ('Both the Greek and the Latin texts in the copy must be corrected very carefully. The Latin text has to be compared diligently with the Sixtine edition; the Greek text with a Plantin edition: either from an independent edition or, better still, with the one in the *Biblia regia*'): MPM, Arch. 135, *Copie de Lettres 1607–1615*, pp. 66–7.

[12] Imhof, *Jan Moretus* (n. 4 above), no. B-27.

[13] MPM, Arch. 12, *Copie de lettres de Jean Moretus I, 1598–1607*, p. 79. The verse with the word 'Oethaea' occurs on p. 121 of Bernaerts's commentary (USTC 407060).

[14] MPM, Arch. 135, *Copie de Lettres 1607–1615*, p. 17. Transcription in J. Fabri, 'La correspondance de Pierre Pantin avec Balthasar Moretus', *De Gulden Passer*, 43/4, 1965, pp. 166–247 (201–2). For this edition, see Imhof, *Jan Moretus* (n. 4 above), no. B-23.

[15] In this text only examples from the years that Balthasar Moretus worked for his father are given. There are numerous other examples of (sometimes extensive) lists of 'dubia' that he sent to his authors when he managed the press between 1610 and 1641.

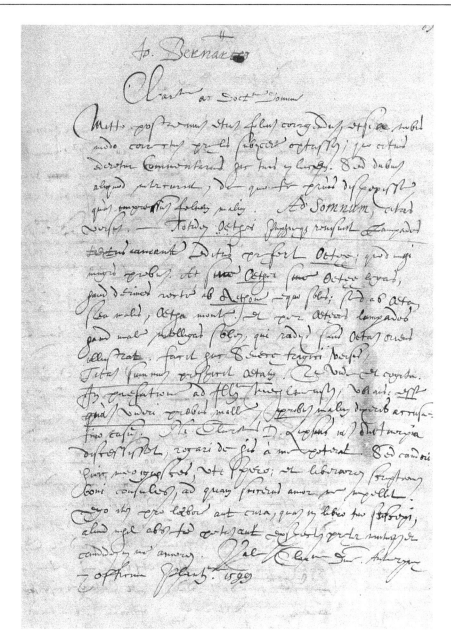

FIG. 9.2. Letter by Balthasar Moretus to Jan Bernaerts from June or July 1599. Antwerp, Museum Plantin-Moretus, Arch. 12, *Copie de lettres de Jean Moretus I, 1598–1607*, p. 79.

back by the same. I send a new one with him now and I will not let go any opportunity for a courier whenever a sheet will be ready'.[16]

---

[16] 'Quod per Petrum Colibrant hac ipsa septimana misi, D[ominationem] T[uam] folium corrigendum accepisse, et per eundem remissurum spero. Aliud per hunc nunc mitto; nec porro occasionem

204   PRINTING AND MISPRINTING

Even if an author did not have privileges such as Lipsius had and the opportunity to correct errors before printing, he could still read his text when the completed gatherings were sent. He could then note the errors and send the list back to Moretus to have them added at the end of the book. In that case, the list of errata had to arrive in time. For example, the Jesuit Martín Anton Delrio carefully compiled all the errata for his *Syntagma tragoediae Latinae*, a work on the Latin tragedy with an edition of *Seneca Tragicus*.[17] On 6 August 1593, he wrote that while he was working on compiling the indices that would be published as the third part, he was also collecting the errata.[18] Delrio was thus able to send the errata on time to the press. However, in other instances, such as an edition of Latin and Greek poems by the French physician Frédéric Jamot, the *Varia poëmata Graeca & Latina* from 1593, this was not the case.[19] The last payment for printing of Jamot's text was recorded on 3 October 1592 (Fig. 9.3).[20] Indeed, as of 30 September, dozens of copies were sent to various book dealers, including one to Andreas Sassenus in Leuven on 30 September, or to Ascanius de Renialme in London, to whom fifty copies were shipped on 23 October.[21] On 11 November 1592, more than a month after the printing had been completed, twelve copies were sent to the Jesuit Aegidius Schoondonck at the Jesuit college in Kortrijk.[22] This Jesuit acted as a mediator between the author and Jan Moretus. Soon thereafter, on 21 November 1592, the printing of errata for Jamot's collection of poems was noted (Fig. 9.3).[23] New shipments of the edition followed from then on, including 200 copies sent to the Frankfurt Fair of 1593. As a result, there are copies with and without errata.[24]

THE COST OF REPRINTING

From the payments to compositors and pressmen it appears that sometimes entire sheets had to be reprinted. This probably only happened when there was no other solution, because

---

ullius tabellarii omittam quandoque paratum folium erit'; the translation in the text is mine. The letter is published in both A. Gerlo, I. Vertessen, and H. D. L. Vervliet (eds), *La correspondance de Juste Lipse conservée au Musée Plantin-Moretus*, Antwerp, 1967, no. 97; *Iusti Lipsi Epistolae*, pars XIII: 1600, ed. J. Papy, Brussels, 2000, no. 00 12 15, XIII, pp. 342–3.

[17] Imhof, *Jan Moretus* (n. 4 above), no. D-14.

[18] MPM, Arch. 81, *Recueils de lettres G. van Dachverlies–H. van Eyck*, pp. 293–4: 'Simul cum indicibus errata colligo, quae ab interpunctis certe multa: ab aliis, non adeo, nec tanti momenti, ut non prorsus lectorem valde morentur: mittam tempestive sub finem operis. Spero pauciora fore in posterum, quia secunda et tertia pars paullo a me diligentius descripta, quam prima' ('Along with the indices I am collecting the errata, which are numerous due to the interpunctuation. The other mistakes are not so important that they will detain the reader. I will send them on promptly by the end of the work. I hope that there will be less in the last part because I have copied the second and third part a little more meticulously than the first').

[19] Imhof, *Jan Moretus* (n. 4 above), no. J-1.

[20] MPM, Arch. 786, *Ouvriers 1590–1610*, fol. 30.

[21] For the first shipment to Andreas Sassenus in Leuven, see MPM, Arch. 69: *Journal 1592*, fol. 116v; for the one to Ascanius de Renialme on 23 October 1592, see MPM, Arch. 69: *Journal 1592*, fol. 124r.

[22] MPM, Arch. 69, *Journal 1592*, fol. 136r.

[23] MPM, Arch. 786, *Ouvriers 1590–1610*, fol. 30.

[24] The copy in Munich, Bayerische Staatsbibliothek (4 P.o.lat. 355), does not have the errata printed on p. 141; the one in Cambridge, University Library (Y.8.22) does.

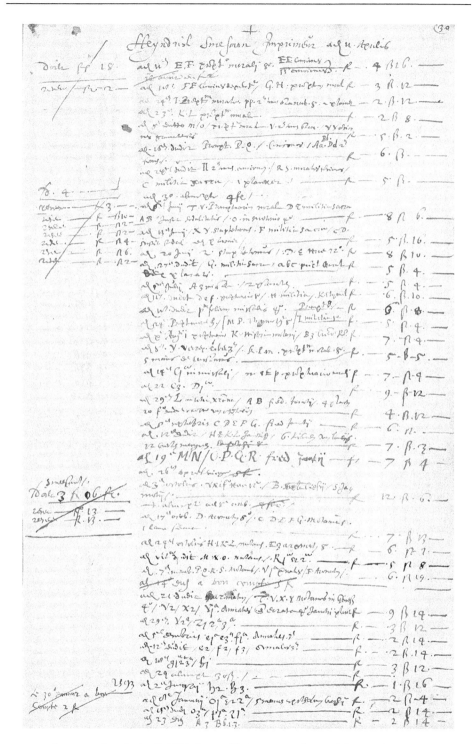

FIG. 9.3. Payments for printing Frédéric Jamot, *Varia poëmata Graeca & Latina*, Antwerp, Jan Moretus, 1593, 4° (USTC 406950) between 29 August and 3 October 1592 and for the errata on 21 November 1592. Antwerp, Museum Plantin-Moretus, Arch. 786, *Ouvriers 1590–1610*, fol. 30r.

206   PRINTING AND MISPRINTING

it implied wasting paper — a costly component of each book. This form of correction is evident, for example, in a little book that Jan Moretus printed for the Capuchins in 1589, the *Regula et testamentum S. Francisci*.[25] In addition to the rule of the Franciscans and St Francis's testament, this also comprised a treatise on poverty, as well as a number of litanies and prayers. Evidently, once the entire text had been printed the first four gatherings of the introductory 'Regula et testamentum' had to be reprinted. Unfortunately, the new text did not fit neatly within four gatherings, so an extra quarter of a sheet, oddly signed with three dots, was added between the new gathering D and the remaining bulk of the text, starting with the existing gathering E. Because the printing of this book was financed by the Capuchins, it was easy for Jan Moretus to charge the extra costs to the order. There are, consequently, two variants of this edition, most readily distinguished by the presence (or absence) of this extra gathering.

If a mistake was made by the press itself and a sheet had to be reprinted, the costs had to be covered by Jan Moretus himself. In the records of payments to his compositors and pressmen there are sometimes references to sheets that had to be reset or printed a second time. When a sheet had to be reset this was only a waste of time, in addition to the cost of extra wages, but no paper had been used; but, if it had to be reprinted the incorrect sheets were useless. If no correspondence concerning the edition is known, it is not easy to determine if a second payment for printing one or more sheets implied that it was printed all over again or that the printer was paid a second time for some other reason (for example, if there was a discussion on his fee). Therefore, such second payments have to be considered with care. Only if there is an explicit reference to resetting the text ('refaict') or printing a sheet again ('réimprimer'), can one safely assume that a sheet was reset or reprinted. For instance, more than a year after the completion of a breviary in octavo in two volumes, two or three gatherings were completely reprinted.[26] Other examples, without further documentation from correspondence, include *La vie et les fables d'Esope* from 1593, for which half of gathering B was reset; the Dutch edition of Peter Canisius's *Manuale catholicorum* from 1604, for which several gatherings had to be reprinted; and the *Graduale Romanum* from 1599.

Sometimes curious mistakes were made when a word was misread. In 1596, the court in Brussels asked Jan Moretus to print an ordinance concerning the use of coats of arms and titles by the nobility, the *Edict et ordonnance du roy* [...] *touchant les armories, tymbres et autres usurpations*.[27] An attentive secretary of the Secret Council had noticed that at one point the text had *homme de guerre* instead of *homme d'eglise*, certainly not an insignificant error in such a text.[28]

---

[25] Imhof, *Jan Moretus* (n. 4 above), no. R-4.

[26] MPM, Arch. 786, *Ouvriers 1590–1610*, fol. 199. Payments for reprinting gatherings D and E were noted on 7 and 14 June 1608 (and perhaps also gathering A on 21 June 1608), while the last payment for printing had been noted on 6 October and 10 November 1607.

[27] Imhof, *Jan Moretus* (n. 4 above), nos Ord-17 and Ord-18.

[28] Letter by François de le Hele from 28 January 1596: 'saulf que prendrez garde de corriger *homme de guerre* mectant *homme d'eglise*, et en laultre <u>Comme la raison</u> doibt estre un nouvel ar[tic]le [...]. De plus il conviendra corriger et mectre *armoiries tymbrees* au lieu de *armories tymbres*' ('Be careful and be certain that you change *homme de guerre* to *homme d'eglise* and further on, <u>Comme la raison</u> should start a new paragraph [...]. Additionally, you should replace *armories tymbres* with *armoiries tymbrees*'): MPM, Arch. 1179, *Privilèges plantiniens, 1554–1802*, no. 305, i.e. a letter added to the privilege for this ordinance.

Intervening on the Printed Text

Despite all efforts to prevent errors — reading the text in advance carefully, asking the author to check the printed sheets, and adding a list of errata — a perfect, error-free edition remained a mirage. However, the Plantin-Moretus press never gave up and resorted to various means to correct printed sheets. One option was to cover an error with a corrected paper slip. This was done in Moretus's 1596 edition of Roberto Bellarmino's Hebrew grammar. The permission of the Jesuit Provincial of the Belgian Province, George Duras, to publish this book was printed at the end (p. [198]). However, the first name of the provincial 'Georgius' is printed on a small piece of paper that is pasted onto the page. Was it just forgotten or misspelled? Regrettably, this is impossible to determine on the basis of the few copies with this correction that I have been able to examine.[29]

More common instruments for making corrections were a scalpel and a pen. Recall Pantin's edition of Basil's life of St Thecla in Greek and his commentary. As I mentioned earlier, the printed gatherings were sent to Pantin so that he could inspect them and note the errors. This list of errors was then printed at the end of the book. However, while the text was still being printed, Balthasar Moretus suggested to Pantin that some errors could be corrected with a pen. For example, on 28 May 1607, he sent for correction the sheet comprising gathering G together with the finished sheet comprising gathering E, and promised Pantin that the 'pueri', namely, the apprentices, would correct two words in Greek with a pen.[30] Other errors that could not be corrected easily would be printed in the errata at the end.[31] On 31 May 1608, Balthasar reported that the apprentices were indeed working with scalpel and pen to correct errors in the text, as was done, for example, on p. 191 with the word 'attentarant' on line 11. Of this edition, 1,000 copies were printed and the handwritten corrections had to be made in all of these copies — it was probably not the most exciting work for these young men! While it is not always easy to find these corrections, one is readily apparent. On the page marking the start of St Thecla's life by the Byzantine hagiographer

---

[29] See, e.g., the copy in the Plantin-Moretus Museum, A 1413.

[30] 'De errore in Δημᾶν et ὑπεπλέθη, haud frustra R[everentia] V[estra] me monuit et curabo a pueris nostris, cum vacant, calamo emendari. Circa puncta item media et finalia diligentius posthac attendam, quae nec in autographo satis distincte ponuntur' ('Not in vain you have warned me about the errors in Δημᾶν et ὑπεπλέθη. I will see that they will be corrected by our boys when they have a moment. About the stops in the middle and at the end I will pay more attention from now on; they were not clearly indicated in the manuscript'): MPM, Arch. 12, p. 351. The letter is not included in Fabri, 'La correspondance de Pierre Pantin' (n. 14 above). The misspelled words, which were printed on p. 26, were actually not corrected. See the description of this edition in Imhof, *Jan Moretus* (n. 4 above), no. B-23, with a list of copies detailing those I have inspected.

[31] MPM, Arch. 135, *Copie de Lettres 1607–1615*, pp. 12–13, end of December 1607: 'Mitto semiduernionem recusum, in quo operae nostrae gravius peccarunt [...]. Menda item typographica, si qua calamo emendari haud possunt, aptissime sub finem indicis apponentur' ('I am sending you the reprinted half sheet in which our workmen made serious mistakes [...]. If there would be typographical errors that cannot be corrected with a pen, we will add them most conveniently at the end of the index'): transcription in Fabri, 'La correspondance de Pierre Pantin' (n. 14 above), no. 2). As appears from this letter, half of gathering m was also reprinted. In the payments to the pressmen, a record was noted for printing gathering m on 1 December 1607 and for half of this gathering on 22 December 1608 (MPM, Arch. 786, *Ouvriers 1590–1610*, fol. 193).

208   PRINTING AND MISPRINTING

Simeon Metaphrastes, the letter R in 'Martyris' was forgotten and was subsequently added by hand.

Pantin's edition was not the only one in which corrections were made by hand. In Delrio's collection of sermons, *Florida Mariana*, published in 1598, there is a poem by Justus Lipsius written in honour of this book (Fig. 9.4).[32] After Delrio had received his copies, Balthasar Moretus wrote him that the Jesuits in Antwerp had noticed that a word was missing from one line of Lipsius's poem ('Abite, vindex: huic mystae suo') and asked Delrio to add the word 'ipsa' after the word 'vindex' with a pen to his copies.[33] Balthasar assured him that they would do the same with the copies that were still available at the press. Consequently, in some copies you will see the word 'ipsa' added by hand, while in others, presumably those that had already been distributed, it is not. Only a quibbling Jesuit could have noticed the missing word.

Corrections with a pen were similarly made to a poem by Gislain Bulteel, councillor of Ypres, part of Jan Moretus's commemorative edition in honour of Justus Lipsius, the *Iusti Lipsii sapientiae et litterarum antistitis fama postuma* from 1607.[34] By the end of March 1607, many copies had already been distributed, including 200 copies sent to the Frankfurt book fair. In a letter to Bulteel from 2 August 1607, Balthasar Moretus apologised for his long silence and the delay in sending Bulteel's copy. Balthasar wrote that one mistake was corrected by pen before the copies were distributed, but another one, which had been overlooked, was corrected thereafter.[35] However miniscule these corrections in the poems by Lipsius and Bulteel may seem, they clearly reveal the extreme attention the Moretuses paid to the accuracy of their editions.

The printing of a manual for priests for the diocese of Cambrai in 1606, the *Manuale parochorum ad usum ecclesiarum civitatis & dioecesis Cameracensis*, was more problematic

[32] Imhof, *Jan Moretus* (n. 4 above), no. D-13. Lipsius's poem, 'In panegyres Marianas Martini Ant. Delrii' is printed on p. 12.

[33] 'Panegyricos tuos Marianos opinor te iampridem accepisse atque impressionem spero placuisse; labori enim et sumptui non peperci quo gratiores a praelo meo exirent in lucem. At nescio quis in carmine D. Lipsii admissus est error quem prime invenerunt Societatis hic patres: 'Abite, vindex: huic mystae suo'. Deest vocabula ad supplendum versum [...]. Quare ut doctissimi viri voto fiat satis R[everentia] T[ua] rogo exemplaria sua pariter corrigere ne gravetur [...]' ('I assume that you have already received the copies of your *Florida Mariana* and I hope that you are pleased with the printing. I did not skimp on labour and costs so that they would be all the more elegantly finished on my presses. Nevertheless, I do not know who made a mistake in Lipsius's poem, which the fathers of the [Jesuit] Society here pointed out to me first: the line 'Abite, vindex: huic mystae suo' is incomplete as a word is missing [...]. I would consequently like to ask you if you would not mind correcting your copies at once, according to the wish of this learned man [...]'): MPM, Arch. 12, *Copie de lettres de Jean Moretus I, 1598–1607*, p. 12.

[34] Imhof, *Jan Moretus* (n. 4 above), no. I-7. For Bulteel's poem, see pp. 75–7 in the *Fama postuma*.

[35] 'Agnosco culpam diuturni huius ad litteras tuas silentii, item moram in mittendi *Famae postumae* exemplari, quo mendi in trochaeis tuis emendationem certo cognosceris. Mendi, inquam, nam alterum istud sine pro sive, in omnibus exemplis corrigi curaram priusquam emitterem. Illud Pandronius suavius irrepserat, quia autographum sic praeferret, nec relegenti postea occurrit. At de silentio et mori ignosci mihi rogo' ('I plead guilty for my long silence following your letter, as well as for the delay in sending your copy of the *Fama postuma*, in which you certainly saw the correction of the mistake in your trochees. Mistakes, I say, because the one with 'sine' instead of 'sive', I had corrected in all copies before they were distributed. The other one, 'Pandronius', had slipped in because it appeared this way in the manuscript and the one who was reading it afterwards, did not catch it'): MPM, Arch. 12, *Copie de lettres de Jean Moretus I, 1598–1607*, p. 362. The correct reading for 'Pandronius' is 'Pandionius', i.e. from Athens.

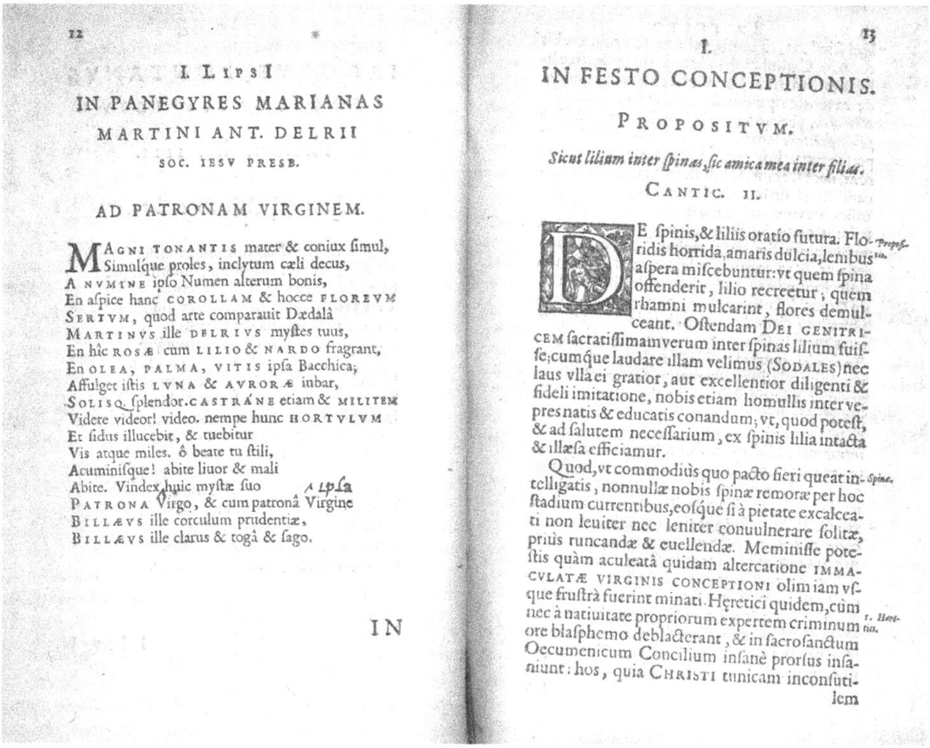

12

I. LIPSI
IN PANEGYRES MARIANAS
MARTINI ANT. DELRII
SOC. IESV PRESB.

AD PATRONAM VIRGINEM.

MAGNI TONANTIS mater & coniux ſimul,
Simulque proles, inclytum cæli decus,
A NVMINE ipſo Numen alterum bonis,
En aſpice hanc COROLLAM & hocce FLOREVM
SERTVM, quod arte comparauit Dædalâ
MARTINVS ille DELRIVS myſtes tuus,
En hîc ROSÆ cum LILIO & NARDO fragrant,
En OLEA, PALMA, VITIS ipſa Bacchica;
Affulget iſtis LVNA & AVRORÆ iubar,
SOLISQ. ſplendor. CASTRÁNE etiam & MILITEM
Videre videor! video. nempe hunc HORTVLVM
Et ſidus illucebit, & tuebitur
Vis atque miles. ô beate tu ſtili,
Acuminiſque! abite liuor & mali
Abite. Vindex huic myſtæ ſuo ʌ ipſa
PATRONA Virgo, & cum patronâ Virgine
BILLÆVS ille corculum prudentiæ,
BILLÆVS ille clarus & togâ & ſago.

IN

13

I.
IN FESTO CONCEPTIONIS.

PROPOSITVM.

Sicut lilium inter ſpinas, ſic amica mea inter filias.

CANTIC. II.

DE ſpinis, & liliis oratio futura. Floridis horrida, amaris dulcia, lenibus aſpera miſcebuntur: vt quem ſpina offenderit, lilio recreetur; quem rhamni mulcarint, flores demulceant. Oſtendam DEI GENITRICEM ſacratiſſimam verum inter ſpinas lilium fuiſſe; cumque laudare illam velimus (SODALES) nec laus vlla ei gratior, aut excellentior diligenti & fideli imitatione, nobis etiam homullis inter vepres natis & educatis conandum; vt, quod poteſt, & ad ſalutem neceſſarium, ex ſpinis lilia intacta & illæſa efficiamur. *Propoſitum.*

Quod, vt commodiùs quo pacto fieri queat intelligatis, nonnullæ nobis ſpinæ remoræ per hoc ſtadium currentibus, eoſque ſi à pietate excalceati non leuiter nec leniter conuulnerare ſolitæ, priùs runcandæ & euellendæ. Meminiſſe poteſtis quàm aculeatâ quidam altercatione IMMACVLATÆ VIRGINIS CONCEPTIONI olim iam vſque fruſtrà fuerint minati. Hęretici quidem, cùm nec à natiuitate propriorum expertem criminum ore blaſphemo deblacterant, & in ſacroſanctum Oecumenicum Concilium inſanè prorſus inſaniunt: hos, quia CHRISTI tunicam inconſutilem *Spinæ.* *1. Hæretici.*

FIG. 9.4. Justus Lipsius's poem in Martín Anton Delrio, *Florida Mariana*, Antwerp, Jan Moretus, 1598, 8° (USTC 4070391598), p. 12. Antwerp, Museum Plantin-Moretus, A 1230.

for Jan Moretus.[36] The whole text had already gone under the press when he received (or paid attention to) three letters from the bishop's secretary with a list of errors. Unfortunately, the secretary's letters are not preserved. Jan Moretus replied that, although he recognised that his employees had been inaccurate, the scribe who had transcribed the copy had made many spelling mistakes as well. His son Balthasar — it was in fact Balthasar himself who wrote the letter for his father — had read the copy carefully before it was printed and had corrected some mistakes; by contrast, he had not altered anything in the music, though the priest-musician ('phonascus') of the Antwerp cathedral had suggested otherwise. While the apprentices could correct the smaller mistakes with a pen in all 1,100 copies, for some *Responsoria* there was no other solution than to reprint them and add them at the end of the book.[37] There are indeed some corrections by hand to the music, but other pages with more errors were reprinted and added at the end of the book. A payment for printing these pages was recorded on 30 December 1606, more than a month after the completion of the book.[38] The result was not ideal because, in at least some surviving copies, there is no indication

[36] Imhof, *Jan Moretus* (n. 4 above), no. M-3.
[37] MPM, Arch. 12, *Copie de lettres de Jean Moretus I, 1598–1607*, p. 339.
[38] MPM, Arch. 786, *Ouvriers 1590–1610*, fol. 185.

at the misprinted pages that the correct music is printed at the end of the book.[39] It was perhaps because he knew it was not such an elegant solution that Jan Moretus generously did not charge the bishop for this extra printing. He claimed in his letter that he preferred financial loss to a blemished reputation.[40]

I would like to conclude this overview with one last example of correction by hand after the completion of the printing of a book, this time in the list of errata itself. Jan Moretus published several books by the Jesuit Johannes David with emblematic illustrations. Only for his last work, the *Duodecim specula Deum aliquando videre desideranti concinnata*, is some correspondence preserved. When the book was finally printed in April 1610 and David had received his twelve presentation copies, he noticed that there were two errors in the list of errata. He corrected these erroneous page numbers by hand in his copies and asked Balthasar to do the same in the remaining 1,200 copies. Balthasar apparently agreed to this ultimate endeavour to perfect even the printed corrections. In each copy that I have seen thus far, the two page numbers have indeed been corrected by removing the old number and rewriting it by hand.[41]

Conclusions

For the production of books with a very limited number of misprints, Jan Moretus was largely indebted to his son Balthasar Moretus. Through his careful preparation of the copy and preliminary reduction of the potential errors as much as possible, the compositors and pressmen could start with a superior copy with a minimal number of faults. During the printing of the book, finished sheets were sent to the authors, if at all possible, to enable them to inspect their text and sum up the errors. Jan Moretus used several approaches to resolve these errors. Besides printing a list of errata at the end of the publication, he sometimes had corrections made with pen and scalpel in as many as a thousand or more copies if there were still errors. As a last resort, part of the text was reprinted. If this was a practice that was regularly used at the Plantin press, this was probably also done at other presses that took correct printing seriously. In most cases, we cannot rely on vast correspondences and archival material such as those related to the Plantin press. Nevertheless, copy-specific analysis often compensates for this gap in documentation, helping to pinpoint mistakes and in-house corrections and understand who instigated them.[42] Albeit a time-consuming operation, careful scrutiny of editions is always revealing, since no publisher was capable of avoiding misprints altogether, not even Jan Moretus.

---

[39] E.g., the copy in the Plantin-Moretus Museum, A 1395.

[40] 'Itaque pecuniae detrimentum me pati malle profiteor quam famae' ('I declare that I would rather suffer a loss in money than reputation'): MPM, Arch. 12, *Copie de lettres de Jean Moretus I, 1598–1607*, p. 339.

[41] For example, the copies in the Plantin-Moretus Museum (A 1236 A and A 1236 B), Cambridge, University Library (Syn.7.61.11), and London, British Museum, Prints & Drawings (157.a.26).

[42] See Della Rocca de Candal' and Sachet's contributions to this Companion.

BIBLIOGRAPHY

PRIMARY SOURCES

MANUSCRIPTS AND ARCHIVAL DOCUMENTATION

Antwerp, MPM, Arch. 10, *Copie de lettres de Plantin 1579–1589.*
Antwerp, MPM, Arch. 12, *Copie de lettres de Jean Moretus I, 1598–1607.*
Antwerp, MPM, Arch. 69, *Journal 1592.*
Antwerp, MPM, Arch. 81, *Recueils de lettres G. van Dachverlies–H. van Eyck.*
Antwerp, MPM, Arch. 93, *Recueils de lettres Aug. Sabbetius–Ger. Symont.*
Antwerp, MPM, Arch. 135, *Copie de Lettres 1607–1615.*
Antwerp, MPM, Arch. 786, *Ouvriers 1590–1610.*
Antwerp, MPM, Arch. 1179, *Privilèges plantiniens, 1554–1802,* no. 305.

PRINTED BOOKS

Basilius of Seleucia, *De vita ac miraculis S. Theclae*, Antwerp, *Jan Moretus*, 1608, 4° (Imhof, *Jan Moretus*, B-23; USTC 1003497).

Bellarmino, Roberto, *Institutiones linguae Hebraicae*, Antwerp, Jan Moretus, 1596, 8° (Imhof, *Jan Moretus*, B-25; USTC 440895).

Bernaerts, Jan, *Ad P. Statii Papinii, Silvarum libros, commentarius*, Antwerp, Jan Moretus, 1599, 8° (Imhof, *Jan Moretus*, B-27; USTC 407060).

David, Joannes, *Duodecim specula Deum aliquando videre desideranti concinnata*, Antwerp, Jan Moretus, 1610, 8° (Imhof, *Jan Moretus*, D-2; USTC 1009428 and 1035933).

Delrio, Martín Anton, *Florida Mariana*, Antwerp, Jan Moretus, 1598, 8° (Imhof, *Jan Moretus*, D-13; USTC 407039).

Delrio, Martín Anton, *Syntagma tragoediae Latinae*, Antwerp, Jan Moretus, 1593–1595, 4° (Imhof, *Jan Moretus*, D-14; USTC 402286).

Edict et ordonnance du roy [...] *touchant les armories, tymbres et autres usurpations*, Antwerp, Jan Moretus, 1596, 4° (Imhof, *Jan Moretus*, Ord-17 and 18; USTC 80865 and 56515).

Jamot, Frédéric, *Varia poëmata Graeca & Latina*, Antwerp, Jan Moretus, 1593, 4° (Imhof, *Jan Moretus*, J-1; USTC 406950).

Iusti Lipsii sapientiae et litterarum antistitis fama postuma, Antwerp, Jan Moretus, 1607, 4° (Imhof, *Jan Moretus*, I-7; USTC 1003255).

Manuale parochorum ad usum ecclesiarum civitatis & dioecesis Cameracensis, Antwerp, Jan Moretus, 1606, 4° (Imhof, *Jan Moretus*, M-3; USTC 1009797).

Regula et testamentum [...] *S. Francisci*, Antwerp, Jan Moretus, 1589, 24° (Imhof, *Jan Moretus*, R-4; USTC 430623).

SECONDARY LITERATURE

Arias Montano, B., *Correspondencia conservada en el Museo Plantin-Moretus de Amberes*, ed. A. Dávila Pérez, Madrid, 2002.

Correspondance de Christophe Plantin, ed. M. Rooses and J. Denucé, 9 vols, Antwerp and Gent, 1883–1920.

Denucé, J., *Inventaire des archives Plantiniennes*, Antwerp, 1926.

Fabri, J., 'La correspondance de Pierre Pantin avec Balthasar Moretus', *De Gulden Passer*, 43/4, 1965, pp. 166–247.

Imhof, D., '*Ex arte et decore typographica*: Balthasar Moretus I, Publisher of Baroque Books', in D. Imhof (ed.), *Balthasar Moretus and the Passion of Publishing*, Kontich, 2018, pp. 12–28.

Imhof, D., *Jan Moretus and the Continuation of the Plantin Press: A Bibliography of the Works Published and Printed by Jan Moretus I in Antwerp (1589–1610)*, 2 vols, Leiden, 2014.

Iusti Lipsi Epistolae, pars XIII: 1600, ed. J. Papy, Brussels, 2000.

La correspondance de Juste Lipse conservée au Musée Plantin-Moretus, ed. A. Gerlo, I. Vertessen, and H. D. L. Vervliet, Antwerp, 1967.

PART III

RELIGION

CHAPTER 10

MISPRINTING THE WORD AND THE IMAGE OF GOD (PARIS, 1498–1538)

FRANÇOIS DUPUIGRENET DESROUSSILLES

MISPRINTS in Bibles are famous, and the most famous of all is certainly that of the seventh commandment in the 1631 Authorised Version printed in London by Robert Barker and Martin Lucas: 'Thou shalt commit adultery'.[1] When the error was discovered, the Star Chamber deprived Barker and Lucas of their license and most of the print run of a thousand copies was destroyed, making it one of the rarest printed books in the world. A recently acquired copy now occupies a post of honour in the Museum of the Bible that opened in Washington, DC.[2] What is less known is that the then-archbishop of Canterbury, George Abbot, railed against the infamous Wicked Bible, as it came to be known: 'I knew the time when great care was had about printing, the Bibles especially, good compositors and the best correctors were gotten being grave and learned men, the paper and the letter rare and faire every way of the best, but now the paper is nought, the composers boys, and the correctors unlearned […]. They heretofore spent their whole time in printing but these looke to gaine, gaine, gaine, nothing els'.[3]

Was there ever a golden age for printed Bibles, as the archbishop suggested, his resentment owing maybe as much to his Puritan rigour as to his role, twenty-odd years before, as one of the translators of the Authorised Version that was so rudely defaced?[4] After all,

---

[1] *The Holy Bible containing the Old Testament and the New*, London, Robert Barker for John Bill, 1631, 8° (USTC 3015715).

[2] The American press paid a lot of attention to the display of the 'Wicked Bible' at the time of the opening of the museum. For example, *The Washington Post*, 18 November 2017, revelled in another misprint in Deuteronomy 5:24. Instead of 'greatnesse' of God, Barker printed 'great-asse'. 'The Bible Museum's "Wicked Bible": Thou Shalt Commit Adultery', *The Washington Post*, 18 November 2017, https://www.washingtonpost.com/news/retropolis/wp/2017/11/17/the-new-bible-museums-wicked-bible-thou-shalt-commit-adultery/, accessed 17 March 2021.

[3] D. Daniel, *The Bible in English: Its History and Influence*, New Haven (CT), 2003, p. 307.

[4] George Abbot was appointed to the second Oxford Company of revisers, which dealt with the Four Gospels, the Acts of the Apostles, and Revelation. See A. Nicolson, *God's Secretaries: The Making of the King James Bible*, New York, Harper Perennial, 2005, pp. 156–62.

François Dupuigrenet Desroussilles, *Misprinting the Word and the Image of God (Paris, 1498–1538)*. In: *Printing and Misprinting*. Edited by Geri Della Rocca de Candal, Anthony Grafton, and Paolo Sachet, Oxford University Press. © François Dupuigrenet Desroussilles (2023). DOI: 10.1093/oso/9780198863045.003.0011

216   PRINTING AND MISPRINTING

the Bible is a big book, in excess of 780,000 words for the Authorised Version, and statistically it is the absence of misprints that would be surprising. The forty-two-line Gutenberg Bible, which certainly benefitted from 'good compositors and the best correctors', is not exempt from them, inverted lines in particular, just as errors in copying were frequent in manuscript Bibles.[5] As early as 1612, in the first edition of the Authorised Version made for private study, Robert Barker, the usual suspect, had printed verse 161 in Psalm 119 as 'printers have persecuted me without a cause', instead of 'princes have persecuted me without a cause'.[6]

This chapter discusses two early cases of printers as persecutors: both biblical, both from Paris, both exceptional because of the rarity and spectacular quality of the copies involved, connected as they were to four kings, the French Charles VIII and Francis I, as well as Henry VII and Henry VIII of England. The first case focuses on a major imposition error in the printing of woodblocks at the end of the incunabula era. While such inaccuracies were common,[7] this one severely needed correction because of its political implications. The second case took place in the 1530s, which is generally regarded as the heyday of the Parisian book industry, and concerns so staggering a mix of errors related to text and illustrations as to call into question the very nature of the publication: the first example of *Figures de la Bible* to be printed in Paris.

REMOVING A CORONATION SCENE
FROM A ROYAL COPY

In 1991, I organised at the Bibliothèque nationale an exhibition about the Bible during the Ancien Régime, with major emphasis given to the representation of French kings in relation to their biblical models from David onwards.[8] In selecting the items from the library's outstanding collection, I stumbled upon a woodcut coronation scene in a *Bible historiée*, printed in c. 1498 by Pierre Le Rouge for Antoine Vérard at the request of Charles VIII, the first printed Bible in French (Fig. 10.1).[9] The illustration was, however, located in a

---

[5] A thorough account of misprints found by comparing copies of the Gutenberg Bibles at the Bodleian Library in Oxford and the Vatican Library is available online under the title 'Printing Errors and Corrections in the Gutenberg Bible' on the site of the Polonsky Foundation Digitization Project: https://www.bodleian.ox.ac.uk/our-work/conservation/case-studies/polonsky-foundation-digitization-project.

[6] *The Holy Bible, conteining the Olde Testament and the New*, London, Robert Barker, 1612, 8° (USTC 3005284).

[7] See in this Companion the passage about misplaced blocks in the contribution by Ilaria Andreoli, Caroline Duroselle-Melish, and Roger Gaskell.

[8] F. Dupuigrenet Desroussilles, *Dieu en son royaume: la Bible dans la France d'autrefois, XIIIᵉ–XVIIIᵉ siècle*, Paris, 1991.

[9] *La bible historiée*, ed. Jean de Rély, Paris, Antoine Vérard, [between 8 May 1498 and 25 Oct. 1499], f° (ISTC ib00623000), f. 87r. The date of publication is variably given within the span 1494–1499. Cf.: D. Hillard, 'Les éditions de la *Bible* en France au XVᵉ siècle', in B. E. Schwarzbach (ed.), *La Bible imprimée dans l'Europe moderne*, Paris, 1999, pp. 68–82; M. Delaveau and D. Hillard, *Les Bibles imprimées du XVᵉ au XVIIIᵉ siècle conservées à Paris, Bibliothèque nationale de France, Bibliothèque Sainte-Geneviève*,

FIG. 10.1. Woodcut representing the coronation of an English king in *Bible historiée*, ed. Jean de Rély, Paris, Antoine Vérard, [between 8 May 1498 and 25 Oct. 1499], f° (ISTC ib00623000), fol. 87r. Paris, Bibliothèque nationale de France, A 270.

rather unusual position, at the beginning of Leviticus, a book that does not discuss kings but is entirely dedicated to the Levites in ancient Israel, considered as the forerunners of the Catholic church.

Subject and position appeared certainly odd, but could have been explained in light of the royal patronage enjoyed by the publisher. At first glance the image seems indeed to portray a French monarch, and in the numerous editions Vérard dedicated to Charles VIII, he invariably had printers insert woodcuts showing the king in the act of receiving a copy of the book itself. This, however, usually happened in the opening gathering, not as deep in the volume as in this particular *Bible historiée* (fol. 87r). It should also be noted that this edition already contains an opening dedication woodcut with the editor, the royal chaplain Jean de Rély, offering the book to the archbishop of Sens, Tristan de Salazar, a major political figure who had been twice ambassador to Henry VII (sig. a2r).

Seeking an explanation for this apparent mistake, I decided to compare the standard paper copy against the presentation copy for Charles VIII, printed on vellum and lavishly illuminated (BnF, Vélins 100).[10] It turned out that, in the latter, the woodcut in the Leviticus was covered by a tempera illumination depicting the payment of the tithe, a subject clearly more in line with the prescriptive content of this biblical book, and commonly found in illustrated manuscripts of the *Bible historiée* (Fig. 10.2).[11]

At the time, I thought that this inconsistency was probably caused by the lack of a woodblock representing this specific biblical scene in Pierre Le Rouge's workshop, and that Le Rouge had picked, as a second choice, a coronation scene from an earlier printing commissioned by Vérard, the *Chroniques de France*, without paying much attention to its iconography and relation to the text.[12] This tentative explanation seemed all the more plausible since it was not uncommon for Vérard to provide the printers who worked for him with woodblocks from different sources and contexts.[13]

Bibliothèque de la Sorbonne, Bibliothèque Mazarine, Bibliothèque de la Société de l'histoire du protestantisme français, Bibliothèque de la Société biblique, Paris, 2002, p. 251; M. B. Winn, Anthoine Vérard, Parisian Publisher (1485–1512): Prologues, Poems and Presentations, Geneva, 1997, pp. 104, 120–3. A recent study, limited to the text, identified a fourteenth-century manuscript from the Bibliothèque municipale of Soissons, 210–12, as the source of Vérard's edition: P. Nobel, 'Du manuscrit à l'imprimé: le traitement des gloses dans l'*editio princeps* de la "Bible historiée" publiée par Antoine Vérard', *Le français préclassique 1500–1650*, 19, 2017, pp. 85–100.

[10] J. Van Praet, *Catalogue des livres imprimés sur vélin de la Bibliothèque du Roi*, Paris, 1822, p. 122. Only three other illuminated copies on vellum are known today: Lyon, Bibliothèque municipale, Inc. 57–8; New York, The Morgan Library and Museum, PML 28379–82; and one sold at Christie's London, *Printed Books and Manuscripts from Longleat*, 13 June 2002, lot. 12. The Lyon copy was analysed by students of the École nationale supérieure des sciences de l'information et des bibliothèques (ENSSIB): L. Barbizet et al., *Textes et images dans la Bible historiée d'Antoine Vérard, mémoire de recherches de l'Enssib*, June 2004 (available at the school, not digitised). Unfortunately, no one pursued their research.

[11] E. P. Spencer, 'Antoine Vérard's Illuminated Vellum Incunables', in J. B. Trapp (ed.), *Manuscripts in the Fifty Years After the Inventions of Printing: Some Papers Read at a Colloquium at the Warburg Institute on 12–13 March 1982*, London, 1983, pp. 62–5. On the manuscript tradition, see E. Fournié, 'Les manuscrits de la Bible historiale. Présentation et catalogue raisonné d'une oeuvre médiévale', *L'Atelier du Centre de recherches historiques*, 3/2, 2009, https://journals.openedition.org/acrh/1408, and her, *L'iconographie de la Bible historiale*, Turnhout, 2012.

[12] Dupuigrenet Desroussilles, *Dieu en son royaume* (n. 8, above), p. 113. *Chroniques de France*, Paris, Jean Maurand (vol. II only) for Antoine Vérard, 1493, f° (ISTC ic00484000).

[13] J. MacFarlane, *Antoine Vérard*, London, 1900, p. 52; D. Sansy, 'Texte et image dans les incunables français', *Médiévales*, 22–3, 1992, pp. 47–70.

10: MISPRINTING THE WORD AND THE IMAGE OF GOD   219

O cōmancement de leuitique met le maiſtre en hiſtoires vne diuiſion moult prouffitable pour entē dre leuitique et dit ainſi. Le liure leui/ tique eſt la tierce hyſtoire que moyſes eſcripſt. Si eſt appellee en grec leuitiq̄ pour ce quil parle de seſectionet du mi/ niſtre des leuites. Ceſt a dire de ceulx qui eſtoient de la lignee leui/ ſicomme aaron et ſes freres. Et ſi eſt appelle ce liure en latin offertoires ou ſacrifie/ ries/pour ce quil parle des ſacrifices et

FIG. 10.2. Tempera painting representing the payment of the tithe. *Bible historiée* (see Fig. 10.1), fol. 87r. Paris, Bibliothèque nationale de France, Vélins 100.

As a result of a more extensive investigation of illuminated and non-illuminated copies of this *Bible historiée*, I can now explain, thirty years later, why it was important, if not crucial, that, in the dedication copy, the coronation scene was replaced by a completely different, overpainted, image.

Examining more closely BnF, Vélins 100, one notices that alteration of images concerned not only the opening of Leviticus, but also Exodus, Numbers, and Deuteronomy, i.e. the whole Pentateuch except for Genesis. Standard paper copies show the original woodcuts, which were similarly drawn, as the coronation scene, from the same edition of the *Chroniques de France*, and all represent scenes in which a French king is the main character; the one in Numbers, repeated in Kings 1 and Ezra, even shows a monarch on horseback clearly identified with the inscription 'Charles roy'. Yet in the presentation copy, they were all erased and painted over with episodes from the life of Moses, which, like the payment of the tithe for Leviticus, conform to the content of the text.

Re-establishing the connection between word and image (and thus correcting errors) seems to be the main reason for these alterations.[14] This was possible because Vérard, originally a bookseller of illuminated manuscripts, regularly ordered the printing of vellum copies of his illustrated publications, not only for the French king but for other high-ranking patrons such as his sister Anne of Beaujeu; Queen Anne of Brittany; John III, king of Navarre; Louis XII, the successor to Charles VIII; as well as Henry VII of England. Vérard had these copies illuminated by artists working for the French court. The most notable of them, Jacques de Besançon, had corrected a few years before another incoherent sequence of woodcuts in the presentation copy to Charles VIII of the first French translation of Josephus's *Jewish War*; here, too, numerous small woodcuts, entirely unrelated to the text, were erased and painted over with illustrations of the events narrated by Josephus.[15]

The same happened in the royal copy of the *Bible historiée*, where the representations of Charles VIII in the Pentateuch were replaced by scenes from the life of Moses. Just like in the royal copy of Josephus, we can here observe the coexistence of mixed technologies, with the earlier, painting, employed as a means to correct the inconsistencies of the most recent one, printing woodcuts in the same form as moveable type.[16]

The correction of the Leviticus illustration may have a further, subtler explanation. On the standard to the right of the woodcut, one can easily spot the three English lions — a clear pointer that this is a coronation not of a French but of an English king, with the fleur-de-lys on the left as a reminder of the long-lasting pretension of the English sovereigns to the throne of France, which were not entirely buried even after the end of the Hundred Years' War in 1475 (Fig. 10.2). When this *Bible historiée* was printed, France and England had recently reached a peaceful understanding. In 1492, they signed the Peace of Étaples,

---

[14] They are not mentioned in the census provided in E. Fournié, 'Les éditions de la *Bible historiale*. Présentation et catalogue raisonné d'éditions de la première moitié du xvie siècle', *L'Atelier du Centre de recherches historiques*, 3/2, 2009, https://journals.openedition.org/acrh/1832?lang=en#tocto3n18'

[15] Flavius Josephus, *De la bataille judaïque*, [transl. Claude de Seyssel?], Paris, Antoine Vérard, [after 7 Dec. 1492], f° (ISTC ij00489000). Paris, BnF, Vélins 696. On Jacques de Besançon, see M. Deldicque, 'L'enluminure à Paris à la fin du xve siècle: Maître François, le Maître de Jacques de Besançon et Jacques de Besançon identifiés?', *Revue de l'art*, 183, 2014, pp. 9–18.

[16] D. Sansy emphasised the relative liberty of painters illuminating vellum copies of the *Grandes Chroniques* printed for Vérard in her 'Entre manuscrit et imprimé: les représentations de Richard Ier dans les *Grandes Chroniques de France* de Vérard (1493)', *Annales de Normandie*, 64, 2014, pp. 99–116.

by which France renounced supporting Perkin Warbeck in his revolt against Henry VII. And even if hostilities between the two kingdoms would not resume until 1513 as a spin-off of the Italian Wars, the woodblock could have only been regarded as a serious blunder for a French publication and an error to be corrected in the presentation copy to Charles VIII as well as in vellum copies made for other aristocratic patrons with political clout.[17]

Vérard was perfectly aware that a copy for his king required special treatment and adaptation, somehow recreating the idea of uniqueness which stands behind each manuscript, especially as Charles VIII had been for years heavily involved in financial transactions with the publisher.[18] In another revealing instance — the 1493 Boccaccio's *Louenge des nobles et cheres dames* — he went as far as covering with tempera the anonymous prologue dedicated to the queen, Anne of Brittany. The newly supplied illustration features himself reverently offering the book to his king.[19]

AN ELEGANT PICTURE BIBLE
MARRED BY MISPRINTS

In 1538, an octavo picture Bible was printed in Paris for the renowned bookseller François Regnault, active in Paris, Lyon, Caen, Rouen, as well as London. It is entitled *Historiarum veteris instrumenti et Apocalypsis icones ad vivum expressae* (henceforth, *Icones*).[20] This intriguing edition is a bibliographical 'cold case', like the *Bible historiée*, that I propose to reopen, focusing on its misprints.

The *Icones* is an exceedingly rare book, with a single known copy in a public institution, that of the Société d'histoire du Protestantisme francais (André 246).[21] Aside from its rarity, it is the first recorded example of *Figures de la Bible* printed in Paris.[22] Bibliographers have hinted at its existence for a long time, but under a gross misconception. In the 'bible' for historians of Parisian sixteenth-century imprints, the *Inventaire chronologique des éditions parisiennes du 16e siècle*, its description ends with the seemingly conclusive judgement: 'contains woodcuts inspired by the Holbein drawings in the Lyonnaise edition published

---

[17] In the two other illuminated copies mentioned at n. 9, the coronation scene woodcut was covered with paintings representing payment of the tithe or a sacrifice. Unfortunately, their earliest owners could not be identified.

[18] See Winn, *Anthoine Vérard* (n. 9 above).

[19] Spencer, 'Vérard's Illuminated Incunables' (n. 11 above), p. 65. *Les nobles et cleres dames*, Paris, Antoine Vérard, 28 Apr. 1493, f° (ISTC ib00719000). Paris, BnF, Vélins 1223.

[20] USTC 147431. The only full-length study dedicated to this major figure is the dated, unpublished dissertation defended at the École nationale des Chartes by A. Jaulme, *Étude sur François Regnault, libraire et imprimeur à Paris, 1500–1541, suivie d'un catalogue de ses édition*. A summary is given in *Positions des théses*, Paris, 1924, pp. 95–103.

[21] This copy belonged to two famous nineteenth-century bibliophiles, the silk merchant Nicolas Yemeniz (1783–1871) and the Protestant banker and politician Alfred André (1827–1893), whose collection of sixteenth-century books is one of the treasures of the library of the Société d'histoire du Protestantisme francais, founded in 1852. A copy in private hands was sold on 8 March 2007 by Duke's in Dorchester; I was not able to trace its current location.

[22] See M. Engammare, 'Les Figures de la Bible. Le destin oublié d'un genre littéraire en image (XVIe–XVIIe siècles)', *Mélanges de l'Ecole Française de Rome*, 106/2, 1994, pp. 549–91 (561).

222   PRINTING AND MISPRINTING

by Trechsel-Frellon in the same year'.[23] The assertion was only the last in a long series of bibliographical statements that linked the Lyonnaise and the Parisian editions, starting with Ambroise Firmin-Didot (1790–1876), the learned nineteenth-century printer who was also a great collector and connoisseur of French early illustrated books. He maintained that:

> Pierre Regnault published in Paris under the title *Historiarum veteris instrumenti et Apocalypsis icones ad vivum expressae*, Paris (Regnault), sub signo elephantis, 1538, a very similar collection [to the Holbein one]. It is very rare. I could not examine the first edition but I own the second one of 1544.[24]

His assumption that the 1544 book must be a second edition was pure guesswork; yet all subsequent bibliographers, none of whom had seen the volume in question, turned that educated guess into sterling truth, from Baudrier[25] to Brun,[26] up until Ruth Mortimer, who stated in her catalogue of French sixteenth-century illustrated books in Harvard: 'Regnault's blocks first appeared in 1538 under the title *Historiarum veteris instrumenti* [...] in imitation of the first edition of Holbein's *Icones*.'[27] Leaving aside the fact that these illustrious bibliographers all mistook François Regnault for his son Pierre, who in 1538 did not use the imprint 'In signo elephantis' that was at the time reserved to his father's output, their consensus seemed impressive.

The elegant Parisian booklet is in fact completely unrelated to Holbein and the Trechsel, though it has to do, indirectly, with Lyon. It is enough to leaf through the first pages of the *Icones* to recognise some woodcuts that illustrated Genesis in the first authorised edition of the Bible in English, commonly referred to as the Great Bible and printed in 1539, initially in a Parisian shop working for Regnault and then completed in London.[28] For instance, the woodcut representing Jerome on the title-page of the *Icones* is the same one used at the beginning of the Great Bible New Testament; a distinctive Temptation scene — with

---

[23] B. Moreau, *Inventaire chronologique des éditions parisiennes du 16ème siècle d'après les manuscrits de Philippe Renouard, V, 1536–1540*, Paris, 2004. The translation is mine. In 1538, the Trechsel brothers did print for Hugues de La Porte a folio Latin Bible and for François Frellon an octavo picture Bible with the same woodcuts copied from Holbein's drawings (USTC 147352 and USTC 147427).

[24] A. Firmin-Didot, *Essai typographique et bibliographique sur l'histoire de la gravure sur bois [...] servant d'introduction aux 'Costumes anciens et modernes' de César Vercellio*, Paris, 1863, p. 68. The translation is mine.

[25] H. Baudrier, *Bibliographie lyonnaise. Recherches sur les imprimeurs, libraires, relieurs et fondeurs de lettres de Lyon au XVIe siècle*, Paris, 1963–1964 (facsimile of the 1895–1921 original edition), V, p. 261.

[26] R. Brun, *Le livre français illustré de la Renaissance. Étude suivie du catalogue des principaux livres à figures du XVIe siècle*, Paris, 1969, p. 131.

[27] R. Mortimer, *Harvard College Library Department of Printing & Graphic Arts: Catalogue of Books and Manuscripts. French 16th Century Books*, I, Cambridge (MA), 1964, p. 85.

[28] *The Byble in Englysh, that is to say the content of all the holy Scripture, bothe of the Olde and Newe Testament, truly translated after the veryte of the Hebrue and Greke textes, by the dylygent men expert in the forsayde tonges*, [Paris and] London, [François Regnault,] Richard Grafton and Edward Whitchurch, 1539, f° (USTC 503073). The Great Bible was prepared under the aegis of Miles Coverdale, the editor of the text, and the merchants Richard Grafton and Edward Whitchurch, who shouldered the cost of the printing with Thomas Cromwell, Henry VIII's minister. I dwell more extensively on the Great Bible illustrations in 'Holy Images on the Move: Reconsidering the Great Bible Illustrations (1529–1745)', *Bibliothèque d'humanisme et renaissance*, 83, 2021, pp. 210–47. The best bibliographical description is still F. Fry, *A description of the Great Bible, 1539, and the six editions of Cranmer's Bible, 1540 and 1541, printed by Grafton and Whitchurch: also of the editions, in large folio, of the authorized version of the Holy Scriptures, printed in the years 1611, 1613, 1617, 1634, 1640*, London, 1865.

10: MISPRINTING THE WORD AND THE IMAGE OF GOD   223

Adam unusually receiving the forbidden fruit from the serpent before him, and not from Eve — can also be found in both editions (Fig. 10.3); the Expulsion from the Garden of Eden is illustrated by means of the same woodcut, even showing the same imperfection on the right side of the frame (Fig. 10.4).

All in all, of the seventy-two Old Testament woodcuts in the Great Bible (in ninety-eight occurrences),[29] as many as sixty-nine appear in the *Icones*. More precisely, the Paris woodcuts, with the exception of the Temptation mentioned above, closely followed the illustrations of a Lyonnaise Vulgate printed in 1529 by Jean Crespin.[30]

The relation between the *Icones* and the Great Bible, rather than the Trechsel-Frellon book with Holbein's illustrations, is further confirmed by the *Expositio* — the brief Latin text accompanying each woodcut. While Trechsel and Frellon inserted explanatory notes written anew, probably by the latter, the *Icones* rehashed the *casus summarii*, the biblical chapter summaries that had been a common feature of printed Vulgates since 1480. Crespin in 1529 reproduced the version of the *casus* first published by Jacques Sacon in Lyon in 1512; the editor of the *Icones*, whoever he was, chose to use this instead of the shorter version from the 1532 Mareschal edition.[31] Sacon's version was also employed in the Great Bible, though it was translated into English.

In contrast with the *Icones*, we have plenty of external sources about the printing history of the Great Bible in Paris, thanks to John Foxe's *Book of Martyrs*[32] and the diplomatic correspondences published by Alfred W. Pollard.[33] Printing started in June 1538 and was in full swing during the summer. In October French authorities were alerted by members of the Parisian book trade about the endeavour, when printing was probably completed. In December, the fate of the Great Bible in Paris was doomed. François Regnault was summoned to appear before the vicar general of the Inquisitor of France because of the fear of 'scandals' and 'errors' that could come from the fact that Regnault was 'printing these days the Bible in vulgar English language'' as John Foxe informs us.[34] He also noted: (1) that Miles Coverdale, Edward Whitchurch, and Richard Grafton, Regnault's English associates, fled to London, 'leaving behind them all their Bibles which were to the number of 2500'; (2) that some of these Bibles were burned publicly in place Maubert by order of the Lieutenant-Criminal, and some sold to a haberdasher; and (3) that at an unknown date, 'encouraged by the lord Cromwell the said Englishmen went agayne to Paris and there got the presses, letters and servants of the aforesaid printer and brought them to London and there they became printers themselves [...] and printed the said Bible in London'.[35]

---

[29] See R. Samson Luborsky and E. Morley Ingram, *A Guide to English Illustrated Books (1536–1603)*, Tempe (AZ), 1998, p. 97.

[30] *Textus Biblie hoc in opere haec sunt*, Lyon, Jean Crespin and Vincent de Portonariis, 1529, f° (USTC 155829). See M. Engammare, *'Qu'il me baise des baisiers de sa bouche': le Cantique des cantiques à la Renaissance*, Geneva, 1993, p. 402.

[31] See the detailed descriptions in H. Quentin, *Mémoire sur l'établissement du texte de la Vulgate. Ire partie: Octateuque*, Paris, 1922, pp. 78–86.

[32] See the admirably commentated online edition of the *Acts* directed by M. Greengrass and D. Loade: *The Unabridged Acts and Monuments Online* or *TAMO*, Sheffield, 2011, http//www.johnfoxe.org.

[33] A. W. Pollard, *Records of the English Bible: The Documents Relating to the Translation and Publication of the Bible in English, 1525–1611*, Oxford, 1911, pp. 223–32.

[34] Ibid., p. 230.

[35] Without indicating his source, J. A. Kingdon, *Pyntz and Grafton*, London, 1895, p. 58, states that in March 1539 Cromwell bargained the return of the sections of the Bible printed in Paris in exchanged for French ships interned in Calais.

FIG. 10.3. Adam receives the forbidden fruit. *Historiarum veteris instrumenti et Apocalypsis icones ad vivum expressae*, Paris, [François Regnault], 1538, 8° (USTC 147431), sig. a3r. Paris, Bibliothèque de la Société d'histoire du Protestantisme francais, André 246.

10: MISPRINTING THE WORD AND THE IMAGE OF GOD   225

FIG. 10.4. Adam and Eve chased out of the garden of Eden. *Historiarum veteris instrumenti* (see Fig. 10.3), sig. a4r. Paris, Bibliothèque de la Société d'histoire du Protestantisme francais, André 246.

226   PRINTING AND MISPRINTING

In light of what we have seen so far, there could be grounds for arguing that the *Icones* and the Great Bible were part of the same publishing project in 1538, similar to what Parisian and Lyonnaise booksellers routinely did when they printed the same woodcut series both in complete illustrated Bibles and as *Figures de la Bible* accompanied by short Latin or vernacular texts to ensure return on the large investment linked to the production of a series of woodcuts. This is exactly what Trechsel and Frellon had done, also in 1538, with the Holbein series and repeated many times: *Icones* on the one hand, a Latin Vulgate on the other.[36] The *Icones* could have been in the same kind of relationship with the Great Bible. To the objection that the *Icones* display a Latin text while the Great Bible is of course in English, one could answer that multilingualism belongs to the very nature of picture bibles as they developed, particularly in Lyon, with parallel editions in French, Italian, Latin, and Spanish.[37] But the Parisian book, the first picture Bible to have been printed in Paris (just like the Holbein was the first to be printed in Lyon), is so clumsily laid out that it is difficult to imagine it could have been intended for commercial diffusion.

However, is it possible to establish more precisely the relationship between the Great Bible and the *Icones*? The answer seems to lie in misprints, intended, rather broadly, as evidence of unusual as well as downright faulty printing. An inventory of those appearing in the *Icones*, is revealing. I divided this inventory in seven parts — the seven sins, so to speak, of the compositor of the *Icones*.

1. There are printing errors common to the *Icones*, the Great Bible, and the 1529 Crespin Vulgate. For example, Joshua 12 as well as Judges 1 are illustrated by the same woodcut representing Joshua with conquered kings dead at his feet; this is a further proof that the *Icones* is connected with the Great Bible illustrations, and certainly not with the 1538 Lyonnaise edition of Holbein's drawings where Joshua XII and Judges I are illustrated by different woodcuts, as in its clumsy imitation published in 1544 by François Regnault's son, Pierre, partly due to the Basel engraver Jacobus Faber.[38]

2. Text starts abruptly, without a preface or a dedication, whereas *Figures de la Bible*, such as the Lyonnaise edition, always displayed dedication and dedicatory poems. In the *Icones*, text begins on fol. A2v.

3. Titles do not always match biblical illustrations or explanatory notes, starting with Genesis I and II where the creation of the world in six days is illustrated with God the Father *in trono majestatis*. 'JUDICUM I' corresponds to the text and illustration of Ruth 1 (Fig. 10.5). 'II PARALIPO I' is illustrated by the vision of Daniel in Dan. 13. 'TOBIE I' corresponds to the text and illustration of Judith 1. 'SAPIENTIE I' corresponds to a woodcut representing Jerome and the lion.

[36] E. Michael, 'The Iconographic History of Hans Holbein the Younger's *Icones* and Their Reception in the Later Sixteenth Century', *Harvard Library Bulletin*, 2, 1947, pp. 28–47.

[37] See E. Kammerer, 'Entre recréation de l'âme et récréation des yeux: les Figures de la Bible au XVIe siècle', in B. Decharneux, C. Maignant, and M. Watthee-Delmotte (eds), *Esthétique et spiritualité*, II: *Circulation des modèles en Europe*, Louvain-la-Neuve, 2011, pp. 167–79.

[38] *Historiarum Veteris Testamenti icones ad vivum expressæ. Unà cum brevi, sed quoad fieri potuit dilucida, earundem & Latina & Gallica expositione*, Paris, Pierre Regnault, 1544, 4° (USTC 149178). See F. Hieronymus, "'Salutat te Nicolaus Episcopius, Jacobus Faber sculptor aerarius omnisque, ut verbo dicam, familia." Jacobus Faber (c. 1500–c. 1550), un graveur français à Bâle', *Bulletin du bibliophile*, 1, 2005, pp. 64–84.

Elimelech cum vxore Noemi & filiis peregri-
natur i Moab, quo mortuo cũ filiis Noemi vxor
eius in Bęthleem redit cum Ruth nuru sua.

IVDICVM I.

FIG. 10.5. The illustration of Ruth 1 with incorrect heading. *Historiarum veteris instrumenti* (see Fig. 10.3), sig. e8v. Paris, Bibliothèque de la Société d'histoire du Protestantisme francais, André 246.

228 PRINTING AND MISPRINTING

4. Some woodcuts are repeated to illustrate different verses, whereas in the Great Bible different woodcuts are used: e.g., Exodus 19 and 34, as well as Psalms 1 and 38.
5. Two woodcuts left behind in the Old Testament — Exodus 1 and 18 — even had to be added at the end of the New Testament series with the awkward note: '*Quae fuerunt derelictae ex veteri testamenti*' (These were forgotten in the Old Testament) (Fig. 10.6).
6. Patent misprints deface the titles in capital letters of biblical books. 'GENFSIS' for GENESIS (Gn.3). 'GENESIR' for GENESIS (Gn. 41). This happened either because the type letters were out of place in the typecase, or because the compositor went for the wrong box next to the one he intended: F for E and R for S. In 'DETERONOMI' for DEUTERONOMI (Deut. 5) and 'HIEEMIE' for HIEREMIE (Jer. 1), he skipped a U and an R.
7. Titles are sometimes given in lower case instead of capitals, contrary to the use of the rest of the text, for example in Psalms 1 and 109.

What can we make of this festival of misprints? Although the unknown printer showed good command of the visual space — woodcuts are perfectly centred in the page — the inescapable impression is that we are dealing with a set of proofs, or a trial piece done in some haste during the preparation of the Great Bible. Our only certainties are that, due to the transfer to London of Regnault's printing material for the Great Bible, this unique attempt at producing a picture Bible with text and woodcuts lifted from a contemporary Lyonnaise Bible left no lasting traces in Paris, where Pierre Regnault published in 1540 a *Biblia Picturis illustrate* illustrated with a totally new set of metal cuts,[39] or elsewhere for that matter, and that no *Figures de la Bible* show such compositorial inaccuracy.

I thus submit to the judgment of readers the hypothesis that the carelessly produced Parisian *Icones* were not intended for diffusion,[40] and that only a few copies were printed, maybe with the specific aim of presenting the woodcuts that would illustrate the Great Bible to Thomas Cromwell, who had commissioned the printing of this first authorised Bible and kept a close watch on its realisation. On 23 June 1538, a letter from Coverdale and Grafton to Cromwell indicates, for example, that 'we be entred into your worke of the Byble' and that they sent two samples of the printing, 'one in parchment' and 'the seconde in paper'.[41] On 9 August, 'certayne leaves thereof' were sent to Cromwell by Coverdale, Grafton, and William Gray — the polemist and poet; they also promised that 'so will we sende your lord-ship the residue from time to time'.[42] I even venture to propose that the compositor of the *Icones*, if he was not a boy as the archbishop of Canterbury put it in 1631, was a beginner in the trade, and could well have been Grafton, Whitchurch, or both of them, since they most likely learned hands-on in Paris the profession that they would exercise in London for a long time under Henry VIII and Elizabeth I.[43] If they misprinted the word and the image of God in Paris, they certainly redeemed themselves in London.

---

[39] Moreau, *Inventaire chronologique* (n. 23 above), V, p. 457, no. 1598.

[40] If my guess is correct, the *Icones* stands halfway between proofs and a published text, perhaps an early instance of mock-up, or, at any rate, a hybrid type of print product of which I have not yet encountered other sixteenth-century examples.

[41] Pollard, *Records* (n. 33 above), pp. 234–5.

[42] Ibid., p. 239.

[43] E. G. Duff, *A Century of the English Book Trade: Short Notices of All Printers*, Cambridge, 2011, p. 169.

Quæ fuerunt derelictæ ex veteri testamento.

EXODI   I.

FIG. 10.6. The forgotten illustration related to Ex. 1. *Historiarum veteris instrumenti* (see Fig. 10.3), sig. []1r. Paris, Bibliothèque de la Société d'histoire du Protestantisme francais, André 246.

CONCLUSIONS

The mistakes in typography and illustration that marred the two Parisian, royally connected editions I examined in this chapter, were certainly spectacular. And yet they had nothing to do with the bizarre, often hilarious, misprints of the 'Thou-shalt-commit-adultery' type which twisted the theological meaning of biblical verses and have horrified or delighted readers for centuries. Studying them has another object of interest: to half-open for today's readers the doors of Vérard' and Regnault's print shops, so that we can understand better the practices of fifteenth- and sixteenth-century printers and illuminators when they dealt with the Scripture. Ever since Gutenberg's Bible, the Book of God — or the 'God of Books', to quote the Puritan poet Christopher Harvey — proved a highly challenging text to run under the press.

BIBLIOGRAPHY

PRIMARY SOURCES

La bible historiée, ed. Jean de Rély, Paris, Antoine Vérard, [between 8 May 1498 and 25 Oct. 1499], f° (ISTC ib00623000). Illuminated copies: Lyon, Bibliothèque municipale, Inc. 57–8; New York, The Morgan Library and Museum, PML 28379-82; Paris, Bibliothèque nationale, Vélins 100–1.

Biblia utriusque Testamenti juxta vulgatam translationem, et eam, quam haberi potuit, emendatissimam, Lyon, Gaspar Trechsel and Melchior Trechsel apud Hugues de La Porte, 1538, 2° (USTC 147352).

Boccaccio, Giovanni, *Les nobles et cleres dames*, Paris, Antoine Vérard, 28 Apr. 1493, f° (ISTC ib00719000). Illuminated copy: Paris, Bibliothèque nationale de France, Vélins 1223.

The Byble in Englysh, that is to say the content of all the holy Scripture, bothe of the Olde and Newe Testament, truly translated after the veryte of the Hebrue and Greke textes, by the dylygent men expert in the forsayde tonges, [Paris and] London, [François Regnault,] Richard Grafton and Edward Whitchurch, 1539, f° (USTC 503073).

Chroniques de France, Paris, Jean Maurand (vol. II only), for Antoine Vérard, 1493, f° (ISTC ic00484000).

Flavius Josephus, *De la bataille judaïque*, [transl. Claude de Seyssel?], Paris, Antoine Vérard, [after 7 Dec. 1492], f° (ISTC ij00489000). Illuminated copy: Paris, Bibliothèque nationale de France, Vélins 696.

Historiarum veteris instrumenti et Apocalypsis icones ad vivum expressae, Paris, [François Regnault], 1538, 8° (USTC 147431).

Historiarum veteris Instrumenti icones ad vivum expressae. Una cum brevi, sed quoad fieri potuit, dilucida earundem expositione, Lyon, Gaspar and Melchior Trechsel, 1538, 4° (USTC 147427).

Historiarum Veteris Testamenti icones ad vivum expressae. Una cum brevi, sed quoad fieri potuit dilucida, earundem & Latina & Gallica exposition, Paris, Pierre Regnault, 1544, 4° (USTC 149178).

The Holy Bible, conteining the Olde Testament and the New, London, Robert Barker, 1612, 8° (USTC 3005284).

The Holy Bible containing the Old Testament and the New, London, Robert Barker for John Bill, 1631, 8° (USTC 3015715).

Textus Biblie hoc in opere haec sunt, Lyon, Jean Crespin and Vincent de Portonariis, 1529, f° (USTC 155829).

SECONDARY LITERATURE

Barbizet, L., et al., *Textes et images dans la Bible historiée d'Antoine Vérard, mémoire de recherches de l'Enssib*, Villeurbanne, 2004.

Baudrier, B., *Bibliographie lyonnaise. Recherches sur les imprimeurs, libraires, relieurs et fondeurs de lettres de Lyon au XVIe siècle*, Paris, 1963–1964 (facsimile of the 1895–1921 original edition).

Brun, R., *Le livre français illustré de la Renaissance. Étude suivie du catalogue des principaux livres à figures du XVIe siècle*, Paris, 1969.

Daniel, D., *The Bible in English: Its History and Influence*, New Haven (CT), 2003.

Delaveau, M., and Hillard, D., *Les Bibles imprimées du xve au xviiie siècle conservées à Paris, Bibliothèque nationale de France, Bibliothèque Sainte-Geneviève, Bibliothèque de la Sorbonne, Bibliothèque Mazarine, Bibliothèque de la Société de l'histoire du protestantisme français, Bibliothèque de la Société biblique*, Paris, 2002.

Deldicque, M., 'L'enluminure à Paris à la fin du xve siècle: Maître François, le Maître de Jacques de Besançon et Jacques de Besançon identifiés?', *Revue de l'art*, 183, 2014, pp. 9–18.

Dupuigrenet Desroussilles, F., *Dieu en son royaume: la Bible dans la France d'autrefois, xiiie–xviiie siècle*, Paris, 1991.

Dupuigrenet Desroussilles, F., 'Holy Images on the Move: Reconsidering the Great Bible Illustrations (1529–1745)', *Bibliothèque d'humanisme et renaissance*, 83, 2021, pp. 210–47.

Duff, E. G., *A Century of the English Book Trade: Short Notices of All Printers*, Cambridge, 2011 (first published in 1948).

Engammare, M., 'Les Figures de la Bible. Le destin oublié d'un genre littéraire en image (XVIe–XVIIe siècles)', *Mélanges de l'Ecole Française de Rome*, 106/2, 1994, pp. 549–91.

Engammare, M., *'Qu'il me baise des baisiers de sa bouche': le Cantique des cantiques à la Renaissance*, Geneva, 1993.

Firmin-Didot, A., *Essai typographique et bibliographique sur l'histoire de la gravure sur bois [...] servant d'introduction aux "Costumes anciens et modernes" de César Vercellio*, Paris, 1863.

Fournié, E., 'Les éditions de la *Bible historiale*. Présentation et catalogue raisonné d'éditions de la première moitié du xvie siècle', *L'Atelier du Centre de recherches historiques*, 3/2, 2009, https://journals.openedition.org/acrh/1832?lang=en#tocto3n18.

Fournié, E., 'Les manuscrits de la *Bible historiale*. Présentation et catalogue raisonné d'une oeuvre médiévale ', *L'Atelier du Centre de recherches historiques*, 3/2, 2009, https://journals.openedition.org/acrh/1408.

Fournié, E., *L'iconographie de la Bible historiale*, Turnhout, 2012.

Fry, F., *A Description of the Great Bible, 1539, and the six editions of Cranmer's Bible, 1540 and 1541, printed by Grafton and Whitchurch: also of the editions, in large folio, of the authorized version of the Holy Scriptures, printed in the years 1611, 1613, 1617, 1634, 1640*, London, 1865.

Greengrass, M., and Loade, D., *The Unabridged Acts and Monuments Online or TAMO*, Sheffield, 2011, http://www.johnfoxe.org.

Hieronymus, F., '"Salutat te Nicolaus Episcopius, Jacobus Faber sculptor aerarius omnisque, ut verbo dicam, familia". Jacobus Faber (c. 1500–c. 1550), un graveur français à Bâle', *Bulletin du bibliophile*, 1, 2005, pp. 64–84.

Hillard, D., 'Les éditions de la *Bible* en France au xve siècle', in B. E. Schwarzbach (ed.), *La Bible imprimée dans l'Europe moderne*, Paris, 1999, pp. 68–82.

Jaulme, A., *Étude sur François Regnault, libraire et imprimeur à Paris, 1500–1541, suivie d'un catalogue de ses édition*. Unpublished École des Chartes dissertation. Summary in *Positions des thèses*, Paris, 1924, pp. 95–103.

Kammerer, E., 'Entre recréation de l'âme et récréation des yeux: les Figures de la Bible au XVIe siècle', in B. Decharneux, C. Maignant, and M. Watthee-Delmotte (eds), *Esthétique et spiritualité*, II: *Circulation des modèles en Europe*, Louvain-la-Neuve, 2011, pp. 167–79.

Kingdon, J. A., *Pyntz and Grafton*, London, 1895.

Luborsky, R., and Morley Ingram, E., *A Guide to English Illustrated Books (1536–1603)*, Tempe (AZ), 1998.

MacFarlane, J., *Antoine Vérard*, London, 1900.

Michael, E., 'The Iconographic History of Hans Holbein the Younger's *Icones* and Their Reception in the Later Sixteenth Century', *Harvard Library Bulletin*, 2, 1947, pp. 28–47.

Moreau, B., *Inventaire chronologique des éditions parisiennes du 16ème siècle* d'après les manuscrits de Philippe Renouard, *V, 1536–1540*, Paris, 2004.

Mortimer, R., *Harvard College Library Department of Printing & Graphic Arts: Catalogue of Books and Manuscripts. French 16th Century Books*, I, Cambridge (MA), 1964.

Nicolson, A., *God's Secretaries: The Making of the King James Bible*, New York, 2005.

Nobel, P., 'Du manuscrit à l'imprimé: le traitement des gloses dans l'editio princeps de la "Bible historiée" publiée par Antoine Vérard', *Le français préclassique (1500–1650)*, 19, 2017, pp. 85–100.

Pollard, A. W., *Records of the English Bible: The Documents Relating to the Translation and Publication of the Bible in English, 1525–1611*, Oxford, 1911.

Printing Errors and Corrections in the Gutenberg Bible, 2013, https://www.bodleian.ox.ac.uk/our-work/conservation/case-studies/polonsky-foundation-digitization-project.

Quentin, H., *Mémoire sur l'établissement du texte de la Vulgate. Ire partie: Octateuque*, Paris, 1922.

Sansy, D., 'Entre manuscrit et imprimé: les représentations de Richard Ier dans les *Grandes Chroniques de France* de Vérard (1493)', *Annales de Normandie*, 64, 2014, pp. 99–116.

Sansy, D., 'Texte et image dans les incunables français', *Médiévales*, 22–3, 1992, pp. 47–70.

Spencer, E. P., 'Antoine Vérard's Illuminated Vellum Incunables', in J. B. Trapp (ed.), *Manuscripts in the Fifty Years After the Inventions of Printing: Some Papers Read at a Colloquium at the Warburg Institute on 12–13 March 1982*, London, 1983, pp. 62–5.

Van Praet, J., *Catalogue des livres imprimés sur vélin de la Bibliothèque du Roi*, Paris, 1822.

Winn, M. B., *Anthoine Vérard, Parisian Publisher (1485–1512): Prologues, Poems and Presentations*, Geneva, 1997.

CHAPTER 11

THE COLLECTIVE EDITORIAL STRATEGY OF THE UNITY OF THE BRETHREN

VERONIKA SLADKÁ

INTRODUCTION

THE most extensive humanistic translation into Czech is the Kralice Bible (1579–1594), which has similar importance for Czech literature as the King James Bible has for English. This outstanding literary work was produced by a radical Protestant church called the Unity of the Brethren. There is no doubt that the Brethren must have used sophisticated methods of textual corrections. This article traces proofreading practices of the Brethren, who employed the most advanced methods of the day for editing and correcting texts. After a detailed description of the publishing process applied by the Unity of the Brethren, the study will use a corrected copy and proof sheets of two Brethren hymnbooks, as well as their bishops' correspondence, to reveal a collective and highly organised system of editing and proofreading. The cases of two Brethren's bishops (Jan Blahoslav and Izaiáš Cibulka) demonstrate the methods of the Brethren's correctors and clarify from where the Brethren drew their proofreading skills.

To date, most of the evidence regarding proofreading practices in Czech-speaking lands in the sixteenth century is directly linked to the publishing activities of the Unity of the Brethren.[1] This radical Protestant church, following Jan Hus's and Petr Chelčický's views, was established in the middle of the fifteenth century in East Bohemia. During the nearly

---

[1] See M. Bohatcová, 'České korektury z let 1523–1524', *Typografia*, 69, 1966, pp. 334–6; V. Fialová, 'Korrekturabzüge aus dem XVI. Jahrhundert. Ein Beitrag zur Historie der Buchdruckerei der Böhmischen Brüder', *Gutenberg-Jahrbuch*, 39, 1964, pp. 217–23.

Veronika Sladká, *The Collective Editorial Strategy of the Unity of the Brethren*. In: *Printing and Misprinting*.
Edited by Geri Della Rocca de Candal, Anthony Grafton, and Paolo Sachet, Oxford University Press. © Veronika Sladká (2023).
DOI: 10.1093/oso/9780198863045.003.0012

two hundred years of its existence in Bohemia, Moravia, and Poland, the moderate religious community included no more than 2% of the population in Czech lands.[2] Most interestingly, the Brethren also operated an illegal printing press in the Moravian city of Ivančice (1562–1619).[3] Undoubtedly, it was the printed books that helped the Brethren to maintain and spread their ideology, attracting protectors and benefactors. At about the same time, this persecuted group of 'Bohemian Pikarts' transformed into a highly disciplined Protestant church, supported by distinguished Czech noblemen, and earned the respect of European humanists and reformers such as Martin Luther, Philipp Melanchthon, and Theodore Beza.[4]

The literary and publishing activity of the Brethren attracted the attention of generations of scholars in the past.[5] The Unity of the Brethren published several distinguished editions of hymnbooks and Bibles, though they made history when they translated the Scriptures from the original biblical languages into Czech[6] and published the six volumes of the Kralice Bible (1579–1594), setting a model for the Czech language and for its aesthetic and literary norms.[7] It remains unknown how such a modest, persecuted religious group, which had utterly rejected higher education until the middle of the sixteenth century, was subsequently able to produce such high-grade editions, comparable to the humanistic editions of western Europe.

This chapter aims to unravel some of the mysteries surrounding the editing and proofreading activity of the Unity of the Brethren, who operated a small illegal publishing house equipped with a single press. Presenting all known pieces of proofreading connected to the Brethren, it argues that it is possible to trace a foreign influence on the way in which the Brethren edited and corrected the published texts. The paper begins by discussing the Brethren's collective approach to publishing and the Brethren's contacts with western-European humanism. Then it will deal with four pieces of evidence: a printer's copy of the hymnbook *Pjsně* (1561); proof sheets of the hymnbook *Pjsně* (1572); bishops' correspondence (1610–1618); and a corrected copy of the music theory textbook *Musica* (1569).

---

[2] Accounts of the historical context and the Brethren's theology are provided by: C. D. Atwood, *The Theology of the Czech Brethren from Hus to Comenius*, University Park (PA), 2009; R. Říčan, *The History of the Unity of the Brethren: A Protestant Hussite Church in Bohemia and Moravia*, Bethlehem, 1992; and J. Th. Müller, *Geschichte der Böhmischen Brüder*, 3 vols, Herrnhut, 1922–1931. The Brethren's assembly records are published in A. Gindely (ed.), *Dekrety Jednoty bratrské*, Prague, 1865.

[3] On this printing house, see M. Bohatcová, 'Ästhetische Konzeptionen der Drucke der Böhmischen Brüder zur Zeit Jan Blahoslav', *Gutenberg-Jahrbuch*, 46, 1971, pp. 189–99 (190–1).

[4] See Melanchthon'/Luther's prefaces to the editions of the Brethren's *Confession* (USTC 568902, 568912).

[5] See R. Dittmann and J. Just, *Biblical Humanism in Bohemia and Moravia in the 16th Century*, Turnhout, 2016, pp. 290–5, as well as M. Bohatcová, 'The Book and the Reformation in Bohemia and Moravia', in J. F. Gilmont (ed.), *The Reformation and the Book*, Aldershot, 1998, pp. 309–402, 407.

[6] The precise translation source has not yet been identified. The Kralice scholars did not mention any particular Latin, Hebrew, or Greek biblical text. However, the translation variants printed in the margin, labelled by 'H' for a Hebrew source, 'Ř' for a Greek one, and 'G' for others, indicate that the Brethren translators must have used not only the Latin translation of the Old Testament produced by Immanuel Tremellius and Franciscus Junius (1576–1579), but also Hebrew and Greek texts. See Dittmann and Just, *Biblical Humanism* (n. 5 above), p. 109.

[7] Dittmann and Just, *Biblical Humanism* (n. 5 above), pp. 257–9.

Highly Skilled Staff and Strict Self-censorship

To understand how a minor, permanently oppressed and persecuted community could publish superior books, we need to take into account several peculiarities of the Brethren as publishers and printers. First, as the text of the Scriptures represented the ultimate authority for the Brethren, they paid close attention to the quality of all printed texts.[8] Clear evidence of how much care the Brethren put into manufacturing books could be seen even in the philosophical-theological treatises by bishop Jan Amos Comenius (1592–1670). According to Comenius, high-quality publications and, consequently, careful correctors were one of the three critical instruments of universal education necessary for human salvation.[9]

Secondly, it is obvious from the archival documents that the editorial process was unique in many ways, as the community's religious commitments and organisational structure had a direct impact on it. The official records of the Brethren's assembly suggest that all titles had to be read and approved by the Brethren's bishops and elders, members of the Inner Council, the supreme administrative organ of the Unity of the Brethren.[10] All publications were considered the collective works of the Unity. The importance of publishing activity was reflected in the existence of the office of the Bishop-Scribe, whose responsibilities included censorship, editing, proofreading, and supervision of the book manufacturing and distribution.[11]

---

[8] Atwood, *The Theology* (n. 2 above), pp. 223–4.

[9] For the first time, Comenius outlined his reform programme in *Via lucis* (The Path of Light), where he sees books as the most important tool of spreading universal education: 'Fixis Panaugiae finibus, media jam accommodabimus. Quorum quatuor se omni offerunt: libri universales [...]' (Johannes Amos Comenius, *Via lucis*, Amsterdam, 1668, 4°, p. 58). In this treatise, the Brethren's scholar also emphasises the key role of printing: 'Ita ultima lucis [ars typographica] omnia illa conjunget, demumque vere illustria reddet: dum et res contemplandas melius ac unquam in luce sistet, et de illis sermones omnium ad omnes exacuet, et libros si non augebit (aucti enim sunt plus satis), depurabit tamen, ut universalis eruditionis vehicula fiant verssima' (ibid., p. 48). In *Typographeum vivum* (i.e. the fourth part of his *Opera didactica omnia*), Comenius depicts an ideal printing shop with correctors in prominent position: 'Personas plena officina typographica requirit ad minimum sex. Inter quas tres primariae, compositor, corrector, impressor, totidem secundariae, celeritatem adjuvantes, lector, tinctor, lotor' (Johannes Amos Comenius, *Opera didactica omnia IV. pars*, Amsterdam, 1657, f°, p. 90). Additionally, he describes the corrector's tasks: 'Correctoris est 1. exemplar imitans cum imitando (ectypum cum archetypo) conferre, et num per omnia conveniant, examinare, 2. si quid discrepans reperit, corrigere, compositorem, ut emendet, monere, 3. demumque ut imprimatur, permittere; subinde tamen intervisedno, annon aliquid depravetur, attendedo, et si quid vitium facit, emendando et sic perpetuo corruptelas praecavendo' (ibid). Eventually, Comenius outlines how such fine books are created: 'Haec sic ingenere, quomodo libri qualescunque imprimantur. Si specialiter de libris optimis, quomodo fiant, quaestio sit; dicendum erit, requiri hic. 1. Exemplar prototypum sapienter scriptum, luce, non tenebris dignum. 2. Typos elegantes. 3. Papyrum mundam. 4. Operasque attentas, ut omnia usque ad apicem clara, distinctra, correcta sint' ibid., p. 91).

[10] Gindely (ed.), *Dekrety* (n. 2 above), pp. 170, 178–9, 181, 185.

[11] Gindely (ed.), *Dekrety* (n. 2 above), p. 185; see also the Brethren's correspondence in Archive of Bishop Matouš Konečný, Archiv Matouše Konečného (AMK), Muzeum Mladoboleslavska,

The historiographer Jan Łasicki (1534–1605) left a detailed description of the complex process that preceded the publication of any official text.[12] First, it had to be decided whether it was in the interest of the Brethren to publish a given text, and then it had to be decided who should be responsible for its preparation. Each text had to be read by at least one of the seniors, often by the Bishop-Scribe. The publication of works without such prior approval was strictly forbidden. Every text selected for publication was discussed in detail at the Brethren's assembly sessions and had to go through a multiple-level approval process. All bishops and seniors were invited to comment. The political implications for the church were taken into special account. In the case of confessions, another step included sending the text to non-members, such as professors at the University of Wittenberg (e.g. Melanchthon, Luther), who were asked for an endorsement.[13]

Finally, such high-quality production was possible because the employees of the Brethren press were priests trained both in the printing business and in editing and proofreading.[14] Most of them had acquired printing skills before going to university, as learning a craft was considered a crucial part of the education of a priest.[15]

It has to be said that one of the crucial features of the Brethren's approach to publishing was its focus on sending its most talented youth to renowned universities in Protestant Europe (mainly in Germany and Switzerland).[16] The most popular destinations were Goldberg in Mecklenburg, Königsberg, Wittenberg,[17] Heidelberg, and Tübingen.[18] Later, students were more frequently sent to Swiss universities in Basel, Zurich, and Geneva.[19] During their studies, many of the Brethren's leaders developed lifelong friendly connections with leading humanists, philologists, translators, pedagogues, editors, and correctors, including Theodore Beza, Immanuel Tremellius, Heinrich Bullinger, Philipp Melanchthon, Caspar Peucer, and Sigmund Gelenius.

A3251/Lanecký/46, 'letter of Jan Lanecký to Matouš Konečný about the proofreading of the catechism, 2th September 1615'.

[12] Jan Łasicki, *Historiae de origine et rebus gestis fratrum Bohemicorum liber VIII*, [Leszno?, Wiegand Funck?], 1649, 8° (USTC 2064309), pp. 109–13.

[13] See the endorsement written by either Luther or Melanchthon and added to the end of the Brethren's confessions: *Confessio Fratrum Bohemorum*, [Ivančice: Tiskárna bratrská — printer of Czech Brothers], 1564, 8° (USTC 568409) and the 1574 edition (USTC 568912).

[14] V. Fialová, 'Persönlichkeiten und Schicksale der berühmtesten Druckerei der Böhmischen Brüder', *Gutenberg-Jahrbuch*, 42, 1967, pp. 138–43.

[15] Bohatcová, 'Ästhetische Konzeptionen' (n. 3 above), p. 190.

[16] Cf. Łasicki, *Historiae de origine* (n. 12 above), p. 87.

[17] Thirty future Brethren priests studied in Wittenberg in 1572; see Prague, Národní archiv, Acta Unitatis Fratrum (AUF), NA, no. 106, a deposit of the UA: AB II R 1.1 Vol. 12, fol. 138v.

[18] For the list of the Brethren's students at German universities, see F. Menčík, 'Studenti z Čech a Moravy ve Vitenberku od roku 1502–1602', *Časopis Musea Království českého*, 71, 1897, pp. 250–3.

[19] For the Brethren students at Calvinist schools, see L. Rejchrt, 'Bratrští studenti na reformovaných akademiích před Bílou horou', *Acta Universitatis Carolinae: Historia Universitatis Carolinae Pragensis*, 13/1–2, 1973, pp. 43–82.

THE FIRST KNOWN BRETHREN CORRECTOR:
BISHOP JAN BLAHOSLAV (1523–1571)

One of the most prominent leaders to be influenced by humanism and the first known corrector among the Brethren was the bishop Jan Blahoslav, who studied abroad in the 1540s and 1550s. Blahoslav spent a year at the Latin school of Valentin von Trotzendorf in Goldberg (1543–1544), where he learned Latin and Greek and developed an interest in rhetoric and grammar.[20] He became acquainted with the ideas of humanism and the Reformation at the University of Wittenberg in 1544.[21] He often attended the lectures of the *praeceptor communis* Philipp Melanchthon, who deepened his interest in linguistics.

In 1549, Blahoslav continued his studies in Basel, but due to illness he did not study at the university. He underwent treatment in the house of the humanist Sigmund Gelenius.[22] His stay with Gelenius was formative. Gelenius (d. 1554), originally from Bohemia, served as the corrector of classical languages and Hebrew in Froben's printing house. As a member of the Basel intellectual elite, Gelenius was well connected to local printers and correctors. Blahoslav, therefore, had ample opportunity during his stay to meet some of the best-known humanists and editors of his time while he regained his health.

For the rest of his life, Blahoslav championed higher education and the principles of biblical humanism among the Brethren.[23] He became Bishop-Scribe in 1557, and after his relocation to Ivančice in Southern Moravia, he proceeded to invest in the local school. In 1562 he set up the first Brethren's printing house (1562–1578), which he managed for the rest of his life and which published his educational and liturgical treatises,[24] biblical translations,[25] and editions of the hymnbook.[26]

A CORRECTED COPY OF THE HYMNBOOK (1561)

In addition to the New Testament, the Brethren's hymnals were the church's key religious 'instruction manual' and liturgical tool, containing more than 730 monophonic spiritual

---

[20] Dittmann and Just, *Biblical Humanism* (n. 5 above), pp. 66–71.

[21] Blahoslav joined the University of Wittenberg on 21 July 1544 as Joannes Blasius Przeroviensis. See Menčík, 'Studenti z Čecha a Moravy' (n. 18 above), p. 255.

[22] 'Basiliae quoque apud doctissimum et singulari pietate praeditum virum, historicum admirandum Sigismundum Gelenium per semestre sum commoratus [...]' AUF, NA, no. 106, vol. 8., fol. 169r.

[23] For Blahoslav's defence of education, see AUF, NA, no. 106, vol. 5, [Jan Blahoslav] 'Corollarium additum Anno 1567 die 15. Februarii', fols 101r–106r.

[24] Jan Blahoslav, *Musica*, [Ivančice, Tiskárna bratrská — printer of Czech Brothers], 1569, 8° (USTC 567053); *Ewangelia*, [Ivančice, Tiskárna bratrská — printer of Czech Brothers], 1571, f° (USTC 568909).

[25] Within a short period of time Blahoslav prepared two different editions of the *New Testament*: *Nowy zákon*, [Ivančice, Tiskárna bratrská — printer of Czech Brothers], 1564, 12° (USTC 568906) and 1568, 8° (USTC 568908).

[26] *Piesne chwal Bożskych*, [Szamotuły, Aleksander Augezdecki, 1561], f°, (USTC 244676); *Pjsně duchownj ewangelistské*, [Ivančice, Tiskárna bratrská — printer of Czech Brothers], 1562–1564, f° (USTC 568903).

songs, psalms, and hymns for regular Wednesday, Friday, and Sunday gatherings, as well as service hymns and general songs for particular occasions. The lyrics written by the Brethren drew directly from the Bible and captured the major events of salvation history and the Brethren's dogma.[27] Since hymnbooks served as the primary religious and pedagogical texts that played a pivotal role in spreading the Brethren's faith, they were very carefully prepared and only the foremost members of the Brethren were allowed to edit them.[28] It is no coincidence that the earliest evidence of Blahoslav's editorial practices can be found in the hymnbook *Piesne* (1561) preserved in Herrnhut.[29] A note on the title-page confirms that this is Jan Blahoslav's copy of the hymnbook with his editorial comments and corrections.[30] In addition to Blahoslav's remarks in black and brown ink, the copy also retains annotations made in red ink by another hand, with further connections to other two editions of the Brethren hymnbook (1576, 1581).[31]

Blahoslav's comments included various interventions in the text: deleting or adding whole hymns or parts of hymns, making linguistic and stylistic changes to the hymns, including titles, names of hymns, or orthography, as well as fixing minor misprints and typographical errors. The most extensive revisions involved the texts of the hymns. Blahoslav had an aesthetic sense and often suggested deleting or shortening certain hymns (e.g., sig. G1r). He often sharply criticised hymn texts, showing his humanist education, with comments such as 'thoroughly improper hymn' or 'very vulgar hymn' (sigs J5v, Qq1v). However, his primary responsibility was to judge the theological content of the hymns. He also critically evaluated the musical rendering and many of the corrections tackle the type of musical notation or the rhythms of the hymns (sigs B6r, G1v). He was especially careful about using consistent typography for the visualisation of texts because frequently these were lyrics about salvation or texts of important sung prayers such as the Lord's Prayer. For instance, he indicated the inappropriate use of a particular typeface or the size and type of initials (sigs Nn4r, Nn6v). Aside from correcting typographical errors, he also added rubrication and *maniculae* at the beginning of Commandments (sig. Fff4r).

Blahoslav's less essential revisions involved linguistic or stylistic changes to make the text easier to understand (e.g., sig. F5r). He crossed out all offensive or redundant words, poorly phrased rhymes, or inappropriately chosen analogies (sigs G4v, H5v). Some of his comments show a humanistic effort to improve the hymns on a linguistic level by including a greater variety of synonyms and choosing more appropriate words when the term was confusing or unclear (sigs B2v, B5v, L5v, H5v). As a philologist, he also corrected grammar and orthography. In many places he corrected the grammar according to the rules he eventually set out while preparing the translations of the *New Testament* (sigs B5r, G4r).[32]

---

[27] The lyrics in the first hymnal part reminded the faithful of Jesus's life and teachings and, to a lesser extent, about saints and martyrs. The second part involves songs about the church and the sacraments, including several dozen songs dedicated to the Eucharist. The last part contained fundamental prayer and doctrinal texts, as well as eschatological songs for various occasions.

[28] Gindely (ed.), *Dekrety* (n. 2 above), p. 178.

[29] *Piesne chwal Božskych* (n. 26 above), held in Herrnhut, Unitätsarchiv, AB II R 3.19.

[30] The fact that it is Bishop Blahoslav's personal commentary was already brought to scholarly attention by the Herrnhut archivists A. Glitsch and J. Th. Müller at the end of the nineteenth century. See also the calendar records written by the Brethren priest and printer Václav Solín in Paulus Eber, *Calendarium historicum*, Wittenberg, Georg Rhau, 1559 (USTC 617737), preserved in Vienna, ÖNB, 109640-A ALT MAG, p. 99.

[31] USTC 568915 and 568926.

[32] See n. 25 above.

Blahoslav wrote his remarks with two different colours of ink to distinguish his commentary from the text that had to be reset. He uses 'd' to indicate where a syllable or word had to be deleted (e.g. sig. F5*v*). Most often, he underlined the text that had to be corrected and, less frequently, he wrote the corrected text in a 'speech bubble' in the middle of the page (sig. Yy5*v*).

Hymnbook Proof Sheets (1572)

The specimen mentioned above shows the kind of extensive preparations that were necessary before publishing, whereas the following evidence of proofreading practices is directly connected to the printing process itself. Vlasta Fialová was the first to draw attention to some remarkable proof sheets[33] during an archaeological survey of the Kralice area where the printing house was located.[34] The analysis of the twenty-two leaves of paper (206 × 300 mm) indicates that they pertain to one of the hymnbook editions (1572) in octavo without musical notes.[35] Six of them are printed on both sides. Fifty-six pages show corrections of various intensity and a barely legible editorial comment. Whereas some of the leaves are full of proofreaders' signs and cross-outs (e.g., fols 9*v*, 66*r*, 71*v*–72*r*), some of the other pages have corrected initials and do not show any revisions (fols 129*v*–130*r*, 135*v*–136*r*). The majority of the handwritten notes concern typographical corrections indicated in the text with pen strokes and underlining and identified in the margins by means of proofreaders' signs, as in fol. 16*r* (Fig. 11.1).

The variations in the numbers of proofreaders' signs and the level of completion of the book decoration indicate that we are looking at three different stages of correction. Among the twenty-two leaves, four (fols 9*r*, 10*v*, 15*r*–16*v*) bear traces of all three stages of the correction process. It is likely that the largest number of leaves in the group which contain woodcut initials and a minimum of proofreaders' signs represent the final stage of the revision (e.g., fols 49*r*, 56*v*,136*r*).

In the first stage of proofreading, the Brethren correctors highlighted misprints in diacritics, errors in capitalisation and punctuation, horizontal misalignment of letters, upside-down letters such as w, n, u, and missing characters (fols 9*r*–*v*, 16*r*–*v*). In the second stage, they corrected only a small number of errors. The most frequent mistakes were the horizontal misalignment of letters, missing or superfluous spaces between words, inconsistencies in headings, the reference number of hymns in the margin, and occasionally, incorrect woodcut initials. Only minor errors appear in the final stage, usually misprints in diacritics (fols 49*r*, 56*v*).

The name of the corrector remains shrouded in mystery. The corrector could have been Jan Blahoslav himself. Given his bad health and many other responsibilities, however, it is much more likely that the corrector was his successor, the Brethren's Bishop Ondřej Štefan, or some assistant at the printing house, such as the Brethren's priest and printer Zachariáš Solín (d. 1596), who also managed the printing of the Kralice Bible.

---

[33] Brno, Moravský zemský archiv (MZA), fond G 21 Staré tisky, II/181, 'Kancionál Kralický — 22 korekturních listů ke kralickému kancionálu'.

[34] Fialová, 'Korrekturabzüge' (n. 1 above), pp. 217–23.

[35] *Pjsně duchownj ewangelistské*, [Ivančice, Tiskárna bratrská — printer of Czech Brothers], 1572, 8° (USTC 568910).

FIG. 11.1. Proof sheets showing the first stage of corrections of *Pjsně duchownj ewangelistské*, [Ivančice, Tiskárna bratrská — printer of Czech Brothers], 1572, 8° (USTC 568910). Brno, Moravský zemský archiv, Fond G 21 Staré tisky, sign. II/181, fols 9v, 16r.

11: THE COLLECTIVE EDITORIAL STRATEGY OF THE UNITY OF THE BRETHREN

What we do know is that the corrector was a professional who marked the text with specific proofreaders' signs routinely used in large printing houses all over western Europe. To delete a letter or word, just like Blahoslav before him, he used the letter 'd' (*deleatur*) in the margin and crossed out the place in the text (e.g., fol. 123r). To delete a space, he added a hyphen in the text and wrote the letter 'd' (*deleatur*) in the margin (fol. 65v). To indicate a missing punctuation mark (period, slash), he used a vertical line and wrote the punctuation mark in a circle in the margin (fol. 130v). To correct a horizontal misalignment of letters, he would underline (fol. 16r in Fig. 11.1). To indicate a missing letter, he drew a vertical line in the text and wrote the letter in a circle in the margin (fol. 9v). To indicate an upside-down letter or letters that had to be connected, the corrector used the same graphic symbol that we use today — a *vertatur* (fol. 16r, again in Fig. 11.1).

CORRESPONDENCE REGARDING THE EDITORIAL AND PROOFREADING PROCESS (1610–1618)

A unique set of historical sources that shed light on the organisation of the editorial process and describes the Brethren's proofreading practices is to be found in the recently discovered archive of Bishop Matouš Konečný.[36] It contains more than 600 documents from 1609 to 1618, predominantly letters between bishops and priests.[37] The correspondence also provides information about ongoing proofreading.[38] In particular, the letters from Matouš Konečný (Bishop-Scribe), Jan Lanecký (Bishop-Judge, i.e. the first among the four bishops of the Unity of the Brethren, responsible for calling and moderating Inner Council sessions and proposing its agenda), and Jan Cruciger (bishop and administrator of the Ivančice congregation) give us a clear picture of the laborious process preceding the publication of the Kralice Bible in 1613.[39]

What is remarkable about the Brethren's proofreading practices is the complexity of proofreading and the number of people involved in this activity. First, the proof sheets in the form of *sexterni* (i.e. gatherings of twelve leaves) were sent by the bishop's office to individual congregations for editing and proofreading.[40] The leaders of the congregations, seniors, and sometimes even other members would perform a thorough check of the content as well as of style and typography. The proof sheets would then be sent back to the bishop's office.

---

[36] The archive of Bishop Matouš Konečný (AMK) is stored at the Museum of Mlada Boleslav. For further details, see, J. Just, 'Neue Quellen zur Geschichte der Brüderunität in der Zeit vor der Schlacht am Weißen Berg. Der Fund des Archives von Matouš Konečný in Mladá Boleslav', *Acta Comeniana*, 22–3, 2009, pp. 249–86.

[37] See Just, 'Neue Quellen' (n. 36 above).

[38] For the critical edition of the correspondence, see J. Just (ed.), *Archiv Matouše Konečného — Kněžská korespondence Jednoty bratrské z českých diecézí z let 1610–1618*, Prague, 2011, pp. 259, 264, 266.

[39] AMK, A3251/Lanecký/2, 8, 10–12, 14, 19–23, 'eleven letters of Jan Lanecký to Matouš Konečný, 1611–1612' with comments on proofreading and correcting the Kralice Bible.

[40] AMK, A3251/Lanecký/46, 'letter of Jan Lanecký to Matouš Konečný of 2nd September 1615', corrections of the Brethren Catechism 1615.

The Bishop-Scribe had overall responsibility for the whole printing process and wrote prefaces and made indexes, just like humanists and *correctores*.[41] The final version had to be approved by the Inner Council.

A Corrected Copy of the Music Theory Textbook *Musica* (1569)

The latest discovery regarding these editing and proofreading practices was made by the author of this paper during bibliographical studies in Wrocław. The University Library holds the second edition of Blahoslav's textbook *Musica* (1569).[42] This practical handbook was the result of a compilation of humanistic schoolbooks on the subject of music theory. It was intended for users of the hymnbook. The first part contains ten chapters categorised by themes and illustrates the basic principles of music theory. The second part of the textbook includes instructions for singers, while the third addresses hymn writers.

The inscription in the lower margin of the title-page indicates that the Wrocław copy initially belonged to the Brethren's priest Izaiáš Cibulka (*Caepolla*) (d. 1582), who was one of Blahoslav's most talented students (Fig. 11.2). In 1563, Blahoslav sent Cibulka to the University of Wittenberg to study under Esrom Rüdinger. He later entrusted Cibulka with editing, translating, and publishing the Confession of the Brethren in Latin (1573).[43] Cibulka maintained contact with some prominent European scholars (Joachim Camerarius the Elder, Caspar Peucer, and Marcello Squarcialupi). An excellent Hebrew linguist, he was part of the team that was responsible for the translation of the Kralice Bible. Also, as the administrator of the Kralice congregation, he directly supervised the printing of the first three volumes of the Bible.[44]

It is not clear why Cibulka corrected his own copy of the textbook on music theory. Perhaps it was because he saw a need to republish this practical tool for the Brethren's vocalists in an improved edition which was never produced. What is notable, however, is that Cibulka mainly corrected errors in punctuation and incorrect capital letters on the first twenty-five pages, while the remaining corrections are all drawn from the errata list printed in the first edition.

This finding confirms that the Brethren employed proofreaders' signs typically adopted by European humanists. Cibulka marked all the mistakes with a vertical line in the text or with a crossing-out. In the margin, he indicated all the errors to be corrected. In addition to the standard 'd' for the deletion of a letter, word, or space, he also used other proofreaders' signs which were later listed in Hornschuch's *Orthotypographia* (1608);[45] for example, the

---

[41] See A. Grafton, *The Culture of Correction in Renaissance Europe*, London, 2011, pp. 18–19.

[42] Wrocław, Biblioteka Uniwersytecka, Oddział Starych Druków, 330759; Blahoslav, *Musica* (n. 24 above).

[43] *Confessio fidei et religionis christianae*, Wittenberg, [Clemens Schleich and Anton Schöne],1573, 8° (USTC 624509).

[44] Dittmann and Just, *Biblical Humanism* (n. 5 above), p. 88.

[45] Hieronymus Hornschuch, *Orthotypographia*, Leipzig, Michael Lantzenberger, 1608, 8° (USTC 2001806), pp. 15–17.

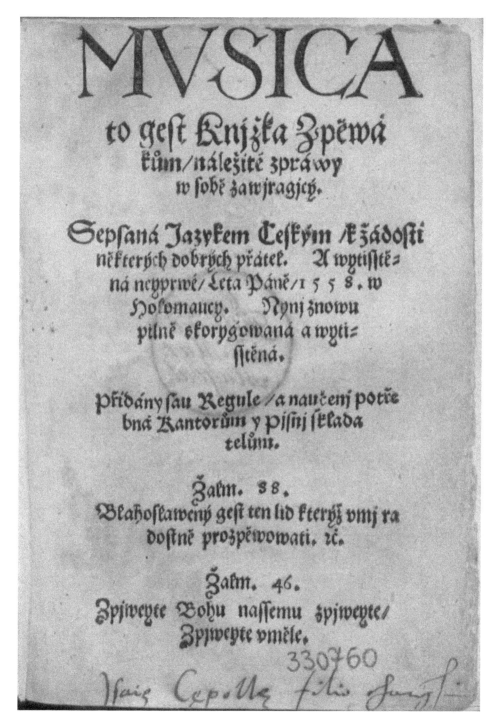

FIG. 11.2. Cibulka's signature on the title-page of Jan Blahoslav, *Musica*, [Ivančice, Tiskárna bratrská—printer of Czech Brothers], 1569, 8° (USTC 567053). Wrocław University Library, 330760.

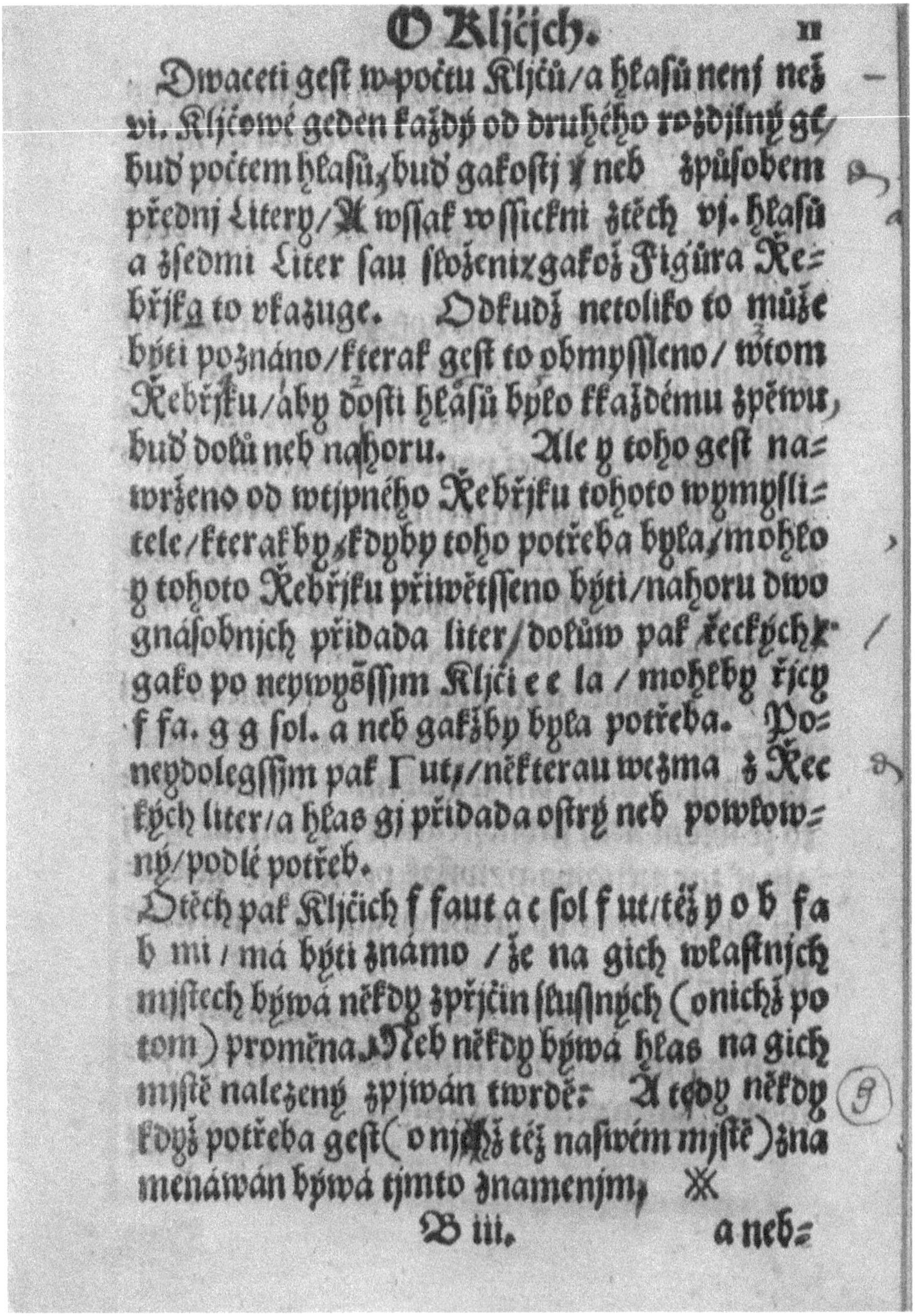

O Klíčích. 11

Dwaceti geſt w poctu Klíčů/a hlaſů není než
vi. Klíčowé geden každý od druhého rozdjlný ge
buď poctem hlaſů/buď gakoſtj ý neb způſobem
přednj Litery/A wſſak wſſickni ztěch vj. hlaſů
a zſedmi Liter ſau ſtoženizgakož Figůra Re=
břjka to vkazuge.   Odkudž netoliko to může
býti poznáno/kterak geſt to obmyſſleno/w tom
Řebřjku/aby doſti hlaſů było kkaždému zpěwu,
buď dolů neb nahoru.   Ale y toho geſt na=
wrženo od wtjpného Řebřjku tohoto wympyſli=
tele/kterak by/kdyby toho potřeba była/mohło
y tohoto Řebřjku přiwětſſeno býti/nahoru dwo
gnáſobnjch přidada liter/dolůw pak řeckých
gako po neywyšſſjm Klíči e e la / mohłby řjcy
f fa. g g ſol. a neb gakžby była potřeba.   Po=
neydolegſſjm pak Γ ut/některau wezma z Řec
kých liter/a hłas gj přidada oſtrý neb powtow=
ný/podlé potřeb.
Otěch pak Klíčich f faut a c ſol f ut/též y o b fa
b mi / má býti známo / že na gich wlaſtnjch
mjſtech býwá někdy zpřjčin ſluſſných (o nichž po
tom) proměna. Neb někdy býwá hłas na gich
mjſtě naleženy zpjwán twrdě: A cždy někdy
kdyż potřeba geſt(o njchž též naſwém mjſtě)zna
menáwán býwá tjmto znamenjm, ✕
                    B iii.   a neb=

FIG. 11.3. Cibulka's corrections in *Musica* (see Fig. 11.2), fol.11r. Wrocław University Library, 330760.

sign for correcting an upside-down letter (fol. *68v*) or the sign for connecting text (fol. *79r*). A missing period after a sentence was indicated with a vertical line in the text, furthermore the missing punctuation mark was marked with a circle in the margin. Two slanted lines were used to indicate where something had to be included, like a preposition, while missing letters and words were carefully reported in the margin.

Upon closer examination, we can see that the corrector mostly paid attention to checking punctuation marks which indicated breathing pauses and were thus intended to help the reader understand the text more clearly.[46] Most often we see the replacement of a virgule (slash) with a comma, sometimes with a colon or parenthesis, as in Fig. 11.3. This is all the more remarkable, since contemporary Czech printed texts did not include commas, which only appeared in Latin publications. Other books published by the Brethren after the second half of the 1570s indicate that the Brethren adopted increasingly clear rules for punctuation marks. Cibulka was one of the first initiators of this trend to which the Brethren remained faithful until the closure of the printing house in 1619.

Thus, this music theory textbook is another piece of evidence unmistakably proving the influence of humanist publishing practices on the Brethren, which consequently contributed to the modernisation and standardisation of the Czech language. Although this church is often associated with traditionalism, everything indicates that its members were keen to use the most recent foreign methods in their highly systematic and sophisticated approach to printing and publishing.

Conclusion

The editorial quality of the Brethren's editions was far beyond the average level of Bohemian print production during the sixteenth century, both from a linguistic and from a typographical perspective. One of the reasons for this high quality was the intense activity of the Brethren's editors and correctors, who used humanistic methods for editing and correcting texts. Historical sources such as the bishops' correspondence indicate that publishing was a highly organised and collective activity, which included close collaboration among the Brethren's seniors, bishops, and members of the Inner Council. Many of these leaders had studied abroad at universities in German-speaking lands where they became acquainted with humanist ideas and the latest innovations in printing and editorial practices. The position of the Bishop-Scribe was directly responsible for editorial supervision and proofreading, as well as for the distribution of the proof sheets to other congregations and the coordination of proofreading practices. It is therefore not surprising that such high-quality publications were printed when Jan Blahoslav was the Bishop-Scribe. As this chapter has shown, he was a passionate proponent of the humanist textual approach, which he had learnt during his studies in Wittenberg and Basel.

---

[46] The topic of punctuation marks and their functions has not yet been studied in depth within the Czech printed books; for a larger picture, see M. B. Parkes, *Pause and Effect: An Introduction to the History of Punctuation in the West*, Berkeley, 1993.

BIBLIOGRAPHY

PRIMARY SOURCES

ARCHIVAL DOCUMENTATION

Brno, Moravský zemský archiv (MZA), fond G 21 Staré tisky, II/181, 'Kancionál Kralický — 22 korekturních listů ke kralickému kancionálu'.

Mlada Boleslav, Archiv Matouše Konečného (AMK), Muzeum Mladoboleslavska, A3251/Lanecký/46, 'letter of Jan Lanecký to Matouš Konečný of 2nd September 1615'; A3251/Lanecký/1, 2, 8, 10–12, 14, 19–23, 'letters of of Jan Lanecký to Matouš Konečný, 1611–1612'.

Prague, Národní archiv, Acta Unitatis Fratrum (AUF), NA, no. 106, deposit of the UA: AB II R 1.1 vol. 8, fol. 169*r*; vol. 12, fol. 138*v*.

PRINTED BOOKS

Blahoslav, Jan, *Musica*, [Ivančice, Tiskárna bratrská — printer of the Czech Brothers], 1569, 8° (USTC 567053).

Comenius, Johannes Amos, *Opera didactica omnia*, Amsterdam, 1657.

Comenius, Johannes Amos, *Via lucis*, Amsterdam, 1668.

Confessio fidei et religionis christianae, Wittenberg, [Clemens Schleich and Anton Schöne], 1573, 8° (USTC 624509).

Confessio Fratrum Bohemicorum, [Ivančice: Tiskárna bratrská — printer of Czech Brothers], 1574, 8° (USTC 568912).

Confessio Fratrum Bohemorum, [Ivančice: Tiskárna bratrská — printer of Czech Brothers], 1564, 8° (USTC 568409).

Eber, Paulus, *Calendarium historicum*, Wittenberg, Georg Rhau, 1559, 8° (USTC 617737).

Ewangelia, [Ivančice, Tiskárna bratrská — printer of Czech Brothers], 1571, f° (USTC 568909).

Hornschuch, Hieronymus, *Orthotypographia*, Leipzig, Michael Lantzenberger, 1608, 8° (USTC 2001806).

Łasicki, Jan, *Historiae de origine et rebus gestis fratrum Bohemicorum liber VIII*, [Leszno?, Wiegand Funck?], 1649, 8° (USTC 2064309).

Nowy zákon, [Ivančice, Tiskárna bratrská — printer of Czech Brothers], 1564, 12° (USTC 568906) and 1568, 80 (USTC 568908).

Piesne chwal Bożskych, [Szamotuły, Aleksander Augezdecki, 1561], f° (USTC 244676).

Pjsně duchownj ewangelistské, [Ivančice, Tiskárna bratrská — printer of Czech Brothers], 1562–1564, f° (USTC 568903).

Pjsně duchownj ewangelistské, [Ivančice, Tiskárna bratrská — printer of Czech Brothers], 1572, 8° (USTC 568910).

Pjsně duchownj ewangelistské, [Ivančice, Tiskárna bratrská — printer of Czech Brothers], 1576, f°
(USTC 568915).

Pjsně duchownj ewangelistské, [Ivančice, Tiskárna bratrská — printer of Czech Brothers], 1581, f°
(USTC 568926).

SECONDARY LITERATURE

Atwood, C. D., *The Theology of the Czech Brethren from Hus to Comenius*, University Park (PA), 2009.

Bohatcová, M., 'Ästhetische Konzeptionen der Drucke der Böhmischen Brüder zur Zeit Jan Blahoslavs', *Gutenberg-Jahrbuch*, 46, 1971, pp. 189–99.

Bohatcová, M., 'The Book and the Reformation in Bohemia and Moravia', in J. F. Gilmont (ed.), *The Reformation and the Book*, Aldershot, 1998, pp. 385–409.

Bohatcová, M., 'České korektury z let 1523–1524', *Typografia*, 69, 1966, pp. 334–6.

Dittmann, R., and Just, J., *Biblical Humanism in Bohemia and Moravia in the 16th Century*, Turnhout, 2016.

Fialová, V., 'Korrekturabzüge aus dem XVI. Jahrhundert. Ein Beitrag zur Historie der Buchdruckerei der Böhmischen Brüder', *Gutenberg-Jahrbuch*, 39, 1964, pp. 217–23.

Fialová, V., 'Persönlichkeiten und Schicksale der berühmtesten Druckerei der Böhmischen Brüder', *Gutenberg-Jahrbuch*, 42, 1967, pp. 138–43.

Gindely, A. (ed.), *Dekrety Jednoty bratrské*, Prague, 1865.

Gindely, A. (ed.), *Quellen zur Geschichte der Böhmischen Brüder*, Vienna, 1856.

Just, J., *Kněžská korespondence Jednoty bratrské z českých diecézí z let 1610–1618*, Prague, 2011.

Just, J., 'Neue Quellen zur Geschichte der Brüderunität in der Zeit vor der Schlacht am Weißen Berg. Der Fund des Archivs von Matouš Konečný in Mladá Boleslav', *Acta Comeniana*, 22–3, 2009, pp. 249–86.

Menčík, F., 'Studenti z Čech a Moravy ve Vitenberku od roku 1502–1602', *Časopis Musea Království českého*, 71, 1897, pp. 250–3.

Müller, J. Th., *Geschichte der Böhmischen Brüder*, 3 vols, Herrnhut, 1922–1931.

Rejchrt, L., 'Bratrští studenti na reformovaných akademiích před Bílou horou', *Acta Universitatis Carolinae: Historia Universitatis Carolinae Pragensis*, 13/1–2, 1973, pp. 43–82.

Parkes, M., *Pause and Effect: An Introduction to the History of Punctuation in the West*, Berkeley, 1993.

Říčan, R., *The History of the Unity of the Brethren: A Protestant Hussite Church in Bohemia and Moravia*, Bethlehem, 1992.

CHAPTER 12

BIBLICAL MISPRINTS

Error and Correction in an Early Yiddish Epic

RACHEL WAMSLEY

INTRODUCTION

THE early Yiddish biblical epic known as *Shmuel Bukh* has come down to us in a variety of manuscripts and printed editions dating from the first half of the sixteenth century onward. An adaptation of the biblical books of I and II Samuel into the metrical and generic conventions of chivalric romance, it depended on a canonical and authoritative text, the Hebrew Bible, and was thus in some sense a reiteration of scriptural, and thence for *Shmuel Bukh*'s Jewish readers, historical truths. At the same time, however, it took many liberties with its sacred source material, freely incorporating rabbinic *midrash*, popular folklore, and lengthy speeches of its own invention. Though the absolute authority of the Tanakh was never called into question, elaboration and fanciful detail embellish virtually every verse.

This tension, between the divine authority of the Scriptures and the imaginative licence of a secular genre, was not only manifest in *Shmuel Bukh*'s literary content; the material text too was substantively reshaped by this tension over the course of its transmission, particularly as it transitioned from manuscript into print. From one textual witness to the next, scribes, correctors, and editors weighed the accurate representation of biblical Hebrew on the page against their own textual aesthetics, aesthetics that were themselves evolving in response to the mechanical exigencies of print. The present essay follows this material strand of *Shmuel Bukh*'s textual history, specifically its typographical aesthetics and the correction of misprints, across two manuscripts and three closely linked printed editions.[1] *Shmuel Bukh*'s

---

[1] I have written elsewhere on the programmatic literary interventions of *Shmuel Bukh*'s later editors, which included thorough copy-editing, narrative emendation, alterations to metre and rhyme, and the interpolation of biblical and midrashic source materials. See R. Wamsley, 'Editorial Policy in *Shmuel Bukh*: Between Augsburg and Kraków', in S. Neuberg and D. Matut (eds), *The Worlds of Old Yiddish*, Oxford, 2022, pp. 60–77, and *Exegetical Poetics: Tanakh and Textuality in Early Modern Yiddish Literature*, PhD dissertation, Berkeley (CA), University of California, 2015, pp. 1–66, available at https://escholarship.org/uc/item/6vc00775.

Rachel Wamsley, *Biblical Misprints*. In: *Printing and Misprinting*. Edited by Geri Della Rocca de Candal, Anthony Grafton, and Paolo Sachet, Oxford University Press. © Rachel Wamsley (2023). DOI: 10.1093/oso/9780198863045.003.0013 treatment of biblical misprints lays bare how the transition to print brought long-established codes of linguistic representation under new pressure.

Shmuel Bukh's typographic challenges result directly from the Hebrew writing system. In contrast to alphabetic languages like Latin, Hebrew was originally a syllabary, written with consonants alone. It was incumbent upon the reader to mentally supply the appropriate vowels. Between the seventh and tenth centuries CE, the Masoretic system of vocalisation (*niqqud*) was introduced to provide exact readings of the Tanakh for liturgical and exegetical purposes: diacritical marks added above, below, or beside the consonant with which they form a syllable. But because the learned Hebrew reader can do without them, virtually all non-biblical Hebrew books are unvocalised, in manuscript as in print, even those with great religious authority such as the Talmud.[2]

The Masoretic system was well designed for a scribal medium: diacritical marks are neat, unobtrusive, and quick to write, nor do they complicate spacing. Often a text was vowelled only after fully written, sometimes by a specialist known as a *naqdan* ('punctuator'). Vowel-points are also, thanks to their diminutive size, easily scraped away in case of error.

Ironically, the very features that made Masoretic vowelling so frictionless in manuscript created a crisis in a movable type. Whereas the compositor ordinarily loads his composing stick with a stack of uniform sorts and spaces, for vocalisation he must also insert, justify, and stabilise, with the help of quads and spacers, the vowel-sorts: spindly, needle-like pieces of type requiring exact alignment. Often all but the last consonant of a word require a diacritic (for example, 'Israel', יִשְׂרָאֵל), so the compositor finds himself composing a word not of five characters, but of nine (and, as usual, upside down and backwards to boot). Even if the compositor does his job in exemplary fashion, vowel-sorts are more vulnerable creatures than their consonant counterparts. Because they are minute, they take ink badly. Because they are delicate, they wear quickly, mashed by the pressure of the platen. Whereas a letter may remain legible even if somewhat deformed, a constellation of points might leave no more than a partial impression, accidentally resemble another vowel, or vanish altogether. Opportunities for error are legion.[3]

The handling of biblical misprints over several successive editions of *Shmuel Bukh* offers a telling case study of this crisis in Hebrew typography and its remediation.[4] The two surviving manuscripts scrupulously vowel all biblical Hebrew words to distinguish them from

---

[2] The single significant exception to this rule is formal Hebrew verse, where vocalisation is the norm.

[3] Though he writes approximately a century after the setting of the Yiddish editions under discussion here, Joseph Moxon describes the mechanics of composition for Hebrew and Greek in the earliest English printer's manual, *Mechanick Exercises on the Whole Art of Printing* (1683). Later still, Simon-Pierre Fournier addresses setting Hebrew with vowel points; see P. S. Fournier, *Fournier on Typefounding: The Text of the* Manuel typographique *(1764–1766)*, transl. H. Carter, London, 1930, pp. 84–5. Taken together, these contemporary accounts offer a picture of the technical challenges posed by Hebrew vocalisation in movable type.

[4] There is as yet no exhaustive study of the transition of Hebrew vocalisation from manuscript to print; however, in-depth examination of individual printers has yielded substantial insights. See, for instance, S. Lubell, *Sixteenth-Century Hebrew Typography: A Typographical and Historical Analysis Based on the Guillaume I Le Bé Documents in the Bibliothèque nationale de France*, PhD dissertation, University of London, 2014, pp. 40–59 and 187–99, available at https://core.ac.uk/download/pdf/33336796.pdf?fbclid=IwAR22Kv6WMQOhRMnFNWZVTQah7xb_oVSiBmmo_7ImOdblfGxAvVYJZCn9Ino, or H. C. Zafren, 'Dyhrenfurth and Shabtai Bass: A typographic profile', in I. E. Kiev and C. Berlin (eds), *Studies in Jewish Bibliography, History and Literature in Honor of I. Edward Kiev*, New York, 1971, pp. 543–80. For a broader consideration of the relationship between Hebrew scribal practices and their realisation in print, see M. Beit-Arié, 'The Relationship between Hebrew Printing and Handwritten

250   PRINTING AND MISPRINTING

the surrounding Yiddish text. The *editio princeps* followed this convention but at the cost of an extremely high rate of misprints.[5] The very next edition dispensed with vocalisation altogether, and it was never revived in any subsequent edition. The incidence of misprints, as one might expect, dropped precipitously. The orthographic conventions of *Shmuel Bukh's* manuscript tradition were thus decisively abandoned in favour of a cleaner (and more practicable) textual aesthetics. New conventions took their place: varied typographic measures to preserve the visual distinction between the biblical word and its vernacular environs. As a survey of these textual witnesses demonstrates, it was evidently more important that a word resemble biblical Hebrew to the eye than to the ear.

WITH VOWELS

The two surviving manuscripts are consistent in their representation of Hebrew words.[6] Unlike the surrounding text (overwhelmingly comprised of Yiddish words of Germanic origin, spelt in an approximately phonetic and relatively standardised orthography), Hebrew words were written with *niqqud*. The Yiddish readership of *Shmuel Bukh*, including women and children as well as men, was not necessarily Hebrew literate, but vocalisation was not, in this instance, an aid to pronunciation. This is evident from the fact that rather than vowelling only rare or ambiguous words in need of clarification, the scribes vowelled *every* occurrence of a word, no matter how frequent or well known. The name David naturally appears hundreds of times throughout the epic; in both manuscripts it is written דָּוִד, or even more pedantically דָּוִֽד.[7] Biblicisms thus stand out against the surrounding text thanks to their halo of (superfluous) diacritics. Further accentuating this visual difference, vowel-points are often calligraphically exaggerated in both manuscripts,

---

Books: Attachment or Detachment', in M. Beit-Arié (ed), *The Makings of the Medieval Hebrew Book*, Jerusalem, 1993, pp. 251–77.

[5] *Sefer Šemûʾel: Dos buch Šemûʾel in taitšer šprach*, Augsburg, [Schwarz], 1544, 4° (not in USTC), Munich, Bayerische Staatsbibliohtek, A.hebr.1070 u#Beibd.1., http://mdz-nbn-resolving.de/urn:nbn:de:bvb:12-bsb10170884-2, accessed 16 December 2020. A second copy resides in London, British Library, 1945.f.17.(3), and is the basis of the fascimile edition, *Das Schmuelbuch des Mosche Esrim Wearba: Ein biblisches Epos aus dem 15. Jahrhundert*, ed. F. Falk and L. Fuks, 2 vols, Assen, 1961. A concise introduction to *Shmuel Bukh's* textual tradition appears in *Early Yiddish Texts*, *1100–1750*, ed. and transl. J. Frakes, Oxford, 2008, pp. 218–20. For *Shmuel Bukh's* generic context, see J. Baumgarten, 'Une chanson de geste en yidich ancien: Le *Shmuel bukh*', *Revue de la Bibliothèque Nationale*, 13, 1984, pp. 24–38, as well as J. Baumgarten, *Le Peuple des Livres*, Paris, 2010. For a prose translation of the *editio princeps*, see *Early Yiddish Epic*, ed. and transl. J. Frakes, Syracuse (NY), 2014, pp. 15–148.

[6] MS Paris, Bibliothèque nationale de France, Hébreu 92 (c. 1530), described and digitised at https://archivesetmanuscrits.bnf.fr/ark:/12148/cc5581x, accessed 16 December 2020; MS Hamburg, Staats- und Universitätsbibliothek (SUB), Cod. hebr. 313 (first quarter of the sixteenth century), described and digitised at https://katalogplus.sub.uni-hamburg.de/vufind/Record/889251401, accessed 16 December 2020.

[7] As this example demonstrates, even those diacritics irrelevant to *Shmuel Bukh's* sixteenth-century readers are included. The *rofeh* over David's final *daled* serves only to indicate that this letter belongs to a group of consonants — the so-called *beged-kefet* class — the phonological behaviour of which had once varied according to position within the word. That the *daled* of sixteenth-century Ashkenaz was pronounced identically irrespective of position seems not to have mattered to the scribe.

whether merely enlarged or taken as the point of departure for a flourish of the pen. Though not as grandiose as the decorative initial words of each verse, the biblical word enjoys graphic pride of place: its pronunciation rendered more precisely, its letters more lavishly.

When the time came to bring *Shmuel Bukh* into print, its earliest editors retained the textual aesthetics established in manuscript. Though less flamboyant in appearance, the *editio princeps* (Augsburg 1544, hereafter *A*) underscores the distinction between Hebrew and Germanic components via *niqqud*.[8] Hebrew words are vowelled, though not with the level of rigour evident in either manuscript. Like the scribe, albeit without his calligraphic flair, the compositor of *A* treated every biblicism as its own miniature enterprise, his labour and concentration intensified in comparison with setting Yiddish, which in this period was written almost entirely without diacritics. Shorn of scribal flourishes, biblical words remained graphically distinct from the surrounding text, catching the reading eye as well as aiding it.

It is no small irony that the very attention to detail lavished on the biblical word by the scribe became such a liability in the print shop. Whatever *A*'s typographic ambitions, misprints are statistically far more frequent among biblicisms. These are high-pressure moments, eye-catching and significant, yet all too often they draw attention to embarrassing fumbles.

A brief statistical survey proves revealing. In the first one hundred verses of *A*, which we will take henceforth as our text sample, biblicisms occur 195 times (comprising a lexicon of forty-five words and phrases.).[9] Whatever his level of literacy, the compositor gets to know the spelling of most of these words very well through practice alone. Of these 195 instances, thirty-five can be taken as misprints of one sort or another: the vowelling may either deviate from the Masoretic standard or the preferred spelling established in the rest of the text, or it may show graphic misadventure (bad inking, damaged type, misalignment, or poor justification).[10] In all, 18% of Hebrew words in this small sample are misprinted; the workers of the print shop (compositors, inkers, pressmen) got every fifth or sixth Hebrew word wrong in one way or another.

How high a rate of error is this? The statistical analysis of errata lists is of limited relevance to us here, but can still be instructive.[11] Errata lists are inherently problematic because they rely on self-reporting. Because I have counted misprints individually, some of these would

---

[8] It should be noted that both manuscripts are approximately contemporary with *A*, which was instead based on an earlier witness now lost. See *Das Schmuelbuch* (n. 3 above), I, p. 20, and *Early Yiddish Texts* (n. 3 above), p. 219.

[9] I have treated collocations, set phrases, and compound words as single items. A religious title such as *kohen gadol* ('high priest'), I count as one item rather than two.

[10] I count as misprints only those instances where, although the text evidences a preferred spelling throughout, a relevant consonant has abruptly appeared or disappeared. A word may thus be written in *ktiv haser* ('spelling without vowels', that is, with only those consonants used if the text were vowelled) or *ktiv male* ('full spelling', unvowelled but with added *matres lectionis*, such as *vav* and *yud*).

[11] See A. Blair, 'Errata Lists and the Reader as Corrector', in S. A. Baron, E. N. Lindquist, and E. F. Shevlin (eds), *Agent of Change: Print Culture Studies after Elizabeth L. Eisenstein*, Amherst (MA), 2007, pp. 21–41. See also L. Repo, *Errors and Corrections: Early Modern English Errata Lists in 1529–1700 and Their Connection to Prescriptivism*, MA thesis, University of Turku, 2018, available online at https://www.utupub.fi/bitstream/handle/10024/146176/Liina_Repo.pdf?sequence=1&isAllowed=y, accessed 16 December 2020.

252   PRINTING AND MISPRINTING

likely not appear on a typical sixteenth-century errata list, which were at any rate often selective rather than exhaustive. Furthermore, analysis of errata lists has usually adopted a per-page model for calculating the frequency of errors. This is also not helpful to us because *Shmuel Bukh* is set in verse surrounded by a considerable amount of white space; it thus contains far fewer words per page than an average prose work from the same period. Even with these caveats, Liina Repo notes that the average frequency of typographical errors recorded in errata lists of English books between 1529–1700 ranged from 0.01 to 1.07 errors per page. In *A*'s case, the errors in Hebrew words alone yield an average frequency of 3.18 per page, nearly triple what we would expect of a book from this period at the maximum — and this without even considering mistakes in the non-Hebrew text! *A* includes no errata list, but even if the non-Hebrew text's average frequency of error were at the high end of the spectrum at 1.07, biblical misprints would constitute three-quarters of all errors. And these were overwhelmingly errors in vowelling: thirty-two of thirty-five misprints (91.4%) concern the diacritics. In sum, though *niqqud* may have lent biblicisms a certain panache in manuscript, they proved a huge liability in print. Everything that could go wrong, did go wrong.

One could imagine that the misapplication of a dot here or there hardly much mattered. *Shmuel Bukh* was after all a vernacular romance printed in a relatively affordable quarto format. Its popular readership may have known little Hebrew if any. Perhaps *A*'s printers were simply not very concerned that *Shmuel Bukh* be a masterpiece of craftsmanship. Closer examination, however, suggests that they were neither subliterate nor indifferent to the quality of their work. Craftsmanship may even have mattered more than biblical accuracy. In a number of instances, the compositor went out of his way to preserve the typographic elegance of the text even if this meant sacrificing correct vocalisation. Vowelling may have been important, but not important enough to warrant disfiguring the surrounding lines of type.

For example, a recurrent conflict arises between vowels appearing below their consonants and the ascenders in the subsequent line of type, which extend above the mean line of the typeface. These ascenders would ordinarily occupy the white space between lines, but proper vowelling likely means that space is already peppered with diacritics. The compositor is thus faced with averting this collision, either by moving the ascender away from the conflicted territory, or by reducing or compressing the vowels. This is, in fact, not a difficult decision to make, and for very practical reasons. The ascender is contiguous with the type's body; it cannot be shifted to make room for the vowels above it. The only way to effect such a change is by inserting hair spaces to push the ascender and its letter further away from the preceding letter, but this risks creating an unsightly gap. Diacritical marks, by contrast, are not contiguous with their respective consonant, and may not even be contiguous with one another (as in the reduced *niqqud* known as *hataf-segol*). They are the obvious place to start when compromise is required.

The ascender of the letter *lamed* (ל) offers a pertinent example. In our 100-verse sample, three of the thirty-three errors in vowelling occur in conjunction with the ascender of a *lamed* in the line below. In each instance, the *lamed* is not shifted away; it either obscures the vowel in the line above or has led the compositor to omit the vowel entirely (as in Fig. 12.1 below). In that case, the name Samuel should be rendered, as it is in the Tanakh and throughout the present text, as שְׁמוּאֵל. Here, however, the first vowel was omitted because the *lamed* of לוייכֿטט ('dawned') in the line below crowds into the available space. In the

FIG. 12.1. *Lamed*-ascender and absent *sheva* below the *shin* in the line above. *Shmuel Bukh*, Augsburg, [Schwarz], 1544, 4° (not in USTC), fol. 5v, v. 64. Munich, Bayerische Staatsbibliothek, A.hebr.1070 u#Beibd.1.

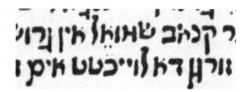

contest between letter and vowel, the compositor sacrifices the diacritic rather than mar the even spacing of the subsequent line.

The same dilemma naturally arises in the case of descenders as well, in which a consonant that descends below the baseline comes into conflict with its own vowel. The most common instances in this sample is the recurrent 'high priest' (*kohen gadol*), which our text attempts to render כּוֹהֵן גָדוֹל [sic], with only limited success. In this edition's typeface, the initial *gimel* of גָדוֹל descends well below the baseline and intrudes on the vowel *qamats*, whose right arm should occupy that very space. As with *lamed*'s ascender, the compositor is forced either to squeeze the vowel tightly and almost illegibly against the descender, cutting off its right arm in the process, or to omit it entirely. The term כּוֹהֵן גָדוֹל appears nineteen times in our 100-verse sample. In the vast majority of cases (sixteen), the compositor opts for including the *qamats*, albeit in mangled or miniaturized form (see Fig. 12.2 below). Diacritics are worth preserving in principle, even at the cost of some unfortunate modification to their size or shape.

Despite this apparent prioritisation of typographic aesthetics over diacritics, there are counter-examples in which the compositor goes to considerable lengths to preserve vowelling, altering the surrounding typography to achieve this goal. The best illustration of this, though it is drawn from a portion of the text beyond our 100-verse sample, has once again to do with the problematic descenders on the *gimel* of *A*'s typeface. In 1 Samuel 15, King Saul goes to war against Agag, king of the Amalekites. The Tanakh spells this name אֲגַג. Thus, in the typeface of our edition, the descender of the central *gimel* threatens to cut off both its own vowel, the *patah*, and the *hataf-patah* of the preceding *alef*, while its left foot is poised to collide with the stem of the *gimel* following it. The compositor resolves this problem with recourse to a different *gimel* altogether (as in Fig. 12.3 below), so that the one word contains two different types of *gimel*. This solution for 'Agag' is used programmatically throughout the text, though oftentimes poor inking results in the loss or partial loss of the vowels regardless.

FIG. 12.2. *Gimel*-descender and partial *qamats*. *Shmuel Bukh* (see Fig. 12.1), fol. 2r, v. 5. Munich, Bayerische Staatsbibliothek, A.hebr.1070 u#Beibd.1.

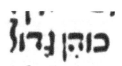

FIG. 12.3. Two types of *gimel* in 'Agag King of Amalek'. *Shmuel Bukh* (see Fig. 12.1), fol. 16v, v. 270. New York, YIVO Institute for Jewish Research Library, Rare Book Collection, Augsburg 1544 (photocopy).

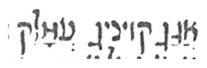

The scrupulous resort to a second, specialised *gimel* suggests that the compositor did feel some responsibility for accurately representing biblical words, both vowels and consonants, and moreover that he ventured innovative, case-by-case solutions when needed.

WITHOUT VOWELS

Despite the valiant efforts of *A*'s compositor to render biblicisms with Masoretic exactitude, later printers were apparently unconvinced that this was a good use of their labour. *A* was never reprinted by its original publishers, but we can establish it was extensively employed for the next edition (Mantua 1562–1564, *m*), of which the only known copy is presumed to have been lost to fire towards the end of World War II. It was from *m* that the two subsequent Kraków editions (1578 and 1593, *k* and *k1* respectively) took their cue.[12] In matters of aesthetics and format, *m* relied heavily on the *editio princeps*: nine four-line stanzas to the page, metrical lines divided by periods, end stanza marked by a colon, final line centre-justified. This layout was maintained in the Kraków editions as well, giving the impression that, in addition to the labour saved by avoiding casting off from scratch, later editors generally approved of *A*'s appearance.[13]

Given everything we have seen so far, it comes as little surprise that *m*'s single sweeping alteration to *A*'s textual aesthetics concerned the use of diacritical vowels. With these it dispensed altogether. As Felix Falk puts it, 'just as in the majority of cases [in *m*] Germanic words appear without Hebrew vowel-points, so too Hebrew words and proper names carry

---

[12] In his critical introduction to the facsimile edition of *A*, Felix Falk argues that the Mantuan editor made use not only of that book, but also of the manuscript tradition, though not necessarily the two surviving manuscripts discussed above: *Das Schmuelbuch*, (n. 3 above) I, p. 22. Falk relied on the lost copy of *m* held in Hamburg, SUB; fortunately, his textual apparatus survives and consistently affirms that *m*'s most direct descendants, *k* and *k1*, resemble it closely. It is now only through these editions and Falk's succinct description and textual apparatus, that we gain some insight into *m*'s composition and appearance. Of the Kraków editions, both printed by Isaac b. Aaron Prostitz, two copies of the first are extant: MS Oxford, Bodleian Library (Bod.), Opp. add. 4° II. 175, and a second, very partial and damaged, held in Jerusalem, National Library of Israel, 990011758100205171, https://www.nli.org.il/en/books/NNL_ALEPH001175810/NLI, accessed 16 December 2020. Of the second edition, two copies are known to me: MS Oxford, Bod., Opp. 4° 171 (1), and Vienna, Österreichishe Nationalbibliothek, 20. H. 27. ALT PRUNK, http://data.onb.ac.at/rep/10A40AD5, accessed 16 December 2020.

[13] Their approval might not have been so easily earned. The founders of this press, Isaac b. Aaron Prostitz and Samuel Boehm, had received impeccable training during Venice's efflorescence of fine Hebrew printing in the first half of the century. Boehm enjoyed particular distinction as the grandson of Elijah Levita, the unparalleled Hebrew grammarian, poet, and translator. Boehm's professional title was *magiah*, literally 'proofreader', but better translated here as 'corrector' (cf. P. Sládek's contribution in this Companion), for he oversaw virtually every aspect of a book's progress through the press: textual emendation, details of typography and page layout, but also final decisions on intellectual content. The sheer scope of Hebrew genres on offer at the Prostitz press — from halakhah to biblical exegesis and Sephardic kabbalah — gives an idea of the breadth of Boehm's expertise. On the history of the Prostitz press, see B. Friedberg, *Toldot ha-defus ha-ivri be-polanyah: Me-reshit hivasdo bi-shenat 294 ve-hitpathuto ad z'manenu*, Tel Aviv, 1950. For a transcription of its printing licences and other pertinent legal sources, see M. Balaban, 'Zur Geschichte der hebraischen Druckerein in Polen', *Soncino-Blätter: Beitrage zur Kunde des jüdischen Buches*, 3/1, 1929, pp. 1–50.

no vowel-points, as they do in A'.[14] The editors of k and $k1$ evidently concurred, as did those of the even later editions p (Prague 1609) and b (Basel 1612).[15] The elimination of vowels proved stunningly effective in reducing the rate of misprints in Hebrew words.[16] Direct comparison between our 100-verse sample from A and the parallel portion of k is complicated by the fact that both extant copies of k are damaged, so that we can only compare the first seventy-two verses of A and k.[17] Nevertheless, of the 160 Hebrew words in k's first seventy-two verses, there are only seven misprints. With an average error rate of 4.3%, about one in twenty-five Hebrew words will fall prey to misprinting. This represents a reduction to the risk of error of approximately two-thirds compared with A (18%). Finally, to rephase in the metric used by Blair and Repo, k now compares reasonably (if not favourably) with other printed books of the sixteenth century at an average frequency of 1.14 errors per page.

In terms of textual aesthetics, then, m's elimination of vowel-points was a resounding success: a cleaner page, fewer errors, more white space. But this innovation necessarily came at the expense of the distinction between Hebraic and Germanic components of Yiddish, a distinction of sufficient cultural significance that it had once warranted constant graphic reiteration on the page. While Falk's description gives us no hint as to whether m's typographic design maintained this distinction, the editors of k made a concerted effort to do so, albeit with mixed results.

In k, Hebrew words are often distinguished from the surrounding text not with vocalisation, but by typeface. Early modern Yiddish books were usually printed in a font, based on Ashkenazic semi-cursive, known as *mashket* or *vaybertaytsh* ('women's writing') in contrast to two typefaces used primarily for high-status texts in Hebrew and Aramaic: 'square' Hebrew type imitating the angular lettering of the Torah scroll and the so-called 'Rashi script', a semi-cursive used for most rabbinic commentaries.[18] As a vernacular book for a wider audience, all editions of *Shmuel Bukh* were naturally printed in *mashket*.

---

[14] *Das Schmuelbuch* (n. 3 above), I, p. 22: '[...] doch sind deutsche Wörter nicht mit hebräischen Vokalzeichen versehen, wie das vielfach bei A der Fall ist, auch die hebräischen Wörter und Eigennamen tragen keine Vokalzeichen wie in A.' The English translation is mine.

[15] See *Das Schmuelbuch* (n. 3 above), I, pp. 24–5. I rely here on the description of Falk because the copy of p which he examined in Hamburg, SUB, has also been missing since the Second World War: Prague, Jacob B. Gershon Bak, 1609, 4° (not in USTC). The Basel edition survives in two copies: Basel, Konrad Waldkirch, 1612, 4° (not in USTC), MS Oxford, Bod., Opp. 4° 166, and Jerusalem, National Library of Israel, 99001175809205171, https://www.nli.org.il/en/books/NNL_ALEPH001175809/NLI accessed 16 December 2020. A third copy, on which Falk based his description, was once housed in Berlin, Staatsbibliothek, but also appears to have been lost in the war.

[16] It is possible that vocalisation was avoided in these editions due to scarcity of vowel-sorts, but this seems unlikely given the consistency with which this practice was adopted in successive editions from different printing houses. The printers of k, for example, published a Yiddish paraphrase of the Song of Songs the following year in which all biblical citations are vowelled: *Sefer Shir Ha-Shirim*, Kraków, Prostitz, 1579, 4° (not in USTC), MS Oxford, Bod., Opp. 4° 171 (3).

[17] In the case of the Bodleian's copy of k, the second and third leaves are missing from gathering 2. In the copy of the National Library of Israel, meanwhile, only the first thirty-six verses (the second and third leaves of gathering 1) are present and the text does not resume until gathering 21.

[18] It should again be noted that, excepting printed editions of the Masoretic text of the Tanakh, Hebrew in both these typefaces was usually unvocalised. On *mashket*, see H. C. Zafren, 'Variety in the Typography of Yiddish, 1535–1635', *Hebrew Union College Annual*, 53, 1982, pp. 137–63, and his 'Early Yiddish Typography', *Jewish Book Annual*, 44, 1986, pp. 106–19.

256   PRINTING AND MISPRINTING

k's innovation over *m* thus seems to have been its institution of a typographic division of labour: square type (with its biblical gravitas) for Hebrew words and *mashket* for everything else. The first seventy-two verses of *k*, those that parallel *A*, contain a total of 160 biblicisms. Of these, eighty-five appear in square type and seventy-five in *mashket*. Later in the edition this typographic distinction between Hebrew and Yiddish appears to be even more consistently implemented. To choose an example at random, fols 12*v*–13*r* contain a total of 55 biblicisms, which are, without a single exception, printed with square type.

The rate of misprints in *k* may even be somewhat inflated. Three of the seven misprints are actually instances in which a letter from one typeface has accidentally migrated into a word in the other typeface.[19] Strictly speaking, these are typographic, as opposed to orthographic, misprints. They would never appear on early modern errata lists and can be hard to see at all unless one is looking for them. Excluding these from the average rate of error, *k* comes out in the middle of the sixteenth-century pack at about 0.5 errors per page.

From the elimination of vowel-points and the introduction of distinct typefaces for Hebrew and Germanic words, one can merely infer that later editors were acting out of a desire to reduce the incidence of misprints. We need not rely solely on inference, however. In addition to removing vowel-points themselves, *k*'s editors also persistently corrected those misprints in *A* that were the *consequence* of flawed vowelling but could have persisted into a resetting of the text without vowels.

A striking example of rigorous copy-editing appears in the spelling of the toponym Aphek, the base camp of the Philistine army (1 Samuel 4:1), printed in *k* at fol. A5*v*, v. 69. In *A*, this toponym has been given an adjectivising suffix: זיא צוהן מיט גיוואלט אין אָפֵּיקָר לנט ('[The Philistines] came into the land of Aphek by force'). The biblical word should properly be spelt אֲפֵק, but we can see the logic of *A*'s vowelling. In Yiddish, this adjectivising suffix typically shifts stress forward; *áfek* should become *afékar*. *A* attempts to reflect this phonological transformation by adding a *patah* to the final *quf*, and by augmenting the length of the vowel in the penultimate syllable with both a diacritical mark (*tsere*) and the letter (*yud*). Finally, *A*'s editor imagines that the already short *hataf-patah* of the initial *alef* must be further reduced to a *sheva* because it now constitutes an unstressed syllable. While none of these are particularly elegant solutions, this last one is egregious because, as a more exacting copy editor would point out, *alef* belongs to a class of guttural consonants that do not generally take a *sheva*, and that *alef* in particular, unlike others of this class, cannot admit one under any circumstances.[20] The editors of *k* (drawing perhaps from the lost *m*) addressed this infelicity not only by omitting the vowels; they also eliminated the stress-shift that created the difficulty in the first place: צוהן מיט גיוואלט אין אפק דער גוים לאנד זיא ('[The Philistines] came by force into the gentile land of Aphek').[21] The normal stress pattern of *áfek* was thus restored, the superfluous and incorrect *yud* removed, the untidy vowelling swept away.

---

[19] Though this could result from running out of a letter in one typeface before the whole forme could be set (cf. J. Misson's chapter on kludging types in this Companion), it occurs here so sporadically that it is more likely due to a foul case.

[20] See, for instance, M. Stuart, *A Grammar of the Hebrew Language*, Oxford, 1831, p. 56, §119c.

[21] The passage in *k* is found at fol. k5*v*, v. 68. Bolding represents square type in contrast to surrounding *mashket* type.

FIG. 12.4. Two square *gimel* in 'Agag' and one *mashket gimel* in 'King'. *Shmuel Bukh*, Kraków, Prostitz, 1593, 4° (not in USTC), fol. 1v, v. 17. 20. Vienna, Österreichishe Nationalbibliothek, 20. H. 27. ALT PRUNK.

The editorial practise used in *k* thus wedded *m*'s sweeping removal of *niqqud* to other methods of correction, reducing the incidence of error in biblical words yet again. At the same time, *k* restored the typographic distinction between Hebrew and Yiddish which had defined the textual aesthetics of *Shmuel Bukh* in manuscript.

Later editions continued this trend, but inconsistently. The second Kraków edition, *k1*, for example, largely abandoned *k*'s mixed typography in favour of an undifferentiated text in *mashket*. The portion of *k1* parallel to fols 12v–13r in *k* (from which I drew the fifty-five-word sample described above), contains fifty-two Hebrew words, all but four of which appear in *mashket*. Of these four, three are instances of the abovementioned 'Agag', in which the two consecutive *gimels*, as we have already seen, made for a collision in this *mashket* typeface, diacritics or no (fol. 1r–v, vv. 9, 11, 17). In square type, no such problem arose (see Fig. 12.4 below).

k1 seems committed first and foremost to a unitary typography, which saved the labour of constant switching between multiple typecases, reducing errors in biblical words yet further. The Prague edition of 1609 emphasised its biblicisms by means of brackets, an improvement over *k1* in that it both maintained the Hebrew–Yiddish distinction, yet conveniently eliminated the risk of mingled typefaces. In Basel 1612, the *mashket*-square distinction was revived, but vocalisation remained a thing of the past.[22] The representation of a biblical word in Yiddish was now determined not by the Masoretic standard, but by its immediate typographic and textual environment. In print, biblical error could be best avoided, not by redoubling the activity of the corrector's pen, but by reconsidering what a Hebrew word should look like in the first place.

A MATTER OF PRINCIPLE

The Kraków editions of *Shmuel Bukh* were neither expensive, nor particularly prestigious. They served, rather, as pleasure reading, accessible to the minds and pockets of a broad audience. Produced in an affordable format, on cheap paper, they were printed without illustration, printer's prefaces, dedications, errata lists, rabbinic approbations, or any other mark of literary esteem. The biblical epic, though poetically ambitious, was no monumental legal codex like the *Shulhan Arukh*, nor an anthology of rabbinic midrash like *Yalkut Shimoni*, nor an esoteric mystical treatise like *Derekh Emunah*.[23] Yet however humble by comparison, these printings of *Shmuel Bukh* bore the imprimatur of reputable houses like

---

[22] See again *Das Schmuelbuch* (n. 3 above), pp. 24–5.
[23] *Shulhan Arukh*, Kraków, Prostitz, 1570–1594, f° (USTC 240016), MS Oxford, Bod., Opp. add. fol. III.52; *Derekh Emunah*, Kraków, Prostitz, 1577, f° (not in USTC), MS Oxford, Bod., Opp. fol. 1089 (1); *Yalkut me-ha-Torah*, Kraków, Prostitz, 1595–1596, f° (not in USTC), MS Oxford, Bod., Opp. fol. 186.

Kraków's Prostitz press, where the aforementioned greater works showcased fine crafts-manship and superlative erudition in massive folio editions. In the product line-up of such a press, *Shmuel Bukh* was undoubtedly low-end. Yet, as the foregoing survey of its corrections has shown, *Shmuel Bukh* could not pass through the hands of such printers untrans-formed: scrupulous textual editing and keen attention to typographic detail are visible on every page.

Whereas the *editio princeps* sought to advertise its quality with a display of Hebraic eru-dition, aspiring to the aesthetics of its manuscript antecedents, *Shmuel Bukh*'s later editors, two and three decades deeper into the evolution of Hebrew typesetting, did not see vocali-sation as a risk worth taking. Their painstaking remediation of misprints, even in a popular, vernacular work like *Shmuel Bukh,* suggests that as a growing body of Yiddish and Hebrew texts were brought into print over the course of the sixteenth century, editorial practice focused more and more intensively on textual aesthetics: pristine editing, typography, and mise-en-page. While the value of Hebraic erudition remained undiminished when a text or genre demanded it, the early modern printer of Hebrew books invested his energy in the aesthetics of the printed page, no matter the language it was printed in.

BIBLIOGRAPHY

PRIMARY SOURCES

MANUSCRIPTS

Paris, Bibliothèque nationale de France, Hébreu 92, *Shmuel Bukh*, [c. 1530].
Hamburg, Staats- und Universitätsbibliothek, Cod. hebr. 313, *Shmuel Bukh*, [early sixteenth c.].

PRINTED BOOKS

Das Schmuelbuch des Mosche Esrim Wearba: Ein biblisches Epos aus dem 15. Jahrhundert, ed. F. Falk and L. Fuks, 2 vols, Assen, 1961.
Derekh Emunah, Kraków, Prostitz, 1577, f° (not in USTC). Copy discussed: Oxford, Bodleian Library, MS Opp. fol. 1089 (1).
Sefer Shir Ha-Shirim, Kraków, Prostitz, 1579, 4° (not in USTC). Copy discussed: Oxford, Bodleian Library, MS Opp. 4° 171 (3).

Shmuel Bukh, Augsburg, [Schwarz], 1544, 4° (not in USTC). Copies discussed: Munich, Bayerische Staatsbibliothek, A.hebr.1070 u#Beibd.1.and London, British Library, 1945.f.17 (3).

Shmuel Bukh, Mantua, [s.n., 1564], 4° (not in USTC). Copy discussed: Hamburg, Staats- und Universitätsbibliothek (presumed lost).

Shmuel Bukh, Kraków, Prostitz, 1578, 4° (not in USTC). Copy discussed: Oxford, Bodleian Library, MS Opp. 4° II. 175.

Shmuel Bukh, Kraków, Prostitz, 1593, 4° (not in USTC). Copies discussed: Oxford, Bodleian Library MS Opp. 4° 171 (1) and Vienna, Österreichishe Nationalbibliothek, 20. H. 27. ALT PRUNK.

Shmuel Bukh, Prague, Bak, 1609, 4° (not in USTC). Copy discussed: Hamburg, Staats- und Universitätsbibliothek (presumed lost).

Shmuel Bukh, Basel, Waldkirch, 1612, 4° (not in USTC). Copy discussed: Oxford, Bodleian Library, MS Opp. 4° 166.

Shulhan Arukh, Kraków, Prostitz, 1570–1594, f° (USTC 240016; BHB 000334729). Copy discussed: Oxford, Bodleian Library, MS Opp. add. fol. III.52.

Yalkut me-ha-Torah, Kraków, Prostitz, 1595–1596, F° (not in USTC; BHB 000176196). Copy discussed: Oxford, Bodleian Library, MS Opp. fol. 186.

SECONDARY LITERATURE

Balaban, M., 'Zur Geschichte der hebraischen Druckerein in Polen', *Soncino-Blätter: Beitrage zur Kunde des jüdischen Buches*, 3/1, 1929, pp. 1–50.

Baumgarten, J., *Le Peuple des Livres*, Paris, 2010.

Baumgarten, J., 'Une chanson de geste en yidich ancien: Le *Shmuel bukh*', *Revue de la Bibliothèque Nationale*, 13, 1984, pp. 24–38.

Beit-Arié, M., 'The Relationship between Hebrew Printing and Handwritten Books: Attachment or Detachment', in M. Beit-Arié (ed), *The Makings of the Medieval Hebrew Book*, Jerusalem, 1993, pp. 251–77.

Blair, A., 'Errata Lists and the Reader as Corrector', in S. A. Baron, E. N. Lindquist, and E. F. Shevlin (eds), *Agent of Change: Print Culture Studies after Elizabeth L. Eisenstein*, Amherst (MA), 2007, pp. 21–41.

Early Yiddish Epic, ed. and transl. J. Frakes, Syracuse (NY), 2014.

Early Yiddish Texts, 1100–1750, ed. and transl. J. Frakes, Oxford, 2008.

Fournier, P. S., *Fournier on Typefounding: The Text of the* Manuel typographique *(1764–1766)*, transl. H. Carter, London, 1930.

Friedberg, B., *Toldot ha-defus ha-ivri be-polanyah: Me-reshit hivasdo bi-shenat 294 ve-hitpathuto ad z'manenu*, Tel Aviv, 1950.

Lubell, S., *Sixteenth-Century Hebrew Typography: A Typographical and Historical Analysis Based on the Guillaume I Le Bé Documents in the Bibliothèque nationale de France*, PhD dissertation, University of London, 2014.

Moxon, J., *Mechanick Exercises on the Whole Art of Printing (1683–4)*, ed. H. Davis and H. Carter, London, 1962.

Repo, L., *Errors and Corrections: Early Modern English Errata Lists in 1529–1700 and Their Connection to Prescriptivism*, MA thesis, University of Turku, 2018.

Stuart, M., *A Grammar of the Hebrew Language*, Oxford, 1831.

Wamsley, R., 'Editorial Policy in *Shmuel Bukh*: Between Augsburg and Kraków', in S. Neuberg and D. Matut (eds), *The Worlds of Old Yiddish*, Oxford, 2022, pp. 60–77.

Wamsley, R., *Exegetical Poetics: Tanakh and Textuality in Early Modern Yiddish Literature*, PhD dissertation, University of California, 2015.

Zafren, H. C., 'Dyhrenfurth and Shabtai Bass: A typographic profile', in I. E. Kiev and C. Berlin (eds), *Studies in Jewish Bibliography, History and Literature in Honor of I. Edward Kiev*, New York, 1971, pp. 543–80.

Zafren, H. C., 'Early Yiddish Typography', *Jewish Book Annual*, 44, 1986, pp. 106–19.

Zafren, H. C., 'Variety in the Typography of Yiddish, 1535–1635', *Hebrew Union College Annual*, 53, 1982, pp. 137–63.

CHAPTER 13

'BEFORE THE LAW'

Jewish Correctors of Early Printed Books

PAVEL SLÁDEK

JEWISH EDITORS AND CORRECTORS OF HEBREW BOOKS

BEGINNING with some of the earliest printed editions, the process of editing and correcting Hebrew books became — not infrequently — the subject of various notes by Jewish editors and correctors.[*][1] They appeared in the editions of those Hebrew texts that aspired to higher religious or cultural status; sometimes — especially towards the end of the sixteenth century — they can also be found in a broader spectrum of editions, often produced by one-time editors. This chapter will focus on the printed production of books in Hebrew script and language, in the period from the dawn of Hebrew printing in the 1460s until the 1620s. It will tackle in particular the books produced with Jewish participation (even if they often were made for Christian publishers) and intended for a readership that included, but was not limited to, Jewish readers. The books aimed primarily for the use of Christian Hebraists, such as Hebrew-Latin editions of biblical texts from Paris, Leiden, and Antwerp, are left aside. In the absence of relevant archival sources, some preliminary insights into the practice of correcting Hebrew printed books will be offered relying on the paratextual evidence, i.e. on the notes by editors and correctors, featured in the same books which they helped to produce.

---

[*] This work was supported by the European Regional Development Fund project Creativity and Adaptability as Conditions of the Success of Europe in an Interrelated World (reg. no.: CZ.02.1.01/0.0/0.0/16_019/0000734) implemented at Charles University, Faculty of Arts. The project is carried out under the ERDF Call "Excellent Research" and its output is aimed at employees of research organizations and Ph.D. students. I am grateful to Olga Sixtová for reading the manuscript and providing valuable comments and suggestions. The responsibility for the text is mine only.

[1] According to Yaakov Shmuel Spiegel, the earliest Hebrew book in which the editor/corrector is mentioned is Salomon Yitshaki, *Commentary on the Torah*, Guadalajara, Salomon ben Alkabets ha-Levi, 1476, f° (ISTC is00625190; BHB 170476). See Yaakov Shmuel Spiegel, *Ammudim be-toldot ha-sefer ha-ivri: Hagahot u-magihim*, Ramat-Gan, 2005, p. 222.

Pavel Sládek, *'Before the Law'*. In: *Printing and Misprinting*. Edited by Geri Della Rocca de Candal, Anthony Grafton, and Paolo Sachet, Oxford University Press. © Pavel Sládek (2023). DOI: 10.1093/oso/9780198863045.003.0014

262 PRINTING AND MISPRINTING

For the purpose of this study, it is essential to bear in mind that terminological confusion often makes it impossible to distinguish between editor and corrector, since Jewish typographers used the same term for both. The verb *lehagiah* means not only 'to read in an intensive way',[2] but also both 'to edit a text', denoting the process of preparing the copy for typesetting, and 'to proofread a text', denoting the process of checking proof sheets and marking typographical errors.[3] As in the non-Jewish environment, 'editor' and 'corrector' could be either the same person or two different 'print professionals';[4] the noun *magiah* (pl. *magihim*) is used for both.

Nevertheless, there is sufficient evidence that, in the production of Hebrew printed books, editing and correcting represented two distinct stages in creating the final text. The 1524 edition of Maimonides's code *Mishneh Torah*, published in Venice by Daniel Bomberg, is instructive. According to the title-page, David ben Eliezer Pizzighettone served as the 'editor of the exemplar' (*magiah ha-heetek*), while Jacob ben Hayyim ibn Adonijah served 'afterwards as the corrector in the course of the printing' (*magiah ahar kakh ba-defus*).[5] Mordecai Tsarfati from Basel wrote in 1489 about the editing and correcting of tractate *Niddah* of the *Babylonian talmud* together with some David ben Elazar: 'He edited (*higiah*) the exemplar (*tofes*) and made it clean and clear. [...] And I humbly came after him to correct (*lehagiah*) the printed sheets, to make them proper and perfect.'[6]

In these rather rare instances, the wording enables us to ascertain that editor and corrector were two different roles — in this case performed by two different scholars — although the Hebrew term '*magiah*' without the specification is typically used for both. In this study, the two roles will be always distinguished whenever sources allow for it.

HALAKHIC CONSIDERATIONS

The early modern print shop issuing books in Hebrew characters did not differ in technology, in craft, and even in the procedures.[7] Employment of gentiles as craftsmen of Hebrew books was so common that it gave rise to a stereotypical excuse used by Jewish correctors,

---

[2] A common wording of owners' inscriptions in books is 'Let the Lord give me the privilege to read through (*lehagot*) it day and night' (e.g., the convoluted annotation in the front pastedown of Oxford, Bodleian Library (Bod.), Opp. 4° 250).

[3] Amnon Raz-Krakotzkin noted that the term also was employed in referring to censorship instead of the more common word *zikkuk* (refinement). A. Raz-Krakotzkin, *The Censor, the Editor, and the Text: The Catholic Church and the Shaping of the Jewish Canon in the Sixteenth Century*, Philadelphia, 2007, pp. 113 and 251, n. 75.

[4] See A. Grafton, *The Culture of Correction in Renaissance Europe*, London, 2011, pp. 13, 16.

[5] Moses Maimonides, *Mishneh Torah*, Venice, Daniel Bomberg, 1524, f° (not in USTC; BHB 150066), I, fol. [1r]. On this edition, see Spiegel, *Ammudim* (n. 1 above), pp. 178–83.

[6] *Babylonian talmud — tractate Niddah*, Soncino, Joshua Salomon ben Israel Nathan Soncino and/or Gershon ben Moses Soncino, 1489, f° (ISTC it00015400; BHB 328583), fol. [96v], also cited in R. N. N. Rabinowitz, *Maamar al hadpasat ha-Talmud*, Munich, 1877, p. 17, n. 18. Rabinowitz identified the editor with David ben Eliezer Pizzighettone, mentioned above.

[7] In the following section, I build on Spiegel, *Ammudim* (n. 1 above), pp. 40–50.

13: 'BEFORE THE LAW'   263

who blamed typographic errors on 'workers who are not Jewish'.[8] Yet it can be argued that the production of Jewish books was, in many respects, culturally specific;[9] this holds particularly true for that which concerns the care for textual correctness. Rabbinic religious law (*halakhah*) meticulously regulates such a production, prescribing the proper use of a valid scroll of Torah (*sefer Torah*) and prohibiting those in which the text had not been 'checked' (*hugah*). The term used here is drawn from the same verb as that used for editing and correcting, and for the roles of editor and corrector. A prooftext is to be found in the *Babylonian talmud*:

> It has been stated: A book (*sefer*) that is not corrected (*hugah*) — R. Ami said: For thirty days, one is allowed to keep it (*leshahoto*). From then onwards, it is forbidden to keep it, because it is said (Job 11:14): 'Let not unrighteousness dwell in thy tents'.[10]

The passage is extant in two versions, one of which speaks more specifically of 'scroll of Torah' (*sefer Torah*), while the other, present in standard editions of the *Talmud*, speaks simply of 'a book'. As demonstrated by Yaakov Shmuel Spiegel, early Sephardic halakhists were inclined to stick to the narrow interpretation, which applied the law only to the Scrolls of Torah, while Ashkenazic authorities starting with Rashi (1040–1105), whose position was later adopted by many Sephardic rabbis, applied the law to all books.[11] In the sixteenth century, the two positions were mirrored in the two most influential halakhic codifications, namely, the *Shulhan arukh* of the Sephardic rabbi Joseph Karo and the correction amendments (*hagahot*) of the Ashkenazic rabbi Moses Isserles. Karo stated: 'The Scroll of Torah, which had not been corrected — it is forbidden to keep it for more than thirty days: Either he must repair it or dispose of it in the *genizah*.'[12] In his gloss, Isserles extended the scope of the law: 'The same law applies to other books too.'[13]

I am not aware of any evidence that this law was codified with any ruling detailing what exactly was necessary to fulfil the obligation. However, the wording of many paratexts, some of which will be cited below, indicates that the Talmudic prooftext was universally known, and that the requirement 'to correct' every book in Jewish use — however vaguely understood — was often behind the production of early Hebrew printed books, and could even underline practices shared with the non-Jewish correctors. For example, Anthony Grafton

---

[8] For a good example, see the 'apology' in Jacob ben Moses Segal (Maharil), *Sheelot u-teshuvot*, Hanau, Hans Jacopo Hena, 1610, 4° (not in USTC; BHB 136198), fol. 71v, which reads: 'Workers who are not sons of Israel, who know neither the language nor the content but only accustomed their hands to perform their job by habit.' This and all subsequent translations from sixteenth-century printed books are mine. The biblical verses are quoted according to the 1917 or 1985 Jewish Publication Society (JPS) translation. See A. Yaari, 'Telunot ha-magihim al hadpasat be-Shabbat al yede ha-goyim', in A. Yaari, *Mehkere sefer: Perakim be-toldot ha-sefer ha-ivri*, Jerusalem, 1958, pp. 170–8.

[9] I argued for a culturally specific approach to the study of the Hebrew printed book in my 'Printing of Learned Literature in Hebrew, 1510–1630: Toward a New Understanding of Early Modern Jewish Practices of Reading', in E. Dillenburg, H. P. Louthan, and D. B. Thomas (eds), *The Printed Book in Central Europe*, Leiden and Boston, 2021, pp. 387–410.

[10] *BT*, Ketubbot 19b, according to the Soncino Translation. (אתמר ספר שאינו מוגה אמר רבי אמי עד) ('ל' יום מותר לשהותו מכאן ואילך אסור לשהותו משום שנא' אל תשכן באהליך עולה).

[11] Spiegel, *Ammudim* (n. 1 above), p. 44.

[12] *ShA*, YD 279:1 (ספר תורה שאינו מוגה אסור להשהותו יותר משלשים יום אלא יתקן או יגנוז).

[13] *ShA*, YD 279:1, *hagahah* (והוא הדין לשאר ספרים).

264   PRINTING AND MISPRINTING

showed that the process of correction was supposed to consist of three stages (readings).[14] The corrector Mordecai Tsarfati, quoted above, relates the same practice to the halakhic prescription, even hinting at the familiar Talmudic dictum:

> I read every page three times and each time I corrected the errors [...] and then I handed it over to be mended for proper printing, so that in the end it was completely corrected. [...] I am certain that only a few errors will be found in it [...] and no buyer and nobody who will keep (*meshaheh*) it in his house will transgress against (Job 11:14): 'Let not unrighteousness dwell in thy tents'.[15]

In this light, the declaration found on many title-pages, with only slight variations, that a text has been 'meticulously edited/corrected' (*hugah be-iyyun rav*) might have been not only a rhetorical device, but rather a formal certificate to reassure readers this book did comply with the halakhic requirement.

CORRECTORS AND THEIR 'APOLOGIES'

The self-presentation of Jewish editors often oscillated between boasting about the excellence of their job and apologising about the flaws of their products.[16] Not infrequently, both attitudes are expressed in the same book. The title-page, which recommends the book to the prospective buyer, would take pride in the fact that the text has been 'refined sevenfold' (Ps. 12:7),[17] while at the back, the correctors would make apologies for 'errors and mistakes that fell into the edition'[18] and invoke God 'to rescue us from mistakes'.[19]

In both their boasting and apologetic attitudes, Jewish correctors did not differ from their non-Jewish counterparts.[20] Yet in Hebrew books, the urge for self-defence brought about a peculiar subgenre of paratext called 'apology' or 'defence' (*hitnatslut*) and typically placed at the end of books. These 'apologies' employed repetitive formulae to voice correctors' frustration about the impossibility of avoiding typos despite their indefatigable efforts, and appealed to the readers' acquaintance with printing technology to elicit their solidarity. The editor Seligman ben Moses Ulma wrote: 'To correct everything is simply ruled out by human nature.'[21] David Nordlingen, the editor of the second edition of *Imre noam* by Jacob

---

[14] Grafton, *The Culture of Correction* (n. 4 above), pp. 8–9, 100, 103, 107.

[15] *Babylonian talmud — tractate Niddah* (n. 6 above), fol. [96*v*], also cited in Rabinowitz, *Maamar* (n. 6 above), p. 17, n. 18.

[16] Cf. Grafton, *The Culture of Correction* (n. 4 above), pp. 23–4 (boasting) and 84–6 (disclaimers).

[17] E.g., Maimonides, *Mishneh Torah* (n. 5 above), I, fol. [1*r*].

[18] E.g., Jacob Weil, *Shehitot u-vdikot*, Kraków, Isaac ben Aaron Prostitz, 1577, 8° (not in USTC; BHB 130965), fol. 38*r*.

[19] *Sefer kinot im perush*, Lublin, Tsvi bar Abraham ben Kalonymos Jaffe, 1617, 4° (not in USTC; BHB 174114), fol. [1*v*].

[20] D. McKitterick, *Print, Manuscript and the Search for Order 1450–1830*, Cambridge, 2003, p. 120.

[21] Shabbetai Sheftel ben Akiba Horowitz, *Sefer shefa tal*, Hanau, Hans Jacopo Hena, 1612, f° (not in USTC; BHB 137592), fol. 94*v*.

di Illescas, stated: 'Printing is a terrible job'.[22] The author of another 'apology' who obviously served as both the editor and corrector of the volume, wrote:

> If a punctilious person finds a mistake or error in this book, let not such a reader put the blame on me, because it happens for two reasons. The first reason: those who understand the matter of printing, will know that it is almost impossible to eschew mistakes. And the second reason: [As a textual source,] I had only one copy, printed in Turkey and full of errors.[23]

The corrector Israel Isaac Mann from Kraków, in his 'apology', reflected on this subgenre and its apologetic mood:

> I saw in all the books an apology by correctors. Each of them would make his own apologies. One says that the workers are 'workers of iniquity' (Is. 31:2), the other says, 'who understands errors?' (Ps. 19:12) Another one blames [the errors] on the text and yet another on the Shabbat or a holiday getting close [...]. When I saw this, I raised my head and I said 'If they who dwell among the cedars of Lebanon cannot escape errors, how could I, the idle?'[24]

The authors of these notes were often not merely regretful. They often express gratefulness to God for completion of their work and a wish 'to print books without end', while sometimes pointing out the books they plan to publish in future. Before resorting to the usual apologies, Meir ben David, who prepared the edition of Israel Isserlein's *Terumat ha-deshen* for Daniel Bomberg in 1519, proudly declared: 'I paid attention that the work is performed properly, removed mistakes and errors as far as possible and according to the limitations of my intellect.'[25] We have seen how Seligman ben Moses Ulma admitted that '[t]o correct everything is simply ruled out by human nature'; at the same time, however, he glorified printing and exclaimed: 'As everybody knows, if printing did not exist, the Torah would have been already forgotten in Israel.'[26]

In the final decades of the period under consideration, the space devoted to remarks on editing and correcting processes grew larger; this appears to be connected with the effort to distinguish new editions of a text from earlier ones and make a case for their superior quality. Among Jewish editors and correctors, the idea of gradual improvement was well rooted. A publisher praised his editor/corrector because 'he improved and extended the work of the corrector who preceded him'.[27] Editors often claimed that their version was 'innovative

---

[22] Jacob di Illescas, *Imre noam*, Cremona, Vincenzo Conti, 1565, 4° (not in USTC; BHB 125,939), fol. 50v.

[23] Judah Kalats, *Sefer ha-musar*, Mantua, Giacomo Ruffinelli and Jacob ben Naphtali ha-Kohen, 1561, 4° (not in USTC; BHB 140167), fol. 139r. The Ottoman edition was printed in Constantinople in 1537 by Eliezer ben Gershom Soncino, 4° (not in USTC; BHB 140166).

[24] Benjamin ben Aaron Slonik, *Masat Binyamin*, Kraków, Menahem Nahum ben Moses Meizels, 1633, 4° (not in USTC; BHB 154278), fol. [169v].

[25] Israel Isserlein, *Terumat ha-deshen*, Venice, Daniel Bomberg, 1519, 4° (not in USTC; BHB 109706), fol. [185v].

[26] Horowitz, *Sefer shefa tal* (n. 21 above), fol. 94v.

[27] Jacob ben Moses ha-Levi (Maharil), *Sheelot u-teshuvot* (n. 8 above), fol. 71v. The previous edition had been printed in 1556 by Vincenzo Conti in Cremona, 8° (not in USTC; BHB 136197).

266   PRINTING AND MISPRINTING

in respect of the earlier printed editions',[28] that it 'has been wonderfully cleared from the stones and snares of errors and mistakes, which existed in earlier printed editions',[29] or that 'if compared to the earlier editions, its superiority will appear like superiority of light over darkness'.[30] Similarly to non-Jewish environments, sometimes the publisher emphasised on the title-page that an eminent scholar prepared the exemplar and corrected the proofs.[31]

In the Ashkenazic realm especially, the interest in improved editions triggered a search for manuscripts and an interest in Jewish literary antiquities.[32] Although the 1579 Kraków edition of *Otyot de-rabbi Akiva* closely followed the earlier Venice edition of 1546, the title-page informed: 'Be it known to the reader, that this book [...] has been already published thirty-three years ago in Venice. And now God, blessed be He, gave to our hands a manuscript, in which there are many novel things which are not in the first edition [...] and so we printed it anew.'[33]

Nissim ben Abba Mari, who edited the second edition of a sought-for Kabbalistic commentary to the Pentateuch by Menahem Recanati, felt compelled to explain that his text was superior to the earlier edition because he could correct the mistakes by using the original Kabbalistic sources, quoted in the commentary. The book was published in 1545, which was the first year of the activity of the press established in Venice by Marco Antonio Giustiniani, and it was supposed to introduce the firm to Jewish readership. Nissim thus had a good reason to explain that his master's print shop was equipped with a rich library of Kabbalistic texts (including 'a major part of the Zohar' still unpublished in print), which enabled him to correct the text satisfactorily. The title-page announced:

> Printed with careful editing and correcting and with much attention, with all errors and mistakes corrected, with some added passages of the Zohar and other texts from the manuscript [...], which were not in the first printed edition.[34]

By the mid sixteenth century in Italy and slightly later in Poland and elsewhere, 'apologies' had increased in length, functioning as a formalised space for the self-expression of Jewish editors and correctors. Composed in convoluted prose, often rhymed, they are usually a

---

[28] *Babylonian talmud — tractate Pesahim*, Venice, Marco Antonio Giustiniani, 1550, f° (not in USTC; BHB 333894), fol. [1r].

[29] Moses mi-Coucy, *Sefer mitswot gadol*, Venice, Daniel Bomberg, 1547, f° (not in USTC; 149,827), fol. 316r; cf. also di Illescas, *Imre noam* (n. 22 above), fol. [1r].

[30] Isaac ben Joseph of Corbeil, *Ammude golah — Sefer mitswot katan*, Kraków, Isaac ben Aaron Prostitz, 1596, 4° (not in USTC; BHB 178203), fol. [1r].

[31] Grafton, *The Culture of Correction* (n. 4 above), pp. 23–4. Cf. Maimonides, *Mishneh Torah* (n. 5 above), I, fol. [1r].

[32] I shall dwell on this phenomenon in 'From Manuscript to Print and Back Again: Two Case Studies in Late Sixteenth-Century Jewish Book Culture', in K. Kogman-Appel and I. Steimann (eds), *The Jewish Book 1400–1600: From Production to Reception*, Turnhout, forthcoming.

[33] *Otyot shel rabbi Akiva*, Kraków, Isaac ben Aaron Prostitz, 1579, 4° (USTC 242319; BHB 108482), fol. [1r]. The earlier Venetian edition is *Otyot shel rabbi Akiva*, Venice, Marco Antonio Giustiniani, 1546, 4° (not in USTC; BHB 108481). The Kraków edition marks where the text follows the Venetian edition and where new text from a manuscript or explicatory glosses were added: see especially fol. 5r, 7r, 9v, 11v.

[34] Menaham Recanati, *Beur al ha-Torah*, Venice, Marco Antonio Giustiniani, 1545, 4° (not in USTC; BHB 167906), fol. 1r–v. On Giustiniani, see D. Amram, *The Makers of Hebrew Books in Italy*, Philadelphia, 1909, pp. 252–76.

mosaic of fragments of biblical verses, often culled from the linguistically terse books, such as Job, Psalms, or Prophets. Their authors used this literary space not only to show off their brilliant mastery of the Hebrew style, but also to explicate their methods of editing and correcting texts. In the absence of a Jewish correspondent to the works of Hornschuch, Paredes, and Moxon, the 'apologies' contain valuable information about the attitudes of early modern Jewish editors and correctors.[35]

LISTS OF CORRIGENDA AND PASSAGES FALLEN OUT

Like their Christian colleagues, Jewish printers sometimes appended to the text errata lists (*luah tauyyot*, lit. 'tablet of errors'). However, such paratext is only infrequently found in the sixteenth-century Hebrew book; even editions of texts which were studied with almost obsessive attention to detail in pre-modern Jewish society do not feature any list of errors. The absence may appear particularly surprising in the second Rabbinic Bible, published in Venice by Daniel Bomberg (1524–1525). The importance of this edition, comprising not only a good number of rabbinic commentaries but also *masorah parva* and *masorah magna*, was proudly declared by its editor, Jacob ben Hayyim ben Isaac ibn Adonijah, who clearly acted as corrector too.[36] In a lengthy introduction, he focused on the many textual intricacies of the Scripture.[37] Instead of the expected errata, however, ibn Adonijah used only the conventional apologetic formulation: 'If some mistake should occur in the print, let it be like an inadvertent (i.e. not intentional and thus graver) error before the Ruler.'[38] The errata are also absent from the sixteenth-century editions of the Babylonian and Jerusalem talmud, although a rich and often animated debate about the minutiae of their textual versions and techniques of emendation had incessantly taken place since the early Middle Ages.[39]

---

[35] See H. Hornschuch, *Orthotypographia 1608*, ed. and transl. P. Gaskell and P. Bradford, Cambridge, 1972; A. V. de Paredes, *Institution, and Origin of the Art of Printing, and General Rules for Compositors [Madrid: ca. 1680]*, ed. and transl. P. Alvarez, Ann Arbor (MI), 2018; J. Moxon, *Mechanick Exercises on the Whole Art of Printing*, ed. H. Davis and H. Carter, New York, 1978.

[36] See Raz-Krakotzkin, *The Censor* (n. 3 above), p. 109.

[37] Jacob ben Chajim ibn Adonijah, *Introduction to the Rabbinic Bible*, ed. and transl. C. D. Ginsburg, London, 1867.

[38] [*Torah, neviim, ketuvim*], part III, *Ketuvim*, Venice, Daniel Bomberg, 1525, f° (not in USTC; BHB 182176), recto of final leaf.

[39] In his notes, David ben Elazar, who prepared several tractates of the Babylonian talmud for the Soncino press, speaks of numerous emendations of the text but also of the haste with which he had to work because of unspecified 'bad occurrences'. He reassured the buyer that he shall find only minor typographic errors, consisting of swapping of letters. See Rabinowitz, *Maamar* (n. 5 above), pp. 13–15, n. 15–16, who transcribed these notes in full drawing from *Babylonian talmud — tractate Bava kama*, Soncino, Joshua Salomon Soncino, 1489, f° (ISTC it00015020; BHB 328576), and *Babylonian talmud — tractate Hullin*, Soncino, Joshua Salomon Soncino, 1489, f° (ISTC it00015220; BHB 328576). Paradoxically, this 'apology' maintained that 'not a word was dropped, nor a letter is missing'.

268 PRINTING AND MISPRINTING

This startling fact can be explained by the Jewish readers' widespread understanding of the errata as compensation for imperfect corrections. The rhetoric with which the errata are presented in Hebrew books indicates that contemporary Jewish buyers did not see them as a sign of diligence on the side of the printers, but rather as an implicit confession that the text was not properly corrected. This may explain why some lists of errata are incomplete or highly uneven. In the Kraków edition of Isaiah Menahem ben Isaac's *Beurim*, consisting of eighty-two leaves, multiple errors are listed for almost every folio between fols 41–76 and one for fol. 33.[40] Similarly to this, a Prague edition of *Kitsur Mizrahi*, covering the Pentateuch, features the errata list only for Numeri and Deuteronomy, which mirrors a decreasing attention paid by the printers (as well as contemporary Jewish scholars in general) to the latter books of the Pentateuch.[41] These partial lists thus seem to cover those portions of the book which for any reason had not been properly corrected rather than the other way around.

Errata in Hebrew books typically list corrections of small-scale errors, from single misprinted letters to short sequences of words. If larger portions of text were affected, the printers resorted to other strategies. In Nathan ben Samson Spira's *Imre shefer*, a missing paragraph was supplemented in print on the verso of the title-page.[42] In Judah Leva ben Betsalel's *Tiferet Yisrael*, a text encompassing two pages was inadvertently dropped: the printers opted for appending it as an extra folio at the end of the volume and adding a note in print in the margin of the very page where the text originally belonged to signal the lacuna; unfortunately, they carelessly made two blatant errors in this note too![43] In the 1524 Venice edition of Maimonides's *Mishneh Torah*, five leaves of Vidal de Tolosa's commentary *Maggid mishneh* were appended at the end of the volume, allegedly because 'what was missing on folio 266 [...] arrived in our hands after the printing was completed'.[44]

Jewish correctors distinguished between serious errors, which might affect the meaning of the text, and minor typographic mistakes resulting from the nature of the craft.[45] Israel Isaac Mann explained:

> And truly, when I was working on the book, I intended to make the errata. But after I did not find any mistakes that would make it impossible to understand the meaning with the help of the context, and because there are no major errors, I said that the remaining [errors] will be regarded as nothing.[46]

---

[40] Isaiah Menahem ben Isaac, *Beurim kabbedu ha-Shem*, Kraków, Isaac ben Aaron Prostitz, 1604, 4° (not in USTC; BHB 178290), fol. 82r-v.

[41] Isaac ben Naftali Kohen Bauking, *Kitsur Mizrahi*, Prague, Moses Schedel's sons, 1604–1608, f° (not in USTC; BHB 136808), fol. 267r-v. On the date of this book, see O. Sixtová, *Hebrejský tisk v Praze 1512–1672*, PhD dissertation, Prague, Charles University, 2017, no. 103.

[42] Nathan ben Samson Spira, *Imre shefer*, Lublin, Kalonymos Jaffe, 1597, f° (not in USTC; BHB 181325), fol. [1v].

[43] Judah Leva ben Betsalel (Maharal), *Tiferet Yisrael*, Venice, Jacob ben Gershon Bak and Daniel Zanetti, 1599, f° (not in USTC; BHB 138996), fols 49v and 65r-v. The note at fol. 49v reads: וע״ש זכרון למעיין שמכאן (נשמנו) [נשמטו] מה שכתו' בסוף (העפר) [הספר].

[44] Maimonides, *Mishneh Torah* (n. 5 above), I, after fol. 389, sigs I I א אא, II I ב אא, III I ג אא, IIII I ד אא.

[45] Cf. Grafton, *The Culture of Correction* (n. 4 above), p. 57.

[46] Slonik, *Masat Binyamin* (n. 24 above), fol. 169v.

13: 'BEFORE THE LAW'   269

When he spoke of 'major errors' (*tauyyot gedolot*), Mann drew a distinction that was probably well understood among Jewish makers of Hebrew books. As a corrector put it: "'Who will understand the errors" (Ps. 19:13) of the press, which result from the similarities between letters! Letters fly from its designated case to the case of the letter next to, underneath or above it.'[47] Mistaking one letter for another, especially in the case of those Hebrew letters which looked similar, was regarded by correctors as a kind of acceptable typographic errors, one which did not have to be corrected or listed in the errata. This is how Hayyim ben Isaac Lifschitz, a cantor who edited the Kraków edition of elegies, detailed the so-called 'well-known/common errors' (*tauyyot mefursamim*) while describing the previous edition of the text:

> The edition itself is full of errors and there are in it letters *kaf* [כ] printed (lit. written) instead of *bet* [ב], *he* [ה] instead of *het* [ח], *waw* [ו] instead of *zayin* [ז], *resh* [ר] instead of *dalet* [ד] and vice versa. This woke me up and 'I shook out the bosom of my garment' (Neh. 5:13) and said to myself, 'do not let injustice reside in your tent' (Job 11:14), 'remove all obstacles' (Is. 57:14). I made a vow to clear rocks of iniquity from the road (after Is. 62:10). [...] The divine art (i.e. printing) should not be 'performed deceitfully' (Ps. 100:7), even though these are 'well-known/common errors'.[48]

Note the central place given to the same verse from Job, which is used by the Talmudic dictum about the obligation to correct Jewish books. True to the dual attitude of Jewish editors and correctors, Lifschitz subsequently switched to an apologetic tone, just to end with an invocation which might sound familiar:

> Judge me lightly because errors are known to occur sometimes in the art of printing from the side of the compositors (*mesadre we-manihe ha-otyot*) — but most of us are the same and I cannot escape a failure, error and ignorance [...]. My request is addressed to the Lord, to whom the hidden is revealed, to clear me from errors because the errors — who can understand them?[49]

Lifschitz's words sound almost as a self-fulfilling prophecy, as the compositor dropped a section of his text, which had to be appended to the end of the book. In another note, placed before the omitted text, the printer labelled it as 'an inadvertent mistake'.[50]

---

[47] Yom-Tov Lipmann Heller, *Tsurat bet ha-mikdash*, Prague, Abraham and Judah Leib and Moses Schedel's sons, 1602, 4° (not in USTC; BHB 127261), fol. 34*v*.

[48] *Sefer kinnot* (n. 19 above), fol. 2*r*. A similar statement is made in Jacob ben Asher, *Arbaah turim*, Part III: *Even ha-ezer*, Venice, Zorzo de' Cavalli, 1565, f° (not in USTC; BHB 313661), fol. 2*v*. Isaac Gershon, corrector of Elyakim ben Naftali's *Tov shem*, Venice, 1606, 4° (not in USTC; BHB 110483), fol. 32*v*, called a mistake consisting of a substitution of similar letters a 'understandable error' (*taut muvan*), in contrast to an 'utter error' (*taut mukhrah*). He listed only the latter in his errata.

[49] *Sefer kinnot* (n. 19 above), fol. 3*r*.

[50] *Sefer kinnot* (n. 19 above), fol. 87*r* ('We forgot to print this comment on its place only by an inadvertent mistake and we decided to put it at the end of the book to make it complete [...] and it belongs to the commentary on the elegy with the incipit *Ekha Eli konenu me-elaw*, there on folio 23*v*, to the lemma [...]'). We cannot rule out completely the possibility that the introductory remarks were printed

Extant errata show that the correctors used the notion of 'common errors', which do not need to be listed in the errata, partly as a rhetorical device. To be sure, they were aware that in Hebrew, quite often the substitution of the pairs of letters mentioned above might result in confusion or a change of meaning. Consequently, errata might also include corrections for this kind of mistakes.[51] In fact, some of them seem to be rather a result of over-mishearing than of misreading the original textual source.[52] A note of Jacob ben Hayyim ibn Adonijah testifies about the employment of assistants reading the text to the compositor or the editor:

> It is impossible to avoid errors in the art of printing, like switching letters and alike, and some-
> times in hearing what the reader pronounces (*bi-shmiat leshon ha-kore*) one can understand
> a different meaning in the given moment, because there is not enough time to go back and
> look over.[53]

The halakhic requirement of not handling an uncorrected book was so projected into the Jewish book culture that often editors and correctors relied on readers as final actors in the emendation process. The editor Hayyim ben Isaac Lifschitz encouraged 'every reader [...] if he finds an error (*shegagah*) or a mistake, to correct it after a scrutiny according to his own erudition and intellect.'[54] Even more symptomatic is the corrector's note preceding the errata in the Kraków edition of Isaac ben Joseph of Corbeil's *Sefer mitswot katan*, hinting clearly at the Talmudic prooftext discussed above:

> Here there is ready for you what must be corrected in this sublime book and if you fail to
> correct each and every one [of these errors] at its place, you will transgress against 'Do not
> let injustice reside in your tent' (Job 11:14).[55]

As shown by Ann Blair, non-Jewish readers were also encouraged to correct mistakes in their own copies.[56] Lifshitz's formulation makes it clear that, in the Jewish environment,

---

after the final note. Foliation, however, seems rather unequivocal: the introduction takes up fols 2–3, while the apology for the omission appears at fol. 87r.

[51] E.g., the errata list in Barukh ben David of Gniezno, *Sefer gedullat Mordekhai*, Hanau, Hans Jacopo Hena, 1615, f° (not in USTC; BHB 114116), fol. 116r, corrects במאכל for כמאכל, חמוציא for המוציא, and עובדען for עוברין.

[52] Cf. P. Gaskell, *A New Introduction to Bibliography*, Oxford, 1985, p. 113.

[53] Maimonides, *Mishneh Torah* (n. 5 above), II, fol. 767v. It should be noted that reading aloud could be occasionally used for deciphering a manuscript in the course of editing. Seligman ben Moses Simon Ulma mentioned that, when editing the *Responsa* of Jacob Segal (n. 8 above) from a manuscript owned originally by his grandfather, a scholar named Meir Fulda agreed to read the text in front of him 'two or three times [...] to arrive at the meaning of the letters' (fols 71v–72r).

[54] *Sefer kinnot im perush* (n. 19 above), fol. 3r.

[55] Isaac of Corbeil, *Sefer mitswot katan* (n. 30 above), fol. 157r. Intriguingly, none of the owners of the four copies that I consulted, either in person or online, followed the corrector's order: Oxford, Bod., Opp. 4°. 677; London, Valmadonna Trust 2379 (scan National Library of Israel, Jerusalem, system number 990018563860205171); Brooklyn (NY), Chabad-Lubavitch Library, card no. 49255 (scan Hebrewbooks.org); Brooklyn (NY), The Chaim Elozor Reich z"l Renaissance Hebraica Collection (scan Hebrewbooks.com).

[56] A. Blair, 'Errata Lists and the Reader as Corrector', in S. A. Baron, E. N. Lindquist, and E. F. Shevlin (eds), *Agent of Change: Print Culture Studies after Elizabeth L. Eisenstein*, Amherst (MA), 2007, pp. 21–41.

13: 'BEFORE THE LAW'   271

the practice shared with Christians was underlined by the halakhic idea; the list of errata as such was not sufficient to comply with that prescription — the corrections ought to be integrated in the text itself.

There is, however, some evidence of an opposite attitude, in which errata lists were presented as satisfactory in respect of the law. A corrector wrote: 'Being that in the art of printing, one cannot escape errors, I wrote here a list of errata, so that "injustice does not reside in your tent" (Job 11:14)'.[57] However, the relatively low occurrence of lists of errata in early modern Jewish printed books and their paradoxical near absence from the editions of the texts endowed with highest degree of sanctity — the Bible and Talmud — indicates that this was not the prevailing position. A list of errata not only 'prompted the reader to seek out yet more errata',[58] but was probably regarded as a sign that the owner still had to fulfil the halakhic requirement and check the text himself, as Lifschitz suggested. In a rare attempt at a halakhic elaboration by a corrector, Jacob ben Hayyim ibn Adonijah reached a very clear conclusion: 'For all these reasons, and based on a received tradition, it is necessary to scrutinise the text in the moment of its editing/correcting (*bi-sheat ha-hagahah*)'.[59]

At times, the process of editing and correcting the text could occur in the form of an epi-text, i.e. outside of the edition itself. In his commentary to Aramaic Targum, Mordecai ben Yehiel Luria promised to 'correct errors, which are in the printed edition of the Targum'.[60] Similarly to this, the compiler of comments and text-critical notes on *Sefer Mordekhai* — a medieval halakhic work and influential source for sixteenth-century legal scholars — explained that 'in the small edition of Riva [di Trento] and in the edition of Venice not a single leaf is without many and many errors'.[61] His compilation cannibalised previous comments, including many text-critical notes from three earlier rabbis, who wrote them in the margins of their copies of *Sefer Mordekhai*. One of the rabbinic marks of approval saw this as the main benefit of the book, claiming that its aim was to 'correct (*lehagiah*) the holy book, *Sefer ha-Mordekhai*'.[62]

The urge for a corrected text could even result in a private new edition of a text. In 1632, a teacher of Hebrew grammar made a neat manuscript copy from the printed editions of

---

See also the example in P. Simpson, *Proof-Reading in the Sixteenth, Seventeenth and Eighteenth Centuries*, Oxford, 1970 (facsimile of the 1935 ed.), pp. 28, 115.

[57] Salomon Luria (Maharshal), *Yeriot Shelomo*, Prague, Moses ben Joseph Betsalel Katz, 1608, 4° (not in USTC; BHB 143807), fol. 38r.

[58] S. Lerer, *Error and the Academic Self: The Scholarly Imagination, Medieval to Modern*, New York, 2002, p. 18.

[59] Maimonides, *Mishneh Torah* (n. 5 above), II, fol. 767v: מכולהו הני טעמי וקהוותן נקיטינן דאיכא לעיוני בשעת ההגהה טובא .

[60] Mordecai ben Yehiel Luria, *Perush ha-millot*, Kraków, Isaac ben Aaron Prostitz, 1580, 4° (not in USTC; BHB 143747), fol. [1r]. The commentary covers the Targum to the Five festive scrolls and to Daniel and Esdras.

[61] Barukh ben David of Gniezno, *Sefer gedullat Mordekhai* (n. 51 above), fol. [2v], misbound after fol. 6 in the copy used here: Oxford, Bod., Opp. fol. 1032 (2).

[62] Ibid.

David ibn Yahya's *Leshon limmudim* and a work on Hebrew prosody. As he explained in the introduction,

> [T]hese books, as the printers release them from the press, are completely marred and full of errors, so that you can almost say *A lack that cannot be made good* (Eccl. 1:15). But they have been completely corrected by the profound wit of two great grammarians [...] Manoah Hendel [...] and the venerable Isaac Katz-Kuskes.[63]

Correctors and Pressmen

Anthony Grafton demonstrated that, although badly paid, print professionals enjoyed a higher status than those who laboured with their bare hands.[64] In Jewish print shops, the hierarchy between these two categories was often blurred. Judah Aryeh Modena, the famous Venetian rabbi and intellectual, had different roles in producing printed Hebrew books. In titling a note for his edition of Mordecai Jaffe's *Levush ha-tekhelet*, he proudly styled himself 'the editor, who is standing above the printer' (*ha-magiah ha-nitsav al ha-mehokek*).[65] However, many complaints by correctors attest that pressmen had the upper hand and that their work rhythm determined how much time editors and correctors had to prepare the exemplar and correct the proofs, since the exemplar was often prepared simultaneously with the printing. As in the non-Jewish environment, economic reasons seem to be at stake. Curiously enough, the complaints as to how manpower affected the final result are to be found in the very same books, so that a compositor could often set a paratext which criticised him.[66]

The corrector of the 1574 Lublin edition of *Shaare Dura* attributed the typographic errors and the need for errata to the printers' hasty work: 'The workers were hasty with their craft and rushed with their work, and because of this speed and hastiness they could not be meticulous enough.'[67] It seems that, most often, publishers and editors gave up and were forced to accept that the quality of their output had been compromised. Moses ben Isaiah, who edited and published his father's work, which, as we have seen, necessitated several hundred errata, forewarned the readers of the presence of typos, warning in his introduction that '[s]ometimes a mistake appeared, as the way of printing is, and so judge the words of the author lightly.'[68] Another corrector wrote in his 'apology':

> The master printer urges the workers to hurry, saying, 'complete your task and get ready for tomorrow before it gets dark'. This pressure forces them to a great haste, in which one cannot

---

[63] MS Oxford, Bod., Opp. Add. 4° 95, fol. 10v.

[64] Grafton, *The Culture of Correction* (n. 4 above), p. 12, as well as pp. 70, 75.

[65] Mordecai Jaffe, *Levush ha-tekhelet*, Venice, Giovanni Cajun, 1620, f° (not in USTC; BHB 136556), fol. 2r.

[66] Grafton, *The Culture of Correction* (n. 4 above), p. 93.

[67] Isaac ben Meir Düren, *Shaare Dura*, Lublin, Kalonymos ben Mordecai Jaffe, 1574, f° (not in USTC; BHB 136795), fol. 109r. See the examples discussed in Simpson, *Proof-Reading* (n. 56 above), pp. 46–9.

[68] Isaiah Menahem ben Isaac, *Beurim* (n. 40 above), fol. [1v].

think of erroneous *defective* or *plene* spelling, so that the expertise of even the most accomplished expert in the correction will not be helpful. His intellect will get dim and errors will remain uncorrected. [...] In spite of this, praised be the wise corrector for his skilled work![69]

Towards the end of the period under discussion, one-time publishers who served also as editors and correctors grew in number. They often had very personal reasons for publishing a text: sons publishing a work of their deceased fathers to honour their memory, or scholars wanting to see an earlier, rediscovered text in print. Expectations of such 'newcomers' in the printing business often clashed with reality. Rabbi Joseph ben Mordecai Gershon Katz of Kraków, a renowned scholar, decided to bring to print the late-medieval halakhic work *Sefer ha-aguddah* by Alexander Süsslin (d. 1349). Despite the fact that Joseph ben Mordecai had on his side an experienced 'print professional', Samuel Boehm, who served as a supervisor of the edition, the money spoke and the pace of the workers overcame non-material considerations. Boehm complained about 'tremendous haste and pressure', and compared the workers to the Egyptian slave masters: 'And the task masters hurried [us], saying, "Fulfil your daily task each day" (Ex 5:13) — and it really is so [...]'.[70] Joseph ben Mordecai was more specific when expressing his frustration. Only during the course of editing the manuscript, which apparently took place simultaneously with printing, did he realise that adding cross references to other halakhic sources would be helpful: 'I started to write and comment on these passages. [...] But I did not have time to do the research because, as it is known, pressmen (*poale mlekhet ha-defus*) coerce, saying, you must complete your assigned task of editing for each day (after Ex 5:15)'.[71]

'Apology' or 'Defence'?

For readers acquainted with the workings of Christian print shops, the material presented in this chapter might seem to bring little new information. The statements of Jewish print professionals we analysed demonstrate that print shops issuing Hebrew books — whether those owned by Christians, such as Bomberg and most other Italian presses, or those completely in Jewish hands, such as the Soncino press or the presses of Prague, Kraków, Lublin, Salonika, and Constantinople — did not in any substantial way differ from printing presses in which non-Jewish workers produced books.

To some extent, this similarity was only to be expected. It is not surprising that the procedures of the production, based on the shared technology of the hand press, were performed in kindred way. But what about the shared '*rhetoric* of error and editorship'?[72] Throughout this chapter it was easy to refer the reader to analogies between the literary figures

---

[69] Maharil, *Sheelot u-teshuvot* (n. 8 above), fol. 71v; the book was edited and corrected by Seligman ben Moses Simon Ulma.

[70] A. Süsslin, *Sefer ha-aguddah*, Kraków, Isaac ben Aaron Prostitz, 1571, f° (not in USTC; BHB 110537), fol. [1v].

[71] Süsslin, *Sefer ha-aguddah* (n. 70 above), fol. 2r. See D. F. McKenzie, 'Printers of the Mind: Some Notes on Bibliographical Theories and Printing-House Practices', in D. F. McKenzie, *Making Meaning: 'Printers of the Mind' and Other Essays*, Amherst (MA) and Boston, 2002, pp. 13–85.

[72] Lerer, *Error and the Academic Self* (n. 58 above), p. 17.

in the 'apologies' of Jewish makers of Hebrew books and in the statements of the Christian 'print professionals'. The similarities in the literary expression, apparent already in the very early editions of the Soncinos (dating back to 1480s), indicate not only shared mental attitudes, but also the acquaintance of the Jewish makers of printed books with the ways their Christian colleagues expressed themselves in the paratexts of non-Jewish books.[73]

Nevertheless, the concern about the halakhic fitness of the printed text represents a specific cultural feature of the Jewish production of printed books. Although it is difficult to pin it down, it seems it gives a distinct momentum to the genre of the 'apologies', as it hovers in a rather indistinct way behind so many statements of editors and correctors. In the absence of a specific legal interpretation of the Talmudic requirement (do not keep uncorrected books), editors and correctors seem to experience a Kafkaesque pain: 'to be ruled by laws that one does not know'.[74] One might even wonder whether it would be more appropriate to understand 'apologies' as 'defences', in consonance with the 'law' being the habitat of pre-modern Jewish culture. For instance, in the colophon of a manuscript *Pentateuch* (1489), the wordy 'apology' by the scribe Matityah ben Jonah of Laun clearly has the form of a defendant's speech before the court:

> And give ear to me, my nation, for the Law shall go forth from Me. (Is. 51:4) [...]. Therefore I have set my face like flint, and I know I shall not be shamed, (Is. 50:7) because the Vindicator is at hand — who dares contend with me (Is. 50:8) and say that here I made a mistake and here is an error? Or that I was not careful enough about the punctuation, in the *plene* and *defective* orthography? [...] I swear that I will never forgive him! And if such a person comes forward and accuses me, I declare his words as completely void. [...] It is almost certain that because of the flaws of my intellect and the weakness of my senses I was seized by forgetfulness. [...] But because I humiliated myself, be this confession of mine also my redemption. Please say 'He is without blemish and clean, devoid and cleared of sin.' Let the merciful God protect us from mistakes![75]

Like contemporary and later editors and correctors of Hebrew printed books, this scribe seems to fluctuate between a pious reverence for the 'law' and a playful hyperbole. To paraphrase Kafka, when they 'seek to adjust themselves somewhat for the present or the future, everything becomes uncertain, and their work seems only an intellectual game.'[76]

---

[73] It should be noted, however, that Gershom Soncino also published books in Italian and Latin: see especially G. Tamani (ed.), *L'attività editoriale di Gershom Soncino*, Soncino, 1997.

[74] F. Kafka, 'The Problem of Our Laws', in F. Kafka, *The Complete Stories*, New York, 1971, pp. 437–8 (437).

[75] MS New York, Yeshiva University, Ms 1247, 3 vols, comprising Pentateuch and Five Festive Scrolls, copied in Prague in 1489 by Matityah ben Jonah for Israel bar Pinhas. The 'apology' can be found at fol. 253r of vol. 3.

[76] Kafka, 'The Problem of Our Laws' (n. 74 above), p. 437.

BIBLIOGRAPHY

PRIMARY SOURCES

MANUSCRIPTS

New York, Yeshiva University, Ms 1247.
Oxford, Bodleian Library, Opp. Add. 4° 95.

PRINTED BOOKS

Babylonian talmud — tractate Bava kama, Soncino, Joshua Salomon Soncino, 1489, f° (ISTC it00015020; BHB 328576).

Babylonian talmud — tractate Hullin, Soncino, Joshua Soncino, 1489, f° (ISTC it00015220; BHB 328576).

Babylonian talmud — tractate Niddah, Soncino, Joshua Salomon ben Israel Nathan Soncino and/or Gershon ben Moses Soncino, 1489, f° (ISTC it00015400; BHB 328583).

Babylonian talmud — tractate Pesahim, Venice, Marco Antonio Giustiniani, 1550, f° (not in USTC; BHB 333894).

Barukh ben David of Gniezno, *Sefer gedullat Mordekhai*, Hanau, Hans Jacopo Hena, 1615, f° (not in USTC; BHB 114116).

Bauking, Isaac ben Naftali Kohen, *Kitsur Mizrahi*, Prague, Abraham and Judah Leib, sons of Moses Schedel, 1604–1608, f° (not in USTC; BHB 136808).

Di Illescas, Jacob, *Imre noam*, Cremona, Vicenzo Conti, 1565, 4° (not in USTC; BHB 125939).

Elyakim Ben Naftali, *Tov shem*, Venice, no printer, 1606, 4° (not in USTC; BHB 110483).

Heller, Yom-Tov Lipmann, *Tsurat bet ha-mikdash*, Prague, Abraham and Judah Leib, sons of Moses Schedel, 1602, 4° (not in USTC; BHB 127261).

Hornschuch, H., *Orthotypographia, 1608*, ed. and transl. P. Gaskell and P. Bradford, Cambridge, 1972.

Horowitz, Sabbatai Sheftel ben Akiba, *Sefer shefa tal*, Hanau, Hans Jacopo Hena, 1612, f° (not in USTC; BHB 137592).

Isaac ben Joseph of Corbeil, *Sefer mitswot katan*, Kraków, Isaac ben Aaron Prostitz, 1596, 4° (not in USTC; BHB 178203).

Isaac ben Meir Düren, *Shaare Dura*, Lublin, Kalonymos ben Mordecai Jaffe, 1574, f° (not in USTC; BHB 136795).

Isaiah Menahem ben Isaac, *Beurim kabbedu ha-Shem*, Kraków, Isaac ben Aaron Prostitz, 1604, 4° (not in USTC; BHB 178290).

Isserlein, Israel, *Terumat ha-deshen*, Venice, Daniel Bomberg, 1519, 4° (not in USTC; BHB 109706).

Jacob ben Asher, *Arbaah turim*, Part III *Even ha-ezer*, Venice, Zorzo de' Cavalli, 1565, f° (not in USTC; BHB 313661).

Jacob ben Chajim ibn Adonijah, *Introduction to the Rabbinic Bible*, ed. and transl. C. D. Ginsburg, London, 1867.

Jacob ben Moses ha-Levi (Maharil), *Sheelot u-teshuvot*, Cremona, Vicenzo Conti, 1556, 8° (not in USTC; BHB 136197).

Jacob ben Moses ha-Levi (Maharil), *Sheelot u-teshuvot*, Hanau, Hans Jacopo Hena, 1610, 4° (not in USTC; BHB 136198).

Jaffe, Mordecai, *Levush ha-tekhelet*, Venice, Giovanni Cajun, 1620, f° (not in USTC; BHB 136556).

Judah Leva ben Betsalel (Maharal), *Tiferet Yisrael*, Venice, Jacob ben Gershon Bak and Daniel Zanetti, 1599, 2° (not in USTC; BHB 138996).

Kafka, Franz, 'The Problem of Our Laws', in F. Kafka, *The Complete Stories*, New York, 1971, pp. 437–8.

Kalats, Judah, *Sefer ha-musar*, Constantinople, Eliezer ben Gershom Soncino, 1537, 4° (not in USTC; BHB 140166).

Kalats, Judah, *Sefer ha-musar*, Mantua, Giacomo Ruffinelli and Jacob ben Naphtali ha-Kohen, 1561, 4° (not in USTC; BHB 140167).

Luria, Mordecai ben Yehiel, *Perush ha-millot*, Kraków, Isaac ben Aaron Prostitz, 1580, 4° (not in USTC; BHB 143747).

Luria, Salomon (Maharshal), *Yeriot Shelomo*, Prague, Moses ben Joseph Betsalel Katz, 1608 4° (not in USTC; BHB 143807).

Moses mi-Coucy, *Sefer mitswot gadol*, Venice, Daniel Bomberg, 1547, f° (not in USTC; BHB 149827).

Moses Maimonides, *Mishneh Torah*, 2 vols, Venice, Daniel Bomberg, 1524, f° (not in USTC; BHB 150066).

Moxon, J., *Mechanick Exercises on the Whole Art of Printing*, ed. H. Davis and H. Carter, New York, 1978.

Otyot shel rabi Akiva, Venice, Marco Antonio Giustiniani, 1546, 4° (not in USTC; BHB 108481).

Otyot shel rabi Akiva, Kraków, Isaac ben Aaron Prostitz, 1579, 4° (USTC 242,319; BHB 108482).

Paredes, A. V. de, *Institution, and Origin of the Art of Printing, and General Rules for Compositors [Madrid: ca. 1680]*, ed. and transl. P. Alvarez, Ann Arbor (MI), 2018.

Recanati, Menahem, *Beur al ha-Torah*, Venice, Marco Antonio Giustiniani, 1545, 4° (not in USTC; BHB 167906).

Sefer kinnot im perush, Lublin, Tsvi bar Abraham ben Kalonymos Jaffe, 1617, 4° (not in USTC; BHB 174114).

Slonik, Benjamin ben Aaron, *Masat Binyamin*, Kraków, Menahem Nahum ben Moses Meizels, 1633, 4° (not in USTC; BHB 154278).

Spira, Natan ben Samson, *Imre shefer*, Lublin, Kalonymos Jaffe, 1597, f° (not in USTC; BHB 181325).

Süsslin, Alexander, *Sefer ha-aguddah*, Kraków, Isaac ben Aaron Prostitz, 1571, f° (not in USTC; BHB 110537).

[Torah, neviim, ketuvim], part III, *Ketuvim*, Venice, Daniel Bomberg, 1525, f° (not in USTC; BHB 182176).

Weil, Jacob, *Shehitot u-vdikot*, Kraków, Isaac ben Aaron Prostitz, 1577, 8° (not in USTC; BHB 130965).

SECONDARY LITERATURE

Amram, D., *The Makers of Hebrew Books in Italy*, Philadelphia, 1909.

Blair, A., 'Errata Lists and the Reader as Corrector', in S. A. Baron, E. N. Lindquist, and E. F. Shevlin (eds), *Agent of Change: Print Culture Studies after Elizabeth L. Eisenstein*, Amherst (MA), 2007, pp. 21–41.

Gaskell, P., *A New Introduction to Bibliography*, Oxford, 1985.

Grafton, A., *The Culture of Correction in Renaissance Europe*, London, 2011.

Lerer, S., *Error and the Academic Self: The Scholarly Imagination, Medieval to Modern*, New York, 2002.

McKenzie, D. F., 'Printers of the Mind: Some Notes on Bibliographical Theories and Printing-House Practices', in D. F. McKenzie, *Making Meaning: 'Printers of the Mind' and Other Essays*, Amherst (MA) and Boston, 2002, pp. 13–85.

McKitterick, D., *Print, Manuscript and the Search for Order 1450–1830*, Cambridge, 2003.

Rabinowitz, R. N. N., *Maamar al hadpasat ha-Talmud*, Munich, 1877.

Raz-Krakotzkin, A., *The Censor, the Editor, and the Text: The Catholic Church and the Shaping of the Jewish Canon in the Sixteenth Century*, Philadelphia, 2007.

Simpson, P., *Proof-Reading in the Sixteenth, Seventeenth and Eighteenth Centuries*, Oxford, 1970 (facsimile of the 1935 ed.).

Sixtová, O., *Hebrejský tisk v Praze 1512–1672*, PhD dissertation, Prague, Charles University, 2017.

Sládek, P., 'From Manuscript to Print and Back Again: Two Case Studies in Late Sixteenth-Century Jewish Book Culture', in K. Kogman-Appel and I. Steimann (eds), *The Jewish Book 1400–1600: From Production to Reception*, Turnhout, forthcoming.

Sládek, P., 'Printing of Learned Literature in Hebrew, 1510–1630: Toward a New Understanding of Early Modern Jewish Practices of Reading', in E. Dillenburg, H. P. Louthan, and D. B. Thomas (eds), *Print Culture at the Crossroads: The Printed Book in Central Europe*, Leiden and Boston, 2021, pp. 387–410.

Spiegel, Y. S., *Ammudim be-toldot ha-sefer ha-ivri: Hagahot u-magihim*, Ramat-Gan, 2005.

Tamani, G. (ed.), *L'attività editoriale di Gershom Soncino*, Soncino, 1997.

Yaari, A., 'Telunot ha-magihim al hadpasat be-Shabbat al yede ha-goyyim', in A. Yaari, *Mehkere sefer: Perakim be-toldot ha-sefer ha-ivri*, Jerusalem, 1958, pp. 170–8.

CHAPTER 14

'*BUT TO WHOSE CHARGE SHALL I LAY IT? YOUR PRINTER IS ALL READIE LOADEN*'

*The Rhetoric of Printers' Errors in Early Modern Religious Disputes**

MATTHEW DAY

INTRODUCTION

IN his moralising text *A Common Whore* (1622), John Taylor, the Thames waterman and poet who gave himself the soubriquet of 'Water Poet', plays with the materiality of textual production and what he deems the characteristics and conduct associated with prostitution. A publication that comprises both the poem called 'A Whore' and a shorter work entitled 'A Comparison betwixt a Whore and a Booke', along with a dedicatory epistle 'To no matter who', *A Common Whore* is a work which Taylor describes as 'honester then some […] wiues or mothers'.[1] The 'Comparison' draws multiple parallels between pimps who 'set forth' prostitutes, and stationers who do the same with books.[2] Taylor claimed that books and prostitutes were both subject to close examination by authority figures, had attractive outward appearances, were used by multiple people, and were often discarded. Prefacing the poem's extended metaphor in the dedicatory epistle, Taylor there included the idea of printers' errors and did so to comment on the sense of dislike derived from public acknowledgement of mistakes.

* The quotation is taken from John Floyd, *Pvrgatories Trivmph over Hell*, Saint Omer, English College Press, 1613, 4° (USTC 3005419), sig. I2*v*.

[1] John Taylor, *A Common Whore*, London, [Edward Allde] for Henry Gosson, 1622, 8° (USTC 3010483), sigs A1*r*-B6*v*, B6*v*-B8*v*, esp. at sig. A2*r*.

[2] Ibid., sig. B6*v*.

Matthew Day, *'But to whose charge shall I lay it? Your Printer is all readie loaden'.* In: *Printing and Misprinting.* Edited by Geri Della Rocca de Candal, Anthony Grafton, and Paolo Sachet, Oxford University Press. © Matthew Day (2023). DOI: 10.1093/oso/9780198863045.003.0015

Both the text and paratext of Taylor's publication are especially concerned with the notions of public display and culpability. In the 'Comparison', Taylor suggested that errata sheets found at the end of books told of 'Errors and offences past', and maintained their late discovery by the reader was akin to 'great Whores' who 'in state survive' and whose 'faults escap'd' and 'Errataes' were only 'made manifest and knowne to men' when they died.[3] Towards the end of the poem Taylor again alluded to the processes of book production and noted that the availability of the book for purchase, meant its 'faults [we]re Printed vnto all mens sight, / Vnpartially declar'd in blacke and white'.[4] Here, the notion of error extended beyond that of technical misprint to include weaknesses in the quality of the poem as judged by the reader. This sense of fault made manifest was also the theme of his allusion to printing errors in his dedicatory epistle. Rather than apologise for literal mistakes, Taylor noted that the 'Printer hath us'd her [*viz.* the "Whore" of his poem's title] as he would be loth to be us'd himselfe': he had 'publish'd and proclaim'd all her faults to the view of the world'.[5] Such conduct, Taylor suggested, however, was acceptable because his publication was intended to teach 'Whoremaisters and Whores to mend' their ways.[6] Taylor thus deployed the motif of printers' errors to draw attention to the idea of post-event discovery, comment on critical and moral judgement, and bring to the fore the issue of public shaming. Implicit in all of these, and evidenced through the moralising nature of the text, is the notion of responsibility for one's actions.

Thanks to scholars such as Anthony Grafton, David McKitterick, Seth Lerer, Ann Blair, and Rachael Stenner, we now have a much better understanding of printers' errors in a variety of different texts and contexts.[7] They have identified the kind of errors that might be made and the range of reasons for their existence. Sources of mistakes included the illegibility of the manuscript, the difficulty of understanding translated texts, works that included unfamiliar words, eye-skip and misreading on the part of compositors, the misplacement or inversion of letters by them, and a lack of oversight by the master printer or author. Errata sheets sought to rectify the problems and told readers how to overcome deficiencies, which they were to consider easily corrected. Readers were also enjoined to show forgiveness.[8] The frequency with which these discourses occur in early modern texts, combined with what seems to have been widespread understanding by authors and readers of the concept of printers' errors, might make us assume that this industry practice was largely uncontentious. Indeed, it seems authors may have *expected* readers to attend to errata sheets.

---

[3] Ibid., sig. B7*v*.
[4] Ibid., sig. B8*v*.
[5] Ibid., sig. A2*r*.
[6] Ibid., sig. A3*v*.
[7] A. Grafton, *The Culture of Correction in Renaissance Europe*, London, 2011; D. McKitterick, *Print, Manuscript and the Search for Order 1450–1830*, Cambridge, 2003, esp. pp. 97–138; S. Lerer, 'Errata: Print, Politics and Poetry in Early Modern England', in K. Sharpe and S. N. Zwicker (eds), *Reading, Society and Politics in Early Modern England*, Cambridge, 2003, pp. 41–71 and the chapter 'Errata: Mistakes and Masters in the Early Modern Book', in S. Lerer, *Error and the Academic Self: The Scholarly Imagination, Medieval to Modern*, New York, 2002, pp. 15–54; A. Blair, 'Errata Lists and the Reader as Corrector', in S. A. Baron, E. N. Lindquist, and E. F. Shelvin (eds), *Agent of Change: Print Culture Studies after Elizabeth L. Eisenstein*, Amherst (MA), 2007, pp. 21–41; R. Stenner, *The Typographic Imaginary in Early Modern English Literature*, London, 2019.
[8] Grafton, *The Culture of Correction*, (n. 7 above), pp. 84–5.

When the Church of England clergyman Richard Parkes appeared not to have noted a correction in the errata list of Andrew Willett's *Limbo-mastix* (1604), he was criticised by the author, who accused him of 'malice'. Willett argued that if Parkes knew about the correction he had ignored it or if, through 'ignorance and rashnesse', he did not know about it but made 'no further search', he was equally at fault.[9] The expectations of close attention to mistakes led to a complex rhetoric around printers' errors, particularly for those involved in the many multifaceted religious disputes of early modern England, which, as Peter Milward has shown, generated multiple textual responses and were a significant feature of early modern religious print culture.[10] Across the sixteenth and seventeenth centuries and regardless of the particular theological dispute at stake, authors largely shared a set of common attitudes about textual errors: the dispute in the 1550s about clerical marriage, the 'Great Controversy' of the 1560s about the legitimacy of the Church of England, the arguments of the 1580s as the Puritans found their voice, the furore under James I about the taking of the oath of supremacy, and the Presbyterian disputes in the 1650s about the interpretation of the Song of Songs all show a common understanding about issues of textual error. As educated men trained in humanist methods, the authors of works about religious matters highlighted flaws in others' texts to undermine the arguments and scholarship of their adversaries. They also used the idea as a defence for defects in their own publications, though such rhetoric came to be regarded as a poor excuse for textual slips.

Though printers' errors were common, it is not the case that they were perceived as an inevitable by-product of a multi-agency and complex process of textual production. Aside from the regular use of correctors in printing houses, and the presence of cancel sheets as tangible evidence of a desire to create accurate texts, there was recognition of the need for care in textual production. Joseph Moxon noted that a good compositor was duty bound to know 'where the Author has been deficient', so that through his care, the compositor 'may not suffer such Work to go out of his Hands as may bring Scandal upon himself, and Scandal and prejudice upon the Master Printer'.[11] Care was particularly to be taken in texts relating to religion. This extended beyond the main body of the text to include paratextual features such as the organisation of the page and the use of different fonts. Thus in 1589 Edmund Bunny attacked the Jesuit Robert Parsons for misprinting part of a citation and commented that both the author and the printer should have 'used more dilige[n]ce in it'.[12] The attention paid to the mise-en-page of the Bible, the text, images, and layout of the various editions of John Foxe's *Actes and Monuments*, and the conscientious use of different fonts to distinguish between authors in pamphlets of religious disputes, all testify to the care that the producers of early modern publications took in presenting work, especially when religion was the theme.[13]

---

[9] Andrew Willett, *Loidoromastix: That is, A Scovrge for a Rayler*, London, Cantrell Legg, 1607, 4° (USTC 3002831), sig. D1r.

[10] Milward's publications are essential guides to the religious controversies of the early modern period. See P. Milward, *Religious Controversies of the Elizabethan Age: A Survey of Printed Sources*, London, 1977, and P. Milward, *Religious Controversies of the Jacobean Age: A Survey of Printed Sources*, London, 1978.

[11] J. Moxon, *Mechanick Exercises*, London, 1677, sig. 2H4v.

[12] Edmund Bunny, *A Briefe Answer, vnto those Idle and Friuolous Quarrels of R.P. against the late Edition of the Resolvtion*, London, John Charlewood, 1589, 8° (USTC 511184), sig. A4r.

[13] For a convenient summary of the layout of the Bible see E. B. Tribble, *Margins and Marginality: The Printed Page in Early Modern England*, Charlottesville (VA), 1993, pp. 11–56; for the care lavished

Books were, as Roger Chartier has reminded us, the product of a collective effort.[14] Yet there is some evidence of differing responsibilities within the process of book production. Moxon's *Mechanick Exercises* made clear that there were separate accountabilities for distinct aspects of the text. Compositors, Moxon noted, should strictly follow their copy, but he allowed that through the 'carelessness of some good Authors and the ignorance of other[s]' it had become incumbent on compositors to 'discern and amend the bad Spelling and Pointing' of their copy if it was in English.[15] If the copy-text was in a foreign language the author was to be left to 'his own Skill and Judgement in Spelling and Pointing', unless the text was in 'Latine, Greek or Hebrew', in which case it was the responsibility of the corrector to check the text.[16] Earlier authors understood this differentiation of labour and responsibility. Thomas Nashe attributed mistakes in *The Vnfortvnate Traveller* (1594) to 'the Printers ouersight and [his] bad writing'.[17] John Taylor's 'Errata, or Faults to the Reader' (1630) acknowledged there might be errors from any of the actors involved in the process of print production and that readers would find imperfections attributable both to himself and the printer.[18] Somewhat ironically, he observed that if the corrector had not also been at fault, then his and the printer's errors would have been erased.[19]

Taylor's claims are to be treated a little tongue in cheek. In neither *A Common Whore* nor his *Collected Works* is an errata sheet to be found and his printers were not made to publish their own mistakes. Rather it was a playful exploitation of a widely understood cultural practice. For Taylor, the concept of printers' errors was a motif through which he could convey a modesty topos in relation to his own writing, moralise about others' conduct, and pass comment on the process of textual scrutiny by the authorities.[20] But if there was levity in Taylor's engagement with the issue, this was not so for those involved in religious controversies, where exploiting errors was part of a rhetorical armoury. Rather than gloss over textual inaccuracies, many authors attacked them in order to undermine the strength of their opponent's argument, show weaknesses in their scholarship, or undermine their credibility. Other writers used the concept as a defence. Drawing on the prefatory material, errata sheets, and the main body of texts published across the sixteenth and seventeenth century, I explore the period's multifaceted engagement with the idea of printing errors. I demonstrate that a discourse emerged which applied across a range of religious disputes and which offers insights into how early modern authors and printers perceived culpability for errors and how they deployed the concept in their scholarly debates.

---

on John Foxe's *Actes and Monuments* see both J. F. King, *Foxe's Book of Martyrs and Early Modern Print Culture*, Cambridge, 2006, pp. 58–200, and E. Evenden and T. S. Freeman, *Religion and the Book in Early Modern England: The Making of Foxe's 'Book of Martyrs'*, Cambridge, 2011, pp. 6–32, 102–34; for the layout of pamphlets of religious disputation see J. M. Lander, *Inventing Polemic: Religion, Print and Literary Culture in Early Modern England*, Cambridge, 2008, pp. 27–31.

[14] R. Chartier, *Inscription and Erasure: Literature and Written Culture from the Eleventh to the Eighteenth Centuries*, trans. A. Goldhammer, Philadelphia, 2007, pp. 28–34.

[15] Moxon, *Mechanick Exercises* (n. 11 above), sig. 2E1*v*.

[16] Ibid.

[17] Thomas Nashe, *The Vnfortvnate Traveller*, London, Thomas Scarlet for Cuthbert Burby, 1594, 4° (USTC 512,608), sig. A3*r*.

[18] John Taylor, *All the Workes of John Taylor the Water Poet*, London, John Beale, Elizabeth Allde, Bernard Alsop, and Thomas Fawcet for James Boler, 1630 (not in USTC), sig. A4*v*.

[19] Ibid.

[20] Taylor, *Common Whore* (n. 1 above), sigs B7*v*–B8*v*.

THE ANXIETY OVER PRODUCING TEXTUAL ERRORS

That textual errors caused anxiety to both authors and printers across the period is clear. The posthumous second edition of Thomas Vicary's *A Profitable Treatise of the Anatomie of Mans Body* (1577) asserted that 'many good and learned men in these our dayes, doe cease to publishe abroade in the English toung' because 'if any one fault or blemishe by fortune be committed, eyther by them or the Printer escaped, they are blamed, yea and condemned for ignoraunt men, and errour holders'.[21] That seven subsequent editions of Vicary's work repeated the observation, suggests it retained its relevance.[22] In short, as Seth Lerer has observed, publishing error-ridden texts — whatever the cause — damaged the author's credit.[23] Some authors were certainly keen to exonerate themselves. The errata sheet of Robert Parker's *A Scholasticall Discovrse against Symbolizing with Antichrist in Ceremonies: Especially in the Signe of the Crosse* (1607) noted that the errors in his text occurred 'through the negligence of the Printer' and 'want of a diligent Correctour'.[24] Joshua Miller's *A Beame of Light Darted Thorough the Clouds* (1650) confidently asserted that the author knew of no errors in his book 'excepting the mistakes of the Printer'.[25]

It was not just authors, however, who were concerned about reputational damage; those in the printing house also felt a sense of opprobrium and showed some tetchiness around accepting responsibility for defects.[26] John Downame's *The Christian Warfare* (1604) excused its mistakes by noting that 'from pag. 371 to pag. 578 was committed to another Printer, who wanting a Corrector suffred [...] faults to escape which are materiall'.[27] In *Lingua Testium* (1651), Edmund Hall provided a list of corrections but 'only the grosse ones'.[28] He claimed he 'durst do no otherwise, lest the Printer should (as those unworthy fellows that printed *Manus Testium*) totally neglect the printing of the *Errata* sent them'.[29] Perhaps aware of the opprobrium that could result from errata lists, Allan Makcouldy's *A Trve Perpetvall*

---

[21] Thomas Vicary, *A Profitable Treatise of the Anatomie of Mans Body*, London, Henry Bamford, 1577, 8° (USTC 508458), sig. 7r.

[22] The work was republished in 1586 under the revised title *The Englishemans Treasvre, or Treasor for Englishemen: with the True Anatomye of Mans Body*, 4° (USTC 510620), and in 1587, 1596, 1613, 1626, 1633, and 1641 as *The Englishmans Treasure. With the True Anatomie of Mans Bodie*, 4° (USTC 510847, 513254, 3005828, 3012819, 3017023, 3041995).

[23] Lerer, 'Errata: Mistakes and Masters' (n. 7 above).

[24] Robert Parker, *A Scholasticall Discovrse against Symbolizing with Antichrist in Ceremonies: Especially in the Signe of the Crosse*, [Middelburg, Richard Schilders], 1607, 2° (USTC 1436545), sig. 2E1v.

[25] Joshua Miller, *A Beame of Light Darted Thorough the Clouds*, London, for H. C. and L. L., 1650, 8° (USTC 3062198), sig. A5v.

[26] Grafton, *The Culture of Correction* (n. 7 above), pp. 85–8.

[27] John Downame, *The Christian Warfare*, London, Felix Kingston for Cuthbert Burby, 1604, 4° (USTC 3001736), unnumbered leaf after sig. 2X1v.

[28] Edmund Hall, *Lingua Testium wherrin Monarchy is Proved*, [s.l.], 1651, unnumbered sheet after sig. G4v. Whether or not, as Hall asserts, the omission was deliberate, it is certainly true that *Manus Testium*, to which *Lingua Testium* was a preface, has no errata sheet. See Edmund Hall, *Manus Testium movens: or, A Presbyteriall Glosse*, [s.l.], 1651.

[29] Hall, *Lingua Testium* (n. 28 above), unnumbered sheet after sig. G4v. Hall was a Presbyterian who was disputing the interpretation which Nathanael Homes, an independent divine, had placed on the

14: 'BUT TO WHOSE CHARGE SHALL I LAY IT?' 283

Prognostication for the Yeare 1632 provided a note 'To' rather than from 'the Printer'. Makcouldy urged him to 'take paines that the faults [...] bee corrected', for that would enable Makcouldy 'to put a more profitable worke in [his] hands'.[30] By implication, the work was well printed and the address 'To the Printer' acted as an advert for the quality of the current publication and a trailer for future ones. At stake, in these discourses, was the coin of early modern culture: credit.

These examples from the prefatory material of books suggest a strong desire to retain credibility. Such concerns are even more apparent within the body of the texts themselves. Here, the voice of the printer is lost, as authors engaged with each other over textual faults. No error was too small for commentary, and critique of textual imperfections spanned minutiae to substantial changes. It encompassed not just the main body of the text but also marginalia and citations. Nor were accusations of mistakes limited to words. Punctuation, fonts, and the textual layout were equally subject to scrutiny: no aspect of the printer's art was immune from condemnation if advantage was to be gained.

Finding Faults in the Texts of Others and Laying Blame

When respondents spotted an error in their opponent's text they had a number of options open to them. One was to overlook minor errors, ascribing them to the printer and engaging with the more serious theological issues at hand. This was the approach Robert Crowley, the Church of England clergyman and polemicist, took in his dispute with Thomas Watson, Bishop of Lincoln, in the mid sixteenth century. Commenting on a mistake in Watson's text, Crowley asserted:

> As for the fault that your printer hath made: I haue amended [*viz.* it] without any more to doe, as in many other places of your printed sermons I haue done: but your own subtile dealing in the translation, I may not passe ouer.[31]

Accepting some mistakes as printers' rather than authorial errors enabled Crowley to focus on what he perceived as the more significant issues. The Jesuit Robert Parsons articulated a similar view in 1609 when he observed that the work of the then Dean of Gloucester, Thomas Morton, *A Preamble vnto an Incovnter with P. R.* (1608), contained a number of errors which Parsons took no notice of, 'hauing more substantiall matters' to write about.[32]

Song of Songs. See E. Clarke *Politics, Religion and the Song of Songs in Seventeenth Century England*, Basingstoke, 2011, p. 126.

[30] Allan Makcouldy, *A Trve Perpetvall Prognostication for the Yeare 1632*, Dublin [i.e. Edinburgh], [s.n.] for my comrades, 1632, (USTC 3015994), verso of title-page.

[31] Robert Crowley, *A Setting Open of the Subtyle Sophistrie of Thomas Watson Doctor of Diuinitie*, London, Henry Denham, 1569, 4° (USTC 506896), sig. Q2v.

[32] Robert Parsons, *A Qviet and Sober Reckoning with M. Thomas Morton*, [Saint Omer, English College Press], 1609, 4° (USTC 1436600), sig. B3r.

284 PRINTING AND MISPRINTING

Other authors, when they spotted a flaw, did not trouble themselves about who was responsible for it. This was especially true when authors did not or could not know the source of the defect. In 1584, Richard Cosin, the Church of England divine and defender of its traditions and practices against Puritan criticism, published *An Answer to the Two Fyrst and Principall Treatises of a Certaine Factious Libell*. It was a response to the anonymously printed and imprint-lacking *An Abstract, of Certain Acts of Parliament* [...] *for the Peaceable Gouernment of the Church* (1583). Commenting on the text's use of particular fonts to distinguish between types of text and unable to differentiate between author and printer, Cosin complained that the author 'or his printer to gratifie him, hath twice changed the forme of the letter from Roman unto Italian, as though they were not the authors onelie words, but some allegation'.[33] The implication being that, through manipulation of font, the author was claiming greater authority for a section of text than it merited by implying it came from a source other than himself. Likewise, John Jewel, Bishop of Salisbury, noted in his dispute with Thomas Harding that in his *A Confutation of a Booke Intituled. An Apologie of the Church of England* (1565) 'M Hardinge [...] in steede of these words, Lulled a sleepe, by erroure hath printed, Lulled a sheepe'.[34] Though the mistake would seem to be almost certainly the printer's rather than authorial, Jewel ascribed it to Harding, collapsing the distinction between printer and author and suggesting Harding had 'printed' the text. It was a tactic that William Fulke, Master of Pembroke College, was to complain about in 1581 when he noted that his opponent had charged him with wrongly printing some words 'in distinct letters'. Fulke defended himself by saying he had not intended the words to be so printed, was not a printer and was '70. miles off at least from the place where they were printed'.[35] Fulke thus sought to preserve a distinction between printer and author, which his adversary had sought to collapse. In doing so, he rejected the accusation of misquotation, and therefore deliberate manipulation of sources, that he was charged with.

If some protagonists sought to unite the idea of printer and author, others emphasised the difference and sought to instigate tension between them. In 1612, the Jesuit and religious controversialist John Floyd published *The Overthrow of the Protestants Pulpit-Babels*. It was part of a long-running set of pamphlets relating to the conversion to Roman Catholicism of Theophilus Higgons, a Protestant minister, and his subsequent recantation. Floyd's work was answered by Sir Edward Hoby in *A Counter-Snarle for Ishmael Rabshacheh* (1613), which Floyd himself responded to with *Purgatories Triumph over Hell* (1613). Floyd began by commenting on Hoby's use of the form 'Razis' instead of 'Razias'.[36] Next, Floyd repudiated Hoby's claim that an error in which the Latin word 'sed' had been printed for the English 'go' was an error of the printer or scribe not the author.[37] He did so on the grounds that, since there was no similarity in the letter forms and the words were from different languages,

---

[33] Richard Cosin, *An Answer to the Two Fyrst and Principall Treatises of a Certaine Factious Libell*, London, Henry Denham for Thomas Chard, 1584, 4° (USTC 509975), sig. L1r.

[34] John Jewel, *A Defence of the Apologie of the Churche of Englande*, London, Henry Wykes, 1567, 2° (USTC 506659), sig. B4r.

[35] William Fulke, *A Reioynder to Bristows Replie*, London, Henry Middleton for George Bishop, 1581, 4° (USTC 509301), sig. E7r.

[36] Floyd, *Pvrgatories Triumph* (n. * above), sig. D4v.

[37] Ibid., sig. H1r–v.

there was little probability that the printer would 'so consequently corrupt the text'.[38] Subsequently, Floyd criticised Hoby's text for printing 'Vt' instead of 'At' and mocked Hoby for blaming the printer again.[39] Floyd wondered whether Hoby's printers would ever work with him again, seeing that he 'returns his falsehoods vpon his Printer, without taking paines to peruse the Authours he citeth'.[40] When Floyd subsequently identified the omission of a citation from Augustine's works, he mocked both Hoby and those who had produced the text, saying he did not know whom to blame. He suggested he could not fault the printers since they were 'all readie laden', and that Hoby would 'rage' if the mistake were attributed to him. Instead, Floyd suggested, he should adopt 'an ancient custome, which was to beat the Minstrall when the Cooke did amisse', ascribing the mistake to whoever it was that advised Hoby.[41] Floyd's close analysis of Hoby's text and his understanding of the kinds of errors that might be attributed to printing-house practices enabled him to attack the author. He was able to charge Hoby with both unreasonable behaviour towards his printers and to attack Hoby's scholarship. Unlike Cosin and Jewel, who sought to collapse printer and author to lay the blame on the latter, Floyd attempted to achieve the same result by distinguishing the two.

Indeed, this approach of separating the printer and author was often deployed to demonstrate that an error was authorial. One means of proving this was to show that failures were not one-offs. John Ponet, Bishop of Winchester's *An Apologie Fvlly Avnsweringe by Scripture and Aunceant Doctors a Blasphemose Book* (1556) engaged with the notion of printer's error in the text of Ponet's opponents only to dismiss it. Ponet was responding to *A Traictise Declaryng and Plainly Prouyng that the Pretensed Marriage of Priests*, [...] *is no Mariage* (1554). It had been published under the name Thomas Martin but drew on works by Stephen Gardiner, the Lord Chancellor, and others, which opposed the marriage of priests. Claiming that Martin's text made a false attribution to the writing of Jerome which demonstrated that the very first married priests were regarded as heretics, Ponet suggested that Martin might claim 'the printer deceaued' him and 'put it in of his own head'.[42] To discount that possibility, Ponet drew attention to a second allusion to the same idea and, accusing his opponents of mendacity, went on to claim that 'by oft telling of there lyes to other[s] / at last they think them true themselues'.[43] That repetition of a mistake was deemed to make it authorial was also evident in Andrew Willett's *Loidoromastix* (1607). Criticising Richard Parkes for using the wrong Greek word 'twice in 10 lines', Willett claimed that this repetition was proof of 'ignorance in the penman' rather than 'ouersight in the Printer'.[44]

It was not, however, only words that led to textual mistakes, for numbers too were acknowledged to be subject to great inaccuracy. As John Jewel observed,

---

[38] Ibid., sig. H1v.
[39] Ibid., sig. H4r.
[40] Ibid.
[41] Ibid., sig. I2v.
[42] John Ponet, *An Apologie Fvlly Avnsweringe by Scripture and Aunceant Doctors a Blasphemose Book*, [Strasbourg, heirs of Wolfgang Köpfel], 1556, 8° (USTC 505370), sig. K2v.
[43] Ibid., sig. K3r.
[44] Willett, *Loidoromastix* (n. 9 above), sig. G4r.

in the heate, and drifte of writinge, when the mind is wholy occupied, and fully bente to the substance of the cause, it is an easy mater [...] to displace a number as to write either 9. for 6. or, 24. for 42.[45]

Such problems were compounded during the printing process when numbers were misread by compositors, or reduced or enlarged by the omission or inclusion of a numeral. As Jewel noted, such errors, though easy to commit, could be of 'great reckoning'.[46]

The recognition that numbers were particularly prone to inaccuracy underpinned the strategies used by authors to prove that defects were authorial and not a result of the process of production. One purpose of this was to attack their adversary's scholarship. The Protestant controversialist Edmund Bunny reproved the Jesuit Robert Parsons for mistaking numbers in his *A Christian Directorie* (1585). Parsons had written 'fiftie' instead of 250 and Bunny noted that the error 'might with some colour, bee laid on the Printer, but that the number is written at large'.[47] It provided him with an opportunity to say that there were so many mistakes of this kind that he assumed Parsons intended to write 'fiftie' since Parsons habitually wrote 'blindly inough'.[48] Likewise, at the start of the seventeenth century the Catholic controversialist Richard Smith criticised Thomas Bell for confusing Pope John XII with Pope John XXII and, like Bunny, Smith asserted 'this error can not be laid vpon the Printer seeing the number is set downe not in cyphers but letters'.[49] By contrast, Robert Crowley ostensibly accepted that his opponent's text did contain a printer's error in its miscitation from Augustine's sermons, but he too turned this into an opportunity to condemn the author's lack of scholarship. Crowley's flamboyantly titled *An Apologie, or Defence, of those Englishe Wryters and Preachers which Cerberus the Three Headed Dog of Hell, Chargeth wyth False Doctryne* (1566) was a response to the anonymous *The Copie of an Answere, Made vnto a Certayne Letter* (1563?). Noting that the author of *The Copie* should have cited the 191st of Augustine's *De tempore* sermons rather than the non-existent 192nd of his *De verbis Apostoli* collection, Crowley attributed the fault to the 'negligence of the printer'.[50] However, he went on to say that there was 'iust cause to ascribe [it] to Cerberus himselfe'. His reasoning was that he had seen a copy of the work with the errors marked up but with this mistake uncorrected. This led Crowley to conclude that the anonymous author 'toke it for no fault' or, not having read the original text of Augustine's sermons, followed a mistake found in Pelagian versions of the text.[51] The rhetoric about printers' errors gave Crowley an opportunity to show his humanist credentials by going back to the original source, while simultaneously undermining the industry, learning, and scholarship of his opponent.

---

[45] Jewel, *Defence* (n. 34 above), sig. B3v.
[46] Ibid., sig. B4r.
[47] Bunny, *Briefe Answer* (n. 12 above), sig. K5r.
[48] Ibid.
[49] Richard Smith, *An Answer to Thomas Bels Late Challeng named by him The Downfal of Popery*, Douai, Laurence Kellam, 1605, 8° (USTC 3002185), sig. K2v; see Thomas Bell, *The Downefall of Poperie*, London, Adam Islip for Arthur Johnson, 1604, 4° (USTC 3001914), sig. F2v.
[50] Robert Crowley, *An Apologie, or Defence, of those Englishe Wryters and Preachers which Cerberus the Three Headed Dog of Hell, Chargeth wyth False Doctryne*, London, Henry Denham, 1566, 4° (USTC 506497), sig. E2v.
[51] Ibid.

The determination to prove that a particular type of error could not be the fault of the printer is also found in relation to mis-citations. Edward Bulkley, in his *An Apologie for the Religion Established in the Church of England* (1608), attacked the Jesuit Thomas Wright's *Certaine Articles or Forcible Reasons* (1600) for mis-citing I Corinthians, Chapter 2, as the source for a reference instead of Chapter 2 of Philippians. Bulkley pre-empted recourse to the discourse of 'Printer's error' by observing it was unlikely that 'the Printer should so much erre'.[52] Similarly, the Catholic priest Thomas Worthington attacked the Church of England theologian John White for his work *The Way to the True Church* (1608). In his *Whyte Dyed Black* (1615), Worthington claimed to list 'Fourty most foule and vniustifiable corruptions and deprauations of Authors' made by White and — anticipating a reply — he sought to set out why these were authorial.[53] Providing a convenient summary about the nature of printers' errors, Worthington observed,

> Whyte can not transferr the fault vpon the printer for heare he standes for the most part chargeable either with adding too, or detracting fro[m] the authority alledged [...] whereas the printers errour commonly resteth in quotations made by figures, or (by mistaking some letter) in placing one woord for another.[54]

In attacking their opponents, then, authors such as Bulkley and Worthington had a clear conception of the type of textual error that was attributable to the printing process. In both cases they were keen to demonstrate that the mistakes they attacked had to be authorial and were eager to argue that such errors revealed poor scholarship or ignorance. Whatever their religious persuasion, Catholic and Protestant controversialists recognised the need to prove that mistakes which could be a result of the printing process should be more appropriately laid at the authors' hands.

Henry Burton's attack on John Cosin's *A Collection of Private Devotions or The Hovres of Prayer* (1627) provides further evidence of the concern in the period with this issue. As L. W. Hanson has shown, Cosin's work, which put into print a number of Elizabethan prayers, had a highly complex and contested publication history.[55] Attacked by both the Puritan-leaning priest Henry Burton and the lawyer William Prynne for being too Catholic, it went through three editions and a reissue. The second edition's added section 'The Printer to the Reader' and Burton's analysis of it highlight a number of aspects of the discourse surrounding the notion of printer's error. Seemingly written by the 'Printer', this address to the reader noted the condemnation that could come to an author for printers' errors and added that in the second edition 'care [wa]s had to amend such escapes, as either by the Printers haste, or the Correctors ouersight were co[m]mitted'.[56] In effect, all changes in the second edition were posited as corrections of printers' errors. Burton, however, was suspicious and,

---

[52] Edward Bulkley, *An Apologie for the Religion Established in the Church of England*, London, George Eld [and Nicholas Okes] for Arthur Johnson, 1608, 4° (USTC 3003462), sig. R1r.

[53] T[homas] P. W[orthington], *Whyte Dyed Black*, [Birchley Hall Press], 1615, 4° (USTC 3006838), sig. A1r.

[54] Ibid., sigs A1v–A2r.

[55] L. W. Hanson, 'John Cosin's *Collection of Private Devotions*, 1627', *The Library*, 5th ser., 13, 1958, pp. 282–7.

[56] John Cosin, *A Collection of Private Devotions or The Hovres of Prayer*, London, Robert Young, 1627, 12° (USTC 3013377), sig. (a)2r.

through careful comparison of the two editions, was able to show that there had been some substantive changes, in particular to the 'Prayer for the Dead'.[57] Claiming that the addition of the words '(with the prayers following)' constituted a 'monstrous' 'Escape or ouersight', Burton asserted 'the Author himselfe [was] the Corrector', claimed that no readers would be fooled, and accused Cosin of 'iuggling tricks'.[58] By doing so, Burton turned the discussion about printer's error into an issue of authorial integrity and deceit.

The narrative around the issue of printers' errors, then, when used by protagonists was one that focused predominantly on seeking to lay the blame for mistakes at the pen of the author. Accusers sought to demonstrate that the nature of some faults meant that they could not be ascribed to the printing house. Such a process allowed writers to draw attention to the scholarly failings of those they attacked, lambasting them for poor scholarship, ignorance, laziness, carelessness, and failure to check their sources. Accusers went on to challenge the personal integrity of the writers they criticised. These approaches were shared across religious differences and over a considerable period of time, showing how well they were understood. If those controversialists who identified errors in others' texts sought to lay the fault on the author, it is perhaps not surprising that those charged with making such mistakes attempted to attribute faulty texts to printers' errors as a form of defence, shifting the blame and protecting their credibility.

DEFENCES AGAINST THE CHARGE
OF MAKING AN ERROR

Although some writers such as John Jewel acknowledged they might have made mistakes themselves, many defendants simply put the blame on the printer.[59] Practically no kind of mistake was exempt from such practice. Robert Crowley blamed the printer for an error in which the phrase 'doe serve' was printed as 'deserve'.[60] Similarly, in his *A Sparing Restraint* (1568), the Puritan-leaning Church of England clergyman Edward Dering explained away a number of mistakes as the fault of the printer. These included mistakes in both the 'wordes' and the 'pointing'.[61] The Catholic John Martiall attributed the misquotation of a phrase in Augustine to his printer and claimed it came about because a correction in the manuscript copy was ignored.[62] Elsewhere, he asserted that the printer omitted a word and that the manuscript was still extant to prove it.[63] William Fulke claimed a mistaken reference was a

---

[57] Henry Burton, *A Tryall of Private Devotions*, London, [Bernard Alsop and Thomas Fawcet and Thomas Cotes], 1628, 4° (USTC 3013746), sig. L1r.

[58] Ibid., sigs L1r–v, L4v.

[59] Jewel, *Defence* (n. 34 above), sig. B2v.

[60] Crowley, *Apologie* (n. 50 above), sig. A1r.

[61] Edward Dering, *A Sparing Restraint of many Lauishe Vntruthes*, London, Henry Denham for Humfrey Toy, 1568, 4° (USTC 506778), sig. *1v.

[62] John Martiall, *A Replie to M. Calfhills Blasphemovs Answer*, Louvain, Jean Bogard, 1566, 4° (USTC 407219), sig. 2A4r.

[63] Ibid., sig. Q4v.

printer's error, as did Thomas Bell, who uncharitably lamented that 'the negligence, ignorance, and ouersight of the Printer, hath beene & often is the cause of many faults extant
in my books'.[64] He made similar complaints in *The Catholique Triumph* (1610), where he
castigated the printer for using the wrong font, reversing numbers in a date, and misquot-
ing a source.[65] George Wharton was even more acerbic, claiming his printer 'maliciously
expunged and altered' content and thereby 'abused' him.[66] Authors, it seems, were keen to
retain a distinction between themselves and their printers — and who had responsibility
for which aspects of the text.

While blaming the printer for textual errors was a common defence among authors who
had been criticised, there were other elements to the rhetoric that sat alongside these replies.
One manoeuvre was to suggest that focusing on printers' errors was petty-minded. At the
same time as John Jewel acknowledged his own mistakes and recognised that printers' errors
were hard to avoid, he attacked his adversary Harding for persistently drawing attention
to them and claiming that they demonstrated Jewel was deceitful.[67] Reiterating a number
of Harding's own mistakes, Jewel concluded, 'If al sutche childishe aduantages shoulde be
taken, then coulde no writer escape uncontrolled'.[68] In 1581, William Fulke complained that
his adversary Richard Bristow had made 'a fonde quarrel of the quotation omitted by the
printer', and in 1614 the Church of England clergyman Richard Harris elaborately developed
this line of thought.[69] His *Concordia Anglicana* (1612) was written to support the Oath of
Supremacy required under James I. It attracted the attention of the Jesuit Martin Becan,
who criticised it and the works of other writers supporting the Church of England stance
in *The English Iarre* (1612). Responding, Harris described both *The English Iarre* and Becan's
Examen of his *English Concord* as containing no 'learning, reading or iudicious discourse'
but being full of

> boy-like wranglings, about either seeming Iarres in wordes or syllables; or escapes of the Tran-
> scriber, Printer, or Corrector in some abcedary letters, in numerall figures, [and] in quoting
> the middle paragraph-word, for the first word of the self same Canon.[70]

In short, Harris dismissed Becan's arguments as trivial and claimed that the points he made
carried no theological or scholarly weight, were childish, and amounted to focusing on
inconsequential printing-house errors. Doing so was an attempt to take the scholarly high
ground and emphasise the gravitas of Harris and his writing.

---

[64] William Fulke, *T. Stapleton and Martiall (Two Popish Heretikes) Confuted*, London, Henry Middleton for George Bishop, 1580, 8° (USTC 509052), sig. H6r; Thomas Bell, *The Golden Ballance of Tryall*,
London, John Windet for Richard Bankworth, 1603, 4° (USTC 3001439), sig. N3r.

[65] [Thomas Bell], *The Catholique Triumph,* London, for the Company of Stationers, 1610, 4° (USTC
3004303), sigs 2T2v–2T3r, 2Y2r.

[66] George Wharton, *Merlini Anglici errata,* [London, s.n.], 1646, 8° (USTC 3055499), sig. D6v.

[67] Jewel, *Defence* (n. 34 above), sig. B3v.

[68] Ibid., sig. B4r.

[69] Fulke, *Reioynder* (n. 35 above), sig. H4r.

[70] Richard Harris, *The English Concord in Answer to Becane's English Iarre*, London, Humfrey Lownes
for Matthew Lownes, 1614, 4° (USTC 3006340), sigs A2v–A3r.

CONCLUSION

I hope to have shown that the notion of printers' errors played a significant part in the publications of English religious controversialists throughout the early modern period. Although many readers dutifully marked up in their copies the corrections listed in errata sheets, there was anxiety among both authors and printers about the need for textual accuracy. Writers were prepared to blame printers, who themselves were willing to criticise their fellow workers, each wishing to preserve their own credit. Yet, it was in religious disputes that the rhetoric of printers' errors was especially apparent. The academic, humanist training that those who entered the church received meant that they were particularly alive both to the practices of the printing house and textual errors. Whatever their religious persuasion, writers recognised not only that textual errors frequently existed but that it was possible to build around them a rhetoric which could strengthen their own arguments. When attacking opponents, disputants sought to apportion blame to the author. Doing so enabled them to highlight an author's lack of learning, diligence, scholarly integrity, or conscientiousness. Such an approach was a common strategy and authors took considerable pains to demonstrate that mistakes should not be ascribed to problems in the printing house. Fundamental to this approach was an understanding of the kinds of imperfections that might occur and how they could be caused in the printing process. The same knowledge lay behind the defence deployed by writers whose works had been attacked. Frequently, they blamed printers for the mistakes and dismissed the errors, denying that they were authorial. To do so was to suggest the mistakes were not of theological or scholarly significance. Indeed, many defenders of texts argued that focusing on such errors was childish and belittling. They did so in a language that was at times vituperative and uncharitable. Though errata slips noted that to err was human and the poet Alexander Pope subsequently suggested that to forgive was divine, when it came to printers' errors it was the divines of early modern England who were some of the least forgiving.[71]

BIBLIOGRAPHY

PRIMARY SOURCES

[Bell, Thomas], *The Catholique Triumph*, London, for the Company of Stationers, 1610, 4° (USTC 3004303).

Bell, Thomas, *The Downefall of Poperie*, London, Adam Islip for Arthur Johnson, 1604, 4° (USTC 3001914).

---

[71] Alexander Pope, *An Essay on Criticism*, London, for W. Lewis, 1711, sig. D3v.

Bell, Thomas, *The Golden Ballance of Tryall*, London, John Windet for Richard Bankworth, 1603, 4° (USTC 3001439).

Bulkley, Edward, *An Apologie for the Religion Established in the Church of England*, London, George Eld [and Nicholas Okes] for Arthur Johnson, 1608, 4° (USTC 3003462).

Bunny, Edmund, *A Briefe Answer, vnto those Idle and Friuolous Quarrels of R. P. against the late Edition of the Resolvtion*, London, John Charlewood, 1589, 8° (USTC 511184).

Burton, Henry, *A Tryall of Private Devotions*, London, [Bernard Alsop and Thomas Fawcet and Thomas Cotes], 1628, 4° (USTC 3013746).

Cosin, John, *A Collection of Private Devotions or The Hovres of Prayer*, London, Robert Young, 1627, 12° (USTC 3013377).

Cosin, Richard *An Answer to the Two Fyrst and Principall Treatises of a Certaine Factious Libell*, London, Henry Denham for Thomas Chard, 1584, 4° (USTC 509975).

Crowley, Robert, *An Apologie, or Defence, of those Englishe Wryters and Preachers which Cerberus the Three Headed Dog of Hell, Chargeth wyth False Doctryne*, London, Henry Denham, 1566, 4° (USTC 506497).

Crowley, Robert, *A Setting Open of the Subtyle Sophistrie of Thomas Watson Doctor of Diuinitie*, London, Henry Denham, 1569, 4° (USTC 506896).

Dering, Edward *A Sparing Restraint of many Lauishe Vntruthes*, London, Henry Denham for Humfrey Toy, 1568, 4° (USTC 506778).

Downame, John, *The Christian Warfare*, London, Felix Kingston for Cuthbert Burby, 1604, 4° (USTC 3001736).

Floyd, John, *Pvrgatories Trivmph over Hell*, Saint Omer, English College Press, 1613, 4° (USTC 3005419).

Fulke, William, *A Reioynder to Bristows Replie*, London, Henry Binneman for George Bishop, 1581, 4° (USTC 509301).

Fulke, William, *T. Stapleton and Martiall (Two Popish Heretikes) Confuted*, London, Henry Middleton for George Bishop, 1580, 8° (USTC 509052).

Hall, Edmund, *Lingua Testium wherrin Monarchy is Proved*, [s.l.], 1651.

Harris, Richard, *The English Concord in Answer to Becane's English Iarre*, London, Humfrey Lownes for Matthew Lownes, 1614, 4° (USTC 3006340).

Jewel, John, *A Defence of the Apologie of the Churche of Englande*, London, Henry Wykes, 1567, 2° (USTC 506659).

Makcouldy, Allan, *A Trve Perpetvall Prognostication for the Yeare 1632*, Dublin [actually Edinburgh], s.n. for my comrades, 1632, unknown (USTC 3015994).

Martiall, John, *A Replie to M. Calfhills Blasphemovs Answer*, Louvain, Jean Bogard, 1566, 4° (USTC 407219).

Miller, Joshua, *A Beame of Light Darted Thorough the Clouds*, London, for H. C. and L. L., 1650, 8° (USTC 3062198).

Moxon, J., *Mechanick Exercises*, London, 1677.

Nashe, Thomas, *The Vnfortvnate Traveller*, London, Thomas Scarlet for Cuthbert Burby, 1594, 4° (USTC 512608).

Parker, Robert, *A Scholasticall Discovrse against Symbolizing with Antichrist in Ceremonies: Especially in the Signe of the Crosse*, [Middelburg, Richard Schilders], 1607, 2° (USTC 1436545).

Parsons, Robert, *A Qviet and Sober Reckoning with M. Thomas Morton*, [Saint Omer, English College Press], 1609, 4° (USTC 1436600).

Ponet, John, *An Apologie Fvlly Avnsweringe by Scripture and Aunceant Doctors a Blasphemose Book*, [Strasbourg, heirs of Wolfgang Köpfel], 1556, 8° (USTC 505370).

Pope, Alexander, *An Essay on Criticism,* London, for W. Lewis, 1711.

Smith, Richard, *An Answer to Thomas Bels Late Challeng named by him The Downfal of Popery*, Douai, Laurence Kellam, 1605, 8° (USTC 3002185).

Taylor, John, *All the Workes of John Taylor the Water Poet*, London, John Beale, Elizabeth Allde, Bernard Alsop, and Thomas Fawcet for James Boler, 1630 (not in USTC).

Taylor, John, *A Common Whore*, London, [Edward Allde] for Henry Gosson, 1622, 8° (USTC 3010483).
Vicary, Thomas, *A Profitable Treatise of the Anatomie of Mans Body*, London, Henry Bamford, 1577, 8° (USTC 508458).
Wharton, George, *Merlini Anglici errata*, [London, s.n.], 1646, 8° (USTC 3055499).
Willett, Andrew, *Loidoromastix: That is, A Scovrge for a Rayler*, London, Cantrell Legg, 1607, 4° (USTC 3002831).
W[orthington], T[homas] P., *Whyte Dyed Black*, [Birchley Hall Press], 1615, 4° (USTC 3006838).

SECONDARY LITERATURE

Blair, A., 'Errata Lists and the Reader as Corrector', in S. A. Baron, E. N. Lindquist, and E. F. Shelvin (eds), *Agent of Change: Print Culture Studies after Elizabeth L. Eisenstein*, Amherst (MA), 2007, pp. 21–41.
Chartier, R., *Inscription and Erasure: Literature and Written Culture from the Eleventh to the Eighteenth Centuries*, trans. A. Goldhammer, Philadelphia, 2007.
Clarke, E., *Politics, Religion and the Song of Songs in Seventeenth Century England*, Basingstoke, 2011.
Evenden, E., and Freeman, T. S., *Religion and the Book in Early Modern England: The Making of Foxe's 'Book of Martyrs'*, Cambridge, 2011.
Grafton, A., *The Culture of Correction in Renaissance Europe*, London, 2011.
Hanson, L. W., 'John Cosin's Collection of Private Devotions, 1627', *The Library*, 5th ser., 13, 1958, pp. 282–7.
King, J. F., *Foxe's Book of Martyrs and Early Modern Print Culture*, Cambridge, 2006.
Lander, J. M., *Inventing Polemic: Religion, Print and Literary Culture in Early Modern England*, Cambridge, 2008.
Lerer, S., 'Errata: Mistakes and Masters in the Early Modern Book', in S. Lerer, *Error and the Academic Self: The Scholarly Imagination, Medieval to Modern*, New York, 2002, pp. 15–54.
Lerer, S., 'Errata: Print, Politics and Poetry in Early Modern England', in K. Sharpe and S. N. Zwicker (eds), *Reading, Society and Politics in Early Modern England*, Cambridge, 2003, pp. 41–71.
McKitterick, D., *Print, Manuscript and the Search for Order 1450–1830*, Cambridge, 2003.
Milward, P., *Religious Controversies of the Elizabethan Age: A Survey of Printed Sources*, London, 1977.
Milward, P., *Religious Controversies of the Jacobean Age: A Survey of Printed Sources*, London, 1978.
Stenner, R., *The Typographic Imaginary in Early Modern English Literature*, London, 2019.
Tribble, E. B., *Margins and Marginality: The Printed Page in Early Modern England*, Charlottesville (VA), 1993.

PART IV

SCIENCE

CHAPTER 15

CONTROLLING ERRORS IN THE FIRST PRINTED BOOK OF ASTRONOMICAL TABLES

Regiomontanus's Ephemerides *(Nuremberg, 1474)*

RICHARD L. KREMER

INTRODUCTION

[…] Master Johannes [Regiomontanus] has left Nuremberg but intends to return; because he wants all his actions to be concealed, he revealed his departure to no one or only a few. Nevertheless he departed in a hurry, in the direction of Italy, desiring, in the opinion of some, to bring back new books. He printed a new calendar of the true motion of the luminaries, the Sun and Moon. It is said to be in 1000 copies, although no one except the pressmen has seen it. The canons will be attached in good time. But now, I hear, he has his pressmen printing an almanac of all the planets for many years. Until now, neither I nor anyone else could gain access to his house; but in the coming days, at the wish of his servants, I will be able to enter and see his labours. Hence if at any time I learn anything about his works, I will share it with you.[*][1]

---

[*] The initial version of this paper, based solely on the London copies, was presented in 2013 at a workshop on printing mathematics in the early modern world, organised by Benjamin Wardhaugh at All Souls College, Oxford. Since then I have benefited greatly from the libraries and their staffs who enabled me to study their copies of Regiomontanus's edition and from the generous assistance of many colleagues, including Geri Della Rocca de Candal, Oliver Duntze, Falk Eisermann, Hans Gaab, Jürgen Hamel, Stephan Heilen, Christoph Mackert, Holger Nickel, Monika Otter, Andreina Rita, Paolo Sachet, Christine Sauer, Michael Shank, Lisa Totzke, and Jarasłow Włodarczyk. For their stimulating questions and suggestions, I thank participants and organisers at the 2018 conference on printing and misprinting at Lincoln College, Oxford.

[1] Hermann Schedel to his cousin Hartmann Schedel, undated, in P. Joachimsohn (ed.), *Hermann Schedels Briefwechsel (1452–1478)*, Tübingen, 1893, pp. 196–7: 'Recessit idem magister Jo[annes] a

---

Richard L. Kremer, *Controlling Errors in the First Printed Book of Astronomical Tables*. In: *Printing and Misprinting*.
Edited by Geri Della Rocca de Candal, Anthony Grafton, and Paolo Sachet, Oxford University Press. © Richard L. Kremer (2023).
DOI: 10.1093/oso/9780198863045.003.0016

Rarely do contemporary sources illuminate the printing of particular incunable editions. In this oft-cited letter, however, the Augsburg physician and bibliophile Hermann Schedel (1410–1485) described one of Nuremberg's first printers, Johannes Regiomontanus (1436–76), and his production of three astronomical editions: a perpetual calendar in Latin and German versions and a Latin ephemerides, or list of daily planetary positions for 'many years' (1475 through 1506). The letter also suggests that Regiomontanus was secretive, had travelled to Italy in search of 'new books', presumably to print, and strictly controlled access to his print shop. And we learn that Schedel and the target of the letter, his cousin, the city physician in nearby Nördlingen, Hartmann Schedel (1440–1514), were keenly interested in the editions then being printed by Regiomontanus. Providing quantitative information for the daily positions of the Sun, Moon, and planets, these imprints would greatly ease the task of casting horoscopes, essential tools for the astrological medicine being practiced by physicians like the Schedels.[2]

The works mentioned by Schedel, three of the nine editions printed by Regiomontanus (Table 15.1), were the first astronomical tables (pages of numbers aligned in rows and columns) to be printed in Europe.[3] The technical challenges of this project would have been considerable (Figs 15.1–3). In addition to developing type-high metal rules (long strips for the horizontal lines, short strips for the vertical lines) to print 'cells' around individual sexagesimal numbers fitted around small woodblock initials,[4] Regiomontanus had to control the typesetting of literally hundreds of thousands of numerical digits. The calendars list the times of new and full moons (syzygies), to minutes, for seventy-six years; the daily positions of the Sun to arcminutes and the Moon to degrees from 1475 to 1534; and the times and magnitudes of all the solar and lunar eclipses from 1475 to 1530. These data are compressed

---

Nur[emberga], causa tamen revertendi, qui cum omnia sua facta occulta esse vult, nulli aut paucis recessum suum manifestavit. Ytaliam tamen versus iter arripuit, opinione quorundam libros novos apportare cupiens. Kalendarium novum super vero motu luminarium solis et lune impressit ad numerum ut dicitur mille, nec est, qui viderit, demptis impressoribus. Canones annectentur tempore suo. Nunc autem, audio, almanach omnium planetarum ad multos annos per impressores suos facit imprimere. Hactenus in domum ego nec quivis alius ingressum habere potuit, in dies tamen ad voluntatem suorum familiarium introibo et labores suos conspiciam, quod si aliqua umquam de operibus suis nactus fuero, vos participem reddam.' Schedel's letter, extant as a draft, is undated; it is known that Regiomontanus travelled from Nuremberg to Italy in the summer of 1472. See E. Zinner, *Leben und Wirken des Joh. Müller von Königsberg genannt Regiomontanus*, 2nd rev. edn, Osnabrück, 1968, pp. 171–2.

[2] R. Stauber, *Die Schedelsche Bibliothek*, Freiburg i. B., 1908; C. Reske, *Die Produktion der Schedelschen Weltchronik in Nürnberg*, Wiesbaden, 2000; B. Wagner, *Worlds of Learning: The Library and World Chronicle of the Nuremberg Physician Hartmann Schedel (1440–1514)*, Munich, 2015; B. Posselt, *Konzeption and Kompilation der Schedelschen Weltchronik*, Wiesbaden, 2015; F. Fuchs (ed.), *Hartmann Schedel (1440–1514): Leben und Werk*, Wiesbaden, 2016; A. Worm, *Geschichte und Weltordnung: Graphische Modelle von Zeit und Raum in Universalchroniken vor 1500*, Berlin, 2021, pp. 371–481.

[3] E. Zinner, *Geschichte und Bibliographie der astronomischen Literatur in Deutschland zur Zeit der Renaissance*, 2nd edn, Stuttgart, 1964, pp. 93–6.

[4] Cf. J. S. Byrne, *The Stars, the Moon and the Shadowed Earth: Viennese Astronomy in the Fifteenth Century*, PhD dissertation, Princeton, Princeton University, 2007, pp. 235–61; R. Baldasso, 'Printing for the Doge: On the First Quire of the First Edition of the *Liber Elementorum Euclidis*', *La Bibliofilia*, 115, 2013, pp. 525–52; E. R. Anderson, 'Printing the Bespoke Book: Euclid's *Elements* in Early Modern Visual Culture', *Nuncius*, 35, 2020, pp. 536–60.

into two pages per month for one year, plus several auxiliary tables. I estimate that the calendar editions required setting about 18,000 numerical digits.[6]

The massive ephemerides, consisting of 448 printed leaves with only three pages of text, also offers two pages per month (Fig. 15.2), with the daily planetary and luminary longitudes, to arcminutes, on the versos and the daily planetary aspects, to hours, listed on the rectos. Printed in one fourteen-leaf gathering per year, the opening recto of each gathering offers a summary of that year's moveable feasts, eclipses, and retrograde motions (Fig. 15.3). Covering thirty-two years, the complete book required that Regiomontanus's compositors set more than 400,000 individual digits to print this edition.[7] The ephemerides is a large quarto volume, the first massive astronomical table to be printed.

As is well known, Regiomontanus had grounded his desire to establish a print shop with humanist rhetoric calling for corrected and improved texts. In a 1471 letter to the Erfurt University rector and mathematician Christian Roder (d. 1478), Regiomontanus urged the Erfurter to join him in a war in which the 'enemies of truth, the errors which defile not

Table 15.1 Regiomontanus's nine Nuremberg editions, in estimated chronological order, issued between about 1472 and 1475. Only the *Ephemerides* is dated, 1474.[5]

Edition	Leaves	Surviving copies	ISTC
Manilius, *Astronomicon*	72	34	im00202000
Peurbach, *Theorica nova planetarum*	20	37	ip01134000
Regiomontanus, [Printing prospectus]	1	5	ir00091800
Regiomontanus, [*Kalendarium*, Latin]	32	37	ir00092000
Regiomontanus, [*Kalender*, German]	30	25	ir00100300
Regiomontanus, [*Ephemerides*]	448	40	ir00104500
Basil, *De legendis libris gentilium*	10	17	ib00272000
Vegius, *Philalethes*	12	28	iv00114000
Regiomontanus, *Disputationes*	10	27	ir00104000

[5] For an earlier inventory of extant copies of Regiomontanus's editions and a reconstruction of the printing order of the editions, see A. Wingen-Trennhaus, 'Regiomontanus als Frühdrucker in Nürnberg', *Mitteilungen des Vereins für Geschichte der Stadt Nürnberg*, 78, 1991, pp. 17–87 (40–5, 57). Based on paper, decorated initials, and information in the broadside printing prospectus, my suggested order differs slightly from Wingen-Trennhaus's. Cf. E. Zinner, 'Die wissenschaftlichen Bestrebungen Regiomontans', *Beiträge zur Inkunabelkunde*, 2nd ser., 1938, pp. 89–103.

[6] Inspection reveals that the tabulated numbers in the twelve typeblocks for the syzygies were not reset between the Latin and German editions; only the headings were reset. Although considered separate editions, the two calendars must have been printed at the same time.

[7] Zinner, *Regiomontanus* (n. 1 above), p. 187, estimates 300,000 'numbers' in the ephemerides. I count 'digits'.

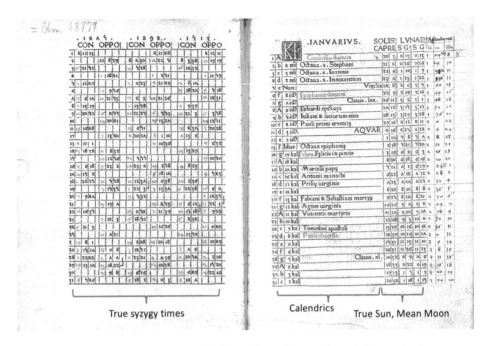

FIG. 15.1. Johannes Regiomontanus, *Kalendarium* [Latin], Nuremberg, Johannes Regiomontanus, c. 1474, 4° (ISTC ir00092000), sigs [a1]v–[a2]r. Munich, Bayerische Staatsbibliothek, 4 Inc.s.a. 1552.

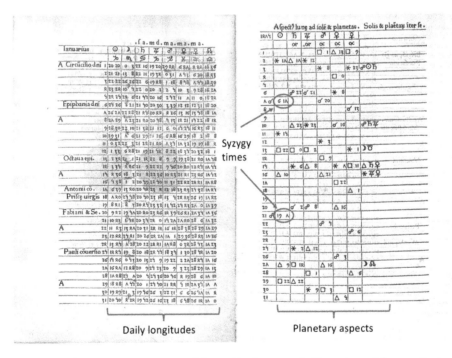

FIG. 15.2. Johannes Regiomontanus, *Ephemerides* [1475–1506], Nuremberg, Johannes Regiomontanus, 1474, 4° (ISTC ir00104500), sigs [a2]v–[a3]r. Munich, Bayerische Staatsbibliothek, Rar. 299.

FIG. 15.3. Regiomontanus, *Ephemerides* (see Fig. 15.2), sig. [a2]r. Munich, Bayerische Staatsbibliothek, Rar. 299.

just astronomy but all of mathematics, must be expunged'.[8] In the preface to his *Disputationes*, printed c. 1475, Regiomontanus emphasised his desire to print 'useful and correct editions, [...] not in order to detract from the authority of others but to enlighten the study of mathematics which has been defiled in many ways for centuries and almost abandoned by all, by wiping off every stain as far as possible'. But he also worried about incompetent translators and 'hungry printers' corrupting works by introducing new errors. Indeed, according to him:

> [...] we are sinning when we obscure the opinions of noble authors by contaminating them with our own ignorance and infecting posterity with erroneous copies of books. For who

---

[8] Regiomontanus to Roder, 4 July 1471, in M. Curtze, 'Der Briefwechsel Regiomontans mit Giovanni Bianchini, Jacob von Speier und Christian Roder', *Abhandlungen zur Geschichte der mathematischen Wissenschaften*, 12, 1902, pp. 187–336 (326). For Regiomontanus and humanism, see N. M. Swerdlow, 'Regiomontanus on the Critical Problems of Astronomy', in T. H. Levere and W. R. Shea (eds), *Nature, Experiment, and the Sciences*, Dordrecht, 1990, pp. 165–95; his 'Science and Humanism in the Renaissance: Regiomontanus's Oration on the Dignity and Utility of the Mathematical Sciences', in P. Horwich (ed.), *World Changes: Thomas Kuhn and the Nature of Science*, Cambridge, 1993, pp. 131–68; and most recently P. D. Omodeo, 'Johannes Regiomontanus and Erasmus Reinhold: Shifting Perspectives on the History of Astronomy', in S. Brentjes and A. Fidora (eds), *Premodern Translation: Comparative Approaches to Cross-Cultural Transformations*, Turnhout, 2021, pp. 165–86. For more on authors eternally complaining about printing errors, see H. Widmann, 'Die Lektüre unendlicher Korrekturen', *Archiv für Geschichte des Buchwesens*, 5, 1962, cols 777–826.

300 PRINTING AND MISPRINTING

does not realise that the admirable art of printing recently devised by our countrymen is as harmful to men if it multiplies erroneous works as it is useful when it publishes properly corrected editions?[9]

Much of Regiomontanus's rhetoric about printing and errors seems directed at printers and editors issuing *editiones principes* of classical or medieval works, which raise philological questions of manuscript collation, emendation, and translation. Regiomontanus, however, was among the first printers to issue contemporary works, and was the first astronomer to print his own works and, as noted above, to organise the printing of large tables of numbers. The surviving copies of his *Ephemerides* offer, therefore, a unique case study of the challenge of controlling errors in an early European print shop.[10]

In the 1930s, Ernst Zinner, the bibliographer and historian of astronomy, had already noticed that Regiomontanus had made hand-entered rather than (in addition to?) stop-press corrections in his print shop. The instructions in the Latin *Kalendarium* for adjusting dates of the moveable feasts in a leap year have been corrected by pasting a slip of paper, bearing nine lines of printed text, over the flawed lines originally printed. In the German edition, this passage was set correctly. The latter, however, misprinted the eclipse desig-nations for 1511 and 1513 and a corrector has cancelled, in multiple copies Zinner and I have seen, the terms 'der Sunnë' and 'des mondes' and added in manuscript above the line 'des mondes' and 'der Sünnen', respectively. Other printing errors in the calendars, Zinner reported, were not corrected.[11] Likewise, Zinner spotted in the *Ephemerides* four manuscript corrections, identically present in four copies he had seen — the one in Bamberg, Staatsbibliothek (SB); copies 1 and 2 in Vienna, Österreichische Nationalbibliothek (ÖNB); and copy 2 in Munich, Bayerische Staatsbibliothek (BSB), as detailed in Table 15.2 — that 'must have been added in the printing shop' and indicate Regiomontanus's desire 'to issue only error-free imprints'.[12]

Prompted by Zinner's preliminary findings, I formulated three questions for this study of how Regiomontanus may have sought to control errors in printing astronomical tables, in particular the *Ephemerides*. First, can stop-press and in-shop manuscript corrections be identified? Second, might the frequency of errors be correlated with the kinds of numbers being printed? Third, does the frequency of errors change diachronically in the thirty-two gatherings of the *Ephemerides*, assuming, that is, that the printers began with the gathering for 1475 and printed the subsequent years sequentially, finishing with the gathering for 1506?

---

[9] Translated in O. Pedersen, 'The Decline and Fall of the *Theorica Planetarum*: Renaissance Astronomy and the Art of Printing', in E. Hilfstein, P. Czartoryski, and F. D. Grande (eds), *Science and History: Studies in Honor of Edward Rosen*, Wrocław, 1978, pp. 157–85 (173, 177, 179).

[10] For a useful typology of incunabula correctors' interventions, beyond the essays in this Companion, see L. Hellinga, 'Proofreading and Printing in Mainz in 1459', in L. Hellinga, *Texts in Transit: Manuscript to Proof and Print in the Fifteenth Century*, Leiden and Boston, 2014, pp. 102–55. She does not, however, consider editions filled with numerical tables.

[11] E. Zinner (ed.), *Der deutsche Kalender des Johannes Regimontan, Nürnberg, um 1474: Faksimiledruck nach dem Exemplar der Preussischen Staatsbibliothek*, Leipzig, 1937, pp. 9–10. See Johannes Regiomon-tanus, *Kalendarium* [Latin], Nuremberg, Johannes Regiomontanus, 1474, 4° (ISTC ir00092000), sig. [C2]r and his *Kalender* [German], Nuremberg, Johannes Regiomontanus, 1474, 4° (ISTC ir00100300), sig. [B9]r.

[12] E. Zinner, *Leben und Wirken des Johannes Müller von Königsberg genannt Regiomontanus*, Munich, 1938, p. 141.

These questions prompt three hypotheses. Given Regiomontanus's complaint, in the 1471 letter to Roder, about the inconvenience of resetting type for numerical tables, and given my challenge of visually identifying (rather than machine-reading) stop-press changes in a work of 400,000 numerical digits, I hypothesise first that in-shop manuscript corrections will be much easier for me to find, and far more numerous, than stop-press corrections.

Those 400,000 digits, however, are not random. The days of each month are printed twice, as decimal numbers ranging from 1 to 31. The hours of the aspects are also decimal numbers, ranging from 1 to 24. And the planetary positions are specified by zodiacal sign (entered by manuscript into the columns on the verso sides) and sexagesimal numbers of degrees and minutes. These types of numbers constrain the digits a compositor or proofreader expects to see as they run their eye down a column in the table. Surely Regiomontanus's compositors and proofreaders would recognise that an entry for day '37' in January, an aspect at hour '26', or a position of Mars at Gemini '33;45' or '13;75' could not be correct. Likewise, they would know that planetary positions generally move smoothly from one day to the next, i.e., that the positions in longitude change smoothly over time.[13] Such constrained sequences of numbers I shall call 'meaningful'. The superior planets move less than 30 arcminutes per day, the Sun, Venus, and Mercury by about 1 degree per day. Columns of sexagesimal numbers for the daily, sequential positions of these planets would thus be 'meaningful'. The Moon, however, moves from between 11 and 15 degrees per day, at a rate that changes dramatically over the month. Likewise, the times of syzygy (new and full moons) vary wildly over the course of the months and year. Numbers marking the Moon's course would thus be 'meaningless' to readers. Controlling their errors could only be achieved by comparison against a source.[14] Hence, I hypothesise that the 'meaningless' lunar data will show considerably more errors than do the 'meaningful' numbers in the *Ephemerides*. To use another metaphor, we are guessing that scribes and pressmen gained tacit knowledge about the expected behaviour of some numbers in astronomical tables.[15]

Finally, given the repetitive nature of printing thirty-two gatherings of the same layout and mise-en-page, we might expect the print shop to gain experience, even efficiency, over time.[16] Surely, they produced the final gathering in less time than they had required for the first gathering. But did the compositors (or scribes) commit fewer errors in the latter gatherings? Or did the readers of the proof sheets catch a greater percentage of the setting

---

[13] Although the compositors worked by lines (rows in the table), I presume that the proof sheet readers and correctors worked by column.

[14] The problem of errors in 'meaningless' numbers exists across all levels of written sources: the (i) initial computation of the astronomical data, presumably on loose sheets; (ii) their scribal transfer to gatherings arranged in the format of an ephemerides (see, e.g., Regiomontanus's autograph ephemerides, with daily planetary positions for the years 1448 and 1451–1463, in MS Vienna, ÖNB, Lat. 4988); (iii) preparation of the printer's copy; (iv) setting the type and pulling proof sheets; (v) post-printing correction of the gatherings before they leave the print shop.

[15] For a fascinating study of nineteenth-century non-Sanskrit reading compositors learning to set type in that language and controlling errors by arm muscle memory, see V. Singh, 'From Handwritten Copy to the Printed Page in Devanagari: Investigating the Curious Case of Friedrich Max Müller', *Journal of the Printing Historical Society*, 26, 2017, pp. 11–22. I thank a referee for suggesting this reference.

[16] Note that the calendrical format for each gathering meant that no casting off was required for the *Ephemerides*. The printers could have started printing with any sheet in a gathering. Cf. L. Hellinga, 'Notes on the Order of Setting a Fifteenth-Century Book', *Quaerendo*, 4, 1974, pp. 64–9.

errors in the latter gatherings? Of course, we might also argue that the printers and correctors became increasingly bored, over time, by all the numbers and thus issued the final gatherings less carefully corrected than the initial gatherings. Without knowing more about the organisation of Regiomontanus's print shop we can hardly evaluate these alternatives. But we might hypothesise, more neutrally, that the printing errors will show some change over time, assuming that the gatherings were printed diachronically in order of the calendar years.

As with most incunabula, we have neither printer's copy nor proof sheets for Regiomontanus's *Ephemerides*.[17] Our investigation of Regiomontanus's efforts to control errors can consider only surviving copies of the edition. I will first characterise the forty surviving copies, then examine stop-press corrections, and finally consider the manuscript corrections. In light of our hypotheses, I will conclude that Regiomontanus's printers, after the formes had been proofed, made no stop-press corrections; that the overwhelming majority of the knife-and-pen corrections were made in the print shop and occur in 'meaningless' numbers; and that the distribution of errors did not change appreciably across the thirty-two gatherings of the edition. On average, Regiomontanus's printers made slightly more than one knife-and-pen correction per folio in the fully corrected copies (roughly three-quarters of the print run) that left the Nuremberg print shop.

THE EXTANT COPIES AND THEIR EXAMINATION

At present, forty copies of the 1474 *Ephemerides* are known (Table 15.2). Of these, nineteen are complete, covering the years 1475–1506; another twelve preserve at least fifteen of the original thirty-two gatherings (or years of data). Four copies consist of a single gathering. I have autopsied twenty-four copies. For the remaining copies I have inspected photographs or digital scans, in a few cases of the entire volume, more usually of only selected pages. Using partial scans means that I have not inspected every folio of every known copy; my quantitative data on corrections are thus relative rather than absolute.

---

[17] Surviving proofs of other incunabula, mostly for pages of text, show that initial type settings were not infrequently modified. Cf. C. Wehmer, 'Ein frühes Korrekturblatt aus der Schöfferschen Offizin', *Gutenberg-Jahrbuch*, 1932, pp. 118–22; F. R. Goff, 'A Few Proof Sheets of the Fifteenth Century', *Gutenberg-Jahrbuch*, 1963, pp. 81–7; E. Dal, 'Einige Korrekturbogen und andere Seltenheiten in der Königlichen Bibliothek Kopenhagen', *Beiträge zur Inkunabelkunde*, 3rd ser., 1, 1965, pp. 105–8; D. Rogers, 'A Glimpse into Zainer's Workshop at Augsburg c. 1475', in L. Hellinga and H. Härtel (eds), *Buch und Text im 15. Jahrhundert*, Hamburg, 1981, pp. 145–63; Hellinga, 'Proofreading' (n. 10 above); P. Needham, 'The Cambridge Proof Sheets of Mentelin's Latin Bible', *Transactions of the Cambridge Bibliographical Society*, 9, 1986, pp. 1–35; O. Duntze and F. Eisermann, 'Fortschritt oder Fidibus? Zur Bestimmung, Bewahrung und Bedeutung von Inkunabelfragmenten', in H.-P. Neuheuser and W. Schmitz (eds), *Fragment und Makulatur: Überlieferungsstörungen und Forschungsbedarf bei Kulturgut in Archiven und Bibliotheken*, Wiesbaden, 2015, pp. 281–307; and, finally, Randall Herz's contribution in this Companion. For amusing commentary on typographical corrections, tucked into colophons, title-pages and dedications issued by Regiomontanus's contemporary Nuremberg printer, Anton Koberger, see O. Hase, *Die Koberger: Eine Darstellung des buchhändlerischen Geschäftsbetriebes in der Zeit des Überganges vom Mittelalter zur Neuzeit*, Leipzig 1885, pp. 81–106.

Table 15.2 Known copies of Regiomontanus, *Ephemerides 1475–1506*

Current location	Shelfmark	Gatherings	Examination	Cor. hand
Uncorrected copies				
Budapest, Eötvös Loránd Library	Inc. 815	1485	Scans complete	
The Hague, Museum Meermanno	4 F 057	Complete	Scans partial	
London, Wellcome Collection	EPB incunabula 3.a.10	1476–1477, 1479–1484, 1487–1492, 1499, 1501, 1504–1505	Physical	
Milan, Ambrosiana	Inc. 1445	1490–1506	Scans partial	
Modena, Estense	Alpha H.7.8	Complete	Scans partial	
Munich, BSB (1)	4 L.impr.c.n.mss. 74	1477–1502	Physical	
Paris, BnF (1)	Res P-V-140 (2)	Complete	Physical	
Paris, BnF (2)	Res P-V-141	1481–1484, 1486–1488, 1490	Physical	
Perugia, Augusta	Inc. 243	Complete	Scans partial	
Rome, Vallicelliana	Inc. 315	1475–1483	Scans partial	
Vatican City, BAV (1)	Stamp.Ross. 1947	Complete	Scans partial	
Corrected copies				
Bamberg, SB	Inc.typ.H.IV.22	1475–1505	Physical	
Budapest, OZK	Inc. 1102	1489–1491, 1493–1506	Scans partial	B
Kraków, MNK	VII-XV.80	1481–1506	Scans complete	A
Halle, ULB	Pd 1897, 8°	Complete	Physical	B
Klosterneuburg, StiftsB	Ct 1367	Complete	Scans partial	A
Leipzig, BSM	Klemm II 24,5a	Complete	Physical	A
Leipzig, UB	Ed.vet. 1474,9	Complete	Physical	A

Continued

Table 15.2 *Continued*

Current location	Shelfmark	Gatherings	Examination	Cor. hand
London, BL	C.16.h.5	Complete	Physical	A
London, RAS	SR 6 A 15	Complete	Physical	A
Madrid, BPR	I/210	1475–1499	Scans complete	A
Manchester, Rylands	Special Collections 17,407	1475, 1491–1506 (lacks Jan–Apr 1494)	Physical	A
Munich, BSB (2)	Rar. 299	Complete	Physical, scans	B
Munich, BSB (3)	Rar. 299a	1475–1489	Physical	
Neuburg, SB	03/Inc. 327	1492–1505	Physical	A
Nuremberg, GNM	Inc. 1327	1491	Physical	B
Nuremberg, SB	Math. 512.4°	1475–1500	Physical	B
Padua, BU	Sec. XV 544	Complete	Scans partial	B
Paris, BnF (3)	Res V-1107	1491–1506	Physical	A
Stuttgart, WLB (1)	Inc.qt. 13,790	Complete	Physical	B
Stuttgart, WLB (2)	HB XI 27	1489–1504	Physical	A
Vatican City, BAV (2)	Inc.IV.286(int.2)	Complete	Scans partial	B
Vatican City, BAV (3)	Inc.IV.570(int.2)	1475–1481	Scans partial	B
Vienna, ÖNB (1)	Ink 19.G.3	Complete	Physical	A
Vienna, ÖNB (2)	Ink 4.H.7	Complete	Physical, scans complete	A
Vienna, ÖNB (3)	Ink 6.H.17 Teil 1	1476–1477, 1479–1481	Physical	
Wrocław, UB (1)	XV.Q.487	Complete	Scans partial	B
Wrocław, UB (2)	XV.Q.421,2	1506	Scans complete	
W"urzburg, UB (1)	I.t.q. 5	Complete	Physical	B
W"urzburg, UB (2)	I.t.q. 6	1475, Dec 1494 (aspects)	Physical	

Furthermore, given the skill with which many of the knife-and-pen emendations were made, many of these changes escape the reader's eye (at least, this reader's eye) when the page is viewed directly from above. Only by scanning the printed surface at an oblique angle can some of the emendation be noticed, not as a manuscript insertion but as a knife disturbance of the paper's surface. Digital scans, of course, do not allow such scrutiny of the physical surfaces.

The completeness and consistency of my quantitative data on the in-shop corrections are limited for several additional reasons. First, since I discovered ever more in-shop corrections (including one after this chapter was in proof) over the course of my multi-year peregrinations to the holding libraries, some of my physical examination reports are partial, since I have not been able to revisit some of the copies.[18] Just as Regiomontanus's pressmen, as I shall argue below, gradually discovered errors over the months of printing the edition, so too did I gradually discover their corrections over the years of conducting this analysis. A complete study of the variations in this edition would require machine-reading all the extant copies and machine-searching for variants, a project I am happy to bequeath to some future scholar of the digital humanities.

Second, as is well known, copies of printed ephemerides quickly became writing diaries for their early owners. By the 1520s, a new genre of the printed *Schreibkalender* would emerge, as printers began arranging astronomical, astrological, and medical information and the feast days for a month on the verso sides of an opening, leaving blank the rectos for readers' insertions.[19] Some of the extant ephemerides in my sample have owners' entries, including corrections, jotted into the margins or across the erroneous typescript. I have ignored all such later manuscript additions and have attempted to consider only changes that are present in more than one copy and thus were undoubtedly added before the gatherings left Regiomontanus's print shop. But occasional owners' corrections may have inadvertently entered my list.

Third, the paper in some of the extant *Ephemerides* has been washed or otherwise treated by conservators (e.g., the Parisian copies). Such interventions can remove manuscript additions, including the print shop emendations. They do not, however, repair the knife damage to the paper surface and in many, but perhaps not all, cases I have been able to identify the knife-and-pen corrections even in the washed copies.

Finally, my analysis of 'errors' in Regiomontanus's *Ephemerides* is aided by the fact that I can repeat his computation of planetary positions and times of the aspects, including syzygies. My computations (Table 15.5) generally match Regiomontanus's to about ± 2–3

---

[18] Cf. the classic study of fifteen copies of an early Aldine by C. F. Bühler, 'Stop-Press and Manuscript Corrections in the Aldine Edition of Benedetti's *Diaria De Bello Carolino*', *Papers of the Bibliographical Society of America*, 43, 1949, pp. 365–73. Presumably, Bühler identified all seventeen of the manuscript emendations in the first copy he inspected; but in a later study he discovered manuscript emendations, as did I, after conducting his initial autopsies. See C. F. Bühler, 'Manuscript Corrections in the Aldine Edition of Bembo's *De aetna*', *Papers of the Bibliographical Society of America*, 45, 1951, pp. 136–42 (137). See also Sachet's and Della Rocca de Candal's contributions to this Companion.

[19] For a recent study of the owner's insertions in one of Regiomontanus's *Ephemerides* (BSB (1)), see M. Michalski, *Dr. Balthasar Mansfeld (1440–1503): Ein Arzt in München an der Wende vom Mittelalter zur Neuzeit*, Munich, 2017. Cf. H. Tersch, *Schreibkalender und Schreibkultur: Zur Rezeptionsgeschichte eines frühen Massenmediums*, Graz and Feldkirch, 2008; R. L. Kremer, 'Readers becoming Authors: Manuscript Entries in Sixteenth-Century Printed *Schreibkalender*', paper presented at the Renaissance Society of America, Chicago, April 2017.

minutes, which means that I can detect his 'errors' (whether computational, scribal, or typographical) when they exceed this amount, especially when consisting of tens of minutes or full degrees. But I have not yet determined which version of the Parisian Alfonsine Tables (henceforth PAT) Regiomontanus employed for computing his ephemerides and calendars. I use the *editio princeps* of PAT, printed by Ratdolt in Venice in 1483, a version not available for Regiomontanus who died in 1476. The PAT, however, exist in hundreds of manuscript copies, most of which transmit very similar numerical material. We do know, however, that in 1456, Regiomontanus and his teacher, Georg Peurbach (1423–1461), computed positions with the tables of Giovanni Bianchini (c. 1400–c. 1469), which are based on the PAT but rearranged to reduce the labour of computation. When their independent results disagreed, they computed again with the PAT. That is, Peurbach and Regiomontanus considered Bianchini's tables equivalent to the PAT. I have not thoroughly compared these table sets; indeed, presumably no one has since 1456. We do know that by 1471 Regiomontanus was comparing his observations against 'Alfonsine computation'. My use of the PAT, when evaluating his *Ephemerides*, surely should be sufficient for a precision of several minutes.[20] As I shall argue below, Regiomontanus's errors suggest that his lunar positions were computed via Bianchini's tables.

STOP-PRESS CORRECTIONS ... OR IMPOSITION PROBLEMS

Indications of what seemed to me to be stop-press corrections appeared in only one copy of Regiomontanus's edition, *viz.*, Munich, BSB (1), acquired in 1478 and heavily annotated by the Munich physician Balthasar Mansfeld (1440–1503).[21] He entered many hand-written corrections, often in red ink, into his copy that do not match the print shop corrections.[22] And he tended to overwrite the printed numbers rather than remove them by scraping.[23]

---

[20] See Peurbach to Johann Bohemus, 1456, in A. Czerny, 'Aus dem Briefwechsel des grossen Astronomen Georg von Peurbach', *Archiv für österreichische Geschichte*, 72, 1888, pp. 281–304 (302); Johannes Schöner, *Scripta clarissimi mathematici M. Ioanis Regiomontani*, Nuremberg, Johann vom Berg and Ulrich Neuber, 1544, 4° (USTC 692614), fols 42v–43r. Regiomontanus's *Nachlaß* includes an autograph copy of Bianchini's tables but not the PAT. See I. Neske, *Die Handschriften der Stadtbibliothek Nürnberg, Bd. V: Die lateinischen mittelalterlichen Handschriften, Varia, 13.–15. und 16.–18. Jahrhundert*, Wiesbaden, 1997, pp. 90–1; J. Chabás and B. R. Goldstein, *The Astronomical Tables of Giovanni Bianchini*, Leiden, 2009. I have reduced all the computational steps of the PAT, including looking up values in tables and interpolating, to a spreadsheet. I use floating-point rather than sexagesimal arithmetic; at a precision of minutes, this change is not noticeable.

[21] Michalski, *Balthasar Mansfeld* (n. 19 above), p. 16.

[22] He also used brown and black ink, and nibs of differing widths, unlike the print shop correctors who corrected an entire exemplar with the same ink and nib. Presumably, Mansfeld entered his corrections as he identified the errors over the course of years.

[23] I find only one example of scraping in BSB (1), for 7 July 1483, where a printed '9' is altered by knife to resemble a '0'.

Mansfeld was thus an early owner who explicitly sought to enhance the quantitative reliability of the *Ephemerides*. But his exemplar also displays two printed features that I have not found in the other copies, features that I initially attributed to stop-press corrections.

Closer analysis, however, reveals that problems of imposition and not stop-press resetting generated the two unusual features of BSB (1): the aspects page for December 1480 is blank; and the December 1484 aspects page instead displays the aspects page for December 1483 (Fig. 15.4). Each gathering of the ephemerides, providing the data for one year in quarto format, requires fourteen leaves printed on three and one-half sheets. The gutter is formed by pages for the June positions and June aspects. The outermost sheet, or wrapper of the gathering, consists of the first leaf, blank on both sides, and the fourteenth leaf, bearing the December aspects and a blank verso. The second half of this sheet is discarded from the gathering. In BSB (1), the wrapper for the 1480 gathering is missing, so the December 1480 aspects are missing. And a wrapper for the 1483 gathering has been incorrectly placed in the gathering for 1484. As can be seen in Fig. 15.4, owner Mansfeld tried to add to his own copy, in brown ink, the missing syzygy times for December 1484. His manuscript times vary slightly from those in the printed gathering; and he failed to add the missing time for 31 December 1484. But he corrected the date at the top of the page (changing '1483' to '1484') and apparently realised that the imposition of his book was incorrect. I have not found imposition problems in any of the other surviving copies of the edition.

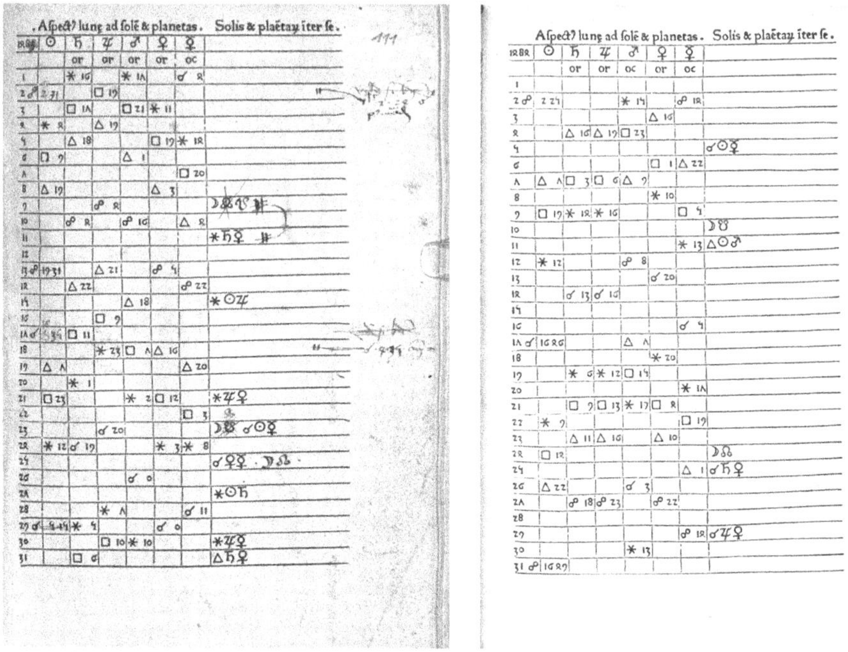

FIG. 15.4. Imposition problem for the December 1484 aspects page in Regiomontanus, *Ephemerides* (see Fig. 15.2). BSB (1) for December 1483, partly corrected by owner to correspond to December 1484 (left); BSB (2) for December 1484 (right). Munich, Bayerische Staatsbibliothek, 4 L.impr.c.n.mss.74 and Rar. 299.

No stop-press resettings were involved in these problems within BSB (1). Although machine reading and analysis would be required to confirm the absence of stop-press changes, it would appear as if Regiomontanus and his pressmen, while printing the 448 leaves of the *Ephemerides* were, indeed, loath to reset a forme after the proofs had been judged satisfactory. Regiomontanus's comment to Roder, in 1471, about the bother of resetting formes seems prophetic.

GLOSSED INSTRUCTIONS FOR CORRECTING SEQUENTIAL 'BATCH ERRORS'

The most apparent print shop corrections are four manuscript glosses placed at the lower margin of a page, instructing readers to add a fixed quantity to a sequential series of lunar positions. In the opening year of 1475, 30 arcminutes (half a degree) are to be added to each lunar longitude from 10 June to 7 July. In 1479, 30 arcminutes must be added from 13 May to 9 June. In 1491, 11 arcminutes must be added from 21 January to 17 February, except for the dates 23, 29, 30, and 31 January and 13 and 14 February. And finally in 1498, 30 arcminutes must be subtracted from 19 to 30 July, except for the date 23 (Fig. 15.5). Together, a total of eighty-nine lunar positions are to be corrected by the reader. Copies that bear these manuscript instructions I shall call 'corrected'; copies lacking these instructions are 'uncorrected'. As can be seen from Table 15.2, eleven copies or roughly one-quarter of my sample, are uncorrected, including BSB (1).

Two hands glossed these instructions, both using the same brown ink and pens of roughly similar nib width (Fig. 15.5); neither seems to make an effort to mimic the neat Roman type used by Regiomontanus. Of the twenty-nine corrected copies, I have photographs or notes for twenty-six of these glosses, fourteen by Hand A, twelve by Hand B. We might guess that

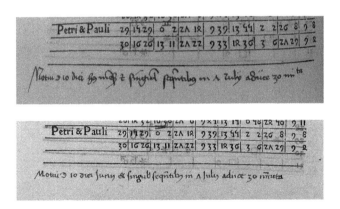

FIG. 15.5. Two hands for the glossed instructions, planetary positions, July 1498 in Regiomontanus, *Ephemerides* (see Fig. 15.2). Hand A, Leipzig BSM (above); Hand B, Padua (below). Leipzig, Deutsches Buch- und Schriftmuseum der Deutschen Nationalbibliothek, Klemm-Sammlung, II 24,5a; Padua, Biblioteca Universitaria, Sec. XV 544.

two correctors evenly divided the work as they glossed the sheets. Generally, the wording of the glosses remains identical in all exemplars. But for the 1491 gloss, Hand A consistently wrote 'Motui lune 21 diei mensis huius in 17 februarii adiice in 11 minuta […]' as Hand B wrote 'Motui lune 21 diei Januarii in 17 februarii adiice 11 minuta […]' (see Table 2 for the distribution of glossing hands in the copies). Several Nuremberg citizens are known to have interacted with Regiomontanus during his few years in that town (1471–1475), but I have not been able to link known Nuremberg hands to the glosses found in the *Ephemerides*.[24] And neither Hand A nor Hand B is Regiomontanus's, which is well known from several large autograph manuscripts.[25]

The nature of these 'batch errors', nearly a month of sequential lunar positions all shifted by the same amount, suggests that these are not the results of 'row slippage', i.e., when a scribe, copying numbers by column, skips one value and shifts all subsequent values up one row before catching the mistake and returning the numbers in their proper rows. A closer look reveals that for three of these sequential errors the period requiring correction was twenty-eight days, the length of the mean lunar month. This suggests that the calculator reckoned lunar positions month by month, looking up the initial mean lunar longitude and then computing the daily intervals for true positions. Further investigation reveals that each of the three 28-day periods, denoted by the two glossators, cover one anomalistic cycle of the Ptolemaic lunar model, as the body moves around the epicycle from apogee to apogee. This strongly suggests that Regiomontanus used the astronomical tables of Bianchini to compute the daily lunar positions.[26] Probably compiled around 1442, Bianchini's tables reconfigure the PAT into a new format based on the number of days a planet has moved from its apogee in the epicycle. The tables are based on the periods of anomaly and were thus designed for

---

[24] The local merchant Bernard Walther (1430–1504), who continued Regiomontanus's astronomical observations from August 1475 until his own death and who was rumoured to have provided financial support for the print shop, jotted weather observations (in German) for 1487 into his copy of the ephemerides, ÖNB (2). His German hand does not match the Latin Hands A or B. Conrad Heinfogel (1450–1517) assisted Walther with the solar observations in 1476–1477 and later copied some of the data into MS Munich, BSB, Clm 24103, fols 47r–54v. He also recorded personal notes from 1502 onward in a later printed almanac (ISTC is00791000, copy at Bamberg, Staatsbibliothek I-IV-21), but his Latin hand does not match those of Regiomontanus's glossators. Perhaps the best candidate is the Nuremberg metal craftsman (*Drahtzieher*) Conrad Scherpp, who had matriculated at the university in Vienna in 1442 and at Regiomontanus's death inherited half of the latter's books and astronomical instruments. Although his name appears not infrequently in Nuremberg archives, no samples of Scherpp's handwriting are known. See H. Petz, 'Urkundliche Nachrichten über den literarischen Nachlass Regiomontans und B. Walthers 1478–1522', *Mitteilungen des Vereins für Geschichte der Stadt Nürnberg*, 7, 1888, pp. 237–62 (242) ; Zinner, *Regiomontanus* (n. 1 above), pp. 176, 246; Wingen-Trennhaus, 'Frühdrucker' (n. 3 above), p. 67; W. von Stromer, 'Meister Konrad Scherp, Regiomontans Experte für Feinmechanik in der Nürnberger Officina und für den wissenschaftlichen Buchdruck', *Mitteilungen des Vereins für die Geschichte der Stadt Nürnberg*, 79, 1992, pp. 123–32, who emphatically suggests, with little evidence, that Scherpp assembled and then operated Regiomontanus's press. Regiomontanus's colophons are terse and provide no information about the personnel in his shop. Cf. G. Reichhart, 'Beiträge zur Incunabelnkunde, 1,1: Alphabetisch geordnetes Verzeichniss der Correctoren der Buchdruckereien des 15. Jahrhunderts', *Zentralblatt für Bibliothekswesen, Beiheft 14*, 1895, pp. 2–185.

[25] For Regiomontanus's hand from 1462 through 1472, see the autograph of his *Defensio Theonis*, reproduced in facsimile at http://regio.dartmouth.edu.

[26] Chabás and Goldstein, *Bianchini* (n. 20 above), pp. 45–59.

computing daily ephemerides like Regiomontanus's; to reduce the labour of tabular inter-polation, Bianchini used velocities to approximate values solved more exactly in the PAT. This explains why Regiomontanus computed the daily lunar positions in twenty-eight-day 'batches'. Errors in the first true longitude would thus be carried through all twenty-eight days of the lunar cycle. Hence the glossators could correct all twenty-eight entries by adding or subtracting a common value.

For the 1475, 1479, and 1491 batch errors, the announced corrections of 30, 30, and -11 arcminutes do nicely reduce the errors. When I compute lunar positions following what I imagine to be the procedures of the PAT[27] (Table 5). I find average errors in the printed values for those batches of, respectively, 29, 28, and -11 arcminutes. Hence, the glossators' corrections would reduce the errors to ± 1–2 arcminutes, i.e., to the precision of the lunar positions generally in the ephemerides (Table 15.5). Note that the 1491 gloss indicates (cor-rectly) that no corrections are required for six days within the twenty-eight, an irregularity that I cannot explain by reference to computational or scribal practices. Likewise, the 1498 batch error covers only twelve days, with one intermediate value exempted from correc-tion. I find the printed errors for this batch to average 9 arcminutes, again matching the announced correction of 10 arcminutes. The fact that this batch does not extend for the full twenty-eight days suggests that Regiomontanus may not have consistently employed his 'batch computation' procedure for all the lunar positions, or perhaps that several different computers had prepared the lunar data for 1498.

We might ask how the correctors in the print shop (Regiomontanus himself?) discov-ered these four batch errors in the printed sheets. Given the amount of labour required to compute a lunar longitude, we would not expect them to have made spot checks, over the full thirty-two years, of independently computed lunar positions. A check of the first differ-ences of the printed daily lunar values (i.e., the distance travelled per day) would not raise a sequential 30-arcminute shift above the computational noise. But a check of second dif-ferences (i.e., the rate of change of the daily lunar travel) might reveal a 30-arcminute shift. Fig. 15.6 displays the second differences across three 28-day intervals in 1475. The red lines

[27] For the lunar computations, I place Nuremberg's meridian 84 minutes of time east of Toledo, follow-ing the 'table of places' given in Regiomontanus's printed calendar editions of 1474. The 1474 ephemerides does not include a table of places. This meridian matches that I extract by least squares from Regiomon-tanus's lunar positions in the ephemerides. A meridian of 84 minutes of time east, for Nuremberg, is not found in any other 'tables of places' I know and does not match the usual Alfonsine meridian of 67 minutes of time east for that town. But it does match the meridian in Biachini's tables. Regiomontanus's earlier ephemerides, computed for 1448 and 1451–1462 (n. 13 above), are for 80 time minutes east, the usual Alfonsine meridian for Vienna (where Regiomontanus lived during those years) and the value Regiomontanus glossed in his autograph of Biachini's tables (MS Nuremberg, Stadtbibliothek, Cent V57, fol. 23v). Regiomontanus had also prepared an ephemerides for 1463, specified for 'Ferrara and Bologna', with the lunar positions computed, according to my least squares analysis, for 84 time minutes east (ÖNB, Lat. 4988, fols 188Ar–188Nr). Note, however, that the true syzygy times in the ephemerides, cor-rected with Peurbach's equation of time, are computed for a meridian 65 minutes of time east. This suggests that (i) Regiomontanus used Bianchini's tables to compute lunar positions for the ephemerides; (ii) Regiomontanus had computed these positions during the 1460s while he was in Italy close to the meridian of Ferrara; (iii) Regiomontanus computed the syzygy times for the ephemerides after he had arrived in Nuremberg. The 1474 ephemerides thus silently combines computations completed for Fer-rara and for Nuremberg. See R. L. Kremer and J. D. Dobrzycki, 'Alfonsine Meridians: Tradition Versus Experience in Astronomical Practice c. 1500', *Journal for the History of Astronomy*, 29, 1998, 187–99 (196); Chabás and Goldstein, *Bianchini* (n. 20 above), p. 37.

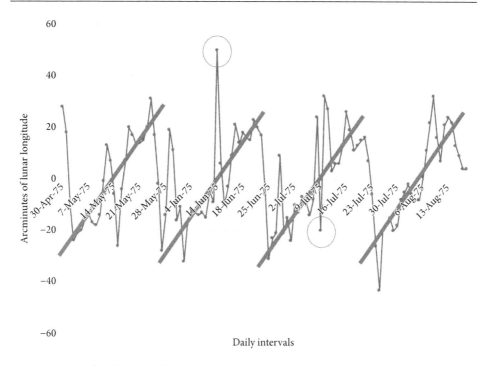

FIG. 15.6. Second differences of daily printed lunar longitudes, 30 April to 18 August 1475.

show the direction of the velocity changes; they cross the horizontal axis at the beginning of each twenty-eight-day interval. At the beginning and end of the 1475 batch error (from 10 June to 7 July), a large deviation occurs in the second difference (marked with red circles). Perhaps the correctors compiled lists of second differences to look for sequential batch errors in the printed sheets? Such a procedure, however, would have required considerable labour and, to my mind at least, would appear rather extravagant since only four batch errors were discovered in the 430 lunations represented in the ephemerides. My recomputation of the lunar positions for selected years (nineteen of the thirty-two) has identified no further twenty-eight-day 'batch errors' in Regiomontanus's work (Table 15.5). Whatever procedure the correctors deployed, it enabled them to detect all the large 'batch errors' in the thirty-two years of lunar positions.

Manuscript Correction of Individual Entries

In addition to the four glossed batch corrections, I have found more than 530 manuscript corrections of individual printed numbers or other symbols, identically entered in multiple copies of the 'corrected' group. This largely common set of corrections must have been inserted in the printed gatherings before they left the print shop. With a total of nearly 900

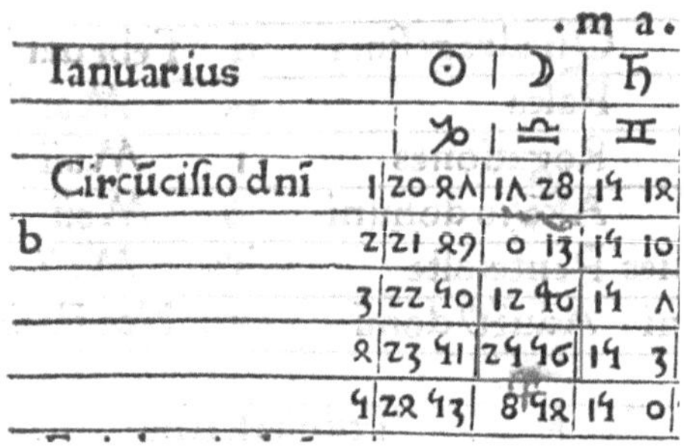

FIG. 15.7. Positions for January 1502 in Regiomontanus, *Ephemerides* (see Fig. 15.2), emending a printed '5' to a manuscript '4', but for the incorrect date. The 10-minute correction is needed for the 4th of the month, not the 3rd. Munich, Bayerische Staatsbibliothek, Rar. 299.

printed pages, Regiomontanus's ephemerides thus have one individual correction for about every two pages.

These individual corrections involve four slightly different types of interventions. First are manuscript additions without overwriting printed marks (twenty-nine cases). The correctors might add missing aspects, cancel an incorrectly placed aspect and write in the correct one, or insert missing digits (e.g., correcting a printed '28 4' to '28 54' with a manuscript '5'). Second are corrections with overwriting but no deleting of printed marks (twenty-three cases). Most common here is overwriting the digit '5', adding a loop to create the digit '4' (Fig. 15.7). Or one could convert the printed zodiacal sign Scorpio to Virgo merely by adding a curved stroke of the pen. Third and most frequent (477 cases) are knife-and-pen interventions. The correctors used a knife to scrape away the printed mark (usually a numerical digit) from the sheet and then overwrote, with a thin nib, the correct mark. Many of these insertions were skilfully executed so that, to the casual eye, all marks on the page look printed (Fig. 15.8). Others involve larger emendations that are quite visible (Fig. 15.9). Finally, in a few cases (three) correctors removed printed marks without inserting manuscript additions, such as scraping off an errantly placed aspects symbol or a superfluous digit (e.g., correcting '21 14' to '21 4'). But the similar appearance of a given correction in all the extant 'corrected' copies suggests that the entire print run for each gathering was corrected by the same hand. I have not noticed different styles for a given knife-and-pen intervention (i.e., a given date) in the extant copies.

The 'batch errors', discussed above, undoubtedly arose from problems in the printer's copy used by the compositors. Errors in individual entries, however, could originate from either the printer's copy or the typesetting. A comparison of the originally printed and the corrected numerical values shows that these individual errors are not generally random. Of the 484 individual numerical corrections, three-quarters correct a single digit in the sexagesimal number. As can be seen in Table 15.3, the most common correction was of 1 degree (164 cases). Since most planets move on average about 1 degree per day or less, we might expect a scribe (inspecting a manuscript copy) or proofreader (inspecting a printed sheet), scanning down the columns of daily planetary positions, to notice most errors of this magnitude (even without comparing the proof against the printer's copy or a scribal copy against a source manuscript) and to signal a need to correct a 1-degree error. The Moon, however, moves between 11 and 15 degrees per day, making it much more difficult to spot 1-degree errors without careful comparison against a source. And indeed, three-quarters (or 128) of the 1-degree corrections are for lunar positions; only nine are for the Sun, another

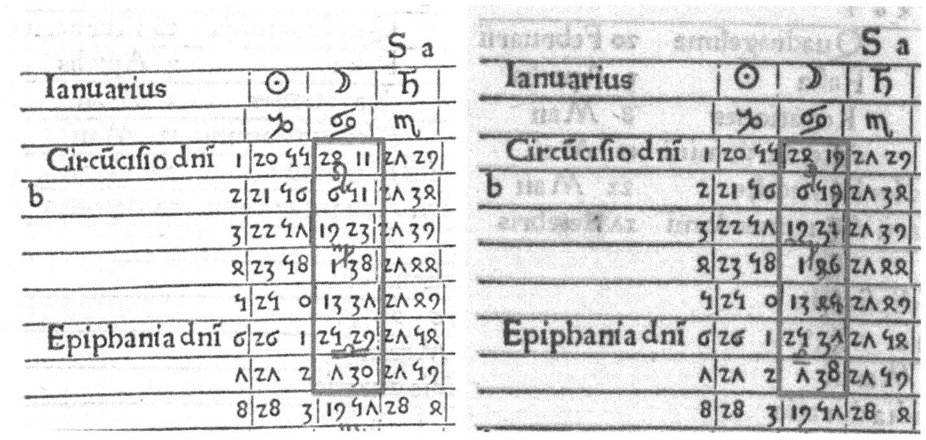

15: CONTROLLING ERRORS IN REGIOMONTANUS'S *EPHEMERIDES*   313

FIG. 15.8. Positions for January 1485 in Regiomontanus, *Ephemerides* (see Fig. 15.2). Budapest ELTE 'uncorrected' (left); Madrid 'corrected' (right). Budapest, ELTE University Library and Archives, Inc. 815; Madrid, Patrimonio Nacional, Real Biblioteca, i/210.

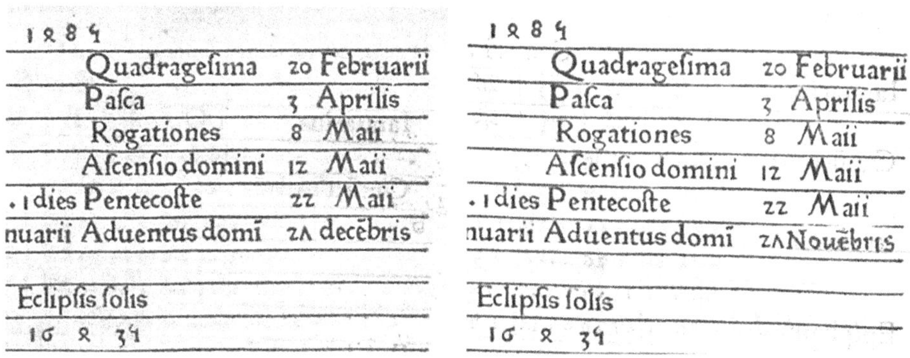

FIG. 15.9. Eclipse page for 1485 in Regiomontanus, *Ephemerides* (see Fig. 15.2). Budapest ELTE 'uncorrected' (left); BSB (2) 'corrected' (right). Budapest, ELTE University Library and Archives, Inc. 815; Munich, BSB Rar. 299.

nine for Mars. Here we see our first evidence supporting my hypothesis about 'meaningless' numbers and error propagation.

Table 15.3 indicates that the next most common one-digit corrections were for 10 minutes. Clearly, the lion's share of the one-digit errors that the correctors chose to correct involved a one-digit shift. Further analysis reveals that the likelihood of such one-digit shifts is roughly similar for all the digits (e.g., confusing 0–1, 1–2, … to 8–9) except for the 2–3 shift which occurs only about one-third as often. Now, if the compositor's type case had been arranged in numerical order, we might expect a higher frequency of single-digit typesetting errors; reaching for a '4' could yield a '3' or a '5' more often than, say, a '9'. Or when breaking up an earlier forme, a digit could be erroneously placed in a neighbouring box. Some one-digit errors might be generated by a scribe copying similarly shaped numerals, e.g., a '2' for a '3' or a '2' for a '1'. But it seems less likely for a fifteenth-century hand to confuse the '6' and '7'

Table 15.3 One–digit corrections

Size of correction	Number found
± 10 degs	8
± 2 degs	9
± 1 deg	164
± 40 mins	3
± 30 mins	19
± 20 mins	57
± 10 mins	119

or the '3' and '4'. Hence, most of the errors recorded in Table 15.3 must have been generated by Regiomontanus's compositors, not the scribes of the printer's copy.

In addition to the relatively large errors summarised in Table 15.3, Regiomontanus's correctors emended forty-four cases of error less than 10 arcminutes, including nine cases less than 5 arcminutes, which approaches the computational 'noise' in Regiomontanus's data. Given that level of noise, I have no way of determining how many errors of less than 10 arcminutes remain uncorrected in the imprint. But these forty-four corrections, 8% of the total set, suggest that Regiomontanus's standards for controlling printing error approached the precision of his standard for computational error!

Another non-random distribution of the individual errors appears when we consider the location of the corrections within the *Ephemerides*. 60% of the individual corrections, regardless of magnitude, appear in the Moon's positions. And these corrections are large; the average absolute value of the 329 lunar corrections is 65 arcminutes. Clearly, the scribes, compositors, and proof sheet readers erred most frequently in the 'meaningless' numbers. And given the central role of the Moon in late medieval astrology, Regiomontanus clearly (and understandably) had decided to focus his correcting energies, in the printed gatherings, on that body (Table 15.4).[28]

'Meaningless' numbers also appear on the eclipse pages placed at the head of each year in the ephemerides. The times and magnitudes of the year's eclipses and the dates of retrogradation for the planets are essentially random numbers. That eleven of the thirty-two eclipse pages bear corrections thus supports our hypothesis about increased chances for printing errors in 'meaningless' material, as do the relatively frequent corrections of syzygy times (two per year) on the aspects pages. Across the entire edition, the correction rate for lunar positions is about 3.5%, for syzygies 1.6%, for Mars only 0.4%.

The text in Regiomontanus's edition is very short, three pages in the first gathering, totalling about one thousand words. I find only one correction there, 'd fferentiis' corrected to 'differentiis'. Given our hypothesis about fewer corrections in 'meaningful' content, we

---

[28] Since I have not systematically checked the printed values for the other planets against my recomputation, I do not know whether they contain a greater percentage of uncorrected errors than do the lunar positions.

15: CONTROLLING ERRORS IN REGIOMONTANUS'S EPHEMERIDES   315

Table 15.4 Locations of the individual corrections

Location	Number	Location	Number
Moon	329	Nodes	13
Mars	42	Aspects	29
Jupiter	23	Syzygies	13
Venus	18	Eclipse pages	11
Sun	14	Column headings	6
Saturn	14	Canon (text)	1
Mercury	14		

should not be surprised to find only one individual correction in the Latin text. Likewise, I found very few corrections in the repeated paratexts for each gathering. The column headings, month names, date numbers from 1 to 31 running down the left side of each page, and year numbers at the top of the aspects pages are essentially never corrected.[29] And I noticed no uncorrected typographical errors in that material, which presumably became increasingly 'meaningful', to say nothing of tedious, as the pressmen produced the thirty-two gatherings.

To explore further the notion of tedium, we turn finally to the diachronic distribution of the 530-plus individual corrections in Regiomontanus's edition. Can we assume that the print shop prepared the gatherings in the order they appear in the bound volume? And that the knife-and-pen correctors worked through the printed gatherings in this order? Might we guess that, in preparing the first printed edition of astronomical tables, a book filled mostly with numbers, the compositors and proof sheet readers gained experience that enabled them, over time, to reduce the number of printing errors requiring knife-and-pen intervention? Or might the tedium of printing 400,000 numerical digits have made them increasingly careless over time and prone to introducing more typographical errors that required knife-and-pen intervention? Fig. 15.10 consolidates the individual corrections into two sets, lunar and all others, and displays the frequency of each over the thirty-two gatherings/years in the edition. The average number of individual corrections per gathering is seventeen, with a maximum of thirty-six corrections in 1490 and a minimum of three in 1506, the book's final gathering. No dramatic trends are visible in Fig. 15.10. The number of lunar corrections per gathering appears to increase slightly, in both relative and absolute terms, over the thirty-two years. The number of all other corrections decreases over time. But the number of corrections remains roughly constant from 1475 until 1505; only the final

---

[29] The only exceptions: '1480' is corrected once to '1490' and '1492' once to '1491'. Planetary signs as headers on the aspects pages are corrected twice and zodiacal signs, at the top of the columns for planetary positions, are corrected in four cases. Slight variations in the headers indicate that this material was reset for each gathering.

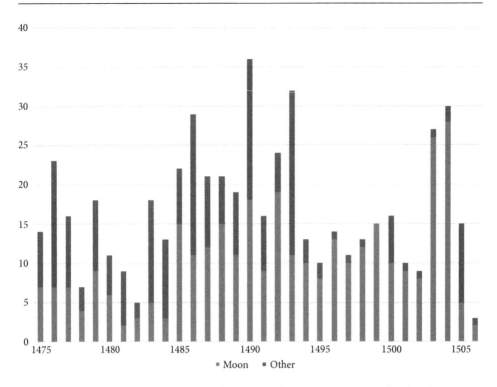

FIG. 15.10. Individual errors by year. Note the decline, after 1494, in errors unrelated to the Moon.

gathering shows a small number of corrections, perhaps the result of a demand to finally complete the project by rushing the last gathering through the process.

Given our minimal knowledge of the workflow in Regiomontanus's print shop, we should not over-interpret Fig. 15.10. However, the lack of a trend over time might indicate that the introduction and correction of errors, especially in the 'meaningless' numerical material, was random and hence impervious to enhanced experience or disciplined procedures inside the print shop. To explore this hypothesis I have recomputed the daily lunar positions for about half of the thirty-two years, seeking to explore how conscientiously Regiomontanus's procedures corrected those data. This exercise allows me to evaluate, together, the computational consistency of the computers who prepared the printer's source and the printing consistency of his compositors, proof sheet readers, and correctors in the shop. My recomputation, of course, cannot distinguish between these two different sites for error propagation; but it does enable me to estimate the size and number of the 'Alfonsine errors' remaining in the gatherings after they had passed through Regiomontanus's print shop.

Each year in Table 15.5 represents 365 (or 366) lunar positions. The second column indicates the number of positions, in the 'corrected' gatherings, that differ by more than 10 arcminutes from my PAT recomputation. The third column shows the three 'batch corrections' in the years, cases not included in the second column. Columns four and five list by year the average residuals (Regiomontanus-Kremer) and their standard deviations, after dropping the cases in columns two and three. Column six gives the meridians I extract by least squares from the residuals (after the drops) and suggests that Regiomontanus or his computers, for whatever reasons, were not always consistent in locating their meridian

Table 15.5 Residuals (daily corrected lunar positions − recomputed PAT positions) for selected years of Regiomontanus's *Ephemerides*

Year	≥10 minute outliers	Batch corrections dropped	Average residuals (minutes)	Stand. dev residuals (minutes)	Meridian (time minutes east of Toledo)
1475	4	28	0.1	2.3	84
1476	14	0	−0.4	2.5	84
1477	7	0	−0.3	2.4	84
1478	6	0	−0.3	2.3	84
1479	4	28	−0.1	2.0	84
1480	2	0	−0.02	2.2	84
1489	3	0	−0.1	2.6	85
1490	3	0	−0.2	2.3	84
1491	10	18	−0.2	2.6	84
1492	17	0	−0.3	2.9	84
1493	20	0	−0.1	2.8	86
1494	2	0	−0.05	2.2	85
1498	2	6	−0.05	2.3	84
1501	3	0	0.05	2.5	86
1502	3	0	0.5	2.3	84
1503	1	0	−0.2	2.3	85
1504	3	0	−0.2	2.3	84
1505	1	0	0.2	2.5	84
1506	1	0	−0.04	2.1	85

relative to Toledo (the meridian of the PAT). The standard deviations also correlate with the number of large outliers (see 1476, 1491, 1492, 1493), and we might wonder whether a different computer prepared those years. Over the other years, however, the standard deviations remain fairly constant (Fig. 15.11).[30]

Over the nineteen years I recomputed, Regiomontanus's printed lunar positions exhibit an average of six large outliers per year. Most of these errors are 10 or 20 arcminutes and presumably were created by the compositor, as argued above, but were not detected by the correctors. In four of the years, sequential sets of these large errors (ranging from three

---

[30] After completing this paper, I partially automated Bianchini's lunar tables and computed true positions for the first twenty-three days of January 1475. As can be seen in Fig. 15.11, Regiomontanus's positions match Bianchini's more closely than they match the PAT values, which further supports my hypothesis that Regiomontanus employed the former tables to compute his ephemerides. Elsewhere I will extend this quantitative analysis of Bianchini's tables and the PAT.

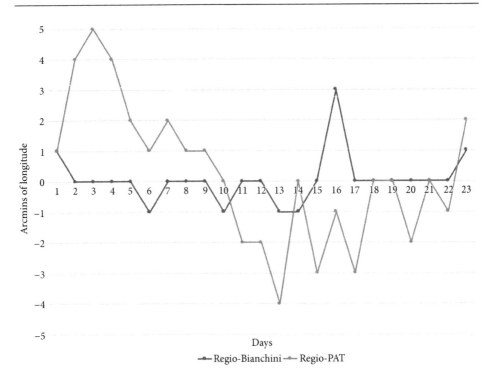

FIG. 15.11. Seeking Regiomontanus's computational algorithm for lunar positions, 1–23 January 1475.

to nine days) appear in the residuals.[31] Clearly, Regiomontanus's correcting protocols did not find all the errors greater than ± 10 arcminutes in his printed lunar positions. Above, I argued that his goal was to find and correct errors down to a few arcminutes. Table 15.5 suggests that he did not consistently realise this goal for the 'meaningless' numbers of the lunar positions.

Consistency and Process in Regiomontanus's Print Shop Correcting

Our analysis divided the surviving copies of the *Ephemerides* into two groups, those corrected by hundreds of knife-and-pen operations and four manuscript instructions for 'batch corrections' (twenty-nine copies) and those lacking these interventions (eleven copies).

---

[31] Large lunar error sequences: 12–18 August 1476, 16–23 April 1491, 7–15 July 1492, 8–16 January 1493. The first three of these sequences do not begin with the twenty-eight-day cycle noted above; if Regiomontanus's error detection protocol were built around that cycle, this would explain why it missed these three cycles. The 1493 sequence, however, does extend over twenty-eight days if errors down to ± 8 arcminutes are included. But the errors from 6 January–2 February 1493 show a sinusoidal pattern that suggests a different computational irregularity than we found in the four 'batch errors' discussed above. I cannot explain the January 1493 errors; in any case, they were not discovered by Regiomontanus's correctors.

15: CONTROLLING ERRORS IN REGIOMONTANUS'S EPHEMERIDES   319

A closer examination reveals that Regiomontanus's correctors did not work consistently within either of these groups. Not all 'corrected' copies listed in Table 15.2 carry identical corrections and not all 'uncorrected' copies are entirely uncorrected.

Consider first the corrected 'uncorrected' copies. I have found a very small number of in-shop corrections in both 'corrected' and 'uncorrected' copies. For example, the three aspects for 30 June 1483 were mistakenly printed one line lower, with the date printed as '31'. This 'meaningful' error obviously caught someone's eye. In every copy I have seen, the '31' has been scraped off, the three printed aspects cancelled (in black or brown ink, by at least two different hands) and entered by hand on the line above (Fig. 15.12).

Another knife-and-pen correction on the aspects page for 12 March 1488, correcting a syzygy time from '12 23' to '23 7', appears in every copy I inspected, as does the knife-and-pen correction of a Venus position for 25 August 1488. Other interventions are less consistent. The time of the solar aspect for 29 August 1476 is knife-and-pen corrected from '21' to '19' in four of the 'uncorrected' copies but not in the Perugia and Rome Vallicelliana 'uncorrected' copies; likewise, it is corrected in only four (Munich, BSB, copies 2 and 3; Vatican City, Biblioteca Apostolica Vaticana (BAV), copies 2 and 3) of the sixteen 'corrected' copies I have seen.[32] And a set of eight sequential solar longitudes, in August 1476, are knife-and-pen corrected in some 'uncorrected' copies (Paris, Bibliothèque nationale de France (BnF), copy 1; Vatican City, BAV, copy 1; and the single copies in London, Wellcome Collection and Modena, Biblioteca Estense Universitaria) but not in others (Perugia, Biblioteca Augusta; Rome, Biblioteca Vallicelliana; The Hague, Museum Meermanno). This set of solar corrections appears consistently, however, in all the 'corrected' copies I have seen.

Alas, these examples of corrections in the 'uncorrected' copies are too few to afford many insights into the correcting process for the edition. But we do note that the five examples cited above (the only cases of corrections found in at least four 'uncorrected' copies) appear

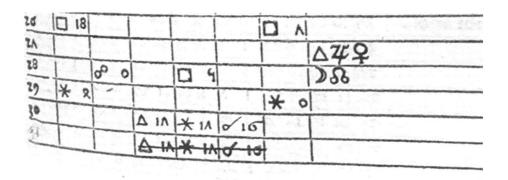

FIG. 15.12. Knife-and-pen correction for 30 June 1483, in an 'uncorrected' copy of Regiomontanus, *Ephemerides* (see Fig. 15.2). Vatican City, Biblioteca Apostolica Vaticana, Stamp.Ross. 1947.

---

[32] ÖNB (3) has the '21' removed but no number has been inserted by hand, so that the correction was left, most likely inadvertently, unfinished.

in the early gatherings of the *Ephemerides*, from 1476 to 1488. This fact prompts us to imagine a two-phase scenario for the in-shop correction of gatherings after their completed printing. Perhaps the gatherings for the early years, through 1488, were sparingly knife-and-pen corrected (fewer than a dozen interventions) for the entire run. Presumably these errors were discovered over time, so that as sets of these gatherings started leaving the shop, the earlier departures contained fewer, the later departures more, of the early knife-and-pen corrections. During this phase, perhaps a quarter of the print run left the shop, comprising our 'uncorrected' copies. Then at some point someone discovered that the gatherings, both before and after 1488, contained many more typographical errors, and a massive knife-and-pen correction process (more than 530 separate interventions) was launched, with few or none of the remaining copies leaving the shop before all had been corrected. Only after all the copies had been corrected did sales resume, creating our 'corrected' copies. Hence, rather than instigating many stop-press interruptions during printing, Regiomontanus (or his printers) made instead a single 'stop-sales' interruption, during which they knife-and-pen corrected three-quarters of the print run. Such a scenario would explain many of the correction patterns I have found in the forty surviving copies of the edition.

Finally, consider the variations in the 'corrected' copies, produced during the second phase proposed above. Given the way I collected my sample of corrections over time (undoubtedly a time considerably longer than that spent by the correctors in Regiomontanus's shop), I cannot fully evaluate the 'efficiency' of corrections in individual exemplars. But we can gain a general impression of how much variation remains in the set of 'corrected' copies. Of the nineteen known complete copies, I have autopsied ten. In those ten, the number of corrections in a given copy ranges from a maximum of 514 to a minimum of 467; and the number of corrections not made (i.e., found in other exemplars) ranges from nine to twenty-one. Hence, of the 530-plus in-shop corrections I found, the correction rates in the ten complete copies range from 96 to 98%. Several correctors failed to insert sets of sequential knife-and-pen corrections (Stuttgart (1), Würzburg (1), Halle), which lowered their correction rates to 96%. But on average, the correctors during the second phase inserted, in any given 'corrected' volume, about 97% of the corrections, with the missed corrections (3 out of every 100) scattered randomly across the gatherings and, presumably, inadvertently skipped. Since the lion's share of these corrections, as noted above, concern 'meaningless' numbers, we might conclude that Regiomontanus's procedures for controlling errors in this, the first printed edition of astronomical tables, deserve high praise. But until other early editions of numerical tables have been similarly studied, such praise might be premature.[33]

---

[33] Bühler, 'Stop-Press' (n. 18 above), p. 333, and 'Manuscript Corrections' (n. 18 above), p. 138, also found that not all manuscript emendations had been entered into every copy of the two Aldine editions he studied. Indeed, the Aldine Bembo edition, with 13 in-shop manuscript corrections, has seven copies with only 1–5 corrections, six with 6–9 corrections, and seven with 10–13 corrections, suggesting that books left the shop continuously while the 13 errors gradually were identified. Kindred findings are illustrated in Della Rocca de Candal' and Sachet's contributions to this Companion.

CONCLUSION

This paper has investigated the first correcting author/printer who attempted to control errors in the edition of an astronomical table, a large work consisting mostly of numbers. Contemporary sources tell us next to nothing about Regiomontanus's computational procedures or the operations within his Nuremberg print shop in the early 1470s. No printer's copy or proof sheets have been found. Our analysis was restricted, therefore, to the forty surviving copies of the ephemerides.

Two of our initial hypotheses have been confirmed. We found no cases of stop-press corrections; the overwhelming majority of common corrections were knife-and-pen emendations in the printed gatherings. Likewise, a large majority of these corrections are in the 'meaningless' numbers of the lunar positions. But our third hypothesis about diachronic corrections proved false; the correction rates per gathering remained roughly constant over the thirty-two gatherings. This suggests that the production of errors and their identification in the print shop was a random process that did not become more efficient or precise over time.

On the other hand, we did find a major break in the correction process inside the print shop that yielded two sets of copies, the 'uncorrected' quarter and the 'corrected' three-quarters.[34] A stop-sale decision to knife-and-pen correct the entire edition, made after someone discovered errors on about half of the printed pages, would explain the pattern of corrections we found in the surviving copies. And we found that the knife-and-pen correctors managed to insert about 97% of the common corrections into any given 'corrected' copy.

Finally, we found evidence strongly suggesting that Regiomontanus used Bianchini's tables rather than the PAT to compute at least the lunar positions in the ephemerides and that his correctors could have employed second differences to look for 'batch errors' in the lunar positions, the part of the work most filled with errors. We noticed knife-and-pen corrections for errors as small as 5 arcminutes, which indicates that Regiomontanus desired precision at that level, just above the 'noise' of his computation. And we found that a large majority of the numerical errors involved displacements of a single digit by ± 1 digit, a pattern that we attribute to the placement of the type in the compositor's boxes or, indeed, the misplacement of type. The ± 1 digit errors were typographical, not scribal.

These correcting procedures in Regiomontanus's print shop nicely align with the values expressed in his programmatic statements about printing to remove 'errors' from mathematics and astronomy. The printed ephemerides embodied computational precision and

---

[34] Interestingly, we can track the movement of the 'corrected' and 'uncorrected' copies by examining later editions of Regiomontanus's *Ephemerides*. Ratdolt and Benalius copied from 'corrected' copies; Emerich, Hamann, and Stöffler and Pflaum from 'uncorrected' copies. Regiomontanus, *Ephemerides [1484–1506]*, Venice, Erhard Ratdolt, 1484, 4° (ISTC ir00107000); *Ephemerides accuratissime calculata [1492–1506]*, Venice, Vincentius Benalius, 1492, 4° (ISTC ir00109000); *Ephemerides astronomicae [1492–1506]*, Venice, Johann Hamann, 1492, 4° (ISTC ir00109500); *Ephemerides [1494–1506]*, Venice, Johann Emerich, 1494, 4° (ISTC ir00109750); Johannes Stöffler and Jacob Pflaum, *Almanach nova plurimis annis venturis inservientia [1499–1531]*, Ulm, Johann Reger, 1499, 4° (ISTC is00791000).

aimed at Eisenstein's 'fixity' of content. Yes, the post-printing corrections, first in the 'uncorrected' and then in the 'corrected' copies, introduced manuscript interventions and hence some variation into the fixity Regiomontanus may have sought, a mutability that Johns has taught us to expect. On the other hand, Regiomontanus's process of computing, printing, and correcting introduced only about 530 print shop corrections that were subject to variation; the other 399,470 digits printed in the edition were reproduced without variation. We might say that Eisenstein was mostly right for the first printed edition of a large astronomical table.[35]

BIBLIOGRAPHY

PRIMARY SOURCES

MANUSCRIPT

Munich, BSB, Clm 24,103.
Nuremberg, Stadtbibliothek, Cent V 57.
Vienna, ÖNB, Lat. 4988.

PRINTED BOOKS

Regiomontanus, Johannes, *Ephemerides [1475–1506]*, Nuremberg, Johannes Regiomontanus, 1474, 4° (ISTC ir00104500).
Regiomontanus, Johannes, *Ephemerides [1484–1506]*, Venice, Erhard Ratdolt, 1484, 4° (ISTC ir00107000).
Regiomontanus, Johannes, *Ephemerides accuratissime calculata [1492–1506]*, Venice, Vincentius Benalius, 1492, 4° (ISTC ir00109000).
Regiomontanus, Johannes, *Ephemerides Astronomicae [1492–1506]*, Venice, Johann Hamann, 1492, 4° (ISTC ir00109500).

---

[35] E. L. Eisenstein, *The Printing Press as an Agent of Change: Communication and Cultural Transformation in Early-Modern Europe*, 2 vols, Cambridge, 1979; A. Johns, *The Nature of the Book: Print and Knowledge in the Making*, Chicago, 1998.

Regiomontanus, Johannes, *Ephemerides [1494–1506]*, Venice, Johann Emerich, 1494, 4° (ISTC ir00109750).

Regiomontanus, Johannes, *Der Deutsche Kalender Des Johannes Regimontan, Nürnberg, Um 1474. Faksimiledruck Nach Den Exemplar Der Preussischen Staatsbibliothek*, Leipzig, 1937.

Regiomontanus, Johannes, *Kalendarium* [Latin], Nuremberg, Johannes Regiomontanus, c. 1474, 4° (ISTC ir00092000).

Regiomontanus, Johannes, *Kalender* [German], Nuremberg, Johannes Regiomontanus, c. 1474, 4° (ISTC ir00100300).

Schöner, Johannes, *Scripta clarissimi mathematici M. Ioanis Regiomontani*, Nuremberg, Johann vom Berg and Ulrich Neuber, 1544, 4° (USTC 692614).

Stöffler, Johannes, and Pflaum, Jacob, *Almanach nova plurimis annis venturis inservientia [1499–1531]*, Ulm, Johann Reger, 1499, 4° (ISTC is00791000).

SECONDARY LITERATURE

Anderson, E. R., 'Printing the Bespoke Book: Euclid's *Elements* in Early Modern Visual Cullture', *Nuncius*, 35, 2020, pp. 536–60.

Baldasso, R., 'Printing for the Doge: On the First Quire of the First Edition of the *Liber Elementorum Euclidis*', *La Bibliofilia*, 115, 2013, pp. 525–52.

Bühler, C. F., 'Stop-Press and Manuscript Corrections in the Aldine Edition of Benedetti's Diaria *De Bello Carolino*', *Papers of the Bibliographical Society of America*, 43, 1949, pp. 365–73.

Byrne, J. S., *The Stars, the Moon and the Shadowed Earth: Viennese Astronomy in the Fifteenth Century*, PhD dissertation, Princeton, Princeton University, 2007.

Chabás, J., and Goldstein, B. R., *The Astronomical Tables of Giovanni Bianchini*, Leiden, 2009.

Curtze, M., 'Der Briefwechsel Regiomontans mit Giovanni Bianchini, Jacob von Speier und Christian Roder', *Abhandlungen zur Geschichte der mathematischen Wissenschaften*, 12, 1902, pp. 187–336.

Czerny, A., 'Aus dem Briefwechsel des grossen Astronomen Georg von Peurbach', *Archiv für österreichische Geschichte*, 72, 1888, pp. 281–304.

Dal, E., 'Einige Korrekturbogen und andere Seltenheiten in der Königlichen Bibliothek Kopenhagen', *Beiträge zur Inkunabelkunde*, 3rd ser., 1, 1965, pp. 105–8.

Duntze, O., and Eisermann, F., 'Fortschritt oder Fidibus? Zur Bestimmung, Bewahrung und Bedeutung von Inkunabelfragmenten', in H.-P. Neuheuser and W. Schmitz (eds), *Fragment und Makulatur: Überlieferungsstörungen und Forschungsbedarf bei Kulturgut in Archiven und Bibliotheken*, Wiesbaden, 2015, pp. 281–307.

Eisenstein, E. L., *The Printing Press as an Agent of Change: Communication and Cultural Transformation in Early-Modern Europe*, 2 vols, Cambridge, 1979.

Fuchs, F. (ed.), *Hartmann Schedel (1440–1514): Leben und Werk*, Wiesbaden, 2016.

Goff, F. R., 'A Few Proof Sheets of the Fifteenth Century', *Gutenberg-Jahrbuch*, 1963, pp. 81–7.

Hellinga, L., 'Notes on the Order of Setting a Fifteenth-Century Book', *Quaerendo*, 4, 1974, pp. 64–9.

Hellinga, L., 'Proofreading and Printing in Mainz', in L. Hellinga, *Texts in Transit: Manuscript to Proof and Print in the Fifteenth Century*, Leiden and Boston, 2014, pp. 102–44.

Joachimsohn, P. (ed.), *Hermann Schedels Briefwechsel (1452–1478)*, Tübingen, 1893.

Johns, A., *The Nature of the Book: Print and Knowledge in the Making*, Chicago, 1998.

Michalski, M., *Dr. Balthasar Mansfeld (1440–1503): Ein Arzt in München an der Wende vom Mittelalter zur Neuzeit*, Munich, 2017.

Needham, P., 'The Cambridge Proof Sheets of Mentelin's Latin Bible', *Transactions of the Cambridge Bibliographical Society*, 9, 1986, pp. 1–35.

Neske, I., *Die Handschriften der Stadtbibliothek Nürnberg, Bd. V: Die lateinischen mittelalterlichen Handschriften, Varia, 13.–15. und 16.–18. Jahrhundert*, Wiesbaden, 1997.

Omodeo, P. D., 'Johannes Regiomontanus and Erasmus Reinhold: Shifting Perspectives on the History of Astronomy', in S. Brentjes and A. Fidora (eds), *Premodern Translation: Comparative Approaches to Cross-Cultural Transformations*, Turnhout, 2021, pp. 165–86.

Pedersen, O., 'The Decline and Fall of the *Theorica Planetarum*: Renaissance Astronomy and the Art of Printing', in E. Hilfstein, P. Czartoryski, and F. D. Grande (eds), *Science and History: Studies in Honor of Edward Rosen*, Wrocław, 1978, pp. 157–85.

Petz, H., 'Urkundliche Nachrichten über den literarischen Nachlass Regiomontans und B. Walthers 1478–1522', *Mitteilungen des Vereins für Geschichte der Stadt Nürnberg*, 7, 1888, pp. 237–62.

Posselt, B., *Konzeption and Kompilation der Schedelschen Weltchronik*, Wiesbaden, 2015.

Reichhart, G., 'Beiträge zur Incunabelnkunde, 1,1: Alphabetisch geordnetes Verzeichniss der Correctoren der Buchdruckereien des 15. Jahrhunderts', *Zentralblatt für Bibliothekswesen, Beiheft* 14, 1895, pp. 2–158.

Reske, C., *Die Produktion der Schedelschen Weltchronik in Nürnberg*, Wiesbaden, 2000.

Rogers, D., 'A Glimpse into Zainer's Workshop at Augsburg c. 1475', in L. Hellinga and H. Härtel (eds), *Buch und Text im 15. Jahrhundert: Arbeitsgespräch in der Herzog August Bibliothek Wolfenbüttel vom 1. bis 3. März 1978*, Hamburg, 1981, pp. 145–63.

Singh, V., 'From Handwritten Copy to the Printed Page in Devanagari: Investigating the Curious Case of Friedrich Max Müller', *Journal of the Printing Historical Society*, 26, 2017, pp. 11–22.

Stauber, R., *Die Schedelsche Bibliothek: Ein Beitrag zur Geschiche der Ausbreitung der italienischen Renaissance, des deutschen Humanismus und der medizinischen Literatur*, ed. H. Grauert, Freiburg i. B., 1908.

Stromer, W. von, 'Meister Konrad Scherp, Regiomontans Experte für Feinmechanik in der Nürnberger Officina und für den wissenschaftlichen Buchdruck', *Mitteilungen des Vereins für die Geschichte der Stadt Nürnberg*, 79, 1992, pp. 123–32.

Swerdlow, N. M., 'Regiomontanus on the Critical Problems of Astronomy', in T. H. Levere and W. R. Shea (eds), *Nature, Experiment, and the Sciences*, Dordrecht, 1990, pp. 165–95.

Swerdlow, N. M., 'Science and Humanism in the Renaissance: Regiomontanus's Oration on the Dignity and Utility of the Mathematical Sciences', in P. Horwich (ed.), *World Changes: Thomas Kuhn and the Nature of Science*, Cambridge, 1993, pp. 131–68.

Tersch, H. *Schreibkalender und Schreibkultur: Zur Rezeptionsgeschichte eines frühen Massenmediums*, Graz and Feldkirch, 2008.

Wagner, B., *Worlds of Learning: The Library and World Chronicle of the Nuremberg Physician Hartmann Schedel (1440–1514)*, Munich, 2015.

Wehmer, C., 'Ein frühes Korrekturblatt aus der Schöfferschen Offizin', *Gutenberg-Jahrbuch*, 7, 1932, pp. 118–22.

Widmann, H., 'Die Lektüre unendlicher Korrekturen', *Archiv für Geschichte des Buchwesens*, 5, 1962, pp. 777–826.

Wingen-Trennhaus, A., 'Regiomontanus als Frühdrucker in Nürnberg', *Mitteilungen des Vereins für Geschichte der Stadt Nürnberg*, 78, 1991, pp. 17–87.

Worm, A., *Geschichte und Weltordnung: Graphische Modelle von Zeit und Raum in Univesalchroniken vor 1500*, Berlin, 2021.

Zinner, E., 'Die wissenschaftlichen Bestrebungen Regiomontans', *Beiträge zur Inkunabelkunde*, 2nd ser., 1938, pp. 89–103.

Zinner, E., *Geschichte und Bibliographie der astronomischen Literatur in Deutschland zur zeit der Renaissance*. 2nd edn, Stuttgart, 1964.

Zinner, E., *Leben und Wirken des Johannes Müller von Königsberg genannt Regiomontanus*, Munich, 1938.

Zinner, E., *Leben und Wirken des Joh. Müller von Königsberg genannt Regiomontanus*, 2nd rev. edn, Osnabrück, 1968.

CHAPTER 16

MISPRINTING ARISTOTLE

The Birth and Life of a Frankenstein's Fish

GRIGORY VOROBYEV

INTRODUCTION

Due to the introduction of neologisms, the vocabulary of Neo-Latin has constantly grown, and it keeps expanding.[*][1] A particularly fast-growing field is the nomenclature of animals and plants. Indeed, when biologists name a new species, they mostly have to introduce a new Latin word. In this process, well described only for the period after Carl von Linné (aka Linnaeus, in Neo-Latin), many mistakes, including typographical ones, occurred. Some of them remained long unnoticed, so that not a few names containing a typo are still valid in the scientific animal nomenclature.[2]

If a word with such an undetected typographical mistake is widely used, it can be regarded as a neologism (sometimes called pseudo-neologism or phantom word).[3] In her article devoted to neologisms born from mistakes, Silvia Rizzo considers those originating from

---

[*] This is a revised and extended version of a paper I published in Russian: G. Vorobyev, 'O prirode latinskogo nazvaniya ryby *sargiacus* (Arist. *Hist. an.* 610b6)', *Indoevropeiskoe yazykoznanie i klassicheskaya filologiya*, 22, 2018, pp. 333–45.

[1] See H. Helander, 'On Neologisms in Neo-Latin', *Renæssanceforum*, 10, 2016, pp. 9–34.

[2] E.g., a typographical mistake is suggested as a possible reason for the spelling of at least the following components of binomial bird names: *arausiaca* (< *aurantiaca*), *coccyzus* (< *coccygus*), *perenopterus* (<*percnopterus*), *pindalus* (James A. Jobling suggests a corruption of *Pindarus*), *pulpa* (< *pulla*), *tigus/tygus* (< *tympanistrugus*), *subhemachalana* / *subhemalacha* / *subhimachala* / *subhimachalana*. See J. A. Jobling, *The Helm Dictionary of Scientific Bird Names: From Aalge to Zusii*, London, 2010, *sub vocibus*. An early instance has recently been studied by D. Berrens, 'Naming an Unknown Animal: The Case of the Sloth', *Archives of Natural History*, 47/2, 2020, pp. 325–43 (331). Namely, for the American animal now called sloth, Conrad Gessner in 1560 introduced the name *arctopithecus* (literally 'bear-ape'), but Jan Jonston, a Polish naturalist of Scottish origin, spelled Gessner's word as *archopithecus* in his 1632 *Thaumatographia naturalis* (rather than a deliberate change, perhaps a mistake of the author or the compositor), and the latter variant was then adopted in some further works (at least Gaspar Schott's 1662 *Physica curiosa* and the appendix to the later editions of Wolfgang Franz's *Historia animalium*).

[3] See S. Rizzo, 'Neologismi nati da corruttele', in L. Gamberale et al. (eds), *Le strade della filologia. Per Scevola Mariotti*, Rome, 2012, pp. 277–88 (278), with earlier bibliography on these terms.

Grigory Vorobyev, *Misprinting Aristotle*. In: *Printing and Misprinting*. Edited by Geri Della Rocca de Candal, Anthony Grafton, and Paolo Sachet, Oxford University Press. © Grigory Vorobyev (2023). DOI: 10.1093/oso/9780198863045.003.0017 corrupted manuscripts and also touches upon compounds born from false word-division. Namely, she remembers the *fistulae clauditibiae*, a would-be kind of ancient flute mentioned by Leon Battista Alberti, who borrowed it from the *didascalia* to Terence's *Eunuchus*, where originally stood 'Modos fecit Flaccus Claudi tibiis duabus dextris' (The music was composed by Flaccus, the slave of Claudius, with two treble flutes).[4] A similar case from the zoological literature will be now introduced, though born in a printer's shop rather than on a scribe's desk.

SARGIACUS IN LATIN AND GREEK EDITIONS OF ARISTOTLE'S *HISTORIA ANIMALIUM*

Numerous neologisms designating animal species were coined by the Byzantine scholar Theodore Gaza in his Latin translation of Aristotle's *Historia animalium*, made in Italy between 1454 and 1473/1474. It was first printed in 1476 and enjoyed great success in the sixteenth century.[5] Many of the words introduced by Gaza made their way into the period after Linnaeus.[6]

Sargiacus was considered a fish name originating from Theodore Gaza's translation, like numerous other peculiar words he introduced. Although it did not enter the binomial nomenclature of fishes, it was discussed in early modern zoological writings and what was probably its last appearance on a printed page dates back to 1874. Its existence was also implicitly accepted in the 2002 edition of the Greek text of the *Historia animalium*. However, as it turns out, the word *sargiacus* is a phantom born from a typographical error.

---

[4] Ibid., p. 280.

[5] Aristoteles, *De animalibus*, transl. Theodorus Gaza, Venice, Johannes de Colonia and Johannes Manthen, 1476, f° (ISTC ia00973000). See: S. Perfetti, '*Cultius atque integrius*. Teodoro Gaza, traduttore umanistico del *De partibus animalium*', *Rinascimento*, 35, 1995, pp. 253–86; J. Monfasani, 'The Pseudo-Aristotelian *Problemata* and Aristotle's *De Animalibus* in the Renaissance', in A. Grafton and N. Siraisi (eds), *Natural Particulars: Nature and the Disciplines in Renaissance Europe*, Cambridge (MA) and London, 1999, pp. 205–47; P. Beullens and A. Gotthelf, 'Theodore Gaza's Translation of Aristotle's *De animalibus*: Content, Influence and Date', *Greek, Roman and Byzantine Studies*, 47, 2007, pp. 469–513.

[6] The role of the translations of Aristotle in the formation of modern fish nomenclature has been studied by P. Beullens, 'Aristotle, his Translators, and the Formation of Ichthyologic Nomenclature', in M. Goyens et al. (eds), *Science Translated: Latin and Vernacular Translations of Scientific Treatises in Medieval Europe*, Leuven, 2008, pp. 105–22. He states that only one neologism of Gaza's coinage, *cernua*, might have survived in Linnaean ichthyological nomenclature (still, the word *cernua* must have been a neologism of sense rather than a true neologism, for Gaza, apparently, modified the Italian *cerna/cernia* so that it could sound like the form of the Latin adjective *cernuus* 'inclined forwards'). I found further cases of Gaza's fish names used by Carl von Linné and later biologists, such as *hiatula*, *spinax*, and *squatinoraia*; see G. Vorobyev, 'Neologizmy Feodora Gazy iz ego latinskogo perevoda *De animalibus* Aristotelya v sovremennoy zoologischeskoy nomenklature', *Indoevropeiskoe yazykoznanie i klassicheskaya filologiya*, 19/1, 2015, pp. 158–68. For the bird names invented by Gaza and used by today's ornithologists, see also my '*Sylvia*: Zur Entstehung des wissenschaftlichen Namens der Grasmücke (Arist. *Hist. an.* 592b22)', *Philologia Classica*, 13/2, 2018, pp. 247–64, and 'Theodore Gaza's Neologisms in *-cilla*/*-cula* and the Role of Sixteenth-Century Reference Books in the Formation of Ornithological Nomenclature', *Indoevropeiskoe yazykoznanie i klassicheskaya filologiya*, 24/1, 2020, pp. 794–818.

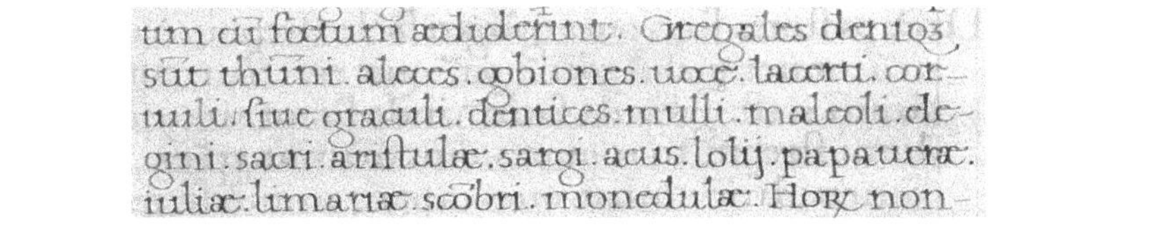

16: MISPRINTING ARISTOTLE 327

> tim aī foctum addiderint. Gregales denique,
> sūt thūni. aleces. gobiones. uoce. lacerti. cor-
> uuli. fiue graculi. dentices. mulli. maleoli. ele-
> gini. sacri. arīstulae. sargi. acus. lolij. papauerae.
> iuliae. limariae scōbri. monedulae. Horæ non

FIG. 16.1. Gaza's translation of Aristotle's *Historia*, 610b3–7. MS Vatican City, Biblioteca Apostolica Vaticana, Vat. lat. 2094, fol. 135r, ll. 18–22.

The lines 610b3–7 of Aristotle's *Historia animalium* contain a list of shoal-fishes:

Ὅλως δ'ἀγελαῖά ἐστι τὰ τοιάδε, θυννίδες, μαινίδες, κωβιοί, βῶκες, σαῦροι, κορακῖνοι, συνόδοντες, τρίγλαι, σφύραιναι, ἀνθίαι, ἐλεγῖνοι, ἀθερῖνοι, *σαργῖνοι*, *βελόναι*, τευθοί, ἰουλίδες, πηλαμύδες, σκόμβροι, κολίαι (here and hereafter, the emphasis is mine).[7]

Σαργῖνοι is a rare name of an unidentified fish; βελόναι, literally 'needle', is a well-attested fish name, standing for garfish. In the splendid dedication copy that Gaza presented to Pope Sixtus IV,[8] his translation reads: 'Gregales denique sunt thunni, aleces, gobiones, vocae, lacerti, corvuli, sive graculi, dentices, mulli, maleoli, elegini, sacri, aristulae, *sargi*, *acus*, lolii, papaverae, iuliae, limariae, scombri, monedulae'(Fig. 16.1).[9]

The plural σαργῖνοι is clearly rendered as *sargi* and the plural βελόναι as a u-declension plural *acus*. In Gaza's translation, these two Latin words are attested elsewhere, so there is no doubt about their correct spelling here.[10] In the Vatican codex, the elements of the cited fish list are separated by dots. In the 1476 *editio princeps*,[11] double dots, looking like colons and set without spaces, assume the same function. Between *sargi* and *acus* this separation mark is skipped: 'aristulae:sargiacus:lolii' (Fig. 16.2).[12]

---

[7] The Greek text of Aristotle's *Historia animalium* is consistently quoted throughout this chapter after: Aristotle, *Historia animalium*, I: *Books I–X: Text*, ed. D. M. Balme, prepared for publication by A. Gotthelf, Cambridge, 2002. Ibid., pp. 397–8 for this passage ('The following are shoaling fishes generally: tunnies, mainis, gobies, bogues, saurus, coracinus, synodon, red mullet, sphyraena, anthias, eleginus, atherines, sarginus, belone, squids, rainbow wrasse, pelamyds, mackerel, coly-mackerel', as in Aristotle, *History of Animals*, III: *Books 7–10*, ed. and transl. D. M. Balme, Cambridge (MA), 1991, pp. 233–5).

[8] On the MS Vatican City, Biblioteca Apostolica Vaticana (BAV), Vat. lat. 2094, see J. Monfasani, 'Aristotle as Scribe of Nature: The Title-Page of MS Vat. lat. 2094', *Journal of the Warburg and Courtauld Institutes*, 69, 2006, pp. 193–205. Cf. Beullens and Gotthelf, 'Theodore Gaza's Translation' (n. 5 above), p. 482.

[9] MS Vat. lat. 2094, fol. 135r, ll. 18–22. Oscillations in the spelling of geminates (*lolii/lollii*, *graculi/gracculi*, *maleoli/malleoli* etc.), often appearing in two different forms in the same page of Gaza's translation, should not be considered significant.

[10] 543a7, 543b8, 570a32, 570b3, 570b19; 506b9, 543b11, 567b23, 571a2, 616a32. On the Latin *sargus* see below.

[11] The editor of the *princeps*, Ludovico Podocataro, states in the colophon that he drew the text 'ex archetypo ipsius Theodori' (sig. ff[4]v). Monfasani, 'Aristotle as Scribe of Nature' (n. 8 above), p. 202, n. 39, suggests that the *Druckvorlage* of the *princeps* could have been a copy of the MS Vat. lat. 2094, made when the latter was borrowed from the Vatican library by the papal official Francesco da Toledo, who kept it from 10 July 1475 until 16 February 1476. On the meanings of *archetypus* see S. Rizzo, *Il lessico filologico degli umanisti*, Roma, 1973, pp. 308–17.

[12] Aristoteles, *De animalibus*, 1476 (n. 5 above), sig. n2v. The typo is also present in other four digitised copies that I could access (Barcelona, Biblioteca de Catalunya, Inc. 10-Fol and Mar. 30-4°; Boston Public Library, Q.403.81 FOLIO; Paris, Bibliothèque Sainte-Geneviève, OEXV 181 RES).

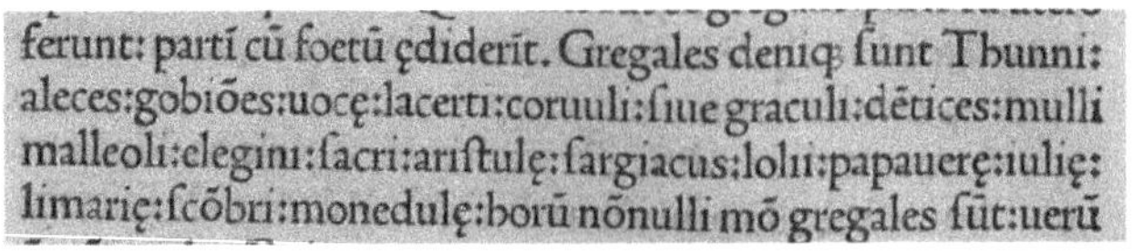

328 PRINTING AND MISPRINTING

> ferunt: partí cū foetū ędiderit. Gregales deniq̃ funt Thunni:
> aleces:gobióes:uoce:lacerti:coruuli:fiue graculi:dētices:mulli
> malleoli:elegini:facri:ariftulę:fargiacus:lolii:papauerę:iulię:
> limarię:fcóbri:monedulę:borū nōnulli mō gregales fūt:uerū

FIG. 16.2. Aristoteles, *De animalibus*, Venice, Johannes de Colonia and Johannes Manthen, 1476, f°
(ISTC ia00973000), sig. n2v, ll. 3–6. Munich, Bayerische Staatsbibliothek, 2 Inc.c.a. 448 m.

All further editions of Gaza's translation apparently descend, directly or not, from the
princeps and do not depend on any different branch of the tradition.[13] Thus, no editor seems
to have recurred to the Vatican codex. In any case, the three incunable editions that followed
the *princeps* contain the same mistake.[14]

The fifth edition of Gaza's translation, prepared in 1504 by Aldus Manutius, derived from
the previous printed ones and offered numerous emendations. Still, instead of correcting
the typo *sargiacus*, Aldus, on the contrary, promoted its acceptance. He did not detect the
loss of a separation sign and decided that the fish name *sargiacus* should belong to the o-
rather than u-declension, so, in the list of fish names all put in plural, he emended *sargiacus*
replacing it by an o-declension plural, *sargiaci*: 'aristulae:sargiaci:lolii'.[15] Moreover, Aldus's
edition is the first one provided with an alphabetical glossary of animal names.[16] It contains
an entry 'sargiaci pisces', 'the fishes *sargiaci*' (Fig. 16.3.a–b).[17]

The only case that I could find where 'sargi, acus' is printed correctly is the commentary
to the *Historia animalium* compiled by Agostino Nifo in 1534. It was printed in 1546 and
accompanied an edition of Gaza's Latin version. Even though Nifo highly appreciated Gaza,
he did not blindly follow his text and included critical remarks in the commentary.[18] Citing
the list of shoal-fishes, Nifo tacitly emends the printed text of Gaza's version, without giving

---

[13] Though not stated explicitly, this can be deduced from Beullens and Gotthelf, 'Theodore Gaza's
Translation' (n. 5 above), especially pp. 481–3 and 495–6.

[14] Aristoteles, *De animalibus*, Venice, Johannes and Gregorius de Gregoriis, 1492, f° (ISTC
ia00974000), fol. 46r; Aristoteles, *De animalibus*, [Venice, Simon Bevilaqua, about 1495], f° (ISTC
ia00975000), sig. L2v; Aristoteles, *De animalibus*, Venice, Bartholomaeus de Zanis for Octavianus
Scotus, 1498, f° (ISTC ia00976000), fol. 39r.

[15] Aristoteles and Theophrastus, *Habentur hoc volumine haec Theodoro Gaza interprete. Aristotelis De
natura animalium, liber IX. Eiusdem De partibus animalium, lib IIII. Eiusdem De generatione animalium,
libri V. Theophrasti De historia plantarum, liber IX Alexandri Aphrodisiensis Problemata duobus libris*,
Venice, Aldo Manuzio, 1504, f° (USTC 810862), fol. 47r.

[16] On the importance of such forms of apparatus as a tool of information transmission in early
modern time, see at least: A. Blair, 'Annotating and Indexing Natural Philosophy', in N. Jardine and
M. Frasca-Spada (eds), *Books and the Sciences in History*, Cambridge, 2000, pp. 69–89; A. Blair, *Too
Much to Know: Managing Scholarly Information before the Modern Age*, New Haven (CT) and London,
2010; B. W. Ogilvie, 'The Many Books of Nature: Renaissance Naturalists and Information Overload',
Journal of the History of Ideas, 64/1, 2003, pp. 29–40.

[17] Aristoteles and Theophrastus, *De natura animalium* (n. 15 above), sig. a4r.

[18] On Nifo's treatment of Gaza's version, see S. Perfetti, 'Metamorfosi di una traduzione: Agostino
Nifo revisore dei *De animalibus* gaziani', *Medioevo*, 22, 1996, pp. 259–301, and Monfasani, 'The Pseudo-
Aristotelian' (n. 5 above), p. 214.

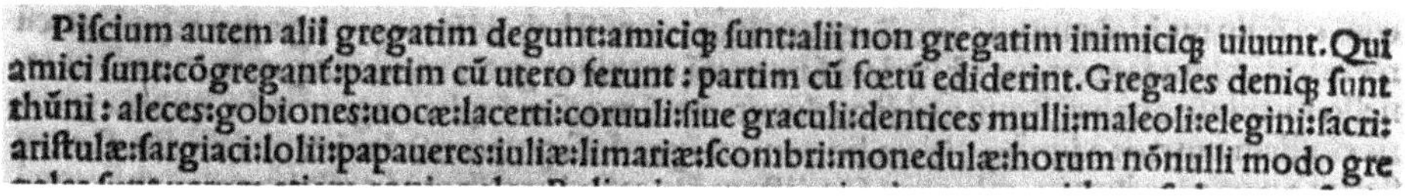

> Piſcium autem alii gregatim degunt:amiciq; ſunt:alii non gregatim inimiciq; uiuunt.Qui
> amici ſunt:cógregant:partim cū utero ferunt : partim cū fœtū ediderint.Gregales deniq; ſunt
> thūni : aleces:gobiones:uocæ:lacerti:coruuli:ſiue graculi:dentices mulli:maleoli:elegini:ſacri:
> ariſtulæ:ſargiaci:lolii:papaueres:iuliæ:limariæ:ſcombri:monedulæ:horum nōnulli modo gre

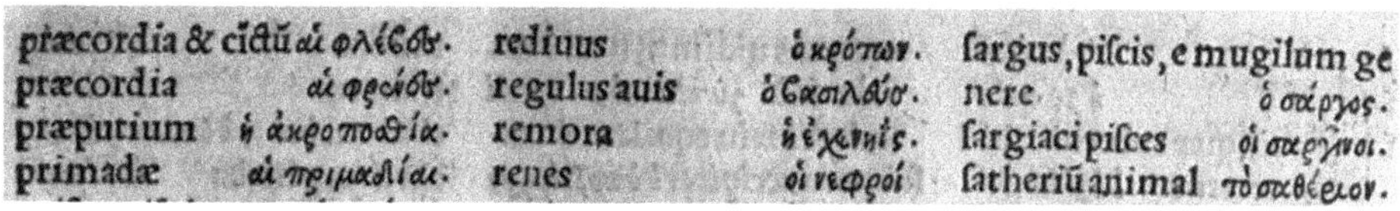

præcordia & ciātū αἰ φλίβόϑ.		rediuus	ὁ κρότων .	ſargus,piſcis,e mugilum ge	
præcordia	αἰ φρςίόϑ.	regulus auis	ὁ βασιλθύσ.	nere	ὁ σάρρχος.
præputium	ἡ ἀκρο ποϑ ία·	remora	ἡ ἐχανίς.	ſargiaci piſces	οἱ σαρχινοι.
primadæ	αἰ προίμακλίαι·	renes	οἱ νεφροί	ſatheriū animal	τὸ σκθίεχον.

FIG. 16.3. a-b. Aristoteles and Theophrastus, *De natura animalium* [...] *De historia plantarum*, Venice, Aldo Manuzio, 1504, f° (USTC 810,862), fol. 47r and sig. a4r. Vienna, Österreichische Nationalbibliothek, 22.L.2 ALT PRUNK.

any comment: 'aristulae, sargi, acus, papaverae, loligines'.[19] Fortunately for the *sargiacus*, Nifo's correction did not influence the further tradition of Gaza's text.

The reading *sargiaci* was maintained, apparently, in all further editions of Gaza's translation.[20] The 1783 edition of the Greek text with parallel French version, prepared by Albert-Gaston Camus, contained an index of animal names and mentioned Gaza's variant *sargiacus* beside an alternative one, *sarginus*.[21] The latter originated from a newer Latin version, made in the 1530s by Julius Caesar Scaliger, who rendered our passage in the following way:

> Summa autem gregalium haec est. Thunnides, maenulae, gobii, boces, lacerti, coracini, dentices, muli, sphyrenae, anthiae, elegini, atherini, *sargini*, *aciculae*, mecones, lolligines, iulides, pelamydes, scombri, graculi.[22]

Thus, Scaliger rendered σαργῖνοι as *sargini* and βελόναι as *aciculae*. In the commentary that accompanies his translation, he constantly criticised Gaza's version and did not fail to point out dubious renderings, but he never mentioned the word *sargiacus*. Scaliger's translation was published long after his death, in 1619, and could not eclipse the authority of Gaza's text,

[19] Agostino Nifo, *Expositiones in omnes Aristotelis libros De historia animalium. liber IX. De partibus animalium, & earum causis. liber IV. Ac De generatione animalium. libri V. Adiecto utili indice*, Venice, Girolamo Scoto, 1546, f° (USTC 844719), p. 265. Remarkably, Nifo corrects Gaza's *vocae* as *bocae*, *mulli* as *nulli* (Nifo also uses this spelling elsewhere) and *lolii* as *loligines*, also swapping it with the word *papaverae*, so that the order corresponds better to the Greek text (on the respective transposition carried out by Gaza, see below). On the oscillations in the spelling of geminates, see n. 9 above.

[20] E.g. Aristoteles, *De historia animalium libri IX. De partibus animalium et earum causis libri IIII. De generatione animalium libri V*, Paris, Simon de Colines, 1524, f° (USTC 180946), fol. 85v; Aristoteles, *Ta sōzomena = Operum, nova editio. Graece et Latine*, ed. I. Casaubon, 2 vols, Lyon [i.e., Geneva], Guillaume de Laimarie, 1590, f° (USTC 142711), I, p. 567; Aristoteles, *Opera quae extant omnia*, 6 vols, Rome, 1668, III, p. 985.

[21] Aristote, *Histoire des animaux*, 2 vols, Paris, 1783, II, pp. 26–7.

[22] Aristoteles, *Peri zōōn historias: Historia de animalibus*, Toulouse, Dominique and Pierre Bosc, 1619, f° (USTC 6808360), p. 1012.

330 PRINTING AND MISPRINTING

which had been seen through the press over forty times by the end of the sixteenth century.[23] When Scaliger's version was printed for a second time, in 1811, the editor, Johann Gottlob Schneider, considered it necessary to mention in his commentary that Gaza's rendering of σαργῖνοι was *sargiaci*.[24]

While Scaliger's version, revised by Schneider, was reprinted in the Latin edition of the *Corpus Aristotelicum* issued in 1831 by the Prussian Academy of Sciences,[25] Aristotle's bilingual Greek–Latin *opera omnia* published between 1848 and 1874 in Paris, by Ambroise Firmin-Didot, contained the *Historia animalium* in Gaza's translation, now considerably revised by Ulco Cats Bussemaker (1810–1865).[26] Among other improvements, the latter followed Scaliger's replacement of Gaza's *sargiacus* by *sarginus*.[27] The detailed *Index rerum and nominum*, with mixed Latin and Greek lemmas, compiled by Bussemaker for the whole Aristotelian corpus, included, consequently, the word *sarginus*, not *sargiacus*.[28] Still, a separate index of Greek animal, plant, and mineral names, prepared for the same volume by Emil Heitz (*Index naturalis historiae*),[29] provided both variants: 'σαργῖνος (*sarginus*), *sargiacus* Gaza. Definiri non potest'.[30]

The typo was not noticed by David Balme either, the author of the last critical edition of the *Historia animalium*, which was prepared for publication after his death by Allan Gotthelf. When listing the variant readings of the word βελόναι in his *apparatus criticus*, Balme specifies that Gaza omitted it, whereas we have seen from the Vatican codex that Gaza translated it as *acus*.[31] Therefore, Balme understood Gaza's *sargiacus* as the rendering of σαργῖνοι and not as an accidental merging of translations for σαργῖνοι and for βελόναι.

SARGIACUS IN EARLY MODERN ZOOLOGICAL TREATISES

The fish name *sargiacus*, firmly established in the Aristotelian tradition since the 1504 Aldine, also enjoyed a certain acceptance in zoological treatises. Nikolaus Marschalk, one of the first ichthyologists of the early modern period, cites the word *sargiacus* as a translation of the Greek σαργῖνος.[32] Among other Latin fish names beginning with 's', he mentions

---

[23] Monfasani, 'The Pseudo-Aristotelian' (n. 5 above), p. 216. For the list of these editions, see Beullens and Gotthelf, 'Theodore Gaza's Translation' (n. 5 above), pp. 508–13.

[24] Aristoteles, *De animalibus historiae Graece et Latine*, 4 vols, Leipzig, 1811, III, p. 287.

[25] *Aristotelis opera, edidit Academia regia Borussia*, III, Berlin, 1831, p. 301.

[26] *Aristotelis opera omnia Graece et Latine*, 5 vols, Paris, 1848–1874. Bussemaker was responsible for the third volume of the edition, issued in 1854: see the preface to vol. V, p. V.

[27] Ibid., III, p. 175.

[28] Ibid., V, p. 736.

[29] Which index was prepared by Bussemaker and which by Heitz is reported ibid., V, pp. VII–VIII.

[30] Ibid., V, p. 914 ('σαργῖνος (*sarginus*), <rendered as> *sargiacus* <by> Gaza. Cannot be defined'). In case of a concurrent index of Aristotle's vocabulary, the *Index Aristotelicus* compiled by Hermann Bonitz for the edition of the Prussian Academy, the entry σαργῖνος mentions neither Gaza nor *sargiacus*: *Aristotelis opera, edidit Academia regia Borussica*, V, Berlin, 1870, p. 671.

[31] Aristotle, *Historia animalium*, 2002 (n. 7 above), p. 398.

[32] On early modern ichthyology see, e.g.: C. Hünemörder, 'Geschichte der Fischbücher von Aristoteles bis zum Ende des 17. Jahrhunderts', *Deutsches Schiffahrtsarchiv*, 1, 1975, pp. 185–200 (193–8); Ä. Bäumer,

sargiacus and *sarginus*, but does not comment upon them, providing only the Greek equivalent, σαργῖνος, for both.[33] The Latin variant *sarginus*, a transliteration of the Greek word, was most probably drawn from the thirteenth-century translation of Aristotle's *Historia animalium* made by William of Moerbeke.

In the important ichthyological treatises by Guillaume Rondelet and Pierre Belon, the fish name σαργῖνος is either not reported at all or mentioned without Latin translation.[34] In the ichthyological volume of his milestone *Historia animalium*, Conrad Gessner uses the transliteration, *sarginus*, but cites the variant *sargiacus*, too: 'Gaza pro *sargino sargonem* vertit, in eiusdem translatione *sargiaci* alicubi legitur, pro *sargini*.'[35]

Ulisse Aldrovandi, in the posthumously published ichthyological volume of his animal encyclopaedia, conceived as an attempt to supersede Gessner's work,[36] comments upon Aristotle's list of shoal-fishes and mentions the Latin word *sargiacus* several times, but always in a modified form, *sardiacus*. The Greek word σαργῖνος became, respectively, σαρδῖνος:

> [...] Enumerans enim pisces gregales, inter eos nominat σαρδῖνους [sic], βελόνας, μηκώνες, legendum βελόνας, σαρδῖνους [sic], μύξωνες, id est *acus* (in aliis codicibus legitur τεῦθοι, id est *lollii*, et sic Theodorus quoque legit), *sardiacos* (ne a Gazae voce recedamus, quanquam rectius nomen Graecum reservari possit) et *myxones* qui tertia *mugilum* sunt species.[37]

Geschichte der Biologie, II: *Zoologie der Renaissance — Renaissance der Zoologie*, Frankfurt am Main, 1991, pp. 346–81; Beullens, 'Aristotle, his Translators' (n. 6 above).

[33] Nikolaus Marschalk, *Historia aquatilium Latine ac Grece cum figuris*, [Rostock, Nikolaus Marschalk, 1517], f° (USTC 663330), sig. L2r.

[34] Cf. Pierre Belon, *De aquatilibus libri duo*, Paris, Charles Estienne, 1553, 8° (USTC 151230), and Guillaume Rondelet, *Libri de piscibus marinis*, Lyon, Macé Bonhomme, 1554, f° (USTC 151588), p. 124. Rondelet mostly cited the Greek original and did not recur to Gaza's version as often as his contemporary zoologists did (e.g., Ippolito Salviani, or Conrad Gessner, on which see below).

[35] Conrad Gessner, *Historiae animalium liber IIII. qui est de piscium & aquatilium animantium natura*, Zürich, Christoph Froschauer, 1558, f° (USTC 624828), p. 996 ('Instead of *sarginus*, Gaza translates *sargo*, <and> at another place in his translation *sargiaci* is written instead of *sargini*'). The rendering *sargo* refers to a passage at line 543b15, where Gaza selected the Greek variant reading σάργων attested in several manuscripts, instead of σάργος, whereas Gessner, following Rondelet (as cited above, n. 34), deemed it necessary to emend σάργος/σάργων as σαργῖνος. In the ichthyological volume of Gessner's *Icones animalium*, a work where he gives less space to philological discussion, only the variant *sarginus* is mentioned: Conrad Gessner, *Nomenclator aquatilium animantium. Icones animalium aquatilium*, Zürich, Christoph Froschauer, 1560, f° (USTC 678237), pp. 44 and 68–9. On Gessner's zoological books see C. Riedl-Dorn, *Wissenschaft und Fabelwesen. Ein kritischer Versuch über Conrad Gessner und Ulisse Aldrovandi*, Wien and Köln, 1989; U. Friedrich, *Naturgeschichte zwischen* artes liberales *und frühneuzeitlicher Wissenschaft. Conrad Gessners* Historia animalium *und ihre volkssprachliche Rezeption*, Tübingen, 1995; K. A. E. Enenkel, 'Zur Konstruierung der Zoologie als Wissenschaft in der Frühen Neuzeit: Diskursanalyse zweier Großprojekte (Wotton, Gesner)', in K. A. E. Enenkel and P. J. Smith (eds), *Early Modern Zoology. The Construction of Animals in Science, Literature and the Visual Arts*, Leiden and Boston, 2007, pp. 15–74.

[36] See Riedl-Dorn, *Wissenschaft und Fabelwesen* (n. 35 above) and Bäumer, *Geschichte der Biologie* (n. 32 above), pp. 74–119.

[37] Ulisse Aldrovandi, *De piscibus libri V et de cetis lib. unus. Ioannes Cornelius Uterverius collegit*, Bologna, Giovanni Battista Bellagamba for Girolamo Tamburini, 1613, f° (USTC 4027422), p. 179 ('For, when he lists the shoal-fishes, he names among them σαρδῖνοι, βελόναι, μηκώνες; it should be read as βελόναι, σαρδῖνοι, μύξωνες, i.e. *acus* (other codices read τεῦθοι, i.e. *lollii*, and Theodore reads thus, too),

Since Aldrovandi does not provide any commentary concerning the spelling with δ/d either here or in the chapter on the fish *sarda/sardina*,[38] it should be perhaps considered a correction carried out at line 610b6 in one of the Greek or bilingual editions of Aristotle, based apparently on the better-known fish name σαρδῖνος.[39] Either Aldrovandi (or perhaps his students who finished his work after his death) or the particular edition of Gaza's Latin text[40] that he used modified the Latin accordingly, replacing 'g' with 'd'. Still, it remains unclear why, in three further instances, Aldrovandi's text identifies *sardiaci* with the correctly spelled σαργῖνοι, not σαρδῖνοι:

> [...] μήκονες pro *myxones*, quam tamen vulgarem lectionem Gaza secutus *papaveres* convertit, et pro *sarginis sardiacos* [...].[41]
>
> [...] σαργῖνος, quem Aristoteles in *mugilum* genere habuisse videtur (ubi Gaza transtulit *sardiacum*) [...].[42]
>
> [...] et pro σαργός σαργῖνος legendum, quam postremam vocem ille *sardiacum* vertit [...].[43]

In any case, the form *sardiacus* does not, as far as I can see, appear in later sources and remains, thus, Aldrovandi's idiosyncratic spelling. It is noteworthy that Aldrovandi considered the transliteration of the Greek word a better solution, yet accepted as the main variant the word *sardiacus* that, as he thought, was introduced by Gaza — so important was the latter's opinion to him.

Peter Artedi, one of the most influential ichthyologists of the eighteenth century, often cites Gaza's variants in his 1738 *Synonymia nominum piscium* but mentions neither *sarginus*

---

sardiaci (let us not depart from Gaza's word, even though one could keep to the more correct Greek name), and *myxones*, which make up the third species of the *mugiles*').

[38] Aldrovandi, *De piscibus* (n. 37 above), pp. 219–22.

[39] According to the text accepted in modern editions of the *Historia animalium* (*Hist. an.*), Aristotle does not use any fish name beginning with σαρδ-. Still, the fish name σαρδῖνος is mentioned by one ancient author, namely Athenaeus (Ath. 7, 137, 28), who explicitly quotes the fifth book of Aristotle's *Hist. an.* as the source of this word: Ἀριστοτέλης δ'ἐν πέμπτῳ ζῴων ἱστορίας σαρδίνους αὐτὰς [*scil.* τὰς ἐριτίμους] καλεῖ ('Aristotle, in the fifth book of the *History of animals*, calls them [*scil.* the fish ἐρίτιμοι] σαρδῖνοι'). Indeed, in modern editions of the *Hist. an.*, the abovementioned σαργός (or σάργος) does appear three times in the fifth book (543a8, 543b8, 543b15). In the first occurrence ('τίκτει δὲ καὶ ὁ σαργὸς δίς, ἔαρος καὶ μετοπώρου', 'the σαργός breeds twice, in spring and in autumn'), several manuscripts, in fact, read σάρδος (Aristotle, *Historia animalium*, 2002 (n. 7 above), p. 221; Gaza follows the reading σαργὸς and translates it as *sargus*). Athenaeus must have been referring to this instance, but in his source text the reading σάρδος should have been replaced by yet another form, σαρδῖνος. The passage from Athenaeus could, therefore, have been the source for the conjecture in the Aristotelian text that Aldrovandi tacitly took over: the emendation might have been implemented at line 543a8 as well as in other occurrences of σαργός (or σάργος).

[40] I could not find any edition containing this spelling so far.

[41] Aldrovandi, *De piscibus* (n. 37 above), p. 505 ('[...] μήκονες for *myxones*, which Gaza, though, rendered as *papaveres*, following the common reading, and for *sargini* <he has> *sardiaci*').

[42] Ibid., p. 179 ('[...] σαργῖνος that Aristotle seems having considered one of the *mugiles* (where Gaza translated *sardiacum*) [...]').

[43] Ibid., p. 173 ('[...] and instead of σαργός it should be read σαργῖνος, which latter word he rendered as *sardiacus*'). The same spelling of these passages is maintained in the second edition: U. Aldrovandi, *De piscibus libri V et de cetis lib. unus. Ioannes Cornelius Uterverius collegit*, Bologna, Nicolò Tebaldini for Marco Antonio Bernia, 1638, f° (USTC 4008088), also at pp. 173, 179 and 505.

nor *sargiacus*.[44] Still, in its extended edition prepared posthumously by the aforementioned Johann Gottlob Schneider, the name *sarginus*, as well as *sargiacus* as its alternative variant, is cited: '<Aristoteles> IX.2. gregatilem facit *sarginum*, ubi Gazae versio *sargiacum* nominat'.[45]

SARGIACUS IN DICTIONARIES

An attempt to track the appearance of the word *sargiacus* in all early modern dictionaries does not seem necessary; for the mainstream of Latin lexicography, clearly non-classical words like *sargiacus* were irrelevant. Still, it is symptomatic that some influential Greek lexicographical tools of the sixteenth and seventeenth centuries cite it, relying, of course, on the editions of Aristotle.

The 1512 Greek–Latin dictionary prepared by Girolamo Aleandro, one of the collaborators of Aldus Manutius, does not include the word σαργῖνος as a lemma. Still, the dictionary has Latin–Greek glossaries of animal and plant names based on Gaza's versions of Aristotle's zoological treatises and Theophrastus's *De plantis*. There, an entry 'sargiaci pisces – οἱ σαργῖνοι' is present, surely based on the aforementioned glossary in the Aldine edition of Gaza's translation.[46]

In the 1552 dictionary of Jacques Toussain, which constituted an important step in the Greek lexicographical tradition,[47] the word σαργῖνοι does appear in the main word list and is commented in the following way: 'σαργῖνοι – *sargiaci* pisces gregales, Aristotel. lib. 9. animal. Gaza Graecam vocem relinquit'.[48] The dictionary of Robert Constantin, depending on the one compiled by Toussain, repeats this entry verbatim, the only difference being the spelling *sargiani* instead of *sargiaci*.[49] In contrast with Aldrovandi's *sardiaci*, this *sargiani* must have been a mere misprint.

---

[44] P. Artedi, *Synonymia nominum piscium*, Leiden, 1738, p. 58.

[45] P. Artedi and J. G. Schneider, *Synonymia piscium Graeca et Latina*, Leipzig, 1789, p. 91 ('<Aristotle> <in Book> IX <chapter> 2 calls *sarginus* a shoal-fish, where Gaza's translation mentions *sargiacus*').

[46] Girolamo Aleandro et al., *Lexicon Graecolatinum multis et preclaris additionibus locupletatum*, [Paris, Gilles de Gourmont] and Matthieu Bolsec, 1512, f° (USTC 143982), sig. aa[7]*v*.

[47] M. Mund-Dopchie, 'Le *Lexicon Graecolatinum* de Jacques Toussain (1552): choix de vocabulaire et méthodes de traduction', in M. Fumaroli (ed.), *Les origines du Collège de France*, Paris, 1998, pp. 405–20; R. Jimenes, 'Un monument lexicographique: le dictionnaire gréco-latin de Jacques Toussain (1552)', in Y. Sordet (ed.), *Passeurs de texte: imprimeurs, éditeurs et lecteurs humanistes*, Turnhout, 2009, pp. 140–3.

[48] Jacques Toussain, *Lexicon Graecolatinum*, Paris, Charlotte Guillard, Claude Chevallon's widow, and Guillaume Merlin, 1552, f° (USTC 151147), sig. TTt5*v* ('σαργῖνοι – shoal-fishes *sargiaci*, Aristotle, book 9 of the <History> of animals; Gaza leaves the Greek word'). The information that Gaza merely transliterated the Greek word must have been mistakenly interpolated in this entry from the next one, 'σάργος', where it is also reported that 'Gaza Graecam vocem relinquit' ('Gaza leaves the Greek word'). In the latter case it is true, for Gaza renders the Greek σάργος (now usually accepted as σαργός) as *sargus* (see below).

[49] Robert Constantin and Francesco Porto, *Lexicon Græcolatinum. Secunda editio*, 2 vols, [Geneva], Héritiers d'Eustache Vignon and Jacob Stoer, 1592, f° (USTC 451309), II, p. 606.

Why the Word *Sargiacus* has not been Explicitly Rejected

Unclear denotatum and Gaza's conjecture σαργῖνος > σαργός

Apparently, the only person who expressed doubts about the existence of the word *sargiacus* was Edward Wotton. In his 1552 treatise *On the differences of animals*,[50] he suspected *sargiacus* might have originated as an error: '*Sarginus*. Theodorus *sargiacum* vocavit, nisi mendosus sit codex'.[51] Still, he did not explain his thought and his suspicion was not supported by later scholars.

One of the reasons for the longevity of the word *sargiacus* is the obscurity of its allegedly existing denotatum. The Greek word σαργῖνος is very rare. Apart from our case at line 610b6 of the *Historia animalium* (*Hist. an.*), it is attested only in the catalogue of fish in Athenaeus' *Deipnosophistae*, where the fish σαργός is discussed: Athenaeus quotes Epicharmus and Dorion who mention σαργῖνος, but these fragments hardly facilitate its identification:

Ἐπίχαρμος δ'ἐν Ἥβας γάμῳ· "αἱ δὲ λῇς, σαργοί τε χαλκίδες τε καὶ τοὶ πόντιοι [...]" ὡς διαφόρους δὲ τοὺς σαργίνους ἐν τοῖσδε καταλέγει· "ἦν δὲ σαργῖνοί <τε> μελάνουροί τε καὶ ταὶ φίνταται ταινίαι λεπταὶ μέν, ἀδεῖαι δέ". ὁμοίως δὲ καὶ Δωρίων ἐν τῷ περὶ ἰχθύων φησὶ σαργίνους διὰ τοῦτ' αὐτοὺς καλῶν καὶ χαλκίδας.[52]

The impossibility of identifying the *sargiacus* with any known fish was clear to the sixteenth-century ichthyologist Ippolito Salviani:

> Ab eodemque [*scil.* Aristotele] inter gregales pisces σαργῖνον, sive (ut vertit Theodorus) *sargiacum* numerari. Quem quidem σαργῖνον sive *sargiacum*, uti Athenaeo authore a *sargo* diversum esse scimus, sic quis piscium sit, neque scimus neque sciri posse arbitramur, cum praeter Aristotelem, qui eum inter gregales (ut diximus) tantum connumerat, ac Epicharmum in nuptiis Hebae, et Dorionem in libro de piscibus, qui nudam tantum mentionem eius fecerunt, nemo veterum eius meminit amplius.[53]

---

[50] On this fundamental treatise, see Enenkel, 'Zur Konstruierung' (n. 35 above).

[51] Edward Wotton, *De differentiis animalium*, Paris, Michel de Vascosan, 1552, f° (USTC 151058), fol. 153r ('*Sarginus*. Theodore called <it> *sargiacus*, if the manuscript is not faulty').

[52] Ath. 7, 117, 10–16; cf. also Ath. 7, 93, 6–8 and Ath., epitome 2, 1, 148, 17–20 ('Epicharmus, in The Marriage of Hebe: "And if thou desire, *sargs* there be, and *sardines*, and those deep-sea creatures [...]" But the *Sargini* he lists in the following lines as something different: "There were *gar-fish* and *black-tails* too, and the beloved *ribbon-fish*, thin but sweet." A similar statement is found in Dorion's work *On Fishes*; hence he calls them *chalcides* (sardines) as well as *sargini*'). The translation is taken from Athenaeus, *The Deipnosophists*, 7 vols, transl. Ch. B. Gulick, III, Cambridge (MA) and New York, 1957, p. 443.

[53] Ippolito Salviani, *Aquatilium animalium historiae liber primus*, Roma, Ippolito Salviani, 1554–1557, f° (USTC 854346), fol. 179r ('<We know that> he [*scil.* Aristotle] mentions, among the shoal-fishes, the σαργῖνος, or (as Gaza translated) *sargiacus*. Though, on the one hand, we know from Athenaeus that this σαργῖνος, or *sargiacus*, is different from the <fish> *sargus*, on the other, we do not know and we think that it is impossible to know, what kind of fish it is, for apart from Aristotle, who (as we said) just names

Evidently Gaza did not know that σαργῖνος appeared in Athenaeus; therefore, when he encountered it just once in Aristotle's text, he considered it a scribal error. Indeed, another fish name, σαργός, is mentioned several times in the *Hist. an.* (543a7, 543b15, 570a32, 591b19) and constantly rendered by Gaza as *sargus*. At line 610b6, consequently, he deemed it justifiable to emend the text, substituting the form σαργῖνοι — that was, for him, a *hapax legomenon* — with σαργοί. That is why Gaza's translation, in the manuscript Vat. lat. 2094, reads *sargi* here.

Though it was known to some sixteenth-century scholars (e.g., Gessner) that Gaza's version was based on his numerous implicit conjectures to the Greek text, his emendation σαργῖνοι > σαργοί remained unnoticed. Indeed, the unique word *sargiacus* seemed an adequate translation of the Greek σαργῖνος. Just as the rare word σαργῖνος was interpreted as a derivate of the well-attested fish name σαργός[54], thus the Latin *sargiacus* appeared as a derivate of *sargus*. Among many other neologisms introduced by Gaza, the pseudo-neologism *sargiacus* — in fact born, like Frankenstein's monster, from other fish names — did not look too strange[55].

Gaza's interpolation of μήκονες/μηκόναι

The disclosure of the incidental origin of the word *sargiacus* was hampered by yet another circumstance. While the Greek text reads 'σαργῖνοι, βελόναι, τευθοί, ἰουλίδες', Gaza has one word more, 'sargi, acus, lolii, papaverae, iuliae' (the unnoticed intruder is *papaverae*); when *sargi* and *acus* are read as one word, the number of words becomes equal. Certainly, not only the number but also the nature of these words was favourable for the persistence of the misprint *sargiacus*. The explanation lies in the manuscript tradition of the word βελόνη.

In the above list of shoal-fishes, at line 610b6, the word βελόνη 'needle', is present. This word occurs as a fish name several times in the *Hist. an.*, always rendered by Gaza as *acus* 'needle',[56] probably based on Pliny the Elder (Plin. *HN* 9, 166, 1–2), who supplies the Latin

---

it among the shoal-fishes, and from Epicharmus, in the *Nuptiae Hebae*, and Dorion, in his book *On Fish*, who merely mentioned it, nobody else of the ancients referred to it').

[54] This etymology is confirmed by Pierre Chantraine, the same pattern being represented by the fish names κεστρῖνος (cf. κέστρα, κεστρεύς), κορακῖνος (cf. κόραξ), ἐρυθρῖνος (cf. ἐρυθρός), φοξῖνος (cf. φοξός), ἀθερίνη (probably from ἀθήρ), as well as, of unclear etymology, σαρδῖνος/σαρδίνη, ἐλεγῖνος, and μαρῖνος: P. Chantraine, *La formation des noms en grec ancien*, Paris, 1933, p. 204 and his *Dictionnaire étymologique de la langue grecque. Histoire des mots*, Paris, 1999, p. 988.

[55] An attempt to identify the name σαργῖνος with a real fish species was made much later, based on a comparison with Modern Greek. Namely, D'Arcy Thompson identifies σαργῖνος with the garfish, *Belone belone* (Linnaeus, 1760), referring to the fact that the latter species is called in Modern Greek σαργάννος, σαργώνη, ζαργάνα. Thompson hypothesises that the word σαργῖνος, standing near βελόνη 'garfish', could have been therefore an interpolated gloss, explaining the meaning of Aristotle's βελόνη to a medieval reader. Still, the identification of σαργῖνος as garfish is questionable, for the forms σαργάννος and σαργώνη could have been independent derivates of σαργός. According to Thompson, σαργός probably stood for quite a different fish, *Diplodus sargus* (Linnaeus, 1758). See D. W. Thompson, *A Glossary of Greek Fishes*, London, 1947, pp. 29–32 and 227–8.

[56] 506b9, 543b11, 567b23, 571a2, 571a5, 616a32; the latter instance was also cited by Gaza in the margin of a manuscript bearing Pliny's *Natural history*: see A. Grafton, *The Culture of Correction in Renaissance*

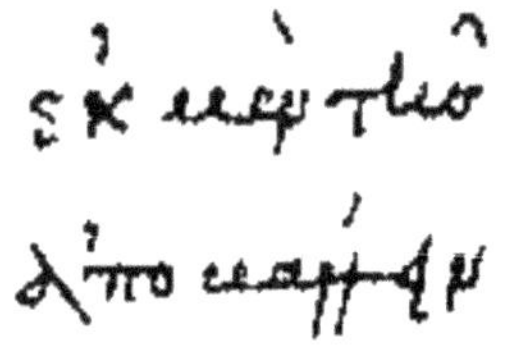

FIG. 16.4.a-b. Similar execution of *mu* and *beta* in MS Vatican City, Biblioteca Apostolica Vaticana, Vat. gr. 1339, a: 'ἐκ μὲν τῆς' ('from the'), fol. 109v, l. 16; b: 'ἀποβάλλειν' ('to throw away'), ibid., l. 10.

equivalent to this Greek fish name in his *Natural history*: 'Acus sive *belone* unus piscium dehiscente propter multitudinem utero parit'.[57]

Still, according to Balme's *apparatus criticus*, the form βελόναι in the passage 610b6 is transmitted in different variants: μηλόναι in codex P; μελοναι in m; μήκονη βελόνη in n; βελόναι μήκονες in L^c and the Aldine.[58]

The readings with μ-, to my mind, are due to a clearly explicable scribal error, for the early minuscule *beta*, looking somewhat like modern Latin *u*, could be easily mixed up with the letter *mu*, since the latter was frequently executed without any protraction of the first vertical element below the line; moreover, the first vertical element of the *mu* often leaned closely on the subsequent curve. Thus, the probability of confusing a *beta* with such a *mu* was rather high. A clear example of their similarity can be seen precisely in the codex P, a mid-fourteenth-century manuscript containing a set of Aristotle's scientific writings and bearing the reading μηλόναι (Fig. 16.4.a–b).

Apparently, one of Gaza's Greek *Vorlagen* combined both variants, interpolating, as it happens, a *varia lectio* into the text.[59] Namely, that supposed *Vorlage* must have contained both readings, βελόναι and μηκόναι (or μήκονες), the latter an emendation from μηλόναι, μελοναι, or similar.[60] That is why Gaza rendered βελόναι as *acus* and μηκόναι, or maybe μήκονες, as *papaverae*. The latter is a neologism coined *ad hoc* for translating this phantom fish name μηκόναι/μήκονες. The Greek word μήκων 'poppy, poppy-head, poppy-seed' is used in Aristotle's zoological treatises a few times, in a special sense, denoting an internal organ of the molluscs (in most cases the hepatopancreas or the ink-bag).[61] Whether Gaza kept in mind this meaning of μήκων or its better-known use as a plant name, he most probably saw the word μηκόναι, not μήκονες, in his Greek *Vorlage*, because

---

Europe, London, 2011, pp. 46–7. Another occurrence is to be found in the *De generatione animalium*, at 755a33.

[57] 'The pipefish or garfish is the only fish so prolific that its matrix is ruptured when it spawns'. The translation is taken from Pliny, *Natural History*, 10 vols, transl. H. Rackham, III, 2nd edn, Cambridge (MA), 1983, p. 277.

[58] Aristotle, *Historia animalium*, 2002 (n. 7 above), p. 398.

[59] That *Vorlage* must have been a manuscript close to codex n, i.e., MS Vatican City, Biblioteca Apostolica Vaticana, Urb. gr. 39, where both readings are integrated in the text, without any comments or peculiarities, at fol. 79v, l. 5. On this manuscript, see G. Vorobyev, 'Iz istorii vatikanskogo kodeksa Urb. gr. 39: Angelo Vadio da Rimini – chitatel Istorii zhivotnykh Aristotelya', *Vspomogatelnye istoricheskie distsipliny*, 35, 2016, pp. 359–85, with earlier literature.

[60] It could also have been Gaza himself who came forth with such an emendation, which would mean that his conjectures influenced codex n; it is not impossible, indeed, that n was transcribed from one of Gaza's working copies of the Greek text. Codex L^c and the Aldine were definitely dependant on Gaza's version. On Gaza's possible propensity to the contaminative insertion of two *variae lectiones* of a single Greek word in his translation, see Vorobyev, 'Theodore Gaza's neologisms in *-cilla/-cula*' (n. 6 above), pp. 800–1, with examples from ll. 592b22 and 593b5.

[61] Chantraine, *Dictionnaire etymologique* (n. 54 above), p. 693.

the respective Latin fish name he introduced was not *papaveres* (which, a plural-form of the third-declension word *papaver* 'poppy', would correspond to Greek μήκονες, correctly μήκωνες), but *papaverae*, as if the Greek word he was translating belonged to the first declension. Apparently, Gaza suspected the Greek derivation ἡ μήκων > ἡ μήκωνα/μήκονα and repeated that pattern in Latin as *papaver* > *papavera*.[62]

Now, if one looks again at Aristotle's list of shoal-fishes, one is struck by seeing that, while Gaza's Greek *Vorlage* must have read 'σαργῖνοι, βελόναι, μήκοναι, τευθοί, ἰουλίδες', Gaza's Latin text transposes words inside it. *Lolius* being Gaza's usual rendering of τευθός, a name of a cephalopod (calamary or squid),[63] he swapped his Latin equivalents of μήκοναι and τευθοί: 'sargi, *acus*, lolii, *papaverae*, iuliae' (not 'sargi, *acus*, *papaverae*, lolii, iuliae'). The only explanation I see for this is Gaza's striving to create a rhetorically elaborate text: he wanted *lolii* and *iuliae* to be distant from each other, so as to prevent the alliteration. In a broader context, the transposition also created a certain rhythmical (of course, non-quantitative) pattern: 'lolii, papaverae, iuliae, limariae'.[64]

The form *papaverae*, first declension, ostensibly appeared erroneous to Aldus, who intervened with a correction that was probably another disimprovement (technically a *Verschlimmbesserung*) of Gaza's text. He replaced that plural form (spelled only in the *editio princeps* as *papaverę* and in the next incunable editions as *papavere*) with the third-declension *papaveres*, making the fish name sound completely homonymous to that of the flower and the organ of the molluscs (cf. Figs 16.2 and 16.3a). That is why Gessner, in his alphabetical overview of existing fishes, cites one called *papaver* ('*Papaver* (μήκων) pro pisce

---

[62] The earlier translators of the *Hist. an.* apparently did not either know or take into consideration the reading with μ-: *balona* (Michael Scot), *acus* (William of Moerbeke and George of Trebizond). Further examples of this derivation pattern, namely change of declension, are Gaza's neologisms *voca* < *vox* 'voice', *junco* < *juncus* 'rush or similar plant', *florus* < *flos* 'flower'. The latter represents a case quite close to that of *papavera*. In the *Hist. an.*, a bird called ἄνθος is mentioned seven times (592b25, 609b14, 609b18, 609b16, 610a6, 610a7, 615a27), unmistakably as a second-declension masculine, ὁ ἄνθος, -ου, in contrast with the well-known word τὸ ἄνθος, -ους 'flower'. Greek etymological dictionaries do not mention this bird name. Whether it derives from the word 'flower' or not, it was surely perceived as such. Twice (609b16 and 609b18) Gaza omits the bird name ἄνθος, so as not to repeat the word that has been just mentioned (609b14); in five other instances, 592b25, 609b14, 610a6, 610a7, 615a27, he renders it as *florus*. Clearly, in doing so, Gaza follows the derivation pattern of the Greek word, coining a second-declension word from a third-declension one: *flos, floris* > *florus, flori*. This new word, rather than a neologism of form, was a neologism of sense. Indeed, the adjective *florus* 'light-coloured, fair, bright', although rare, is attested in Naevius, Aulus Gellius, and in a few other authors (P. G. W. Glare, *Oxford Latin dictionary*, Oxford, 2012, p. 784). Besides, a well-known personal name *Florus/Flora* is derived from the adjective. The adjective *florus* might in fact be connected with *flos*, but probably rather with *flavus* (A. Ernout and A. Meillet, *Dictionnaire étymologique de la langue latine. Histoire des mots*, Paris, 2001, pp. 239, 241). Gaza's use of this word as a bird name was a merely purist innovation, designed so as to avoid transliterating Greek, because he surely knew that Plin. *HN* 10, 116, 7 used the transliterated form *anthus*, after which Gessner, even though citing Gaza's translation, entitled his chapter on the respective bird *De antho* (Conrad Gessner, *Historiae animalium liber III. qui est de avium natura*, Zürich, Christoph Froschauer, 1555, fᵒ (USTC 624829), pp. 159–60, 576). It is, therefore, no wonder that in the modern nomenclature there is a passerine genus named *Anthus* (Bechstein, 1805), known in English as pipits, and no bird taxon bears the name *Florus*. The genus name *Florus* (Distant, 1884) existing in the *Hemiptera* order of the insects must have been introduced independently from the bird name discussed here.

[63] The appearance of a cephalopod in the list of shoal-fishes is strange. If a scribal error, it must have been a very old one, because all extant Greek manuscripts read it unanimously.

[64] Gaza carried out a similar transposition, also for the sake of euphony, in a list of birds at line 592b22: see Vorobyev, '*Sylvia*' (n. 6 above), pp. 253–4.

338 PRINTING AND MISPRINTING

quodam accipitur'), as well as 'Mecones, μήκονες (penultima per o breve), pisces gregales, nominantur ab Aristotele Historiae 9.2., Gaza vertit *papaveres*.'[65]

In any case, given that *papaverae/papaveres* are not mentioned, as far as I know, in any commentary on this Aristotelian passage, Gaza's contaminative interpolation apparently did not arouse any suspicions from Scaliger up until D'Arcy Thompson.[66] Moreover, David Balme thought, as has been shown above by a quotation from his apparatus, that Gaza merely omitted βελόναι (or its alternative reading). Why no attention has been paid to the peculiar *papavera/papaver* 'poppy-fish', remains unclear.[67]

CONCLUSION

Turning back to *sargiacus*, the interpolation of the phantom 'poppy-fish' committed by Gaza was perhaps one of the factors that prevented his readers from discerning the fish name *acus* in *sargiacus*. Indeed, they saw the word *papaverae*, thought that Gaza had read μήκονες, or μήκοναι, instead of βελόναι and had no reason to look for a Latin rendering of the latter *inside* the word *sargiacus*, which authoritative editors since Aldus had considered legitimate. Besides, this blunting of their philological sagacity could have been facilitated by the transposition of *papaverae* and *lolii*.

A sort of typographical mondegreen, the phantom word *sargiacus* entered sixteenth-century ichthyological nomenclature without meeting resistance and, remaining at its periphery, aroused almost no suspicion in early modern scholars. Indeed, they were accustomed to bizarre animal names, i.e. those born from the experiments that the humanist translator Theodore Gaza had carried out on Aristotle's *Historia animalium*: his creations were frequently discussed in sixteenth-century books on animals. In case of *sargiacus*, though, it was not Gaza but his printer who, a Frankenstein *ante nomen*, in the mid 1470s merged two fish names, *sargi* and *acus*, into one, by merely skipping a punctuation mark. Grammatically healed by Aldus Manutius in 1504, *sargiacus* easily passed itself off as a true word and even underwent further spelling mutations, becoming *sardiacus* and *sargianus*.

In general, early modern philological discussions of problematic scientific terms were frequently reduced to the question of whether the word was a true *hapax legomenon* or an error committed by a scribe (or, more seldom, printer). The nature of the humanist method itself, which underpinned most encyclopaedic works on animals in the sixteenth century, implied consideration of the corrupt manuscript tradition of ancient texts, i.e. much attention was paid to the detection and correction of possible scribal errors. Early modern zoologists were therefore also on the alert for mistakes made by printers, especially in cases where modern

---

[65] Gessner, *Historiae animalium liber IIII* (n. 35 above), pp. 776 and 637 ('*Papaver* (μήκων) is considered a certain fish'; '*Mecones*, μήκονες (the former with a short o), shoal-fishes, are mentioned by Aristotle, History <of animals>, 9.2., Gaza renders as *papaveres*').

[66] Thompson, *A Glossary of Greek Fishes* (n. 55 above), does not mention any similar Greek fish name.

[67] In Aristoteles, *Peri zōōn historias* (n. 22 above), Scaliger included both the β- and the μ-reading, but rendered the latter with a mere transliteration *mecones* ('Summa autem gregalium haec est: thunnides, maenulae, gobii, boces, lacerti, coracini, dentices, mulli, sphyrenae, anthiae, elegini, atherini, *sargini*, *aciculae*, *mecones*, lolligines, iulides, pelamydes, scombri, gracculi', p. 1012).

authors were cited and no manuscript tradition existed.[68] All the more surprising is the long life of the would-be fish *sargiacus*. Maybe one day a zoologist seeking an appropriate Latin name for a newly discovered fish species, a particularly monstrous one, will adopt this word for it.

APPENDIX MONSTRUOSA

Among other misprints in rare animal names from Gaza's translation, at least the following two enjoyed an afterlife comparable to that of *sargiacus*.

First, *squatiraia*, a compound Gaza coined for the Greek ῥινόβατος. The fish was described by Aristotle at 566a28 as a hybrid of two species, or as a truly Frankenstein's fish:

> Τῶν μὲν οὖν ἄλλων ἰχθύων παρὰ τὰς συγγενείας οὐδὲν ὦπται συνδυαζόμενον, ῥίνη δὲ μόνη δοκεῖ τοῦτο ποιεῖν καὶ βάτος· ἔστι γάρ τις ἰχθὺς ὃς καλεῖται ῥινόβατος· ἔχει γὰρ τὴν μὲν κεφαλὴν καὶ τὰ ἔμπροσθεν βάτου, τὰ δ᾽ ὄπισθεν ῥίνης, ὡς γινόμενος ἐξ ἀμφοτέρων τούτων τῶν ἰχθύων.

Or, in Balme's translation:

> No instance has been observed of fishes uniting outside their own kind except for the angel-fish (rhinē) only, which appears to mate with the batos, for there is a fish known as the rhinobatos, which has the head and foreparts of a batos, and the rear parts of a rhinē, as though it were composed of these two fishes.[69]

Gaza reads (MS Vat. lat. 2094, fol. 90r, l. 14):

> Piscium caeterorum diversa genera coire visum a nemine est. Squatinam solam et raiam hoc facere creditur, argumento piscis cuiusdam, qui nomen ex utroque compositum trahit *rhinobati*, quasi *squatiraiam* appelles. Est enim parte priore raiae similis, posteriore squatinae.

---

[68] In early modern books on animals, *librarii* or *scriptores* 'scribes' are blamed more often than *typographi*, for the obvious reason that, during the centuries of ancient texts' manuscript transmission, many more errors had been accumulated than those caused by the printers. And yet, Latin formulas shifting the responsibility for a mistake from the author of the cited book onto a scribe and onto the printer are similar, e.g.: 'librarii vero monedulam etiam in nicedulam perverterunt' ('but the scribes distorted *monedula* as *nicedula*'), Gessner, *Historiae animalium liber III* (n. 62 above), p. 505; 'Theodorus (nisi culpa sit librariorum) hanc avem confudit cum gnaphalo' ('If it is not the scribes' fault, Theodore mixed up this bird with *gnaphalus*'), Wotton, *De differentiis animalium* (n. 51 above), fol. 129r; '[...] quomodo et apud Horatium hanc vocem scribi invenimus, nisi typographorum forte incuria' ('[...] in which way we find this word spelled in Horace, too, if it is not perhaps due to the negligence of the printers'), Aldrovandi, *De piscibus* (n. 37 above), p. 307; 'Gesnerus pro Amia (nisi sit error typographi) habet Lamia' ('Gessner reads *lamia* instead of *amia*, if it is not the printer's error'), Ibid., p. 328; '[...] in Latina Theodori versione non tamen ipsius, sed typographi errore pro Rana perperam legitur Raia' ('[...] Theodore's Latin version reads erroneously *raia* instead of *rana*, though this is not due to his mistake, but the printer's'), Ibid., p. 448.

[69] Balme, *History of Animals* (n. 7 above), p. 265.

Squatiraia was distorted as *squatraia* in the 1476 *princeps*.[70] The same holds true for the 1495 edition (sig. G[5]*r*, second paragraph, l. 4) and the 1498 edition (fol. 26*r*, second paragraph, l. 4), while the 1492 edition reads *squatroraia* at fol. 30*v*, ll. 8–9.[71]

In the 1504 Aldine, it was 'emended' to *squatinoraia*[72] — as if derived from *squatina*, not from the related word *squatus* — and entered, in this latter form, the binomial nomenclature, namely as *Raia squatinoraia*.[73] This species name is not used in today's taxonomy though.

Similarly, Gaza coined the neologism *montifringilla* for the Greek ὀρόσπιζος at 592b25: 'ὀρόσπιζος· οὗτος σπίζῃ ὅμοιος καὶ τὸ μέγεθος παραπλήσιος, πλὴν ἔχει τὸν αὐχένα κυανοῦν, καὶ διατρίβει ἐν τοῖς ὄρεσιν', translated by David Balme as 'Mountain-finch: this is like a chaffinch and is comparable in size but has blue on the neck; it spends its time in the mountains',[74] and rendered by Gaza (MS Vat. lat. 2094, fol. 117*r*, l. 3) as: '[…] *montifringilla* quae fringillae similis et magnitudine proxima est, sed collo coeruleo et in montibus degit, unde nomen accepit'.

In the *princeps*, this became erroneously *monti fringilla*, with a clear blank space in the middle (sig. l[9]*r*, l. 4), repeated also in the 1492 (fol. 39*v*, l. 10), 1495 (sig. I[4]*r*, l. 7), and 1498 editions (fol. 34*r*, l. 15). The Aldine restored Gaza's original variant *montifringilla*, both in the text (fol. 40*v*, l. 12) and in the accompanying Greek–Latin glossary ('ὁ ὀροσπίζης [sic] – *montifringilla*', sig. a[8]*r*). Still, the Latin–Greek glossary, printed in the same gathering, reads, at sig. a3*r*, '*montisfringilla* avis – ὁ ὀροσπίζης', with the insertion of a superfluous 's'. This corrupt reading was repeated, for instance, in Conrad Gessner et al., *Lexicon Graecolatinum*, Basel, [Hieronymus Curio], 1545, f° (USTC 671,853), sig. zz4*r*): 'ὀροσπίζης – *montisfringilla* avis, ut Gaza vertit ex Aristot(ele)' ('ὀροσπίζης – bird *montisfringilla*, as Gaza translates from Aristotle').[75] The correct reading eventually won, so that today's zoologists use Gaza's original form *montifringilla*: the brambling's valid scientific name is currently *Fringilla montifringilla* (Linnaeus, 1758), and the white-winged snow finch is known as *Montifringilla nivalis* (Linnaeus, 1766). Incidentally, for the impact of a blank space, one should also recall the Greek bird name ἀείσκωψ, spelled together in many editions, though not in the most recent one, Aristotle, *Hist. An.* 617b32: 'σκῶπες δ'οἱ μὲν ἀεὶ πᾶσαν ὥραν εἰσί, καὶ καλοῦνται ἀεὶ σκῶπες', translated as 'Of scops, some are always present at every season and are called *ever-scops*'.[76] Gaza, however, rendered this ἀείσκωψ as *semperasio*, with the explicit comment that it is a solid compound word: 'asiones aliqui omnibus anni temporibus patent et ob eam rem *peremnes* [pro *perennes*] et *semperasiones* vocabulo composito appellantur' (MS Vat. lat. 2094, fol. 143*r*, ll. 10–12).

---

[70] Aristoteles, *De animalibus* (n. 5 above, sig. i5*r*, l. 6).

[71] See above n. 14 for these editions.

[72] See n. 15 above, fol. 31*r*, second paragraph, l. 4.

[73] C. F. Stephan, *De Raiis. Shediasma* [sic] *primum*, Leipzig, 1779, p. 21.

[74] Balme, *History of animals* (n. 7 above), pp. 101–3.

[75] On the sources of that edition see M. Sergeev, 'Tsitaty i ssylki na istochniki v gumanisticheskoy grechesko-latinskoy leksikografii (Henri Estienne i ego predshestvenniki)', *Journal of Applied Linguistics and Lexicography*, 2/1, 2020, pp. 37–46 (42–3).

[76] Aristotle, *Hist. an.* (n. 7 above), p. 421; Balme, *History of animals* (n. 7 above), p. 291.

BIBLIOGRAPHY

PRIMARY SOURCES

MANUSCRIPTS

Vatican City, Biblioteca Apostolica Vaticana, Vat. lat. 2094 (Aristotle, *De animalibus*).
Vatican City, Biblioteca Apostolica Vaticana, Vat. gr. 1339 (Aristotle, scientific writings).
Vatican City, Biblioteca Apostolica Vaticana, Urb. gr. 39 (Aristotle, scientific writings).

PRINTED BOOKS

Aldrovandi, Ulisse, *De piscibus libri V et de cetis lib. unus. Ioannes Cornelius Uterverius collegit*, Bologna, Giovanni Battista Bellagamba for Girolamo Tamburini, 1613, f° (USTC 4027422).
Aldrovandi, Ulisse, *De piscibus libri V et de cetis lib. unus. Ioannes Cornelius Uterverius collegit*, Bologna, Nicolò Tebaldini for Marco Antonio Bernia, 1638, f° (USTC 4008088).
Aleandro, Girolamo, et al., *Lexicon Graecolatinum multis et preclaris additionibus locupletatum*, [Paris, Gilles de Gourmont] and Matthieu Bolsec, 1512, f° (USTC 143982).
Aristoteles Latine interpretibus variis (Aristotelis opera, edidit Academia regia Borussica, 3), Berlin, 1831.
Aristoteles, *De animalibus*, transl. Theodorus Gaza and ed. Ludovicus Podocatharus, Venice, Johannes de Colonia and Johannes Manthen, 1476, f° (ISTC ia00973000).
Aristoteles, *De animalibus*, transl. Theodorus Gaza, [Venice, Simon Bevilaqua, about 1495], f° (ISTC ia00975000).
Aristoteles, *De animalibus*, transl. Theodorus Gaza and ed. Sebastianus Manilius, Venice, Johannes and Gregorius de Gregoriis, 1492, f° (ISTC ia00974000).
Aristoteles, *De animalibus*, transl. Theodorus Gaza, Venice, Bartholomaeus de Zanis for Octavianus Scotus, 1498, f° (ISTC ia00976000).
Aristoteles, *De animalibus historiae Graece et Latine*, transl. J. C. Scaliger and ed. J. G. Schneider, 4 vols, Leipzig, 1811.
Aristoteles, De historia animalium libri IX. De partibus animalium et earum causis libri IIII. De generatione animalium libri V, transl. Theodorus Gaza and Pietro Alcionio, Paris, Simon de Colines, 1524, f° (USTC 180946).
Aristoteles, *Histoire des animaux*, ed. and transl. A.-G. Camus, 2 vols, Paris, 1783.
Aristoteles, *Opera quae extant omnia brevi paraphrasi, ac litterae perpetuo inhaerente explanatione illustrata*, 6 vols, Rome, 1668.
Aristoteles, *Peri zōōn historias: Historia de animalibus*, ed. and transl. Julius Caesar Scaliger, Toulouse, Dominique and Pierre Bosc, 1619, f° (USTC 6808360).

PRINTING AND MISPRINTING

Aristoteles, *Ta sōzomena = Operum, nova editio. Graece et Latine. Accesserunt ex libris Aristotelis, qui hodie desiderantur, fragmenta quaedam. Indices duo perutiles*, ed. Isaac Casaubon, 2 vols, Lyon [i.e., Geneva], Guillaume de Laimarie, 1590, f° (USTC 142711).

Aristoteles and Theophrastus, *Habentur hoc volumine haec Theodoro Gaza interprete. Aristotelis De natura animalium, liber IX. Eiusdem De partibus animalium, lib IIII. Eiusdem De generatione animalium, libri V. Theophrasti De historia plantarum, liber IX Alexandri Aphrodisiensis Problemata duobus libris*, Venice, Aldo Manuzio, 1504, f° (USTC 810862).

Aristotelis opera omnia Graece et Latine, 5 vols, Paris, 1848–1874.

Aristotelis qui ferebantur librorum fragmenta. Scholiorum in Aristotelem supplementum. Index Aristotelicus (Aristotelis opera, edidit Academia regia Borussica, 5), Berlin, 1870.

Aristotle, *Historia animalium*, I: *Books I–X: Text*, ed. D. M. Balme, prepared for publication by A. Gotthelf, Cambridge, 2002.

Aristotle, *History of Animals*, III: *Books 7–10*, ed. and transl. D. M. Balme, Cambridge (MA), 1991.

Artedi, P., and Schneider, J. G., *Synonymia piscium Graeca et Latina*, Leipzig, 1789.

Artedi, P., *Synonymia nominum piscium*, Leiden, 1738.

Athenaeus, *The Deipnosophists*, 7 vols, III, Cambridge (MA) and New York, 1957 (first ed. 1929).

Belon, Pierre, *De aquatilibus libri duo*, Paris, Charles Estienne, 1553, 8° (USTC 151230).

Constantin, Robert, and Porto, Francesco, *Lexicon Græcolatinum. Secunda editio*, 2 vols, [Geneva], Héritiers d'Eustache Vignon and Jacob Stoer, 1592, f° (USTC 451309).

Gessner, Conrad, *Historiae animalium liber III. qui est de avium natura*, Zürich, Christoph Froschauer (I), 1555, f° (USTC 624829).

Gessner, Conrad, *Historiae animalium liber IIII. qui est de piscium & aquatilium animantium natura*, Zürich, Christoph Froschauer, 1558, f° (USTC 624828).

Gessner, Conrad, *Nomenclator aquatilium animantium. Icones animalium aquatilium*, Zürich, Christoph Froschauer, 1560, f° (USTC 678237).

Gessner, Conrad, et al., *Lexicon Graecolatinum*, Basel, [Hieronymus Curio], 1545, f° (USTC 671853).

Marschalk, Nikolaus, *Historia aquatilium Latine ac Grece cum figuris*, [Rostock, Nikolaus Marschalk, 1517], f° (USTC 663330).

Nifo, Agostino, *Expositiones in omnes Aristotelis libros De historia animalium. libri IX. De partibus animalium, & earum causis. libri IV. Ac De generatione animalium. libri V*, Venice, Girolamo Scoto, 1546, f° (USTC 844719).

Pliny, *Natural History*, 10 vols, III, 2nd edn, Cambridge (MA), 1983 (first ed. 1940).

Rondelet, Guillaume, *Libri de piscibus marinis*, Lyon, Macé Bonhomme, 1554, f° (USTC 151588).

Salviani, Ippolito, *Aquatilium animalium historiae liber primus*, Rome, Ippolito Salviani, 1554–1557, f° (USTC 854346).

Stephan, C. F., *De Raiis. Shediasma* [sic] *primum*, Leipzig, 1779.

Toussain, Jacques, *Lexicon Graecolatinum*, Paris, Charlotte Guillard, Claude Chevallon's widow and Guillaume Merlin, 1552, f° (USTC 151147).

Wotton, Edward, *De differentiis animalium*, Paris, Michel de Vascosan, 1552, f° (USTC 151058).

SECONDARY LITERATURE

Bäumer, Ä., *Geschichte der Biologie*, II: *Zoologie der Renaissance — Renaissance der Zoologie*, Frankfurt am Main, 1991.

Berrens, D., 'Naming an Unknown Animal: The Case of the Sloth', *Archives of Natural History*, 47/2, 2020, pp. 325–43.

Beullens, P., 'Aristotle, his Translators, and the Formation of Ichthyologic Nomenclature', in M. Goyens et al. (eds), *Science Translated: Latin and Vernacular Translations of Scientific Treatises in Medieval Europe*, Leuven, 2008, pp. 105–22.

Beullens, P., and Gotthelf, A., 'Theodore Gaza's Translation of Aristotle's *De animalibus*: Content, Influence and Date', *Greek, Roman and Byzantine Studies*, 47, 2007, pp. 469–513.

Blair, A., 'Annotating and Indexing Natural Philosophy', in N. Jardine and M. Frasca-Spada (eds), *Books and the Sciences in History*, Cambridge, 2000, pp. 69–89.

Blair, A., *Too Much to Know: Managing Scholarly Information before the Modern Age*, New Haven (CT) and London, 2010.

Chantraine, P., *Dictionnaire étymologique de la langue grecque. Histoire des mots*, Paris, 1999.

Chantraine, P., *La formation des noms en grec ancien*, Paris, 1933.

Enenkel, K. A. E., 'Zur Konstruierung der Zoologie als Wissenschaft in der Frühen Neuzeit: Diskursanalyse zweier Großprojekte (Wotton, Gesner)', in K. A. E. Enenkel and P. J. Smith (eds), *Early Modern Zoology. The Construction of Animals in Science, Literature and the Visual Arts*, Leiden and Boston, 2007, pp. 15–74.

Ernout, A., and Meillet, A., *Dictionnaire étymologique de la langue latine. Histoire des mots*, Paris, 2001.

Friedrich, U., *Naturgeschichte zwischen* artes liberales *und frühneuzeitlicher Wissenschaft. Conrad Gessners* Historia animalium *und ihre volkssprachliche Rezeption*, Tübingen, 1995.

Glare, P. G. W., *Oxford Latin Dictionary*, Oxford, 2012.

Grafton, A., *The Culture of Correction in Renaissance Europe*, London, 2011.

Helander, H., 'On Neologisms in Neo-Latin', *Renæssanceforum*, 10, 2016, pp. 9–34.

Hünemörder, C., 'Geschichte der Fischbücher von Aristoteles bis zum Ende des 17. Jahrhunderts', *Deutsches Schiffahrtsarchiv*, 1, 1975, pp. 185–200.

Jimenes, R., 'Un monument lexicographique: le dictionnaire gréco-latin de Jacques Toussain (1552)', in Y. Sordet (ed.), *Passeurs de texte: imprimeurs, éditeurs et lecteurs humanistes*, Turnhout, 2009, pp. 140–3.

Jobling, J. A., *The Helm Dictionary of Scientific Bird Names: From Aalge to Zusii*, London, 2010.

Monfasani, J., 'Aristotle as Scribe of Nature: The Title-Page of MS Vat. lat. 2094, *Journal of the Warburg and Courtauld Institutes*, 69, 2006, pp. 193–205.

Monfasani, J., 'The Pseudo-Aristotelian *Problemata* and Aristotle's *De Animalibus* in the Renaissance', in A. Grafton and N. Siraisi (eds), *Natural Particulars: Nature and the Disciplines in Renaissance Europe*, Cambridge (MA) and London, 1999, pp. 205–47.

Mund-Dopchie, M., 'Le *Lexicon Graecolatinum* de Jacques Toussain (1552): choix de vocabulaire et méthodes de traduction', in M. Fumaroli (ed.), *Les origines du Collège de France*, Paris, 1998, pp. 405–20.

Ogilvie, B. W., 'The Many Books of Nature: Renaissance Naturalists and Information Overload', *Journal of the History of Ideas*, 64/1, 2003, pp. 29–40.

Perfetti, S. 'Metamorfosi di una traduzione: Agostino Nifo revisore dei *De animalibus* gaziani', *Medioevo*, 22, 1996, pp. 259–301.

Perfetti, S., '*Cultius atque integrius*. Teodoro Gaza, traduttore umanistico del *De partibus animalium*', *Rinascimento*, 35, 1995, pp. 253–86.

Riedl-Dorn, C., *Wissenschaft und Fabelwesen. Ein kritischer Versuch über Conrad Gessner und Ulisse Aldrovandi*, Wien and Köln, 1989.

Rizzo, S. *Il lessico filologico degli umanisti*, Rome, 1973.

Rizzo, S., 'Neologismi nati da corruttele', L. Gamberale et al. (eds), *Le strade della filologia. Per Scevola Mariotti*, Rome, 2012, pp. 277–88.

Sergeev, M., 'Tsitaty i ssylki na istochniki v gumanisticheskoy grechesko-latinskoy leksikografii (Henri Estienne i ego predshestvenniki)', *Journal of Applied Linguistics and Lexicography*, 2/1, 2020, pp. 37–46 (in Russian).

Thompson, D. W., *A Glossary of Greek Fishes*, London, 1947.

Vorobyev, G., 'Iz istorii vatikanskogo kodeksa Urb. gr. 39: Angelo Vadio da Rimini — chitatel Istorii zhivotnykh Aristotelya', *Vspomogatelnye istoricheskie distsipliny*, 35, 2016, pp. 359–85 (in Russian).

Vorobyev, G., 'Neologizmy Feodora Gazy iz ego latinskogo perevoda *De animalibus* Aristotelya v sovremennoy zoologischeskoy nomenklature', *Indoevropeiskoe yazykoznanie i klassicheskaya filologiya*, 19/1, 2015, 1, pp. 158–68 (in Russian).

Vorobyev, G., 'O prirode latinskogo nazvaniia ryby *sargiacus* (Arist. *Hist. an.* 610b6)', *Indoevropeiskoe yazykoznanie i klassicheskaya filologiya*, 22, 2018, pp. 333–45 (in Russian).

Vorobyev, G., '*Sylvia*: Zur Entstehung des wissenschaftlichen Namens der Grasmücke (Arist. *Hist. an.* 592b22)', *Philologia Classica*, 13/2, 2018, pp. 247–64.

Vorobyev, G., 'Theodore Gaza's neologisms in *-cilla/-cula* and the role of sixteenth-century reference books in the formation of ornithological nomenclature', *Indoevropeiskoe yazykoznanie i klassicheskaya filologiya*, 24/1, 2020, pp. 794–818.

CHAPTER 17

CONRAD GESSNER AS CORRECTOR

How to Deal with Errors in Images

ANTHONY GRAFTON

CONRAD GESSNER: MAN OF THE PRINTING HOUSE

CONRAD Gessner was a scholar, a medical man, a bibliographer, and a natural historian, but he also knew his way around printers' shops better than most.[*][1] He worked closely with their owners. When he needed to send letters or books to friends, he had Christoph Froschauer, the Zurich publisher with whom he worked most often, pack them in the barrels of books that he shipped to colleagues in other cities.[2] Gessner understood the deadline pressures imposed by bookfairs and other factors, and when it was necessary, he timed his writing projects to meet their needs.[3] And he cultivated equally close working relationships with their employees. Froschauer's corrector, for example, helped Gessner send and receive

---

[*] Many thanks to Ann Blair for comments and corrections.

[1] On Gessner's work with publishers see esp. U. Leu, *Conrad Gessner (1515–1565): Universalgelehrter und Naturforscher der Renaissance*, Zurich, 2016; A. M. Blair, 'Conrad Gessner's Paratexts', *Gesnerus*, 73/1, 2016, pp. 73–123; A. M. Blair, 'The dedication strategies of Conrad Gessner', in G. Manning and C. Klestinec (eds), *Professors, Physicians and Practices in the History of Medicine: Essays in Honor of Nancy Siraisi*, Cham, 2017, pp. 169–209; and A. M. Blair, 'Printing and Humanism in the Work of Conrad Gessner', *Renaissance Quarterly*, 70/1, 2017, pp. 1–43.

[2] Conrad Gessner to Achilles Pirmin Gasser, 20 October 1564, in K. H. Burmeister, *Achilles Pirmin Gasser, 1505–1577: Artzt und Naturforscher, Historiker und Humanist*, III: *Briefwechsel*, Wiesbaden, 1975, p. 327; Gessner to Gasser, 6 November 1564, ibid., p. 332; Gessner to Gasser, 15 January 1565, ibid., p. 338.

[3] Conrad Gessner to Jean Bauhin, 24 August 1561, in Jean Bauhin, *De plantis a divis sanctisve nomen habentibus*, Basel, Conrad Waldkirch, 1591, 8° (USTC 88526), pp. 107–8: 'Plura nunc non vacat. Libellum enim ad praelum scribo, quem hodie absolvam' ('This is all for now. I am writing this little book at the press, and will finish it today'). The Frankfurt book fair took place in October: hence the pressure in this case.

Anthony Grafton, *Conrad Gessner as Corrector*. In: *Printing and Misprinting*. Edited by Geri Della Rocca de Candal, Anthony Grafton, and Paolo Sachet, Oxford University Press. © Anthony Grafton (2023). DOI: 10.1093/oso/9780198863045.003.0018 letters.[4] He befriended block cutters, both in Zurich and in Basel, who helped him to collect and study images of animals and plants as well as to produce his own illustrated books. Collaboration with artisans did not always run smoothly. Gessner tried to send his friend Jean Bauhin, a medical man who shared his interest in natural history, sample proofs of the images of plants being cut for his *Herbarium*. But the publisher knew Gessner too well and refused permission to share the proofs, since he feared that doing so might result in errors in the eventual book: 'The block cutter', Gessner explained, 'says that Froschauer forbade him to turn over to me more than one proof from each block, which I am to insert in the right place in the copy to be printed so they cannot make a mistake'.[5] Evidently, Gessner's skilled collaborators feared — or knew from experience — that he might confuse images or place them on the wrong page unless he was carefully overseen. But Gessner never lost his deep enthusiasm for their craftsmanship and knowledge. When he heard that one of the two Wyssenbach brothers, who were both renowned block cutters from Zurich, was at work making illustrations for an edition of Theophrastus in Basel, he asked Bauhin for help in making a connection that would enable the two men, scholar and artisan, to exchange images: 'Please greet him for me and ask him to grant me two or three pictures, or one at least, to examine, and if he wishes I will send him the same number of ours'.[6]

GESSNER AS A CORRECTOR

Gessner, moreover, knew one of the crafts of the printing house from personal experience. He was a skilled corrector in his own right. In 1543–1544, during a stay in Venice, he met a New Christian medical man, Manuel Brudo, who would eventually have a very successful career in Istanbul. Brudo was working on a treatise on the proper way to maintain one's diet when suffering from a fever, in which he examined the views of Hippocrates and later medical writers.[7] Gessner was impressed. Once back in Zurich, he sent Brudo a revealing letter. He began by making Brudo a generous offer. If Brudo would entrust him with the book, he wrote, 'we will use the utmost care and effort to see to it that it is published in

---

[4] Gessner to Bauhin, April 5, 1564, ibid., p. 137, and Gessner to Bauhin, 1564, ibid., p. 142; cf. also Gessner to Bauhin, probably October 1561, ibid., p. 110.

[5] Gessner to Bauhin, 11 July 1563, ibid., p. 117: 'Icones vero nostri herbarij nullas mittere possum. Sculptor enim sibi interdictum ait a Froschouero, ne amplius quam singulas de singulis mihi traderet, quas ego exemplari imprimendo insero, ne possint errare.' Translation from K. Reeds, 'Publishing Scholarly Books in the Sixteenth Century', *Scholarly Publishing*, 14/1, 1982, pp. 259–74 (266–7), slightly altered.

[6] Gessner to Bauhin, 19 July 1563, in Bauhin, *De plantis* (n. 3 above), p. 120: 'D. Constantinum lubentissime vidi. Audio formas pro Theophrasto eius sculpi apud vos a sculptore Tigurino, nomine Vuyssenbachio: quem meo nomine salutari velim, & rogari ut duas aut tres picturas, aut unicam, quamcunque, picturas mihi videndas concedat: totidem, si voluerit, de nostris mittam.'

[7] Manuel Brudo, *De ratione victus in singulis febribus secundum Hippocratem in genere et singillatim libri III*, Venice, heirs of Pietro Ravani, 1544, 8° (USTC 816961). On this work and Brudo's career see A. M. L. Andrade, 'Conrad Gessner Edits Brudus Lusitanus: The Trials and Tribulations of Publishing a Sixteenth Century Treatise on Dietetics', in C. B. Stuckzynski and B. Feitler (eds), *Portuguese Jews, New Christians and 'New Jews': A Tribute to Roberto Bachmann*, Leiden and Boston, 2018, pp. 189–205.

handsome type, on elegant paper, with no errors'.[8] He also promised to bring the book out quickly and to provide as many author's copies as Brudo wanted.[9] And he took care to give Brudo grounds for trusting his authority to make these promises:

> I wanted to send you these massages both in my name and in that of our printer Christoph Froschauer. In mine, since I desire that this learned and useful book be published quickly and well, and that can scarcely be done more conveniently than in our city. In that of the printer, since he generally follows my advice and prints the books that I think will be saleable.[10]

Like many other learned correctors, in other words, Gessner acted as an intermediary between a major printer and potential authors.[11] Like them too, he used his expertise to make his promises precise and attractive. He even took the time to explain that the bookseller Vincenzo Valgrisi or the scholar and corrector Arnoldus Arlenius could advise Brudo on how to send his manuscript to Frankfurt.[12]

Instead of accepting Gessner's offer, Brudo published his book in Venice in 1544, adroitly including Gessner's letter, with its official invitation to publish with a prestigious Swiss printer, as a sort of blurb. Unfortunately, his Swiss friend's last name appeared as 'hesnerus'.[13] But Gessner did not lose interest. In 1555, he published a small collection of introductory works on medicine, including his own *Enchiridion rei medicae triplicis* and Brudo's *De ratione victus*. In his dedicatory letter to another learned medical man, Achilles Pirmin Gasser, he explained that the latter book 'was so corrupted and mistreated by very ignorant scribes that every page was full of errors, not only the more or less tolerable sort that affect spelling, but also those that have to do with the separation of sentences by full stops and commas. Very often neither the beginning nor the end of the sentence could be discerned'.[14] Punctuation, he noted, was a serious matter: 'After all, it's proverbial that a

---

[8] Gessner to Brudo, 1544, in Brudo, *De ratione victus* (n. 7 above), sig. [*viiir]: 'Si librum tuum de ratione victus iam absolvisti, & apud nos eum imprimi placet, dabis huic tabellioni, curabimus summa fide ac diligentia ut egregiis characteribus, elegante charta, sine ullis mendis in publicum exeat, ita ut te nunquam poeniteat librum nostro praelo commisisse.'

[9] Ibid.: 'Exemplaria quot quot voles tibi dono mittemus, & sine mora aeditionem maturabimus.'

[10] Ibid., sig. [*viiir-v]: 'Haec ad te cum meo tum typographi nostri Christophori Froschoueri nomine scribere volui. Meo quidem, quoniam librum adeo doctum & utilem cito ac bene publicari cupio, quod commodius atque in urbe nostra fieri vix potest. Typographi autem, quoniam ille meis consilijs uti solet in excudendis libris quos vendibiles fore existimem.'

[11] On the tasks of correctors see, e.g., A. Goldgar, *Impolite Learning: Conduct and Community in the Republic of Letters*, New Haven (CT) and London, 1995; B. Richardson, *Printing, Writers, and Readers in Renaissance Italy*, Cambridge, 1999; and A. Grafton, *The Culture of Correction in Renaissance Europe*, London, 2011.

[12] Gessner to Brudo, in Brudo, *De ratione victus* (n. 7 above), sig. [*viiir]: 'Tunc ad nos commode mitti poterit per mercatores, qui FrancFordiam petunt, qua de re ex domino Vincentio bibliopola ad signum Erasmi Roterodami certior fieri potes [ed. potest], vel ex domino Arlenio nostro' ('Then it can be conveniently sent to us via the merchants who head for Frankfurt: on this you can seek information from the bookseller Vincenzo at the sign of Erasmus of Rotterdam or from our friend Arlenius').

[13] Ibid., sig. [*viiiv].

[14] Gessner to Gasser, August 1554, in Burmeiser, *Gasser*, III (n. 2 above), p. 134: 'Nam Brudi Lusitani ante annos decem excusi, adeo ab imperitissimis librariis depravati et male tractati erant, ut nulla non

348   PRINTING AND MISPRINTING

book with good punctuation is equipped with a commentary.'[15] Gessner had corrected the typographical errors in passing as he read the book, pen in hand, in the hope that it might eventually be reprinted.[16]

As a good corrector, however, he also told Gasser that when he had the chance to reissue Brudo's book himself he set out to do more than eliminate misprints. The author had made mistakes in Latin, which Gessner purged from his edition — not, he explained to Gasser, from stylistic purism, but to prevent the reader from being distracted: 'In addition, since the author often used verbs in the infinitive in place of the indicative, as is sometimes the custom of Greeks, I changed that as well, so that there would be nothing to delay the reader.'[17]

In this case, Gessner — like many other correctors — tried to convey a somewhat inflated view of his expertise as a copy editor. Brudo's book appeared with a printed list of errata, three pages long. Its anonymous author — the corrector working for Pietro Ravani's heirs? — wrote:

> As I was about to list the errors and all the omissions that came about through the carelessness of the printer, honourable reader, I wanted to warn you at the outset that our author had a singular habit of often using infinitive absolutes in place of the indicative. It is obvious that you should change individual instances to the indicative, or understand 'constat' or 'manifestum est'. Thus, when he says at the start '*varias esse apud medicos opiniones*' (literally: the views of medical men to be varied), you must understand '*variae sunt*' (they are varied) or '*varias esse constat*' (it is clear that they are varied).[18]

The mistake singled out here was hard to miss, since it occurred in the first sentence of Book I, Chapter 1.[19] But even if Gessner gave himself modest airs by suppressing any mention of the original corrector, in preparing a new copytext of Brudo's work he performed one of the corrector's basic tasks. Gessner's experience with printers also enabled him to advise friends whether their projects would fit a particular list, and whether 'the printers' compositors, as

---

pagina multis scateret mendis, non modo qui orthographiam attinent et tolerari facilius possunt, innumeris, sed etiam quod ad sententiarum per punctos et commata distinctionem, ita ut saepissime nec initium nec finis sententiae appareret.'

[15] Ibid.: 'Atqui vulgo fertur librum bene distinctum vice commentarii esse.' On the role of correctors in divising and imposing new forms of punctuation see M. B. Parkes, *Pause and Effect: An Introduction to the History of Punctuation in the West*, Aldershot, 1992, and more recently J. Richards, *Voices and Books in the English Renaissance: A New History of Reading*, Oxford, 2019.

[16] Ibid., pp. 134–5: 'Ego igitur, cum superioribus annis libros hos legendos mihi in manus sumpsissem, ut eorum lectione me exercerem atque proficerem, obiter etiam istis vitiis mederi volui, ut typographis aliquando diligentioribus traderem' ('Accordingly, when I had taken these books in hand in earlier years to read them in order to master and learn from their study, I also wanted to correct those errors in passing, so that I might someday pass them to more careful printers').

[17] Ibid., p. 135: 'Ad haec cum auctor verbis infinitivis loco indicativorum frequenter uteretur, ut Graeci interdum solent, hoc quoque mutavi, ut nihil esset, quod lectorem remoraretur, isque ita facilius iucundiusque in solam ipsam rerum contemplationem incumberet.'

[18] 'Ad lectorem', in Brudo, *De ratione victus* (n. 7 above), sig. [*viv]: 'Errata et quaecunque incuria typographi omissa sunt numeraturus candide lector, volui te primum admonere peculiare esse autori infinitivis absolutis loco indicativi crebro uti. Quorum singula ad indicativum reducito aut subintelligito constat aut manifestum est. Vt cum in initio ait, varias esse apud medicos opiniones, variae sunt aut varias esse constat intelligere oportet.'

[19] Ibid., sig. Aivr.

they are called', would be able to read their handwriting — services that correctors regularly performed for authors.[20]

ILLUSTRATING NATURAL HISTORY

As an author who hoped to see his own works appear in a correct and elegant form, Gessner faced special difficulties when he began publishing the great series of illustrated natural histories that won him the title of the Pliny of the sixteenth century — a role he has played not only in histories of science, but also in Robertson Davies's novel *The Rebel Angels*. A great philologist, Gessner emphasised in his first *Historia animalium* the seemingly endless webs of textual references that he could weave around every imaginable animal, bird, fish, and insect. But even this first entry into natural history had illustrations. In the next few years, as his project to provide the world with its first comprehensive, up-to-date history of nature advanced, images played a larger and larger part in his work and took up more and more space in his books.

Sharp-eyed historians of science — Brian Ogilvie, Laurent Pinon, Sachiko Kusukawa, Florike Egmond, Holger Funk, and others — have traced the complex ways by which Gessner obtained the thousands of images of animals, and later of plants, which he collected, organised, and printed.[21] He drew, critically and carefully, on a vast range of sources, from curious woodcuts in books whose authority he did not always accept — such as Olaus Magnus's *Description of the Northern Peoples* — through the more precise work of fellow natural historians like Pierre Belon, to the coloured drawings, made from the life, that colleagues around Europe sent him and that he himself learned to make. When Gessner could, he directly supervised the work of the artisan he called 'my painter'. In the words of his biographer, Josias Simler,

> [when working on his final project,] on plants, he regularly spent time with the painter. And he took great care, first, that a fixed order was maintained in all things, so that the painter did

---

[20] Reeds, 'Publishing Scholarly Books' (n. 5 above), p. 261; Gessner to Bauhin, 1 August 1563, in Bauhin, *De plantis* (n. 3 above), p. 122: 'Manum tuam non ubique assequerentur Typographorum compositores, quos vocant, ut timeo: & oporteret prius transcribere, transcriptum conferre' ('I'm afraid that the printers' compositors, as they are called, could not follow your writing at all points, and it would be necessary first to copy it and then to collate the copy').

[21] B. Ogilvie, *The Science of Describing: Natural History in Renaissance Europe*, Chicago and London, 2006, chap. 5; L. Pinon, 'Conrad Gessner and the Historical Depth of Renaissance Natural History', in G. Pomata and N. Siraisi (eds), Historia: *Empiricism and Erudition in Early Modern Europe*, Cambridge (MA) and London, 2005, pp. 241–67; S. Kusukawa, 'The sources of Gessner's pictures for the *Historia animalium*', *Annals of Science*, 67/3, 2009, pp. 303–28; S. Kusukawa, *Picturing the Book of Nature: Image, Text, and Argument in Sixteenth-Century Human Anatomy and Medical Botany*, Chicago and London, 2011, chaps 7–8; F. Egmond, 'A Collection within a Collection: Rediscovered Animal Drawings from the Collections of Conrad Gessner and Felix Platter', *Journal of the History of Collections*, 25/2, 2013, pp. 149–70; F. Egmond and S. Kusukawa, 'Circulation of Images and Graphic Practices in Renaissance Natural History: The Example of Conrad Gessner', *Gesnerus*, 73/1, 2016, pp. 29–72; H. Funk, 'John Caius's contributions to Conrad Gessner's *Historia animalium* and "*Historia plantarum*": A Survey with Commentaries', *Archives of Natural History*, 44/2, 2017, pp. 334–51.

not show off his artistry, but imitated nature and approached it as closely as he could. When it came to the fibres of leaves and the little lines in flowers, the painter represented not what he himself preferred, but what nature had made in them, as exactly as possible.[22]

Gessner turned his study, with its windows engraved with images of fish, into a massive archive, which contained hundreds of images, organised on special shelving.[23]

Confronted, as Gessner often was, with multiple, conflicting images of a single animal or fish, he carefully adapted and corrected the images he had collected. Often he covered handsome paintings with detailed annotations, before he decided how he would mix and match his visual sources for a given woodblock. But if he was always critical in his response to images, he was anything but consistent in his ways of using them. The illustrations that irradiated his printed books were woodcuts, black and white. For those who wanted them, a painter provided coloured copies, which he executed in batches, presumably without checking the original coloured images that Gessner had examined and emended so systematically. In many cases, as Gessner explained to Caius, he had no evidence about the colouring of the actual animal.[24] The most expensive copies of Gessner's books on animals were also, in one sense at least, the least reliable.

Like other naturalists, Gessner soon boiled his big books down into much shorter, slimmer forms, in which images played the central role: the *Icones animalium* (first published in 1553); the *Icones avium* (1555); and the *Nomenclator aquatilium* (1560).[25] These were not coffee-table books: Gessner took them seriously. The first one, the *Icones animalium* of 1553, contained virtually no text. Yet he organised the images by the different orders of animals, a pioneering step and one that others would emulate. And he soon repealed his self-denying ordinance. From 1555, when he published the first *Icones avium*, onwards, he embedded the

[22] Josias Simler, *Vita clarissimi philosophi et medici excellentissimi Conradi Gesneri*, Zurich, Christoph Froschauer, 1566, 4° (USTC 701427), p. 15: 'Antequam vero in morbum incideret, figurae plantarum quam plurimae ligno insculptae fuerunt, in quibus depingendis ipse frequens pictori aderat: & curabat sedulo, primum, ut certa servaretur in omnibus proportio, ut pictor non artem suam ostentaret, sed naturam imitaretur & ad illam quam proxime accederet, & in foliis fibras, in floribus lineolas, non quas ipsi collibuisset, sed quas natura in his finxisset quam exactissime repraesentaret.' For a rich study of Gessner's views on the representation of nature see S. Kusukawa, 'Conrad Gessner on an "Ad Vivum" Image', in P. H. Smith, A. R. W. Meyers and H. J. Cook (eds), *Ways of Making and Knowing: The Material Culture of Empirical Knowledge*, Ann Arbor (MI), 2014, pp. 330–56.

[23] Leu, *Gessner* (n. 1 above), pp. 194–5 and plate 34; for more details see U. Leu and M. Ruoss (eds), *Conrad Gessner 1516-2016: Facetten eines Universums*, Zurich, 2016.

[24] Gessner to Caius, 19 August 1561, in Conrad Gessner, *Epistolarum medicinalium* [...] *libri III*, Zurich, Christoph Froschauer, 1577, 4° (USTC 651725), fol. 135r: 'Typographus noster iam diu pictorem habet, qui libris nostris de animalibus omnibus picturas addit: atque ita pictos vendit: sed parum accurate. Simul autem duodenos aut plures pictor depingere solet. Quod si unicum exemplar, idque diligentius depingendum ei foret, nimium forte precium posceret. Faciam tamen in tuam gratiam quicquid iusseris & fieri poterit. Plurimorum quidem picturae & colores veri nobis desiderant: ita ut eorum icones vel sine coloribus relinquendae sint, vel ex coniectura, aut temere etiam pingendae' ('Our printer has for a long time employed a painter, who adds all the pictures to our books on animals. And he sells them with these illustrations, which are not very accurate. The painter usually colours twelve or more at once. If he were to do a very careful job of colouring a single copy, it would be too expensive. For your sake I will do whatever you demand and can be done. In many cases we lack the images and true colours. Hence their images must either be left without colours, or painted by conjecture or at random').

[25] L. Pinon, *Livres de zoologie à la Renaissance: une anthologie (1450–1700)*, Paris, 1995, p. 98.

17: CONRAD GESSNER AS CORRECTOR   351

images in ever-thicker masses of new text — much of it excerpted from recent letters from such expert informants as John Caius and bulging with fresh information about animal behaviour.[26] In 1560, Gessner published revised editions of the works on animals and birds as well as the first edition of the *Nomenclator aquatilium animantium* — which, despite its title, offered up a rich virtual banquet of images of sea creatures of every kind.[27]

PREPARING THE 'THREE BOOKS OF IMAGES'

Gessner saw these three books as a coherent unit. He took pains to arrange for his friend Gasser to purchase coloured copies of what he referred to as 'the three books of images'.[28] Once he had his own copies in hand, he revised them, inserting both printed addenda and handwritten marginalia that were seemingly intended for the preparation of further editions. A handwritten note on the title-page of his 1560 *Icones avium* records that 'I have put some emendations and additions to this book at the end of the *Images of Four-footed Animals* (the *Icones animalium*)'.[29] At the end of the *Icones animalium* a page of printed notes appears, under a revealing heading: 'I decided to put here a few emendations and additions to the book that contains the images and names of birds, which should have been placed at its conclusion but were omitted by carelessness'.[30] Like many correctors before him, in other words, Gessner found himself compelled to repair the errors of compositors who worked in haste — as well, no doubt, as his own.

The printed notes themselves are also revealing. They show that Gessner continued to gather information and images even as his books went through the press. In a set of printed additions to his *Icones avium*, rather than in the original text, Gessner provided readers with an image of a *Caprimulgus* (a species of nightjar). The woodcut, he explained, was based

---

[26] A. Grafton, 'Philological and Artisanal Knowledge Making in Renaissance Natural History: A Study in Cultures of Knowledge', *History of Humanities*, 3/1, 2018, 39–55.

[27] Digital facsimiles of Gessner's working copies of all three books, now held in the Zentralbibliothek Zurich, are available at www.e-rara.ch: Conrad Gessner, *Icones animalium quadrupedum viviparorum et oviparorum, quae in historiae animalium Conradi Gesneri libro I. et II. describuntur*, Zurich, Christoph Froschauer, 1560, f° (USTC 664935; Gessner's working copy: Zentralbibliothek Zurich NNN 44 / F, http://dx.doi.org/10.3931/e-rara-1668), hereafter Gessner, *Icones animalium* (1560); his *Icones avium omnium, quae in historia avium Conradi Gesneri describuntur*, Zurich, Christoph Froschauer, 1560, f° (USTC 664938; Gessner's working copy: Zentralbibliothek Zurich, NNN 44, 2, http://dx.doi.org/10.3931/e-rara-1694), hereafter Gessner, *Icones avium* (1560); his *Nomenclator aquatilium animantium*, Zurich, Christoph Froschauer, 1560, f° (USTC 678237; Gessner's working copy: Zentralbibliothek Zurich NNN 44, 3, http://dx.doi.org/10.3931/e-rara-1693), hereafter Gessner, *Nomenclator* (1560).

[28] Gessner to Gasser, 4 March 1565, in Burmeister, *Gasser*, III (n. 2 above), pp. 345–6: 'Pretium etiam trium librorum iconum perscripseram florenos vi. Tanti enim vendit bibliopolis' ('I had written out the price of the three books of images at 6 florins. That is what he charges the booksellers for them'). See also ibid., pp. 288, 299–300, 319, 327, 332, 335, 338–9.

[29] Gessner, *Icones avium* (1560) (n. 27 above), note on title-page: 'Emendationes et additiones aliquot in hunc librum posui ad finem Iconum quadrupedum.'

[30] Gessner, *Icones animalium* (1560) (n. 27 above), sig. [aaa4vv]: 'In librum, qui Avium eicones & nomenclaturas continet, emendationes & additiones pauculas, quae ad eius finem ponendae fuerant, incuria quadam omissas: huc referre libuit.'

352   PRINTING AND MISPRINTING

on a skeleton that Pierre Belon had given him and was, as shown, half life size.[31] In the additional notes that he printed in the *Icones animalium*, Gessner added further information about the *Caprimulgus* from a letter sent him by the British naturalist William Turner, which had arrived after he had already added the former passage to his bird book.[32] In the printed additions to the bird book, Gessner illustrated and described the *Passer solitarius*, a sparrow.[33] In the additional notes that he drew up for the *Icones animalium*, he thanked Claude, the son of the distinguished Genevan doctor Benedict Textor, for sending him two further images of sparrows, which he described but evidently could not include in the space available.[34]

The situation revealed by these examples is confirmed by both the printed texts of Gessner's three books of images and the manuscript notes that he added to his copies of them. Gessner's study was a node on multiple correspondence networks as well as a workplace: indeed, the letters formed a substantial part of his workflow. While he finished one text and put it through the press, new images and new letters continued to arrive. So he cut up the letters, made them into additions to his original text, and had Froschauer add them in new sections at the end of each book. In each case, space remained at the end of the original text (which suggests that Froschauer, knowing his author, expected addenda). All three of Gessner's illustrated natural histories were folios in sixes. In the *Icones animalium* the original text ended, with his account of frogs, at L*r*. The new material that Gessner added stretched from L*v* to [Li*vr*], making six pages of text and leaving a blank page before the index began. In the *Icones avium*, Gessner's *Accessiones* began at [Li*vv*] and reached Mii*r*, making ten pages in total. The index began on Mii*iv*. The *Nomenclator*, exceptionally, wound up with a gathering of eight. Gessner's *Emendanda* began at h2*v* and ended at [h7*v*], making eleven pages and leaving room for a page of pious verses in six languages on h8*r* and a blank h8*v*. Gessner, in other words, treated printing as a continuous, additive process, and his publisher indulged him.

Yet even as the additions were being printed, the flow of visual and verbal information continued. Gessner, accordingly, made each of his working copies into a unique historical record of the ways in which he tried to control and improve images and the text that explained them. He corrected the texts that he had already printed, and turned their margins into tiny archives of natural history, in which he recorded what he had seen and learned since he submitted his original and supplementary copy. These notes — and the printed texts they refer to — preserve Gessner's struggle to bring his images to a standard of visual precision that approximated the quality of the new images, made from life, that piled up in his study, and to supplement his texts with the new information he had received.[35]

---

[31] Gessner, *Icones avium* (1560) (n. 27 above), p. 130.

[32] Gessner, *Icones animalium* (1560) (n. 27 above), sig. [aaa4*vv*]: 'Post ea quae de Caprimulgo scripsi addantur haec: His scriptis, doctissimi viri Gul. Turneri ex Anglia literas accepi [...]' ('After what I wrote about the Caprimulgus add the following: "After this was written, I received a letter from England from the most learned gentleman William Turner" [...]').

[33] Gessner, *Icones avium* (1560) (n. 27 above), p. 132.

[34] Gessner, *Icones animalium* (1560) (n. 27 above), sig. [aaa4*vv*].

[35] Gessner describes his image files in a letter to Caius, *Epistolarum medicinalium* [...] *libri* (n. 24 above), fol. 135*r*: 'Quae antehac picta ad me suis coloribus misisti animalia, una cum caeteris, quae accuratius picta habebam plurimis, in librum quendam scite digessi: & pleraque inter se agglutinavi, ita ut separari non possint: si tamen volueris, denuo tibi depingenda curabo' ('The animals that you sent me,

CORRECTION: GESSNER'S PRACTICES

At every point in the process of publication, Gessner's corrections took many forms. Sometimes all that was required was the correction of an obvious slip — as when Gessner stated in his text that Aristotle had claimed that frogs were viviparous, a polar error in textual terms, and set matters right in the margin (Fig. 17.1).[36] But he often added fresh matter to the texts in which he discussed his images. As he explained to Gasser, he sometimes lost letters from friends as they hid among his 'Sibylline leaves'.[37] But he managed to use many of them as sources for first-hand information, integrating passages from older letters into the printed texts of his picture books and adding material from new ones in the margins. At the end of his account of the buffalo, for example, he added in the margin a new observation that Caius had sent him after his book appeared: 'At Rome, buffalos pull rafts against the current. Their bodies are firmer and larger than those of bulls. They look like bulls, and they have horns that turn backwards, almost like those of rams. John Caius'.[38] Another note recorded the exact source of his information: 'see at the end of Caius's letter to me (July 1561)'.[39] Corrections and additions like these were the basic work of the corrector, easy and straightforward to enter in his books, even though he did not live long enough to reprint them.

In many cases, though, Gessner made clear that he was chiefly concerned with the core content of these books, their images, and bent on ensuring their reliability and utility. When he drew images from other printed sources, he had them cut directly into new wood blocks. He did not worry about the fact that they were reversed, perhaps because he could rely on this nearly mechanical process of reproduction to ensure what he saw as basic accuracy. This is how he dealt, for example, with André Thevet's famous image of an opossum.[40] Thevet's book appeared in 1557. Gessner slotted his striking image of the opossum, and a long discussion, not into the text he first gave Froschauer but into a later set of *Additiones* (Fig. 17.2):

Once Gessner saw the text and image in print, however, he noticed problems. Here as elsewhere he paid no attention to small discrepancies between his image and its source, such as the omission of the plants depicted by Thevet.

What worried Gessner in this case was rather, in the first instance, the accompanying text. Following Thevet, he had described the 'Giants', as they were called in the Patagonian

---

painted in their true colours, along with many others, of which I had precise paintings, I cleverly arranged in a particular notebook. And I glued many of them together, so that they can't be separated. But if you wish, I will have them painted again for you').

[36] Gessner, *Nomenclator* (1560) (n. 27 above), p. 117.

[37] Gessner to Gasser, 11 November 1563, in Burmeister, *Gasser*, III (n. 2 above), p. 247: 'Literas tuas nuper accepi, quae nunc mihi respondenti non sunt ad manum et inter mea Sibyllae folia alicubi latitant' ('I recently received your letter. Now, as I reply, it is not accessible, and hiding somewhere amid my Sibylline leaves').

[38] Gessner, *Icones animalium* (1560) (n. 27 above), p. 13: 'Buffali Romae trahunt adverso flumine cymbas. Corpus illis firmius et amplius quam tauris: taurorum aspectus, et repanda cornua instar arietum pene. Io. Caius.'

[39] Ibid.: 'V. in fine epistolae Caij ad me (1561 Iulio) et Buselaphium.'

[40] André Thevet, *Les singularitez de la France antartique*, Paris, heirs of Maurice de la Porte, 1558, 4° (USTC 14262), fol. 109r. Leu suggests that this is actually an anteater: his *Gessner* (n. 1 above), p. 206.

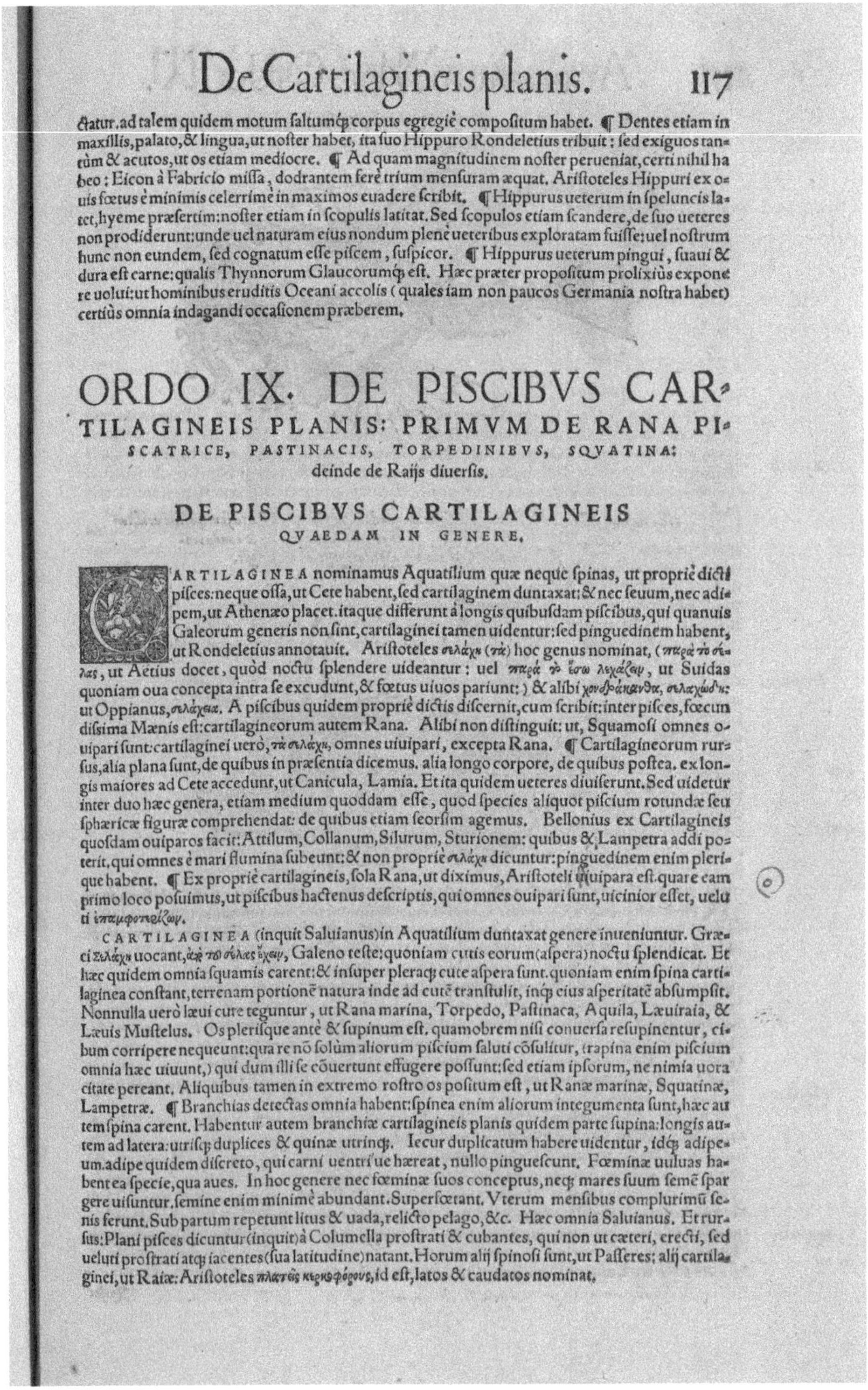

De Cartilagineis planis. 117

ctatur,ad talem quidem motum saltumép corpus egregie compositum habet. ¶ Dentes etiam in maxillis,palato,& lingua,ut noster habet, ita suo Hippuro Rondeletius tribuit : sed exiguos tan= tùm & acutos,ut os etiam mediocre. ¶ Ad quam magnitudinem noster perueniat,certi nihil ha beo : Eicon à Fabricio missa , dodrantem ferè trium mensuram æquat. Aristoteles Hippuri ex o= uis fœtus è minimis celerrimè in maximos euadere scribit. ¶ Hippurus ueterum in speluncis la= tet,hyeme præsertim:noster etiam in scopulis latitat. Sed scopulos etiam scandere,de suo ueteres non prodiderunt:unde uel naturam eius nondum plenè ueteribus exploratam fuisse:uel nostrum hunc non eundem, sed cognatum esse piscem , suspicor. ¶ Hippurus ueterum pingui , suaui & dura est carne:qualis Thynnorum Glaucorumép est. Hæc præter propositum prolixiùs exponè re uolui:ut hominibus eruditis Oceani accolis (quales iam non paucos Germania nostra habet) certiùs omnia indagandi occasionem præberem.

ORDO IX. DE PISCIBVS CAR=
TILAGINEIS PLANIS: PRIMVM DE RANA PI=
SCATRICE, PASTINACIS, TORPEDINIBVS, SQVATINA:
deinde de Raijs diuersis.

DE PISCIBVS CARTILAGINEIS
QVAEDAM IN GENERE.

CARTILAGINEA nominamus Aquatilium quæ neque spinas, ut propriè dicti pisces:neque ossa,ut Cete habent,sed cartilaginem duntaxat:& nec seuum,nec adi= pem,ut Athenæo placet.itaque differunt à longis quibusdam piscibus,qui quanuis Galeorum generis non sint,cartilaginei tamen uidentur:sed pinguedinem habent, ut Rondeletius annotauit. Aristoteles σελάχη (τὰ) hoc genus nominat, (πιρὰ τὸ σί= λας, ut Aetius docet, quòd noctu splendere uideantur : uel πιρὰ τὸ ἴσω λυχάζειν, ut Suidas quoniam oua concepta intra se excudunt,& fœtus uiuos pariunt:) & alibi χονδράκανδρα, σελαχώδης: ut Oppianus,σελάχεα. A piscibus quidem propriè dictis discernit,cum scribit:inter pisces,fœcun dissima Mænis est:cartilagineorum autem Rana. Alibi non distinguit: ut, Squamosi omnes o= uipari sunt:cartilaginei uerò, τὰ σελάχη, omnes uiuipari, excepta Rana. ¶ Cartilagineorum rur= sus,alia plana sunt,de quibus in præsentia dicemus, alia longo corpore, de quibus postea. ex lon= gis maiores ad Cete accedunt,ut Canicula, Lamia. Et ita quidem ueteres diuiserunt. Sed uidetur inter duo hæc genera, etiam medium quoddam esse, quod species aliquot piscium rotundæ seu sphæricæ figuræ comprehendat: de quibus etiam seorsim agemus. Bellonius ex Cartilagineis quosdam ouiparos facit:Attilum,Collanum,Silurum, Sturionem: quibus & Lampetra addi po= terit,qui omnes è mari flumina subeunt:& non propriè σελάχη dicuntur:pinguedinem enim pleri= que habent. ¶ Ex propriè cartilagineis,sola Rana,ut diximus,Aristoteli uiuipara est.quare eam primo loco posuimus,ut piscibus hactenus descriptis,qui omnes ouipari sunt,uicinior esset, uelu ti ἰπαμφοτερίζων.

CARTILAGINEA (inquit Saluianus)in Aquatilium duntaxat genere inueniuntur. Græ= ci σελάχη uocant,ἐπὶ τῶ σέλας ἔχειν, Galeno teste:quoniam cutis eorum(aspera)noctu splendicat. Et hæc quidem omnia squamis carent:& insuper pleraçp cute aspera sunt. quoniam enim spina carti= laginea constant,terrenam portionè natura inde ad cutè transtulit, inçp eius asperitatè absumpsit. Nonnulla uerò læui cute teguntur , ut Rana marina, Torpedo, Pastinaca, Aquila, Læuiraia, & Læuis Mustelus. Os plerisque antè & supinum est. quamobrem nisi conuersa resupinentur, ci= bum corripere nequeunt:qua re nõ solùm aliorum piscium saluti cõsulitur, (rapina enim piscium omnia hæc uiuunt,) qui dum illi se cõuertunt effugere possunt:sed etiam ipsorum, ne nimia uora citate pereant, Aliquibus tamen in extremo rostro os positum est , ut Ranæ marinæ, Squatinæ, Lampetræ. ¶ Branchias detectas omnia habent:spinea enim aliorum integumenta sunt,hæc aut tem spina carent. Habentur autem branchiæ cartilagineis planis quidem parte supina:longis au= tem ad latera:utrisçp duplices & quinæ utrinçp. Iecur duplicatum habere uidentur, ideçp adipe= um.adipe quidem discreto, qui carni uentri ue hæreat, nullo pinguescunt. Fœminæ uuluas ha= bent ea specie,qua aues. In hoc genere nec fœminæ suos conceptus,neçp mares suum semè spar gere uisuntur,semine enim minimè abundant.Superscœtant, Vterum mensibus complurimũ se= nis ferunt.Sub partum repetunt litus & uada,relicto pelago,&c. Hæc omnia Saluianus. Et rur= sus:Plani pisces dicuntur(inquit)à Columella prostrati & cubantes, qui non ut cæteri, erecti, sed ueluti prostrati atçp iacentes(sua latitudine)natant.Horum alij spinosi sunt,ut Passeres; alij cartila= ginei,ut Raiæ:Aristoteles πλατεῖς κερκοφόρους,id est,latos & caudatos nominat.

FIG. 17.1. This marginal correction to Gessner's *Nomenclator* is by the author. Where he had written that frogs were viviparous, he changes this to oviparous in the margin. Conrad Gessner, *Nomenclator aquatilium animantium*, Zurich, Christoph Froschauer, 1560, f° (USTC 678237), p. 117. Zurich, Zentralbibliothek, NNN 44, 3.

FIG. 17.2. In his working copy, Gessner notes problems in his figure of the opossum, drawn from André Thevet. Conrad Gessner, *Icones animalium quadrupedum viviparorum et oviparorum*, Zurich, Christoph Froschauer, 1560, f° (USTC 6649365), p. 127. Zurich, Zentralbibliothek, NNN 44/F.

356   PRINTING AND MISPRINTING

language, who dressed in the skins of this monstrous creature, as well as the animal's own ability to carry its young, and the furious clamour with which it killed its young rather than let them be taken by hunters.[41] But he had forgotten to provide a philologically appropriate name for this newly discovered animal from the New World. Gessner raised possibilities in the margin: 'Could it be called Myrmecoleon [ant-lion] from its form?'[42] But he made no decision. It seems that he also began to wonder if readers would think him credulous to believe in a creature that looked so strange. In the printed text, he had cited Thevet's book as the source of his description of the animal. In an additional note entered in the bottom margin, he observed that 'we also borrowed this image from it'.[43] In this case, Gessner seems to have cast about for a way to reassure future critical readers.

In other cases, Gessner's concerns were narrower. He worried about the source of his image of a panther: 'Where did this image come from? I will record it'.[44] In other cases — perhaps those where he had multiple sources — he queried small visual details. 'Are the fingers well depicted?' he asked, looking at an image of a squirrel with anthropomorphic front paws.[45] More than once he noted that his images were contradicted by his text. Examining an image of a merops (bee-eater), he realised that the caption stated that two of the four digits on each of its feet pointed backwards and two forwards. In his image, however, only one pointed backwards, and three forwards.[46] A manuscript annotation called attention to the discrepancy (Fig. 17.3).

Even as Gessner approved his image of a simivulpa — 'fox-ape' — for print, he noticed that it did not match his prose description (Fig. 17.4). He added a printed caption, awkwardly inserted above the image, that called attention to the discrepancy: 'The simivulpa has the tail of a monkey, which this image does not show. That may lead one to suspect that the other features are also not correctly represented'.[47] In the margin Gessner suggested a solution: 'this can be emended in accordance with the description. But the reader must be informed'.[48] But he did not show how to make the changes he desired, offer an alternative image, or raise any question about the reality about the animal.[49]

In other cases as well, Gessner found himself stuck, unable to provide a definitive correction and forced to notify the reader that his image did not deserve trust. He recorded that he thought his image of a tiger had been made 'at Florence, from the living animal', and that a friend had given it to him. But he recorded immediately after that, 'I received another

---

[41] Gessner, *Icones animalium* (1560) (n. 27 above), p. 127.
[42] Ibid.: 'An a figura Myrmecoleon dici posset?'
[43] Ibid.: 'Ex qua hanc etiam Iconem mutuati sumus.'
[44] Ibid., p. 67: 'Vnde haec icon? Adscribo.'
[45] Ibid., p. 110: 'an digiti bene picti?'
[46] Gessner, *Icones avium* (1560) (n. 27 above), p. 98.
[47] Gessner, *Icones animalium* (1560) (n. 27 above), p. 90: 'Simivulpa caudam Cercopithi habet, quod haec icon non ostendit: ut inde caetera etiam non probe expressa aliquis suspicetur.'
[48] Ibid.: '[e]mendari potest ad descriptionem n[ecesse] tamen ut admoneatur lector.'
[49] See also his printed note on the image of a scomber in *Nomenclator* (1560) (n. 27 above), p. 107: 'Scombri haec effigies Venetijs facta non satis probe exprimit pinnulas illas versus caudam. nam & plures, & supra infraque esse debebant: tales omnino, quales in Amia, Colia & Thynnorum genere spectantur' ('This image of a scomber, made at Venice, does not accurately represent those little fins near the tail, for there should be more of them, both above and below: like those observed in the bonito, the coly-mackerel, and a kind of tuna').

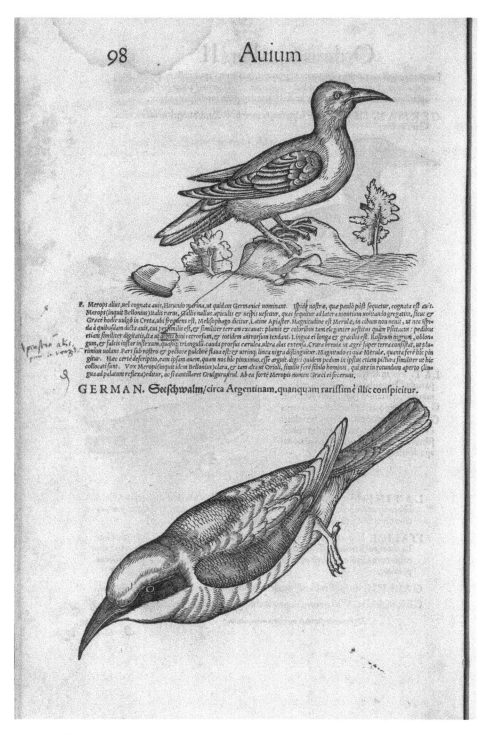

FIG. 17.3. The feet are wrongly depicted in Gessner's image of a merops (bee-eater), as his note indicates. Conrad Gessner, *Icones avium omnium, quae in historia avium Conradi Gesneri describuntur*, Zurich, Christoph Froschauer, 1560, f° (USTC 6649378), p. 98. Zurich, Zentralbibliothek, NNN 44, 2.

FIG. 17.4. Gessner indicates that his image of a simivulpa (fox-ape) does not match the description in his text. Gessner, *Icones animalium* (see Fig. 17.2), p. 90. Zurich, Zentralbibliothek, NNN 44/F.

depiction of a tiger made at Constantinople in the court of the emperor'.[50] Sometimes the new image came in time, but still could not be fully integrated into his text.

Layers of comment, printed and handwritten, reveal Gessner's struggles to eliminate as many errors as possible from his woodcuts. An image of a civet in the *Icones animalium* bore the printed caption: 'a certain learned and noble man at Milan had this painted for us once upon a time'. But a continuation, also printed, informed the reader that 'we will give another, more accurate one at the end of this book' (Fig. 17.5).[51] Gessner, in other words, illustrated his text with a woodcut made from a painting which he himself thought was not entirely accurate. When he received another image, he could not replace the original, faulty one, so he inserted it in the printed *Additiones* that he drew up for the whole text (Fig. 17.6). He had room to add a reference, in the original printed caption, to the better image — but not to provide its page number, which he added, accordingly, by hand, perhaps in the hope that it could be entered in the text of the next edition.

In the printed commentary that Gessner added to the new image, he repeated that his first image 'was not so accurately represented as this one, which the most learned and diligent John Caius sent me from England'.[52] He also remarked that the Torgau medical man Johannes Kentmann, another of his correspondents and informants, had sent him an exactly similar one.[53] Even then, however, Gessner was not finished. An apothecary in Antwerp, Pieter van Coudenberghe, who often sent him material, informed him that the second image of the civet was 'not well represented, nor is the first', as he wrote by the second one.[54] He also told Gessner that the first image 'was not well represented', as Gessner had thought, though, 'the skin is well done'.[55]

The book, with its two printed, captioned images of the civet and its further handwritten notes, documents multiple exchanges — between Gessner and his Milanese informant, Gessner and Caius, Gessner and Kentmann, Gessner and van Coudenberghe. It also reveals the complexity of what Gessner was trying to do. He could not eliminate the first image, however faulty he came to think it, since the sheets of the first part of his book were already printed when new images arrived. Caius and Kentmann sent him paintings in which the animal's outlines were rendered more accurately than in the Milanese painting, and he managed to use a block made from the first of these in a new section, newly printed. In the end, though, van Coudenberghe told him that even the new images were not well drawn and

---

[50] Gessner, *Icones animalium* (1560) (n. 27 above), p. 72: 'Haec icon Florentiae puto ad animal vivum facta, ab amico mihi donata est [...] . Tigridis aliam effigiem accepi a magnifico d. Bonero, factam Constantinopoli in aula imperatoris.'

[51] Ibid., p. 72: 'Hanc iconem doctus & nobilis quidam vir Mediolani nobis olim pingendam curavit. accuratiorem aliam ad finem huius libri dabimus.'

[52] Ibid., p. 126: 'Pag. 72. iconem Felis Zibethi dedimus, non ita accurate expressam atque haec est, a doctissimo diligentissimoque viro Io. Caio ex Anglis ad me missa.'

[53] Ibid.: 'Alteram quoque, huic per omnia similem, Io. Kentmanus medicus eximius ad me dedit' ('Johannes Kentmann, that excellent medical man, gave me another which is similar to this one in all respects'). For Kentmann's practices as a botanical illustrator see S. Kusukawa, 'Image, Text and "Observatio": the "Codex Kentmanus"', *Early Science and Medicine*, 14/4, 2009, pp. 445–75.

[54] Gessner, *Icones animalium* (1560) (n. 27 above), p. 126: 'Zibethi effigies nec ultima bene expressa est, neque prima, Coldenbergius.'

[55] Ibid., p. 72: 'Male expressa est haec icon. Sed pellis bene, Coldenbergius.'

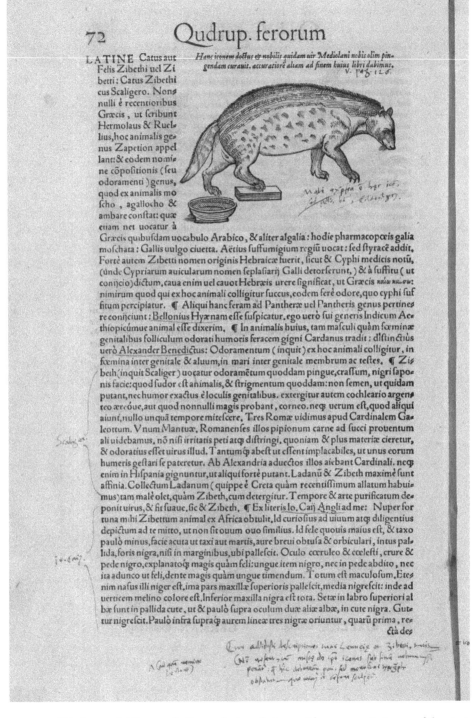

FIG. 17.5. This image vividly records Gessner's struggle to provide an accurate image of the civet. Gessner, *Icones animalium* (see Fig. 17.2), p. 72. Zurich, Zentralbibliothek, NNN 44/F.

126 Additiones.

ma. Sectas enim ungulas habet: quanquam & quæ solidas haberent, repertæ sint, sed id perrarum est. Animal est altius Ceruo, auribus & naribus prominulis, cornibus à Ceruo nonnihil diuersis, colore item magis ad albedinem tendente. Cursus est uelocissimi: non quo cætera animalia modo, sed (Equi) gradarij instar. Vngulæ, tanquam amuletum, contra morbum caducum gestari solent.

AD QVADRVPEDVM FERORVM
ORDINEM II.

DE Pardalide seu Leopardo diximus pag. 67. cui hæc addes. Pardalin Persæ (inquit Scaliger) Barbuct uocant: Leænæ similem pilo ruffo, maculis oblongis picto, nigris ex transuerso. Faciem habet subrubram, nigris uariam maculis, & candidis: uentrem album, caudam Leonis. Sunt & quædam dorso minùs fuluo, & maculis minùs uegetis. Oculos eis glaucos esse scit, qui uidit, ut nos. ¶ Pardalis (seu Panthera) Oppiano, maior & minor est. hæc quidem uiribus & animo nihil inferior maiore, unde apparet Pantheras minores, alias esse quàm Pantheres (πάνθηρας) ab eo dictos sub finem secundi de uenatione: [ubi eos θῶας ὀτελλανούς, id est, nullius precij uel nullarum uirium feras: & χερεπούς nominans, cum Felibus & Gliribus numerat.] Cæterum ut Thoês, sic etiam Pantheres duorum generum statuuntur: & forsan Thos minor, Panther minor fuerit: qui & Lycopantheros, Pantherium, & Lupus canarius dicitur. ¶ Leopardi (inquit Io. Leo Africanus) degunt in syluis Barbariæ, neque homini, cum robusti sint & crudeles, nocent: nisi alicui (quod raro contingit) in angusto calle obuij, illi aut cedere non possint, aut redarguantur, fastidioǽ afficiantur. in hunc enim irruentes unguibus uultum comprehendunt, tantumǽ carnis auferunt, quantū prendunt: & plerunǽ cerebrum homini perfringunt. Gregem inuadere non solent: Canibus alioqui infestissimi, quos occidunt ac deuorant. Monticolæ Constantinæ regionis equestrem uenationem aduersus illos instruunt, exitus uiarum occludentes. Leopardus autem hac illac fugiens, dum uia equitibus obsessa se nequaquam euasurum perspicit, in crebros flexus gyros confodiendum se præbet. At si Leopardum effugere contingat, qui incautius eam partem obseruauit, conuiuium cæteris uenatoribus, recepta consuetudine, præparare tenetur, Sic ille.

Pag. 72. iconem Felis Zibethi dedimus, non ita accuratè expressam atǽ hæc est, à doctissimo diligentissimoǽ uiro Io. Caio ex Anglia ad me missa. Alteram quoǽ, huic

per omnia similem Io. Kentmanus medicus eximius ad me dedit. Zibetti liquorem, umbilico impositum uteri strangulationibus mirum in modum mederi, alijsǽ multis remedijs pollere aiunt.

Pag. 74. Lyncis imaginem proposuimus, nō inscitè factā, capite excepto. quamobrem aliam à Io. Caio mihi cōmunicatam, & probè expressam, hîc adijcere uolui. Vngues
Lynx

FIG. 17.6. In the *additiones* to his *Icones animalium* (see Fig. 17.2), p. 126, Gessner gives a second, improved image of the civet, but remarks that it too is imperfect. Zurich, Zentralbibliothek, NNN 44/F.

that the first one had given a better impression of the animal's skin. Gessner recorded this comment too — only to cross it out, for reasons that he did not state.

Gessner himself did not always pin down the sources of his images with absolute clarity. Caius described at length in a letter the hyperactive lynx that he had seen in the menagerie at the Tower of London. A woodpecker's song had seemingly bewitched it, making it keep still and enabling Caius's painter to take an accurate likeness. Gessner incorporated Caius's vivid account, with an image of the animal, into his text (Fig. 17.7). Even an alert reader could have assumed that the image, as well as the description, came from Caius. Gessner's own commentary was ambiguous. In his printed caption, he told the reader that 'this image is good, except for the face, which ought to look like a cat. You may find a better one at the end of this book'.[56] A second image, with a somewhat more plausible image of the animal's face, appeared in the new printed material at the end of the book. This time Gessner made clear that Caius had sent it: 'I provided an image of the Lynx, which was quite skilfully made, except for the head. Therefore, I decided to add another one, sent to me by Caius and accurately represented, here' (Fig. 17.8).[57] Still disappointed by the first image, Gessner wrote 'emenda' — correct! — above it, but made no effort to carry out his own command even in his working copy — far less to identify its source or to explain why he had not used Caius's image in the first place. As he tried to improve his images by iteration and correction, in other words, Gessner frequently found himself trying to keep multiple plates spinning in the air — and failing, by his own standards, to arrive at a substantively improved final product.

When it came to correcting images of animals, after all, Gessner faced a daunting task. He wanted to provide his readers with images that gave an accurate impression of the animal's body shape — even such elusive portions of it as the face and tail. To improve such images, he needed better paintings — which friends sometimes sent him — as well, perhaps, as better block cutters. But these did not always arrive on time. Further, he also wanted to depict in his woodcuts aspects of the animal's appearance less amenable to correction than its outlines — for example, the patterns of its fur, which a painting could depict in full colour and texture, but a woodcut could only suggest. Each house of cards that he erected, tongue between his teeth and breath held, could be knocked down in an instant by a new letter from an expert informant who had a better painting to offer or had seen the original beast. The visual information that made Gessner's books — and those of other mid-sixteenth-century naturalists so richly informative — was too rich and multivalent for the available techniques of correction to maintain its accuracy, even by the standards of the time. Even the endless, iterative practice of correction that Gessner used on his books yielded, in the end, not an immaculate visual natural history but a rich record of why it was impossible to produce one.

---

[56] Ibid., p. 74: 'Icon haec proba est, excepta facie, quae Felem referre debebat. Meliorem quaeres sub finem huius libri.'

[57] Ibid., p. 126: 'Lyncis imaginem proposuimus, non inscite factam, capite excepto. Quamobrem aliam a Io. Caio mihi commmunicatam, & probe expressam, hic adijcere volui.'

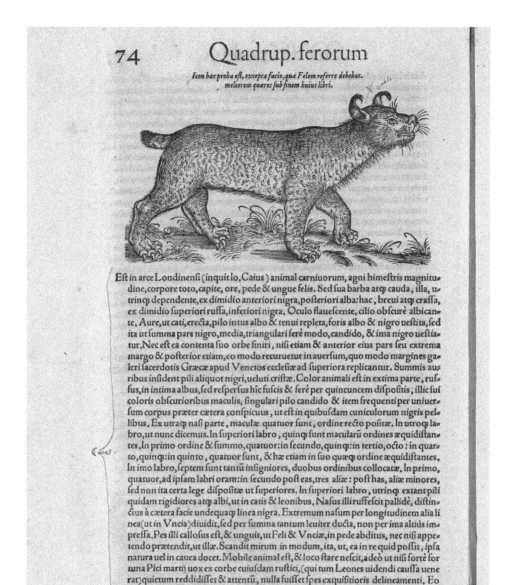

FIG. 17.7. Gessner included this image of a lynx in the text of the *Icones animalium* (see Fig. 17.2), p. 74, though he considered its face inaccurate. Zurich, Zentralbibliothek, NNN 44/F.

FIG. 17.8. This improved image of the lynx, supplied by John Caius, found its place in Gessner's additions to the *Icones animalium* (see Fig. 17.2), p. 127. Zurich, Zentralbibliothek, NNN 44/F.

BIBLIOGRAPHY

PRIMARY SOURCES

Bauhin, Jean, *De plantis a divis sanctisve nomen habentibus*, Basel, Conrad Waldkirch, 1591, 8° (USTC 88526).

Brudo, Manuel, *De ratione victus in singulis febribus secundum Hippocratem in genere et singillatim libri III*, Venice, heirs of Pietro dei Ravani, 1544, 8° (USTC 816961).

Gessner, Conrad, *Icones animalium quadrupedum viviparorum et oviparorum, quae in historiae animalium Conradi Gesneri libro I. et II. describuntur*, Zurich, Christoph Froschauer, 1560, f° (USTC 6649365; Gessner's working copy: Zentralbibliothek Zurich NNN 44/F, http://dx.doi.org/10.3931/e-rara-1668).

Gessner, Conrad, *Icones avium omnium, quae in historia avium Conradi Gesneri describuntur*, Zurich, Christoph Froschauer, 1560, f° (USTC 6649378; Gessner's working copy: Zentralbibliothek Zurich, NNN 44, 2, http://dx.doi.org/10.3931/e-rara-1694).

Gessner, Conrad, *Nomenclator aquatilium animantium*, Zurich, Christoph Froschauer, 1560, f° (USTC 678237; Gessner's working copy: Zentralbibliothek Zurich NNN 44, 3, http://dx.doi.org/10.3931/e-rara-1693).

Simler, Josias, *Vita clarissimi philosophi et medici excellentissimi Conradi Gesneri*, Zurich, Christoph Froschauer, 1566, 4° (USTC 701427).

Thevet, André, *Les singularitez de la France antartique*, Paris, heirs of Maurice de la Porte, 1558, 4° (USTC 14262).

SECONDARY LITERATURE

Andrade, A. M. L., 'Conrad Gessner Edits Brudus Lusitanus: The Trials and Tribulations of Publishing a Sixteenth Century Treatise on Dietetics', in C. B. Stuckzynski and B. Feitler (eds), *Portuguese Jews, New Christians and 'New Jews': A Tribute to Roberto Bachmann*, Leiden and Boston, 2018, pp. 189–205.

Blair, A. M., 'Conrad Gessner's Paratexts', *Gesnerus*, 73/1, 2016, pp. 73–123.

Blair, A. M., 'The dedication strategies of Conrad Gessner', in G. Manning and C. Klestinec (eds), *Professors, Physicians and Practices in the History of Medicine: Essays in Honor of Nancy Siraisi*, Cham, 2017, pp. 169–209.

Blair, A. M., 'Printing and Humanism in the Work of Conrad Gessner', *Renaissance Quarterly*, 70/1, 2017, pp. 1–43.

Burmeister, K. H., *Achilles Pirmin Gasser, 1505–1577: Artzt und Naturforscher, Historiker und Humanist*, III: *Briefwechsel*, Wiesbaden, 1975.

Egmond, F., 'A Collection within a Collection: Rediscovered Animal Drawings from the Collections of Conrad Gessner and Felix Platter', *Journal of the History of Collections*, 25/2, 2013, pp. 149–70.

Egmond, F., and Kusukawa, S., 'Circulation of Images and Graphic Practices in Renaissance Natural History: The Example of Conrad Gessner', *Gesnerus*, 73/1, 2016, pp. 29–72.

Funk, H., 'John Caius's contributions to Conrad Gessner's *Historia animalium* and "*Historia plantarum*": A Survey with Commentaries', *Archives of Natural History*, 44/2, 2017, pp. 334–51.

Goldgar, A., *Impolite Learning: Conduct and Community in the Republic of Letters*, New Haven (CT) and London 1995.

Grafton, A., *The Culture of Correction in Renaissance Europe*, London, 2011.

Grafton, A., 'Philological and Artisanal Knowledge Making in Renaissance Natural History: A Study in Cultures of Knowledge', *History of Humanities*, 3/1, 2018, 39–55.

Kusukawa, S., 'Conrad Gessner on an "Ad Vivum" Image', in P. H. Smith, A. R. W. Meyers, and H. J. Cook (eds), *Ways of Making and Knowing: The Material Culture of Empirical Knowledge*, Ann Arbor (MI), 2014, pp. 330–56.

Kusukawa, S., 'Image, Text and "Observatio": the "Codex Kentmanus"', *Early Science and Medicine*, 14/4, 2009, pp. 445–75.

Kusukawa, S., *Picturing the Book of Nature: Image, Text, and Argument in Sixteenth-Century Human Anatomy and Medical Botany*, Chicago and London, 2011.

Kusukawa, S., 'The Sources of Gessner's Pictures for the *Historia animalium*', *Annals of Science*, 67/3, 2090, pp. 303–28.

Leu, U., *Conrad Gessner (1515–1565): Universalgelehrter und Naturforscher der Renaissance*, Zurich, 2016.

Leu, U., and Ruoss, M. (eds), *Conrad Gessner 1516–2016: Facetten eines Universums*, Zurich, 2016.

Ogilvie, B., *The Science of Describing: Natural History in Renaissance Europe*, Chicago and London, 2006.

Parkes, M. B., *Pause and Effect: An Introduction to the History of Punctuation in the West*, Aldershot, 1992.

Pinon, L., 'Conrad Gessner and the Historical Depth of Renaissance Natural History', in G. Pomata and N. Siraisi (eds), Historia: *Empiricism and Erudition in Early Modern Europe*, Cambridge (MA) and London, 2005, pp. 241–67.

Pinon, L., *Livres de zoologie à la Renaissance: une anthologie (1450–1700)*, Paris, 1995.

Reeds, K., 'Publishing Scholarly Books in the Sixteenth Century', *Scholarly Publishing*, 14/1, 1982, pp. 259–74.

Richards, J., *Voices and Books in the English Renaissance: A New History of Reading*, Oxford, 2019.

Richardson, B., *Printing, Writers, and Readers in Renaissance Italy*, Cambridge, 1999.

PART V

POETRY, MUSIC, AND THEATRE

CHAPTER 18

FERNANDO DE HERRERA *CONTRA ERRATA*

A Re-evaluation of his Edition of Garcilaso de la Vega

PABLO ALVAREZ

INTRODUCTION

THE Sevillian poet Fernando de Herrera published his extensively annotated edition of the poetry of Garcilaso de la Vega, *Obras de Garcilasso de la Vega con anotaciones de Fernando de Herrera*, in Seville in 1580.[*1] A close examination of multiple copies of this edition reveals that Herrera was thoroughly involved as a corrector in the course of publication. Most notably, he inserted two consecutive errata lists, being directly responsible for numerous emendations undertaken during printing and immediately afterwards. This chapter attempts to contribute to the discussion about the role of errata lists and corrections as tools to convey to readers the ideal of textual accuracy. Valuable information about the dynamics of the art of correction in the printing house are provided in Alonso Víctor de Paredes' *Institution, and Origin of the Art of Printing, and General Rules for Compositors* (Madrid, c. 1680). This printing manual helps elucidate the emendations which can be found in numerous copies of Herrera's edition.

---

[*] I wish to thank the editors for giving me the opportunity to share an early version of this essay at the conference 'Printing and Misprinting: Typographical Mistakes and Publishers' Corrections (1450–1650)', Oxford, 20 April 2018. I also appreciate their meticulous editing. Similarly, I am grateful to Cathleen A. Baker, Julia Miller, and the anonymous reviewer for their suggestions. Funding for this research was provided through a 'Research & Creative Project Grant', University of Michigan Library. Finally, I also want to thank the University of Michigan Library, the Biblioteca Nacional de España, and the Biblioteca Histórica Marqués de Valdecilla for granting permission to publish images from their collections.

[1] Garcilaso de la Vega, *Obras con Anotaciones de Fernando de Herrera*, Seville, Alonso de la Barrera, 1580, 4° (USTC 336469). The collation formula is as follows: 4°: πA⁴ (πA4+ πA5, πA6) A-C⁸ D⁶ E-N⁸ O⁴ P-Aa⁸ Bb⁴ Cc-Xx⁸ Yy⁴, 350/352 leaves. The first state of the edition is reproduced in Garcilaso de la Vega, *Obras con Anotaciones de Fernando de Herrera*, ed. J. Montero, 2 vols, Seville, 1998, while the third is the model followed in Fernando de Herrera, *Anotaciones a la poesía de Garcilaso*, ed. I. Pepe and J. M. Reyes, Madrid, 2001.

Pablo Alvarez, *Fernando de Herrera Contra Errata*. In: *Printing and Misprinting*. Edited by Geri Della Rocca de Candal, Anthony Grafton, and Paolo Sachet, Oxford University Press. © Pablo Alvarez (2023). DOI: 10.1093/oso/9780198863045.003.0019

370   PRINTING AND MISPRINTING

Indeed, the broad scope and complexity of Herrera's edition contrasted with previous efforts to establish the text of such a significant author, who was at that time widely acknowledged as part of the elite group of poets who had Italianised Spanish poetry. Following Garcilaso's death in 1536, his friend Juan Boscán began the onerous task of editing a rather chaotic body of work that, for years, had been transmitted in various manuscript forms, including fragmentary drafts and later copies transcribed by friends of the poet. However, Boscán died in September 1542 before he could revise, or even complete, his promised edition, which only a few months later, still unfinished and marred by errors, was hastily published along with Boscán's poetry by the latter's widow, Ana Girón de Rebolledo, in 1543. It is therefore not surprising that subsequent editors included in their prefaces proud announcements of how errors had been duly emended, even though in reality these claims were mostly marketing tools to attract buyers. For a truly scholarly edition, when the poetry of Garcilaso first appeared without Boscán's, we need to wait until that compilation was published in Salamanca in 1569. It was the result of the efforts of several scholars of the University of Salamanca, probably including the collaboration of the Chair of Rhetoric, Francisco Sánchez de las Brozas. In 1574, Sánchez formally began the literary canonisation of Garcilaso by publishing a critical edition with commentaries in the humanistic fashion of the time. In essence, Sánchez emended the text of Garcilaso by comparing the readings of various manuscripts that, he claimed, were in his possession, also adding a systematic identification of Garcilaso's literary sources.[2]

Herrera must have been mortified by the fact that Sánchez's edition, which appeared when Herrera migh have been working on the text of Garcilaso for at least three years, was the first of its kind.[3] Although Sánchez is never mentioned by name, Herrera's editorial project was gradually shaped as a strong implicit criticism of Sánchez's readings and notes. Certainly, in scope and method, both editions differ entirely. While Sánchez is fairly moderate in his commentaries, philologically focusing on text and sources, Herrera's edition is rather digressive, even pedantic, often using the text of Garcilaso as a model for a new vernacular poetics.[4]

HERRERA IN THE PRINTING HOUSE

Although there is no record of the contract between Herrera and the printer, Alonso de la Barrera, evidence shows that the former played a prominent role in the printing process, and that he may have funded this publication. For instance, Herrera arranged the casting of special types to reflect his orthographic idiosyncrasies, such as vowels with dieresis and the letters 'j' and 'i' without the tilde, and it is very likely that he also dictated the design of the

---

[2] M. Rosso Gallo, *La poesía de Garcilaso de la Vega. Análisis filológico y texto crítico*, Madrid, 1990, pp. 5–26.

[3] In the *Anotaciones*, Herrera refers to his friend Juan de Mal Lara, who died in 1571, as the person who most strongly persuaded him to continue his work on Garcilaso. De la Vega, *Obras*, ed. Montero (n. 1 above), p. 14.

[4] J. V. Núñez Rivera, 'Garcilaso según Herrera. Aspectos de crítica textual en las *Anotaciones*', in B. López Bueno (ed.), *Las 'Anotaciones' de Fernando de Herrera: doce estudios* (IV Encuentro Internacional sobre Poesía del Siglo de Oro, Seville and Córdoba, 18–21 November 1996), Seville, 1997, pp. 107–34 (111–18).

title-page, a witty emblematic reference to the military and humanist values of Garcilaso (Fig. 18.1).[5]

Most importantly, Herrera was the main corrector, though likely with the assistance of other Sevillian scholars.[6] In his brief treatise on printing, Juan Caramuel y Lobkowitz alludes to the kind of scenario in which Herrera might have found himself:

> If the book is printed at the expense of the printer, it is corrected with care; if at the expense of the author or the bookseller, with little or no care. Why? If it is corrected well the price is higher and the book has many buyers. Therefore, the printer is diligent if his investment is at stake and negligent if somebody else's.[7]

One of the most remarkable bibliographical features of this edition is the existence of three states, as manifested by three different preliminary sections (A^1, A^2, A^3), which included the legal apparatus that authorised publication, as typical of Spanish books of the time.[8] In Herrera's edition, the first state included a single quarto sheet containing the title-page; the license, issued by Juan Gallo de Andrada on 5 September 1579; the approval by Alonso de Ercilla; and a dedication to the Marquis of Ayamonte, D. Antonio de Guzmán (A^1). But shortly after the death of Antonio de Guzmán on 20 April 1580, there was an important addition to this preliminary section: a half quarto sheet containing a new dedication, now addressed to D. Francisco de Guzmán, the son of the deceased marquis, and a list of thirteen errata preceded by a statement of the editor inviting readers to emend the mistakes that still remained uncorrected in some of the copies (A^2):

> Despite all the diligence applied to the printing of this edition, it was not possible to avoid a few mistakes in some of the copies. However, these mistakes have been corrected in the rest of them. Thus, omitting the mention of insignificant errors, which can be easily identified, here is the list of some.[9]

---

[5] Garcilaso took part in numerous military campaigns led by Charles V across Europe. The meaning of the woodcut illustration is as follows: the motto, 'non minus praeclarum hoc, quam illud' (is not to be accounted less illustrious than his), is drawn from a passage in Cicero, *De officiis*, I. 22.75, where it is argued that the political career of Solon is comparable to the military achievements of Themistocles. Inside the circle, the helmet and the book further emphasise the idea that arms and letters should be equally praised. And the vegetation surrounding these two objects, that is, the laurel (outer) and the ivy (inner), symbolise epic and lyric poetry respectively. See De la Vega, *Obras*, ed. Montero (n. 1 above), pp. 25–9. Afterwards, Alonso de la Barrera reused this allegorical woodblock for two other publications. See A. Castillejo Benavente, *La imprenta en Sevilla en el siglo XVI (1521–1600)*, ed. C. López Lorenzo, 2 vols, Seville, 2019, pp. 1219–20, 1262–3.

[6] S. B. Vranich, 'Génesis y significado de las *Anotaciones a Garcilaso*', in S. B. Vranich, *Ensayos Sevillanos del Siglo de Oro*, Valencia and Chapel Hill (NC), 1981, pp. 29–41; G. Lazure, 'Fashioning Fame: Fernando de Herrera's *Anotaciones* as a Space of Knowledge', in *Calíope*, 2, 2018, pp. 69–92.

[7] 'Si liber Typographi impensis imprimitur, magna cura corrigitur: si Authoris aut Bibliopolae, parva, aut nulla: et cur? si sit bene correctus, majori pretio, et a pluribus emitur; et ideo Typographus, si rem suam agat, est diligens: si alienam, negligens.' J. Caramuel y Lobkowitz, *Syntagma de arte typographica* in his *Theologia praeterintentionalis* [...] *est Theologiae Fundamentalis Tomus IV*, Lyon, 1664, pp. 185–200, reproduced in *Syntagma de arte typographica*, ed. and transl. P. A. Escapa, Salamanca, 2004, pp. 132–3.

[8] De la Vega, *Obras*, ed. Montero (n. 1 above), pp. 33–56; Castillejo, *Imprenta* (n. 5 above), pp. 1197–200.

[9] 'Con toda la diligencia, que se à puesto en esta impression, no se an podido escusar en algunos libros unos pocos errores; porque en los demas van corregidos. i assi dexando de señalar los de menos importancia, i que facilmente se pueden conocer, se pondran aqui algunos'.

FIG. 18.1. Title-page of Garcilaso de la Vega, *Obras con Anotaciones de Fernando de Herrera*, Alonso de la Barrera, Seville, 1580, 4° (USTC 336,469). Ann Arbor (MI), University of Michigan Library, PQ 6391 .A1 1580.

However, some time later, an entirely new preliminary gathering was produced: a quarto sheet was reset bearing no trace of the special types originally commissioned by Herrera, suggesting that at that point they had already been melted down and recast (A³). This new gathering consisted of the title-page, the old dedication, and five errata pages comprising 149 entries, nine of which were repeated from the first list; the remaining four were eliminated with no apparent rationale. It is remarkable that the records of the license and approval were removed, being now replaced by a single statement on the title-page: *Con Licensia de los SS del Consejo Real*. Additionally, it is even more remarkable that the privilege, the errata list prepared by an official corrector (*fe de erratas*), and the fixed minimum sale price (*tassa*) were never included in any of the three states of the preliminary gatherings. As Juan Montero argues, the absence of a privilege would support the thesis that Herrera was responsible for the cost of the edition: Alonso de la Barrera did not have to worry about asking for exclusive rights to help him recover an invested capital. As for the lack of the obligatory *fe de errata* and *tassa*, many books printed in Seville at that time also appeared without them because printers and booksellers often preferred the risk of paying a fine, rather than facing the financial burden of waiting for the official corrector to complete his job.[10]

Undoubtedly, these two errata lists reveal Herrera's anxiety to regain control over the text of an edition that he had so carefully prepared. While the first list mostly focuses on typographical mistakes, the second contains a wide range of errors, numerous stylistic changes, and even some highly revealing comments such as the one on a passage at p. 309, where Herrera says that it had been wrongly inserted by the professional scribe who copied this autograph manuscript: 'all this should not be read because it was written in this place due to the scribe's error.'[11] In fact, it was not uncommon that, despite the pressure of having to adjust to the pace dictated by the press, some editors were able to implement important stylistic changes during printing; such was the case of Beatus Rhenatus, who managed to introduce extensive changes in his edition of Seneca while the sheets were being printed.[12] Similarly, a close examination of multiple copies of Herrera's *Anotaciones* shows that corrections were implemented in the course of printing or shortly afterwards.[13] In the following

---

[10] De la Vega, *Obras*, ed. Montero (n. 1 above), p. 16; F. de los Reyes Gómez, 'La tasa en el libro antiguo español', *Pliegos de Bibliofilia*, 4, 1998, pp. 35–52 (44–6).

[11] 'Todo esto no se à de leer; que entrò en este lugar por descuido del que lo trasladò.'

[12] Beatus Rhenanus to Erasmus, Basel, 17 April 1515, available in the English translation in *The Correspondence of Erasmus: Letters 298 to 445*, ed. R. A. B. Mynors and D. F. S. Thompson, III, Toronto, 1976, no. 328.

[13] Considering the scope and complexity of the *Anotaciones*, we assume that Herrera and the printer anticipated a fairly small readership of educated humanists. Thus, we can conjure up a modest print run of 500 copies. According to WorldCat, there are thirty-four libraries worldwide holding this 1580 edition. However, we need to add seventeen libraries mentioned in Montero's edition that do not appear in WorldCat as repositories of the *Anotaciones*. De la Vega, *Obras*, ed. Montero (n. 1 above), pp. 9–11. Therefore, taking into account that some libraries hold two or more copies, as my study shows, there are sixty-seven extant copies held in libraries around the world. For my research, I have closely examined twenty-two copies of the *Anotaciones*, including examples from each of the three states: A¹: U/1110 (Biblioteca Nacional de España), 88-5-10 (Biblioteca Capitular y Colombina de Sevilla); A²: R/5850, R/12817 (Biblioteca Nacional de España), R.M. 6835, C-3860 (Biblioteca de la Real Academia Española), Ra. 275 (Biblioteca de las Facultades de Filología y Geografía e Historia, Universidad de Sevilla), PQ 6391 .A1 1580 (Special Collections Research Center, University of Michigan Library); A³: R/1408, R/3697, R/12798, R/3707 (Biblioteca Nacional de España), BH FL 26159, BH FG 1750 (Biblioteca Histórica Marqués de Valdecilla, Universidad Complutense, Madrid), S.Com. 7-A-138 (Biblioteca de la

pages, I argue that the nature of the corrections help us understand not only the role of Herrera as a corrector inside the printing house but also the position of this extraordinary edition in the context of Spanish printing in the second half of the sixteenth century. While previous works have almost exclusively focused on identifying the errors in Herrera's *Anotaciones*, examining this edition in isolation,[14] little has been said about what these corrections can reveal about printing-house practices in early modern Spain, and in Europe in general, raising, therefore, broader questions about the transmission and reception of vernacular literary texts edited in the humanistic tradition.

As stated by Herrera at the beginning of the first errata list, the intention was to address errors that had been corrected in some sheets of each print run. In fact, the editor is implicitly referring to stop-press corrections and other emendations made in the printing house (Fig. 18.2). For instance, the wrongly spelt ἐκλογίξω was properly retyped into ἐκλογίζω in the course of printing in six out of the twenty-two examined copies (p. 405);[15] πάλλειν was wrongly printed with 'η' instead of 'ει', but was press-corrected by using a common manuscript abbreviation of 'ει', so the resulting printed abbreviation for 'ει' is found in twenty of those copies (p. 669).[16] However, most of the recommended emendations were hand-corrected in some of the sheets when they were still in the printing house: δαώφονη to δαωφονῆ in three copies (p. 142);[17] *resplandecian* to *resplandescan* in all twenty-two copies (p. 171); *por quem das causas* to *cousas* in seven copies (p. 260).[18]; *undosa* to *umbrosa* in two copies by means of a printed paste slip (p. 312);[19] *i no paxaro* to *i no al paxaro* in all twenty-two copies (p. 359); *tienenme* to *tieneme* in nineteen copies, the 'n' being crossed out;[20] and *ruestiqueza* to *rustiqueza* in seven copies, the first 'e' being crossed out (p. 549).[21]

Nevertheless, there were stop-press corrections and other emendations unrecorded in the errata lists, suggesting that Herrera might not have had full control over the task of emendation (Fig 18.3). For example, the verb *tiene* was added to complete the verse *o Betis, cual mi Sorga, tiene a Laura*, by a stop-press correction in eighteen out of the twenty-two copies, the remaining four with the missing word added by hand (p. 255).[22] More dramatically, a whole verse was added by using something like a type holder at the bottom of p. 376.[23] This page originally, and wrongly, ended with the line *Parte consume d'aquesta agua el fuego*, followed

---

Real Academia Española). In some copies of A², the additional half sheet, or two leaves, has been nested within the first gathering, thus the second dedication appears as the recto and verso of sig. A3, and the first errata list as the recto of sig. A4: R/5850, R.M. 6835, C-3860, PQ 6391 .A1 1580. Moreover, there are some copies that cannot be described as belonging to any of the three states, because the preliminary gathering is either partly or completely, missing, or it was made up of leaves drawn from other copies: R/5853, R/30901, R/5384, R/5063, R/9120, R/9138, (Biblioteca Nacional de España), R. 11.5.11 (Biblioteca Rector Machado y Núñez, Universidad de Sevilla).

[14] J. M. Blecua, 'Las Obras de Garcilaso con anotaciones de Fernando de Herrera', in J. M. Blecua, *Sobre poesía de la edad de oro: ensayos y notas eruditas*, Madrid, 1970, pp. 100–5; De la Vega, *Obras*, ed. Montero (n. 1 above), pp. 50–61; De Herrera, *Anotaciones*, ed. Pepe and Reyes (n. 1 above), pp. 95–128.

[15] R/3697, R/30901, R/5063, R/5384, BH FLL 26159, BH FG 1750.

[16] R/9120 and R/9138 were not press-corrected.

[17] R/3707, R/9120, S.Com. 7-A-138, but R/3697 was likely corrected by a reader.

[18] R.M. 6835, R/5063, U/1110, R/9138, BH FG 1750, C-3860, Ra. 275. R/12817 was corrected by a reader.

[19] R/1408, 88-5-10.

[20] R/30901, U/1110, and R/9138 were not corrected.

[21] R/3697, R/30901, R/5063, R/5384, BH FLL 26159, BH FG 1750, S. Coms. 7-A-138. R. 11.5.11 was erased by a reader.

[22] R/12817, R/30901, R/9138, Ra. 275.

[23] One or more lines of type could be set in a type holder, similar to the ones used by binders to stamp a line of type on a label. Cathleen A. Baker, personal communication with the author.

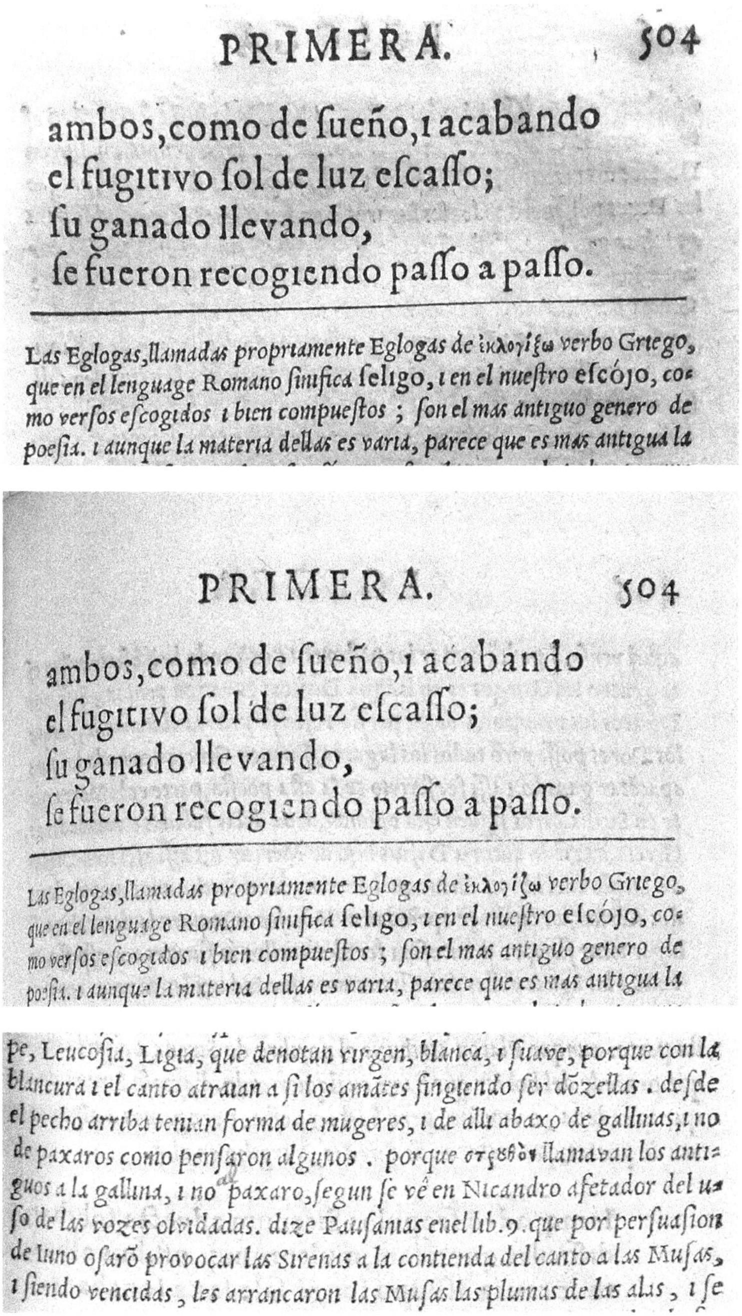

PRIMERA. 504

ambos, como de sueño, i acabando
el fugitivo sol de luz escasso;
su ganado llevando,
se fueron recogiendo passo a passo.

Las Eglogas, llamadas propriamente Eglogas de ἐκλογίζω verbo Griego, que en el lenguage Romano sinifica seligo, i en el nuestro escójo, como versos escogidos i bien compuestos ; son el mas antiguo genero de poesia. i aunque la materia dellas es varia, parece que es mas antigua la

PRIMERA. 504

ambos, como de sueño, i acabando
el fugitivo sol de luz escasso;
su ganado llevando,
se fueron recogiendo passo a passo.

Las Eglogas, llamadas propriamente Eglogas de ἐκλογίζω verbo Griego, que en el lenguage Romano sinifica seligo, i en el nuestro escójo, como versos escogidos i bien compuestos ; son el mas antiguo genero de poesia. i aunque la materia dellas es varia, parece que es mas antigua la

pe, Leucosia, Ligia, que denotan virgen, blanca, i suave, porque con la blancura i el canto atraian a si los amantes fingiendo ser dozellas . desde el pecho arriba tenian forma de mugeres, i de alli abaxo de gallinas, i no de paxaros como pensaron algunos . porque οτσηδόι llamavan los antiguos a la gallina, i no paxaro, segun se vé en Nicandro afetador del uso de las vozes olvidadas. dize Pausanias en el lib. 9. que por persuasion de Iuno osarõ provocar las Sirenas a la contienda del canto a las Musas, i siendo vencidas, les arrancaron las Musas las plumas de las alas, i se

FIG. 18.2.a–c. In-house corrections in de la Vega, *Obras* (see Fig. 18.1). a: p. 504 [i.e., 405]. Madrid, Biblioteca Nacional de España, U/1110. b–c: pp. 504 [i.e., 405] and 359. Madrid, Biblioteca Histórica Marqués de Valdecilla, Universidad Complutense, FLL 26159.

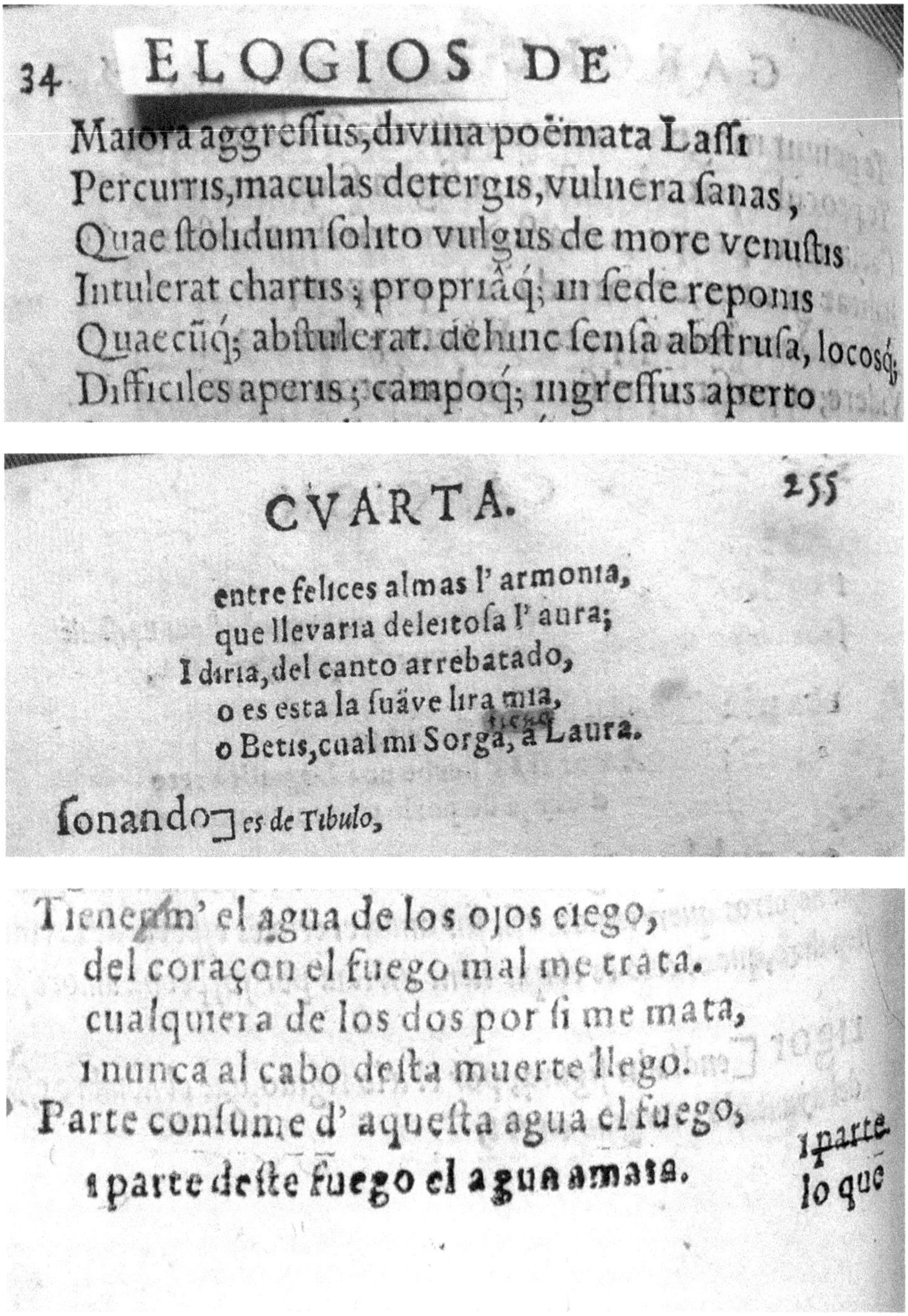

34   ELOGIOS DE

Maiora aggreſſus, diuina poëmata Laſſi
Percurris, maculas detergis, vulnera ſanas,
Quae ſtolidum ſolito vulgus de more venuſtis
Intulerat chartis; propriaq́; in ſede reponis
Quaecūq́; abſtulerat: dehinc ſenſa abſtruſa, locoſq́;
Difficiles aperis; campoq́; ingreſſus aperto

CVARTA.   255

entre felices almas l' armonia,
que llevaria deleitoſa l' aura;
I diria, del canto arrebatado,
o es esta la ſuáve lira mia,
o Betis, cual mi Sorga, à Laura.

ſonando⌉ es de Tibulo,

Tienen in' el agua de los ojos ciego,
del coraçon el fuego mal me trata.
cualquiera de los dos por ſi me mata,
i nunca al cabo deſta muerte llego.
Parte conſume d' aqueſta agua el fuego,
i parte deſte fuego el agua amaia.

i parte
lo que

FIG. 18.3.a–c. In-house corrections in de la Vega, *Obras* (see Fig. 18.1). a: p. 34. Madrid, Biblioteca Nacional de España, R/5384. b: p. 255. Madrid, Biblioteca Nacional de España R/30901. c: p. 376, Madrid, Biblioteca Histórica Marqués de Valdecilla, Universidad Complutense, FLL 26159.

by the catchword *i parte*, which obviously did not match the beginning of the verse of the next page, *lo qu'el*. Appropriately, the missing line, *i parte deste fuego el agua amata*, along with the correct catchword, *lo que*, appears in fifteen copies, with the incorrect catchword being systematically crossed out (p. 376).[24] Furthermore, the repetition *que la que la* (p. 47) is amended in all twenty-two copies. Finally, printed paste slips were employed in two cases: the running title, *Vida de Garcilasso* to *Elogios de Garcilasso*, in two copies (pp. 36–7);[25] and the emendation of *qnanto* into *cuanto* in fourteen copies (p. 144).[26]

However, the errata of the *Anotaciones* seem to have failed to achieve their claimed goal: out of the twenty-two examined copies, only one shows the marks of a diligent reader who consistently followed the second errata list to emend the errors (Fig. 18.4).[27] Here are some examples: *eram* to *erat* (p. 19); *enel lib.20* to *enel lib. 21* (p. 180); *cuanto de sus senores* to *por sus señores* (p. 499); and *bāco* to *blanco* (p. 641). The case of πάλλην to πάλλειν (p. 669) is striking because the second errata list displays as 'wrong' the version that had already and rightly been press-corrected with the abbreviation of 'ει', recommending, therefore, the unnecessary correction into 'ει', which this reader made. Additionally, when this reader inserted the prescribed emendation *umores frios* to *frios humores* and *Frācisco d'Figueroa;* to *Francisco de Cuevas;* (p. 376), he expressed his disagreement with it, questioning the new attribution of the sonnet to Francisco de Cuevas by adding a note acknowledging the authority of Dr. Alcocer and others: 'en las erratas dice Cuevas mal el Dr. Alcocer y otros dicen del divino Figueroa'. Finally, on the same page, this critical reader added the missing verse, correcting the wrong catchword, a mistake that was never recorded in any of the errata lists, suggesting not only a lack of communication between the compositor and Herrera, but also that the latter might have overlooked this error.

The Task of Correction According to Alonso Víctor de Paredes

In addition to the bibliographical analysis of the errors, we need to examine Herrera's efforts, and limitations, as an author turned corrector in the context of what we know about well-established practices in the printing house. For this purpose, it seems appropriate to look at some passages in Chapter 10 of the *Institucion, y origen del arte de la imprenta y reglas generals para los componedores,* a seventeenth-century Spanish printing manual written by Alonso Víctor de Paredes, a compositor with more than thirty years of experience.[28] While

---

[24] R.M. 6835, R/12798, R/5384, BH FG 1750, and C-3860 remained uncorrected, and in R/5063 and Ra. 275 a reader added the missing verse by hand.

[25] R.M. 6835, R/5384.

[26] R/5850, R/1408, and R/5063 show signs that a small printed correction slip had been pasted in earlier on. R/30901 was hand-corrected to *quanto*, and R/9138, S. Coms. 7-A-138, Ra.275, and PQ 6391 .A1 1580 were not corrected.

[27] R/5063.

[28] A. V. de Paredes, *Institucion, y origen del arte de la imprenta, y reglas generales para los componedores* [Madrid, c. 1680] 4° (USTC 5033068), translated into English in A. V. de Paredes, *Institution, and Origin of the Art of Printing, and General Rules for Compositors [Madrid: ca. 1680],* ed. and transl. P. Alvarez, Ann Arbor (MI), 2018, pp. 18–22.

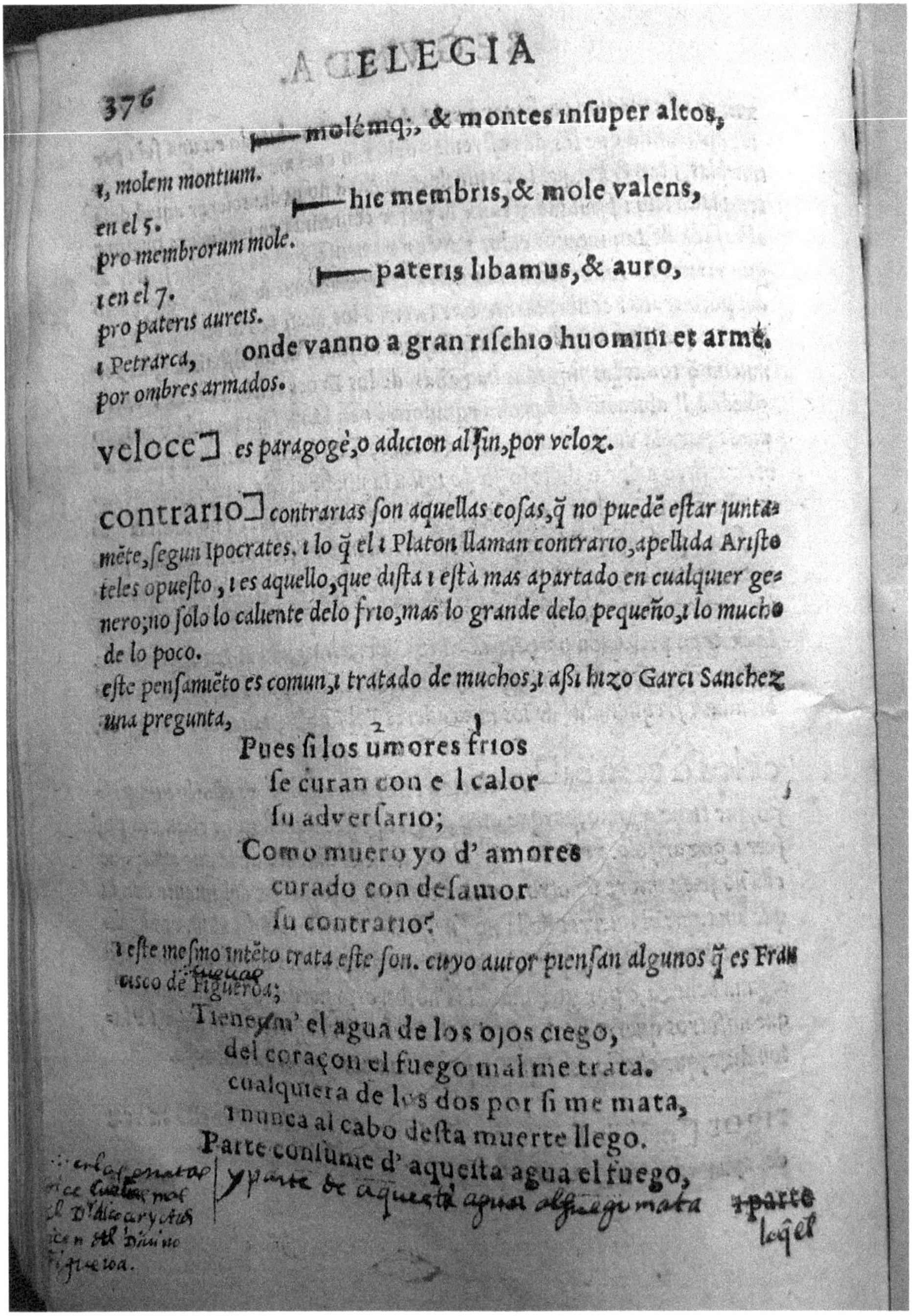

ELEGIA

376

molémq;, & montes insuper altos,

i, molem montium.

hic membris,& mole valens,

en el 5.

pro membrorum mole.

pateris libamus,& auro,

i en el 7.

pro pateris aureis.

i Petrarca, onde vanno a gran rischio huomini et arme.

por ombres armados.

veloce] es paragogè,o adicion al fin,por veloz.

contrario] contrarias son aquellas cosas,q̃ no puedẽ estar juntamẽte,segun Ipocrates. i lo q̃ el i Platon llaman contrario,apellida Aristoteles opuesto, i es aquello,que dista i està mas apartado en cualquier genero;no solo lo caliente delo frio,mas lo grande delo pequeño,i lo mucho de lo poco.

este pensamiẽto es comun,i tratado de muchos,i assi hizo Garci Sanchez una pregunta,

Pues si los [2] umores frios
se curan con el calor
su adversario;
Como muero yo d' amores
curado con desamor
su contrario?

i este mesmo intẽto trata este son. cuyo autor piensan algunos q̃ es Francisco de Figueroa;

Tiene m' el agua de los ojos ciego,
del coraçon el fuego mal me trata.
cualquiera de los dos por si me mata,
i nunca al cabo desta muerte llego.
Parte consume d' aquesta agua el fuego,
i parte

FIG. 18.4. A reader's correction in de la Vega, *Obras* (see Fig. 18.1), p. 376. Madrid, Biblioteca Nacional de España, R/5063.

other sources offer us the idealised image of the corrector as an accomplished scholar who is fluent in many ancient and vernacular languages, Paredes paints a broader and more realistic picture by listing the different kinds of correctors according to the nature of the text to be printed and the resources available in the printing house:

> The first is when the corrector is a good grammarian, and learned in theology, law, or other such sciences, but he has not been a printer. He will admirably correct Latin and the vernacular with all perfection. But if they give him a misplaced page, an erroneous leaf, or an altered signature, how will he correct it if he does not understand it? The second is when the corrector is a printer and a Latinist as well, sufficiently read in history and in other books, as I have known some; and there is no doubt that they are the most suitable. The third is when the slight relevance of the editions does not require anything special, and it is enough to entrust the correction to the most expert compositor that the master printer can find in his printing house, even if he is not a Latinist; any problem can be overcome if, when encountering some difficulty with the Latin, he consults with the author, or with those who know, and submits to the best opinion. The fourth is when the owner of the printing house is not a printer, but a book trader, or a widow, or someone who does not understand printing. And, nevertheless, they want to correct or entrust it to people who hardly know how to read. Regarding this sort, who could call them correctors? What works requiring care can be entrusted to them?[29]

Acknowledging the existence of error as an inherent element of printing, Paredes strives to offer useful advice:

> To avoid this problem, then, it is sound advice that the corrector listen to the reading of the copy, and that he revise the proof afterwards. And if necessary, because there are too many errors, he should ask for a second proof to recheck it, and see if it is corrected well. In other words, the corrector should do the second proofreading of the first sheet coming from the press, not allowing the compositor to do this second proofreading unless he has a lot of faith in him. And before beginning to correct, it is necessary to make sure that the leaves are right according to the signatures, and whether there are any errors in the running titles of the pages.[30]

Admittedly, Paredes idealises the task of proofreading by suggesting that it should be completed before the print run begins, when, in fact, as we have seen in the emendations of the

---

[29] Ibid., pp. 199, 201. Conversely, see the idealistic portrait drawn by J. I Moretus in Antwerp, Museum Plantin-Moretus, Archives Plantiniennes, vol. 118, fol. 1r–v, transcribed in H. D. L. Vervliet, 'Une instruction Plantinienne à l'intention des correcteurs', *Gutenberg-Jahrbuch*, 1959, pp. 99–103 (100), and partly rediscussed in Dirk Imhof's contribution in this Companion; J. Moxon, *Mechanick Exercises: Or, the Doctrine of Handy-Works. Applied to the Art of Printing. The Second Volume*, London, 1683, commented on in his *Mechanick Exercises on the Whole Art of Printing (1683–1684)*, ed. H. Davis and H. Carter, 2nd edn, London, 1958. p. 246.

[30] Paredes, *Institution* (n. 28 above), p. 201. Evidence suggests that proof sheets were meant to be checked two or three times, with one person reading aloud from the printer's copy while the corrector checked the proof sheet. However, it is also likely that this practice was Paredes' ideal goal. Realistically, only a few prestigious printing houses were able to do two or three rounds of proofs. See the letter from Wigle van Aytta van Zwichem to Dooitzen Wiarda, Dülmen, 1 July 1534, published in J. Gerritsen, 'Printing at Froben's: An Eye-Witness Account', *Studies in Bibliography*, 44, 1991, pp. 144–63 (150, 162), as well as Moxon, *Mechanick Exercises on the Whole Art of Printing* (n. 29 above), p. 250.

380   PRINTING AND MISPRINTING

Anotaciones and as evidenced in most of the textual variants of copies within an edition during the hand-press period, mistakes were mostly corrected in the course of printing or shortly afterwards. To confirm this, we have additional information about how corrections were implemented at printing houses in early modern Spain through the evidence provided by five extant printer's copies that include annotations and corrections by the authors.[31] For instance, an examination of two manuscript printer's copies used by Fray Pedro de Vega to correct the second and third parts of his *Declaración de los Siete Psalmos Penitenciales* can serve as a parallel to Herrera's textual anxieties. Indeed, Fray Pedro turned these two manuscripts, fair copies prepared by professional scribes and approved by the Council of Castile, into tools to guide the compositor to implement numerous changes regarding both the content and layout of the text. More importantly, one of the author's main concerns was the elaboration of a comprehensive index, a task that he kept postponing until the very end, as the complicated printing history of the *Declaración* reveals. Consisting of the interpretation of the first four Penitential Psalms, the first part of the *Declaración* was printed by Juan Íñiguez de Lequerica in Alcalá de Henares in 1599, and then republished, with numerous corrections, by Luis Sánchez in Madrid in 1602. The second part, which deals with the fifth psalm, was printed by Miguel Serrano de Vargas in Madrid in 1602. And the third part, an exegesis of the sixth and seventh psalms, was printed also by Serrano de Vargas in 1603. Undoubtedly, the disastrous edition of 1599 was the main reason why the author made a great effort to regain control over his own text: Íñiguez de Lequerica had introduced numerous mistakes and, without consulting with the author, had foliated the commentaries for each of the four psalms independently, making Fray Pedro's index useless. This experience was so traumatic that he prefaced the final index for the third part with a memorable apologetic paragraph that aptly summarises one of the main challenges that an author like Herrera had to face in the printing house:

> When the first part was being printed in Alcalá, the pressmen did not stop while I was correcting the sheet, so those being printed during the short time I spent in the correction could include errors, differing from what is cited in our index.[32]

Returning to Paredes' manual, we must cite a passage that helps us understand the potential misunderstanding between the author and the journeymen of the printing house:

> It is customary in the profession that the first three sheets of any book that come from the press are given to the journeymen. The first to the corrector, because if any error, or errors, are found in the printed sheet, he should rectify it, or blame others for it, showing them his sheet. The second to the compositor so that, after seeing any error that has occurred, he shows his proof, and sheet, in order to find out whether it has been corrected or not. The third to the pressman so that it can be seen if, by mischance, the error was caused by a type that was pulled out by the ink balls, and which was then displaced, or if the sheet was put on the tympan the

---

[31] P. A. Escapa, 'Autores en la oficina del impresor. Tres reimpresiones del Siglo de Oro español y un aplazamiento', *Boletín de la Real Academia Española*, 79, 1999, pp. 249–66 (251–9).

[32] Ibid., p. 253: 'Quando se imprimía la Primera parte de Alcalá, no paravan los impressores mientras yo emendava el pliego, y assí los que se estampavan en aquel poco tiempo que yo me detenía en la enmienda, podrían yr errados y no venir con lo que cita esta nuestra tabla.'

wrong way round. And with these three sheets (which are called 'proof sheets'), it should be discovered who was responsible so that he emends it or reprints it on his own.[33]

Certainly, Paredes' suggestion that the task of correction should be shared between the corrector, the compositor, and the pressman, is relevant to understanding the position of Herrera: how would a sophisticated scholar like Herrera detect, or even correct, errors such as a misplaced page, an erroneous leaf, or an altered signature, if he does not understand these things? Therefore, as seen in the mistakes that were not listed in the errata lists, an incorrect running title is the pressman's responsibility, and a missing line and catchword, or an upside-down letter, are typical compositor's mistakes. As Paredes prescribes, the compositor and the pressman should take responsibility for those and correct them on their own, possibly without even consulting with the corrector or the author. This separation of tasks would explain the fact that, for instance, the compositor never realised that Herrera listed errata with their wrong pagination in the first list: p. 237 is actually p. 273, and the correction listed for p. 664 should be on p. 669. It is also remarkable that Herrera correctly listed the errata for p. 405, whereas this page wrongly shows as p. 504 in all the examined copies. It is therefore understandable that compositors and pressmen were suspicious of the role of authors as correctors, as indicated by the note on the margin that Paredes intended to add for the future publication of his manual, 'do not trust the correction of the author only', and by the following anecdote:

> I know someone who found such a mistake in a very distinguished author, whom I could name along with the book and the chapter, and having consulted with him, had it emended. In the emendation, however, the author put it badly; and, not being satisfied, the compositor for a second time presented his doubt to the author, who, recognising that it was legitimate, and examining it more carefully, made the correction as it needed to be, so that the person who printed it received no little praise.[34]

In his manual for correctors, Hieronymus Hornschuch goes even further by being skeptical about the role of the author as a corrector, suggesting that the author will generate more mistakes if he checks the proofs:

> For it is impossible for anyone not fully trained in this school not to go wrong. Therefore, it will be best to entrust the work to the corrector who is in duty bound to check and examine everything two or three times.[35]

---

[33] Paredes, *Institution* (n. 28 above), pp. 201, 203.
[34] Ibid., p. 205.
[35] Hieronymus Hornschuch, Ὀρθοτυπογραφία, *Hoc Est: Instructio, operas typographicas correcturis; Et Admonitio, scripta sua in lucem edituris Utilis [et] necessaria: Adiecta Sunt Sub Finem Varia Typorum Sive Scripturarum typographis usitatarum genera [et] appellationes* [...], Leipzig, Michael Lantzenberger, 1608, 8° (USTC 2001806), translated into English in his *Orthotypographia, 1608*, ed. and transl. P. Gaskell and P. Bradford, Cambridge, 1972, p. 34.

CONCLUSION

Herrera's role as a corrector, and particularly his obsessive intervention in the correction of the text through emendations undertaken in the printing house and the production of two errata lists, are not particularly unique in the context of early modern printing in Europe.[36] Herrera must have understood that printing was a compromise. There were too many stages beyond his control, from the moment his autograph manuscript was professionally copied for official approval to the complexity of the mechanics of the printing house. Despite the idealised image that printing manuals convey, the press did not stop during the production of a book. Moreover, the evidence from Paredes' printing manual, which often displays a picture based on actual experience, as opposed to the rosy idealisation of other manuals, is confirmed by the nature of the emendations in the twenty-two examined copies, suggesting that Herrera found himself unable to communicate with others involved in the task of correction. To put it succinctly, Paredes describes the task of correction as being rather compartmentalised, establishing a clear distinction between presswork errors, which should be corrected by the compositor and the pressman, and textual mistakes, which should be addressed by a professional corrector or the author. It is therefore unsurprising that Paredes states that correction should not be entrusted to the author alone. Indeed, this division of expertise, along with the obvious anxiety to keep the press running, prevented Herrera from having a full picture of the extent to which his edition was being misprinted. Moreover, Herrera must have been aware that it was rather difficult to implement all the corrections in every single copy, particularly since it was challenging to reconstruct the exact chronological order in which the sheets were printed: they could be arbitrarily nested in gatherings, which meant that these gatherings were not necessarily bound in an order that matched the timeline of the three states (A^1, A^2, A^3). If the errors were known before folding the sheets, or after folding them but before their collation, it would have been a fairly manageable task. Conversely, if the mistakes were detected only after folding the sheets and collating them into gatherings, the task of correction would have been extremely hard. It is even plausible that some copies of the first state (A^1) had been already distributed for sale before some late corrections could be implemented.

Nevertheless, despite of all these challenges, Herrera and his colleagues still pursued the endless duty of correcting, producing a comprehensive errata list that was perhaps designed as the ultimate proof of the editor's commitment to both his future readers and his ambitious literary project.

---

[36] For fairly recent studies on the task of correction and the unavoidable existence of error in early modern printing, see T. J. Dadson, 'La corrección de pruebas (y un libro de poesía)', in P. A. Escapa and S. Garza Merino (eds), *Imprenta y crítica textual en el siglo de oro*, Valladolid, 2000, pp. 97–128; D. McKitterick, *Print, Manuscript and the Search for Order, 1450–1830*, Cambridge, 2003, pp. 97–138; A. Grafton, *The Culture of Correction in Renaissance Europe*, London, 2011.

BIBLIOGRAPHY

PRIMARY SOURCES

Aytta van Zwichem, Wigle van, to Dooitzen Wiarda, Dülmen, 1 July 1534, transcribed in J. Gerritsen, 'Printing at Froben's: An Eye-Witness Account', *Studies in Bibliography*, 44, 1991, pp. 144–63.

Caramuel y Lobkowitz, J., *Syntagma de arte typographica* in his *Theologia praeterintentionalis […] est theologiae fundamentalis tomus IV*, Lyon, 1664, pp. 185–200.

Caramuel y Lobkowitz, J., *Syntagma de arte typographica*, ed. and transl. P. A. Escapa, Salamanca, 2004.

Herrera, F. de, *Anotaciones a la poesía de Garcilaso*, ed. I. Pepe and J. M. Reyes, Madrid, 2001.

Hornschuch, Hieronymus, Ὀρθοτυπογραφία, *Hoc Est: Instructio, operas typographicas correcturis; Et Admonitio, scripta sua in lucem edituris Utilis [et] necessaria: Adiecta Sunt Sub Finem Varia Typorum Sive Scripturarum typographis usitatarum genera [et] appellationes […]*, Leipzig, Michael Lantzenberger, 1608, 8° (USTC 2001806).

Hornschuch, H., *Orthotypographia, 1608*, ed. and transl. P. Gaskell and P. Bradford, Cambridge, 1972.

Moxon, J., *Mechanick Exercises: Or, the Doctrine of Handy-Works. Applied to the Art of Printing. The Second Volume*, London, 1683.

Moxon, J., *Mechanick Exercises on the Whole Art of Printing (1683–1684)*, ed. H. Davis and H. Carter, 2nd edn, London, 1958.

Paredes, A. V. de, *Institucion, y origen del arte de la imprenta, y reglas generales para los componedores* [Madrid, c. 1680] 4° (USTC 5033068).

Paredes, A. V. de, *Institution, and Origin of the Art of Printing, and General Rules for Compositors [Madrid: ca. 1680]*, ed. and transl. P. Alvarez, Ann Arbor (MI), 2018.

Rhenanus, Beatus, to Erasmus, Basel, 17 April 1515, translated into English in *The Correspondence of Erasmus: Letters 298 to 445*, ed. R. A. B. Mynors and D. F. S. Thompson, III, Toronto, 1976, no. 328.

Vega, Garcilaso de la, *Obras con Anotaciones de Fernando de Herrera*, Seville, Alonso de la Barrera, 1580, 4° (USTC 336469).

Vega, G. de la, *Obras con Anotaciones de Fernando de Herrera*, ed. J. Montero, 2 vols, Seville, 1998.

SECONDARY LITERATURE

Blecua, J. M., 'Las Obras de Garcilaso con anotaciones de Fernando de Herrera', in Blecua, J. M., *Sobre poesía de la edad de oro: ensayos y notas eruditas*, Madrid, 1970, pp. 100–5.

Dadson, T. J., 'La corrección de pruebas (y un libro de poesía)', in P. A. Escapa and S. Garza Merino (eds), *Imprenta y crítica textual en el siglo de oro*, Valladolid, 2000, pp. 97–128.

Castillejo Benavente, A., *La imprenta en Sevilla en el siglo XVI (1521–1600)*, ed. C. López Lorenzo, 2 vols, Seville, 2019.

Escapa, P. A., 'Autores en la oficina del impresor. Tres reimpresiones del Siglo de Oro español y un aplazamiento', *Boletín de la Real Academia Española*, 79, 1999, pp. 249–66.

Grafton, A., *The Culture of Correction in Renaissance Europe*, London, 2011.

Lazure, G., 'Fashioning Fame: Fernando de Herrera's *Anotaciones* as a Space of Knowledge', *Calíope*, 2, 2018, pp. 69–92.

McKitterick, D., *Print, Manuscript and the Search for Order, 1450–1830*, Cambridge, 2003.

Núñez Rivera, J. V., 'Garcilaso según Herrera. Aspectos de crítica textual en las *Anotaciones*', in B. López Bueno (ed.), *Las 'Anotaciones' de Fernando de Herrera: doce estudios* (IV Encuentro Internacional sobre Poesía del Siglo de Oro, Seville and Córdoba, 18–21 November 1996), Seville, 1997, pp. 107–34.

Reyes Gómez, F. de los, 'La tasa en el libro antiguo español', *Pliegos de Bibliofilia*, 4, 1998, pp. 35–52.

Rosso Gallo, M., *La poesía de Garcilaso de la Vega. Análisis filológico y texto crítico*, Madrid, 1990.

Vervliet, H. D. L., 'Une instruction Plantinienne à l'intention des correcteurs', *Gutenberg-Jahrbuch*, 1959, pp. 99–103.

Vranich, S. B., 'Génesis y significado de las *Anotaciones a Garcilaso*', in S. B. Vranich, *Ensayos Sevillanos del Siglo de Oro*, Valencia and Chapel Hill (NC), 1981, pp. 29–41.

CHAPTER 19

MARKETING A MISPRINT

Christopher Tye's The Actes of the Apostles
and Early English Music Publishing

ANNE HEMINGER

INTRODUCTION

SHORTLY before the death of Edward VI in 1553, the English printer William Seres issued a small octavo containing four-part polyphonic settings of the first fourteen chapters of the biblical book of Acts in metrical verse.* Written by the Chapel Royal composer Christopher Tye, the volume was likely inspired by contemporary publications of English-texted biblical verse, and in particular the popular, unnotated psalm translations of Thomas Sternhold and John Hopkins.[1] Tye and Seres could not possibly have known, of course, that in a few short months their publication would be rendered obsolete, deemed heretical by the Catholic government of Edward's half-sister, Queen Mary. Indeed, the existence of Tye's *The Actes of the Apostles, translated into Englyshe metre* in not one, but two distinct versions, each containing different music printing errors, not only offers valuable evidence about how printed books containing musical notation were conceptualised, created, and marketed in mid-Tudor England, but also speaks to the significance that both composer and publisher believed the volume could have for the still-reforming English populace.

The primary difference between these two versions of Tye's *Actes* is significant: one contains all fourteen of Tye's texts but only music to accompany two and a half of the composer's translations, while the other features fourteen distinct musical settings. A detailed study of

---

* I would like to thank Stefano Mengozzi, Theresa Tinkle, Andrew Kohler, Samantha Arten, Paolo Sachet, and Geri Della Rocca de Candal for their feedback at various stages in the writing process, as well as Andrew Kohler, Alyssa Wells, and Samantha Arten for their aid in obtaining sources during the COVID-19 pandemic. An earlier version of this chapter was presented at the 46th Medieval and Renaissance Music Conference in Maynooth, Ireland, in July 2018.

[1] For an overview of the metrical psalm tradition, see B. Quitslund, *The Reformation in Rhyme: Sternhold, Hopkins and the English Metrical Psalter, 1547–1603*, Burlington (VT), 2008, pp. 59–110.

Anne Heminger, *Marketing a Misprint.* In: *Printing and Misprinting.* Edited by Geri Della Rocca de Candal, Anthony Grafton, and Paolo Sachet, Oxford University Press. © Anne Heminger (2023). DOI: 10.1093/oso/9780198863045.003.0020 printing errors in these copies of the *Actes* indicates that music publishing in mid-sixteenth-century England was hampered by printers' (and publishers') lack of musical literacy, but shows that printing errors might be salvaged if a music volume could be repurposed. The considerable errors in both versions also offer a compelling explanation as to why most biblical metrical song was printed without musical notation. In addition, the musical changes made prior to the second edition's printing indicate that Tye was involved throughout the printing process. In highlighting which categories of musical mistakes printers (and the public) were willing to overlook in mid-Tudor England, I furthermore suggest that the cost of correcting notational errors may have been a mitigating factor in whether a music book might be sold despite its mistakes.[2] The extant copies of Tye's *Actes* thus offer an opportunity to examine a range of possible errors in the process of printing musical notation in the sixteenth century, and demonstrate that the level of functionality required by contemporary amateur audiences was considerably lower than that which professional singers typically expected from music manuscripts.[3]

Musical notation, in which the placement of a series of notes on a staff of four or five lines corresponds to an audible pattern of pitches and rhythms, posed particular challenges to the printing process. Though the first printed musical notation appeared in fifteenth-century liturgical books, it was not until Ottaviano Petrucci's publication in 1501 of *Harmonice musices odhecaton* (USTC 801634) that printers began to create books of polyphony using moveable type.[4] The music-printing industry in early sixteenth-century England, meanwhile, was well behind its continental counterparts in terms of technical expertise, size, and commercial output.[5] Yet England was the site of the first known use of single-impression musical type, in which each piece of type contains a single note and a set of five staff lines: in c. 1520, John Rastell included three pages employing this notational font in gathering E of *The Nature of the Four Elements* (USTC 501608).[6] Five further examples of this font have survived: one book and two fragmentary song sheets printed around the same time

---

[2] Large-scale errors, such as the omission of several notes or an incorrect page layout, required reprinting of an entire sheet. Since paper was the most expensive element of book production, accounting for 60 to 75% of the total direct costs, corrections of this scale were expensive. See I. Fenlon, 'Music, Print and Society in Sixteenth-Century Europe', in J. Haar (ed.), *European Music, 1520–1640*, Woodbridge, 2006, p. 286. In England, the prices of imported materials such as type and paper increased over the course of Edward VI's reign, so the cost of paper was an important consideration for printers operating in this period. P. W. M. Blayney, *The Stationers' Company and the Printers of London, 1501–1557*, Cambridge, 2013, p. 652.

[3] Small errors in music manuscripts were common, but issues of the magnitude discussed here were rare.

[4] In the 1501 *Odhecaton*, Petrucci employed a double- (or possibly triple-) impression printing method, in which the staves, notes, and text were printed separately; while high quality, these editions were expensive to produce. The more common technique of printing music in the fifteenth and early sixteenth centuries was to use woodcuts, which allowed notes and their staves to be printed simultaneously. For an overview of Petrucci's techniques, see S. Boorman, *Ottaviano Petrucci: Catalogue Raisonné*, New York, 2006, pp. 160–4. Further insight into fifteenth-century music printing is provided by M. K. Duggan, *Italian Music Incunabula: Printers and Type*, Berkeley, 1992.

[5] J. L. Smith, *Thomas East and Music Publishing in Renaissance England*, Oxford, 2003, p. 21.

[6] Blayney, *The Stationers' Company* (n. 2 above), pp. 264–5. It was not until 1528 that single-impression music printing became widespread, with its adoption by the Parisian printer Pierre Attaingnant; on this topic, see D. Heartz, *Pierre Attaingnant, Royal Printer of Music: A Historical Study and Bibliographical Catalogue*, Berkeley, 1969.

by Rastell, another imperfect song sheet printed by his son William c. 1533, and Miles Coverdale's *Goostly psalmes and spirituall songes* (c. 1536, USTC 502754).[7] Rastell's only contemporary rival in the field of music printing was the unidentified printer who produced *Twenty Songs* (USTC 502221), a set of quarto partbooks dated 10 October 1530.[8] Following *Twenty Songs*, no further volumes of polyphonic music appeared on the market until Tye's *Actes*, making the *Actes* only the second known edition of polyphony printed in England.

Christopher Tye was already well known as a musician by the end of Henry VIII's reign in 1547. Although his name does not appear in extant lists of Chapel Royal staff from 1545–1560, it is probable that he served there at some point during the 1550s, as he participated in Mary Tudor's coronation in 1553.[9] He thus had some connection to court, possibly even spending several years there, while also serving as *Magister choristarum* of Ely Cathedral. Shortly after the accession of Elizabeth I, Tye took religious orders, becoming an ordained priest in November of 1560.[10] When combined with his decision to issue a printed volume of reformist music in 1553, his ordination suggests that he held reasonably strong Protestant convictions by the end of Edward VI's reign.

Tye's *Actes* has suffered considerably from scholarly neglect, despite its significant place in the history of English music printing as the earliest collection of a single composer's works as well as the first publication of entirely sacred polyphony produced in the country. In his formative study of music and the English Reformation, for example, Peter le Huray dismisses Tye's *Actes* as 'of no great distinction. The word accentuation is stiff and the imitative points are rather mechanically contrived'.[11] What scholarship exists on the *Actes*, moreover, often rests on incomplete knowledge of extant copies of the work, leading to incorrect assertions about the volume's function, Tye's contributions, and the book's potential audiences. Beth Quitslund, for example, concludes that Tye 'composed only three tunes for the fourteen verses of text',[12] a statement that not only obscures the musical qualities of Tye's settings — to characterise them as 'tunes' ignores their polyphonic nature — but is also incorrect. Quitslund clearly only examined the copy of the *Actes* that is incomplete. Robert Weidner's 1972 article on the print, meanwhile, focuses only on the two copies now found in the British Library, whose contents are virtually identical.[13]

---

[7] Blayney, *The Stationers' Company* (n. 2 above), pp. 268, 456–8. Blayney gives a date of late 1536 or 1537 for Coverdale's *Goostly psalmes*. Robin Leaver, in his study of the volume, posits 1535 or 1536 as the book's print date; see R. Leaver, *'Goostly Psalmes and Spirituall Songes': English and Dutch Metrical Psalms from Coverdale to Utenhove, 1535–1566*, Oxford, 1991, p. 66.

[8] Blayney, *The Stationers' Company* (n. 2 above), p. 268. For an overview of this volume see J. Milsom, 'Songs and Society in Early Tudor London', *Early Music History*, 16, 1997, pp. 235–93.

[9] P. Doe and D. Mateer, 'Tye, Christopher', *Grove Music Online*, https://doi-org.proxy.lib.umich.edu/10.1093/gmo/9781561592630.article.28665, accessed 17 April 2018. Not only does Tye identify himself as 'one of the Gentylmen of hys grace's most honourable chappell' on the title-page of the *Actes*, but a mandate for his livery allowance for Mary's coronation likewise describes him as one of the 'gentylmen of our Chapell'.

[10] Doe and Mateer, 'Tye, Christopher' (n. 9 above).

[11] P. le Huray, *Music and the Reformation in England, 1549–1660*, Cambridge, 1978, p. 384.

[12] Quitslund, *The Reformation in Rhyme* (n. 1 above), p. 107.

[13] R. W. Weidner, 'Tye's *Actes of the Apostles*: A Reassessment', *The Musical Quarterly*, 58/2, 1972, pp. 242–58.

388 PRINTING AND MISPRINTING

Table 19.1 Known copies of Tye's Actes.

Cambridge University Library, Syn.8.55.85 (I ed.)

British Library, G.12146. (II ed.)

British Library, K.4.c.4. (II ed.)

Boston Public Library, M.Cab.2.52 (II ed.)

Lambeth Palace Library, MS. 1160 (II ed.)

New York Public Library, *KC 1553 Tye (II ed.)

There are six known copies of Tye's *Actes*, as outlined in Table 19.1.[14] Except for the copy in Cambridge, all contain only minor variants, suggesting they were part of the same print run.[15] The publisher of Tye's *Actes* was William Seres, a newcomer to the trade. Like Tye, Seres was a reformer with connections to the English court: from at least 1548 he was a valued servant of William Cecil, who himself served as private secretary to the Duke of Somerset, Lord Protector of England. Although Seres is often referred to as a printer in colophons for his publications, Blayney notes he was not himself a printer.[16] Instead, Tye's *Actes* was printed on Seres's behalf by Nicholas Hill, who is credited in four of the Tye colophons and who also probably printed Francis Segar's *Certayne Psalmes* for Seres in the same year.[17]

Except for the Cambridge copy, Tye's *Actes* contains metrical translations of the first fourteen chapters of the Book of Acts, each of which is set to its own music, for a total of fourteen distinct musical compositions. Although partbooks were the preferred format for printed polyphony on the continent, Tye's *Actes* is laid out in choirbook format (Fig. 19.1): each opening contains all four parts, so that — at least in theory — a group of four singers might need only one copy to perform the pieces.[18] Although its contents were produced by an eminent composer whose ties to the court are highlighted in its preface, the book's small size (approximately three and a half by five inches, or roughly 9×13 cm) and choirbook layout, combined with its general lack of ornamentation and single-colour printing, indicate that it was made with affordability in mind, intended for a wide audience. Despite its musical notation, it resembles no other print of the period so much as Sternhold and Hopkins's

---

[14] My thanks to Samantha Arten for tracking down and confirming the presence of the copy in the New York Public Library, and to the library's staff for allowing her to sharing her research photographs with me.

[15] One of the British Library copies (K.4.c.4.) has its own record in USTC (504886), though as far as I have been able to determine the only difference between it and the other complete copies (USTC 504928) is a slight variation in the colophon. The Cambridge copy is correctly catalogued as a separate edition: USTC 504933. Such an arrangement derives from ESTC: see record nos S91049, S115612, S124640.

[16] Blayney, *The Stationers' Company* (n. 2 above), pp. 664–5.

[17] Hill appears to have been the only printer during the Edwardine period in possession of musical type. Although attributed to John Kingston in the USTC, Hill also printed Richard Beard's *A Godly Psalme of Marye Queene* for William Griffith in 1553 (USTC 504825). See Blayney, *The Stationers' Company* (n. 2 above), p. 751.

[18] In practice, the volume seems a bit small for this purpose, and I would suggest that two singers per book would have been a more comfortable arrangement. It was also common for informal performances of polyphony such as Tye's *Actes* to omit one of the vocal lines if only three singers were available.

19: MARKETING A MISPRINT   389

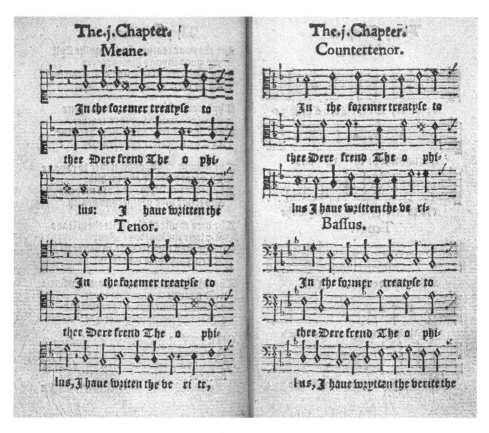

FIG. 19.1. Beginning of the musical setting for Chapter 1 in the second edition of Christopher Tye, *The Actes of the Apostles, translated into Englyshe Metre*, London, William Seres, 1553, 8° (USTC 504928 and 504886). London, British Library, K.4.c.4.

Al suche psalmes (1549): each chapter is prefaced first with a four-line introductory verse in Roman type, and Tye uses common meter, also known as Sternhold's meter, throughout.

TYE'S *ACTES*: THE FIRST EDITION

The Cambridge copy of Tye's *Actes* is unique, and unlike the remaining copies, it is undated. Despite its lack of even an imprint year, I argue that it was printed earlier than the remaining five copies. Whereas each of the variant copies of the *Actes* contains a different printed musical setting for each chapter, the Cambridge copy includes settings only for the first two chapters, with a truncated opening (featuring only the first lines of the mean and the countertenor) for the third chapter. There are no indications that the two complete settings ought to be used to sing the remaining texts. A close examination of the printed music shows a substantial error in the first two settings that must have been noticed only after the first two gatherings (A and B) had been printed, and which accounts for this striking disparity.

In the Cambridge *Actes*, Hill's alignment of the *text* of each system of music with its counterparts in all voices, rather than aligning the *music* in all parts, posed significant problems for performers. For four singers to share a single book in performance, each singer's part would need to contain the same number of beats on each opening — that is, the same duration of music. In sixteenth-century polyphony, it was common for the same text to be set to a different number of beats in each part. Hill's alignment of the text rather than the music in these settings thus resulted in unequal lines of music, as each respective section of text often contained a number of beats unequal to the same section of text in another voice part. The problem is compounded, moreover, by each piece's presentation over three openings. In the first setting, for example, neither page turn works for all singers: in the first opening, the tenor contains only twenty-seven minims (the fundamental note value in the piece), while the remaining parts have twenty-nine, so that by the end of the second opening none of the parts lines up correctly over the page turn. In other words, while performing this first setting, the tenor would have tried to turn the first page before the remaining singers were ready; by the *next* page turn, *each* singer would have needed to turn the page at a different time. The second setting, 'When that the fyfte daye was cume', suffers from a similar layout problem; if anything, the issue is worse: since Tye's setting of the text 'They came together', occurring over the page turn, features imitative entries, where each singer's entrance follows the previous voice at a delay (rather than all voices beginning at the same time), by the end of the first opening all four singers would need to turn the page at different moments (Fig. 19.2). The four singers, then, would have been unable to sing from a single copy of the *Actes* in this format without considerable practice.

Hill's error here is identical to one he made in a similar publication, Francis Segar's *Certayne Psalmes select out of the Psalter of Dauid* (USTC 504860), also printed in 1553 for William Seres. Hill's name does not appear in the colophon of Segar's *Certayne Psalmes*. However, a close comparison of this volume with copies of the *Actes* indicates that both use the same musical font, and Hill is listed as its printer in USTC. Segar's psalm collection includes two four-part musical settings, one for the first twelve and a second for the last seven psalms. The first setting suffers from the same problems as the Cambridge copy of Tye's *Actes*: in its first opening the treble and tenor have thirty-five minims, the mean has thirty-four, and the bassus has thirty-seven, making the use of a single copy difficult. In each subsequent psalm that uses this music, moreover, this problem persists; the music and text are presented in the same manner as they are for Segar's first psalm.

Although the aforementioned errors might not have been enough to prevent these two books from being used, they do suggest a lack of musical literacy — or at least inexperience with music — on behalf of the publisher, William Seres, and his printer Nicholas Hill.[19] Such problems with the music likely would have necessitated singers purchasing multiple

---

[19] Setting music in choirbook format such that each singer needed to turn the page at a different time is akin to providing a facing, direct translation of a text where the original text and its translation are misaligned; no literate musician would make such an error. Manuscript sources of music in choirbook format, moreover, show the lengths to which copyists often went to avoid this particular blunder: those transcribing music into a choirbook regularly left staves devoid of notation, squished extra notes messily onto a staff, and even extended an existing staff into the margins to ensure the music would align correctly, rather than continue with music misaligned on the following opening. No musicologist I have consulted over the course of my research, moreover, could think of a single example of the same error existing in a music manuscript.

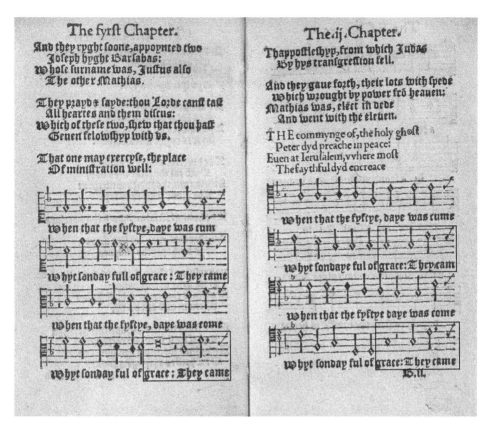

FIG. 19.2. Beginning of the musical setting for Chapter 2 in the first edition of Christopher Tye, *The Actes of the Apostles, translated into Englyshe Metre*, London, William Seres, 1553, 8° (USTC 504933). Cambridge, Cambridge University Library, Syn.8.55.85.

copies of the books in question, making these prints more expensive to use than their publisher had planned.[20] If Seres had wanted singers to need multiple books to sing the *Actes*, for example, he could have produced the collection in partbook format, which had long since become the standard for polyphonic music on the Continent. That partbooks were not used strongly indicates Seres and Tye planned for users to need only one copy. These errors also suggest a possible reason so much of the English-texted biblical metrical song of this period was printed without musical notation: not only did the lack of tunes make the publications more flexible (in that each text might be sung to a number of different

---

[20] It is impossible to pinpoint an exact price for Tye's *Actes*. F. R. Johnson, 'Notes on English Retail Book-Prices, 1550–1640', *The Library*, 5th ser., 5/2, 1950, pp. 83–112, has estimated that in the early 1550s, the normal price for new books was approximately one-third of a penny per sheet. As Tye's *Actes* used four and a half sheets (thirteen gatherings (A-M) plus four leaves of gathering N), using Johnson's figures we might approximate a cost of five pence for an unbound copy of Tye's *Actes*. Since Hill was the only printer in possession of a musical font in London, however, he may have been be able to charge a premium for his services, making the expense of printing the *Actes* higher than for a 'standard' volume. Regardless of its absolute price, a need for multiple copies would double, triple, or even quadruple the cost of Tye's *Actes* for the consumer.

melodies), but if the only publisher and printer available in London for issuing notated editions had difficulty reproducing music properly, many of those capable of writing polyphonic music might have decided that the risk was not worth the potential reward. It was better, in other words, to publish a book without notation than to risk that the music might be set incorrectly, rendering it difficult to use.

Whereas in Segar's *Certayne Psalmes* these music-typesetting errors appear to have gone unnoticed, such was not the case in Tye's *Actes*. The first two settings in the Cambridge *Actes* are printed on gatherings A and B of the volume, with the truncated opening of setting three beginning on the verso of the last leaf. At the beginning of gathering C, however, rather than a continuation of printed music, Hill instead begins with the text of Chapter 3 (Fig. 19.3). It is clear that at this point in the printing process, someone — possibly even Tye himself — noticed that the edition, though technically useable, was likely to require singers to purchase multiple copies, thus limiting its affordability (and marketability) to a broader audience. This abrupt break in the Cambridge copy, I posit, indicates that this volume predates the remaining extant variants. It is highly unlikely that Hill would have made such typesetting errors *after* printing at least one run of the *Actes* correctly.

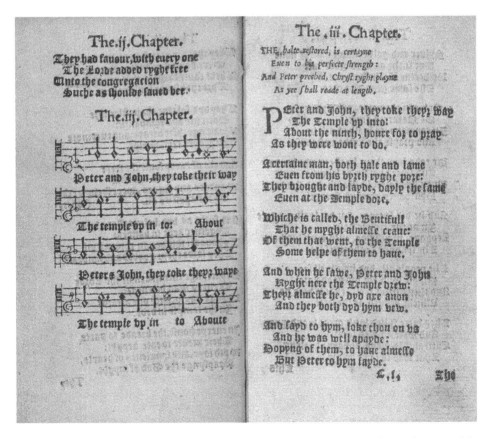

FIG. 19.3. Beginning of the musical setting for Chapter 3 in the first edition of Tye, *The Actes of the Apostles* (see Fig. 19.2). Cambridge, Cambridge University Library, Syn.8.55.85.

Evidence from the Second Edition

Differences between the music of the settings for Chapter 1 and Chapter 2 in the Cambridge *Actes* and that found in the remaining copies, moreover, offer additional corroboration that the Cambridge *Actes* is the earliest extant copy of Tye's print. Furthermore, these musical changes strongly suggest Tye himself remained directly involved throughout the printing process.[21] The overwhelming majority of the musical differences between the two versions

EXAMPLES 1. a–b. 'In which the Sprite up him did feach' (mm. 13–14) from the musical setting for Chapter 1. a: first edition (Cambridge copy); b: second edition (remaining copies as listed in Table 19.1).

---

[21] Since the proportion of unauthorised to authorised editions was approximately ninety to one throughout the sixteenth century, Tye's direct involvement in this process is atypical. See A. Johns, *The Nature of the Book: Print and Knowledge in the Making*, Chicago, 1998, p. 31.

EXAMPLES 2. a–b. 'To dwell aboue for aye' (mm. 16–17) from the musical setting for Chapter 1. a: first edition (Cambridge copy); b: second edition (remaining copies as listed in Table 19.1).]

of the *Actes* are found in the setting for Chapter 1, and some are minor, such as an E-natural on two words in the countertenor which are changed to E-flats in the later copies. In a similar manner, the tenor B-flat and A-natural on 'did feach', both minims, are replaced in the other copies with a sequence of B-flat (semi-minim), A-natural (semi-minim), and G-natural (minim), altering the sonority in the third beat of that bar from a first-inversion A minor to a root position C minor chord, so to speak (cf. Examples 1.a–b). These changes do not correct errors; that is, there is nothing wrong with the voice-leading or the sonorities in the Cambridge copy in these instances. Instead, these alterations must have been made for one of two reasons: either they were mistakes made in translating the manuscript source into print which were caught and subsequently corrected, or they were compositional second thoughts; the latter implies that Tye himself decided to make musical alterations to the score, having been presented with the opportunity.

One change more significant than those described above further verifies the possibility that Tye himself was involved in the publication process: before the next edition of the *Actes* went to press, he apparently rewrote the last phrase of the setting for Chapter 1, such that only the bass line remains the same on the phrase 'To dwell aboue for aye'. As shown in Example 2.a–b, the ornamentation of the Cambridge copy has been stripped away in favour of a strictly homophonic setting. The style in the Cambridge copy, of course, is typical of English anthems of this period, with efficient text underlay, chordal texture, and a carefully controlled use of dissonances. A rare exception in the Cambridge copy are the passing notes E-flat and C against D in the bass on the second syllable of 'above', which create harsh dissonances leading into the final cadence. Not only that, these dissonances do not resolve down by step as they should, and the E-flat in the countertenor leads to a seventh (C against D). In order to detect such contrapuntal subtleties, however, an individual would have had to possess more than basic musical literacy. The most expedient solution to fixing this impropriety would have been simply to rewrite the single problematic beat. This is, in fact, the only alteration made to the harmonic structure. The simplification of the upper three voices that occurs in conjunction with this change, however, suggests that Tye decided to rewrite the entire phrase, perhaps determining the leap in the mean to be more difficult than necessary; the resulting music is cleaner, albeit less rhythmically interesting.

Rather than consigning the faulty pages of the Cambridge copy to binding material — a typical answer to such a problem — Seres (and perhaps Tye) chose instead to rescue Hill's first two gatherings by incorporating them into a text-only edition of the *Actes*, which allows us to draw three important conclusions regarding this volume and its history. First, it stands to reason that Hill had to have already printed a full complement of gathering A, and most likely gathering B as well, by the time his errors came to light; otherwise, the existing gatherings presumably would have been discarded. Second, the choice to go ahead with a text-only edition indicates that Seres had enough confidence in the market for biblical metrical song to risk the cost of printing the rest of the volume without music, assuming that it would in fact be purchased by willing consumers. Finally, and perhaps most importantly for modern scholars of sixteenth-century books, this copy's existence suggests that what we might see as irredeemable faults according to present-day standards were less concerning to sixteenth-century publishers, printers, and even consumers. Notably, however, such errors were evidently unacceptable to composers. Given the general irregularity of the printing process in this period, it is possible that these individuals might not even have acknowledged such problems as errors in the same way a modern audience might; they are furthermore of a magnitude and type not found in music manuscripts from the same period. Thus, while the musical errors in the Cambridge copy were clearly of enough concern that Seres halted the printing process and corrected them in a subsequent edition, he nevertheless did not see these problems as completely insurmountable. Rather, they might be overcome by directing the finished product to a slightly different audience.

Although the issue of musical layout in the Cambridge copy is corrected in the subsequent second edition of Tye's *Actes*, these volumes contain a new error that would likewise have necessitated singers purchasing multiple copies of the book. In gatherings C and D, which contain most of the setting for Chapter 3, as well as those for Chapters 4 and 5, the voice parts are printed consecutively, rather than in the choirbook format found throughout the remaining settings. As a result, just one individual might be able to sing from a single volume at a time; note in Fig. 19.4 that the parts begin in choirbook format on the last leaf of gathering B, but sig. C1r contains only the treble for Chapter 3. This change in format cannot have been intentional, as in Chapter 6 (gathering E) the layout reverts to the choirbook format of Chapters 1 and 2 and remains consistent throughout the rest of the book. Why Seres and Hill decided to proceed with the remainder of this edition but did *not* print corrected versions of gatherings C and D is impossible to know; perhaps Seres simply could not afford the cost of reprinting two gatherings in their entirety for a second time. Robert Weidner's hypothesis that Seres was under pressure to finish the printing

FIG. 19.4. Beginning of the musical setting for Chapter 3 in Tye, *The Actes of the Apostles*, second edition (see Fig. 19.1). London, British Library, G.12146.

quickly is likely: as the year is printed on the title-page rather than in the colophon and the volume is dedicated to Edward VI, this edition of Tye's *Actes* was probably produced between 25 March (the beginning of 1553) and late May, when Edward VI's declining health was widely known. Seres would have been pressed for time to produce a finished product if he (and Tye) hoped to have the book on the market once news of the king's illness had begun to spread.[22] Further supporting Weidner's suggestion is the presence of a small number of more minor errors in the music in the remaining copies.[23] Although the accidental omission of two or three notes in a single line or the printing of an incorrect pitch here or

---

[22] Weidner, 'Tye's *Actes*' (n. 13 above), pp. 256–7.
[23] In the setting of Chapter 1, for example, at the beginning of the third opening (sig. A7), four notes and their text ('daye In whych the') were omitted from the bassus part in the second edition (USTC 504928 and 504886). British Library G.12146. and the copy at Lambeth Palace both contain later, hand-written corrections, suggesting that copies of the first edition must have been available to those noting this error in later centuries. In other instances, accidentals have been written into the extant copies of the second edition; the inconsistency with which they are applied across editions, the flexibility of the rules governing the use of *musica ficta* (altered notes) in the sixteenth century, and the lack of an original manuscript source for the *Actes*, make it difficult to tell which of these are true errors and which were 'corrected' due to matters of taste.

there is common in printed music of this period, the fact that these problems were not corrected lends credence to Weidner's conclusion that Seres and Hill were in a hurry to finish production.

Conclusion

By including new musical settings for use alongside metrical translations of the first fourteen chapters of the book of Acts, Christopher Tye created a unique publication, though it shared much in common with other contemporary biblical metrical song. The extant copies of this publication demonstrate that difficulties with the music printing process may, at least in part, account for the general lack of similar volumes being produced in England at this time: not only was Hill the only Edwardine printer who owned musical type, but his shop made substantial errors in setting music delivered to him in manuscript. Thus, we should not be surprised that most biblical metrical song of the period was published in text-only editions. These copies of Tye's *Actes* also shed light on the creative ways publishers and printers sought to recoup their losses when musical typesetting mistakes had been made. Indeed, both the decision to finish the first edition of the *Actes* as a text-only volume and Seres's choice to use the imperfect C and D gatherings in the subsequent edition suggest that mid-sixteenth-century English amateur musicians were willing to overlook problems that later consumers — and their professional contemporaries — would have found insurmountable. Unfortunately, the death of Edward VI on 6 July 1553, and his half-sister Mary's official reintroduction of Catholicism only a few months later, also cut the life of Tye's publication abruptly short, and even its second, more complete edition most likely never saw widespread use. Nevertheless, the extant copies highlight the challenges composers faced in England's nascent music printing industry. And despite the publication's relative obscurity, the top melody for Chapter 8, known as Winchester Old, still survives in the current English hymnal, demonstrating that Tye's music had a lasting impact on the musical life of the Church of England.[24]

[24] Winchester Old is used for hymn #42, 'While Shepherds Watched Their Flocks by Night', in G. Timms (ed.), *The New English Hymnal, Second Edition*, Norwich, 1994. The melody of Tye's Chapter 3 (known as Windsor) remained in the English hymnal until its most recent edition (first published in 1986).

BIBLIOGRAPHY

PRIMARY SOURCES

Beard, Richard, *A Godly Psalme, of Marye Queene, which brought vs comfort al, Through God, whom we of dewtye prayse, that giues her foes a fal*, London, William Griffith, 1553, 4° (USTC 504825).

Coverdale, Miles, *Goostly psalmes and spirituall songes drawen out of the holy Scripture, for the comforte and consolacyon of soch as loue to reioyse in God and his worde*, London, John Gough, c. 1535–1536, 4° (USTC 502754).

Harmonice musices odhecaton, Venice, Ottaviano Petrucci, 1501, 4° (USTC 801634).

Rastell, John, *A new iuterlude and a mery of the nature of the .iiii. element declarynge many proper poynt of phylosophy naturall*, London, John Rastell, 1520, 8° (USTC 501608).

Seager (Segar), Francis, *Certayne Psalmes select out of the Psalter of Dauid, and drawen into Englyshe Metre, with Notes to euery Psalme in iiij. partes to Synge, by F. S*, London, William Seres, 1553, 8° (USTC 504860).

Tye, Christopher, *The Actes of the Apostles, translated into Englyshe Metre*, London, William Seres, 1553, 8° (USTC 504933).

Tye, Christopher, *The Actes of the Apostles, translated into Englyshe Metre*, London, William Seres, 1553, 8° (USTC 504928 and 504886).

XX songes.ix.of.iiii.ptes, and xi.of thre ptes, London, 1530, 4° oblong (USTC 502221).

SECONDARY LITERATURE

Blayney, P. W. M, *The Stationers' Company and the Printers of London, 1501–1557*, Cambridge, 2013.

Boorman, S., *Ottaviano Petrucci: Catalogue Raisonné*, New York, 2006.

Doe, P., and Mateer, D., 'Tye, Christopher', in *Grove Music Online: Oxford Music Online*, at https://doi-org.proxy.lib.umich.edu/10.1093/gmo/9781561592630.article.28665.

Duggan, M. K., *Italian Music Incunabula: Printers and Type*, Berkeley, 1992.

Fenlon, I., 'Music, Print and Society in Sixteenth-Century Europe', in J. Haar (ed.), *European Music, 1520–1640*, Woodbridge, 2006, pp. 280–303.

Heartz, D., *Pierre Attaingnant, Royal Printer of Music: A Historical Study and Bibliographical Catalogue*, Berkeley, 1969.

le Huray, P. *Music and the Reformation in England, 1549–1660*, Cambridge, 1978.

Johns, A., *The Nature of the Book: Print and Knowledge in the Making*, Chicago, 1998.

Johnson, F. R., 'Notes on English Retail Book-Prices, 1550–1640'. *The Library*, 5th ser., 5/2, 1950, pp. 83–112.

Leaver, R. A., '*Goostly Psalmes and Spirituall Songes*': *English and Dutch Metrical Psalms from Coverdale to Utenhove, 1535–1566*, Oxford, 1991.

Milsom, J., 'Songs and Society in Early Tudor London', *Early Music History*, 17, 1997, pp. 235–93.

Quitslund, B., *The Reformation in Rhyme: Sternhold, Hopkins and the English Metrical Psalter, 1547–1603*, Burlington (VT), 2008.

Smith, J. L., *Thomas East and Music Publishing in Renaissance England*, Oxford, 2003.

Timms, G. (ed.), *The New English Hymnal, Second Edition*, Norwich, 1994.

Weidner, R. W., '*Tye's Actes of the Apostles*: A Reassessment', *The Musical Quarterly*, 58/2, 1972, pp. 242–58.

CHAPTER 20

MISPRINTING AND MISREADING IN *THE COMEDY OF ERRORS*

ALICE LEONARD

INTRODUCTION

IN *The schollers purgatory* (1624), George Wither laments that in printing, the printer 'cares not how vnworkmanlike it be parformed; nor how many faults he lett goe to the Authors discredit, & the readers trouble'.[1] Wither joins a long line of Renaissance authors who complained about the errors or inaccuracies the mechanics of the press made with their work, much to the 'Authors discredit'.[2] Yet the 'readers trouble' over these misprints, as Wither terms it, was not as frequently worried over. The reader's difficulty and their consequent misdirection does not feature loudly in the history of reading. This chapter argues that misunderstanding is a common state of literary encounter and deserves much fuller examination. It examines a set of small printing errors in Shakespeare's *The Comedy of Errors* from its first appearance in print, in the First Folio (1623, henceforth F1), which repeatedly confused early readers.

The Comedy of Errors is itself about error: the plot centres on the unstoppable mistaken identity of two sets of homonymous twins. F1 only adds to this, as the most notable print errors mix up the twins. While the play is wickedly bent on dramatising the complete

---

[1] George Wither, *The schollers purgatory discouered in the Stationers common-wealth*, London, [G. Wood for] the Stationers' Company, [1624], 8° (USTC 3011498), pp. 120–1. On the various struggles between George Wither and the Stationers Company, see W. W. Greg, *Some Aspects and Problems of London Publishing between 1550 and 1650*, Oxford, 1956, and J. Doelman, 'George Wither, the Stationers Company and the English Psalter', *Studies in Philology*, 90/1, 1993, pp. 74–82. My thanks go to Ben Higgins for his insightful comments.

[2] For example, Erasmus famously complained of the poor education and sloppiness of those at work in printer's shops. He claimed that books are 'published to the world by men so ill-educated that they cannot so much as read, so idle that they are not prepared to read over what they print'. D. Erasmus, *The Adages of Erasmus,* transl. W. Barker, Toronto, 2001, p. 144. For more on disputes between printers and authors over error in early modern England, see Matthew Day's contribution in this Companion.

Alice Leonard, *Misprinting and Misreading in The Comedy of Errors.* In: *Printing and Misprinting.* Edited by Geri Della Rocca de Candal, Anthony Grafton, and Paolo Sachet, Oxford University Press. © Alice Leonard (2023). DOI: 10.1093/oso/9780198863045.003.0021 confusion of all characters, the earliest printed text inadvertently replicates this for the reader by inserting errors in the twins' speech prefixes and stage directions. The annotations left by seventeenth- and early eighteenth-century readers demonstrate that they fell into a state of error, sometimes significantly, in simply attempting to follow the play. The censorious eighteenth-century editorial tradition initiated with Nicholas Rowe (1709) developed the instinct to correct, and initiated the process that produced the clean, well-ordered *Errors* we read today. Yet there exists a neglected history of reading as it responds to an earlier, erroneous text that is almost entirely absent in our present-day editions. It is largely assumed today that the audience's experience of watching the play is that of knowledgeable superiority, that part of our pleasure is watching the chaotic mistakes unfold in front of us while we remain in control of which twin is which. For some early readers, however, this was not the case, as they struggled and often failed to manage the mistaken identity exacerbated by the unclear and misleading F1 and the following seventeenth-century editions. This chapter, then, argues that in *Errors*, misprints are consequential for the reception of early Shakespeare in a way that extends beyond their 'accidental' status and silent correction.

THE TEXTUAL MISPRINTS

At the beginning of *The Comedy of Errors*, a shipwreck breaks up a family and separates two pairs of homonymous twins who are on board. These are the Antipholuses and the Dromios. One master Antipholus is paired off with one servant Dromio and are distinguished exclusively by their supposed hometown, Syracuse and Ephesus. In the city of Ephesus, where the play is set, the two sets of twins are brought back together, unknown to everyone else. The play is set around the continual mistaken identity that follows. Dromio of Ephesus is viciously beaten for stealing his master's money, which he was never given (1.2), and Antipholus of Syracuse is greatly surprised when he is suddenly presented with a gold chain, which in fact his brother ordered (3.2). The same Antipholus wonders, '[W]as I married to her in my dream?' when Adriana unwittingly addresses him as 'my husband', because she is married to his brother (2.2.183).[3] Every character senses some deep problem in the reality around them and the reliability of their senses to discern it; as Antipholus of Syracuse asks, 'What error drives our eyes and ears amiss?' (2.2.185).

The twins' physical similarity is such that they are indistinguishable. The main job of the audience is to keep up with the complex plot twists and maintain the twins as distinct, correcting their own inevitable slips. Egeon describes his sons as 'the one so like the other | As could not be distinguish'd but by names' (1.1.51–2). Names are, in fact, the only tool to

---

[3] For the ease of the reader, the standard edition used throughout the chapter is W. Shakespeare, *The Norton Shakespeare*, ed. S. Greenblatt, London, 2016, 3rd edn. When the earliest texts are discussed, the edition is: William Shakespeare, *Mr. William Shakespeares comedies, histories, & tragedies. Published according to the true originall*, London, Isaac Jaggard and Edward Blount at the expenses of William Jaggard, Edward Blount, John Smethwicke and William Aspley, 1623, f° (USTC 301070). This according to Charlton Hinman's Through Line Numbering (henceforth TLN) in the *Internet Shakespeare Editions* (*ISE*), ed. Matthew Steggle, http://internetshakespeare.uvic.ca/, accessed 8 May 2020.

20: MISPRINTING AND MISREADING IN *THE COMEDY OF ERRORS*   401

distinguish between them.[4] Yet Egeon's faith in the naming function is misplaced in the world of the early modern print shop, aptly described as a 'house of error' by David McKitterick.[5] F1 refers to the character we know as Antipholus of Syracuse as 'Antipholis Erotes' or 'Antipholis Errotis'.[6] This variant naming continues until the third act. The alternative name emphasises Antipholus's status as a wanderer, from the etymology of *errare*, as he travels far to find his lost family. 'Erotes' is, however, an error for 'Erraticus' or 'Errans'. In his speech prefix, F1 then abbreviates his name to 'E. Ant.' — a straightforward shorthand. Yet this is in confusion with Antipholus of Ephesus who is also abbreviated as 'E. Anti' in 3.1, and introduces a distinct possibility that the reader will take one twin for another.[7] The only distinguishing feature between the twins vanishes and they both become 'E. Anti'. These coincidental misprints, however, have been overlooked by editors.[8]

Just as Antipholus of Syracuse becomes 'E. Anti', so Antipholus of Ephesus is given as 'Antipholis Sereptus' (2.1).[9] 'Sereptus' is a misprint for 'Surreptus', meaning 'stolen', as he was taken from his father in the shipwreck. The variant name emphasises an aspect of character, yet at first glance, 'Sereptus' could easily be read as 'Syracuse': the wrong twin. Both Antipholuses are referred to only as some abbreviation of 'Antipholus', leaving the reader to decide who is who. When they are distinguished beyond 'Ant.' or 'Antipholus', it is unhelpfully sometimes under multiple names. The early printed texts of *Errors* consistently fail to differentiate the twins in speech prefixes and stage directions, and sometimes even confuse them, risking an even greater loss of identity of the twins than the play intends.[10] While the temporary, comic uncertainties stemming from the plot are always pleasurably corrected, the misprints in the early texts multiply this, plunging the reader into genuine, sustained confusion.[11]

The second pair of twins, the Dromio brothers, are also mostly undistinguished by F1. When Dromio of Syracuse first enters, he is only referred to as: 'Enter Antipholis Erotes, a Marchant, and Dromio' (TLN 162). So too in the speech prefixes, which are also fairly often

---

[4] On a specific case of misprint and misinterpretation of (animal) names, see Grigory Vorobyev's contribution in this Companion.

[5] D. McKitterick, *Print, Manuscript and the Search for Order, 1450–1830*, Cambridge, 2003, pp. 97–138.

[6] TLN 163 and 394. P. Werstine discusses these errors in "'Foul Papers' and 'Prompt-Books': Printer's Copy for Shakespeare's 'Comedy of Errors'", *Studies in Bibliography*, 41, 1988, pp. 232–46.

[7] TLN 409 (p. 88) and TLN 619 (p. 90). On the impact of typography on our understanding of early modern drama, see C. M. L. Bourne, *Typographies of Performance in Early Modern England*, Oxford, 2020.

[8] R. A. Foakes sees this as no more than a 'nice confusion' in his, 'Introduction', in William Shakespeare, *The Comedy of Errors*, ed. R. A. Foakes, London, 1991, p. xii.

[9] TLN 273, 617, and onwards.

[10] On editing Shakespeare's speech prefixes, see R. B. McKerrow, 'A Suggestion Regarding Shakespeare's Manuscripts', *The Review of English Studies*, 11/44, 1935, pp. 459–65; P. Werstine, 'McKerrow's "Suggestion" and W. W. Greg', in G. W. Williams (ed.), *Shakespeare's Speech-Headings: Speaking the Speech in Shakespeare's Plays*, Newark (DE), 1997, pp. 11–16; A. Murphy, '"Tish ill done": Henry the Fifth and the Politics of Editing', in M. T. Burnett and R. Wray (eds), *Shakespeare and Ireland: History, Politics, Culture*, London, 1997, pp. 217–34; L. P. Wilder, 'Changeling Bottom: Speech Prefixes, Acting, and Character in A Midsummer Night's Dream"', *Shakespeare*, 4/1, 2008, pp. 41–58; and L. Marcus, *How Shakespeare Became Colonial: Editorial Tradition and the British Empire*, Abingdon, 2017, pp. 121–30.

[11] On error in early modern print see A. Smyth, *Material Texts in Early Modern England*, Cambridge, 2018, pp. 75–136, and A. Smyth, 'Errata Lists', in D. Duncan and A. Smyth (eds), *Book Parts*, Oxford, 2019, pp. 251–63, as well as the present Companion.

left as 'Dromio'. 64% of the twins' speech prefixes hang unspecified, either as 'Dro.' or 'Ant.', or some similar form.[12] While critical editions today *always* standardise and distinguish the twins, F1's system of signification is more complex. It demands that the reader refer back to the character's entrance or previous scene to ascertain the identity of the twin. This builds uncertainty into the experience of reading, but also promotes a particular way of reading, one that is attentive to context and other dramaturgical cues to help us keep hold of the coherency of the play.

Dromio of Ephesus is joined in origin and bondage with Antipholus of Ephesus, but F1 also disrupts and confuses this pairing of the twins. In 2.2, rather than Dromio being identified alongside his master, Antipholus 'Errotis', he is described as 'Siracufia', breaking his association with Antipholus and emphasising his existence not as a wanderer but instead as a foreigner (TLN 401). While the master and servant are united in their shared experience, their names divide them, with one being 'E. Anti' and the other 'S. Dro'. Their shared origin is a tool of distinction for the audience to help control misreading, but F1 makes this treacherous. At 5.1, the stage direction states: 'Enter Antipholus and Dromio againe', with Antipholus's speech prefixed only by 'Ant.' (TLN 1473). Rather than clarifying identity, 'again' is a confusion generator because it is unclear to which part of the previous act or scene it refers. This 'again' is further destabilised by the whirl of entrances and exits, with characters appearing in the street, at the marketplace, before the house of Antipholus of Ephesus, the house of the Courtesan, and the priory.

Textual criticism has interpreted the sometimes violently shifting naming conventions in F1 as nevertheless linked to the unfolding narrative. R. B. McKerrow argues that the 'names by which the characters are indicated, instead of being the same throughout, frequently depend, much as they do in a novel, on the progress of the story'.[13] McKerrow claims that as Egeon's status as father to the missing twins is revealed, his prefixes change from 'Merchant' to 'Father'. The print variants and potential confusions are made to fit the story. Yet the seemingly arbitrary naming system of the twins is unattached to their journey through Ephesus and the frights and shocks they experience. Rather than developing a broader understanding of character, as McKerrow argues, the print variants of the twins only add to the 'readers trouble'.[14] These misprints first appeared in F1, but as each subsequent edition was based on the last, these same errors were perpetuated in the Second (1632), Third (1663–1664), and Fourth (1685) Folios (henceforth F2, F3 and F4 respectively), before Nicholas Rowe in his *The works of Mr. William Shakespear* (1709) corrected a large amount. Thus, there is a pre-correction period of eighty-six years, where readers would have accessed the play through these faulty editions. A significant number of these early copies carry the marks of confused readers misreading the play. These annotations from seventeenth- and early eighteenth-century readers demonstrate that attempting to understand and even correct error was a crucial mode of interaction with the play.

---

[12] Of the 170 speech prefixes belonging to any of the four Antipholuses or Dromios, sixty-nine specify in some way which twin is referred to.

[13] McKerrow, 'A Suggestion Regarding Shakespeare's Manuscripts' (n. 10 above), p. 460. For more on names in *The Comedy of Errors*, see L. Maguire, *Shakespeare's Names*, Oxford, 2007.

[14] Wither, *The schollers purgatory* (n. 1 above), pp. 120–1.

MISREADING *THE COMEDY OF ERRORS*

The earliest printed copies of *The Comedy of Errors* bear witness to readers through marks or names left behind. From these annotations, it is clear that one of the most common experiences of reading the play was confusion. Copies which carry these marks include the so-called Nursery copy of F1 held in Edinburgh University Library (EUL JY 438); a copy of F1 owned by Lucy Hutchinson, or at least her family (Folger Shakespeare Library, Fo. 1 no. 54);[15] the Douai manuscript, transcribed, possibly from F2, (MS 787 in the Bibliothèque municipale of Douai); a copy of F2 annotated by Lewis Theobald held in the Folger Shakespeare Library (Fo. 2 no. 20);[16] a copy of F2 owned by John Prater and held in the Bodleian Library (Arch G c 9);[17] an F3 copy known as the Smock Alley promptbook held in the Folger Shakespeare Library (PROMPT 3d Folio Com. Err. Smock Alley);[18] and a copy of F4 held in the Bodleian Library (Arch G c 13).[19]

This chapter focuses on two of these, the Nursery copy and the Douai manuscript, because they demonstrate some of the highest levels of confusion of all the annotated copies identified, and their associations with the theatre set up expectations of rectitude and order which they, interestingly, do not support. Were early performances really as chaotic as these texts suggest? It is difficult to know whether these faulty emendations led to incorrect staging. Something that is much more certain is that being in error or at least uncertainty was one of the defining experiences of reading the play.[20] While readerly marks are fleeting and not every moment of the struggle to follow the text is recorded, the interventions follow a pattern with the same problems being addressed.

The first example is the Nursery promptbook.[21] Here, *The Comedy of Errors* was separated from F1 and bound individually, forming a manageable theatrical script. Amongst the extensive annotations are several names that refer to one of the two theatre companies licensed by Charles II on his return to the monarchy.[22] G. Blakemore Evans suggests that the copy was used by a part of the King's Company, the Nursery Company of younger players,

---

[15] The annotator attempted here to clarify the twins' identity. They use 'E' or 'S', for example adding 'E' next to 'Dro.' (p. 93), amongst other interventions.

[16] Theobald made annotations which tried to order the twins throughout his copy of F2, some of which are signed 'L.T.'

[17] This copy contains annotations by two hands, one which adds the label 'of Syracuse' to 'Antipholis Erotes' (p. 88, 2.1, TLN 162).

[18] The 'Smock Alley' promptbook was annotated for performances at Dublin's Smock Alley Theatre in the 1670s and 1680s: it carries the marks of a reader struggling to distinguish the twins.

[19] An eighteenth-century hand has heavily annotated the copy. For example, they clarify the 'Ant.' speech prefixes by adding 'S' seven times over (p. 82).

[20] On the literary and textual status of error, see J. Yates, *Error, Misuse, Failure*, Minneapolis, 2002; S. Lerer, *Error and the Academic Self: The Scholarly Imagination, Medieval to Modern*, New York, 2002; D. Wakelin, *Scribal Correction and Literary Craft: English Manuscripts 1375–1510*, Cambridge, 2014; and A. Williams, *Reading it Wrong*, Princeton, forthcoming.

[21] See G. B. Evans (ed.), *Shakespearean Prompt-Books of the Seventeenth Century*, III, Charlottesville (VA), 1964, http://bsuva.org/bsuva/promptbook/ShaComP.html, accessed 2 May 2020.

[22] These include 'Mr Biggs', 'Mr Disney', and 'Mrs Cooke'. Emma Smith argues that they were all members of Thomas Killigrew's King's Company, who performed at Drury Lane Theatre in London, in the 1660s and 1670s. E. Smith, *Shakespeare's First Folio: Four Centuries of an Iconic Book*, Oxford, 2016, p. 241.

possibly in the 1660s and 1670s.[23] The substantial annotations throughout the play attempt to enforce the distinction between the Antipholus twins that the printed copy only makes clear in the final act. The annotator adds 'S' or 'E' to each speech prefix of the Antipholus brothers to distinguish them. Similarly, in the stage directions, one of the Antipholuses is associated with 'Ephesus', and the other with 'Seracuse', to mark one as different from the other. Yet while we can recognise a sustained desire to order the text, the annotator is in complete confusion about which twin is which.

Beginning with good intentions, the corrector emends one of the most confusing misprints, deleting 'Erotes' and inserting 'Seracuse' above at Act One, Scene Two, and adding 'Se' after 'Dromio' to specify this is Dromio of Syracuse (see Fig. 20.1).[24] The annotator uses geographical origin as an addition to specify the characters clearly, using 'Ephesus' or 'Seracuse', as is standard editorial practice today. In the speech prefixes which follow the opening of the scene, however, this desire to clarify slips into mistake. The same hand adds 'E:' to all the speech prefixes of Antipholus, presumably for 'Erotes' (see also Fig. 20.1). This, in fact, refers to the wrong twin, as it is Antipholus of Syracuse who is speaking. These 'corrections' only re-establish the confusion that has just been clarified. It then seems that the annotator realised that 'E:' was ambiguous as it could refer to either 'Erotes' or 'Ephesus', and subsequently and systematically deletes all the 'E:'s and adds 'S', for Syracuse. This occurs twelve times.[25] Later in the play, the annotator falls into the same trap. In the opening stage direction of 2.2, they replace 'Errotis'. with 'Seracus:' (see Fig. 20.2). Yet this emendation conflicts with their changes to the speech prefixes in this scene. The annotator added 'E:' to all the speech prefixes of Antipholus (of Syracuse), then realised that this was wrong and corrected them twenty-two times to 'S'. This represents a significant intervention in the text, centred around misprinting, misreading, and correction, as the reader struggles and fails to keep up with the text.[26]

By the middle of the play, the annotator is not attempting to regularise the names but suspects the printed text to be fundamentally mistaken. At the opening stage direction of Act Three, Scene One, the annotator believes the wrong twin has been referred to, and writes 'Sera' above 'Ephesus'.[27] Yet this is incorrect. At some point the mistake is realised and 'Sera' is crossed out. From line 25, the annotator adds 'E:' to the speech prefix 'Anti.', referring to Ephesus, adopting a different means of distinguishing the twins than they started with, using 'E' to refer to 'Ephesus' and 'S' to 'Syracuse'.[28] For anyone reading the copy back over, the annotations are not consistent with themselves, adding to the sense of mistake. The opening stage direction of Act Three, Scene Two demonstrates that, by now, the annotator was thoroughly lost in the play. 'Siracusia' is deleted with 'Ephe:' added above, but then

---

[23] Evans (ed.), *Shakespearean Prompt-Books* (n. 20 above), http://bsuva.org/bsuva/promptbook/images/ce12open.jpg. For all images see http://bsuva.org/bsuva/promptbook/images/, accessed 2 May 2020.

[24] Ibid.

[25] At ll. 9, 19, 30, 33, 53, 58, 68, 72, 77, 87, 91, 95. See Evans (ed.), *Shakespearean Prompt-Books* (n. 20 above), http://bsuva.org/bsuva/promptbook/images/ce-p88a.jpg, accessed 2 May 2020.

[26] At ll. 1, 14, 17, 22, 41, 43, 46, 51, 54, 58, 60, 62, 65, 149, 157, 162, 165, 168, 183, 198, 200, 214. See Evans (ed.), *Shakespearean Prompt-Books* (n. 20 above), http://bsuva.org/bsuva/promptbook/images/ce-p88b.jpg, accessed 2 May 2020.

[27] See Evans (ed.), *Shakespearean Prompt-Books* (n. 20 above).

[28] This occurs another twelve times, at ll. 27, 40, 42, 54, 57, 59, 63, 69, 73, 80, 84, 123.

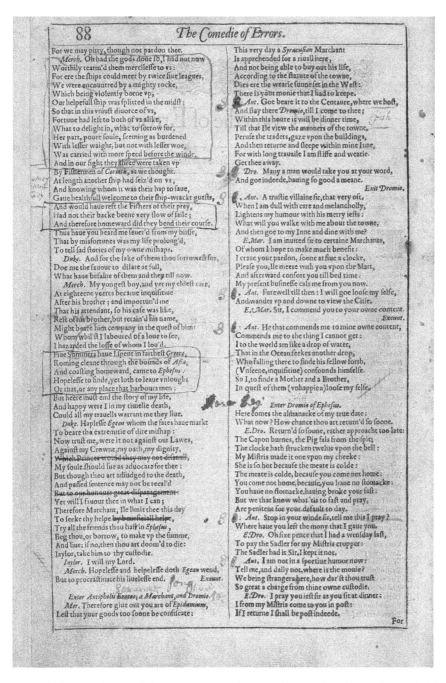

FIG. 20.1. The 'Nursery' Copy of Shakespeare First Folio, p. 86 (misnumbered as p. 88). Hand 1 deletes 'Erotes', adds 'Seracuse' above, and places 'Se' after 'Dromio'. On this page, the same hand adds an 'E:' to all the speech prefixes of Antipholus, presumably for 'Erotes'. Realising that 'E:' was ambiguous and would be confused with 'Ephesus', Hand 1 deleted 'E:' and added 'S', presumably for 'Syracuse'. Edinburgh, Edinburgh University Library, EUL JY 438.

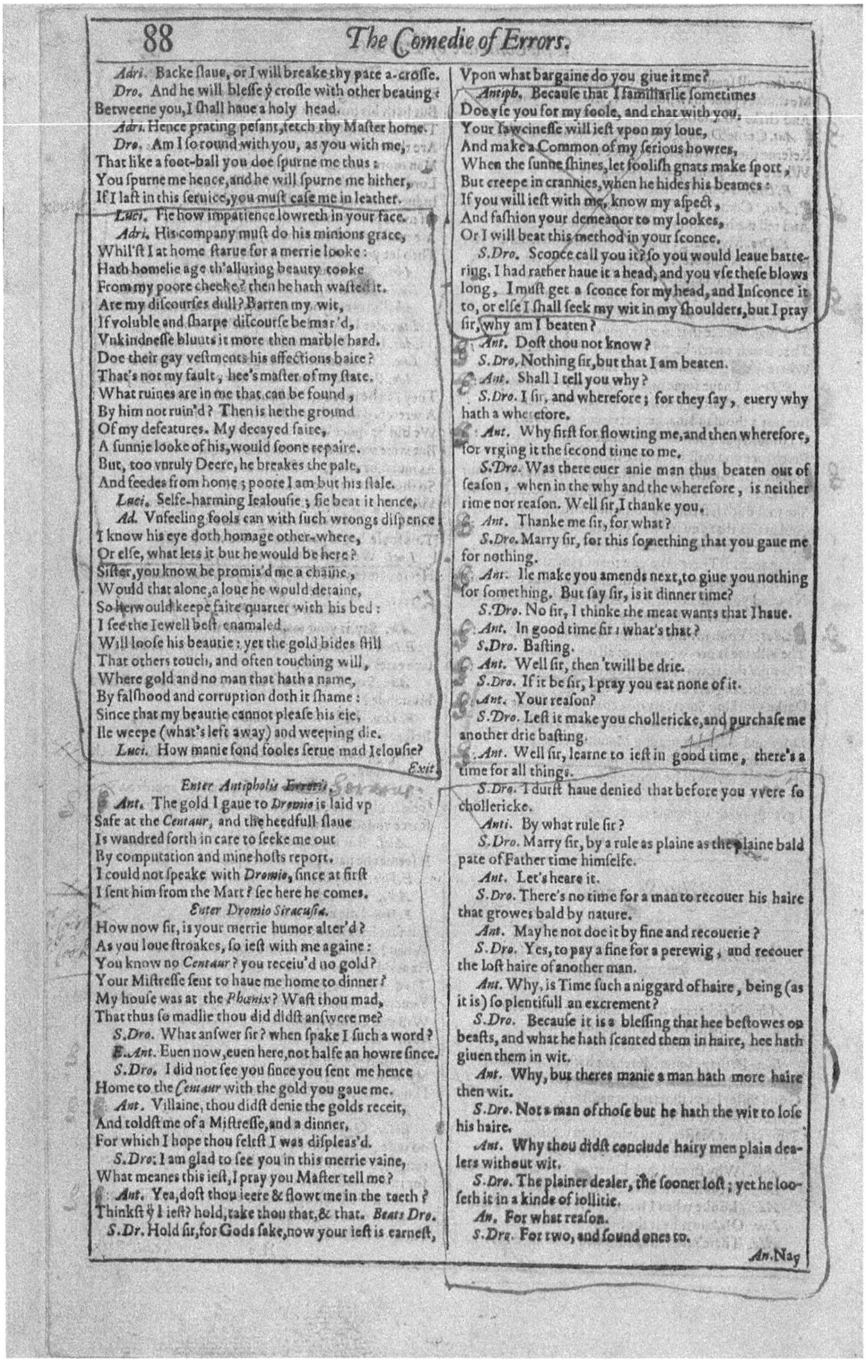

88 *The Comedie of Errors.*

Adri. Backe slaue, or I will breake thy pate a-crosse.
Dro. And he will blesse ý crosse with other beating:
Betweene you, I shall haue a holy head.
Adri. Hence prating pesant, fetch thy Master home.
Dro. Am I so round with you, as you with me,
That like a foot-ball you doe spurne me thus:
You spurne me hence, and he will spurne me hither,
If I last in this seruice, you must case me in leather.
Luci. Fie how impatience lowreth in your face.
Adri. His company must do his minions grace,
Whil'st I at home starue for a merrie looke:
Hath homelie age th'alluring beauty tooke
From my poore cheeke? then he hath wasted it.
Are my discourses dull? Barren my wit,
If voluble and sharpe discourse be mar'd,
Vnkindnesse blunts it more then marble hard.
Doe their gay vestments his affections baite?
That's not my fault, hee's master of my state.
What ruines are in me that can be found,
By him not ruin'd? Then is he the ground
Of my defeatures. My decayed faire,
A sunnie looke of his, would soone repaire.
But, too vnruly Deere, he breakes the pale,
And feedes from home; poore I am but his stale.
Luci. Selfe-harming Iealousie; fie beat it hence.
Ad. Vnfeeling fools can with such wrongs dispence:
I know his eye doth homage other-where,
Or else, what lets it but he would be here?
Sister, you know he promis'd me a chaine,
Would that alone, a loue he would detaine,
So he would keepe faire quarter with his bed:
I see the Iewell best enamaled
Will loose his beautie: yet the gold bides still
That others touch, and often touching will,
Where gold and no man that hath a name,
By falshood and corruption doth it shame:
Since that my beautie cannot please his eie,
Ile weepe (what's left away) and weeping die.
Luci. How manie fond fooles serue mad Ielousie?
Exit.

Enter Antipholis Errotis.

Ant. The gold I gaue to *Dromio* is laid vp
Safe at the *Centaur*, and the heedfull slaue
Is wandred forth in care to seeke me out
By computation and mine hosts report.
I could not speake with *Dromio*, since at first
I sent him from the Mart? see here he comes.

Enter Dromio Siracusia.

How now sir, is your merrie humor alter'd?
As you loue stroakes, so iest with me againe:
You know no *Centaur*? you receiu'd no gold?
Your Mistresse sent to haue me home to dinner?
My house was at the *Phœnix*? Wast thou mad,
That thus so madlie thou did didst answere me?
S.Dro. What answer sir? when spake I such a word?
E.Ant. Euen now, euen here, not halfe an howre since.
S.Dro. I did not see you since you sent me hence
Home to the *Centaur* with the gold you gaue me.
Ant. Villaine, thou didst denie the golds receit,
And toldst me of a Mistresse, and a dinner,
For which I hope thou feltst I was displeas'd.
S.Dro. I am glad to see you in this merrie vaine,
What meanes this iest, I pray you Master tell me?
Ant. Yea, dost thou ieere & flowt me in the teeth?
Thinkst ý I iest? hold, take thou that, & that. *Beats Dro.*
S.Dr. Hold sir, for Gods sake, now your iest is earnest,
Vpon what bargaine do you giue it me?
Antiph. Because that I familiarlie sometimes
Doe vse you for my foole, and chat with you,
Your sawcinesse will iest vpon my loue,
And make a Common of my serious howres,
When the sunne shines, let foolish gnats make sport,
But creepe in crannies, when he hides his beames:
If you will iest with me, know my aspect,
And fashion your demeanor to my lookes,
Or I will beat this method in your sconce.
S.Dro. Sconce call you it? so you would leaue battering, I had rather haue it a head, and you vse these blows long, I must get a sconce for my head, and Insconce it to, or else I shall seek my wit in my shoulders, but I pray sir, why am I beaten?
Ant. Dost thou not know?
S.Dro. Nothing sir, but that I am beaten.
Ant. Shall I tell you why?
S.Dro. I sir, and wherefore; for they say, euery why hath a wherefore.
Ant. Why first for flowting me, and then wherefore, for vrging it the second time to me.
S.Dro. Was there euer anie man thus beaten out of season, when in the why and the wherefore, is neither rime nor reason. Well sir, I thanke you.
Ant. Thanke me sir, for what?
S.Dro. Marry sir, for this something that you gaue me for nothing.
Ant. Ile make you amends next, to giue you nothing for something. But say sir, is it dinner time?
S.Dro. No sir, I thinke the meat wants that I haue.
Ant. In good time sir: what's that?
S.Dro. Basting.
Ant. Well sir, then 'twill be drie.
S.Dro. If it be sir, I pray you eat none of it.
Ant. Your reason?
S.Dro. Lest it make you chollericke, and purchase me another drie basting.
Ant. Well sir, learne to iest in good time, there's a time for all things.
S.Dro. I durst haue denied that before you vvere so chollericke.
Anti. By what rule sir?
S.Dro. Marry sir, by a rule as plaine as the plaine bald pate of Father time himselfe.
Ant. Let's heare it.
S.Dro. There's no time for a man to recouer his haire that growes bald by nature.
Ant. May he not doe it by fine and recouerie?
S.Dro. Yes, to pay a fine for a perewig, and recouer the lost haire of another man.
Ant. Why, is Time such a niggard of haire, being (as it is) so plentifull an excrement?
S.Dro. Because it is a blessing that hee bestowes on beasts, and what he hath scanted them in haire, hee hath giuen them in wit.
Ant. Why, but theres manie a man hath more haire then wit.
S.Dro. Not a man of those but he hath the wit to lose his haire.
Ant. Why thou didst conclude hairy men plain dealers without wit.
S.Dro. The plainer dealer, the sooner lost; yet he looseth it in a kinde of iollitie.
An. For what reason.
S.Dro. For two, and sound ones to.
An. Nay

FIG. 20.2. The 'Nursery' Copy of Shakespeare First Folio, p. 88. Hand 1 substituted 'Errotis' with 'Seracus:' and also added 'E:' to all the speech prefixes related to Antipholus (of Syracuse). Realising the mistake, Hand 1 either wrote 'S' over 'E:' or deleted 'E:' and wrote 'S' next to it. Edinburgh, Edinburgh University Library, EUL JY 438.

this is crossed through with 'Sera:' reinstated. Again at 4.1.13 (s.d), another deletion has to be restored, where the annotator crosses out the print 'Ephes.' and writes 'Serac.' above, before realising their error and deleting 'Serac.', letting the suspicious print stand.[29] At the penultimate act, we can observe that the annotator has spent most of the play in complete confusion over the Antipholus twins.[30]

The annotator continues the attempt to order the text by adding 'E:' or 'S:' to every moment of speech by the Antipholuses. This type of annotation is the dominant mode of interaction by this reader, and the copy is covered with attempted corrections. Yet the desire to correct leads only to further mistakes, demonstrating the level of complex error that the world of the play creates, augmented by its material state. The Nursery copy witnesses a committed reader making a sustained effort to understand and improve the text, but in fact often correcting things that are not wrong and introduce further obfuscation. Previous critics have assumed that texts designed for or coming from the theatre must demonstrate a higher level of accuracy as a working text, whereas, implicitly, texts created for reading can tolerate a higher level of mistake.[31] Yet this copy does not support this theory, not only with the faulty interventions regarding the Antipholuses, but with the neglect of the Dromios, the second set of twins, where the annotator lets the print confusions stand. The Nursery copy falls short of the expected textual rectitude for a reliable guide to performance, as does the Douai manuscript.

MS 787 in the Bibliothèque municipal of Douai, Northern France, originates from one of the local foundations of English Roman Catholics.[32] At the end of the seventeenth century, six Shakespeare plays were copied and bound together, including *The Comedy of Errors*. They are thought to be transcribed from F2, and may have been used by the students in dramatic performance.[33] Like the Nursery copy, the Douai manuscript is heavily annotated

---

[29] See Evans (ed.), *Shakespearean Prompt-Books* (n. 20 above).

[30] See also 3.2.54, where Hand 1 prefixes the F speech-head 'Ant.' with 'S:', as well as: ll. 56, 58, 60, 60, 66, 71, 75, 79, 84, 90, 95, 103, 107, 110, 114, 118, 122, 125, 128, 133, 136, 142, 152, 161, 170, 174, 176, 181, 184; 4.1.15 where Hand 1 prefixes the F speech-head 'Ant.' with 'E:'; ll. 34, 41, 43, 48, 54, 57, 62, 64, 66, 74, 80, 93, 96, 100; 4.3.15 where Hand 1 prefixes the F speech-head 'Ant.' with 'S:'; ll. 21, 29, 34, 42, 48, 50, 63, 66, 80; 4.4.1 where Hand 1 prefixes the F speech-head 'An.' with 'E:'; and ll. 11, 13, 15, 17, 24,27, 43, 47, 56, 61, 63, 71, 73, 75, 77, 79, 85, 90, 98, 104, 112, 127, 129. See Evans (ed.), *Shakespearean Prompt-Books* (n. 20 above), http://bsuva.org/bsuva/promptbook/images/, accessed on 2 May 2020.

[31] Smith claims that the troubled and misprinted speech prefixes 'only emerge[s] as an ambiguity when using the Folio as a performance text.' Smith, *Shakespeare's First Folio* (n. 21 above), p. 241. R. B. McKerrow, 'A Suggestion Regarding Shakespeare's Manuscripts' (n. 10 above), p. 464, states: 'a copy intended for use in the theatre would surely, of necessity, be accurate and unambiguous in the matter of the character-names.' Pushing against this, Werstine argues that 'in one way or another, all three theatrical texts compound such confusions'. P. Werstine, *Early Modern Playhouse Manuscripts*, Cambridge, 2013, p. 117.

[32] On the Douai manuscript, see J.-C. Mayer, 'Annotating and Transcribing for the Theatre: Shakespeare's Early Modern Reader-Revisers at Work', in M. Kidnie and S. Massai (eds), *Shakespeare and Textual Studies*, Cambridge, 2015, pp. 163–76; A. Marotti and L. Estill, 'Manuscript Circulation', in A. F. Kinney (ed.), *The Oxford Handbook of Shakespeare*, Oxford, 2012, pp. 53–70; and A.-M. Hedbäck, 'The Douai Manuscript Reexamined', *Papers of the Bibliographical Society of America*, 73/1, 1979, pp. 1–18.

[33] The manuscript now resides in the Douai Public Library. The *Catalogue général des manuscrits des bibliothèques publiques des départements*, VI: *Douai*, Paris, 1878, pp. 477–8, states: 'Provient sans doute de l'un des couvents anglais de Douai' ('Undoubtedly coming from one of the English monasteries in Douai').

and displays the desire — along with the inability — to correct error. It uses the following speech prefixes: 'A:E' for Antipholis Erotes, (Antipholus of Syracuse); 'D:E' for Dromio of Ephesus; 'D:S' for Dromio of Syracuse; and 'A:S' for Antipholus Sereptus, (Antipholus of Ephesus). When transcribing the play, the scribe used 'Erotes' and 'Sereptus' and applied them to the Antipholuses but not the Dromios. This unevenness has the effect of removing the point of place around which the characters can be organised: each coupling of one Antipholus with one Dromio who come from the same place and understand each other fully are distinguished by different referents, 'Erotes' or 'Siracusia'. The scribe uses 'S' to designate the Syracusan Dromio and the Ephesian Antipholis; and 'E' for the Ephesian Dromio and the Syracusan Antipholus. 'Erotes' and 'Siracusia' are employed in an attempt to order the play, but as we have seen in F1 already, these are the names which cause the greatest confusion in the play.[34]

The Douai manuscript inflates identity confusion. But at the same time, it invents an alternative method of reading and ordering the play that is consistently applied, which tolerates error and complexity even within performance. It does so whilst contemporary eighteenth-century editors were worrying over what they saw as the problem of error in Shakespeare, and its eradication. In the Nursery copy and the Douai manuscript, reading and altering the play is a treacherous activity, where the minor confusions on which the play thrives can easily turn into major ones. Critics and editors have tended to explain error straightforwardly, an impulse which fails to capture the messy reality and incorrigibility of *Errors*, and its afterlife. The repeated interaction between textual and readerly error raises questions about editorial intervention, as correcting error moves us much further away from the play as it was first experienced.

THE EDITORIAL TRADITION: INVENTING ERROR

With the eighteenth century began the tradition of editing and publishing Shakespeare's complete plays. These include: Rowe (1709), Pope (1723–1725, 1728), Theobald (1733), Hanmer (1743–1744), Warburton (1747), Johnson (1765), Capell (1767–1768), Johnson-Steevens (1773, 1778), Johnson-Steevens-Reed (1785), and Malone (1790).[35] These editors (and readers) believed that the print errors and confusion found in F1 *Errors* required urgent action. Rowe stated that his principal motivation for the edition was to 'redeem' Shakespeare 'from the injuries of former impressions'.[36] F1 itself participates in this tradition of error-correction, with John Heminge and Henry Condell's famous claim to have rescued with

---

[34] As Werstine argues, this 'theatrical text introduces complication that exceeds anything to be found in the F version'. Werstine, *Early Modern Playhouse Manuscripts* (n. 31 above), p. 118.

[35] Massai examines the editorial practices of pre-1709 annotating readers, challenging Rowe's dominance as the first editor of Shakespeare. S. Massai, *Shakespeare and the Rise of the Editor*, Cambridge, 2007, p. 2.

[36] N. Rowe, 'Dedication', in W. Shakespeare, *The Works of Mr. William Shakespear*, ed. N. Rowe, I, London, 1709.

plays from their 'maimed and deformed' copies.[37] Yet Rowe's 1709 *Works* initiated the standardisation of Shakespeare's material copies that still forms a significant part of the editorial task today.

Rowe first corrected the two confusing stage directions that refer to 'Antipholus Erotes', printed in F1, F2, F3 and F4 (1.2.0, 2.2.0).[38] He replaced 'Erotes' with 'of Syracuse', introducing a new standardisation of names that has been followed ever since. Two partial exceptions are George Lyman Kittredge's 1936 edition and the *Riverside Shakespeare* (1997), which retain 'of Syracuse' in square brackets, after 'Erotes'.[39] Rowe adds 'Dro. Eph.' to the F1–4 stage direction that fails to distinguish which Dromio has entered (4.1.13); Capell, Johnson and Steevens, and Malone replicate this correction in their editions.[40] Rowe also was the first to insert a *Dramatis Personae* list, which attempted to sort the confusion of names, introducing 'Antipholis *of* Ephesus' and 'Antipholis *of* Syracuse'.[41] His standardisation only goes so far, however, and he does not correct the F1–4 reference to 'Antipholis Sereptus' in the opening of 2.1 (stage direction). He simply removes any reference to Antipholus altogether. Where F1–4 refers to 'E. Ant.', in confusion with Antipholus of Ephesus, Rowe again removes rather than clarifies, excising 'E.' to leave just 'Ant.' (2.2.14). This is followed through twelve editions by Pope, Theobald, and up to Samuel Johnson, until Edward Capell regularises the stage directions and speech prefixes from the beginning, using 'A.S' or 'D.S', leaving no twin unspecified.

It is only with Edmund Malone in 1790 that the speech prefixes take the familiar form that we recognise today. In Act Five, the F1 stage direction states: 'Enter Antipholus and Dromio againe'. Rowe alters this to: 'Enter Antipholis and Dromio of Syracuse', but it is Capell who distinguishes each twin with their own locative descriptor: '*Enter* Antiphilus Syracusan, *and* Dromio Syracusan' (5.1.9).[42] Just as Massai argues against the dominance of 1709 in Shakespearean editing, *The Comedy of Errors* demonstrates the complexities of print emendation that spread out across time.[43] Rather than being a straightforward, single action that alters obvious mistakes, correction was in fact an incremental process over eighty-one years, characterised by attempt and revision.

Since the eighteenth century, no modern edition lets these various textual errors and ambiguities stand.[44] 'Print error' is synonymous with 'careless mistake', which therefore

---

[37] Shakespeare, *Comedies* (n. 1 above), sig. A3r; London, British Library, C.39.k.15, available at https://www.bl.uk/collection-items/, accessed 16 February 2021.

[38] At 2.2.0, this is spelled 'Antipholus Errotis' in F1 and 'Erotes' F2–4.

[39] W. Shakespeare, *The Complete Works*, ed. G. L. Kittredge, Boston, 1936 and W. Shakespeare, *The Riverside Shakespeare*, ed. G. B. Evans, Boston, 1997.

[40] Cf.: W. Shakespeare, *Mr William Shakespeare: His Comedies, Histories, and Tragedies*, ed. E. Capell, II, London, 1768, p. 35 ('Dromio Ephesian'); W. Shakespeare, *The Plays of William Shakespeare: With the Corrections and Illustrations of Various Commentators*, ed. S. Johnson and G. Steevens, II, London, 1773, p. 188 ('Dromio of Ephesus'); W. Shakespeare, *The Plays and Poems of William Shakespeare*, ed. E. Malone, II, London, 1790, p. 172 ('Dromio of Ephesus').

[41] W. Shakespeare, *The Works*, ed. Rowe (n. 36 above), p. 272.

[42] Ibid., p. 309; W. Shakespeare, *His Comedies, Histories, and Tragedies*, ed. Capell (n. 39 above), p. 50.

[43] Massai, *Shakespeare and the Rise* (n. 35 above).

[44] This includes the *Variorum Shakespeare*, which does not record emendations to the speech prefixes but silently corrects them. *Variorum Shakespeare*, ed. S. Henning, New York, 2011. Similarly, the *Oxford Shakespeare* also silently alters the text, despite Charles Whitworth's claim that disputable speech prefixes

warrants correction. It can be corrected without fuss because it is a mistake in a mechanical process of replication, rather than of interpretation, such as confusing one twin with another. But in *The Comedy of Errors*, what we see as print errors are complex and suggest semantic confusion of one character with another. I would argue that these misprints are not mindless or insignificant, but are small radical units that have affected understanding of the play over time.[45] They are distinct from an upside down letter that cannot be read much beyond its mistake. For example, in F1, Dromio of Syracuse refers to the 'chalkle Cliffes', where the 'i' in 'chalkie' is misprinted as an 'l'.[46] 'Chalkie' can easily be guessed, and the word is corrected in F2–4. The alternative 'chalkle' is not particularly meaningful in itself, whereas the set of misprints in *Errors* concerning the twins could represent an alternative text, where the audience is placed in a position of sustained mistaken identity. Their systematic correction by the editorial tradition, however, suggests they are worth very little. The body of evidence from early readers' marks in copies of the early printed editions demonstrates that, rather than being accidental or insignificant, the printing errors that originate with F1 have a direct impact on the experience and understanding of the play. Uniquely for *The Comedy of Errors,* the editorial response has obscured a history of reading where printing error precipitates the type of confusion the play itself creates.

Recent scholarship has paid little attention to these misinterpretations. As Adam Smyth argues, the close analysis of Lisa Jardine and Anthony Grafton on Gabriel Harvey, or William Sherman on Sir Julius Caesar, 'has meant that the history of reading, as a field, has often been organized around biography precisely at a time when early modern studies more generally has been moving away from the individual as the unit of cultural analysis'.[47] Katherine Acheson, for example, explores the construction of identity through Anne Clifford's various forms of marginalia, where she argues that '[b]ooks gave women access to spaces within which to write, within which to enlarge their senses of themselves'.[48] Similarly, Emma Smith argues that through the annotations in a collection of books owned by Isabella and Thomas Hervey at the end of the seventeenth century, we 'gain a glimpse of marital and familial relationship enacted and authorized via books'.[49] For Harvey, Caesar, Clifford, Isabella and Thomas Hervey, annotation reveals personal identity. These readers'

---

are in square brackets. C. Whitworth, 'Editorial Procedures', in W. Shakespeare, *The Comedy of Errors*, ed. C. Whitworth, Oxford, 2002, p. 82.

[45] On the discrimination between meaningful difference and error, see, John Jowett's proposition that error, as opposed to difference, occurs 'where the text fails to maintain its own standards of consistency.' J. Jowett, 'Full Pricks and Great P's: Spellings, Punctuation, Accidentals', in M. Kidnie and S. Massai (eds), *Shakespeare and Textual Studies*, Cambridge, 2015, pp. 317–31 (331).

[46] TLN 917; p. 91 in F1. F2 has 'chalky Cliffes' (p. 92); F3 has 'chalky Cliffes' (p. 92); F4 has 'chalky Cliffs' (p. 83). Rowe has 'chalky Cliffs' (p. 295).

[47] A. Smyth, 'Book Marks: Object Traces in Early Modern Books', in K. Acheson (ed.), *Early Modern English Marginalia*, London, 2018, pp. 51–69 (64). See L. Jardine and A. Grafton, '"Studied for Action": How Gabriel Harvey Read His Livy', *Past & Present*, 129, 1990, pp. 30–78, and W. H. Sherman, *John Dee: The Politics of Reading and Writing in the English Renaissance*, Amherst (MA), 1995. Although it is a biographical study, Sherman also deals with anonymous readers and multiple forms of annotation.

[48] K. Acheson, 'The Occupation of the Margins: Writing, Space, and Early Modern Women', in K. Acheson (ed.), *Early Modern English Marginalia*, London, 2018, pp. 70–89 (86).

[49] E. Smith, 'Marital Marginalia: The Seventeenth-Century Library of Thomas and Isabella Hervey', in K. Acheson (ed.), *Early Modern English Marginalia*, London, 2018, pp. 155–72 (155–6). For a wider study of marginalia, see H. J. Jackson, *Marginalia: Readers Writing in Books*, New Haven (CT), 2001.

deep reading, cross-referencing, and displays of knowledge make these heavily individualised historical readers 'good', but this leaves little space for often anonymous, mistaken, or superficial attempts on the text. The reader behind each set of annotations in copies of Shakespeare's early folios discussed in this chapter is, instead, the self to hide. Most of the copies are anonymously annotated; no one wants to take ownership of these shaky, wayward, misdirected marks that cannot be erased.

Shakespeare's first readers approached *Errors* not as a poetic entity to be commonplaced, treasured, or remembered.[50] The dominant way of reading was to attempt to correct the printing errors that affected comprehension of the plot. Readers engaged in acts of rewriting and correction where they felt the text was either wrong or would benefit from improvement. This earliest approach runs directly counter to the reification of both Shakespeare's now revered language, in the hands of careful and scrutinising editors, and the highly valuable earliest texts, mostly in endowed libraries and research institutions. These lax, stymied readings are not the kind we hope to see inside a Shakespeare First Folio, but instead represent the messy reality of reading *Errors*. Shakespeare's earliest readers felt none of the pressure we do today to make great effort to grasp it, or assume it was even correct.

Mistaken identity in the play is an 'offer'd fallacy', not contained to the stage for the audience to consume knowingly, as it is often interpreted, but 'offer'd' to those looking back in the theatre or gazing down at the page (2.2.187). Mistake has been 'sympathizèd' by the characters, as Emilia announces at the end of the play, but also by readers (5.1.399). It is often assumed that the audience only witnesses the mistakes of the on-stage characters for entertainment, but the material world of manuscript annotations in books reminds us that misprints can precipitate our own mistakes. As such, genuine audience confusion is the historical condition of reading the play, both in the theatre and in the book. In folio copies, such as the Nursery Copy and the Douai copy, readers bump up against a reality of the text. The jumbled speech prefixes are in some sense a printing-house echo of the stage issue of doubling, where an audience feels a sense of uncanny recognition alongside a problem of differentiation. Yet these misprints and misreadings are perhaps not what we expect to see in a Shakespeare folio and often do not because of careful editors. Early readers who did encounter these slips and faults experience a very different play, one that seems almost booby-trapped for printers and readers alike. The earliest text risks a level of mistake for the reader from which we are severely distanced today. The Rowean impulse to correct that is germane to modern editorial policy is in tension with the history of reading *Errors* in early printed editions and manuscripts which retain this comic, performative, residual interaction with error. The correction of these textual mistakes in *Errors* is not straightforward as their dispersal through print writes them into the history of the play.

The faulty readings of these faulty printings have been mainly ignored, which raises the question: how committed are we to recovering past reading practices? Historians of reading repeatedly emphasise the absence of evidence of most readers, as '[m]any instances of marginalia have surely been lost, and many more readers never left annotations at all'.[51]

---

[50] Laura Estill argues that the majority of early modern readers were commonplacing readers. L. Estill, 'Commonplacing Readers', in M. Kidnie and S. Massai (eds), *Shakespeare and Textual Studies*, Cambridge, 2015, pp. 149–62 (149).

[51] H. Brayman Hackel, *Reading Material in Early Modern England: Print, Gender and Literacy*, Cambridge, 2005, p. 141. As William G. Rowland observes, 'we simply do not know and cannot find out what

Despite this, typical editorial strategies and conventions leave no space for the history of mistaken reading, and very little for misprinting. This chapter encourages reading error while resisting the urge to correct. To take seriously the idea of reading F1–4 and approach them as correct opens our experience to a pre-standardised textual world of flawed readers and playful mistakenness, which exists in concert with a play all about *Error*. The value, then, of these annotations lies in revealing an alternative history of reading and misunderstanding; reading the misprints as being a correct version enables the riskier possibility that we too might seriously misunderstand Shakespeare.

BIBLIOGRAPHY

PRIMARY SOURCES

MANUSCRIPTS

Douai, Bibliothèque municipale, MS 787 Anglais.
Edinburgh, University Library, EUL JY 438 (the 'Nursery' playhouse copy *The Comidie of Errors*).

PRINTED BOOKS

F1 = Shakespeare, William, *Mr. William Shakespeares comedies, histories, & tragedies. Published according to the true originall*, London, Isaac Jaggard and Edward Blount at the expenses of William Jaggard, Edward Blount, John Smethwicke and William Aspley, 1623, f° (USTC 3010710). Copies discussed: London, British Library, C.39.k.15, and Washington DC, Folger Shakespeare Library, STC 22273 Fo. 1 no. 54, West 112

F2 = Shakespeare, William, *Mr. VVilliam Shakespeares comedies, histories, and tragedies. Published according to the true originall*, London, Thomas Cotes for Robert Allot John Smethwick William Aspley Richard Hawkins and Richard Meighen, 1632, f°, (USTC 3015914). Copies discussed: Washington DC, Folger Shakespeare Library, STC 22274 Fo. 2 no. 2, and Oxford, Bodleian Library, Arch G c 9.

F3 = Shakespeare, W., *The Comedie of Errors*, London, 1663–1664, pp. 85–100. H⁶, I². Copy discussed: Washington DC, Folger Shakespeare Library, Prompt 3d Folio Com. Err. Smock Alley.

most readers of the past thought about a particular book'. W. G. Rowland, *Literature and the Marketplace: Romantic Writers and their Audiences in Great Britain and the United States*, Lincoln (NE), 1996, p. ix.

F4 = Shakespeare, W., *Mr. William Shakespear's comedies, histories, and tragedies, publ. [by J. Heminge and H. Condell], unto which is added seven plays*, London, 1685. Copy discussed: Oxford, Bodleian Library, Arch G c 13.

Shakespeare, W., *The Comedy of Errors*, ed. C. Whitworth, Oxford, 2002.

Shakespeare, W., *The works of Mr. William Shakespear*, ed. N. Rowe, I, London, 1709.

Shakespeare, W., *The Works of Shakespear*, ed. A. Pope, I, London, 1725.

Shakespeare, W., *The works of Shakespear. In six volumes*, ed. T. Hanmer, London, 1743–1744.

Shakespeare, W., *The Works of Shakespear. In Eight Volumes*, ed. W. Warburton, London, 1747.

Shakespeare, W., *The Plays of William Shakespeare in Eight Volumes*, ed. S. Johnson, London, 1765.

Shakespeare, W., *Mr William Shakespeare: His Comedies, Histories, and Tragedies*, ed. E. Capell, II, London, 1768.

Shakespeare, W., *The Plays of William Shakespeare: With the Corrections and Illustrations of Various Commentators*, ed. S. Johnson and G. Steevens, II, London, 1773.

Shakespeare, W., *The plays of William Shakspeare: In ten volumes*, ed. S. Johnson, G. Steevens, and I. Reed, London, 1785.

Shakespeare, W., *The plays and poems of William Shakespeare*, ed. E. Malone, II, London, 1790.

Shakespeare, W., *The Complete Works*, ed. G. L. Kittredge, Boston, 1936.

Shakespeare, W., *The Riverside Shakespeare*, ed.G. B. Evans, Boston, 1997.

Shakespeare, W., *The Norton Shakespeare*, ed. S. Greenblatt, London, 2016, 3rd edn.

Shakespeare, W., *Internet Shakespeare Editions (ISE)*, ed. M. Steggle, http://internetshakespeare.uvic.ca/.

Variorum Shakespeare, ed. S. Henning, New York, 2011.

Wither, George, *The schollers purgatory discouered in the Stationers common-wealth*, London, [G. Wood for] the Stationers' Company, [1624], 8° (USTC 3011498).

SECONDARY LITERATURE

Acheson, K., 'The Occupation of the Margins: Writing, Space, and Early Modern Women', in K. Acheson (ed.), *Early Modern English Marginalia*, London, 2018, pp. 70–89.

Bourne, C. M. L., *Typographies of Performance in Early Modern England*, Oxford, 2020.

Brayman Hackel, H., *Reading Material in Early Modern England: Print, Gender and Literacy*, Cambridge, 2005.

Catalogue général des manuscrits des bibliothèques publiques des départements, VI: *Douai*, Paris, 1878.

Doelman, J., 'George Wither, the Stationers Company and the English Psalter', *Studies in Philology*, 90/1, 1993, pp. 74–82.

Erasmus, D., *The Adages of Erasmus*, transl. W. Barker, Toronto, 2001.

Estill, L., 'Commonplacing Readers', in M. Kidnie and S. Massai (eds), *Shakespeare and Textual Studies*, Cambridge, 2015, pp. 149–62.

Evans, G. B. (ed.), *Shakespearean Prompt-Books of the Seventeenth Century*, III, Charlottesville (VA), 1964, online edition available: http://bsuva.org/bsuva/promptbook/ShaComP.html,

Evans, G. B., 'The Douai Manuscript — Six Shakespearean Transcripts (1694–95)', *Philological Quarterly*, 41, 1962, pp. 158–72.

Foakes, R. A., 'Introduction', in William Shakespeare, *The Comedy of Errors*, ed. R. A. Foakes, London, 1991.

Greg, W. W., *The Shakespeare First Folio*, Oxford, 1955.

Greg, W. W., *Some Aspects and Problems of London Publishing between 1550 and 1650*, Oxford, 1956.

Hedbäck, A.-M., 'The Douai Manuscript Reexamined', *Papers of the Bibliographical Society of America*, 73/1, 1979, pp. 1–18.

Jackson, H. J., *Marginalia: Readers Writing in Books*, New Haven (CT), 2001.

Jardine, L., and Grafton, A., '"Studied for Action": How Gabriel Harvey Read His Livy', *Past & Present*, 129, 1990, pp. 30–78.

Jowett, J., 'Full Pricks and Great P's: Spellings, Punctuation, Accidentals', in M. J. Kidnie and S. Massai (eds), *Shakespeare and Textual Studies*, Cambridge, 2015, pp. 317–31.

Lerer, S., *Error and the Academic Self: The Scholarly Imagination, Medieval to Modern*, New York, 2002.

McKerrow, R. B., 'A Suggestion Regarding Shakespeare's Manuscripts', *The Review of English Studies*, 11/44, 1935, Vol. 11, pp. 459–65.

McKitterick, D., *Print, Manuscript and the Search for Order, 1450–1830*, Cambridge, 2003.

McLeod, R., 'What's the Bastard's Name? Random Cloud', in G. W. Williams (ed.), *Shakespeare's Speech-Headings: Speaking the Speech in Shakespeare's Plays*, Newark (DE), 1997, pp. 133–209.

Maguire, L., *Shakespeare's Names*, Oxford, 2007.

Marcus, L., *How Shakespeare Became Colonial: Editorial Tradition and the British Empire*, Abingdon, 2017.

Marotti, A., and Estill, L., 'Manuscript Circulation', in A. F. Kinney (ed.), *The Oxford Handbook of Shakespeare*, Oxford, 2012, pp. 53–70.

Massai, S., *Shakespeare and the Rise of the Editor*, Cambridge, 2007.

Mayer, J.-C., 'Annotating and Transcribing for the Theatre: Shakespeare's Early Modern Reader-Revisers at Work', in M. J. Kidnie and S. Massai (eds), *Shakespeare and Textual Studies*, Cambridge, 2015, pp. 163–76.

Murphy, A., '"Tish ill done": Henry the Fift and the Politics of Editing', in M. T. Burnett and R. Wray (eds), *Shakespeare and Ireland: History, Politics, Culture*, London, 1997, pp. 217–34.

Orgel, S., 'Marginal Maternity: Reading Lady Anne Clifford's *A Mirror for Magistrates*', in D. A. Brooks (ed.), *Printing and Parenting in Early Modern England*, Aldershot, 2005, pp. 267–90.

Rowland, W. G., *Literature and the Marketplace: Romantic Writers and their Audiences in Great Britain and the United States*, Lincoln (NE), 1996.

Sherman, W. H., *John Dee: The Politics of Reading and Writing in the English Renaissance*, Amherst (MA), 1995.

Smith, E., 'Marital Marginalia: The Seventeenth-Century Library of Thomas and Isabella Hervey', in K. Acheson (ed.), *Early Modern English Marginalia*, London, 2018, pp. 155–72.

Smith, E., *Shakespeare's First Folio: Four Centuries of an Iconic Book*, Oxford, 2016.

Smyth, A., 'Book Marks: Object Traces in Early Modern Books', in K. Acheson (ed.), *Early Modern English Marginalia*, New York, 2018, pp. 51–69.

Smyth, A., 'Errata Lists', in D. Duncan and A. Smyth (eds), *Book Parts*, Oxford, 2019, pp. 251–63.

Smyth, A., *Material Texts in Early Modern England*, Cambridge, 2018, pp. 75–136.

Wakelin, D., *Scribal Correction and Literary Craft: English Manuscripts 1375–1510*, Cambridge, 2014.

Werstine, P., *Early Modern Playhouse Manuscripts*, Cambridge, 2013.

Werstine, P., '"Foul Papers" and "Prompt-Books": Printer's Copy for Shakespeare's "Comedy of Errors"', *Studies in Bibliography*, 41, 1988, pp. 232–46.

Werstine, P., 'McKerrow's "Suggestion" and W. W. Greg', in G. W. Williams (ed.), *Shakespeare's Speech-Headings: Speaking the Speech in Shakespeare's Plays*, Newark (DE), 1997, pp. 11–16.

Wilder, L. P., 'Changeling Bottom: Speech Prefixes, Acting, and Character in *A Midsummer Night's Dream*', *Shakespeare*, 4/1, 2008, pp. 41–58.

Williams, A., *Reading it Wrong*, Princeton, forthcoming.

Yates, J., *Error, Misuse, Failure*, Minneapolis, 2002.

CHAPTER 21

MAKING SENSE OF ERROR IN COMMERCIAL DRAMA

The case of *Edward III*

AMY LIDSTER

INTRODUCTION

> I[n] steed of the Trumpets sounding thrice, before the Play begin: it shall not be amisse (for him that will read) first to beholde this short Comedy of Errors, and where the greatest enter, to giue them in stead of a hisse, a gentle correction.[1]

WHILE the sounding of trumpets marks the beginning of a play in the theatre, error announces the start of a play reader's experience — so says the 'Ad Lectorem' in *Satiromastix,* a rather neglected paratext that in fact contains the very first errata list in a printed play from the commercial stages in England (Fig. 21.1). It provides, after the statement above, a list of seven errors and their corrections, all of which appear on the verso (sig. A4*v*) opposite the first scene of the play (sig. B1*r*), and serves as a kind of print prologue that requests the reader's participation. Error is a character — not only in the sense that it is signified through the characters or type on the page, but also in a theatrical sense. Error enters a printed play like an actor on the stage; it requires attention and demands a response. This unsigned, perspicacious address to readers offers a useful commentary on how a play (to adapt Genette) makes a book of itself: it is conditioned by error, and it assigns its new readerly audience an active role to engage with error through 'gentle correction'.[2]

This chapter is concerned with the coexistence of error and correction, of misprinting and proofreading, in plays that were first performed on the commercial stages in England before

---

[1] 'Ad Lectorem' in Thomas Dekker, *Satiro-mastix*, London, Edward White, 1602, 4° (USTC 3000771), sig. A4*v*.

[2] G. Genette, 'Introduction to the Paratext', transl. M. Maclean, *New Literary History*, 22, 1991, pp. 261–72 (261).

Amy Lidster, *Making Sense of Error in Commercial Drama*. In: *Printing and Misprinting*. Edited by Geri Della Rocca de Candal, Anthony Grafton, and Paolo Sachet, Oxford University Press. © Amy Lidster (2023). DOI: 10.1093/oso/9780198863045.003.0022

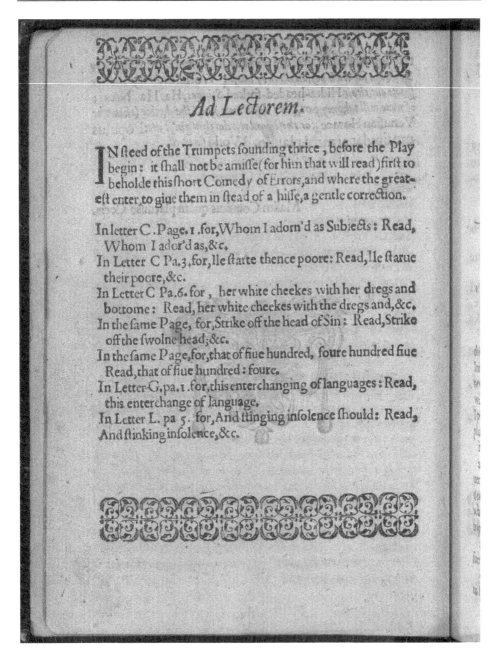

FIG. 21.1. Thomas Dekker, *Satiro-mastix*, London, Edward White, 1602, 4° (USTC 3000771), sig. A4v. Austin, The Harry Ransom Center, University of Texas, Wh D39 602s WRE.

being re-presented as printed books, a process that was not regularly overseen by the plays' dramatists. Within these parameters, I offer a case study on the two early quarto editions (henceforth Q1 and Q2) of the anonymously issued *Edward III* to explore how the play was prepared for publication and to highlight the ubiquity of silent error in playbooks.[3] The term 'commercial' is used to refer to plays that were performed by professional adult and children's companies in front of paying audiences. Playscripts (meaning any handwritten manuscript of a play) originating from these companies offered distinctive challenges during the printing process: the manuscripts were not often prepared with publication in mind, and they represent a wide range of provisional texts, from authors' papers, to scribal copies, to playhouse scripts (by no means an exhaustive or clear-cut list). As Julie Stone Peters has discussed, when plays were printed, their existence played out in two arenas: on the stage and on the page.[4] Error, I suggest, is one of the features that distinguishes the printed play from its theatrical incarnation. Both incarnations are provisional in different and overlapping ways. In the theatre, plays are subject to revision, adaptation, and improvisation — as Tiffany Stern has argued, playscripts existed as a series of fragments, rather than having a single, stable identity.[5] Through publication, these theatrical fragments assemble and are witness to the processes of print preparation, error, and correction — occasionally overseen by dramatists, but most often by publication agents — that reshape and 'materialise' the experience of play-watching into play-reading.

These integral processes are mostly silent in *playbooks* (meaning, throughout this chapter, the physical printed book of a play). It is useful therefore to propose two broad categories of error that relate to the presentation of playbooks: announced error and silent error. As I will consider briefly in this chapter, the former category applies to error that is explicitly referred to — perhaps, one could argue, advertised — in errata lists and errata commentary, often accompanied by instructions for correction. The second — and main — part of the chapter concentrates on silent error: the processes of error and correction that are nowhere discussed in playbooks but that take place silently, are overseen by communities of agents connected to the publication process, and can be studied through a comparison of extant editions that sometimes suggest readings of the plays themselves. For all genres of text, as Adam Smyth discusses, error is 'not a rare anomaly but a defining trait of print' and material texts from the period reveal 'an expectation that the printed book would be error-stuffed'.[6] Drawing on examples of announced error (as Smyth's study emphasises) and silent error, this chapter argues that error and correction position (early modern and modern) readers of commercial playbooks as new 'authorisers', required to navigate the sometimes blurred boundaries of textual 'erratics', misprints, and emendation that draw attention to the play's continued provisionality in print.[7]

---

[3] Anon., *The Raigne of King Edward the Third*, London, [Thomas Scarlet] for Cuthbert Burby, 1596, 4° (USTC 513018) = Q1; Anon., *The Raigne of King Edward the Third*, London, Simon Stafford for Cuthbert Burby, 1599, 4° (USTC 513866) = Q2. See also A. Grafton, *The Culture of Correction in Renaissance Europe*, London, 2011, and J. Jowett, 'Shakespeare and the Kingdom of Error', in *The New Oxford Shakespeare: Critical Reference Edition*, ed. G. Taylor et al., II.1, Oxford, 2017, pp. xlix–lxiii.

[4] J. S. Peters, *Theatre of the Book, 1480–1880: Print, Text and Performance in Europe*, Oxford, 2000.

[5] T. Stern, *Documents of Performance in Early Modern England*, Cambridge, 2009, p. 7.

[6] A. Smyth, *Material Texts in Early Modern England*, Cambridge, 2018, pp. 78–9.

[7] See Jowett, 'Kingdom' (n. 3 above), p. xlix, who describes the 'casual erratics of an early modern printed playbook — variable speech prefixes, unsystematic stage directions, unpredictable spelling, uneven punctuation, and so on'.

Discourses of Error in Commercial Playbooks

Detection and correction of errors — as paratextually discussed features of texts — came late to commercial playbooks printed in England, which is probably owing in part to the novelty and uncertain status of these publications. When playbooks from the commercial stages started to be printed during the 1580s, they did not adopt the errata lists and errata commentaries that featured in non-dramatic texts and other types of plays (such as translations of Seneca published during the 1560s), as well as in a range of continental publications that made their way to England.[8] The 'Ad Lectorem' in *Satiromastix*, printed in 1602, is, as I identified earlier, the first errata list to appear. But this precedent did not lead to the widespread incorporation of errata lists in commercial playbooks. Between the first list in 1602 and 1650, only five playbook editions contain a list of errors and corrections: *Satiromastix* (1602), John Day's *Isle of Gulls* (1606), Samuel Daniel's *Philotas* (1611), James Shirley's *The Bird in a Cage* (1633), and Thomas Nabbes's *Hannibal and Scipio* (1637).[9] These errata lists are all unsigned. They may have been prepared by a printing agent or an overseeing dramatist. They tend to concentrate on word substitutions and do not make reference to mechanical faults or outline errors of style and judgement. According to the lists, error is specific and local; it can be easily identified and corrected by the reader. *The Isle of Gulls*, for example, contains only one erratum — 'for Lord, read loue cannot be saued' — a correction that is, in fact, wrong.[10] It should read 'lover', rather than 'love', which the reader's marginalia added to the copy held by the Harry Ransom Center demonstrates, as does the play's second edition in 1633.[11] One effect of including a single erratum might be to advertise the playbook's precision and correctness. It is, however, silent about other examples of 'error'. Notoriously, Day's play was censored on stage because it was seen to offer disparaging representations of the Stuart monarchy. Silent corrections are witnessed in the printed text. The King and Queen become the Duke and Duchess (providing distance from the Jacobean court), and the title-page exists in two states — one with the publisher's name, John Trundle, and the other with it removed.[12] For playbooks, the few examples of errata lists seem to reflect not only on a play's textual state, but on some of its thematic and theatrical concerns: one minor

---

[8] See the errata lists ('Faultes escaped') in the English translations of Seneca's *Oedipus*, transl. Alexander Neville, London, Thomas Colwell, 1563, 8° (USTC 506179), and *Agamemnon*, transl. John Studley, London, Thomas Colwell, 1566, 8° (USTC 506576). The first 'commercial' drama in England was published in 1584: Robert Wilson's *Three Ladies of London*, Roger Ward, 1584, 4° (USTC 510134), George Peele's *The Arraignment of Paris*, Henry Marsh, 1584, 4° (USTC 510099), and John Lyly's *Sappho and Phao*, [Thomas Dawson] for Thomas Cadman, 1584, 4° (USTC 510068) and *Campaspe*, [Thomas Dawson] for Thomas Cadman, 1584, 4° (USTC 510077).

[9] In my count, I am only considering playbooks from the commercial theatres that specify at least one error. *Philotas* was printed in its fourth edition in Samuel Daniel, *Certain Small Works*, London, I. L. for Simon Waterson, 1611, 12° (USTC 3004748); earlier editions do not include an errata list.

[10] John Day, *The Isle of Gulls*, London, John Trundle, 1606, 4° (USTC 3002388), sig. H4v.

[11] Austin (TX), Harry Ransom Center, PFORZ 269 PFZ, sig. B4v.

[12] See USTC 3002387 and 3002388, as well as W. W. Greg, 'The Two Issues of Day's *Isle of Gulls*, 1606', *The Library*, 4th ser., 3/4, 1923, pp. 307–9.

erratum renders Day's censored play 'correct', while the satiric portrayal of Ben Jonson in *Satiromastix* that defines the play's interest in 'correction' spills over, as Harry Newman has explored, into the errata list.[13]

More playbooks contain paratexts that discuss error and correction but do not provide a specific errata list. It is difficult to quantify patterns and numbers of inclusion because of the variety within this category. Should title-page claims of correction (such as *Locrine*'s 'Newly set foorth, ouerseene and corrected') be counted alongside more extensive discussions of error, as in the address 'To the Reader and Hearer' in Edward Sharpham's *The Fleer* (1607), which discusses the author's absence and excuses the errors in the book that users may correct or neglect?[14] This issue leads to some inconsistencies in resources that provide errata finding aids: under the category of 'errata', the *Database of Early English Playbooks* counts most playbooks that contain errata lists and some (but not all) that include errata commentary; for example, the note about errors escaped in John Ford's *'Tis Pity She's a Whore* is counted, but the similar note in the second edition of John Marston's *Parasitaster* is not.

Overall, errata commentaries tend to cast a wider net than errata lists in suggesting the parameters of error: it not only involves misprints, but also faults in style and dramatic judgement, which can be corrected in the playbook. Indeed, the first paratextual address ever to be attached to a commercial playbook in England — publisher Richard Jones's signed address 'To the Gentlemen Readers' in Marlowe's *Tamburlaine* (1590) — broadly discusses ideas of error as they relate to dramatic judgement. In this unprecedented paratext, Jones claims to have improved Marlowe's play: he has '(purposely) omitted and left out some fond and friulous Iestures, digressing (and in my poore opinion) far vnmeet for the matter, which I thought, might seeme more tedious vnto the wise'.[15] Jones does not adopt a deferential pose towards Marlowe, who is nowhere named in a playbook that was clearly prepared without his involvement. The address emphasises the role of a publication agent in the correction of a play, a process that is presented as much more extensive than attending to ambiguities and inconsistencies in the playscript. Jones's practices and paratextual commentaries are, however, somewhat unrepresentative for commercial playbooks at this time.[16]

In other cases, errata commentaries focus on misprints, rather than ideas of wholesale revision. A common concern that emerges, witnessed also in Jones's paratext, is the representation of a play as a text to be read. In the second edition of Marston's *Parasitaster* (1606), the author (probably Marston) of an unsigned address claims to 'haue perused this coppy to make some satisfaction for the first faulty impression: yet so vrgent hath been my busines, that some errors haue styll passed, which thy discretion may amend'.[17] The reader is presented as an authoriser of the printed play — one who takes on the role of correction — and, as demonstrated earlier through the marginalia added to a copy of *The Isle of Gulls*, readers sometimes used their 'discretion' to improve the specific readings suggested in errata lists. The address in *Parasitaster* goes on to express concern about the play's new existence as a book, pointing out that '[c]omedies are writ to be spoken, not read: Remember the life

---

[13] H. Newman, 'Reading Metatheatre', *Shakespeare Bulletin*, 36/1, 2018, pp. 89–110 (96–7).

[14] Anon. ('W. S.'), *Locrine*, London, Thomas Creede, 1595, 4° (USTC 512975), sig. A2r; Edward Sharpham, *The Fleer*, London, Francis Burton, 1607, 4° (USTC 3003081), sig. A2r–v.

[15] Christopher Marlowe, *Tamburlaine*, London, Richard Jones, 1590, 8° (USTC 511597), sig. A2r.

[16] K. Melnikoff, 'Jones's Pen and Marlowe's Socks: Richard Jones, Print Culture, and the Beginnings of English Dramatic Literature', *Studies in Philology*, 102/2, 2005, pp. 184–209.

[17] John Marston, *Parasitaster*, London, William Cotton, 1606, 4° (USTC 3002367), sig. A2v.

of these things consists in action'.[18] An apology for local errors and misprints is bound up with a concern about the merits of reading plays and the additional errors of judgement that might be levelled at those who oversee a play's transmission into this new medium. As in *Satiromastix*, one of the ways of repurposing the activity of play-watching is by enlisting the reader as an annotator and participant in the printed text.

In most commercial playbooks, however, error is silent. Five errata lists exist for the entire period, while errata commentaries such as those mentioned above appear infrequently. Indeed, it was not until the late Jacobean period that prominent print paratexts such as addresses to the reader, dedications, and commendatory verses became a regular feature of playbooks. None of Shakespeare's single-text playbooks contain dedications or commendatory verses and only two — *Troilus and Cressida* (1609) and *Othello* (1622) — contain an address to readers (both contributed by their publishers). None feature errata lists or discuss error. This silence is only, however, a paratextual one. Most of the stationers involved in the publication of Shakespeare's plays issued errata lists in their non-dramatic texts.[19] And, as the second part of this chapter considers, processes of error and correction were integral to the representation of *all* plays as printed books.

EXPLORING ERROR IN *EDWARD III*

The two early quartos of *Edward III* offer a useful case study: both are silent on the issue of error, but a contrastive analysis of the editions reveals the work of a careful corrector or, to use the term proposed by Sonia Massai, an 'annotating reader' in the preparation of Q2.[20] J. K. Moore's survey of manuscripts and printed texts used in the printing house does not yield any dramatic examples, suggesting that, in order to understand the processes of preparation and proofreading for playbooks, comparisons '*within* and *between* early printed editions' are necessary.[21] In the case of *Edward III*, the variants *between* the two editions indicate that the preparation of Q2 did not involve the consultation of a new manuscript or, it seems, the original manuscript used to set Q1.[22] The two editions do not differ significantly from each other, unlike, for example, the two quarto and folio editions of *Hamlet* (respectively 1603, 1604, and 1623), which clearly involve different manuscript sources. The early editions of *Edward III* are not witness to a complicated textual history and this simplicity

---

[18] Ibid.

[19] The printer of Q1 *Edward III*, Thomas Scarlet, included an errata list in one of his first printed texts — Richard Alison's *Plain Confutation of a Treatise of Brownism*, 1590, London, Thomas Scarlet for William Wright, 4° (USTC 511383) — and in the Inns of Court play *Tancred and Gismund*, 1591, 4° (USTC 511941). See also Jowett, 'Kingdom' (n. 3 above), p. liii.

[20] See Massai's account of annotating readers as 'a previously overlooked category of textual agents' involved in the preparation of copy for publication; see her *Shakespeare and the Rise of the Editor*, Cambridge, 2007, pp. 10–30, esp. p. 10.

[21] S. Massai, 'Scholarly Editing and the Shift from Print to Electronic Cultures', in L. Erne and M. J. Kidnie (eds), *Textual Performances: The Modern Reproduction of Shakespeare's Drama*, Cambridge, 2004, pp. 94–108 (94); J. Moore, *Primary Materials Relating to Copy and Print in English Books of the Sixteenth and Seventeenth Centuries*, Oxford, 1992.

[22] *King Edward III*, ed. G. Melchiori, Cambridge, 1998, p. 175.

facilitates a close examination of the work undertaken in the correction of copy. So-called 'derivative editions' are often overlooked in modern criticism because they are seen as moving further away from the author and the stage — to use a standard critical phrase, they have no independent authority. But an examination of Q2 makes it possible to profile the agent(s) involved and understand, in the absence of extant proof sheets, the process of correction that took place during publication — a type of authorisation extended to professional readers of the play and, as suggested by errata lists, to all readers.

The identity of the corrector remains unknown, although it is clear that the play's dramatists did not oversee either edition. Unlike those associated with prominent continental printing houses, such as those of Aldus Manutius and Christopher Plantin, the correctors of English playbooks are anonymous — perhaps one of the reasons why they are regularly overlooked.[23] Indeed, the editions of *Edward III* are anonymous in several ways: neither of them names a dramatist on its title-page (though the play is now usually attributed in part to Shakespeare), nor do they include playing company origins (which remain unclear); Q1 does not even give the name of its printer, who has been identified as Thomas Scarlet.[24] Only the publisher — Cuthbert Burby — is named on the title-page imprints of both editions, while Simon Stafford is specified as the printer of Q2. Both quartos are silent on some of the most pressing questions of agency — a condition regularly encountered in playbooks. While dramatists could have assisted in the initial provision of a playscript to Scarlet and Burby for Q1, misprints in both editions indicate that they were not involved in proofreading copy. Particularly revealing is the continuation of errors in proper nouns between the editions, which suggests that the printing agents were unfamiliar with these names and aimed to reproduce, as exactly as possible, what appeared in the manuscript. For example, when Edward III is attempting to seduce the Countess of Salisbury, he compares his desire, somewhat ominously, to the story of Hero and Leander, claiming he will — as Q1 prints it — 'throng a hellie spout of bloud | To arryue at Cestus'.[25] The compositor clearly did not recognise the classical name for the Dardanelles — the Hellespont — and the misprint is not corrected during the publication process. This error is maintained in Q2, though the individual who prepared the new edition has attempted, rather unsuccessfully, to make sense of this line by rendering it as 'I will through a helly spoute of blood | To arriue at Cesttus'.[26] The fact that most other obvious misprints are carefully attended to indicates that the plays' dramatists did not act as correctors and that a publication agent — someone at the nexus of Stafford's printing house and Burby's publishing–bookselling business — was responsible for the preparation of the second edition. Attempting to pinpoint agency, John Jowett identifies the printing-house corrector as 'usually the master printer or an experienced employee', while Massai proposes that substantive changes to the fictive world of a play (involving speech prefixes, stage directions, and dialogue) were undertaken by publishers acting as annotating readers.[27] Given the impossibility of clear identification, the term 'corrector' is, as Massai argues, more usefully function-specific than agent-specific.

---

[23] Grafton, *The Culture* (n. 3 above), Chapter 1, as well as the contributions by Geri Della Rocca de Candal, Paolo Sachet, and Dirk Imhof in this Companion.

[24] For authorship claims, see *King Edward III*, ed. R. Proudfoot and N. Bennett, London, 2017, pp. 49–89.

[25] Q1 *Edward III*, sig. D4v.

[26] Q2 *Edward III*, sig. D2v. *Edward III*, ed. Melchiori (n. 22 above), pp. 118–19.

[27] Jowett, 'Kingdom' (n. 3 above), p. lv; Massai, *Shakespeare and the Rise* (n. 20 above), pp. 1–30.

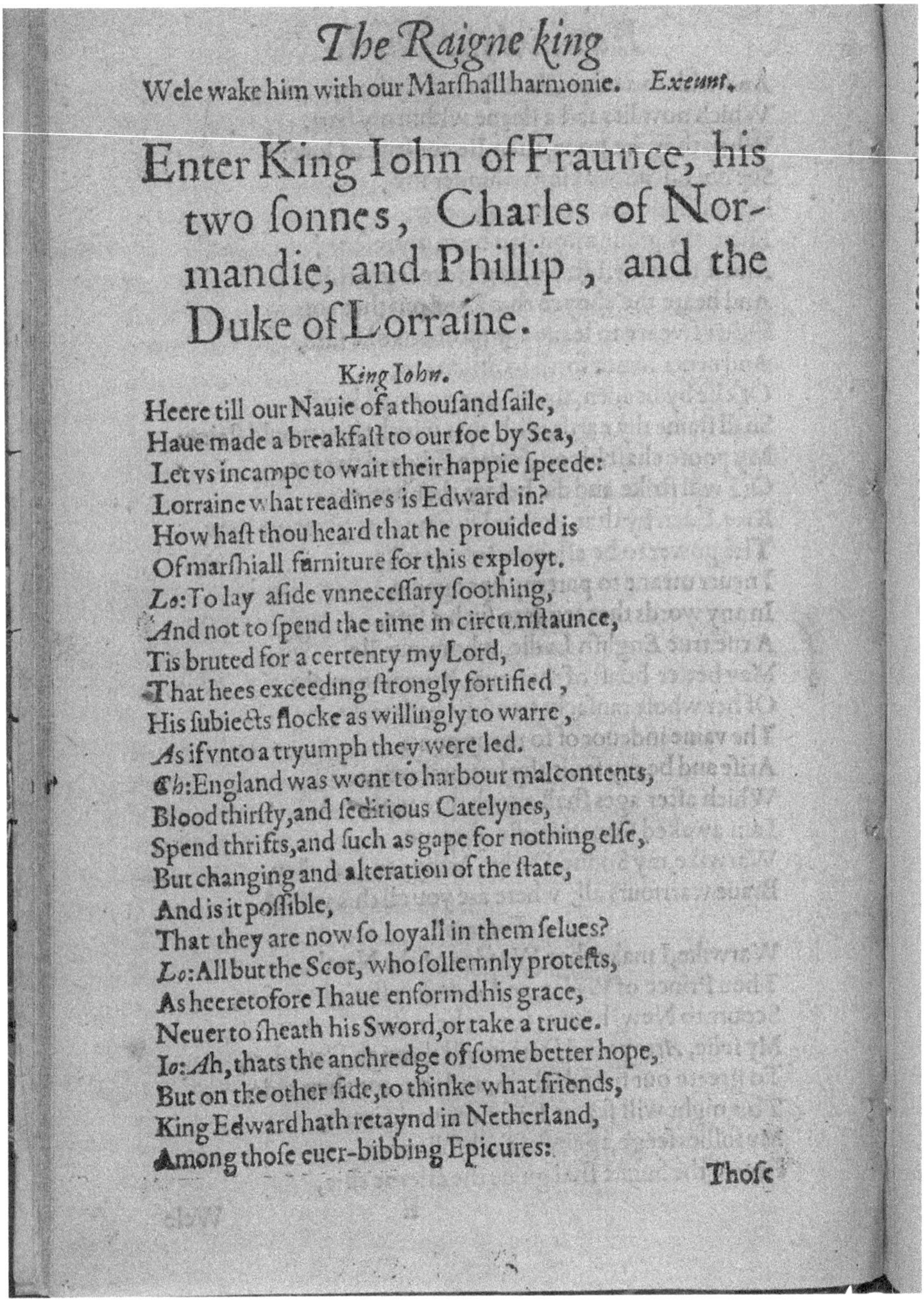

PRINTING AND MISPRINTING

FIG. 21.2. Anon., *The Raigne of King Edward the Third*, London, [Thomas Scarlet] for Cuthbert Burby, 1596, 4° (USTC 513018) = Q1 *Edward III*, sig. E1v. Washington, DC, Folger Shakespeare Library, STC 7501.

The primary concern of this figure was to correct errors arising from the distinctive challenges of the playscript used to set the first edition and to clarify the play for a readerly, rather than theatrical, audience. Aside from preserving a few misprints involving place names and introducing some new errors, the corrector attended carefully to the play. A casting-off miscalculation in Q1 led the compositors to render two stage directions on sigs E1v–E2r in very large type, which is the edition's most visually striking error (Fig. 21.2) and is corrected in Q2. Obvious misprints and word substitutions — similar to those that appear in the few playbook errata lists from the period — are also corrected: 'proffered' for 'poffered' (sigs E3v and F1v); 'wind' for 'wine' (sigs E2r and E4r); 'houres' for 'owers' (sigs E3v and F2r). More significant is the corrector's extensive revisions to punctuation and misplaced, missing, and incorrect speech prefixes. As it seems to have been common practice for dramatists and scribes to write out the lines of speech in the central page and then add in speech prefixes in the left margin, playscripts often witness problems with incorrectly aligned or missing prefixes.[28] The corrector resolves most of these issues: for example, in Q1 a speech prefix for King Edward on sig. C2v is given one line earlier than it should be, which Q2 corrects at sig. C1r, an error that likely originated from confusion in the manuscript about the alignment of dialogue and speech heading. Q2 also standardises and expands abbreviated speech prefixes. One of the distinctive features of the playscript used to set Q1 was unusually short speech prefixes of just one or two letters, which the compositors mostly followed: King Edward is sometimes identified, in Q1, as 'K' or 'Ki' and the Countess of Salisbury as 'Co'. These short prefixes lead in some cases to confusion between different characters, such as the English and French princes — both at times introduced as 'Pr'. An interesting example that draws attention to the range of printing agents acting on a text can be seen with the character Lodowick, Edward's secretary, who is often abbreviated in Q1 as 'Lo'. This designation introduces confusion with the French Duke of Lorraine and, within the same scene in Q1, Lodowick is sometimes given ambiguously as 'Lo', but sometimes incorrectly as 'Lor' (sigs B4v–C2v). Giorgio Melchiori has shown convincingly that all of the incorrect prefixes appear on the same formes and proposes that the two compositors thought to have set Q1 alternated formes; one of them attempted to expand the manuscript's characteristically short prefixes, but did so incorrectly.[29] Q2 fixes the error and expands the prefixes. Indeed, the editorial attention typically demanded by speech headings highlights their new permanence in printed playbooks: on stage, prefixes are theatrical paratexts, never spoken and somewhat outside of the play itself; but within a playbook, they acquire new importance and are one of the key features to be edited for readers.

Changes appear in Q2 that are not obvious corrections of misprints or confusion in Q1, which suggests a desire to improve the text for readers. Most notably, the positions of stage directions are moved to make more sense for the play-reading experience. During its representation of the siege of Calais (part of the Hundred Years' War), Q1 contains the following direction at sig. I3v: 'Enter six Citizens in their Shirts, barefoote, with halters about their necks. Enter King Edward, Queene Phillip, Derby, soldiers'. The first lines of dialogue are given to Edward III, who enters in the middle of a conversation with his queen, before the attention of the English party is directed towards the citizens of Calais. The stage direction suggests that two separate groups of characters enter the stage at the same time, but

---

[28] A. Lidster and S. Massai, 'Textual Introduction', *Edward III*, Internet Shakespeare Editions, https://internetshakespeare.uvic.ca/doc/Edw_TextIntro/index.html, paragraph 13, accessed 1 Febraury 2022.

[29] *Edward III*, ed. Melchiori (n. 22 above), pp. 172–3.

424 PRINTING AND MISPRINTING

do not interact immediately. Q1's presentation probably reflects how the play was staged in the theatre and could have involved the use of the upper stage.[30] For readers, however, it is less suitable because the citizens are introduced and then ignored. Q2 rearranges the lines: the scene begins with the entry for the English party, while the direction for the citizens of Calais appears immediately before their first line (sig. I1r; Fig. 21.3).

Although the variants in Q2 do not amount to substantial revision and are mostly word substitutions — e.g., Q2's 'foolish part' (sig. A3r) for Q1's 'childish part' (sig. A4r) — some could advance a specific reading or interpretative agenda. Q2 alters many pronouns and articles, some of which have the effect of reinforcing England's successional claim to France during the Hundred Years' War. When Edward the Black Prince spurns the advice from King John of France to surrender at the battle of Poitiers, his instruction to the French herald in Q1 (sigs H2v–H3r) to 'returne and tell the king | My tongue is made of steele' is changed to 'thy king' in Q2, at sig. G4r. The meaning is clear in Q1, but the variant in Q2 underscores Prince Edward's dismissal of King John, who is not his king or *the* king, but only the king of this misguided herald. When Edward complains in Q1 that the people of Calais 'will not ope their gates and let vs in' (sig. G3r), it appears in Q2 as 'the gates' (sig. F4v) — a variant which tempers the suggestion that the town and its defences belong to the people and complements the sections of the play where even the French characters admit the correctness of Edward's claim, as recounted in Q2, sigs E2r–E3r. Similarly, when Queen Phillipa of England recommends mercy for the people of Calais after they surrender, she advises Edward in Q1: 'As thou intendest to be king of Fraunce, | So let her people liue to call thee king' (sig. I4r). A different pronoun appears in Q2 (sig. I1v) — Edward should 'let thy people liue to call thee king'. The people of France therefore already belong to Edward, and his victory is cast in a providential, predetermined light. Similar substitutions of pronouns and articles occur throughout the text in relation to monarchical ownership of territories and people, and tend to favour England's claim, which could indicate the political sympathies and reading of the corrector. An interest in the play's martial events is also suggested by the substitution in Q2 (sig. F4r) of 'Private soliders' for Q1's 'Common soliders' at sig. G2v. This description is part of Prince Edward's account of those who lost their lives in battle and could, in the war-wearied context of its 1599 publication, be designed to remove a contemptuous or depreciatory application — that is, that soldiers are disposable and of little value.[31]

The variants in *Edward III*, however, draw attention to a blurred interplay of 'erratics', misprints, and emendation.[32] It is sometimes difficult to tell if a specific variant in Q2 represents a correction of a supposed misprint, the deliberate emendation of the text to offer an improved reading, or an unintentional variant that could either represent a new error, or simply reflect the erratics of plays and publication in terms of spelling, punctuation, speech prefixes, and so on. Instances of pronoun and article substitution might not be the work of a corrector, but instead represent new errors introduced by the compositor(s) — the/their is a common misprint. Q2's description of the Scottish nobles' discourse as 'rabble, blunt and full of pride' (sig. A4v) differs from Q1's 'babble' (sig. B1v) — which is the reading preferred by modern editions. As 'rabble' can carry the same meaning as 'babble' (that is, foolish, disorderly speech), but with an additional derogatory application to an unruly, threatening

---

[30] *Edward III*, ed. Proudfoot and Bennett (n. 24 above), p. 335.
[31] See *OED*: 'common, *adj.* and *adv.*', (see meanings A12 and A14).
[32] See also Jowett, 'Kingdom' (n. 3 above), pp. xlix, lviii.

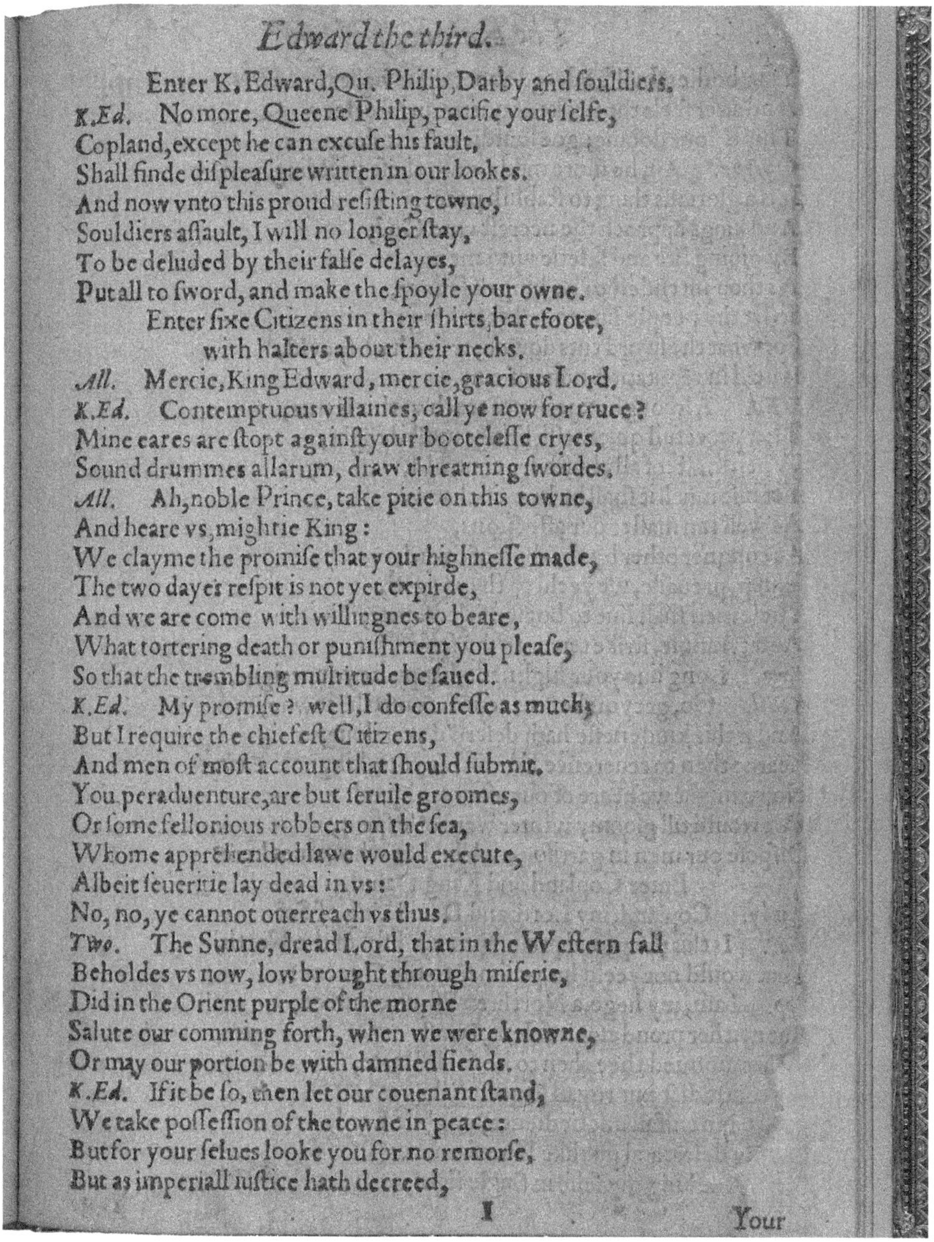

21: MAKING SENSE OF ERROR IN COMMERCIAL DRAMA 425

Edward the third.

Enter K. Edward, Qu. Philip, Darby and fouldiers.
K.Ed. No more, Queene Philip, pacifie your felfe,
Copland, except he can excufe his fault,
Shall finde difpleafure written in our lookes.
And now vnto this proud refifting towne,
Souldiers affault, I will no longer ftay,
To be deluded by their falfe delayes,
Put all to fword, and make the fpoyle your owne.
    Enter fixe Citizens in their fhirts barefoote,
        with halters about their necks.
All. Mercie, King Edward, mercie, gracious Lord.
K.Ed. Contemptuous villaines, call ye now for truce?
Mine eares are ftopt againft your bootelefle cryes,
Sound drummes allarum, draw threatning fwordes.
All. Ah, noble Prince, take pitie on this towne,
And heare vs, mightie King:
We clayme the promife that your highnefle made,
The two dayes refpit is not yet expirde,
And we are come with willingnes to beare,
What tortering death or punifhment you pleafe,
So that the trembling multitude be faued.
K.Ed. My promife? well, I do confefle as muck,
But I require the chiefeft Citizens,
And men of moft account that fhould fubmit,
You peraduenture, are but feruile groomes,
Or fome fellonious robbers on the fea,
Whome apprehended lawe would execute,
Albeit feueritie lay dead in vs:
No, no, ye cannot ouerreach vs thus.
Two. The Sunne, dread Lord, that in the Weftern fall
Beholdes vs now, low brought through miferie,
Did in the Orient purple of the morne
Salute our comming forth, when we were knowne,
Or may our portion be with damned fiends.
K.Ed. If it be fo, then let our couenant ftand,
We take poffeffion of the towne in peace:
But for your felues looke you for no remorfe,
But as imperiall iuftice hath decreed,
                I   Your

FIG. 21.3. Anon., *The Raigne of King Edward the Third*, London, Simon Stafford for Cuthbert Burby, 1599, 4° (USTC 513866) = Q2 *Edward III*, sig. I1r. Washington, DC, Folger Shakespeare Library, STC 7502.

crowd, the variant in Q2 could be deliberate — to expand the resonances of the original word in a way that further condemns the Scottish attack — or unintentional, a misprint on the part of the Q2 compositor.[33] The fact that the work of the corrector reveals careful

---

[33] See *OED*: 'rabble, *n.1* and *adj.*', (see meanings A1 and A5).

revisions of punctuation, speech prefixes, and clearly incorrect pronouns (e.g., Q2's 'your ayde' at sig. F4r for Q1's 'our aide' at sig. G2v) suggests that some of the ambiguous variants could be deliberate changes. In contrast to errata lists which advertise specificity and the possibility of definitive correction, error is a typically silent condition of playbooks that often eschews clarity. Error is not always a 'self-identifying dysfunctionality'; it is in the eye of the beholder.[34] As suggested by some errata commentaries, it is also widely grounded, incorporating misprints, inconsistencies, and textual confusion, as well as perceived faults in style, phrasing, and content. At one extreme, Jones's edition of *Tamburlaine* claims to have substantially revised the play's theatrical text, but this approach was exceptional rather than representative. The conservative local changes witnessed in Q2 *Edward III* that aim to clarify the text for readers are perhaps more useful for understanding the process of preparing commercial drama for publication.

Conclusions

An erratum in Samuel Daniel's *Delia and Rosamond* (1594) seems to offer a metatextual comment — 'lyne 3. for error, reade terror' — but error is everywhere a part of printed texts.[35] My emphasis on English playbooks highlights the distinctive challenges posed by playscripts from the commercial theatres (including problems related to speech prefixes, stage directions, and the fragmented texts that arrive and are reassembled in the printing house), and the strategies for approaching these issues and re-presenting a play for readers. Most playbooks do not, however, announce the defining processes of error and correction that they silently witness. While critics regularly study multiple editions of a play as they relate to different stages in its theatrical life, the study of 'derivative' editions that primarily reveal the work of publication agents is much less widespread, but should prompt a shift in focus that is also crucial for non-dramatic texts. Rather than, to use Fredson Bowers's outdated phrase, stripping the veil of print to access underlying 'authorial' versions, it is vital to consider the *books* themselves (and especially derivative editions) because they reveal the life of texts in print and the readings of those who oversaw their publication. As this chapter has argued, the publication of plays — and, indeed, of all texts — is a process conditioned by error. Printing introduces error and sometimes underlines its visibility by announcing misprints or acknowledging a process of revision and improvement, especially through errata lists and errata commentary. But it is also vital to pay attention to silent error and silent correction, including the porous conceptual boundary between them. A close evaluation of a text's different editions clarifies how it changes and helps us to consider how individuals connected to publication have evaluated its error — the extent to which the text has 'wandered' from its course and could be improved or re-presented through correction. For editions that lack paratextual materials that comment directly on the text, silent error and correction can reveal readings of it — both in relation to its content and perceived value as a book. The printing process invites a range of individuals — authors, publication agents, and readers — to become collaborators in the book and to leave their marks in and on it.

---

[34] Jowett, 'Kingdom' (n. 3 above), p. l.

[35] Samuel Daniel, *Delia and Rosamond*, London, Simon Waterson, 1594, 16° (USTC 512533), sig. A2v.

BIBLIOGRAPHY

··

PRIMARY SOURCES

Alison, Richard, *Plain Confutation of a Treatise of Brownism*, London, Thomas Scarlet for William Wright, 1590, 4° (USTC 511383).

Anon., *The Raigne of King Edward the Third*, London, [Thomas Scarlet] for Cuthbert Burby, 1596, 4° (USTC 513018) = Q1 *Edward III*.

Anon., *The Raigne of King Edward the Third*, London, Simon Stafford for Cuthbert Burby, 1599, 4° (USTC 513866) = Q2 *Edward III*.

Anon. ('W. S.'), *Locrine*, London, Thomas Creede, 1595, 4° (USTC 512975).

Daniel, Samuel, *Certain Small Works*, London, I. L. for Simon Waterson, 1611, 12° (USTC 3004748).

Daniel, Samuel, *Delia and Rosamond Augmented; Cleopatra*, London, Simon Waterson, 1594, 16° (USTC 512533).

Day, John, *The Isle of Gulls*, London, John Trundle, 1606, 4° (USTC 3002387 and 3002388).

Dekker, Thomas, *Satiro-mastix*, London, Edward White, 1602, 4° (USTC 3000771).

Lyly, John, *Campaspe*, London, [Thomas Dawson] for Thomas Cadman, 1584, 4° (USTC 510077).

Lyly, John, *Sappho and Phao*, London, [Thomas Dawson] for Thomas Cadman, 1584, 4° (USTC 510068).

Marlowe, Christopher, *Tamburlaine*, London, Richard Jones, 1590 8° (USTC 511597).

Marston, John, *Parasitaster*, London, William Cotton, 1606, 4° (USTC 3002367).

Nabbes, Thomas, *Hannibal and Scipio*, London, Richard Oulton for Charles Greene, 1637, 4° (USTC 3019430).

Peele, George, *The Arraignment of Paris*, London, Henry Marsh, 1584, 4° (USTC 510099).

Seneca, *Agamemnon*, transl. John Studley, London, Thomas Colwell, 1566, 8° (USTC 506576).

Seneca, *Oedipus*, transl. Alexander Neville, London, Thomas Colwell, 1563, 8° (USTC 506179).

Shakespeare, William, *Hamlet*, London, [Valentine Summes] for N. L. [Nicholas Ling] and John Trundell, 1603, 4° (USTC 3001209).

Shakespeare, William, *Hamlet*, London, I. R. [James Roberts] for N. L. [Nicholas Ling], 1604, 4° (USTC 3001644).

Shakespeare, William, *Hamlet* in *Comedies, Histories, & Tragedies*, London, Isaac [and William] Jaggard for Edward Blount, John Smethwick, [Isaac] Jaggard, and William Aspley, 1623, 2° (USTC 3010710).

Sharpham, Edward, *The Fleer*, London, Francis Burton, 1607, 4° (USTC 3003081).

Shirley, James, *The Bird in a Cage*, London, Bernard Alsop and Thomas Fawcet for William Cooke, 1633, 4° (USTC 3016864).

Wilmot, Robert ('R. W.') [and others], *Tancred and Gismund*, London, Thomas Scarlet and sold by Robert Robinson, 1591, 4° (USTC 511941).

Wilson, Robert, *Three Ladies of London*, London, Roger Ward, 1584, 4° (USTC 510134).

SECONDARY LITERATURE

··

Farmer, A., and Lesser, Z., (eds), *DEEP: Database of Early English Playbooks*, created in 2007, http://deep.sas.upenn.edu.

Genette, G., 'Introduction to the Paratext', transl. M. Maclean, *New Literary History*, 22, 1991, pp. 261–72.

Grafton, A., *The Culture of Correction in Renaissance Europe*, London, 2011.

Greg, W. W., 'The Two Issues of Day's *Isle of Gulls*, 1606', *The Library*, 4th ser., 3/4, 1923, pp. 307–9.

Jowett, J., 'Shakespeare and the Kingdom of Error', in *The New Oxford Shakespeare: Critical Reference Edition*, ed. G. Taylor et al., II.1, Oxford, 2017, pp. xlix–lxiii.

King Edward III, ed. G. Melchiori, Cambridge, 1998.

King Edward III, ed. R. Proudfoot and N. Bennett, London, 2017.

Lidster, A., and, Massai, S., 'Textual Introduction', *Edward III*, Internet Shakespeare Editions, https://internetshakespeare.uvic.ca/doc/Edw_TextIntro/index.html.

Massai, S., 'Scholarly Editing and the Shift from Print to Electronic Cultures', in L. Erne and M. J. Kidnie (eds), *Textual Performances: The Modern Reproduction of Shakespeare's Drama*, Cambridge, 2004, pp. 94–108.

Massai, S., *Shakespeare and the Rise of the Editor*, Cambridge, 2007.

Melnikoff, K., 'Jones's Pen and Marlowe's Socks: Richard Jones, Print Culture, and the Beginnings of English Dramatic Literature', *Studies in Philology*, 102/2, 2005, pp. 184–209.

Moore, J., *Primary Materials Relating to Copy and Print in English Books of the Sixteenth and Seventeenth Centuries*, Oxford, 1992.

Newman, H., 'Reading Metatheatre', *Shakespeare Bulletin*, 36/1, 2018, pp. 89–110.

OED Online, Oxford, www.oed.com.

Peters, J. S., *Theatre of the Book, 1480–1880: Print, Text and Performance in Europe*, Oxford, 2000.

Smyth, A., *Material Texts in Early Modern England*, Cambridge, 2018.

Stern, T., *Documents of Performance in Early Modern England*, Cambridge, 2009.

PART VI

WIDESPREAD AND EPHEMERAL CIRCULATION

CHAPTER 22

DRAWN CORRECTIONS AND PICTORIAL INSTABILITY IN DEVOTIONAL BOOKS FROM THE WORKSHOP OF GERARD LEEU

ANNA DLABAČOVÁ

INTRODUCTION

IMAGES in early printed books are generally seen as holding a somewhat flexible relationship to the texts they accompany; therefore, possible practices of correcting images have hitherto received little to no attention.* To have woodcuts made was a substantial investment: once a printer was in the possession of a series of woodblocks, he would exploit them in a variety of texts, so that the same woodblocks would end up serving multiple purposes in numerous editions and even sometimes in several printing shops. There were, however, instances in which text and image were so closely connected that the printer felt he needed to preserve this association. One such case comes from the workshop of Gerard Leeu (d. 1492). On 16 February 1488 he published the edition of a Middle Dutch text under the title *Van die gheestlike kintscheÿt Ihesu ghemoraliseert* (On Jesus's Spiritual Childhood Moralised),[1] which serves as a case study for the present chapter. The edition shows that drawn corrections made to secure a correct text–image relation occurred in devotional works too, and not only — as one might expect — in scientific or technical manuals. Moreover, the case

---

* This chapter was written as part of the project 'Leaving a Lasting Impression. The Impact of Incunabula on Spirituality in the Low Countries' (Veni, 2018–2022, grant number 275-30-036) funded by NWO (Dutch Research Council).

[1] *Van die gheestlike Kintscheÿt ihesu ghemoraliseert*, Antwerp, Gerard Leeu, 16 Feb. 1488, 8° (ISTC ik00022000).

Anna Dlabačová, *Drawn corrections and pictorial instability in devotional books from the workshop of gerard leeu.* In: *Printing and Misprinting.* Edited by Geri Della Rocca de Candal, Anthony Grafton, and Paolo Sachet, Oxford University Press. © Anna Dlabačová (2023). DOI: 10.1093/oso/9780198863045.003.0023

PRINTING AND MISPRINTING

study points to an important phenomenon that should be taken into account when studying woodcuts in incunabula editions: pictorial instability.

GERARD LEEU

Gerard Leeu was one of the most productive and prolific printers of the fifteenth-century Low Countries, and yet he is neither widely known nor considered a national figure.[2] He started his business in 1477 in the town of Gouda with the publication of a Dutch translation of the *Epistolae et Evangelia* as well as religious texts in the Dutch vernacular; Leeu's mother tongue, in fact, would remain an important part of his publisher's list throughout his career.[3] In 1484, Leeu decided to move his business to Antwerp, where he became the first printer to join the artist's guild of St Luke.[4] In 1489 we find him visiting his hometown of Gouda and meeting Erasmus, who joined him for a walk from the monastery of Steyn — just outside the city — to the IJssel river. Erasmus reported this encounter to Jacob Canter, a young humanist who had just returned from Italy and who worked for Leeu as an editor. Erasmus believed that Canter and he were kindred spirits and was particularly interested in establishing contact with the young humanist. Erasmus uses flattering words to address Canter, such as 'excellent scholar' or 'most learned sir'. Then he writes:

> it was in the first place a printer named Gerard Leeuw, a very clever fellow, who told me your whole story. For as he was departing from us [the convent of Steyn where Erasmus was still a regular canon at this time] I escorted him to the bank of the IJssel which he had to cross, and it was then that he told me a great deal about you, while I listened eagerly.[5]

In December 1492, Leeu's life ended prematurely. One of his workmen, Henric van Symmen, a punchcutter ('lettersteker') from Holland, threatened to walk out and to set up his own independent shop in order 'to make more money' ('om meerder winningen te doen'). Leeu was not amused and tried to stop Henric, first with words, but the argument would quickly escalate into a physical fight during which Henric gave Gerard 'a slight stab' ('een cleyn

---

[2] On Gerard Leeu, see: K. Goudriaan, 'Een drukker en zijn markt. Gheraert Leeu (Gouda 1477— Antwerpen 1492/1493)', *Madoc. Tijdschrift over de Middeleeuwen*, 6, 1992, pp. 194–205; L. Hellinga-Querido, 'De betekenis van Gheraert Leeu', in K. Goudriaan et al. (eds), *Een drukker zoekt publiek. Gheraert Leeu te Gouda*, Delft, 1993, pp. 12–30; L. Hellinga, 'Gheraert Leeu, Claes Leeu, Jacob Bellaert, Peter van Os van Breda', in *De vijfhonderdste verjaring van de boekdrukkunst in de Nederlanden*, Brussels, 1973, pp. 283–308; J.-W. Klein, 'The Leeu[w] van Gouda: new facts, new possibilities', *Quaerendo*, 33, 2003, pp. 175–90.

[3] *Epistolae et Evangelia* [Dutch], [Gouda, Gerard Leeu], 24 May 1477, f° (ISTC ie00064700).

[4] See J. van der Stock, 'De Antwerpse Sint-Lucasgilde en de drukkers-uitgevers: "middeleeuws" achterhoedegevecht of paradigma van cultureel-politieke machtsverschuivingen?', in J. M. M. Hermans and K. van der Hoek (eds), *Boeken in de late middeleeuwen. Verslag van de Groningse Codicologendagen 1992*, Groningen, 1994, pp. 155–65.

[5] Desiderius Erasmus, *The Correspondence of Erasmus: Letters 1 to 141, 1484 to 1500*, transl. R. A. B. Mynors and D. F. S. Thomson and annotated by W. K. Ferguson, Toronto and Buffalo (NY), 1974, letter 32, p. 61, ll. 36–9. Cf. Hellinga, 'Gheraert Leeu' (n. 2 above), p. 288.

22: DRAWN CORRECTIONS AND PICTORIAL INSTABILITY IN DEVOTIONAL BOOKS   433

steecxken') in the head. The stab turned out to be a lethal wound: Leeu passed away two or three days later.[6]

During his life, Leeu did not produce only texts: from 1480 onward, the printer started to enrich his books by adding images to his publications through the use of woodcuts. According to Ina Kok, his more than 220 editions contain impressions of no less than 936 original woodcuts, making him by far the top producer of woodcuts in the Low Countries.[7] With this vast amount of pictorial material inserted into his books, it does not come as a surprise that sometimes things did not go entirely as planned and corrections became necessary.

On Jesus's Spiritual Childhood Moralised (Antwerp, 1488)

The printing of this book was finished on 16 February 1488 in Leeu's Antwerp printing office, situated next to Our Lady's Pand, the city's art market. The book was printed in octavo; plus, a series of thirty-eight woodcuts were made specifically for this text.[8] As with most Netherlandish woodcuts, these 'rather small woodcuts' were religious in nature, designed and cut by the so-called 'Haarlem woodcutter', with whom Leeu had already worked on several occasions. The style was identical to the larger cuts made for the *Hoofkijn van devotion* (Garden of Devotion), which Leeu had published only a few months earlier, in November 1487.[9]

In order to understand and fully appreciate the close relationship between text and image in this edition of *Jesus's Spiritual Childhood*, we need to briefly scrutinise the structure, design, and content of the book, which consists of three sections preceded by an elaborated table of contents presenting the sections briefly ('summatim').[10] In the first section the reader, imagined as the devout, loving Soul, is encouraged to nurture and bring up the Christ Child by way of twenty ladies or virgins acting in pairs. These personifications of virtues wash and dry the Christ Child's swaddling clothes, in addition to guarding, bathing, entertaining, feeding, and putting him to sleep. Every chapter closes with a prayer to the Child. The woodcuts in this first section, placed before the start of each chapter, portray the interactions — to be emulated by the reader — between the Christ Child and successively Contritio and Confessio, Puritas and Caritas, Tranquillitas and Cumulatio, and so forth. Each prayer is also preceded by an image of a lady (the Soul) praying to the Child, who

---

[6] Hellinga, 'Gheraert Leeu' (n. 2 above), p. 308, no. 139.

[7] I. Kok, *Woodcuts in Incunabula Printed in the Low Countries*, I, Houten, [2013], pp. xxi–xxii.

[8] Ibid., pp. 247–51, nos 89.1–37. As we will see below, one woodcut is missing in Kok's inventory, making the total number of woodcuts in the series thirty-eight.

[9] Petrus de Alliaco, *Le Jardin amoureux* [Dutch] *Thoofkijn van devotien*, Antwerp, Gerard Leeu, 28 Nov. 1487, 4° (ISTC ia00478250). Kok, *Woodcuts* (n. 7 above), pp. 244–5, nos 87.1–12. W. M. Conway, *The Woodcutters of the Netherlands in the Fifteenth Century: In Three Parts*, I, Cambridge, 1884, pp. 77–9.

[10] The most elaborate study of this edition to date is F. van Buuren, 'Van die gheestelike kintsheyt Jhesu ghemoraliseeret. Een verkenning', in K. Goudriaan et al. (eds), *Een drukker zoekt publiek. Gheraert Leeu te Gouda 1477–1484*, Delft, 1993, pp. 111–32.

appears to her in a crown of thorns. Once the Christ Child has grown up, and after a short conversation with the Soul, he flees from the Soul to his heavens.

The central section, in which the Soul pursues Christ, consists of a love dialogue set in verse between the Soul and the Christ Child, who eventually guides the Soul towards mystical union.[11] The Soul is again portrayed as a lady, often with her senses and faculties represented as hounds; the Christ Child is depicted on top of a stag or deer. In this section the woodcuts function as vignettes: while showing part of the action — as happens for example when one of the Soul's hounds hunts Jesus down and the Soul finally pierces her dear Christ — they mainly signal the shift of voice in the dialogue. This explains their frequent repetition as well as the fact that up to four nearly identical woodblocks were made to ensure there would be enough material to repeat an image in a single gathering.[12] Such endeavour points towards a careful planning of the gatherings and placement of the woodcuts: printer and woodcutter must have worked closely together to ensure that the right number of woodblocks with the correct image would be available for the compositors.

In the last section, the Soul wants to ensure that her chase will not be in vain and, with the help of seven maidens, she nails Christ to the Tree of Life. A relatively rare tradition of images of the 'virtue crucifixion' — an allegory of Christ's sacrifice — started around the middle of the thirteenth century in the Rhineland.[13] Yet, although the woodcut designer did draw inspiration from this tradition, these woodcut images deviate from earlier examples in many aspects; most notably, they form a narrative series in which the action of each virtue is shown separately. Here again, the needs of the book had a profound impact on the production of images.

Due to their accurate design and placement, the images played an important role in the reader's experience. It seems that the woodcut designer, who had the text at his disposal, was asked to follow it closely in his compositions: in this sense, he truly seems to 'penetrate into the spirit of the book', as Conway wrote about the *Hoofkijn* woodcuts.[14] With regard to the design and layout of the book, it is also interesting to note that while the second, dialogic section is the only part of the text that was transmitted in manuscript, the manuscripts were not illustrated.[15] Thus, the edition transformed the text not only through compilation, but also through the addition of a pictorial programme that was invented and designed by both the printer and the woodcutter working for him.[16] Leeu ensured this transformation would be flawless by taking measures to maintain the close rapport between text and image whenever it was at risk.

---

[11] For the text in this section see G. Roth and V. Honemann, 'Die "Geistliche Minnejagd". Ein niederdeutsche geistliche Minneallegorie', in V. Bok et al. (eds), Magister et amicus. *Festschrift für Kurt Gärtner zum 65. Geburtstag*, Vienna, 2003, pp. 175–239 (188–9).

[12] Four nearly identical woodcuts were made of the Soul blowing a horn with a hound on a leash: Kok, *Woodcuts* (n. 7 above), p. 249 (nos 89.19–22).

[13] H. Kraft, *Die Bildallegorie der Kreuzigung Christi durch die Tugenden*, Frankfurt, 1976. See also P. Parshall, 'The Art of Memory and the Passion', *The Art Bulletin*, 81, 1999, pp. 456–72 (462–3), and B. Newman, *God and the Goddesses: Vision, Poetry, and Belief in the Middle Ages*, Philadelphia, 2003, pp. 159–65.

[14] Conway, *The Woodcutters*, I (n. 9 above), p. 78.

[15] In one manuscript, the dialogue starts with a historiated initial: MS Darmstadt, Universitäts- und Landesbibliothek (ULB), Hs 2667, fol. 217r.

[16] On Leeu's transformation of the design of the *Dialogus creaturarum*, see Hellinga, 'De betekenis' (n. 2 above), p. 23.

A New Fifteenth-Century Netherlandish Woodcut

According to the sixth chapter of the final section of *Jesus' Spiritual Childhood Moralised*, Love (Amor), dressed in red, thrusts a lance into the Christ Child's side. In 1884 Conway catalogued a woodcut of '*Amor*, clothed in red, piercing the Child's Side' on the basis of the copy held at the Royal Library in The Hague (Fig. 22.1).[17] In her 2013 comprehensive inventory of woodcuts in incunabula printed in the Low Countries, Kok indicated that this entry ought 'to be deleted'.[18] This is due to the fact that the image of Amor in the The Hague copy is in fact an impression of the woodcut of 'The Soul kneeling before the Christ Child nailed to the Tree of the Cross'.[19] This woodcut was not meant to accompany the chapter on Amor; rather, the image was designed to precede a prayer at the end of the third section, after the crucifixion of the Christ Child by way of the virtues was completed (Fig. 22.2). Thus, the same woodblock was used twice — once on sig. n1*v* and a second time on sig. o1*v*. This would not be significant at all, had it not been for the lance and banderol that were drawn onto the first of these impressions: these details are in fact manuscript corrections, in this case not attempting to emend a text, but an image.

In the chapter about Amor, the woodcut of 'The Soul kneeling before the Christ Child crucified in the Tree' was transformed into an image of 'Amor piercing the Child's side': a lance, drawn with brown ink, was placed in the hands of the Soul, pointing ominously at the Child's right side, and a banderol with the word '*Amor*' was drawn to the right of her face in the style of the other woodcuts in the series. While in the The Hague copy the lower part of the lance is almost entirely concealed by the red colour added to the dress, in other copies, such as the one held at the British Library, we can still see that the lance had a much longer haft and was elegantly positioned in the Soul's — now Amor's — hands (Fig. 22.3). As the colouring in the copy held at The Hague was applied on top of the ink drawing (which is also the case of other copies where colouring was added to the woodcuts), the correction of the image must have taken place at an earlier stage. In some copies the colouring even enhances the details added by hand. This happens, for instance, in exemplars where blood is dripping from the lance, indicating that Amor has already wounded the Saviour.[20] Even though the various copies show some conventional similarities (e.g. Amor's dress is red), the colouring of the woodcuts is different for each copy and was therefore likely added at the discretion of individual buyers.[21]

The hand-drawn emendations, however, were supplemented before the books left Leeu's workshop. The meaning of the image was altered in the same way in all extant copies that

---

[17] Conway, *The Woodcutters*, II (n. 9 above), p. 252, no. 12.6:35. The Hague, Koninklijke Bibliotheek (KB), 150 F 10, sig. n1*v*.

[18] Kok, *Woodcuts* (n. 7 above), p. 250, no. 227.

[19] Ibid., p. 248, no. 89.37.

[20] Haarlem, Stadsbibliotheek (SB), 56 D 10, sig. n1*v*, and Utrecht, Museum Catharijne Convent (MCC), I 14.304, sig. n1*v*.

[21] It is unclear whether Leeu had woodcuts coloured in his workshop. Cf. Van der Stock, 'De Antwerpse Sint-Lucasgilde' (n. 4 above), who suggests that Leeu joined the guild because he used painters' materials in his workshop.

FIG. 22.1. Woodcut of 'The Soul kneeling before the Christ Child nailed to the Tree of the Cross' converted into 'Amor piercing the Child's Side' through details added by hand in this copy of *Van die gheestlike Kintscheÿt ihesu ghemoraliseert*, Antwerp, Gerard Leeu, 16 Feb. 1488, 8° (ISTC ik00022000), sig. n1v. The drawn emendations are partly concealed by the red paint. The Hague, Koninklijke Bibliotheek, 150 F 10.

22: DRAWN CORRECTIONS AND PICTORIAL INSTABILITY IN DEVOTIONAL BOOKS 437

FIG. 22.2. Woodcut of 'The Soul kneeling before the Christ Child nailed to the Tree of the Cross' at the start of the final prayer of the Soul to the Child in *Van die gheestlike Kintscheÿt ihesu ghemoraliseert* (see Fig. 22.1), sig. o1v. The Hague, Koninklijke Bibliotheek, 150 F 10.

FIG. 22.3. Woodcut of 'The Soul kneeling before the Christ Child nailed to the Tree of the Cross' converted into 'Amor piercing the Child's Side' in a copy of *Van die gheestlike Kintscheÿt ihesu ghemoraliseert* (see Fig. 22.1), sig. n1v. The details added by hand are fully visible. Washington, DC, Library of Congress, Incun. 1488 .V3.

FIG. 22.4. Woodcut of 'Amor piercing the Christ Child's side' in a copy of *Van die gheestlike Kintscheÿt ihesu ghemoraliseert* (see Fig. 22.1), sig. n1v. Gouda, Streekarchief Midden-Holland, 2306 G 5.

still retain the relevant leaf — with the exception of one copy to which I will return shortly — in order to safeguard the close connection between text and image.[22] The drawings added

[22] According to ISTC, a total of fifteen copies survive. The manuscript corrections can be found in the following eleven copies: London, British Library (BL), IA 49776; Cambridge, University Library,

PRINTING AND MISPRINTING

to the impressions can be classified as corrections because they are meant to suggest that the reader is looking at another woodcut, the *correct* one. While the vast majority of extant copies, ten in total, contain the emendated image, the correct woodcut can be found in a single copy only (Fig. 22.3).[23] The copy once belonged to the Gouda city library and is currently still kept in Leeu's birthplace. It contains the only extant impression of the woodblock of 'Amor piercing the Christ Child's side' that was originally designed and cut as part of the series for the edition of *On Jesus' Spiritual Childhood Moralised*. The woodcut described in Conway's 1884 inventory can therefore be reinstated, even though the image was slightly different from the amended woodcut Conway had seen and described: Amor stands (rather than kneels) next to the tree and, with her hands at a distance, grips the lance, preparing to pierce the Christ Child's torso (Fig. 22.4).[24] Her position resembles the one adopted by Amor in a thirteenth-century manuscript painting.[25]

POSSIBLE SCENARIOS

If Leeu did possess a woodblock to place at the start of the chapter about Amor's wounding of Christ, why is there only one extant copy containing an impression of the correct woodblock? What happened in Leeu's printing office, and what — if anything — can this incident tell us about the printing of richly illustrated books in the fifteenth century, and about research methods with regards to woodcuts in incunabula? Although it is impossible to point to a conclusive explanation, three scenarios should be considered.

A possible explanation for the exclusive appearance of the Amor woodcut in one copy is that the woodblock broke or was heavily damaged early on during the printing process.[26] This seems unlikely, however, since it was brand new and the one available impression does not show any signs of premature damage or breakage (Fig. 22.4). Moreover, the rest of the forme, including text, remained intact, which would not be the case if, for example, something heavy had fallen onto it and damaged the woodblock beyond repair. The correct

---

Inc.7.F.6.2[3368]; Brussels, Royal Library of Belgium, INC A 1.415; Antwerp, Museum Plantin-Moretus, R 48.2; Paris, Bibliothèque nationale de France (BnF), D-35928 and D-26417 [2]; Haarlem, SB, 56 D 10 and 56 D 6 (3); The Hague, KB, 150 F 10; Utrecht, MCC, I 14.304; Washington, DC, Library of Congress, Rosenwald 544. Gent, University Library, BHSL.RES.1432, and New Haven (CT), Yale University, Beinecke Library, call no. 1972 269, both lack sig. n1v. In the copy Antwerp, Erfgoedbibliotheek Hendrik Conscience, B 35754 [C2-536 f], the image has been cut out.

[23] Gouda, Streekarchief Midden-Holland (SAMH), 2306 G 5, sig. n1v. In an earlier article I wrote about this edition and the hand-drawn additions to the woodcut, I was not aware of the existence of the *Amor* woodcut. I am indebted to Eleanor Goerss (Department of History of Art and Architecture, Harvard University) for both pointing me to the copy held in Gouda and for the stimulating discussion about the edition. The article in question is A. Dlabačová, 'De houtsnede die niet bestond. Een gecorrigeerde afbeelding in het werk van Gerard Leeu', *Madoc. Tijdschrift over de Middeleeuwen*, 30, 2016, pp. 28–40.

[24] Since the woodcut is placed between the *Veritas* and *Pax* — nos 89.34–5 in Kok's *Woodcuts* (n. 7 above), p. 248 — I suggest adding a new woodcut to Kok's inventory as no. 89.34*bis* 'The Christ Child, nailed to the Tree of the Cross, pierced in his side with a lance by Lady *Amor*'.

[25] Newman, *God and the Goddesses* (n. 13 above), p. 161, fig. 4.1.

[26] Kok also suggested that '[The woodcut] may have existed originally, and have been destroyed somehow': Kok, *Woodcuts* (n. 7 above), p. 250.

Amor woodcut is placed in exactly the same position as the woodcut of 'The Soul kneeling before the crucified Child' in all other extant copies. No changes or shifts appear in types and woodblocks set in this forme (the inner forme of gathering n comprising sigs n1v–n2r, n4r, n5v–n6r, n7v–n8r): all types remain in the exact same position and no other (textual) correction was made, even though typos do occur.[27]

A second possibility is that the Amor woodcut was not available when the compositor worked on the inner forme of gathering n. This might have had several explanations: the woodblock, for some reason, was not shipped to Leeu's office together with the other woodblocks of the series; perhaps it was simply forgotten or it was not yet ready because the woodcarver had failed to produce one of the designs. It may also be possible that the woodcut was delivered, but got lost in Leeu's workshop. And since the compositor could not find the correct block, he settled for 'the next best thing', i.e. the woodcut of 'The Soul kneeling before the Christ Child crucified in the Tree'. When the block was found, or when it was finally delivered, it was carefully replaced by temporarily suspending printing operations. In both the first and second scenario the 'misprint' would have been intentional, as an alternative woodblock had to be found, possibly in consultation with Leeu; likewise, the drawn emendations would have been planned.

A last possibility is that the compositor made a mistake: he mixed up the two woodblocks and mislaid them. Since the small blocks have exactly the same size, a similar composition, and were both supposed to go on the verso of the first folio of subsequent gatherings (n and o), it is not unlikely that one block was mistaken for the other. When a corrector noticed the mistake, or when the compositor setting the inner forme for gathering o found the Amor woodcut amongst the materials, the press was halted, and the woodblock replaced. By then, most copies had already been printed, and Leeu had the copies with the wrong image corrected.[28]

Such corrections were likely made by one of his employees, someone with a steady hand who drew the lance and the banderol in all copies with the misplaced image; yet we cannot rule out the possibility that Leeu himself performed these corrections. Remarkably, it was not an option to distribute copies with an incorrect image. The care that was taken in executing the corrections suggests that the severity of the error was comparable to a serious misprint in a number of copies of the first 1487 edition of the *Boeck vanden leven Jhesu Christi*, a dialogic text based on Ludolf of Saxony's *Vita Christi*.[29] Here we find another rare

---

[27] I have compared the text in the Gouda copy (SAMH, 2306 G 5) to the one held in The Hague (RL, 150 F 10). On sig. n7v, for example, 'saechtmoedigen' is incorrectly spelled as 'saethtmoedigen' in both copies.

[28] This hypothesis could be corroborated by the sixteenth-century case of a misplaced woodcut that was brought to my attention by Andrea van Leerdam (Utrecht University), whom I thank for sharing the information with me. During the printing of the 1514 *Den groten herbarius* the compositors mixed up the woodcuts for chapters 10 and 11. By the time they noticed the mistake, all leaves with the start of chapter 10 were already printed. The error was solved by adding an erratum to the text below the image at the start of chapter 11, pointing the reader to the correct image at the start of chapter 10. In the next 1526 edition, the woodcuts appear in the correct order. See Johannes von Cuba, *Den groten herbarius met al sijn figueren, die Ortus sanitatis ghenaemt is*, Antwerp, Nicolaes Grapheus, 1514, f° (USTC 400329), sig. b2r and Johannes von Cuba, *Den groten herbarius met al sijn figueren die Ortus sanitatis ghenaemt is*, Antwerp, Nicolaes Grapheus, 1526, f° (USTC 437309).

[29] Ludolphus de Saxonia, *Vita Christi* [Dutch] *Tboeck vanden leven Jhesu Christi*, Antwerp, Gerard Leeu, 3 Nov. 1487, f° (ISTC il00353000). The misprint can be found at sig. kk1r in at least three

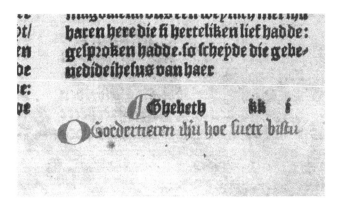

FIG. 22.5. In-house correction in a copy of the *Boeck vanden leven Jhesu Christi*, Antwerp, Gerard Leeu, 3 Nov. 1487, f° (ISTC il00353000), sig. kk1r. Maastricht, Stadsbibliotheek, 6000 E 6.

instance of an in-house correction made in Leeu's workshop to an edition of a vernacular, religious work. As with the drawn correction in the woodcut, the textual correction appears to have been carefully considered and executed. The space at the end of the page, left blank after the ommission of three text lines with the beginning of a prayer, was filled with five handwritten words (Fig. 22.5).[30] The words were added in all copies by the same steady and neat hand. In one of them, the ruling made with a hardpoint to ensure the corrector would write in a straight line is still clearly visible.[31]

Pictorial Instability

A final point based on the present case study can be made with regard to the study of woodcuts in incunabula and early printed books in general. Scholars working on woodcuts in Netherlandish incunabula can now take advantage of Kok's *Woodcuts in Incunabula printed in the Low Countries*, published in four substantial volumes in 2013. Kok based her inventory of woodcuts on editions rather than copies, and understandably so.[32] A consequence of this approach, however, is that changes that were made to the images in a book *during* the printing process will pass unnoticed.

On Jesus' Spiritual Childhood Moralised is not the only edition from Leeu's workshop with individual copies showing what we might call pictorial instability, i.e. variation in woodcuts in the copies of a single edition. In June 1491, Leeu published a Middle Dutch translation

copies: Maastricht, Stadsbibliotheek (SB), 6000 E 6; New York, The Morgan Library and Museum, PML 651/ChL1702; Paris, BnF, D-672.

[30] The correct text ('O aldergoedertierenste heere, o alder suetste meester, hoe goet bestu den genen die oprecht sijn van herten, hoe suete') appearing, for instance, in The Hague, KB, 171 E 39, sig. kk1r, was truncated into '[O] Goedertieren Ihesu hoe suete bistu' in copies with a misprint (see n. 29 above).

[31] Paris, BnF, D-672, sig. kk1r.

[32] Kok, *Woodcuts* (n. 7 above), pp. XVII–XVIII. Kok often consulted several copies of an edition when copies were incomplete.

of the *Life and Passion of Christ and his Mother*. The text, originally published in Latin, was extracted and compiled from St Bridget's *Revelations* and the Gospels. The editor was the humanist Jacob Canter, to whom the young Erasmus would write a letter as a way to come into contact with the former's intellectual circles.[33] In the edition, the text is preceded by a prologue, printed as a gathering of eight leaves together with the title-page showing the only fifteenth-century Netherlandish woodcut image of St Bridget, which was originally made for the 1489 Latin edition of Canter's work.[34] Canter's prologue, however, ends at the top of sig. [a]8*r*, leaving most of the page and the entire verso side blank. To avoid this much blank space, and because sig. [a]8*v* faces the start of the first chapter dealing with Adam's transgression against God's commandments, a decision was made during the printing process to insert a woodcut of the Fall from Eden, with Eve taking the forbidden fruit from the serpent. The woodblock had previously belonged to the Haarlem printer Jacob Bellaert.[35] The change during the printing process resulted in copies with and without this woodcut.[36] Such differences also seem to hint at the ad hoc addition of images to some devotional books. In contrast to the edition of *On Jesus' Spiritual Childhood Moralised*, which had a finely thought-out set of images, the Dutch translation of Canter's compilation appears to have been supplied with images gradually, as setting continued, with compositors using already available images from various woodcut series.[37]

Final Remarks

Bibliographers, editors, and virtually all scholars dealing with the printed word are well aware of the considerable amount of textual variations found in different copies of a book, but have overlooked the alterations that can also be found in images throughout an edition. Pictorial instability must have occurred more frequently than in just *On Jesus' Spiritual Childhood Moralised* and the *Life and Passion of Christ and his Mother*. It is not unlikely that 'new' fifteenth-century Netherlandish woodcuts, not yet inventoried by Kok, will be found as research and online availability of individual copies increases. To reach a truly comprehensive census of (the use of) woodcuts, ideally all copies of every edition should be consulted. The question is, of course, whether to do this manually would be worth the time and the effort. Thanks to the increasing digitisation of early printed books, such a comprehensive approach might start to come within the bounds of possibility.

Beside pictorial instability — variation in woodcuts in the copies of a single edition — a practice of correcting images must have existed in the fifteenth century. As happens

---

[33] Saint Birgitta, *Opusculum vitae et passionis Christi eiusque genitricis Mariae ex Revelationibus* [Dutch] *Leven en passie van Christus en zijn moeder, getrokken uit de Revelacien van S. Birgitten. Add: Bonifacius IX: Bulle der canonizacien van S. Birgitten; Petrus Olavi: Leven Katarinen*, Antwerp, Gerard Leeu, 4 June and 21 June 1491, 8° (ISTC ib00676700).

[34] Kok, *Woodcuts* (n. 7 above), p. 256, no. 94.

[35] Kok, *Woodcuts* (n. 7 above), pp. 392–3; 197–8; 246, no. 170.1. It is the only occurrence of this woodcut in Netherlandish incunabula.

[36] Paris, BnF, D-27253 has no woodcut on sig. [a]8*v* while, for example, Stockholm, RL, Ink 224, does have an impression of the woodcut. These differences were not observed by Kok.

[37] The Latin edition contains the woodcut of St Bridget only: see n. 33 above.

with pictorial instability, this practice was much more limited than the culture of correction regarding texts. In devotional texts such as *On Jesus' Spiritual Childhood Moralised*, where text and image were equally important both in conveying meaning and in serving as tools for prayer and meditation based on the book, the need to preserve a close connection between text and image led to drawn emendations. These interventions, in turn, confirm the importance allocated to the images in the readers' devotional practice. From an aesthetical point of view, it seems that buyers and readers apparently accepted drawn emendations as perfectly adequate. After all, printed books were still relatively close to the manuscript world and their own aesthetics had not yet fully developed.[38] Copy-specific investigations of the whole print run of early modern illustrated editions can shed new light on this and many other aspects connected to correction by means of drawing, not only in devotional literature, but certainly in all genres where images played an important role in the transmission of knowledge.

BIBLIOGRAPHY

PRIMARY SOURCES

MANUSCRIPTS

Darmstadt, Universitäts- und Landesbibliothek (ULB), Hs 2667.

PRINTED EDITIONS

Alliaco, Petrus de, *Le Jardin amoureux* [Dutch] *Thoofkijn van devotien*, Antwerp, Gerard Leeu, 28 Nov. 1487, 4° (ISTC ia00478250).
Cuba, Johannes von, *Den groten herbarius met al sijn figueren, die Ortus sanitatis ghenaemt is*, Antwerp, Nicolaes Grapheus, 1514, f° (USTC 400329).
Cuba, Johannes von, *Den groten herbarius met al sijn figueren die Ortus sanitatis ghenaemt is*, Antwerp, Nicolaes Grapheus, 1526, f° (USTC 437309).
Epistolae et Evangelia [Dutch], [Gouda, Gerard Leeu], 24 May 1477, f° (ISTC ie00064700).
Erasmus, Desiderius, *The Correspondence of Erasmus: Letters 1 to 141, 1484 to 1500*, transl. R. A. B. Mynors and D. F. S. Thomson and annotated by W. K. Ferguson, Toronto and Buffalo (NY), 1974.

---

[38] See, e.g., D. McKitterick, *Print, Manuscript and the Search for Order, 1450–1830*, Cambridge, 2003.

Saint Birgitta, *Opusculum vitae et passionis Christi eiusque genitricis Mariae ex Revelationibus* [Dutch] *Leven en passie van Christus en zijn moeder, getrokken uit de Revelacien van S. Birgitten. Add: Bonifacius IX: Bulle der canonizacien van S. Birgitten; Petrus Olavi: Leven Katarinen*, Antwerp, Gerard Leeu, 4 June and 21 June 1491, 8° (ISTC ib00676700).

Saxonia, Ludolphus de, *Vita Christi* [Dutch] *Tboeck vanden leven Jhesu Christi*, Antwerp, Gerard Leeu, 3 Nov. 1487, f° (ISTC il00353000).

Van die gheestlike Kintscheÿt ihesu ghemoraliseert, Antwerp, Gerard Leeu, 16 Feb. 1488, 8° (ISTC ik00022000).

SECONDARY LITERATURE

Conway, W. M., *The Woodcutters of the Netherlands in the Fifteenth Century: In Three Parts*, I, Cambridge, 1884.

Dlabačová, A., 'De houtsnede die niet bestond. Een gecorrigeerde afbeelding in het werk van Gerard Leeu', *Madoc. Tijdschrift over de Middeleeuwen*, 30, 2016, pp. 28–40.

Goudriaan, K., 'Een drukker en zijn markt. Gheraert Leeu (Gouda 1477—Antwerpen 1492/1493)', *Madoc. Tijdschrift over de Middeleeuwen*, 6, 1992, pp. 194–205.

Hellinga, L., 'Gheraert Leeu, Claes Leeu, Jacob Bellaert, Peter van Os van Breda', in *De vijfhonderdste verjaring van de boekdrukkunst in de Nederlanden*, Brussels, 1973, pp. 283–308.

Hellinga-Querido, L., 'De betekenis van Gheraert Leeu', in K. Goudriaan et al. (eds), *Een drukker zoekt publiek. Gheraert Leeu te Gouda*, Delft, 1993, pp. 12–30.

Klein, J.-W., 'The Leeu[w] van Gouda: new facts, new possibilities', *Quaerendo*, 33, 2003, pp. 175–90.

Kok, I., *Woodcuts in Incunabula Printed in the Low Countries*, I, Houten, [2013].

Kraft, H., *Die Bildallegorie der Kreuzigung Christi durch die Tugenden*, Frankfurt, 1976.

McKitterick, D., *Print, Manuscript and the Search for Order, 1450–1830*, Cambridge, 2003.

Newman, B., *God and the Goddesses: Vision, Poetry, and Belief in the Middle Ages*, Philadelphia, 2003.

Parshall, P., 'The Art of Memory and the Passion', *The Art Bulletin*, 81, 1999, pp. 456–72.

Roth, G., and Honemann, V., 'Die "Geistliche Minnejagd". Ein niederdeutsche geistliche Minneallegorie', in V. Bok et al. (eds), Magister et amicus. *Festschrift für Kurt Gärtner zum 65. Geburtstag*, Vienna, 2003, pp. 175–239.

Van Buuren, F., 'Van die gheestelike kintsheyt Jhesu ghemoraliseeret. Een verkenning', in K. Goudriaan et al. (eds), *Een drukker zoekt publiek. Gheraert Leeu te Gouda 1477–1484*, Delft, 1993, pp. 111–32.

Van der Stock, J., 'De Antwerpse Sint-Lucasgilde en de drukkers-uitgevers: "middeleeuws" achterhoedegevecht of paradigma van cultureel-politieke machtsverschuivingen?', in J. M. M. Hermans and K. van der Hoek (eds), *Boeken in de late middeleeuwen. Verslag van de Groningse Codicologendagen 1992*, Groningen, 1994, pp. 155–65.

CHAPTER 23

LEARNING FROM MISTAKES

Paper and Printing Defects in Sixteenth-Century Italian Popular Books

LAURA CARNELOS

INTRODUCTION

PUBLICATIONS aimed at a wide audience and sold at the lowest price or even given for free through various channels — in bookshops, from street stalls, by itinerant sellers — are generally defined as popular.* In the early modern period, they were often the only books which people of every social status could actually possess: hornbooks from which children learnt their first words, devotional prayers leafed through by devout women, almanacs used by farmers to calculate when to sow or harvest.

As David Atkinson and Steve Roud said, 'cheap to buy means cheap to print'.[1] The cheapness of these books was strictly connected to the materials used and methods adopted to produce them. Nevertheless, their materiality is largely understudied, even though it is a determining factor in popular print and a crucial key to a deeper understanding of the practices adopted in typography in early printing.[2] This neglect is partially due to the rarity of these books, often surviving only in one copy (if they survived at all), but mainly to the lack of a scientific method with which to explore the materiality of the production in relation to book history (as well as social history).

In this paper, I present the results of a systematic analysis of paper quality and printing defects conducted on a relevant corpus of sixteenth-century Italian popular books through

---

* I am deeply grateful to all the librarians who so generously sent me pictures of the books in their collections, allowing me to continue my research during the pandemic.

[1] D. Atkinson and S. Roud (eds), *Cheap Print and the People: European Perspectives on Popular Literature*, Newcastle upon Tyne, 2019, p. 3.

[2] D. Bellingradt and J. Salman, 'Books and Book History in Motion: Materiality, Sociality and Spatiality', in D. Bellingradt, P. Nelles, and J. Salman (eds), *Books in Motion in Early Modern Europe: Beyond Production, Circulation and Consumption*, London, 2017, pp. 1–11.

Laura Carnelos, *Learning from Mistakes*. In: *Printing and Misprinting*. Edited by Geri Della Rocca de Candal, Anthony Grafton, and Paolo Sachet, Oxford University Press. © Laura Carnelos (2023). DOI: 10.1093/oso/9780198863045.003.0024 a database specifically created to collect this information (PATRIMONiT).[3] Based on the assumption that the definition of what it is to be 'popular' is also linked to materiality, I discuss what can we learn from these faults and how this evidence influences what we know about popular books. Owing to the scarcity of contemporary archival evidence, documentation from the seventeenth and eighteenth centuries will be used to elucidate the different qualities of the sixteenth-century Italian paper industry.

Tears, Tongues, and Feet: Early Modern Paper Flaws

Paper analysis is fundamental to investigating the printer's mind and understanding his/her intentions. Paper represented the costliest item in the production of a book, and consequently, choosing cheap paper meant limiting the expenses and addressing the product to customers who did not require quality and beauty in printed materials.

According to a recent study, paper composition and, in particular, calcium and gelatine concentrations and paper thickness changed over the centuries.[4] While thickness depended on the quality and quantity of pulp used for each sheet, calcium and gelatine were substances added in two fundamental processes of papermaking. Calcina or lime water helped the rags retting and fermenting in preparation for their reduction into pulp. Gelatine, which resulted from boiling innards and leftover carcassas (*carniccio*), was instead used on the sheet, already formed and dried, to 'size' it (make it impermeable to ink).[5] During the sixteenth century, the increasing demand for books pushed European papermakers to cut back on calcium and gelatine specifically and produce thinner paper to speed work and lower expenses.[6] Beside this general degradation in quality and local differences, early modern paper was available in various grades depending on materials and workmanship. To calculate these variabilities and collect quantitative data on printing paper, T. Barrett, M. Ormsby, and J. B. Lang adopted a range of five numbers, in which grade 1 was assigned

---

[3] The data was collected as part of my Marie S. Curie Individual Fellowship project, 'PATRIMONiT. From Cheap Print to Rare Ephemera: 16th-Century Italian "Popular" Books at the British Library', supervised by Prof. Cristina Dondi and based at the Consortium of European Research Libraries (CERL), London (H2020-MSCA-IF-2014, grant agreement No 659625, 2016-2018), in collaboration with Stephen Parkin, Curator at the British Library, and the Italian Agency for Cataloguing (ICCU). Developed by Alexander Jahnke of Data Conversion Group (University of Göttingen), the database PATRIMONiT has been operational since December 2016 and is available at http://data.cerl.org/patrimonit/_search (accessed 08/05/2020). To locate an individual record in the database, please add the PT number given in the citations below to the URL, e.g., https://data.cerl.org/patrimonit/PT00000067.

[4] T. Barrett, M. Ormsby, and J. B. Lang, 'Non-Destructive Analysis of 14th–19th Century European Handmade Papers', *Restaurator*, 37/2, 2016, pp. 93–135 (105–11).

[5] S. Rodgers Albro, *Fabriano: City of Medieval and Renaissance Papermaking*, New Castle (DE) and Washington, 2016, pp. 61 and 72–3.

[6] 'The average gelatine concentration in the poorest quality paper from before 1500 was comparable or greater than the average gelatine content for the highest quality paper in all other periods.' Barrett, Ormsby, and Lang, 'Non-Destructive Analysis' (n. 4 above), p. 111.

to the worst quality paper and grade 5 to the best one. They describe the poorest paper having 'stray foreign fibres, straw, bits of debris, lumps, clumps, and signs of quick or unskilled sheet forming or couching'.[7] What publications were printed on such paper and why?

Usually offered on the street at very low prices, ordinary publications, such as schoolbooks, devotional texts, almanacs, and ballads, are generally described as printed on bad paper. However, little is known about the characteristics of this paper as yet.

During my Marie S. Curie project, I analysed a corpus of 330 sixteenth-century Italian popular books (religious plays and small histories mainly printed in Florence and Siena) at the British Library (BL) and the Bodleian Library (Bod). In order to examine paper quality, I adopted the above-mentioned five grades, observing the sheets with a back and raking light and recording the data in a specific area within PATRIMONiT. To assign grades more objectively, I designed a grid (Table 23.1) with questions to be answered 'book in hand'. Of the examined corpus, not one booklet was printed on very good quality paper (grade 5) and only one was printed on good paper (grade 4). Most of them (99.7%) were produced on *retree* paper (i.e. defective) with structural and manufacturing defects, with a higher concentration of paper ranked at grade 2.[8]

Materially, these specimens were characterised by the presence of lumps and coloured fibres, and by a clumpy or mottled appearance when checked against the light. These flaws are structural: they are caused by a pulp of uneven texture produced cheaply, using low-quality raw materials, and quickly, shortening beating times.[9] Different rags needed different times for fermenting. If they were removed too early from the fermentation process, they created a lumpy and crude paper.[10] Obviously, the more refined the pulp was, the more expensive the paper. Therefore, papermakers usually offered a well-assorted choice of paper of different qualities and prices, depending on the raw materials employed, their mixture, and beating times. For example, in an edict on the production and sale of paper published in Parma in 1762, eighteen different kinds of paper are clustered into four groups based on the pulp (*pesto*): fine (*fino*), ordinary (*ordinario*), third-choice rags (*fiorettone*), and black (*nero*).[11] Excluding fine and dark pulps, which were employed for high-quality paper and wrapping sheets respectively, we can assume that paper made of ordinary and third-choice pulps was probably used for the majority of publications, with a tendency to use the latter for the cheapest ones.

Structural defects in paper are frequently coupled with manufacturing mishaps, resulting in signs of unskilled forming and couching.[12] In 9.4% of the 330 editions taken into examination, i.e. in thirty-one cases, a significant presence of circular spots or splashes was observed. These were caused by water drops that had accidentally fallen on the paper while it was still soft, either in the process of forming the sheet (when the vatman dipped a mould into a vat, a large container filled with water and pulp) or laying it (when the coucher

---

[7] Ibid., p. 96.

[8] Overall figures stand at: grade 5 (0%), grade 4 (0.3%), grade 3 (47.7%), grade 2 (51%), grade 1 (0.9%).

[9] Barrett, Ormsby, and Lang, 'Non-Destructive Analysis' (n. 4 above), pp. 118–19, fig. 26.

[10] In fourteenth-century Fabriano, the price of rags was based on their quality: *boni*, clean and white; *vergati*, possibly striped or coloured; *grossi*, inferior quality; *neri*, dark coloured. Rodgers Albro, *Fabriano* (n. 5 above), pp. 59–61.

[11] The edict was published in 1762. Z. Campanini, *Istruzioni pratiche ad un novello capo-stampa o sia regolamento per la direzione di una tipografica officina (1789)*, ed. C. Fahy, Florence, 1998, pp. 373–4.

[12] Barrett, Ormsby, and Lang, 'Non-Destructive Analysis' (n. 4 above), pp. 96 and 118.

grasped the mould and flipped the newly formed sheet onto a woollen felt). Drops dispersed the fibres in a circle, creating spots with a thinner, sometimes transparent, surface inside and thicker edges around. Known as a 'papermaker's tear' or 'chestnut', this flaw could be produced by either the vatman (on the felt side of the sheet) or the coucher (on the wire side of it), dripping from their hands or tools.[13]

Even more frequent — present in nearly 47% of the items (154 cases) — are wrinkles and blisters of various forms and dimensions on which some text was printed. Also called 'goat's feet' and 'cow's tongues', respectively, they could be easily generated on a fresh sheet, for example if the vatman struck his form against the drainer, or the coucher was too quick in laying the sheet, occasioning air bubbles on the paper.[14]

With a rhythm of between 1,500 and 3,000 sheets per day or more, imperfect paper was inevitably part of the process.[15] While the most ruined and heavily damaged sheets were recycled in playing cards or cartons,[16] defective yet exploitable sheets were used for the two or three outer quires — the ones most likely to be damaged — of each ream when packing and storing paper.[17] If the price per ream depended on the balance between perfect, good, and faulty quires, it comes as no surprise that publishers and printers used as much as possible of each purchased ream, consequently printing on paper with flaws too.[18]

The Venetian documentation regarding the guild of printers and booksellers gives evidence of the use of low-quality paper among publishers and printers. In 1537 the Senato,

---

[13] Also called 'vatman's drips' (or 'coucher's drips'). D. Farnsworth, *Handmade Paper Method Cinquecento: Renaissance Paper Textures*, Oakland, 2019, p. 54. 'Chestnuts' is a form attested in L. N. Rosenband, *Papermaking in Eighteenth-Century France: Management, Labor, and Revolution at the Montgolfier Mill 1761–1805*, Baltimore and London, 2000, p. 11. See also A. Honey, '"Torn, wrinckled, stained, and otherwise naughty sheets": How should we interpret paper faults in seventeenth century paper?', paper presented at the Conservators Together At Home series organised by the Institute of Conservation Book and Paper Group, 26 March 2020; the script is available at https://ora.ox.ac.uk/objects/uuid:7842dddb-09f1-484f-add4-d06b1d314bbd, accessed 29 November 2020.

[14] Blisters were also called andouilles, sausages, or, more colourfully, shit. Rosenband, *Papermaking* (n. 13 above), p. 11. Wrinkes (in this case called 'back marks') could be also created when flattening out the back of a sheet after drying it on waxed horsehair, cow-hair ropes, or wooden poles, though this is to be regarded as the shortcoming of a process rather than a human mistake. Farnsworth, *Handmade* (n. 13 above), pp. 19–37.

[15] At least twenty posts of paper (containing six quires of paper each) were regularly made per day according to the apothecary J. Houghton, *Husbandry and Trade Improv'd: Being a Collection of Many Valuable Materials*, II, London, 1727, no. CCCLVIII, 2 June 1698, pp. 415–16. In seventeenth-century Italy, a vatman and a coucher together could produce a maximum of 4,500 sheets per day: C. M. Cipolla, *Before the Industrial Revolution: European Society and Economy 1000–1700*, London, 2005, p. 82.

[16] Rosenband, *Papermaking* (n. 13 above), p. 12.

[17] They were called *cassie* or cording quires. P. Gaskell, *A New Introduction to Bibliography*, Oxford, 1979, p. 59; C. Fahy, 'Paper Making in Seventeenth-Century Genoa: The Account of Giovanni Domenico Peri (1651)', *Studies in Bibliography*, 56, 2003–2004, pp. 243–59 (254). This is also attested in eighteenth-century Venice: Venice, Archivio di Stato, Riformatori dello Studio di Padova, env. 370, report on the printing press, 1 January 1741, partially transcribed in L. Carnelos, *I pirati dei libri. Stampa e contraffazione a Venezia tra Sei e Settecento*, Venice, 2012, pp. 19–22. In the papermaking industry, a quire represents a set of twenty-four or twenty-five sheets; twenty quires formed a ream of 480 or 500 sheets.

[18] See the different prices based on the quality of the quires (*mazzetti*) in *Bando dell'appalto generale della carta, cenci, e carnicci*, Florence, nella stamperia di S.A.R. per i Tartini e Franchi, 1722.

one of the major Venetian institutions which, among other tasks, supervised the book market, discussed the 'pernicious and outrageous habit' ('dannosa e vituperosa usanza') that Venetian printers had of saving money by using such a bad quality paper in books that one could barely write on them.[19] The Senato decided that, from then onwards (the same law was reprinted at the end of the eighteenth century), printers were prohibited from using paper in which ink would sink through the page and the margins would be so thin as to dissolve. The prohibition, however, did not apply to works printed on ten or fewer paper sheets. Therefore, devotional booklets, schoolbooks, histories, miracles, prayer books, news reports, letters, and songs which were usually printed on less than ten sheets were printed on the lowest quality paper.[20] In north-eastern Italy, this paper was produced without fine gelatine and with mixed pulps derived from cheaper raw materials, such as hemp and tow.[21] It was called 'corsiva' or, if of lower quality, 'corsivetta'. These were the two low-quality kinds of paper that the Remondini, the biggest chapbooks publishers in eighteenth-century Italy, employed in their cheapest publications, sold unbound at a fixed price per ream.[22]

To draw two preliminary conclusions, we can see that, first, through a non-destructive analysis, we are able to rate, with some degree of caution, the quality of western paper in early modern printed material. The five-grade division is so far the most accurate representation of part of the selection process of paper qualities for printing runs in early modern paper mills.[23] Secondly, defective yet usable paper sheets, commonly found in printing shops, were suitable for printing any publications whose low price was more important than the aesthetics of their pages. It is conceivable that similar laws and strategies to those found in north-east Italy existed and were applied also in other early modern Italian states.

---

[19] '[...] quasi tutti i libri che hora s'imprimono in questa terra, non ritengono l'inchiostro da chi vol nottar, et scriver alcuna cosa in essi, [...] et per il più scompissono di sorte' ('[...] nearly all books currently printed in these lands cannot withhold the ink when people try to annotate or write something on them [...] and in most cases the paper is extremely fragile'). Venice, Biblioteca del Museo Correr, Mariegola MS iv 119, Report on the printing press, 4 June 1537, fols 20*r*–21*v*.

[20] For a comparison, in England 'a pamphlet typically consisted of between one sheet and a maximum of twelve sheets, or between eight and ninety-six pages in quarto': J. Raymond, *Pamphlets and Pamphleteering in Early Modern Britain*, Cambridge, 2003, p. 5.

[21] Venice, Archivio di Stato, Arti, env. 164, Atti VIII, Report on the printing press, 6 June 1766, pp. 205–7, partially transcribed in Carnelos, *I pirati* (n. 17 above), pp. 25–9. On the production of paper in Veneto, see A. Fedrigoni, *L'industria veneta della carta dalla II dominazione austriaca all'Unità*, Turin, 1966, pp. 88–9; I. Mattozzi, *Produzione e commercio della carta nello stato veneziano settecentesco. Lineamenti e problemi*, Bologna, 1975, pp. 43–59.

[22] The specific paper was detailed on their sale catalogues; e.g., the *Catalogus librorum amplissimus in typographia Remondiniana Impressorum*, Venice, Joseph Remondini, & Filios, 176[1], contains the lists of the 'Libri da risma in carta corsiva che si vendono a contanti senza sconto alcuno al ristrettissimo prezzo di L. 14 la risma' and 'Libri in carta corsivetta, che si vendono per contanti al ristrettissimo prezzo di L. 12 la risma' (sig. N6*v*). The books sold per ream are analysed in depth in L. Carnelos, *I libri da risma. Catalogo delle edizioni Remondini a larga diffusione (1650–1850)*, Milan, 2008.

[23] In early modern French paper mills, women were usually in charge of separating paper into five grades: good (white, intact, spotless, of equal thickness), inferior (speckled, uneven, hence inconsistently absorbent), moitié (cloudy, stained, wrinkled, highly irregular edges), cassé (broken sheets with tears and perforations), déchet (ruined paper to be recycled often for producing cardboard). Rosenband, *Papermaking* (n. 13 above), p. 14.

'Monks', Smudges, and Other Dirty Stuff: Printing Defects

Beside low-quality paper, what made a book cheap was the way it was produced. Finding one or more mistakes in an early modern publication is far from being an exception. Workers generally printed thousands of sheets per day and some faults could easily happen.[24] However, in publications intended for wide dissemination the number of mistakes is remarkably high. These materials were sold cheaply because they were produced cheaply. The final result depended on various factors — from the conditions of tools, to the quality of materials (we have seen paper quality, but also inks), to workers' skills — and how meticulously each operation was handled.[25]

The study of 'side-effects of printing processes' is a growing field in analytical bibliography.[26] However, further research is needed to establish the frequency and causes of these side effects.[27] Were they caused by a process that needed refinement, or by a slip in attention, or were they the result of market strategies?

We have seen how publishers and printers economised on paper when printing ordinary material. This alone had some consequences for the output: the presence of creases or water drops in sheets could not but create misalignments and ink bleed on printed pages. Yet these are not the only defects observed in early modern popular books.

The systematic analysis of the corpus in PATRIMONiT shows that printing imperfections are a significant feature of these publications, with a combination in average of at least three defects per book. The most common ones are uneven inking (90%, 294 items), a poor register (77.6%, 254 items), inked shoulders (65%, 213 items) and smudged types (48%, 157 items).[28]

Although, strictly speaking, it cannot be considered a mistake, an uneven distribution of ink suggests that something during the printing process did not quite work: whether it

---

[24] The Venetian *Soprintendente alle stampe* (superintendent of printing) Antonio Prata wrote in 1781 that printers produced up to 3,700 sheets per day. Venice, Archivio di Stato, Riformatori dello Studio di Padova, env. 369, Report on the printing press, 25 November 1781, partially transcribed in Carnelos, *I pirati* (n. 17 above), pp. 29–35 (31). In his manual for printing, Campanini mentioned that two workers could print up to four reams per day (2,000 paper sheets) of works that did not require great attention and care. Other sources suggest 2,500 impressions per day. See Campanini, *Istruzioni pratiche* (n. 11 above), p. 219 n. 111.

[25] L. Carnelos, 'Popular Print Under the Press: Strategies, Practices and Materials', *Quaerendo*, 51 (2021), pp. 8–35.

[26] G. T. Tanselle, 'The Treatment of Typesetting and Presswork in Bibliographical Description', *Studies in Bibliography*, 52, 1999, pp. 1–57, and Neil Harris's list of 'devices and desires', with bibliography, available at http://ihl.enssib.fr/en/analytical-bibliography-an-alternative-prospectus/devices-and-desires, accessed 7 May 2020. An important work on printing practices is by C. Bolton, *The Fifteenth-Century Printing Practices of Johann Zainer, Ulm 1473–1478*, Oxford and London, 2016.

[27] Examples of set-off are discussed in N. Harris, 'L'*Hypnerotomachia Poliphili* e le contrastampe', *La Bibliofilia*, 100, 1998, pp. 201–51.

[28] For this analysis, I examined each page of the corpus with a back and raking light after having prepared a glossary of printing defects with Claire Bolton's help. I am also truly grateful to Michael Twyman, Martin Andrews, and Geoff Wyeth (all from the Department of Typography and Graphic Communication, University of Reading), and the Oxford letterpress printer Richard Lawrence.

was due to haste, negligence, coarse raw materials, or the combination of the three factors is hard to tell. Beside being unaesthetic, uneven inking strained readers' eyes and, in some cases, limited text comprehension. It was such a huge issue in early modern Italian books that Venetian documents give evidence of it. In 1766 two printers of the Venetian Guild of Printers and Booksellers were asked by the Riformatori dello Studio di Padova (one of the major institutions supervising the printing press in Venice as well as the University in Padua) to explain the poor quality of Venetian printed books.[29] The printers mentioned the unevenness of ink as one of their main concerns. Causes could be various. For example, it occurred when the compositor did not perfectly set each line to the same tension as the others or correctly justify the page. He would hand an uneven forme (in Venetian, such a forme was called *stravacata*, not flattened down correctly) over to the beater. Once the forme was locked up, some lines of type could rise, causing uneven inking. This would result in some lines of text being too inked, while others would appear pale and less visible.[30] It could also happen that individual pieces of type, including spaces, were not at the right height in the forme.[31] If a single piece of type stuck up too high — possibly during setting or inking — it could cause a sort of blank circle around it, preventing the ink from reaching the neighbouring types. This occurred in some copies of *La rapresentatione di santa Agata vergine & martire* (Firenze, 1558; Fig 23.1).[32] On the last page, the second 'i' in the word 'eccelsitudine' emerges black and thick from the sheet, hiding other letters in the word, which reads 'eccelsitu', and extending its blank shadow on the lines above and below. Single spacing could also rise and be printed. The result is a more or less black vertical line interrupting the fluidity of the text, such as in the verse 'donzel|son del palazzo assai divoto', with a black line unifying the first two word, in the BL copy of the *Rappresentatione di santa Eufrosina Vergine*, printed in Florence in 1561 (sig. B1r).[33]

[29] Venice, Archivio di Stato, Arti, env. 164, Atti VIII, Report on the printing press, 20 May 1766, pp. 204–5, partially transcribed in Carnelos, *I pirati* (n. 17 above), pp. 25–9.

[30] '[Il] compositore, che non spieghi le righe perfetamente e che tra parola e parola non proporzioni il spazio, e che quando consegna la forma al torchiaio tintore sia stravacata [—] termine di stamparia, che vuol dire non ben ritta [...] quando il torchiaio la serra [...] le righe che crescono in lunghezza si alzano e levano l'impressione alle altre' ('When the compositor does not set each line perfectly to the same tension or correctly allocate spaces between words, or hands over to the beater a forme which is *stravacata* — a term used in print shops to mean not flattened down correctly [...] once the beater locks this forme up [...] some lines rise up preventing others from being properly printed'). Ibid.

[31] See Bolton's contribution in this Companion.

[32] *La rapresentatione di santa Agata vergine & martire. Nuouamente ristampata*, Florence, s.n., 1558, 4° (PT00000067; USTC 801089), sig. A6v. Nine copies of this edition are known. The defect is clearly visible in the copies in London, British Library (BL), C.34.h.5 (27); Venice, Fondazione Giorgio Cini, FOAN TES 1061; Florence, Biblioteca Nazionale Centrale (BNCF), RARI.B.R. 179./9; Cambridge, Fitzwilliam Museum 32.G.4.(1); Paris, Bibliothèque nationale de France (BnF), RES-YD-376 and RES-YD-496; in the copy Wolfenbüttel, Herzog August Bibliothek, A: 12.2 Eth. (33), the letters 'di' in 'eccelsitudine' are badly printed, the 'd' is not entirely visible and the 'i' is blurry. The defect is absent in the copy in Oxford, Bodleian Library (Bod.), Mortara Adds. 9. I have not been able to inspect the copy in Berlin, Staatliche Museen, Sign. 3124, Stück 6.

[33] *Rappresentatione di santa Eufrosina vergine*, Florence, Paolo Bigio, 1561, 4° (PT00000041; USTC 801237), sig. B1r. Three copies of this edition are known. I consulted the copy in London, BL, 111426.f.37. The difect is also visible in Rome, Biblioteca dell'Accademia Nazionale dei Lincei e Corsiniana (Bibl. Cors.), 92 F 23 (19) and Paris, BnF, RES-YD-394.

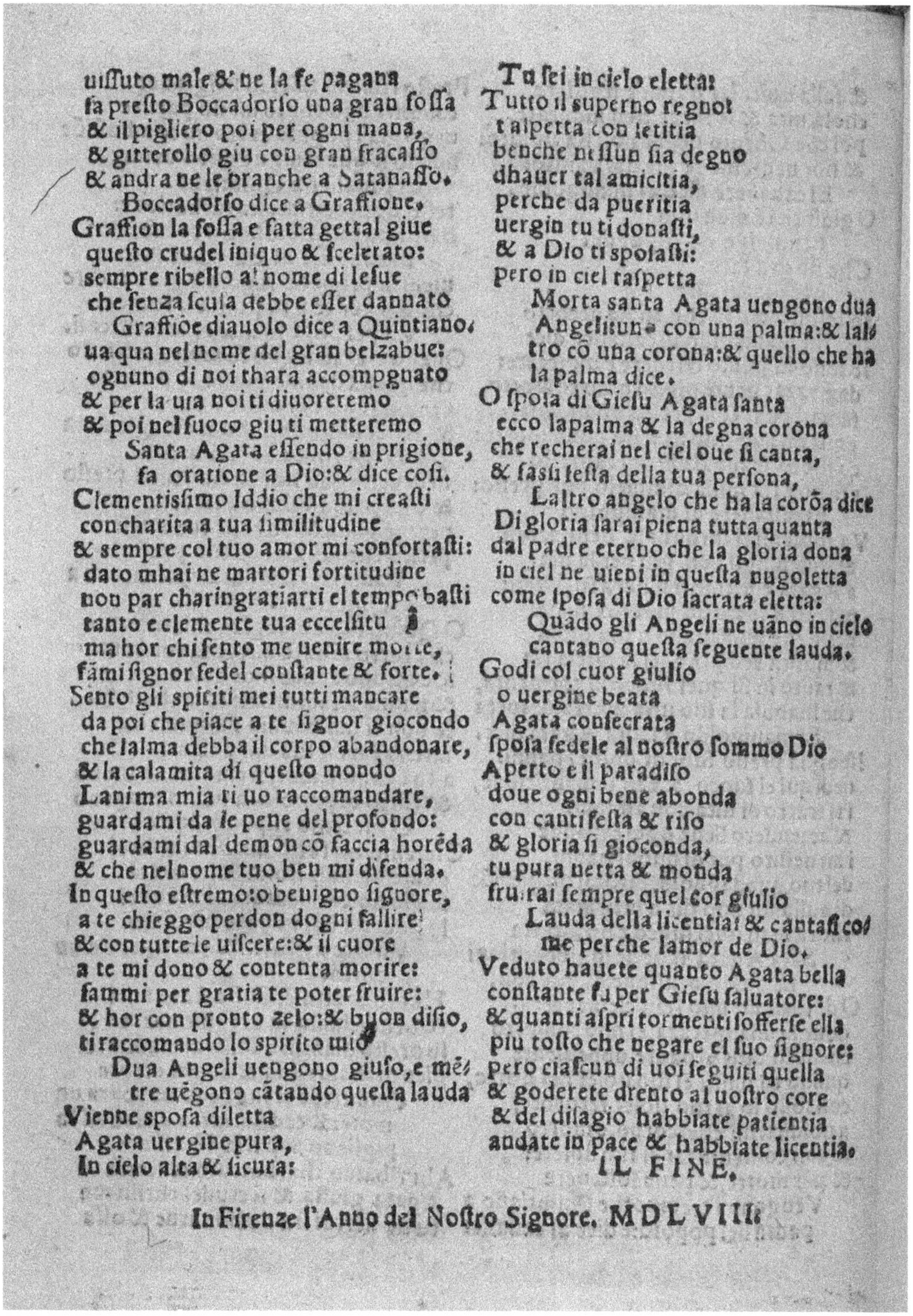

23: LEARNING FROM MISTAKES

uiſſuto male & ne la fe pagana
fa preſto Boccadorſo una gran foſſa
& il pigliero poi per ogni mana,
& gitterollo giu con gran fracaſſo
& andra ne le branche a Satanaſſo,
   Boccadorſo dice a Graſſione,
Graſſion la foſſa e fatta gettal giue
queſto crudel iniquo & ſceletrato:
ſempre ribello al nome di Ieſue
che ſenza ſcuſa debbe eſſer dannato
   Graſſide diauolo dice a Quintiano,
ua qua nel nome del gran belzabue:
ognuno di noi thara accompguato
& per la uia noi ti diuoreremo
& poi nel ſuoco giu ti metteremo
   Santa Agata eſſendo in prigione,
   fa oratione a Dio:& dice coſi.
Clementisſimo Iddio che mi creaſti
con charita a tua ſimilitudine
& ſempre col tuo amor mi confortaſti:
dato mhai ne martori fortitudine
non par charingratiarti el tempo baſti
tanto e clemente tua eccelſitu ſ̃
ma hor chi ſento me uenire morte,
fãmi ſignor fedel conſtante & forte. ¦
Sento gli ſpiriti mei tutti mancare
   da poi che piace a te ſignor giocondo
che lalma debba il corpo abandonare,
& la calamita di queſto mondo
Lanima mia ti uo raccomandare,
guardami da le pene del profondo:
guardami dal demon cõ faccia horéda
& che nel nome tuo ben mi diſenda.
In queſto eſtremo:o benigno ſignore,
   a te chieggo perdon dogni fallire¦
& con tutte ie uiſcere:& il cuore
a te mi dono & contenta morire:
fammi per gratia te poter ſruire:
& hor con pronto zelo:& buon diſio,
ti raccomando lo ſpirito mio
   Dua Angeli uengono giuſo, e mẽ
   tre uegono cãtando queſta lauda
Vienne ſpoſa diletta
Agata uergine pura,
In cielo alta & ſicura:

Tu ſei in cielo eletta:
Tutto il ſuperno regno:
t aſpetta con letitia
benche neſſun ſia degno
dhauer tal amicitia,
perche da pueritia
uergin tu ti donaſti,
& a Dio ti ſpoſaſti:
pero in ciel raſpetta
   Morta santa Agata uengono dua
   Angeli tun= con una palma:& lal
tro cõ una corona:& quello che ha
la palma dice,
O ſpoſa di Gieſu Agata ſanta
ecco la palma & la degna corona
che recherai nel ciel oue ſi canta,
& ſaſſi feſta della tua perſona,
   Laltro angelo che ha la corõa dice
Di gloria ſarai piena tutta quanta
dal padre eterno che la gloria dona
in ciel ne uieni in queſta nugoletta
come ſpoſa di Dio ſacrata eletta:
   Quãdo gli Angeli ne uãno in cielo
   cantano queſta ſeguente lauda,
Godi col cuor giulio
o uergine beata
Agata conſecrata
ſpoſa fedele al noſtro ſommo Dio
Aperto e il paradiſo
doue ogni bene abonda
con canti feſta & riſo
& gloria ſi gioconda,
tu pura netta & monda
fru rai ſempre quel cor giulio
   Lauda della licentia: & cantaſi co
   me perche lamor de Dio,
Veduto hauete quanto Agata bella
conſtante ſi per Gieſu ſaluatore:
& quanti aſpri tormenti ſofferſe ella
piu toſto che negare el ſuo ſignore:
pero ciaſcun di uoi ſeguiti quella
& goderete drento al uoſtro core
& del diſagio habbiate patientia
andate in pace & habbiate licentia,
    IL FINE,

In Firenze l'Anno del Noſtro Signore, MDLVIII,

FIG. 23.1. A raised type in the middle of the page preventing the ink from reaching the adjacent types. Note also the imperfect register in the last line. *La rapresentatione di santa Agata vergine & martire. Nuouamente ristampata*, Florence, s.n., 1558, 4° (PT00000067; USTC 801089), sig. A6v. Venice, Fondazione Giorgio Cini, FOAN TES 1061.

454 PRINTING AND MISPRINTING

On the contrary, if types were too low — for example, if they were too worn out to receive ink — they would not be properly printed. An example is visible in the BL copy of *La rapresentatione duno* [sic] *miracolo di due pellegrini che andauano a San Iacopo di Galitia* [1550?].[34] Here a few letters are almost completely invisible; they are so pale that the text comprehension is severely compromised. The last verse of the first column on sig. B1*r* should read '& della patria ci porta il disio', but the two central letters of the word 'patria' and the first in 'porta' are so weak that the verse reads '& della pa ia ci orta il disio'.

So far we have blamed the compositor. However, uneven inking — as pointed out in in the 1766 Venetian document — could also be caused by a puller unable to prepare a perfectly flat surface above the forme and correctly balance the platen.[35] This was a delicate operation.[36] The platen could tilt and leave an unbalanced impression on the sheet if the packing material, which was either inserted between the tympan and the inner tympan or leant directly onto the sheet before printing, was not even or some parts were too worn out. As a result, parts would be too inked, parts almost invisible.[37]

The third cause of uneven inking mentioned in the Venetian document concerns ink balls. If ink was not carefully distributed on their external skin, the skin had some wear, or the ink balls were unevenly stuffed, these could easily leave spots and lumps of ink on the page.[38]

Although not listed in the document, other factors influenced the distribution of ink on the page. Uneven paper could only absorb ink unevenly, and ink that was not ground sufficiently or was not produced with the best materials could leave 'monks' and 'friars' on the sheet, i.e. black spots on the paper and white spots on the letters, respectively.[39] Whatever the cause, the presence of uneven inking in a large majority of ordinary publications strongly suggests that they were produced without strict quality control.

---

[34] *La rapresentatione duno* [sic] *miracolo di due pellegrini che andauano a San Iacopo di Galitia*, [Florence?], s.n., [1550?], 4° (PT00000150, not in USTC). The BL copy (11426.f.51) is the only one known at present.

[35] 'Il tiratore che non sapia fare il suo arte cioè un buon registro, [...] vale a dire un perfetto piano sopra la forma, questo lavoro riuscirà storto, e con un'impressione parte caricata e parte non visibile' ('If a puller is unable to do his job, i.e., a good register, [...] which is a perfectly flat surface above the forme, his work would turn out unbalanced, with parts overinked and others not visible'). See 'Report on the printing press', 20 May 1766 (n. 29 above).

[36] Harris, 'Devices and desires' (n. 26 above), *sub vocem* 'bearing type (blind impressions)'. See also Bolton, *The Fifteenth-Century Printing Practices* (n. 26 above), pp. 119–58.

[37] This is the case in the BL copy (11426.f.33) of *La rappresentatione di Costantino imperatore, et di san Siluestro papa, & di santa Elena imperatrice*, Siena and Orvieto, Antonio Colaldi, [circa 1600], 4°, (PT00000153; USTC 807465), sig. A13*r*. Two copies are known. In the second one (Rome, Bibl. Cors., 92 F 15 (13)), the defect is visible but it is less dramatic.

[38] 'Se tanto il tiratore che il battitore non tirano l'inchiostro sottile sopra la pelle del mazzo, o che questa abbia consumata la superfizie [...], la stampa riuscirà piena di sporchi' ('If either the puller or the beater is unable to spread the ink thinly over the ink balls, or these balls are worn out [...], the impression would be full of dirty areas'). See 'Report on the printing press', 20 May 1766 (n. 29 above). Spots are well visible in the BL copy, C.34.h.5 (22), of *La rappresentatione di santa Apollonia vergine: & martire*, Siena, [Luca Bonetti, c. 1580], 4° (PT00000110; USTC 805599), sig. A2*r*. Four copies are known. Similar spots are visible on this and other pages also in the copies in Florence, BNCF, Pal. E.6.7.56.I.13; Rome, Bibl. Cors., 93 L 14 (7); and Perugia, Biblioteca Dominicini, III B 378/25.

[39] C. H. Bloy, *A History of Printing Ink: Balls and Rollers, 1440–1850*, London, 1972, p. 90.

The 'book in hand' analysis also makes it possible to shed some light on the frequency of four other typical defects: poor register, inked shoulders (Fig. 23.2), smudged types and inked smudges in margins (Fig. 23.3).

I am inclined to consider them mainly as drawbacks of procedures aimed at reducing time and costs. In 77.6% of the inspected items, the paper sheet was incorrectly imposed on the press, resulting in a poor register.[40] Inked shoulders were detected in 65% of the items, most usually at the head and foot of the text block. They could be caused by very soft packing, by not filing down the shoulders of type letters, or both. The third common defect is smudged type, occurring in 48% of the items. This happened when the paper was not either laid on or lifted off the forme cleanly, though it can possibly be due to the unstableness of some parts of a press. Finally, even though the figure is rounded down because of the paucity of copies in which the margins were not completely trimmed, 12% of the analysed specimens show inked smudges of different sizes and forms around the text area. Ink could get spread on the furniture surrounding text blocks while the forme was inked with ink balls. To protect the book pages from picking up extraneous ink, a frisket should be placed on the tympan with windows cut as neatly as possible to fit just around the text blocks. The frisket helped support the floppy paper as well as protecting the sheet from ink. If the frisket was not used or one with a bigger window was reused, the margins could be marked, usually with long black stripes on the margins.[41] Without using the frisket, some pieces of furniture, accidentally risen, could also be impressed on paper, as with the piece of wooden furniture visible on a page of the Bodleian copy of the *Rappresentazione di s. Agata*, (Florence, 1558).[42]

Although my investigation is at an early stage, the high percentage of these side effects not only suggests lack of care, but also that the printing procedure was simplified in the case of ordinary publications: the continuous opening and closing of the frisket and tympan and/or the preparation of a new frisket ostensibly slowed work down and cost money.[43] As these

---

[40] If the second side (the reiteration) was not put back exactly in the same position of the first side (the white sheet), the lines of text on the two sides would not perfectly overlap. See Bolton, *The Fifteenth-Century Printing Practices* (n. 26 above), pp. 192–219.

[41] Such as in Giulio Cesare Croce, *Lamento di tutte le arti del mondo*, Modena, Paolo Gadaldini, 1588, 8°, (USTC 824892), sig. A3r, of which the only copy known is in London, BL, 1071.c.63 (8); the *Litera de tutti li successi di Roma*, [Rome?], s.n., [1534], 4° (Edit16 79603; not in USTC), sig. A2r, of which the only copy known is in London, BL, C.32.g.7 (4); and *La rappresentatione d'un miracolo di dua pellegrini*, Florence, alle Scalee di Badia, [1580?], 4° (PT00000055, PT00000071; USTC 804756). Five copies of this edition are known. The defect is visible in the copies held in London, BL, C.34.h.33, sig. A4r, and C.34.h.6 (12), sigs A3v–A4r, and in Florence, BNCF, Pal. E.6.7.56.VI.16, sig. A3v. It is not visible in the copies in Yale, Beinecke Library, 2008 1340, and Chicago, Newberry Library, VAULT Case Y 7134 .735 no. 31.

[42] *Rappresentazione di s. Agata* (n. 32 above). Oxford, Bod., Mortara Adds. 9, sig. A5v. The defect is visible in the copy in Wolfenbüttel, Herzog August Bibliothek, A: 12.2 Eth. (33) and partially visible in the copy in Cambridge, Fitzwilliam Museum, 32.G.4.(1).

[43] Alternatively, printers could reuse an old frisket, patching up the extra space if too large or cutting a bigger window if too small. In this case, if the frisket had a smaller window or the register was not perfect, some lines or letters were not printed, causing a defect known as the frisket bite. Harris, 'Devices and desires' (n. 26 above), *sub vocem* 'frisket bite'. Frisket bites are visible in *La rappresentatione di Abraam e di Sarra sua moglie*, Florence, s.n., 1556, 4° (PT00000068; USTC 801073), sig. A4r (out of the nine copies currently known, the defect being visible only in the BL copy C.34.h.5 (28)), and in *Il Malatesta. Comedia spirituale*, Florence, s.n., 1575, 4° (PT00000098; USTC 805219), p. 5. Ten copies of the latter are known. The defect is clearly visible in London, BL, C.34.h.5 (2), while the last letter in the bottom left corner is partially not visible in the copies in Milan, Biblioteca del Museo Poldi Pezzoli, C III n. 4/3 (inv.

FIG. 23.2. Inked shoulders are particularly marked on the last two letters of 'rapresentatione' and 'vergine'. Most probably, the sheet was slightly moved during printing, leaving a sort of double impression (smudged types). The woodcut is also crooked. *La rapresentatione di santa Agata* (see Fig. 23.1), sig. A1r. Venice, Giorgio Cini Foundation, FOAN TES 1061.

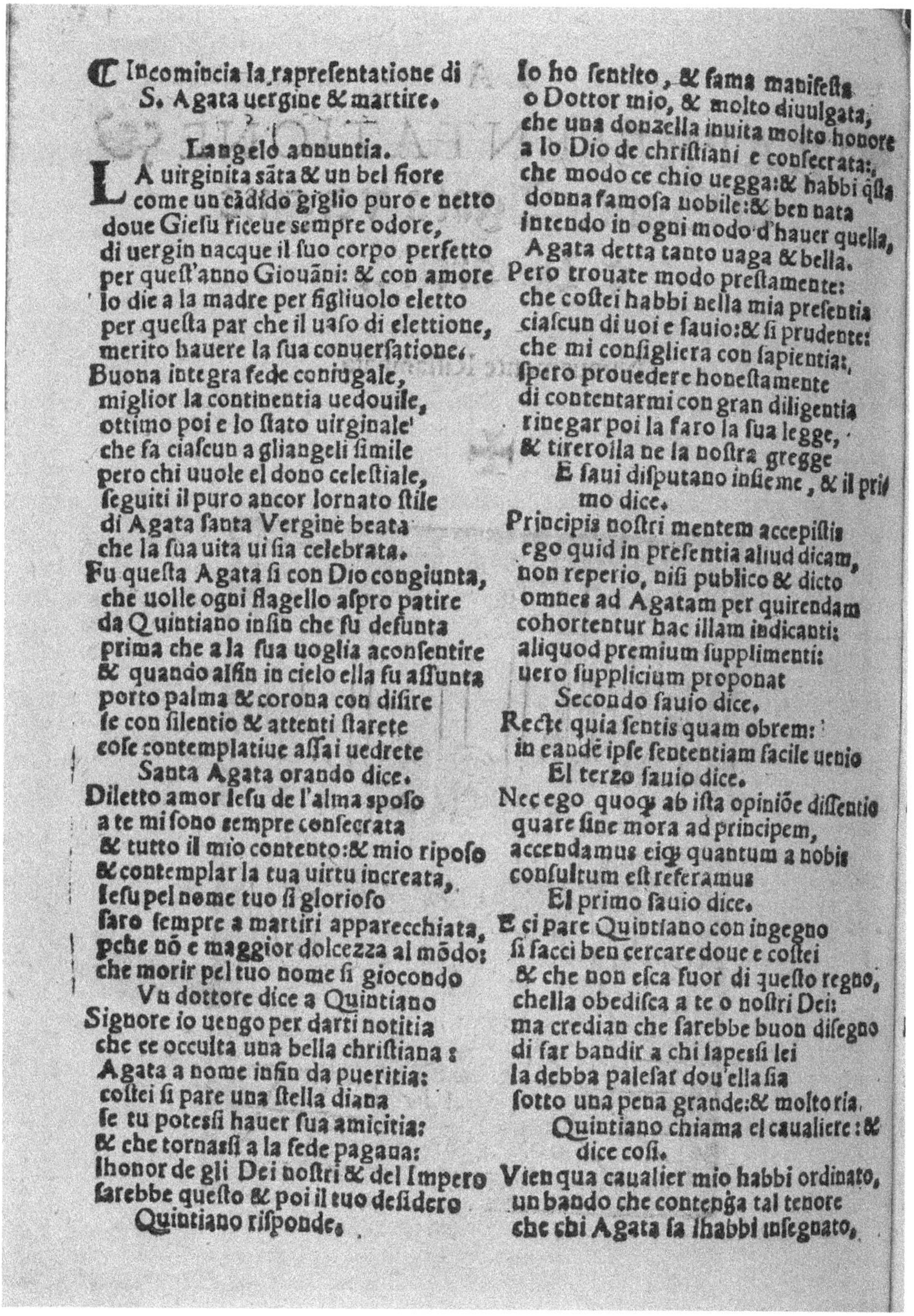

*Incomincia la rapresentatione di
S. Agata uergine & martire.*

L'angelo annuntia.

LA uirginita sàta & un bel fiore
come un càdido giglio puro e netto
doue Giesu riceue sempre odore,
di uergin nacque il suo corpo perfetto
per quest'anno Giouàni: & con amore
lo die a la madre per figliuolo eletto
per quella par che il uaso di elettione,
merito hauere la sua conuersatione.
Buona integra fede coniugale,
miglior la continentia uedouile,
ottimo poi e lo stato uirginale
che fa ciascun a gliangeli simile
pero chi uuole el dono celestiale,
seguiti il puro ancor lornato stile
di Agata santa Vergine beata
che la sua uita ui sia celebrata.
Fu questa Agata si con Dio congiunta,
che uolle ogni flagello aspro patire
da Quintiano infin che fu defunta
prima che a la sua uoglia aconsentire
& quando alfin in cielo ella fu assunta
porto palma & corona con disire
se con silentio & attenti starete
cose contemplatiue assai uedrete
Santa Agata orando dice.
Diletto amor Iesu de l'alma sposo
a te mi sono sempre consecrata
& tutto il mio contento:& mio riposo
&contemplar la tua uirtu increata,
Iesu pel nome tuo si glorioso
saro sempre a martiri apparecchiata,
pche nò e maggior dolcezza al mòdo:
che morir pel tuo nome si giocondo
Vn dottore dice a Quintiano
Signore io uengo per darti notitia
che ce occulta una bella christiana:
Agata a nome infin da pueritia:
costei si pare una stella diana
se tu potessi hauer sua amicitia:
& che tornassi a la fede pagana:
lhonor de gli Dei nostri & del Impero
sarebbe questo & poi il tuo desidero
Quintiano risponde.

Io ho sentito, & fama manifesta
o Dottor mio, & molto diuulgata,
che una donzella inuita molto honore
a lo Dio de christiani e consecrata:
che modo ce chio uegga:& habbi qsta
donna famosa nobile:& ben nata
intendo in ogni modo d'hauer quella,
Agata detta tanto uaga & bella.
Pero trouate modo prestamente:
che costei habbi nella mia presentia
ciascun di uoi e sauio:& si prudente:
che mi consigliera con sapientia:
spero prouedere honestamente
di contentarmi con gran diligentia
rinegar poi la faro la sua legge,
& tireroila ne la nostra gregge
E saui disputano insieme, & il pri
mo dice.
Principis nostri mentem accepistis
ego quid in presentia aliud dicam,
non reperio, nisi publico & dicto
omnes ad Agatam per quirendam
cohortentur hac illam indicanti:
aliquod premium supplimenti:
uero supplicium proponat
Secondo sauio dice.
Recte quia sentis quam obrem:
in eandè ipse sententiam facile uenio
El terzo sauio dice.
Nec ego quoqs ab ista opinióe dissentio
quare sine mora ad principem,
accendamus eiqs quantum a nobis
consultum est referamus
El primo sauio dice.
E si pare Quintiano con ingegno
si facci ben cercare doue e costei
& che non esca fuor di questo regno,
chella obedisca a te o nostri Deii
ma credian che sarebbe buon disegno
di far bandir a chi sapessi lei
la debba palesar dou'ella sia
sotto una pena grande:& molto ria.
Quintiano chiama el caualiere:&
dice così.
Vien qua caualier mio habbi ordinato,
un bando che contenga tal tenore
che chi Agata sa lhabbi insegnato,

FIG. 23.3. The ink bled from the recto giving a dirty aspect to the page. The margin on the left side shows an inked smudge running along the text. *La rapresentatione di santa Agata* (see Fig. 23.1), sig. A1v. Venice, Giorgio Cini Foundation, FOAN TES 1061.

parts of the printing press were detachable, it is possible that printers removed them when in a rush and/or when printing materials that would be sold at a low price.[44] This speeded up work, but could easily lead to such defects as those analysed in this chapter.

The resulting quality of a book was therefore determined by many factors other than the abilities of a printer, and faults could easily occur in any case. What was the printer's reaction to flaws, if any? The extremely low survival rate of popular material makes it difficult to answer this question. Nevertheless, the fact that same defects can be frequently found in more than one surviving copy hints at a slow reaction from printers, if not intentional disregard.[45] For example, in at least five copies of *La rappresentatione di Iudith hebrea* (Florence, 1568), spacing material or furniture near the foot of the type block area was inked and printed at the bottom left corner of sig. A3*v*.[46] It probably took some time to correct the issue, or it was not considered significant enough a defect to warrant fixing it, as the text legibility was not compromised.

As already discussed, if each line was not set to the same tension as the others, loose types could rise and move during setting, transferring, inking, or printing. In the worst cases they could also fall.[47] In two copies of the *Rapresentatione di s. Tomaso apostolo. Composta per m. Castellano Castellani* printed in Florence in 1561, a type close to the external margin is missing.[48] The first verse of the second column on sig. A2*r* should read 'Giugne Abbane in Cesarea, & ua', but the final letter 'a' probably fell out of the forme. As a consequence, the two 'o's in the lines below crept up into the created space. It is not known whether or when the printer noticed the mistake, but surely the reaction (if ever there was one) must not have been too prompt, since two out of six surviving copies have the two flying 'o's.

It should be noted, however, that unnoticed and uncorrected defects could sometimes get increasingly worse during the operation of printing the whole print run of a forme. A page in the BL copy of *Il Malatesta. Comedia spirituale* (Florence, 1575) literally froze the moment when most letters fell out the forme.[49] The incident involved the three bottom lines of the

---

451); Rome, Bibl. Cors., 92.F.15(5); Venice, Biblioteca Nazionale Marciana (Bibl. Marc.), RARI 496.7 and Berkeley, Bancroft Library, PQ4561.A1 M25 1575.

[44] They could lean the packing material directly on the paper sheet before pushing the forme under the platen. I have experimented with this procedure with letterpress printers in the Department of Typography and Graphic Communication, University of Reading. See also Harris, 'Devices and desires' (see n. 26 above), *sub vocem* 'bearing type (blind impressions)'.

[45] See *Rappresentazione di s. Agata* (n. 32 above) and *La rappresentatione d'un miracolo* (n. 41 above).

[46] *La rappresentatione di Iudith hebrea*, Florence, alle Scalee di Badia, 1568, 4° (PT00000047; USTC 801228), sig. A3*v*. Six copies are known. The defect is visible in London, BL, 11426.f.57; Florence, BNCF: Pal. E.6.7.56.V.12; Florence, Biblioteca Riccardiana, Ed.R.674.25; Milan, Biblioteca Trivulziana, TRIV.H 564; Paris, BnF, RES-YD-346.

[47] See Bolton, *The Fifteenth-Century Printing Practices* (n. 26 above), pp. 81–92, as well as her contribution in this Companion.

[48] *Rapresentatione di s. Tomaso apostolo. Composta per m. Castellano Castellani*, Florence, Paolo Bigio, 1561, 4°, sig. A2*r* (PT00000296; USTC 819333). Six copies are known. The defect is visible in all known copies: Oxford, Bod., Mortara Adds. 17; Florence, BNCF, Pal. E.6.5.1.V.22; Siena, Biblioteca degli Intronati, FP LXXXVII [22]; Paris, BnF, RES-YD-391; Yale, Beinecke Library, 2001 1092; New York, New York Public Library, Spencer Coll. Ital. 1561.

[49] *Il Malatesta* (n. 43 above), p. 4. The last three lines should read 'Di guardar più che mai, hoggi t'ingegna| Bianca, del viver mio vera colonna, | Tu'l mio parlare intendi, & donde vegna [...]'. The letters are falling off in the BL copy C.34.h.5(2). Preliminary stages with letters only partially printed can be

first column on p. 4. The letter 'D' at the beginning of the second verse is printed almost two lines below; the first four letters of the word 'bianca' disappear into the margin; there is no sign of the first four letters of the final verse as well. How long did it take to get to this point? According to the defects found in other extant copies, it took a while. In this case, the printer pressed his luck too much.

The massive presence of paper and printing defects demonstrates that printers and publishers economised on materials and time when printing publications intended for wide dissemination. They sacrificed quality to speed up work, whenever possible. The result of this low investment was consequently modest, as modest as the price asked for the final output. Rather than mistakes, material flaws are therefore intrinsic features of these products, resulting from a specific strategy for reducing expenses in order to cope with the incessant demand for a kind of publication which ought to be cheap and rapidly available at the same time.

seen in other copies: at the last line the 'T' has only one bar and the 'u' is ill-printed in the copies Venice, Bibl. Marc., RARI 496.7, and Siena, Biblioteca degli Intronati, Misc. FP LXXXVII [21]; the 'T' has only half bar and the 'l' is almost invisible in Florence, BNCF, Pal. E.6.7.56/VI.3; same defects in the copies in Milan, Biblioteca Trivulziana, TRIV. H 579, Wellesley, Wellesley College, Spec. Coll. Plimpton P1021, and Venice, Bibl. Marc., RARI 501.2, possibly with the addition of a frisket bite covering the last four letters in the word 'parlare'; the letters 'Tu' and the second shoulder of 'm' on the last line are barely visible in Milan, Biblioteca del Museo Poldi Pezzoli, C III n. 4/3 (inv. 451), Rome, Bibl. Cors., 92.F.15(5), and Berkeley, Bancroft Library, PQ4561.A1 M25 1575.

460   PRINTING AND MISPRINTING

Table 23.1 Analysing paper quality in early modern books.

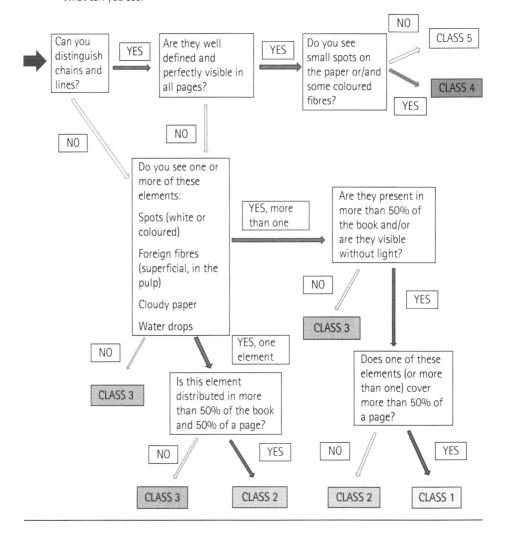

BIBLIOGRAPHY

PRIMARY SOURCES

ARCHIVAL DOCUMENTATION

Venice, Archivio di Stato, Arti, env. 164.
Venice, Archivio di Stato, Riformatori dello Studio di Padova, envs 369–370.
Venice, Biblioteca del Museo Correr, Mariegola MS iv 119.

PRINTED BOOKS

Bando dell'appalto generale della carta, cenci, e carnicci, Florence, nella stamperia di S.A.R. per i Tartini e Franchi, 1722.

Catalogus librorum amplissimus in typographia Remondiniana Impressorum, Venice, Joseph Remondini, & Filios, 176[1].

Croce, Giulio Cesare, *Lamento di tutte le arti del mondo*, Modena, Paolo Gadaldini, 1588, 8° (USTC 824892).

Houghton, J., *Husbandry and Trade Improv'd: Being a Collection of Many Valuable Materials*, II, London, 1727.

Litera de tutti li successi di Roma, [Rome?], s.n., [1534], 4° (not in USTC; see Edit16 79603).

Il Malatesta. Comedia spirituale, Florence, s.n., 1575, 4° (USTC 805219).

La rappresentatione di Abraam e di Sarra sua moglie, Florence, s.n., 1556, 4° (USTC 801073).

La rappresentatione di Costantino imperatore, et di san Siluestro papa, & di santa Elena imperatrice, Siena and Orvieto, Antonio Colaldi, [c. 1600], 4° (USTC 807465).

La rappresentatione di Iudith hebrea, Florence, alle Scalee di Badia, 1568, 4° (USTC 801228).

Rapresentatione di s. Tomaso apostolo. Composta per m. Castellano Castellani, Florence, Paolo Bigio, 1561, 4° (USTC 819333).

La rappresentatione di santa Agata vergine & martire. Nuouamente ristampata, Florence, s.n., 1558, 4° (USTC 801089).

La rappresentatione di santa Apollonia vergine: & martire, Siena, [Luca Bonetti, c. 1580], 4° (USTC 805599).

Rappresentatione di santa Eufrosina vergine, Florence, Paolo Bigio, 1561, 4° (USTC 801237).

La rappresentatione d'un miracolo di dua pellegrini, Florence, alle Scalee di Badia, [1580?], 4° (USTC 804756).

La rappresentatione duno [sic] miracolo di due pellegrini che andauano a San Iacopo di Galitia, [Florence?], s.n., [1550?], 4° (not in USTC; see PT00000150).

SECONDARY LITERATURE

Atkinson, D., and Roud, S. (eds), *Cheap Print and the People: European Perspectives on Popular Literature*, Newcastle upon Tyne, 2019.

Barrett, T., Ormsby, M., and Lang, J. B., 'Non-Destructive Analysis of 14th–19th Century European Handmade Papers', *Restaurator*, 37/2, 2016, pp. 93–135.

Bellingradt, D., and Salman, J., 'Books and Book History in Motion: Materiality, Sociality and Spatiality', in D. Bellingradt, P. Nelles, and J. Salman (eds), *Books in Motion in Early Modern Europe: Beyond Production, Circulation and Consumption*, London, 2017, pp. 1–11.

Bloy, C. H., *A History of Printing Ink: Balls and Rollers 1440–1850*, London, 1972.

Bolton, C., *The Fifteenth-Century Printing Practices of Johann Zainer, Ulm 1473–1478*, Oxford and London, 2016.

Campanini, Z., *Istruzioni pratiche ad un novello capo-stampa o sia regolamento per la direzione di una tipografica officina (1789)*, ed. C. Fahy, Florence, 1998.

Carnelos, L., *I libri da risma. Catalogo delle edizioni Remondini a larga diffusione (1650–1850)*, Milan, 2008.

Carnelos, L., *I pirati dei libri. Stampa e contraffazione a Venezia tra Sei e Settecento*, Venice, 2012.

Carnelos, L., 'Popular Print Under the Press: Strategies, Practices and Materials', *Quaerendo*, 51 (2021), pp. 8–35.

Cipolla, C. M., *Before the Industrial Revolution: European Society and Economy 1000–1700*, London, 2005.

Fahy, C., 'Paper Making in Seventeenth-Century Genoa: The Account of Giovanni Domenico Peri (1651)', *Studies in Bibliography*, 56, 2003–2004, pp. 243–59.

Farnsworth, D., *Handmade Paper Method Cinquecento: Renaissance Paper Textures*, Oakland, 2019.

Fedrigoni, A., *L'industria veneta della carta dalla II dominazione austriaca all'Unità*, Turin, 1966.

Gaskell, P., *A New Introduction to Bibliography*, Oxford, 1979.

Harris, N., 'L'*Hypnerotomachia Poliphili* e le contrastampe', *La Bibliofilia*, 100/2–3, 1998, pp. 201–51.

Mattozzi, I., *Produzione e commercio della carta nello stato veneziano settecentesco. Lineamenti e problemi*, Bologna, 1975.

Ornato, E. [et al.], *La carta occidentale nel tardo Medioevo*, I, Rome, 2001.

Raymond, J., *Pamphlets and Pamphleteering in Early Modern Britain*, Cambridge, 2003.

Rodgers Albro, S., *Fabriano: City of Medieval and Renaissance Papermaking*, New Castle (DE) and Washington, 2016.

Rosenband, L. N., *Papermaking in Eighteenth-Century France: Management, Labor, and Revolution at the Montgolfier Mill 1761–1805*, Baltimore and London, 2000.

Tanselle, G. T., 'The Treatment of Typesetting and Presswork in Bibliographical Description', *Studies in Bibliography*, 52, 1999, pp. 1–57.

ONLINE SOURCES

Edit16: http://edit16.iccu.sbn.it/.

Neil Harris, 'Devices and desires', available at http://ihl.enssib.fr/en/analytical-bibliography-an-alternative-prospectus/devices-and-desires.

PATRIMONiT: http://data.cerl.org/patrimonit/_search.

CHAPTER 24

PRINTING UNDER PRESSURE

Mistakes in the Earliest Newspapers

JAN HILLGÄRTNER

INTRODUCTION

FEW other forms of print were more prone to contain printer's errors than the newspapers of the seventeenth century. They first appeared at the turn of the century, published at weekly intervals and later more often, comprising one to two sheets of paper per issue in quarto. Newspapers were relatively cheap products, produced at speed, usually with little attention to detail, which led to a staggering amount of printer's errors. Much of the reason for this lay in the hasty production process. Already in 1609, Johann Carolus, printer of the first newspaper in Strasbourg, mentioned in a foreword that '[w]e print the newspapers with the greatest urgency during the night'.[1] This chapter explores the type of mistakes and errors that were often made by newspaper printers and seeks to elucidate the ways in which they sought to control the problem.

To understand why newspapers were riddled with printer's errors it is important to understand the context of their production. News had enjoyed some currency in the world of print almost since the beginning of printing with moveable types. In Germany publishing news peaked for the first time around 1550 and throughout the latter half the sixteenth century with the *Newe Zeytung*. The blanket term covers broadsheets and short pamphlets containing news which were published irregularly and usually confined to reporting on one topic only. The genre of the newspaper was invented when the young and aspiring printer Johann Carolus had put one and one together and began to use the potential of the printing press to disseminate news in 1605.[2] He had been active as a purveyor of written newsletters, a job that required him to collect and bundle the news that arrived at the doorstep of his workshop, reproduce it manually, and send the written products to his

---

[1] *Relation aller Fuernemmen und Gedenckwürdigen Historien*, [Strasbourg, Johann Carolus, 1609], 4° (USTC N60-1), p. [3]: 'vnnd das bey der Nacht eylend gefertigt werden muß/ zum besten verstehn/ auff vnd annemmen/'.

[2] J. Weber, 'Strassburg, 1605: The Origins of the Newspaper in Europe', *German History*, 24/3, 2006, pp. 387–412 (388–92).

Jan Hillgärtner, *Printing under Pressure*. In: *Printing and Misprinting*. Edited by Geri Della Rocca de Candal, Anthony Grafton, and Paolo Sachet, Oxford University Press. © Jan Hillgärtner (2023). DOI: 10.1093/oso/9780198863045.003.0025

464   PRINTING AND MISPRINTING

subscribers. Carolus, who had taken over the print shop of Tobias Jobin in August 1604, saw the opportunity to drastically lower the price of his wares and thus increase the circle of potential buyers if he was able to print periodicals, rather than have the news copied by hand.[3] The idea quickly caught on across the Holy Roman Empire and elsewhere, and by the middle of the seventeenth century more than 100 newspapers had appeared across the country in cities large and small.

The sometimes grotesque and absurd mistakes were the result of production under extreme time pressure that more often than not prevented printers from correcting even the most obvious mistakes. Newspapers had a quick turnaround time and printers gave little attention to the correction of mistakes. This was precisely part of their economic appeal to printers: the production of a newspaper was a relatively modest job that even minor work-shops could easily take on. In most cases, the print run did not exceed 300 to 500 copies per issue. Printing newspapers was often a side project between larger printing undertakings, requiring only a limited amount of paper, not much type, and little press time. A printer with a single press was thus able to produce around 600 copies of one newspaper per day. Given that the actual print run for most will have been significantly lower, we can assume that printers must have been able to print all copies of a weekly newspaper in less than a day.[4] In order to keep up with the pace of the events, printers had to sacrifice important steps such as the production of proof sheets, their correction by a professional proofreader, and changes to the formes once errors had been found and corrected in the proof sheets.

THE CONSEQUENCES OF QUICK AND CHEAP PRODUCTION: PRINTERS' ERRORS

The usually hasted production of newspapers meant that printers were left with little to no time to correct simple errors and typos. Misprints of this type, as well as scrambled letters and instances of misplaced types, were by far the most common type of errors we find in the earliest newspapers. They regularly happened to almost every printer. Evidence presented in this chapter suggests that printers who were pressed for time saw no need to rectify these mistakes and many would tolerate even shocking mistakes on the title-pages of their periodicals.

In Altona, just outside of Hamburg, Anna de Löw published the *Altonaische Relation* in collaboration with the publisher Heinrich Heuss from the early 1680s onward.[5] The peri-odical was founded in 1673 by her late husband Victor and appeared in two weekly issues of

---

[3] C. Reske, *Die Buchdrucker des 16. und 17. Jahrhunderts im deutschen Sprachgebiet. Auf der Grundlage des gleichnamigen Werkes von Josef Benzing*, Wiesbaden, 2007, p. 898.

[4] M. Welke, 'Die Entwicklung der frühen Zeitungsdrucktechnik (17. und 18. Jahrhundert)', in M. Welke and B. Fuchs (eds), *Zeitungsdruck. Die Entwicklung der Technik vom 17. bis zum 20. Jahrhundert*, Munich, 2000, pp. 9–28.

[5] On the history of this newspaper, see E. Bogel and E. Blühm, *Die deutschen Zeitungen des 17. Jahrhunderts. Ein Bestandsverzeichnis mit historischen und bibliographischen Angaben. Band 1: Text*, Bremen, 1971, pp. 206–12, and P. T. Hoffmann, 'Victor de Löw, Altonas ältester Buch- und Zeitungsdrucker', *Altonaische Zeitschrift für Geschichte und Heimatkunde*, 1, 1931, pp. 191–6.

eight pages each. Often, the printer's desire to purvey promptly the latest news to her paying customers meant that she sacrificed diligence and artisanal attention to details. Printing errors and negligence haunted the *Altonaische Relation* for much of its existence, indicating that the compositors, journeymen, and printers produced the newspaper quickly and with little care. The pagination for example, which usually appeared centred at the top of the newspaper page, was inserted the wrong way round in the printing block in this issue of 31 March 1691 (Fig. 24.1).[6] The printer typically used a slightly smaller type for pagination compared to the set of body text. The page number was inserted last into the printing block. In this specific case, the manual pencil correction was not carried out in the workshop itself, but added by a reader or librarian.

Another obvious yet absurd mistake crept into the title of the *Europaeische Zeitung* from 5 February 1684 (Fig. 24.2) The letter 'R' in the title of the issue had either been set incorrectly or fallen out of the text block during the printing process. It was rotated by 90 degrees clockwise before the frame containing the set text went to press. The printer or journeyman entered the letter the wrong way round into the composing stick.[7] It would have been simple to correct this error, given that German printers in the seventeenth century typically used type with a little nick at one side of the foot. This was a safeguard against precisely such mistakes: if the line of text was set correctly, those nicks would join together and create a line. Compositors would then run their fingernails along the line to ensure that no type was set upside down or had been otherwise twisted. This misprint was a minor mishap that could have been avoided, had the composition and printing block been handled with care and had printer or journeymen checked their work thoroughly and made the necessary corrections in time. Neither Justus Böff, the publisher and printer of the newspaper, nor one of his employees in the Hanau workshop seems to have been bothered by the obvious mistake, which, due to its more than prominent position directly in the newspaper's title, must have been noticed immediately.

Mistakes such as the pagination turned upside down, letters inserted wrongly, and inconsistent use of type size that we will encounter later in this chapter were legion in the early press, though most printers seem to have paid attention to eliminating these at least in the titles of their periodicals. What they had no control over were the constraints of the format of usually one sheet per issue. The amount of text a printer had to accommodate within this space often varied wildly. It was not uncommon for a newspaper that contained around 2,000 words per issue on average to grow by around 50% if the amount of news that had to be included in the issue was particularly large. A closer look at the distribution of text on the three pages depicted in Fig. 24.3.a–b reveals the inconsistencies that came with this.

---

[6] *Vom 31 Marty. Fol. 201 Die Europäische RELATION No 26 1693*, [Altona, Anna de Löw and Heinrich Heuss, 1693], 4° (USTC N214-4305), p. 208. I am grateful to the Staats- und Universitätsbibliothek Bremen for granting the right to use this and the other images in my contribution.

[7] It may have also been the case that the type letter had come loose during the printing process and was dislocated from its original position. Such cases of misplaced types, however, are relatively uncommon in newspaper printing.

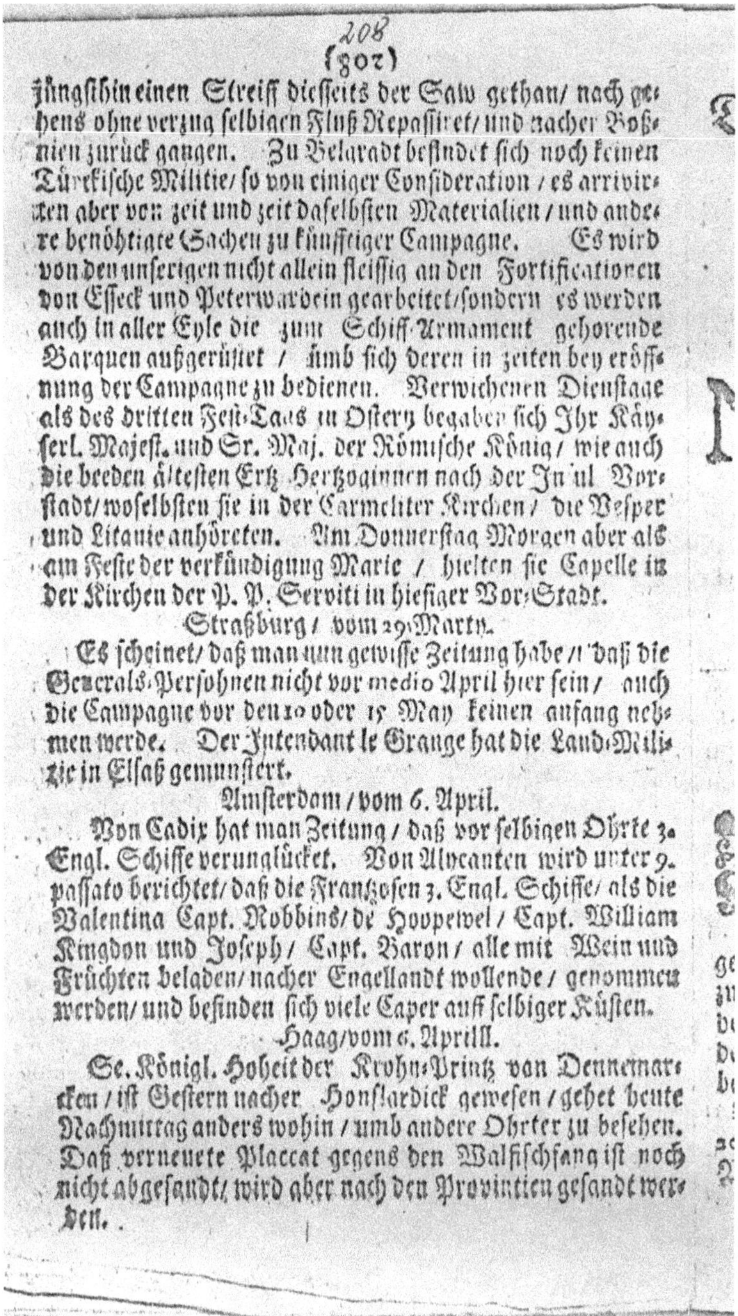

208

(807)

Jüngsthin einen Streiff dießseits der Saw gethan/ nach ge-
hens ohne verzug selbigen Fluß Repassiret/ und nacher Boß-
nien zurück gangen. Zu Belaradt befindet sich noch keinen
Türckische Militie/ so von einiger Consideration / es arrivir-
ten aber von zeit und zeit daselbsten Materialien/ und andere benöhtigte Sachen zu künfftiger Campagne. Es wird
von den unserigen nicht allein fleissig an den Fortificationen
von Esseck und Peterwardein gearbeitet/sondern es werden
auch in aller Eyle die zum Schiff-Armament gehörende
Barquen außgerüstet / umb sich deren in zeiten bey eröff-
nung der Campagne zu bedienen. Verwichenen Dienstage
als des dritten Fest-Taus in Ostern begaben sich Jhr Käy-
serl. Majest. und Sr. Maj. der Römische König/ wie auch
die beeden ältesten Ertz-Hertzoginnen nach der Jn ul Vor-
stadt/woselbsten sie in der Carmeliter Kirchen/ die Vesper
und Litanie anhöreten. Am Donnerstag Morgen aber als
am Feste der verkündigung Marie / hielten sie Capelle in
der Kirchen der P. P. Serviti in hiesiger Vor-Stadt.
                    Straßburg / vom 29 Marty.
Es scheinet/ daß man um gewisse Zeitung habe/ daß die
Generals-Persohnen nicht vor medio April hier sein/ auch
die Campagne vor den 10 oder 15 May keinen anfang neh-
men werde. Der Jntendant le Grange hat die Land-Mili-
tie in Elsaß gemunstert.
                    Amsterdam / vom 6. April.
Von Cadix hat man Zeitung / daß vor selbigen Ohrte 3.
Engl. Schiffe verunglücket. Von Alycanten wird unter 9.
passato berichtet/ daß die Frantzosen 3. Engl. Schiffe/ als die
Valentina Capt. Robbins/ de Hoopewel / Capt. William
Kingdon und Joseph / Capt. Baron / alle mit Wein und
Früchten beladen/nacher Engellandt wollende / genommen
werden/ und befinden sich viele Caper auff selbiger Küsten.
                    Haag/vom 6. Aprill.
Se. Königl. Hoheit der Krohn-Printz von Dennemar-
cken / ist Gestern nacher Honslardick gewesen/ gehet heute
Nachmittag anders wohin / umb andere Ohrter zu besehen.
Daß verneuete Placcat gegens den Walfischfang ist noch
nicht abgesandt/ wird aber nach den Provintien gesandt wer-
den.

FIG. 24.1. Pagination inserted upside down in *Vom 31 Marty. Fol. 201 Die Europäische RELATION No 26 1693*, [Altona, Anna de Löw and Heinrich Heuss, 1693], 4° (USTC N214-4305), p. 208.

EU **⊼** OPÆische Zeitung.

Den 5. Februarij. 1684.

Crakau/vom 23 Januarij st n.

Auß Ungarn kompt Bericht ein / daß der Petrorzi die in Ungarn ligende Fuß-Völcker blocquirt halte/ und Töckelo den Grafen Humanen beängstige / diese zu entsetzen hat der General Rabatta 7000. Mann auß den Quartieren zusammen gezogen/und ist dieser Tagen der General Major Scherffenberg vom Kayserlichen Hof per Posta hier angelangt/ mit dem ansuchen / daß einige Polnische oder Littbauische Treuppen/ zu besagtem Corpo Kayserl. Völcker stossen möchten. Dieser Tagen hat der Herr Krovczo Torczzeiewitz seine Lebens-Comœdie geendigt / welcher als ein Galant Homme vom Frauenzimmer sehr beklagt wird. Zum Außbruch dieses Hofes ist noch keine Zeit bestimbt. Sonst wird geredet/daß Ihre Majest. denen Cosacken/ umb sie desto mehr zu encouragiren, 100000. fl. baar Geld/1000. Stück blau Tuch/ und so.stück Holländisch fein Lacken für die Staros-cona / wie auch etliche stück Sammet und Seiden / auch mit Zobeln und Luchs Futter staffirte Röcke/für den Zaporewischen Feld-Haupt Mann Kunicko/nebenst einem neuen Siegel/ womit er als Cosackischer Feld-Herr seine Universalien und Ordres expediren soll/geschickt haben : Gewester Herr Graf Scherffenberg hat vor den Königl. Printzen den güldnen Fluß mitgebracht/ ob aber solcher hier wird angenommen werden/ kan man noch nicht wissen.

Copenhagen/vom 22. Januarij st.v.

Unsere Milicz bestehet in 12000. Reutern und Dragonern / und 21000. Mann zu Fuß ; und ob schon diese grosse Armatur zu einem Krieg angesehen zu seyn scheinet / so hat doch der Herr Cantzler Alefeld gesagt / daß Ihro Königliche Majestät nicht die geringste Gedancken darzu hätte / und Sie allein werden tiessen/ umb dero Authorität zu erhalten/ weilen alle benachbarte Fürsten in Woffen wären. Der Herr Gioe gehet nach dem Haag / umb daselbst das Friedens-Werck zu recommendiren. Man solle dieses Jahr allhier keine Flotte zur See außrüsten.

Paris/vom 2. Februarij st n.

Der Chevalier de Seppeville,so zu Tevion in Arrest gesessen/ ist auf Königl Beseich wieder loß gelassen worden/ weilen Se.Kön.Maj.nicht haben wollen/ daß er dem Kriegs-Rath untergeben werden sollen. Als der König den 25.paßato mit Monsieur in sein Cabinet gienge/ließ Se.Majest. Mademoiselle/des Hertzogen von Orleans Tochter/ dahin ruffen/ als diese erschiene/ sagte Seine Majestät daß der Hertzog von Savoyen/ Sie zu heurathen begehrte / aber Seine Majestät und Monsieur hätten solchen Heurath / ohne zuvor ihren Consens und Einwilligung deßhalben zu haben/ nicht schliessen wollen / daß Sie glücklich mit einem jungen Printzen seyn würde/mit welchem Sie sich verliebte/weiln weder Se Maj.noch Sie/keinen greissen Unterscheid zwischen dem Frantzösis.u.d Savoyschen Hof finden würden/indem solche fast einerley Manieren hätten ; Herr auf versicherte diese junge Princessin mit vergiessung einiger Thränen/ daß Sie resolvirt wäre / in allem deme/ was Se.Maj.und Monsieur vor genehm halten und gut befinden thäten / zu gehorsamen / worauf dann der Heurath declarirt , und bey der Abend-Mahlzeit Mademoiselle zur lincken Hand von Monseigneur gesetzt ward/wäheender Mahlzeit/liesse Sie viel Thränen lauffen/ und empfieng von dem gantzen Hof/und auch selbsten von Madame,die Visite ; der Savoysche Ambassadeur legte auch seine schuldigkeit ab. und complimentirte Sie/Nahmens seines Herrn. Man versichert/dz die Hochzeits-Ceremonien, zwischen Mademoiselle und dem Hertzogen von Savoyen/zu Fontainebleau beschehen sollen/und daß der König hernach nacher Lion gehen/ allwo sich der Hertzog von Savoyen auch einfinden / und daselbst Mademoiselle als seine Gemahlin empfangen werde. Sonsten verlautet auch daß/wann Se.Aller-Christl.Maj die Infantin von Portugall heurathen werde/der König von Portugall hingegen Mademoiselle de Bourbon, Mr.le Prince Tochter heurathen würde/und daß/indeme dieser Printz noch nicht 40 Jahr alt seye/ Er sich auch bald wieder verheurathen werde/umb Erben zu überkommen. Man glaubt / daß Monsr. de la Feuillade von seiner langwürigen Kranckheit nicht wieder auffstehen werde ; dieser hat den König gebetten / ihme doch die Einkünfften von vier Jahren hero von seinem Gouvernement Dauphine bezahlen zu lassen/ damit er das Hauß Seneterre, allwo er deß Königs Bildnüß/ so er hat machen lassen/dismalen lässet, vollends bezahlen könte/welches ihm auch vere williget worden ist. Alle Oerter in Flandern/thun anjetzo die jenige Contributiones, worzu man sie angesetzt hat/ erlegen / welches sie aber ein wenig zu spat gerhan haben / indeme schon gar viel eingeäschert worden seynd. Man schicket 25000. Mann in Navarra und in Catalonien/also daß sich der Krieg dorthin ziehen wird/nichts desto weniger redet man noch sehr starck vom Frieden. Einem Page, so einem Herrn von Hof von Versailles biß nach Pariß eine Fackel getragen/ist die eine Arm dergestalten er froren/daß man ihm selbigen abhauen muss sen. Vergangene Woche seynd wieder 5. Kirchen/so denen Reformirten in Dausiné, wie auch 5.in denen Ce-

FIG. 24.2. Example of a misplaced type in the *Europaeische Zeitung* from 5 February 1684.

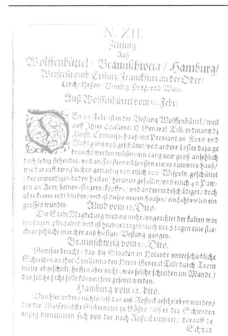

FIG. 24.3.a–b. Varying type sizes in the main body of text in a newspaper issue from 1620.

Part of the difficulty of printing a visually pleasing newspaper was trying to predict correctly how much text had to be set and to select the type size accordingly. Failures at this were the main reasons for inconsistency in the typography of the early newspapers. Theoretically, for any issue the compositor or printer somehow had to anticipate the amount and length of incoming reports. News often trickled in letter by letter and not in bulk. When the compositors began their work, they were often still waiting for the last report destined for inclusion into the newspaper to arrive at the workshop. Compositors needed to select the type size accordingly to ensure size consistency in the main body of text. In theory, the reports would then fill the issue evenly until the last page. In reality, the constraints of speedy production meant that those tasked with the composition of the pages used widely varying type sizes.

Studying one issue of the *Zeitung Auß Wolfenbüttel/ Braunschweig/* of 1620 allows us to understand just how rushed the production of newspapers must have been.[8] The compositor began his work using a mid-sized type. On the subsequent pages, he then reduced the type size as he realised that he would otherwise be unable to include all reports. He started with 26 lines of text on the second page and gradually reduced the size so that he could print up to 38 lines of text on page 7. At the end, he reverted to a type size even larger than the one he had begun with in order to fill the last page.

---

[8] *N. XII. Zeitung Auß Wolfenbüttel/ Braunschweig/ Hamburg/ Weserstromb/ Erffurt/ Franckfurt an der Oder/ Lorch/ Heßen/ Venedig/ Prag/ vnd Wien*, [s.l., s.n., 1620], 4° (USTC N114-12), pp. [1], [6].

Dealing with Shortfalls and Mistakes

Newspaper printers in the seventeenth century were by no means ignorant of the many mistakes they made in their newspapers. Most errors stemmed from the rushed production of the issues. The reasons behind this were manifold. For one, printers relied on the steady stream of news that came in by way of post. Disruptions to the postal system, such as weather events, conflicts, or the breakdown of an important link somewhere in the chain, were common and resulted in a delayed arrival of the news at the workshop. News in the press was arranged according to the respective place of origin, and when publishers failed to include the news from one place, they would often include apologetic passages in their periodicals, promising that the readers could expect the missing news in one of the following issues.

Yet what seems to have mattered to printers and publishers even more were errors and inconsistencies in the spelling of names of people and places. Whereas they had no control over shortfalls in the supply of news, here they could be held accountable. Printers and publishers often showed a certain amount of repentance for this kind of mistake. Many included forewords in their first issues of the year. Besides the standard good wishes for the new year, they sought to create an understanding of the circumstances they found themselves subjected to when printing their periodicals. Whether done openly or not, they sought to ask for clemency from their readers regarding mistakes. Once again it was Johann Carolus who, in the preface of the first issue of his *Relation aller Fürnemmen und gedenckwürdigen Historien*, showed clear awareness of the numerous mistakes and variations in the spellings of proper nouns and titles:

> Whenever there are occasional mistakes and inconsistencies in the spelling of names of individuals and their respective titles or in place names, these mistakes stem either from the ignorance of the editor or it has been impossible to rectify them during the correction phase of the printing process. Thus, we urge the generous reader to correct himself such errors and the mistakes that come from the speedy production of the newspaper, using his knowledge and good judgement.[9]

Careful readers will have surely noticed the irony these few lines contained, for Carolus or his compositor had spelled the conjunction 'and' differently in the space of only a few lines of text. Similar evidence from many other newspapers suggests that these were only cautious words that were part of a rhetorical discourse around the newspaper. This did not suggest that the printers made considerable efforts to improve the situation. Apologetic statements comparable to Carolus's can be found in the opening paragraphs of many other early newspapers. Yet it should be noted that the outbreak of the Thirty Years War shortly after the

---

[9] *Relation* (n. 1 above), p. [3]: 'Wann aber bißweilen Errata vnd vngleichheiten/ die so wol wegen der vnbekandten Ort/ als auch der Persohnen Namen/ dero authoritet Erbämpter oder dergleichen Singulariteten vnd Proprieteten fürfallen/ so aus vnwissenheit nicht recht geschrieben/ in der Correctur auch angeregter vrsachen halben nicht zu ändern müglich/ etc. Als wolte der großgünstige Leser solcher/ wie auch/ was in der Eyl vbersehen/ seinem vernüfftigen wissen nach/ vnbeschwert selbsten corrigiren/ Endern vnd verbessern/.'

inception of the newspaper quickly shifted the focus in the forewords away from delving into mistakes. Now, wishes for peace and prayers replaced all considerations of mistakes and inconsistencies.

Those who published newspapers appear to have accepted small mistakes and inconsistencies as part of the business. After all, publishing presumably false news and political bias in the reporting had far more severe consequences for the business of the printer than the occasional spelling mistake.[10] The eminent Hamburg author and publisher of the *Nordischer Mercurius,* Georg Greflinger, remarked in the foreword of the first issue of 1667:

> The sympathetic reader will have mercy on the printer's errors that have crept into the issues of this year as well as in the issues of the preceding years. For he must consider that the printing of an issue takes place under great time pressure. Curious readers expect their newspapers quickly, especially during the short winter days, which leaves little room for correction.[11]

Actuality became the guiding principle in newspaper publishing and Greflinger seemed to stipulate a deal between him as the editor and publisher and his readers of the *Nordischer Mercurius.* For, if they wanted to read the news as soon as it became available, they would surely have to cope with the mistakes the reports contained.[12]

A Genre Riddled with Inconsistencies

By far the most common type of errors were simple printer's mistakes and typos that affected all newspapers of the seventeenth century. They appeared all over the press, most prominently in the main body of text but also with some regularity in the titles of the newspapers. Just as common were inconsistencies in the spelling of titles and variations in the design of a newspaper. Strictly speaking, these were anomalies in the mise-en-page rather than straightforward mistakes. Readers, however, perceived them as flaws.

Variations in the spelling of titles were common and almost all newspapers that existed for more than just a few years underwent title changes at one or several points during their

---

[10] We are aware of several legal cases in which one printer pressed charges of false reporting against his competitor with the goal of squeezing him out of the market. Perhaps the best-known examples are the series of trials that took place around the monopoly to print a newspaper in Frankfurt and that involved the imperial postmaster Johann von den Birghden. The case is documented in W. Behringer, *Im Zeichen des Merkur. Reichspost und Kommunikationsrevolution in der Frühen Neuzeit,* Göttingen, 2003, pp. 198–201.

[11] *Nordischer MERCURIUS. Welcher kürzlich vorstellet/ was in diesem 1667. Jahr an Novellen aus Europa eingekommen ist,* Hamburg, Friedrich Conrad Greflinger for Georg Greflinger, 1667, 4° (USTC N196-178), p. 3: 'Die einschleichende[n] Druckfehler/ so in diesem/ als andern Jahren/ wird der geneigte Leser nicht so gar scheel besehen/ wann er bedencket/ daß solche Arbeit allezeit schleunig beschehen müsse/ und die Neubegierige oftmals/ sonderlich in den kurzen Tagen/ so vieler Zeit nicht erwarten/ um die andere Correctur zu thun.'

[12] For a more extensive discussion of the repercussions of this attitude, see J. Gieseler, 'Vom Nutzen und richtigen Gebrauch der frühen Zeitungen. Zur sogenannten Pressedebatte des 17. Jahrhunderts', in G. Fritz and E. Straßner (eds), *Die Sprache der ersten deutschen Wochenzeitungen im 17. Jahrhundert,* Tübingen, 1996, pp. 259–85 (281–2).

lifetimes. In the earliest years of the newspaper printers did not pay too much attention to the titles of their periodicals. Christoph Reusner and Moritz Sachs of Rostock published the third newspaper to appear, the *Newe Zeitung(en)*.[13] Rather than give their periodical a standardised title that would be used in issue after issue, they summarised the news in the title of each respective issue. This in turn led to long and winding titles for each issue that resembled those of intermittently published news broadsheets and pamphlets. Only in the period after the 1620s did rising competition in the market for newspapers lead the way to more standardised titles across Germany. Printers and publishers increasingly began to see the titles of their newspaper as a distinctive feature that was recognisable and could serve as a marketing tool.[14]

The *Wochentliche Zeitung auß Hamburg* provides a good case in which to study the inconsistencies in the title and the design of a newspaper that could inevitably be found similarly in almost all other periodicals. This newspaper was the first German-language periodical printed in Copenhagen by Peter Hake.[15] Hake had come to the Danish capital to serve as the official printer to the university, a job that must have taken up most of the capacity of his workshop. From 1657 onward, he essentially published his newspaper for the diaspora of German-speaking readers in Denmark and in the northern stretches of the Holy Roman Empire. Soon after its inception, he began to face local competition. The Danish printer Peder Jensen Morsing started his own newspaper in Danish two years later, clearly borrowing from his German competitor while addressing a Danish-speaking audience.[16] Hake undertook no legal action against Morsing, for copying and translating news at the time was not a punishable offence.[17] The survival of the *Wochentliche Zeitung auß Hamburg* is relatively patchy. Yet extant issues suggest that the production quality of Peter Hake's newspaper gradually declined once his wife Catharina took over the business after his death in 1659.

As with many other newspapers of the time, the *Wochentliche Zeitung auß Hamburg* changed its title frequently. A closer look at the annual run of 1659, however, shows that fluctuation in titling may not have been the result of sloppiness on the part of the printer, but rather of a series of attempts to create a marketable product. Twelve of the 104 weekly issues of this newspaper from 1658 and 1659 have come down to us. A closer inspection of them allows us to understand how haphazardly the printer and publisher approached the title and design of the newspaper. The first issue from 1658 bears the title *Ordinarie Wochentliche Zeitung auß Hamburg.* Hake changed it into *Ordinarie Wochentliche Zeitung/*

---

[13] For an extended discussion of newspaper publishing history, see J. Hillgärtner, *German Newspapers 1605–1650: A Bibliography*, Leiden and Boston, 2023.

[14] See, e.g., the work of C. Prange on the naming principles of the two leading Hamburg newspapers in C. Prange, *Die Zeitungen und Zeitschriften des 17. Jahrhunderts in Hamburg und Altona. Ein Beitrag zur Publizistik der Frühaufklärung*, Hamburg, 1978, pp. 152–5.

[15] See Bogel and Blühm, *Die deutschen Zeitungen des 17. Jahrhunderts* (n. 5 above), pp. 151–2.

[16] J. Weber, 'Neue Funde aus der Frühgeschichte des deutschen Zeitungswesens', *Archiv für Geschichte des Buchwesens*, 39, 1993, pp. 321–60 (349).

[17] Printers could obtain privileges from a governmental body that granted them the exclusive right to publish a newspaper in a given locality, though use, reuse, and translation of news was not affected by this; see B. Haube, 'Der Leipziger Privilegienstreit. Die erste Tageszeitung der Welt', *Post und Telekommunikationsgeschichte*, 1, 2000, pp. 101–7 and, more broadly, U. Eisenhardt, *Die kaiserliche Aufsicht über Buchdruck, Buchhandel und Presse im Heiligen Römischen Reich Deutscher Nation (1496–1806)*, Karlsruhe, 1970, pp. 170–5.

auß Deutschlandt in the following issue that appeared in mid March. Over the course of the following months, Hake had second thoughts and dropped the 'Zeitung' part of the title altogether. The next surviving issue from October appeared as *Warhafftige RELATION, Von Unter schiedenen* [sic] *Oertern/ aus Deutschlandt* (Fig. 24.4). Whereas the title in the previous issues appeared at the top of the first page, it now prominently occupied a separate

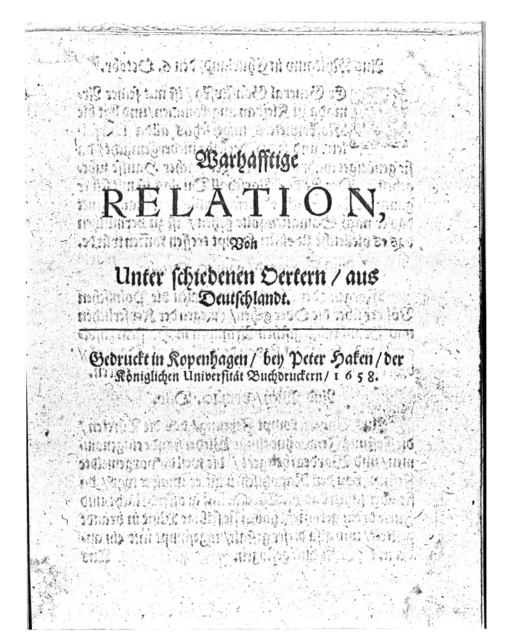

FIG. 24.4. Mistakes on a title-page of Hake's newspaper.

title-page. Interestingly enough, the relatively large space between 'Unter' and 'schiedenen' drew attention to it. Either this was a straightforward textual error (the adjective *unter-schiedenen* should be written as single word), or the separation was intentional, but too much blind material was inserted in between.

The new title must have had a strangely old-fashioned ring to it. For it had last been in 1634 that another printer used the term 'warhaftig', or 'truthful', in a newspaper's title on a regular basis.[18] Claims to the veracity of the news and adjectives that underlined the reliability of a newspaper were relatively uncommon in the world of German periodicals. They were more often found in news pamphlets and broadsheets — two genres that contemporaries often criticised for their biased and often downright false reporting. Hake dropped this new title shortly afterwards. The title of the following issue from 16 November 1658 highlighted the fact that the news had been gathered 'from several foreign places'.[19] The first surviving issue of 1659 appeared on 27 January, again as *Europæische RELATION, Auß Unterschiedlichen frembden Oertern*. The title was plainly inserted at the top of the first page. A large initial letter decorated the first report. The following undated issue carried almost the same title. The printer only changed the umlaut in 'Oertern' to 'Ortern' — a rather unusual phrasing in the context of seventeenth-century German orthography — and framed the title with a border made out of typographical decorative material. Following on from this, the next issues appeared again without the frame. The printer had the choice of at least two sets of initial letters and selected randomly one for each issue. Within the space of just about two years, the *Wochentliche Zeitung auß Hamburg* had undergone several title changes and Peter and Catharina Hake had significantly altered the design of the newspaper.

IMPROMPTU AND RETROSPECTIVE CORRECTIONS IN THE HAMBURG PRESS

Mistakes such as misspelled titles in the newspapers from Hanau, Altona, and Copenhagen were common. The time constraints printers were subjected to meant that they had little to no margin for correction. However, scattered evidence from a small number of newspapers shows that printers occasionally did indeed halt the production of an issue to make stop-press corrections in the set text when they spotted evident mistakes during the printing process. Only a small handful of issues that document this practice have survived and it seems that some printers were very careful to correct even the slightest mistakes, if they came across them early enough. One report dated 4 September 1648 appeared under the headline 'From Bohemia'. It contained a misspelled name that had found its way into the *Wöchentliche Zeitung auß mehrerley örther* from Hamburg in 1648. The report in the first copies of the newspaper informed the reader about the latest activities of the Swedish army in Tábor, southern Bohemia. 'General Wenberg and his 300 foot soldiers and 200 cavalry

---

[18] This was the case in the anonymously published *Warhafftiger Bericht*, which must have been published in eighteen issues, see Hillgärtner, *German Newspapers* (n. 13 above).

[19] 'Aus Unterschiedlichen frembden Orten'.

474   PRINTING AND MISPRINTING

quickly returned to Prague after they besieged Tábor and other places'.[20] In the earliest copies this relatively short text alone contained three mistakes: firstly, it lacked the date of the report. In the earliest newspapers it was customary to sort news chronologically and according to the place of its geographical origin. This meant that a headline had to comprise the date and place from which a report had been sent. In this instance, the date information was lacking; a flaw that the printer or compositor must have become aware of at some point during the printing process. He fixed this in the later copies and added the correct information.

Furthermore, he had made a mistake in the spelling of the Swedish general's name. The commander in question was Arvid Wittenberg, not 'Wenberg', as the earlier copies of the issue claimed. Wittenberg had been commanding one wing of the Swedish army since the Battle of Breitenfeld in 1642. He soon became known as an ambitious commander who enjoyed a good standing within the military.[21] Reports, however, made only fleeting references to him in the second half of the 1640s and only very avid newspaper readers could be expected to have a good sense of the composition of the Swedish military hierarchy. A small number of reports from the beginning of 1648 talk about him, but he was by no means a clearly distinguishable figure to readers of newspapers. Lastly, the report contained a significant typo in the word *marschieren* (to march). The earlier copies of the issue used the nonsensical spelling 'mairet' and it was later corrected to 'marchiret'.

The person responsible for the printing of the issue must have been so dissatisfied with the amount of mistakes that he decided to fix the errors before carrying out the remaining part of the print run. However, this did not mean that the earlier copies containing the mistakes were discarded, for we could not otherwise study the corrections made. Evidently, the printer decided to distribute even the copies of the newspaper he had found fault with.[22] We can trace only a handful of such cases in the extant body of early German newspapers and it is noteworthy that the printers in the workshop of the Meyer firm in Hamburg appeared to have been especially prone to correcting their errors as they were printing the newspaper issues. Yet it is almost impossible to establish how many other printers applied the same principle. The poor survival of newspapers is one of the idiosyncrasies of this genre of print. Only about half of the total of around 24,300 issues that must have been printed in the first half of the seventeenth century have come down to us today.[23] News was a perishable good and readers seldom kept their issues. The majority of all surviving specimens resurface from the collections of contemporary rulers, royal houses, and local councils. They often received several dozen copies of a single periodical: the majority of them were intended for distribution among the elites and a small part went directly into the archive, where they have been preserved until today.[24] It is due to this factor that over 95% of extant newspapers

---

[20] *Ordentliche Zeitung Ao.: 1648. Prima von No. 38*, [Hamburg, Meyer, 1648], 4° (USTC N67-2507 and N67-2508), p. [3]: 'Nachdem der Herr Gen. Wenberg [sic] Tabor mit 300. Mann zu Fuß vnd 200. Pferden besetzt/ vnd ander mehr Oerther occupiret/ ist er in aller eyl zurück vff Prag mairet [sic] [...]'.

[21] On Wittenberg's involvement in the army and his reputation among the Swedish elites and rulers, see M. Roberts, 'Charles X and the Great Parenthesis. A Reconsideration', in M. Roberts, *From Oxenstierna to Charles XII: Four Studies*, Cambridge, 1991, pp. 100–43 (119–21).

[22] The earlier copy of the issue survived in the city archive of Stralsund and the latter was found in the Royal Library in Stockholm.

[23] On the bibliographic details of this newspaper, see Hillgärtner, *German Newspapers* (n. 13 above).

[24] See: G. Hagelweide, 'Geschichte und Entwicklung des Zeitungssammelns in Deutschland', in G. Hagelweide (ed.), *Zeitung und Bibliothek. Ein Wegweiser zu Sammlungen und Literatur*, Pullach, 1974,

have survived in only one copy. This makes it plausible to think that other printers too corrected mistakes on the spot as they oversaw their current issue in production. The massive loss of source material, however, makes it impossible to establish how common this form of corrections was.

A few printers adopted another strategy and occasionally discussed the printing errors in their own newspapers. Once again, it was the firm of the Meyers in Hamburg where we find examples of retrospective corrections of printer's mistakes, in other words a belated errata list. One issue of the *Wöchentliche Zeitung auß mehrerley örther* from 1674 contained a small but curious correction: 'A typesetting error occurred in my last issue of the *Appendix*. The report from Amsterdam speaks of one "Steinern Berg", whereas it should have read "Steinern Behren".[25] The report from Amsterdam in the previous issue dealt with minor military operations in the region around Nijmegen. Soldiers had captured part of a fortified construction and the report did not give the exact name of the building or its location.[26] The confusion between 'Steinern Berg', literally 'stony mountain', and 'Steinern Behren', or 'stony bear', stemmed from the fact that the latter was part of the terminology of fortifications. The compositor was in all likelihood not familiar with the specialist jargon. He thought to improve what he perceived to be a mistake in the incoming report.

The exact reasons why the printer saw a need to correct his mistake retrospectively remains unclear. After all, this was only a minor mistake by any standard. Most readers will have been unfamiliar with the correct term. They will have understood the core message of the report that a part of defensive building has been occupied by a military unit. Furthermore, the mistake had no political implications whatsoever. Printers feared the loss of their right to publish a newspaper should authorities take offence with the reporting. Here, however, news spoke of an unimportant event in the Franco-Dutch War in which Hamburg officially did not have any interest. Only a handful of experts with a solid knowledge of the architectural features of defensive buildings could spot this slight alteration to the meaning of the report; at best, such expert readers would have chuckled at it.

Pre-emptive Corrections: Johann Jakob Gabelkover as Proofreader and Censor

Most printers tolerated printer's errors to a certain degree. Only a few outriders such as the firm of the Meyers in Hamburg made the effort to halt the production process and correct the mistakes they had noticed. In most cases, errors were inevitable and born out of the production logic of the newspapers. Almost invariably, newspapers were set and printed

---

pp. 15–51; E. Blühm, 'Adlige Bezieher des Wolfenbütteler "Aviso". Bericht über einen Archivfund von Wilhelm Hartmann', *Publizistik*, 1, 1971, pp. 64–7; and K. Bücher, 'Zur Geschichte des Zeitungs-Abonnements', *Zeitschrift für die gesamte Staatswissenschaft*, 78/1, 1924, pp. 3–18.

[25] *Ordinari Diengstags Zeitung Anno 1674. Prima von Num. 43.*, [Hamburg, Meyer, 1674], 4° (USTC N67-6603), p. [4]: 'N.B. Jn meinem letzten Appendice sub Num. 42. ist unter andern im Druck versehen/ daß in dem Amsterdammer Brieff vom 23. October Steinern Berg statt Steinern Behren gesetzt'.

[26] The report can be found in the *Appendix der Wochenlichen Zeitung 1674. Von Numero 42.*, [Hamburg, Meyer, 1674], 4° (USTC N67-6602), p. [4].

476   PRINTING AND MISPRINTING

in consecutive steps, without first producing proof issues that correctors in the workshop checked for errors. In addition, not being subjected to censorial control of the authorities set them apart from other genres of printed books which were closely read by correctors and censors.

One notable exception to this approach was the *Zeitungen*, a Stuttgart periodical published by Johann Weyrich Rößlin the elder and his son, presumably between 1619 and 1665.[27] The Württembergisches Landesarchiv holds a series of 486 issues of the *Zeitungen*, some of them retaining extensive annotations. They were penned by Johann Jakob Gabelkover, a former cleric who had become the royal archivist to Duke John Frederick at his court in Stuttgart. Some of the surviving issues were not the final product but the proof sheets that the printer had to submit to Gabelkover to check before the final issue went into production. Gabelkover's intimate knowledge of political affairs and his connection to the court led Duke John Frederick to appoint him as official corrector of the newspaper.[28] According to Helmut Fischer, John Frederick required that Rößlin made proof sheets of each issue of the *Zeitungen*. He then had to deliver them to Gabelkover to check for factual errors and printer's mistakes. A study of the annotations reveals that Gabelkover took this duty very seriously and soon found himself both correcting and editing the reports for clarity and readability. He helped to produce a newspaper, which explained difficult legal cases using the vernacular, rather than relying on complicated legal terminology.[29] Fischer identified Rößlin as a Jew. He argued that his background must have affected his trustworthiness at the court and effectively disqualified him from printing a periodical without pre-publication censorship. John Frederick may have only granted him the privilege to print his newspaper in Stuttgart if Rößlin submitted all issues to censorship to verify the contents of every forthcoming issue.

In his work as a censor, Gabelkover did not simply restrict himself to correcting factual errors. He also ordered the printer to delete passages he perceived to be too speculative and he thought could clash with the interest of other rulers. Perhaps more than anything else, he carefully corrected the spellings of the names of rulers, monarchs, and places.[30] In furious handwriting, he corrected a passage where the printer had mistakenly used the capital letter 'T' instead of an 'R' for the word 'Rome'.[31]

Less frequently, his annotations were intended to facilitate understanding, usually adding the full names of persons mentioned in the reports. One news item from Amsterdam in 1624 related that 'Admiral Eremite [sic] is said to have taken control of a thirty-mile-long island in the West Indies, fought a number of skirmishes with the Spaniards and conquered two

---

[27] For bibliographical details, see Hillgärtner, *German Newspapers* (n. 13 above).

[28] H. Fischer, *Die ältesten Zeitungen und ihre Verleger. Nach archivalischen und sonstigen Quellen dargestellt*, Augsburg, 1936, pp. 111–12; on Gabelkover's work, see also Johannes Weber, 'Kontrollmechanismen im deutschen Zeitungswesen des 17. Jahrhunderts. Ein kleiner Beitrag zur Geschichte der Zensur', *Jahrbuch für Kommunikationsgeschichte*, 6, 2004, pp. 66–7, and J. O. Opel, 'Ueber eine bisher unbekannte süddeutsche Zeitung. Mit drei photographischen Abbildungen', *Archiv für Geschichte des deutschen Buchhandels*, 10, 1886, pp. 207–24.

[29] H. Böning, *Dreißigjähriger Krieg und Öffentlichkeit. Zeitungsberichte als Rohfassung der Geschichtsschreibung*, Bremen, 2018, p. 218. This was far from the standard in the context of the seventeenth century. Newspapers frequently presented the news in a language interspersed with complex legal terminology.

[30] Weber, 'Kontrollmechanismen im deutschen Zeitungswesen' (n. 28 above), p. 66.

[31] This was the case in *XVI*, [Stuttgart, Johann Weyrich Rößlin, 1625], p. [4].

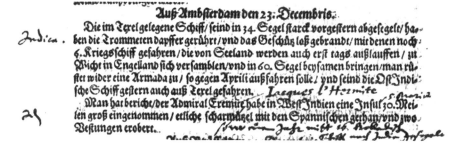

FIG. 24.5. Gabelkover's corrections to the proof sheets of the *Zeittung*.

fortifications'.[32] Gabelkover apparently was not happy with the relatively imprecise information. He corrected the spelling of the Admiral's last name and added his first name as well, so that the published, final version of the report would read 'Jacques L'Hermite' and not just 'Eremite' (Fig. 24.5.).

The admiral led an armada of eleven ships on their voyage from Amsterdam to South America.[33] Their goal was to intercept Spanish ships carrying silver to Europe and eventually establish a Dutch colony in the area of today's Peru and Chile. In his comments, Gabelkover identified the previously unnamed islands as 'Santa Maria' in the southern part of the Peruvian coast and instructed the printer via his comments to add this information.

A LONG-LASTING TOLERATION FOR PRINTER'S ERRORS

In comparison to other printed material, early newspapers had to be produced quickly. As news is a highly perishable good, sending out the issues on time was crucial to the success of a printer in the increasingly competitive market. This left very little room to check for printer's errors, with the result that they ended up being tolerated and regarded as a drawback readers would surely understand. Only rarely was a periodical systematically, regularly, and carefully checked for errors, as happened to the *Zeittung* from Stuttgart. In this special case, however, the focus was not primarily on correcting obvious printing errors, this being a side effect of Johann Jakob Gabelkover's censorship control. Typographical errors and inconsistencies remained uncorrected in most newspapers throughout early modern times. The attitude expressed in the forewords by Johann Carolus and Georg Greflinger — that readership would be forgiving — was widespread. The vast majority of printing errors

---

[32] *I. [Zeittungen]*, [Stuttgart, Johann Weyrich Rößlin, 1624], 4° (USTC N75-231), p. [3]: 'Man hat bericht/ der Admiral Eremite habe in West Indien eine Jnsul 30. Meilen groß eingenommen/ etliche Scharmützel mit den Spannischen gethan/ vnd zwo Vestungen erobert.'

[33] P. T. Bradley, *The Lure of Peru: Maritime Intrusion into the South Sea, 1598–1701*, Basingstoke, 1989, pp. 49–71.

appear to be testimony to the rapid and less careful production of newspapers and were largely tolerated by both printers and readers as intrinsic to the genre. It was not until around 1850 that it became increasingly common practice among publishers to include a section entitled 'Druckfehler', or 'printer's mistakes', at the end of a newspaper issue, in which errors in the previous issue were corrected.

BIBLIOGRAPHY

PRIMARY SOURCES

Appendix der Wochentlichen Zeitung 1674. Von Numero 42, [Hamburg, Meyer, 1674], 4° (USTC N67-6602).

Nordischer MERCURIUS. Welcher kürzlich vorstellet/ was in diesem 1667. Jahr an Novellen aus Europa eingekommen ist, [Hamburg, Friedrich Conrad Greflinger for Georg Greflinger, 1667], 4° (USTC N196-178).

Ordentliche Zeitung Ao.: 1648. Prima von No. 38, [Hamburg, Meyer, 1648], 4° (USTC N67-2507 and N67-2508).

Ordinari Diengstags Zeitung Anno 1674. Prima von Num. 43, [Hamburg, Meyer, 1674], 4° (USTC N67-6603).

Relation aller Fuernemmen und Gedenckwürdigen Historien, [Strasbourg, Johann Carolus, 1609], 4° (USTC N60-1).

Vom 31 Marty. Fol. 201 Die Europäische RELATION No 26 1693, [Altona, Anna de Löw and Heinrich Heuß, 1693], 4° (USTC N214-4305).

N. XII. Zeitung Auß Wolfenbüttel/ Braunschweig/ Hamburg/ Weserstromb/ Erffurt/ Franckfurt an der Oder/ Lorch/ Heßen/ Venedig/ Prag/ vnd Wien [s.l., s.n., 1620], 4° (USTC N114-12).

I. [Zeittungen], [Stuttgart, Johann Weyrich Rößlin, 1624], 4° (USTC N75-231).

XVI. [Zeittungen], [Stuttgart, Johann Weyrich Rößlin, 1625], 4° (USTC N75-298).

SECONDARY LITERATURE

Behringer, W., *Im Zeichen des Merkur. Reichspost und Kommunikationsrevolution in der Frühen Neuzeit*, Göttingen, 2003.

Blühm, E., 'Adlige Bezieher des Wolfenbütteler "Aviso". Bericht über einen Archivfund von Wilhelm Hartmann', *Publizistik*, 1, 1971, pp. 64–7.

Bogel, E., and Blühm, E., *Die deutschen Zeitungen des 17. Jahrhunderts. Ein Bestandsverzeichnis mit historischen und bibliographischen Angaben. Band 1: Text*, Bremen, 1971.

Böning, H., *Dreißigjähriger Krieg und Öffentlichkeit. Zeitungsberichte als Rohfassung der Geschichts-schreibung*, Bremen, 2018.

Bradley, P. T., *The Lure of Peru: Maritime Intrusion into the South Sea, 1598–1701*, Basingstoke, 1989.

Bücher, K., 'Zur Geschichte des Zeitungs-Abonnements', *Zeitschrift für die gesamte Staatswissenschaft*, 78/1, 1924, pp. 3–18.

Eisenhardt, U., *Die kaiserliche Aufsicht über Buchdruck, Buchhandel und Presse im Heiligen Römischen Reich Deutscher Nation (1496–1806)*, Karlsruhe, 1970.

Fischer, H., *Die ältesten Zeitungen und ihre Verleger. Nach archivalischen und sonstigen Quellen dargestellt*, Augsburg, 1936.

Gieseler, J., 'Vom Nutzen und richtigen Gebrauch der frühen Zeitungen. Zur sogenannten Pressedebatte des 17. Jahrhunderts', in G. Fritz and E. Straßner (eds), *Die Sprache der ersten deutschen Wochenzeitungen im 17. Jahrhundert*, Tübingen, 1996, pp. 259–85.

Hagelweide, G., 'Geschichte und Entwicklung des Zeitungssammelns in Deutschland', in G. Hagelweide (ed.), *Zeitung und Bibliothek. Ein Wegweiser zu Sammlungen und Literatur*, Pullach, 1974, pp. 15–51.

Haube, B., 'Der Leipziger Privilegienstreit. Die erste Tageszeitung der Welt', *Post und Telekommunikationsgeschichte*, 1, 2000, pp. 101–7.

Hillgärtner, J., *German Newspapers 1605–1650: A Bibliography*, Leiden and Boston, 2022.

Hoffmann, P. T., 'Victor de Löw, Altonas ältester Buch- und Zeitungsdrucker', *Altonaische Zeitschrift für Geschichte und Heimatkunde*, 1, 1931, pp. 191–6.

Opel, J. O., 'Ueber eine bisher unbekannte süddeutsche Zeitung. Mit drei photographischen Abbildungen', *Archiv für Geschichte des deutschen Buchhandels*, 10, 1886, pp. 207–24.

Prange, C., *Die Zeitungen und Zeitschriften des 17. Jahrhunderts in Hamburg und Altona. Ein Beitrag zur Publizistik der Frühaufklärung*, Hamburg, 1978.

Reske, C., *Die Buchdrucker des 16. und 17. Jahrhunderts im deutschen Sprachgebiet. Auf der Grundlage des gleichnamigen Werkes von Josef Benzing*, Wiesbaden, 2007.

Roberts, M., 'Charles X and the Great Parenthesis: A Reconsideration', in M. Roberts, *From Oxenstierna to Charles XII: Four Studies*, Cambridge, 1991, pp. 100–43.

Weber, J., 'Kontrollmechanismen im deutschen Zeitungswesen des 17. Jahrhunderts. Ein kleiner Beitrag zur Geschichte der Zensur', *Jahrbuch für Kommunikationsgeschichte*, 6, 2004, pp. 56–73.

Weber, J., 'Neue Funde aus der Frühgeschichte des deutschen Zeitungswesens', *Archiv für Geschichte des Buchwesens*, 39, 1993, pp. 321–60.

Weber, J., 'Strassburg, 1605: The Origins of the Newspaper in Europe', *German History*, 24/3, 2006, pp. 387–412.

Welke, M., 'Die Entwicklung der frühen Zeitungsdrucktechnik (17. und 18. Jahrhundert)', in M. Welke and B. Fuchs (eds), *Zeitungsdruck. Die Entwicklung der Technik vom 17. bis zum 20. Jahrhundert*, Munich, 2000, pp. 9–28.

APPENDIX A

GLOSSARY OF PRINTING AND MISPRINTING

This short glossary is intended to provide a basic degree of terminological standardisation for early modern misprinting and in-house correcting practices. For the sake of *brevitas*, typographical jargon has been included only insofar as it helps understand the causes of some particular categories of misprints. However, five technical drawings have been included in the next opening to help the reader visualise and understand other components of a hand press and a printing forme mentioned in this book but not necessarily described in the glossary.

We based our work on M. Suarez and H. Woudhuysen (eds), *The Oxford Companion to the Book*, Oxford, 2010 (henceforth *OCB*), where a much broader range of entries, also covering a substantially larger timespan, may be found. Further information on the inner workings of early modern and modern print shops is provided in G. T. Tanselle, 'The Treatment of Typesetting and Presswork in Bibliographical Description', *Studies in Bibliography*, 52 (1999), pp. 1–57, as well as N. Harris, *Analytical Bibliography: An Alternative Prospectus*, published online at http://ihl.enssib.fr/analytical-bibliography-an-alternative-prospectus.

Entries by the following authors were specifically written for this glossary:

*GDR+PS	Geri Della Rocca de Candal and Paolo Sachet
*LC	Laura Carnelos
*NH	Neil Harris
*JM	James Misson
*PWN	Paul W. Nash

Entries signed by the following authors are extracted directly from *OCB*, and, as such, they have not been edited, except for minor spelling and punctuation for internal consistency. Passages not immediately relevant to the early modern period, however, have been omitted.

ABRW	A. B. R. Weiner	LH	Lotte Hellinga
ASR	Adam Rounce	MMS	Margaret M. Smith
DCC	Daven C. Chamberlain	OCB	Unsigned entry in *OCB*
DRSP	David Pearson	RMR	R. M. Ritter
ETK	Eric Kindel	RWO	Richard Ovenden
IG	Ian Gadd	SK	Stephen Karian
JAL	John A. Lane	TK	Tim Killick
KEA	Karen Attar		

Entries signed by Neil Harris [NH] and Paul W. Nash [PWN] were revised by the authors from their *OCB* entries, with the exception of 'Duplicate setting', drawn from N. Harris, *Analytical Bibliography: An Alternative Prospectus*. We take this opportunity to express our gratitude to Neil Harris and Paul W. Nash for revising the contents of this glossary.

1. Printing press

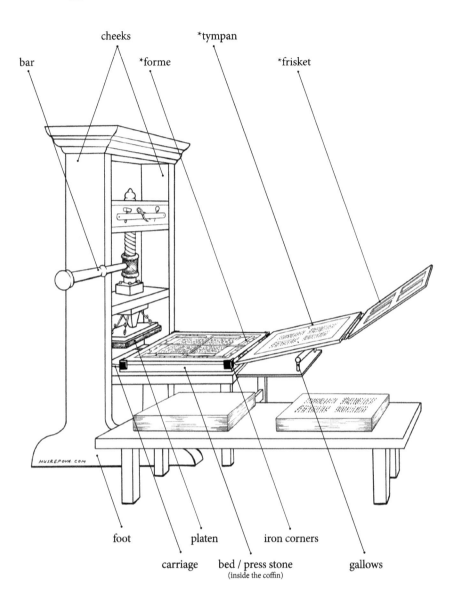

entries defined in the glossary

APPENDIX A: GLOSSARY   483

2. *Composing stick

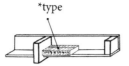

3. *Galley

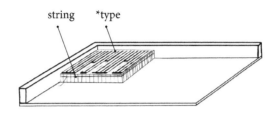

4. * 'Skeleton' forme

The 'skeleton' forme is a bibliographical abstraction coined by Fredson Bowers. It describes the forme stripped of the text block but retaining elements that are frequently recycled in the next forme, e.g. signatures, headlines, furniture, quoins, etc.

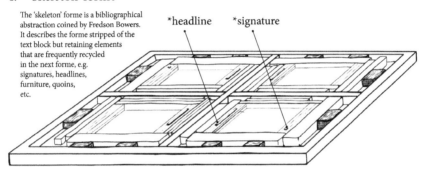

5. *Forme

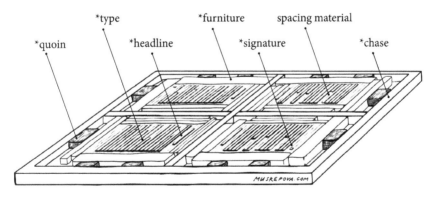

FIG. A.1. The printing press and the forme.

484   PRINTING AND MISPRINTING

Allography   Variation in the graphic representation of the same sound. More common in non-Latin alphabets (e.g., in medieval and renaissance Greek), it can occasionally lead to mistakes in typesetting. [*GDR+PS]

Apologies   A rhetorical expedient increasingly used by early modern printers, editors, and occasionally authors, to justify the textual imperfections the reader may still encounter in an *edition. It was not uncommon to turn these apologies into an opportunity to shift the blame onto other parties involved in the production. [*GDR+PS]

Archetype   The MS or text posited at the head of the tree or stemma, after *recension. The archetype is the source from which all other witnesses descend; being usually not extant, it is the focus of editorial attempts hypothetically to reconstruct its details, using the surviving witnesses. [ASR]
See also *copy-text, *exemplar, *printer's copy.

Bearer type   For pages with sizeable blank areas, *types were placed in the *forme to bear the platen's weight. Intended to be blind, they were neither inked nor masked. Bearers are most frequently observed in *incunabula, although the practice has been reported in some sixteenth-century books. Lines of text that had already been printed were sometimes used as bearers. [MMS]
See also *spacing material.

Beater   The press operator responsible for keeping the *ink soft, by working his ink balls together, and for inking the *forme (inserting the paper and pulling the *impression being undertaken by a separate 'puller'). The beater was also usually responsible for examining the printed sheet to check for defects. [PWN]

Bibliography   The study of books. Bibliography has five branches that often overlap: (1) enumerative bibliography; (2) analytical bibliography; (3) descriptive bibliography; (4) textual bibliography; (5) historical bibliography.
1) In its attempts to synthesize knowledge, enumerative bibliography provides the foundation for scholarship. The basic function of enumerative bibliography (also known as systematic bibliography) is to list all titles of books that fall within specified parameters: geographic, linguistic, chronological, thematic, or some combination thereof. In its highest form, an enumerative bibliography strives for completeness, although that standard is rarely met. The tradition of enumerative bibliography extends from the Alexandrian Library to online public-access catalogues, and includes many impressive feats of scholarship [...]. Unlike analytical and descriptive bibliography, enumerative bibliography is not necessarily concerned with the physical makeup of books.
2) Analytical bibliography refers to the practice of reconstructing the physical processes by which printed books came to be produced. In this respect, the focus of analytical bibliography has a narrower scope than enumerative bibliography, which may encompass both MSS and printed books. Analytical bibliographers pursue this historical inquiry for various reasons: to identify a book's printers and publishers; to assign a date to a book; to distinguish between variant *states of the same *edition; and to understand how a book's text was altered in the process of printing. The physical evidence examined by analytical bibliographers includes: typography, paper (including *watermarks and chain lines), patterns of *imposition, and the printed marks themselves (including printers' ornaments, damaged *type, *running titles, and press figures) [...].
3) Like analytical bibliography, descriptive bibliography is concerned with books as material objects, and indeed these two branches of bibliography overlap at many points. Yet, while analytical bibliography has various purposes, descriptive bibliography has the single goal of describing the physical structure of books in a clear and concise way. At the heart of a bibliographical description is a statement of format and a collational formula [...]. Anyone familiar with the system of notation used in descriptive bibliography can mentally reconstruct the physical makeup of a book without having it before them [...]. In addition to a book's *format and *collational formula, a

descriptive bibliography contains other information, such as the number and priority of the various states, *issues, and editions; the paper used; references to known advertisements; price; copyright registration; *press runs; binding; and published responses to the book [...].

4) Textual bibliography refers to any bibliographical endeavour that attempts to reconstruct the transmission of texts, with the possible goal of establishing or editing a specific work. In this respect, textual bibliography is often synonymous with textual criticism. Yet the term textual bibliography highlights the need for the textual scholar to study how the material forms of texts have affected their transmission. The fields of analytical and descriptive bibliography inform textual bibliography, as do the study of handwriting (palaeography), linguistic study, and literary scholarship in general.

5) Historical bibliography refers to the historical study of books, and as a term it has been displaced by history of the book or *histoire du livre*. Historical bibliography encompasses topics as various as copyright, censorship, authorship, reading and reception, the technologies of printing, the economics of publishing, and the cultural impact of the written word. The overlap between historical bibliography and both analytical and descriptive bibliography should be clear; anyone who studies books as material objects needs to do so with an awareness of particular historical patterns of printing and publishing. Similarly, the physical production of books is very much a part of their history.

Despite the various branches of bibliography and their different methods of inquiry, bibliographers of all types are united around a shared object of study and a desire to understand the cultural and physical conditions that produced books. Ultimately, all the various branches of bibliography intersect, and thorough scholars employ multiple methods and avail themselves of all known forms of evidence [...]. [SK]

For a broader overview, see N. Harris, 'Definitions of Bibliography, and in Particular of the Variety Called Analytical', available at: http://ihl.enssib.fr/analytical-bibliography-an-alternative-prospectus/definitions-of-bibliography-and-in-particular-of-the-variety-called-analytical.

Blind impression Inkless *impression occasionally visible on a page, especially in copies printed on parchment. It often resulted from the use of lines of text (often already printed) reused as *bearer type. [*GDR+PS]

Cancel Best defined as a disturbance in the physical structure of a book, a cancel is usually executed after the completion of the original *press run and sometimes after the distribution of the first copies. From the fifteenth to the nineteenth century, compositors worked for the most part with small quantities of *type in the case, so that any *forme, after printing, was immediately *distributed, rather than being kept standing for a further *impression [...]. Cancels, as they were known in the trade, went from a tiny piece of paper containing, for example, a single punctuation mark pasted over the error (see *paste slip) to recomposing one or more sheets of an edition. A single *leaf cancel is recognisable because it is glued to the *stub left by the original, while a double-leaf cancel, folded and sewn in the centre, is often detected by irregularities in the paper structure of the *gathering and by differences in typographical work. A full-sheet cancel, however, can be all but invisible [...].

To avoid ambiguity in describing cancels, bibliographers employ the following terminology, established by R. W. Chapman: [folium] *cancellandum* (Lat., 'that which is to be cancelled'; pl. [folia] *cancellanda*) for the cancelled leaf/sheet that has nevertheless survived; and [folium] *cancellans* (Lat., 'that which cancels'; pl. [folia] *cancellantia*) for the leaf/sheet introduced into the book. There is also a term [folium] *cancellatum* (Lat., 'that which has been cancelled'; pl. [folia] *cancellata*) for any example of the *cancellandum* that has been removed but has nonetheless survived, obviously a rare occurrence. In formulas of *collation, where *cancellandum* and *cancellans* have the same physical shape, cancels are indicated by combined plus and minus (±) signs [...]. [NH]

Caret See *signe de renvoi.

Cartouche See *paste slip.

Case See *type case.

Castigationes In early modern *editions of classical texts, *castigationes* or *lectiones* are alternative readings of specific passages obtained through the comparison of different manuscript witnesses (*collatio*) or by conjecture (*divinatio*). While usually listed in an appendix to a volume, they should not be confused with *errata. [*GDR+PS]

Casting off copy Estimating a book's length by counting the words in the copy and computing the length of the whole, based on the size of paper, the *format, and the *size of type to be used. This process allows the printer to estimate costs and order the right amount of paper; it also permits *composition by formes. *Printer's copy [...] sometimes has the ends of cast-off pages marked. However, a *compositor might similarly mark the copy to indicate the ends of pages as he has finished composing them. [MMS]

Catchword A word at the end of a page or *gathering of a MS or printed book, normally in the direction line, providing the next page's first word. It aided binders in assembling gatherings in the correct order (related to the *signature), printers in the *imposition of pages in the *forme, and readers in anticipating the following page [...]. [MMS]

Chase Solid frame of wood or (more commonly) iron into which the *type and other matter making up a *forme are locked, usually using *quoins. [OCB]

Collation Five senses of the word may be distinguished. (1) The act of checking that the gathered printed *sheets are correctly ordered and oriented prior to folding and sewing [...]. (2) In a related but more modern sense, the construction of a *collational formula: a bibliographical description of the book detailing the *format, the order of *gatherings, any inserted or omitted *leaves, and the number of leaves [...]. (3) The bibliographical comparison of a specific copy of a book with another copy or with a collational formula in a reference work to establish whether the number and order of gatherings is complete. (4) The editorial comparison of a specific copy of a book with another copy to identify textual *variants [...]. (5) A list of such variants. [IG]

Colophon [Gr., 'summit', 'finishing stroke'] Originally a closing statement written at the end of a text by a scribe or rubricator, sometimes providing his name and the date and place of production [...]. The colophon was retained at the end of the book by some printers of *incunabula, who often placed their printer's device nearby [...]. The information provided in a colophon gradually migrated to the developing *title-page at the front of the book, which sometimes also acquired the printer's device, or the publisher's [...]. [MMS]

Composing stick A small (often adjustable) hand-held tray, originally of wood (later metal), in which the *compositor arranges *type and *spacing material during *composition. The composing stick is usually large enough to accommodate several lines, which are set before the type is transferred to a *galley. [PWN]

Composition The act or process of setting *type. The hand *compositor would stand (or sometimes sit) at the *type cases, with a *copy-text before him (or, rarely, her), sometimes displayed on a *visorum [...]. The compositor would normally begin with the main text, leaving until later any *preliminaries (e.g. foreword, dedication, title-page). With a *composing stick in his left hand, he would pick the first piece of type, or *sort, from the case with his right hand, and place it, upside down with the face towards him, at the left end of the stick, holding it there with his left thumb. He might look at the sort as he picked it up, or work largely by feel with his eyes on the copy, knowing which way up to place each sort by the nick in its body. Equal spaces would be placed between words until the end of the line of type neared the stick's right end. The compositor would then judge whether to break a word (usually using a hyphen), and whether more or less space between words would be needed to justify the line. When setting verse, or other unjustified text, this last consideration was unnecessary, and the line could be completed with spaces and quads. In early printing, *justification was aided by the free use of contractions and abbreviations, and sometimes variant characters. Careless composition could result in obvious, uneven spacing (*rivers) between words, while the best compositors made word spaces visually uniform (though this could require subtly different spacing between words). Upon completing one line, the compositor would begin the next, placing the first sort at the left-hand end of the stick, on top of the line already set. A *setting rule might be inserted first, to stabilise the new line and aid the movement of type during justification (the rule was removed once the line was complete). *Leading could be inserted at this stage by laying a strip of type-metal, card, or *reglet atop the first line, before beginning the second. Once the stick was full […], the contents were carefully removed, often into a *galley. Composition would continue with the next stick-full, and so on, until sufficient type had been set to print the first *gathering or *forme. It was not uncommon for two or more compositors to work on different parts of the same book, sometimes even in different printing shops, when accurate *casting off would be essential, so that each compositor knew where to begin and end […]. Composition might be carried out *seriatim* or by formes. *Seriatim* is the simplest method of composition, in which the entire text of a *gathering is composed before *imposition. One of its advantages is that the text can easily be divided into pages with the correct number of lines, and the *casting off of copy is not needed. However, it can be slow and requires more type. The other method entails progression by formes: standard sixteenth- and seventeenth-century practice in some print shops, it requires less type than setting *seriatim*, and may allow printing to begin and progress more quickly. It demands accurate casting off to predict page-breaks. A gathering containing multiple *sheets could be worked from the outer forme inwards or vice versa […]. [PWN]

Compositor Worker employed, usually within printing offices, to set *type. The compositor was responsible also for *distribution, and usually for making *corrections following *proofreading […]. [PWN]

Conjugate leaves Two *leaves of a book that form a single bifolium. In a *collational formula a point indicates conjugacy, e.g. 'B1.8'. [OCB]

Copy census A *bibliographical methodology building on *copy-specific information and entailing the comparative study of as many copies of an *edition as possible. It has two main purposes: understanding the circulation and use of the *edition and detecting textual *variants, regardless of their philological value. Compared to analytical bibliography, it provides a more nuanced and multifaceted history of a printed text. [*GDR+PS]

Copy-specific analysis A *bibliographical methodology describing single copies, their material evidence, and other provenance information (e.g. archival documentation). [*GDR+PS]

Copy-text (1) Sometimes used to refer to the original authorial MS from which a *compositor sets a text to be printed. (2) The particular text chosen as the basis for a critical edition of a work. It may be an authorial or non-authorial MS, or that printed *edition which is thought most closely to reflect authorial intention, whether the first or a later (usually in the author's lifetime) edition embodying authorial revision. Editors follow the copy-text in accidentals (i.e. capitalisation, punctuation, spelling), with, in the case of a printed edition, the printers' customary normalisations from the MS, according to house rules and style. Editors may adopt variant authorial readings for substantives (anything that affects the sense), or may provide conjectural *emendation where no witnessed reading makes adequate sense. For texts not intended for publication, such as correspondence or diaries, copy-text normally follows the author's accidentals. This is also the case in instances where the author paid particular attention to such matters. Where there are two or more collateral printed texts set from the MS, editors may select one as a copy-text, follow its accidentals, and choose substantive variants from either version. In cases of extensive authorial revision, an editor may choose to ignore one version or to produce a parallel-text edition [...]. [KEA]

See also *archetype, *exemplar, *printer's copy.

Correction A revision made to a text to suppress faults of the author, editor, *compositor, printer, or scribe. The term may also refer to the mark that indicates the error or that provides the proper text or other insertion. [ETK]

See also *cancel, *erasure, *errata, *manuscript correction, *proofreading, *proofs, *overprinting.

Corrector See *proofs, proofreading.

Corrigenda See *errata.

Coucher In papermaking, [a coucher] transfers the newly formed *sheet from the hand *mould on to a felt blanket so that the water can be pressed out. [OCB]

See also *vatman.

Damping One of various intermediate processes in printing. During the hand-press period [...], paper was dampened with water or another solution before printing to increase its receptivity to printer's *ink and to decrease *set-off. [MMS]

Distribution The process of returning *type to the *type case, the opposite of *composition [...]. Once the *forme is washed, and the type extracted, several lines of type are picked up by the compositor and held upside down in the left hand, or sometimes in a *composing stick. As much type as can be held between the thumb and forefinger of the right hand is taken from the right-hand end of the uppermost line, read, and each character dropped back into place, the hand moving swiftly between the boxes of the case. Distribution is normally substantially faster than composition. [PWN]

Drag lines *Ink marks that result from paper being inadvertently dragged across the inked letters instead of being lifted off cleanly. In early printing, in particular, drag lines may also have been caused by a piece of string used to support a *damp *sheet of paper when on the press. [*LC]

Drying/hanging Between the completion of printing and storage, newly printed *sheets were hung until they dried in the print shop, where space allowed, commonly in the attic. This fundamental passage of the printing process is often overlooked, but it had a more crucial impact on the final arrangement of sheets in copies than the actual order of printing. Contrary to what is stated in some *printing manuals, sheets were not usually hung to dry between the printing of the first and second *formes. [*GDR+PS]

Druckvorlage See *printer's copy.

Duplicate setting At times bibliographers discover that the same text has been set twice over. Several explanations are possible. First, that a 'second *edition' was set and printed as an exact duplicate of the *princeps*. Second, that, after a certain point in printing, the run was increased, so the early *gatherings had to be *reset.

APPENDIX A: GLOSSARY   489

Third, that *leaves were reset at a later date in order to make up incomplete copies. Nevertheless cases have been discovered in which the bibliographical evidence suggests that both settings of *type were extant at the same time in the same shop, or in different shops (perhaps to allow more copies to be printed rapidly), and in which no really convincing explanation of the fact is forthcoming. [NH]

Edition   The total number of copies of a book printed, at any time, from substantially the same setting of *type [...]. Type was set up by printers in *formes; it would not normally remain thus for very long, as this tied up the investment in type and meant that other books could not be printed from it. Accordingly, printers usually *distributed the type from a forme once it had been used to print the *sheets. If the original *print run sold out, the book would need to be *reset with a new setting of type — thus, a new edition would be created. Complications emerge when considering books that have been printed from *standing type. Sometimes, a printer would deliberately leave type standing in formes in the expectation of using it to print additional copies. Alternatively, a printer may have kept only a few pages in standing type (for instance, if the decision to reprint was made towards the end of the first printing, when most of the type from other pages had already been distributed) [...]. The identification of different editions requires specialised bibliographical analysis and close examination of the differences between copies (often by using devices such as collating machines). For instance, by identifying damaged types that have been reused, bibliographers may chart the redistribution of type; by measuring the space between the words on a line of type, they may determine where resetting has occurred [...]. [RWO]

Emendation   The *correction of a text where it is thought to have been corrupted by *transmission, or is otherwise incoherent [...]. In the editing of many classical texts, for example, the extant documents could be incomplete, or lacking in specific places; the solution was to emend, and where evidence was absent, the onus fell on editorial conjecture (sometimes called divination), in order to ascertain the possible or probable meanings [...]. [ASR]
See also *castigationes.

Erasure   The removal of one or more letters thorough scraping or rubbing from parchment or, involving more damage, paper. A traditional form of correcting in the manuscript world, its use declined with printing due to mistakes often being repeated in a hardly manageable number of copies. It was usually performed with a scalpel or pumice. [*GDR+PS]

Errata   Errors in a text, or a printed list of errors and their *corrections in an *edition. They could include instructions on how to *emend the text and *apologies for the presence of errors, with or without hopeful remarks that the mistakes not listed would be so obvious that they could be corrected by the readers themselves. Errata lists are often found in the final *leaves of a volume and frequently on a distinct *sheet or *gathering since they had to be prepared towards the end of the printing process, but they could also be produced later. On rare occasions, multiple errata lists were produced for the same edition. Strictly speaking, the term *erratum* represents a single mistake, while *errata* are also referred to as *corrigenda*, though they should not be confused with *castigationes. [*GDR+PS]

Exemplar   The text from which a particular copy is made, generally used in relation to MS copying and also for *printer's copy. [Also, a] particular copy of a book. [OCB]
See also *archetype, *copy-text, *printer's copy.

490   PRINTING AND MISPRINTING

Fallen type A loose letter, usually pulled out by the *ink balls during the inking of a *forme, which falls on top of the *type, blocks, or in the margins, and is printed along with the forme, leaving an *impression in the paper. Depending on whether it was inked or not, fallen type would leave either an inked profile or a *blind impression. The thickness of the *sort would determine the extent of the unprinted 'halo' left around the fallen type, and the damage to the type beneath. [*LC]

Filler See *spacing material.

Foliation The sequential numbering of the *leaves of a book, usually on the recto of each leaf [...]. In late medieval MSS and early printed books, [...] Roman numerals were often used, sometimes with the Latin word 'folio'. Around the mid sixteenth century, foliation was succeeded by *pagination, when the use of Arabic numerals also became predominant. The numbering of openings or double-page spreads supplied a short-lived alternative system. More radically, in place of numbering leaves, pages, or columns, the parts of a text might be numbered: the most common examples of this are the Bible's chapters and verses (as in Robert Estienne's Geneva Bible), and the acts and scenes in a play. In the printing trade a folio is a page number, and can also signify a *format and, loosely, a book size. [MMS]

Font/Fount *Type acquired or consistently used as a single entity [...]. A fount may change in the printing office by wear, damage, or the mixing of type from different founts, but a character from one fount accidentally set with another is a 'wrong fount' [...]. Founts are products, while *typefaces are abstractions: one produces, sells, buys, and downloads founts, but designs (and sells rights to) typefaces [...]. [JAL]
See also *sort.

Format Often used in a generic fashion to describe the size and appearance of a book, format is the technical and bibliographical term for the shape of the book, defined by the number of times each *sheet has been folded. During the Middle Ages and Renaissance, four basic sizes were available, as defined on the Bologna stone (c.1389, reproduced in Briquet): *imperialle* (imperial, 74 × 50cm); *realle* (royal, 61.5 × 44.5cm); *meçane* (median, 51.5 × 34.5cm); and *reçute* (chancery, 45 × 31.5cm). These sizes conform to the ratio $1:\sqrt{2}$, meaning that the proportions remain the same no matter how many times the sheet is folded. The same principle applies in modern A3, A4 formats, conforming to ISO 216. From Aldus onwards, however, printers have sometimes experimented with differently shaped sheets, obtaining taller, narrower folios and squarer quartos. When a sheet is folded once, to make a folio, the chain lines are vertical, the wire lines are horizontal, and the *watermark generally falls in the centre of the *leaf. When the sheet is folded twice, to make a quarto, the chain lines are horizontal, the wire lines vertical, and the watermark shifts into the inner margin. When making an octavo, the sheet is folded three times: the chain lines return to vertical, the wire lines to horizontal, and the watermark disappears to the top, inner corner. In *incunabula, mixed formats are not unusual, i.e. full sheets of chancery and half-sheets of royal [...]. Folio-size books dominated until the 1490s, only to be overtaken by quarto. By 1540, in Italy, octavo represented more than half of the printed output, while even smaller formats, including duodecimo, became common in the second half of the century. [NH]

Forme The *chase and its contents (*type, *furniture, etc.) prepared for printing. Once a forme has been made up on the imposing stone or bed of the press, *corrections and adjustments can be made before, or during, printing. When using a hand press, each *sheet of a book is usually printed from two formes (one for each side of the paper), the inner and outer formes. The outer includes the first page of the resulting *gathering, plus those other pages necessary for the correct *imposition of the appropriate *format; the inner forme includes the remaining pages of the gathering. Occasionally, a single forme is used for printing two half sheets, by a practice known as 'work-and-turn'. [PWN]

Foul case   A *typo caused by inaccurate *distribution: the *compositor drew from the correct compartment of the *type case but picked a *sort that had been misplaced. [*GDR+PS]

Frisket   A flat frame, usually of iron, covered with a sheet of paper or parchment (sometimes sheets of both, pasted together), which folds down over the *tympan of a hand press, holding the paper in position and keeping the margins clean. Parts of the frisket *sheet are cut away to allow the inked *type to meet the paper as required. [PWN]

Frisket bite   A missing part of printed matter, caused by a poorly cut *frisket or by the *frisket moving, stretching, or otherwise intervening between inked *type and the paper. [PWN]

Furniture   Blocks and strips of wood (latterly also metal or plastic) of standard dimensions, used to surround *type etc. in a *forme. [OCB]
See also *reglet, *spacing material.

Galley   A flat tray with one or two open sides for accumulating or storing composed *type. Galleys (so-called because they are vessels in which type is held or transported) were originally made of wood, were the same sizes as book pages, and often had a false bottom called a 'slice' which allowed the type to be withdrawn easily [...]. [PWN]

Gathering   A group of one or more *conjugate leaves sewn together before binding. Depending on *format, a gathering is made from one folded *sheet, from a fraction of a sheet, or from several folded sheets tucked one inside another (i.e. quired). Sewing folios as single units is labour-intensive and thickens the spine of a binding, while sewing twenty-fourmo or thirty-twomo foldings in one gathering strains the thread and results in an awkward text block. A folio gathering consisted of between two and five sheets in the fifteenth century [and] normally had three sheets in the next two centuries [...]. Quartos might be quired in sixes, tens, or twelves in the fifteenth century, but were more commonly gathered in eights; quarto in eights remained common in English printing until the seventeenth century [...]. Beyond the *incunable period, when an octavo gathering might comprise two sheets, octavos were rarely quired [...]. As a guide to binders, gatherings were identified by *signatures up to their halfway point or one *leaf beyond it [...]. [KEA]

Hand stamping   The practice of transferring text or image from a relief surface by means of a handheld, inked stamp, used in a few MSS and early printed books to add initials, *corrections, *signatures, *catchwords, and most notably borders, the last especially in Venice in the early 1470s. [MMS]

Haplography   During transcription or *type setting, the accidental skipping of a single letter or a group of letters within a word caused by the proximity of similar phonetic elements in the source text. E.g. 'philogy' for philology. Cases involving more than one word fall under the broader category of *saut du même au même. [*GDR+PS]

Headline   A line at the top of each page of a book containing information about the book (its title or author), the chapter (its title), or the page (its contents). Sometimes called a running head [...]. [MMS]
See also *skeleton forme, *running title.

492 PRINTING AND MISPRINTING

Hypercorrection A correction that is ultimately unnecessary or, in fact, plainly wrong, caused by overzealousness or overapplication of grammatical rules. Mainly affecting exceptions and highly unusual words, it occurs daily in spoken languages, though a few amusing instances can be found in early printed books, involving particularly pedantic printers, correctors, editors (such as us), and readers. Hypercorrection can overlap with the philological notion of *Verschlimmbesserung*, a wishful improvement that only results in disimprovement. [*GDR+PS]

Ideal copy [...] As individual copies from a single *issue, *impression, or *edition might vary (particularly during the hand press era), descriptive bibliographers generalise from the evidence present in surviving copies to reconstruct the intended form of that specific issue, impression, or edition at the moment of publication. Because such evidence may be inconclusive or incomplete, the ideal copy is often conjectural, and it is possible, especially when few copies survive, that no one copy matches the projected ideal copy. Bowers was the first to define the term at length; Tanselle refined the definition to include 'all the states of each *sheet as they were issued'. Ideal copy is usually described using *collational formulas. [IG]

Imposition The correct arrangement or layout of the *type or other matter of a printer's *forme, usually achieved on an imposing stone or on the bed of the press. The details of imposition depend on the *format of the book or other job. In an octavo book, for example, the printer would have to lay out sixteen pages, along with any necessary *headlines, direction lines, and *pagination, in such a way that, when the *sheet was printed and folded, all would appear in the correct position and orientation within the *gathering. An experienced printer would know the correct manner of imposition so well that setting up the two formes necessary for each octavo sheet would be a quick and simple matter, and one in which he would seldom err. Errors of imposition do occur, however, and may give rise to pages appearing with incorrect *pagination, in the wrong sequence, or, less commonly, upside down [...]. [PWN]

Impression All copies of an *edition printed at any one time. In the hand press period, an impression usually equates with an edition, as type from each *forme was normally distributed as it was printed off. Features indicating new impressions may include new *signatures, altered press figures, or variant paper stock.
Also, the act or process ('taking an impression'), or the quality (a 'good', 'bad', 'light', or 'heavy impression'), of printing, usually letterpress. [KEA]
See also *print run.

Incunabula *[Lat., 'swaddling-clothes', 'cradle']*. European printing with movable *type produced between the mid 1450s — when Gutenberg invented it in Mainz and the first printed items appeared (indulgences, the Gutenberg Bible) — and 1501. Block-books and engravings, although mechanically reproduced in the same period, are not incunabula. Some 27,000 separate *editions of incunabula are now on record as surviving. The *press run of each edition could vary according to available investment and expected market. Records of edition sizes are scarce, but they seem to have increased over the years, from about 175 in the 1450s, to 300 in the 1460s and 1470s, 600 in the 1490s, and even 1,400 for the Latin Nuremberg Chronicle (1493), an exceptional book. It is therefore hazardous to give a reasonable estimate of the total number of books and items printed in the fifteenth century. Much of what was printed is now lost. The term 'incunabula' was initially applied only to the first products of the invention of printing, which for centuries was hotly disputed [...]. The first *bibliography was van Beughem's *Incunabula Typographiae* (1688), listing c. 3,000 works. From then on, incunabula were treated as a distinct category of books. [LH]

APPENDIX A: GLOSSARY 493

Ink A pigment-bearing substance used for writing or printing. The scribe's ink is water-based to flow from a pen, and can use lampblack or iron-gall for the black. The printer's ink, oil-based and more viscous, is distributed on the *type by ink balls or rollers. [MMS]

Ink bleed Poor quality or poorly prepared oil in printing *ink took longer to dry and caused brown or yellow staining through the paper behind the text and its surroundings. The same happened if the *type had been over inked. [*LC]

Inked hair A hair that was inked either whilst lying on the *type or because inadvertently locked up in the *forme. [*LC]

Integrans [Lat., pl. *integrantia*] A *sheet or sheets *reset and reprinted to make up, rather than to correct, an *edition. Unlike *cancels, it was usually the consequence of an error in calculating the number of copies of a *sheet or the accidental spoiling of part of a *print run, or, in some instances, a belated decision to increase the print run after the first sheets had been printed off. [*GDR+PS] See also *duplicate setting.

Inverted type A piece of *type erroneously turned 180° in the *forme. On the page, this results in an inverted letter or numeral, e.g. 'p' for 'd', 'u' for 'n', or '6' for '9'. [*GDR+PS]

Issue All copies identifiable within an *edition as a consciously planned printed unit for sale, distinct from the basic form of the *ideal copy. An issue may be a separate issue or a *reissue […]. [KEA]

Justification The process of setting *type […] so that each line is the same length, usually filling the measure […]. Visually consistent spacing and well-judged hyphenation to achieve justification are important skills for a *compositor. Justified text is usually used for prose, while verse is generally unjustified. Prose may be unjustified when, for example, it is set with a ragged right or ragged left margin, or is centred on the measure. [PWN]

Kern The part of a metal *type projecting beyond its body; also, the action of adjusting space within certain combinations of characters for aesthetic reasons. [OCB]

Kludge A creative solution to a problem that reappropriates equipment to a purpose for which it was not designed. Having run out of a certain letter, a *compositor might resort to a kludge by using another letter as a substitute: an upside-down 'A' could become a 'V', for instance, or the tail of a 'Q' could be concealed to form an 'O'. At first glance, a kludge may appear to be a mistake; they are in fact ingenious safeguards against error. [*JM]

Lay of the case The disposition of characters in the compartments of a *type case, differing in detail between eras, countries, languages, and alphabets. Learning the lay of the case was an important duty of the apprentice *compositor. The earliest lays had all the characters in one large case. Before 1600, however, a standard divided lay had developed, with the majuscules, small capitals, and other less-used characters (accented vowels, for example) in alphabetical order in the upper case (placed uppermost on the *frame) and the minuscules arranged in a separate lower case in such a way as to bring the most commonly used characters closest to the compositor's hand […]. [PWN]

Layout See *mise-en-page.

Leaf Double-sided piece of paper, parchment, or similar material capable of being written or printed on, comprising two pages, recto and verso. [OCB]

Manuscript correction Any kind of manual *emendation in a text. In printed books, it can include interlinear and *marginal insertions, pen cancellations, and *erasures. Palaeographical analysis, together with the comparison of multiple copies (ideally a *copy census), can help understand whether the *correction

494   PRINTING AND MISPRINTING

was made directly at the print shop (i.e. in-house correction), by the author, or by the reader of a specific copy. [*GDR+PS]

Marginalia   Notes in the margins of texts containing short comments, keywords, or references. A centuries-old practice, they can be found in both manuscripts and printed books. In the latter case, it was usually readers who added marginalia, but a few instances are known in which printers employed them as a means of *emendation. The later collectors' habit of washing their books to obtain the cleanest possible copies could thus unwittingly result in the removal of precious in-house *corrections. [*GDR+PS]

Master printer   The person in charge of running the daily activities of a print shop and coordinating its work force. In early printing, the master printer may or may not have partaken in the ownership of the business, the editorial choices, or the *correction processes. [*GDR+PS]

Misalignment   Imperfect *justification of one or more printed elements on the page. It may affect text, images, or their mutual relation. It resulted from poor typesetting, inaccurate preparation and positioning of a *sheet (*register), or poor *imposition. [*GDR+PS]

Miscalculation   In *composition by *formes, the inaccurate calculation of line and page distribution within a *gathering, caused either by the *master printer in dividing the source text or by a *compositor in reading the *printer's copy. It may result in the addition or, more rarely, removal of a few lines in page. In particularly serious cases, however, a whole page or more could be missing. [*GDR+PS] See also *casting off copy.

Misnumbering   Mistakes concerning numerals, such as *leaf or page numbers, but also wrong digits in scientific books. [*GDR+PS]

Mise-en-page   A French phrase without a good English equivalent, internationally used in relation to book and typographical design to refer to a book's general layout: its page layout, column structure, and methods of textual articulation and presentation. The related term *mise en texte* concerns the structural subdivisions of the text into chapters or scenes and their subsections, such as paragraphs or acts [...]. When printed books began to appear in the fifteenth century, design conventions initially followed those established for handwritten books. Most legal, medical, biblical, and encyclopaedic books (which had very long texts and benefited from smaller *type sizes) were laid out in two columns, whereas classical texts were invariably printed in long lines [...]. The scribal habit of *justification of lines of prose was reinforced by the need for movable *type to be tightly wedged into the *forme, so justified prose became the norm [...]. [MMS]

Misprint   A broad term to indicate a variety of mistakes resulting from imperfections in the printing process and affecting its final outcome. Although the definition includes defective illustrations, *misalignment, *miscounting, and *misnumbering, it is often used in relation to text as a more serious mistake than a *typo. [*GDR+PS]

Mock-up   A sketch positioning the *type and images on a page spread, allowing its final appearance to be visualised before layout work is executed. [OCB] See also *mise-en-page.

Mould   In typefounding, the two-part hand mould used to cast individual *sorts. In the papermaking industry, a metal mesh in a wooden frame, with a separate deckle (a second frame), usually containing a *watermark, used to screen fibers and produce a *sheet. The organization of papermaking at the vat, with two men, the *vatman and the *coucher, meant that two moulds were used in

APPENDIX A: GLOSSARY   495

alternation, always with the same deckle. This gives rise to twin *watermarks, usually distinguished by being placed in the opposite left- and right-hand halves of their respective moulds. [*GDR+PS]

Offset See *set-off.

Overprinting A rudimentary means of *correction involving a second run under the press. The solution seems to have been seldom adopted due to the high risks of increasing the magnitude of the problem. [*GDR+PS]

Overslip See *paste slip.

Pagination The sequential numbering of a book's pages, usually with odd numbers on rectos of *leaves. Pagination is rare in medieval books, which sometimes have numbered leaves (*foliation). Few *incunables used either method of numbering, although W. Rolewinck's *Sermo in Festo Presentationis Beatissime Marie* (Cologne, 1470) was paginated. By the late sixteenth century, pagination with Arabic numerals had become nearly universal [...]. Numbers are often carried in the *skeleton forme of a book. A pagination statement is usually part of a *collation, with indications of disturbances and *misprints in the sequences. Contents tables and indexes use page numbers as locators. [MMS]

Paper crease A crease in a *sheet of paper over which *type or a block has been printed. The crease would have been flattened out, perhaps during the binding process, leaving a gap in the printed text or image. [*LC]

Paratext The nonce word 'paratext', coined by the French literary scholar and professor at the Sorbonne, Gérard Genette (1930–2018), and first used in *Palimpsestes* (1982), usefully labels several elements of a book and endows them with theoretical status. In his subsequent *Seuils*, or 'thresholds' (1987) [...], Genette defines paratext as the sum of two subordinate definitions: the 'peritext' is whatever is in the book and communicates a message, without necessarily forming part of the authorial text; the 'epitext' is the information emanating from the book, but not actually part of its physical structure, such as advertising, publisher's catalogues, reviews, etc. [...]. Paratextual elements include, for example, the title-page, which in many printed books served as an advertisement, and dedication, which helps to define the cultural context of the work [...]. [NH]

Paste slip A method of *correction that involves printing, *hand stamping, or writing the corrected text on a *sheet or piece of paper, cutting it to size, and pasting the slip over the incorrect version. This method may also be used to alter text for other purposes (censorship, change of publisher). Pasting-in was occasionally employed as a way of adding enlarged initials, miniatures, or other illustrations to a MS or printed book. [MMS]

Pin/point holes In Western printing, unlike earlier processes, the *sheet was impressed on both sides, making it suitable for diffusion in codex form. Proper *register of the sheet was obtained by placing pins on the *tympan, which left small holes when the sheet received an *impression on one side; when the sheet was printed on the other side, the pressman inserted the holes onto the pins, thus obtaining an exact placement. Early printed artefacts show up to six pinholes, due to the use of the one-*pull press, but standard practice soon meant two, in — but not always exactly on — the sheet's central fold. When books were sewn up and bound, the pinholes usually disappeared, but where copies have remained in sheets, the pinholes can provide useful *bibliographical evidence. [NH]

Press run See *print run.

Print run The total number of *sheets printed from a *forme, or pair of formes, and, by extension, the number of copies of an *edition, regardless of *states and *variants. Early modern print runs are almost invariably a matter of estimation, if not dangerous guesswork, though scattered evidence survives for a few editions. [*GDR+PS]

See also *impression.

Printer's copy The MS or printed text, sometimes with *corrections, handed to the printer; because this *exemplar — from which *type was composed — was usually disbound to facilitate the work of the *compositor(s), printer's copy is a rare source of evidence. In a number of instances, rather than destroy a valuable manuscript, a copy was made to be employed and destroyed in the printing shop. [NH]

See also *archetype, *copy-text, *exemplar.

A degree of terminological overlap between *archetype, *copy-text, *exemplar and *printer's copy is inevitable. The use of 'archetype', ideally, should be confined to ecdotic and MS studies, as it almost inevitably involves a degree of speculation towards the reconstruction of a lost original (*Urtext*). Similarly, the use of 'printer's copy' should be limited to MSS and printed books used to prepare a printed edition. 'Copy-text' and 'exemplar', however, are broader in meaning, and thus more exposed to overlapping interpretations, and occasionally to inconsistent or confusing uses. This problem is less frequent in non-English contexts: for instance, while 'printer's copy' translates in German as *Druckvorlage* (a term also frequently used in Italian and other languages), 'copy-text' and 'exemplar' both translate as *Vorlage* (equally used in Italian and other languages), thus reducing the overlap and potential confusion.

Printer's manual Guide designed for printers and members of the publishing trade. Historically, printers' manuals were produced for apprentice or journeyman printers, as an introduction to the trade. These manuals dealt with many aspects of the printer's trade, including setting up a printing press, typefounding and typography, *composition, and maintaining good business relations with publishers and authors. Some manuals pertained specifically to a particular printing house or publisher, and provided details of house rules and style and *impositions [...]. Because printers' manuals are often so precise and exhaustive, the study of them can be invaluable in helping modern *bibliographers to understand the way a particular text has been assembled. Manuals often include extensive diagrams and illustrations, and their anecdotal components can powerfully evoke the atmosphere of the printer's workshop [...]. [TK]

Proofreader's marks The traditional marks used by proofreaders are derived ultimately from the *obeli* and other notations used by ancient scribes. Later, the marks employed to correct printed matter showed remarkable uniformity throughout Europe; they persisted, with only minor variations, from the early sixteenth century down to the present day [...]. [RMR]

Proofs; Proofreading One or more sets of trials pulled at different stages between the initial typesetting and the final *print run in order to minimize *typos and *misprints and/or include textual revisions. Unlike manuscripts, the complexity of *composing and printing a text with moveable *type generally resulted in a larger number of mistakes which could potentially multiply over hundreds of copies and, in the worst cases, make them unusable. To avert this risk, printers started to produce proofs which were more or less attentively read, marked, and corrected so as to implement the required changes in the *forme. Over time and in larger print shops, proofs were increasingly handled by specialized workers known as *correctores*. Often scholars in their own right, these precursors of modern proofreaders were usually entrusted with additional tasks, such as drafting *errata lists and *paratextual elements (titles, dedications and addresses to readers, tables of contents, etc.).

From Zwinger's *Methodus apodemica* (1577) to Hornschuch's *Orthotypographia* (1608), from Paredes' *Institucíon y origen* (c. 1680) to Moxon's *Mechanick exercises* (1683–1684), early modern *printer's manuals describe different rounds of proofs, usually three. However, caution on such a clearcut distinction in early printing is advisable and the very existence of these manuals suggests that such high standards were perhaps not as established as one might think. Depending on the specific circumstances of an *edition (date, size, purpose, genre, authorship, etc.), proofs may be loosely classified as: first proofs, taken immediately after *composition and usually for in-house *correction; author/editor's proofs, an improved version for the author/editor — if there was one — to check the text (this practice, however, developed over time, and during the Renaissance was fairly rare); final proofs, pulled by some printers for counterchecks just before the *impression of the *print run, often involved printing a small nucleus of *sheets on both sides, also as a check on the *register for the second forme. Canny printers would not discard them, even if they bore *manuscript corrections, since they could be used in the last resort to make up copies. Proofs could be obtained by contact, i.e. placing a sheet of paper directly on the forme and rubbing it with a brush (this solution was useful to obtain proofs of single pages still in the galley without waiting for whole formes to be set up), or by using an old press kept for that purpose. Galley proofs, printed on slips, were particularly useful for newspaper articles, and thus only spread from the mid seventeenth century onwards. A major obstacle to a good understanding of the whole process is the lack of any significant number of surviving proofs for the same edition, let alone the same sheet. Proof sheets are indeed extremely rare; they usually survive in archives, crop up in early bindings where they were inserted as endleaves or fillers, and can even be found in some copies in place of correctly printed sheets. [*GDR+PS]

See also *proofreader's marks.

Pull   The act of pulling the bar of a printing press, or (informally) the resulting printed matter. The 'puller' was, traditionally, the senior operator of a hand press, who worked with the more junior *beater. The puller's job was to place paper on the *tympan, fold down the *frisket, and then fold them both down to meet, or almost meet, the *inked *forme, turn the rounce to move the bed under the platen, and pull on the bar to make the *impression. The earliest wooden presses were 'one-pull', meaning that they were mechanically capable of printing only one pull from each *forme, so that each *sheet of paper or parchment could only be printed on half of one side at a time. 'Two-pull' presses, which allowed the carriage, bed, and forme of the press to be advanced to print both halves of a full forme with two successive pulls, were introduced during the 1470s and were the norm until the introduction of iron presses around 1800. Once the pull or pulls had been made, the puller would then turn the rounce in the opposite direction to bring the carriage out from beneath the platen, raise the tympan and frisket together, fold the frisket up, remove the printed sheet, and lay it on a separate pile [...]. [PWN]

Puller   See *pull.

Quad   See *spacing material.

Quire   A twentieth part of a ream of paper. While sizes could vary to some extent, quires of twenty-five *sheets, in the case of full reams, or twenty-four sheets, in the case of 'short' reams, were the norm. In the latter case, the two outermost quires were known as 'cording quires' or 'cassie quires' (from the French *cassé*,

498 PRINTING AND MISPRINTING

	broken), and were formed with defective sheets, for which it was no matter if they were damaged in transport. In manuscript studies, quire is also used as a synonym for *gathering, the latter term being preferred for printed books. [*GDR+PS]
Quoin	Small, expanding device for locking up *formes. Originally wooden wedges, later quoins have two metal cheeks, expanded with a screw via a '*quoin* key'. [OCB]
Raised furniture	A piece of *furniture accidentally leaving a trace, either *inked or blind, on the page. It could result from furniture being turned on its edge or raised up by a foreign element underneath. [*LC]
Raised type	*Type or *spacing material drawn up by mistake and then stuck in such position, preventing the adjacent letters from being properly *inked and/or printed. [*LC]
Ream	See *quire.
Recension	The procedure whereby the relationship between surviving MSS or texts is established. In the genealogical tradition of editing associated with Lachmann, the original purpose of recension was to discover the ancestral claims of the texts, whether any source could be found to be a common point of origin, or indeed if such an origin or *archetype was lost, and would therefore need to be reconstructed from the surviving documents. Recension involved the collection of all authoritative evidence, including *collation of sources and the analysis of *variants and their relative *states of agreement or otherwise, in order to create the tree, or stemma, that would reveal the relationship of texts and produce the ancestral text (whether extant or reconstructed) that could then be *emended and *corrected. Critical awareness of the drawbacks of the genealogical editing tradition has meant that 'recension' is sometimes used pejoratively, given its historical connotations. It has, however, retained its place in general editorial parlance, although it is used as a neutral term (when not associated with a particular editorial tradition) to describe the process of textual assessment and collation in editing, or to denote the product of this process, such as a stemma. [ASR]
Register	Sometimes applied to the series of *signatures in a printed book but, more properly, the list of the signatures, usually preceding the *colophon, included as an instruction to the binder. Registers antedate printing, but printed *sheets, sold unbound, especially required indications about structure. Early examples, usually in *editions without signatures, contain lists of the opening word in each sheet. Once signatures became commonplace in the mid 1470s, the register became a summary of the same. The practice of including a register grew rarer from the end of the sixteenth century. Register also refers to the precise positioning of printed text or images on a sheet of paper, important when perfecting or printing in several colours. Failure results in printing being 'out of register'. [NH]
Reglet	A strip of oil-soaked wood used when printing with movable *type, placed between lines of letters to create interlinear spacing […]. [DRSP] Not to be confused with a *setting rule.
Reissue	Early printed books very often remained in *sheets up to the moment of purchase. If a title sold poorly, it was common practice to reissue it by reprinting the sheet(s) containing the title and/or *colophon with a new date and perhaps the name of another publisher. Examples are known of books, usually *incunabula, in which a blank *leaf acquires a title or a *colophon by passing it through the press again; but reissue usually involves physical substitution. A reissue is still part of the same *edition, but constitutes a new *issue, or unit of sale. [NH]

APPENDIX A: GLOSSARY   499

Reset A broad term indicating the partial or full recomposition of one or more *formes. It may usually be divided into three subcategories serving different purposes: inserting *corrections during printing (*stop-press emendation); replacing one or more *leaves during or after printing (*cancellans); making up for missing sheets when the original forme is no longer available (*integrans). [*GDR+PS]

River Irregular white space running vertically through several lines of text. Associated with the *justification of typesetting, in which the widths of word spaces are not consistent. [OCB]

Running title Title of book or section of book at the top of each page or opening, as part of the *headline. [OCB]
See also *skeleton forme.

Saut du même au même During transcription or typesetting, the accidental skipping of one or more words caused by the proximity of similar or identical words in the source text. If the similarity concerns the beginning of words, lines, or verses it is called 'homeoarchy', if it concerns the end 'homeoteleuton'. [*GDR+PS]

Set-off Oil-based printer's *ink, which reacts with oxygen, has residual elements that do not dry immediately. Printers therefore have had to deal with freshly printed *sheets that will set off — transfer an impression to the next sheet — especially if the ink is cheap or 'soft' (i.e. the oil has not been boiled long enough). Since paper was *dampened for printing, moisture impeded most setting off [...]. In printing the second *forme of a sheet (also known as 'perfecting', or 'reiteration'), printers often caught the set-off with a smut-sheet, usually a piece of waste, regularly changed. Set-offs sometimes show that two *editions were being printed at the same time, though instances have been found in which smut-sheets from an earlier printing were recycled. Taking account of the fact that the word 'set-off' appears earlier and seems to be the trade term, it is to be preferred to 'off-set'; there is also the advantage of distinguishing it with respect to the more recent rotary printing process. [NH]

Setting rule A piece of (usually brass) rule of standard length [...] used to set the measure of a *composing stick. [OCB]
Not to be confused with a *reglet.

Sheet The printer's unit of paper, manufactured in various sizes, weights, and qualities. A sheet in the handpress period printed two folio *leaves, four quarto leaves, eight octavo, and so forth. It was printed in two stages: usually, first the outer, then the inner, *forme. Until the introduction of wove paper in the late eighteenth century, sheets had deckle edges, chain and wire lines, and sometimes *watermarks. Sheets were sold in *quires and reams, with a ream comprising twenty quires of twenty-four or twenty-five sheets each. In most *bibliographical study, the sheet or forme is the basic unit of analysis. [KEA]

Shoulder The non-printing surface of a piece of *type on which the printing surface (the face) sits; it also supports *kerns from adjacent typeset letters. [OCB]

Show-through Printed marks visible from the wrong side of a *leaf, caused by excessive *ink penetration or pressure during printing, or insufficient paper opacity. [OCB]

Signature Alphanumeric indicator for the binder of the *gathering [...] and of the gathering's place in the sequence of gatherings [...]. [OCB]

Signe de renvoi [Fr., 'sign of return']. A pair of kindred, graphic signs that can take different shapes (e.g. carets): the first marks the position in the text where a *correction or insertion is to be made, while the second, usually in the margins (or very occasionally omitted), introduces the correction or insertion. *Signes de renvoi* may also be used to highlight cross references. Common in manuscripts, the practice was also adopted in printed books, added either in the print shop or, later on, by a reader. On rare occasions, one may also find printed examples. [*GDR+PS]

Singleton A single (i.e. non-*conjugate) *leaf, either one whose pair has been severed for insertion elsewhere in the publication, or an additional leaf printed separately. [OCB]

Skeleton forme A *forme from which the *type for the text block has been removed. It contains items that show up on the printed page (*headlines, rules, ornaments, and *signatures) and others that do not (*furniture, *quoins, and the *chase). These items, being common to all of or part of the book, are available for reuse after the first *sheet has been printed and the text in the forme is available for *distribution. By holding the components of the skeleton together at this stage and in a configuration that keeps the relative positions of each intact, and then reusing them when making up the next group of pages in the chase, *compositors save time and ensure that the page layout (see *mise-en-page) remains consistent throughout the book. Skeleton formes have been used by *bibliographers to study certain problems of textual transmission, such as compositorial analysis and *cancels. [ABRW]

Slipped type *Type could slip (move between lines or beyond the margins) from the *forme when lines had not been set each to the same tension and properly locked up, or when making up the forme. When one or more letters slipped, the adjacent ones usually crept into the empty space more and more during the printing process. This could affect legibility and layout. [*LC]

Smudged type This can occur when the paper is not laid on or lifted off the *type cleanly, or there is some movement of the *sheet during printing. It usually results from carelessness or a poor method of keeping the paper *pinned. [*LC]

Smudges/thumbing Traces of *ink or dirt on the printed page, most commonly in the margins, often caused by inaccurate handling in the print shop or, at a later stage, by readers' carelessness. The former tend to be heavier and darker due to the difference in viscosity between printing and writing ink. The presence, in some manuscripts, of a particular concentration of thumbing, smudges, and other marks in printer's ink, may provide additional evidence that they were used as *printer's copy. [*GDR+PS]

Sort An individual piece of physical *type. The term is precise, unlike *type which can have multiple meanings. [*PWN]
See also *font/fount.

Spacer See *spacing material.

Spacing material Type sorts used to separate words, to justify to the right margin, and to fill out lines at the end of a paragraph or blank lines between paragraphs. It was generally cast shorter than letter sorts, since it was not intended to be inked; it does happen, however, that spaces between words were not sufficiently pushed down by the compositor and caught ink, sometimes creating variants of state if the error is corrected. Spacing sorts existed in various sizes from half-spaces through to quads and double-quads. A trick of the trade was to use strips of paper, the same size as a sort, to fill very narrow spaces, but the practice was frowned upon in the better printing shops. [*NH]
See also *bearer type.

Stamping See *hand stamping.

APPENDIX A: GLOSSARY   501

Standing type Composed *type which is not *distributed but remains set after it has been printed, either because the type is not needed immediately for another job, or in order to allow a planned (or hoped for) new *impression. [*PWN]

State In *bibliography, state only has meaning when one or more *variant states of an *edition exist. Each state displays a particular variation or group of variations in the setting of the *type, or more rarely in the *imposition. Variant states may result from *stop-press corrections, *fallen-type, and other accidents in the *forme which cause the removal or movement of *sorts, or from the printer intervening, for example to change the dedication, date, or publisher's name in a title-page or *colophon (the alteration of a publisher's name is sometimes said to give rise to a variant *issue rather than a state). If an increase in *print run necessitates two or more editions of certain pages, then the edition as a whole is said to exist in different states. The term is sometimes also applied to type, in an attempt to indicate the chronological development of the character set of a particular typeface (usually with the identification of early and late states of a type). [*PWN]

Stop-press correction A *correction made to a *forme on the press while printing an *edition. Stop-press corrections may be the result of delayed *proofreading, of pressmen noticing errors (or missing or broken types) during printing, or of late decisions about the text made by the master printer, publisher, or author. Such corrections always give rise to a *variant *state. [*PWN]

Stub A narrow strip of paper, visible in the gutter of a book. In a *cancel, the stub represents the remains of a *cancellandum, after the *leaf has been cut away, to which a *cancellans* may be attached. Stubs are also characteristic of endpapers, when the latter are wrapped around the first and last *gatherings of a book in order to reinforce the binding. [NH]

Transmission errors A variety of mistakes that occur during the replication of a text in manuscript or print and often caused by cognitive biases towards oversimplification or, more rarely, overcomplication. Some of the most common instances are related to specific features of the source text. Transmission errors may loosely be divided into four major categories: (1) omissions (eyeskip, *haplography, *saut du même au même — including homeoteleuton and homeoarchy); (2) additions (dittography, contamination); (3) transpositions (metathesis); (4) alterations (unwitting or deliberate, including interpolation and *hypercorrection). [*GDR+PS]

Tympan [Lat. *tympanum*, 'drum'] A frame, usually covered with taut parchment, upon which paper is placed in a hand press. The tympan usually has an inner frame, also covered with parchment, which can be removed from the back to allow cloth and/or paper packing to be inserted between the two frames. Make-ready, usually in the form of pieces of thin paper, may be passed to the tympan to provide additional pressure in certain areas of the *forme. In operation, the *frisket is folded over the paper and tympan, and both are folded down to rest just above the *inked *forme prior to printing. [PWN]

Type The most general term for letters and other characters repeatedly used together to form texts or decorations [...]. Traditional and modern usage suggest distinctions between type, *typeface, and *fount, often at odds with attempts to rationalize terminology (see also *sort). Type, usually a collective noun, formerly referred primarily to the pieces of cast metal used for letterpress printing, but was also used more broadly [...]. Typeface and fount more specifically emphasize, respectively, the design or form, and the product acquired or used by the compositor. One designs type or a typeface, casts [...] type or a fount, and sets type [...]. [JAL]

Type case A subdivided tray (originally wooden, subsequently metal or plastic) for storing *type and displaying it during *composition. [OCB]
See also *lay of the case.

Typeface The entire set of characters, considered for their design or form, intended to be used together repeatedly to produce texts or decorations. Various sizes, weights, or even styles such as Roman, Italic, [...] when intended as a family, may therefore constitute a single typeface. [JAL]
See also *font/fount, *sort, *type.

Typo Abbreviation of 'typographical error': a small mistake involving a single typographical *sort or two adjacent ones caused by a *compositorial slip (e.g 'q'/'p' for 'p' or 'nu' for 'un'). Anything major should considered, more generally, a *misprint. [*GDR+PS]

Typographical lacuna Missing portion of a printed text, usually caused by a piece of paper fallen on the *forme and preventing the correct printing of the page. [*LC]

Variant [...] Variant *issues arise through a difference on a title-page, typically in the *imprint. Variant *states arise through *corrections made after printing [...] has begun. They result from: intentional or unintentional alterations not affecting page makeup, such as *stop-press corrections of letters or words; *resetting following accidental damage to the *type, or the resetting of *distributed matter following a decision made during printing to increase the *print run; addition, deletion, or substitution of matter affecting page makeup but made during printing; and errors of *imposition [...]. [KEA]

Vatman The person who makes a *sheet of paper by dipping the *mould into the vat and lifting it out, forming the *sheet on its surface. [OCB]
See also *coucher.

Visorium/Visorum A wooden clasp or board with a spiked foot which, attached to the edge of a *type case, was used by *compositors to display *copy-text, often with the addition of a moveable ruler to indicate which line was being set. The etymology is uncertain: the French term is *visorium*; German printers called the clasp a *Tenakel*, but with the confusing *Divisorium* used for the moveable ruler; the English form ('visorum') is probably derived from the French. [*PWN]

Vorlage See *printer's copy.

Water drop In papermaking, when the deckle is removed from the *mould, no matter how careful the *vatman is, it sometimes happens that a drop of water falls on the freshly made *sheet. Also known as 'vatman's tears', they can occasionally affect legibility. [*GDR+PS]

Watermark Any non-random repetitive decoration or identification mark introduced deliberately into a *sheet or web of paper when wet — such that it causes a variation in optical density and becomes visible in transmitted or reflected light — is commonly called a watermark. More correctly, the term applies to a main image, such as a decorated shield, while subsidiary impressions are called countermarks. The earliest watermarks appeared around the thirteenth century in Italy, although current research suggests they may have been an extension of a development pioneered at earlier times in Asia [...]. [DCC]

Woodblock printing Printing images, text, or patterns by means of wooden blocks, usually *inked on the relief surface. The block can be rubbed, used as a stamp (for printing cloth), or placed face up in a press (for book illustrations, printed simultaneously and juxtaposed with text). Woodcut illustration was the preferred method for the early printed book using metal *type; *block printing of text and image yields a blockbook. Fruitwood blocks cut along the grain with a knife produce woodcuts; denser blocks of boxwood cut on the end-grain with a burin produce wood engravings. Blocks of metal produce metalcuts. [MMS]

APPENDIX B

··

GLOSSARY TRANSLATION TABLES

··

The following pages provide translations of the glossary's headwords in eighteen different languages. When a direct translation could not be found, tentative suggestions have been offered with question marks or in square brackets. Synonyms are separated by commas, while different meanings are separated by semicolons. The names and affiliations of the translators — usually three or more, but at any rate never fewer than two — are listed under each table. The network of librarians and book historians of the Consortium of European Research Libraires (CERL) has been instrumental in connecting us to experts in various languages, and we are particularly grateful to Falk Eisermann and Oliver Duntze (Berlin, Staatsbibliothek) for their support in this endeavour.

ARABIC

	English	Arabic
1	Allography	تعدد الرسم، تعدد الإملاء
2	Apologies	تنويه واعتذار
3	Archetype	الأصل، النص الأساسي
4	Bearer type	حرف حامل، محرف حامل (لدعم المناطق الفارغة في الصفحة)
5	Beater	خافق الحبر، عاجن الحبر
6	Bibliography	بيليوغرافيا، دراسة الكتب: ١)بيليوغرافيا تعدادية؛ ٢) بيليوغرافيا تحليلية؛ ٣) بيليوغرافيا وصفية؛ ٤) بيليوغرافيا نصيّة؛ ٥) بيليوغرافيا تاريخية
7	Blind impression	انطباع أعمى
8	Cancel	تصويب مادي (عادة إعادة طبع ورقة لاستبدال أخرى معيبة)
9	*Castigationes*	بدائل، قراءات بديلة
10	Casting off copy	تقدير المتن، تقدير الأصول
11	Catchword	تعقيبة
12	Chase	طوق، شاسيه
13	Collation	١) التحقق من أن الأوراق المطبوعة المجمعة مرتبة وموجهة بشكل صحيح قبل الطي والخياطة. ٢) لائحة التجميع: وصف بيليوغرافي للكتّاب يوضح بالتفصيل تنسيق وترتيب الملازم وأي أوراق مدرجة أو محذوفة وعدد الأوراق. ٣) المقارنة البليوغرافية لنسخة معينة من كتّاب بنسخة أخرى أو مع لائحة التجميع في عمل مرجعي لتحديد ما إذا كان عدد الملازم وترتيبها كاملين. ٤) العرض أو المقارنة التحريرية لنسخة معينة من كتّاب بنسخة أخرى لتحديد المتغيرات النصية. ٥) قائمة بهذه المتغيرات.
14	Colophon	كولوفون، معلومات الناسخ، حرد المتن، قيد الفراغ
15	Composing stick	مصَفّ، مصَفّ المحارف
16	Composition	تنضيد، صفّ، جمع
17	Compositor	منضّد، منضد المحارف
18	Conjugate leaves	الأوراق المترافقة
19	Copy census	إحصائيات النص
20	Copy-specific analysis	تحليل النَسخ، تحليل معلومات النَسخ
21	Copy-text	النسخة الأساس، النص المعتمد
22	Correction	تصويب، تصحيح
23	Coucher	ناقل شرائح الورق
24	Damping	ترطيب
25	Distribution (of type)	توزيع (المحارف)، إعادة التوزيع (على الصندوق)، تفريق
26	Drag lines	خطوط السحب، علامات السحب، مصري: سنيوهات من الكلمة الفرنسية (signet)

27	Drying/hanging	تجفيف/تعليق
28	Duplicate setting	تنضيد مكرر، جمع مكرر
29	Edition	طبعة، إصدار
30	Emendation	تنقيح، تكميل
31	Erasure	محو
32	Errata	تصويب، جدول الخطأ والصواب
33	Exemplar	النموذج الأم، النموذج الأصلي
34	Fallen type	حرف ساقط، محرف ساقط
35	Foliation	ترقيم، ترقيم الأوراق
36	Font/Fount	نسقة الحروف الطباعية، الخط الطباعي
37	Format	قطع الكتاب وشكله العام
38	Forme	فُرمة، فورم
39	Foul case	صندوق مغلوط
40	Frisket	قناع الوقاية
41	Frisket bite	عضة القناع (جزء مفقود من المادة المطبوعة نتيجة خطأ في الإطار)
42	Furniture	البياض، مربعات وشرائح البياض، تواضيب
43	Galley	صينية، صينية الصف
44	Gathering	تجميع الأوراق، ملزمة
45	Hand stamping	خَتْم يدوي، طبع يدوي
46	Haplography	هابلوغرافيا: سقط الحروف في النسخ أو الطبع
47	Headline	ترويس، ترويسة
48	Hypercorrection	فرط التصحيح
49	Ideal copy	نسخة مثالية
50	Imposition	ترتيب الصفحات للطبع، التوليف، رمي الصفحات
51	Impression	طبعة، كامل النسخ المطبوعة في مرة واحدة؛ مقدار ضغط السطح المحبّر على ورقة معدة للطبع
52	Incunabula	إنكونابولا، أوائل المطبوعات (الكتب المطبوعة بالمحارف المتحركة في فترة ١٤٥٠ ١٥٠١)
53	Ink	حبر، مداد
54	Ink bleed	نزيف الحبر، تبقيع الحبر (إما بالظهور على الطرف الآخر للصفحة أو حول المحارف المطبوعة)
55	Inked hair	شعرة محبّرة
56	*Integrans*	إنتغران: أوراق إضافية صُفّت وطبعت لإكمال طبعة كتاب (من اللاتيني)
57	Inverted type	حرف مقلوب، محرف مقلوب

APPENDIX B: GLOSSARY TRANSLATION TABLES   ARABIC   507

58	Issue	إصدار(جميع نسخ طبعات الكِتاب)
59	Justification	محاذاة الأسطر، ضبط الأسطر، ملء الأسطر(بحيث تكون جميعها بنفس الطول)
60	Kern	القرن، تعديل المسافة بين بعض الحروف؛ جزء من المحرف المعدني خارج عن جسمه
61	Kludge	استعاضة (حل مبتكر لمشكلة بإعادة استخدام المعدات، مثلاً المحارف، لغير غرضها الأصلي)
62	Lay of the case	ترتيب الصندوق، ترتيب المحارف في عيون صندوق الحروف
63	Leaf	ورقة
64	Manuscript correction	تصحيح المخطوطة؛ تعديل يدوي على الكِتاب المطبوع
65	Marginalia	ملاحظات هامشية (من تعليقات أو كلمات رئيسية أو مراجع)
66	Master printer	رئيس المطبعة، رئيس الطابعين
67	Misalignment	عدم المحاذاة (للعناصر المطبوعة على الصفحة)
68	Miscalculation	سوء تقدير
69	Misnumbering	خطأ الترقيم
70	Mise-en-page	ميز أون باج، تصميم الكتب (عبارة فرنسية تُستخدم دولياً فيما يتعلق بتصميم الكِتاب والتصميم المطبعي للإشارة إلى التخطيط العام للكِتاب: تخطيط الصفحة، وهيكل العمود، وطرق التعبير النصي والعرض)
71	Misprint	خطأ مطبعي
72	Mock-up	نموذج (رسم لترتيب النص والصور على الصفحة)
73	Mould	قالب، في صب الحروف: قالب يدوي مكون من جزئين لصب المحارف الفردية؛ في صنع الورق: شبكة معدنية في إطار خشبي
74	Overprinting	طبع فوقي (طريقة لإصلاح خطأ مطبعي بإجراء الطبع مرة أخرى)
75	Pagination	ترقيم الصفحات
76	Paper crease	تحزيز الورق
77	Paratext	العناصر شبه النصية في الكِتاب (مثل صفحة العنوان والإهداء، مما يساعد على تحديد السياق الثقافي للعمل)
78	Paste slip	قُصاصة ملصوقة (تُستخدم لعمل تصليحات أو تعديلات على نص مطبوع)
79	Pin/point holes	ثقوب الدبوس
80	Print run	عدد الطبعة
81	Printer's copy	نسخة الطابع، نسخة عامل المطبعة
82	Printer's manual	دليل الطابع، دليل عامل المطبعة
83	Proofreader's marks	علامات المصحح
84	Proofs; Proofreading	تجربة، بروفة، تصحيح
85	Pull	سحب، تجربة، بروفة (ناتجة عن السحب)

86	Quire	رزمة من ٢٤ أو ٢٥ ورقة، ملزمة مجموعة. كرّاسة، جزء في دراسات المخطوطات.
87	Quoin	قفل الفورمة، قفل ربط الصفحات، تجليّة
88	Raised furniture	بياض بارز، بياض مرتفع
89	Raised type	حرف بارز، محرف مرتفع
90	Recension	تحديد الأصل
91	Register	سجل الملازم؛ انتظام واتّساق عناصر الصفحة
92	Reglet	رقيقة خشبية (للفصل بين السطور)
93	Reissue	إعادة إصدار
94	Reset	إعادة التنضيد، إعادة الصفّ
95	River	نهر (شريط أبيض يمتد شاقولياً داخل عدة أسطر من النص)
96	Running title	عنوان جاري، عنوان متكرر
97	*Saut du même au même*	كلمات ساقطة (بسبب التشابه)
98	Set-off	تلويث، تلطيخ (الورقة التالية). مصري: ورقة مبصمة.
99	Setting rule	مسطرة التنضيد (عادة من النحاس الأصفر)
100	Sheet	ورقة (صفحتان)، فرخ
101	Shoulder	كتف، كتف الحرف، كتف المحرف
102	Show-through	علامات الطباعة الشاقّة (المرئية من الوجه الآخر للصفحة)
103	Signature	التوقيع، رقم الملزمة، رقم ترتيب الملزمة (ضمن الملازم المجلدة)
104	*Signe de renvoi*	علامة التخريج، خَرجة، علامة التعديل (زوج من العلامات المتشابهة لتحديد مكان التعديل في النص وكتابة التعديل في الهامش)
105	Singleton	ورقة وحيدة
106	Skeleton forme	فورمة هيكلية، فورمة مشتركة
107	Slipped type	حرف منزلق، محارف منزلقة، محارف مُزاحة
108	Smudged type	نص ملطخ، طباعة ملطخة (بها بقع)
109	Smudges/thumbing	لطخات/بصمات
110	Sort	حرف معدني، محرف
111	Spacing material	مواد فصل، فواصل
112	Standing type	حرف محفوظ (لم يتم توزيعه بعد الطبع)، صفحات محفوظة (لم يتم توزيعها بعد الطبع)
113	State	حالة (عند وجود عدة تنويعات على النص)
114	Stop-press correction	تصحيح وقف الطبع (تصحيح تم أثناء الطبع)
115	Stub	أرومة (شريط ورق ضيق يبقى بعد القص)
116	Transmission errors	أخطاء النسخ أو النقل
117	Tympan	حشو
118	Type	حرف طباعي، حرف مطبعي
119	Type case	صندوق الحروف
120	Typeface	خط طباعي

121	Typo	اختصار لـ خطأ مطبعي
122	Typographical lacuna	نص مفقود، ثغرة في النص المطبوع
123	Variant	نسخة مغايرة
124	Vatman	عامل الراقود (الراقود وعاء كبير لخلط عجينة الورق)
125	Visorium/Visorum	حامل النص (على صندوق الحروف)
126	Water drop	قطرة ماء (عند صناعة الورق)
127	Watermark	علامة مائية
128	Woodblock printing	طرش، طبع بالقوالب الخشبية

Arabic translation by: Mamoun Sakkal (Seattle); Ahmed Mansour (Bibliotheca Alexandrina, Alexandria, Egypt); Joel Mitchell (London); Lutfallah Gari (Yanbu, Saudi Arabia).

CHINESE

	English	Chinese
1	Allography	字素變體, 字位變體
2	Apologies	道歉, 致歉
3	Archetype	原型(文稿或文本)
4	Bearer type	用作承受壓板重量的活字
5	Beater	上墨員
6	Bibliography	文獻學, 圖書學, 書志學
7	Blind impression	平壓印, 素壓印
8	Cancel	經修正的版面
9	*Castigationes*	校勘不同文稿後發現的異文
10	Casting off copy	版面預估
11	Catchword	下頁首詞, 導字, 渡字
12	Chase	版框
13	Collation	查帖; 配頁, 配帖; 版本校勘; 書籍稽核項
14	Colophon	書末題記; 書末出版說明; 版權頁; 牌記 (printer's colophon)
15	Composing stick	排字盤
16	Composition	排版, 排字
17	Compositor	排版工, 排字工
18	Conjugate leaves	和合頁
19	Copy census	抄本或印本調查
20	Copy-specific analysis	特定抄本或印本分析
21	Copy-text	原稿; 評注版的底本
22	Correction	改正, 修正, 勘誤
23	Coucher	負責使紙張脫模落在毛布氈上的造紙工人
24	Damping	潤濕
25	Distribution (of type)	拆版, 散字還盤
26	Drag lines	曳痕
27	Drying/hanging	印張吊晾
28	Duplicate setting	重複排版
29	Edition	版本; 一版印刷總數
30	Emendation	校訂
31	Erasure	擦除
32	Errata	勘誤表
33	Exemplar	樣本, 範本
34	Fallen type	掉落在印版上的活字
35	Foliation	張數編碼; 標記頁數; 標記葉碼
36	Font/Fount	字型
37	Format	版式; 開本
38	Forme	印版
39	Foul case	因使用字盤中錯置的活字而造成的排印錯誤
40	Frisket	夾紙框
41	Frisket bite	因夾紙框放置不當而漏印的部分
42	Furniture	裝版用的木製間隔材料, 置於文字版塊外
43	Galley	活版盤
44	Gathering	書帖
45	Hand stamping	手壓印

46	Haplography	掉字, 字母脫誤
47	Headline	頁眉, 書眉
48	Hypercorrection	矯枉過正
49	Ideal copy	理想本
50	Imposition	拼版
51	Impression	印次
52	Incunabula	搖籃本
53	Ink	油墨
54	Ink bleed	滲墨
55	Inked hair	上了墨的毛髮
56	*Integrans*	補充印張
57	Inverted type	倒置活字
58	Issue	發行印次
59	Justification	齊行
60	Kern	活字的出格部分; 為了美觀而調整特定字母的距離
61	Kludge	臨時應急方案
62	Lay of the case	字盤活字的排列
63	Leaf	張; 頁; 葉
64	Manuscript correction	文稿修正
65	Marginalia	邊注
66	Master printer	印坊主
67	Misalignment	排列不齊
68	Miscalculation	書帖頁面行數分佈的誤算
69	Misnumbering	數字錯誤
70	Mise-en-page	版面配置, 版面設計, 版式
71	Misprint	印刷錯誤
72	Mock-up	樣張
73	Mould	字模; 造紙模
74	Overprinting	套印, 重印, 疊印
75	Pagination	頁碼
76	Paper crease	紙上的皺褶
77	Paratext	副文本, 超文本, 輔文
78	Paste slip	修訂或勘誤用紙貼
79	Pin/point holes	在紙上穿的孔, 用以把頁面固定在壓紙格上
80	Print run	印數
81	Printer's copy	印刷用原稿
82	Printer's manual	印刷業者指南
83	Proofreader's marks	校對符號
84	Proofs; Proofreading	Proofs: 校樣, 稿樣, 校稿 ; Proofreading: 校對
85	Pull	拉動(印刷機的手柄)壓印, 或由此而成的印刷品; 稿樣
86	Quire	一刀 : 紙張數量單位, 相等於二十分之一令; 紙摺, 對頁
87	Quoin	版楔
88	Raised furniture	凸起的裝版用木製間隔材料
89	Raised type	因誤拔而卡住的活字
90	Recension	校訂
91	Register	帖號表; 印刷套准
92	Reglet	排版用的木嵌條

93	Reissue	未經改版再度發行
94	Reset	重新排版
95	River	川流: 因字詞間空白過多, 造成內文從上向下的白色條子
96	Running title	逐頁題名, 簡略題目, 眉題
97	*Saut du même au même*	因跳讀而產生的字詞遺漏
98	Set-off	蹭髒, 背印, 反印
99	Setting rule	排字尺
100	Sheet	張, 單頁
101	Shoulder	(活字的)字肩
102	Show-through	透印, 濾損
103	Signature	帖碼; 折標
104	*Signe de renvoi*	勘誤或插入文字的標記
105	Singleton	單頁; 單葉
106	Skeleton forme	鏤空版
107	Slipped type	從印版上滑落的活字
108	Smudged type	被弄髒的活字
109	Smudges/thumbing	印刷頁上的墨水漬或污漬
110	Sort	活字
111	Spacing Material	裝版用的金屬間隔材料, 置於文字版塊內
112	Standing type	存版
113	State	(同一個版本的不同) 印樣
114	Stop-press correction	印刷過程中, 因故停止印刷後對印版所作的改正
115	Stub	紙頭
116	Transmission errors	文本傳抄或印刷過程中出現的舛誤
117	Tympan	壓紙格
118	Type	活字; 鉛字; 印刷字體
119	Type case	字盤
120	Typeface	字體
121	Typo	打字或排印的小錯誤
122	Typographical lacuna	缺漏
123	Variant	異文
124	Vatman	撈紙工, 抄紙工, 抄造工, 紙漿工人
125	Visorium/Visorum	排版員的文件閱讀架, 用以放置預備排版的文本原稿
126	Water drop	殘留在紙上的水滴痕跡, 源於造紙過程中滴落在未乾透紙張上的水滴
127	Watermark	水印
128	Woodblock printing	木版印刷

Chinese translation by: George Kam Wah Mak (Hong Kong Baptist University); Nan Xu (Nanjing University Press).

CZECH

	English	Czech
1	Allography	Alografie
2	Apologies	Omluva tiskaře za chyby
3	Archetype	Archetyp, Nejstarší předloha
4	Bearer type	Podpůrná sazba
5	Beater	Navalovač barvy
6	Bibliography	Bibliografie
7	Blind impression	Otisk podpůrné sazby
8	Cancel	Tisková oprava, tektura
9	*Castigationes*	Cenzurní zásah (odstranění závadných míst)
10	Casting off copy	Textová předloha s rozvržením sazby
11	Catchword	Kustod, Reklamant
12	Chase	Rám Tiskové formy
13	Collation	Kolace
14	Colophon	Kolofon
15	Composing stick	Sázítko
16	Composition	Sazba
17	Compositor	Sazeč
18	Conjugate leaves	Dvojlist, Bifolium
19	Copy census	Soupis exemplářů vydání
20	Copy-specific analysis	Exemplářový průzkum
21	Copy-text	Textová předloha
22	Correction	Korektura
23	Coucher	Skladač
24	Damping	Vlhčení (papíru)
25	Distribution (of type)	Rozmetání sazby
26	Drag lines	Šmouhy (vzniklé chybným vyjmutím papíru z lisu)
27	Drying/hanging	Sušení (tiskařský archů)
28	Duplicate setting	Duplicitní sazba, Přesazba
29	Edition	Vydání
30	Emendation	Emendace
31	Erasure	Razura
32	Errata	Erata, Opravy tiskových chyb
33	Exemplar	Textová předloha
34	Fallen type	Uvolněná litera omylem vytištěná napříč textem
35	Foliation	Foliace
36	Font/Fount	Písmová sada
37	Format	Formát
38	Forme	Tisková forma; Sazba v tiskové formě
39	Foul case	Chybně zařazená litera v sazečské kase
40	Frisket	Nátisková maska
41	Frisket bite	Posun nátiskové masky
42	Furniture	Obložky
43	Galley	Loďka
44	Gathering	Složka papíru
45	Hand stamping	Razítkový tisk

46	Haplography	Haplografie, přehození písmen
47	Headline	Nadpis; záhlaví
48	Hypercorrection	Hyperkorektnost
49	Ideal copy	Úplný exemplář
50	Imposition	Vyřazení sazby
51	Impression	Tisk; Náklad; Vydání
52	Incunabula	Prvotisk; Inkunábule
53	Ink	Tiskařská barva
54	Ink bleed	Rozpíjení tiskařské barvy
55	Inked hair	Vlas omylem otištěný spou se sazbou
56	*Integrans*	Dotisk stran; Dotisk archů
57	Inverted type	Otočené písmeno, Převrácené písmeno
58	Issue	Vydání, Náklad
59	Justification	Úprava sazby
60	Kern	Přesah litery přes písmovou kuželku
61	Kludge	[Kludge]
62	Lay of the case	Naložení sazečské kasy
63	Leaf	List
64	Manuscript correction	Rukopisná oprava
65	Marginalia	Marginálie
66	Master printer	Tiskařský mistr, Faktor
67	Misalignment	Nevyrovnané účaří
68	Miscalculation	Chybný propočet (textu pro sazbu)
69	Misnumbering	Chybná paginace, Chybné stránkování; Chybná foliace
70	Mise-en-page	Zrcadlo sazby
71	Misprint	Chyba v sazbě, Chyba v tisku
72	Mock-up	Maketa
73	Mould	Ruční licí strojek
74	Overprinting	Přetisk
75	Pagination	Paginace, Stránkování
76	Paper crease	Vráska na papíře
77	Paratext	Paratext
78	Paste slip	Přelep, Tektura
79	Pin/point holes	Punktura
80	Print run	Náklad
81	Printer's copy	Předloha k sazbě
82	Printer's manual	Příručka pro knihtisk
83	Proofreader's marks	Korekturní znaménko, Korekturní značka
84	Proofs; Proofreading	Korektura; Zkušební obtah
85	Pull	Zátah lisu; Nátisk; Obtah
86	Quire	Složka papíru
87	Quoin	Uzávěr formy
88	Raised furniture	Přečnívající písmový výplněk
89	Raised type	Přečnívající litera
90	Recension	Textová kritika
91	Register	Rejstřík signatur složek; Rejstřík stránkový, řádkový (soutisk)
92	Reglet	Proložka
93	Reissue	Obálkové vydání; Titulové vydání

APPENDIX B: GLOSSARY TRANSLATION TABLES   CZECH   515

94	Reset	Přesazba
95	River	Řeka
96	Running title	Záhlaví
97	*Saut du même au même*	Vynechaná část textu při opisu či sazbě
98	Set-off	Zrcadlový otisk
99	Setting rule	Sázecí linka
100	Sheet	Arch
101	Shoulder	Hlava litery
102	Show-through	Prosvítání tisku, Propíjení tisku (skrz papír)
103	Signature	Složková signatura
104	*Signe de renvoi*	Korekturní značka
105	Singleton	Vevázaný samostatný list
106	Skeleton forme	Kostra tiskové formy (po odstranění tiskového bloku)
107	Slipped type	Vypadlá litera
108	Smudged type	Rozmazané písmo
109	Smudges/thumbing	Šmouhy, Skvrny, Otisky prstů (od tiskařské barvy nebo inkoustu na stránkách knihy)
110	Sort	Kovová litera
111	Spacing Material	Písmové výplňky
112	Standing type	Stojatá sazba
113	State	Variantní exemplář; Variantní vydání
114	Stop-press correction	Oprava sazby během tisku
115	Stub	Papírové křidélko
116	Transmission errors	Chyby v transmisi textů
117	Tympan	Tympán
118	Type	Tiskové písmo
119	Type case	Sazečská kasa
120	Typeface	Písmový řez
121	Typo	Tisková chyba
122	Typographical lacuna	Lakuna, Mezera v tisku
123	Variant	Exemplářová varianta (úprava knihy po vytištění, ale před prodejem)
124	Vatman	Čerpač
125	Visorium/Visorum	Divizor (přidržuje sazečskou předlohu)
126	Water drop	Vodní stopy, poškození vodou
127	Watermark	Filigrán
128	Woodblock printing	Deskotisk

Czech translation by: Richard Šípek (National Museum Library, Prague); Veronika Sladká (Library of Czech Academy of Sciences, Prague); Petr Voit (Institute of Information Studies and Librarianship, Prague); Kamil Boldan (National Library, Prague).

DANISH

	English	Danish
1	Allography	Allografi
2	Apologies	Undskyldning
3	Archetype	Arketype
4	Bearer type	[Bæretype]
5	Beater	[Den ene trykker]
6	Bibliography	Bibliografi
7	Blind impression	Tørtryk, Blindtryk
8	Cancel	Omtryk, Karton
9	*Castigationes*	Tekstforbedringer
10	Casting off copy	Manuskriptberegning
11	Catchword	Kustode, Bladviser
12	Chase	Ramme, Slutteramme
13	Collation	Kollation
14	Colophon	Kolofon
15	Composing stick	Vinkelhage
16	Composition	Sats, Sætning, Satsarbejde
17	Compositor	Sætter
18	Conjugate leaves	Sammenhørende blade, Konjunkte blade, Sammenhængende dobbeltblad
19	Copy census	Eksemplarundersøgelse
20	Copy-specific analysis	Eksmplarspecifik undersøgelse
21	Copy-text	Originalmanuskript; Grundtekst
22	Correction	Rettelse
23	Coucher	Gusker, Gausker
24	Damping	Fugte, Anfugte
25	Distribution (of type)	Aflægning
26	Drag lines	Slæbelinjer, Slæbeudtværing
27	Drying/hanging	Tørring
28	Duplicate setting	Dobbelttryk
29	Edition	Udgave
30	Emendation	Emendation, Tekstrettelse, Tekstforbedring
31	Erasure	Radering
32	Errata	Trykfejlsfortegnelse, Trykfejlsliste, Errata
33	Exemplar	Forlæg; Eksemplar
34	Fallen type	Udfalden type
35	Foliation	Foliering
36	Font/Fount	Skrift, Skriftgarniture
37	Format	Format
38	Forme	Trykform
39	Foul case	Fisk, Svibelfisk
40	Frisket	Ræmmeke
41	Frisket bite	Ræmmekebid
42	Furniture	Steg
43	Galley	Skib, Satsskib
44	Gathering	Læg
45	Hand stamping	Håndstemple

APPENDIX B: GLOSSARY TRANSLATION TABLES   DANISH   517

46	Haplography	Haplografi
47	Headline	Sideoverskrift
48	Hypercorrection	Hyperkorrektion
49	Ideal copy	Idealeksemplar
50	Imposition	Udskydning, Formatlægning
51	Impression	Oplag; Trykning
52	Incunabula	Inkunabler
53	Ink	Farve, trykfarve
54	Ink bleed	Udblødning af farve, Udflydende farve
55	Inked hair	[Hår med trykfarve]
56	*Integrans*	*Integrans*
57	Inverted type	Omvendt type
58	Issue	Oplag
59	Justification	Justering
60	Kern	Overhæng [n.], udfile [v.]
61	Kludge	Anvendelse af forhåndenværende materiale
62	Lay of the case	Kasseinddeling
63	Leaf	Blad
64	Manuscript correction	Håndskreven rettelse
65	Marginalia	Marginalier, Randnote, Marginalnote
66	Master printer	Bogtrykkermester, Bogtrykker, Principal
67	Misalignment	Skævhed, Dårlig justering
68	Miscalculation	Fejlberegning
69	Misnumbering	Fejlnummerering
70	Mise-en-page	Ombrydning, Layout, *Mise en page*
71	Misprint	Trykfejl, Fejltryk
72	Mock-up	Prøvebog
73	Mould	Støbeform
74	Overprinting	Overtryk
75	Pagination	Paginering, Pagination
76	Paper crease	Papirfold
77	Paratext	Paratekst
78	Paste slip	Overklæbning
79	Pin/point holes	Punkturhuller
80	Print run	Oplag, Antal trykte eksemplarer
81	Printer's copy	Trykmanuskript, Trykforlæg
82	Printer's manual	Håndbog i bogtrykkerkunsten
83	Proofreader's marks	Korrekturtegn
84	Proofs; Proofreading	Korrektur; Korrekturlæsning
85	Pull	Trykke
86	Quire	Bog; Læg
87	Quoin	Kile, Sluttekile
88	Raised furniture	Spis, Spies
89	Raised type	[Hævet type]
90	Recension	Recension
91	Register	Register
92	Reglet	Reglet
93	Reissue	Optryk (uforandret)
94	Reset	Sætte på ny, Omsætte

95	River	Flod
96	Running title	Kolumnetitel, Klummetitel
97	*Saut du même au même*	*Saut du même au même*, Overspringelse, Begravelse
98	Set-off	Afsmitning
99	Setting rule	Sættelinje, Udhævespån
100	Sheet	Ark
101	Shoulder	Skulder
102	Show-through	Gennemtryk
103	Signature	Arksignatur, Arktæller
104	*Signe de renvoi*	Henvisningstegn
105	Singleton	Enkeltblad
106	Skeleton forme	Skabelonform
107	Slipped type	Udfalden type
108	Smudged type	Udtværet type
109	Smudges/thumbing	Sværteaftryk/fingeraftryk
110	Sort	Type, Typelegeme
111	Spacing Material	Spatierings- og udslutningsmateriale
112	Standing type	Stående sats
113	State	Stat
114	Stop-press correction	Rettelse under trykningen
115	Stub	Fals
116	Transmission errors	Transmissionsfejl
117	Tympan	Dækkel, Tympan
118	Type	Type
119	Type case	Skriftkasse
120	Typeface	Skriftsnit
121	Typo	Trykfejl
122	Typographical lacuna	Typografisk lakune
123	Variant	Variant
124	Vatman	Former
125	Visorium/Visorum	Tenakel
126	Water drop	Vanddryp
127	Watermark	Vandmærke
128	Woodblock printing	Trætryk, Træsnit, Xylografi

Danish translation by: Anders Toftgaard (Royal Danish Library, Copenhagen); Jens Jørgen Hansen (Holsted).

DUTCH

	English	Dutch
1	Allography	Allografie
2	Apologies	[Verantwoording]
3	Archetype	Archetype
4	Bearer type	Drager
5	Beater	Opgever
6	Bibliography	Bibliografie (list of titles); Boekwetenschap (study of the book)
7	Blind impression	Blinddruk
8	Cancel	Cancel
9	*Castigationes*	*Castigationes*
10	Casting off copy	Voorberekening
11	Catchword	Custode, Bladwachter
12	Chase	Insluitraam, Raam
13	Collation	Collatie
14	Colophon	Colofon
15	Composing stick	Zethaak
16	Composition	Zetsel
17	Compositor	Zetter
18	Conjugate leaves	Conjuncte bladen
19	Copy census	Census van exemplaren
20	Copy-specific analysis	Exemplaargebonden analyse
21	Copy-text	Basistekst
22	Correction	Correctie
23	Coucher	Koetser
24	Damping	Natten
25	Distribution (of type)	Distributie
26	Drag lines	[Smet]
27	Drying/hanging	Drogen/ophangen
28	Duplicate setting	Zetten in duplicaat
29	Edition	Editie, Druk
30	Emendation	Emendatie
31	Erasure	Rasuur, Ratuur
32	Errata	Errata
33	Exemplar	Kopij (printed books), Legger (manuscripts)
34	Fallen type	Uitgevallen letter
35	Foliation	Foliëring
36	Font/Fount	Font
37	Format	Formaat
38	Forme	Vorm
39	Foul case	Vuile kast
40	Frisket	Verschet, Frisket
41	Frisket bite	Afbijtsel
42	Furniture	Formaatgoed
43	Galley	Galei
44	Gathering	Katern
45	Hand stamping	Stempeling met de hand

46	Haplography	Haplografie
47	Headline	Kopregel, Hoofdregel
48	Hypercorrection	Hypercorrectie
49	Ideal copy	Ideal copy
50	Imposition	Formaatmaken, Inslag
51	Impression	Oplage
52	Incunabula	Incunabelen, Wiegendrukken
53	Ink	Inkt
54	Ink bleed	Wegslaan van de inkt
55	Inked hair	Ingeïnkte haar
56	*Integrans*	[Bijdrukken]
57	Inverted type	Omgekeerde letter
58	Issue	Uitgave
59	Justification	Uitvulling, uitvullen
60	Kern	Overhang
61	Kludge	Noodoplossing
62	Lay of the case	Indeling van de letterkast
63	Leaf	Blad
64	Manuscript correction	Correctie in handschrift
65	Marginalia	Marginalia, randnoten
66	Master printer	Drukkerspatroon, Meesterdrukker
67	Misalignment	Verkeerde uitlijning
68	Miscalculation	Verkeerde voorberekening
69	Misnumbering	Fout in paginering
70	Mise-en-page	Opmaak, Layout
71	Misprint	Misdruk
72	Mock-up	Model, Ontwerp
73	Mould	Gietvorm (type); Schepvorm (paper)
74	Overprinting	Overdruk
75	Pagination	Paginering
76	Paper crease	Vouw in het papier
77	Paratext	Paratekst
78	Paste slip	[Overplakking]
79	Pin/point holes	Punctuurgaatjes
80	Print run	Oplage
81	Printer's copy	Drukkerskopij
82	Printer's manual	Drukkershandboek
83	Proofreader's marks	Correctietekens
84	Proofs; Proofreading	Proeven/ Drukproeven; Proeflezen
85	Pull	Teug
86	Quire	Boek
87	Quoin	Kooi
88	Raised furniture	Gerezen wit
89	Raised type	Gerezen letter
90	Recension	Recensio
91	Register	Registrum, Register; Registeren
92	Reglet	Reglet
93	Reissue	Titeluitgave
94	Reset	Herzetten

APPENDIX B: GLOSSARY TRANSLATION TABLES   DUTCH   521

95	River	Rivier
96	Running title	Sprekende hoofdregel
97	*Saut du même au même*	*Saut du même au même*
98	Set-off	Overzetten
99	Setting rule	Zetlijn
100	Sheet	Vel
101	Shoulder	Schouder
102	Show-through	Doorschijnen
103	Signature	Katernsignatuur, Signatuur
104	*Signe de renvoi*	Verwijzingsteken
105	Singleton	Los blad
106	Skeleton forme	Skeleton
107	Slipped type	Losgeraakte letter
108	Smudged type	Smet
109	Smudges/thumbing	Smet/smet
110	Sort	Letterstaafje
111	Spacing Material	Spaties
112	Standing type	Staand zetsel
113	State	Staat
114	Stop-press correction	Perscorrectie, Correctie op de pers
115	Stub	Oortje, Kim, Onglet
116	Transmission errors	Transmissiefouten
117	Tympan	Timpaan
118	Type	Drukletter
119	Type case	Letterkast
120	Typeface	Lettertype
121	Typo	Zetfout
122	Typographical lacuna	Tekstverlies
123	Variant	Variant
124	Vatman	Schepper
125	Visorium/Visorum	Visorium, Divisorium
126	Water drop	[Water drop]
127	Watermark	Watermerk
128	Woodblock printing	Blokdruk

Dutch translation by: Marieke van Delft (National Library of the Netherlands, The Hague); Frans Janssen (University of Amsterdam).

FRENCH

	English	French
1	Allography	Allographie
2	Apologies	[Apologies]
3	Archetype	Archétype
4	Bearer type	Lingot
5	Beater	Encreur
6	Bibliography	Bibliographie
7	Blind impression	Impression aveugle
8	Cancel	Carton
9	*Castigationes*	Leçons
10	Casting off copy	Calibrage de la copie
11	Catchword	Réclame
12	Chase	Châssis
13	Collation	Collation
14	Colophon	Colophon
15	Composing stick	Composteur
16	Composition	Composition
17	Compositor	Compositeur
18	Conjugate leaves	Feuillets conjoints
19	Copy census	Relevé d'exemplaires
20	Copy-specific analysis	Analyse des particularités d'exemplaires
21	Copy-text	Texte-source
22	Correction	Correction
23	Coucher	Coucheur
24	Damping	Tremperie
25	Distribution (of type)	Distribution
26	Drag lines	Maculatures
27	Drying/hanging	Sèchage/suspension
28	Duplicate setting	Composition double
29	Edition	Édition
30	Emendation	Correction
31	Erasure	Grattage
32	Errata	Errata
33	Exemplar	Exemplar
34	Fallen type	Caractère couché, Chien
35	Foliation	Foliotation
36	Font/Fount	Fonte
37	Format	Format
38	Forme	Forme
39	Foul case	Cassetin empoisonné
40	Frisket	Frisquette
41	Frisket bite	Morsure de frisquette
42	Furniture	Garnitures
43	Galley	Galée
44	Gathering	Cahier
45	Hand stamping	Estampage à la main

46	Haplography	Haplographie
47	Headline	Titre courant
48	Hypercorrection	Hypercorrection
49	Ideal copy	Exemplaire théorique
50	Imposition	Imposition
51	Impression	Impression
52	Incunabula	Incunables
53	Ink	Encre
54	Ink bleed	Auréole
55	Inked hair	Trace de cheveu
56	*Integrans*	*Integrans*
57	Inverted type	Caractère inversé
58	Issue	Émission
59	Justification	Justification
60	Kern	Crénage
61	Kludge	[Kludge]
62	Lay of the case	Disposition de la casse
63	Leaf	Feuillet
64	Manuscript correction	Correction manuscrite
65	Marginalia	Annotations marginales
66	Master printer	Maître imprimeur
67	Misalignment	Justification imparfaite
68	Miscalculation	Erreur de distribution
69	Misnumbering	Erreur de numérotation
70	Mise-en-page	Mise en page
71	Misprint	Erreur d'impression
72	Mock-up	Maquette
73	Mould	Moule
74	Overprinting	Surimpression
75	Pagination	Pagination
76	Paper crease	Larron
77	Paratext	Paratexte
78	Paste slip	Papillon
79	Pin/point holes	Pointures
80	Print run	Tirage
81	Printer's copy	Modèle d'impression, Copie, Exemplar
82	Printer's manual	Manuel typographique
83	Proofreader's marks	Signe de correction
84	Proofs; Proofreading	Épreuves; Relecture des épreuves
85	Pull	Tirage
86	Quire	Main
87	Quoin	Coin
88	Raised furniture	Garniture en relief
89	Raised type	Caractère en relief
90	Recension	Recension
91	Register	Registre
92	Reglet	Réglette
93	Reissue	Nouvelle émission

94	Reset	Recomposition
95	River	Lézarde, Cheminée
96	Running title	Titre courant
97	*Saut du même au même*	Saut du même au même
98	Set-off	Décharge
99	Setting rule	Réglette de longueur
100	Sheet	Feuille
101	Shoulder	Épaule
102	Show-through	Transparence
103	Signature	Signature
104	*Signe de renvoi*	Signe de renvoi
105	Singleton	Singulion
106	Skeleton forme	Forme désossée
107	Slipped type	Caractère couché, Bourdon
108	Smudged type	Caractères maculés
109	Smudges/thumbing	Tâches/traces
110	Sort	Sorte
111	Spacing Material	Espace (une)
112	Standing type	Caractères mis de côté (en vue d'une réimpression)
113	State	État
114	Stop-press correction	Correction en cours de tirage
115	Stub	Onglet
116	Transmission errors	Erreur à la transmission du texte
117	Tympan	Tympan
118	Type	Caractère d'imprimerie
119	Type case	Casse
120	Typeface	Caractère, Police
121	Typo	Coquille
122	Typographical lacuna	Lézarde, Moine
123	Variant	Variante
124	Vatman	Ouvreur
125	Visorium/Visorum	Visorion
126	Water drop	Goutte d'eau
127	Watermark	Filigrane
128	Woodblock printing	Impression/Gravure sur bois

French translation by: Florine Levecque-Stankiewicz, Yann Sordet (Mazarine Library, Paris); Alexandre Vanautgaerden (Warwick University); Renaud Adam (University of Liège).

GERMAN

	English	German
1	Allography	Allographie
2	Apologies	Apologie
3	Archetype	Archetyp
4	Bearer type	Stützsatz
5	Beater	Ballenmeister
6	Bibliography	Bibliographie
7	Blind impression	Blinddruck
8	Cancel	Karton, Austauschblatt
9	*Castigationes*	*Castigationes,* Lesarten
10	Casting off copy	Abschätzung des Satzumfangs
11	Catchword	Kustode
12	Chase	Schließrahmen
13	Collation	Kollationierung
14	Colophon	Kolophon
15	Composing stick	Winkelhaken
16	Composition	Setzen
17	Compositor	Setzer
18	Conjugate leaves	Doppelblatt
19	Copy census	Census
20	Copy-specific analysis	Exemplarspezifische Beschreibung
21	Copy-text	Textvorlage; Leittext
22	Correction	Korrektur
23	Coucher	Gautscher
24	Damping	Feuchten
25	Distribution (of type)	Ablegen
26	Drag lines	Schmierstreifen
27	Drying/hanging	Trocknen/Aufhängen der Druckbögen
28	Duplicate setting	Doppelsatz
29	Edition	Auflage
30	Emendation	Emendation (Textkritik)
31	Erasure	Rasur
32	Errata	Errata
33	Exemplar	Vorlage, Druckvorlage
34	Fallen type	Aus dem Satz gefallene Type
35	Foliation	Foliierung, Blattzählung
36	Font/Fount	Schriftart
37	Format	Format
38	Forme	Druckform
39	Foul case	Zwiebelfisch
40	Frisket	Frisquette, Rähmchen (Druckerpresse)
41	Frisket bite	Druckfehler durch verrutschtes Rähmchen
42	Furniture	Schließzeug
43	Galley	Setzschiff
44	Gathering	Lage
45	Hand stamping	Stempeln

46	Haplography	Haplografie
47	Headline	Kolumnentitel
48	Hypercorrection	Hyperkorrektur
49	Ideal copy	Ideales Exemplar
50	Imposition	Ausschießen
51	Impression	Auflage
52	Incunabula	Inkunabel, Wiegendruck
53	Ink	Tinte, Druckfarbe
54	Ink bleed	Durchschlagen der Farbe
55	Inked hair	Mitgedrucktes Haar
56	*Integrans*	*Integrans*
57	Inverted type	Auf den Kopf gestellte Letter
58	Issue	Ausgabe
59	Justification	Ausschließen
60	Kern	Unterschneidung (Schrift)
61	Kludge	[Kludge]
62	Lay of the case	Setzkastenschema, Setzkastenaufteilung
63	Leaf	Blatt
64	Manuscript correction	Handschriftliche Korrektur
65	Marginalia	Marginalien
66	Master printer	Buchdrucker(-herr)
67	Misalignment	Schlechtes Ausrichten
68	Miscalculation	Fehlerhaftes Ausschießen; Fehlerhafte Satzberechnung
69	Misnumbering	Fehlzählung
70	Mise-en-page	*Mise en page,* Layout
71	Misprint	Druckfehler
72	Mock-up	Rohlayout
73	Mould	Gußform, Handgießinstrument
74	Overprinting	Überdrucken
75	Pagination	Paginierung / Seitenzählung
76	Paper crease	Papierfalte, Knick
77	Paratext	Paratext
78	Paste slip	Eingeklebter Korrekturstreifen
79	Pin/point holes	Punkturlöcher
80	Print run	Auflagenhöhe
81	Printer's copy	Druckvorlage
82	Printer's manual	Druckerhandbuch
83	Proofreader's marks	Korrekturzeichen
84	Proofs; Proofreading	Druckfahnen, Korrekturfahnen; Korrekturlesen
85	Pull	Bengelanziehen (Druckvorgang); Abzug
86	Quire	Buch (Papiermengenmaß); Lage
87	Quoin	Keil
88	Raised furniture	Hochstehendes Schließzeug
89	Raised type	Hochstehende Letter
90	Recension	*Recensio* (Textkritik)
91	Register	Registrum; Register
92	Reglet	Reglette
93	Reissue	Neuauflage

94	Reset	Neusatz
95	River	Fluss
96	Running title	Lebender Kolumnentitel
97	*Saut du même au même*	Augensprung
98	Set-off	Abklatsch
99	Setting rule	Setzlinie
100	Sheet	Bogen
101	Shoulder	Schulterfläche, Achselfläche
102	Show-through	Durchscheinender Druck
103	Signature	Signatur
104	*Signe de renvoi*	*Signe de renvoi,* Verweisungszeichen
105	Singleton	Einzelblatt
106	Skeleton forme	[Skeleton forme]
107	Slipped type	Herausgezogene Typen
108	Smudged type	Verschmierte Typen
109	Smudges/thumbing	Verschmutzter Bogen
110	Sort	Letter
111	Spacing Material	Ausschussmaterial
112	Standing type	Stehender Satz
113	State	Zustand
114	Stop-press correction	Presskorrektur
115	Stub	Blattrest, Stummelfalz
116	Transmission errors	Überlieferungsfehler
117	Tympan	Tympanon, Deckel (Druckerpresse)
118	Type	Type
119	Type case	Setzkasten
120	Typeface	Schriftart
121	Typo	Druckfehler
122	Typographical lacuna	Lacuna, Lakune
123	Variant	Variante
124	Vatman	Büttknecht
125	Visorium/Visorum	Manuskripthalter, Tenakel und Divisorium
126	Water drop	Wassertropfen im Papier, Papiermacherträne
127	Watermark	Wasserzeichen
128	Woodblock printing	Blockdruck

German translation by: Oliver Duntze, Falk Eisermann (State Library, Berlin).

GREEK

	English	Greek
1	Allography	Αλλογραφία
2	Apologies	[Apologies]
3	Archetype	Πρωτόγραφο, Αρχέτυπο χειρόγραφο
4	Bearer type	Τυπογέμισμα
5	Beater	Μελανωτής
6	Bibliography	Βιβλιολογία-βιβλιογραφία
7	Blind impression	Αποτύπωμα τυπογεμίσματος
8	Cancel	Διόρθωση με αφαίρεση και αντικατάσταση φύλλων
9	*Castigationes*	Εναλλακτικές αναγνώσεις
10	Casting off copy	Υπολογισμός έκτασης βιβλίου
11	Catchword	Παραπεμπτική λέξη, Συνδετική λέξη
12	Chase	Πλαίσιο τυπογραφικής φόρμας
13	Collation	Αντιβολή
14	Colophon	Κολοφώνας
15	Composing stick	Συνθετήριο, Στοιχειάγρα
16	Composition	Στοιχειοθεσία, Σύνθεση
17	Compositor	Στοιχειοθέτης, Τυποθέτης
18	Conjugate leaves	Τευχοδίφυλλο
19	Copy census	Απογραφή αντιτύπων
20	Copy-specific analysis	Μελέτη ιδιαιτερότητας αντιτύπων
21	Copy-text	Πρότυπο κείμενο για στοιχειοθεσία
22	Correction	Διόρθωση
23	Coucher	Στοιβαχτής χαρτοποιείου
24	Damping	Διαβροχή, Ύγρανση
25	Distribution (of type)	Διάλυση
26	Drag lines	Τυπομουτζούρες
27	Drying/hanging	Στέγνωμα/κρέμασμα εκτυπωμένου φύλλου
28	Duplicate setting	Πιστή επαναστοιχειοθέτηση
29	Edition	Έκδοση
30	Emendation	Διόρθωση, Emendatio
31	Erasure	Σβήσιμο
32	Errata	Παροράματα, Errata
33	Exemplar	Αντίβολο
34	Fallen type	Πλαγιασμένο στοιχείο
35	Foliation	Φυλλαρίθμηση
36	Font/Fount	Στοιχειοσειρά
37	Format	Σχήμα
38	Forme	Τυπογραφική φόρμα
39	Foul case	Παρατοποθέτηση στη στοιχειοθήκη
40	Frisket	Μάσκα προστασίας περιθωρίων
41	Frisket bite	Μασκοφάγωμα
42	Furniture	Βοηθητικά εξαρτήματα τυπογραφικής φόρμας
43	Galley	Σελιδοθέτης
44	Gathering	Τεύχος
45	Hand stamping	Σφραγιδοτύπωμα

APPENDIX B: GLOSSARY TRANSLATION TABLES   GREEK   529

46	Haplography	Απλογραφία
47	Headline	Κεφαλίδα
48	Hypercorrection	Περιττή διόρθωση
49	Ideal copy	Ιδεατό αντίτυπο
50	Imposition	Διάταξη σελίδων
51	Impression	Εκτύπωση
52	Incunabula	Αρχέτυπα
53	Ink	Μελάνι
54	Ink bleed	Μελανολεκές
55	Inked hair	Τριχοτύπωμα
56	*Integrans*	Φύλλα συμπληρωματικών εκτυπώσεων
57	Inverted type	Ανεστραμμένο στοιχείο
58	Issue	Τράβηγμα
59	Justification	Αμφίπλευρη στοίχιση, Πλήρης στοίχιση
60	Kern	Διαστοιχείωση
61	Kludge	[Kludge]
62	Lay of the case	Διάταξη στοιχειοθήκης
63	Leaf	Φύλλο
64	Manuscript correction	Χειρόγραφη διόρθωση
65	Marginalia	Σημειώσεις στο περιθώριο
66	Master printer	Αρχιτυπογράφος
67	Misalignment	Κακή ευθυγράμμιση
68	Miscalculation	Λάθος υπολογισμός σελίδων
69	Misnumbering	Λάθος αρίθμησης
70	Mise-en-page	Σελιδοποίηση
71	Misprint	Λάθος εκτύπωσης
72	Mock-up	Προσχέδιο
73	Mould	Καλούπι (type mould, paper mould); Τελάρο (paper mould)
74	Overprinting	Πανωτύπωμα
75	Pagination	Σελιδαρίθμηση
76	Paper crease	Κακοτύπωμα από τσάκιση χαρτιού
77	Paratext	Παρακείμενα, Κείμενα προκαταρκτικών σελίδων
78	Paste slip	Τυποεπίθεμα, Επικολλημένη διόρθωση
79	Pin/point holes	Οπές καρφίδων σύμπτωσης
80	Print run	Αριθμός αντιτύπων, Τιράζ
81	Printer's copy	"Χειρόγραφο" προς στοιχειοθεσία
82	Printer's manual	Τυπογραφικό εγχειρίδιο
83	Proofreader's marks	Σύμβολα διόρθωσης
84	Proofs; Proofreading	Δοκίμια. Διόρθωση
85	Pull	Τράβηγμα μοχλού πιεστηρίου
86	Quire	Δεσμίδα φύλλων χαρτιού
87	Quoin	Σφήνα, Σφιγκτήρας
88	Raised furniture	Αποτύπωμα ανυψωμένου μετάλλου
89	Raised type	Ανυψωμένο στοιχείο
90	Recension	Κατάρτιση στέμματος
91	Register	Κατάλογος δεικτών ακολουθίας των τυπογραφικών φύλλων (list of signatures)
92	Reglet	Ξύλινο παρέμβλημα διαστίχωσης
93	Reissue	Τεχνητός εκσυγχρονισμός, Ψευδοεπανέκδοση
94	Reset	Επαναστοιχειοθεσία

95	River	Λευκό ποτάμι
96	Running title	Τρέχων τίτλος
97	*Saut du même au même*	Λιπογραφία
98	Set-off	Οπισθοείδωλο
99	Setting rule	Οδηγός πλάτους στήλης
100	Sheet	Φύλλο χαρτιού
101	Shoulder	Υποφθάλμιο στοιχείου
102	Show-through	Διαπερασμένοι χαρακτήρες
103	Signature	Δείκτης ακολουθίας τυπογραφικών φύλλων
104	*Signe de renvoi*	Σύμβολο προσθήκης, Σύμβολο διόρθωσης
105	Singleton	Πρόσθετο φύλλο
106	Skeleton forme	Φόρμα με τα επαναλαμβανόμενα στοιχεία των σελίδων
107	Slipped type	Παραπεσμένο στοιχείο
108	Smudged type	Μουτζουρωμένο στοιχείο
109	Smudges/thumbing	Μουτζούρα
110	Sort	Τυπογραφικό στοιχείο
111	Spacing Material	Βοηθητικά εξαρτήματα τυπογραφικής φόρμας
112	Standing type	Στοιχειοθετημένο κείμενο σε αναμονή
113	State	Διακριτή ομάδα αντιτύπων
114	Stop-press correction	Διόρθωση επί του πιεστηρίου
115	Stub	Προέκταση/γλωσσίδα στερέωσης φύλλου
116	Transmission errors	Λάθη μεταφοράς κειμένου
117	Tympan	Τύμπανο
118	Type	Τυπογραφικά στοιχεία
119	Type case	Στοιχειοθήκη, Τυπογραφική κάσα
120	Typeface	Σειρά τυπογραφικών στοιχείων
121	Typo	Τυπογραφικό λάθος
122	Typographical lacuna	Τυπογραφικό χάσμα
123	Variant	Παραλλαγή
124	Vatman	Χαρτοποιός
125	Visorium/Visorum	Αναλόγιο στοιχειοθεσίας
126	Water drop	Υδατοκηλίδα
127	Watermark	Υδατόσημο, Υδατογράφημα
128	Woodblock printing	Ξυλοτυπία

Greek translation by: Vera Andriopoulou, Kleopatra Kyrtata, Aggeliki Papadopoulou (Aikaterini Laskaridis Foundation, Piraeus); Yannis Kokkonas (Ionian University, Corfu); Georgios Matthiopoulos (University of West Attica, Athens).

APPENDIX B: GLOSSARY TRANSLATION TABLES   HEBREW

HEBREW

	English	Hebrew
1	Allography	אלוגרפיה
2	Apologies	[?]התנצלויות
3	Archetype	אב טיפוס
4	Bearer type	משטח תמיכה
5	Beater	מושח דיו
6	Bibliography	ביבליוגרפיה
7	Blind impression	הטבעה עיוורת
8	Cancel	ביטול
9	*Castigationes*	תיקונים
10	Casting off copy	טקסט סֵדֶר סופי
11	Catchword	מֵימְרָה
12	Chase	מִסְגֶרֶת
13	Collation	איסוף
14	Colophon	קוֹלוֹפוֹן
15	Composing stick	מְשׂוּרָה
16	Composition	סְדוּר דְפוּס
17	Compositor	סַדָר
18	Conjugate leaves	עלים מצומדים
19	Copy census	סֵקֶר עותקים
20	Copy-specific analysis	ניתוח מדויק של העותקים
21	Copy-text	טקסט סֵדֶר
22	Correction	תיקון
23	Coucher	משטח העיסה
24	Damping	לחלוח
25	Distribution (of type)	מיון
26	Drag lines	גרירת שורות
27	Drying/hanging	יבּוּשׁ
28	Duplicate setting	סְדוּר מוכפל
29	Edition	מַהֲדוּרָה
30	Emendation	תיקון
31	Erasure	מְחִיקָה
32	Errata	רשימת טעויות
33	Exemplar	עותק
34	Fallen type	אות שנשמטה
35	Foliation	עמוּד
36	Font/Fount	גוֹפָן
37	Format	פורמט
38	Forme	תבנית
39	Foul case	אות שגויה
40	Frisket	מִסְגְרוֹנִית
41	Frisket bite	שגיאת דפוס עקב החלקת מסגרונית
42	Furniture	כְּפִיסִים
43	Galley	מגש
44	Gathering	קונטרס
45	Hand stamping	הדפסה ביד
46	Haplography	הפלוגרפיה

HEBREW — PRINTING AND MISPRINTING

47	Headline	כותרת
48	Hypercorrection	תיקון יתר
49	Ideal copy	עותק אידיאלי
50	Imposition	הַטָלָה
51	Impression	דְפוּס
52	Incunabula	דפוס ערש ;אִינְקוּנָבּוּלָה
53	Ink	דְיוֹ
54	Ink bleed	בליד ;דימום דיו
55	Inked hair	-
56	*Integrans*	[*Integrans*]
57	Inverted type	כתב הפוך
58	Issue	מַהֲדוּרָה
59	Justification	יישור
60	Kern	מרווח בין שני תווים צמודים
61	Kludge	[Kludge]
62	Lay of the case	תיבת סדר
63	Leaf	עַמוּד
64	Manuscript correction	תיקון כתב יד
65	Marginalia	הֶעָרַת שׁוּלַיִם
66	Master printer	סַדָר רָאשִׁי
67	Misalignment	יציאה מחוץ לשורה
68	Miscalculation	חישוב מוטעה
69	Misnumbering	טעות במספור
70	Mise-en-page	עַמוּד
71	Misprint	טָעוּת דְפוּס
72	Mock-up	דֶגֶם
73	Mould	תַבְנִית
74	Overprinting	הדפסת יתר
75	Pagination	מִסְפּוּר
76	Paper crease	קפל נייר
77	Paratext	פאראטקסט
78	Paste slip	רצועת נייר מודבקת
79	Pin/point holes	חורי נקודה
80	Print run	מספר עותקים
81	Printer's copy	עותק המדפיס
82	Printer's manual	מדריך למדפיס
83	Proofreader's marks	הערות המגיה
84	Proofs; Proofreading	הגהות ;הגהה
85	Pull	דפוס
86	Quire	קונטרס
87	Quoin	טריז עץ/עוֹפֶרֶת
88	Raised furniture	תבליט גבוה
89	Raised type	אות מוגבהת
90	Recension	הערכה ואיסוף טקסטואלי
91	Register	רגיסטרציה
92	Reglet	מפריד
93	Reissue	הנפקה מחודשת
94	Reset	אתחול
95	River	שביל

APPENDIX B: GLOSSARY TRANSLATION TABLES HEBREW 533

96	Running title	כותר רץ
97	*Saut du même au même*	השמטה מחמת הדומות
98	Set-off	קזוז
99	Setting rule	קַו הַסְּדָר
100	Sheet	גִלְיוֹן
101	Shoulder	כָּתֵף שֶׁל הָאוֹת
102	Show-through	סימנים מודפסים הנראים מהצד הלא נכון של הדף, הנגרמים מחדירת דיו או לחץ מוגזם במהלך ההדפסה, או אטימות נייר לא מספקת
103	Signature	חתימת קיפול של גיליון דפוס
104	*Signe de renvoi*	סימן הפניה
105	Singleton	דַף בּוֹדֵד
106	Skeleton forme	שבלונה
107	Slipped type	-
108	Smudged type	אות מרוחה
109	Smudges/thumbing	כְּתָמִים
110	Sort	גופן
111	Spacing Material	-
112	Standing type	-
113	State	וַאריאנט
114	Stop-press correction	עצירת הדפסה לתיקונים
115	Stub	גודל ספח
116	Transmission errors	שגיאת שידור
117	Tympan	טימפן
118	Type	אוֹת
119	Type case	מְגֵרַת אוֹתִיוֹת
120	Typeface	גופן
121	Typo	שְׁגִיאַת דְפוּס
122	Typographical lacuna	לקונה טיפוגרפית
123	Variant	וַרְיָאנט
124	Vatman	אוסף העיסה
125	Visorium/Visorum	-
126	Water drop	-
127	Watermark	סִימָן מַיִם
128	Woodblock printing	דפוס גלופת עץ

Hebrew translation by: Alexander Gordin (National Library of Israel, Jerusalem); Dorit Raines (Università Ca' Foscari, Venice). David Malkiel (Bar-Ilan University, Tel Aviv); Ishai Mishory (Columbia University, New York)

HUNGARIAN

	English	Hungarian
1	Allography	Allográfia, Átírás
2	Apologies	Apológia, Védőbeszéd
3	Archetype	Archetípus, Őstípus
4	Bearer type	Vakanyag, Töltelékanyag
5	Beater	Festékező legény, Labdamester
6	Bibliography	Bibliográfia, Irodalomjegyzék
7	Blind impression	Vaknyomás
8	Cancel	Rendellenesség az ívfüzetben
9	*Castigationes*	Hibajavítás
10	Casting off copy	Szedő példány
11	Catchword	Őrszó
12	Chase	Zárókeret
13	Collation	Kolláció, Bibliográfiai leírás, Kollációs lista
14	Colophon	Kolofón
15	Composing stick	Szedővas, Vinkel, Sorzó
16	Composition	Szedés
17	Compositor	Szedő
18	Conjugate leaves	Oldalpár
19	Copy census	Teljes példány-nyilvántartás
20	Copy-specific analysis	Példányspecifikus vizsgálat
21	Copy-text	Nyomdai példány
22	Correction	Korrekció
23	Coucher	Rakosólegény
24	Damping	Nyirkosítás
25	Distribution (of type)	Visszaosztás
26	Drag lines	Festéknyomok
27	Drying/hanging	Szárítás/felakasztás
28	Duplicate setting	Ikernyomat
29	Edition	Kiadás
30	Emendation	Emendálás, Javítás
31	Erasure	Törlés
32	Errata	Errata, Hibajegyzék
33	Exemplar	Mintapéldány
34	Fallen type	Szedésből kiesett betű
35	Foliation	Levélszámozás
36	Font/Fount	Betűgarnitúra
37	Format	Formátum
38	Forme	Szedés
39	Foul case	Rosszul visszaosztott betűk, Fisch
40	Frisket	Ívtartó keret
41	Frisket bite	Ívtartó keret elmozdulása
42	Furniture	Fa stég, Űrkitöltő
43	Galley	Szedőhajó, Szedőlemez
44	Gathering	Ívfüzet
45	Hand stamping	Dörzsnyomás, Dörzsnyomat

APPENDIX B: GLOSSARY TRANSLATION TABLES   HUNGARIAN   535

46	Haplography	Haplográfia, Betű/szókihagyás
47	Headline	Élőfej
48	Hypercorrection	Hiperkorrekció, Túljavítás
49	Ideal copy	Ideális példány
50	Imposition	Kilövés
51	Impression	Lenyomat
52	Incunabula	Ősnyomtatványok
53	Ink	Tinta (ink); Nyomdafesték (printing ink)
54	Ink bleed	Tintafolt, Festékfolt
55	Inked hair	Szedésbe került szőrszál
56	*Integrans*	Újraszedés
57	Inverted type	Fejjel lefelé álló betű
58	Issue	Lenyomat
59	Justification	Sorkizárás
60	Kern	A nyomdai betű azon része, amely túlnyúlik a betű testén
61	Kludge	Betűhelyettesítés (kényszerűségből)
62	Lay of the case	Alfabétumszétválasztás (a szedőszekrényben)
63	Leaf	Levél
64	Manuscript correction	Kéziratjavítás
65	Marginalia	Marginália, Széljegyzet
66	Master printer	Mesternyomdász
67	Misalignment	Téves kilövés
68	Miscalculation	Kilövési hiba
69	Misnumbering	Félreszámozás
70	Mise-en-page	Szedéstükör beosztása, Drucksatz
71	Misprint	Sajtóhiba
72	Mock-up	Sablon (szedés beosztása)
73	Mould	Öntőforma
74	Overprinting	Felülnyomás
75	Pagination	Lapszámozás
76	Paper crease	Papírgyűrődés
77	Paratext	Segédszöveg
78	Paste slip	Átragasztás
79	Pin/point holes	Punktúra
80	Print run	Példányszám
81	Printer's copy	Nyomdai példány
82	Printer's manual	Nyomdász kézikönyv
83	Proofreader's marks	Korrektúrajel
84	Proofs; Proofreading	Korrektúra; Korrektúrázás
85	Pull	Próbanyomat
86	Quire	Ív, Ívfüzet, Konc
87	Quoin	Ívfogó
88	Raised furniture	Űrkitöltő anyag kiemelkedik a szedésből
89	Raised type	Betű kiemelkedik a szedésből
90	Recension	Recenzió, Ismertetés
91	Register	Regiszter, Soregyen
92	Reglet	Fatérző, Regletta
93	Reissue	Újrakiadás

94	Reset	Újraszedés
95	River	utca
96	Running title	Élőfej
97	*Saut du même au même*	Hasonló szóra való átugrás
98	Set-off	Ofszet nyomás
99	Setting rule	Elválasztó vonalzó
100	Sheet	Ív, Levél
101	Shoulder	Abstand, azaz a betű vállfelülete
102	Show-through	Nyomás átüt
103	Signature	Füzetjel, Ívjelzés
104	*Signe de renvoi*	Korrektúrajel
105	Singleton	Egy kettéhajtott ív fele (csonka ív)
106	Skeleton forme	Szedés sablon
107	Slipped type	Elcsúszott betű
108	Smudged type	Elcsúszott nyomtatás
109	Smudges/thumbing	Elcsúszás, Elkenődés
110	Sort	Ólombetű
111	Spacing Material	Spácium
112	Standing type	Állva hagyott szedés
113	State	Variáns (példány)
114	Stop-press correction	Nyomás közbeni javítás
115	Stub	Csonk
116	Transmission errors	Átnyomási hibák
117	Tympan	Tempó, Nyomófedél
118	Type	Betűtípus
119	Type case	Casta, Azaz betűtartó szekrény
120	Typeface	Betűkép, Betűtípus
121	Typo	Betűhiba
122	Typographical lacuna	Tipográfiai hiány, Lakúna
123	Variant	Változat, Variáns
124	Vatman	Merítőlegény
125	Visorium/Visorum	Kétágú csippentyű
126	Water drop	Vízcsepp
127	Watermark	Vízjel
128	Woodblock printing	Táblanyomat

Hungarian translation by: Eszter Konrád (Eötvös Loránd University Library, Budapest); István Monok (Library and Information Centre of the Hungarian Academy of Sciences, Budapest); Judit V. Ecsedy, Zsuzsanna Bakonyi (National Széchényi Library, Budapest); Melinda Simon (University of Szeged).

ITALIAN

English	Italian
1	Allography	Allografia
2	Apologies	Note apologetiche
3	Archetype	Archetipo
4	Bearer type	Sostegni
5	Beater	Battitore
6	Bibliography	Bibliografia
7	Blind impression	Impressione cieca / in bianco
8	Cancel	*Cancellans*
9	*Castigationes*	*Castigationes*
10	Casting off copy	Calibrazione, Casting off dell'esemplare / modello di tipografia
11	Catchword	Richiamo, Parola guida
12	Chase	Cornice, Telaio
13	Collation	Collazione
14	Colophon	Colophon
15	Composing stick	Compositoio
16	Composition	Composizione
17	Compositor	Compositore
18	Conjugate leaves	Carte solidali (stampa); Bifolio (manoscritto)
19	Copy census	Censimento delle copie
20	Copy-specific analysis	Analisi dei dati di esemplare
21	Copy-text	Testo base
22	Correction	Correzione
23	Coucher	Ponitore
24	Damping	Bagnatura
25	Distribution (of type)	Redistribuzione
26	Drag lines	Sbavature
27	Drying/hanging	Asciugatura/stenditura
28	Duplicate setting	Composizione simultanea
29	Edition	Edizione
30	Emendation	Emendazione
31	Erasure	Cancellatura
32	Errata	Errata
33	Exemplar	Archetipo di (stampa); *Exemplar* (manoscritto)
34	Fallen type	Carattere caduto
35	Foliation	Foliazione (stampa); Cartulazione (manoscritto)
36	Font/Fount	Font
37	Format	Formato
38	Forme	Forma
39	Foul case	Errore di cassa
40	Frisket	Fraschetta
41	Frisket bite	Smangio della fraschetta
42	Furniture	Marginatura
43	Galley	Vantaggio
44	Gathering	Fascicolo (stampa)
45	Hand stamping	Stampigliatura

46	Haplography	Aplografia
47	Headline	Intestazione
48	Hypercorrection	Ipercorrettismo
49	Ideal copy	Copia ideale
50	Imposition	Imposizione
51	Impression	Impressione
52	Incunabula	Incunaboli
53	Ink	Inchiostro
54	Ink bleed	Trapasso dell'inchiostro
55	Inked hair	Capello inchiostrato
56	*Integrans*	*Integrans*
57	Inverted type	Carattere capovolto
58	Issue	Emissione
59	Justification	Giustificazione
60	Kern	Crenatura
61	Kludge	[Kludge]
62	Lay of the case	Disposizione della cassa
63	Leaf	Carta
64	Manuscript correction	Correzione manoscritta
65	Marginalia	Marginalia
66	Master printer	Mastro tipografo, Proto
67	Misalignment	Disallineamento
68	Miscalculation	Errore di calcolo
69	Misnumbering	Errore di numerazione
70	Mise-en-page	Impaginazione, Layout, *Mise-en-page*
71	Misprint	Errore di stampa
72	Mock-up	Menabò
73	Mould	Forma (tipografia), Telaio (carta), Modulo (carta)
74	Overprinting	Sovrastampa
75	Pagination	Paginazione
76	Paper crease	Grinza
77	Paratext	Paratesto
78	Paste slip	Cartiglio
79	Pin/point holes	Fori d'imposizione
80	Print run	Tiratura
81	Printer's copy	Esemplare / modello di tipografia
82	Printer's manual	Manuale tipografico
83	Proofreader's marks	Segni di correzione
84	Proofs; Proofreading	Bozze; Correzione delle bozze
85	Pull	Colpo di barra
86	Quire	Fascicolo (manoscritto)
87	Quoin	Cuneo, Morsetto
88	Raised furniture	Marginatura sporgente
89	Raised type	Carattere sporgente
90	Recension	*Recensio*
91	Register	Registro
92	Reglet	Bianco d'interlinea
93	Reissue	Riemissione

APPENDIX B: GLOSSARY TRANSLATION TABLES   ITALIAN   539

94	Reset	Nuova composizione
95	River	Canaletto
96	Running title	Titolo corrente
97	*Saut du même au même*	*Saut du même au même*, pesce, drone
98	Set-off	Controstampa
99	Setting rule	Righello
100	Sheet	Foglio
101	Shoulder	Spalletta
102	Show-through	Impressione in trasparenza
103	Signature	Segnatura
104	*Signe de renvoi*	*Signe de renvoi*
105	Singleton	Carta singola
106	Skeleton forme	Gabbia
107	Slipped type	Caratteri slittati
108	Smudged type	Impressione sbavata
109	Smudges/thumbing	Sbavature/spolliciature
110	Sort	Carattere
111	Spacing Material	Spazi
112	Standing type	Standing type
113	State	Stato
114	Stop-press correction	Correzione in corso di tiratura
115	Stub	Tallone
116	Transmission errors	Errore di tradizione
117	Tympan	Timpano
118	Type	Tipo
119	Type case	Cassa
120	Typeface	Famiglia tipografica, Typeface
121	Typo	Refuso
122	Typographical lacuna	Lacuna tipografica
123	Variant	Variante
124	Vatman	Lavorente
125	Visorium/Visorum	Visorium
126	Water drop	Lacrima del cartaio
127	Watermark	Filigrana
128	Woodblock printing	Stampa xilografica

Italian translation by: Paolo Sachet (University of Geneva); Geri Della Rocca de Candal (Milan); Neil Harris (University of Udine); Edoardo Barbieri (Catholic University, Milan).

JAPANESE

	English	Japanese
1	Allography	異表記 (letter variations); 異形活字 (typographical variations)
2	Apologies	弁明
3	Archetype	原型, アーキタイプ
4	Bearer type	込め物として空印の活字を使うこと
5	Beater	インクボール専門の印刷工
6	Bibliography	書誌学 (bibliography); 列挙書誌学 (enumerative bibliography); 分析書誌学 (analytical bibliography); 記述書誌学 (descriptive bibliography); 本文書誌学 (textual bibliography); 本文批評 (textual criticism); 歴史書誌学 (historical bibliography)
7	Blind impression	空印
8	Cancel	削除, 差し替え
9	*Castigationes*	異読
10	Casting off copy	組み頁に見積もる
11	Catchword	捕語, キャッチワード
12	Chase	チェース
13	Collation	校合; 丁調べ, 落丁調べ; 印刷中異同の一覧
14	Colophon	奥付, 刊記, コロフォン
15	Composing stick	植字ステッキ
16	Composition	植字
17	Compositor	植字工
18	Conjugate leaves	二枚一続きになった紙葉
19	Copy census	現存本の総体調査
20	Copy-specific analysis	個々の書物の特徴分析
21	Copy-text	印刷用自筆原稿; 底本
22	Correction	訂正, 修正
23	Coucher	クーチャー
24	Damping	印刷前に紙を湿らせること
25	Distribution (of type)	解版
26	Drag lines	線状のインクの跡
27	Drying/hanging	乾燥, 印刷後に紙を干して乾燥させること
28	Duplicate setting	活字を組み直して組版を複製すること; 増刷
29	Edition	版
30	Emendation	校訂
31	Erasure	削除
32	Errata	正誤表
33	Exemplar	印刷用原稿, イグゼンプラー (text from which a particular copy is made); 現存本, 部 (a particular copy of a book)
34	Fallen type	活字が倒れた跡
35	Foliation	丁付け
36	Font/Fount	フォント, 活字一式
37	Format	判型
38	Forme	組版, 版
39	Foul case	活字の戻し間違い
40	Frisket	フリスケット, 紙押さえ

APPENDIX B: GLOSSARY TRANSLATION TABLES　JAPANESE　541

41	Frisket bite	フリスケットのずれ又は正確に切られなかったために頁の一部が脱落すること
42	Furniture	込め物, フォルマート
43	Galley	ゲラ
44	Gathering	折り丁
45	Hand stamping	手による押印, スタンプ
46	Haplography	重字脱落
47	Headline	欄外標題
48	Hypercorrection	過剰修正
49	Ideal copy	理想本
50	Imposition	組付け, 面付け
51	Impression	刷り, 一度に印刷されたある版の全てのコピー (all copies of an edition); 印刷する (act or process of printing); 押印の質 (quality of printing)
52	Incunabula	揺籃期本, インキュナブラ
53	Ink	インク
54	Ink bleed	インクの滲み
55	Inked hair	インクのついた毛の跡
56	*Integrans*	印刷数が足りない本の一部分のみ, 活字を組み直して再び組版をすること
57	Inverted type	上下反転の文字
58	Issue	刷り, ある版に属するものとして印刷された全てのコピー (issue); 別版 (separate issue)
59	Justification	両端揃え, 行を追い込む又は言葉の間隔を空けて行を揃えること
60	Kern	カーン, 活字の飾りひげ (part of a metal type projecting beyond its body); 文字間の間隔を読み易いように調整すること (adjustment of space between characters for aesthetic reasons)
61	Kludge	応急処置, 特定の活字が足りない場合に他の活字を使うこと
62	Lay of the case	活字の配列
63	Leaf	紙葉
64	Manuscript correction	手書きの訂正
65	Marginalia	余白の書き込み; 傍注
66	Master printer	印刷工房の親方
67	Misalignment	印刷のずれ
68	Miscalculation	組み頁の見積りの計算違い
69	Misnumbering	番号の間違い
70	Mise-en-page	頁の割付, レイアウト, ミザンパージュ
71	Misprint	誤植
72	Mock-up	印刷レイアウトの指定図
73	Mould	鋳型 (typefounding); 簀 (papermaking)
74	Overprinting	印刷を重ねて訂正すること
75	Pagination	頁付け
76	Paper crease	紙のしわの上に印刷されること
77	Paratext	パラテクスト
78	Paste slip	貼り付けられた訂正票
79	Pin/point holes	見当針の穴
80	Print run	印刷部数

81	Printer's copy	印刷用原稿
82	Printer's manual	印刷者のための手引書
83	Proofreader's marks	校正記号
84	Proofs; Proofreading	校正刷り (proofs); 校正 (proofreading)
85	Pull	印刷機のバーを引く (action); 刷り (impression); 校正刷り (proof pull); 試し刷り (trial pull)
86	Quire	帖 (unit of paper quantity); 折り丁 (synonym for gathering)
87	Quoin	締め金, くさび, クォイン
88	Raised furniture	高めの込め物, 字面よりも高い込め物のために紙にインクの跡が残ることがある
89	Raised type	高めの活字, 字面よりも高い活字のためにその周りの活字が正しく印刷されないことがある
90	Recension	現存写本又は本文の関係を確立する過程, 校訂作業の一部
91	Register	折丁記号表 (list of the signatures); 見当 (positioning of printed text or images)
92	Reglet	木インテル
93	Reissue	再発行, 重版
94	Reset	活字の組み直し, 新組み
95	River	河川, 両端揃えで印刷すると言葉の間の余白部分が縦に流れるように見える現象
96	Running title	通し書名, 通し柱
97	*Saut du même au même*	似ている単語間での飛ばし読みによる脱語
98	Set-off	裏移り
99	Setting rule	植字定規, セッテン
100	Sheet	全紙
101	Shoulder	肩
102	Show-through	透き通し, ショースルー
103	Signature	折丁記号
104	*Signe de renvoi*	参照記号
105	Singleton	一枚紙葉
106	Skeleton forme	組版の骨組み
107	Slipped type	脱字
108	Smudged type	活字の歪み
109	Smudges/thumbing	インクの汚れや染み
110	Sort	一本の活字
111	Spacing material	スペーサー (スペース, クワタ)
112	Standing type	組置き版
113	State	異刷
114	Stop-press correction	印刷中に施された訂正
115	Stub	足, スタブ

116	Transmission errors	本文が伝播する際の誤り
117	Tympan	チンパン
118	Type	活字
119	Type case	活字箱
120	Typeface	活字書体
121	Typo	誤植
122	Typographical lacuna	脱字又は脱文
123	Variant	異版
124	Vatman	紙漉業者
125	Visorium/Visorum	ヴィゾルム, 印刷用原稿台
126	Water drop	紙の水滴の跡
127	Watermark	透かし
128	Woodblock printing	木版印刷

Japanese translation by: Takako Kato (De Montfort University, Leicester); Akihiko Watanabe (Otsuma Women's University, Tokyo).

POLISH

	English	Polish
1	Allography	Alograf
2	Apologies	Usprawiedliwienie
3	Archetype	Archetyp
4	Bearer type	Rodzaj justunku wypełniającego dużą powierzchnię
5	Beater	Nakładacz farby, nadawacz farby
6	Bibliography	Bibliografia
7	Blind impression	Ślepe odbicie
8	Cancel	Kasacja
9	*Castigationes*	Oczyszczanie, *Castigationes*
10	Casting off copy	Obliczanie znaków
11	Catchword	Kustosz
12	Chase	Rama
13	Collation	Kolacjonowanie, Kolacja, Zestawienie
14	Colophon	Kolofon
15	Composing stick	Wierszownik, Winkielak
16	Composition	Składanie
17	Compositor	Składacz, Zecer
18	Conjugate leaves	Podwójna karta w składce
19	Copy census	Cenzus, Wykaz egzemplarzy
20	Copy-specific analysis	Analiza cech indywidualnych egzemplarza
21	Copy-text	Podstawa wydania
22	Correction	Korekta
23	Coucher	Wykładacz
24	Damping	Zwilżanie
25	Distribution (of type)	Rozbieranie składu
26	Drag lines	Smugi
27	Drying/hanging	Suszenie, Wieszanie
28	Duplicate setting	Skład oboczny
29	Edition	Wydanie, Edycja
30	Emendation	Emendacja
31	Erasure	Razura
32	Errata	*Errata*, Corrigenda
33	Exemplar	*Źródło*, Exemplar
34	Fallen type	Ślad przewróconej czcionki
35	Foliation	Foliacja
36	Font/Fount	Garnitur
37	Format	Format
38	Forme	Forma drukowa
39	Foul case	Kaszta z pomieszanymi czcionkami
40	Frisket	Ramka maskująca
41	Frisket bite	Uszczerbek w druku z powodu defektu ramki maskującej
42	Furniture	Obsadnik
43	Galley	Szufla zecerska
44	Gathering	Składka
45	Hand stamping	Ręczne dobijanie elementów typograficznych

APPENDIX B: GLOSSARY TRANSLATION TABLES   POLISH   545

46	Haplography	Haplografia
47	Headline	Nagłówek
48	Hypercorrection	Hiperpoprawność, Hiperkorekta
49	Ideal copy	Egzemplarz wzorowy
50	Imposition	Impozycja
51	Impression	Odbicie
52	Incunabula	Inkunabuły
53	Ink	Farba drukarska; Atrament
54	Ink bleed	Wżery atramentowe
55	Inked hair	Włos w druku
56	*Integrans*	*Integrans*, dodruk i ponowne scalenie arkusza
57	Inverted type	Czcionka odbita do góry nogami
58	Issue	Nakład
59	Justification	Justowanie
60	Kern	Przewieszka; Regulacja odstępów międzyznakowych
61	Kludge	Podmiana czcionki
62	Lay of the case	Rozkład kaszty
63	Leaf	Karta
64	Manuscript correction	Odręczna korekta
65	Marginalia	Marginalia
66	Master printer	Mistrz drukarski
67	Misalignment	Błędne justowanie
68	Miscalculation	Błędne obliczenie
69	Misnumbering	Błędna numeracja
70	Mise-en-page	Układ typograficzny
71	Misprint	Błąd drukarski
72	Mock-up	Makieta, Szablon
73	Mould	Forma odlewnicza; Forma papiernicza
74	Overprinting	Naddruk, Nadruk
75	Pagination	Paginacja
76	Paper crease	Zagniecenie papieru
77	Paratext	Paratekst
78	Paste slip	Naklejone paski korektorskie
79	Pin/point holes	Punktura
80	Print run	Nakład
81	Printer's copy	Egzemplarz drukarski
82	Printer's manual	Podręcznik drukarski
83	Proofreader's marks	Znak korektorski
84	Proofs; Proofreading	Odbitki próbne; Korekta drukarska
85	Pull	Pociągnięcie drąga (w prasie drukarskiej); Odbitka
86	Quire	Libra, Składka
87	Quoin	Klin
88	Raised furniture	Wystający obsadnik
89	Raised type	Wystająca czcionka
90	Recension	Rewizja
91	Register	Register; Pasowanie
92	Reglet	Ryga (rodzaj justunku)
93	Reissue	Reedycja, Wznowienie
94	Reset	Przeskład
95	River	Rynna

96	Running title	Żywa pagina
97	*Saut du même au même*	*Saut du même au même*, tzw. rybka
98	Set-off	Ślad odbicia z sąsiedniego arkusza
99	Setting rule	Składaczka, Zeclinia
100	Sheet	Arkusz
101	Shoulder	Odsadka
102	Show-through	Przebijanie
103	Signature	Sygnatura
104	*Signe de renvoi*	*Signe de renvoi*
105	Singleton	Pojedyncza karta
106	Skeleton forme	Forma szkieletowa
107	Slipped type	Przesunięty materiał typograficzny
108	Smudged type	Rozmazana czcionka
109	Smudges/thumbing	Smugi/ślady palców
110	Sort	Pojedyncza czcionka
111	Spacing material	Justunek
112	Standing type	Skład stojący, Skład zatrzymany
113	State	Odbicie wariantowe; Stan (materiału zecerskiego)
114	Stop-press correction	Korekta naniesiona w trakcie druku
115	Stub	Falc, Zagiętka
116	Transmission errors	Skażenie tekstu
117	Tympan	Dekiel, Tympan
118	Type	Czcionka; Materiał zecerski
119	Type case	Kaszta zecerska
120	Typeface	Krój pisma
121	Typo	Literówka
122	Typographical lacuna	Lakuna typograficzna
123	Variant	Wariant
124	Vatman	Czerpalnik
125	Visorium/Visorum	Dywizorek, Dywizor
126	Water drop	Kropla wody, tzw. łzy czerpalnika
127	Watermark	Znak wodny, Filigran
128	Woodblock printing	Druk drzeworytowy

Polish translation by: Agnieszka Franczyk-Cegła (Ossolineum, Wrocław); Martyna Osuch, Izabela Wiencek-Sielska (University of Warsaw Library, Warsaw).

PORTUGUESE

	English	Portuguese
1	Allography	Alografia
2	Apologies	Apologias
3	Archetype	Arquétipo, Modelo
4	Bearer type	Letra em branco, Branco
5	Beater	Batedor, Batedor de tinta, Bate-balas
6	Bibliography	Bibliografia
7	Blind impression	Impressão a seco
8	Cancel	Cancelamento
9	*Castigationes*	Correção, Revisão
10	Casting off copy	Cálculo de edição, Medir a composição
11	Catchword	Reclamo
12	Chase	Caixilho
13	Collation	Colação, Colacionamento [Br]
14	Colophon	Colofão
15	Composing stick	Componedor
16	Composition	Composição
17	Compositor	Compositor
18	Conjugate leaves	Folhas conjugadas
19	Copy census	Recensão
20	Copy-specific analysis	Exemplar em mão, Análise de exemplar
21	Copy-text	Texto-fonte
22	Correction	Correção
23	Coucher	[Coucher]
24	Damping	Molhagem, Umidificação [Br]
25	Distribution (of type)	Distribuição dos tipos
26	Drag lines	Erro tipográfico
27	Drying/hanging	Secagem pós-impressão
28	Duplicate setting	Duplicação
29	Edition	Edição
30	Emendation	Correção
31	Erasure	Rasura, Raspagem [Br]
32	Errata	Errata
33	Exemplar	Exemplar
34	Fallen type	Letra perdida
35	Foliation	Foliação
36	Font/Fount	Fonte
37	Format	Formato
38	Forme	Forma
39	Foul case	Letra perdida
40	Frisket	Frasqueta
41	Frisket bite	Mordido
42	Furniture	Guarnição
43	Galley	Galé
44	Gathering	Caderno
45	Hand stamping	Estampagem manual

46	Haplography	Haplografia
47	Headline	Título corrente
48	Hypercorrection	Hipercorrecção
49	Ideal copy	Exemplar ideal
50	Imposition	Imposição
51	Impression	Impressão
52	Incunabula	Incunábulos
53	Ink	Tinta
54	Ink bleed	Borrão
55	Inked hair	Fio de tinta
56	*Integrans*	Interpolação
57	Inverted type	Letra invertida
58	Issue	Emissão, Edição
59	Justification	Justificação
60	Kern	Espaçamento entre letras, Creno
61	Kludge	[Kludge]
62	Lay of the case	Distribuição, Organizar os tipos na caixa
63	Leaf	Folha
64	Manuscript correction	Correção manuscrita
65	Marginalia	Marginália
66	Master printer	Mestre-impressor
67	Misalignment	Desalinhamento
68	Miscalculation	Erro de cálculo
69	Misnumbering	Erro de paginação/ foliação
70	Mise-en-page	Mise en page, Empaginação, Diagramação [Br]
71	Misprint	Erros de impressão
72	Mock-up	Esquisso, Boneca
73	Mould	Molde (type mould); Forma (paper mould)
74	Overprinting	Sobreimpressão
75	Pagination	Paginação
76	Paper crease	Dobra, Vinco
77	Paratext	Paratexto
78	Paste slip	Emenda colada
79	Pin/point holes	Perno de fixação
80	Print run	Tiragem
81	Printer's copy	Cópia de impressão (padrão)
82	Printer's manual	Manual do impressor (ou de impressão)
83	Proofreader's marks	Sinais de revisão ou correção de provas
84	Proofs; Proofreading	Prova; Revisão
85	Pull	Prensagem
86	Quire	Caderno, Mão de papel
87	Quoin	Cunho
88	Raised furniture	Guarnição em relevo
89	Raised type	Tipo sobrelevado (em relevo)
90	Recension	Recensão
91	Register	Registo, Registro [Br]
92	Reglet	Guarnição
93	Reissue	Reedição
94	Reset	Reimpressão
95	River	Canal, Goteira

APPENDIX B: GLOSSARY TRANSLATION TABLES   PORTUGUESE   549

96	Running title	Título corrente
97	*Saut du même au même*	Salto do mesmo ao mesmo, Homeoteleuto
98	Set-off	Transferência de tinta, Repinte
99	Setting rule	Regreta, Régua de composição
100	Sheet	Folha
101	Shoulder	Talude, Rebarba [Br]
102	Show-through	Repasse, Atravessamento [Br]
103	Signature	Assinatura
104	*Signe de renvoi*	Sinal de intercalação
105	Singleton	Folha avulsa
106	Skeleton forme	Armação da página.
107	Slipped type	Letra inclinada
108	Smudged type	Letra suja, Letra manchada
109	Smudges/thumbing	Mancha, Nódoa
110	Sort	Sorte, Tipo móvel de metal
111	Spacing material	Caracteres de espaçamento, Claros
112	Standing type	Composição de tipos não desfeita
113	State	Variante
114	Stop-press correction	Interrupção para correção
115	Stub	Pestana
116	Transmission errors	Erros
117	Tympan	Tímpano
118	Type	Tipo
119	Type case	Caixotim
120	Typeface	Fonte
121	Typo	Gralha
122	Typographical lacuna	Lacuna
123	Variant	Variante
124	Vatman	Papeleiro
125	Visorium/Visorum	Divisório, Visor
126	Water drop	Auréola, Gota d´água [Br]
127	Watermark	Marca de água, Marca d´água [Br]
128	Woodblock printing	Impressão xilográfica, Xilogravura

Portuguese translation by: Fabiano Cataldo de Azevedo (Universidade Federal da Bahia); Silvio Costa (Public Library, Porto).

RUSSIAN

	English	Russian
1	Allography	Аллография
2	Apologies	Извинения
3	Archetype	Архетип
4	Bearer type	Несущий набор (литеры, использованные в качестве пробельного материала)
5	Beater	Батырщик
6	Bibliography	Библиография
7	Blind impression	Слепой оттиск, Блинт, Бескрасочное тиснение
8	Cancel	Частичная перепечатка (перепечатка слова, листа и т. д.)
9	*Castigationes*	Критические примечания (разночтения, конъектуры)
10	Casting off copy	Расчет набора по рукописи, Расчет объема издания
11	Catchword	Кустод(а)
12	Chase	Рама для заключки, Формная рама
13	Collation	Коллация, Колляция
14	Colophon	Колофон
15	Composing stick	Верстатка
16	Composition	Набор
17	Compositor	Наборщик
18	Conjugate leaves	Парные (смежные) листы
19	Copy census	Учет всех доступных экземпляров
20	Copy-specific analysis	Поэкземплярный анализ, Анализ специфики экземпляра
21	Copy-text	Оригинал (*Druckvorlage*); Основной текст/список (basis for a critical edition)
22	Correction	Правка, Корректура
23	Coucher	Валяльщик
24	Damping	Смачивание, Мочка
25	Distribution (of type)	Разбор (шрифта)
26	Drag lines	Следы смазанной краски
27	Drying/hanging	Сушка/развешивание
28	Duplicate setting	Повторный набор
29	Edition	Издание
30	Emendation	Эмендация, Исправление
31	Erasure	Стирание, Выскабливание
32	Errata	Опечатки, Ошибки; Список опечаток
33	Exemplar	Оригинал, Антиграф (text from which a particular copy is made); Экземпляр (a particular copy of a book)
34	Fallen type	Упавшая поверх набора литера
35	Foliation	Фолиация

36	Font/Fount	Шрифт (in general); Гарнитура (a set of various sizes or styles intended as a family)
37	Format	Формат
38	Forme	Печатная форма
39	Foul case	Ошибка сортировки шрифта (a typo caused by innacurate distribution)
40	Frisket	Рашкет, Бумажная рамка
41	Frisket bite	Рашкетное пятно (непропечатанный текст из-за смещения рашкета)
42	Furniture	Обкладочный материал
43	Galley	Наборная доска, Уголок
44	Gathering	Тетрадь
45	Hand stamping	Ручное штемпелевание, Клиширование
46	Haplography	Гаплография
47	Headline	Колонтитул
48	Hypercorrection	Гиперкоррекция
49	Ideal copy	Идеальный экземпляр
50	Imposition	Спуск полос, Раскладка листа
51	Impression	Тираж, Завод (all copies of an edition); Оттиск, Печать (act of printing)
52	Incunabula	Инкунабулы
53	Ink	Чернила, Типографская краска
54	Ink bleed	Расплывание чернил, Растекание краски
55	Inked hair	Отпечаток волоса
56	*Integrans*	Повторный набор
57	Inverted type	Перевернутая литера
58	Issue	Издание, Тираж
59	Justification	Выключка, Выравнивание
60	Kern	Свисающий элемент очка (projecting part of a type); Кернинг (action of adjusting space)
61	Kludge	Клудж
62	Lay of the case	Раскладка кассы
63	Leaf	Лист (двусторонняя единица писчего материала, в т.ч. доля сфальцованного печатного листа)
64	Manuscript correction	Рукописная правка
65	Marginalia	Маргиналии
66	Master printer	Мастер-типограф, Типографский мастер
67	Misalignment	Неправильное выравнивание
68	Miscalculation	Ошибка расчета
69	Misnumbering	Ошибка нумерации (в т. ч. пагинации или фолиации)
70	Mise-en-page	Мизанпаж, Компоновка страницы
71	Misprint	Типографская ошибка, Опечатка
72	Mock-up	Макет
73	Mould	Матрица
74	Overprinting	Надпечатка, Впечатывание
75	Pagination	Пагинация

76	Paper crease	Складка, Морщина
77	Paratext	Паратекст
78	Paste slip	Наклейка
79	Pin/point holes	Пунктуры, Точечные отверстия
80	Print run	Тираж
81	Printer's copy	Типографский оригинал, Оригинал для набора
82	Printer's manual	Руководство по типографскому делу, Руководство для типографа
83	Proofreader's marks	Корректурные знаки
84	Proofs; Proofreading	Корректура, Корректурный оттиск; Чтение корректуры
85	Pull	Тиснение, Натиск (act); Оттиск (result)
86	Quire	Десть
87	Quoin	Заключка, Клин для заключки
88	Raised furniture	Приподнявшийся обкладочный материал
89	Raised type	Приподнявшаяся литера, Марашка
90	Recension	*Recensio*, Рецензия
91	Register	Регистр/перечень сигнатур (list of signatures); Приводка (positioning on a sheet)
92	Reglet	Реглет, Шпон
93	Reissue	Титульное издание
94	Reset	Переборка, Заборка, Повторный (вторичный) набор
95	River	Коридор
96	Running title	Колонтитул
97	*Saut du même au même*	*Saut du même au même*, Прыжок от сходного к сходному
98	Set-off	Отмарывание (перенос краски с оттиска на другой лист)
99	Setting rule	Наборная линейка
100	Sheet	Лист (печатный лист, подвергающийся фальцовке)
101	Shoulder	Заплечико
102	Show-through	Просвечивание
103	Signature	Сигнатура
104	*Signe de renvoi*	Знак выноски
105	Singleton	Одинарный лист (in general); Вкладной лист, Вкладка (an additional leaf printed separately)
106	Skeleton forme	Каркасная форма (форма без литерного блока)
107	Slipped type	Выпавшая литера
108	Smudged type	Смазанный оттиск, Дробление формы
109	Smudges/thumbing	Пятна типографской краски, Чернильные отпечатки пальцев
110	Sort	Литера гарнитуры
111	Spacing material	Пробельный материал
112	Standing type	Неотработанный набор, Неразобранная форма
113	State	Вариант
114	Stop-press correction	Исправление в процессе печати
115	Stub	Полоска бумаги на сгибе между двумя соседними листами
116	Transmission errors	Ошибки в передаче текста (рукописного или печатного), Ошибки копирования

117	Tympan	Тимпан, Декель
118	Type	Литера (a single sort); Шрифт (collective noun referred to the pieces of cast metal for letterpress printing)
119	Type case	Наборная касса, Шрифт-касса
120	Typeface	Шрифт (in general); Гарнитура (a set of various sizes or styles intended as a family)
121	Typo	Опечатка
122	Typographical lacuna	Типографская лакуна, Непропечатанный текст
123	Variant	Вариант
124	Vatman	Черпальщик
125	Visorium/Visorum	Визорий, Дивизорий
126	Water drop	Водяное пятно
127	Watermark	Водяной знак, Филигрань
128	Woodblock printing	Ксилографическая печать

Russian translation by: Grigory Vorobyev (University of Innsbruck); Mikhail Sergeev (National Library of Russia, St Petersburg); Viktorija Vaitkevičiūtė (Martynas Mažvydas National Library of Lithuania, Vilnius); Sondra Rankelienė, Aušra Rinkūnaitė (Vilnius University Library).

SPANISH

	English	Spanish
1	Allography	Alografía
2	Apologies	Apologías, Aviso al lector
3	Archetype	Arquetipo
4	Bearer type	Impresión en blanco, Imposición de altura
5	Beater	Batidor
6	Bibliography	Bibliografía
7	Blind impression	Impresión en seco
8	Cancel	Supresión, Reposición
9	*Castigationes*	*Castigationes*
10	Casting off copy	Cuenta del original
11	Catchword	Reclamo
12	Chase	Rama
13	Collation	Colación
14	Colophon	Colofón
15	Composing stick	Componedor
16	Composition	Composición
17	Compositor	Componedor, Cajista
18	Conjugate leaves	Hojas conjugadas
19	Copy census	Lista de ejemplares
20	Copy-specific analysis	Análisis del ejemplar
21	Copy-text	Original, Ejemplar de base textual
22	Correction	Corrección
23	Coucher	Ponedor
24	Damping	Mojadura
25	Distribution (of type)	Distribución
26	Drag lines	Borrón, Ensuciado
27	Drying/hanging	Tendido
28	Duplicate setting	Composición duplicada
29	Edition	Edición
30	Emendation	*Emendatio*
31	Erasure	Raspado
32	Errata	Lista de erratas, Fe de erratas
33	Exemplar	Original, Ejemplar
34	Fallen type	Tipo caído
35	Foliation	Foliación
36	Font/Fount	Fuente
37	Format	Formato
38	Forme	Forma
39	Foul case	Caja empastelada
40	Frisket	Frasqueta
41	Frisket bite	Lardón
42	Furniture	Guarnición
43	Galley	Galera
44	Gathering	Cuaderno
45	Hand stamping	Estampar a mano

APPENDIX B: GLOSSARY TRANSLATION TABLES   SPANISH   555

46	Haplography	Haplografía
47	Headline	Cabecera
48	Hypercorrection	Hipercorrección
49	Ideal copy	Ejemplar ideal
50	Imposition	Imposición
51	Impression	Impresión
52	Incunabula	Incunables
53	Ink	Tinta
54	Ink bleed	Sangrado
55	Inked hair	Pelo entintado
56	*Integrans*	*Integrans*
57	Inverted type	Tipo volteado
58	Issue	Emisión
59	Justification	Justificación
60	Kern	Parte sobresaliente del tipo
61	Kludge	[Kludge]
62	Lay of the case	División de la caja
63	Leaf	Hoja
64	Manuscript correction	Corrección a mano
65	Marginalia	Notas marginales
66	Master printer	Impresor
67	Misalignment	Error en la justificación
68	Miscalculation	Error de cuenta
69	Misnumbering	Error de numeración
70	Mise-en-page	Diseño, Compaginación
71	Misprint	Error de imprenta
72	Mock-up	Maqueta
73	Mould	Molde
74	Overprinting	Sobreimpresión
75	Pagination	Paginación
76	Paper crease	Agujeta
77	Paratext	Paratexto
78	Paste slip	Banderilla
79	Pin/point holes	Puntizones
80	Print run	Tirada
81	Printer's copy	Original de imprenta
82	Printer's manual	Manual de imprenta
83	Proofreader's marks	Signos del corrector de pruebas
84	Proofs; Proofreading	Pruebas; Corrección de pruebas
85	Pull	Tiro, Tirar
86	Quire	Mano, Cuaderno
87	Quoin	Cuña
88	Raised furniture	Guarnición alzada
89	Raised type	Tipo alzado
90	Recension	*Recensio*
91	Register	Registro
92	Reglet	Regleta, Interlinea
93	Reissue	Reemisión
94	Reset	Recomposición
95	River	Calle

96	Running title	Titulillo
97	*Saut du même au même*	Mochuelo, Salto por *homoioteleuton*
98	Set-off	Repintado
99	Setting rule	Regla de composición
100	Sheet	Pliego
101	Shoulder	Hombro
102	Show-through	Transparencia
103	Signature	Signatura
104	*Signe de renvoi*	Llamadas
105	Singleton	Hoja suelta
106	Skeleton forme	Armazón
107	Slipped type	Encaballado
108	Smudged type	Remosqueado
109	Smudges/thumbing	Maculaturas
110	Sort	Tipo, Suerte
111	Spacing material	Espacios
112	Standing type	Composición guardada
113	State	Estado
114	Stop-press correction	Corrección en prensa
115	Stub	Cartivana
116	Transmission errors	Errores de transmisión
117	Tympan	Tímpano
118	Type	Tipo
119	Type case	Caja
120	Typeface	Ojo
121	Typo	Errata tipográfica
122	Typographical lacuna	Laguna tipográfica
123	Variant	Variante
124	Vatman	Laurente
125	Visorium/Visorum	Divisorio
126	Water drop	Gota de agua
127	Watermark	Filigrana, Marca de agua
128	Woodblock printing	Xilografía, Impresión en madera

Spanish translation by: Pablo Alvarez (University of Michigan); Benito Rial Costas, José Luis Gonzalo Sánchez-Molero (Complutense University, Madrid).

SWEDISH

	English	Swedish
1	Allography	Allografi
2	Apologies	Apologi
3	Archetype	Arketyp
4	Bearer type	Löpsteg
5	Beater	Uppdragare
6	Bibliography	Bibliografi
7	Blind impression	Blindtryck
8	Cancel	Kancellans
9	*Castigationes*	*Castigationes*
10	Casting off copy	Omfångsberäkning (anskjutning, tilltryckning)
11	Catchword	Kustod
12	Chase	Ram
13	Collation	Kollationering
14	Colophon	Kolofon
15	Composing stick	Sätthake, Vinkelhake
16	Composition	Sats, Sättning
17	Compositor	Sättare
18	Conjugate leaves	Konjugata blad
19	Copy census	Exemplarcensus
20	Copy-specific analysis	Exemplarspecifik analys
21	Copy-text	Bastext
22	Correction	Rättelse
23	Coucher	Guskare
24	Damping	Fuktning
25	Distribution (of type)	Avläggning
26	Drag lines	Hyssjning, smetning
27	Drying/hanging	Torkning, upphängning
28	Duplicate setting	Parallellsats
29	Edition	Edition upplaga, utgåva
30	Emendation	Emendation
31	Erasure	Radering
32	Errata	Errata
33	Exemplar	Exemplar
34	Fallen type	Lös typ
35	Foliation	Foliering
36	Font/Fount	Font
37	Format	Format
38	Forme	Tryckform
39	Foul case	Svibel
40	Frisket	Remmika
41	Frisket bite	Remmikaskada
42	Furniture	Steg
43	Galley	Skepp
44	Gathering	Lägg
45	Hand stamping	Handprägling

46	Haplography	Haplografi
47	Headline	Rubrik
48	Hypercorrection	Hyperkorrektion
49	Ideal copy	Idealexemplar
50	Imposition	Utskjutning
51	Impression	Tryckning
52	Incunabula	Inkunabeln
53	Ink	Bläck
54	Ink bleed	Blödande bläck
55	Inked hair	Spis
56	*Integrans*	*Integrans*
57	Inverted type	Upp och nedvänd typ
58	Issue	Emission
59	Justification	Utslutning
60	Kern	Överhäng, Uppstapel, Underskärning
61	Kludge	[Kludge]
62	Lay of the case	Kastindelning
63	Leaf	Blad
64	Manuscript correction	Handskriven rättelse
65	Marginalia	Marginalanteckningar
66	Master printer	Boktryckarmästare
67	Misalignment	Felplacering, Felinställning
68	Miscalculation	Felräkning
69	Misnumbering	Felnumrering
70	Mise-en-page	Komposition, Sidkomposition, Ombrytning
71	Misprint	Feltryck
72	Mock-up	Modell
73	Mould	Gjutform (typography); Form (paper)
74	Overprinting	Påtryck
75	Pagination	Paginering
76	Paper crease	Pappersveck
77	Paratext	Paratext
78	Paste slip	Inklistrad lapp (med rättelse)
79	Pin/point holes	Punkturhål
80	Print run	Upplaga
81	Printer's copy	Sättningsförlaga
82	Printer's manual	Tryckmanual
83	Proofreader's marks	Korrekturläsartecken
84	Proofs; Proofreading	Korrektur; Korrekturläsning
85	Pull	Dra, Klappavdrag
86	Quire	Bok, Lägg
87	Quoin	Slutsteg, Slutkil
88	Raised furniture	Upphöjt steg
89	Raised type	Upphöjd typ
90	Recension	Recension
91	Register	Register
92	Reglet	Reglett
93	Reissue	Nyemission
94	Reset	Nysättning
95	River	Flod

APPENDIX B: GLOSSARY TRANSLATION TABLES   SWEDISH   559

96	Running title	Kolumntitel, Löpande titel
97	*Saut du même au même*	Ögonhoppsfel
98	Set-off	Smetning
99	Setting rule	Sättlinje
100	Sheet	Ark
101	Shoulder	Skuldra
102	Show-through	Genomslag
103	Signature	Signatur
104	*Signe de renvoi*	Nottecken
105	Singleton	Enkelblad
106	Skeleton forme	Konturform
107	Slipped type	Lös typ
108	Smudged type	Utsmetad typ
109	Smudges/thumbing	Fläckar/tumning
110	Sort	Typsort
111	Spacing material	Utslutning, Lågmaterial
112	Standing type	Stående sats
113	State	Stat
114	Stop-press correction	Rättelse under tryckningen
115	Stub	Fals
116	Transmission errors	Överföringsfel
117	Tympan	Däckel
118	Type	Typ
119	Type case	Kast, Stilkast, Sättkast, Typkast
120	Typeface	Typsnitt
121	Typo	Tryckfel
122	Typographical lacuna	Typografisk lakun
123	Variant	Variant
124	Vatman	Formare
125	Visorium/Visorum	Tenakel
126	Water drop	Vattendroppe
127	Watermark	Vattenmärke
128	Woodblock printing	Blocktryck

Swedish translation by: Peter Sjökvist (Uppsala University); Jonas Nordin, Arina Stoenescu (Lund University); Patrik Åström, Wolfgang Undorf (Royal Library, Stockholm).

TURKISH

	English	Turkish
1	Allography	Yazısal değişke
2	Apologies	Özür metni, özürname, özür beyanı
3	Archetype	Sahih nüsha
4	Bearer type	Hâmil harf
5	Beater	Mürekkep dövücü usta
6	Bibliography	Kitap bilimi, bibliyografya
7	Blind impression	Mürekkepsiz intiba, kör baskı
8	Cancel	İptal
9	*Castigationes*	Ekte verilen mukabele ve kıyas metinleri
10	Casting off copy	Sayfa ayarlama, kalibraj
11	Catchword	Reddade, ayak
12	Chase	Çember
13	Collation	Harmanlama; Karşılaştırma, tahkik
14	Colophon	Ferağ kaydı; Kolofon
15	Composing stick	Kumpas, dizgi harf yatağı
16	Composition	Dizgi
17	Compositor	Mürettip, dizgici
18	Conjugate leaves	Mütehhid varaklar, birleşik yapraklar
19	Copy census	Nüshaların tetkiki
20	Copy-specific analysis	Nüsha bazlı inceleme
21	Copy-text	Nüsha metni
22	Correction	Düzeltme, tashih
23	Coucher	Kağıdı tekneden eleğe aktaran işçi
24	Damping	Nemleme
25	Distribution (of type)	Harflerin kasaya geri konması
26	Drag lines	Çekme izi
27	Drying/hanging	Kurutma/asma
28	Duplicate setting	Mükerrer dizgi
29	Edition	Basım, edisyon
30	Emendation	Tashih
31	Erasure	Silinti
32	Errata	Hata cetveli
33	Exemplar	Asıl nüsha
34	Fallen type	Kaymış harf
35	Foliation	Sayfa sayılandırma
36	Font/Fount	Font, yazı karakteri takımı
37	Format	Kitabın boyu
38	Forme	Baskı kalıbı
39	Foul case	[Hurufat kasasına yanlış harf konmasına bağlı] Hatalı dizgi
40	Frisket	Örtücü kağıt
41	Frisket bite	Örtücü kağıt hatası
42	Furniture	Aralık tahtası, tertib tahtası, garnitür
43	Galley	Gale, tabakanın dizildiği tezgah
44	Gathering	Forma, cüz
45	Hand stamping	Elle baskı

APPENDIX B: GLOSSARY TRANSLATION TABLES   TURKISH   561

46	Haplography	Tekleşmeli yazım
47	Headline	Başlık
48	Hypercorrection	Lüzumsuz düzeltme
49	Ideal copy	Mükemmel nüsha
50	Imposition	Sayfa atmak, baskısı yapılacak sayfaların kalıba dizilmesi
51	Impression	İntiba; tab etme
52	Incunabula	Beşikdevri basmaları, inkunabel, 1500 yılı ve öncesinde basılan eserler
53	Ink	Mürekkep
54	Ink bleed	Mürekkebin arka yapması
55	Inked hair	Saç izi
56	*Integrans*	Sonradan tamamlanan eksik tabakalar
57	Inverted type	Ters dönmüş harf
58	Issue	Baskı
59	Justification	Hizalama
60	Kern	Harf çıkıntısı; harf aralığı
61	Kludge	Yama
62	Lay of the case	Harf kasası düzeni
63	Leaf	Yaprak
64	Manuscript correction	Elle düzeltme
65	Marginalia	Haşiye; derkenar; talika
66	Master printer	Usta matbaacı, mahir basmacı
67	Misalignment	Hizalama hatası
68	Miscalculation	Hesaplama hatası
69	Misnumbering	Hatalı sayfa sayısı verme
70	Mise-en-page	Sayfa düzeni, mizanpaj
71	Misprint	Hatalı basım
72	Mock-up	Baskı provası
73	Mould	Kalıp
74	Overprinting	Aynı tabakaya tekrar baskı yapılması
75	Pagination	Sayfa sayısı
76	Paper crease	Kağıdın kırışıp baskıda boşluk oluşması
77	Paratext	Yan metin
78	Paste slip	Yapıştırma yöntemi ile düzeltme
79	Pin/point holes	İğne deliği
80	Print run	Baskı adedi
81	Printer's copy	Müsvedde
82	Printer's manual	Basmacının elkitabı, matbaacının kılavuzu
83	Proofreader's marks	Musahhihin işaretleri, düzelticinin imleri
84	Proofs; Proofreading	Düzeltme; Redaksiyon
85	Pull	Çekme işlemi
86	Quire	24 veya 25 tabakalık kağıt destesi
87	Quoin	Takoz
88	Raised furniture	Tertib tahtasının yüksekte kalması
89	Raised type	Harfin yüksekte kalıp yakınındaki harflerin basımını engellemesi
90	Recension	Düzeltilmiş metin
91	Register	Forma rakamlarının künyesi
92	Reglet	Satır aralarına konan ahşap çıta

93	Reissue	Önceden basılmış bir eserin yeni bir kapakla tekrar piyasaya sürülmesi
94	Reset	Tekrar dizgi
95	River	Nehir, satırlar arası dikey boşluk
96	Running title	Dizi başlık
97	*Saut du même au même*	Sayfada benzer veya aynı kelimenin olması nedeniyle gözün kayıp satır atlaması
98	Set-off	Baskı mürekkebinin sonraki sayfaya bulaşması
99	Setting rule	Gönye
100	Sheet	Tabaka
101	Shoulder	Huruf yüzü
102	Show-through	Mürekkebin sayfanın arkasına çıkması
103	Signature	Forma rakamı
104	*Signe de renvoi*	Düzeltme yapılacak yere konan işaret
105	Singleton	Tek sayfa
106	Skeleton forme	Baskı kalıbı şablonu
107	Slipped type	Kaymış harf
108	Smudged type	Lekeli harf
109	Smudges/thumbing	Mürekkep bulaşması, mürekkep izi
110	Sort	Metal döküm harf
111	Spacing material	Espas, ara boşu
112	Standing type	Yerine geri konmamış harf
113	State	Baskı evresi
114	Stop-press correction	Baskı esnasında yapılan düzeltme
115	Stub	Dip koçanı
116	Transmission errors	Nakil hataları, aktarımda yanlışlık
117	Tympan	Baskı kağıdının üzerine konduğu iç ve dış çerçeve
118	Type	Hurufat
119	Type case	Hurufat kasası
120	Typeface	Harf
121	Typo	Hata
122	Typographical lacuna	Baskıda boşluk kalması
123	Variant	Değişken
124	Vatman	Kağıt hamurunu eleğe döken işçi
125	Visorium/Visorum	Dizilecek satırı gösteren metal imleç
126	Water drop	Su lekesi
127	Watermark	Filigran
128	Woodblock printing	Ahşap baskı, ağaç baskısı

Turkish translation by: Nil Palabıyık (Queen Mary, University of London), with special thanks to İsmail Erünsal (Marmara University, Istanbul) and Orlin Sabev (Bulgarian Academy of Sciences, Sofia).

INDEX OF SUBJECTS

Note: this index does not include references to the Glossary (Appendix A)

Allography 173–4, 176n, 180

Apologies vi, 70, 84, 263n, 264–74, 380, 420, 469

Archetype 24, 111, 166, 168n, 173, 235, 327n

Bearer type 134, 161n, 174–5, 189–93, 454n

Blind impression 43, 48, 66, 145n, 174–5, 454n

Cancel 2, 17, 94–6, 99, 124, 137, 145–6, 149, 152–4, 159–62, 280

Casting off copy 65, 111, 254, 301n, 423

Catchword 123, 129, 131, 134, 137–8, 145–6, 153, 172n, 178n, 377, 381

Chase 52

Collation 17n, 52, 121n, 123, 125, 129, 131, 158, 183, 300, 349n, 369n, 382

Colophon 72, 114, 131, 137, 146, 154, 160, 170, 274, 302n, 309n, 327n, 388, 396

Composing stick 42, 52, 249, 465

Composition 52, 100, 122n, 124, 132, 159, 172, 174, 175n, 176, 249n, 465, 468

Compositor vii, 6–7, 51–2, 55, 57–8, 65–6, 71–8, 81, 92, 137, 151–2, 168, 172–80, 184, 186, 204, 206, 210, 215–16, 226, 228, 235n, 249, 251–4, 269–70, 272, 279–81, 286, 297, 301, 312–17, 321, 325n, 348, 349n, 351, 377, 379–82, 421, 423–5, 434, 441, 443, 452, 454, 465, 468–9, 474–5

Conjugate leaves 51, 58, 137, 144n, 147, 167, 172–80

Copy census 82n, 100n, 159, 171, 188–93, 220n, 303, 443

Copy-text 3n, 78, 281

Damping 36, 46, 48, 92

Distribution (of type) vii, 57, 73, 76, 174

Drying/hanging 48, 184, 447, 449n

Erasure 2, 113, 122–4, 133, 135, 144, 150, 151n, 153n, 160, 207, 210, 220, 249, 302, 305–6, 312, 315, 318–21, 374n

Errata vi, 2, 4, 9–10, 20, 80–9, 92, 96, 99–100, 122–4, 127, 129, 131, 142–3, 146, 149n, 153–58, 199, 204–5, 207, 210, 242, 251–2, 256–7, 267–72, 279–82, 290, 348, 369–82, 415–23, 426, 441n, 469n, 475

Exemplar 1, 15, 67, 184, 186, 199n, 200n, 202n, 208n, 235n, 262, 266, 272, 346n, 347n, 350n

Fallen type 33–48, 146, 159

Foliation 123, 129, 131, 136–8, 162, 170, 174, 178–80, 198, 270n, 380

Forme 6, 33–5, 42–3, 46, 52, 57–8, 66, 73, 76, 123n, 124, 134, 137, 138n, 144, 147, 149, 153n, 161n, 172–5, 180, 187, 256n, 284, 302, 308, 313, 423, 440–41, 452–8, 464

Foul case 56–7, 73, 80n, 256n

Frisket 134n, 138n, 175, 455, 459n

Furniture 455, 458

Gathering 21, 53, 55, 58, 66, 95n, 112, 129, 131, 137–8, 142n, 147, 149, 152, 154, 156–7, 159, 161, 172–4, 178, 184, 202, 204, 206–7, 218, 238, 241, 255n, 297, 300–5, 307, 311–16, 320–1, 352, 373, 374n, 382, 386, 389, 391n, 392, 395, 397, 434, 441, 443

Hand stamping 122–4, 144n, 157, 160n

Haplography 173

Headline 22, 53, 95, 473–4

Hypercorrection 337

Imposition 51, 80n, 81, 84–5, 94–5, 100, 216, 306–7, 455

Impression 2, 34, 38, 41, 43, 47–8, 51, 73, 80n, 82n, 86, 95, 99, 124–5, 131, 146, 149, 175, 184n, 208n, 249, 371n, 386, 408, 419, 433, 435, 440, 443, 451n, 452n, 454–5

Ink bleed 451, 457

Integrans 123, 133, 137, 145–9, 152–4, 159, 161–2, 174, 184n

Inverted type 72n

Justification 93, 251, 254

Kludge 70–9, 136, 152n, 180n, 256n

Lay of the case 176, 313

Layout *see* Mise-en-page

Manuscript correction 2, 10, 54–5, 81, 99, 108, 110–12, 114, 117, 122–62, 171–8, 185, 187, 208–10, 238, 300–13, 319, 320n, 348, 351, 359, 374, 377n, 403–7, 435, 438–9, 440n, 441–2, 465

Misalignment 174n, 239, 241, 251, 390n, 451

Miscalculation 53, 122, 137, 142, 149, 159, 178–81, 377, 423

Mise-en-page vi, 4, 22–3, 63–6, 85, 130, 165, 169n, 182, 254, 258, 280, 281n, 283, 301, 380, 386n, 390, 395, 434, 465, 470

Misnumbering 210, 308–22, 405

Mock-up 60–7, 221–9

INDEX OF SUBJECTS 567

Overprinting 2, 124

Pagination 12, 21n, 170, 179, 381, 465–6
Paper crease 449
Paste slip vii, 17, 85, 94–7, 122–4, 133, 137, 158–9, 207, 374, 377
Print run 46, 53, 86, 123n, 147, 150, 170–1, 174, 177, 179, 186–7, 215, 302, 312, 320, 373n, 374, 379, 444, 458, 464, 474
Printer's copy 65, 66n, 87, 111–2, 123, 129, 131, 141n, 171, 174, 176–7, 183–4, 234, 301n, 302, 312, 314, 321, 379n, 401n
Printer's manual 37n, 51–2, 58n, 242n, 249n, 267, 280–1, 369, 377–82, 451n
Proofreader's marks 57, 65–6, 241, 245
Proofs; Proofreading vii, 1–5, 9, 16, 20, 51–67, 81, 99, 110–14, 123, 126–7, 135, 144n, 147–8, 152, 161, 166, 172, 174–7, 183–4, 185–7, 228, 233–6, 239–42, 245, 262, 266, 272, 301–2, 308, 314–16, 321, 346, 379, 381, 415, 420–1, 464, 476–7
Pull vi, 52–3, 60, 66, 172n, 175, 184n, 301n, 454

Raised furniture 452, 455
Raised type 452–3
Register 123, 129, 131, 172n, 177n, 451, 453, 454n, 455
Reissue 287, 348
Reset 112, 122, 124–5, 132, 135, 137–8, 143–52, 154n, 160–1, 172–4, 188–93, 206, 239, 256, 297n, 301, 307–8, 315n, 373
Running title 72n, 122n, 123, 131, 136, 158, 377, 379, 381

Saut du même au même 173
Set-off 149, 451n
Sheet 4, 9, 11, 16, 36, 44n, 51–67, 76, 82, 84n, 87n, 94n, 95, 96n, 100, 111–12, 114, 117, 122n, 123–31, 134–8, 145–54, 159n, 160–1, 170, 172–4, 176, 179–80, 184, 202–3, 206–7, 210, 233–4, 239–41, 245, 262, 279–82, 290, 301–2, 307, 309–12, 314–16, 321, 359, 371, 373–4, 379–82, 386, 387, 391n, 421, 447–58, 463–5, 476–7
Shoulder 451, 455–6
Signature 20n, 95, 134, 136–8, 145–7, 149, 151–3, 157–8, 379, 381
Signe de renvoi 147, 187
Singleton 44n, 94n, 96n, 100, 137–8, 154
Slipped type 57, 458
Smudged type 34, 451, 455–7
Smudges/thumbing 455
Spacing material 35, 38, 45, 57, 174, 253, 452, 458
Standing type 76
State 21, 24, 55, 60, 94–5, 132, 134, 151n, 152–3, 156, 160, 369n, 371, 373, 374n, 382, 418
Stop-press correction 82, 107–12, 117, 122, 124–7, 132–62, 166, 174, 177, 179, 186, 300–2, 305–8, 320–1, 374, 473

Transmission errors (see also haplography, hypercorrection, and saut du même au même) 8, 13–4, 20, 56–8, 66, 73–4, 82, 87n, 89, 94, 111, 115, 124n, 126, 135, 137, 158, 173, 175, 220, 228, 248, 252–4, 269, 270n, 282, 285–9, 309, 320, 329n, 330, 333–9, 348, 351, 353, 386n, 395–6, 420, 475
Type case 52, 57n, 73–4, 76, 269, 313
Typographical lacuna 268

Variant 3n, 54n, 112–13, 114n, 121n, 122n, 123, 125, 129, 131–3, 134n, 136n, 137, 138n, 139n, 142, 144n, 145n, 146, 149, 151n, 152–4, 155n, 156, 159, 160n, 161–2, 173n, 174, 177n, 179n, 180–1, 183n, 186, 206, 234n, 305, 380, 388–9, 392, 420, 424–5

Water drop 448–9, 451, 460

Index of Names

Note: fictitious and fictionalised characters are not included, while authors of secondary literature appear only when they are either mentioned in the main text or critically discussed in footnotes.

Abba Mari, Nissim ben 266
Abbot, George 215
Acheson, Katherine 410
Acworth, George 22–3
Aelfric of Eynsham 9
Aesop 53, 60, 62, 65, 67, 91
Agag, King of Amalek 253, 257
Alamanus, Nicolaus *see* Della Magna, Niccolò
Alberti, Leon Battista 111–12, 326
Alcocer, Hernando de 377
Aldrovandi, Ulisse 331–3, 339n
Aleandro, Girolamo 333
Alfred, King of England 9
Alighieri, Dante *see* Dante
Alopa, Lorenzo 167, 168n
Amaseo, Girolamo 130, 132–4, 141
Ambergau, Adam de 85
Amerbach, Johann 34, 39
Ami, rabbi 263
Amman, Jost 52
André, Alfred 221n
Anne of Brittany, Queen of France 220–1
Antinori, Carlo 167
Antonio di Luca di Berto 113
Apollonius of Perga 85
Apostolios (Aristoboulos), Arsenios 167n
Arias Montano, Benito 9, 200
Ariosto, Ludovico 98, 122n
Aristophanes 130, 134, 156
Aristotle 122n, 128, 135–9, 144n, 149n, 153n, 158–9, 161, 166, 168–9, 178, 179n, 180n, 325–40
Arlenius, Arnoldus 347
Arnulf, Holy Roman Emperor 22
Artedi, Peter 332
Artus, Thomas 45
Ashley, Anthony 93
Asser, Bishop of Sherborne 9, 20
Athenaeus 122n, 138–9, 332n, 334–5
Atkinson, David 446
Audin, Maurice 34, 42
Augustine of Canterbury 12, 13n, 16, 21–3
Augustine of Hippo v, 285–6, 288
Aulus Gellius 337n
Aytta van Zwichem, Wigle van 379n

Baldasso, Renzo 54
Baldini, Baccio 117
Bale, John 11, 35
Balme, David 330, 336, 338–40
Barbarigo, Pierfrancesco 127
Barbaro, Daniele 95–6
Barbieri, Edoardo 2
Barclay, Alexander 75
Barker, Robert 215–16
Barker, William 74
Barnes, Robert v
Baronio, Cesare 199
Barrera, Alonso de la 370, 371n, 373
Barrett, Timothy 447
Bartolo di Domenico di Guido 110n
Basil of Seleucia 207
Baudrier, Henri 222
Bauhin, Jean 345n, 346, 349n
Baxter, William 1n
Beaujeu, Anne of 220
Becan, Martin 289
Becchi, Gentile 109
Becket, Thomas 10
Bede 12, 21
Bell, Thomas 286, 289
Bellaert, Jacob 443
Bellarmino, Roberto 207
Belon, Pierre 331, 349, 352
Bembo, Pietro 125, 128, 132, 139–41, 320n
Benali, Vincenzo 34n, 321n
Benedetti, Alessandro 128, 132, 134, 140–2, 149n
Bennett, H. S. 81, 100
Bentley, Richard 1
Bergmann, Johann 38, 40
Berlinghieri, Francesco 116
Bernaerts, Jan 202
Besançon, Jacques de 220
Besson, Jacques 82, 86, 100
Betsalel, Judah Leva ben (Maharal) 268
Beughem, Cornelius van 492
Bevilaqua, Simone 34, 40, 45
Beza, Theodore 234, 236
Bianchini, Giovanni 306, 309–10, 317n, 321
Bibliander, Theodor 9, 22

Billingsley, Henry 84–5
Birghden, Johann von den 470n
Blackwood, William vin
Blahoslav, Jan 233, 237–9, 241–2, 245
Blair, Ann M. 2, 87n, 100, 255, 270, 279
Blayney, Peter W. M. 72, 387n, 388
Boccaccio, Giovanni 98, 221
Boehm, Samuel 254n, 273
Böff, Justus 465
Bohemus, Johann 306n
Bolzanio, Urbano 124, 128, 142–3, 149n, 168–9, 183
Bomberg, Daniel 262, 265, 267, 273
Boniface, archbishop of Mainz 21
Bonitz, Hermann 330n
Boscán, Juan 370
Botticelli, Sandro 100n, 117
Bowers, Fredson 2–3, 426, 492
Brant, Sebastian 45, 75
Bridget of Sweden 443
Bringhurst, Robert 74n
Briquet, Charles-Moïse 490
Bristow, Richard 70, 289
Brudo, Manuel 346–8
Brun, Robert 222
Budé, Guillaume 8, 175n
Bühler, Curt F. 171
Bulkley, Edward 287
Bulle, Johannes 109
Bullinger, Heinrich 236
Bulteel, Gislain 208
Bunny, Edmund 280, 286
Burby, Cuthbert 421
Burchiello 87
Burghley, Baron see Cecil, William
Burton, Henry 287–8
Bussemaker, Ulco Cats 330
Byron, George Gordon vi

Caesar 12, 94
Caesar, Julius, Sir 410
Caius, John 350–1, 352n, 353, 359, 362
Calvin, John 101
Camerarius, Joachim 7–8, 242
Campanini, Zefirino 451n
Camus, Albert-Gaston 329
Canisius, Peter 206
Canter, Jacob 432, 443
Capell, Edward 408–9
Caramuel y Lobkowitz, Juan 371
Carolus, Johann 463–4, 469, 477
Carter, Harry 41
Carteromaco (Fortiguerri), Scipione 122n, 130, 149, 168
Catherine of Siena 125n, 127, 130, 143, 178, 179n
Caxton, William 36, 38, 40, 53
Cecil, William, Baron Burghley 9–11, 16, 23, 388
Cervini, Marcello 166n
Chapman, R.W. 485

Charles II, King of England, Scotland, and Ireland 403
Charles V, Holy Roman Emperor 371n
Charles VIII, King of France 216, 218, 220–1
Chartier, Roger 281
Chelčický, Petr 233
Cibulka, Izaiáš 233, 242, 245
Cicero vi, 8, 122n, 130, 143, 371n
Clifford, Anne 410
Cochlaeus, Johannes 22
Colibrant, Peter 202, 203n
Colonna, Francesco 124, 130, 132, 135n, 143–6, 149, 161
Comenius, Jan Amos 235
Condell, Henry 408
Connolly, Cyril 10n
Constantin, Robert 333
Conway, William Martin 434–5, 440
Copernicus, Nicolaus 87–91, 100n
Corbeil, Isaac ben Joseph of 270
Cosin, John 287–8
Cosin, Richard 284–5
Coudenberghe, Pieter van 359
Cousin, Jean 97
Coverdale, Miles 222n, 223, 228, 387
Crastone, Giovanni 128, 146
Crespin, Jean 223, 226
Cromwell, Thomas 222n, 223, 228
Crowley, Robert 283, 286, 288
Cruciger, Jan 241
Cuevas, Francisco de 377

Daniel, Samuel 418, 426
Dante 86, 100n, 117
Darleriis, Carolus de 38, 40
Darnton, Robert 5
Dausque, Claude 200
David, Johannes 210
David, King of Judah 216, 250
David, Meir ben 265
Davies, Hugh W. 94
Davies, Robertson 349
Day, John, dramatist 418–9
Day, John, printer 16, 22, 72, 84
Della Magna, Niccolò 108–13, 116–7
Della Rocca de Candal, Geri 171, 183
Deloignon, Olivier 37, 48n
de L'Orme, Philibert 92
Delrio, Martín Anton 204, 208
Dering, Edward 288
Didot, Firmin 37
Dinckmut, Conrad 58
Dioscorides 123, 127, 130, 147
Dolce, Lodovico 97–8
Dolman, John vi
Dorion 334
Downame, John 282
Drake, Samuel 17, 23
Drayton, Michael vin

570 INDEX OF NAMES

Duntze, Oliver 54
Dupré, Jean 38, 40
Duras, George 207

Edward VI, King of England and Ireland 385, 386n, 387, 388n, 396–7
Edwards, A. S. G. 2
Egmond, Florike 349
Eisenstein, Elizabeth 322
Eisermann, Falk 54
Elazar, David ben 262, 267n
Eleutherius, Pope 12
Elizabeth I, Queen of England and Ireland 11, 228, 387
Elzevir, family 184
Emerich, Johann 321n
Epicharmus 334
Erasmus, Desiderius 7–8, 127n, 143, 147, 185, 373, 399, 432, 443
Ercilla, Alonso de 371
Essling, Prince d' see Masséna, Victor
Estienne, family 184
Estienne, Robert 490
Euclid 84
Eusebius of Caesarea 21–2
Eustathius 167, 169

Faber, Jacobus 226
Fabricius, Johann Albert 169
Falk, Felix 254–5
Farnese, Alessandro 199n
Favorino, Guarino 167–9, 174, 176, 183, 186
Ferdinand I, King of Naples 109
Ferretti, Francesco 95
Fialová, Vlasta 239
Fienus, Thomas 201n
Figueroa, Francisco de 377
Fine, Olivier a 200
Finé, Oronce 85
Firmicus Maternus 130–1, 148–9
Firmin-Didot, Ambroise 222, 330
Fischer, Helmut 476
Fisher, John 20
Flacius Illyricus, Matthias 11, 24
Fleming, Richard v, vii
Floyd, John 284–5
Fonzio, Bartolomeo 110
Ford, Henry 5
Ford, John 419
Fortiguerri, Scipione see Carteromaco, Scipione
Fournier, Pierre 249n
Foxe, John 223, 280
Francis I, King of France 216
Francis of Assisi 206
Frankfordia, Nicolaus de 38, 40
Franz, Wolfgang 325n
Frederick Louis, Prince of Wales 2
Frellon, François 222n

Friburgensis, Johannes 35
Froben, press 237
Froschauer, Christoph 25–6, 345–7, 352–3
Fuchs, Leonhart 92
Fulda, Meir 270n
Fulke, William 70, 284, 288–9
Füllmaurer, Heinrich 92n
Funk, Holger 349
Fust, Johann 38, 51

Gabelkover, Johann Jakob 475–7
Gallo de Andrada, Juan 371
Gardiner, Stephen 285
Gaskell, Philip 2
Gasser, Achilles Pirmin 345n
Gaza, Theodore 128, 151, 326–40
Gelenius, Sigmund 236–7
Genette, Gérard 415, 495
Gérard, Pierre 38, 40
Gervase of Canterbury 13
Gessner, Conrad 169–70, 325n, 331, 335, 337, 339n, 340, 345–62
Gheesdael, Jan 199
Giolito, Gabriele 98
Giunta, press 92
Giustiniani, Marco Antonio 266
Glanvill, Gilbert 20
Gotthelf, Allan 330
Götz, Nicolaus 38, 40
Graesse, Johann Georg Theodor 170
Grafton, Anthony 263, 272, 279, 410
Grafton, Richard 223, 228
Granholm, Jackson W. 71, 74
Gray, William 228
Greetham, David C. 2
Greflinger, Georg 470, 477
Greg, W. W. 3
Gregori, Giovanni and Gregorio, de 38, 40, 45
Gregory I, Pope 13n, 21, 113
Griffo, Francesco 180
Guest, Edmund 14–15
Gunzenhauser Ashkenazi, Azriel ben Joseph 38, 40
Gutenberg, Johannes 2, 51, 216, 230, 492
Guthlac of Crowland 12
Guzmán, Antonio de 371
Guzmán, Francisco de 371

Haddon, Walter 17
Haebler, Konrad 2, 54
Hake, Catharina 473
Hake, Peter 471–3
Hall, Edmund 282
Hamann, Johann 321n
Hanmer, Thomas 408
Hanson, L. W. 287
Harding, Thomas 284, 289
Harduinus, François 200

Harris, Neil 2, 126, 145n, 146
Harris, Richard 289
Harvey, Christopher 230
Harvey, Gabriel 410
Heinfogel, Conrad 309n
Heitz, Emil 330
Hele, François de le 206n
Hellinga, Lotte 2, 54, 72
Heminge, John 408
Hendel, Manoah 272
Henry VII, King of England 216, 218, 220–1
Henry VIII, King of England and Ireland 216, 222n, 228, 387
Herodianus 169
Herrera, Fernando de 369–82
Hervey, Isabella 410
Hervey, Thomas 410
Hessus, Helius Eobanus 7–8
Heuss, Heinrich 464
Higgons, Theophilus 284
Hill, Nicholas 388, 390, 391n, 392, 395, 397
Hinman, Charlton 3, 400n
Hippocrates 346
Hoby, Edward 284–5
Hoffman, George 3
Holbein, Hans, the Younger 221–3, 226
Homer 2, 5, 167, 169, 173n, 186
Homes, Nathanael 282n
Hopkins, John 385, 388
Horace 1, 10–11, 186, 339n
Hornschuch, Hieronymus 58, 242, 267, 381, 497
Houghton, John 449n
Hovius, Mathias 199n
Hrabanus Maurus 13, 15
Hunt, John vi
Huray, Peter le 387
Hus, Jan 233
Huss, Matthias 36–8, 40, 45
Hutchinson, Lucy 403

Ibn Adonijah, Jacob ben Hayyim 262, 267, 270–1
Ibn Yahya, David 272
Illescas, Jacob di 264–5
Íñiguez de Lequerica, Juan 380
Isaac, Isaiah Menaham ben 268
Isaiah, Moses ben 272
Isserlein, Israel 265
Isserles, Moses 263

Jaffe, Mordecai 272
Jamblichus 128, 136n, 153
James I, King of England, Scotland, and Ireland 280, 289
Jamot, Frédéric 204
Jardine, Lisa 410
Jerome of Stridon 22, 222, 226, 285
Jewel, John 284–6, 288–9

Jobin, Tobias 464
John Frederick, Duke of Württemberg 476
John III, King of Navarre 220
John XII, Pope 286
John XXII, Pope 286
Johns, Adrian 322
Johnson, Samuel 408–9
Jonah, Matityah ben 274
Jones, Richard 419, 426
Jonson, Ben 419
Jonston, Jan 325n
Joscelyn, John 11–13, 23–4, 26
Josephus, Flavius 220
Jowett, John 410n, 421
Jugge, Richard 9, 16

Kafka, Franz 274
Karo, Joseph 263
Katz-Kuskes, Isaac 272
Katz, Joseph ben Mordecai Gershon 273
Keerbergen, Jan van 199n
Kentmann, Johannes 359
Kermode, Frank vii
Ketelaar, Nicolaus 38, 40
Kiliaan, Corneliis 199
Kingston, John 388n
Kittredge, George Lyman 409
Koberger, Anton 55–7, 302n
Kok, Ina 433, 435, 440n, 442–3
Kölhoff, Johann 38, 40, 44
Konečný, Matouš 235n, 236n, 241
Kusukawa, Sachiko 349

Lachmann, Karl 184, 498
Lambarde, William 9–10
Lambillon, Antoine 36, 38, 40, 44
Landino, Cristoforo 117
Lanecký, Jan 236n, 241
Lanfranc, archbishop of Canterbury 13, 16, 20
Lang, Joseph B. 447
La Porte, Hugues de 222n
Lascaris, Costantinos 124, 128, 138n, 150, 153–4
Lascaris, Janos 167–8
Łasicki, Jan 236
Le Rouge, Pierre 216, 218
Leempt, Gerard de 38, 40
Leeu, Gerard 431–44
Leo X, Pope 168n
Leonard, Alice 3
Leoniceno, Niccolò 124, 127–8, 130, 154
Lerer, Seth 279, 282
Levita, Elijah 254n
L'Hermite, Jacques 477
Lifschitz, Hayyim ben Isaac 269–71
Linné (Linnaeus), Carl von 325, 326n
Lipsius, Justus 1, 199–200, 202, 204, 208
Locke, John 1

INDEX OF NAMES

Louis XII, King of France 220
Löw, Anna de 464
Löw, Victor de 464
Lucas, Martin 215
Lucian 178
Lucius, King of Britain 12
Lucretius 127, 130, 155
Luria, Mordecai ben Yehiel 271
Luther, Martin 234, 236
Lyon, John 70

Madden, J. P. A. 34
Magnus, Olaus 98, 349
Maimonides 262, 268
Maioli, Lorenzo 124, 128–9, 132, 155–6
Makcouldy, Allan 282–3
Mal Lara, Juan de 370n
Malermi, Niccolò 85
Malmesbury, William of 12, 13n, 20–1
Malone, Edmund 408–9
Manassi, Niccolò 185n
Manetti, Antonio 86, 87n, 99
Manilius, Marcus 131, 149n, 297
Mann, Israel Isaac 265, 268
Manni, Angelo 143, 268
Mansfeld, Balthasar 306–7
Manutius, Aldus 38, 40, 94, 121–62, 165–93, 305n, 320n, 328, 330, 333, 336–8, 340, 421, 490
Manuzio, Aldo the Younger 185
Manuzio, Paolo 170n
Marcolini, Francesco 41n
Mareschal, Jean 223
Margócsy, Dániel 82
Marlowe, Christopher 419
Marschalk, Nikolaus 330
Marston, John 419
Martiall, John 288
Martin, Thomas 285
Mary, Queen of England and Ireland 385, 387, 397
Massai, Sonia 408n, 409, 420–1
Masséna, Victor, Prince d'Essling 85
Mauss, Detlef 35
McKenzie, Donald F. 3
McKerrow, Ronald B. 2, 402
McKitterick, David 3, 81, 94n, 279, 401
McLeod, Randall 2, 126
Medici, de', family 108–10, 114, 117, 168
Medici, Giovanni di Lorenzo de' see Leo X, Pope
Medici, Giuliano di Piero de' 108
Medici, Lorenzo di Piero de' 108–10, 116–17, 167
Medici, Piero di Lorenzo de' 167
Melanchton, Philipp 234, 236–7
Melchiori, Giorgio 423
Mentelin, Johann 36–8, 40, 44, 48n
Mercuriale, Girolamo 92
Metaphrastes, Simeon 208
Meyer, Albertus 92n

Meyers, press 475
Mignanelli, Fabio 166n
Miller, Joshua 282
Milward, Peter 280
Modena, Judah Aryeh 272
Moerbeke, William of 331, 337n
Montaigne, Michel de 185n
Montero, Juan 373
Moore, J. K. 420
More, Thomas v
Moretus, Balthasar 1, 200–3, 207–10
Moretus, Jan I 185n, 198–210, 379n
Moretus, Jan II 200
Morsing, Peder Jensen 471
Mortimer, Ruth 81, 91, 94–6, 222
Morton, Thomas 283
Moxon, Joseph 249n, 267, 280–1, 497
Münster, Sebastian 16n
Münzer, Heinrich 24
Musaeus 124, 128, 132, 157–8
Musurus, Marcus 157, 185
Mynors, Roger A. B. 6

Nabbes, Thomas 418
Naevius 337n
Nashe, Thomas 281
Needham, Paul 54
Nelson, Stan 42
Newman, Harry 419
Nider, Johann 34
Nifo, Agostino 328–9
Nordlingen, David 264
Nutius, Martin 199n

Ogilvie, Brian 349
Oporinus, Johann 9, 99
Oppeln, Pelegrinus de 58
Origen 178
Ormsby, Mark 447
Ortelius, Abraham 199
Ovid 91, 97–8

Pachel, Leonhard 38, 40
Pantaleon, Heinrich 22
Pantin, Peter 202, 207–8
Paredes, Alonso Víctor de 267, 369, 377–82, 497
Paris, Matthew 9
Parker, John 23–4
Parker, Matthew 8–26
Parker, Robert 282
Parkes, Richard 280, 285
Parsons, Robert 280, 283, 286
Paul of Thebes 12
Pazzi, family 108–10, 113, 115, 117
Perotti, Niccolò 124, 130, 158, 179n
Peters, Julie Stone 417
Petrarca, Francesco 179n

INDEX OF NAMES 573

Petreius, Johannes 87
Petrucci, Ottaviano 386
Peucer, Caspar 236, 242
Peurbach, Georg 306, 310n
Pflaum, Jacob 321n
Philippi, Nicolaus 37–40, 43–4
Pine, John 1–2
Pinhas, Israel bar 274n
Pinon, Laurent 349
Pistoia, Domenico da 110n
Pizzighettone, David ben Eliezer 262
Planche, Jean de 10
Plantin, Christopher 95n, 199–200, 202n, 421
Plantin, press 185n, 199, 202n, 207, 210
Platter, Thomas 5
Pliny the Elder 349, 355
Podocataro, Ludovico 327n
Pole, Reginald 17
Poliziano (Politianus), Angelo 107–17, 130, 143, 146, 158–9, 167–9
Pollard, Alfred W. 223
Ponet, John 285
Pope, Alexander 290
Prata, Antonio 451n
Prater, John 403
Pray, György 170
Printer of the 1481 *Legenda Aurea* 38, 40, 44
Prostitz, Isaac ben Aaron 254n
Prostitz, press 254n, 258
Prynne, William 287
Pynson, Richard 72, 74–7

Quentell, Heinrich 55n
Quitslund, Beth 387

Rashi 255, 263
Rastell, John 386–7
Rastell, William 387
Ratdolt, Erhard 38–40, 48, 306, 321n
Ravani, Pietro, heirs of 348
Rebolledo, Ana Girón de 370
Recanati, Menahem 266
Reed, Isaac 408
Regiomontanus, Johannes 295–322
Regnault, François 221–3, 226, 228, 230
Regnault, Pierre 222, 226, 228
Reinhart, Marcus 37–40, 43–44
Rély, Jean de 218
Remondini, press 450
Renialme, Ascanius de 204
Renouard, Antoine-Augustin 170
Repo, Liina 252, 255
Reuchlin, Johannes 130, 132, 159–60
Reusner, Christoph 471
Rhenanus, Beatus 373n
Rheticus, Georg Joachim 87, 90
Richards, Jennifer 3

Richardson, Brian 3
Ripoli, press 109–10
Rizzo, Silvia 325
Roberti, Jean 202n
Roder, Christian 297, 299n, 301, 308
Rolewinck, Werner 39, 53, 495
Rondelet, Guillaume 331
Rood, Theodoric 38, 40
Rossi, Giovan Girolamo de' 165n
Rößlin, Johann Weyrich, the Elder 476
Rößlin, Johann Weyrich, the Younger 476
Roud, Steve 446
Rowe, Nicholas 400, 402, 408–9, 410n, 411
Rüdinger, Esrom 242
Ruppel, Berthold 38, 40, 44
Rusch, Adolf 38–40, 44
Rusconi, Giorgio 91
Rusconi, Giovanni Antonio 98

Sachs, Hans 92
Sachs, Moritz 471
Sacon, Jacques 223
Salazar, Tristan de 218
Salviani, Ippolito 331n, 334
Sánchez de las Brozas, Francisco 370
Sánchez, Luis 380
Sappho 183
Sassenus, Andreas 204
Saxony, Ludolph of 441
Scala, Bartolomeo 109
Scaliger, Julius Caesar 329–30, 338
Scarlet, Thomas 420n, 421
Schedel, Hartmann 24, 65, 295n, 296
Schedel, Hermann 295n, 296
Scherpp, Conrad 309n
Schmidt, Adolf 35
Schneider, Johann Gottlob 330, 333
Schobsser, Johann 94
Schöffer, Peter 38, 51
Schönsperger, Johann 36, 38, 40, 44–5
Schoondonck, Aegidius 204
Schott, Gaspar 325n
Schreiber, Wilhelm Ludwig 94
Scinzenzeler, Ulrich 38, 40
Segar, Francis 388, 390, 392
Selden, John vin
Seneca 204, 373, 418
Seres, William 72, 385, 388–91, 395–7
Serrano de Vargas, Miguel 380
Seymour, Edward, Duke of Somerset 388
Shakespeare, William 4–5, 399–412, 420–1
Sharpham, Edward 419
Shirley, James 418
Simler, Josias 349
Simpson, Percy 3, 84n
Sixtus IV, Pope 109, 327
Sixtus V, Pope 9

Smith, Emma 403n, 407n, 410
Smith, Richard 286
Smyth, Adam 3, 410, 417
Solín, Václav 238n
Solín, Zachariáš 239
Solon 371n
Somerset, Duke of *see* Seymour, Edward
Soncino, Gershom 274n
Soncino, press 267n, 273–4
Speckle, Vitus Rudolph 92n
Speranzi, David 183
Speyer (Spira), Wendelin de 85
Spiegel, Yaakov Shmuel 261n, 263
Spira, Nathan ben Samson 268
Squarcialupi, Marcello 242
Stafford, Simon 421
Stammheim, Melchior von 43
Stapleton, Thomas 198
Statius 202
Steevens, George 408–9
Štefan, Ondřej 239
Steinhöwel, Henrich 53, 60–2, 65–7
Stenner, Rachael 279
Stern, Tiffany 417
Sternhold, Thomas 385, 388–9
Stöffler, Johannes 321
Stratton, Alexander 200
Stubbe, John 25–6
Süsslin, Alexander 273
Swerdlow, Noel 87
Symmen, Henric van 432

Talbot, James 1
Tanselle, G. Thomas 2, 492
Taylor, Frederick Winslow 5
Taylor, John 278–9, 281
Terence 326
Textor, Benedict 352
Textor, Claude 352
Thecla of Iconium 202, 207
Themistocles 371n
Theobald, Lewis 403, 408–9
Theocritus 125, 128, 135n, 144n, 160–1
Theophrastus 333, 346
Thevet, André 353, 356
Thompson, D'Arcy Wentworth 335n, 338
Toledo, Francesco da 327n
Tolosa, Vidal de 268
Torresano, Andrea 127, 151, 167n, 178
Tortis, Baptista de 36, 38, 40
Toussain, Jacques 333
Trechsel, Gaspar and Melchior 222–3
Tremellius, Immanuel 234n, 236
Trotzendorf, Valentin von 237
Trovato, Paolo 3
Trundle, John 418
Tsarfati, Mordecai 262, 264

Tschichold, Jan 70
Tucher, Hans 53
Turner, William 352
Tye, Christopher 385–97
Tyndale, William v

Ulma, Seligman ben Moses Simon 264–5, 270n, 273n
Urban V, Pope 21
Urceo Codro, Antonio 166n
Ussher, James 24

Valgrisi, Vincenzo 347
Valturio, Roberto 100
Vega, Garcilaso de la 369–82
Vega, Pedro de 380
Vérard, Antoine 216, 218, 220–1, 230
Vergil 6, 16, 44, 145
Vesalius, Andreas 82, 99
Vicary, Thomas 282
Virgili, Polidoro 22
Vitruvius 95

Wagenaer, Lucas 93
Wakelin, David 26
Wallis, John 84n, 85n
Walther, Bernard 309n
Warbeck, Perkin 221
Warburton, William 408
Waters, Michael 96
Watson, Thomas 283
Weidner, Robert 387, 395–7
Weiss, Adrian 73
Werner, Sarah 3n, 76
Wharton, George 289
Whitchurch, Edward 222n, 223, 228
White, John 287
Whytstons, James 77
Wiarda, Dooitzen 379n
Willeboirts Bosschaert, Thomas 201
Willett, Andrew 280, 285
William I, King of England 15
Winters, Conrad 38–40, 44
Wither, George 399
Wittenberg, Arvid 474
Wolf, Georges 38, 40
Wolfe, Reginald 9, 72
Worthington, Thomas 287
Wotton, Edward 334
Wotton, Thomas 9
Wright, Thomas 287
Wyclif, John v
Wyssenbach, family 346

Yale, doctor 24
Yemeniz, Nicolas 221n
Yitshaki, Salomon 261n
York, Thomas of 20

Zainer, Günther 35–6, 38, 40, 44
Zainer, Johann 36, 38, 40, 44, 60, 65–7
Zangwill, Israel vin
Zemon Davis, Natalie 5

Zeno, Apostolo 169
Zephyrinus, Pope 21
Zinner, Ernst 300
Zwinger, Theodor 497